Nagraj (Raju) Balakrishnan, Barry Ren[...]
Managerial Decision Modeling

Nagraj (Raju) Balakrishnan, Barry Render,
Ralph M. Stair, Chuck Munson

Managerial Decision Modeling

Business Analytics with Spreadsheets

Fourth Edition

DE
G
PRESS

ISBN 978-1-5015-1510-1
e-ISBN (PDF) 978-1-5015-0620-8
e-ISBN (EPUB) 978-1-5015-0631-4

Library of Congress Cataloging-in-Publication Data
A CIP catalog record for this book has been applied for at the Library of Congress.

Bibliographic information published by the Deutsche Nationalbibliothek
The Deutsche Nationalbibliothek lists this publication in the Deutsche Nationalbibliografie; detailed bibliographic data are available on the Internet at http://dnb.dnb.de.

© 2017 Walter de Gruyter Inc., Boston/Berlin
Printing and binding: CPI books GmbH, Leck
♾ Printed on acid-free paper
Printed in Germany

www.degruyter.com

To my children, Nitin and Nandita, and most of all to my darling wife, Meena, my rock – N.B.

To Donna, Charlie, and Jesse – B.R.

To Ken Ramsing and Alan Eliason – R.M.S.

To my wife Kim and my sons Christopher and Mark
for their unwavering support and encouragement – C.M

Acknowledgments

The authors would like to thank Howard Weiss for his outstanding job in developing ExcelModules, and for adding a new Mac version. Raju Balakrishnan would like to thank his daughter Nandita for her diligent help in reviewing and revising many of the end-of-chapter exercises, Nesreen El-Rayes for her research in updating the *Decision Modeling In Action* boxes, and Megan Seccombe for her valuable assistance with the revised figures and Excel screenshots.

Several people worked very hard to bring the book through the publication process. We would like to gratefully acknowledge the outstanding help provided by Jeffrey Pepper, Megan Lester, Caitlyn Nardozzi, John Woolsey, Angie MacAllister, and Mark Watanabe who worked on the book for De|G PRESS. Thank you all!

It is no secret that unlike courses in functional areas such as finance, marketing, and accounting, decision modeling courses always face an uphill battle in getting students interested and excited about the material (despite its increased value in today's business world). We hope that this book will be an ally to all in this endeavor.

About the Authors

Raju Balakrishnan serves as Dean of the College of Business (COB) at the University of Michigan-Dearborn. Prior to that, he was Senior Associate Dean in the College of Business and Behavioral Science at Clemson University, where he served on the faculty and administration for nearly 19 years. He has also served on the faculty at Tulane University and has taught in the Executive MBA program at Tulane and the University of Georgia.

Dr. Balakrishnan earned his Ph.D. in Management from Purdue University, M.S. in Mechanical Engineering from the University of Kentucky, and a B.E. with honors in Mechanical Engineering from the University of Madras in India.

He has published extensively in leading academic journals such as *Decision Sciences*, *Production and Operations Management*, *European Journal of Operational Research*, *IIE Transactions*, and *Computers & Operations Research*. His teaching interests include spreadsheet-based decision modeling, statistics, and operations management. He serves as senior departmental editor of *Production and Operations Management* and served as secretary of the *Production and Operations Management Society* during 2006–08. He has been recognized multiple times for teaching excellence at both Clemson and Tulane, and has received several research awards including best paper awards from the D*ecision Sciences Institute and the Institute of Industrial Engineers*.

Barry Render is the Charles Harwood Professor of Management Science Emeritus at the Crummer Graduate School of Business at Rollins College. He received his M.S. in Operations Research and his Ph.D. in Quantitative Analysis at the University of Cincinnati. He previously taught at George Washington University, the University of New Orleans, Boston University, and George Mason University, where he held the GM Foundation Professorship in Decision Sciences and was Chair of the Decision Science Department. Dr. Render also worked in the aerospace industry.

Professor Render has co-authored ten textbooks with Pearson/Prentice Hall, including *Quantitative Analysis for Management, Operations Management, Principles of Operations Management, Service Management, Introduction to Management Science,* and has published more than one hundred articles on a variety of management topics.

Dr. Render has also been honored as an AACSB Fellow and named as a Senior Fulbright Scholar in 1982 and in 1993. He was twice vice-president of the Decision Science Institute Southeast Region and served as Software Review Editor for Decision Line from 1989 to 1995. He was Editor of the *New York Times* Operations Management special issues from 1996 to 2001. Finally, Professor Render has been involved in consulting for for many organizations, including NASA; the FBI; the U.S. Navy; Fairfax County, Virginia; and C&P Telephone.

Before retiring in 2009, he taught operations management courses in Rollins College's MBA programs. In 1995 and in 2009 he was named as that school's Professor of the Year, and in 1996 was selected by Roosevelt University to receive the St. Claire Drake Award for Outstanding Scholarship.

Ralph Stair is Professor Emeritus of Management Information Systems in the College of Business at Florida State University. He received a B.S. in Chemical Engineering from Purdue University and an MBA from Tulane University. He received his Ph.D. in operations management from the University of Oregon.

He has taught at the University of Oregon, the University of Washington, the University of New Orleans, and Florida State University. He has twice taught in Florida State University's Study Abroad Program in London.

Dr. Stair has published numerous articles and books, has funded a student scholarship at St. Johns Northwestern Military Academy, and endowed a faculty prize in innovative education at Florida State University.

Chuck Munson is a Professor of Operations Management and Ph.D. Program Director in the Carson College of Business at Washington State University. His received his BSBA *summa cum laude* in finance, along with his MSBA and Ph.D. in operations management, from Washington University in St. Louis. For two years, he served as Associate Dean for Graduate Programs in Business at Washington State U. He also worked for three years as a financial analyst for Contel Telephone Corporation.

Professor Munson serves as a senior editor for *Production and Operations Management*, and he serves on the editorial review board of four other journals. He has published more than 25 articles in such journals as *Production and Operations Management, IIE Transactions, Decision Sciences, Naval Research Logistics, European Journal of Operational Research, Journal of the Operational Research Society, International Journal of Production Economics,* and *Annals of Operations Research*. He is a coauthor of *Operations Management: Sustainability and Supply Chain Management* (12 ed.). He is also editor of *The Supply Chain Management Casebook: Comprehensive Coverage and Best Practices in SCM,* and he has co-authored the research monograph *Quantity Discounts: An Overview and Practical Guide for Buyers and Sellers*.

Dr. Munson teaches Business Modeling with Spreadsheets, along with operations management courses at the undergraduate, MBA, and Ph.D. levels at Washington State U. His major awards include winning the Sahlin Faculty Excellence Award for Instruction, the top teaching award at Washington State University 2016); being a Founding Board Member of the Washington State University President's Teaching Academy (2004); winning the WSU College of Business Outstanding Teaching Award (2001 and 2015), Research Award (2004), and Service Award (2009 and 2013); and being named the WSU MBA Professor of the Year (2000 and 2008).

Contents

Chapter 1: Introduction to Managerial Decision Modeling —— 1
1.1 What is Decision Modeling? —— 2
1.2 Types of Decision Models —— 3
 Deterministic Models —— 3
 Probabilistic Models —— 4
 Quantitative versus Qualitative Data   5
 Using Spreadsheets in Decision Modeling —— 5
1.3 Steps Involved in Decision Modeling —— 6
 Step 1: Formulation —— 7
 Step 2: Solution 9
 Step 3: Interpretation and Sensitivity Analysis —— 10
1.4 Spreadsheet Example of a Decision Model: Tax Computation —— 11
1.5 Spreadsheet Example of a Decision Model: Break-Even Analysis —— 16
 Using Goal Seek to Find the Break-Even Point —— 18
1.6 Possible Problems in Developing Decision Models —— 21
 Defining the Problem —— 21
 Developing a Model —— 22
 Acquiring Input Data —— 22
 Developing a Solution —— 23
 Testing the Solution —— 23
 Analyzing the Results —— 23
1.7 Implementation—Not Just the Final Step —— 24
1.8 Summary —— 24
1.9 Exercises —— 27

Chapter 2: Linear Programming Models: Graphical and Computer Methods —— 33
2.1 Introduction —— 34
2.2 Developing a Linear Programming Model —— 35
 Formulation —— 35
 Solution —— 35
 Interpretation and Sensitivity Analysis —— 36
 Properties of a Linear Programming Model —— 36
 Basic Assumptions of a Linear Programming Model —— 37
2.3 Formulating a Linear Programming Problem —— 38
 Linear Programming Example: Flair Furniture Company —— 38
 Decision Variables —— 39
 The Objective Function —— 39
 Constraints —— 40
 Nonnegativity Constraints and Integer Values —— 41
 Guidelines for Developing a Correct LP Model —— 41

2.4	Graphical Solution of a Linear Programming Problem with Two Variables —— 43
	Graphical Representation of Constraints —— 43
	Painting Time Constraint —— 46
	Feasible Region —— 47
	Identifying an Optimal Solution by Using Level Lines —— 48
	Identifying an Optimal Solution by Using All Corner Points —— 51
	Comments on Flair Furniture's Optimal Solution —— 52
	Extension to Flair Furniture's LP Model —— 52
2.5	A Minimization Linear Programming Problem —— 54
	Holiday Meal Turkey Ranch —— 55
	Graphical Solution of the Holiday Meal Turkey Ranch Problem —— 56
2.6	Special Situations in Solving Linear Programming Problems —— 58
	Redundant Constraints —— 58
	Infeasibility —— 59
	Alternate Optimal Solutions —— 60
	Unbounded Solution —— 61
2.7	Setting Up and Solving Linear Programming Problems Using Excel's Solver —— 62
	Using Solver to Solve the Flair Furniture Problem —— 63
	The Objective Cell —— 65
	Creating Cells for Constraint RHS Values —— 67
	Entering Information in Solver —— 68
	Using Solver to Solve Flair Furniture Company's Modified Problem —— 76
	Using Solver to Solve the Holiday Meal Turkey Ranch Problem —— 77
2.8	Algorithmic Solution Procedures for Linear Programming Problems —— 79
2.9	Summary —— 80
2.10	Exercises —— 85

Chapter 3: Linear Programming Modeling Applications with Computer Analyses in Excel —— 101

3.1	Using Linear Programming to Solve Real-World Problems —— 102
3.2	Manufacturing Applications —— 103
	Product Mix Problem —— 103
	Make-Buy Decision Problem —— 108
3.3	Marketing Applications —— 112
	Media Selection Problem —— 112
	Marketing Research Problem —— 113
3.4	Finance Applications —— 118
	Portfolio Selection Problem —— 118
	Alternate Formulations of the Portfolio Selection Problem —— 121
3.5	Employee Staffing Applications —— 123
	Labor Planning Problem —— 123

	Extensions to the Labor Planning Problem —— 127
	Assignment Problem —— 127
3.6	Transportation Applications —— 127
	Vehicle Loading Problem —— 127
	Expanded Vehicle Loading Problem—Allocation Problem —— 132
	Transportation Problem —— 133
3.7	Blending Applications —— 134
	Diet Problem —— 134
	Blending Problem —— 136
3.8	Multiperiod Applications —— 141
	Production Scheduling Problem —— 141
	Sinking Fund Problem —— 147
3.9	Summary —— 151
3.10	Exercises —— 153

Chapter 4: Linear Programming Sensitivity Analysis —— 181

4.1	Importance of Sensitivity Analysis —— 182
	Why Do We Need Sensitivity Analysis? —— 182
4.2	Sensitivity Analysis Using Graphs —— 183
	Types of Sensitivity Analysis —— 185
	Impact of Changes in an Objective Function Coefficient —— 185
	Impact of Changes in a Constraint's Right-Hand-Side Value —— 187
4.3	Sensitivity Analysis Using Solver Reports —— 193
	Solver Reports —— 194
	Sensitivity Report —— 195
	Impact of Changes in a Constraint's RHS Value —— 196
	Impact of Changes in an Objective Function Coefficient —— 198
4.4	Sensitivity Analysis for a Larger Maximization Example —— 200
	Anderson Home Electronics Example —— 200
	Some Questions We Want Answered —— 203
	Alternate Optimal Solutions —— 205
4.5	Analyzing Simultaneous Changes by Using the 100% Rule —— 206
	Simultaneous Changes in Constraint RHS Values —— 206
	Simultaneous Changes in OFC Values —— 207
4.6	Pricing Out New Variables —— 207
	Anderson's Proposed New Product —— 207
4.7	Sensitivity Analysis for a Minimization Example —— 211
	Burn-Off Diet Drink Example —— 211
	Burn-Off's Excel Solution —— 212
	Answering Sensitivity Analysis Questions for Burn-Off —— 213
4.8	Summary —— 216
4.9	Exercises —— 218

Chapter 5: Transportation, Assignment, and Network Models —— 239
5.1 Types of Network Models —— 239
 Transportation Model —— 240
 Transshipment Model —— 240
 Assignment Model —— 240
 Maximal-Flow Model —— 241
 Shortest-Path Model —— 241
 Minimal-Spanning Tree Model —— 241
 Implementation Issues —— 241
5.2 Characteristics of Network Models —— 242
 Types of Arcs —— 242
 Types of Nodes —— 243
 Common Characteristics —— 243
5.3 Transportation Model —— 244
 LP Formulation for Executive Furniture's Transportation Model —— 246
 Solving the Transportation Model Using Excel —— 247
 Unbalanced Transportation Models —— 249
 Alternate Optimal Solutions —— 251
 An Application of the Transportation Model: Facility Location —— 251
5.4 Transportation Models with Max-Min and Min-Max Objectives —— 252
5.5 Transshipment Model —— 256
 Executive Furniture Company Example—Revisited —— 256
 LP Formulation for Executive Furniture's Transshipment Model —— 256
 Lopez Custom Outfits—A Larger Transshipment Example —— 258
 LP Formulation for Lopez Custom Outfits Transshipment Model —— 259
5.6 Assignment Model —— 262
 Fix-It Shop Example —— 263
 Solving Assignment Models —— 264
 LP Formulation for Fix-It Shop's Assignment Model —— 266
5.7 Maximal-Flow Model —— 268
 Road System in Waukesha, Wisconsin —— 268
 LP Formulation for Waukesha Road System's Maximal-Flow Model —— 269
5.8 Shortest-Path Model —— 272
 Ray Design Inc. Example —— 273
 LP Formulation for Ray Design Inc.'s Shortest-Path Model —— 274
5.9 Minimal-Spanning Tree Model —— 276
 Lauderdale Construction Company Example —— 276
5.10 Summary —— 279
5.11 Exercises —— 282

Chapter 6: Integer, Goal, and Nonlinear Programming Models —— 303
6.1 Models That Relax Linear Programming Conditions —— 304

	Integer Programming Models —— 304
	Goal Programming Models —— 305
	Nonlinear Programming Models —— 305
6.2	Models with General Integer Variables —— 305
	Harrison Electric Company —— 306
	Using Solver to Solve Models with General Integer Variables —— 309
	Solver Options —— 313
	Should We Include Integer Requirements in a Model? —— 315
6.3	Models with Binary Variables —— 317
	Portfolio Selection at Simkin and Steinberg —— 317
	Set-Covering Problem at Sussex County —— 322
6.4	Mixed Integer Models: Fixed-Charge Problems —— 325
	Locating a New Factory for Hardgrave Machine Company —— 326
6.5	Goal Programming Models —— 331
	Goal Programming Example: Wilson Doors Company —— 331
	Solving Goal Programming Models with Weighted Goals —— 335
	Solving Goal Programming Models with Ranked Goals —— 338
	Comparing the Two Approaches for Solving GP Models —— 344
6.6	Nonlinear Programming Models —— 344
	Why Are NLP Models Difficult to Solve? —— 345
	Solving Nonlinear Programming Models Using Solver —— 347
	Computational Procedures for Nonlinear Programming Problems —— 354
6.7	Summary —— 354
6.8	Exercises —— 357

Chapter 7: Project Management —— 383

7.1	Planning, Scheduling, and Controlling Projects —— 384
	Phases in Project Management —— 384
	Use of Software Packages in Project Management —— 387
7.2	Project Networks —— 387
	Identifying Activities —— 388
	Identifying Activity Times and Other Resources —— 389
	Project Management Techniques: PERT and CPM —— 389
	Project Management Example: General Foundry, Inc. —— 391
	Drawing the Project Network —— 392
7.3	Determining the Project Schedule —— 394
	Forward Pass —— 396
	Backward Pass —— 398
	Calculating Slack Time and Identifying the Critical Path(s) —— 399
	Total Slack Time versus Free Slack Time —— 401
7.4	Variability in Activity Times —— 402
	PERT Analysis —— 403

Probability of Project Completion —— 406
Determining Project Completion Time for a Given Probability —— 408
Variability in Completion Time of Noncritical Paths —— 409
7.5 Managing Project Costs and Other Resources —— 410
Planning and Scheduling Project Costs: Budgeting Process —— 410
Monitoring and Controlling Project Costs —— 413
Managing Other Resources —— 415
7.6 Project Crashing —— 417
Crashing General Foundry's Project (Hand Calculations) —— 418
Crashing General Foundry's Project Using Linear Programming —— 421
Using Linear Programming to Determine Earliest and Latest Starting Times —— 424
7.7 Summary —— 425
7.8 Exercises —— 429

Chapter 8: Decision Analysis —— 449
8.1 What is Decision Analysis? —— 450
8.2 The Five Steps in Decision Analysis —— 450
Thompson Lumber Company Example —— 451
8.3 Types of Decision-Making Environments —— 453
8.4 Decision Making Under Uncertainty —— 454
Maximax Criterion —— 455
Maximin Criterion —— 455
Criterion of Realism (Hurwicz) —— 456
Equally Likely (Laplace) Criterion —— 457
Minimax Regret Criterion —— 457
Using Excel to Solve Decision-Making Problems under Uncertainty —— 458
8.5 Decision Making Under Risk —— 461
Expected Monetary Value —— 461
Expected Opportunity Loss —— 462
Expected Value of Perfect Information —— 463
Using Excel to Solve Decision-Making Problems under Risk —— 464
8.6 Decision Trees —— 466
Folding Back a Decision Tree —— 467
8.7 Decision Trees for Multistage Decision-Making Problems —— 469
A Multistage Decision-Making Problem for Thompson Lumber —— 469
Expanded Decision Tree for Thompson Lumber —— 470
Folding Back the Expanded Decision Tree for Thompson Lumber —— 472
Expected Value of Sample Information —— 474
8.8 Estimating Probability Values Using Bayesian Analysis —— 475
Calculating Revised Probabilities —— 476
Potential Problems in Using Survey Results —— 478
8.9 Utility Theory —— 478

Measuring Utility and Constructing a Utility Curve —— 479
Utility as a Decision-Making Criterion —— 483
8.10 Summary —— 485
8.11 Exercises —— 488

Chapter 9: Queuing Models —— 509
9.1 The Importance of Queuing Theory —— 510
Approaches for Analyzing Queues —— 510
9.2 Queuing System Costs —— 511
9.3 Characteristics of a Queuing System —— 513
Arrival Characteristics —— 513
Queue Characteristics —— 516
Service Facility Characteristics —— 516
Measuring the Queue's Performance —— 519
Kendall's Notation for Queuing Systems —— 520
Variety of Queuing Models Studied Here —— 520
9.4 M/M/1 Queuing System —— 521
Assumptions of the M/M/1 Queuing Model —— 521
Operating Characteristic Equations for an M/M/1 Queuing System —— 522
Arnold's Muffler Shop Example —— 523
Using ExcelModules for Queuing Model Computations —— 524
Cost Analysis of the Queuing System —— 527
Increasing the Service Rate —— 528
9.5 M/M/s Queuing System —— 529
Operating Characteristic Equations for an M/M/s Queuing System —— 530
Arnold's Muffler Shop Revisited —— 531
Cost Analysis of the Queuing System —— 533
9.6 M/D/1 Queuing System —— 533
Operating Characteristic Equations for an M/D/1 Queuing System —— 534
Garcia-Golding Recycling, Inc. —— 535
Cost Analysis of the Queuing System —— 536
9.7 M/G/1 Queuing System —— 536
Operating Characteristic Equations for an M/G/1 Queuing System —— 537
Meetings with Professor Crino —— 537
Using Excel's Goal Seek to Identify Required Model Parameters —— 539
9.8 M/M/S/∞/N Queuing System —— 540
Operating Characteristic Equations for the Finite Population Queuing System —— 542
Department of Commerce Example —— 543
Cost Analysis of the Queuing System —— 544
9.9 More Complex Queuing Systems —— 546
9.10 Summary —— 547
9.11 Exercises —— 551

Chapter 10: Simulation Modeling — 565

- 10.1 Why Create a Simulation? — 566
  - Simulation Basics — 566
  - Advantages and Disadvantages of Simulation — 568
- 10.2 Monte Carlo Simulation — 569
  - Step 1: Establish a Probability Distribution for Each Variable — 570
  - Step 2: Simulate Values from the Probability Distributions — 571
  - Step 3: Repeat the Process for a Series of Replications — 573
- 10.3 Role of Computers in Simulation — 574
  - Types of Simulation Software Packages — 575
  - Random Generation from Some Common Probability Distributions Using Excel — 575
- 10.4 Simulation Model to Compute Expected Profit — 582
  - Setting Up the Model — 583
  - Replication by Copying the Model — 585
  - Replication Using Data Table — 586
  - Analyzing the Results — 587
- 10.5 Simulation Model of an Inventory Problem — 591
  - Simkin's Hardware Store — 591
  - Setting Up the Model — 593
  - Computation of Costs — 596
  - Replication Using Data Table — 596
  - Analyzing the Results — 597
  - Using Scenario Manager to Include Decisions in a Simulation Model — 598
  - Analyzing the Results — 601
- 10.6 Simulation Model of a Queuing Problem — 601
  - Denton Savings Bank — 601
  - Setting Up the Model — 602
  - Replication Using Data Table — 604
  - Analyzing the Results — 604
- 10.7 Simulation Model of a Revenue Management Problem — 605
  - Judith's Airport Limousine Service — 605
  - Setting Up the Model — 606
  - Replicating the Model Using Data Table and Scenario Manager — 608
  - Analyzing the Results — 609
- 10.8 Other Types of Simulation Models — 610
  - Operational Gaming — 610
  - Systems Simulation — 610
- 10.9 Summary — 611
- 10.10 Exercises — 615

Chapter 11: Forecasting Models — 647

- 11.1 What is Forecasting? — 648

11.2	Types of Forecasts —— 649	
	Qualitative Models —— 650	
	Time-Series Models —— 650	
	Causal Models —— 650	
11.3	Qualitative Forecasting Models —— 650	
11.4	Measuring Forecast Error —— 651	
11.5	Basic Time-Series Forecasting Models —— 652	
	Components of a Time Series —— 653	
	Stationary and Nonstationary Time-Series Data —— 654	
	Moving Averages —— 654	
	Using ExcelModules for Forecasting Model Computations —— 655	
	Weighted Moving Averages —— 659	
	Exponential Smoothing —— 664	
11.6	Trend and Seasonality in Time-Series Data —— 668	
	Linear Trend Analysis —— 668	
	Scatter Chart —— 669	
	Least-Squares Procedure for Developing a Linear Trend Line —— 672	
	Seasonality Analysis —— 676	
11.7	Decomposition of a Time Series —— 678	
	Multiplicative Decomposition Example: Sawyer Piano House —— 678	
	Using ExcelModules for Multiplicative Decomposition —— 679	
11.8	Causal Forecasting Models: Simple and Multiple Regression —— 684	
	Causal Simple Regression Model —— 684	
	Causal Simple Regression Using ExcelModules —— 686	
	Causal Simple Regression Using Excel's Analysis ToolPak (Data Analysis) —— 692	
	Causal Multiple Regression Model —— 696	
	Causal Multiple Regression Using ExcelModules —— 696	
	Causal Multiple Regression Using Excel's Analysis ToolPak (Data Analysis) —— 700	
11.9	Summary —— 705	
11.10	Exercises —— 710	

Appendix A: Probability Concepts and Applications —— 731

A.1	Fundamental Concepts —— 731	
	Types of Probability —— 732	
A.2	Mutually Exclusive and Collectively Exhaustive Events —— 733	
	Adding Mutually Exclusive Events —— 734	
	Law of Addition for Events that Are Not Mutually Exclusive —— 735	
A.3	Statistically Independent Events —— 736	
A.4	Statistically Dependent Events —— 737	
A.5	Revising Probabilities with Bayes' Theorem —— 740	
	General Form of Bayes' Theorem —— 741	
A.6	Further Probability Revisions —— 742	

- A.7 Random Variables —— 743
- A.8 Probability Distributions —— 745
  - Probability Distribution of a Discrete Random Variable —— 745
  - Expected Value of a Discrete Probability Distribution —— 747
  - Variance of a Discrete Probability Distribution —— 747
  - Probability Distribution of a Continuous Random Variable —— 748
- A.9 The Normal Distribution —— 750
  - Area under the Normal Curve —— 751
  - Using the Standard Normal Table —— 752
  - Haynes Construction Company Example —— 753
- A.10 The Exponential Distribution —— 756
- A.11 The Poisson Distribution —— 757
- A.12 Summary —— 758
- A.13 Exercises —— 760

Appendix B: Useful Excel 2016 Commands and Procedures for Installing ExcelModules —— 767

- 1B.1 Introduction —— 767
- B.2 Getting Started —— 767
  - Organization of a Worksheet —— 768
  - Navigating through a Worksheet —— 769
- B.3 The Ribbon, Toolbars, and Tabs —— 769
  - Excel Help —— 774
- B.4 Working with Worksheets —— 775
- B.5 Using Formulas and Functions —— 775
  - Copying Formulas —— 779
  - Errors in Using Formulas and Functions —— 779
- B.6 Printing Worksheets —— 780
- B.7 Excel Options and Add-Ins —— 781
- B.8 ExcelModules —— 784
  - Installing ExcelModules —— 784
  - Running ExcelModules —— 784
  - ExcelModules Help and Options —— 786

Appendix C: Areas Under The Standard Normal Curve —— 787

Appendix D: Brief Solutions to All Odd-Numbered End-Of-Chapter Problems —— 789

Index —— 795

Preface

In recent years, the use of spreadsheets to teach decision modeling (alternatively referred to as *business analytics, management science, operations research,* and *quantitative analysis*) has become standard practice in many business programs. This emphasis has revived interest in the field significantly, and several books have attempted to discuss spreadsheet-based decision modeling. However, some of these books have become too spreadsheet oriented, focusing more on the spreadsheet commands to use than on the underlying decision model. Other books have maintained their algorithmic approach to decision modeling, adding spreadsheet instructions almost as an afterthought. In the fourth edition of *Managerial Decision Modeling: Business Analytics with Spreadsheets*, we have continued to build on our success with the first three editions in trying to achieve the perfect balance between the decision modeling process and the use of spreadsheets to set up and solve decision models. In so doing, the book not only serves the needs of students but those of professionals who wish to use the techniques presented here. In keeping with the growing emphasis on *business analytics* and the use of many of the decision modeling techniques in this field, we have retitled the book.

It is important that books that support decision modeling try to combine the power to logically model and analyze diverse decision-making scenarios with software-based solution procedures. Therefore, this edition continues to focus on teaching the reader the skills needed to apply decision models to different kinds of organizational decision-making situations. The discussions are very application oriented and software based, with a view toward how a manager can effectively apply the models learned here to improve the decision-making process. The target audiences for this book are students in undergraduate and graduate level introductory decision modeling courses in business and engineering schools and professionals who need to use the content delivered in this book every day. However, this book will also be useful in other introductory courses that cover some of the core decision modeling topics, such as linear programming, network modeling, project management, decision analysis, and simulation.

Although the emphasis in this edition continues to be on using spreadsheets for decision modeling, the book remains, at heart, a *decision modeling* book. That is, while we use spreadsheets as a tool to quickly set up and solve decision models, our aim is not to teach students how to blindly use a spreadsheet without understanding how and why it works. To accomplish this, we discuss the fundamental concepts, assumptions, and limitations behind each decision modeling technique, show how each decision model works, and illustrate the real-world usefulness of each technique with many applications from both for-profit and not-for-profit organizations.

Basic knowledge of algebra and Excel are the only prerequisites. For your convenience, we have included brief introductions to Excel 2016 and probability in the appendices.

This book's chapters, supplements, and software package cover virtually every major topic in the decision modeling field and are arranged to provide a distinction between techniques that deal with deterministic environments and those that deal with probabilistic environments. We have included more material than most instructors can cover in a typical first course. We hope that the resulting flexibility of topic selection is appreciated by instructors who need to tailor their courses to different audiences and curricula.

Overall Approach

While writing this fourth edition, we have continued to adhere to certain themes that have worked very well in the first three editions:

- First, we have tried to separate the discussion of each decision modeling technique into three distinct issues:
  1. Formulation or problem setup
  2. Model solution
  3. Interpretation of the results and what-if analysis

  In this three-step framework, steps 1 and 3 (formulation and interpretation) call upon the manager's expertise. Mastering these steps now will give readers a competitive advantage later, in the marketplace, when it is necessary to make business decisions.
- Second, that most business and engineering professionals or students are not developers. Hence, to deal with step 2 (model solution), we have fully integrated Excel into our discussions so that readers can take full advantage of the wide availability and acceptability of spreadsheet-based software for decision modeling techniques.

  Excel is a very important part of what would be considered the two main topics in any *basic* decision modeling book: linear programming and simulation. However, we recognize that some topics are not well suited for spreadsheet-based software, such as project management, where Excel is generally not the best choice.
- Third, we try to ensure that readers focus on *what* they are doing and *why* they are doing it, rather than just mechanically learning which Excel formula to use, or button to press. To facilitate this, we also *briefly* discuss the steps and rationale of the solution process in many cases.
- Finally, we note that most of the students in decision modeling courses are likely to specialize in *other* functional areas, such as finance, marketing, accounting, operations, and human resources. In addition, we expect that a wide array of professionals will find the book a best solution. We therefore try to integrate decision modeling techniques with problems drawn from these different areas so that readers can recognize the importance of what they are learning and the potential benefits of using decision modeling in real-world settings. In addition, we have included summaries of selected articles from journals such as *Interfaces* that discuss the actual application of decision modeling techniques to real-world problems.

Features in This Book

The features of the first three editions of this book that have been well received as effective aids to the learning process have been updated and expanded in this fourth edition.

In creating this edition, we not only updated the content, we analyzed how we could best present the content from a learning point of view. Readers benefit from being able to deep dive into a chapter filled with examples and exercises, carefully explained, so that they can master the content. But readers also need quick review whether it be for a student cramming for a test or a professional wanting to recall something not used in a while. So, we created a Summary section that includes an overview of the chapter, then dozens of detailed Key Points, backed up with a Glossary of the terms used in the chapter, highlighted in red in the text as they appear.

We hope that the features listed below will continue to elp readers better understand the material:
- *Consistent layout and format for creating effective Excel models*—The consistent layout and format for creating spreadsheet models for all linear, integer, goal, and nonlinear programming problems is best suited to the beginner in using these types of decision models.
- *Functional use of color*—We have standardized the use of colors so that the various components of the models are easily identifiable.
- *Excel Notes and Excel Extra boxes*—We have added separate Excel Notes *boxes to provide simple Excel tips to make the spreadsheet usage as easy and error-free as possible. In addition, in each chapter, we have provided an* Excel Extra *box that illustrate advanced Excel techniques or commands.*
- *Description of the algebraic formulation and its spreadsheet implementation for all examples*—For each model, we first discuss the algebraic formulation so that the reader can understand the logic and rationale behind the decision model. The spreadsheet implementation then closely follows for ease of understanding.
- *Numerous screen captures of Excel outputs, with detailed callouts*—We have included numerous screen captures of Excel files with detailed callouts explaining the important entries and components of the model. Excel files are located at *degruyter.com/view/product/486941* and, for your convenience, the callouts are shown as comments on appropriate cells in these Excel files.
- *Ability to teach topics without the use of additional software*—Several topics can be studied using only Excel's standard built-in add-ins and commands. For example, we have discussed how Excel's Data Table and Scenario Manager procedures can be used to analyze and replicate even large simulation models.
- *Extensive discussion of linear programming sensitivity analysis, using the Solver report*—The discussion of linear programming sensitivity analysis in this book is more comprehensive than that in any competing book.
- *Decision Modeling In Action boxes*—These boxes summarize published articles that illustrate how real-world organizations have used decision models to solve problems.
- *ExcelModules*—This software package from Professor Howard Weiss of Temple University solves problems in queuing models (Chapter 9), forecasting models (Chapter 11), and inventory control models (in an optional Chapter 12 found online and downloadable from the Companion Website). Readers can see the power of this software package in modeling and solving problems in these chapters. ExcelModules is menu driven and easy to use, and it is available at *degruyter.com/view/product/486941*. A Mac version of the program is also available for the first time.

Major Changes in the FOURTH Edition

We have made the following major changes in this fourth edition—All spreadsheet applications have been fully updated to Excel 2016. The software program ExcelModules that accompanies this book has also been updated to suit Excel 2016 as well as 32-bit and 64-bit systems. In addition a Mac version of this software is now available.
- *Significant number of new end-of-chapter exercises*—We have added at least eight new exercises in each chapter. On average, there are now more than 45 end-of-chapter exercises per chapter.

- *More challenging chapter examples and end-of-chapter exercises*—Many of the chapter examples and end-of-chapter exercises have been revised to make them more current, rigorous, and better suited to a computer-based solution environment inviting readers to modify the Excel models contained in the chapters to incorporate new constraints or conditions. This requires readers to first thoroughly understand the original Excel models before attempting to modify them.
- *New Excel Extra Boxes*—In addition to the Excel Notes boxes that provide quick tips on Excel commands and procedures relevant to the topic being discussed, we have added new Excel Extra boxes. These boxes illustrate advanced Excel techniques and commands including descriptions of cell comments; locking cells; data validation; drop-down lists; linked charts; VBA for user interaction; sorting; identifying the owner of a max or min search; hiding rows, columns, sheets, and formulas; automating with macros; conditional formatting; and scroll bars and other form controls.
- *Updated Decision Modeling In Action boxes*—Decision Modeling In Action boxes illustrate the use of decision modeling in real-world scenarios. Many of these examples are from recent issues of *Interfaces*.
- *Streamlined network problem formulations*—We have modified the algebraic formulation and Excel implementation of certain network problems in Chapters 5 and 6 to provide a more streamlined presentation.
- *Excel functions*—We have added an extensive list of common Excel functions for your reference in Appendix B.
- *Better introductions*—Set expectations in each chapter.

Companion Website

The following items can be downloaded at *degruyter.com/view/product/486941*:
1. *Data Files*—Excel files for all examples discussed in the book. (For easy reference, the relevant file names are printed below the titles of the corresponding figures at appropriate places in the book.)
2. *Online Chapter*—The electronic-only Chapter 12: Inventory Control Models (PDF).
3. *ExcelModules Software*—This program solves problems and examples in the queuing models (Chapter 9), forecasting models (Chapter 11), and the downloadable inventory control models (Chapter 12) chapters in this book. Available in both Windows and Mac versions.
4. *Solutions to End-of-Chapter Exercises*—Detailed Excel solutions for all end-of-chapter exercises. Access is available to faculty adopters only.

Raju Balakrishnan
313-593-5462 (phone)
rajub@umich.edu (e-mail)

Barry Render
brender@rollins.edu (e-mail)

Ralph Stair
ralphmstair@cs.com (e-mail)

Chuck Munson
509-335-3076 (phone)
munson@wsu.edu (e-mail)

Chapter 1
Introduction to Managerial Decision Modeling

Do you frequently struggle to make decisions? Some people argue incessantly over relatively trivial choices, such as where to go for lunch. More life-altering decisions, such as where to go to college, whether or not to take that new job offer, or whether or not to say yes to a marriage proposal, can hound us for days and keep us up at night. And when we make a wrong decision, the regret that we feel can haunt us for weeks, months, or even years.

Managers face similar dilemmas as they struggle to make the best decisions for their respective organizations. Great decisions can lead to millions of extra dollars for the company and personal promotions or bonuses for the decision maker. Poor decisions can lead to huge financial losses for the company and potential job loss for the decision maker. People make many decisions on a personal level and even for their companies based on "gut feel." That may be the best approach for some decisions. But for many decisions, decision-making tools can provide tremendous guidance by illustrating the pros and cons of various alternatives. This is the essence of decision modeling.

We begin this chapter by defining decision modeling and then delineating the two major types of decision models. Next, we discuss the three major steps involved in decision modeling. The vast majority of the models covered in this book are quantitative in nature. Fortunately, these generally *do not* require the skills of a professional mathematician to set up or solve. Most of these models require only standard algebra and arithmetic, along with little bit of statistical background. An important reason for this is that we let the computer do most of the "heavy mathematical lifting" for us. And while many specialized computer optimization packages exist to solve large-scale decision models, it turns out that the standard spreadsheet, Microsoft Excel, can solve many types of modeling problems of reasonable size. We focus exclusively in this book on using Excel to solve the models that we present.

Most managers around the globe have Excel on their computers, and many use Excel frequently. As such, Excel can be a great tool for modeling because co-workers may be more comfortable with spreadsheets than they would be with unfamiliar specialized programs. Excel has allowed the "common manager" to use and even build his or her own decision models without the need to hire a specialist.

We introduce two models in this chapter that illustrate the standard approach for modeling with Excel that we will use for the rest of the book. The first illustrates how to compute estimated income taxes, and the second utilizes the Excel feature Goal Seek to perform a simple profit break-even analysis for a small firm. We conclude Chapter 1 by describing certain pitfalls that may arise in the modeling process and some challenges with implementation.

Chapter Objectives

After completing this chapter, you will be able to:
1. Define *decision model* and describe the importance of such models.
2. Understand the two types of decision models: deterministic and probabilistic models.
3. Understand the steps involved in developing decision models in practical situations.
4. Understand the use of spreadsheets in developing decision models.
5. Discuss possible problems in developing decision models.

1.1 What is Decision Modeling?

Although there are several definitions of *decision modeling*, we define it here as a scientific approach to managerial decision making. Alternatively, we can define it as the development of a *model* (usually mathematical) of a real-world problem scenario or environment. The resulting model typically should be such that the decision-making process is not affected by personal bias, whim, emotions, or guesswork. This model can then be used to provide insights into the solution of the managerial problem. Decision modeling is also commonly referred to as *quantitative analysis*, *management science*, or *operations research*. In this book, we prefer the term *decision modeling* because we will discuss all modeling techniques in a managerial decision-making context.

You may have heard about the explosion of "big data" or "data analytics" in the business world. The increasing power of technology to collect massive amounts of data from customers and other sources, along with never-ending comments appearing in social media, have opened possibilities for companies that were heretofore unimaginable. Just imagine the amount of data being collected daily by companies such as Google, Facebook, Twitter, and Yahoo, and the wealth of useful information contained in that data. The term "analytics" is being used in many ways, but at its core it describes transforming data into information, hopefully leading to sound business decisions. This is exactly what decision modeling encompasses. In fact, "data analytics" is now considered by many to be synonymous with decision modeling, quantitative analysis, management science, and operations research. Firms are searching for employees with these skills like never before. If you can master the skills, you will be highly valued by the marketplace.

Organizations such as American Airlines, United Airlines, IBM, Google, UPS, FedEx, and AT&T frequently use decision modeling to help solve complex problems. Although mathematical tools have been in existence for thousands of years, the formal study and application of quantitative (or mathematical) decision modeling techniques to practical decision making is largely a product of the twentieth century. The decision modeling techniques studied here have been applied successfully to an increasingly wide variety of complex problems in business, government, health care, education, and many other areas. Many such successful uses are discussed throughout this book.

It isn't enough, though, just to know the mathematical details of how a particular decision modeling technique can be set up and solved. It is equally important to be familiar with the limitations, assumptions, and specific applicability of the model. The correct use of decision modeling techniques usually results in solutions that are timely, accurate, flexible, economical, reliable, easy to understand, and easy to use.

1.2 Types of Decision Models

Decision models can be broadly classified into two categories, based on the type and nature of the decision-making problem environment under consideration: (1) deterministic models and (2) probabilistic models. We define each type in the following sections.

Deterministic Models

Deterministic models assume that all the relevant input data values are known with certainty; that is, they assume that all the information needed for modeling a decision-making problem environment is available, with fixed and known values. An example of such a model is the case of Dell Corporation, which makes several different types of PC products (e.g., desktops, laptops), all of which compete for the same resources (e.g., labor, hard disks, chips, working capital). Dell knows the specific amounts of each resource required to make one unit of each type of PC, based on the PC's design specifications. Further, based on the expected selling price and cost prices of various resources, Dell knows the expected profit contribution per unit of each type of PC. In such an environment, if Dell decides on a specific production plan, it is a simple task to compute the quantity required of each resource to satisfy that production plan. For example, if Dell plans to ship 50,000 units of a specific laptop model, and each unit includes a pair of 8.0 GB DDR4 memory chips, then Dell will need 100,000 units of these memory chips. Likewise, it is easy to compute the total profit that will be realized by this production plan (assuming that Dell can sell all the laptops it makes).

Perhaps the most common and popular deterministic modeling technique is linear programming (LP). In Chapter 2, we first discuss how small LP models can be set up and solved. We extend our discussion of LP in Chapter 3 to more complex problems drawn from a variety of business disciplines. In Chapter 4, we study how the solution to LP models produces, as a byproduct, a great deal of information useful for managerial interpretation of the results. Finally, in Chapters 5 and 6, we study a few extensions to LP models. These include several different network flow models (Chapter 5), as well as integer, nonlinear, and multi-objective (goal) programming models (Chapter 6).

As we demonstrate during our study of deterministic models, a variety of important managerial decision-making problems can be set up and solved using these techniques.

Probabilistic Models

In contrast to deterministic models, probabilistic models (also called *stochastic models*) assume that some *input data* values are not known with certainty. That is, they assume that the values of some important variables will not be known *before* decisions are made. It is therefore important to incorporate this "ignorance" into the model. An example of this type of model is the decision of whether to start a new business venture. As we have seen with the high variability in the stock market during the past several years, the success of such ventures is uncertain. However, investors (e.g., venture capitalists, founders) have to make decisions regarding this type of venture based on their expectations of future performance. Clearly, such expectations are not guaranteed to occur. In recent years, we have seen several examples of firms that have yielded (or are likely to yield) great rewards to their investors (e.g., Google, Facebook, Twitter) and others that have either failed (e.g., eToys.com, Pets.com) or been much more modest in their returns.

Another example of probabilistic modeling to which students may be able to relate easily is their choice of a major when they enter college. Clearly, there is a great deal of uncertainty regarding several issues in this decision-making problem: the student's aptitude for a specific major, his or her actual performance in that major, the employment situation in that major in four years, etc. Nevertheless, a student must choose a major early in his or her college career. Recollect your own situation. In all likelihood, you used your own assumptions (or expectations) regarding the future to evaluate the various alternatives (i.e., you developed a "model" of the decision-making problem). These assumptions may have been the result of information from various sources, such as parents, friends, and guidance counselors. The important point to note here is that none of this information is guaranteed, and no one can predict with 100% accuracy what exactly will happen in the future. Therefore, decisions made with this information, while well thought out and well intentioned, may still turn out not to be the best choices. For example, how many of your friends changed majors during their college careers?

Because their results are not guaranteed, does this mean that probabilistic decision models are of limited value? As we will see later in this book, the answer is an emphatic no. Probabilistic modeling techniques provide a structured approach for managers to incorporate uncertainty into their models and to evaluate decisions under alternate expectations regarding this uncertainty. They do so by using probabilities on the "random," or unknown, variables. Probabilistic modeling techniques discussed in this book include decision analysis (Chapter 8), queuing (Chapter 9), simulation (Chapter 10), and forecasting (Chapter 11). Two other techniques, project management (Chapter 7) and inventory control (Chapter 12), include aspects of both deterministic and probabilistic modeling. For each modeling technique, we discuss what kinds of criteria can be used when there is uncertainty and how to use these models to identify the preferred decisions.

Because uncertainty plays a vital role in probabilistic models, some knowledge of basic probability and statistical concepts is useful. Appendix A provides a brief overview of this topic. It should serve as a good refresher while studying these modeling techniques.

Quantitative versus Qualitative Data

Any decision modeling process starts with data. Like raw material for a factory, these data are manipulated or processed into information valuable to people making decisions. This processing and manipulating of raw data into meaningful information is the heart of decision modeling.

In dealing with a decision-making problem, managers may have to consider both qualitative and quantitative factors. For example, suppose we are considering several different investment alternatives, such as certificates of deposit, the stock market, and real estate. We can use *quantitative* factors, such as rates of return, financial ratios, and cash flows, in our decision model to guide our ultimate decision. In addition to these factors, however, we may also wish to consider *qualitative* factors, such as pending state and federal legislation, new technological breakthroughs, and the outcome of an upcoming election. It can be difficult to quantify these qualitative factors.

Due to the presence (and relative importance) of qualitative factors, the role of quantitative decision modeling in the decision-making process can vary. When there is a lack of qualitative factors, and when the problem, model, and input data remain reasonably stable and steady over time, the results of a decision model can automate the decision-making process. For example, some companies use quantitative inventory models to determine automatically when to order additional new materials and how much to order. In most cases, however, decision modeling is an aid to the decision-making process. The results of decision modeling should be combined with other (qualitative) information while making decisions in practice.

Using Spreadsheets in Decision Modeling

In keeping with the ever-increasing presence of technology in modern times, computers have become an integral part of the decision modeling process in today's business environments. Until the early 1990s, many of the modeling techniques discussed here required specialized software packages in order to be solved using a computer. However, spreadsheet packages such as Microsoft Excel have become increasingly capable of setting up and solving most of the decision modeling techniques commonly used in practical situations. For this reason, the current trend in many college courses on decision modeling focuses on spreadsheet-based instruction. In keeping with this trend, we discuss the role and use of spreadsheets (specifically Microsoft Excel) during our study of the different decision modeling techniques presented here.

In addition to discussing the use of some of Excel's built-in functions and procedures (e.g., Goal Seek, Data Table, Chart Wizard), we also discuss a few add-ins for Excel. The Data Analysis and Solver add-ins come standard with Excel. A custom add-in called ExcelModules is included on the Companion Website and used in Chapter 9 (Queuing Models), Chapter 11 (Forecasting Models), and the online Chapter 12 (Inventory Control Models).

Because a knowledge of basic Excel commands and procedures facilitates understanding the techniques and concepts discussed here, we recommend reading Appendix B, which provides a brief overview of the Excel features that are most useful in decision modeling. In addition, at appropriate places throughout this book, we discuss several Excel functions and procedures specific to each decision modeling technique.

Decision Modeling In Action

IBM Uses Decision Modeling to Improve the Productivity of Its Sales Force

IBM is a well-known multinational computer technology, software, and services company with more than 380,000 employees and revenue of more than $79 billion. A majority of IBM's revenue comes from services, including outsourcing, consulting, and systems integration.

Recognizing that improving the efficiency and productivity of this large sales force can be an effective operational strategy to drive revenue growth and manage expenses, IBM Research developed two broad decision modeling initiatives to explore this issue. The first initiative provides a set of analytical models designed to identify new sales opportunities at existing IBM accounts and at noncustomer companies. The second initiative allocates sales resources optimally based on field-validated analytical estimates of future revenue opportunities in market segments. IBM estimates the revenue impact of these two initiatives to be in the several hundreds of millions of dollars each year.

Source: Based on R. Lawrence et al. "Operations Research Improves Sales Force Productivity at IBM," *Interfaces* 40, 1 (January-February 2010): 33–46.

1.3 Steps Involved in Decision Modeling

Regardless of the size and complexity of the decision-making problem at hand, the decision modeling process involves three distinct steps: (1) formulation, (2) solution, and (3) interpretation. Figure 1.1 provides a schematic overview of these steps, along with the components, or parts, of each step. We discuss each of these steps in the following sections.

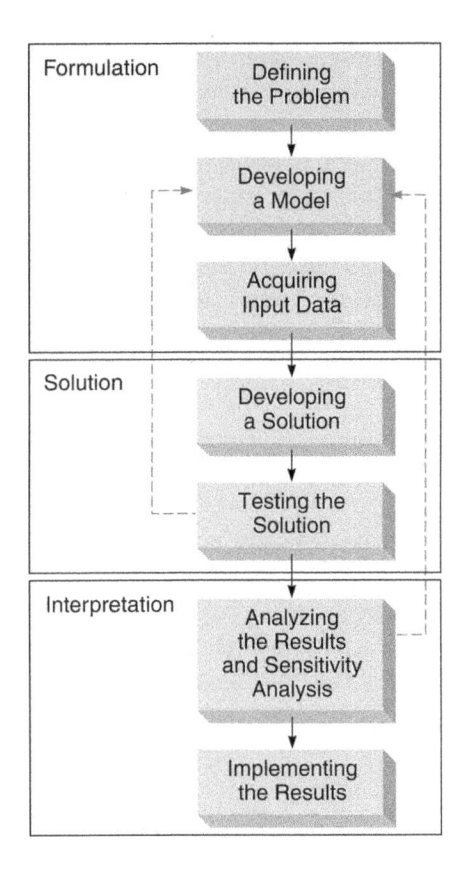

Figure 1.1: The Decision Modeling Approach

It is important to note that it is common to have an iterative process between these three steps before obtaining the final solution. For example, testing the solution (see Figure 1.1) might reveal that the model is incomplete or that some of the input data are being measured incorrectly. This means that the formulation needs to be revised. That, in turn, causes all the subsequent steps to be changed.

Step 1: Formulation
Formulation is the process by which each aspect of a problem scenario is translated and expressed in terms of a mathematical model. This is perhaps the most important and challenging step in decision modeling because the results of a poorly formulated problem will almost surely be incorrect. It is also in this step that the decision maker's ability to analyze a problem rationally comes into play. Even the most sophisticated software program will not automatically formulate a problem. The aim in formulation is to ensure that the mathematical model completely addresses all the issues relevant

to the problem at hand. Formulation can be further classified into three parts: (1) defining the problem, (2) developing a model, and (3) acquiring input data.

Defining the Problem The first part in formulation (and in decision modeling) is to develop a clear, concise statement of the problem. This statement gives direction and meaning to all the parts that follow it.

In many cases, defining the problem is perhaps the most important, and the most difficult, part. It is essential to go beyond just the symptoms of the problem at hand and identify the true causes behind it. One problem may be related to other problems, and solving a problem without regard to its related problems may actually worsen the situation. Thus, it is important to analyze how the solution to one problem affects other problems or the decision-making environment in general. Experience has shown that poor problem definition is a major reason for failure of management science groups to serve their organizations well.

When a problem is difficult to quantify, it may be necessary to develop *specific*, *measurable* objectives. For example, say a problem is defined as inadequate health care delivery in a hospital. The objectives might be to increase the number of beds, reduce the average number of days a patient spends in the hospital, increase the physician-to-patient ratio, and so on. When objectives are used, however, the real problem should be kept in mind. It is important to avoid obtaining specific and measurable objectives that may not solve the real problem.

Developing a Model Once we select the problem to be analyzed, the next part is to develop a decision model. Even though you might not be aware of it, you have been using models most of your life. For example, you may have developed the following model about friendship: Friendship is based on reciprocity, an exchange of favors. Hence, if you need a favor, such as a small loan, your model would suggest that you ask a friend.

Of course, there are many other types of models. An architect may make a physical model of a building he or she plans to construct. Engineers develop scale models of chemical plants, called pilot plants. An analog model, e.g., a thermometer measuring temperature or an oil dipstick signaling the level of oil remaining in a car, represents a phenomenon but does not look like it. A schematic model is a picture or drawing of reality. Automobiles, lawn mowers, circuit boards, typewriters, and numerous other devices have schematic models (drawings and pictures) that reveal how these devices work.

What sets decision modeling apart from other modeling techniques is that the models we develop here are mathematical. A *mathematical model* is a set of mathematical relationships. In most cases, these relationships are expressed as equations and inequalities, as they are in a spreadsheet model that computes sums, averages, or standard deviations.

Although there is considerable flexibility in the development of models, most of the models presented here contain one or more variables and parameters. A variable, as the name implies, is a measurable quantity that may vary or that is subject to change. Variables can be controllable or uncontrollable. A controllable variable is also called a *decision variable*. An example is how many inventory items to order. A problem parameter is a measurable quantity that is inherent in the problem, such as the cost of placing an order for more inventory items. In most cases, variables are unknown quantities, whereas parameters (or input data) are known quantities.

All models should be developed carefully. They should be solvable, realistic, and easy to understand and modify, and the required input data should be obtainable. A model developer must be careful to include the appropriate amount of detail for the model to be solvable yet realistic.

Acquiring Input Data   Once we have developed a model, we must obtain the input data to be used in the model. Obtaining accurate data is essential because even if the model is a perfect representation of reality, improper data will result in misleading results. This situation is called *garbage in, garbage out (GIGO)*. For larger problems, collecting accurate data can be one of the most difficult aspects of decision modeling.

Several sources can be used in collecting data. In some cases, company reports and documents can be used to obtain the necessary data. Another source is interviews with employees or other persons related to the firm. These individuals can sometimes provide excellent information, and their experience and judgment can be invaluable. A production supervisor, for example, might be able to tell you with a great degree of accuracy the amount of time it takes to manufacture a particular product. Sampling and direct measurement provide other sources of data for the model. You may need to know how many pounds of a raw material are used in producing a new photochemical product. This information can be obtained by going to the plant and actually measuring the amount of raw material being used. In other cases, statistical sampling procedures can be used to obtain data.

Step 2: Solution

The solution step is when the mathematical expressions resulting from the formulation process are solved to identify the optimal solution. Until the mid-1990s, typical courses in decision modeling focused a significant portion of their attention on this step because it was the most difficult aspect of studying the modeling process. As stated earlier, thanks to computer technology, the focus today has shifted away from the detailed steps of the solution process and toward the availability and use of software packages. The solution step can be further classified into two parts: (1) developing a solution and (2) testing the solution.

Developing a Solution   Developing a solution involves manipulating the model to arrive at the best (or optimal) solution to the problem. In some cases, this may require that a set of mathematical expressions be solved to determine the best decision. In other cases, you can use a trial-and-error method, trying various approaches and picking the one that results in the best decision. For some problems, you may wish to try all possible values for the variables in the model to arrive at the best decision; this is called *complete enumeration*. For problems that are quite complex and difficult, you may be able to use an algorithm. An *algorithm* consists of a series of steps or procedures that we repeat until we find the best solution. Regardless of the approach, the accuracy of the solution depends on the accuracy of the input data and the decision model itself.

Testing the Solution Before a solution can be analyzed and implemented, it must be tested completely. Because the solution depends on the input data and the model, both require testing. There are several ways to test input data. One is to collect additional data from a different source and use statistical tests to compare these new data with the original data. If there are significant differences, more effort is required to obtain accurate input data. If the data are accurate but the results are inconsistent with the problem, the model itself may not be appropriate. In this case, the model should be checked to make sure that it is logical and represents the real situation.

Step 3: Interpretation and Sensitivity Analysis
Assuming that the formulation is correct and has been successfully implemented and solved, how does a manager use the results? Here again, the decision maker's expertise is called upon because it is up to him or her to recognize the implications of the presented results. We discuss this step in two parts: (1) analyzing the results and sensitivity analysis and (2) implementing the results.

Analyzing the Results and Sensitivity Analysis Analyzing the results starts with determining the implications of the solution. In most cases, a solution to a problem will result in some kind of action or change in the way an organization is operating. The implications of these actions or changes must be determined and analyzed before the results are implemented.

Because a model is only an approximation of reality, the sensitivity of the solution to changes in the model and input data is an important part of analyzing the results. This type of analysis is called *sensitivity*, *post-optimality*, or *what-if analysis*. *Sensitivity analysis* is used to determine how much the solution will change if there are changes in the model or the input data. When the optimal solution is very sensitive to changes in the input data and the model specifications, additional testing must be performed to make sure the model and input data are accurate and valid.

The importance of sensitivity analysis cannot be overemphasized. Because input data may not always be accurate or model assumptions may not be completely appropriate, sensitivity analysis can become an important part of decision modeling.

Implementing the Results The final part of interpretation is to *implement* the results. This can be much more difficult than one might imagine. Even if the optimal solution will result in millions of dollars in additional profits, if managers resist the new solution, the model is of no value. Experience has shown that numerous decision modeling teams have failed in their efforts because they have failed to implement a good, workable solution properly.

After the solution has been implemented, it should be closely monitored. Over time, there may be numerous changes that call for modifications of the original solution. A changing economy, fluctuating demand, and model enhancements requested by managers and decision makers are examples of changes that might require an analysis to be modified.

1.4 Spreadsheet Example of a Decision Model: Tax Computation

Now that we have discussed what a decision model is, let us develop a simple model for a real-world situation we all face each year: paying taxes. Sue and Robert Miller, a newly married couple, will be filing a joint tax return for the first time this year. Because both work as independent contractors (Sue is an interior decorator, and Rob is a painter), their projected income is subject to some variability. However, because their earnings are not taxed at the source, they know that they have to pay estimated income taxes on a quarterly basis, based on their estimated taxable income for the year. To help calculate this tax, the Millers would like to set up a spreadsheet-based decision model. Assume that they have the following information available:

- Their only source of income is from their jobs.
- They would like to put away 7% of their total income in a retirement account, up to a maximum of $8,000. Any amount they put in that account can be deducted from their total income for tax purposes.
- They are entitled to a personal exemption of $4,050 each. This means that they can deduct $8,100 (= 2 × $4,050) from their total income for tax purposes.
- The standard deduction for married couples filing taxes jointly this year is $12,700. This means that $12,700 of their income is free from any taxes and can be deducted from their total income.
- They do not anticipate having any other deductions from their income for tax purposes.
- The tax brackets for this year are 10% for the first $18,650 of taxable income, 15% between $18,651 and $75,900, and 25% between $75,901 and $153,100. The Millers don't believe that tax brackets beyond $153,100 are relevant for them this year.

EXCEL NOTES

- The Companion Website for this book, at *degruyter.com/view/product/486941*, contains the Excel file for each sample problem discussed here. The relevant file/sheet name is shown below the title of the corresponding figure in this book.
- In each of our Excel layouts, for clarity, we color code the cells as follows:
  - Variable input cells, in which we enter specific values for the variables in the problem, are shaded yellow.
  - Output cells, which show the results of our analysis, are shaded green.
- We have used callouts to annotate the screenshots in this book to highlight important issues in the decision model.
- Wherever necessary, many of these callouts are also included as comments in the Excel files themselves, making it easier for you to understand the logic behind each model.

Figure 1.2 shows the formulas that we can use to develop a decision model for the Millers. Just as we have done for this Excel model (and all other models in this book), we strongly recommend that you get in the habit of using descriptive titles, labels, and comments in any decision model you create. The reason for this is very simple: In many real-world settings, decision models that you create are likely to be passed on to others. In such cases, the use of comments will help them understand your thought process. Perhaps an appropriate question you should always ask yourself is, "Will I understand this model a year or two after I first write it?" If appropriate labels and comments are included in the model, the answer should always be yes.

In Figure 1.2, the known problem parameter values (i.e., constants) are shown in the box labeled Known Parameters. Rather than use these known constant values directly in the formulas, we recommend that you develop the habit of entering each known value into a cell and then using that cell reference in the formulas. In addition to being more "elegant," this way of modeling has the advantage of making any future changes to these values easy. *This is one of the most important Excel practices to implement!* Many expensive spreadsheet mistakes are made in companies because numbers are hard-coded into formulas in multiple places throughout spreadsheets—and these spreadsheets originally may have been developed by managers long retired from the firm. When formulas reference easily identifiable cells for all their parameters, users can be confident that parameter changes need to be made only once and that all formulas will be correctly updated.

Cells B13 and B14 denote the only two variable data entries in this decision model: Sue's and Rob's estimated incomes for this year. When we enter values for these two variables, the results are computed in cells B17:B26 and presented in the box labeled "Tax Computation."

Spreadsheet Example of a Decision Model: Tax Computation — 13

	A	B	C	D	E
1	**Millers' Tax Computation**		This box shows		
2			all the known		
3	Known Parameters		input parameter		
4	Retirement Savings %	0.07	values.		
5	Maximum savings	8000			
6	Personal exemption	4050	per person		
7	Standard deduction	12700			
8	Tax rates	0.1	1	to	18650
9		0.15	18651	to	75900
10		0.25	75901	to	153100
11					
12	Variables				
13	Sue's estimated income		This box shows the		
14	Rob's estimated income		two input variables.		
15					
16	Tax Computation				
17	Total income	=B13+B14	Minimun of (7% of		
18	Retirement savings	=MIN(B4*B17,B5)	total income $8,000)		
19	Personal exemptions	=2*B6			
20	Standard deduction	=B7	Maximum of		
21	Taxable income	=MAX(0,B17-SUM(B18:B20))	(0, taxable income)		
22	Tax @ 10% rate	=B8*MIN(B21,E8)			
23	Tax @ 15% rate	=IF(B21>E8,B9*(MIN(B21,E9)-E8),0)	10% tax up to $18,650		
24	Tax @ 25% rate	=IF(B21>E9,B10*(MIN(B21,E10)-E9),0)			
25	Total tax	=SUM(B22:B24)			
26	Estimated tax per quarter	=B25/4			

25% tax between $75,901 and $153,100. This tax is calculated only if taxable income exceeds $75,900.

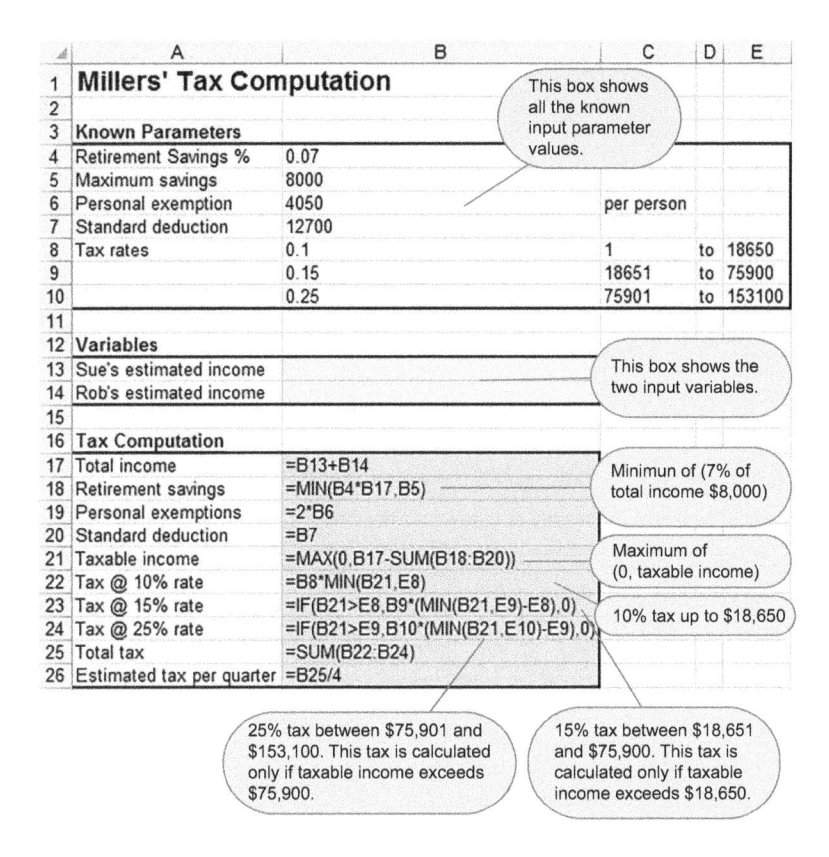

15% tax between $18,651 and $75,900. This tax is calculated only if taxable income exceeds $18,650.

Figure 1.2: Formula View of Excel Layout for the Millers' Tax Computation

File: Figure 1.2.xlsx; Sheet: Figure 1.2

Cell B17 shows the total income. The MIN function is used in cell B18 to specify the tax-deductible retirement contribution as the smaller value of 7% of total income and $8,000. Cells B19 and B20 set the personal exemptions and the standard deduction, respectively. The net taxable income is shown in cell B21, and the MAX function is used here to ensure that this amount is never below zero. The taxes payable at the 10%, 15%, and 25% rates are then calculated in cells B22, B23, and B24, respectively. In each of these cells, the MIN function is used to ensure that only the incremental taxable income is taxed at a given rate. (For example, in cell B23, only the portion of taxable income above $18,650 is taxed at the 15% rate, up to an upper limit of $75,900.) The IF function is used in cells B23 and B24 to check whether the taxable income exceeds the lower limit for the 15% and 25% tax rates, respectively. If the taxable income does not exceed the relevant lower limit, the IF function sets the tax payable at that rate to zero. Finally, the total tax payable is computed in cell B25, and the estimated quarterly tax is computed in cell B26.

EXCEL EXTRA

Cell Comments

The most useful spreadsheets are self-documenting. You can create descriptive callout boxes similar to those describing certain cells in Figure 1.2 by using the built-in Excel feature that allows you to document cell entries with *comment boxes*. Any cell can have an associated comment box. Similar to how messages appear in Word or Excel when you place the mouse over certain command buttons, your cell comment will appear when the user places the mouse over that particular cell. A small red triangle in the upper right-hand side of the cell indicates that the cell contains a comment. Alternatively, you can set the comment box to be displayed at all times. Comment boxes can be resized by editing the comment and dragging one of the eight squares on the outside of the box as desired. Font size and comment contents can also be changed by editing the comment.

- To create a comment: Right click on the cell and select Insert Comment [then enter text]

- To change or resize: Right click on the cell and select Edit Commen

- To show constantly: Right click on the cell and select Show/Hide Comments

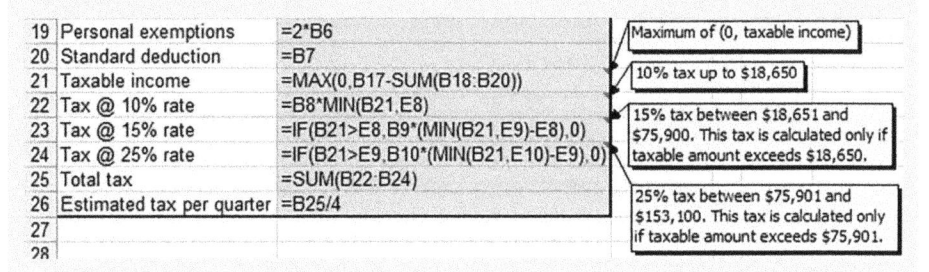

19	Personal exemptions	=2*B6
20	Standard deduction	=B7
21	Taxable income	=MAX(0,B17-SUM(B18:B20))
22	Tax @ 10% rate	=B8*MIN(B21,E8)
23	Tax @ 15% rate	=IF(B21>E8,B9*(MIN(B21,E9)-E8),0)
24	Tax @ 25% rate	=IF(B21>E9,B10*(MIN(B21,E10)-E9),0)
25	Total tax	=SUM(B22:B24)
26	Estimated tax per quarter	=B25/4
27		
28		

Callouts:
- Maximum of (0, taxable income)
- 10% tax up to $18,650
- 15% tax between $18,651 and $75,900. This tax is calculated only if taxable amount exceeds $18,650.
- 25% tax between $75,901 and $153,100. This tax is calculated only if taxable amount exceeds $75,901.

- To remove "Show Comment:" Right click on the cell and select Hide Comment

- To remove the comment completely: Right click on the cell and select Delete Comment

- Three options for printing comments:

  Click Page Layout|Print Titles|Sheet|Comments

  (1) (None)—none will be printed (default)

  (2) At end of sheet—all comments will be printed

  (3) As displayed on sheet—only comments set to "show" are printed on the spreadsheet

---

Now that we have developed this decision model, how can the Millers actually use it? Suppose Sue estimates her income this year at $65,000, and Rob estimates his at $60,000. We enter these values into cells B13 and B14, respectively. The decision model immediately lets us know that the Millers have a taxable income of $96,200 and that they should pay estimated taxes of $3,881.88 each quarter. These input values, and the resulting computations, are shown in Figure 1.3. We can use this decision model in a similar fashion with any other estimated income values for Sue and Rob.

	A	B	C	D	E
1	**Millers' Tax Computation**				
2					
3	Known Parameters				
4	Retirement Savings %	7.0%			
5	Maximum savings	$8,000			
6	Personal exemption	$4,050	per person		
7	Standard deduction	$12,700			
8	Tax rates	10.0%	$1	to	$18,650
9		15.0%	$18,651	to	$75,900
10		25.0%	$75,901	to	$153,100
11					
12	Variables				
13	Sue's estimated income	$65,000.00			
14	Rob's estimated income	$60,000.00			
15					
16	Tax Computation				
17	Total income	$125,000.00			
18	Retirement savings	$8,000.00			
19	Personal exemptions	$8,100.00			
20	Standard deduction	$12,700.00			
21	Taxable income	$96,200.00			
22	Tax @ 10% rate	$1,865.00			
23	Tax @ 15% rate	$8,587.50			
24	Tax @ 25% rate	$5,075.00			
25	Total tax	$15,527.50			
26	Estimated tax per quarter	$3,881.88			

Annotations: Estimated income (B13:B14). Total income of $125,000 has been reduced to taxable income of only $96,200. The Millers should pay $3881.88 in estimated taxes each quarter.

Figure 1.3: Excel Decision Model for the Millers' Tax Computation

File: Figure 1.2.xlsx; Sheet: Figure 1.3

Decision Modeling In Action

Using Decision Modeling to Combat Spread of Hepatitis B Virus in the United States and China

Hepatitis B is a vaccine-preventable viral disease that is a major public health problem, particularly among Asian populations. Left untreated, it can lead to death from cirrhosis and liver cancer. More than 350 million people are chronically infected with the hepatitis B virus (HBV) worldwide. In the United States (US), although about 10% of Asian and Pacific Islanders are chronically infected, about two-thirds of them are unaware of their infection. In China, HBV infection is a leading cause of death.

During several years of work conducted at the Asian Liver Center at Stanford University, the authors used combinations of decision modeling techniques to analyze the cost effectiveness of various intervention schemes to combat the spread of the disease in the US and China. The results of these analyses have helped change US public health policy on hepatitis B screening, and they have helped encourage China to enact legislation to provide free vaccination for millions of children.

> These policies are an important step in eliminating health disparities and ensuring that millions of people can now receive the hepatitis B vaccination they need. The Global Health Coordinator of the Asian Liver Center states that this research "has been incredibly important to accelerating policy changes to improve health related to HBV."
>
> **Source:** Based on D. W. Hutton, M. L. Brandeau, and S. K. So. "Doing Good with Good OR: Supporting Cost-Effective Hepatitis B Interventions," *Interfaces* 41, 3 (May-June 2011): 289–300.

Observe that the decision model we have developed for the Millers' example does not optimize the decision in any way. That is, the model simply computes the estimated taxes for a given income level. It does not, for example, determine whether these taxes can be reduced in some way through better tax planning. Later in this book, we discuss decision models that not only help compute the implications of a specified decision, but also help identify the optimal decision, based on some objective or goal.

1.5 Spreadsheet Example of a Decision Model: Break-Even Analysis

Let's now develop another decision model—this one to compute the total profit for a firm, as well as the associated break-even point. We know that profit is simply the difference between revenue and expense. In most cases, we can express revenue as the selling price per unit multiplied by the number of units sold. Likewise, we can express expense as the sum of the total fixed and variable costs. In turn, the total variable cost is the variable cost per unit multiplied by the number of units sold. Thus, we can express profit using the following mathematical expression:

$$\text{Profit} = (\text{Selling price per unit}) \times (\text{Number of units}) - (\text{Fixed cost}) \\ - (\text{Variable cost per unit}) \times (\text{Number of units}) \qquad (1\text{--}1)$$

Let's use Bill Pritchett's clock repair shop to demonstrate the creation of a decision model to calculate profit and the associated break-even point. Bill's company, Pritchett's Precious Time Pieces, buys, sells, and repairs old clocks and clock parts. Bill sells rebuilt springs for a unit price of $10. The fixed cost of the equipment to build the springs is $1,000. The variable cost per unit is $5 for spring material. If we represent the number of springs (units) sold as the variable X, we can restate the profit as follows:

$$\text{Profit} = \$10X - \$1{,}000 - \$5X$$

Figure 1.4 shows the formulas used in developing the decision model for Bill Pritchett's example. Cells B4, B5, and B6 show the known problem parameter values—namely, revenue per unit, fixed cost, and variable cost per unit, respectively. Cell B9 is the lone variable in the model, and it represents the number of units sold (i.e., X). Using these entries, the total revenue, total variable cost, total cost, and profit are computed in cells B12, B14, B15, and B16, respectively. For example, if we enter a value of 1,000 units for X in cell B9, the profit is calculated as $4,000 in cell B16, as shown in Figure 1.5.

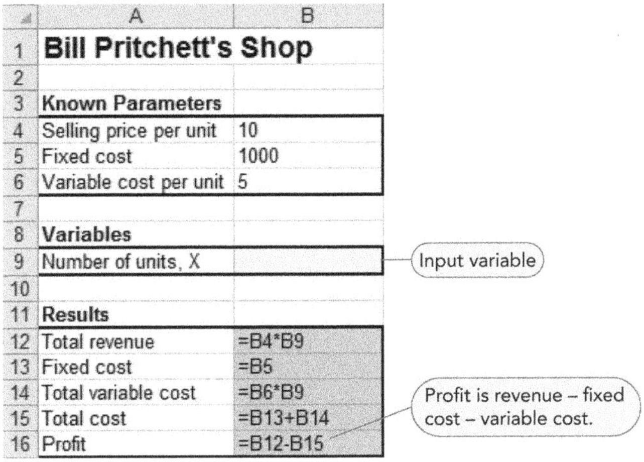

	A	B
1	**Bill Pritchett's Shop**	
2		
3	**Known Parameters**	
4	Selling price per unit	10
5	Fixed cost	1000
6	Variable cost per unit	5
7		
8	**Variables**	
9	Number of units, X	← Input variable
10		
11	**Results**	
12	Total revenue	=B4*B9
13	Fixed cost	=B5
14	Total variable cost	=B6*B9
15	Total cost	=B13+B14
16	Profit	=B12-B15

Profit is revenue − fixed cost − variable cost.

Figure 1.4: Formula View of Excel Layout for Pritchett's Precious Time Pieces

File: Figure 1.4.xlsx; Sheet: Figure 1.4

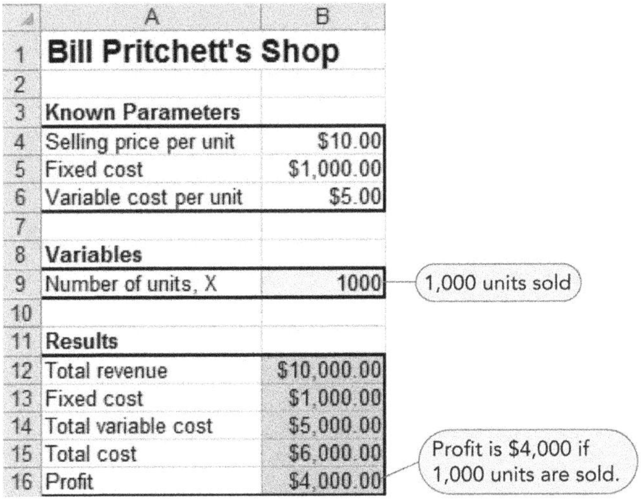

	A	B
1	**Bill Pritchett's Shop**	
2		
3	**Known Parameters**	
4	Selling price per unit	$10.00
5	Fixed cost	$1,000.00
6	Variable cost per unit	$5.00
7		
8	**Variables**	
9	Number of units, X	1000 ← 1,000 units sold
10		
11	**Results**	
12	Total revenue	$10,000.00
13	Fixed cost	$1,000.00
14	Total variable cost	$5,000.00
15	Total cost	$6,000.00
16	Profit	$4,000.00

Profit is $4,000 if 1,000 units are sold.

Figure 1.5: Excel Decision Model for Pritchett's Precious Time Pieces

File: Figure 1.4.xlsx; Sheet: Figure 1.5

In addition to computing the profit, decision makers are often interested in the break-even point (BEP). The BEP is the number of units sold that will result in total revenue equaling total costs (i.e., profit is $0). We can determine the BEP analytically by setting profit equal to $0 and solving for X in Bill Pritchett's profit expression. That is

$$0 = \text{(Selling price per unit)} \times \text{(Number of units)} - \text{(Fixed cost)} \\ - \text{(Variable cost per unit)} \times \text{(Number of units)}$$

which can be mathematically rewritten as

$$\text{Break-even point (BEP)} = \text{Fixed cost}/(\text{Selling price per unit} \\ - \text{Variable cost per unit}) \quad (1\text{--}2)$$

For Bill Pritchett's example, we can compute the BEP as $1,000/($10 - $5) = 200 springs. The BEP in dollars (which we denote as $BEP_\$$) can then be computed as

$$BEP_\$ = \text{Fixed cost} + \text{Variable costs} \times BEP \quad (1\text{--}3)$$

For Bill Pritchett's example, we can compute $BEP_\$$ as $1,000 + $5 × 200 = $2,000.

Using Goal Seek to Find the Break-Even Point

While the preceding analytical computations for BEP and $BEP_\$$ are fairly simple, an advantage of using computer-based models is that many of these results can be calculated automatically. For example, we can use a procedure in Excel called Goal Seek to calculate the BEP and $BEP_\$$ values in the decision model shown in Figure 1.5. The Goal Seek procedure allows us to specify a desired value for a *target cell*. This target cell should contain a formula that involves a different cell, called the *changing cell*. Once we specify the target cell, its desired value, and the changing cell in Goal Seek, the procedure automatically manipulates the changing cell value to try and make the target cell achieve its desired value.

In our case, we want to manipulate the value of the number of units X (in cell B9 of Figure 1.5) such that the profit (in cell B16 of Figure 1.5) takes on a value of zero. That is, cell B16 is the target cell, its desired value is zero, and cell B9 is the changing cell. Observe that the formula of profit in cell B16 is a function of the value of X in cell B9 (see Figure 1.4).

Figure 1.6 shows how the Goal Seek procedure is implemented in Excel. As shown in Figure 1.6 (a), we invoke Goal Seek by clicking the Data tab on Excel's main menu bar, followed by the What-If Analysis button (found in the Data Tools group within the Data tab), and then finally on Goal Seek. The window shown in Figure 1.6 (b) is displayed. We specify cell B16 in the Set cell box, a desired value of zero for this cell in the To value box, and cell B9 in the By changing cell box. When we now click OK, the Goal Seek Status window shown in Figure 1.6 (c) is displayed, indicating that the target of $0 profit has been achieved. Cell B9 shows the resulting BEP value of 200 units. The corresponding $BEP_\$$ value of $2,000 is shown in cell B15.

Spreadsheet Example of a Decision Model: Break-Even Analysis — 19

(a), **(b)**, **(c)** [screenshots of Excel Data tab, Goal Seek dialog, and spreadsheet for Bill Pritchett's Shop]

Annotations:
- Data tab in Excel
- Goal Seek is part of What-If Analysis in the Data Tools group.
- Cell denoting profit.
- Set profit to 0.
- Cell denoting number of units.
- Goal Seek result window
- BEP is 200 units.
- Profit target of $0 has been achieved.
- BEP$ is $2,000.

Spreadsheet contents:

	A	B
1	Bill Pritchett's Shop	
3	Known Parameters	
4	Selling price per unit	$10.00
5	Fixed cost	$1,000.00
6	Variable cost per unit	$5.00
8	Variables	
9	Number of units, X	200
11	Results	
12	Total revenue	$2,000.00
13	Fixed cost	$1,000.00
14	Total variable cost	$1,000.00
15	Total cost	$2,000.00
16	Profit	$0.00

Goal Seek dialog:
- Set cell: $B$16
- To value: 0
- By changing cell: $B$9

Goal Seek Status: Goal Seeking with Cell B16 found a solution. Target value: 0; Current value: $0.00

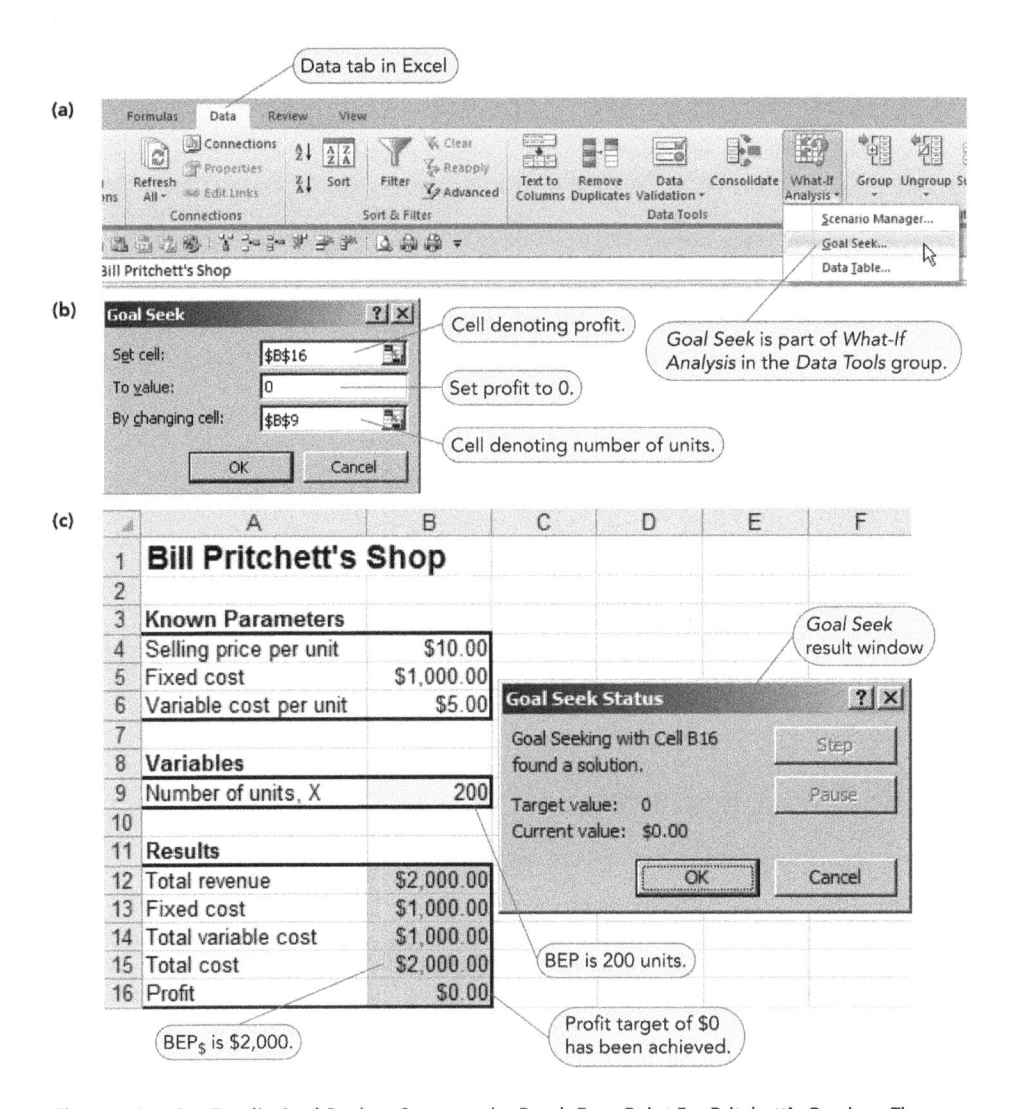

Figure 1.6: Using Excel's Goal Seek to Compute the Break-Even Point For Pritchett's Precious Time Pieces

File: Figure 1.4.xlsx; Sheet: Figure 1.6

Observe that we can use Goal Seek to compute the sales level needed to obtain any desired profit. For example, see if you can verify that in order to get a profit of $10,000, Bill Pritchett would have to sell 2,200 springs. We will use the Goal Seek procedure again in Chapter 9.

EXCEL NOTES

- Bear in mind that, for more complicated functions, if an equation has multiple roots, Goal Seek will return only one of those roots. The answer may represent the closest root to the starting point in the changing cell, so choose carefully. Try this experiment. Insert the number 5 into cell A1 and the formula =A1^2 into cell A2. Invoke Goal Seek, where the Set cell is A2, To value is 36, and By changing cell is A1. You should get an answer of 6 in cell A1. Now insert the number −3 into cell A1 and repeat the same Goal Seek procedure. You should get an answer of −6 in cell A1. If your answer was supposed to represent, for example, a nonnegative production quantity, that could be a problem!
- Goal Seek should be able to indicate if there is no solution that will give you the target value that you are seeking. Try the above experiment again by setting the target value as −49. Goal Seek should search for a short time and then return the message, "Goal Seeking with cell A2 may not have found a solution" (because no number that is squared would produce a negative number). Goal Seek will place a value from the last iteration into cell A1, but that number is meaningless and does not produce the desired result. Thus, always check the message in the Goal Seek Status box carefully.

Decision Modeling In Action

Operations Research Increases Revenues at HP

After the internet revolution, Hewlett Packard (HP) decided to change its marketing strategy and enter the online consumer sales business. This was done through the creation of an "HPDirect.com" portal that enables direct customers or retailers to buy HP products online. HP had some initial problems in the e-commerce value chain process, and the firm faced fierce competition from Dell's online portal.

To help HP increase the accuracy of predicting the number of customers who are willing to buy its products, which products will be bought, through which channels, and when, the data scientists at HP Global Analytics (GA) used mathematical programming, Bayesian modeling, regression analysis, and time-series forecasting models to develop solutions for customer acquisition, development, and retention. The operations-research-based solutions that were implemented helped increase the annual portal traffic by 2.6%, resulting in $44 million in incremental sales. In addition, average order size increased by 15%, resulting in $63 million in additional revenues and savings of $2 million through cost reduction from better inventory management.

Source: Based on S. Subramanian, D. Hill, and P. Dhore. "Hewlett Packard: Delivering Profitable Growth for HPDirect.com Using Operations Research," *Interfaces* 43, 1 (January – February 2013): 48–61.

1.6 Possible Problems in Developing Decision Models

We present the decision modeling approach as a logical and systematic means of tackling decision-making problems. Even when these steps are followed carefully, however, many difficulties can hurt the chances of implementing solutions to real-world problems. We now look at problems that can occur during each of the steps of the decision modeling approach.

Defining the Problem
In the worlds of business, government, and education, problems are, unfortunately, not easily identified. Decision analysts typically face four roadblocks in defining a problem. We use an application, inventory analysis, throughout this section as an example.

Conflicting Viewpoints Analysts often may have to consider conflicting viewpoints in defining a problem. For example, in inventory problems, financial managers usually believe that inventory is too high because inventory represents cash not available for other investments. In contrast, sales managers often believe that inventory is too low because high levels may be needed to fill unexpected orders. If analysts adopt either of these views as the problem definition, they have essentially accepted one manager's perception. They can, therefore, expect resistance from the other manager when the "solution" emerges. So, it's important to consider both points of view before stating the problem.

Impact on Other Departments Problems do not exist in isolation and are not owned by just one department of a firm. For example, inventory is closely tied with cash flows and various production problems. A change in ordering policy can affect cash flows and upset production schedules to the point that savings on inventory are exceeded by increased financial and production costs. The problem statement should therefore be as broad as possible and include inputs from all concerned departments.

Beginning Assumptions People often tend to state problems in terms of solutions. For example, the statement that inventory is too low implies a solution: that its levels should be raised. An analyst who starts off with this assumption will likely find that inventory should be raised! From an implementation perspective, a "good" solution to the right problem is much better than an "optimal" solution to the wrong problem.

Solution Outdated Even if a problem has been specified correctly at present, it can change during the development of the model. In today's rapidly changing business environment, especially with the amazing pace of technological advances, it is not unusual for problems to change virtually overnight. The analyst who presents solutions to problems that no longer exist can't expect credit for providing timely help.

Developing a Model
Even with a well-defined problem statement, a decision analyst may have to overcome hurdles while developing decision models for real-world situations. Some of these hurdles are discussed in the following sections.

Fitting the Textbook Models A manager's perception of a problem does not always match the textbook approach. For example, most textbook inventory models involve minimizing the sum of holding and ordering costs. Some managers view these costs as unimportant; instead, they see the problem in terms of cash flow, turnover, and levels of customer satisfaction. The results of a model based on holding and ordering costs are probably not acceptable to such managers.

Understanding a Model Most managers simply do not use the results of a model they do not understand. Complex problems, though, require complex models. One trade-off is to simplify assumptions to make a model easier to understand. The model loses some of its reality but gains some management acceptance. For example, a popular simplifying assumption in inventory modeling is that demand is known and constant. This allows analysts to build simple, easy-to-understand models. Demand, however, is rarely known and constant, so these models lack some reality. Introducing probability distributions provides more realism but may put comprehension beyond all but the most mathematically sophisticated managers. In such cases, one approach is for the decision analyst to start with the simple model and make sure that it is completely understood. More complex models can then be introduced slowly as managers gain more confidence in using these models.

Acquiring Input Data
Gathering the data to be used in the decision modeling approach to problem solving is often not a simple task. Frequently, the data are buried in several different databases and documents, making it very difficult for a decision analyst to gain access to the data.

Using Accounting Data One problem is that most data generated in a firm come from basic accounting reports. The accounting department collects its inventory data, for example, in terms of cash flows and turnover. But decision analysts tackling an inventory problem need to collect data on holding costs and ordering costs. If they ask for such data, they may be shocked to find that the data were simply never collected for those specified costs.

Validity of Data A lack of "good, clean data" means that whatever data are available must often be distilled and manipulated (we call it "fudging") before being used in a model. Unfortunately, the validity of the results of a model is no better than the validity of the data that go into the model. You cannot blame a manager for resisting a model's "scientific" results when he or she knows that questionable data were used as input.

Developing a Solution
An analyst may have to face two potential pitfalls while developing solutions to a decision model. These are discussed in the following sections.

Hard-To-Understand Mathematics The first concern in developing solutions is that although the mathematical models we use may be complex and powerful, they may not be completely understood. The aura of mathematics often causes managers to remain silent when they should be critical.

The Limitation of Only One Answer The second concern in developing solutions is that decision models usually give just one answer to a problem. Most managers would like to have a range of options and not be put in a take-it-or-leave-it position. A more appropriate strategy is for an analyst to present a range of choices, indicating the effect that each solution has on the objective function. This gives managers a choice, as well as information on how much it will cost to deviate from the optimal solution. It also allows problems to be viewed from a broader perspective because it means that qualitative factors can also be considered.

Testing the Solution
The results of decision modeling often take the form of predictions of how things will work in the future if certain changes are made in the present. To get a preview of how well solutions will really work, managers often are asked how good a solution looks to them. The problem is that complex models tend to give solutions that are not intuitively obvious. And such solutions tend to be rejected by managers. Then a decision analyst must work through the model and the assumptions with the manager in an effort to convince the manager of the validity of the results. In the process, the analyst must review every assumption that went into the model. If there are errors, they may be revealed during this review. In addition, the manager casts a critical eye on everything that went into the model, and if he or she can be convinced that the model is valid, there is a good chance that the solution results are also valid.

Analyzing the Results
Once a solution has been tested, the results must be analyzed in terms of how they will affect the total organization. You should be aware that even small changes in organizations are often difficult to bring about. If results suggest large changes in organizational policy, the decision analyst can expect resistance. In analyzing the results, the analyst should ascertain who must change and by how much, whether the people who must change will be better or worse off, and who has the power to direct the change.

1.7 Implementation—Not Just the Final Step

We have just presented some of the many problems that can affect the ultimate acceptance of decision modeling in practice. It should be clear now that implementation isn't just another step that takes place after the modeling process is over. Each of these steps greatly affects the chances of implementing the results of a decision model.

Even though many business decisions can be made intuitively, based on hunches and experience, there are more and more situations in which decision models can assist. Some managers, however, fear that the use of a formal analytical process will reduce their decision-making power. Others fear that it may expose some previous intuitive decisions as inadequate. Still others feel uncomfortable about having to reverse their thinking patterns with formal decision making. These managers often argue against the use of decision modeling.

Many action-oriented managers do not like the lengthy formal decision-making process and prefer to get things done quickly. They prefer "quick and dirty" techniques that can yield immediate results. However, once managers see some quick results that have a substantial payoff, the stage is set for convincing them that decision modeling is a beneficial tool.

We have known for some time that management support and user involvement are critical to the successful implementation of decision modeling processes. A Swedish study found that only 40% of projects suggested by decision analysts were ever implemented. But 70% of the modeling projects initiated by users, and fully 98% of projects suggested by top managers, were implemented.

1.8 Summary

Decision modeling is a scientific approach to decision making in practical situations faced by managers. Decision models can be broadly classified into two categories, based on the type and nature of the problem environment under consideration: (1) deterministic models and (2) probabilistic models. Deterministic models assume that all the relevant input data and parameters are known with certainty. In contrast, probabilistic models assume that some input data are not known with certainty. The decision modeling approach includes three major steps: (1) formulation, (2) solution, and (3) interpretation. It is important to note that it is common to iterate between these three steps before the final solution is obtained. Spreadsheets are commonly used to develop decision models.

In using the decision modeling approach, however, there can be potential problems, such as conflicting viewpoints, disregard of the impact of the model on other departments, outdated solutions, misunderstanding of the model, difficulty acquiring good input data, and hard-to-understand mathematics. In using decision models, implementation is not just the final step. There can be a lack of commitment to the approach and resistance to change that must be addressed.

Key Points
- Decision modeling is a scientific approach to decision making.
- Deterministic models assume that all input data are known with complete certainty.
- The most commonly used deterministic modeling technique is linear programming.
- In probabilistic models, some or all of the input data may be unknown.
- Probabilistic models use probabilities to incorporate uncertainty.
- The decision modeling process starts with data.
- Both qualitative and quantitative factors must be considered when dealing with a decision making problem.
- Spreadsheet packages can handle many decision modeling techniques.
- ExcelModules, an add-in for Excel, is included on the Companion Website for this book and helps solve decision models in Queuing (Chapter 9), Forecasting (Chapter 11), and Inventory Control (Chapter 12).
- The decision modeling process involves three steps: (1) formulation, (2) solution, and (3) interpretation and sensitivity analysis.
- It is common to iterate between the three steps of the decision modeling process.
- Formulation is the most challenging step in decision modeling, and is the process by which each aspect of a problem scenario is translated and expressed in terms of a mathematical model.
- Clearly defining the problem is a critical part of formulation.
- Types of models include physical, scale, analog, schematic, and mathematical.
- A variable is a measurable quantity that is subject to change.
- A decision variable is a variable whose value can be controlled.
- A parameter is an input to a decision model that usually has a known value.
- Garbage in, garbage out means that improper data will result in misleading results.
- In the solution step of decision modeling, we solve the mathematical expressions in the model's formulation.
- An algorithm is a series of steps that are repeated until the best solution is found.
- The quality of the input data and the accuracy of the model's formulation determine the accuracy of the solution.
- Analysts test the data and model assumptions before analyzing and implementing the results.
- Sensitivity analysis determines how the solution will change with different input data values and/or model assumptions.
- The solution should be closely monitored even after implementation.
- Wherever possible, titles, labels, and comments should be included in an Excel model to make them easier to understand.
- In Excel, rather than including constants directly in formulas, it is preferable to make them cell references to allow for easy changes in future to the model.

- Excel's MAX, MIN, and IF functions commonly appear in decision models.
- The break-even point results in a profit of $0.
- Excel's Goal Seek can be used to automatically find the break-even point.
- Many real-world problems are not easily identifiable or definable.
- A problem needs to be examined from several viewpoints.
- All inputs to a problem must be considered.
- Managers will typically not use the results of a decision model they do not understand.
- The results of a model are only as good as the input data used.
- Two potential problems in developing and implementing a solution are: (1) hard-to-understand mathematics, and (2) having only one answer.
- Model assumptions should be reviewed when evaluating the validity of a model.
- Management support and user involvement are important in decision modeling.

Glossary

Break-Even Point (BEP) The number of units sold that will result in total revenue equaling total costs (i.e., profit is $0).

Break-Even Point in Dollars ($BEP_\$$) The sum of fixed and total variable cost if the number of units sold equals the break-even point.

Business Analytics Process by which data are transformed into information that can be used for decision making.

Decision Analyst An individual who is responsible for developing a decision model.

Decision Modeling A scientific approach that uses quantitative (mathematical) techniques as a tool in managerial decision making; also known as *quantitative analysis*, *management science*, and *operations research*.

Deterministic Model A model that assumes all the relevant input data and parameters are known with certainty.

Formulation The process by which each aspect of a problem scenario is translated and expressed in terms of a mathematical model.

Goal Seek A feature in Excel that allows users to specify a goal or target for a specific cell and automatically manipulate another cell to achieve that target.

Input Data Data that are used in a model in arriving at the final solution.

Model A representation (usually mathematical) of a practical problem scenario or environment.

Probabilistic Model A model that assumes some input data are not known with certainty.

Problem Parameter A measurable quantity inherent in a problem. It typically has a fixed and known value (i.e., a constant).

Sensitivity Analysis A process that involves determining how sensitive a solution is to changes in the formulation of a problem.

Variable A measurable quantity that may vary or that is subject to change.

1.9 Exercises

Discussion Questions

1-1. Define *decision modeling*. Identify some organizations that support the use of the scientific approach.
1-2. What is the difference between deterministic and probabilistic models? Give several examples of each type of model.
1-3. What are the differences between quantitative and qualitative factors that may be present in a decision model?
1-4. Why might it be difficult to quantify some qualitative factors in developing decision models?
1-5. What steps are involved in the decision modeling process? Give several examples of this process.
1-6. Why is it important to have an iterative process between the steps of the decision modeling approach?
1-7. In what ways do you think that corporations or governments could abuse their access to big data? What types of safeguards can governments, corporations, and individuals implement to try to mitigate these risks?
1-8. What types of models are mentioned in this chapter? Give examples of each.
1-9. List some sources of input data.
1-10. Define *decision variable*. Give some examples of variables in a decision model.
1-11. What is a problem parameter? Give some examples of parameters in a decision model.
1-12. List some advantages of using spreadsheets for decision modeling.
1-13. What is implementation, and why is it important?
1-14. Describe the use of sensitivity analysis, or post-optimality analysis, in analyzing the results of decision models.
1-15. Managers are quick to claim that decision modelers talk to them in a jargon that does not sound like English. List four terms that might not be understood by a manager. Then explain in nontechnical terms what each means.
1-16. Why do you think many decision analysts don't like to participate in the implementation process? What could be done to change this attitude?
1-17. Should people who will be using the results of a new modeling approach become involved in the technical aspects of the problem-solving procedure?
1-18. C. W. Churchman once said that "mathematics tends to lull the unsuspecting into believing that he who thinks elaborately thinks well." Do you think that the best decision models are the ones that are most elaborate and complex mathematically? Why?

Problems

1–19. A website has a fixed cost of $15,000 per day. The revenue is $0.06 each time the website is accessed. The variable cost of responding to each hit is $0.02.
   (a) How many times must this website be accessed each day to break even?
   (b) What is the break-even point, in dollars?

1–20. An electronics firm is currently manufacturing an item that has a variable cost of $0.60 per unit and selling price of $1.10 per unit. Fixed costs are $15,500. Current volume is 32,000 units. The firm can improve the product quality substantially by adding a new piece of equipment at an additional fixed cost of $8,000. Variable cost would increase to $0.70, but volume is expected to jump to 50,000 units due to the higher quality of the product.
   (a) Should the company buy the new equipment?
   (b) Compute the profit with the current equipment and the expected profit with the new equipment.

1–21. A manufacturer is evaluating options regarding his production equipment. He is trying to decide whether he should refurbish his old equipment for $70,000, make major modifications to the production line for $135,000, or purchase new equipment for $230,000. The product sells for $10, but the variable costs to make the product are expected to vary widely, depending on the decision to be made regarding the equipment. If the manufacturer refurbishes, the variable costs will be $7.20 per unit. If the firm modifies or purchases new equipment, the variable costs are expected to be $5.25 and $4.75, respectively.
   (a) Which alternative should the manufacturer choose if the demand is expected to be between 30,000 and 40,000 units?
   (b) What will be the manufacturer's profit if the demand is 38,000 units?

1–22. St. Joseph's School has 1,200 students, each of whom pays $8,000 per year to attend. In addition to revenues from tuition, the school receives an appropriation from the church to sustain its activity. The budget for the upcoming year is $15 million, and the church appropriation will be $4.8 million. By how much will the school have to raise tuition per student to keep from having a shortfall in the upcoming year?

1–23. Refer to Problem 1–22. Sensing resistance to the idea of raising tuition from members of St. Joseph's Church, a board member suggested that the 960 children of church members could pay $8,000 as usual. Children of nonmembers would pay more. What would the nonmember tuition per year be if St. Joseph's wanted to continue to plan for a $15 million budget?

1–24. Refer to Problems 1–22 and 1–23. Another board member believes that if church members pay $8,000 in tuition, the most St. Joseph's can increase nonmember tuition is $1,000 per year. She suggests that another solution might be to cap nonmember tuition at $9,000 and attempt to recruit more nonmember

1-25. students to make up the shortfall. Under this plan, how many new nonmember students will need to be recruited?

1-25. Great Lakes Automotive is considering producing, in-house, a gear assembly that it currently purchases from Delta Supply for $6 per unit. Great Lakes estimates that if it chooses to manufacture the gear assembly, it will cost $23,000 to set up the process and then $3.82 per unit for labor and materials. At what volume would these options cost Great Lakes the same amount of money?

1-26. A start-up publishing company estimates that the fixed costs of its first major project will be $190,000, the variable cost will be $18, and the selling price per book will be $34.
   (a) How many books must be sold for this project to break even?
   (b) Suppose the publishers wish to take a total of $40,000 in salary for this project. How many books must be sold to break even, and what is the break-even point, in dollars?

1-27. The electronics firm in Problem 1-20 is now considering purchasing the new equipment and increasing the selling price of its product to $1.20 per unit. Even with the price increase, the new volume is expected to be 50,000 units. Under these circumstances, should the company purchase the new equipment and increase the selling price?

1-28. A distributor of prewashed shredded lettuce is opening a new plant and considering whether to use a mechanized or manual process to prepare the product. The manual process will have a fixed cost of $43,400 per month and a variable cost of $1.80 per 5-pound bag. The mechanized process would have a fixed cost of $84,600 per month and a variable cost of $1.30 per bag. The company expects to sell each bag of shredded lettuce for $2.50.
   (a) Find the break-even point for each process.
   (b) What is the monthly profit or loss if the company chooses the manual process and sells 70,000 bags per month?

1-29. A fabrication company must replace its widget machine and is evaluating the capabilities of two available machines. Machine A would cost the company $75,000 in fixed costs for the first year. Each widget produced using Machine A would have a variable cost of $16. Machine B would have a first-year fixed cost of $62,000, and widgets made on this machine would have a variable cost of $20. Machine A would have the capacity to make 18,000 widgets per year, approximately double the capacity for Machine B.
   (a) If widgets sell for $28 each, find the break-even point for each machine. Consider first-year costs only.
   (b) If the fabrication company estimates a demand of 6,500 units in the next year, which machine should be selected?
   (c) At what level of production do the two production machines cost the same?

1-30. Bismarck Manufacturing intends to increase capacity through the addition of new equipment. Two vendors have presented proposals. The fixed cost for proposal A is $65,000, and for proposal B, $34,000. The variable cost for A is $10, and for B, $14. The revenue generated by each unit is $18.
   (a) What is the break-even point for each proposal?
   (b) If the expected volume is 8,300 units, which alternative should be chosen?

1-31. Jianli Hu, regional manager of Drones, Drones, Drones, wishes to have a model to evaluate the profit impact of various pricing strategies for the firm's newest product, the Drone3000. Monthly fixed costs for the Drone3000 are $60,000. The variable cost per unit is $50.00. Jianli's marketing manager believes that the following monthly demand curve represents the product: $D = 8,000 - 40P$, where D is the monthly demand, and P is the sales price.
   (a) Set up an Excel model, similar to Bill Pritchett's clock repair shop in Figure 1.4, to compute monthly profit. Here the sales price will be the decision variable, and quantity produced will be a function of sales price. (Designate the quantity as one of the "Results.")
   (b) What is the monthly profit for a sales price of $100?
   (c) Try a few different values for the price. Does it appear that the current price of $100 is too high or too low?
   (d) Use Goal Seek to find the price that would lead to a monthly profit of $161,000.

1-32. (a) Modify the Millers' Tax Computation program in Figure 1.2 to include the next higher tax bracket: 28% for earnings between $153,101 and $233,350.
   (b) Suppose that Sue's estimated income is now $120,000, and Rob's is $80,200. What will be their new estimated tax per quarter?

1-33. (a) Modify the Millers' Tax Computation program in Figure 1.2 to include a tax deduction for educator expenses.
   (b) Next modify the program to account for a growing family. In particular, instead of having two personal exemptions hard-coded in the Tax Computation formula for "Personal exemptions," create a parameter for "Number of exemptions." Refer to that parameter in the Tax Computation formula for "Personal exemptions."
   (c) Suppose Rob has educator expenses of $200, and the couple now has one child. Compute their updated estimated tax per quarter.

1-34. Create an Excel model to provide the answer for Problem 1–19.

1-35. Suppliers frequently provide quantity discounts to customers who place large orders. An *all-units* quantity discount applies a discount to all units purchased once the applicable price breaks have been reached. Consider the following all-units quantity discount schedule:

Size of Order	Price per Unit
0–499 units	$40.00
500–1199 units	$38.00
≥ 1200 units	$35.00

(a) Using IF functions, build an Excel model that returns the price per unit and the total purchase amount for any supplied order size.

(b) Modify your model from part (a) to find the product price using the VLOOKUP function.

1–36. Suppliers frequently provide quantity discounts to customers who place large orders. An *incremental* quantity discount provides a discount to all units purchased beyond the applicable price breaks, but units purchased before the price breaks still pay their respective higher prices. Consider the following incremental quantity discount schedule:

Size of Order	Price per Unit
0–400 units	$40.00
401–1200 units	$40.00 for the first 400, and $38.00 after that
≥ 1201 units	$40.00 for the first 400, $38.00 for the next 800, and $30.00 for any purchased beyond 1200

Build an Excel model that returns the total purchase amount and the average price per unit for any supplied order size.

1–37. Consider a machine that fills bottles with beer. Output is known to be normally distributed with a standard deviation σ of 0.2 ounces. The bottle labels state that the bottles contain 10 ounces of beer. (Thus, consider 10 to be the lower specification limit, or LSL.) Management can calibrate the machine to fill each bottle with a specified mean μ amount of beer. Management wants to keep μ relatively close to the LSL so that the company does not spend too much money filling bottles with extra beer. At the same time, management hopes to exceed the LSL most of the time so that customers are not shortchanged and so that the company does not find itself in legal trouble. Using the standard normal distribution, a Z-value can be computed to indicate the number of standard deviations that the LSL is below the mean: $Z = (LSL - \mu)/\sigma$. This will be a negative value. Using Excel, the probability of output being less than the LSL is then =NORMSDIST(Z).

(a) Create an Excel model to calculate the probability of output being below the lower specification limit for any given value of μ.

(b) What is the probability of output being below the LSL for $\mu = 10.1$ ounces?

(c) Use Goal Seek to find the value of μ that will cause output to fall below the LSL only 5% of the time.

1–38. Download the spreadsheet for Bill Pritchett's shop in Figure 1.5.

(a) Using Goal Seek, how many units must be sold to earn a profit of $18,000?

(b) Suppose that Bill believes he can sell up to 1800 units at the $10.00 price, but he wants to earn $10,000. He believes that he can make some adjustments to his process to lower his variable cost. Using Goal Seek, determine what the new variable cost per unit needs to be in order to earn $10,000 by selling 1800 units.

Chapter 2
Linear Programming Models: Graphical and Computer Methods

Have you ever wondered how to allocate your time during the week to accomplish all of your goals and still have some fun? Have you wondered how to spend your monthly income in the best way to satisfy your goals and needs without running out of money? Have you wondered which items to pack for your international trip while keeping the weight of your suitcase below the 50-pound maximum? These questions and many others could be answered by using a technique called *linear programming*.

Beginning with this chapter and continuing through Chapter 6, we will show numerous examples where linear programs can help companies make great decisions. Writing a linear program has a lot of similarities with high school algebra, where we are given a word problem that we convert to a mathematical expression that hopefully has a solution. A linear program takes several (perhaps thousands) of such expressions and combines them into a single mathematical problem. We can then place those expressions into Excel, quickly set up the model parameters, press the Solve button, and, in an instant, have what is guaranteed to be the very best decision for the problem we have formulated. Excel can often find that answer almost instantaneously in what would take a human minutes, hours, or weeks to solve by hand. In essence, a linear program examines an uncountable (essentially infinite) number of possible solutions and returns the very best one. Linear programming is truly one of the most powerful decision tools available.

We begin by defining linear programming and describing its properties and assumptions. Next, we describe how to formulate a typical linear programming problem known as a *product mix problem*. Then we illustrate how to solve a two-variable problem by hand, using the *graphical method*. While managers would seldom solve a linear program by hand in practice, the study of the graphical approach provides significant insight into the properties of these models and how computers solve them. After providing an example of a cost-minimization *blending problem*, we move on to discuss four special situations that arise with linear programs: *redundant constraints, infeasibility, alternate optimal solutions,* and *unbounded solutions.* Next, we illustrate how to solve linear programming using Excel and its built-in solution tools called Solver. The process basically involves entering relevant data into the spreadsheet in an organized fashion and then clicking on appropriate parts of dialog boxes. We end the chapter with a very brief description of the standard solution processes that computers utilize.

Chapter Objectives

After completing this chapter, readers will be able to:
1. Understand the basic assumptions and properties of linear programming (LP).
2. Use graphical procedures to solve LP problems with only two variables to understand how LP problems are solved.
3. Understand special situations, such as redundancy, infeasibility, unboundedness, and alternate optimal solutions in LP problems.
4. Understand how to set up LP problems on a spreadsheet and solve them using Excel's Solver.

2.1 Introduction

Management decisions in many organizations involve trying to make the most effective use of resources. Resources typically include machinery, labor, money, time, warehouse space, and raw materials. These resources can be used to manufacture products (e.g., computers, automobiles, furniture, clothing) or provide services (e.g., package delivery, health services, advertising policies, investment decisions).

In all resource allocation situations, the manager must sift through several thousand decision choices or alternatives to identify the best, or optimal, choice. The most widely used decision modeling technique designed to help managers in this process is called mathematical programming. The term *mathematical programming* is somewhat misleading because this modeling technique requires no advanced mathematical ability (it uses basic algebra) and has nothing whatsoever to do with computer software programming! In the world of decision modeling, *programming* refers to setting up and solving a problem mathematically.

Within the broad topic of mathematical programming, the most widely used modeling technique designed to help managers in planning and decision making is linear programming (LP). We devote this and the next two chapters to illustrating how, why, and where LP works. Then, in Chapter 5, we explore several special LP models called *network flow problems*. We follow that with a discussion of a few other mathematical programming techniques (i.e., integer programming, goal programming, and nonlinear programming) in Chapter 6.

When developing LP-based decision models (and other mathematical programming), we assume that all the relevant input data and parameters are known with certainty. For this reason, these types of decision modeling techniques are classified as *deterministic* models.

Computers, of course, have played an important role in the advancement and use of LP. Real-world LP problems are too cumbersome to solve by hand or with a calculator, and computers have become an integral part of setting up and solving LP models in today's business environments. As noted in Chapter 1, over the past decade, spreadsheet packages such as Microsoft Excel have become increasingly capable of handling many of the decision modeling techniques (including LP and other mathematical programming models) that are commonly encountered in practical situations. So, throughout the chapters on mathematical programming techniques, we discuss the role and use of Microsoft Excel in setting up and solving these models.

2.2 Developing a Linear Programming Model

Since the mid-twentieth century, LP has been applied extensively to medical, transportation, operations, financial, marketing, accounting, human resources, and agricultural problems. Regardless of the size and complexity of the decision-making problem at hand in these diverse applications, the development of all LP models can be viewed in terms of the three distinct steps, as defined in Chapter 1: (1) formulation, (2) solution, and (3) interpretation. We now discuss each with regard to LP models.

HISTORY

How Linear Programming Started

Linear programming was conceptually developed before World War II by the outstanding Soviet mathematician A. N. Kolmogorov. Another Russian, Leonid Kantorovich, won the Nobel Prize in Economics for advancing the concepts of optimal planning. An early application of linear programming, founded by George Stigler in 1945, was in the area we today call "diet problems."

Major progress in the field, however, took place in 1947 and thereafter, when George B. Dantzig developed the solution procedure known as the *simplex algorithm*. Dantzig, then a U.S. Air Force mathematician, was assigned to work on logistics problems. He noticed that many problems involving limited resources and more than one demand could be set up in terms of a series of equations and inequalities. Although early LP applications were military in nature, industrial applications rapidly became apparent with the spread of business computers. In 1984, Narendra Karmarkar developed an algorithm that is superior to the simplex method for many very large applications.

Formulation

Formulation is the process by which each aspect of a problem scenario is translated and expressed in terms of simple mathematical expressions. The aim in LP formulation is to ensure that the set of mathematical equations, taken together, completely address all the issues relevant to the problem situation at hand. We demonstrate a few examples of simple LP formulations in this chapter. Then we introduce several more comprehensive formulations in Chapter 3.

Solution

The *solution* step is where the mathematical expressions resulting from the formulation process are solved to identify *an* optimal (or best) solution to the model.[1] In

---

[1] We refer to the best solution as *an* optimal solution rather than as *the* optimal solution because, as we shall see later, the problem could have more than one optimal solution.

this book, the focus is on solving LP models using spreadsheets. However, we briefly discuss graphical solution procedures for LP models involving only two variables. The graphical solution procedure is useful in that it allows us to provide an intuitive explanation of the procedure used by most software packages to solve LP problems of any size.

Interpretation and Sensitivity Analysis

Assuming that a formulation is correct and has been successfully implemented and solved using an LP software package, how does a manager use the results? In addition to just providing the solution to the current LP problem, the computer results also allow the manager to evaluate the impact of several types of what-if questions. We discuss this subject, called *sensitivity analysis*, in Chapter 4.

In this book, our emphasis is on formulation (Chapters 2 and 3) and interpretation (Chapter 4), along with detailed descriptions of how spreadsheets can be used to efficiently set up and solve LP models.

Properties of a Linear Programming Model

All LP models have the following properties in common:

1. All problems seek to maximize or minimize some quantity, often profit or cost. We refer to this property as the objective function of an LP problem. For example, the objective of a typical manufacturer is to maximize profits. In the case of a trucking or railroad distribution system, the objective might be to minimize shipping costs. In any event, this objective must be stated clearly and defined mathematically. It does not matter whether profits and cost are measured in cents, dollars, euros, or millions of dollars. An *optimal solution* to the problem is the solution that achieves the best value (maximum or minimum, depending on the problem) for the objective function.

2. LP models usually include restrictions, or constraints, that limit the degree to which we can pursue our objective. For example, when we are trying to decide how many units to produce of each product in a firm's product line, we are restricted by available machinery time. Likewise, in selecting food items for a hospital meal, a dietitian must ensure that minimum daily requirements of vitamins, protein, and so on are satisfied. We want, therefore, to maximize or minimize a quantity (the objective) subject to limited resources (the constraints).

    An LP model usually includes a set of constraints known as nonnegativity constraints. These constraints ensure that the variables in the model take on only nonnegative values (i.e., ≥ 0). This is logical because negative values of physical quantities are impossible; you simply cannot produce a negative number of chairs or computers.

3. There must be alternative courses of action from which we can choose. For example, if a company produces three different products, management could use LP to decide how to allocate limited production resources (of personnel, machi-

nery, and so on) among these products. Should it devote all manufacturing capacity to make only the first product, should it produce equal numbers or amounts of each product, or should it allocate the resources in some other ratio? If there were no alternatives from which to select, we would not need LP.

4. The objective and constraints in LP problems must be expressed in terms of *linear* equations or inequalities. In linear mathematical relationships, all variables used in the objective function and constraints appear just once, are separable (i.e., not multiplied or divided by each other), and are of the first degree (i.e., not squared, raised to the third or higher power, or appearing in a denominator). Hence, the equation $2A + 5B = 10$ is a valid linear function, whereas the equation $2A^2 + 5B^3 + AB = 10$ is not linear because the variable A is squared, the variable B is cubed, and the two variables appear as a product in the third term. Similarly, the equation $72A - 32B + 56C = 0$ is linear, but the equations $5A + 6\sqrt{B} = 130$ and $(A / B) + C = 92$ are not linear.

You will see the term inequality quite often when we discuss LP problems. By *inequality* we mean that not all LP constraints need be of the form $A + B = C$. This particular relationship, called an equation, implies that the sum of term A and term B exactly equals term C. In most LP problems, we see inequalities of the form $A + B \leq C$ or $A + B \geq C$. The first of these means that A plus B is less than or equal to C. The second means that A plus B is greater than or equal to C. This concept provides a lot of flexibility in defining problem limitations.

Basic Assumptions of a Linear Programming Model

Technically, there are four additional requirements of an LP problem of which you should be aware:

1. We assume that conditions of *certainty* exist. That is, numbers used in the objective function and constraints are known with certainty and do not change during the period being studied.
2. We also assume that *proportionality* exists in the objective function and constraints. This means that if production of 1 unit of a product uses 3 hours of a particular resource, then making 10 units of that product uses 30 hours of the resource.
3. The third assumption deals with *additivity*, meaning that the total of all activities equals the sum of the individual activities. For example, if an objective is to maximize profit = $8 per unit of the first product made plus $3 per unit of the second product made, and if 1 unit of each product is actually produced, the profit contributions of $8 and $3 must add up to produce a sum of $11.
4. We make the *divisibility* assumption that solutions need not necessarily be in whole numbers (integers). That is, they may take any fractional value. If a fraction of a product cannot be produced (e.g., one-third of a submarine), an integer programming problem exists. We discuss integer programming in more detail in Chapter 6.

2.3 Formulating a Linear Programming Problem

One of the most common LP applications is the product mix problem. In many manufacturing firms, two or more products are usually produced using limited resources, such as personnel, machines, raw materials, and so on. The profit that the firm seeks to maximize is based on the profit contribution per unit of each product. (Profit contribution, you may recall, is the selling price per unit minus the variable cost per unit.[2]) The firm would like to determine how many units of each product it should produce so as to maximize overall profit, given its limited resources.

We begin our discussion of LP formulation with a simple product mix problem that involves only two variables (one for each product, in this case). We recognize that in most real-world situations, there is very little chance we will encounter LP models with just two variables. Such LP models therefore have little *real-world* value. We nevertheless consider it worthwhile to study these models for two reasons. First, the compact size of these models makes it easier for a beginner to understand the structure of LP models and the logic behind their formulation. As we will see, the same structure and logic carry forward to problems of larger size. Second, and more importantly, as we will see in section 2.4, we can represent a two-variable model in a graphical form, which allows us to visualize the interaction between various issues in the problem.

Linear Programming Example: Flair Furniture Company

Flair Furniture Company produces inexpensive tables and chairs. The production process for each is similar in that both require a certain number of labor hours in the carpentry department and a certain number of labor hours in the painting department. Each table takes 3 hours of carpentry work and 2 hours of painting work. Each chair requires 4 hours of carpentry and 1 hour of painting. During the current month, 2,400 hours of carpentry time and 1,000 hours of painting time are available. The marketing department wants Flair to make no more than 450 new chairs this month because there is a sizable existing inventory. However, because the existing inventory of tables is low, the marketing department wants Flair to make at least 100 tables this month. Each table sold results in a profit contribution of $7, and each chair yields $5.

Flair Furniture's problem is to determine the best possible combination of tables and chairs to manufacture this month in order to attain the maximum profit. The firm would like this product mix situation formulated (and subsequently solved) as an LP problem.

---

[2] Technically, we maximize total contribution margin, which is the difference between unit selling price and costs that vary in proportion to the quantity of the item produced. Depreciation, fixed general expense, and advertising are excluded from calculations.

To provide a structured approach for formulating this problem (and any other LP problem, irrespective of size and complexity), we present a three-step process in the following sections: (1) define decision variables, (2) state the objective function to be maximized or minimized, and (3) write out the constraints that restrict values of the decision variables.

Decision Variables

Decision variables (or choice variables) represent the unknown entities in a problem—that is, what we are solving for in the problem. For example, in the Flair Furniture problem, there are two unknown entities: the number of tables and the number of chairs to be produced this month. Note that all other unknowns in the problem (e.g., the total carpentry time needed this month) can be expressed as linear functions of the number of tables produced and the number of chairs produced.

Decision variables are expressed in the problems using alphanumeric symbols. When writing the formulation on paper, it is convenient to express the decision variables using simple, easy-to-understand names. For example, the number of tables to be produced can be denoted by names such as T, *Tables*, or X_1, and the number of chairs to be produced can be denoted by C, *Chairs*, or X_2.

Throughout this book, to the extent possible, we use self-explanatory names to denote the decision variables in our formulations. For example, in Flair Furniture's problem, we use T and C to denote the number of tables and chairs to be produced this month, respectively.

Although the two decision variables in Flair's model define similar entities (in the sense that they both represent the number of units of a product to make), this need not be the case in all LP (and other) decision models. It is perfectly logical for different decision variables in the same model to define completely different entities and be measured in different units. For example, variable X can denote the amount of labor to use (measured in hours), while variable Y can denote the amount of paint (measured in gallons).

The Objective Function

The objective function states the goal of a problem—that is, why we are trying to solve the problem. An LP model must have a single objective function. In most business-oriented LP models, the objective is to either maximize profit or minimize cost. The goal in this step is to express the profit (or cost) in terms of the decision variables defined earlier. In Flair Furniture's problem, the total profit can be expressed as

$$\text{Profit} = (\$7 \text{ profit per table}) \times (\text{number of tables produced}) \\ + (\$5 \text{ profit per chair}) \times (\text{number of chairs produced})$$

Using the decision variables T and C defined earlier, the objective function can be written as

$$\text{Maximize } \$7T + \$5C$$

Constraints

Constraints denote conditions that prevent us from selecting any value we please for the decision variables. An LP model should have as many constraints as necessary to accurately describe the problem scenario. Each constraint is expressed as a mathematical expression and can be independent of the other constraints in the model.

In Flair's problem, we note that there are four restrictions on the solution. The first two have to do with available carpentry and painting times. The third and fourth constraints deal with marketing-specified production conditions on the numbers of chairs and tables to make, respectively.

With regard to the carpentry and painting times, the constraints must ensure that the amount of the resource (time) required by the production plan is less than or equal to the amount of the resource (time) available. For example, in the case of carpentry, the total time used is

$$(3 \text{ hours per table}) \times (\text{number of tables produced})$$
$$+ (4 \text{ hours per chair}) \times (\text{number of chairs produced})$$

There are 2,400 hours of carpentry time available. Using the decision variables T and C defined earlier, this constraint can be stated as

$$3T + 4C \leq 2,400$$

Likewise, the second constraint specifies that the painting time used is less than or equal to the painting time available. This can be stated as

$$2T + 1C \leq 1,000$$

Next, there is the marketing-specified constraint that no more than 450 chairs be produced. This can be expressed as

$$C \leq 450$$

Finally, the second marketing-specified constraint is that at least 100 tables must be produced. Note that, unlike the first three constraints, this constraint involves the $\geq$ sign because 100 is a minimum requirement. It is very common in practice for a single LP model to include constraints with different signs (i.e., $\leq, \geq,$ and $=$). The constraint on the production of tables can be expressed as

$$T \geq 100$$

All four constraints represent restrictions on the numbers that we can make of the two products and, of course, affect the total profit. For example, Flair cannot make 900 tables because the carpentry and painting constraints are both violated if $T = 900$. Likewise, it cannot make 500 tables and 100 chairs, because that would require more than 1,000 hours of painting time. Hence, we note one more important aspect of LP models: Certain interactions exist between variables. The more units of one product a firm makes, the fewer it can make of other products. We show how this concept of interaction affects the solution to the model as we tackle the graphical solution approach in the next section.

Nonnegativity Constraints and Integer Values

Before we consider the graphical solution procedure, we need to address two other issues. First, because Flair cannot produce negative quantities of tables or chairs, the nonnegativity constraints must be specified. Mathematically, these can be stated as

$$T \geq 0 \quad \text{(number of tables produced} \geq 0)$$
$$C \geq 0 \quad \text{(number of chairs produced} \geq 0)$$

Second, it is possible that the optimal solution to the LP model will result in fractional values for T and C. Because the production plan in Flair's problem refers to a month's schedule, we can view fractional values as work-in-process inventory carried over to the next month. However, in some problems, we may require the values for decision variables to be whole numbers (integers) in order for the solution to make practical sense. A model in which some or all the decision variables are restricted only to integer values is called an integer programming (IP) model. We will study IP models in detail in Chapter 6. In general, as we will see in Chapter 6, it is considerably more difficult to solve an IP problem than an LP problem. Further, LP model solutions allow detailed sensitivity analysis (the topic of Chapter 4) to be undertaken, whereas IP model solutions do not. For these reasons, we do not specify the integer requirement in LP models, and we permit fractional values in the solution. Fractional values can often be rounded off appropriately, if necessary.

Guidelines for Developing a Correct LP Model

We have now developed our first LP model. Before we proceed, let us address a question that many users have, especially at the early stages of their experience with LP formulation: "How do I know if my LP model is right?" There is, unfortunately, no simple magical answer for this question. Instead, we offer the following guidelines to judge whether a model does what it is intended to do. Note that these guidelines do not guarantee that your model is correct. Formulation is still an art that you master only through repeated application to several diverse problems. (We will practice this over the next few chapters.) However, by following these guidelines, you can hopefully avoid the common errors that many beginners commit:

- Recognizing and defining the decision variables is perhaps the most critical step in LP formulation. In this endeavor, one approach we have often found useful and effective is to assume that you have to communicate your result to someone else. When you tell that person "The answer is to do _____," what exactly do you need to know to fill in the blank? Those entities are usually the decision variables.

- Remember that it is perfectly logical for different decision variables in a single LP model to be measured in different units. That is, all decision variables in an LP model need not denote similar entities.
- All expressions in the model (the objective function and each constraint) must use *only* the decision variables defined for the model. For example, in the Flair Furniture problem, the decision variables are T and C. Notice that all expressions involve only T and C. It is, of course, permissible for a decision variable to not be part of a specific expression. For example, the variable T is not part of the constraint $C \leq 450$.
- At any stage of the formulation, if you find yourself unable to write a specific expression (the objective function or a constraint) using the defined decision variables, it is a pretty good indication that you either need more decision variables or you've defined your decision variables incorrectly.
- All terms within the same expression must refer to the same entity. Consider, for example, the expression for the carpentry constraint $3T + 4C \leq 2,400$. Notice that each term (i.e., $4T$, $3C$, and 2,400) measures an amount of carpentry time. Likewise, in the objective function, each term (i.e., $\$7T$ and $\$5C$) in the expression measures profit.
- All terms within the same expression must be measured in the same units. That is, if the first term in an expression is in hours, all other terms in that expression must also be in hours. For example, in the carpentry constraint $3T + 4C \leq 2,400$, the $4T, 3C,$ and 2,400 are each measured in hours.
- Address each constraint separately. That is, there is no single "mega" expression that will take care of all constraints in the model at one time. Each constraint is a separate issue, and you must write a separate expression for each one. While writing one constraint (e.g., carpentry time), do not worry about other constraints (e.g., painting time).
- Try "translating" the mathematical expression back to words. After all, writing a constraint is just a matter of taking a problem scenario that is in words (e.g., "the amount of the carpentry time required by the production plan should be less than or equal to the carpentry time available") and translating it to a simple linear mathematical expression (e.g., $3T + 4C \leq 2,400$). To make sure the translation has been done correctly, do the reverse. That is, try explaining in words (to yourself) what the expression you have just written is saying. While doing so, make sure you remember the previous guidelines about all terms in an expression dealing with the same issue and being measured in the same units. If your "reverse translation" yields exactly the situation you were trying to express in mathematical form, chances are your expression is correct.

2.4 Graphical Solution of a Linear Programming Problem with Two Variables

As noted earlier, there is little chance of encountering LP models with just two variables in real-world situations. However, a major advantage of two-variable LP models (such as Flair Furniture's problem) is that they can be graphically illustrated using a two-dimensional graph. This graph can then be used to identify the optimal solution to the model. Although this graphical solution procedure has limited value in real-world situations, it is invaluable in two respects. First, it provides insights into the properties of solutions to *all* LP models, regardless of their size. Second, even though we use a computerized spreadsheet-based procedure to solve LP models in this book, the graphical procedure allows us to provide an intuitive explanation of how this more complex solution procedure works for LP models of any size. For these reasons, we first discuss the solution of Flair's problem using a graphical approach.

Decision Modeling In Action

Linear Programming Helps Intel Improve Project Portfolio Planning

Portfolio selection is a complicated decision at Intel due to the complex interactions between projects and products. Intel developed a decision support tool that uses linear programming, simulation, and other operations research techniques to identify the best portfolio from the proposed projects, and resulting products. The tool then helps decision makers make the final decision through analysis and visualization tools along with their own intuition.

The tool was first implemented in Intel's Data Center Group (DCG) in parallel with their standard process of portfolio selection to compare the level of improvement achieved in the decision making by the tool. The set of project portfolios produced by the tool had overall NPV 10% higher than the project portfolios produced by the standard process. The tool helped classify the projects that were overfunded, underfunded, and the ones that should be avoided. The improvement witnessed in the DCG encouraged the decision makers in other Intel groups to put the tool through an evaluation process for possible implementation.

Source: Based on S. Sampath, E. Gel, J. Fowler, K. Kempf. "A Decision-Making Framework for Project Portfolio Planning at Intel Corporation," *Interfaces 45, 5* (September – October 2015): 391–408.

Graphical Representation of Constraints

The complete LP model for Flair's problem can be restated as follows:

$$\text{Maximize profit} = \$7T + \$5C$$

subject to the constraints

$$
\begin{aligned}
3T + 4C &\leq 2{,}400 &&\text{(carpentry time)} \\
2T + 1C &\leq 1{,}000 &&\text{(painting time)} \\
C &\leq 450 &&\text{(maximum chairs allowed)} \\
T &\leq 100 &&\text{(minimum tables required)} \\
T, C &\geq 0 &&\text{(nonnegativity)}
\end{aligned}
$$

To find an optimal solution to this LP problem, we must first identify a set, or region, of feasible solutions. The first step in doing so is to plot each of the problem's constraints on a graph. We can plot either decision variable on the horizontal (X) axis, and the other variable on the vertical (Y) axis. In Flair's case, let us plot T (tables) on the X-axis and C (chairs) on the Y-axis. The nonnegativity constraints imply that we are working only in the first (or positive) quadrant of the graph.

Carpentry Time Constraint To represent the carpentry constraint graphically, we first convert the expression into a linear equation (i.e., $3T + 4C = 2,400$) by replacing the inequality sign ($\leq$) with an equality sign ($=$).

As you may recall from elementary algebra, the solution of a linear equation with two variables represents a straight line. The easiest way to plot the line is to find any two points that satisfy the equation and then draw a straight line through them. The two easiest points to find are generally the points at which the line intersects the horizontal (T) and vertical (C) axes.

If Flair produces no tables (i.e., $T = 0$), then $3(0) + 4C = 2,400$, or $C = 600$. That is, the line representing the carpentry time equation crosses the vertical axis at $C = 600$. This indicates that if the entire carpentry time available is used to make only chairs, Flair could make 600 chairs this month.

To find the point at which the line $3T + 4C = 2,400$ crosses the horizontal axis, let us assume that Flair uses all the carpentry time available to make only tables. That is, $C = 0$. Then $3T + 4(0) = 2,400$, or $T = 800$.

The nonnegativity constraints and the carpentry constraint line are illustrated in Figure 2.1. The line running from point ($T = 0$, $C = 600$) to point ($T = 800$, $C = 0$) represents the carpentry time equation $3T + 4C = 2,400$. We know that any combination of tables and chairs represented by points on this line (e.g., $T = 400$, $C = 300$) will use up all 2,400 hours of carpentry time.[3]

---

[3] Thus, we have plotted the carpentry constraint equation in its most binding position (i.e., using all of the resource).

Graphical Solution of a Linear Programming Problem with Two Variables — 45

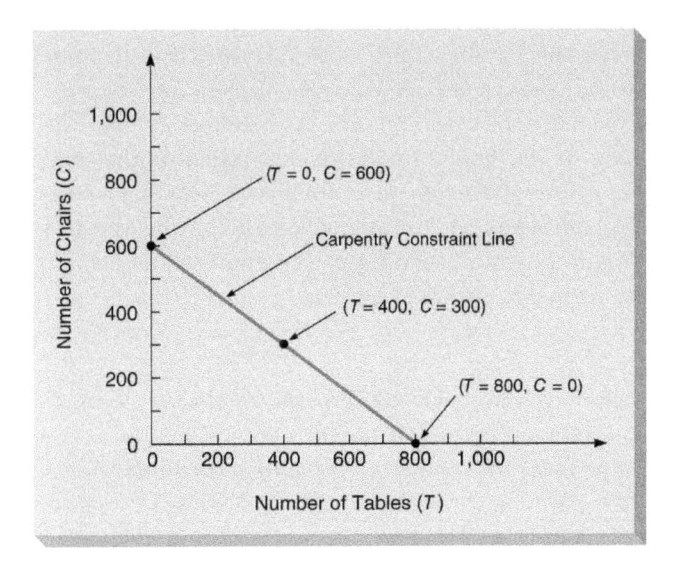

Figure 2.1: Graph of the Nonnegativity Constraint and the Carpentry Constraint Equation

Recall, however, that the actual carpentry constraint is the inequality $3T + 4C \leq 2{,}400$. How do we identify all the points on the graph that satisfy this inequality? To do so, we check any possible point in the graph. For example, let us check $(T = 300, C = 200)$. If we substitute these values in the carpentry constraint, the result is $3 \times 300 + 4 \times 200 = 1{,}700$. Because 1,700 is less than 2,400, the point $(T = 300, C = 200)$ satisfies the inequality. Further, note in Figure 2.2 that this point is below the constraint line.

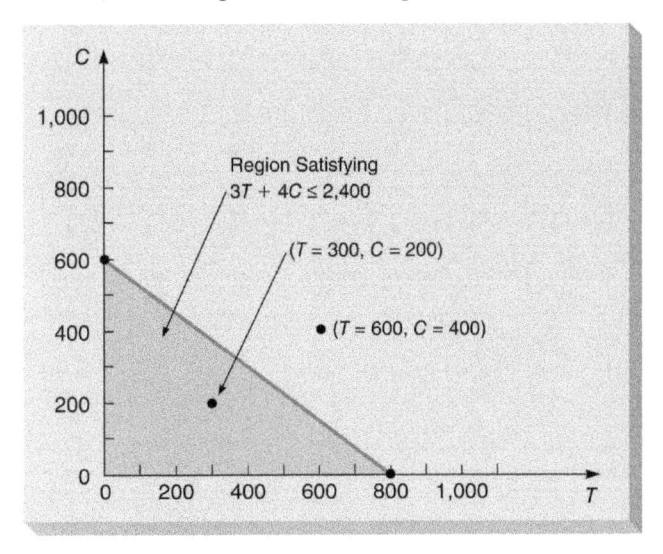

Figure 2.2: Region That Satisfies the Carpentry Constraint

In contrast, let's say the point we select is $(T = 600, C = 400)$. If we substitute these values in the carpentry constraint, the result is $3 \times 600 + 4 \times 400 = 3{,}400$. Because 3,400 exceeds 2,400, this point violates the constraint and is, therefore, an unacceptable production level. Further, note in Figure 2.2 that this point is above the constraint line. As a matter of fact, any point above the constraint line violates that restriction (test this yourself with a few other points), just as any point below the line does not violate the constraint. In Figure 2.2, the shaded region represents all points that satisfy the carpentry constraint inequality $3T + 4C \leq 2{,}400$.

Painting Time Constraint

Now that we have identified the points that satisfy the carpentry constraint, we recognize that the final solution must also satisfy all other constraints. Therefore, let us now add to this graph the solution that corresponds to the painting constraint.

Recall that we expressed the painting constraint as $2T + 1C \leq 1{,}000$. As we did with the carpentry constraint, we start by changing the inequality to an equation and identifying two points on the line specified by the equation $2T + 1C = 1{,}000$. When $T = 0$, then $2(0) + 1C = 1{,}000$, or $C = 1{,}000$. Likewise, when $C = 0$, then $2T + 1(0) = 1{,}000$, or $T = 500$.

The line from the point $(T = 0, C = 1{,}000)$ to the point $(T = 500, C = 0)$ in Figure 2.3 represents all combinations of tables and chairs that use exactly 1,000 hours of painting time. As with the carpentry constraint, all points on or below this line satisfy the original inequality $2T + 1C \leq 1{,}000$.

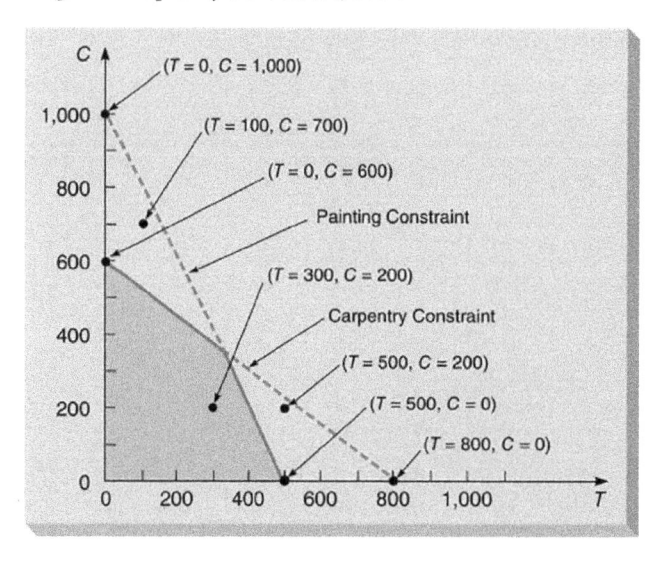

Figure 2.3: Region That Satisfies the Carpentry and Painting Constraints

In Figure 2.3, some points, such as ($T = 300$, $C = 200$), are below the lines for both the carpentry equation and the painting equation. That is, we have enough carpentry and painting time available to manufacture 300 tables and 200 chairs this month. In contrast, there are points, such as ($T = 500, C = 200$) and ($T = 100$, $C = 700$), that satisfy one of the two constraints but violate the other. (See if you can verify this statement mathematically.) Because we need the solution to satisfy both the carpentry and painting constraints, we will consider only those points that satisfy both constraints simultaneously. The region that contains all such points is shaded in Figure 2.3.

Production Constraint for Chairs We must make sure the final solution requires us to produce no more than 450 chairs ($C \leq 450$). As before, we first convert this inequality to an equation ($C = 450$). This is relatively easy to draw because it is just a horizontal line that intersects the vertical (C) axis at 450. This line is shown in Figure 2.4, and all points below this line satisfy the original inequality ($C \leq 450$).

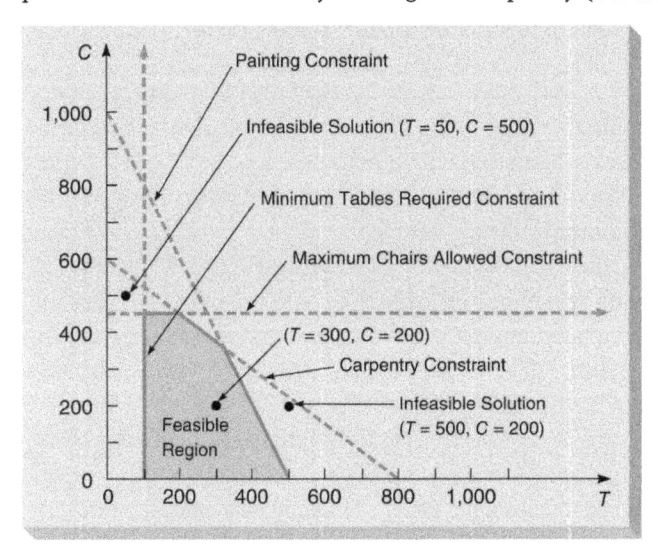

Figure 2.4: Feasible Solution Region for the Flair Furniture Company Problem

Production Constraint for Tables Finally, we have to ensure that the final solution makes at least 100 tables ($T \geq 100$). In this case, the equation ($T = 100$) is just a vertical line that intersects the horizontal (T) axis at 100. This line is also shown in Figure 2.4. However, because this constraint has the $\geq$ sign, it should be easy to verify that all points to the *right* of this line satisfy the original inequality ($T \geq 100$).

Feasible Region
The feasible region of an LP problem consists of those points that simultaneously satisfy all constraints in the problem; that is, it is the region where all the problem's constraints overlap.

Consider a point such as $(T = 300, C = 200)$ in Figure 2.4. This point satisfies all four constraints, as well as the nonnegativity constraints. This point, therefore, represents a feasible solution to Flair's problem. In contrast, points such as $(T = 500, C = 200)$ and $(T = 50, C = 500)$ each violate one or more constraints. They are, therefore, not feasible solutions. The shaded area in Figure 2.4 represents the feasible region for Flair Furniture's problem. Any point outside the shaded area represents an infeasible solution (or production plan).

Identifying an Optimal Solution by Using Level Lines

When the feasible region has been identified, we can proceed to find the optimal solution to the problem. In Flair's case, the *optimal solution* is the point in the feasible region that produces the highest profit. But there are many, many possible solution points in the feasible region. How do we go about selecting the optimal one, the one that yields the highest profit? We do this by essentially using the objective function as a "pointer" to guide us toward an optimal point in the feasible region.

Drawing Level Lines In the level, or iso, lines method, we begin by plotting the line that represents the objective function (i.e., $\$7T + \$5C$) on the graph, just as we plotted the various constraints.[4] However, note that we do not know what $\$7T + \$5C$ equals in this function. In fact, that's what we are trying to find out. Without knowing this value, how do we plot this equation?

To get around this problem, let us first write the objective function as $\$7T + \$5C = Z$. We then start the procedure by selecting *any* arbitrary value for Z. In selecting this value for Z, the only recommended guideline is to select one that makes the resulting equation easy to plot on the graph. For example, for Flair's problem, we can choose a profit of $\$2,100$. We can then write the objective function as $\$7T + \$5C = \$2,100$.

Clearly, this expression is the equation of a line that represents all combinations of (T, C) that would yield a total profit of $\$2,100$. That is, it is a *level line* corresponding to a profit of $\$2,100$. To plot this line, we proceed exactly as we do to plot a constraint line. If we let $T = 0$, then $\$7(0) + \$5C = \$2,100$, or $C = 420$. Likewise, if we let $C = 0$, then $\$7T + \$5(0) = \$2,100$, or $T = 300$.

The objective function line corresponding to $Z = \$2,100$ is illustrated in Figure 2.5 as the line between $(T = 0, C = 420)$ and $(T = 300, C = 0)$. Observe that if any points on this line lie in the feasible region identified earlier for Flair's problem, those points represent *feasible production plans* that will yield a profit of $\$2,100$.

---

[4] Iso means "equal" or "similar." Thus, an isoprofit line represents a line with all profits the same, in this case $\$2,100$.

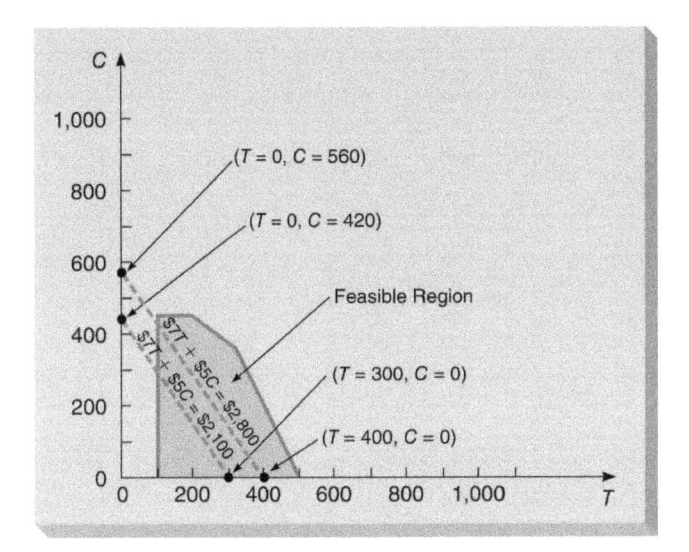

Graphical Solution of a Linear Programming Problem with Two Variables — 49

[Graph showing feasible region with labeled points (T=0, C=560), (T=0, C=420), (T=300, C=0), (T=400, C=0), and level profit lines $7T + 5C = 2100$ and $7T + 5C = 2800$]

Figure 2.5: Level Profit Lines for $Z=\$2,100$ and $Z=\$2,800$

What if we had selected a different Z value, such as $2,800, instead of $2,100? In that case, the objective function line corresponding to $Z = \$2,800$ would be between the points $(T = 0, C = 560)$ and $(T = 400, C = 0)$, also shown in Figure 2.5. Further, because there are points on this line that lie within the feasible region for Flair's problem, it is possible for Flair to find a production plan that will yield a profit of $2,800 (obviously, better than $2,100).

Observe in Figure 2.5 that the level lines for $Z = \$2,100$ and $Z = \$2,800$ are parallel to each other. This is a very important point. It implies that regardless of which value of Z we select, the objective function line that we draw will be parallel to the two level lines shown in Figure 2.5. The exact location of the parallel line on the graph will, of course, depend on the value of Z selected.

We know now that Flair can obtain a profit of $2,800. However, is $2,800 the highest profit Flair can get? From the preceding discussion, we note that as the value we select for Z gets larger (which is desirable in Flair's problem because we want to maximize profit), the objective function line moves in a *parallel* fashion away from the origin. Therefore, we can "draw" a series of parallel level lines (by carefully moving a ruler in a plane parallel to the $Z = \$2,800$ line). However, as we visualize these parallel lines, we need to ensure that at least one point on each level line lies within the feasible region. The level line that corresponds to the highest profit but still touches some point of the feasible region pinpoints an optimal solution.

From Figure 2.6, we can see that the level profit line that corresponds to the highest achievable profit value will be tangential to the shaded feasible region at the point denoted by ④. Any level line corresponding to a profit value higher than that of this line will have no points in the feasible region. For example, note that a level line corresponding to a profit value of $4,200 is entirely outside the feasible region (see Figure 2.6). This implies that a profit of $4,200 is not possible for Flair to achieve.

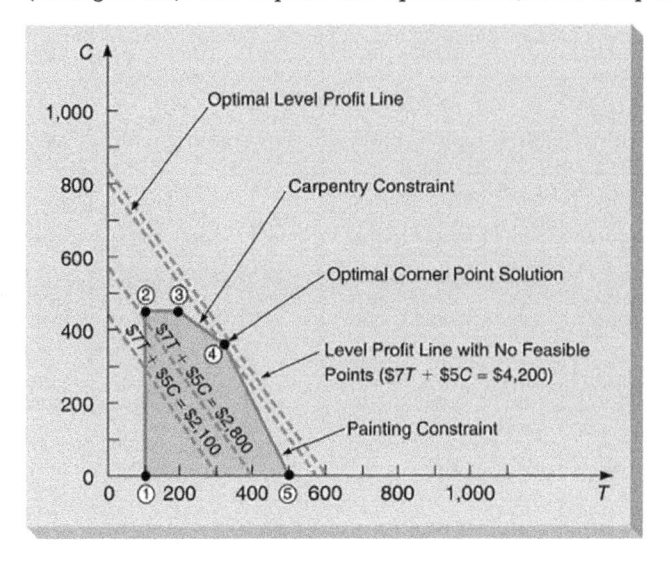

Figure 2.6: Optimal Corner Point Solution to the Flair Furniture Company Problem

Observe that point ④ defines the intersection of the carpentry and painting constraint equations. Such points, where two or more constraints intersect, are called corner points, or extreme points. In Figure 2.6, note that the other corner points in Flair's problem are points ①, ②, ③, and ⑤.

Corner Point Property   The preceding discussion reveals an important property of LP problems, known as the *corner point property*. This property states that an optimal solution to an LP problem will always occur at a corner point of the feasible region. In Flair's problem, this means that the optimal solution has to be one of the five corner points (i.e., ①, ②, ③, ④, or ⑤). For the specific objective function considered here (Maximize $7T + 5C$), corner point ④ turns out to be optimal. For a different objective function, one of the other corner points could be optimal.

Calculating the Solution at an Optimal Corner Point

Now that we have identified point ④ in Figure 2.6 as an optimal corner point, how do we find the values of T and C, and the profit at that point? Of course, if a graph is perfectly drawn, you can always find point ④ by carefully examining the intersection's coordinates. Otherwise, the algebraic procedure shown here provides more precision. To find the coordinates of point ④ accurately, we have to solve for the intersection of the two constraint equations intersecting at that point. Recall from your last course in algebra that you can apply the simultaneous equations method to the two constraint equations:

$$3T + 4C = 2{,}400 \quad \text{(carpentry time equation)}$$
$$2T + 1C = 1{,}000 \quad \text{(painting time equation)}$$

To solve these equations simultaneously, we need to eliminate one of the variables and solve for the other. One way to do this would be to first multiply the first equation by 2 and the second equation by 3. If we then subtract the modified second equation from the modified first equation, we get

$$6T + 8C = 4{,}800$$
$$-(6T + 3C = 3{,}000)$$
$$\overline{5C = 1{,}800} \quad \text{implies } C = 360$$

We can now substitute 360 for C in either of the original equations and solve for T. For example, if $C = 360$ in the first equation, then $3T + (4)(360) = 2{,}400$ or $T = 320$. That is, point ④ has the coordinates $(T = 320, C = 360)$. Hence, in order to maximize profit, Flair Furniture should produce 320 tables and 360 chairs. To complete the analysis, we can compute the optimal profit as $\$7 \times 320 + \$5 \times 360 = \$4{,}040$.

Identifying an Optimal Solution by Using All Corner Points

Because an optimal solution to any LP problem always occurs at a corner point of the feasible region, we can identify an optimal solution by evaluating the objective function value at every corner point in the problem. While this approach, called the corner point method, eliminates the need for graphing and using level objective function lines, it is somewhat tedious because we end up unnecessarily identifying the coordinates of many corner points. Nevertheless, some people prefer this approach because it is conceptually much simpler than the level lines approach.

To verify the applicability of this approach to Flair's problem, we note from Figure 2.6 that the feasible region has five corner points: ①, ②, ③, ④, and ⑤. Using the procedure discussed earlier for corner point ④, we find the coordinates of each of the other four corner points and compute their profit levels. They are as follows:

Point ①	$(T = 100, C = 0)$	Profit $= \$7 \times 100 + \$5 \times 0 = \$700$
Point ②	$(T = 100, C = 450)$	Profit $= \$7 \times 100 + \$5 \times 450 = \$2{,}950$
Point ③	$(T = 200, C = 450)$	Profit $= \$7 \times 200 + \$5 \times 450 = \$3{,}650$
Point ④	$(T = 320, C = 360)$	Profit $= \$7 \times 320 + \$5 \times 360 = \$4{,}040$
Point ⑤	$(T = 500, C = 0)$	Profit $= \$7 \times 500 + \$5 \times 0 = \$3{,}500$

Note that corner point ④ produces the highest profit of any corner point and is therefore the optimal solution. As expected, this is the same solution we obtained using the level lines method.

Comments on Flair Furniture's Optimal Solution

The result for Flair's problem reveals an interesting feature. Even though chairs provide a smaller profit contribution ($5 per unit) than tables ($7 per unit), the optimal solution requires us to make more units of chairs (360) than tables (320). This is a common occurrence in such problems. We cannot assume that we will always produce greater quantities of products with higher profit contributions. We need to recognize that products with higher profit contributions may also consume larger amounts of resources, some of which may be scarce. Hence, even though we may get smaller profit contributions per unit from other products, we may more than compensate for this by making more units of these products.

Notice, however, what happens if the profit contribution for chairs is only $3 per unit instead of $5 per unit. The objective now is to maximize $7T + $3C instead of $7T + $5C. Although Figure 2.6 does not show the profit line corresponding to $7T + $3C, you should be able to use a straight edge to represent this revised profit line in this figure and verify that the optimal solution will now correspond to corner point ⑤. That is, the optimal solution is to make 500 tables and 0 chairs, for a total profit of $3,500. Clearly, in this case, the profit contributions of tables and chairs are such that we should devote all our resources to making only the higher profit contribution product, tables.

The key point to note here is that in either situation (i.e., when the profit contribution of chairs is $5 per unit or when it is $3 per unit), there is no easy way to predict *a priori* what the optimal solution is going to be with regard to the numbers of tables and chairs to make. We can determine these values only after we have formulated the LP model and solved it in each case. This clearly illustrates the power and usefulness of such types of decision models. As you can well imagine, this issue will become even more prominent when we deal in subsequent chapters with models that have more than two decision variables.

Extension to Flair Furniture's LP Model

As noted in Chapter 1, the decision modeling process is iterative in most real-world situations. That is, the model may need to be regularly revised to reflect new information. With this in mind, let us consider the following revision to the Flair Furniture model before we move on to the next example.

Suppose the marketing department has informed Flair that all customers purchasing tables usually purchase at least two chairs at the same time. While the existing inventory of chairs may be enough to satisfy a large portion of this demand, the marketing department would like the production plan to ensure that at least 75 more chairs than tables are made this month. Does this new condition affect the optimal solution? If so, how?

Using the decision variables T and C we have defined for Flair's model, we can express this new condition as

$$C \geq T + 75$$

Notice that unlike all our previous conditions, this expression has decision variables on both sides of the inequality. This is a perfectly logical thing to have in an expression, and it does not affect the model's validity in any way. We can, of course, manipulate this expression algebraically if we wish and rewrite it as

$$C - T \geq 75$$

The revised graphical representation of Flair's model reflecting the addition of this new constraint is shown in Figure 2.7. The primary issue noticeably different in drawing the new constraint when compared with the carpentry and painting constraints is that it has a positive slope. All points above this line satisfy the inequality $(C - T \geq 75)$.

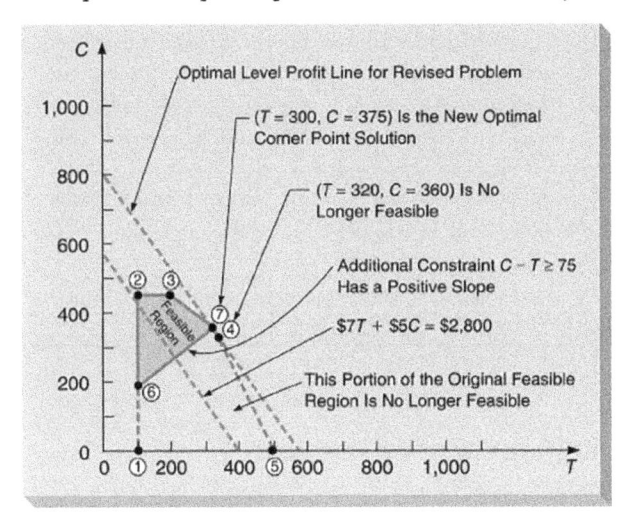

Figure 2.7: Optimal Corner Point Solution to the Extended Flair Furniture Company Problem

Notice the dramatic change in the shape and size of the feasible region just because of this single new constraint. This is common in LP models, and it illustrates how each constraint in a model is important because it can significantly affect the feasible region (and, hence, the optimal solution). In Flair's model, the original optimal corner point ④ $(T = 320, C = 360)$ is no longer even feasible in the revised problem. In fact, of the original corner points, only points ② and ③ are still feasible. Two new corner points, ⑥ and ⑦, now exist.

To determine which of these four corner points (②, ③, ⑥, and ⑦) is the new optimal solution, we use a level profit line as before. Figure 2.7 shows the level line for a profit value of $2,800. Based on this line, it appears that corner point ⑦ is the new optimal solution. The values at this corner point can be determined to be $T = 300$ and $C = 375$, for a profit of $3,975. (See if you can verify these yourself.) Note that the profit has decreased because of this new constraint. This is logical because each new constraint can never improve the solution and may worsen it by making the feasible region more restrictive. In fact, the best we can hope for when we add a new constraint is that our current optimal solution continues to remain feasible (and, hence, optimal).

Decision Modeling In Action

Using Linear Programming to Improve Capacity Management at Indian Railways

Indian Railways (IR) operates more than 1,600 long-distance trains and carries more than 7 million passengers daily. Reserved tickets are booked through IR's passenger reservation system, which reserves a specific seat in a specific class on a specific train per booking. A major problem is deciding how many seats to allocate in a given class of a train to multiple travel segments, including segments traveled by en route passengers (i.e., those not traveling from the train's origin to its destination). A train's capacity must therefore be distributed among various intermediate stations by allocating specific quotas to ensure that the twin objectives of maximizing the number of confirmed seats and increasing the seat utilization are met.

IR personnel used a linear programming model to determine the optimal capacity allocation on multiple travel segments. The model, which uses a simple, effective capacity management tool, has helped IR reduce its overall seat requirements and has increased the availability of confirmed seats for the various en route passenger demands on several trains. A spokesperson for IR notes, "The model and software developed have been used in over 50 long-distance trains originating on Western Railway with considerable success."

Source: Based on R. Gopalakrishnan and N. Rangaraj. "Capacity Management on Long-Distance Passenger Trains of Indian Railways," *Interfaces* 40, 4 (July-August 2010): 291–302.

2.5 A Minimization Linear Programming Problem

Many LP problems involve minimizing an objective such as cost instead of maximizing a profit function. A restaurant, for example, may wish to develop a work schedule to meet staffing needs while minimizing the total number of employees. A manufacturer may seek to distribute its products from several factories to its many regional warehouses in a way that minimizes total shipping costs. A hospital may want to provide patients with a daily meal plan that meets certain nutritional standards while minimizing food purchase costs.

To introduce the concept of minimization problems, we first discuss a problem that involves only two decision variables. As before, even though such problems may have limited applicability in real-world situations, a primary reason to study them is that they can be represented and solved graphically. This will make it easier for us to understand the structure and behavior of such problems when we consider larger minimization problems in subsequent chapters.

Let's look at a common LP problem, referred to as the *diet problem*. This situation is similar to one that a hospital faces in feeding its patients at the least cost.

Holiday Meal Turkey Ranch

The Holiday Meal Turkey Ranch is planning to use two brands of turkey feed—brand A and brand B—to provide a good diet for its turkeys. Each feed contains different quantities (in units) of the three nutrients (protein, vitamin, and iron) essential for fattening turkeys. Table 2.1 summarizes this information and shows the minimum unit of each nutrient required per month by a turkey. Brand A feed costs $0.10 per pound, and brand B costs $0.15 per pound. The owner of the ranch wants to use LP to determine the quantity of each feed in a turkey's diet that would meet the minimum monthly requirements for each nutrient at the lowest cost.

Table 2.1: Data for Holiday Meal Turkey Ranch

Nutrient	Brand A Feed	Brand B Feed	Minimum Required Per Turkey Per Month
Protein (units)	5	10	45.0
Vitamin (units)	4	3	24.0
Iron (units)	0.5	0	1.5
Cost per pound	$0.10	$0.15	

If we let A denote the number of pounds of brand A feed to use per turkey each month and B denote the number of pounds of brand B, we can proceed to formulate this LP problem as follows:

$$\text{Minimize cost} = \$0.10A + \$0.15B$$

subject to the constraints

$$
\begin{aligned}
5A + 10B &\geq 45 \quad \text{(protein required)} \\
4A + 3B &\geq 24 \quad \text{(vitamin required)} \\
0.5A &\geq 1.5 \quad \text{(iron required)} \\
A, B &\geq 0 \quad \text{(nonnegativity)}
\end{aligned}
$$

Before solving this problem, note two features that affect its solution. First, as the problem is formulated, we will be solving for the optimal amounts of brands A and B to use per month *per turkey*. If the ranch houses 5,000 turkeys in a given month, we can simply multiply the A and B quantities by 5,000 to decide how much feed to use overall. Second, we are now dealing with a series of greater than or equal to constraints. These cause the feasible solution area to be above the constraint lines, a common situation when handling minimization LP problems.

Graphical Solution of the Holiday Meal Turkey Ranch Problem

We first construct the feasible solution region. To do so, we plot each of the three constraint equations as shown in Figure 2.8. In plotting constraints such as $0.5\,A \geq 1.5$, if you find it more convenient to do so, you can multiply both sides by 2 and rewrite the inequality as $A \geq 3$. Clearly, this does not change the position of the constraint line in any way.

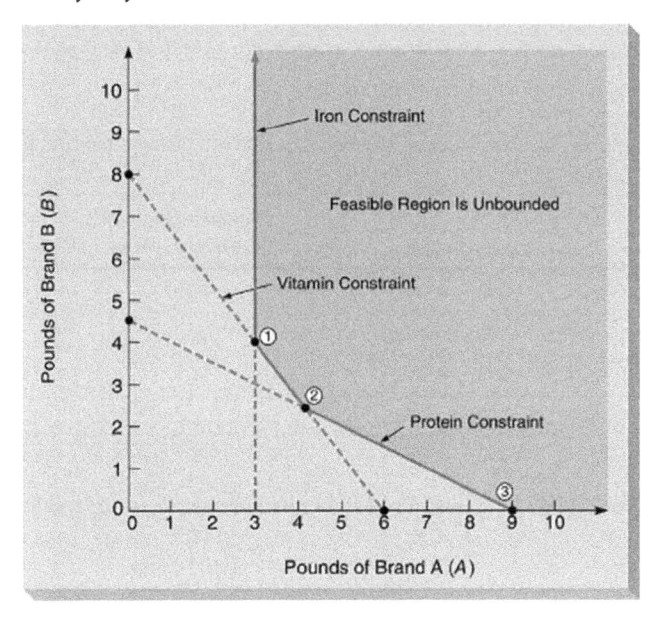

Figure 2.8: Feasible Region for the Holiday Meal Turkey Ranch Problem

The feasible region for Holiday Meal's problem is shown by the shaded space in Figure 2.8. Notice that the feasible region has explicit boundaries inward (i.e., on the left side and the bottom) but is unbounded outward (i.e., on the right side and on top). Minimization problems often exhibit this feature. This causes no difficulty in solving them as long as an optimal corner point solution exists on the bounded side. (Recall that an optimal solution will lie at one of the corner points, just as it did in a maximization problem.)

In Figure 2.8, the identifiable corner points for Holiday Meal's problem are denoted by points ①, ②, and ③. Which, if any, of these corner points is an optimal solution? To answer this, we write the objective function as $\$0.10A + 0.15B = Z$ and plot this equation for *any* arbitrary value of Z. For example, we start in Figure 2.9 by drawing the level cost line corresponding to $Z = \$1.00$. Obviously, there are many points in the feasible region that would yield a lower total cost. As with the parallel level lines we used to solve the Flair Furniture maximization problem, we can draw a series of parallel level cost lines to identify Holiday Meal's optimal solution. The lowest level cost line to touch the feasible region pinpoints an optimal corner point.

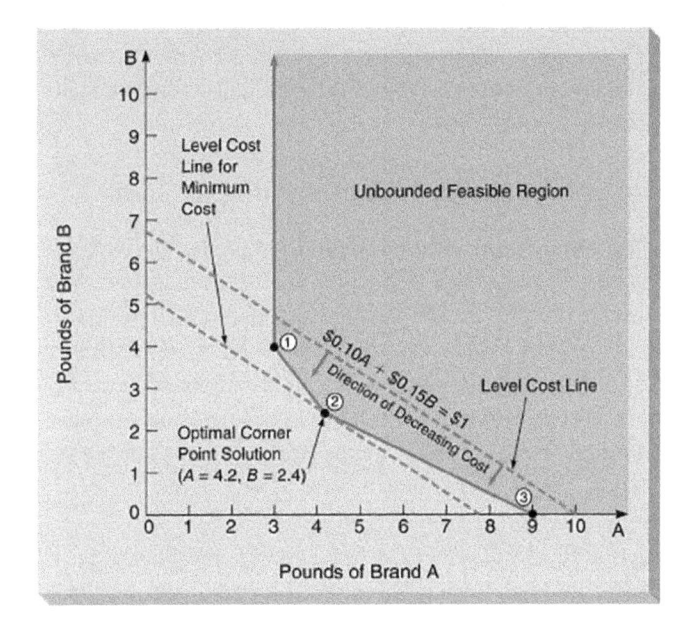

Figure 2.9: Graphical Solution to the Holiday Meal Turkey Ranch Problem Using the Level Cost Line Method

Because Holiday Meal's problem involves minimization of the objective function, we need to move our level cost line toward the lower left in a plane parallel to the $1.00 level line. Note that we are moving toward the bounded side of the feasible region and that there are identifiable corner points on this side. Hence, even though the feasible region is unbounded, it is still possible to identify an optimal solution for this problem.

As shown in Figure 2.9, the last feasible point touched by a level cost line as we move it in a parallel fashion toward the lower left is corner point ②. To find the coordinates of this point algebraically, we proceed as before by eliminating one of the variables from the two equations that intersect at this point (i.e., $5A+10B=45$ and $4A+3B=24$) so that we can solve for the other. One way would be to multiply the first equation by 4, multiply the second equation by 5, and subtract the second equation from the first equation, as follows:

$$4(5A+10B=45) \quad \text{implies} \quad 20A+40B=180$$
$$-5(4A+3B=24) \quad \text{implies} \quad -(20A+15B=120)$$
$$25B=60 \quad \text{implies } B=2.40$$

Substituting $B=2.40$ into the first equation yields $4A+(3)(2.40)=24$, or $A=4.20$. The cost at corner point ② is $0.10 \times 4.20 + $0.15 \times 2.40 = 0.78. That is, Holiday Meal should use 4.20 pounds of brand A feed and 2.40 pounds of brand B feed, at a cost of $0.78 per turkey per month. Observe that this solution has fractional values. In this case, however, this is perfectly logical because turkey feeds can be measured in fractional quantities.

As with the Flair Furniture example, we could also identify an optimal corner point in this problem by using the corner point method (i.e., evaluating the cost at all three identifiable corner points ①, ②, and ③).

2.6 Special Situations in Solving Linear Programming Problems

In each of the LP problems discussed so far, all the constraints in the model have affected the shape and size of the feasible region. Further, in each case, there has been a *single* corner point we can identify as the optimal corner point. There are, however, four special situations that may be encountered when solving LP problems: (1) redundant constraints, (2) infeasibility, (3) alternate optimal solutions, and (4) unbounded solutions. We illustrate the first three using the Flair Furniture example as the base model and the last one using the Holiday Meal Turkey Ranch example.

Redundant Constraints

A redundant constraint is one that does not affect the feasible region in any way. In other words, other constraints in the model are more restrictive and thereby negate the need to even consider the redundant constraint. The presence of redundant constraints is quite common in large LP models with many variables. However, it is typically impossible to determine whether a constraint is redundant just by looking at it.

Let's consider the LP model for the Flair Furniture problem again. Recall that the original model is

$$\text{Maximize profit} = \$7T + \$5C$$

subject to the constraints

$$
\begin{aligned}
3T + 4C &\leq 2{,}400 &&\text{(carpentry time)} \\
2T + 1C &\leq 1{,}000 &&\text{(painting time)} \\
C &\leq 450 &&\text{(maximum chairs allowed)} \\
T &\geq 100 &&\text{(minimum tables required)} \\
T, C &\geq 0 &&\text{(nonnegativity)}
\end{aligned}
$$

Now suppose that the demand for tables has become quite weak. Instead of specifying that at least 100 tables need to be made, the marketing department is now specifying that a *maximum* of 100 tables should be made. That is, the constraint should be $T \leq 100$ instead of $T \geq 100$, as originally formulated. The revised feasible region for this problem due to this modified constraint is shown in Figure 2.10. From this figure, we see that the production limit constraints on chairs and tables are so restrictive that they make the carpentry and painting constraints redundant. That is, these two time constraints have no effect on the feasible region.

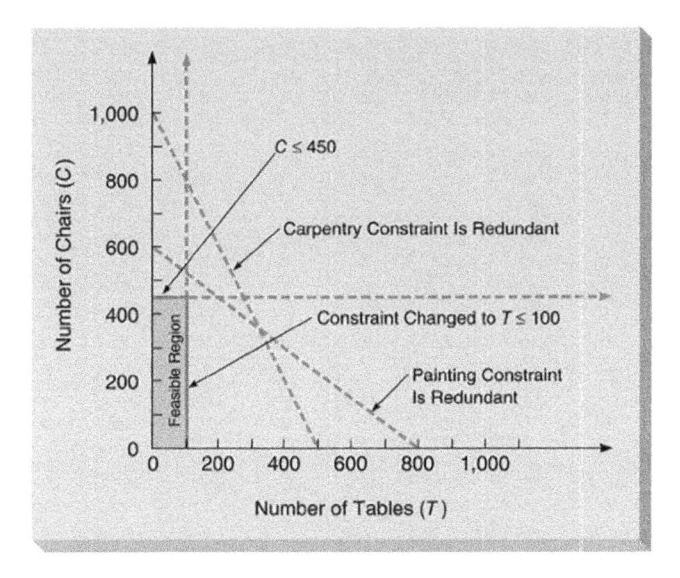

Figure 2.10: Problem with a Redundant Constraint

Redundant constraints are not bad to include in a formulation per se in the sense that their presence will not affect the optimal solution. Plus, it can be a good idea to leave them in the model in case at some future date other constraints are removed that might cause the redundant constraints to no longer be redundant. On the other hand, the removal of redundant constraints reduces problem size and can possibly speed up solution time, especially for large problems.

Infeasibility

Infeasibility is a condition that arises when no single solution satisfies all of an LP problem's constraints. That is, no feasible solution region exists. Such a situation might occur, for example, if the problem has been formulated with conflicting constraints. As a graphical illustration of infeasibility, consider the Flair Furniture problem again (please refer back to the formulation of this problem). Now suppose that Flair's marketing department has found the demand for tables has become very strong. To meet this demand, it is now specifying that at least 600 tables should be made. That is, the constraint should now be $T \geq 600$ instead of $T \geq 100$. The revised graph reflecting this modified constraint is shown in Figure 2.11. From this figure, we see that there is no feasible solution region for this problem because of the presence of conflicting constraints.

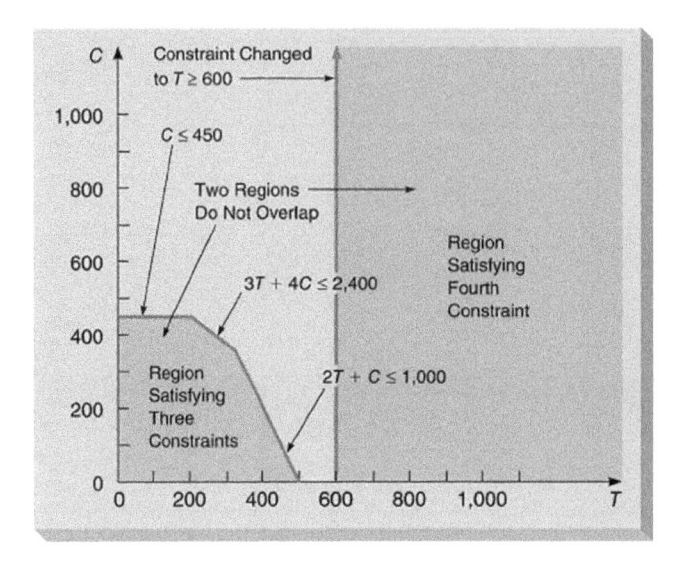

Figure 2.11: Example of an Infeasible Problem

Infeasibility is not uncommon in real-world, large-scale LP problems that involve hundreds of constraints. In such situations, the decision analyst coordinating the LP problem must resolve the conflict between the constraints causing the infeasibility and revise them appropriately. In particular, at least one of the constraints will have to be relaxed (loosened) or eliminated for a feasible answer to exist for the problem.

Alternate Optimal Solutions

An LP problem may, on occasion, have alternate optimal solutions (i.e., more than one optimal solution). Graphically, this is the case when the level profit (or cost) line runs parallel to a constraint in the problem that lies in the direction in which the profit (or cost) line is being moved—in other words, when the two lines have the same slope. To illustrate this situation, let us consider the Flair Furniture problem again.

Suppose the marketing department has indicated that due to increased competition, profit contributions of both products have to be revised downward to $6 per table and $3 per chair. That is, the objective function is now $6T + $3C$ instead of $7T + $5C$. The revised graph for this problem is shown in Figure 2.12. From this figure, we note that the level profit line (shown here for a profit of $2,100) runs parallel to the painting constraint equation. At a profit level of $3,000, the level profit line will rest directly on top of this constraint line. This means that any point along the painting constraint equation between corner points ④ $(T = 320, C = 360)$ and ⑤ $(T = 500, C = 0)$ provides an optimal T and C combination.

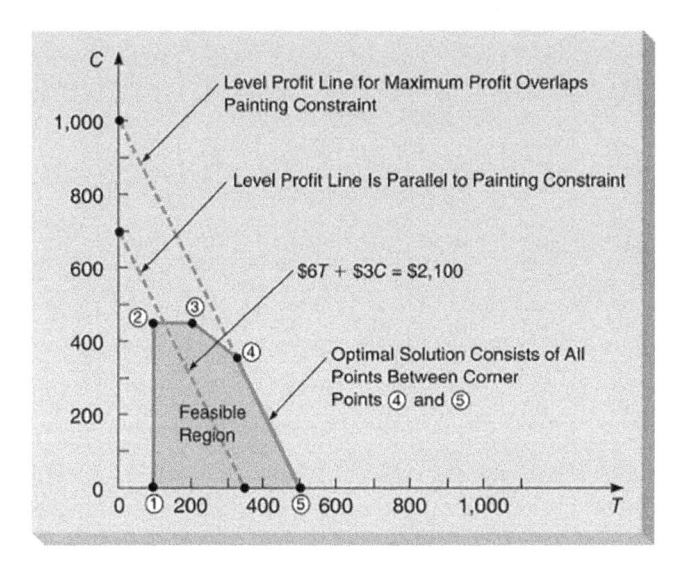

Figure 2.12: Example of a Problem with Alternate Optimal Solutions

Far from causing problems, the presence of more than one optimal solution actually allows management greater flexibility in deciding which solution to select. The optimal objective function value remains the same at all alternate solutions.

Unbounded Solution

When an LP model has a bounded feasible region, as in the Flair Furniture example (i.e., it has an explicit boundary in every direction), it has an identifiable optimal corner point solution. However, if the feasible region is unbounded in one or more directions, as in the Holiday Meal Turkey Ranch example, depending on the objective function, the model may or may not have a finite solution. In the Holiday Meal problem, for example, we could identify a finite solution because the optimal corner point existed on the bounded side (refer to Figure 2.9). However, what happens if the objective function is such that we have to move our level profit (or cost) lines away from the bounded side?

To study this, let us again consider the Holiday Meal example (please refer back to the formulation of this problem). Suppose that instead of minimizing cost, the ranch owner wants to use a different objective function. Specifically, based on his experience with the feeds and their fattening impact on his turkeys, assume the owner estimates that brand A feed yields a "fattening value" of 8 per pound, while brand B feed yields a fattening value of 12 per pound. The owner wants to find the diet that maximizes the total fattening value.

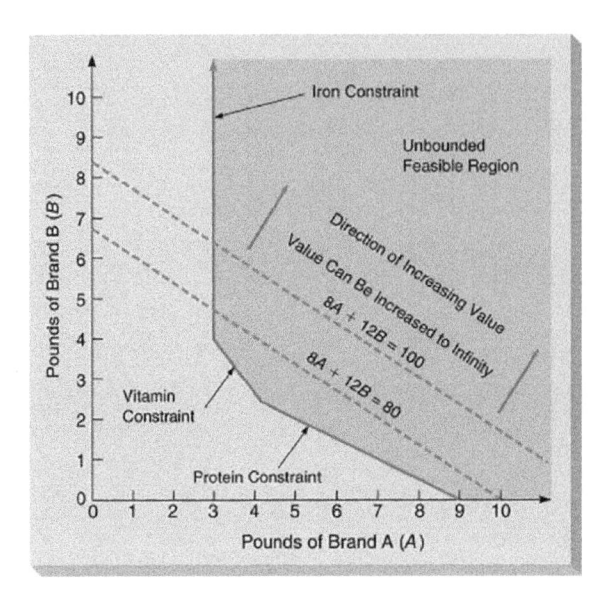

Figure 2.13: Example of a Problem with an Unbounded Solution

The objective function now changes from "Minimize $0.10A + 0.15B$" to "Maximize $8A + 12B$." Figure 2.13 shows the graph of this problem with the new objective function. As before, the feasible region (which has not changed) is unbounded, with three identifiable corner points on the bounded side. However, because this is now a maximization problem and the feasible region is unbounded in the direction in which profit increases, the solution itself is unbounded. That is, the profit can be made infinitely large without violating any constraints. In real-world situations, the occurrence of an unbounded solution usually means the problem has been formulated improperly. That is, either one or more constraints have the wrong sign or values, or some constraints have been overlooked. In Holiday Meal's case, it would indeed be wonderful to achieve an infinite fattening value, but that would have serious adverse implications for the amount of feed the turkeys must eat each month!

2.7 Setting Up and Solving Linear Programming Problems Using Excel's Solver

Although graphical-solution approaches can handle LP models with only two decision variables, more complex solution procedures are necessary to solve larger LP models. Fortunately, such procedures exist. (We briefly discuss them in section 2.8.) However, rather than use these procedures to solve large LP models by hand, the focus in this book is on using Excel to set up and solve LP problems. Excel and other spreadsheet programs offer users the ability to analyze large LP problems by using built-in problem-solving tools.

There are two main reasons why this book's focus on Excel for setting up and solving LP problems is logical and useful in practice:
- The use of spreadsheet programs is now very common, and virtually every organization has access to them.
- Because you likely are using Excel in many other contexts, you are probably already familiar with many of its commands. Therefore, there is no need to learn any specialized software to set up and solve LP problems.

Excel uses a Microsoft add-in program named Solver to find the solution to LP-related problems. Solver is available when you install Microsoft Office or Excel. The standard version included with Excel can handle LP problems with up to 200 decision variables and 100 constraints, not including simple lower and upper bounds on the decision variables (e.g., nonnegativity constraints). Larger versions of Solver are available for commercial use from Frontline Systems, Inc. (www.solver.com) which has developed and marketed this add-in for Excel (and other spreadsheet packages). We use Solver to solve LP problems in Chapters 2 to 5 and integer and nonlinear programming problems in Chapter 6.

Several other software packages (e.g., LINDO, GAMS) can handle very large LP models. Although slightly different in terms of input and output formats, each program takes basically the same approach toward handling LP problems. Hence, once you are experienced in dealing with computerized LP procedures, you can easily adjust to minor differences among programs.

Using Solver to Solve the Flair Furniture Problem

Recall that the decision variables T and C in the Flair Furniture problem denote the number of tables and chairs to make, respectively. The LP formulation for this problem is as follows:

$$\text{Maximize profit} = \$7T + \$5C$$

subject to the constraints

$$
\begin{aligned}
3T + 4C &\leq 2{,}400 &&\text{(carpentry time)} \\
2T + 1C &\leq 1{,}000 &&\text{(painting time)} \\
C &\leq 450 &&\text{(maximum chairs allowed)} \\
T &\geq 100 &&\text{(minimum tables required)} \\
T, C &\geq 0 &&\text{(nonnegativity)}
\end{aligned}
$$

Just as we discussed a three-step process to formulate an LP problem (i.e., decision variables, objective function, and constraints), setting up and solving a problem using Excel's Solver also involves three parts: changing variable cells, objective cell, and constraints. We discuss each in the following sections.

In practice, there are no specific guidelines regarding the layout of an LP model in Excel. Depending on your personal preference and expertise, any model that satisfies the basic requirements discussed subsequently will work. However, for purposes of convenience and ease of explanation, we use (to the extent possible) the same layout for all problems in this book. Such a consistent approach is more suited to an LP beginner. As you gain experience with spreadsheet modeling of LP problems, we encourage you to try alternate layouts.

In our suggested layout, we use a separate column for each decision variable in the problem to represent all of its parameters (e.g., solution value, profit contribution, and constraint coefficients). The objective function and each constraint in the problem is then modeled on separate rows of the Excel worksheet. Although not required to solve the model, we also add several labels in our spreadsheet to make the entries as self-explanatory as possible.

EXCEL NOTE

The Companion Website for this book, at *degruyter.com/view/product/486941* contains the Excel file for each sample problem discussed here. The relevant file/sheet name is shown below the title of the corresponding figure in this book.

Changing Variable Cells

Solver refers to decision variables as changing variable cells. Each decision variable in a formulation is assigned to a unique cell in the spreadsheet. Although there are no rules regarding the relative positions of these cells, it is typically convenient to use cells that are next to each other.

In the Flair Furniture example, two decision variables need to be assigned to any two cells in the spreadsheet. In Figure 2.14, we use cells B5 and C5 to represent the number of tables (T) and the number of chairs (C) to make, respectively.

The initial entries in these two cells can be blank or any value of our choice. At the conclusion of the Solver run, the optimal values of the decision variables will automatically be shown here (if an optimal solution is found).

It is possible, and often desirable, to format these cells using any of Excel's formatting features. For example, we can choose to specify how many decimal points to show for these values. Likewise, the cells can be assigned any name (instead of B5 and C5), using the naming option in Excel. Descriptive titles for these cells (such as those shown in cells A5, B4, and C4 of Figure 2.14) are recommended to make the model as self-explanatory as possible, but they are not required to solve the problem.

Setting Up and Solving Linear Programming Problems Using Excel's Solver — 65

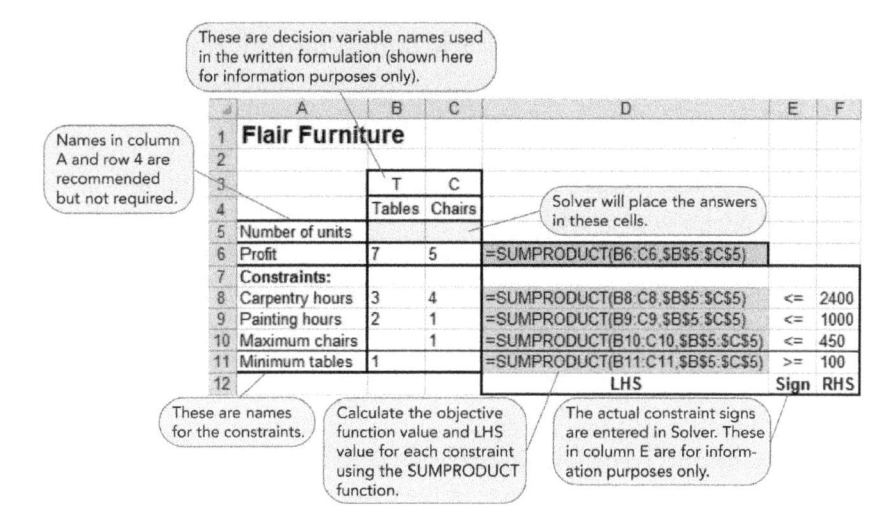

	A	B	C	D	E	F
1	Flair Furniture					
2						
3		T	C			
4		Tables	Chairs			
5	Number of units					
6	Profit	7	5	=SUMPRODUCT(B6:C6,$B$5:$C$5)		
7	Constraints:					
8	Carpentry hours	3	4	=SUMPRODUCT(B8:C8,$B$5:$C$5)	<=	2400
9	Painting hours	2	1	=SUMPRODUCT(B9:C9,$B$5:$C$5)	<=	1000
10	Maximum chairs		1	=SUMPRODUCT(B10:C10,$B$5:$C$5)	<=	450
11	Minimum tables	1		=SUMPRODUCT(B11:C11,$B$5:$C$5)	>=	100
12				LHS	Sign	RHS

- Names in column A and row 4 are recommended but not required.
- These are decision variable names used in the written formulation (shown here for information purposes only).
- Solver will place the answers in these cells.
- These are names for the constraints.
- Calculate the objective function value and LHS value for each constraint using the SUMPRODUCT function.
- The actual constraint signs are entered in Solver. These in column E are for information purposes only.

Figure 2.14: Formula View of the Excel Layout for Flair Furniture

File: Figure 2.14.xlsx, Sheet: Figure 2.14

EXCEL NOTES

- In all our Excel layouts, for clarity, the changing variable cells (decision variables) are shaded yellow.
- In all our Excel layouts, we show the decision variable names (such as *T* and *C*) used in the written formulation of the model (see cells B3 and C3). These names have no role or relevance in using Solver to solve the model and can therefore be ignored. We show these decision variable names in our models so that the equivalence of the written formulation and the Excel layout is clear.

The Objective Cell

We can now set up the objective function, which Solver refers to as the objective cell. We select any cell in the spreadsheet (other than the cells allocated to the decision variables). In that cell, we enter the formula for the objective function, referring to the two decision variables by their cell references (B5 and C5 in this case). In Figure 2.14, we use cell D6 to represent the objective function. Although we could use the unit profit contribution values ($7 per table and $5 per chair) directly in the formula, it is preferable to make the $7 and $5 entries in some cells in the spreadsheet and refer to them by their cell references in the formula in cell D6. This is a more elegant way of setting up the problem and is especially useful if subsequent changes in parameter values are necessary.

In Figure 2.14, we have entered the 7 and 5 in cells B6 and C6, respectively. The formula in cell D6 can therefore be written as

$$= B6*B5+C6*C5$$

The = at the start of the equation lets Excel know that the entry is a formula. This equation corresponds exactly to the objective function of the Flair Furniture problem. If we had left cells B5 and C5 blank, the result of this formula would initially be shown as 0. As with cells B5 and C5, we can format the objective cell (D6) in any manner. For example, because D6 denotes the profit, in dollars, earned by Flair Furniture, we can format it to show the result as a dollar value.

If there are several decision variables in a problem, however, formulas can become somewhat long, and typing them can become quite cumbersome. In such cases, you can use Excel's SUMPRODUCT function to express the equation efficiently and to minimize typographical errors. The syntax for the SUMPRODUCT function requires specifying two cell ranges of equal size, separated by a comma.[5] One of the ranges defines the cells containing the profit contributions (cells B6:C6), and the other defines the cells containing the decision variables (cells B5:C5). The SUMPRODUCT function computes the products of the first entries in each range, second entries in each range, and so on. It then sums these products.

Based on the preceding discussion, as shown in Figure 2.14, the objective function for Flair Furniture can be expressed as

=SUMPRODUCT(B6:C6,$B$5:$C$5)

Note that this is equivalent to =B6*B5+C6*C5 . Also, the use of the $ symbol while specifying the cell references (in the second cell range) keeps those cell references fixed in the formula when we copy this cell to other cells. This is especially convenient because, as we show next, the formula for each constraint in the model also follows the same structure as the objective function.

EXCEL NOTE

In each of our Excel layouts, for clarity, the objective cell (objective function) has been shaded green.

Constraints

We must now set up each constraint in the problem. To achieve this, let us first separate each constraint into three parts: (1) a *left-hand-side (LHS)* part consisting of every term to the left of the equality or inequality sign, (2) a *right-hand-side (RHS)* part consisting of all terms to the right of the equality or inequality sign, and the (3) equality or inequality sign itself. The RHS in most cases may just be a fixed number—that is, a constant.

---

[5] The SUMPRODUCT function also can be used with more than two cell ranges. And it is especially useful in LP problems when decision variables are represented in Excel in two-dimensional blocks (e.g., the network models in Chapter 5). See Excel's help feature for more details on this function.

Creating Cells for Constraint LHS Values We now select a unique cell for each constraint LHS in the formulation (one for each constraint) and type in the relevant formula for that constraint. As with the objective function, we refer to the decision variables by their cell references. In Figure 2.14, we use cell D8 to represent the LHS of the carpentry time constraint. We have entered the coefficients (i.e., 3 and 4) on the LHS of this constraint in cells B8 and C8, respectively. Then, either of the following formulas would be appropriate in cell D8:

$$=B8*B5+C8*C5$$

or

$$=SUMPRODUCT(B8:C8,\$B\$5:\$C\$5)$$

Here again, the SUMPRODUCT function makes the formula compact in situations in which the LHS has many terms. Note the similarity between the objective function formula in cell D6 [=SUMPRODUCT(B6:C6,$B$5:$C$5)] and the LHS formula for the carpentry constraint in cell D8 [=SUMPRODUCT(B8:C8,$B$5:$C$5)]. In fact, because we have anchored the cell references for the decision variables (B5 and C5) using the $ symbol in cell D6, we can simply copy the formula in cell D6 to cell D8.

The LHS formula for the painting hours constraint (cell D9), chairs production limit constraint (cell D10), and tables minimum production constraint (cell D11) can similarly be copied from cell D6. As you have probably recognized by now, the LHS cell for virtually every constraint in an LP formulation can be created in this fashion.

EXCEL NOTE
In each of our Excel layouts, for clarity, cells denoting LHS formulas of constraints have been shaded blue.

Creating Cells for Constraint RHS Values
When all the LHS formulas have been set up, we can pick unique cells for each constraint RHS in the formulation. Although the Flair Furniture problem has only constants (2,400, 1,000, 450, and 100, respectively) for the four constraints, it is perfectly valid in Solver for the RHS to also have a formula like the LHS. In Figure 2.14, we show the four RHS values in cells F8:F11.

Constraint Type In Figure 2.14, we also show the sign ($\leq, \geq,$ or $=$) of each constraint between the LHS and RHS cells for that constraint (see cells E8:E11). Although this makes each constraint easier to understand, note that the inclusion of these signs here is for information purposes only. As we show next, the actual sign for each constraint is entered directly in Solver.

Nonnegativity Constraints It is not necessary to specify the nonnegativity constraints (i.e., $T \geq 0$ and $C \geq 0$) in the model using the previous procedure. As we will see shortly, there is a simple option available in Solver to automatically enforce these constraints.

Entering Information in Solver

After all the constraints have been set up, we invoke the Solver Parameters window in Excel by clicking the Data tab and then selecting Solver in the Analysis group, as shown in Figure 2.15(a).[6] The Solver Parameters window is shown in Figure 2.15(b).

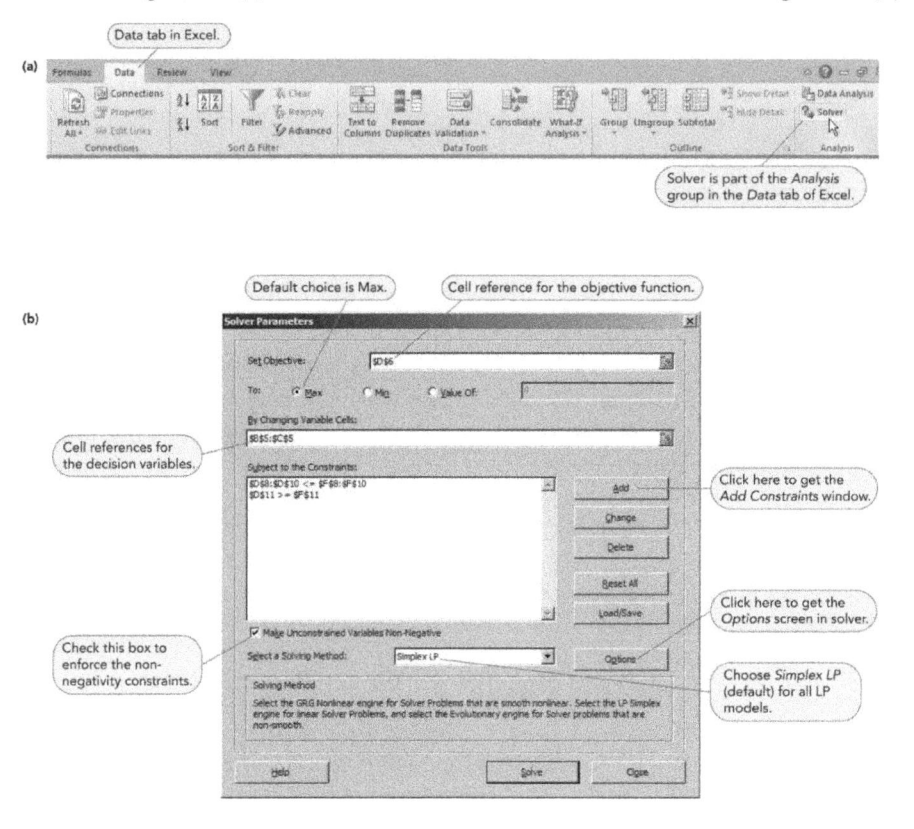

Figure 2.15: Solver Parameters Window for Flair Furniture

Specifying the Objective Cell We first enter the relevant cell reference (i.e., cell D6) in the Set Objective box. The default in Solver is to maximize the objective value.

---

[6] If you do not see Solver in the Analysis group within the Data tab in Excel, refer to Appendix B, section B.6, *Installing and Enabling Excel Add-Ins*, for instructions on how to fix this problem. Alternatively, type Solver in Excel's help feature and select Load the Solver Add-in for detailed instructions.

(Note that the Max option is already selected.) For a minimization problem, we must click the Min option to specify that the objective function should be minimized. The third option (Value Of) allows us to specify a value that we want the objective cell to achieve, rather than obtain the optimal solution. (We do not use this option in our study of LP and other mathematical programming models.)

Specifying the Changing Variable Cells We now move the cursor to the box labeled By Changing Variable Cells. We enter the cell references for the decision variables in this box. If the cell references are next to each other, we can simply enter them as one block. For example, we could enter B5:C5 for Flair Furniture's problem. (If we use the mouse or keyboard to highlight and select cells B5 and C5, Excel automatically puts in the $ anchors, as shown in Figure 2.15.) If the cells are not contiguous (i.e., not next to each other), we can enter the changing variable cells by placing a comma between noncontiguous cells (or blocks of cells). So, we could enter B5,C5 in the By Changing Variable Cells window for this specific problem.

Specifying the Constraints Next, we move to the box labeled Subject to the Constraints and click the Add button to enter the relevant cell references for the LHS and RHS of each constraint. The Add Constraint window (shown in Figure 2.16) has a box titled Cell Reference in which we enter the cell reference of the constraint's LHS, a drop-down menu in which we specify the constraint's sign, and a second box titled Constraint in which we enter the cell reference of the constraint's RHS. The drop-down menu has six choices: $\leq$, $\geq$, $=$, Int (for integer), Bin (for binary), and dif (for all different). (We discuss the last three choices in Chapter 6.)

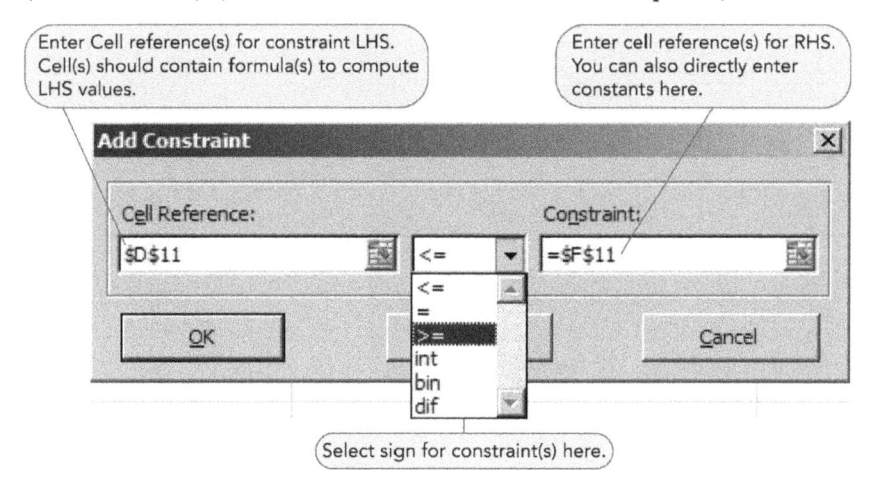

Figure 2.16: Solver Add Constraint Window

We can either add constraints one at a time or add blocks of constraints that have the same sign ($\leq$, $\geq$, or $=$) at the same time. For instance, we could first add the carpentry constraint by entering D8 in the LHS input box, entering F8 in the RHS input box, and selecting the ≤ sign from the drop-down menu. As noted earlier, the ≤ sign shown in cell E8 is not relevant in Solver, and we must enter the sign of each constraint by using the Add Constraint window. We can now add the painting constraint by entering D9 and F9 in the LHS and RHS input boxes, respectively. Next, we can add the chairs limit constraint by entering D10 and F10 in the LHS and RHS input boxes, respectively. Finally, we can add the minimum table production constraint by entering D11 and F11 in the LHS and RHS input boxes, respectively. Note that in this constraint's case, we should select the ≥ sign the from the drop-down menu.

Alternatively, because the first three constraints have the same sign (≤), we can input cells D8 to D10 in the LHS input box (i.e., enter D8:D10) and correspondingly enter F8:F10 in the RHS input box. We select ≤ as the sign between these LHS and RHS entries. Solver interprets this as taking each entry in the LHS input box and setting it ≤ to the corresponding entry in the RHS input box (i.e., D8 ≤ F8, D9 ≤ F9, and D10 ≤ F10).

Using the latter procedure, note that it is possible to have just three entries in the constraints window: one for all the ≤ constraints in the model, one for all the ≥ constraints in the model, and one for all the = constraints in the model. This, of course, requires that the spreadsheet layout be such that the LHS and RHS cells for all constraints that have the same sign are in contiguous blocks, as in Figure 2.14. However, as we demonstrate in several examples in Chapter 3, this is quite easy to do.

At any point during or after the constraint input process, we can use the Change or Delete buttons in the Subject to the Constraints box to modify one or more constraints, as necessary. It is important to note that we *cannot* enter the formula for the objective function and the LHS and/or RHS of constraints from within the Solver Parameters window. The formulas must be created in appropriate cells in the spreadsheet before using the Solver Parameters window. Although it is possible to directly enter constants (2,400, 1,000, 450, and 100 in our model) in the RHS input box while adding constraints, it is preferable to make the RHS also a cell reference (F8, F9, F10, and F11 in our model).

Specifying the Nonnegativity Constraints Directly below the box labeled Subject to the Constraints (Figure 2.15), there is a box labeled Make Unconstrained Variables Non-Negative. This box is checked by default in Excel; for most LP models, it should remain this way. The checked box automatically enforces the nonnegativity constraint for all the decision variables in the model.

Solving Method Next, we move to the box labeled Select a Solving Method. To solve LP problems, we should choose the option called Simplex LP. Selecting this setting directs Solver to solve LP models efficiently and provide a detailed Sensitivity Report, which we cover in Chapter 4. Clicking the down arrow in this box reveals two other method choices: GRG Nonlinear and Evolutionary. We will discuss the GRG Nonlinear procedure in Chapter 6.

Solver Options After all constraints have been entered, we are ready to solve the model. However, before clicking the Solve button on the Solver Parameters window, we click the Options button to open the Solver Options window (shown in Figure 2.17) and focus on the choices available in the All Methods tab. (The options in the GRG Nonlinear and Evolutionary tabs are not relevant for LP models.) For solving most LP problems, we do not have to change any of the default parameters for these options. The options related to Evolutionary and Integer Constraints are not relevant for LP models. To see details of each iteration taken by Solver to go from the initial solution to the optimal solution (if one exists), we can check the Show Iterations Results box.

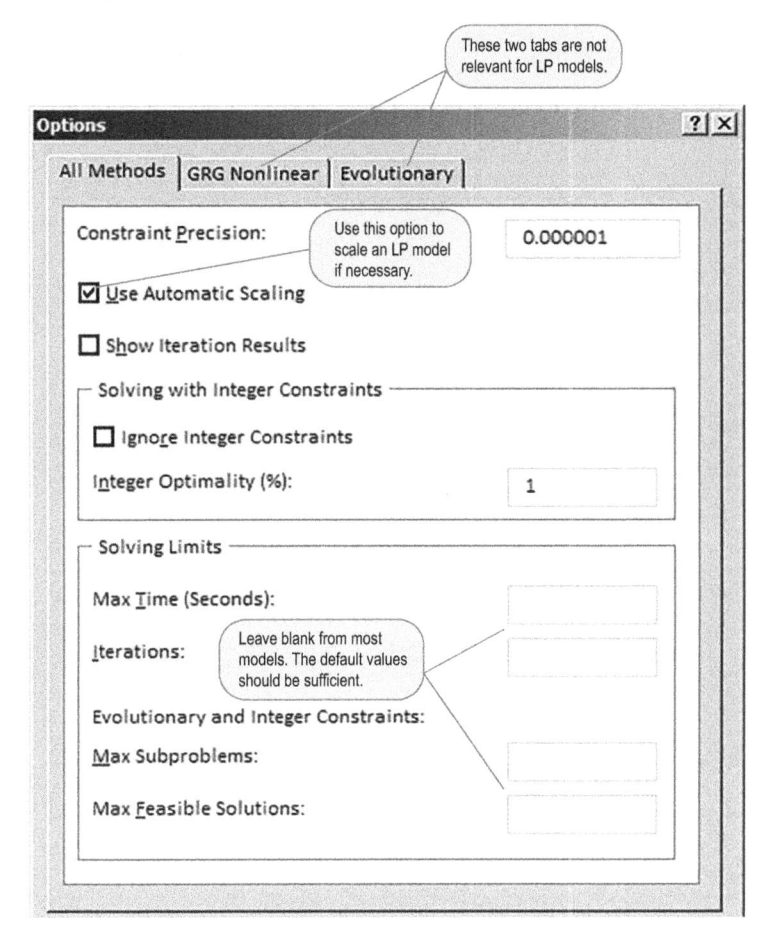

Figure 2.17: Solver Options Window

With regard to the option called Use Automatic Scaling (see Figure 2.17), it is a good idea in practice to scale problems in which values of the objective function coefficients and constraint coefficients of different constraints differ by several orders of magnitude. For instance, a problem in which some coefficients are in millions while others have fractional values would be considered a poorly scaled model. Due to the effects of a computer's finite precision arithmetic, such poorly scaled models could cause difficulty for Solver, leading to fairly large rounding errors. Checking the automatic scaling box directs Solver to scale models it detects as poorly scaled and possibly avoid such rounding problems.

Solving the Model When the Solve button is clicked, Solver executes the model and displays the results, as shown in Figure 2.18.

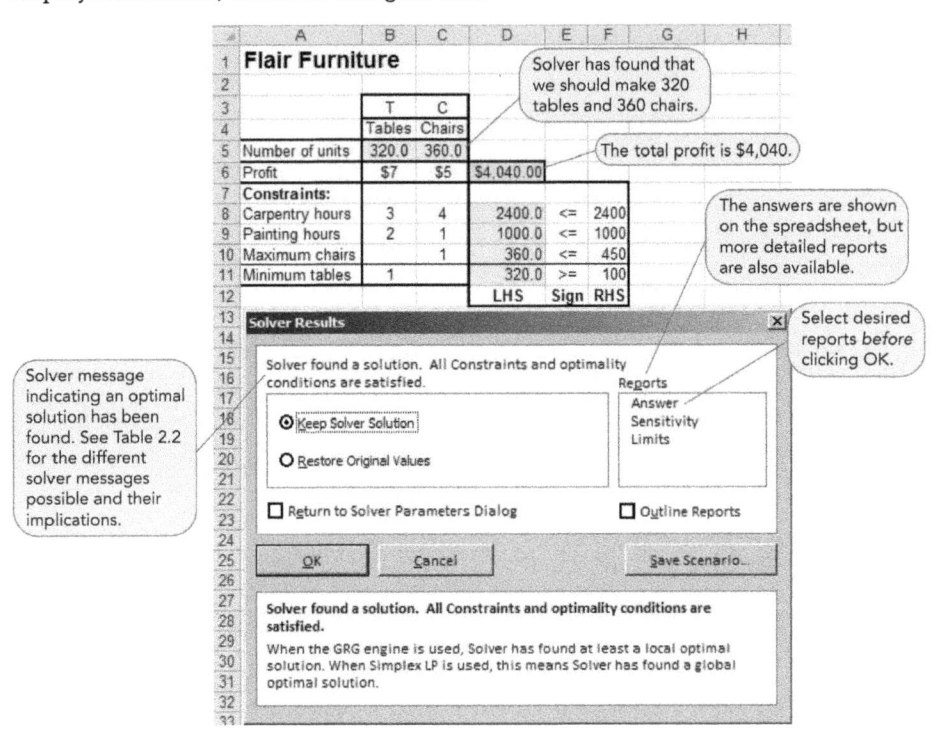

Figure 2.18: Excel Layout and Solver Solution for Flair Furniture (Solver Results Window Also Shown)

File: Figure 2.14.xlsx, Sheet: Figure 2.18

Before looking at the results, it is important to read the message in the Solver Results window to verify that Solver found an optimal solution. In some cases, the window indicates that Solver is unable to find an optimal solution (e.g., when the formulation is infeasible or the solution space is unbounded). Table 2.2 shows several different Solver messages that could result when an LP model is solved, the meaning of each message, and a possible cause for each message.

Table 2.2: Possible Messages in the Solver Results Window

Message	Meaning	Possible Cause
Solver found a solution. All Constraints and optimality conditions are satisfied.	Ideal message!	*Note:* This does *not* mean the formulation and/or solution is correct. It just means there are no syntax errors in the Excel formulas and Solver entries.
Solver could not find a feasible solution.	There is no feasible region.	Incorrect entries in LHS formulas, signs, and/or RHS values of constraints.
The Objective Cell values do not converge.	Unbounded solution.	Incorrect entries in LHS formulas, signs, and/or RHS values of constraints.
Solver encountered an error value in the Objective Cell or a Constraint cell.	Formula error in the objective cell or a constraint cell. At least one of the cells in the model becomes an error value when Solver tries different values for the changing variable cells.	Most common cause is division by zero in some cell.
The linearity conditions required by this LP Solver are not satisfied.	The Simplex LP method has been specified in Solver to solve this model, but one or more formulas in the model are not linear.	Multiplication or division involving two or more variables in some cell. *Note:* Solver sometimes gives this error message even when the formulas are linear. This occurs especially when both the LHS and RHS of a constraint have formulas. In such cases, we should manipulate the constraint algebraically to make the RHS a constant.

The Solver Results window also indicates that there are three reports available: Answer, Sensitivity, and Limits. We discuss the Answer Report in the next section and the Sensitivity Report in Chapter 4. The Limits Report is not useful for our discussion here, and we therefore ignore it. Note that to get these reports, we must click on the relevant report names to highlight them before clicking OK on the Solver Results window.

Cells B5 and C5 show the optimal quantities of tables and chairs to make, respectively, and cell D6 shows the optimal profit. Cells D8 to D11 show the LHS values of the four constraints. For example, cell D8 shows the number of carpentry hours used.

EXCEL EXTRA

Locking Cells

Especially when you are creating spreadsheets for other people to use, it can pay off significantly to make the spreadsheets as mistake-proof as possible. One helpful technique is to *lock certain cells you don't want changed*. This may be particularly important when you don't want users accidently overwriting formulas. For example, in Figure 2.18, you might want to ensure that the formulas in cells D6 and D8:D11 can't be changed in case the user wants to solve the model using different inputs—say, different profit values for tables and chairs. In fact, many end-user worksheets should have all cells locked except parameter input and decision variable cells.

- First select the entire worksheet and then click:
  Home|Format|Lock Cell [the lock icon will remain pressed]

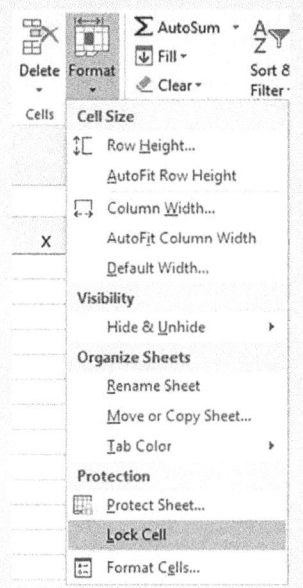

- Next, select each range that you don't want protected and then click:
  Home|Format|Lock Cell [the lock icon will no longer remain pressed]

- Then click Home|Format|Protect Sheet...|OK (optional password)

- To unlock the sheet, click:
  Home|Format|Unprotect Sheet...

- If the user tries to enter something into a protected cell, an error message appears:

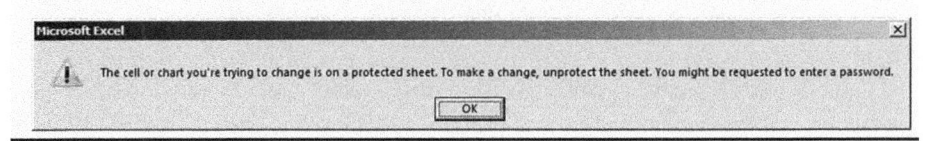

Answer Report If requested, Solver provides the Answer Report in a separate worksheet. The report for Flair's problem is shown in Figure 2.19. (We have added grid lines to this report to make it clearer.) The report essentially provides the same information as that discussed previously but in a more detailed and organized manner. In addition to showing the initial and final (optimal) values for the objective function and each decision variable, it includes a column titled Integer, which indicates whether the decision variable was specified as continuous valued or integer valued in the model. (We will discuss integer-valued variables in Chapter 6). The report also includes the following information for each constraint in the model:

```
Microsoft Excel 14.0 Answer Report
Worksheet: [Figure 2.14.xlsx]Figure 2.19
Result: Solver found a solution. All Constraints and optimality conditions are satisfied.
Solver Engine
   Engine: Simplex LP
   Solution Time: 0.015 Seconds.
   Iterations: 3 Subproblems: 0
Solver Options
   Max Time 100 sec, Iterations 100, Precision 0.000001
   Max Subproblems 5000, Max Integer Sols 5000, Integer Tolerance 0.05%, Assume NonNegative
```

Objective Cell (Max)

Cell	Name	Original Value	Final Value
$D$6	Profit	$0.00	$4,040.00

The initial and final solution values are shown here.

Variable Cells

Cell	Name	Original Value	Final Value	Integer
$B$5	Number of units Tables	0.0	320.0	Contin
$C$5	Number of units Chairs	0.0	360.0	Contin

Indicates decision variables are continuous valued in this LP model.

Constraints

Cell	Name	Cell Value	Formula	Status	Slack
$D$8	Carpentry hours	2400.0	$D$8<=$F$8	Binding	0.0
$D$9	Painting hours	1000.0	$D$9<=$F$9	Binding	0.0
$D$10	Maximum chairs	360.0	$D$10<=$F$10	Not Binding	90.0
$D$11	Minimum tables	320.0	$D$11>=$F$11	Not Binding	220.0

Calculate slack as the difference between the RHS and LHS of a ≤ constraint.

All names can be overwritten if desired.

These are the final values of the constraint LHS.

Calculate surplus as the difference between the LHS and RHS of a ≥ constraint.

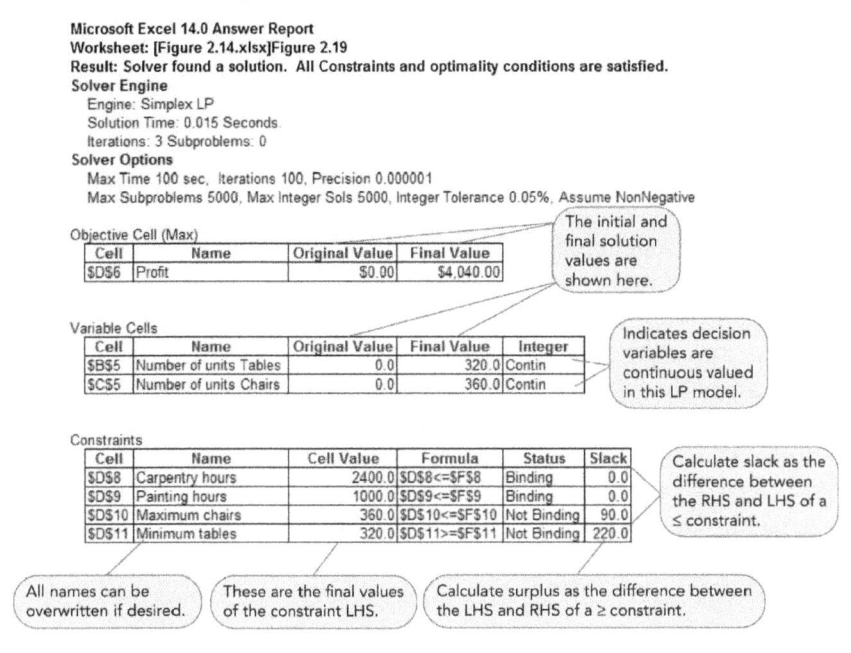

Figure 2.19: Solver's Answer Report for Flair Furniture

📊 File: Figure 2.14.xlsx, Sheet: Figure 2.19

1. Cell. Cell reference corresponding to the LHS of the constraint. For example, cell D8 contains the formula for the LHS of the carpentry constraint.
2. Name. Descriptive name of the LHS cell. We can use Excel's naming feature to define a descriptive name for any cell (or cell range) simply by typing the desired name in the Name box (which is at the left end of the formula bar in any Excel worksheet and has the cell reference listed by default). If we do so, the cell name is reported in this column. If no name is defined for a cell, Solver extracts the name shown in this column from the information provided in the spreadsheet layout. Solver simply combines labels (if any) to the left of and above the LHS cell to create the name for that cell. Note that these labels can be overwritten manually, if necessary. For example, the name Profit for the objective cell (cell D6) can be overwritten to say Total Profit. Observe that the Excel layout we have used here ensures that all names automatically generated by Solver are logical.

3. Cell Value. The final value of the LHS of the constraint at the optimal solution. For example, the cell value for the carpentry time constraint indicates that we are using 2,400 hours at the optimal solution.
4. Formula. The formula specified in Solver for the constraint. For example, the formula entered in Solver for the carpentry time constraint is D8 ≤ F8 .
5. Status. Indicates whether the constraint is binding or nonbinding. Binding means that the constraint becomes an equality (i.e., LHS = RHS) at the optimal solution. For a ≤ constraint, this typically means that all the available amounts of that resource are fully used in the optimal solution. In Flair's case, the carpentry and painting constraints are both binding because we are using all the available hours in either case.

For a ≥ constraint, binding typically means we are exactly satisfying the minimum level required by that constraint. In Flair's case, the minimum tables required constraint is nonbinding because we plan to make 320 as against the required minimum of 100.

6. Slack. Magnitude (absolute value) of the difference between the RHS and LHS values of the constraint. Obviously, if the constraint is binding, slack is zero (because LHS = RHS). For a nonbinding ≤ constraint, slack typically denotes the amount of resource that is left unused at the optimal solution. In Flair's case, we are allowed to make up to 450 chairs but are planning to make only 360. The absolute difference of 90 between the RHS and LHS (=|450 − 360|) is the slack in this constraint.

For a nonbinding ≥ constraint, we call this term surplus (even though Solver refers to this difference in all cases as slack). A surplus typically denotes the extent to which the ≥ constraint is oversatisfied at the optimal solution. In Flair's case, we are planning to make 320 tables even though we are required to make only 100. The absolute difference of 220 between the RHS and LHS (=|100 − 320|) is the surplus in this constraint.

Using Solver to Solve Flair Furniture Company's Modified Problem

Recall that after solving Flair Furniture's problem using a graphical approach, we added a new constraint specified by the marketing department. Specifically, we needed to ensure that the number of chairs made this month is at least 75 more than the number of tables made. The constraint was expressed as

$$C - T \geq 75$$

The Excel layout and Solver entries for Flair's modified problem are shown in Figure 2.20. Note that the constraint coefficient for T is entered as −1 in cell B12 to reflect the fact that the variable T is subtracted in the expression. The formula in cell D12 is the same SUMPRODUCT function used in cells D8:D11. The optimal solution now is to make 300 tables and 375 chairs, for a profit of $3,975, the same solution we obtained graphically in Figure 2.7.

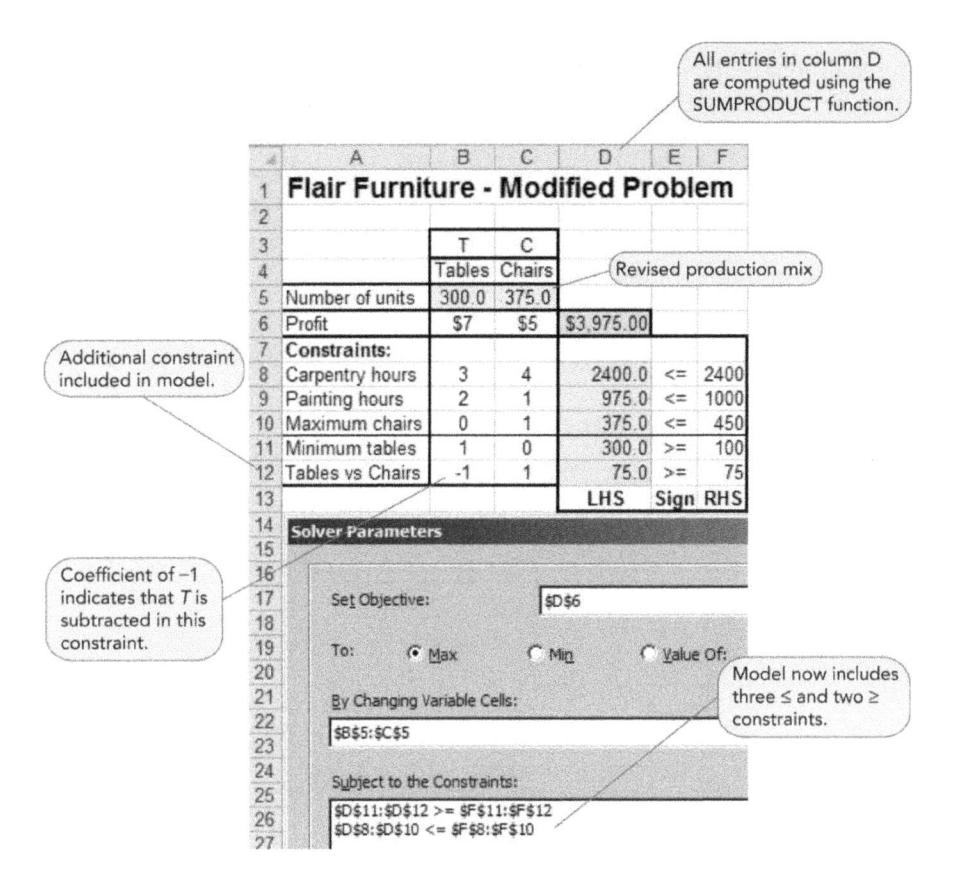

Setting Up and Solving Linear Programming Problems Using Excel's Solver — 77

Figure 2.20: Excel Layout and Solver Entries for Flair Furniture—Revised Problem

File: Figure 2.20.xlsx

Using Solver to Solve the Holiday Meal Turkey Ranch Problem

Now that we have studied how to set up and solve a maximization LP problem using Excel's Solver, let us consider a minimization problem—the Holiday Meal Turkey Ranch example. Recall that the decision variables A and B in this problem denote the number of pounds of brand A feed and brand B feed to use per month, respectively. The LP formulation for this problem is as follows:

$$\text{Minimize cost} = \$0.10A + \$0.15B$$

subject to the constraints

$$5A + 10B \geq 45 \quad \text{(protein required)}$$
$$4A + 3B \geq 24 \quad \text{(vitamin required)}$$
$$0.5A \geq 1.5 \quad \text{(iron required)}$$
$$A, B \geq 0 \quad \text{(nonnegativity)}$$

The formula view of the Excel layout for the Holiday Meal Turkey Ranch LP problem is shown in Figure 2.21. The solution values and the Solver Parameters window are shown in Figure 2.22. Note that Solver shows the problem as being solved as a Min problem. As with the Flair Furniture example, all problem parameters are entered as entries in different cells of the spreadsheet, and Excel's SUMPRODUCT function is used to compute the objective function as well as the LHS values for all three constraints (corresponding to protein, vitamin, and iron).

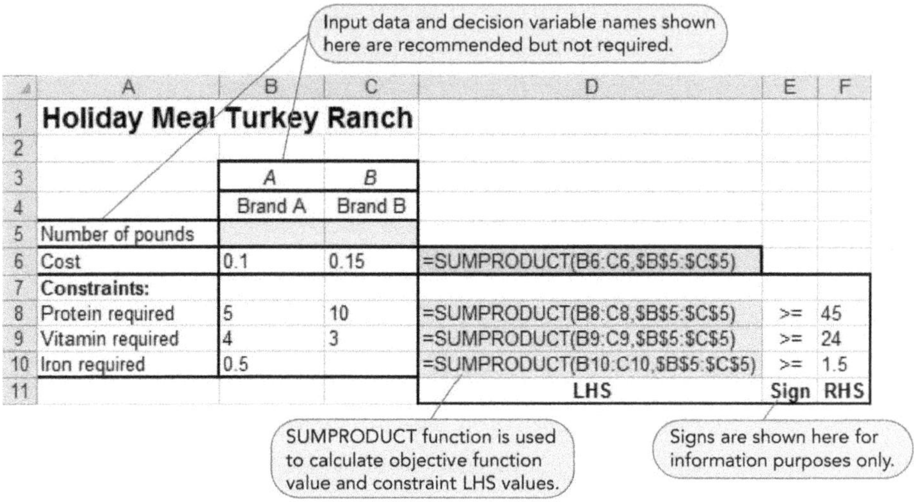

Input data and decision variable names shown here are recommended but not required.

	A	B	C	D	E	F
1	Holiday Meal Turkey Ranch					
2						
3		A	B			
4		Brand A	Brand B			
5	Number of pounds					
6	Cost	0.1	0.15	=SUMPRODUCT(B6:C6,$B$5:$C$5)		
7	Constraints:					
8	Protein required	5	10	=SUMPRODUCT(B8:C8,$B$5:$C$5)	>=	45
9	Vitamin required	4	3	=SUMPRODUCT(B9:C9,$B$5:$C$5)	>=	24
10	Iron required	0.5		=SUMPRODUCT(B10:C10,$B$5:$C$5)	>=	1.5
11				LHS	Sign	RHS

SUMPRODUCT function is used to calculate objective function value and constraint LHS values.

Signs are shown here for information purposes only.

Figure 2.21: Formula View of the Excel Layout for Holiday Meal

📊 File: Figure 2.21.xlsx, Sheet: Figure 2.21

As expected, the optimal solution is the same as the one we obtained using the graphical approach. Holiday Meal should use 4.20 pounds of brand A feed and 2.40 pounds of brand B feed, at a cost of $0.78 per turkey per month. The protein and vitamin constraints are binding at the optimal solution. However, we are providing 2.1 units of iron per turkey per month even though we are required to provide only 1.5 units (i.e., an oversatisfaction, or *surplus*, of 0.6 units).

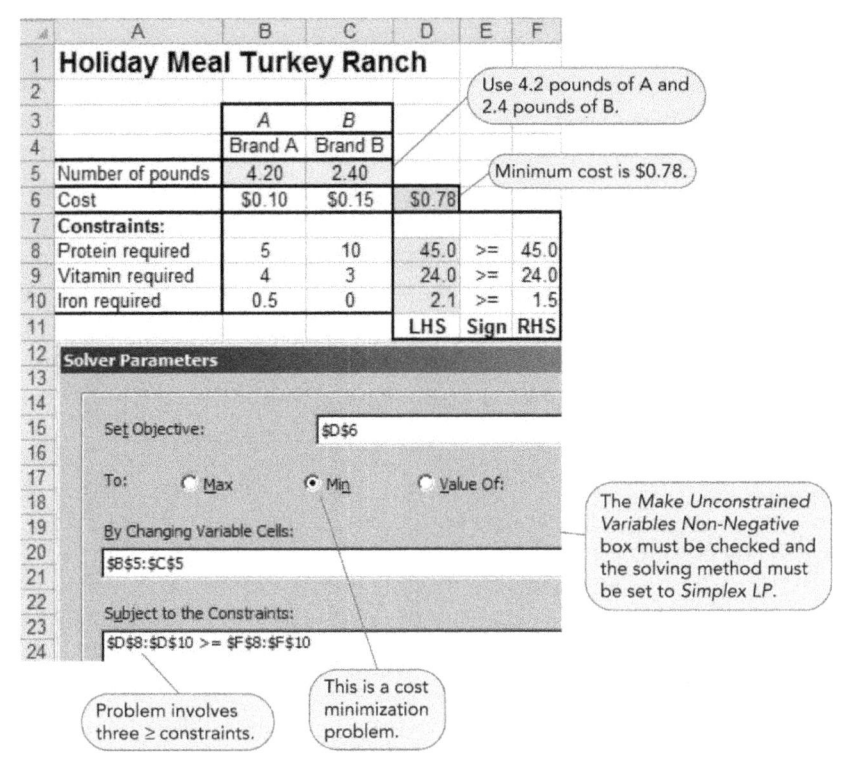

Figure 2.22: Excel Layout and Solver Entries for Holiday Meal

	A	B	C	D	E	F
1	**Holiday Meal Turkey Ranch**					
2					Use 4.2 pounds of A and 2.4 pounds of B.	
3		A	B			
4		Brand A	Brand B			
5	Number of pounds	4.20	2.40		Minimum cost is $0.78.	
6	Cost	$0.10	$0.15	$0.78		
7	Constraints:					
8	Protein required	5	10	45.0	>=	45.0
9	Vitamin required	4	3	24.0	>=	24.0
10	Iron required	0.5	0	2.1	>=	1.5
11				LHS	Sign	RHS

Solver Parameters

Set Objective: $D$6

To: ○ Max ● Min ○ Value Of:

By Changing Variable Cells:
$B$5:$C$5

Subject to the Constraints:
$D$8:$D$10 >= $F$8:$F$10

Problem involves three ≥ constraints.

This is a cost minimization problem.

The Make Unconstrained Variables Non-Negative box must be checked and the solving method must be set to Simplex LP.

Figure 2.22: Excel Layout and Solver Entries for Holiday Meal

File: Figure 2.21.xlsx, Sheet: Figure 2.22

2.8 Algorithmic Solution Procedures for Linear Programming Problems

So far, we have looked at examples of LP problems that contain only two decision variables. With only two, it is possible to use a graphical approach. We plotted the feasible region and then searched for an optimal corner point and corresponding profit or cost. This approach provides a good way to understand the basic concepts of LP. Most real-life LP problems, however, have more than two variables and are thus too large for the simple graphical solution procedure. Problems faced in business and government can have dozens, hundreds, or even thousands of variables. We need a more powerful method than graphing; for this we turn to a procedure called the simplex method.

How does the simplex method work? The concept is simple and similar to graphical LP in one important respect: In graphical LP, we examine each of the corner points; LP theory tells us that an optimal solution lies at one of them. In LP problems containing several variables, we may not be able to graph the feasible region, but an optimal solution still lies at a corner point of the many-sided, many-dimensional figure (called an n-dimensional polyhedron) that represents the area of feasible solutions. The simplex method systematically examines the corner points using basic algebraic concepts. It does so in an iterative process—that is, it repeats the same set of steps time after time until it reaches an optimal solution. Each iteration of the simplex method brings a value for the objective function that is no worse (and usually better) than the current value, progressively moving closer to an optimal solution.

In most software packages, including Excel's Solver, the simplex method has been coded in a very efficient manner to exploit the computational capabilities of modern computers. As a result, for most LP problems, the simplex method identifies an optimal corner point after examining just a tiny fraction of the total number of corner points in the feasible region.

2.9 Summary

In this chapter, we introduce a mathematical modeling technique called linear programming (LP). Analysts use LP models to find an optimal solution to problems that have a series of constraints binding the objective value. We discuss how to formulate LP models and then show how models with only two decision variables can be solved graphically. The graphical solution approach of this chapter provides a conceptual basis for tackling larger, more complex real-life problems. However, solving LP models that have numerous decision variables and constraints requires a solution procedure such as the simplex algorithm.

The simplex algorithm is embedded in Excel's Solver add-in. We describe how LP models can be set up on Excel and solved using Solver. The structured approach presented in this chapter for setting up and solving LP problems with just two variables can be easily adapted to problems of larger size. We address several such problems in Chapter 3.

Key Points
— Linear programming helps in resource allocation decisions.
— Formulation involves expressing a problem scenario in terms of simple mathematical expressions.
— Solution involves solving the mathematical expressions to find values for the decision variables.
— Sensitivity analysis allows a manager to answer "what-if" questions regarding a problem's solution.
— First LP property: Problems seek to maximize or minimize an objective.
— Second LP property: Constraints limit the degree to which the objective can be achieved.
— Third LP property: There must be alternatives available for the solution.
— Fourth LP property: All mathematical expressions in the model are linear.

Summary

- An inequality has a ≤ or ≥ sign.
- Four technical requirements of an LP problem are certainty, proportionality, additivity, and divisibility.
- Product mix problems use LP to decide how much of each product to make, given a series of resource restrictions.
- Decision variables are the unknown entities in a problem. The problem is solved to find values for the decision variables.
- Different decision variables in the same model can be measured in different units.
- The objective function represents the motivation for solving a problem.
- Constraints represent restrictions on the values that the decision variables can take.
- It is common for different constraints in an LP model to have different signs (≤, =, or ≥).
- A key principle of LP is that interactions exist between variables.
- Nonnegativity constraints specify that decision variables cannot have negative values.
- In LP models, we do not explicitly specify that decision variables should have only integer values.
- Recognizing and defining the decision variables properly is perhaps the most critical step in LP formulation.
- All mathematical expressions in the model (the objective function and each constraint) must use only the decision variables that have been defined for the model.
- All terms within the same expression must refer to the same entity.
- All terms within the same LP mathematical expression must be measured in the same units.
- The graphical method works only when there are two decision variables, but it provides valuable insight into how larger problems are solved.
- Nonnegativity constraints in a two-variable LP problem mean we are always in the first quadrant of the graphical area.
- Plotting a constraint in a two-variable LP problem involves finding points at which the line intersects both axes.
- In all problems, we are interested in satisfying all constraints at the same time.
- The feasible region is the overlapping area of all constraints.
- In the graphical solution method, we use the objective function to point us toward the optimal solution.
- In the graphical solution method, we draw a series of parallel level lines to the objective function until we find the one that corresponds to the optimal solution.
- An important property of all LP models is that the optimal solution must be at one of the corner points in the feasible region.
- Solving for the coordinates of a corner point requires the use of simultaneous equations, an algebraic technique.
- Adding a constraint to an LP problem cannot improve the solution and may actually worsen it.

- Minimization LP problems typically deal with trying to reduce costs.
- The feasible region of minimization problems is often unbounded (i.e., open outward).
- A redundant constraint is one that does not affect the feasible solution region.
- Lack of a feasible solution region can occur if constraints conflict with one another.
- Alternate optimal solutions are possible in LP problems.
- When a problem has an unbounded feasible region, it may not have a finite solution.
- When the solution is unbounded in a maximization problem, the objective function value can be made infinitely large without violating any constraints.
- Excel has a built-in solution tool called Solver for solving LP problems.
- The standard version of Solver is included with all versions of Excel.
- There is no prescribed layout for setting up LP problems in Excel.
- In the Excel implementations of an LP model, it is convenient to represent all parameters associated with a decision variable in the same column.
- The By Changing Variable Cells entries in the Solver Parameters box in Excel are the decision variables in the problem.
- The objective cell in Excel contains the formula for the objective function to which Solver refers.
- Excel's SUMPRODUCT function makes it easy to enter even long expressions.
- Constraints in Solver include three entries: LHS, RHS, and sign.
- In Solver, the RHS of a constraint can also include a formula.
- The actual sign for each constraint is entered directly in Solver.
- The default in Solver is to maximize the objective cell.
- The By Changing Variable Cells entries in the Solver Parameters box can be entered as a block or as individual cell references separated by commas.
- The Add Constraint window in Solver is used to enter constraints.
- Constraints with the same sign can be entered as a block in the Add Constraint window in Solver.
- Check the Make Unconstrained Variables Non-Negative box in Solver to enforce the nonnegativity constraints.
- Select Simplex LP as the solving method in Solver to solve LP models.
- It is a good idea to check Use Automatic Scaling in the Options box of Solver to avoid rounding problems with problems that are poorly scaled.
- Solver provides options to obtain different reports.
- The Answer Report presents the Solver results in a more detailed manner.
- Names in Solver reports can be edited, if desired.
- Binding means that the constraint is exactly satisfied and LHS = RHS.
- Slack typically refers to the amount of unused resource in a $\leq$ constraint.
- Surplus typically refers to the amount of over-satisfaction of a $\geq$ constraint.

— For large LP problems, the feasible region cannot be graphed because it has many dimensions, but the concept that the optimal solution will lie at a corner point of the feasible region is the same.
— The simplex method systematically examines corner points, using algebraic steps, until an optimal solution is found.

Glossary

Alternate Optimal Solution A situation in which more than one optimal solution is possible. It arises when the angle or slope of the objective function is the same as the slope of the constraint.

Answer Report A report created by Solver when it solves an LP model. This report presents the optimal solution in a detailed manner.

Binding The constraint becomes an equality (i.e., LHS = RHS) at the optimal solution.

Changing Variable Cells Cells that represent the decision variables in Solver.

Constraint A restriction (stated in the form of an inequality or an equation) that inhibits (or binds) the value that can be achieved by the objective function.

Constraint LHS The cell that contains the formula for the left-hand side of a constraint in Solver. There is one such cell for each constraint in a problem.

Constraint RHS The cell that contains the value (or formula) for the right-hand side of a constraint in Solver. There is one such cell for each constraint in a problem.

Corner (or Extreme) Point A point that lies on one of the corners of the feasible region. This means that it falls at the intersection of two constraint lines.

Corner Point Method The method of finding the optimal solution to an LP problem that involves testing the profit or cost level at each corner point of the feasible region. The theory of LP states that the optimal solution must lie at one of the corner points.

Decision Variables The unknown quantities in a problem for which optimal solution values are to be found.

Feasible Region The area that satisfies all of a problem's resource restrictions—that is, the region where all constraints overlap. All possible solutions to the problem lie in the feasible region.

Feasible Solution Any point that lies in the feasible region. Basically, it is any point that satisfies all of the problem's constraints.

Inequality A mathematical expression that contains a greater-than-or-equal-to relation ($\geq$) or a less-than-or-equal-to relation ($\leq$) between the left-hand and right-hand sides of the expression.

Infeasible Solution Any point that lies outside the feasible region. It violates one or more of the stated constraints.

Infeasibility A condition that arises when there is no solution to an LP problem that satisfies all of the constraints.

Integer Programming A mathematical programming model in which some or all decision variables are restricted only to integer values.

Iterative Process A process (algorithm) that repeats the same steps over and over.

Level (or Iso) Line A straight line that represents all nonnegative combinations of the decision variables for a particular profit (or cost) level.

Linear Programming (LP) A mathematical technique used to help management decide how to make the most effective use of an organization's resources.

Make Unconstrained Variables Nonnegative An option available in Solver that automatically enforces the nonnegativity constraint.

Mathematical Programming The general category of mathematical modeling and solution techniques used to allocate resources while optimizing a measurable goal; LP is one type of programming model.

Nonnegativity Constraints A set of constraints that requires each decision variable to be nonnegative; that is, each decision variable must be greater than or equal to 0.

Objective Cell The cell in Solver that contains the formula for the objective function.

Objective Function A mathematical statement of the goal of an organization, stated as an intent to maximize or minimize some important quantity, such as profit or cost.

Product Mix Problem A common LP problem that involves a decision about which products a firm should produce, given that it faces limited resources.

Redundant Constraint A constraint that does not affect the feasible solution region.

Simplex Method An iterative procedure for solving LP problems.

Simplex LP An option available in Solver that forces it to solve the model as a linear program by using the simplex procedure.

Simultaneous Equation Method The algebraic means of solving for the intersection point of two or more linear constraint equations.

Slack The difference between the right-hand side and left-hand side of a ≤ constraint. Slack typically represents the unused resource.

Solver An Excel add-in that allows LP problems to be set up and solved in Excel.

SUMPRODUCT An Excel function that allows users to easily model formulas for the objective function and constraints while setting up a linear programming model in Excel.

Surplus The difference between the left-hand side and right-hand side of a ≥ constraint. Surplus typically represents the level of oversatisfaction of a requirement.

Unbounded Solution A condition that exists when the objective value can be made infinitely large (in a maximization problem) or small (in a minimization problem) without violating any of the problem's constraints.

2.10 Exercises

Solved Problems
Below are the solutions to problems featured in this chapter to help you with upcoming exercises.

Solved Problem 2-1. Solve the following LP model graphically and then by using Excel:

$$\text{Maximize profit} = \$30X + \$40Y$$

subject to the constraints

$$4X + 2Y \leq 16$$
$$Y \leq 2$$
$$2X - Y \geq 2$$
$$X, Y \geq 0$$

Solution Figure 2.23 shows the feasible region, as well as a level profit line for a profit value of $60. Note that the third constraint $(2X - Y \geq 2)$ has a positive slope.

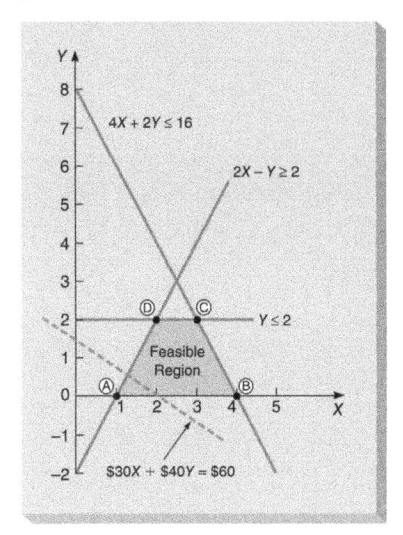

Figure 2.23: Graph for Solved Problem 2-1

As usual, to find the optimal corner point, we need to move the level profit line in the direction of increased profit—that is, up and to the right. Doing so indicates that corner point Ⓒ yields the highest profit. The values at this point are calculated to be $X = 3$ and $Y = 2$, yielding an optimal profit of $170.

The Excel layout and Solver entries for this problem are shown in Figure 2.24. As expected, the optimal solution is the same as the one we found by using the graphical approach $(X = 3, Y = 2, \text{profit} = \$170)$

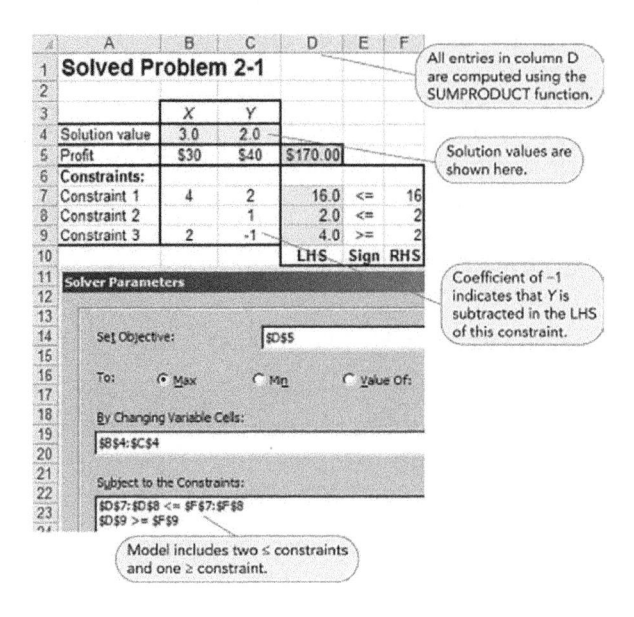

Figure 2.24: Excel Layout and Solver Entries for Solved Problem 2-1

File: Figure 2.24.xlsx

Solved Problem 2-2 Solve the following LP formulation graphically and then by using Excel:

$$\text{Minimize cost} = \$24X + \$28Y$$

subject to the constraints

$$5X + 4Y \leq 2{,}000$$
$$X + Y \geq 300$$
$$X \geq 80$$
$$Y \geq 100$$
$$X, Y \geq 0$$

Solution Figure 2.25 shows a graph of the feasible region along with a level line for a cost value of $10,000.

The arrows on the constraints indicate the direction of feasibility for each constraint. To find the optimal corner point, we need to move the cost line in the direction of lower cost—that is, down and to the left. The last point where a level cost line touches the feasible region as it moves toward the origin is corner point Ⓓ. Thus Ⓓ, which represents $X = 200, Y = 100$, and a cost of $7,600, is the optimal solution.

The Excel layout and Solver entries for this problem are shown in Figure 2.26. As expected, we get the same optimal solution as we do by using the graphical approach ($X = 200, Y = 100$, cost $= \$7{,}600$).

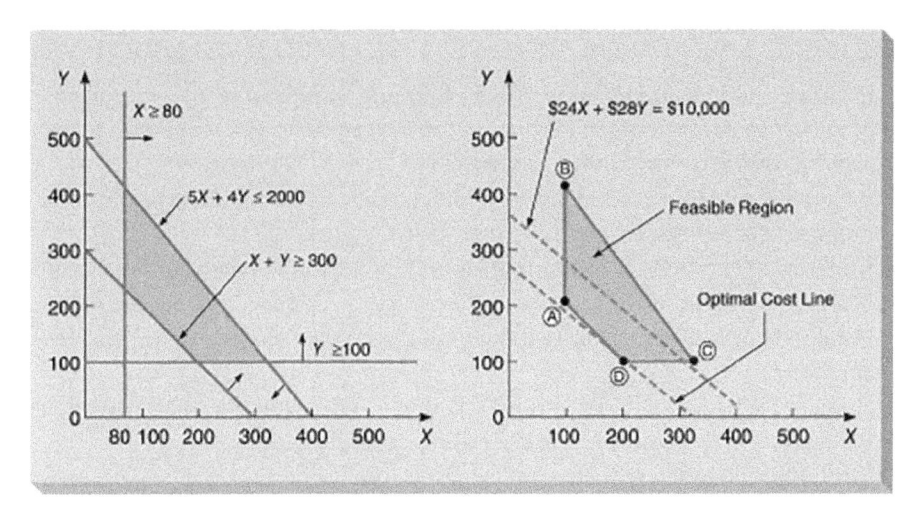

Figure 2.25: Graphs for Solved Problem 2-2

	A	B	C	D	E	F
1	**Solved Problem 2-2**					
2						
3		X	Y	Solution values		
4	Solution value	200.0	100.0			
5	Cost	$24	$28	$7,600.00		
6	Constraints:					
7	Constraint 1	5	4	1400.0	<=	2000
8	Constraint 2	1	1	300.0	>=	300
9	Constraint 3	1	0	200.0	>=	80
10	Constraint 4	0	1	100.0	>=	100
11				LHS	Sign	RHS

Solver Parameters

Set Objective: $D$5

To: ○ Max   ● Min   ○ Value Of:

By Changing Variable Cells:
$B$4:$C$4

Subject to the Constraints:
$D$7 <= $F$7
$D$8:$D$10 >= $F$8:$F$10

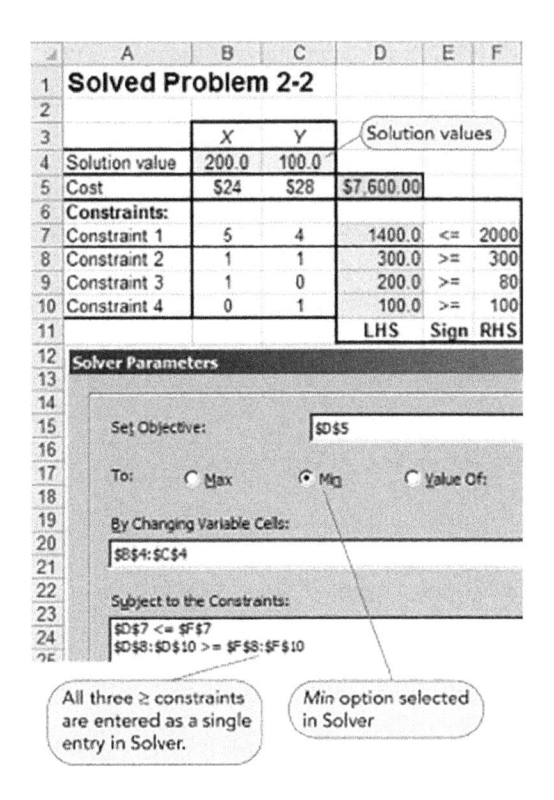

All three ≥ constraints are entered as a single entry in Solver.

Min option selected in Solver

Figure 2.26: Excel Layout and Solver Entries for Solved Problem 2-2

File: Figure 2.26.xlsx

Discussion Questions

2–1. It is important to understand the assumptions underlying the use of any quantitative analysis model. What are the assumptions and requirements for an LP model to be formulated and used?

2–2. It has been said that each LP problem that has a feasible region has an infinite number of solutions. Explain.

2–3. Under what condition is it possible for an LP problem to have more than one optimal solution?

2–4. Under what condition is it possible for an LP problem to have an unbounded solution?

2–5. Develop your own set of constraint equations and inequalities and use them to illustrate graphically each of the following conditions:
   (a) An unbounded problem.
   (b) An infeasible problem.
   (c) A problem containing redundant constraints.

2–6. The production manager of a large Cincinnati manufacturing firm once made the statement, "I would like to use LP, but it's a technique that operates under conditions of certainty. My plant doesn't have that certainty; it's a world of uncertainty. So, LP can't be used here." Do you think this statement has any merit? Explain why the manager may have said it.

2–7. The mathematical relationships that follow were formulated by an operations research analyst at the Smith-Lawton Chemical Company. Which ones are invalid for use in an LP problem? Why?

$$\text{Maximize profit} = 4X_1 + 3X_1X_2 + 8X_2 + 5X_3$$

subject to the constraints

$$2X_1 + X_2 + 2X_3 \leq 50$$
$$X_1 - 4X_2 \geq 6$$
$$1.5X_1^2 + 6X_2 + 3X_3 \geq 21$$
$$19X_2 - 0.33X_3 = 17$$
$$5X_1 + 4X_2 + 3\sqrt{X_3} \leq 80$$

2–8. How do computers aid in solving LP problems today?

2–9. Explain why knowing how to use Excel to set up and solve LP problems may benefit a manager.

2–10. What are the components of defining a problem in Excel so that it can be solved using Solver?

2–11. How is the slack (or surplus) calculated for a constraint? How is it interpreted?

2–12. What is an unbounded solution? How does Solver indicate that a problem solution is unbounded?

2–13. What is the optimal solution (X, Y, Z) to the following linear program? *Hint: You should be able to solve this question by inspection, i.e., without graphing or using Excel.*

$$\text{Max } 2X + 4Y + 6Z$$

subject to the constraints

$$Z \leq 0$$
$$X + Y + Z \leq 20$$
$$X, Y, Z, \geq 0$$

2–14. Consider the following constraints from a two-variable linear program.
(1) $X \geq 0$
(2) $Y \geq 0$
(3) $10X + 4Y \leq 110$
(4) $5X - Y \leq 90$
If constraints (2) and (3) are binding, what is the optimal solution (X, Y)?

Problems

2–15. Solve the following LP problem by using the graphical procedure and by using Excel:

$$\text{Maximize profit} = 2X + Y$$

subject to the constraints

$$3X + 6Y \leq 32$$
$$7X + Y \leq 20$$
$$3X - Y \geq 3$$
$$X, Y \geq 0$$

2–16. Solve the following LP problem by using the graphical procedure and by using Excel:

$$\text{Maximize profit} = 4X + 5Y$$

subject to the constraints

$$5X + 2Y \leq 40$$
$$3X + 6Y \leq 30$$
$$X \leq 7$$
$$2X - Y \geq 3$$
$$X, Y \geq 0$$

2–17. Solve the following LP problem by using the graphical procedure and by using Excel:

$$\text{Maximize profit} = 4X + 3Y$$

subject to the constraints

$$2X + 4Y \leq 72$$
$$3X + 6Y \geq 27$$
$$-3X + 10Y \geq 0$$
$$X, Y \geq 0$$

2-18. Solve the following LP problem by using the graphical procedure and by using Excel:

$$\text{Minimize cost} = 4X + 7Y$$

subject to the constraints

$$2X + 3Y \geq 60$$
$$4X + 2Y \geq 80$$
$$X \leq 24$$
$$X, Y \geq 0$$

2-19. Solve the following LP problem by using the graphical procedure and by using Excel:

$$\text{Minimize cost} = 3X + 7Y$$

subject to the constraints

$$9X + 3Y \geq 36$$
$$4X + 5Y \geq 40$$
$$X - Y \leq 0$$
$$2X \leq 6$$
$$X, Y \geq 0$$

2-20. Solve the following LP problem by using the graphical procedure and by using Excel:

$$\text{Minimize cost} = 4X + 7Y$$

subject to the constraints

$$3X + 6Y \geq 100$$
$$10X + 2Y \geq 160$$
$$2Y \geq 40$$
$$2X \leq 75$$
$$X, Y \geq 0$$

2-21. Solve the following LP problem, which involves three decision variables, by using Excel:

$$\text{Maximize profit} = 20A + 25B + 30C$$

subject to the constraints

$$10A + 15B - 8C \leq 45$$
$$0.5(A + B + C) \leq A$$
$$A \leq 3B$$
$$B \geq C$$
$$A, B, C \geq 0$$

2-22. Consider the following four LP formulations. Using a graphical approach in each case, determine
   (a) which formulation has more than one optimal solution.
   (b) which formulation has an unbounded solution.
   (c) which formulation is infeasible.
   (d) which formulation has a unique optimal solution.

Formulation 1	Formulation 3
maximize: $3X + 7Y$	maximize: $2X + 3Y$
subject to: $2X + Y \leq 6$	subject to: $X + 2Y \geq 12$
$4X + 5Y \leq 20$	$8X + 7Y \geq 56$
$2Y \leq 7$	$2Y \geq 5$
$2X \geq 7$	$X \leq 9$
$X, Y \geq 0$	$X, Y \geq 0$
Formulation 2	**Formulation 4**
maximize: $3X + 6Y$	maximize: $3X + 4Y$
subject to: $7X + 6Y \leq 42$	subject to: $3X + 7Y \leq 21$
$X + 2Y \leq 10$	$2X + Y \leq 6$
$X \leq 4$	$X + Y \geq 2$
$2Y \leq 9$	$2X \geq 2$
$X, Y \geq 0$	$X, Y \geq 0$

Note: *Problems 2–23 to 2–38 each involve only two decision variables. Therefore, at the discretion of the instructor, they can be solved using the graphical method, Excel, or both.*

2–23. A decorating store specializing in do-it-yourself home decorators must decide how many information packets to prepare for the summer decorating season. The store managers know they will require at least 400 copies of their popular painting packet. They believe their new information packet on specialty glazing techniques could be a big seller, so they want to prepare at least 300 copies. Their printer has given the following information: Each painting packet will require 2.5 minutes of printing time and 1.8 minutes of collating time. The glazing packet will require 2 minutes for each operation. The store has decided to sell the painting packet for $5.50 a copy and to price the glazing packet at $4.50. At this time, the printer can devote 36 hours to printing and 30 hours to collation. He will charge the store $1 for each packet prepared. How many of each packet should the store order to maximize the revenue associated with information packets, and what is the store's expected revenue?

2–24. The Coastal Tea Company sells 60-pound bags of blended tea to restaurants. To be able to label the tea as South Carolina Tea, at least 55% of the tea (by weight) in the bag must be Carolina grown. For quality, Coastal requires that the blend achieve an average aroma rating of at least 1.65. Carolina tea, which costs Coastal $1.80 per pound, has an aroma rating of 2; other teas likely to be blended with Carolina tea are rated only at 1.2, but they are available for only $0.60 per pound. Determine the best mix of Carolina and regular tea to achieve Coastal's blending goals, while keeping the costs as low as possible.

2-25. The advertising agency promoting a new product is hoping to get the best possible exposure in terms of the number of people the advertising reaches. The agency will use a two-pronged approach: focused Internet advertising, which is estimated to reach 200,000 people for each burst of advertising, and print media, which is estimated to reach 80,000 people each time an ad is placed. The cost of each Internet burst is $3,000, as opposed to only $900 for each print media ad. It has been agreed that the number of print media ads will be no more than five times the number of Internet bursts. The agency hopes to launch at least 5 and no more than 15 Internet bursts of advertising. The advertising budget is $75,000. Given these constraints, what is the most effective advertising strategy?

2-26. A small manufacturer makes two types of motors, models A and B. The assembly process for each is similar in that both require a certain amount of wiring, drilling, and assembly. Each model A takes 3 hours of wiring, 2 hours of drilling, and 1.5 hours of assembly. Each model B must go through 2 hours of wiring, 1 hour of drilling, and 0.5 hours of assembly. During the next production period, 240 hours of wiring time, 210 hours of drilling time, and 120 hours of assembly time are available. Each model A sold yields a profit of $22. Each model B can be sold for a $15 profit. Assuming that all assembled motors can be sold, find the best combination of motors to yield the highest profit.

2-27. The manufacturer in Problem 2-26 now has a standing order of 24 model A motors for each production period. Resolve Problem 2-26 to include this additional constraint.

2-28. A furniture cabinet maker produces two types of cabinets that house and hide plasma televisions. The Mission-style cabinet requires $340 in materials and 15 labor hours to produce, and it yields a profit of $910 per cabinet. The Rustic-style cabinet requires $430 in materials and 20 hours to produce, and it yields a profit of $1,200. The firm has a budget of $30,000 to spend on materials. To ensure full employment, the firm wishes to maximize its profit but at the same time to keep all 30 workers fully employed, so all 1,200 available labor hours available must be used. What is the best combination of furniture cabinets to be made?

2-29. Members of a book club have decided, after reading an investment book, to begin investing in the stock market. They would like to achieve the following: Their investment must grow by at least $6,000 in the long term (over three years) and at least $900 in the short term, and they must earn a dividend of at least $300 per year. They are consulting with a stockbroker, who has narrowed their search to two stocks: Carolina Solar Power and South West Steel. The data on each stock, per $1 invested, are as follows:

	Carolina Solar Power	South West Steel
Short-term appreciation	$0.46	$0.26
Long-term appreciation	$1.72	$1.93
Dividend income	9%	13%

Assuming that these data indicate what will happen to these stocks over the next three years, what is the smallest investment, in dollars, that the members would have to make in one or both of these two stocks to meet their investment goals?

2–30. Treetops Hammocks produces lightweight nylon hammocks designed for campers, scouts, and hikers. The hammocks come in two styles: double and single. The double hammocks sell for $225 each. They incur a direct labor cost of $101.25 and a production cost of $38.75, and they are packed with hanging apparatus and storage bags, which cost $20. The single hammocks sell for $175 each. Their direct labor costs are $70 and production costs are $30, and they, too, are packed with the same hanging apparatus and storage bags, which cost $20. Each double hammock uses 3.2 hours of production time; each single hammock uses 2.4 hours of production time. Treetops plans for no more than 960 labor hours per production cycle. Treetops wants to maximize its profit while making no more than 200 single hammocks and no more than 400 total hammocks per production cycle.
(a) How many of each hammock should Treetops make?
(b) If the restriction on single hammocks were removed, what would be the optimal production plan?

2–31. A commuter airline makes lattes in the galley and sells them to passengers. A regular latte contains a shot of espresso, 1 cup of 2% milk, steamed, and 0.5 cup of whipped cream. The low-fat latte contains a shot of espresso, 1.25 cups of skim milk, frothed, and no whipped cream. The plane begins its journey with 100 shots of espresso, 60 cups of skim milk, 60 cups of 2% milk, and 30 cups of whipped cream. The airline makes a profit of $1.58 on each regular latte and $1.65 on each low-fat latte. Assuming that all lattes that are made can be sold, what would be the ideal mix of regular and low-fat lattes to maximize the profit for the airline?

2–32. A warehouse storage-building company must determine how many storage sheds of each size—large or small—to build in its new 8,000-square-foot facility to maximize rental income. Each large shed is 150 square feet, requires $1 per week in advertising, and rents for $50 per week. Each small shed is 50 square feet, requires $1 per week in advertising, and rents for $20 per week. The company has a weekly advertising budget of $100 and estimates that it can rent no more than 40 large sheds in any given week.

2-33. A bank is retrofitting part of its vault to hold safety deposit boxes. It plans to build safety deposit boxes approximately 6 feet high along the walls on both sides of a 20-foot corridor. Hence, the bank will have 240 square feet of wall space to use. It plans to offer two sizes of safety deposit box: large and small. Large boxes (which consume 122.4 square inches of wall space) will rent for $40 per year. Small boxes (which consume 72 square inches of wall space) will rent for $30 per year. The bank believes it will need at least 350 total boxes, at least 80 of which should be large. It hopes to maximize revenue for safety deposit boxes. How many boxes of each size should the bank's design provide?

2-34. An investment broker has received $250,000 to invest in a 12-month commitment. The money can be placed in Treasury notes (with a return of 8% and a risk score of 2) or in municipal bonds (with a return of 9% and a risk score of 3). The broker's client wants diversification to the extent that between 50% and 70% of the total investment must be placed in Treasury notes. Also, because of fear of default, the client requests that the average risk score of the total investment should be no more than 2.42. How much should the broker invest in each security so as to maximize return on investment?

2-35. A wooden furniture company manufactures two products, benches and picnic tables, for use in yards and parks. The firm has two main resources: its carpenters (labor force) and a supply of redwood for use in the furniture. During the next production cycle, 1,000 hours of labor are available. The firm also has a stock of 3,500 board-feet of good-quality redwood. Each bench that Outdoor Furniture produces requires 4 labor hours and 10 board-feet of redwood; each picnic table takes 6 labor hours and 35 board-feet of redwood. Completed benches will yield a profit of $9 each, and tables will result in a profit of $20 each. Since most customers usually buy tables and benches at the same time, the number of benches made should be at least twice as many as the number of tables made. How many benches and tables should be produced to obtain the largest possible profit?

2-36. A plumbing manufacturer makes two lines of bathtubs, model A and model B. Every tub requires blending a certain amount of steel and zinc; the company has available a total of 24,500 pounds of steel and 6,000 pounds of zinc. Each model A bathtub requires a mixture of 120 pounds of steel and 20 pounds of zinc, and each yields a profit of $90. Each model B tub can be sold for a profit of $70; it requires 100 pounds of steel and 30 pounds of zinc. To maintain an adequate supply of both models, the manufacturer would like the number of model A tubs made to be no more than 5 times the number of model B tubs. Find the best product mix of bathtubs.

2-37. A technical college department head must plan the course offerings for the next term. Student demands make it necessary to offer at least 20 core courses (each of which counts for 3 credit hours) and 20 elective courses (each of which counts for 4 credit hours) in the term. Faculty contracts dictate that a total of at least

60 core and elective courses and at least 205 total credit hours be offered. Each core course taught costs the college an average of $2,600 in faculty salaries; each elective course costs $3,000. How many each of core and elective courses should be scheduled so that total faculty salaries are kept to a minimum?

2-38. The size of the yield of olives in a vineyard is greatly influenced by a process of branch pruning. If olive trees are pruned, trees can be planted more densely, and output is increased. (However, olives from pruned trees are smaller in size.) Obtaining a barrel of olives in a pruned vineyard requires 5 hours of labor and 1 acre of land. Obtaining a barrel of olives by the normal process requires only 2 labor hours but takes 2 acres of land. A barrel of olives produced on pruned trees sell for $20, whereas a barrel of regular olives has a market price of $30. An olive grower has 250 hours of labor available and a total of 150 acres available to plant. He has determined that because of uncertain demand, no more than 40 barrels of pruned olives should be produced. Find the combination of barrels of pruned and regular olives that will yield the maximum possible profit. Also, how many acres should the olive grower devote to each growing process?

Note: *Problems 2-39 to 2-45 are straightforward extensions of the two-variable problems we have seen so far and involve more than two variables. They therefore cannot be solved graphically. They are intended to give you an excellent opportunity to get familiar with formulating larger LP problems and solving them using Excel.*

2-39. Cattle are sent to a feedlot to be grain-fed before being processed into beef. The owners of a feedlot seek to determine the amounts of cattle feed to buy so that minimum nutritional standards are satisfied to ensure proper weight gain, while total feed costs are minimized. The feed mix used is made up of three grains that contain the following nutrients per pound of feed:

	Nutrient (ounces per pound of feed)			
Feed	A	B	C	D
Feed mix X	3	2	1	6
Feed mix Y	2	3	0	8
Feed mix Z	4	1	2	4

Feed mixes X, Y, and Z cost $3, $4, and $2.25 per pound, respectively. The minimum requirement per cattle per day is 4 pounds of nutrient A, 5 pounds of nutrient B, 1 pound of nutrient C, and 8 pounds of nutrient D. The ranch faces one additional restriction: It can obtain only 500 pounds of feed mix Z per day from the feed supplier regardless of its need. Because there are usually 100 cattle at the feed lot at any given time, this means that no more than 5 pounds of stock Z can be counted on for use in the feed of each cattle per day. Formulate this problem as a linear program and solve it by using Excel.

2-40. The production department for an aluminum valve plant is scheduling its work for next month. Each valve must go through three separate machines during the fabrication process. After fabrication, each valve is inspected by a human being, who spends 15 minutes per valve. There are 525 inspection hours available for the month. The time required (in hours) by each machine to work on each valve is shown in the following table. Also shown are the minimum number of valves that must be produced for the month and the unit profit for each valve.

Product	V231	V242	V784	V906	Capacity (hours)
Drilling	0.40	0.30	0.45	0.35	700
Milling	0.60	0.65	0.52	0.48	890
Lathe	1.20	0.60	0.5	0.70	1,200
Unit profit	$16	$12	$13	$8	
Minimum needed	200	250	600	450	

Determine the optimal production mix for the valve plant to make the best use of its profit potential.

2-41. The bank in Problem 2-33 now wants to add a mini-size box, which will rent for $17 per year and consume 43.2 square inches of wall space. The bank still wants a total of at least 350 total boxes; of these, at least 100 should be mini boxes and at least 80 should be large boxes. However, the bank wants the total area occupied by large boxes and miniboxes to be at most 50% of the available space. How many boxes of each type should be included to maximize revenue? If all the boxes can be rented, would the bank make more money with the addition of the miniboxes?

2-42. A photocopy machine company produces three types of laser printers—the Print Jet, the Print Desk, and the Print Pro—the sale of which earn profits of $60, $90, and $73, respectively. The Print Jet requires 2.9 hours of assembly time and 1.4 hours of testing time. The Print Desk requires 3.7 hours of assembly and 2.1 hours of testing. The Print Pro requires 3 hours of assembly and 1.7 hours of testing. The company wants to ensure that Print Desk constitutes at least 15% of the total production and Print Jet and Print Desk together constitute at least 40% of the total production. There are 3,600 hours of assembly time and 2,000 hours of testing time available for the month. What combination of printers should be produced to maximize profits?

2-43. An electronics corporation manufactures four highly technical products that it supplies to aerospace firms. Each of the products must pass through the following departments before being shipped: wiring, drilling, assembly, and inspection. The time requirement (in hours) for each unit produced, the available time in each department each month, minimum production levels for each product, and unit profits for each product are summarized in the following table:

Product	EC221	EC496	NC455	NC791	Capacity (hours)
Wiring	0.5	1.5	1.5	1.0	15,000
Drilling	0.3	1.0	2.0	3.0	17,000
Assembly	0.2	4.0	1.0	2.0	10,000
Inspection	0.5	1.0	0.5	0.5	12,000
Unit profit	$9	$12	$15	$11	
Minimum needed	150	100	300	400	

Formulate this problem and solve it by using Excel. Your solution should honor all constraints and maximize the profit.

2–44. A snack company packages and sells three different 1-pound canned party mixes: Plain Nuts, Mixed Nuts, and Premium Mix. Plain Nuts sell for $2.25 per can, Mixed Nuts sell for $3.37, and Premium Nuts sell for $6.49. A can of Plain Nuts contains 0.8 pound of peanuts and 0.2 pound of cashews. A can of Mixed Nuts consists of 0.5 pound of peanuts, 0.3 pound of cashews, 0.1 pound of almonds, and 0.1 pound of walnuts. A can of Premium Nuts is made up of 0.3 pound of cashews, 0.4 pound of almonds, and 0.4 pound of walnuts. The company has on hand 500 pounds of peanuts, 225 pounds of cashews, 100 pounds of almonds, and 80 pounds of walnuts. Past demand indicates that customers purchase at least twice as many cans of Plain Nuts as Premium Nuts. What production plan will maximize the total revenue?

2–45. An investor is considering three different television news stocks to complement his portfolio: British Broadcasting Company (BBC), Canadian Broadcasting Company (CBC), and Australian Broadcasting Company (ABC). His broker has given him the following information:

	Short-Term Growth (per $ invested)	Intermediate Growth (per $ invested)	Dividend Rate
BBC	0.39	1.59	8%
CBC	0.26	1.70	4%
ABC	0.42	1.45	6%

The investor's criteria are as follows: (1) The investment should yield short-term growth of at least $1,000; (2) the investment should yield intermediate-term growth of at least $6,000; and (3) the dividends should be at least $250 per year. Determine the least amount the investor can invest and how that investment should be allocated among the three stocks.

2-46. Find the intersection of each of the following sets of constraints.
(a) $10X + 8Y = 800$ and $X + 4Y = 100$
(b) $2X + 4Y \leq 28$ and $3X - 12Y \geq 6$
(c) $4X + 9Y \leq 180$ and $8X + 2Y \leq 240$
(d) $4X - 7Y \geq 75$ and $5X - 9Y \leq 35$

2-47. Consider the linear programming formulation below. Which constraint is redundant?

Maximize profit = $4X + 4Y$

subject to the constraints

$$6X + 4Y \leq 120$$
$$3X + 8Y \leq 120$$
$$2X + 2.5Y \leq 100$$
$$X, Y \geq 0$$

2-48. Consider the linear programming formulation below, where X and Y represent units of production of two different products. As currently written, the formulation is infeasible. The formulation can become feasible if one of the constraints (other than nonnegativity) is removed. Which single constraint must be removed?

Maximize profit = $2X + Y$

subject to the constraints

$$5X + 4Y \geq 200$$
$$4X + 6Y \leq 120$$
$$16X + 8Y \leq 320$$
$$20X - 10Y \geq 200$$
$$X, Y \geq 0$$

2-49. Consider the linear programming formulation below.

Minimize cost = $5X + 4Y$

subject to the constraints

$$5X + 4Y \geq 200$$
$$4X + 6Y \geq 360$$
$$8X + 4Y \leq 160$$
$$X \geq 20$$
$$Y \leq 50$$
$$X, Y \geq 0$$

(a) Try to solve the problem in Excel. What error message do you get?
(b) The error can be eliminated by removing one of the constraints. Remove that constraint and resolve the model. What is the optimal solution?

2-50. Consider the linear programming formulation below.

$$\text{Maximize profit} = 50X + 42Y$$

subject to the constraints

$$5X - 4Y \leq 200$$
$$X \leq 60$$
$$Y \geq 10$$
$$X, Y \geq 0$$

(a) Try to solve the problem in Excel. What error message do you get?
(b) *Add* a single constraint that would eliminate the error message. What constraint did you add, and what is the value of the optimal solution?

2-51. Solve the following LP problem by using the graphical procedure and by using Excel:

$$\text{Maximize } 40X + 50Y$$

subject to the constraints

$$X + 2Y \leq 80$$
$$4X + 3Y \leq 240$$
$$X \leq 51$$
$$X, Y \geq 0$$

2-52. Consider the linear programming formulation below.

$$\text{Maximize } 9T + 10S + 2P$$

subject to the constraints

$$T + S + P = 6$$
$$S \geq 3$$
$$T \geq 1$$
$$P \leq 3$$
$$T, S, P \geq 0$$

This is a linear program with 3 variables. Rewrite this as an algebraically equivalent linear program that only has 2 variables. Then solve the problem graphically. What is the optimal solution (T, S, P), and what is the objective function value?

2-53. Solve the following LP problem, which involves three decision variables, by using Excel:

$$\text{Minimize cost} = 10.50X + 4.60Y + 12.20Z$$

subject to the constraints

$$5X + 4Y \geq 200$$
$$4X - 6Y + 8Z \geq 360$$
$$X \leq 0.40(X + Y + Z)$$
$$Z \geq Y$$
$$X, Y, Z \geq 0$$

2-54. Modify the Holiday Meal Turkey Ranch Problem in Figure 2.22 to include a third brand (Brand C). Brand C feed costs $0.12 per pound. Each pound of Brand C feed contains 12 protein units, 2 vitamin units, and 0.20 iron units. Use Excel to solve the problem.

2–55. Solve the following LP problem, which involves four decision variables, by using Excel:

$$\text{Maximize profit} = 210A + 400B + 320C + 280D$$

subject to the constraints

$$5A + 14B + 6C + 8D \leq 200$$
$$A \geq 10$$
$$B \leq 0.25(A + B + Y + Z)$$
$$D \geq B$$
$$A, B, C, D \geq 0$$

Chapter 3
Linear Programming Modeling Applications with Computer Analyses in Excel

Suppose that you won $1 million in the lottery. Rather than spending all of it now, you would like to invest it wisely so that you can retire early. Where should your money be placed? You know that some stocks have high expected returns but carry a lot of risk. Money market investments are much safer, but those returns alone wouldn't let you retire before your kids finish college. What is the best combination of risk and return? Or suppose instead that you didn't win the lottery, but your 12-year-old daughter plans to go to college in six years, followed by medical school. You have promised to fund her education. You need to make safe investments now that will ensure that you have adequate income to cover her expenses in each of those schooling years. Which investments with which maturity dates should you select so that you don't have to work a second job while your daughter earns her degrees?

Corporate finance officers make such decisions regularly, and linear programming (LP) can help to determine the best ones. In fact, managers can apply LP to numerous different functional areas within their organizations. Service firms such as restaurants with peak demand times (breakfast, lunch, and dinner) can apply LP to determine how many employees to bring in on each shift to cover demand needs while minimizing idle time during off hours. Marketing managers can employ LP to help them select the best mix of advertisements or to determine which customers to survey. Manufacturing managers can determine the best mix of products to produce in order to most fully utilize available resources while maximizing profit or minimizing cost. They can also develop LP models to select suppliers or even produce some supplies themselves. Production planning LP models enable managers to determine how much to produce each period and when to carry inventory. Transportation managers can determine which items to load on which vehicles by using LP. Finally, for products created by blending ingredients together (e.g., cereal, gasoline, or fruit juice), linear programs can determine the cheapest way to formulate the product while ensuring that the various minimum or maximum requirements of its features (e.g., protein, octane level, or vitamin C, respectively) are met.

We present LP models for each of these decisions in this chapter. The collection of examples provides a picture of the wide variety of possible LP applications, and it provides a good beginning set of core examples. The process of formulating linear programs is part "art" and part "science." Sometimes, creativity is required to convert the stated constraints into linear expressions. Familiarizing yourself with a variety of LP applications is perhaps the best way to expand your "creative toolbox."

Chapter Objectives

After completing this chapter, you will be able to:
1. Model a wide variety of linear programming (LP) problems.
2. Understand major business application areas for LP problems, including manufacturing, marketing, finance, employee staffing, transportation, blending, and multiperiod planning.
3. Gain experience in setting up and solving LP problems using Excel's Solver.

3.1 Using Linear Programming to Solve Real-World Problems

The purpose of this chapter is to illustrate how linear programming (LP) can be used to model real-world problems in several managerial decision-making areas. In our discussion, we use examples from areas such as product mix, make–buy decisions, media selection, marketing research, financial portfolio selection, labor planning, shipping and transportation, allocation decisions, ingredient blending, and multiperiod scheduling.

For each example discussed, we first briefly describe the development of the written mathematical model and then illustrate its solution using Excel's Solver. Although we use Solver to solve these models, it is critical that you understand the logic behind a model before implementing it on a computer. Remember that the solution is only as good as the model itself. If the model is incorrect or incomplete from a logical perspective (even if it is correct from a mathematical perspective), Excel has no way of recognizing the logical error. Too many, especially those at the early stages of instruction in LP, hit roadblocks when they try to implement an LP problem directly in Excel without conceptualizing the model on paper first. So we highly recommend that, until you become very comfortable with LP formulations (which takes many hours of practice), you sketch out the layout for each problem on paper first. Then, you can translate your written model to the computer.

In developing each written mathematical model, we use the approach discussed in Chapter 2. This means first identifying the decision variables and then writing out linear expressions for the objective function and each constraint in terms of these decision variables. Although some of the models discussed in this chapter are relatively small numerically, the principles developed here are definitely applicable to larger problems. Moreover, the structured formulation approach used here should provide enough practice in "paraphrasing" LP model formulations and help in developing skills to apply the technique to other, less common applications.

When implementing these models in Excel, to the extent possible, we employ the same layout presented in Chapter 2. That is, all parameters (i.e., the solution value, objective coefficient, and constraint coefficients) associated with a specific decision variable are modeled in the same column. The objective function and each constraint in the problem are shown on separate rows of the worksheet. Later in this chapter (section 3.8), however, we illustrate an alternate implementation that may be more compact and efficient for some problems. As noted in Chapter 2, we encourage you to try alternative layouts based on your personal preference and expertise with Excel.

EXCEL NOTES

– The Companion Website for this book, at *degruyter.com/view/product/486941*, contains the Excel file for each sample problem discussed here. TThe relevant file/sheet name is shown below the title of the corresponding figure in this book.

– In each of our Excel layouts, for clarity, changing variable cells are shaded yellow, the objective cell is shaded green, and cells denoting left-hand-side formulas of constraints are shaded blue. If the right-hand side of a constraint also includes a formula, that cell is also shaded blue.

– To make the equivalence of the written formulation and the Excel layout clear, the Excel layouts show the decision variable names used in the written formulation of the model. Note that these names have no role in using Solver to solve the model.

3.2 Manufacturing Applications

Product Mix Problem

A fertile field for the use of LP is in planning for the optimal mix of products that a company should produce. A company must meet a myriad of constraints, ranging from financial concerns to sales demands to material contracts to union labor demands. Its primary goal is either to generate the largest profit (or revenue) possible or to keep the total manufacturing costs as low as possible. We have already studied a simple version of a product mix problem (the Flair Furniture problem) involving just two products in Chapter 2. Let's now look at a more detailed version of a product mix problem.

Fifth Avenue Industries, a nationally known manufacturer of menswear, produces four varieties of ties. One is an expensive, all-silk tie, one is an all-polyester tie, and two are blends of polyester and cotton. Table 3.1 illustrates the cost and availability (per monthly production planning period) of the three materials used in the production process.

Table 3.1: Material Data for Fifth Avenue Industries

Material	Cost Per Yard	Material Available per Month (YARDS)
Silk	$20	1,000
Polyester	$ 6	2,000
Cotton	$ 9	1,250

Decision Modeling In Action

Canada Achieves Transportation Asset Management Excellence Through Operations Research

The New Brunswick Department of Transportation (NBDoT) is the public agency charged with the management, maintenance, and repair of roads and highways in New Brunswick, Canada. NBDoT maintains more than 18,000 kilometers of roads, 2,900 bridges, and various ferry crossings and assets. The department wanted to create a comprehensive asset management system to rehabilitate its infrastructure assets, worth billions of dollars. The rehabilitation process includes highway maintenance, preservation, and reconstruction.

Faced with a limited budget available to rehabilitate its assets, NBDoT needed an optimal and smart way to use its budget for long-term rehabilitation activities, in addition to the short-term plans and quick fixes. NBDoT allocated $2 million toward consulting, software development, and software purchase to support its goal of asset management. The software solution enabled the operations research team to develop different models and evaluate different scenarios and alternatives based on a combination of linear programming and heuristic techniques.

The solution that was created addressed all the constraints faced by NBDot, including but not limited to cost, time, the life cycle of different assets, and treatment choices. NBDoT could save about $72 million annually using the model developed by the operations research team, and the agency expects to save about $1.4 billion over the next 20 years.

Source: Based on U. Feunekes, S. Palmer, A. Feunekes, J. MacNaughton, J. Cunningham, K. Mathisen. "Talking the Politics Out of Paving: Achieving Transportation Asset Management Excellence Through OR," *Interfaces* 41, 1 (January – February 2011): 51–65.

The firm has fixed contracts with several major department store chains to supply ties each month. The contracts require that Fifth Avenue Industries supply a minimum quantity of each tie but allow for a larger demand if Fifth Avenue chooses to meet that demand. (Most of the ties are not shipped with the name Fifth Avenue on their label, incidentally, but with "private stock" labels supplied by the stores.) Table 3.2 summarizes the contract demand for each of the four styles of ties, the selling price per tie, and the fabric requirements of each variety. The production process for all ties is almost fully automated, and Fifth Avenue uses a standard labor cost of $0.75 per tie (for any variety). Fifth Avenue must decide on a policy for product mix in order to maximize its monthly profit.

Formulating the Problem As is usual with product mix problems, in this case, the decision variables represent the number of units to make of each product. Let

S = number of all-silk ties to make per month
P = number of all-polyester ties to make per month
B_1 = number of poly-cotton blend 1 ties to make per month
B_2 = number of poly-cotton blend 2 ties to make per month

Table 3.2: Product Data for Fifth Avenue Industries

Variety of Tie	Selling Price per Tie	Monthly Contract Minimum	Monthly Demand	Total Material Required per Tie (yards)	Material Requirements
All-silk	$6.70	6,000	7,000	0.125	100% silk
All-polyester	$3.55	10,000	14,000	0.08	100% polyester
Poly-cotton blend 1	$4.31	13,000	16,000	0.10	50% polyester/50% cotton
Poly-cotton blend 2	$4.81	6,000	8,500	0.10	30% polyester/70% cotton

Unlike the Flair Furniture example in Chapter 2, where the unit profit contribution for each product was given directly (e.g., $7 per table and $5 per chair), the unit profits must be first calculated in this example. We illustrate the net profit calculation for all-silk ties (S). Each all-silk tie requires 0.125 yards of silk, at a cost of $20 per yard, resulting in a material cost of $2.50. The selling price per all-silk tie is $6.70, and the labor cost is $0.75, leaving a net profit of $6.70 − $2.50 − $0.75 = $3.45 per tie. In a similar fashion, we can calculate the net unit profit for all-polyester ties (P) to be $2.32, for poly-cotton blend 1 ties (B_1) to be $2.81, and for poly-cotton blend 2 ties (B_2) to be $3.25. Try to verify these calculations for yourself.

The objective function can now be stated as

$$\text{Maximize profit} = \$3.45S + \$2.32P + \$2.81B_1 + \$3.25B_2$$

subject to the constraints

$0.125S$	$\leq$	$1,000$	(yards of silk)
$0.08P + 0.05B_1 + 0.03B_2$	$\leq$	$2,000$	(yards of polyester)
$0.05B_1 + 0.07B_2$	$\leq$	$1,250$	(yards of cotton)
S	$\geq$	$6,000$	(contract minimum for all silk)
S	$\leq$	$7,000$	(maximum demand for all silk)
P	$\geq$	$10,000$	(contract minimum for all polyester)
P	$\leq$	$14,000$	(maximum demand for all polyester)
B_1	$\geq$	$13,000$	(contract minimum for blend 1)
B_1	$\leq$	$16,000$	(maximum demand for blend 1)
B_2	$\geq$	$6,000$	(contract minimum for blend 2)
B_2	$\leq$	$8,500$	(maximum demand for blend 2)
S, P, B_1, B_2	$\geq$	0	(nonnegativity)

Instead of writing the objective function by using the profit coefficients directly, we can optionally choose to split the profit into its three components: a revenue component, a labor cost component, and a material cost component. For example, the objective (profit) coefficient for all-silk ties (S) is $3.45. However, we know that the $3.45 is obtained by subtracting the labor cost ($0.75) and material cost ($2.50) from the revenue ($6.70) for S. Hence, we can rewrite the objective function as

$$\text{Maximize profit} = (\$6.70S + \$3.55P + \$4.31B_1 + \$4.81B_2)$$
$$- \$0.75(S + P + B_1 + B_2) - (\$2.50S + \$0.48P + \$0.75B_1 + \$0.81B_2)$$

Whether we model the objective function by using the profit coefficients directly or by using the selling prices and cost coefficients, the final solution will be the same. However, in many problems it is convenient, and probably preferable, to have the model show as much detail as possible.

Solving the Problem The formula view of the Excel layout for this problem is shown in Figure 3.1. Cell F6 defines the revenue component, cell F7 defines the labor cost component, and cell F8 defines the material cost component of the objective function. Cell F9 (the objective cell in Solver) is the difference between cell F6 and cells F7 and F8.

Titles, such as the ones shown in row 4 and column A, are included to clarify the model. They are recommended but not required.

These are the decision variable names used in the written LP formulation. They are shown here for information purposes only.

	A	B	C	D	E	F	G	H	I
1	Fifth Avenue Industries								
2									
3			S	P	B₁	B₂			
4			All silk	All poly	Blend-1	Blend-2			
5	Number of units								
6	Selling price	6.7	3.55	4.31	4.81	=SUMPRODUCT(B6:E6,$B$5:$E$5)			
7	Labor cost	0.75	0.75	0.75	0.75	=SUMPRODUCT(B7:E7,$B$5:$E$5)			
8	Material cost	2.5	0.48	0.75	0.81	=SUMPRODUCT(B8:E8,$B$5:$E$5)			
9	Profit	=B6-B7-B8	=C6-C7-C8	=D6-D7-D8	=E6-E7-E8	=F6-F7-F8			
10	Constraints:								Cost/Yd
11	Yards of silk	0.125				=SUMPRODUCT(B11:E11,$B$5:$E$5)	<=	1000	20
12	Yards of polyester		0.08	0.05	0.03	=SUMPRODUCT(B12:E12,$B$5:$E$5)	<=	2000	6
13	Yards of cotton			0.05	0.07	=SUMPRODUCT(B13:E13,$B$5:$E$5)	<=	1250	9
14	Maximum all silk	1				=SUMPRODUCT(B14:E14,$B$5:$E$5)	<=	7000	
15	Maximum all poly		1			=SUMPRODUCT(B15:E15,$B$5:$E$5)	<=	14000	
16	Maximum blend-1			1		=SUMPRODUCT(B16:E16,$B$5:$E$5)	<=	16000	
17	Maximum blend-2				1	=SUMPRODUCT(B17:E17,$B$5:$E$5)	<=	8500	
18	Minimum all silk	1				=SUMPRODUCT(B18:E18,$B$5:$E$5)	>=	6000	
19	Minimum all poly		1			=SUMPRODUCT(B19:E19,$B$5:$E$5)	>=	10000	
20	Minimum blend-1			1		=SUMPRODUCT(B20:E20,$B$5:$E$5)	>=	13000	
21	Minimum blend-2				1	=SUMPRODUCT(B21:E21,$B$5:$E$5)	>=	6000	
22						LHS		Sign	RHS

Objective function terms and constraint LHS values are computed using the SUMPRODUCT function.

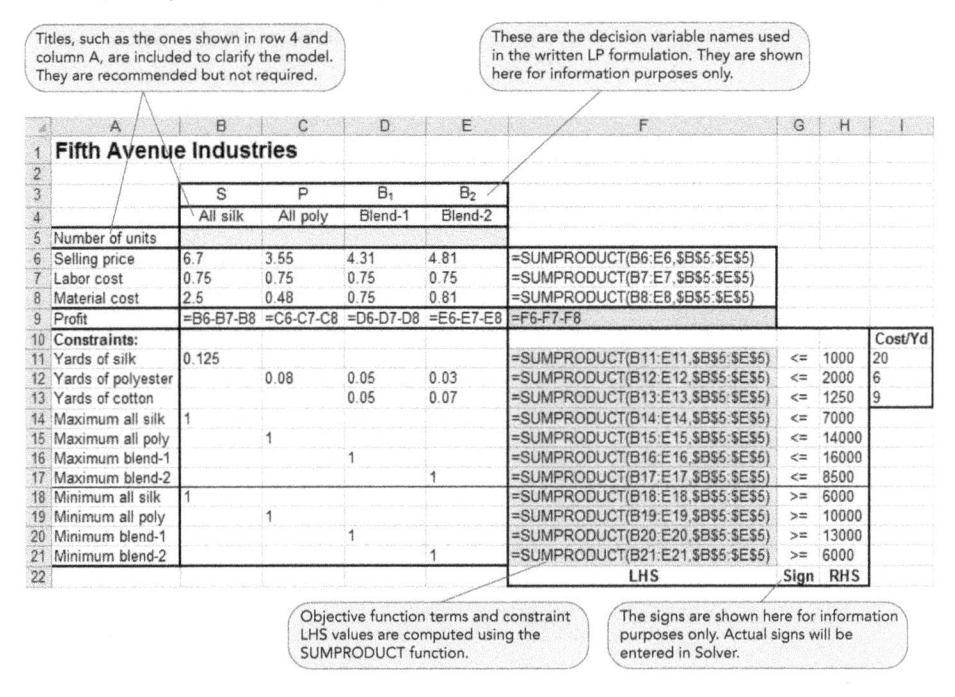

The signs are shown here for information purposes only. Actual signs will be entered in Solver.

Figure 3.1: Formula View of the Excel Layout for Fifth Avenue Industries

File: Figure 3.1.xlsx, Sheet: Figure 3.1

Observe that in this spreadsheet (as well as in all other spreadsheets discussed in this chapter), the primary Excel function we have used to model all formulas is the SUM-PRODUCT function (discussed in section 2.7). We have used this function to compute the objective function components (cells F6:F8), as well as the LHS values for all constraints (cells F11:F21).

As noted earlier, we have adopted this type of Excel layout for our models to make it easier for the LP beginner to understand them. Further, an advantage of this layout is the ease with which all the formulas in the spreadsheet can be created. Observe that we have used the $ sign in cell F6 to anchor the cell references for the decision variables (i.e., $B$5:$E$5). This allows us to simply copy this formula to cells F7:F8 for the other components of the objective function, and to cells F11:F21 to create the corresponding LHS formulas for the constraints.

Interpreting the Results The Solver entries and optimal solution values for this model are shown in Figure 3.2. As discussed in Chapter 2, before solving the LP model using Solver, we ensure that the box labeled Make Unconstrained Variables Non-Negative is checked (it is set this way by default in Solver) and the Select a Solving Method box is set to Simplex LP.

The results indicate that the optimal solution is to produce 7,000 all-silk ties, 13,625 all-polyester ties, 13,100 poly-cotton blend 1 ties, and 8,500 poly-cotton blend 2 ties. This results in total revenue of $192,614.75, labor cost of $31,668.75, and total material cost of $40,750, yielding a net profit of $120,196. Polyester and cotton availability are binding constraints, while 125 yards (=1,000−875) of silk will be left unused. Interestingly, the availability of the two cheaper resources (polyester and cotton) is more critical to Fifth Avenue than the availability of the more expensive resource (silk). Such occurrences are common in practice. That is, the more expensive resources need not necessarily be the most important or critical resources from an availability or need point of view. Fifth Avenue will satisfy the full demand for all-silk and poly-cotton blend 2 ties, and it will satisfy a little over the minimum contract level for the other two varieties.

Fifth Avenue Industries

	A	B	C	D	E	F	G	H	I
1	Fifth Avenue Industries								
2									
3		S	P	B₁	B₂				
4		All silk	All poly	Blend-1	Blend-2				
5	Number of units	7000.0	13625.0	13100.0	8500.0				
6	Selling price	$6.70	$3.55	$4.31	$4.81	$192,614.75			
7	Labor cost	$0.75	$0.75	$0.75	$0.75	$31,668.75			
8	Material cost	$2.50	$0.48	$0.75	$0.81	$40,750.00			
9	Profit	$3.45	$2.32	$2.81	$3.25	$120,196.00			
10	Constraints:								Cost/Yd
11	Yards of silk	0.125				875.00	<=	1000	$20
12	Yards of polyester		0.08	0.05	0.03	2000.00	<=	2000	$6
13	Yards of cotton			0.05	0.07	1250.00	<=	1250	$9
14	Maximum all silk	1				7000.00	<=	7000	
15	Maximum all poly		1			13625.00	<=	14000	
16	Maximum blend-1			1		13100.00	<=	16000	
17	Maximum blend-2				1	8500.00	<=	8500	
18	Minimum all silk	1				7000.00	>=	6000	
19	Minimum all poly		1			13625.00	>=	10000	
20	Minimum blend-1			1		13100.00	>=	13000	
21	Minimum blend-2				1	8500.00	>=	6000	
22						LHS	Sign	RHS	

Solver Parameters

Set Objective: $F$9

To: ● Max   ○ Min   ○ Value Of: 0

By Changing Variable Cells:
$B$5:$E$5

Subject to the Constraints:
$F$11:$F$17 <= $H$11:$H$17
$F$18:$F$21 >= $H$18:$H$21

☑ Make Unconstrained Variables Non-Negative

Select a Solving Method: Simplex LP

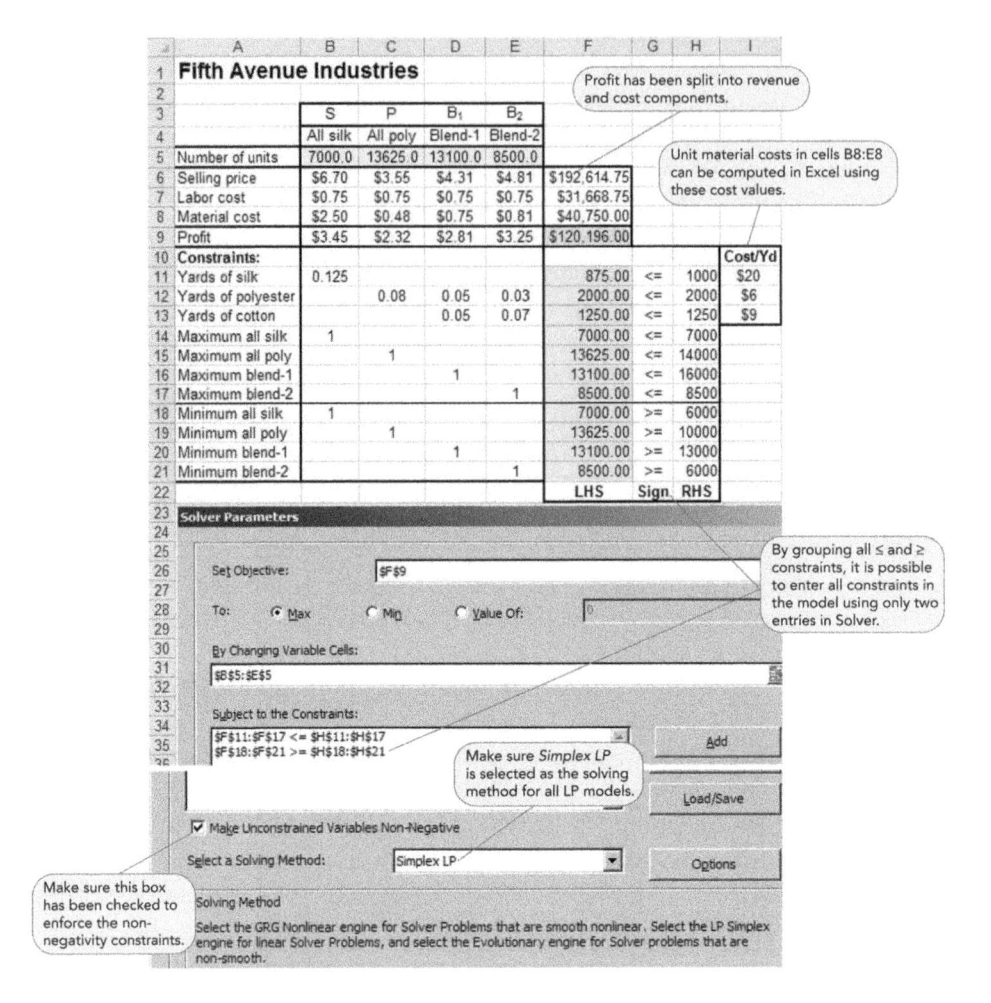

Solving Method
Select the GRG Nonlinear engine for Solver Problems that are smooth nonlinear. Select the LP Simplex engine for linear Solver Problems, and select the Evolutionary engine for Solver problems that are non-smooth.

Annotations: Profit has been split into revenue and cost components. Unit material costs in cells B8:E8 can be computed in Excel using these cost values. By grouping all ≤ and ≥ constraints, it is possible to enter all constraints in the model using only two entries in Solver. Make sure Simplex LP is selected as the solving method for all LP models. Make sure this box has been checked to enforce the non-negativity constraints.

Figure 3.2: Excel Layout and Solver Entries for Fifth Avenue Industries

📄 File: Figure 3.1.xlsx, Sheet: Figure 3.2

Make-Buy Decision Problem

An extension of the product mix problem is the make-buy decision problem. In this situation, a firm can satisfy the demand for a product by making some of it in-house ("make") and by subcontracting or outsourcing the remainder to another firm ("buy"). For each of its products, then, the firm needs to determine how much of the product to make and how much to buy. (*Note:* Under the scenario considered here, it is possible for the firm to use *both* the in-house and outsourcing options simultaneously for a product. That is, it is not necessary for the firm to choose either the in-house option or the outsourcing option exclusively. The situation where the firm has to choose only one of the two options for a given product is an example of a binary integer programming model, which we will address in Chapter 6.)

To illustrate this type of problem, let's consider the Fifth Avenue Industries problem again. As in the product mix example, Tables 3.1 and 3.2 show the relevant data for this problem. However, let's now assume that the firm *must* satisfy all demand exactly. That is, the monthly contract minimum numbers in Table 3.2 are now the same as the monthly demands. In addition, assume that Fifth Avenue now has the option to outsource part of its tie production to Ties Unlimited, another tie maker. Ties Unlimited has enough surplus capacity to handle any order that Fifth Avenue may place. It has provided Fifth Avenue with the following price list per tie: all-silk, $4.25; all-polyester, $2.00; poly-cotton blend 1, $2.50; and poly-cotton blend 2, $2.20. (Ties Unlimited is selling poly-cotton blend 2 ties for a lower price than poly-cotton blend 1 ties because it has obtained its cotton at a much cheaper cost than Fifth Avenue.) What should Fifth Avenue do under this revised situation to maximize its monthly profit?

Formulating the Problem   As before, let

S = number of all-silk ties to make (in-house) per month
P = number of all-polyester ties to make (in-house) per month
B_1 = number of poly-cotton blend 1 ties to make (in-house) per month
B_2 = number of poly-cotton blend 2 ties to make (in-house) per month

In this case, however, Fifth Avenue must decide on a policy for the product mix that includes both the make and buy options. To accommodate this feature, let

S_0 = number of all-silk ties to outsource (buy) per month
P_0 = number of all-polyester ties to outsource (buy) per month
B_{10} = number of poly-cotton blend 1 ties to outsource (buy) per month
B_{20} = number of poly-cotton blend 2 ties to outsource (buy) per month

Note that the total number of each variety of tie equals the sum of the number of ties made in-house and the number of ties outsourced. For example, the total number of all-silk ties equals $S + S_0$. The total revenue from all ties can now be written as

$$\text{Revenue} = \$6.70(S + S_0) + \$3.55(P + P_0) + \$4.31(B_1 + B_{10}) + \$4.81(B_2 + B_{20})$$

To compute the profit, we need to subtract the labor cost, material cost, and outsourcing cost from this revenue. As in the previous product mix example, the total labor and material costs may be written as

$$\text{Labor cost} = \$0.75(S + P + B_1 + B_2)$$
$$\text{Material cost} = \$2.50S + \$0.48P + \$0.75B_1 + \$0.81B_2$$

Note that the labor and material costs are relevant only for the portion of the production that occurs in-house. The total outsourcing cost may be written as

$$\text{Outsourcing cost} = \$4.25S_0 + \$2.00P_0 + \$2.50B_{10} + \$2.20B_{20}$$

The objective function can now be stated as

$$\text{Maximize profit} = \text{revenue} - \text{labor cost} - \text{material cost} - \text{outsourcing cost}$$

subject to the constraints

$0.125S$	$\leq$	$1,000$	(yards of silk)
$0.08P + 0.05B_1 + 0.03B_2$	$\leq$	$2,000$	(yards of polyester)
$0.05B_1 + 0.07B_2$	$\leq$	$1,250$	(yards of cotton)
$S + S_0$	$=$	$7,000$	(required demand for all-silk)
$P + P_0$	$=$	$14,000$	(required demand for all-polyester)
$B_1 + B_{10}$	$=$	$16,000$	(required demand for blend 1)
$B_2 + B_{20}$	$=$	$8,500$	(required demand for blend 2)
$S, P, B_1, B_2, S_0, P_0, B_{10}, B_{20}$	$\geq$	0	(nonnegativity)

Because all demand must be satisfied in this example, we write a single demand constraint for each tie variety. Note that we have written all the demand constraints as = constraints in this model. Could we have used the ≤ sign for the demand constraints without affecting the solution? In this case, the answer is yes because we are trying to maximize profit, and the profit contribution of each tie is positive, regardless of whether it is made in-house or outsourced (as shown in cells B10:I10 in the Excel layout for this model in Figure 3.3).

Likewise, could we have used the ≥ sign for the demand constraints? In this case, the answer is no. Why? (*Hint:* Because the selling price of each tie variety is greater than its outsourcing cost, what will the solution suggest if we write the demand constraints as ≥ equations?)

Solving the Problem The Solver entries and optimal solution values for this model are shown in Figure 3.3. Cell J6 defines the revenue component of the profit, cells J7 and J8 define the labor and material cost components, respectively, and cell J9 defines the outsourcing cost component. The profit shown in cell J10 (the objective cell in Solver) is the difference between cell J6 and cells J7, J8, and J9.

Interpreting the Results The results show that the optimal solution is to make in-house 7,000 all-silk ties, 12,589.30 all-polyester ties, 16,000 poly-cotton blend 1 ties, and 6,428.60 poly-cotton blend 2 ties. The remaining demand (i.e., 1,410.70 all-polyester ties and 2,071.40 poly-cotton blend 2 ties) should be outsourced from Ties Unlimited. This results in total revenue of $206,445, total labor cost of $31,513.39, total material cost of $40,750, and total outsourcing cost of $7,378.57, yielding a net profit of $126,803.04.

It is interesting to note that the presence of the outsourcing option changes the product mix for in-house production (compare Figure 3.2 with Figure 3.3). Also, Fifth Avenue's total profit increases as a result of outsourcing because it is now able to satisfy more of the demand (profit is now $126,803.04 versus only $120,196 earlier).

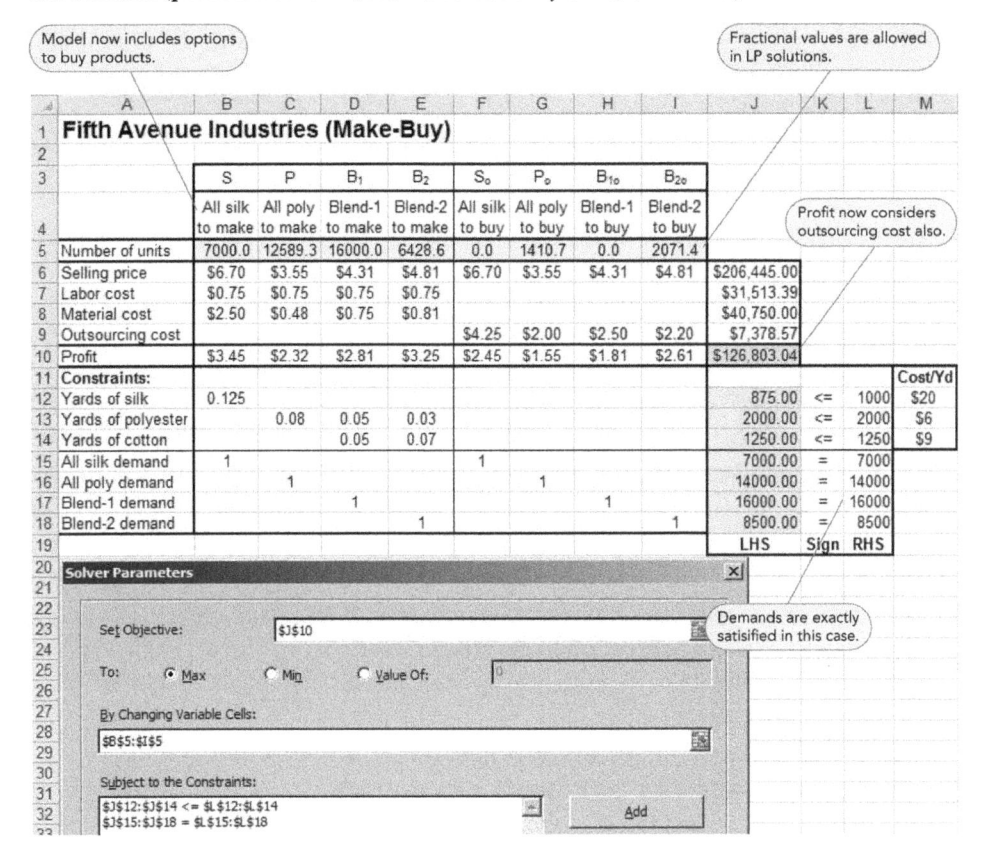

Figure 3.3: Excel Layout Solver Entries for Fifth Avenue Industries—Make-Buy Problem

File: Figure 3.3.xlsx

Observe that this solution turns out to have some fractional values. As noted in Chapter 2, because it is considerably more difficult to solve an integer programming model than an LP model, it is quite common to not specify the integer requirement in many LP models. We can then attempt to round the resulting solution appropriately if it turns out to have fractional values. In product mix problems that have many ≤ constraints, the fractional values for production variables should typically be rounded down. If we round up these values, we might potentially violate a binding constraint for a resource. In Fifth Avenue's case, the company could probably round down P and B_2 to 12,589 and 6,428, respectively, and it could correspondingly round up the outsourced values P_0 and B_{20} to 1,411 and 2,072, respectively, without affecting the profit too much.

In some situations, however, rounding may not be an easy task. For example, there is likely to be a huge cost and resource impact if we round a solution that suggests making 10.71 Boeing 787 aircraft to 10 versus rounding it to 11. In such cases, we need to solve the model as an integer programming problem. We discuss such problems (i.e., problems that require integer solutions) in Chapter 6.

3.3 Marketing Applications

Media Selection Problem

LP models have been used in the advertising field as a decision aid in selecting an effective media mix. Sometimes the technique is employed in allocating a fixed or limited budget across various media, which might include radio or television commercials, newspaper ads, direct mailings, magazine ads, and so on. In other applications, the objective is to maximize audience exposure. Restrictions on the allowable media mix might arise through contract requirements, limited media availability, or company policy. An example follows.

Win Big Gambling Club promotes gambling junkets from a large Midwestern city to casinos in The Bahamas. The club has budgeted up to $8,000 per week for local advertising. The money is to be allocated among four promotional media: TV spots, newspaper ads, and two types of radio advertisements. Win Big's goal is to reach the largest possible high-potential audience through the various media. Table 3.3 presents the number of potential gamblers reached by making use of an advertisement in each of the four media. It also provides the cost per advertisement placed and the maximum number of ads that can be purchased per week.

Table 3.3: Data for Win Big Gambling Club

Medium	Audience Reached per Ad	Cost per Ad	Maximum Ads per Week
TV spot (1 minute)	5,000	$800	12
Daily newspaper (full-page ad)	8,500	$925	5
Radio spot (30 seconds, prime time)	2,400	$290	25
Radio spot (1 minute, afternoon)	2,800	$380	20

Win Big's contractual arrangements require that at least five radio spots be placed each week. To ensure a broad-scoped promotional campaign, management also insists that no more than $1,800 be spent on radio advertising every week.

Formulating and Solving the Problem This is somewhat like the product mix problem we discussed earlier in this chapter, except that the "products" here are the various media that are available for use. The decision variables denote the number of times each of these media choices should be used. Let

T = number of 1-minute television spots taken each week
N = number of full-page daily newspaper ads taken each week
P = number of 30-second prime time radio spots taken each week
A = number of 1-minute afternoon radio spots taken each week

Objective:

$$\text{Maximize audience coverage} = 5{,}000T + 8{,}500N + 2{,}400P + 2{,}800A$$

subject to the constraints

T	$\leq$	12	(maximum TV spots/week)
N	$\leq$	5	(maximum newspaper ads/week)
P	$\leq$	25	(maximum 30-second radio spots/week)
A	$\leq$	20	(maximum 1-minute radio spots/week)
$800T + 925N + 290P + 380A$	$\leq$	8,000	(weekly advertising budget)
$P + A$	$\geq$	5	(minimum radio spots contracted)
$290P + 380A$	$\leq$	1,800	(maximum dollars spent on radio)
T, N, P, A	$\geq$	0	(nonnegativity)

The Excel layout and Solver entries for this model, and the resulting solution, are shown in Figure 3.4.

Interpreting the Results The optimal solution is found to be 1.97 television spots, 5 newspaper ads, 6.21 30-second prime time radio spots, and no 1-minute afternoon radio spots. This produces an audience exposure of 67,240.30 contacts. Here again, this solution turns out to have fractional values. Win Big would probably round down P to 6 spots and correspondingly round up T to 2 spots. A quick check indicates that the rounded solution satisfies all constraints even though T has been rounded up.

Marketing Research Problem
LP has been applied to marketing research problems and the area of consumer research. The next example illustrates how LP can help statistical pollsters make strategic decisions.

	A	B	C	D	E	F	G	H
1	**Win Big Gambling Club**							
2							Fractional values can be rounded off appropriately, if desired.	
3		T	N	P	A			
		TV spots	Newspaper ads	Prime-time radio spots	Afternoon radio spots			
5	Number of units	1.97	5.00	6.21	0.00			
6	Audience	5000	8500	2400	2800	67240.30		
7	Constraints:							
8	Maximum TV	1				1.97	<=	12
9	Maximum newspaper		1			5.00	<=	5
10	Max prime-time radio			1		6.21	<=	25
11	Max afternoon radio				1	0.00	<=	20
12	Total budget	$800	$925	$290	$380	$8,000.00	<=	$8,000
13	Maximum radio $			$290	$380	$1,800.00	<=	$1,800
14	Minimum radio spots			1	1	6.21	>=	5
15						LHS	Sign	RHS

Solver Parameters

Set Objective: $F$6

To: ● Max ○ Min ○ Value Of: 0

By Changing Variable Cells:
$B$5:$E$5

Subject to the Constraints:
$F$14 >= $H$14
$F$8:$F$13 <= $H$8:$H$13

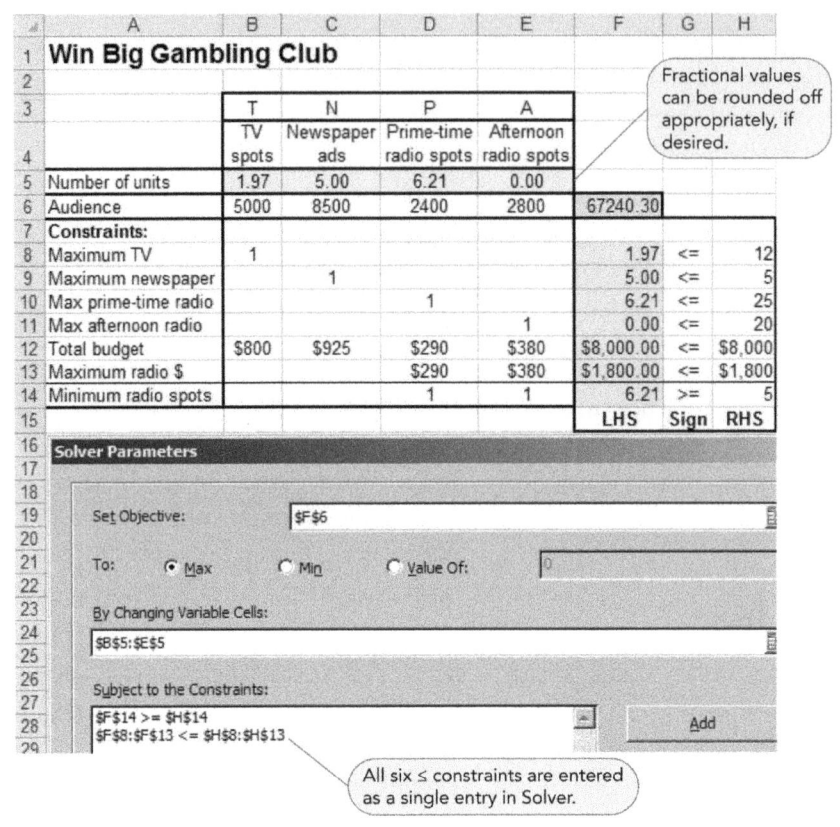

All six ≤ constraints are entered as a single entry in Solver.

Figure 3.4: Excel Layout and Solver Entries for Win Big Gambling Club

File: Figure 3.4.xlsx

Management Sciences Associates (MSA) is a marketing and computer research firm based in Washington, DC, that handles consumer surveys. One of its clients is a national press service that periodically conducts political polls on issues of widespread interest. In a survey for the press service, MSA determines that it must fulfill several requirements in order to draw statistically valid conclusions on the sensitive issue of new U.S. immigration laws:

1. Survey at least 2,300 people in total in the United States.
2. Survey at least 1,000 people who are 30 years of age or younger.
3. Survey at least 600 people who are between 31 and 50 years old.
4. Ensure that at least 15% of those surveyed live in a state that borders Mexico.
5. Ensure that at least 50% of those surveyed who are 30 years of age or younger live in a state that does not border Mexico.
6. Ensure that no more than 20% of those surveyed who are 51 years of age or older live in a state that borders Mexico.

MSA decides that all surveys should be conducted in person. Its estimates of the costs of reaching people in each age and region category are as shown in Table 3.4. MSA's goal is to meet the six sampling requirements at the least possible cost.

Table 3.4: Data for Management Sciences Associates

Region	Age ≤ 30	Age 31–50	Age ≥ 51
State bordering Mexico	$7.50	$6.80	$5.50
State not bordering Mexico	$6.90	$7.25	$6.10

Cost per Person Surveyed

Formulating the Problem The first step is to decide what the decision variables are. We note from Table 3.4 that people have been classified based on their ages (three categories) and regions (two categories). There is a separate cost associated with a person based on his or her age as well as his or her region. That is, for example, the cost for all persons from the ≤30 group is not the same and depends explicitly on whether the person is from a border state ($7.50) or from a nonborder state ($6.90). The decision variables, therefore, need to identify each person surveyed based on his or her age as well as region. Because we have three age categories and two regions, we need a total of 6 (= 3×2) decision variables. We let

B_1 = number surveyed who are ≤ 30 years of age and live in a border state
B_2 = number surveyed who are 31–50 years of age and live in a border state
B_3 = number surveyed who are ≥ 51 years of age and live in a border state
N_1 = number surveyed who are ≤ 30 years of age and do not live in a border state
N_2 = number surveyed who are 31–50 years of age and do not live in a border state
N_3 = number surveyed who are ≥ 51 years of age and do not live in a border state

Objective function:

$$\text{Minimize total interview cost} = \$7.50 B_1 + \$6.80 B_2 + \$5.50 B_3 + \$6.90 N_1 + \$7.25 N_2 + \$6.10 N_3$$

subject to the constraints

$B_1 + B_2 + B_3 + N_1 + N_2 + N_3 \geq 2{,}300$		(total number surveyed)
$B_1 + N_1$	$\geq 1{,}000$	(persons 30 years or younger)
$B_2 + N_2$	≥ 600	(persons 31–50 in age)
$B_1 + B_2 + B_3 \geq 0.15 (B_1 + B_2 + B_3 + N_1 + N_2 + N_3)$		(border states)
N_1	$\geq 0.5 (B_1 + N_1)$	(≤ 30 years and not border state)
B_3	$\leq 0.2 (B_3 + N_3)$	(51+ years and border state)
$B_1, B_2, B_3, N_1, N_2, N_3$	≥ 0	(nonnegativity)

Solving the Problem The Excel layout and Solver entries for this model are shown in Figure 3.5. In implementing this model for constraints 4 (border states), 5 (≤ 30 years and not border state), and 6 (51 + years and border state), we have chosen to include Excel formulas for both the left-hand-side (LHS) and right-hand-side (RHS) entries. For example, for the border states constraint (4), cell H11 in Figure 3.5 represents the formula $(B_1 + B_2 + B_3)$ and is implemented in Excel by using the SUMPRODUCT function, as usual:

$$= \text{SUMPRODUCT}(B11:G11,\$B\$5:\$G\$5)$$

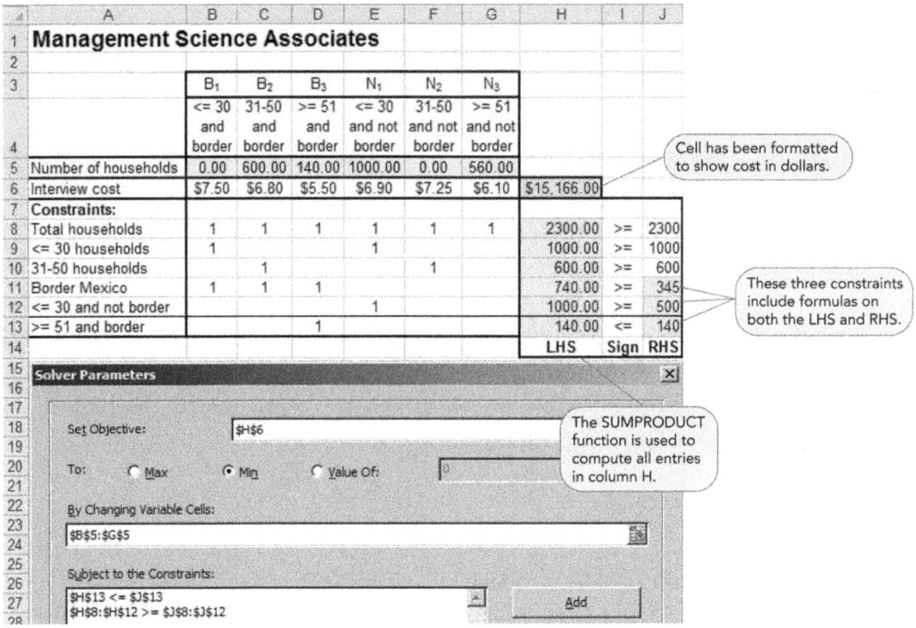

Figure 3.5: Excel Layout and Solver Entries for Management Sciences Associates

File: Figure 3.5.xlsx

Cell J11 represents the formula $0.15(B_1 + B_2 + B_3 + N_1 + N_2 + N_3)$ in the RHS of constraint 4. For this cell, we can write the Excel formula as

$$=0.15*\text{SUM}(B5:G5) \quad \text{or} \quad =0.15*H8$$

To be consistent with our layout format, we have colored both cells H11 and J11 blue to indicate the presence of Excel formulas in both cells. In a similar fashion, the formula in cells J12 (RHS for constraint 5) and J13 (RHS for constraint 6) would be

Cell J12: $=0.5*(B5+E5)$
Cell J13: $=0.2*(D5+G5)$

Alternatively, if we prefer, we can algebraically modify constraints 4, 5, and 6 to bring all the variables to the LHS and just leave a constant on the RHS. For example, constraint 4 is currently modeled as

$$B_1 + B_2 + B_3 \geq 0.15(B_1 + B_2 + B_3 + N_1 + N_2 + N_3)$$

This can be rewritten as

$$B_1 + B_2 + B_3 - 0.15(B_1 + B_2 + B_3 + N_1 + N_2 + N_3) \geq 0$$

which simplifies to

$$0.85B_1 + 0.85B_2 + 0.85B_3 - 0.15N_1 - 0.15N_2 - 0.15N_3 \geq 0$$

Likewise, constraints 5 and 6 would be

Constraint 5: $-0.5B_1 + 0.5N_1 \geq 0$ (≤ 30 years and not border state)
Constraint 6: $0.8B_3 - 0.2N_3 \leq 0$ (51+ years and border state)

Note that such algebraic manipulations are not required to implement this model in Excel. In fact, in many cases it is probably not preferable to make such modifications because the meaning of the revised constraint is not intuitively obvious. For example, the coefficient 0.85 for B_1 in the modified form for constraint 4 has no direct significance or meaning in the context of the problem.

Decision Modeling In Action

Optimization Models for Production Planning in LG Display

LG Display use different types and quantities of light-emitting diode (LED) arrays based on the type of product it produces. In that capacity, LG Display had three main problems related to the storage and usage of LED arrays: determining the different types and quantities of array bars that should be available in inventory, determining the optimal combination of LED arrays to be used in each product in order to minimize cost while sustaining high quality levels, and minimizing the scrap rate and damage of LED array parts that result from high inventory levels.

LG Display used an application, based on linear programming and multirank mixing (MRM) optimization, in two of its manufacturing facilities in South Korea to handle these three problems. The application determines the best combination of LED parts used at each assembly step to reduce the inventory level of these parts for various electronic devices, while meeting customer demands. The implementation of the application resulted in a massive reduction in inventory levels, enabling LG Display to save about $50 million annually in the two facilities.

Source: Based on S. Chang, J. Chung. "Optimization Models for Production Planning in LG Display," *Interfaces* 43, 6 (November-December 2013): 518–529.

Interpreting the Results The optimal solution to MSA's marketing research problem costs $15,166 and requires the firm to survey people as follows:

People who are 31–50 years of age and live in a border state = 600
People who are ≥ 51 years of age and live in a border state = 140
People who are ≤ 30 years of age and do not live in a border state = 1,000
People who are ≥ 51 years of age and do not live in a border state = 560

3.4 Finance Applications

Portfolio Selection Problem

A problem frequently encountered by managers of banks, mutual funds, investment services, and insurance companies is the selection of specific investments from among a wide variety of alternatives. A manager's overall objective is usually to maximize expected return on investment, given a set of legal, policy, or risk constraints.

Consider the example of International City Trust (ICT), which invests in trade credits, corporate bonds, precious metal stocks, mortgage-backed securities, and construction loans. ICT has $5 million available for immediate investment and wishes to maximize the interest earned on its investments over the next year. The specifics of the investment possibilities are shown in Table 3.5. For each type of investment, the table shows the expected return over the next year as well as a score that indicates the risk associated with the investment. (A lower score implies less risk.)

Table 3.5: Data for International City Trust

Investment	Interest Earned	Risk Score
Trade credits	7%	1.7
Corporate bonds	10%	1.2
Gold stocks	19%	3.7
Platinum stocks	12%	2.4
Mortgage securities	8%	2.0
Construction loans	14%	2.9

To encourage a diversified portfolio, the board of directors has placed several limits on the amount that can be committed to any one type of investment: (1) No more than 25% of the total amount invested may be in any single type of investment, (2) at least 30% of the funds invested must be in precious metals, (3) at least 45% must be invested in trade credits and corporate bonds, and (4) the average risk score of the total investment must be 2 or less.

Formulating the Problem The decision variables in most investment planning problems correspond to the amount that should be invested in each investment choice. In ICT's case, to model the investment decision as an LP problem, we let

T = dollars invested in trade credit
B = dollars invested in corporate bonds
G = dollars invested in gold stocks
P = dollars invested in platinum stocks
M = dollars invested in mortgage securities
C = dollars invested in construction loans

The objective function may then be written as

Maximize dollars of interest earned = $0.07T + 0.10B + 0.19G + 0.12P + 0.08M + 0.14C$

The constraints control the amounts that may be invested in each type of investment. ICT has $5 million available for investment. Hence the first constraint is

$$T + B + G + P + M + C \leq 5{,}000{,}000$$

Could we express this constraint by using the = sign rather than ≤? Because any dollar amount that is not invested by ICT does not earn any interest, it is logical to expect that, under normal circumstances, ICT would invest the entire $5 million. However, it is possible in some unusual cases that the conditions placed on investments by the board of directors are so restrictive that it is not possible to find an investment strategy that allows the entire amount to be invested. To guard against this possibility, it is preferable to write the preceding constraint using the ≤ sign. Note that if the investment conditions do permit the entire amount to be invested, the optimal solution will automatically do so because this is a maximization problem.

The diversification constraints are

$$T \leq 0.25\,(T + B + G + P + M + C)$$
$$B \leq 0.25\,(T + B + G + P + M + C)$$
$$G \leq 0.25\,(T + B + G + P + M + C)$$
$$P \leq 0.25\,(T + B + G + P + M + C)$$
$$M \leq 0.25\,(T + B + G + P + M + C)$$
$$C \leq 0.25\,(T + B + G + P + M + C)$$

If we are sure that the investment conditions will permit the entire $5 million to be invested, we can write the RHS of each of these constraints as a constant $1,250,000 (= 0.25 \times \$5,000,000)$. However, for the same reason discussed for the first constraint, it is preferable to write the RHS for these constraints (as well as all other constraints in this problem) in terms of the sum of the decision variables rather than as constants.

As in the marketing research problem, we can, if we wish, algebraically modify these constraints so that all variables are on the LHS and only a constant is on the RHS. (*Note:* Such algebraic manipulations are not required for Excel to solve these problems, and we do not recommend that they be done.) For example, the constraint regarding trade credits would then be written as

$$0.75T - 0.25B - 0.25G - 0.25P - 0.25M - 0.25C \leq 0 \quad \text{(no more than 25\% in trade credits)}$$

The constraints that at least 30% of the funds invested must be in precious metals and that at least 45% must be invested in trade credits and corporate bonds are written, respectively, as

$$G + P \geq 0.30\,(T + B + G + P + M + C)$$
$$T + B \geq 0.45\,(T + B + G + P + M + C)$$

Next, we come to the risk constraint, which states that the average risk score of the total investment must be 2 or less. To calculate the average risk score, we need to take the weighted sum of the risk and divide it by the total amount invested. This constraint may be written as

$$\frac{1.7T + 1.2B + 3.7G + 2.4P + 2.0M + 2.9C}{T + B + G + P + M + C} \leq 2$$

Finally, we have the nonnegativity constraints:

$$T, B, G, P, M, C \geq 0$$

EXCEL NOTES

- Although the previous expression for the risk constraint is a valid linear equation, Excel's Solver sometimes misinterprets the division sign in the expression as an indication of nonlinearity and gives the erroneous message, "The linearity conditions required by this LP Solver are not satisfied."

- Likewise, if Solver sets all decision variable values to zero at any stage during the solution process, the denominator in the previous expression becomes zero. This causes a division-by-zero error, which could sometimes lead to a "Solver encountered an error value in the Objective Cell or a Constraint cell" message.

- If a constraint with a denominator that is a function of the decision variables causes either of these situations to occur in your model, we recommend that you algebraically modify the constraint before implementing it in Excel. For example, in ICT's problem, the risk constraint could be implemented as
$$1.7T + 1.2B + 3.7G + 2.4P + 2.0M + 2.9C \leq 2(T + B + G + P + M + C)$$

Solving the Problem The Excel layout and Solver entries for this model are shown in Figure 3.6. Because we have chosen to express the RHS values for most constraints in terms of the decision variables rather than as constants, we have formulas on both sides for all but one of the constraints. The only exception is the constraint specifying that $5 million is available for investment. As usual, cells representing the LHS values of constraints (cells H8:H17) use the SUMPRODUCT function. Cells representing RHS values are modeled using simple Excel formulas, as in the marketing research problem. For example, the RHS (cell J9) for the constraint specifying no more than 25% in trade credits would contain the formula

$$= 0.25 * \text{SUM}(B5:G5) \quad \text{or} \quad = 0.25 * H8$$

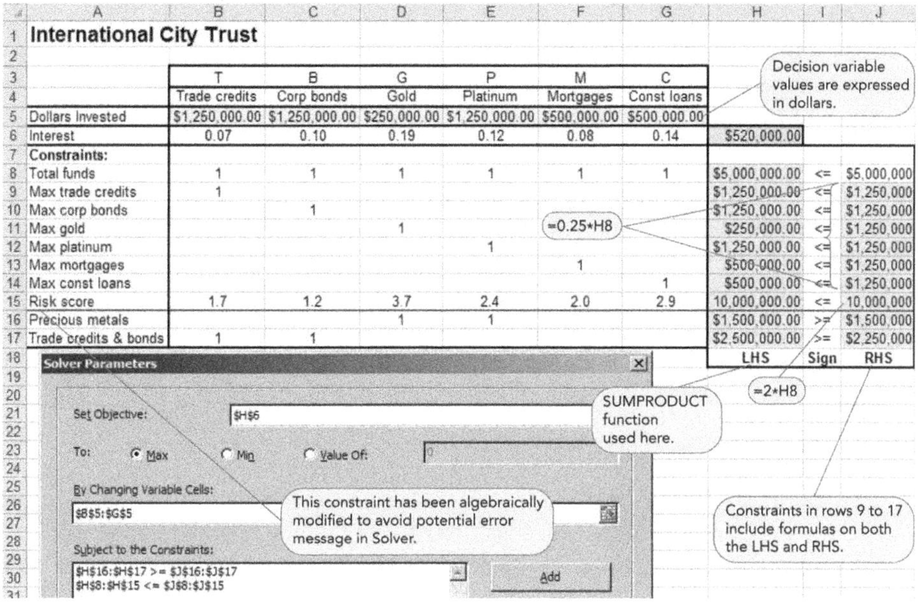

Figure 3.6: Excel Layout and Solver Entries for International City Trust

File: Figure 3.6.xlsx, Sheet: Figure 3.6

Likewise, the RHS (cell J15) for the risk score constraint would contain the formula =2*H8 to reflect the algebraic manipulation of this constraint (see **EXCEL NOTES** above).

Interpreting the Results The optimal solution is to invest $1.25 million each in trade credits, corporate bonds, and platinum stocks; $500,000 each in mortgage-backed securities and construction loans; and $250,000 in gold stocks—earning a total interest of $520,000. In this case, the investment conditions do allow the entire $5 million to be invested, meaning that we could have expressed the RHS values of all constraints by using constants without affecting the optimal solution.

Alternate Formulations of the Portfolio Selection Problem
In our discussion of the portfolio selection problem, we have chosen to express the decision variables as the number of dollars invested in each choice. However, for this

problem (as well as many other problems), we can define the decision variables in alternate fashions. We address two alternatives here.

First, we could set up the decision variables to represent the number of dollars invested in *millions*. As noted in Chapter 2, it is usually a good idea in practice to scale problems in which values of the objective function coefficients and constraint coefficients of different constraints differ by several orders of magnitude. One way to do so would be to click the Use Automatic Scaling option available in Solver, discussed in Chapter 2. In ICT's problem, observe that the only impact of this revised definition of the decision variables on the written formulation would be to replace the $5,000,000 in the total funds available constraint by $5. Likewise, cell J8 in Figure 3.6 would show a value of $5. Because all other RHS values are functions of the decision variables, they will automatically reflect the revised situation. The optimal solution will show values of $1.25 each for trade credits, corporate bonds, and platinum stocks; $0.50 each for mortgage-backed securities and construction loans; and $0.25 for gold stocks—earning a total interest of $0.52.

Second, if we assume that the $5 million represents 100% of the money available, we could define the decision variables as the portion (or percentage) of this amount invested in each investment choice. For example, we could define

T = portion (or percentage) of the $5 million invested in trade credit

We could do likewise for the other five decision variables (B, G, P, M, and C). The interesting point to note in this case is that the actual amount available ($5 million) is not really relevant and does not figure anywhere in the formulation. Rather, the idea is that if we can decide how to distribute 100% of the funds available among the various choices, we can apply those percentage allocations to any available amount.

The revised Excel layout and solution for this problem is shown in Figure 3.7. In ICT's problem, we note that the only impact of this revised definition of decision variables is to replace the $5 million in the total funds available constraint by 1 (or 100%). Other constraint RHS values (cells J9:J14 and J16:J17) no longer show dollar values but instead show total portions invested. The RHS for the constraint in row 15 (cell J15) shows the average risk score of the investment strategy. Figure 3.7 indicates that the optimal solution now shows 0.25 each for trade credits, corporate bonds, and platinum stocks; 0.10 each for mortgage-backed securities and construction loans; and 0.05 for gold stocks—earning a total return of 0.104. If we multiply each of these portions by the amount available ($5 million), we get the same dollar values as in the solution to the original formulation (Figure 3.6).

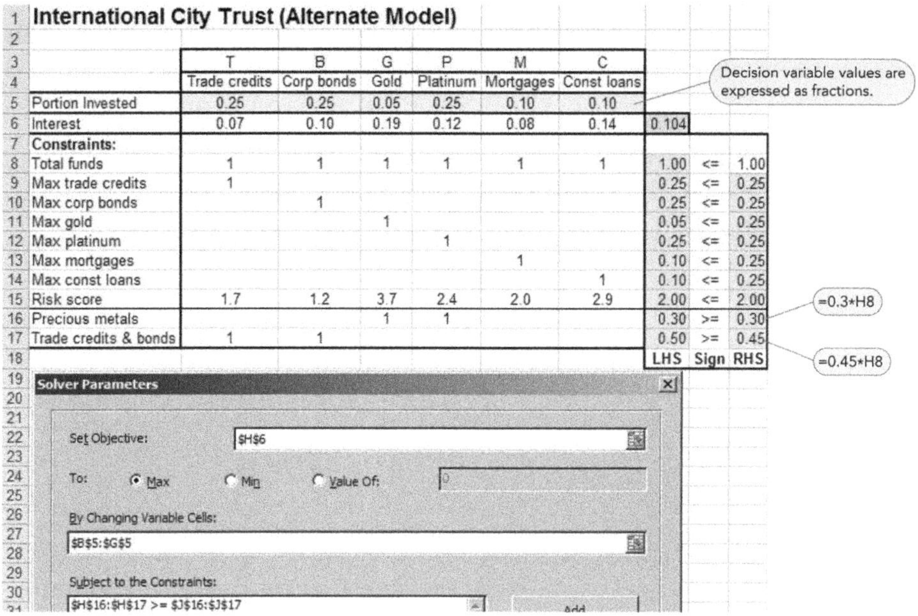

International City Trust (Alternate Model)

	T	B	G	P	M	C				
	Trade credits	Corp bonds	Gold	Platinum	Mortgages	Const loans				
Portion Invested	0.25	0.25	0.05	0.25	0.10	0.10				
Interest	0.07	0.10	0.19	0.12	0.08	0.14	0.104			
Constraints:										
Total funds	1	1	1	1	1	1	1.00	<=	1.00	
Max trade credits	1						0.25	<=	0.25	
Max corp bonds		1					0.25	<=	0.25	
Max gold			1				0.05	<=	0.25	
Max platinum				1			0.25	<=	0.25	
Max mortgages					1		0.10	<=	0.25	
Max const loans						1	0.10	<=	0.25	
Risk score	1.7	1.2	3.7	2.4	2.0	2.9	2.00	<=	2.00	=0.3*H8
Precious metals			1	1			0.30	>=	0.30	
Trade credits & bonds	1	1					0.50	>=	0.45	=0.45*H8
							LHS	Sign	RHS	

Decision variable values are expressed as fractions.

Solver Parameters

Set Objective: $H$6

To: ● Max   ○ Min   ○ Value Of: 0

By Changing Variable Cells:
$B$5:$G$5

Subject to the Constraints:
$H$16:$H$17 >= $J$16:$J$17

Figure 3.7: Excel Layout and Solver Entries for International City Trust—Alternate Model

File: Figure 3.6.xlsx, Sheet: Figure 3.7

The preceding discussion reinforces the need to define the decision variables in an LP problem as precisely as possible. As we observed, depending on how the decision variables have been defined, the constraints and, hence, the resulting optimal solution values will be different.

3.5 Employee Staffing Applications

Labor Planning Problem

Labor planning problems address staffing needs over a specific planning horizon, such as a day, week, month, or year. They are especially useful when staffing needs are different during different time periods in the planning horizon and managers have some flexibility in assigning workers to jobs that require overlapping or interchangeable talents. Many service businesses (e.g., restaurants with high demand at lunchtime but little demand at 3:00 p.m. or call centers responding to built-up overnight concerns between 8:00 and 9:00 a.m. the following day) experience wildly fluctuating customer demand patterns daily. Large banks frequently use LP to tackle their labor staffing problem.

Hong Kong Bank of Commerce and Industry is a busy bank that has requirements for between 10 and 18 tellers, depending on the time of day. The afternoon time, from noon to 3 P.M., is usually heaviest. Table 3.6 indicates the workers needed at various hours that the bank is open.

Table 3.6: Tellers Required for Hong Kong Bank

Time Period	Number Required
9 a.m.–10 a.m.	10
10 a.m.–11 a.m.	12
11 a.m.–Noon	14
Noon–1 p.m.	16
1 p.m.–2 p.m.	18
2 p.m.–3 p.m.	17
3 p.m.–4 p.m.	15
4 p.m.–5 p.m.	10

The bank now employs 12 full-time tellers but also has several people available on its roster of part-time employees. A part-time employee must put in exactly 4 hours per day but can start anytime between 9 A.M. and 1 P.M. Part-timers are a fairly inexpensive labor pool because no retirement or lunch benefits are provided for them. Full-timers, on the other hand, work from 9 A.M. to 5 P.M. but are allowed 1 hour for lunch. (Half of the full-timers eat at 11 A.M. and the other half at noon.) Each full-timer thus provides 35 hours per week of productive labor time.

The bank's corporate policy limits part-time hours to a maximum of 50% of the day's total requirement. Part-timers earn $7 per hour (or $28 per day) on average, and full-timers earn $90 per day in salary and benefits, on average. The bank would like to set a schedule that would minimize its total personnel costs. It is willing to release one or more of its full-time tellers if it is cost-effective to do so.

Formulating and Solving the Problem In employee-staffing problems, we typically need to determine how many employees need to start their work at the different starting times permitted. For example, in Hong Kong Bank's case, we have full-time tellers who all start work at 9 A.M. and part-timers who can start anytime between 9 A.M. and 1 P.M. Let

F = number of full-time tellers to use (all starting at 9 A.M.)
P_1 = number of part-timers to use, starting at 9 A.M. (leaving at 1 P.M.)
P_2 = number of part-timers to use, starting at 10 A.M. (leaving at 2 P.M.)
P_3 = number of part-timers to use, starting at 11 A.M. (leaving at 3 P.M.)
P_4 = number of part-timers to use, starting at noon (leaving at 4 P.M.)
P_5 = number of part-timers to use, starting at 1 P.M. (leaving at 5 P.M.)

The objective function is

Minimize total daily personnel cost = $90F + $28(P_1 + P_2 + P_3 + P_4 + P_5)$

Next, we write the constraints. For each hour, the available number of tellers must be at least equal to the required number of tellers. This is a simple matter of counting which of the different employees (defined by the decision variables) are working during a given time period and which are not. It is also important to remember that half the full-time tellers break for lunch between 11 A.M. and noon and the other half break between noon and 1 P.M.:

$$F + P_1 \geq 10 \quad \text{(9 A.M.–10 A.M. requirement)}$$
$$F + P_1 + P_2 \geq 12 \quad \text{(10 A.M.–11 A.M. requirement)}$$
$$0.5F + P_1 + P_2 + P_3 \geq 14 \quad \text{(11 A.M.–12 noon requirement)}$$
$$0.5F + P_1 + P_2 + P_3 + P_4 \geq 16 \quad \text{(12 noon–1 P.M. requirement)}$$
$$F + P_2 + P_3 + P_4 + P_5 \geq 18 \quad \text{(1 P.M.–2 P.M. requirement)}$$
$$F + P_3 + P_4 + P_5 \geq 17 \quad \text{(2 P.M.–3 P.M. requirement)}$$
$$F + P_4 + P_5 \geq 15 \quad \text{(3 P.M.–4 P.M. requirement)}$$
$$F + P_5 \geq 10 \quad \text{(4 P.M.–5 P.M. requirement)}$$

Only 12 full-time tellers are available, so

$$F \leq 12$$

Part-time worker hours cannot exceed 50% of total hours required each day, which is the sum of the tellers needed each hour. Hence

$$4(P_1 + P_2 + P_3 + P_4 + P_5) \leq 0.5(10 + 12 + 14 + 16 + 18 + 17 + 15 + 10)$$

or

$$4P_1 + 4P_2 + 4P_3 + 4P_4 + 4P_5 \leq 56$$
$$F, P_1, P_2, P_3, P_4, P_5 \geq 0$$

The Excel layout and Solver entries for this model are shown in Figure 3.8.

Interpreting the Results Figure 3.8 reveals that the optimal solution is to employ 10 full-time tellers, 7 part-time tellers at 10 A.M., 2 part-time tellers at 11 A.M., and 5 part-time tellers at noon, for a total cost of $1,292 per day. Because we are using only 10 of the 12 available full-time tellers, Hong Kong Bank can choose to release up to 2 of the full-time tellers.

It turns out that there are several alternate optimal solutions that Hong Kong Bank can employ. In practice, the sequence in which you present constraints in a model can affect the specific solution that is found. We revisit this example in Chapter 4 (Solved Problem 4–1) to study how we can use the Sensitivity Report generated by Solver to detect and identify alternate optimal solutions.

Hong Kong Bank

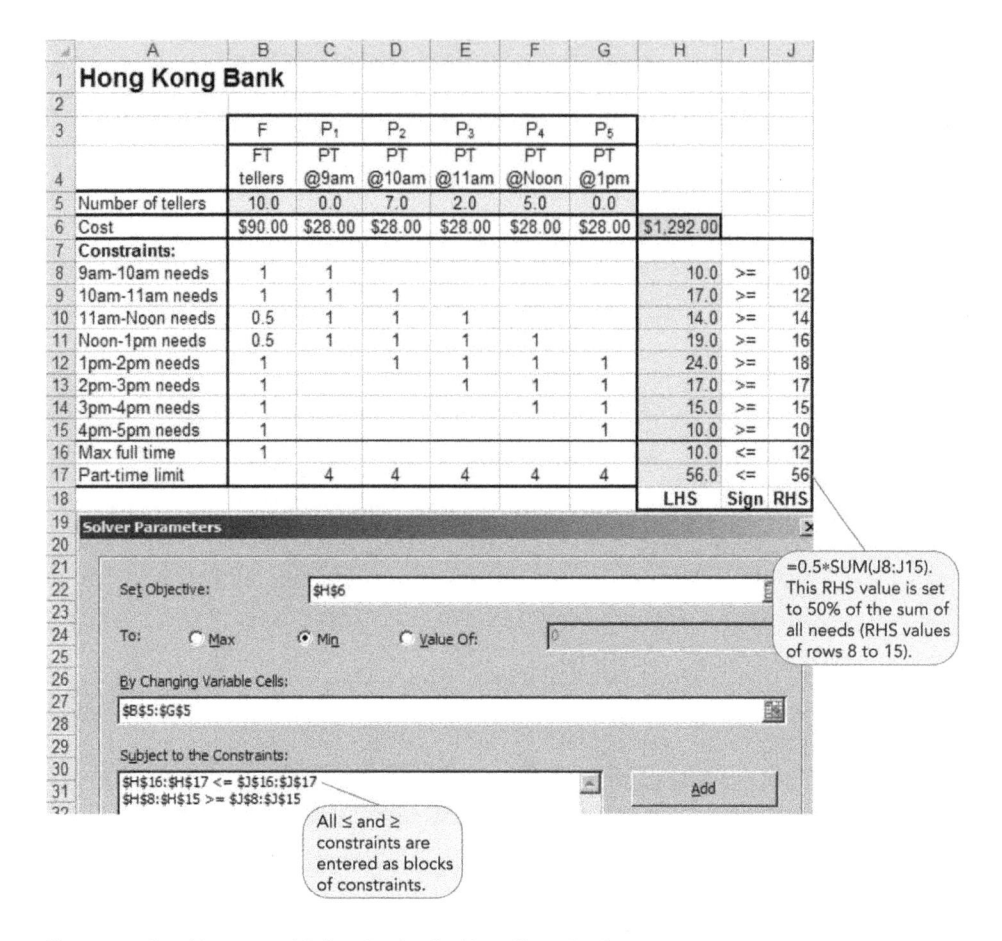

	A	B	C	D	E	F	G	H	I	J
1	Hong Kong Bank									
2										
3		F	P_1	P_2	P_3	P_4	P_5			
4		FT tellers	PT @9am	PT @10am	PT @11am	PT @Noon	PT @1pm			
5	Number of tellers	10.0	0.0	7.0	2.0	5.0	0.0			
6	Cost	$90.00	$28.00	$28.00	$28.00	$28.00	$28.00	$1,292.00		
7	Constraints:									
8	9am-10am needs	1	1					10.0	>=	10
9	10am-11am needs	1	1	1				17.0	>=	12
10	11am-Noon needs	0.5	1	1	1			14.0	>=	14
11	Noon-1pm needs	0.5	1	1	1	1		19.0	>=	16
12	1pm-2pm needs	1		1	1	1	1	24.0	>=	18
13	2pm-3pm needs	1			1	1	1	17.0	>=	17
14	3pm-4pm needs	1				1	1	15.0	>=	15
15	4pm-5pm needs	1					1	10.0	>=	10
16	Max full time	1						10.0	<=	12
17	Part-time limit		4	4	4	4	4	56.0	<=	56
18								LHS	Sign	RHS

Solver Parameters

Set Objective: $H$6

To: ○ Max ● Min ○ Value Of: 0

By Changing Variable Cells:
$B$5:$G$5

Subject to the Constraints:
$H$16:$H$17 <= $J$16:$J$17
$H$8:$H$15 >= $J$8:$J$15

All ≤ and ≥ constraints are entered as blocks of constraints.

*=0.5*SUM(J8:J15). This RHS value is set to 50% of the sum of all needs (RHS values of rows 8 to 15).*

Figure 3.8: Excel Layout and Solver Entries for Hong Kong Bank

File: Figure 3.8.xlsx

For this problem, one alternate solution is to employ 10 full-time tellers, 6 part-time tellers at 9 A.M., 1 part-time teller at 10 A.M., 2 part-time tellers at 11 A.M., and 5 part-time tellers at noon. The cost of this policy is also $1,292.

Note that we are setting up the teller requirement constraints as ≥ constraints rather than as = constraints. The reason for this should be obvious by now: If we try to *exactly* satisfy the teller requirements every period, the fact that each teller (full or part time) works more than one hour at a stretch may make it impossible to simultaneously satisfy all requirements as = constraints. In fact, if you replace the ≥ sign with = for the teller requirement constraints in Hong Kong Bank's model (rows 8 to 15) and resolve the problem, Solver returns a "Solver could not find a feasible solution" message.

Extensions to the Labor Planning Problem

The previous example considered the labor requirements during different time periods of a single day. In other labor planning problems, the planning horizon may consist of a week, a month, or a year. In this case, the decision variables will correspond to the different work schedules that workers can follow and will denote the number of workers who should follow a specific work schedule. Solved Problem 3–1 at the end of this chapter illustrates an example where the planning horizon is a week and the time periods are days of the week. The worker requirements are specified for each of the seven days of the week.

In extended versions of this problem, the time periods may also include specific shifts. For example, if there are two shifts per day (day shift and night shift), there are then 14 time periods (seven days of the week, two shifts per day) in the problem. Worker requirements need to be specified for each of these 14 time periods. In this case, the work schedules need to specify the exact days and shifts that the schedule denotes. For example, an available work schedule could be "Monday to Friday on shift 1, Saturday and Sunday off." Another available work schedule could be "Tuesday to Saturday on shift 2, Sunday and Monday off." The decision analyst would need to specify all available work schedules before setting up the problem as an LP model.

Assignment Problem

Assignment problems involve determining the most efficient assignment of people to jobs, machines to tasks, police cars to city sectors, salespeople to territories, and so on. The assignments are done on a one-to-one basis. For example, in a people-to-jobs assignment problem, each person is assigned to exactly one job, and, conversely, each job is assigned to exactly one person. Fractional assignments are not permitted. The objective might be to minimize the total cost of the assignments or maximize the total effectiveness or benefit of the assignments.

The assignment problem is an example of a special type of LP problem known as a network flow problem, and we study this type of problem in greater detail in Chapter 5.

3.6 Transportation Applications

Vehicle Loading Problem

Vehicle loading problems involve deciding which items to load on a vehicle (e.g. truck, ship, aircraft) to maximize the total value of the load shipped. The items loaded may need to satisfy several constraints, such as weight and volume limits of the vehicle, minimum levels of certain items that may need to be accepted, etc. As an example, we consider Goodman Shipping, an Orlando, Florida, firm owned by Steven Goodman. One of his trucks, with a weight capacity of 15,000 pounds and a volume capacity of 1,300 cubic feet, is about to be loaded. Awaiting shipment are the items shown in

Table 3.7. Each of these six items, we see, has an associated total dollar value, available weight, and volume per pound that the item occupies. The objective is to maximize the total value of the items loaded onto the truck without exceeding the truck's weight and volume capacities.

Table 3.7: Shipments for Goodman Shipping

Item	Value	Weight (pounds)	Volume (cu. ft. per pound)
1	$15,500	5,000	0.125
2	$14,400	4,500	0.064
3	$10,350	3,000	0.144
4	$14,525	3,500	0.448
5	$13,000	4,000	0.048
6	$ 9,625	3,500	0.018

Formulating and Solving the Problem The decision variables in this problem define the number of pounds of each item that should be loaded on the truck. There would be six decision variables (one for each item) in the model. In this case, the dollar value of each item needs to be appropriately scaled for use in the objective function. For example, if the total value of the 5,000 pounds of item 1 is $15,500, the value per pound is then 3.10 (= 15,500 / 5,000 pounds). Similar calculations can be made for the other items to be shipped.

Let W_i be the weight (in pounds) of each item i loaded on the truck. The LP model can then be formulated as follows:

$$\text{Maximize load value} = \$3.10W_1 + \$3.20W_2 + \$3.45W_3 + \$4.15W_4 + \$3.25W_5 + \$2.75W_6$$

subject to the constraints

$W_1 + W_2 + W_3 + W_4 + W_5 + W_6 \leq 15{,}000$ (weight limit of truck)

$0.125 W_1 + 0.064 W_2 + 0.144 W_3 + 0.0448 W_4 + 0.048 W_5 + 0.018 W_6 \leq 1{,}300$ (volume limit of truck)

$W_1 \leq 5{,}000$ (item 1 availability)
$W_2 \leq 4{,}500$ (item 2 availability)
$W_3 \leq 3{,}000$ (item 3 availability)
$W_4 \leq 3{,}500$ (item 4 availability)
$W_5 \leq 4{,}000$ (item 5 availability)
$W_6 \leq 3{,}500$ (item 6 availability)
$W_1, W_2, W_3, W_4, W_5, W_6 \geq 0$ (nonnegativity)

Figure 3.9 shows the Excel layout and Solver entries for Goodman Shipping's LP model.

Goodman Shipping

LP solution allows fractional quantities to be shipped.

	A	B	C	D	E	F	G	H	I	J
1	Goodman Shipping									
2										
3		W_1	W_2	W_3	W_4	W_5	W_6		Decision variable values expressed in pounds.	
4		Item 1	Item 2	Item 3	Item 4	Item 5	Item 6			
5	Weight in pounds	3,037.38	4,500.00	3,000.00	0.00	4,000.00	462.62			
6	Load value	$3.10	$3.20	$3.45	$4.15	$3.25	$2.75	$48,438.08		
7	Constraints:									
8	Weight limit	1	1	1	1	1	1	15000.00	<=	15000
9	Volume limit	0.125	0.064	0.144	0.448	0.048	0.018	1300.00	<=	1300
10	Item 1 limit (pounds)	1						3037.38	<=	5000
11	Item 2 limit (pounds)		1					4500.00	<=	4500
12	Item 3 limit (pounds)			1				3000.00	<=	3000
13	Item 4 limit (pounds)				1			0.00	<=	3500
14	Item 5 limit (pounds)					1		4000.00	<=	4000
15	Item 6 limit (pounds)						1	462.62	<=	3500
16								LHS	Sign	RHS

Solver Parameters

Set Objective: $H$6

To: ● Max ○ Min ○ Value Of: 0

By Changing Variable Cells:
$B$5:$G$5

Subject to the Constraints:
$H$8:$H$15 <= $J$8:$J$15

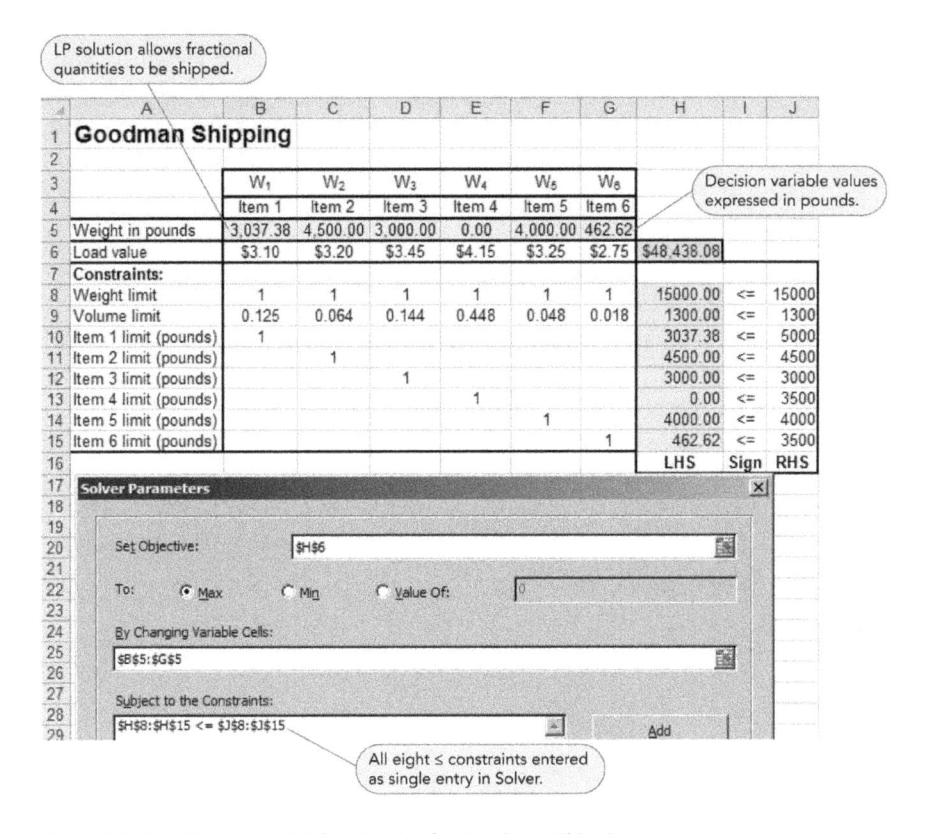

All eight ≤ constraints entered as single entry in Solver.

Figure 3.9: Excel Layout and Solver Entries for Goodman Shipping

File: Figure 3.9.xlsx, Sheet: Figure 3.9

Interpreting the Results The optimal solution in Figure 3.9 yields a total value of $48,438.08 and requires Goodman to ship 3,037.38 pounds of item 1; 4,500 pounds of item 2; 3,000 pounds of item 3; 4,000 pounds of item 5; and 462.62 pounds of item 6. The truck is fully loaded from both weight and volume perspectives. As usual, if shipments have to be integers, Goodman can probably round down the totals for items 1 and 6 without affecting the total dollar value too much. Interestingly, the only item that is not included for loading is item 4, which has the highest dollar value per pound. However, its relatively high volume (per pound loaded) makes it an unattractive item to load.

Alternate Formulations As in the portfolio selection problem we studied previously, there are alternate ways in which we could define the decision variables for this problem. For example, the decision variables could denote the portion (or percentage) of each item that is accepted for loading. Under this approach, let P_i be the portion of each item i loaded on the truck. Figure 3.10 shows the Excel layout and solution for the alternate model, using these revised decision variables. The layout for this model is identical to that shown in Figure 3.9, and you should be able to recognize its written formulation easily. The coefficients in the volume constraint show the volume occupied by the entire quantity of an item. For example, the volume coefficient for item 1 is 625 cubic feet ($=0.125$ cubic feet per pound $\times 5{,}000$ pounds). Likewise, the coefficient for item 2 is 288 cubic feet ($=0.064$ cubic feet per pound $\times 4{,}500$ pounds).

The final six constraints reflect the fact that at most one "unit" (i.e., a proportion of 1) of an item can be loaded onto the truck. In effect, if Goodman can load a *portion* of an item (e.g., item 1 is a batch of 1,000 folding chairs, not all of which need to be shipped together), the proportions P_i will all have values ranging from 0 (none of that item is loaded) to 1 (all of that item is loaded).

The solution to this model shows that the maximum load value is $48,438.08. This load value is achieved by shipping 60.748% of item 1 ($0.60748 \times 5{,}000 = 3{,}037.4$ pounds) of item 1; all available quantities (i.e., 100%) of items 2, 3, and 5; and 13.218% (462.63 pounds) of item 6. As expected, this is the same solution we obtained in Figure 3.9, using the original model for this problem.

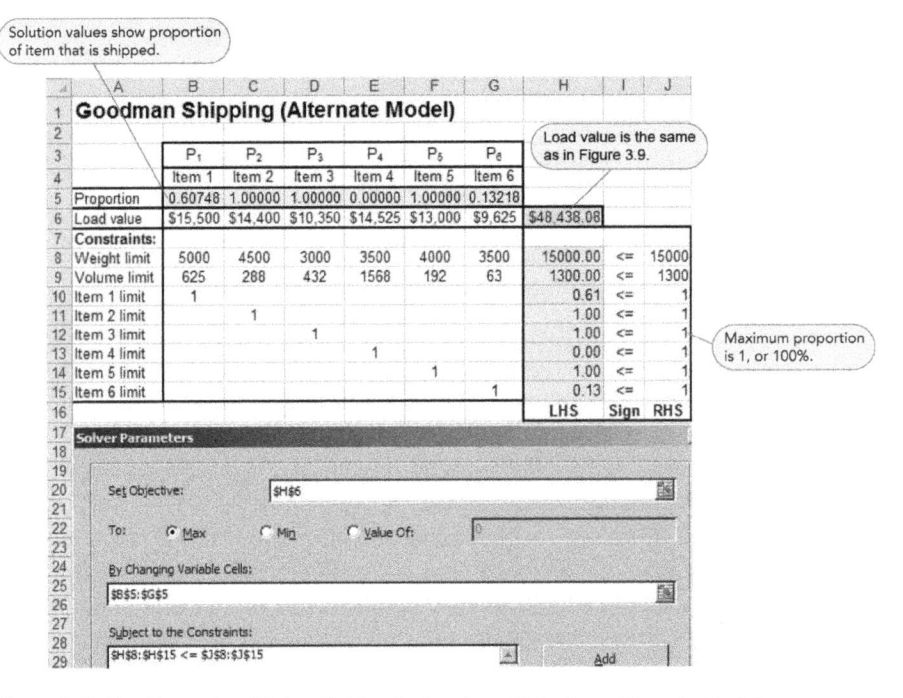

Figure 3.10: Excel Layout and Solver Entries for Goodman Shipping—Alternate Model

File: Figure 3.9.xlsx, Sheet: Figure 3.10

EXCEL EXTRA

Data Validation

Especially when you are creating spreadsheets for other people to use, it can pay off significantly to make the spreadsheets as mistake-proof as possible. One helpful technique is to set *data validation* limits on certain cells. With data validation, only legitimate values can be used as inputs for a cell or range of cells. For example, in Figure 3.9, you might want to ensure that only values between $2 and $5 can be inserted to represent the respective "load values."

To create a data validation criterion, highlight the cell or cells involved and select:

Data|Data Validation

Under Settings|Allow:, you can restrict the entry to be a Whole number, a Decimal, a selection from a List, a Date, a Time, or even subject to a Custom formula. If you select Text length, you can specify the number of characters within a text entry. For numbers, dates, times, and text lengths, you can choose parameters for the data to be between, not between, equal to, not equal to, greater than, less than, greater than or equal to, or less than or equal to.

There are also tabs at the top of the Data Validation dialog box (shown below) to create either an Input Message or an Error Alert (or both). The input message appears whenever the cell is selected and provides instructions regarding which types of entries are valid. The input message is informational only and will not prevent invalid entries. On the other hand, three Styles of error alerts are available, and each requires a response from the user:

(1) Stop will not allow the entry and forces the user to either Retry or Cancel.

(2) Warning, shown in the lower screen below, allows the entry for Yes, puts the cell in edit mode for No, or deletes the entry for Cancel.

(3) Information allows the entry for OK or deletes the entry for Cancel.

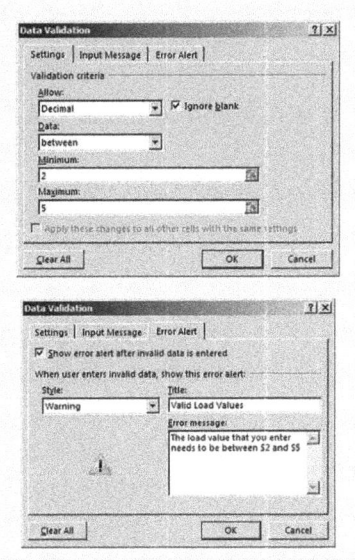

Expanded Vehicle Loading Problem—Allocation Problem

In the previous example, Goodman had only a single truck and needed to load all items on the same truck. Let's now assume that Goodman has the option of replacing his single truck (with a weight capacity of 15,000 pounds and a volume capacity of 1,300 cubic feet) with two smaller trucks (each with a weight capacity of 10,000 pounds and a volume capacity of 900 cubic feet). Item availabilities and other data are still as shown in Table 3.7. If he uses two trucks, Goodman wants to ensure that they are loaded in an equitable manner. That is, the same total weight should be loaded on both trucks. Total volumes loaded in the two trucks can, however, be different. If the fixed cost of operating the two smaller trucks is $5,000 more than the current cost of operating just a single truck, should Goodman go with the two trucks?

In this revised model, Goodman has to decide how to allocate the six items between the two trucks. Note that it is possible for the total quantity of an item to be split between the two trucks. That is, we can load a portion of an item in the first truck and load part or all the remaining portion in the other truck. Because the decision involves an allocation (of items to trucks, in Goodman's case), this type of problem is called an *allocation* problem.

Formulating the Problem The decision variables here need to specify how much of each item should be loaded on each truck. Let the double-subscripted variable W_{i1} be the weight (in pounds) of each item i loaded on the first truck and W_{i2} be the weight (in pounds) of each item i loaded on the second truck. The LP model for this expanded vehicle loading problem can then be formulated as follows:

$$\text{Maximize load value} = \$3.10(W_{11} + W_{12}) + \$3.20(W_{21} + W_{22}) + \$3.45(W_{31} + W_{32})$$
$$+ \$4.15(W_{41} + W_{42}) + \$3.25(W_{51} + W_{52}) + \$2.75(W_{61} + W_{62})$$

subject to the constraints

$$W_{11} + W_{21} + W_{31} + W_{41} + W_{51} + W_{61} \leq 10{,}000 \quad \text{(weight limit of truck 1)}$$

$$0.125\,W_{11} + 0.064\,W_{21} + 0.144\,W_{31} +$$
$$0.448\,W_{41} + 0.048\,W_{51} + 0.018\,W_{61} \leq 900 \quad \text{(volume limit of truck 1)}$$

$$W_{12} + W_{22} + W_{32} + W_{42} + W_{52} + W_{62} \leq 10{,}000 \quad \text{(weight limit of truck 2)}$$

$$0.125\,W_{12} + 0.064\,W_{22} + 0.144\,W_{32} +$$
$$0.448\,W_{42} + 0.048\,W_{52} + 0.018\,W_{62} \leq 900 \quad \text{(volume limit of truck 2)}$$

$$W_{11} + W_{12} \leq 5{,}000 \quad \text{(item 1 availability)}$$
$$W_{21} + W_{22} \leq 4{,}500 \quad \text{(item 2 availability)}$$
$$W_{31} + W_{32} \leq 3{,}000 \quad \text{(item 3 availability)}$$
$$W_{41} + W_{42} \leq 3{,}500 \quad \text{(item 4 availability)}$$
$$W_{51} + W_{52} \leq 4{,}000 \quad \text{(item 5 availability)}$$
$$W_{61} + W_{62} \leq 3{,}500 \quad \text{(item 6 availability)}$$
$$W_{11} + W_{21} + W_{31} + W_{41} + W_{51} + W_{61} = W_{12} + W_{22} + W_{32} + W_{42} + W_{52} + W_{62}$$
$$\text{(same weight in both trucks)}$$

All variables ≥ 0 (nonnegativity)

Solving the Problem Figure 3.11 shows the Excel layout and Solver entries for Goodman Shipping's allocation LP model. For the constraint that ensures the same total weight is loaded on both trucks, the Excel layout includes formulas for both the LHS (cell N18) and RHS (cell P18) entries. While the formula in cell N18 uses the usual SUMPRODUCT function, the formula in cell P18 is

$$\text{Cell P18:} \quad =\text{SUM(H5:M5)}$$

Figure 3.11: Excel Layout and Solver Entries for Goodman Shipping—Allocation

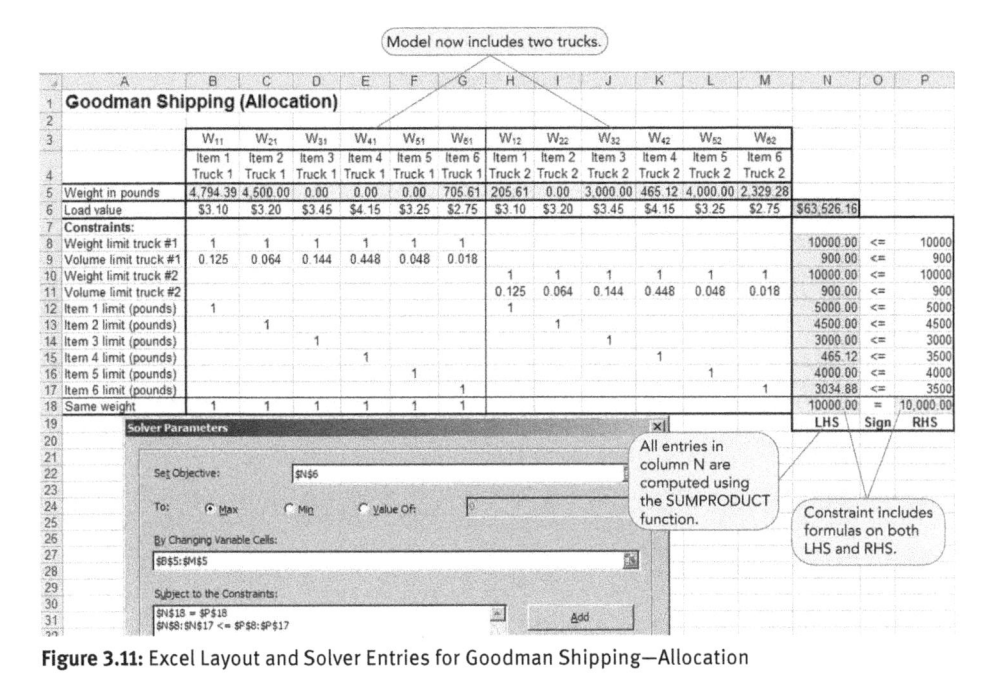

File: Figure 3.11.xlsx

Interpreting the Results Figure 3.11 indicates that the optimal solution to Goodman Shipping's allocation problem yields a total value of $63,526.16. This is an increase of $15,088.08 over the load value of $48,438.08 realizable with just the single truck. Because this more than compensates for the increased $5,000 operating cost, Goodman should replace his single truck with the two smaller ones. Both trucks are fully loaded from both weight and volume perspectives. All available quantities of items 1, 2, 3, and 5 are loaded. Most of item 6 is loaded (3,034.88 of 3,500 pounds available), while only about 13.29% (465.12 of 3,500 pounds available) of item 4 is loaded.

Transportation Problem

A transportation, or shipping, problem involves determining the amount of goods or number of items to be transported from a number of origins (or supply locations) to a number of destinations (or demand locations). The objective usually is to minimize total shipping costs or distances. Constraints in this type of problem deal with capacities or supplies at each origin and requirements or demands at each destination.

Like the assignment problem, the transportation problem is also an example of a network flow problem. We will study this type of problem in greater detail in Chapter 5.

Decision Modeling In Action

Optimizing Chevron's Refineries

Chevron's upstream operations focus on the exploration and production of crude oil and natural gas, while their downstream operation refines and markets transportation fuels, chemicals, and lubricants. Over the past 30 years, Chevron has continually improved its systems and business processes using different operations research tools and techniques. Recently, Chevron has developed a software modeling tool called "Petro" to improve its downstream operations. The tool is based on linear programming with distributive recursion mathematics and is used to support operations and strategic planning in seven refineries owned by Chevron.

Petro and other operations research tools are used to select the most profitable raw materials, optimize crude oil selection, evaluate product options, optimize refinery processes, and promote efficient capital investments. In addition, the tools are used to optimize the way the refining processing units are run, as crude oil prices, raw material availability, product prices, product specifications, and equipment capabilities change.

The implementation and continuous improvement done using Petro and other operations research tools yield around $1 billion annually to Chevron, with around $600 million coming from improvements in the downstream business and the remaining generated from improved capital efficiency.

Source: Based on T. Kutz, M. Davis, R. Creek, N. Kenaston, C. Stenstrom, M. Connor. "Optimizing Chevron's Refineries," *Interfaces* 44, 1 (January – February 2014): 39–54.

3.7 Blending Applications

Diet Problem

The diet problem, one of the earliest applications of LP, was originally used by hospitals to determine the most economical diet for patients. Known in agricultural applications as the feed-mix problem, the diet problem involves specifying a food or feed ingredient combination that satisfies stated nutritional requirements at a minimum cost level. An example follows.

The Whole Food Nutrition Center uses three different types of bulk grains to blend a natural breakfast cereal that it sells by the pound. The store advertises that each 2-ounce serving of the cereal, when taken with $1/2$ cup of whole milk, meets an average adult's minimum daily requirement for protein, riboflavin, phosphorus, and magnesium. The cost of each bulk grain and the protein, riboflavin, phosphorus, and magnesium units per pound of each are shown in Table 3.8.

Table 3.8: Requirements for Whole Food Nutrition Center's Natural Cereal

Grain	Cost per Pound (cents)	Protein (units/lb)	Riboflavin (units/lb)	Phosphorus (units/lb)	Magnesium (units/lb)
A	33	22	16	8	5
B	47	28	14	7	0
C	38	21	25	9	6

The minimum adult daily requirement (called the U.S. Recommended Daily Allowance, or USRDA) for protein is 3 units, for riboflavin is 2 units, for phosphorus is 1 unit, and for magnesium is 0.425 units. Whole Food Nutrition Center wants to select the blend of grains that will meet the USRDA at a minimum cost.

Formulating and Solving the Problem The decision variables in blending applications typically define the amount of each ingredient that should be used to make the product(s). It is interesting to contrast this with product mix problems, where the decision variables define the number of units to make of each product. That is, blending problems typically make decisions regarding amounts of each *input* (resource) to use, while product mix problems make decisions regarding numbers of each *output* to make.

In Whole Food Nutrition's case, the ingredients (inputs) are the three different types of bulk grains. We let

A = pounds of grain A to use in one 2-ounce serving of cereal
B = pounds of grain B to use in one 2-ounce serving of cereal
C = pounds of grain C to use in one 2-ounce serving of cereal

This is the objective function:

Minimize total cost of mixing a 2-ounce serving of cereal = $\$0.33A + \$0.47B + \$0.38C$

subject to the constraints

$$22A + 28B + 21C \geq 3 \quad \text{(protein units)}$$
$$16A + 14B + 25C \geq 2 \quad \text{(riboflavin units)}$$
$$8A + 7B + 9C \geq 1 \quad \text{(phosphorus units)}$$
$$5A + 6C \geq 0.425 \quad \text{(magnesium units)}$$
$$A + B + C = 0.125 \quad \text{(total mix is 2 ounces, or 0.125 pound)}$$
$$A, B, C \geq 0$$

Figure 3.12 shows the Excel layout and Solver entries for this LP model.

Whole Food Nutrition Center

	A	B	C
	Grain A	Grain B	Grain C
Number of pounds	0.025	0.050	0.050
Cost	$0.33	$0.47	$0.38

Solution values are in pounds. Cost total: $0.05

Constraints:

	Grain A	Grain B	Grain C	LHS	Sign	RHS
Protein	22	28	21	3.00	>=	3
Riboflavin	16	14	25	2.35	>=	2
Phosphorus	8	7	9	1.00	>=	1
Magnesium	5	5	6	0.425	>=	0.425
Total Mix	1	1	1	0.125	=	0.125

This constraint uses the = sign.

Solver Parameters

Set Objective: $E$6

To: ○ Max ● Min ○ Value Of: 0

By Changing Variable Cells:
$B$5:$D$5

Subject to the Constraints:
$E$12 = $G$12
$E$8:$E$11 >= $G$8:$G$11

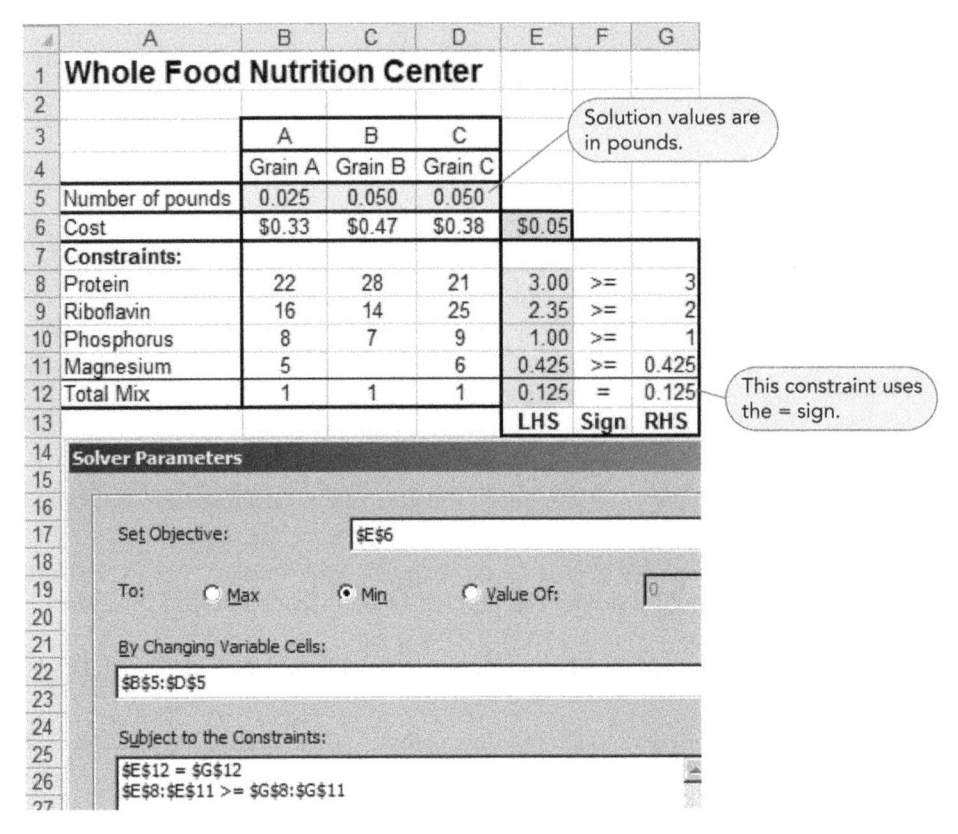

Figure 3.12: Excel Layout and Solver Entries for Whole Food Nutrition Center

📄 File: Figure 3.12.xlsx

Interpreting the Results The solution to Whole Food Nutrition Center's problem requires mixing together 0.025 pounds of grain A, 0.050 pounds of grain B, and 0.050 pounds of grain C. Another way of stating this solution is in terms of a 2-ounce serving of each grain: 0.4 ounces of grain A, 0.8 ounces of grain B, and 0.8 ounces of grain C in each 2-ounce serving of cereal. The cost per serving is $0.05.

Blending Problem

In the preceding diet problem, the ingredients (grains) had to be mixed to create just a single product (cereal). Diet and feed-mix problems are actually special cases of a more general class of LP problems known as *blending problems*. Blending problems are very common in chemical industries, and they arise when a decision must be made regarding the blending of two or more ingredients (or resources) to produce two or more products (or end items). The ingredients must be blended in such a manner that each final product satisfies specific requirements regarding its composition. In addition, ingredients may have limitations regarding their availabilities, and products may have conditions regarding their demand. The following example deals with an application frequently seen in the petroleum industry: the blending of crude oils to produce different grades of gasoline.

The Low Knock Oil Company produces three grades of gasoline for industrial distribution. The three grades—premium, regular, and economy—are produced by refining a blend of three types of crude oil: type $X100$, type $X200$, and type $X300$. Each crude oil differs not only in cost per barrel, but in its composition as well. Table 3.9 indicates the percentage of three crucial compounds found in each of the crude oils, the cost per barrel for each, and the maximum weekly availability of each.

Table 3.9: Ingredient Data for Low Knock Oil

Crude Oil Type	Compound A (%)	Compound B (%)	Compound C (%)	Cost/Barrel ($)	Avail. (barrels)
X100	35	25	35	86	15,000
X200	50	30	15	92	32,000
X300	60	20	15	95	24,000

Table 3.10 indicates the weekly demand for each grade of gasoline and the specific conditions on the amounts of the different compounds that each grade of gasoline should contain. The table shows, for example, that in order for gasoline to be classified as premium grade, it must contain at least 55% of compound A. Low Knock's management must decide how many barrels of each type of crude oil to buy each week for blending to satisfy demand at minimum cost.

Table 3.10: Gasoline Data for Low Knock Oil

Gasoline Type	Compound A	Compound B	Compound C	Demand (barrels)
Premium	≥ 55%	≤ 23%		14,000
Regular		≥ 25%	≤ 35%	22,000
Economy	≥ 40%		≤ 25%	25,000

Formulating the Problem As noted in the diet problem, the decision variables in blending applications typically denote the amount of each ingredient that should be used to make the product(s). In Low Knock's case, the ingredients are the crude oils, and the products are the grades of gasoline. Because there are three ingredients that are blended to create three products, we need a total of $9 (= 3 \times 3)$ decision variables. We let

P_1 = barrels of $X100$ crude blended to produce the premium grade
P_2 = barrels of $X200$ crude blended to produce the premium grade
P_3 = barrels of $X300$ crude blended to produce the premium grade
R_1 = barrels of $X100$ crude blended to produce the regular grade
R_2 = barrels of $X200$ crude blended to produce the regular grade
R_3 = barrels of $X300$ crude blended to produce the regular grade
E_1 = barrels of $X100$ crude blended to produce the economy grade
E_2 = barrels of $X200$ crude blended to produce the economy grade
E_3 = barrels of $X300$ crude blended to produce the economy grade

We can calculate the total amount produced of each gasoline grade by adding the amounts of the three crude oils used to create that grade. For example,

$$\text{Total amount of premium grade gasoline produced} = P_1 + P_2 + P_3$$

Likewise, we can calculate the total amount used of each crude oil type by adding the amounts of that crude oil used to create the three gasoline grades. For example,

$$\text{Total amount of crude oil type } X100 \text{ used} = P_1 + R_1 + E_1$$

The objective is to minimize the total cost of the crude oils used and can be written as

$$\text{Minimize total cost} = \$86(P_1 + R_1 + E_1) + \$92(P_2 + R_2 + E_2) + \$95(P_3 + R_3 + E_3)$$

subject to the constraints

$$\begin{aligned}
P_1 + R_1 + E_1 &\leq 15{,}000 \quad &&\text{(availability of } X100 \text{ crude oil)} \\
P_2 + R_2 + E_2 &\leq 32{,}000 \quad &&\text{(availability of } X200 \text{ crude oil)} \\
P_3 + R_3 + E_3 &\leq 24{,}000 \quad &&\text{(availability of } X300 \text{ crude oil)} \\
P_1 + P_2 + P_3 &\geq 14{,}000 \quad &&\text{(demand for premium gasoline)} \\
R_1 + R_2 + R_3 &\geq 22{,}000 \quad &&\text{(demand for regular gasoline)} \\
E_1 + E_2 + E_3 &\geq 25{,}000 \quad &&\text{(demand for economy gasoline)}
\end{aligned}$$

Observe that we have written the demand constraints as $\geq$ conditions in this problem. The reason is that the objective function in this problem is to minimize the total cost. If we write the demand constraints also as $\leq$ conditions, the optimal solution could result in a trivial "don't make anything, don't spend anything" situation.[1] As we have seen in several examples before now, if the objective function is a minimization

---

[1] This, of course, assumes that the total availability of the three crude oils is sufficient to satisfy the total demand for the three gasoline grades. If total availability is less than total demand, we need to write the demand constraints as $\leq$ expressions and the availability constraints as = expressions.

function, there must be at least one constraint in the problem that forces the optimal solution away from the origin (i.e., zero values for all decision variables).

Next, we come to the blending constraints that specify the amounts of the different compounds that each grade of gasoline can contain. First, we know that at least 55% of each barrel of premium gasoline must be compound A. To write this constraint, we note that:

$$\text{Amount of compound A in premium grade gasoline} = 0.35P_1 + 0.50P_2 + 0.60P_3$$

If we divide this amount by the total amount of premium grade gasoline produced ($= P_1 + P_2 + P_3$), we get the total portion of compound A in this grade of gasoline. Therefore, the constraint may be written as:

$$(0.35P_1 + 0.50P_2 + 0.60P_3)/(P_1 + P_2 + P_3) \geq 0.55 \quad \text{(compound A in premium grade)}$$

The other compound specifications may be written in a similar fashion, as follows:

$$(0.25P_1 + 0.30P_2 + 0.20P_3)/(P_1 + P_2 + P_3) \leq 0.23 \quad \text{(compound B in premium grade)}$$
$$(0.25R_1 + 0.30R_2 + 0.20R_3)/(R_1 + R_2 + R_3) \geq 0.25 \quad \text{(compound B in regular grade)}$$
$$(0.35R_1 + 0.15R_2 + 0.15R_3)/(R_1 + R_2 + R_3) \leq 0.35 \quad \text{(compound C in regular grade)}$$
$$(0.35E_1 + 0.50E_2 + 0.60E_3)/(E_1 + E_2 + E_3) \geq 0.40 \quad \text{(compound A in economy grade)}$$
$$(0.35E_1 + 0.15E_2 + 0.15E_3)/(E_1 + E_2 + E_3) \leq 0.25 \quad \text{(compound C in economy grade)}$$

Finally, we have the nonnegativity constraints:

$$P_1, P_2, P_3, R_1, R_2, R_3, E_1, E_2, E_3 \geq 0 \quad \text{(nonnegativity)}$$

Solving the Problem Figure 3.13 shows the Excel layout and Solver entries for this LP model. As in the portfolio selection problem, to avoid potential error messages from Solver (see the **EXCEL NOTES**), we have algebraically modified all the compound specification constraints in our Excel implementation of this model. For example, the constraint specifying the portion of compound A in premium grade gasoline is modified as

$$0.35P_1 + 0.50P_2 + 0.60P_3 \geq 0.55(P_1 + P_2 + P_3)$$

The six compound specification constraints, therefore, have Excel formulas in both the LHS cells (K11:K13, K17:K19) and RHS cells (M11:M13, M17:M19). The LHS cells use the usual SUMPRODUCT function.

140 — Chapter 3: Linear Programming Modeling Applications with Computer Analyses in Excel

	A	B	C	D	E	F	G	H	I	J	K	L	M
1	Low Knock Oil Company										Optimal blending values		
2													
3		P_1	P_2	P_3	R_1	R_2	R_3	E_1	E_2	E_3			
4		X100 in premium	X200 in premium	X300 in premium	X100 in regular	X200 in regular	X300 in regular	X100 in economy	X200 in economy	X300 in economy	=0.55*SUM(B5:D5)		
5	Number of barrels	2,500.00	0.00	11,500.00	0.00	22,000.00	0.00	12,500.00	10,000.00	2,500.00			
6	Cost	$86.00	$92.00	$95.00	$86.00	$92.00	$95.00	$86.00	$92.00	$95.00	$5,564,000.00		
7	Constraints:												
8	Premium demand	1	1	1							14000.00	>=	14000
9	Regular demand				1	1	1				22000.00	>=	22000
10	Economy demand							1	1	1	25000.00	>=	25000
11	A in premium	0.35	0.50	0.60							7775.00	>=	7700
12	B in regular				0.25	0.30	0.20				6600.00	>=	5500
13	A in economy							0.35	0.50	0.60	10875.00	>=	10000
14	X100 available	1			1			1			15000.00	<=	15000
15	X200 available		1			1			1		32000.00	<=	32000
16	X300 available			1			1			1	14000.00	<=	24000
17	B in premium	0.25	0.30	0.20							2925.00	<=	3220
18	C in regular				0.35	0.15	0.15				3300.00	<=	7700
19	C in economy							0.35	0.15	0.15	6250.00	<=	6250
20											LHS	Sign	RHS

Solver Parameters

Set Objective: $K$6

To: ○ Max ● Min ○ Value Of: 0

By Changing Variable Cells:
$B$5:$J$5

Subject to the Constraints:
$K$14:$K$19 <= $M$14:$M$19
$K$8:$K$13 >= $M$8:$M$13

Constraints in rows 11 to 13 and 17 to 19 include formulas on RHS also.

Constraints in rows 11 to 13 and 17 to 19 have been algebraically modified to avoid potential error message in Solver.

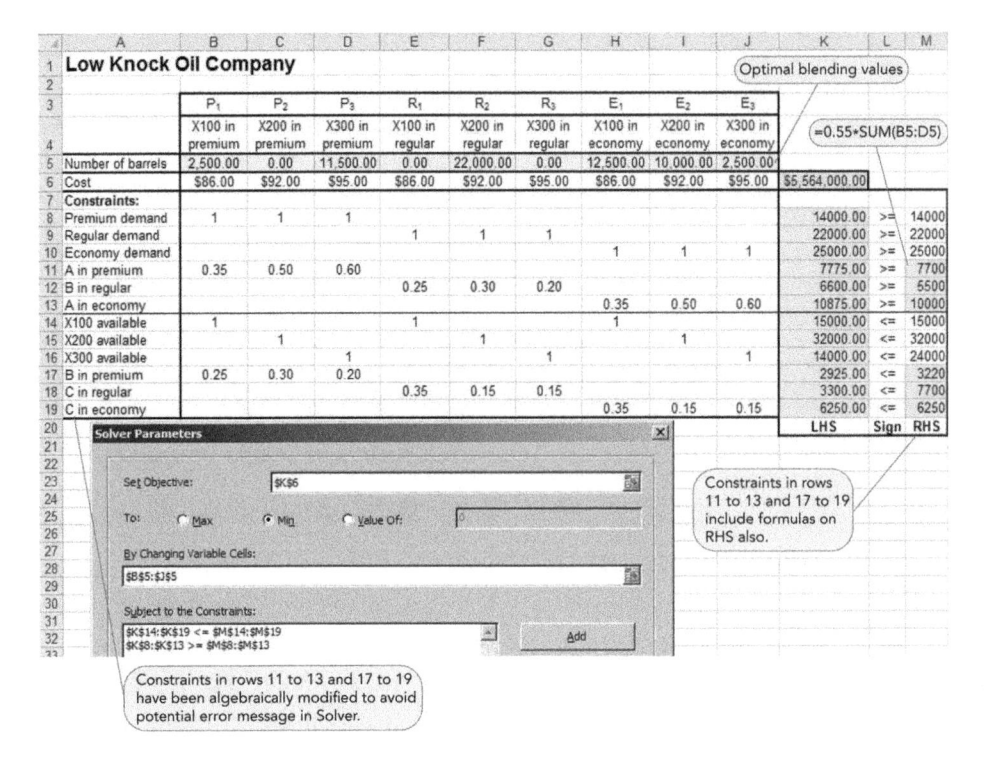

Figure 3.13: Excel Layout and Solver Entries for Low Knock Oil

File: Figure 3.13.xlsx

Interpreting the Results Figure 3.13 indicates that the blending strategy will cost Low Knock Oil $5,564,000 and require it to mix the three types of crude oil as follows:

$P_1 = 2,500$ barrels of $X100$ crude oil to make premium grade gasoline
$P_3 = 11,500$ barrels of $X300$ crude oil to make premium grade gasoline
$R_2 = 22,000$ barrels of $X200$ crude oil to make regular grade gasoline
$E_1 = 12,500$ barrels of $X100$ crude oil to make economy grade gasoline
$E_2 = 10,000$ barrels of $X200$ crude oil to make economy grade gasoline
$E_3 = 2,500$ barrels of $X300$ crude oil to make economy grade gasoline

The entire demand for the three gasoline grades is met. Low Knock should buy all available barrels of crude oil types $X100$ and $X200$ and only 14,000 barrels of the 24,000 barrels available of type $X300$. (Note: This model has multiple optimal solutions.)

3.8 Multiperiod Applications

Perhaps the most challenging application of LP is in modeling multiperiod scenarios. These are situations in which the decision maker must determine the optimal decisions for several periods (e.g., weeks, months). What makes these problems especially difficult is that the decision choices in later periods are directly dependent on the decisions made in earlier periods. We discuss two examples in the following sections to illustrate this feature. The first example deals with a multiperiod production scheduling problem. The second example involves the establishment of a multiperiod financial sinking fund.

Production Scheduling Problem

Setting a low-cost production schedule over a period of weeks or months is a difficult and important management problem in most plants. Because most companies produce more than one product, the scheduling process is often quite complex. The production manager has to consider several factors, such as labor capacity, inventory and storage costs, space limitations, product demand, and labor relations. These factors often conflict with each other. For example, it is desirable to produce the same number of each product each period in order to simplify planning and scheduling of workers and machines. However, the need to keep inventory carrying costs down suggests producing in each period only what is needed that period. As we shall see in the following problem, LP is an effective tool for resolving such conflicts and identifying a production schedule that will minimize the total cost of production and inventory holding. Production scheduling is especially amenable to solution by LP because it is a problem that must be solved on a regular basis. When the objective function and constraints for a firm are established, the inputs easily can be changed each period to provide an updated schedule.

Basically, a multiperiod problem resembles the product mix model for each period in the planning horizon, with the additional issue of inventory from one period to the next to be considered. The objective is to either maximize profit or to minimize the total cost (production plus inventory) of carrying out the task. As noted earlier, production decision choices in later periods are directly affected by decisions made in earlier periods. An example follows.

Greenberg Motors, Inc., manufactures two different electrical motors for sale under contract to Drexel Corp., a well-known producer of small kitchen appliances. Its model GM3A is found in many Drexel food processors, and its model GM3B is used in the assembly of blenders.

Three times each year, the procurement officer at Drexel contracts Irwin Greenberg, the founder of Greenberg Motors, to place a monthly order for each of the coming four months. Drexel's demand for motors varies each month, based on its own sales forecasts, production capacity, and financial position. Greenberg has just received the January–April order and must begin his own four-month production plan. The demand for motors is shown in Table 3.11.

Table 3.11: Four-Month Order Schedule for Greenberg Motors

Model	January	February	March	April
GM3A	800	700	1,000	1,100
GM3B	1,000	1,200	1,400	1,400

The following additional data are available regarding Greenberg's problem:
1. Production costs are currently $10 per GM3A motor produced and $6 per GM3B unit. However, a planned wage increase going into effect on March 1 will raise each figure by 10%.
2. Each GM3A motor held in stock costs $0.18 per month, and each GM3B has a holding cost of $0.13 per month. Greenberg's accountants allow monthly ending inventories as an acceptable approximation to the average inventory levels during the month.
3. Greenberg is starting the new four-month production cycle with a change in design specifications that has left no old motors of either type in stock on January 1.
4. Greenberg wants to have ending inventories of 450 GM3As and 300 GM3Bs at the end of April.
5. The storage area can hold a maximum of 3,300 motors of either type (they are similar in size) at any one time. Additional storage space is very expensive and is therefore not available as an option.
6. Greenberg has a no-layoff policy, which has been effective in preventing unionization of the shop. The company has a base employment level of 2,240 labor hours per month, and, by contract, this level of labor must be used each month. In busy periods, however, the company has the option of bringing on board two skilled former employees who are now retired. Each of these employees can provide up to 160 labor hours per month.
7. Each GM3A motor produced requires 1.3 hours of labor, and each GM3B takes a worker 0.9 hours to assemble.

Formulating the Problem Just as in the product mix problem, the primary decision variables here define the number of units of each product (motors) to make. However, because production of motors occurs in four separate months, we need to define decision variables to determine the production of each motor in each month. Using double-subscripted variables is a convenient way of defining the decision variables in this LP model. We let

P_{At} = number of model GM3A motors produced in month t ($t = 1, 2, 3, 4$ for January–April)
P_{Bt} = number of model GM3B motors produced in month t

Using these variables, the total production cost may be written as follows (recall that unit costs go up 10% in March):

$$\text{Cost of production} = \$10P_{A1} + \$10P_{A2} + \$11P_{A3} + \$11P_{A4} + \$6P_{B1}$$
$$+ \$6P_{B2} + \$6.60P_{B3} + \$6.60P_{B4}$$

To keep track of the inventory carried over from one month to the next, we introduce a second set of decision variables. Let

I_{At} = level of on-hand inventory for GM3A motors at end of month t ($t = 1, 2, 3, 4$)
I_{Bt} = level of on-hand inventory for GM3B motors at end of month t ($t = 1, 2, 3, 4$)

Using these variables, the total inventory carrying costs may be written as:

$$\text{Cost of carrying inventory} = \$0.18I_{A1} + 0.18I_{A2} + 0.18I_{A3} + 0.18I_{A4}$$
$$+ 0.13I_{B1} + 0.13I_{B2} + 0.13I_{B3} + 0.13I_{B4}$$

The objective function is then:

Minimize total costs = cost of production + cost of carrying inventory

$$= 10P_{A1} + 10P_{A2} + 11P_{A3} + 11P_{A4} + 6P_{B1} + 6P_{B2} + 6.60P_{B3}$$
$$+ 6.60P_{B4} + 0.18I_{A1} + 0.18I_{A2} + 0.18I_{A3} + 0.18I_{A4} + 0.13I_{B1}$$
$$+ 0.13I_{B2} + 0.13I_{B3} + 0.13I_{B4}$$

In all multiperiod problems, we need to write a *balance equation*, or *constraint*, for each product for each period. Each balance equation specifies the relationship between the previous period's ending inventory, the current period's production, the current period's sales, and the current period's ending inventory. Specifically, the balance equation states that the inventory at the end of the current period is given by

$$\begin{pmatrix} \text{inventory} \\ \text{at end} \\ \text{of previous} \\ \text{period} \end{pmatrix} + \begin{pmatrix} \text{current} \\ \text{period's} \\ \text{production} \end{pmatrix} - \begin{pmatrix} \text{current} \\ \text{period's} \\ \text{sales} \end{pmatrix} = \begin{pmatrix} \text{inventory} \\ \text{at end} \\ \text{of current} \\ \text{period} \end{pmatrix}$$

In Greenberg's case, we are starting with no old motors in stock on January 1. Recalling that January's demand for GM3As is 800 and for GM3Bs is 1,000, we can write the balance constraints for January as

$$0 + P_{A1} - 800 = I_{A1} \quad \text{(GM3A motors in January)}$$
$$0 + P_{B1} - 1{,}000 = I_{B1} \quad \text{(GM3B motors in January)}$$

In a similar fashion, the balance constraints for February, March, and April may be written as follows:

$$I_{A1} + P_{A2} - 700 = I_{A2} \quad \text{(GM3A motors in February)}$$
$$I_{B1} + P_{B2} - 1{,}200 = I_{B2} \quad \text{(GM3B motors in February)}$$
$$I_{A2} + P_{A3} - 1{,}000 = I_{A3} \quad \text{(GM3A motors in March)}$$
$$I_{B2} + P_{B3} - 1{,}400 = I_{B3} \quad \text{(GM3B motors in March)}$$
$$I_{A3} + P_{A4} - 1{,}100 = I_{A4} \quad \text{(GM3A motors in April)}$$
$$I_{B3} + P_{B4} - 1{,}400 = I_{B4} \quad \text{(GM3B motors in April)}$$

If Greenberg wants to have ending inventories of 450 GM3As and 300 GM3Bs at the end of April, we add the constraints

$$I_{A4} = 450$$
$$I_{B4} = 300$$

Although the balance constraints address demand, they do not consider storage space or labor requirements. First, we note that the storage area for Greenberg Motors can hold a maximum of 3,300 motors of either type. Therefore, we write

$$I_{A1} + I_{B1} \leq 3{,}300$$
$$I_{A2} + I_{B2} \leq 3{,}300$$
$$I_{A3} + I_{B3} \leq 3{,}300$$
$$I_{A4} + I_{B4} \leq 3{,}300$$

Second, we note that Greenberg must use at least 2,240 labor hours per month and could potentially have up to 2,560 labor hours ($=2{,}240+160\times 2$) per month. Because each GM3A motor produced requires 1.3 hours of labor and each GM3B takes a worker 0.9 hours to assemble, we write the labor constraints as:

$$1.3P_{A1} + 0.9P_{B1} \geq 2{,}240 \quad \text{(January labor minimum)}$$
$$1.3P_{A1} + 0.9P_{B1} \leq 2{,}560 \quad \text{(January labor maximum)}$$
$$1.3P_{A2} + 0.9P_{B2} \geq 2{,}240 \quad \text{(February labor minimum)}$$
$$1.3P_{A2} + 0.9P_{B2} \leq 2{,}560 \quad \text{(February labor maximum)}$$
$$1.3P_{A3} + 0.9P_{B3} \geq 2{,}240 \quad \text{(March labor minimum)}$$
$$1.3P_{A3} + 0.9P_{B3} \leq 2{,}560 \quad \text{(March labor maximum)}$$
$$1.3P_{A4} + 0.9P_{B4} \geq 2{,}240 \quad \text{(April labor minimum)}$$
$$1.3P_{A4} + 0.9P_{B4} \leq 2{,}560 \quad \text{(April labor maximum)}$$

Finally, we have the nonnegativity constraints:

$$\text{All variables} \geq 0$$

Multiperiod Applications — 145

Solving the Problem There are several ways of setting up the Greenberg Motors problem in Excel. The setup shown in Figure 3.14 follows the usual logic we have used in all problems so far; that is, all parameters associated with a specific decision variable are modeled in the same column.

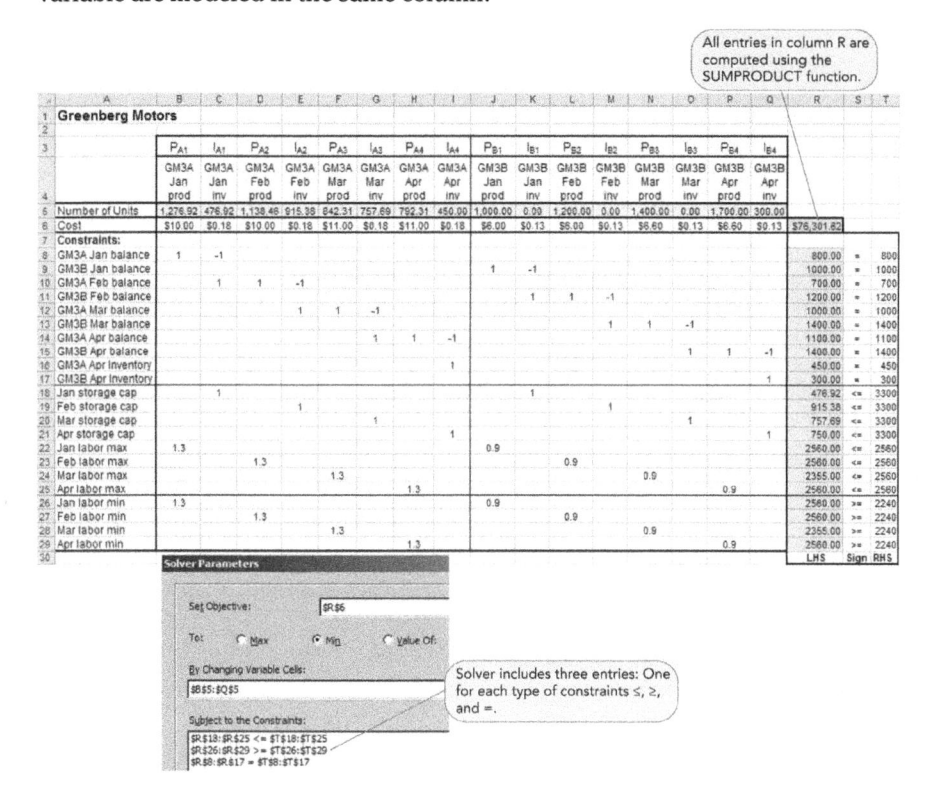

Figure 3.14: Excel Layout and Solver Entries for Greenberg Motors

File: Figure 3.14.xlsx, Sheet: Figure 3.14

In setting up the balance constraints in Figure 3.14, we have algebraically modified each equation by moving all variables to the LHS of the equation and the constants to the RHS. This is a convenient way of implementing these constraints. For example, the balance constraint for GM3A motors in February, which currently reads:

$$I_{A1} + P_{A2} - 700 = I_{A2}$$

is modified as:

$$I_{A1} + P_{A2} - I_{A2} = 700$$

Interpreting the Results The solution to Greenberg's problem, summarized in Table 3.12, indicates that the four-month total cost is $76,301.62. The solution requires Greenberg to use the two former employees to their maximum extent (160 hours each; 320 hours total) in three of the four months and for 115 hours in March (labor usage in March is 2,355 hours as compared to the base employment level of 2,240 hours). This suggests that perhaps Greenberg should consider increasing the base employment level. Storage space is not an issue (at least during the four months in consideration here), with less than one-third of the available space being used each month. The solution does include several fractional values, which may need to be rounded off appropriately before implementation. Alternatively, in such problem scenarios, it may be possible to view fractional production values as work-in-process (WIP) inventories.

Table 3.12: Solution to the Greenberg Motors Problem

Production Schedule	January	February	March	April
Units of GM3A produced	1,276.92	1,138.46	842.31	792.31
Units of GM3B produced	1,000.00	1,200.00	1,400.00	1,700.00
Inventory of GM3A carried	476.92	915.38	757.69	450.00
Inventory of GM3B carried	0.00	0.00	0.00	300.00
Labor hours required	2,560.00	2,560.00	2,355.00	2,560.00

For many multiperiod problems, it may often be convenient to group all the variables for a given month in the same column. Figure 3.15 shows the Excel layout of an alternate model for the Greenberg Motors problem.

Note that in this alternate model, the only decision variables are the production variables (P_{A1} to P_{A4}, P_{B1} to P_{B4}). The inventory variables are no longer explicitly stated as decision variables, and they are not specified as changing variable cells in Solver. Rather, they are calculated as simple byproducts of the other parameters in the problem. Using the standard inventory constraints, the ending inventory each month is calculated as follows:

$$\begin{pmatrix} \text{inventory} \\ \text{at the} \\ \text{end of} \\ \text{last month} \end{pmatrix} + \begin{pmatrix} \text{current} \\ \text{month's} \\ \text{production} \end{pmatrix} - \begin{pmatrix} \text{current} \\ \text{month's} \\ \text{sales} \end{pmatrix} = \begin{pmatrix} \text{inventory} \\ \text{at the} \\ \text{end of} \\ \text{this month} \end{pmatrix}$$

$$\text{Row 5} \quad + \quad \text{Row 6} \quad - \quad \text{Row 7} \quad = \quad \text{Row 8}$$

Because they are no longer decision variables, however, we need to add constraints to ensure that the ending inventories for all products have nonnegative values in each month. Depending on individual preferences and expertise, we can design other layouts for setting up and solving this problem using Excel.

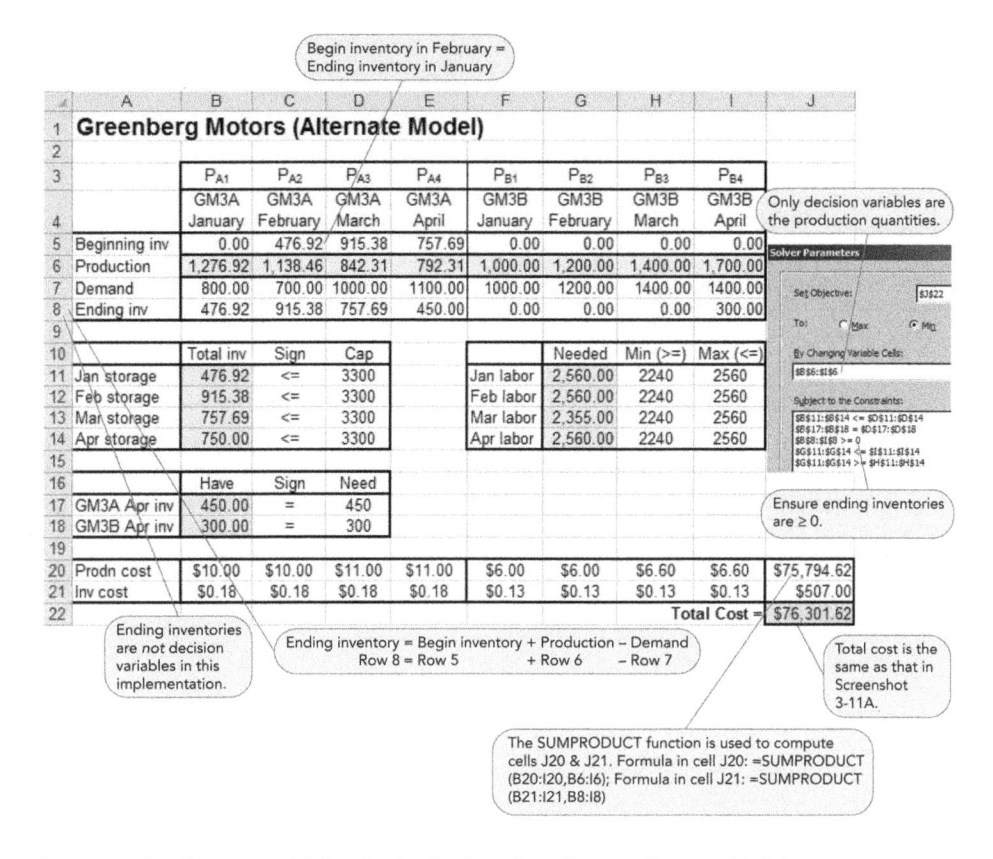

Figure 3.15: Excel Layout and Solver Entries for Greenberg Motors—Alternate Model

📊 File: Figure 3.14.xlsx, Sheet: Figure 3.15

The Greenberg Motors example illustrates a relatively simple production planning problem in that only two products were considered for a four-month planning horizon. The LP model discussed here can, however, be applied successfully to problems with dozens of products, hundreds of constraints, and longer planning horizons.

Sinking Fund Problem

Another excellent example of a multiperiod problem is the sinking fund problem. In this case, an investor or a firm seeks to establish an investment portfolio, using the least possible initial investment, that will generate specific amounts of capital at specific time periods in the future.

Consider the example of Larry Fredendall, who is trying to plan for his daughter Susan's college expenses. Based on current projections (it is now the start of year 1), Larry anticipates that his financial needs at the start of each of the following years is as shown in Table 3.13.

Table 3.13: Financial Needs for Larry Fredendall

Year	$ Needed
3	$20,000
4	$22,000
5	$24,000
6	$26,000

Larry has several investment choices to choose from at the present time, as listed in Table 3.14. Each choice has a fixed known return on investment and a specified maturity date. Assume that each choice is available for investment at the start of every year, and assume that returns are tax free if used for education. Because choices C and D are relatively risky choices, Larry wants no more than 20% of his total investment in those two choices at any point in time.

Table 3.14: Investment Choices for Larry Fredendall

Choice	ROI	Maturity
A	5%	1 year
B	13%	2 years
C	28%	3 years
D	40%	4 years

Larry wants to establish a sinking fund to meet his requirements. Note that at the start of year 1, the entire initial investment is available for investing in the choices. However, in subsequent years, only the amount maturing from a prior investment is available for investment.

Formulating the Problem Let's first define the decision variables. Note that in defining these variables, we need to consider only those investments that will mature by the end of year 5, at the latest, because there is no requirement after 6 years:

$A_1 = \$$ amount invested in choice A at the start of year 1
$B_1 = \$$ amount invested in choice B at the start of year 1
$C_1 = \$$ amount invested in choice C at the start of year 1
$D_1 = \$$ amount invested in choice D at the start of year 1
$A_2 = \$$ amount invested in choice A at the start of year 2
$B_2 = \$$ amount invested in choice B at the start of year 2
$C_2 = \$$ amount invested in choice C at the start of year 2
$D_2 = \$$ amount invested in choice D at the start of year 2
$A_3 = \$$ amount invested in choice A at the start of year 3
$B_3 = \$$ amount invested in choice B at the start of year 3
$C_3 = \$$ amount invested in choice C at the start of year 3
$A_4 = \$$ amount invested in choice A at the start of year 4
$B_4 = \$$ amount invested in choice B at the start of year 4
$A_5 = \$$ amount invested in choice A at the start of year 5

The objective is to minimize the initial investment and this can be expressed as:

$$\text{Minimize } A_1 + B_1 + C_1 + D_1$$

As in the multiperiod production scheduling problem, we need to write balance constraints for each period (year). These constraints recognize the relationship between the investment decisions made in any given year and the investment decisions made in all prior years. Specifically, we need to ensure that the amount used for investment at the start of a given year is restricted to the amount maturing at the end of the previous year, *less* any payments made for Susan's education that year. This relationship can be modeled as:

$$\begin{pmatrix} \text{amount} \\ \text{invested at} \\ \text{start of} \\ \text{year } t \end{pmatrix} + \begin{pmatrix} \text{amount} \\ \text{paid for} \\ \text{education at} \\ \text{start of year } t \end{pmatrix} = \begin{pmatrix} \text{amound} \\ \text{maturing} \\ \text{at end} \\ \text{of year } (t-1) \end{pmatrix}$$

At the start of year 2, the total amount maturing is $1.05A_1$ (investment in choice A in year 1 plus 5% interest). The constraint at the start of year 2 can therefore be written as:

$$A_2 + B_2 + C_2 + D_2 = 1.05A_1 \quad \text{(year 2 cash flow)}$$

Constraints at the start of years 3 through 6 are as follows and also include the amounts payable for Susan's education each year:

$$A_3 + B_3 + C_3 + 20{,}000 = 1.13B_1 + 1.05A_2 \quad \text{(year 3 cash flow)}$$
$$A_4 + B_4 + 22{,}000 = 1.28C_1 + 1.13B_2 + 1.05A_3 \quad \text{(year 4 cash flow)}$$
$$A_5 + 24{,}000 = 1.4D_1 + 1.28C_2 + 1.13B_3 + 1.05A_4 \quad \text{(year 5 cash flow)}$$
$$26{,}000 = 1.4D_2 + 1.28C_3 + 1.13B_4 + 1.05A_5 \quad \text{(year 6 cash flow)}$$

These five constraints address the cash flow issues. However, they do not account for Larry's risk preference with regard to investments in choices C and D in any given year. To satisfy these requirements, we need to ensure that total investment in choices C and D in any year is no more than 20% of the total investment in *all* choices that year. In keeping track of these investments, it is important to also account for investments in *prior* years that may have still not matured. At the start of year 1, this constraint can be written as

$$C_1 + D_1 \le 0.2(A_1 + B_1 + C_1 + D_1) \quad \text{(year 1 risk)}$$

In writing this constraint at the start of year 2, we must take into account the fact that investments B_1, C_1, and D_1 have still not matured. Therefore,

$$C_1 + D_1 + C_2 + D_2 \le 0.2(B_1 + C_1 + D_1 + A_2 + B_2 + C_2 + D_2) \quad \text{(year 2 risk)}$$

Constraints at the start of years 3 through 5 are as follows. Note that there is no constraint necessary at the start of year 6 because there are no investments that year:

$$C_1 + D_1 + C_2 + D_2 + C_3 \le 0.2(C_1 + D_1 + B_2 + C_2 + D_2 + A_3 + B_3 + C_3) \quad \text{(year 3 risk)}$$
$$D_1 + C_2 + D_2 + C_3 \le 0.2(D_1 + C_2 + D_2 + B_3 + C_3 + A_4 + B_4) \quad \text{(year 4 risk)}$$
$$D_2 + C_3 \le 0.2(D_2 + C_3 + B_4 + A_5) \quad \text{(year 5 risk)}$$

Finally, we have the nonnegativity constraints:

$$\text{All variables} \quad \ge 0$$

Solving the Problem and Interpreting the Results Figure 3.16 shows the Excel layout and Solver entries for this model. As with the production scheduling problem, there are several alternate ways in which the Excel layout could be structured, depending on the preference and expertise of the analyst. In our implementation of this model, we have algebraically modified the cash flow constraints for each year so that all variables are on the LHS and the education cash outflows are on the RHS. We have, however, implemented the risk constraints as written in the formulation above. The modified cash flow constraints are as follows:

$$1.05A_1 - A_2 - B_2 - C_2 - D_2 = 0 \quad \text{(year 2 cash flow)}$$
$$1.13B_1 + 1.05A_2 - A_3 - B_3 - C_3 = 20{,}000 \quad \text{(year 3 cash flow)}$$
$$1.28C_1 + 1.13B_2 + 1.05A_3 - A_4 - B_4 = 22{,}000 \quad \text{(year 4 cash flow)}$$
$$1.4D_1 + 1.28C_2 + 1.13B_3 + 1.05A_4 - A_5 = 24{,}000 \quad \text{(year 5 cash flow)}$$
$$1.4D_2 + 1.28C_3 + 1.13B_4 + 1.05A_5 = 26{,}000 \quad \text{(year 6 cash flow)}$$

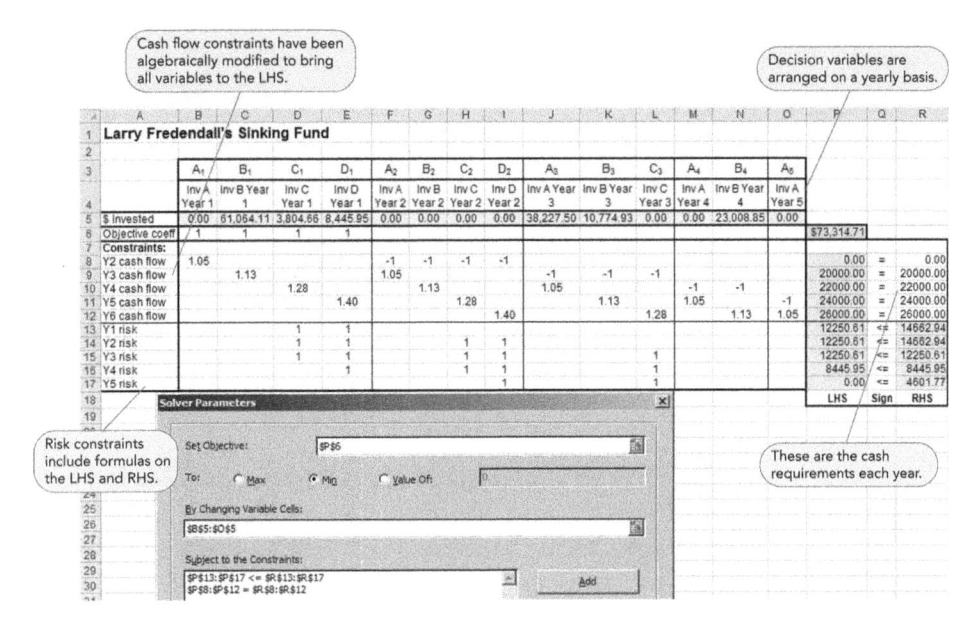

Figure 3.16: Excel Layout and Solver Entries for Larry Fredendall's Sinking Fund

File: Figure 3.16.xlsx

The optimal solution requires Larry to invest a total of $73,314.71 at the start of year 1, putting $61,064.11 in choice B, $3,804.66 in choice C, and $8,445.95 in choice D. There is no money maturing for investment at the start of year 2. At the start of year 3, using the maturing amounts, Larry should pay off $20,000 for Susan's education, invest $38,227.50 in choice A, and invest $10,774.93 in choice B. At the start of year 4, Larry should use the maturing amounts to pay off $22,000 for Susan's education and invest $23,008.85 in choice B. The investments in place at that time will generate $24,000 at the start of year 5 and $26,000 at the start of year 6, meeting Larry's requirements in those years.

3.9 Summary

This chapter continues the discussion of LP models. To show ways of formulating and solving problems from a variety of disciplines, we examine applications from manufacturing, marketing, finance, employee scheduling, transportation, ingredient blending, and multiperiod planning. For each example, we illustrate how to set up and solve all these models by using Excel's Solver add-in. In several cases, we provide alternate ways to formulate the problem and obtain the same optimal solution.

Key Points
- It is a good idea to always develop a written LP model on paper before attempting to implement it on Excel.
- In LP formulation, we first identify decision variables and then write linear mathematical expressions for the objective function and each of the constraints.
- A popular use of LP is in solving product mix problems.
- Decision variables in product mix problems usually represent the number of units to make of each product.
- In a product mix problem, instead of profit contributions, the objective function can include selling prices and cost components.
- It is preferable to have the Excel layout show as much detail as possible for a problem.
- It is often most efficient to have formulas in Excel LP layouts modeled using the SUMPRODUCT function.
- The make-buy decision problem is an extension of the product mix problem, and its objective function includes the outsourcing cost.
- Because integer programming models are much more difficult to solve than LP models, we solve many problems as LP models and attempt to round off any fractional values when it is clear that the rounded solution will remain feasible.
- Media selection problems can be approached with LP from two perspectives: maximizing audience exposure or minimizing advertising costs.
- Selection of survey participants for consumer research is another popular use of LP.
- If desired, constraints can be algebraically modified to bring all variables to the left-hand-side (LHS) of the mathematical expression.
- Such algebraic modifications of constraints are, however, not required for implementation in Excel.
- Maximizing return on investment subject to a set of risk constraints is a popular financial application of LP.
- Decision variables in financial planning models usually define the amounts to be invested in each investment choice.
- Alternate formulations are possible for some LP problems.
- Problems with large variability in the magnitudes of parameter and/or variable values should be scaled.
- It is important to define the decision variables in an LP problem as precisely as possible.
- Labor staffing is a popular application of LP, especially when there is wide fluctuation in labor needs between various periods.
- Labor staffing problems involving multiple shifts per period can also be modeled using LP.
- Alternate optimal solutions are common in many LP applications.

- Assigning people to jobs, jobs to machines, and so on is an application of LP called the assignment problem.
- Loading problems deal with deciding the load mix that maximizes value or minimizes cost.
- Allocation problems involve deciding how much of an item to allocate to the different choices that are available.
- Using double-subscripted variables is a convenient way of formulating many LP models, including allocation problems and multiperiod problems.
- A problem involving transporting goods from several origins to several destinations efficiently is called a transportation problem.
- In blending applications, the decision variables typically denote the amount of each ingredient that should be used to make the product(s).
- In most practical blending problems, the ingredients are usually used to make more than one product.
- Major oil refineries use LP for blending crude oils to produce gasoline grades.
- Blending constraints specify the compositions of each product.
- Multiperiod problems are perhaps the most challenging application of LP.
- Models for multiperiod production planning typically have to include several, often conflicting, factors.
- In a multiperiod production planning model, production decisions in later periods depend directly on decisions made in earlier periods.
- Balance constraints in a multiperiod problem specify the relationship between the previous period's closing inventory, this period's production, this period's sales, and this period's closing inventory.
- Another excellent example of multiperiod LP models involves making investment decisions over several periods.

3.10 Exercises

Solved Problem

Solved Problem 3-1 The Loughry Group has opened a new mall in Gainesville, Florida. Mark Loughry, the general manager of the mall, is trying to ensure that enough support staff is available to clean the mall before it opens each day. The mall operates seven days a week, and the cleaning staff works between 12:30 A.M. and 8:30 A.M. each night. Based on projected mall traffic data for the upcoming week, Mark estimates that the number of cleaning staff required each day will be as shown in Table 3.15.

Table 3.15: Cleaning Staff Requirement Data for Loughry Group's Mall

Day of Week	Number of Staff Required
Monday	22
Tuesday	13
Wednesday	15
Thursday	20
Friday	18
Saturday	23
Sunday	27

Mark can use the work schedules shown in Table 3.16 for the cleaning staff. The wages for each schedule are also shown in Table 3.16. In order to be perceived as being a fair employer, Mark wants to ensure that at least 75% of the workers have two consecutive days off and that at least 50% of the workers have at least one weekend day off. How should Mark schedule his cleaning staff in order to meet the mall's requirements?

Table 3.16: Schedule and Cost Data for Loughry Group's Mall

Work Schedule	Wages Per Week
1. Saturday and Sunday off	$350
2. Saturday and Tuesday off	$375
3. Tuesday and Wednesday off	$400
4. Monday and Thursday off	$425
5. Tuesday and Friday off	$425
6. Thursday and Friday off	$400
7. Sunday and Thursday off	$375
8. Sunday and Wednesday off	$375

Formulating and Solving the Problem   As noted in the previous labor staffing problem, the decision variables typically determine how many employees need to start their work at the different starting times permitted. In Mark's case, because there are eight possible work schedules, we have eight decision variables in the problem. Let:

S_1 = number of employees who need to follow schedule 1 (Saturday and Sunday off)
S_2 = number of employees who need to follow schedule 2 (Saturday and Tuesday off)
S_3 = number of employees who need to follow schedule 3 (Tuesday and Wednesday off)
S_4 = number of employees who need to follow schedule 4 (Monday and Thursday off)
S_5 = number of employees who need to follow schedule 5 (Tuesday and Friday off)
S_6 = number of employees who need to follow schedule 6 (Thursday and Friday off)
S_7 = number of employees who need to follow schedule 7 (Sunday and Thursday off)
S_8 = number of employees who need to follow schedule 8 (Sunday and Wednesday off)

This is the objective function:

$$\text{Minimize total weekly wages} = \$350\,S_1 + \$375\,S_2 + \$400\,S_3 + \$425\,S_4 + \$425\,S_5 \\ + \$400\,S_6 + \$375\,S_7 + \$375\,S_8$$

subject to the constraints:

$$
\begin{aligned}
S_1 + S_2 + S_3 + S_5 + S_6 + S_7 + S_8 &\geq 22 \quad \text{(Monday requirement)} \\
S_1 + S_2 + S_4 + S_6 + S_7 + S_8 &\geq 13 \quad \text{(Tuesday requirement)} \\
S_1 + S_2 + S_4 + S_5 + S_6 + S_7 &\geq 15 \quad \text{(Wednesday requirement)} \\
S_1 + S_2 + S_3 + S_5 + S_8 &\geq 20 \quad \text{(Thursday requirement)} \\
S_1 + S_2 + S_3 + S_4 + S_7 + S_8 &\geq 18 \quad \text{(Friday requirement)} \\
S_3 + S_4 + S_5 + S_6 + S_7 + S_8 &\geq 23 \quad \text{(Saturday requirement)} \\
S_2 + S_3 + S_4 + S_5 + S_6 &\geq 27 \quad \text{(Sunday requirement)}
\end{aligned}
$$

At least 75% of workers must have two consecutive days off each week, and at least 50% of workers must have at least one weekend day off each week. These constraints may be written, respectively, as:

$$
\begin{aligned}
S_1 + S_3 + S_6 &\geq 0.75\,(S_1 + S_2 + S_3 + S_4 + S_5 + S_6 + S_7 + S_8) \\
S_1 + S_2 + S_7 + S_8 &\geq 0.5\,(S_1 + S_2 + S_3 + S_4 + S_5 + S_6 + S_7 + S_8)
\end{aligned}
$$

Finally,

$$S_1, S_2, S_3, S_5, S_6, S_7, S_8 \geq 0$$

The Excel layout and Solver entries for this model are shown in Figure 3.17.

	A	B	C	D	E	F	G	H	I	J	K	L
1	Loughry Group Mall											
2												
3		S_1	S_2	S_3	S_4	S_5	S_6	S_7	S_8			
4		Sat & Sun off	Sat & Tue off	Tue & Wed off	Mon & Thu off	Tue & Fri off	Thu & Fri off	Sun & Thu off	Sun & Wed off			
5	Number of staff	10.00	7.00	20.00	0.00	0.00	0.00	0.00	3.00			
6	Wages	$350	$375	$400	$425	$425	$400	$375	$375	$15,250.00		
7	Constraints:											
8	Monday needs	1	1	1		1	1	1	1	40.00	>=	22
9	Tuesday needs	1			1		1	1	1	13.00	>=	13
10	Wednesday needs	1	1		1	1	1			17.00	>=	15
11	Thursday needs	1	1	1		1			1	40.00	>=	20
12	Friday needs	1	1	1	1			1	1	40.00	>=	18
13	Saturday needs			1	1	1	1	1	1	23.00	>=	23
14	Sunday needs		1	1	1	1	1			27.00	>=	27
15	75% consecutive	1		1				1		30.00	>=	30
16	50% weekend day	1	1					1	1	20.00	>=	20
17										LHS	Sign	RHS

Solver Parameters

Set Objective: $J$6

To: ○ Max ● Min ○ Value Of: 0

By Changing Variable Cells: $B$5:$I$5

Subject to the Constraints: $J$8:$J$16 >= $L$8:$L$16

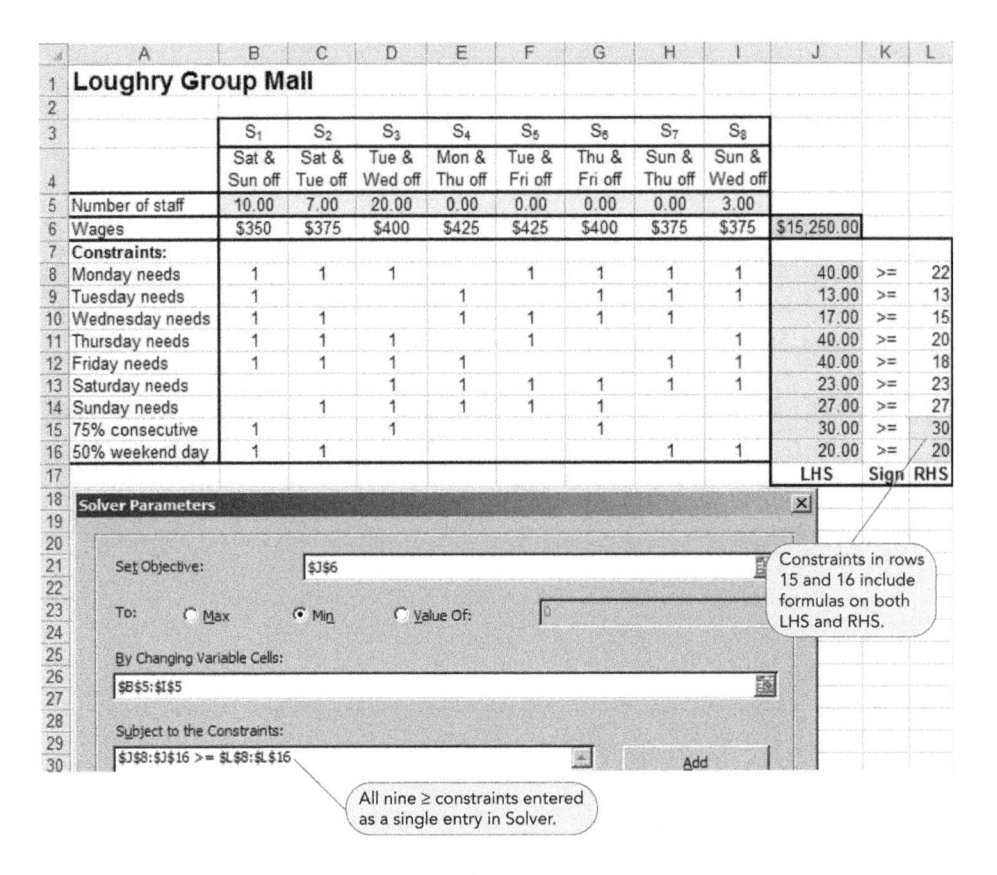

(Constraints in rows 15 and 16 include formulas on both LHS and RHS.)

(All nine ≥ constraints entered as a single entry in Solver.)

Figure 3.17: Excel Layout and Solver Entries for Loughry Group Mall

File: Figure 3.17.xlsx

For the last two constraints, the Excel layout includes formulas for both the LHS (cells J15:J16) and RHS (cells L15:L16) entries. While the formulas in cells J15:J16 use the usual SUMPRODUCT function, the formulas in cells L15:L16 are:

Cell L15: =0.75*SUM($B$5:$I$5)
Cell L16: =0.50*SUM($B$5:$I$5)

Interpreting the Results Figure 3.17 reveals that the optimal solution is to employ 10 people on schedule 1; 7 people on schedule 2; 20 people on schedule 3; and 3 people on schedule 8, for a total cost of $15,250 per week. As in the solution for the Hong Kong Bank problem (see Figure 3.8), it turns out that this problem has alternate optimal solutions, too. For example, we can satisfy the staff requirements at the same cost by employing 10 people on schedule 1; 7 people on schedule 2; 3 people on schedule 3; 17 people on schedule 6; and 3 people on schedule 7.

The solution indicates that while exactly meeting staffing needs for Tuesday, Saturday, and Sunday, Mark is left with way more than he needs on Monday, Thursday, and Friday. He should perhaps consider using part-time help to alleviate this mismatch in his staffing needs.

Problems

3–1. A small backpack manufacturer carries four different models of backpacks, made of canvas, plastic, nylon, and leather. The bookstore, which will sell the backpacks exclusively, expects to be able to sell between 15 and 40 of each model. The store has agreed to pay $35.50 for each canvas backpack, $39.50 for each plastic backpack, $42.50 for each nylon backpack, and $69.50 for each leather backpack that can be delivered by the end of the following week.

One worker can work on either canvas or plastic, can complete a backpack in 1.5 hours, and will charge $7.00 per hour to do the work. This worker can work a maximum of 90 hours during the next week. Another worker can sew backpacks made of nylon fabric. He can complete a bag in 1.7 hours, will charge $8.00 per hour to work, and can work 42.5 hours in the next week. A third worker has the ability to sew leather. He each can complete a book bag in 1.9 hours, will charge $9.00 per hour to work, and can work 80 hours during the next week. The following table provides additional information about each backpack. What is the best combination of backpacks to provide the store to maximize profit?

Backpack Model	Material Required (square yards)	Material Available (square yards)	Cost/ Square Yard
Canvas	2.25	200	$4.50
Plastic	2.40	350	$4.25
Nylon	2.10	700	$7.65
Leather	2.60	550	$9.45

3–2. A contestant on the hit reality television show Top Bartender was asked to mix a variety of drinks, each consisting of 4 fluid ounces. No other ingredients were permitted. She was given the following quantities of liquor:

Liquor	Quantity
Bourbon	128 ounces
Brandy	128 ounces
Vodka	128 ounces
Dry Vermouth	32 ounces
Sweet Vermouth	32 ounces

The contestant is considering making the following four drinks:

- The New Yorker: 25% each of bourbon, brandy, vodka, and sweet vermouth
- The Garaboldi: 25% each of brandy and dry vermouth; 50% sweet vermouth
- The Kentuckian: 100% bourbon
- The Russian: 75% vodka and 25% dry vermouth

The contestant's objective is to make the largest number of drinks with the available liquor. What is the combination of drinks to meet her objective?

3-3. A manufacturer of travel pillows must determine the production plan for the next production cycle. He wishes to make at least 300 of each of the three models that his firm offers and no more than 1,200 of any one model. The specifics for each model are shown in the following table. How many pillows of each type should be manufactured in order to maximize total profit?

Pillow Model	Selling Price	Cutting	Sewing	Finishing	Packing
Junior travel pillow	$5.75	0.10	0.05	0.18	0.20
Travel pillow	$6.95	0.15	0.12	0.24	0.20
Deluxe travel pillow	$7.50	0.20	0.18	0.20	0.20
Available hours		450	550	600	450
Cost per hour		$7.00	$9.00	$8.50	$7.25

3-4. Students who are trying to raise funds have an agreement with a local pizza chain. The chain has agreed to sell them pizzas at a discount, which the students can then resell to families in the local community for a profit. It is expected that of the 500 families in the community, at most 70% will buy pizza. Based on a survey of their personal preferences, the students believe that they should order no more than 120 cheese pizzas, no more than 150 pepperoni pizzas, and no more than 100 vegetarian pizzas. They also want to make sure that at least 20% of the total pizzas are cheese and at least 50% of the pizzas are pepperoni. They make a profit of $1.45, $1.75, and $1.98, respectively, for each cheese, pepperoni, and vegetarian pizza they resell. How many pizzas of each type should they buy?

3-5. A furniture maker sells three different styles of cabinets, including an Italian model, a French Country model, and a Caribbean model. Each cabinet produced must go through three departments: carpentry, painting, and finishing. The table for this problem contains all relevant information concerning production times (hours per cabinet), production capacities for each operation per day, and profit ($ per unit). The owner has an obligation to deliver a minimum of 60 cabinets in each style to a furniture distributor. He would like to determine the product mix that maximizes his daily profit. Formulate the problem as an LP model and solve using Excel.

Cabinet Style	Carpentry	Painting	Finishing	Profit
Italian	3.00	1.50	0.75	$72
French	2.25	1.00	0.75	$65
Caribbean	2.50	1.25	0.85	$78
Available hours	1,360	700	430	

3-6. An electronics manufacturer has an option to produce six styles of cell phones. Each device requires time, in minutes, on three types of electronic testing equipment, as shown in the table for this problem. The first two test devices each are available for 120 hours per week. Test device 3 requires more preventive maintenance and may be used only for 100 hours each week. The market for all six cell phones is vast, so the manufacturer believes that it can sell as many cell phones as it can manufacture. The table also summarizes the revenues and material costs for each type of phone.

In addition, variable labor costs are $15 per hour for test device 1, $12 per hour for test device 2, and $18 per hour for test device 3. Determine the product mix that would maximize profits. Formulate the problem as an LP model and solve it by using Excel.

	Smartphone	Blueberry	Mo Phone	Bold Phone	Lux Phone4G	Tap3G
Test device 1	7	3	12	6	18	17
Test device 2	2	5	3	2	15	17
Test device 3	5	1	3	2	9	2
Revenue per unit	$200	$120	$180	$200	$430	$260
Material cost per unit	$ 35	$25	$ 40	$ 45	$170	$ 60

3-7. A company produces three different types of wrenches: W111, W222, and W333. It has a firm order for 2,000 W111 wrenches, 3,750 W222 wrenches, and 1,700 W333 wrenches. Between now and the order delivery date, the company has only 16,500 fabrication hours and 1,600 inspection hours. The time that each wrench requires in each department is shown in the table for this problem. Also shown are the costs to manufacture the wrenches in-house and the costs to outsource them. For labeling considerations, the company wants to manufacture in-house at least 60% of each type of wrench that will be shipped. How many wrenches of each type should be made in-house and how many should be outsourced? What will be the total cost to satisfy the order?

Wrench	Fabrication Hours	Inspection Hours	In-House Cost	Outsource Cost
W111	2.50	0.25	$17.00	$20.40
W222	3.40	0.30	$19.00	$21.85
W333	3.80	0.45	$23.00	$25.76

3-8. A gear manufacturer is planning next week's production run for four types of gears. If necessary, it is possible to outsource any type of gear from another gear company located nearby. The tables for this problem show next week's demand, revenue per unit, outsource cost per unit, time (in hours) required per unit in each production process, and the availability and costs of these processes. The nearby company can supply a maximum of 300 units of each type of gear next week. What should be the production and/or outsource plan for the next week to maximize profit?

Process	Gear A	Gear B	Gear C	Gear D	Hours Available	Cost per Hour
Forming	0.30	0.36	0.38	0.45	500	$9.00
Hardening	0.20	0.30	0.24	0.33	300	$8.00
Deburring	0.30	0.30	0.35	0.25	310	$7.50

Gear Type	Gear A	Gear B	Gear C	Gear D
Demand	400	500	450	600
Revenue	$12.50	$15.60	$17.40	$19.30
Outsource	$ 7.10	$ 8.10	$ 8.40	$ 9.00

3-9. A political polling organization is to conduct a poll of likely voters prior to an upcoming election. Each voter is to be interviewed in person. It is known that the costs of interviewing different types of voters vary due to the differences in proportion within the population. The costs to interview males, for example, are $10 per Democrat, $9 per Republican, and $13.50 per Independent voter. The costs to interview females are $12, $11 and $13.50 for Democrat, Republican, and Independent voters, respectively. The polling service has been given certain criteria to which it must adhere:
- There must be at least 4,500 total interviews.
- At least 1,000 independent voters must be polled.
- At least 2,000 males must be polled.
- At least 1,750 females must be polled.
- No more than 40% of those polled may be Democrats.
- No more than 40% of those polled may be Republicans.
- No more than one-quarter of those polled may be Republican males.
- Each of the six categories of voters must be represented in the poll by at least 10% of the total interviews.

Determine the least expensive sampling plan and the total cost to carry out the plan.

3-10. The advertising director of a large retail store in Columbus, Ohio, is considering three advertising media possibilities: (1) ads in the Sunday *Columbus Dispatch* newspaper, (2) ads in a local trade magazine that is distributed free to all houses in the city and northwest suburbs, and (3) ads on Columbus' WCC-TV station. She wishes to obtain a new-customer exposure level of at least 50%

within the city and 60% in the northwest suburbs. Each TV ad has a new-customer exposure level of 5% in the city and 3% in the northwest suburbs. The *Dispatch* ads have corresponding exposure levels per ad of 3.5% and 3%, respectively, while the trade magazine has exposure levels per ad of 0.5% and 1%, respectively. The relevant costs are $1,000 per *Dispatch* ad, $300 per trade magazine ad, and $2,000 per TV ad. The advertising policy is that no single media type should consume more than 45% of the total amount spent. Find the advertising strategy that will meet the store's objective at minimum cost.

3–11. A grocery chain wants to promote the sale of a new flavor of ice cream by issuing up to 15,000 coupons by mail to preferred customers. The budget for this promotion has been limited to $12,000. The following table shows the expected increased sales per coupon and the probability of coupon usage for the various coupon amounts under consideration.

Coupon Amount	Increased sales per coupon (cartons)	Probability coupon will be used
$1.00	1.50	0.80
$0.85	1.40	0.75
$0.70	1.25	0.60
$0.55	1.00	0.50
$0.40	0.90	0.42

For example, every $1-off coupon issued will stimulate sales of 1.5 additional cartons. However, since the probability that a $1-off coupon will actually be used is only 0.80, the expected increased sales per coupon issued is $1.2 (= 0.8 \times 1.5)$ cartons.

The selling price per carton of ice cream is $3.50 before the coupon value is applied. The chain wants at least 20% of the coupons issued to be of the $1-off variety and at least 10% of the coupons issued to be of each of the other four varieties. What is the optimal combination of coupons to be issued, and what is the expected net increased revenue from this promotion?

3–12. A political candidate is planning his media budget for an upcoming election. He has $90,500 to spend. His political consultants have provided him with the following estimates of additional votes as a result of the advertising effort:
  – For every small sign placed by the roadside, he will garner 10 additional votes.
  – For every large sign placed by the roadside, he will garner 30 additional votes.
  – For every thousand bumper stickers placed on cars, he will garner 10 additional votes.
  – For every hundred personal mailings to registered voters, he will garner 40 additional votes, and

- For every radio ad heard daily in the last month before the election, he will garner 485 additional votes.

The costs for each of these advertising devices, along with the practical minimum and maximum that should be planned for each, are shown on the following table. How should the candidate plan to spend his campaign money?

Advertising Medium	Cost	Minimum	Maximum
Bumper stickers (thousands)	$ 30	40	100
Personal mailings (hundreds)	$ 81	500	800
Radio ads (per day)	$1,000	3	12
Small roadside signs	$ 25	100	500
Large roadside signs	$ 60	50	300

3-13. A brokerage firm has been tasked with investing $500,000 for a new client. The client has asked that the broker select promising stocks and bonds for investment, subject to the following guidelines:
- At least 20% in municipal bonds
- At least 10% each in real estate stock and pharmaceutical stock
- At least 40% in a combination of energy and domestic automobile stocks, with each accounting for at least 15%
- No more than 50% of the total amount invested in energy and automobile stocks in a combination of real estate and pharmaceutical company stock

Subject to these constraints, the client's goal is to maximize projected return on investments. The broker has prepared a list of high-quality stocks and bonds and their corresponding rates of return, as shown in the following table.

Investment	Annual Rate of Return
City of Miami (municipal) bonds	5.3%
American Smart Car	8.8%
GreenEarth Energy	4.9%
Rosslyn Pharmaceuticals	8.4%
RealCo (real estate)	10.4%

Formulate this portfolio selection problem by using LP and solve it by using Excel.

3-14. An investor wishes to invest some or all of his $12.5 million in a diversified portfolio through a commercial lender. The types of investments, the expected interest per year, and the maximum allowed percentage investment he will consider are shown on the following table. He wants at least 35% of his investments to be in nonmortgage instruments and no more than 60% to be in high-yield (and high-risk) instruments (i.e., expected interest $>8\%$). How should his investment be diversified to make the most interest income?

Investment	Expected Interest	Maximum Allowed
Low-income mortgage loans	7.00%	20%
Conventional mortgage loans	6.25%	40%
Government sponsored mortgage loans	8.25%	25%
Bond investments	5.75%	12%
Stock investments	8.75%	15%
Futures trading	9.50%	10%

3–15. A finance major has inherited $200,000 and wants to invest it in a diversified portfolio. Some of the investments she is considering are somewhat risky. These include international mutual funds, which should earn 12.25% over the next year, and U.S. stocks, which should earn 11.5% over the next year. She has decided, therefore, that she will put no more than 30% of her money in either of these investments and no more than a total of 50% in both investments.

She also wants to keep some of her investment in what is considered a liquid state, so that she can divest quickly if she so chooses. She believes school bonds, which return 5% interest, short-term certificates of deposit, which return 6.25% interest, and tax-free municipal bonds, which return 8.75%, to be reasonably liquid. She will keep no more than 40% of her money in these investments and no more than 15% in any one of these investments. She believes that T-bills are also considered liquid and less risky and that they will return 7.5%. However, she has decided to invest no more than 25% of her investment in T-bills.

She wishes to have experience investing in different types of instruments, so she will invest at least 10% of her money in each of the six types of investment choices. What is the optimal investment strategy for her to follow?

3–16. A couple has agreed to attend a "casino night" as part of a fundraiser for the local hospital, but they believe that gambling is generally a losing proposition. For the sake of the charity, they have decided to attend and to allocate $300 for the games. There are to be four games, each involving standard decks of cards.

The first game, called *Jack in 52*, is won by selecting a jack of a specific suit from the deck. The probability of doing this is, of course, 1 in 52 (=0.0192) Gamblers may place a bet of $1, $2, or $4 on this game. If they win, the payouts are $12 for a $1 bet, $24.55 for a $2 bet, and $49 for a $4 bet.

The second game, called *Red Face in 52*, is won by selecting from the deck a red face card (i.e., red jack, red queen, or red king). The probability of winning is 6 in 52 (=0.1154) Again, bets may be placed in denominations of $1, $2, and $4. Payouts are $8.10, $16.35, and $32.50, respectively.

The third game, called *Face in 52*, is won by selecting one of the 12 face cards from the deck. The probability of winning is 12 in 52 (= 0.2308). Payouts are $4, $8.15, and $16 for $1, $2, and $4 bets.

The last game, called *Red in 52*, is won by selecting a red card from the deck. The probability of winning is 26 in 52 (= 0.50). Payouts are $1.80, $3.80, and $7.50 for $1, $2, and $4 bets.

Given that they can calculate the expected return (or, more appropriately, loss) for each type of game and level of wager, they have decided to see if they can minimize their total expected loss by planning their evening using LP. For example, the expected return from a $1 bet in the game *Jack in 52* is equal to $0.2308 (= $12 × 1/52 + $0 × 51/52). Since the amount bet is $1, the expected loss is equal to $0.7692 (= $1 − $0.2308). All other expected losses can be calculated in a similar manner.

They want to appear to be sociable and not as if they are trying to lose as little as possible. Therefore, they will place at least 20 bets (of any value) on each of the four games. Further, they will spend at least $26 on $1 bets, at least $50 on $2 bets, and at least $72 on $4 bets. They will bet no more than (and no less than) the agreed-upon $300. What should be their gambling plan, and what is their expected loss for the evening?

3–17. A hospital emergency room is open 24 hours a day. Nurses report for duty at 1 A.M., 5 A.M., 9 A.M., 1 P.M., 5 P.M., or 9 P.M., and each works an 8-hour shift. Nurses are paid the same, regardless of the shift they work. The following table shows the minimum number of nurses needed during the six periods into which the day is divided. How should the hospital schedule the nurses so that the total staff required for one day's operation is minimized?

Shift	Time	Nurses needed
1	1–5 a.m.	4
2	5–9 a.m.	13
3	9 a.m.–1 p.m.	17
4	1–5 p.m.	10
5	5–9 p.m.	12
6	9 p.m.–1 a.m.	5

3–18. A nursing home employs attendants who are needed around the clock. Each attendant is paid the same, regardless of when his or her shift begins. Each shift is 8 consecutive hours. Shifts begin at 6 A.M., 10 A.M., 2 P.M., 6 P.M., 10 P.M., and 2 A.M. The following table shows the nursing home's requirements for the numbers of attendants to be on duty during specific time periods.

Shift	Time	Number of attendants
A	2–6 a.m.	8
B	6–10 a.m.	27
C	10 a.m.–2 p.m.	12
D	2–6 p.m.	23
E	6–10 p.m.	29
F	10 p.m.–2 a.m.	23

(a) What is the minimum number of attendants needed to satisfy the nursing home's requirements?

(b) The nursing home would like to use the same number of attendants determined in part (a) but would now like to minimize the total salary paid. Attendants are paid $16 per hour during 8 A.M.–8 P.M., and a 25% premium per hour during 8 P.M.–8 A.M. How should the attendants now be scheduled?

3–19. A hospital is moving from 8-hour shifts for its lab techs to 12-hour shifts. Instead of working five 8-hour days, the lab techs would work three days on and four days off in the first week followed by four days on and three days off in the second week, for a total of 84 hours every two weeks.

Because the peak demand times in the hospital appear to be between 5 A.M. and 7 A.M. and between 5 P.M. and 7 P.M., four 12-hour shifts will be arranged according to the following table.

Shifts	Work Times	Pay Rate/Week
A and A (alt)	5 a.m.–5 p.m.	$756
B and B (alt)	7 a.m.–7 p.m.	$840
C and C (alt)	5 p.m.–5 a.m.	$882
D and D (alt)	7 p.m.–7 a.m.	$924

The shift pay differentials are based on the most and least desirable times to begin and end work. In any one week, techs on shift A might work Sunday through Tuesday, while techs on shift A (alt) would work at the same times but on Wednesday through Saturday. In the following week, techs on shift A would work Sunday through Wednesday, while techs on shift A (alt) would work the corresponding Thursday through Saturday. Therefore, the same number of techs would be scheduled for shift A as for shift A (alt).

The requirements for lab techs during the 24-hour day are shown in the following table. What is the most economical schedule for the lab techs?

	5 A.M.–7 A.M.	7 A.M.–5 P.M.	5 P.M.–7 P.M.	7 P.M.–5 A.M.
Lab techs needed	12	8	14	10

3-20. An airline with operations in San Diego, California, must staff its ticket counters inside the airport. Ticket attendants work 6-hour shifts at the counter. There are two types of agents: those who speak English as a first language and those who are fully bilingual (English and Spanish). The requirements for the number of agents depend on the numbers of people expected to pass through the airline's ticket counters during various hours. The airline believes that the need for agents between the hours of 6 A.M. and 9 P.M. are as follows:

	6 A.M.–9 A.M.	9 A.M.–NOON	NOON–3 P.M.	3 P.M.–6 P.M.	6 P.M.–9 P.M.
Agents Needed	12	20	16	24	12

Agents begin work either at 6 A.M., 9 A.M., noon, or 3 P.M. The shifts are designated as shifts A, B, C, and D, respectively. It is the policy of the airline that at least half of the agents needed in any time period will speak English as the first language. Further, at least one-quarter of the agents needed in any time period should be fully bilingual.

(a) How many and what type of agents should be hired for each shift to meet the language and staffing requirements for the airline, so that the total number of agents is minimized?

(b) What is the optimal hiring plan from a cost perspective if English-speaking agents are paid $25 per hour and bilingual agents are paid $29 per hour? Does the total number of agents needed change from that computed in part (a)?

3-21. A small trucking company is determining the composition of its next trucking job. The load master has his choice of seven types of cargo, which may be loaded in full or in part. The specifications of the cargo types are shown in the following table. The goal is to maximize the amount of freight, in terms of dollars, for the trip. The truck can hold up to 900 pounds of cargo in a 2,500-cubic-foot space. What cargo should be loaded, and what will be the total freight charged?

Cargo Type	Freight per Pound	Volume per Pound (cu. ft.)	Pounds Available
A	$8.00	3.0	210
B	$6.00	2.7	150
C	$3.50	6.3	90
D	$5.75	8.4	120
E	$9.50	5.5	130
F	$5.25	4.9	340
G	$8.60	3.1	250

3-22. The load master for a freighter wants to determine the mix of cargo to be carried on the next trip. The ship's volume limit for cargo is 100,000 cubic meters, and its weight capacity is 2,310 tons. The master has five types of cargo from which to select and wishes to maximize the value of the selected shipment. However, to make sure that none of his customers is ignored, the load master would like to make sure that at least 20% of each cargo's available weight is selected. The specifications for the five cargoes are shown in the following table.

Cargo Type	Tons Available	Value per Ton	Volume per Ton (cu. m.)
A	970	$1,350	26
B	850	$1,675	54
C	1,900	$1,145	28
D	2,300	$ 850	45
E	3,600	$1,340	37

3-23. A cargo transport plane is to be loaded to maximize the revenue from the load carried. The plane may carry any combination and any amount of cargoes A, B, and C. The relevant values for these cargoes are shown in following table.

Cargo Type	Tons Available	Revenue per Ton	Volume per Ton (cu. ft.)
A	10	$700	2,000
B	12	$725	3,500
C	17	$685	3,000

The plane can carry as many as 32 tons of cargo. The plane is subdivided into compartments, and there are weight and volume limitations for each compartment. It is critical for safety reasons that the weight ratios be strictly observed. The requirements for cargo distribution are shown in the following table.

Compartment	Maximum Volume (CU. FT.)	Compartment Weight/Total Weight Ratio
Right fore	16,000	Must equal 18% of total weight loaded
Right center	20,000	Must equal 25% of total weight loaded
Right aft	14,000	Must equal 7% of total weight loaded
Left fore	10,000	Must equal 18% of total weight loaded
Left center	20,000	Must equal 25% of total weight loaded
Left aft	12,000	Must equal 7% of total weight loaded

Which cargoes should be carried, and how should they be allocated to the various compartments?

3-24. The owner of a private freighter is trying to decide which cargo he should carry on his next trip. He has two choices of cargo, which he can agree to carry in any combination. He may carry up to 15 tons of cargo A, which takes up 675 cubic feet per ton and earns revenue of $85 per ton. Or he may carry up to 54 tons of cargo B, with a volume of 450 cubic feet per ton and revenue of $79 per ton.

The freighter is divided into two holds, starboard and port. The starboard hold has a volume of 14,000 cubic feet and a weight capacity of 26 tons. The port hold has a volume of 15,400 cubic feet and a weight capacity of 32 tons. For steering reasons, it is necessary that the weight be distributed equally between the two sides of the freighter. However, the freighter engines and captain's bridge, which together weight 6 tons, are on the starboard side of the freighter. This means that the port side is usually loaded with 6 tons more cargo to equalize the weight. The owner may carry any combination of the two cargoes in the same hold without a problem. How should this freighter be loaded to maximize total revenue?

3-25. A farmer is making plans for next year's crop. He is considering planting corn, tomatoes, potatoes and okra. The data he has collected, along with the availability of resources, are shown in the table for this problem. He can plant as many as 60 acres of land. Determine the best mix of crops to maximize the farm's revenue.

Crop	Yield (bushels/ acre)	Revenue/ Bushel	Planting (hours/ acre)	Tending (hours/ acre)	Harvest (hours/ acre)	Water (units/ acre)	Fertilizer (pounds/ acre)
Corn	50	$55	10	2	6	2.5	50
Tomato	40	$85	15	8	20	3.0	60
Potato	46	$57	12	2	9	2.0	45
Okra	48	$52	18	12	20	3.0	35
Available			775	550	775	300	2,500

3-26. The farmer in Problem 3-25 has an opportunity to take over the neighboring 80-acre farm. If he acquires this farm, he will be able to increase the amounts of time available to 1,600 hours for planting, 825 hours for tending, and 1,400 hours for harvesting. Between the two farms, there are 510 units of water and 6,000 pounds of fertilizer available. However, the neighboring farm has not been cultivated in a while. Therefore, each acre of this farm will take an additional 4 hours to plant and an additional 2 hours to tend. Because of the condition of the new farm, the farmer expects the yields per acre planted there to be only 46 bushels, 37 bushels, 42 bushels, and 45 bushels, respectively, for corn, tomato, potato, and okra. In order to make sure that both farms are used effectively, the farmer would like at least 80% of each farm's acreage to be planted. What is the best combination of crops to plant at each farm in order to maximize revenue?

3-27. A family farming concern owns five parcels of farmland broken into a southeast sector, north sector, northwest sector, west sector, and southwest sector. The farm concern is involved primarily in growing wheat, alfalfa, and barley crops and is currently preparing the production plan for next year. The Water Authority has just announced its yearly water allotment, with this farm receiving 7,500 acre-feet. Each parcel can tolerate only a certain amount of irrigation per growing season, as specified in the following table.0

Parcel	Area (acres)	Water Irrigation Limit (acre-feet)
Southeast	2,000	3,200
North	2,300	3,400
Northwest	600	800
West	1,100	500
Southwest	500	600

Each crop needs a minimum amount of water per acre, and there is a projected limit on sales of each crop, as noted in the following table.

Crop	Maximum Sales	Water Needed per Acre (acre-feet)
Wheat	110,000 bushels	1.6
Alfalfa	1,800 tons	2.9
Barley	2,200 tons	3.5

Wheat can be sold at a net profit of $2 per bushel, alfalfa at $40 per ton, and barley at $50 per ton. One acre of land yields an average of 1.5 tons of alfalfa and 2.2 tons of barley. The wheat yield is approximately 50 bushels per acre. What is the best planting plan for this farm?

3-28. A farmer has subdivided his land into three plots and wants to plant three crops in each plot: corn, rice, and soy. Plot sizes, crop acreage, profit per acre, and manure needed (pounds per acre) are given in the table for this problem.

Plot	Acreage	Crop	Maximum Acreage	Profit per Acre	Manure per Acre (pounds)
A	500	Corn	900	$600	200
B	800	Wheat	700	$450	300
C	700	Soy	1,000	$300	150

The maximum acreage for each crop denotes the total acres of that crop that can be planted over all three plots. Currently there are 450,000 pounds of manure available. To ensure that the plots are used equitably, the farmer wants the same proportion of each plot to be under cultivation. (The proportion of each plot under cultivation must be the same for all three plots.) How much of each crop should be planted at each plot to maximize total profit?

3-29. A fuel cell manufacturer can hire union, nonunion permanent, or temporary help. She has a contract to produce at the rate of 2,100 fuel cells per day and would like to achieve this at minimum cost. Union workers work 7 hours per day and can make up to 10 fuel cells per hour. Their wages and benefits cost the company $15.00 and $7.00 per hour, respectively. Union workers are assured that there will be no more than 80% of their number working in non-union permanent positions and that there will be no more than 20% of their number working in temporary positions.

Non-union permanent workers work 8 hours per day and can also make up to 10 fuel cells per hour. Their wages are the same as the union employees, but their benefits are worth only $3.00 per hour. Temporary workers work 6 hours per day, can make up to 5 fuel cells per hour, and earn only $10 per hour. They do not receive any benefits.

How many union, nonunion, and temporary workers should be hired to minimize the cost to the manufacturer? What is the average cost of producing a fuel cell?

3-30. A chemical company wishes to mix three elements (E, F, and G) to create three alloys (X, Y, and Z). The costs of the elements are as shown in the following table.

Element	Cost per Ton
E	$3.00
F	$4.00
G	$3.50

To maintain the required quality for each alloy, it is necessary to specify certain maximum or minimum percentages of the elements. These are as shown in the following table.

Alloy	Specifications	Selling Price per Ton
X	No more than 30% of E, at least 40% of F, no more than 50% of G	$5.50
Y	No more than 50% of E, at least 10% of F	$4.00
Z	No more than 70% of E, at least 20% of G	$6.00

The usage of each element is limited to 5,000 tons, and the total usage of all three elements is limited to 10,000 tons. Further, due to the relatively uncertain demand for alloy Z, the company would like to ensure that Z constitutes no more than 30% of the total quantity of the three alloys produced. Determine the mix of the three elements that will maximize profit under these conditions.

3-31. An animal feed company is developing a new puppy food. Their nutritionists have specified that the mixture must contain the following components by weight: at least 16% protein, 13% fat, and no more than 15% fiber. The percentages of each nutrient in the available ingredients, along with their cost per pound, are shown in the table for this problem.

	Ingredient					
Nutrient	Beef	Pork	Corn	Lamb	Rice	Chicken
Protein (%)	16.9	12.0	8.5	15.4	8.5	18.0
Fat (%)	26.0	4.1	3.8	6.3	3.8	17.9
Fiber (%)	29.0	8.3	2.7	2.4	2.7	28.8
Cost ($/lb)	0.52	0.49	0.20	0.40	0.17	0.39

What is the mixture that will have the minimum cost per pound and meet the stated nutritional requirements?

3–32. A boarding stable feeds and houses work horses used to pull tourist-filled carriages through the streets of a historic city. The stable owner wishes to strike a balance between a healthy nutritional standard for the horses and the daily cost of feed. This type of horse must consume exactly 5 pounds of feed per day. The feed mixes available are an oat product, a highly enriched grain, and a mineral product. Each of these mixes contains a predictable amount of five ingredients needed daily to keep the average horse healthy. The table for this problem shows these minimum requirements, units of each nutrient per pound of feed mix, and costs for the three mixes.

	Feed Mix			
Nutrient	Oat (units/lb.)	Grain (units/lb.)	Mineral (units/lb.)	Needed (units/day)
A	2.0	3.0	1.0	6
B	0.5	1.0	0.5	2
C	3.0	5.0	6.0	9
D	1.0	1.5	2.0	8
E	0.5	0.5	1.5	5
Cost/lb.	$0.33	$0.44	$0.57	

Formulate this problem and solve for the optimal daily mix of the three feeds.

3–33. Clint Hanks has decided to try a new diet that promises enhanced muscle tone if the daily intake of five essential nutrients is tightly controlled. After extensive research, Clint has determined that the recommended daily requirements of these nutrients for a person of his age, height, weight, and activity level are as follows: between 69 grams and 100 grams of protein, at least 700 milligrams of phosphorus, at least 420 milligrams of magnesium, between 1,000 milligrams and 1,750 milligrams of calcium, and at least 8 milligrams of iron. Given his limited finances, Clint has identified seven inexpensive food items that he can use to meet these requirements. The cost per serving for each food item and its contribution to each of the five nutrients are given in the table for this problem.

Food Item (SERVING SIZE)	Protein (G)	Phosphorus (MG)	Magnesium (MG)	Calcium (MG)	Iron (MG)	Cost per Serving ($)
Chicken Patty (0.25 pound)	17.82	250	29	23	1.14	0.50
Lasagna (300 grams)	24.53	223	56	303	2.52	0.58
2% Milk (1 cup)	8.05	224	27	293	0.05	0.42
Mixed Vegetables (1 cup)	5.21	93	40	46	1.49	0.24
Fruit Cocktail (1 cup)	1.01	26	11	15	0.62	0.37
Orange Juice (1 cup)	1.69	42	27	27	0.32	0.36
Oatmeal (1 packet)	4.19	136	46	142	10.55	0.18

(a) Use LP to identify the lowest cost combination of food items that Clint should use for his diet.
(b) Would you characterize your solution in (a) as a well-balanced diet? Explain your answer.

3-34. A steel company is producing steel for a new contract. The contract specifies the information in the following table for the steel.

Material	Minimum	Maximum
Manganese	2.10%	3.10%
Silicon	4.30%	6.30%
Carbon	1.05%	2.05%

The steel company mixes batches of eight different available materials to produce each ton of steel according to the specification. The following table details these materials.

Material Available	Manganese	Silicon	Carbon	Pounds Available	Cost per Pound
Alloy 1	70.0%	15.0%	3.0%	No limit	$0.12
Alloy 2	55.0%	30.0%	1.0%	300	$0.13
Alloy 3	12.0%	26.0%	0%	No limit	$0.15
Iron 1	1.0%	10.0%	3.0%	No limit	$0.09
Iron 2	5.0%	2.5%	0%	No limit	$0.07
Carbide 1	0%	24.0%	18.0%	50	$0.10
Carbide 2	0%	25.0%	20.0%	200	$0.12
Carbide 3	0%	23.0%	25.0%	100	$0.09

Formulate and solve the LP model that will indicate how much of each of the eight materials should be blended into a 1-ton load of steel so that the company can meet the specifications under the contract while minimizing costs.

3-35. A meat-packing house is creating a new variety of hot dog for the low-calorie, low-fat, low-cholesterol market. This new hot dog will be made of beef and pork, plus either chicken, turkey, or both. It will be marketed as a 2-ounce all-meat hot dog, with no fillers. Also, it will have no more than 6 grams of fat, no more than 27 grams of cholesterol, and no more than 100 calories. The cost per pound for beef, pork, chicken, and turkey, plus their calorie, fat, and cholesterol counts, are shown in the following table.

	Cost/Pound	Calories/Pound	Fat (G/LB.)	Cholesterol (G/LB.)
Beef	$0.76	640	32.5	210
Pork	$0.82	1,055	54.0	205
Chicken	$0.64	780	25.6	220
Turkey	$0.58	528	6.4	172

The packer would like each 2-ounce hot dog to be at least 25% beef and at least 25% pork. What is the most economical combination of the four meats to make this hot dog?

3-36. A distributor imports olive oil from Spain and Italy in large casks. He then mixes these oils in different proportions to create three grades of olive oil that are sold domestically in the United States. The domestic grades include (a) commercial, which must be no more than 35% Italian; (b) virgin, which may be any mix of the two olive oils; and (c) extra virgin, which must be at least 55% Spanish. The cost to the distributor for Spanish olive oil is $6.50 per gallon. Italian olive oil costs him $5.75 per gallon. The weekly demand for the three types of olive oils is 700 gallons of commercial, 2,200 gallons of virgin, and 1,400 gallons of extra virgin. How should he blend the two olive oils to meet his demand most economically?

3-37. A paint company has two types of bases from which it blends two types of paints: Tuffcoat and Satinwear. Each base has a certain proportion of ingredients X, Y, and Z, as shown in the following table, along with their costs.

	Ingredient X	Ingredient Y	Ingredient Z	Cost/Gallon
Paint base A	25%	34%	10%	$4.50
Paint base B	35%	42%	15%	$6.50

The specifications for the two paints are shown in the following table.

Tuffcoat	Satinwear
Must contain at least 33% ingredient X	Must contain at least 30% ingredient X
Must contain at least 35% ingredient Y	Must contain at least 38% ingredient Y
Must contain no more than 14% ingredient Z	Must contain no more than 13% ingredient Z
Demand = 1,600 gallons	Demand = 1,250 gallons

How should the two bases be blended to manufacture the two paints at a minimum cost? What is the cost per gallon for each paint?

3–38. The military has requested a new ready-to-eat meal (MRE) that will provide troops in the field with a very high-protein, low-carbohydrate instant canned breakfast. The can will contain 11 fluid ounces, or 325 mL, of the product. The design specifications are as follows. The drink should have at least 15 grams of protein, no more than 3 grams of fat, no more than 38 grams of carbohydrates, and no more than 310 mg of sodium. To make the drink, a food contractor plans to mix two ingredients it already makes, liquid A and liquid B, together with a new ingredient, liquid protein. The table for this problem describes the costs and the nutritional makeup of the three ingredients. Determine the least-cost mixture for the new MRE.

	Composition of the Ingredients (per liter)				
	Protein (G)	Fat (G)	Carbohydrate (G)	Sodium (MG)	Cost/liter
Liquid A	6	8	147	1770	$ 3.25
Liquid B	9	12	96	720	$ 4.50
Liquid protein	230	2	24	320	$28.00

3–39. A commercial food for caged reptiles is made in 40-pound bags from five potential feeds. For labeling purposes, feed A must constitute at least 20% of each bag by weight, and each of feeds B to E must be at least 5% of the total weight. Further, feeds B and D must together constitute at least 30% by weight, and feeds B, C, and E together must be no more than 50% by weight. The costs per pound for feeds A to E are, respectively, $0.96, $0.85, $0.775, $0.45, and $0.375. How shall this reptile food be made, and what is the cost per bag?

3–40. A power company has just announced the August 1 opening of its second nuclear power-generation facility. The human resources department has been directed to determine how many nuclear technicians will need to be hired and trained over the remainder of the year. The plant currently employs 350 fully trained technicians and projects personnel needs as shown in the following table.

Month	Hours needed
August	40,000
September	45,000
October	35,000
November	50,000
December	45,000

By law, a reactor employee can work no more than 130 hours per month. (Slightly more than 1 hour per day is used for check-in and check-out, record-keeping, and daily radiation health scans.) Company policy at the power company also dictates that layoffs are not acceptable in months when the nuclear power plant is overstaffed. So, if more trained employees are available than are needed in any month, each worker is still fully paid, even though he or she is not required to work the 130 hours.

Training new employees is an important and costly procedure. It takes one month of one-on-one classroom instruction before a new technician is permitted to work alone in the reactor facility. Therefore, trainees must be hired one month before they are actually needed. Each trainee teams up with a skilled nuclear technician and requires 90 hours of that employee's time, meaning that 90 hours less of the technician's time is available that month for actual reactor work.

Human resources department records indicate a turnover rate of trained technicians of 2% per month. In other words, 2% of the skilled technicians at the start of any month resign by the end of that month. A trained technician earns a monthly salary of $4,500, and trainees are paid $2,000 during their one month of instruction.

Formulate this staffing problem by using LP and solve it by using Excel.

3–41. A manufacturer of integrated circuits is planning production for the next four months. The forecast demand for the circuits is shown in the following table.

Circuit	Sep	Oct	Nov	Dec
IC341	650	875	790	1,100
IC256	900	350	1,200	1,300

At the beginning of September, the warehouse is expected to be completely empty. There is room for no more than 1,800 integrated circuits to be stored. Holding costs for both types are $0.05 per unit per month. Because workers are given time off during the holidays, the manufacturer wants to have at least 800 IC341s and 850 IC256s already in the warehouse at the beginning of January.

Production costs are $1.25 per unit for IC341 and $1.35 per unit for IC256. Because demand for raw materials is rising, production costs are expected to rise by $0.05 per month through the end of the year.

Labor to make model IC341 is 0.45 hours per unit; making model IC256 takes 0.52 hours of labor. Management has agreed to schedule at least 1,000 hours per month of labor. As many as 200 extra hours per month are available to management at the same cost, except during the month of December, when only 100 extra hours are possible. What should be the production schedule for IC341 and IC256 for the four months?

3-42. A woman inherited $356,000. As she had no immediate need for the money at the time she inherited, she decided to invest some or all of it on January 1, 201n, with a goal of making the money grow to $500,000 by December 31, 201n + 5. She is considering the investments in the following table.

	Rate	Matures
Fund A	7%	December 31 (at the end of one year)
Fund B	16%	December 31 (at the end of the second year after investment)
Fund C	24%	December 31 (at the end of the third year after investment)
Fund D	32%	December 31 (at the end of the fourth year after investment)

She wants to set up her investment strategy at the start of year 1. If she does not need to invest all the inheritance to have $500,000 at the end of year 6, she will find another purpose for the remainder. She may choose to place a sum of money in any or all of the investments available at the start of year 1. From that point, however, all subsequent investments should come from the matured investments of previous years. To ensure that funds are spread over different investment choices, she does not want any single *new* investment in any year to be over $120,000. (Note that prior investments in a fund do not count toward this limit.)

How much money will she have to invest on January 1, 201n, to meet her goal of $500,000 at the end of the sixth year?

3-43. The Transportation Security Administration (TSA) at a large airport has 175 agents hired and trained for the month of January. Agents earn an average of $3,300 per month and work 160 hours per month. The projection is that 26,400 agent-hours will be required in February, 29,040 agent hours will be required in March, and 31,994 agent hours will be required in each of the months of April and May. Attrition during the month of January is anticipated to be 5%, so only 95% of the agents trained and working in January will be available for work in February. Efforts are being made to improve attrition: The TSA expects to lose only 4% of agents during February, 3% in March, and 2% in May. To ensure that enough agents will be available to meet the demand, new agents must be hired and trained. During the one-month training period, trainees are paid $2,600. Existing agents, who normally work 160 hours per month, are able to work only 80 hours during the months they are training new people. How many agents should be hired during the months of January to May?

3-44. A paper mill sells rolls of paper to newspapers, which usually place orders for rolls of different widths. The mill has just received a large order for 1.5 million feet of 4-foot-wide paper, 6 million feet of 9-foot-wide paper, and 3 million feet of 12-foot-wide paper. It produces rolls of two sizes: (1) 3,000 feet long and 14 feet wide, at a cost of $600 per roll, and (2) 3,000 feet long and 20 feet wide, at a cost of $1,100 per roll. Large cutting machines are then used to cut these rolls to rolls of desired widths.
  (a) What should the paper mill do to satisfy this order at minimum cost? *Hint:* You need to first identify the different ways in which 14-foot-wide and 20-foot-wide rolls can be cut into 4-, 9-, and 12-foot-wide rolls.
  (b) The paper mill is very concerned about the environment. Rather than determining the cheapest way of satisfying the current order, the firm would like to determine the least wasteful way (i.e., minimize the amount of paper wasted). What is the solution with this revised objective, and what is the new cost?

3-45. A company that manufactures products in two plants ships locally using its own transportation system, but it has orders that must be sent to customers too far away to be serviced by the local fleet. It therefore contracts with a middle-distance carrier to complete its shipping. The locations of the two manufacturing plants, the amounts available at each plant to be shipped per week, the locations of the three customers, their weekly requirements, and shipping costs ($ per unit) between each plant and customer are shown in the table for this problem.

| | Customers ($ per unit shipped) | | | |
Plant	Savannah	Mobile	Roanoke	Available
Columbia	$13	$42	$38	450
Greensboro	$25	$48	$17	290
Required	250	225	210	

What is the optimal shipping plan to satisfy the demand at the lowest total shipping cost?

3-46. A school district must determine which students from each of the four attendance zones will attend which of the three high schools. The north attendance zone is 8 miles from Central High School, 4 miles from Northwestern High School, and 16 miles from Southeastern High School. All of the distances (in miles) are shown in the following table.

Attendance Zone	North	South	East	West
Central High School	8	5	5	11
Northwestern High School	4	17	15	6
Southeastern High School	16	6	6	18
Number of Students	903	741	923	793

Each school can have as many as 1,200 students enrolled. The school district would like to make the allocation of students to schools that will minimize the number of miles necessary to transport the students.

3-47. The school district in Problem 3-46 wishes to impose an additional constraint on the problem: It wants to enroll the same number of students in each of the three schools. Solve for the revised allocation of students to schools that will minimize the number of miles necessary to transport the students.

3-48. Consider the International City Trust portfolio selection problem in Section 3.4. In that formulation, we maximized dollars of interest earned subject to a risk constraint (plus other constraints). Problems such as this can alternatively be formulated to *minimize risk* subject to a minimum interest earned constraint. Resolve the International City Trust problem by minimizing total risk score and replacing the risk constraint (regarding the average risk score of 2 or less) with a constraint stating that dollars of interest earned must be at least $500,000. (Here it makes sense to also convert the budget constraint to an equality constraint.) *Hint: Solver may act unstable if the objective function includes a division operation. Thus, it is safer to minimize total risk score (the numerator of average risk score) and then afterwards divide that amount by 5,000,000 to compute the average risk score.*

3-49. Consider the Win Big Gambling Club media selection problem in Section 3.3 (Figure 3.4). In that formulation, we maximized audience coverage subject to an advertising budget constraint (plus other constraints). Problems such as this can alternatively be formulated to *minimize advertising expenditures* subject to a minimum level of audience coverage achieved. Resolve the Win Big Gambling Club problem by minimizing advertising costs and replacing the budget constraint with a constraint stating that audience coverage must be at least 60,000 people.

3-50. College freshman Jon Jackson wants to plan his Saturday night schedule for the next three weekends. In particular, he wants to determine what to do between 8:00 P.M. until 2:00 A.M. each Saturday night. He has narrowed his choices to three possible activities each evening, and he has assigned "utils" (i.e., happiness points on a scale of 1–10, with 10 being best) to each of those activities. Jon loves to watch TV because it relaxes him after a tough week at school, so he assigns 9 utils per hour of television watching. In addition, he is a serious student, so he assigns studying a value of 8 per hour in each of the first two weeks and 10 per hour during week 3 (because there is an exam the following Monday). Finally, Jon hates college parties because he doesn't like loud music, but his girlfriend always wants him to join her at her sorority parties. Jon assigns 2 utils per hour of partying in weeks 1 and 3 and 4 utils during week 2 (because at least ice cream will be served at the week 2 party).

After careful thought, Jon has come up with the following restrictions for his problem:

(1) Total hours spent on activities each night must equal the 6 hours available.
(2) He won't study more than 4 hours per night during either of the first two weeks (he doesn't want to be perceived as being a complete nerd).
(3) He must study at least 3 hours in the third week (he wants to score well on the upcoming exam).
(4) He must study at least 10 hours over the 3-week period (he wants to maintain a high grade-point average).
(5) He must average at least 1 hour per week of TV watching (he is forcing himself to relax).
(6) He must party at least 2 hours over the next 3 weeks (he wants to keep his girlfriend happy).
(7) He will never spend more than 3 hours at a party (he is concerned about long-term hearing loss).

What allocation of time will maximize Jon's happiness while satisfying his various requirements?

3-51. Pullman Tire Company would like to plan production for the next three months. The firm can satisfy demand by using inventory, regular production (at $40 per tire), overtime (at $50 per tire), or subcontracting (at $70 per tire). Any tires held over for one month incur a $2 per tire inventory carrying cost. Pullman Tire has sufficient regular production capacity to produce up to 700 tires each month, and it can produce up to 50 more tires each month using overtime. The subcontracting availability from an alternative supplier is 150 in January and February and 130 in March. Customers will demand 650 tires in January, 1,000 in February, and 890 in March (all demand must be satisfied on time; i.e., no backorders are allowed). The firm begins with 100 tires and wants to have no tires left in inventory at the end of March. Formulate a linear program for this problem, and determine the cheapest tire production plan after solving the problem in Excel.

3-52. The Marketing Club on campus sells three popular mixed soda drinks on campus to raise funds. The drinks are simple mixed blends of pure flavors of grape, orange, and cherry soda. "Starburst" comprises 50% orange, 25% grape, and 25% cherry. "Morning Delight" comprises 75% orange and 25% grape. "Cherry Surprise" comprises 80% cherry, 10% orange, and 10% grape. Based on past demand, the club sets prices of its one-liter products at $2.75 for Starburst, $3.00 for Morning Delight, and $2.00 for Cherry Surprise. On any given sales day (football game days), the club can sell all that it produces, but the supplies are limited. The club receives the pure flavors (and one-liter bottles) free as a donation from a loyal alumnus, who provides 100 liters of grape, 150 liters of cherry, and 250 liters of orange soda before each football game.

(a) Determine the best product mix for the Marketing Club.

(b) Suppose that the loyal donor loves the Morning Delight beverage and wants more customers to try it. She requests that the price for Morning Delight be reduced to $2.40 to entice even higher demand for that flavor. Resolve the Excel model. What happened? Will the Marketing Club sell more liters of Morning Delight? And are any donations now going to waste?

3-53. Some countries impose "local content rules" on products manufactured in their country to try to stimulate the use of local suppliers and presumably to help the local economy. Global Industries, Inc., produces in a country imposing a local content rule stating that 60% of the value of all purchases must be procured from local suppliers. The firm wishes to minimize purchasing costs while satisfying the local content requirement. Demand for the final product is 1,000 units. For each of its five components, Global Industries has identified the cheapest local supplier and cheapest supplier from outside the country. Assume that the quality level between competing suppliers is similar so that price is the only meaningful difference. The following table provides the purchasing cost for each component, along with the amount of each component used in each final product (e.g., a car would have 4 tires). Determine the least-cost purchasing plan. Does it match your intuition?

Component	Cost Per Unit from Local Supplier	Cost Per Unit from Overseas Supplier	Number of Components Used In Each Final Product
A	$0.30	$0.25	20
B	4.00	2.20	2
C	6.20	5.30	4
D	95.00	80.00	1
E	52.00	45.50	1

3-54. Consider the Hong Kong Bank labor planning problem from Section 3.5. Would the solution improve if it were possible to bring in part-time workers for just 3-hour shifts instead of 4-hour shifts? Modify the model and resolve the problem to find out.

3-55. Consider the Management Science Associates marketing research problem from Section 3.3 (Figure 3.5). Suppose that the client has imposed two additional constraints: (1) the same number of people who are between 31 and 50 years of age should be surveyed from states that border Mexico as the number surveyed in that age group from states that do not, and (2) from states that border Mexico, the number of people who are 30 years of age or younger that are surveyed should be at least as large as the number of people who are 51 years of age or over. Modify the model and resolve the problem. What is the new solution?

Chapter 4
Linear Programming Sensitivity Analysis

How often do you ponder "what-if" questions? If I get that bonus, what will I spend the money on? If she answers, "Yes!," to my marriage proposal, how will my life change? If my favorite team wins the Super Bowl, how will I celebrate? If I lose my job, how will I stay in my house?

Professional modelers refer to what-if analysis as sensitivity analysis. Organizations ask the same sorts of questions. Managers don't just want to know the best decisions under the current conditions, but they also want to know what will happen if conditions change. What if costs rise? What if demand falls? What if a new competitor joins our market? What if our estimates were too high? What if tax rates change? What if we purchase a new machine? Sensitivity analysis of a linear programming (LP) solution can help to answer such questions.

After describing the motivation for sensitivity analysis, we illustrate how to use graphical methods to perform sensitivity analysis on a two-variable LP. As we saw in Chapter 2, analyzing small problems via the graphical method provides useful insights into the properties of all LP models, regardless of size. In this chapter, the graphical method helps explain how computers determine what happens when objective function coefficients change and when right-hand-side values of constraints change. Fortunately, optimization software, including Excel's Solver, provide these calculations for us, and this chapter explains how to interpret those sensitivity reports. We provide examples for both a maximization and a minimization problem in Q&A format to illustrate potential uses of sensitivity analysis in practice. While sensitivity reports typically apply only for one change at a time, we explain how managers can sometimes invoke the *100% rule* to consider simultaneous changes. We further provide a special section that illustrates how to use sensitivity reports to "price out new variables" to consider, for example, whether or not to introduce a new product into the product line.

Chapter Objectives
After completing this chapter, you will be able to:
1. Understand, using graphs, the impact of changes in objective function coefficients, right-hand-side values, and constraint coefficients on the optimal solution of a linear programming problem.
2. Generate Answer and Sensitivity Reports using Excel's Solver.
3. Interpret all parameters of these reports for maximization and minimization problems.
4. Analyze the impact of simultaneous changes in input data values using the 100% rule.
5. Analyze the impact of the addition of a new variable using the pricing-out strategy.

4.1 Importance of Sensitivity Analysis

Optimal solutions to linear programming (LP) problems have thus far been found under what are called *deterministic* assumptions. This means that we assume complete certainty in the data and relationships of a problem—namely, prices are fixed, resources' availabilities are known, production time needed to make a unit are exactly set, and so on. That is, we assume that all the coefficients (constants) in the objective function and each of the constraints are fixed and do not change. But in most real-world situations, conditions are dynamic and changing. This could mean, for example, that just as we determine the optimal solution to an LP model that has the profit contribution for a given product set at $10 per unit, we find out that the profit contribution has changed to $9 per unit. What does this change mean for our solution? Is it no longer optimal?

In practice, such changes to input data values typically occur for two reasons. First, the value may have been estimated incorrectly. For example, a firm may realize that it has overestimated the selling price by $1, resulting in an incorrect profit contribution of $10 per unit, rather than $9 per unit. Or it may determine during a production run that it has only 175 pumps in inventory, rather than 200, as specified in the LP model. Second, management is often interested in getting quick answers to a series of what-if questions. For example, what if the profit contribution of a product decreases by 10%? What if less money is available for advertising? What if workers can each stay one hour longer every day at 1.5-times pay to provide increased production capacity? What if new technology will allow a product to be wired in one-third the time it used to take?

Why Do We Need Sensitivity Analysis?

Sensitivity analysis, also known as *postoptimality analysis*, is a procedure that allows us to answer questions such as those posed above, using the current optimal solution itself, without having to resolve the LP model each time. Before we discuss this topic in more detail, let us first address a question that may arise commonly: Why do we need to study sensitivity analysis when we can use the computer to make the necessary changes to the model and quickly solve it again? The answer is as follows.

If, in fact, we know that a change in an input data value is definite (e.g., we know *with certainty* that the profit contribution has decreased from $10 to $9 per unit), the easiest and logical course of action is to do just what the question suggests. That is, we should simply change the input data value in the formulation and solve the model again. Given the ease with which most real-world models can be solved using computers today, this approach should not be too difficult or time-consuming. Clearly, this same approach can be used even if we are making *definite* changes to more than one input data value at the same time.

In contrast, what if changes in input data values are just hypothetical, such as in the various what-if scenarios listed earlier? For example, assume we are just considering lowering the selling price of a product but have not yet decided to what level it should be lowered. If we are considering 10 different selling price values, changing the input data value and resolving the LP model for every proposed value results in 10 separate models. If we expand this argument to consider 10 selling price levels each for two different products, we now have 100 (=10×10) LP models to solve. Clearly, this approach (i.e., changing and resolving the LP model) quickly becomes impractical when we have many input data values in a model and we are considering what-if multiple changes in each of their values.

In such situations, the preferred approach is to formulate and solve a *single* LP model with a given set of input data values. However, after solving this model, we conduct a sensitivity analysis of the optimal solution to see just how *sensitive* it is to changes in each of these input data values. That is, for each input data value, we attempt to determine a *range of values* within which the current optimal solution will remain optimal. For example, if the current selling price for a product is $10 per unit, we identify the extent to which this value can change (both on the higher side and on the lower side) without affecting the optimality of the current solution. We can obtain this information, as we shall see, from the current solution itself without resolving the LP model each time.

As we did previously with LP formulations and solutions, we first study LP sensitivity analysis using a two-variable product mix problem. We recognize here again that we are unlikely to encounter two-variable problems in real-world situations. Nevertheless, a big advantage of studying such models is that we can demonstrate the concepts of sensitivity analysis using a graphical approach. This experience will be invaluable in helping understand the various issues in sensitivity analysis even for larger problems. For these larger problems, because we cannot view them graphically, we will rely on Excel's Solver to generate a Sensitivity Report. We discuss three separate Solver sensitivity reports in this chapter: (1) a report for the two-variable product mix problem that we also first analyze graphically, (2) a report for a larger problem (i.e., more than two variables) with a maximization objective function, and (3) a report for a larger problem with a minimization objective function. The two larger problems allow us to illustrate fully the various types of information we can obtain by using sensitivity analysis.

We will initially study sensitivity analysis by varying only one input data value at a time. Later, we will expand our discussion to include simultaneous changes in several input data values.

4.2 Sensitivity Analysis Using Graphs

To analyze LP sensitivity analysis by using graphs, let us revisit the Flair Furniture problem that we first used in Chapter 2 to introduce LP formulation and solution. Our motivation for using the same problem here is the hope that you are already familiar with that problem and its graphical solution. Nevertheless, you might want to briefly review sections 2.3 and 2.4 in Chapter 2 before proceeding further.

Recall that the Flair Furniture Company problem involved two products: tables and chairs. The constraints dealt with the hours available in the carpentry and painting departments, production limits on chairs, and the minimum production level on tables. If we let T denote the number of tables to make and C denote the number of chairs to make, we can formulate the following LP problem to determine the best product mix:

$$\text{Maximize profit} = \$7T + \$5C$$

subject to the constraints

$$\begin{aligned}
3T + 4C &\leq 2{,}400 & \text{(carpentry time)} \\
2T + 1C &\leq 1{,}000 & \text{(painting time)} \\
C &\leq 450 & \text{(maximum chairs allowed)} \\
T &\geq 100 & \text{(minimum tables required)} \\
T, C &\geq 0 & \text{(nonnegativity)}
\end{aligned}$$

The solution to this problem is illustrated graphically in Figure 4.1 (which is essentially the same information as in Figure 2.6). Recall from Chapter 2 that we can use the level profit lines method to identify the optimal corner point solution. (The level profit line for a profit value of $2,800 is shown in Figure 4.1.) It is easy to see that Flair's optimal solution is at corner point ④. At this corner point, the optimal solution is to produce 320 tables and 360 chairs, for a profit of $4,040.

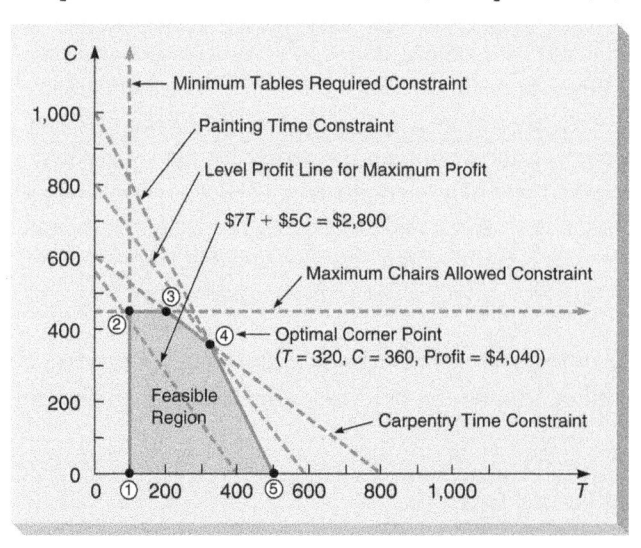

Figure 4.1: Optimal Corner Point Solution for Flair Furniture

Types of Sensitivity Analysis
In the preceding LP formulation, note that there are three types of input parameter values:
1. *Objective function coefficient (OFC).* The OFCs are the coefficients for the decision variables in the objective function (such as the $7 and $5 for T and C, respectively, in Flair's model). In many business-oriented LP models, OFCs typically represent unit profits or costs, and they are measured in monetary units such as dollars, euros, and rupees.

    Are OFCs likely to have any uncertainty in their values? Clearly, the answer is yes because in many real-world situations, selling and cost prices are seldom static or fixed. For this reason, we will study how the optimal solution may be affected by changes in OFC values.

2. *Right-hand-side (RHS) value of a constraint.* The RHS values are constants, such as the 2,400 and 1,000 in Flair's model, that typically appear on the RHS of a constraint (i.e., to the right of the equality or inequality sign). For $\leq$ constraints, they typically represent the amount available of a resource, and for $\geq$ constraints, they typically represent the minimum level of satisfaction needed.

    Are these types of input data subject to uncertainty in practice? Here again, the answer is a clear yes. In many practical situations, companies may find that their resource availability has changed due to, for example, miscounted inventory, broken-down machines, absent labor, additional overtime availability, etc. For this reason, we will study how the optimal solution may be affected by changes in RHS values.

3. *Constraint coefficient.* The constraint coefficients are the coefficients for the decision variables in a model's constraints (such as the 3 and 4 in the carpentry constraint in Flair's model). In many problems, these represent design issues related to the decision variables. For example, needing three hours of carpentry per table is a product design issue that has probably been specified by design engineers.

    Although we could think of specific situations where these types of input parameters also could be subject to uncertainty in their values, such changes are less likely here than in OFC and RHS values. For this reason, we do not usually study the impact of changes in constraint coefficient values on the optimal solution.

Most computer-based LP software packages, including Excel's Solver, provide sensitivity reports only for analyzing the effect of changes in OFC and RHS values.

Impact of Changes in an Objective Function Coefficient
When the value of an OFC changes, the feasible solution region remains the same (because it depends only on the constraints). That is, we have the same set of corner points, and their locations do not change. All that changes is the slope of the level profit (or cost) line.

Let us consider the impact of changes in the profit contribution of tables (*T*). First, what if the demand for tables becomes so high that the profit contribution can be raised from $7 to $8 per table? Is corner point ④ still the optimal solution? The answer is definitely yes, as shown in Figure 4.2. However, even though the decision variable values did not change, the new optimal objective function value (i.e., the profit) does change and increases to $4,360 (= \$8 \times 320 + \$5 \times 360)$.

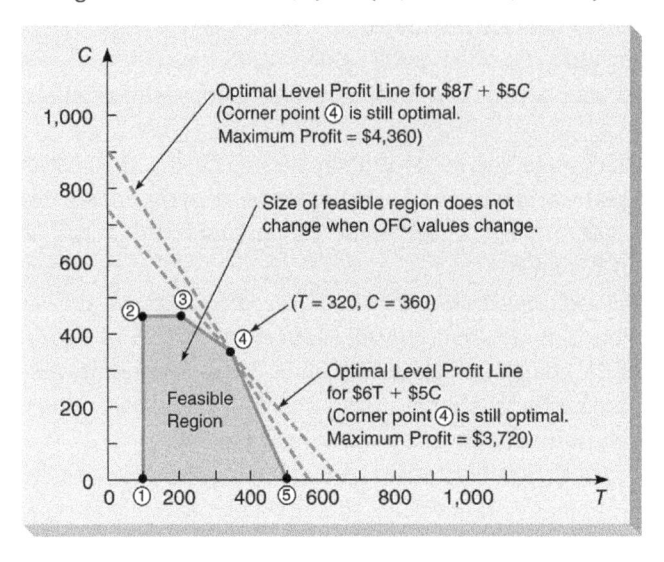

Figure 4.2: Small Changes in Profit Contribution of Tables

In a similar fashion, let us analyze what happens if the demand for tables forces us to reduce the profit contribution from $7 to $6 per table. Here again, we see from the level profit line in Figure 4.2 that corner point ④ continues to remain the optimal solution, and the production plan does not change. The optimal profit, however, is now only $3,720 (= \$6 \times 320 + \$5 \times 360)$.

On the other hand, what if a table's profit contribution can be raised all the way to $11 per table? In such a case, the level profit line, shown in Figure 4.3, indicates that the optimal solution is now at corner point ⑤, instead of at corner point ④. The new solution is to make 500 tables and 0 chairs, for a profit of $5,500. That is, tables are now so profitable compared with chairs that we should devote all our resources to making only tables.

Likewise, what if a table's profit contribution was highly overestimated and should have been only $3 per table? In this case also, the slope of the level profit line changes enough to cause a new corner point ③ to become optimal (as shown in Figure 4.3). That is, tables have now become relatively unattractive compared with chairs, and so we will make fewer tables and more chairs. In fact, the only reason we even make any tables in this case is because we are explicitly constrained in the problem from making more than 450 chairs (we also had to make at least 100 tables). At corner point ③, the solution is to make 200 tables and 450 chairs, for a profit of $2,850 (= \$3 \times 200 + \$5 \times 450)$.

[Figure 4.3 graph: Feasible region with corner points ①, ②, ③, ④, ⑤ on T-C axes. Labels: "Optimal Level Profit Line for $11T + $5C (Corner point ⑤ is optimal. Maximum Profit = $5,500)" and "Optimal Level Profit Line for $3T + $5C (Corner point ③ is optimal. Maximum Profit = $2,850)"]

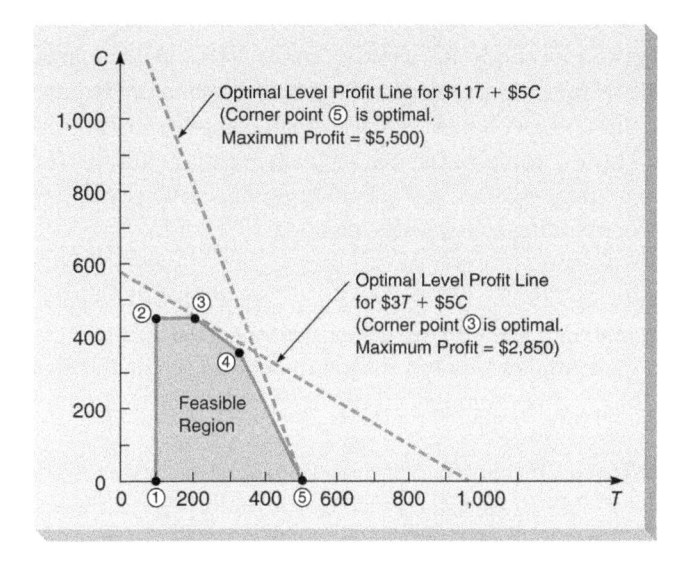

Figure 4.3: Larger Changes in Profit Contribution of Tables

From the preceding discussion regarding the OFC for a table, it is apparent that there is a range of possible values for this OFC for which the *current* optimal corner point solution remains optimal. Any change in the OFC value beyond this range (either on the higher end or the lower end) causes a *new* corner point to become the optimal solution. Clearly, we can repeat the same discussion with regard to the OFC for chairs.

It is algebraically possible to use the graphical solution procedure to determine the allowable range for each OFC within which the current optimal solution remains optimal. However, we use the information provided in the Solver Sensitivity Report to discuss this issue further in the next section.

Again, whenever changes occur in OFC values, the feasible region of the problem (which depends only on the constraints) does not change. Therefore, there is no change in the physical location of each corner point. To summarize, only two things can occur from a change in an OFC: (1) If the current optimal corner point continues to remain optimal, the decision variable values do not change, even though the objective function value may change; and (2) if the current corner point is no longer optimal, the values of the decision variables change, as does the objective function value.

Impact of Changes in a Constraint's Right-Hand-Side Value

Unlike changes in OFC values, a change in the RHS value of a nonredundant constraint results in a change in the size of the feasible region.[1] Hence, one or more corner

---

[1] Recall from section 2.6 in Chapter 2 that a *redundant* constraint does not affect the feasible region in any way.

points may physically shift to new locations. Recall from Chapter 2 that at the optimal solution, constraints can either be binding or nonbinding. Binding constraints intersect at the optimal corner point and are, hence, exactly satisfied at the optimal solution. Nonbinding constraints have a non-zero slack (for $\leq$ constraints) or surplus (for $\geq$ constraints) value at the optimal solution. Let us analyze impacts of changes in RHS values for binding and nonbinding constraints separately.

Impact of Change in RHS Value of a Binding Constraint From Figure 4.1, we know that the two binding constraints in Flair's problem are the carpentry and painting hours. Let us analyze, for example, potential changes in the painting hours available. Flair currently projects an availability of 1,000 hours, all of which will be needed by the current production plan.

Let us first analyze the impact if this value is increased. What happens if, for example, the painting time availability can be increased by 300 hours (to 1,300 hours) by adding an extra painter? Figure 4.4 shows the revised graph for Flair's problem under this scenario.

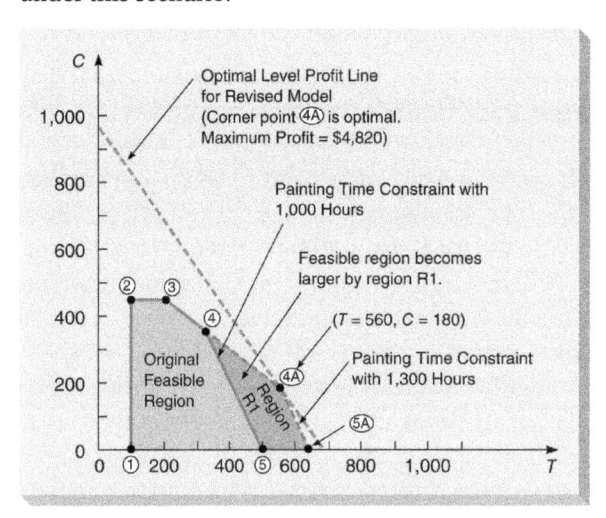

Figure 4.4: Increase in Availability of Painting Hours to 1,300 Hours

The first point to note is that because the painting constraint is a binding $\leq$ constraint, any increase in its RHS value causes the feasible region to become larger, as shown by the region marked R1 in Figure 4.4. As a consequence of this increase in the feasible region's size, the locations of corner points ④ and ⑤ shift to new locations—④A and ⑤A, respectively. However, the level profit lines approach (shown in Figure 4.4) indicates that the intersection of the carpentry and painting constraints (i.e., corner point ④A) is still the optimal solution. That is, the "same" corner point (in the sense that the same two constraints intersect at this point) is still optimal. But it now has a new location and, hence, there are new values for T, C, and profit. The values at corner point ④A can be computed to be $T = 560$ and $C = 180$, for a profit of $4,820. This implies that if Flair can obtain an additional 300 hours of painting time, it can increase profit by $780 (from $4,040 to $4,820) by revising the production plan. This profit increase of $780 for 300 additional hours of painting time translates to a profit increase of $2.60 per additional hour of painting time.

Next, let us analyze the impact if the painting time availability is decreased. What happens if, for example, this value is only 900 hours instead of 1,000 hours? The revised graph, shown in Figure 4.5, indicates that this decrease in the RHS value of a binding ≤ constraint shrinks the size of the feasible region (as shown by the region marked R2 in Figure 4.5). Here again, the locations of corner points ④ and ⑤ have shifted to new locations, ④B and ⑤B, respectively. However, as before, the level profit lines approach indicates that the "same" corner point (i.e., intersection of the carpentry and painting constraints, point ④B) is still optimal. The values of the decision variables and the resulting profit at corner point ④B can be computed to be $T = 240$ and $C = 420$, for a profit of $3,780. That is, the loss of 100 hours of painting time causes Flair to lose $260 in profit (from $4,040 to $3,780). This translates to a decrease in profit of $2.60 per hour of painting time lost.

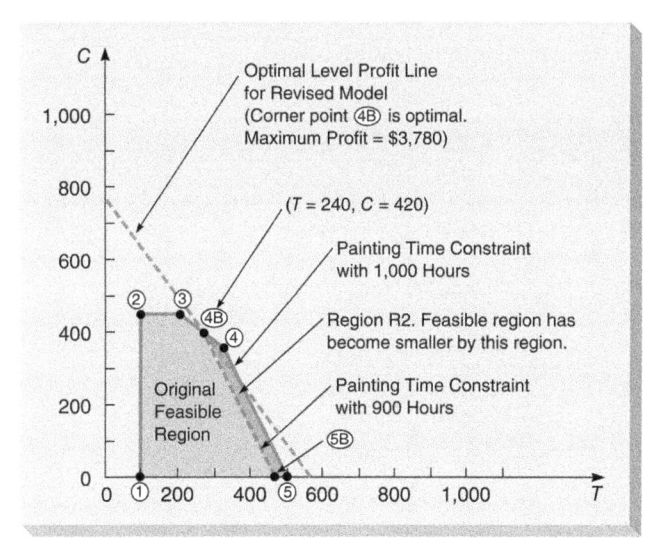

Figure 4.5: Decrease in Availability of Painting Hours to 900 Hours

Observe that the profit increases by $2.60 per each additional hour of painting time gained, and it decreases by the *same* $2.60 per each hour of painting time lost from the current level. This value, known as the shadow price, is an important concept in LP models. The shadow price of a constraint can be defined as the change in the optimal objective function value for a one-unit increase in the RHS value of that constraint. In the case of painting time, the shadow price is $2.60; this implies that each hour of painting time (with respect to the current availability) affects Flair's profit by

$2.60. Because painting time is a binding ≤ constraint, each additional hour obtained increases profit by $2.60, while each hour lost decreases profit by $2.60.

Is this shadow price of $2.60 valid for any level of change in the painting time availability? That is, for example, can Flair keep obtaining additional painting time and expect its profit to keep increasing endlessly by $2.60 for each hour obtained? Clearly, this cannot be true, and we illustrate the reason for this in the following section.

Validity Range for the Shadow Price Consider, for example, what happens if Flair can increase the painting time availability even further, to 1,700 hours. Under this scenario, as shown in Figure 4.6, the feasible region increases by the region marked R3. However, due to the presence of the nonnegativity constraint $C \geq 0$, the corner point defined by the intersection of the carpentry and painting constraints is no longer feasible. In fact, the painting constraint has now become a redundant constraint. Obviously, in such a case, the optimal solution has shifted to a new corner point. The level profit lines approach indicates that the optimal solution is now at corner point ⑤Ⓒ ($T = 800$, $C = 0$, profit = 5,600). Note that this translates to a profit increase of $1,560 (= $5,600 − $4,040) for 700 additional hours, or $2.23 per hour, which is different from the shadow price of $2.60. That is, the shadow price of $2.60 is not valid for an increase of 700 hours in the painting time availability.

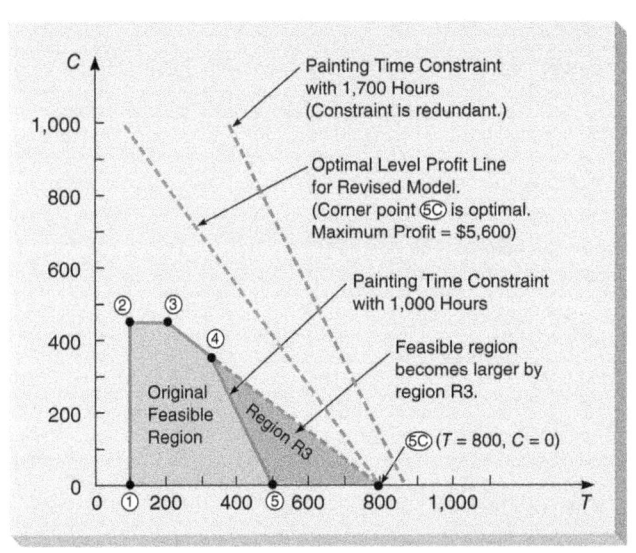

Figure 4.6: Increase in Availability of Painting Hours to 1,700 Hours

What happens if the painting time availability is decreased all the way down to 700 hours? Here again, as shown in Figure 4.7, the intersection point of the carpentry and painting constraints is no longer even feasible. The carpentry constraint is now redundant, and the optimal solution has switched to a new corner point given by corner point ③A ($T = 125, C = 450$, profit = $3,125). This translates to a profit decrease of $915 (= $4,040 − $3,125) for a decrease of 300 hours, or $3.05 per hour, which is again different from the shadow price of $2.60. That is, the shadow price of $2.60 is not valid for a decrease of 300 hours in the painting time availability.

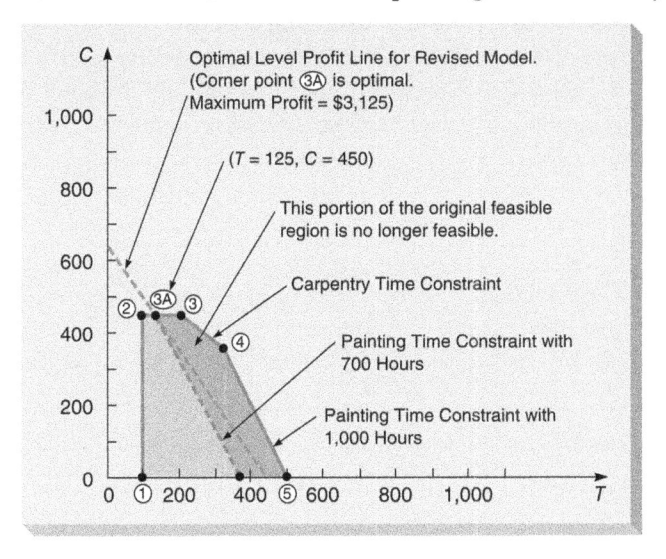

Figure 4.7: Decrease in Availability of Painting Hours to 700 Hours

The preceding discussion based on Figures 4.4 to 4.7 shows that for a certain range of change in the RHS value of a binding constraint, the "same" corner point will continue to remain optimal. That is, the constraints that are currently binding at the optimal solution will continue to remain the binding constraints. The location of this optimal corner point will, however, change, depending on the change in the RHS value. In fact, it turns out that as long as this corner point exists in the feasible region, it will continue to remain optimal. In Flair's case, this means that the corner point where the carpentry and painting constraints intersect will remain the optimal solution *as long as it exists in the feasible region*. Also, the shadow price of $2.60 measures the impact on profit for a unit change in painting time availability as long as this corner point continues to exist in the feasible region. Once this RHS value changes to such an extent that the current binding constraints no longer intersect in the feasible region, the shadow price of $2.60 is no longer valid and changes to a different value. It is algebraically possible to use the graphical solution to determine the RHS range within which the current optimal corner point continues to exist, albeit at a new location. We will, however, use the information provided in the Solver Sensitivity Report to further discuss this issue in a subsequent section.

A similar analysis can be conducted with the RHS value for the other binding constraint in Flair's example—the carpentry constraint.

Impact of Changes in RHS Value of a Nonbinding Constraint Let us now consider a nonbinding constraint such as the production limit on chairs ($C \leq 450$). As shown in Figure 4.8, the gap between corner point ④ and the chairs constraint represents the amount of slack in this nonbinding constraint. At the present solution, the slack is $90 (= 450 - 360)$. What happens now if the marketing department allows more chairs to be produced (i.e., the 450 limit is increased)? As we can see in Figure 4.8, such a change serves only to increase the slack in this constraint and does not affect the optimality of corner point ④ in any way. How far can we raise the 450 limit? Clearly, the answer is infinity.

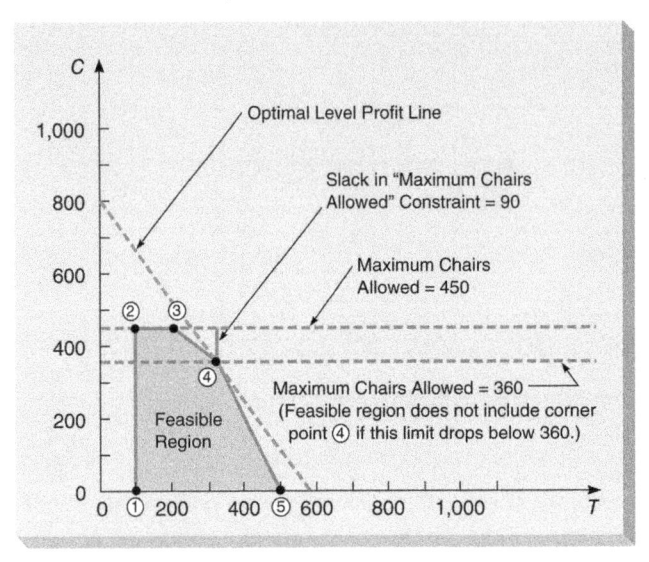

Figure 4.8: Change in RHS Value of a Nonbinding Constraint

Now consider the case where the marketing department wants to make this production limit even more restrictive (i.e., the 450 limit is decreased). As long as we are permitted to make at least 360 chairs, Figure 4.8 indicates that corner point ④ is feasible and still optimal. That is, as long as the change in the RHS value for the chairs constraint is within the slack of 90 units, the current optimal corner point continues to exist and remains optimal. However, if the chairs production limit is reduced below 360, corner point ④ is no longer feasible, and a new corner point becomes optimal. A similar analysis can be conducted with the other nonbinding constraints in the model (i.e., $T \geq 100$).

The preceding discussion illustrates that for nonbinding constraints, the allowable change limit on one side is infinity. On the opposite side, the allowable change limit equals the slack (or surplus).

4.3 Sensitivity Analysis Using Solver Reports

Let us consider Flair Furniture's LP model again. Figure 4.9 shows the Excel layout and Solver entries for this model. Recall that we saw the same information in Chapter 2. Cells B5 and C5 are the entries in the By Changing Variable Cells box and denote the optimal quantities of tables and chairs to make, respectively. Cell D6 is the entry in the Set Objective box and denotes the profit. Cells D8 to D11 contain the formulas for the left-hand sides of each of the four constraints.

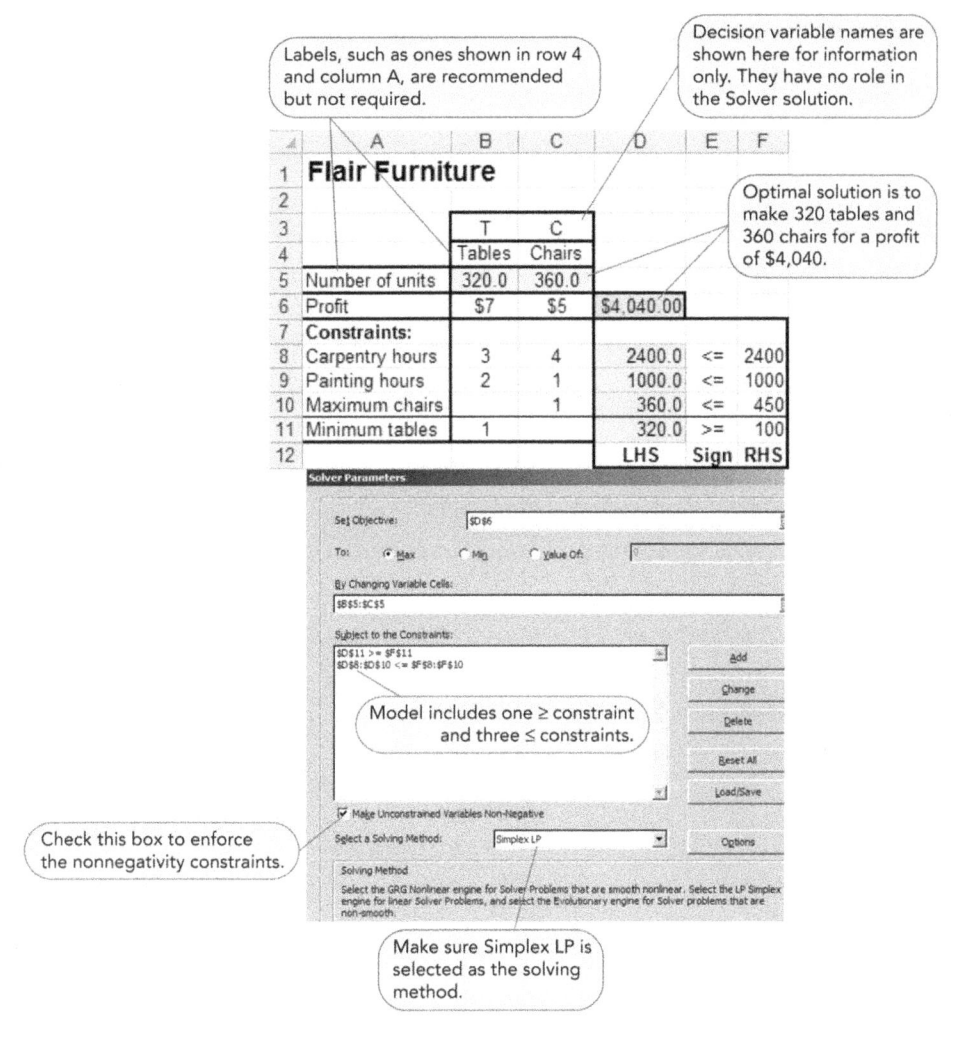

Figure 4.9: Excel Layout and Solver Entries for Flair Furniture

File: Figure 4.9.xlsx, Sheet: Figure 4.9

EXCEL NOTES

- The Companion Website for this book, at *degruyter.com/view/product/486941*, contains the Excel file for each problem in the examples discussed here. The relevant file/sheet name is shown below the title of the corresponding figure in this book.

- In each of our Excel layouts, for clarity, changing variable cells are shaded yellow, the objective cell is shaded green, and cells denoting left-hand-side (LHS) formulas of constraints are shaded blue. If the RHS of a constraint also includes a formula, that cell is also shaded blue.

- Also, to make the equivalence of the *written* formulation and the Excel layout clear, our Excel layouts show the decision variable names used in the written formulation of the model. Note that these names have no role in using Solver to solve the model.

Solver Reports

Before solving the LP model, we need to ensure that Simplex LP has been selected in the Select a Solving Method box in the Solver Parameters window to solve the problem (see Figure 4.9). If a different method is selected, Solver does not solve the model as a linear program, and the resulting Sensitivity Report will look very different from the report we discuss here. Also, recall that we must check the Make Unconstrained Variables Non-Negative option to enforce the nonnegativity constraints.

When Solver finds the optimal solution for a problem, the Solver Results window provides options to obtain three reports: Answer, Sensitivity, and Limits. Note that to obtain the desired reports, we must select them *before* we click OK. In our case, we select Answer and Sensitivity from the available choices in the box labeled Reports, and then we click OK (see Figure 4.10). The Limits Report is relatively less useful, and we therefore do not discuss it here.

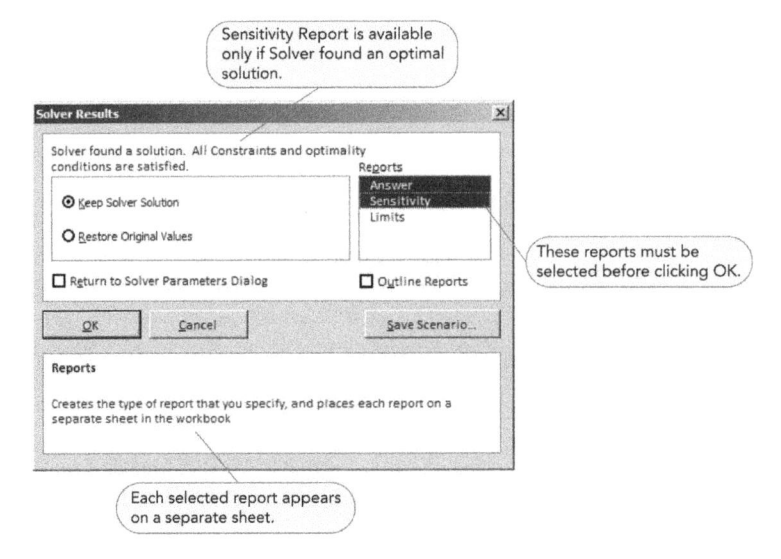

Figure 4.10: Solver Results Window

We discussed the Answer Report extensively in section 2.7 of Chapter 2 and urge you to read that section again now. Recall that this report provides essentially the same information as the original Excel layout (such as in Figure 4.9) but in a more descriptive manner.

We now turn our attention to the information in the Sensitivity Report. Before we do so, it is important to note once again that while using the information in this report to answer what-if questions, we assume that we are considering a change to only a *single* input data value. Later, in section 4.5, we will expand our discussion to include simultaneous changes in several input data values.

Sensitivity Report

The Sensitivity Report for the Flair Furniture example is shown in Figure 4.11. We have added grid lines to this report to make it clearer and have also formatted all values to display a consistent number of decimal points. The Sensitivity Report has two distinct tables, titled Variable Cells and Constraints. These tables permit us to answer several what-if questions regarding the problem solution.

Microsoft Excel 14.0 Sensitivity Report
Worksheet: [Figure 4.9.xlsx]Flair Furniture

Variable Cells

Cell	Name	Final Value	Reduced Cost	Objective Coefficient	Allowable Increase	Allowable Decrease
$B$5	Number of units Tables	320.00	0.00	7.00	3.00	3.25
$C$5	Number of units Chairs	360.00	0.00	5.00	4.33	1.50

Constraints

Cell	Name	Final Value	Shadow Price	Constraint R.H. Side	Allowable Increase	Allowable Decrease
$D$8	Carpentry hours	2400.00	0.60	2400.00	225.00	900.00
$D$9	Painting hours	1000.00	2.60	1000.00	600.00	150.00
$D$10	Maximum chairs	360.00	0.00	450.00	1E+30	90.00
$D$11	Minimum tables	320.00	0.00	100.00	220.00	1E+30

- Two components of the Sensitivity Report
- The shadow prices are valid for this range of change in the RHS values.
- Each additional hour of painting time will increase profit by $2.60.
- The shadow price for a nonbinding constraint is zero.
- Solver's way of showing infinity

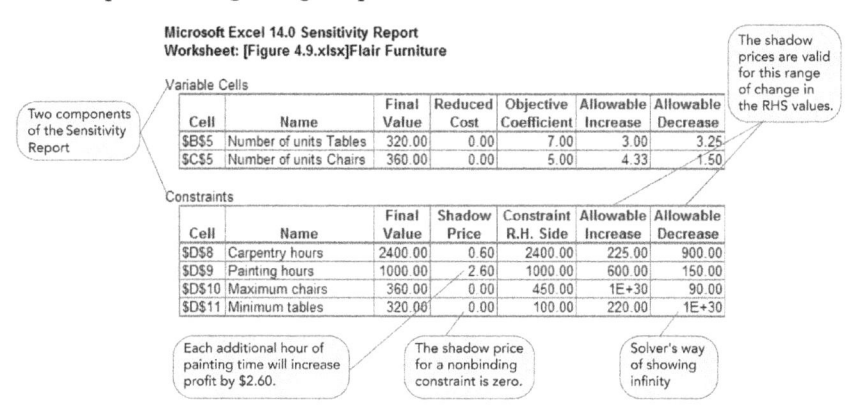

Figure 4.11: Solver Sensitivity Report for Flair Furniture

File: Figure 4.9.xlsx, Sheet: Figure 4.11

EXCEL NOTE

Solver does a rather poor job of formatting the Sensitivity Report. There is no consistency in the number of decimal points shown. While some values are displayed with no decimal points, others are displayed with many decimal points. This could sometimes cause a value such as 0.35 to be displayed (and erroneously interpreted) as 0. For this reason, we urge you to format the Sensitivity Report as needed to display a consistent number of decimal points.

The Variable Cells table presents information regarding the impact of changes to the OFCs (i.e., unit profits of $7 and $5) on the optimal solution. The Constraints table presents information related to the impact of changes in constraint RHS values (such as the 2,400 and 1,000 availabilities in carpentry and painting times, respectively) on the optimal solution. Although different LP software packages may format and present these tables differently, the programs all provide essentially the same information.

Impact of Changes in a Constraint's RHS Value

Let us first discuss the impact on the optimal solution of a change in the RHS value of a constraint. As with the graph-based analysis earlier, we study this issue separately for binding and nonbinding constraints.

Impact of Changes in the RHS Value of a Binding Constraint Recall from the graph-based analysis in section 4.2 that if the RHS value of a binding constraint changes, the size of the feasible region also changes. If the change causes the feasible region to *increase* in size, the optimal objective function value could potentially improve. In contrast, if the change causes the feasible region to *decrease* in size, the optimal objective function value could potentially worsen. The magnitude of this change in the objective function value is given by the shadow price of the constraint, provided that the RHS change is within a certain range. In the Solver Sensitivity Report, this information is shown in the Constraints table in Figure 4.11.

Recall from section 4.2 that the shadow price can be defined as the change in the optimal objective function value for a one-unit increase in the RHS value of a constraint. In Figure 4.11, the entry labeled Shadow Price for the painting constraint shows a value of $2.60. This means that for each *additional* hour of painting time that Flair can obtain, its total profit changes by $2.60. What is the direction of this change? In this specific case, the change is an increase in profit because the additional painting time causes the feasible region to become larger and, hence, the solution to improve.

Validity Range for the Shadow Price For what level of increase in the RHS value of the painting constraint is the shadow price of $2.60 valid? Once again, recall from our discussion in section 4.2 that there is a specific range of possible values for the RHS value of a binding constraint for which the current optimal corner point (i.e., the intersection point of the current binding constraints) exists, even if its actual location has changed. Increasing or decreasing the RHS value beyond this range causes this corner point to be no longer feasible and causes a new corner point to become the optimal solution.

The information to compute the upper and lower limits of this range is given by the entries labeled Allowable Increase and Allowable Decrease in the Sensitivity Report. In Flair's case, these values show that the shadow price of $2.60 for painting time availability is valid for an increase of up to 600 hours from the current value and a decrease of up to 150 hours. That is, the painting time available can range from a low of 850 (=1,000 − 150) to a high of 1,600 (=1,000 + 600) for the shadow price of $2.60 to be valid. Note that the Allowable Decrease value implies that for each hour of painting time that Flair loses (up to 150 hours), its profit decreases by $2.60. Likewise, the Allowable Increase value implies that for each hour of painting time that Flair gains (up to 600 hours), its profit increases by $2.60.

The preceding discussion implies that if Flair can obtain an additional 300 hours of painting time, its profit will increase by $300 \times \$2.60 = \$780$, to $4,820. In contrast, if it loses 100 hours of painting time, its profit will decrease by $100 \times \$2.60 = \$260$, to $3,780. If the painting time availability increases by more than 600 hours (for example, increases by 700 hours, to 1,700 hours) or decreases by more than 150 hours (for example, decreases by 300 hours, to 700 hours) the current corner point is no longer feasible, and the solution has switched to a new corner point. Recall that we made these same observations earlier graphically using Figures 4.4 to 4.7. Note that we cannot know the precise impact of a change beyond the Allowable Increase or Allowable Decrease by examining the Sensitivity Report. In that situation, we would need to resolve the Excel model.

For carpentry time, the shadow price is $0.60, with a validity range of $1,500 (=2,400-900)$ to $2,625 (=2,400+225)$ hours. This means for every hour of carpentry time in this range, Flair's profit changes by $0.60.

Impact of Changes in the RHS Value of a Nonbinding Constraint We note that Flair is planning to make only 360 chairs, even though it could make as many as 450. Clearly, Flair's solution would not be affected in any way if we increased this production limit. Therefore, the shadow price for the chairs limit constraint is zero.

In Figure 4.11, the allowable increase for this RHS value is shown to be infinity (displayed as 1E+30 in Solver). This is logical because any addition to the chair production limit will only cause the slack in this constraint to increase and will have no impact on profit. In contrast, once we decrease this limit by 90 chairs (our current slack), this constraint also becomes binding. Any further reduction in this limit will clearly have an adverse effect on profit. This is revealed by the value of 90 for the allowable decrease in the RHS of the chairs limit constraint. To evaluate the new optimal solution if the production limit decreases by more than 90 chairs from its current value, the problem would have to be solved again.

In a similar fashion, we note that Flair is planning to make 320 tables even though it is required to make only 100. Clearly, Flair's solution would not be affected in any way if we decreased this requirement from 100. This is indicated by the infinity in the Allowable Decrease column for this RHS. The current optimal solution will also not be affected as long as the increase in this RHS value is below 220. However, if Flair increases the RHS by more than 220 (and specifies that more than 320 tables must be made), the current optimal solution is no longer valid, and the model must be resolved to find the new solution.

Impact of Changes in an Objective Function Coefficient

Let us now focus on the information provided in the table titled Variable Cells. For your convenience, we repeat that part of Figure 4.11 here as Figure 4.12. Each row in the Variable Cells table contains information regarding a decision variable in the model.

Microsoft Excel 14.0 Sensitivity Report
Worksheet: [Figure 4.9.xlsx]Flair Furniture

Difference between marginal contribution and marginal worth of resources consumed.

Variable Cells

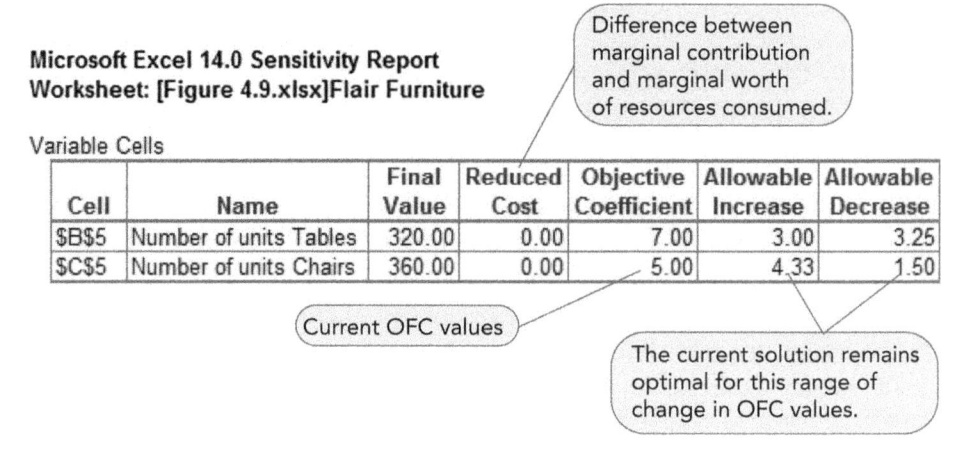

Cell	Name	Final Value	Reduced Cost	Objective Coefficient	Allowable Increase	Allowable Decrease
$B$5	Number of units Tables	320.00	0.00	7.00	3.00	3.25
$C$5	Number of units Chairs	360.00	0.00	5.00	4.33	1.50

Current OFC values

The current solution remains optimal for this range of change in OFC values.

Figure 4.12: Partial Solver Sensitivity Report for Flair Furniture

Allowable Ranges for OFCs In Figure 4.2, repeated here as Figure 4.13, we saw that as the unit profit contribution of either product changes, the slope of the isoprofit line changes. The size of the feasible region, however, remains the same. That is, the locations of the corner points do not change.

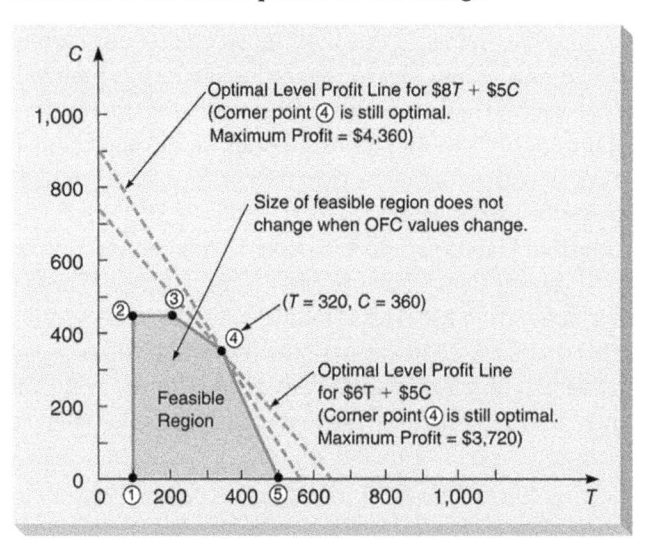

Figure 4.13: Changes in Profit Contribution of Tables Repeated

In the case of tables, as the unit profit increases from the current value of $7, the slope of the profit line in Figure 4.13 changes in a manner that makes corner point ⑤ more and more attractive. At some point, the unit profit of tables is so high as to make corner point ⑤ the optimal solution. On the other hand, as the unit profit decreases, the slope of the profit line changes in a manner that makes corner point ③ become more and more attractive. At some point, the unit profit of tables is so low as to make corner point ③ the optimal solution.

The limits to which the profit coefficient of tables can be changed without affecting the optimality of the current solution (corner point ④) is revealed by the values in the Allowable Increase and Allowable Decrease columns of the Sensitivity Report in Figure 4.12. In the case of tables, their profit contribution per table can range anywhere from a low of $3.75 (= $7 − $3.25) to a high of $10 (= $7 + $3), and the current production plan ($T = 320, C = 360$) will continue to remain optimal. The total profit will, of course, change, depending on the actual profit contribution per table. For example, if the profit contribution is $6 per table, the total profit is $3,720 (= $6 × 320 + $5 × 360). This is the same result we saw earlier in Figure 4.2. Any profit contribution below $3.75 or over $10 per table will result in a different corner point solution being optimal. Note that we cannot know what that new solution would be by examining the Sensitivity Report. In that situation, we would need to resolve the Excel model.

For chairs, the profit contribution per chair can range anywhere from a low of $3.50 (= $5 − $1.50) to a high of $9.33 (= $5 + $4.33), and the current production plan will continue to remain optimal. Here again, the total profit will depend on the actual profit contribution per chair. For example, if the profit contribution is $8 per chair, the total profit is $5,120 (= $7 × 320 + $8 × 360). Any profit contribution below $3.50 or over $9.33 per chair will result in a different corner point solution being optimal.

Reduced Cost The magnitude of the reduced cost tells us the minimum amount by which the OFC of a variable should change in order for that variable to have a non-zero value in the optimal solution. For Flair's example, because 320 tables and 360 chairs are made, both decision variables already have positive optimal values; hence, their respective reduced costs equal 0. In other words, neither product needs to become any more profitable to ensure that at least some units are produced because some units are already being made.

On the other hand, if corner point ⑤ had been optimal (as occurred in Figure 4.3 when the OFC for tables was increased to $11), then no chairs would have been produced, and the decision variable for chairs would have had a positive reduced cost. That reduced cost value would have told us how much more profitable chairs would have to be in order for the optimal corner point to move away from point ⑤ such that some chairs would be made in the optimal solution. We will see non-zero reduced costs appear in later examples in this chapter.

4.4 Sensitivity Analysis for a Larger Maximization Example

Now that we have explained some of the basic concepts in sensitivity analysis, let us consider a larger production mix example that will allow us to discuss some further issues.

Anderson Home Electronics Example

Anderson Home Electronics is considering the production of four inexpensive products for the low-end consumer market: an MP3 player, a satellite radio tuner, an LCD TV, and a Blu-ray DVD player. For the sake of this example, let us assume that the input for all products can be viewed in terms of just three resources: electronic components, non-electronic components, and assembly time. The composition of the four products in terms of these three inputs is shown in Table 4.1, along with the unit selling prices of the products.

Table 4.1: Data for Anderson Home Electronics

	MP3 Player	Satellite Radio Tuner	LCD TV	Blu-ray DVD Player	Supply
Electronic components	3	4	4	3	4,700
Non-electronic components	2	2	4	3	4,500
Assembly time (hours)	1	1	3	2	2,500
Selling price (per unit)	$70	$80	$150	$110	

Electronic components can be obtained at $7 per unit, non-electronic components can be obtained at $5 per unit, and assembly time costs $10 per hour. Each resource is available in limited quantities during the upcoming production cycle, as shown in Table 4.1. Anderson believes the market demand is strong enough that it can sell all the quantities it makes of each product.

By subtracting the total cost of making a product from its unit selling price, the profit contribution of each product can be easily calculated. For example, the profit contribution of each MP3 player is $29 (= selling price of $70 less the total cost of 3 × $7 + 2 × $5 + 1 × $10) Using similar calculations, see if you can confirm that the profit contribution of each satellite radio tuner is $32, each LCD TV is $72, and each Blu-ray DVD player is $54.

Let M, S, T, and B denote the number of MP3 players, satellite radio tuners, LCD TVs, and Blu-ray DVD players to make, respectively. We can then formulate the LP model for this problem as follows:

$$\text{Maximize profit} = \$29M + \$32S + \$72T + \$54B$$

subject to the constraints

$$3M + 4S + 4T + 3B \leq 4{,}700 \quad \text{(electronic components)}$$
$$2M + 2S + 4T + 3B \leq 4{,}500 \quad \text{(non-electronic components)}$$
$$M + S + 3T + 2B \leq 2{,}500 \quad \text{(assembly time, in hours)}$$
$$M, S, T, B \geq 0 \quad \text{(nonnegativity)}$$

Figures 4.14, 4.15, and 4.16 show the Excel layout and Solver entries, Answer Report, and Sensitivity Report, respectively, for Anderson's problem. The results show that Anderson should make 380 satellite radio tuners, 1,060 Blu-ray DVD players, and no MP3 players or LCD TVs, for a total profit of $69,400 in the upcoming production cycle.

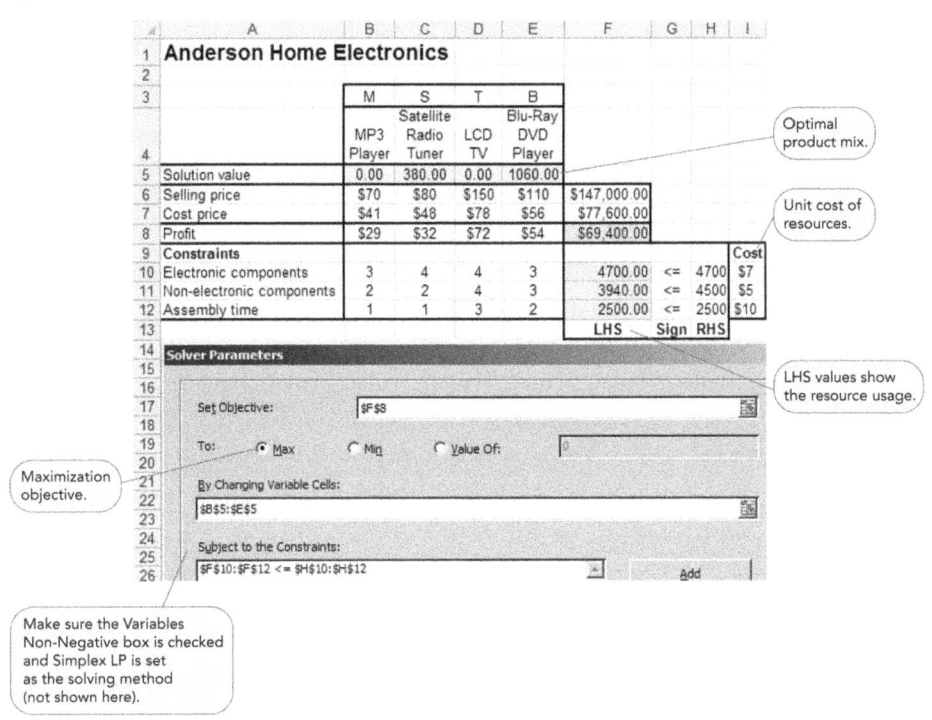

Figure 4.14: Excel Layout and Solver Entries for Anderson Home Electronics

File: Figure 4.14.xlsx, Sheet: Figure 4.14

Microsoft Excel 14.0 Answer Report
Worksheet: [Figure 4.14.xlsx]Anderson Home Electronics
Result: Solver found a solution. All Constraints and optimality conditions are satisfied.
Solver Engine
  Engine: Simplex LP
  Solution Time: 0.016 Seconds.
  Iterations: 3 Subproblems: 0
Solver Options
  Max Time 100 sec, Iterations 100, Precision 0.000001
  Max Subproblems 5000, Max Integer Sols 5000, Integer Tolerance 0.05%, Assume NonNegative

Objective Cell (Max)

Cell	Name	Original Value	Final Value
$F$8	Profit	$0.00	$69,400.00

← Optimal profit

Variable Cells

Cell	Name	Original Value	Final Value	Integer
$B$5	Solution value MP3 Player	0.00	0.00	Contin
$C$5	Solution value Satellite Radio Tuner	0.00	380.00	Contin
$D$5	Solution value LCD TV	0.00	0.00	Contin
$E$5	Solution value Blu-Ray DVD Player	0.00	1060.00	Contin

← Optimal solution does not include MP3 players or LCD TVs.

Constraints

Cell	Name	Cell Value	Formula	Status	Slack
$F$10	Electronic components	4700.00	$F$10<=$H$10	Binding	0.00
$F$11	Non-electronic components	3940.00	$F$11<=$H$11	Not Binding	560.00
$F$12	Assembly time	2500.00	$F$12<=$H$12	Binding	0.00

← There are 560 units of non-electronic components unused.

Figure 4.15: Solver Answer Report for Anderson Home Electronics

📊 File: Figure 4.14.xlsx, Sheet: Figure 4.15

Microsoft Excel 14.0 Sensitivity Report
Worksheet: [Figure 4.14.xlsx]Anderson Home Electronics

← For changes to OFC values in this range, current solution remains optimal.

Variable Cells

Cell	Name	Final Value	Reduced Cost	Objective Coefficient	Allowable Increase	Allowable Decrease
$B$5	Solution value MP3 Player	0.00	-1.00	29.00	1.00	1E+30
$C$5	Solution value Satellite Radio Tuner	380.00	0.00	32.00	40.00	1.67
$D$5	Solution value LCD TV	0.00	-8.00	72.00	8.00	1E+30
$E$5	Solution value Blu-Ray DVD Player	1060.00	0.00	54.00	10.00	5.00

← Allowable decrease is infinity since product is not attractive even at current OFC value.

Constraints

Cell	Name	Final Value	Shadow Price	Constraint R.H. Side	Allowable Increase	Allowable Decrease
$F$10	Electronic components	4700.00	2.00	4700.00	2800.00	950.00
$F$11	Non-electronic components	3940.00	0.00	4500.00	1E+30	560.00
$F$12	Assembly time	2500.00	24.00	2500.00	466.67	1325.00

← Since non-electronic components are nonbinding, shadow price is zero.

← The allowable increase is infinity since there are already 560 units of slack.

Figure 4.16: Solver Sensitivity Report for Anderson Home Electronics

📊 File: Figure 4.14.xlsx, Sheet: Figure 4.16

Some Questions We Want Answered

We now ask and answer several questions that will allow us to understand the shadow prices, reduced costs, and allowable ranges information in the Anderson Home Electronics Sensitivity Report. Each question is independent of the other questions and assumes that only the change mentioned in that question is being considered.

Q: What is the impact on profit of a change in the supply of non-electronic components?

A: The slack values in the Answer Report (Figure 4.15) indicate that of the potential supply of 4,500 units of non-electronic components, only 3,940 units are used, leaving 560 units unused. This implies that additional non-electronic components are of no value to Anderson in terms of contribution to profit; that is, the shadow price is zero.

This shadow price is valid for an unlimited (infinite) increase in the supply of non-electronic components. Further, Anderson would be willing to give up as many as 560 units of these components with no impact on profit. These values are shown in the Allowable Increase and Allowable Decrease columns in Figure 4.16, respectively, for the supply of non-electronic components.

Q: What is the impact on profit if we could increase the supply of electronic components by 400 units (to a total of 5,100 units)?

A: We first look at the Allowable Increase column for electronic components in Figure 4.16 to verify whether the current shadow price is valid for an increase of 400 units in this resource. Because the Allowable Increase column shows a value of 2,800, the shadow price is valid.

Next, we look at the shadow price for electronic components, which is $2 per unit. That is, each additional unit of electronic components (up to 2,800 additional units) will allow Anderson to increase its profit by $2. The impact of 400 units, therefore, will be a net increase in profit of $800. The new profit will be $70,200 (= $69,400 + $800).

It is important to remember that whenever the RHS value of a nonredundant constraint changes, the size of the feasible region changes. Hence, some of the corner points shift locations. In the current situation, because the proposed change is within the allowable change, the current corner point is still *optimal*. That is, the constraints that are binding at present will continue to remain the binding constraints. However, the corner point itself has shifted from its present location. What are the values of the decision variables at the new location of this corner point? Because we know which constraints are binding at the optimal point, we can answer this question by solving those equations simultaneously. Alternatively, we can resolve the LP model.

Q: In the previous question, what would happen if we could increase the supply of electronic components by 4,000 units (to a total of 8,700 units)?

A: From Figure 4.16, we see that the shadow price of $2 per unit is valid only up to 2,800 additional units. This means that the first 2,800 units will cause the total profit to increase by $5,600 (= $2 × 2,800). However, the impact of the last 1,200 units (assuming that we are forced to accept all or nothing of the 4,000 units) cannot be analyzed by using the current report. The problem would have to be resolved using Solver to measure its impact.

The fact that the potential additional supply (4,000) of electronic components is beyond the allowable increase value (2,800) does *not* mean that Anderson's management cannot implement this change. It just means that the total impact of the change cannot be evaluated from the *current* Sensitivity Report in Figure 4.16.

Q: Refer to the question about getting an additional 400 units of electronic components. What would happen if the supplier of these 400 units wanted $8 per unit rather than the current cost of $7 per unit?

A: We know that the shadow price of $2 for electronic components represents the increase in total profit from each additional unit of this resource. This value is net after the cost of this additional unit has been taken into account. That is, it is actually beneficial for Anderson to pay a premium of up to $2 per additional unit of electronic components. In the current situation, getting 400 additional units of electronic components would cost Anderson $8 per unit. This represents a premium of $1 per unit over the current rate of $7 per unit. However, it would still be beneficial to get these units because each additional unit would increase the total profit by $1 (= shadow price of $2 less the premium of $1). The total profit, therefore, would increase by $400, to a new value of $69,800.

This adjusted value of $1 represents the actual increase in profit and can be referred to as the *adjusted shadow price*.

Q: Assume that we have an opportunity to get 250 additional hours of assembly time. However, this time will cost us time and a half (i.e., $15 per hour rather than the current $10 per hour). Should we take it?

A: From Figure 4.16, the shadow price of $24 per hour of assembly time is valid for an increase of up to 466.67 hours. This shadow price, however, assumes that the additional time costs only $10 per hour. The $5-per-hour premium paid on the additional time, therefore, results in an increase of only $19 (= $24 − $5) per each additional hour of assembly time obtained.

The net impact on profit of the additional 250 hours of assembly time is an increase of $4,750 (= 250 × $19). Anderson should definitely accept this opportunity.

Q: If we force the production of MP3 players, what would be the impact on total profit?

A: MP3 players are currently not being recommended for production because they are not profitable enough. You may recall from our discussion in section 4.3 that the reduced cost shows the minimum amount by which the OFC of a variable needs to change in order for it to be included in the optimal solution. The reduced cost for MP3 player is −$1, as shown in Figure 4.16. This implies that the net impact of producing one MP3 player will be to decrease total profit by $1 (to $69,399).

Q: How profitable must MP3 players become before Anderson would consider producing them?

A: We know that each MP3 player produced will cause Anderson's profit to decrease by $1. This implies that if Anderson can find a way of increasing the profit contribution of MP3 players by $1, MP3 players would then become an attractive product. This can be achieved either by increasing the selling price of MP3 players by $1 (to $71 per unit) or by reducing their cost by $1, or a combination of the two.

This information is also seen from the $1 in the Allowable Increase column for the OFC for MP3 players. Not surprisingly, the Allowable Decrease column shows a value of infinity (shown as 1E + 30 in Excel) for the OFC of MP3 players. This is logical because if MP3 players are not attractive at a unit profit of $29, they are clearly not going to be attractive at unit profit values lower than $29.

Q: Assume that there is some uncertainty in the price for Blu-ray DVD players. For what range of prices will the current production be optimal? If Blu-ray DVD players sold for $106, what would be Anderson's new total profit?

A: Blu-ray DVD players currently sell for $110, yielding a profit of $54 per unit. The allowable ranges for the OFC of Blu-ray DVD players in Figure 4.16 shows that this value can increase by up to $10 (to $64; selling price of $120) or decrease by up to $5 (to $49; selling price of $105) for the current production plan to remain optimal.

If Blu-ray DVD players actually sold for $106, the profit per unit would drop to $50. The current values of the decision variables would remain optimal. However, the new total profit would decrease by $4,240 (= $4 per Blu-ray DVD player for 1,060 players), to $65,160.

Alternate Optimal Solutions

Is the optimal solution identified in Figure 4.14 for Anderson Home Electronics (380 satellite radio tuners and 1,060 Blu-ray DVD players, for a total profit of $69,400) unique? Are there alternate production mixes that will also yield a profit of $69,400?

Recall that in Chapter 2 (section 2.6) we saw a graphical example of a situation in which a problem with only two variables had alternate optimal solutions (also referred to as *multiple optimal solutions*). How can we detect a similar condition from the Solver Sensitivity Report for problems involving more than two variables?

In most cases, when the Allowable Increase or Allowable Decrease value for the OFC of a variable is zero in the Variable Cells table, this indicates the presence of alternate optimal solutions. In Anderson's problem, we see from Figure 4.16 that this is not the case.

Note also from Figure 4.16 that the reduced costs for both products currently not being produced in the optimal solution (MP3 players and LCD TVs) are non-zero. This indicates that if Anderson is forced to produce either of these products, the net impact will be a reduction in total profit (as discussed earlier). That is, there is no solution possible involving products other than satellite radio tuners and Blu-ray DVD players that will yield a profit as high as the current solution ($69,400). The current optimal solution is, therefore, unique.

In Solved Problem 4–1 at the end of this chapter, we discuss a problem for which the Solver Sensitivity Report indicates the presence of alternate optimal solutions. We also discuss how Solver can be used to identify these alternate optimal solutions.

4.5 Analyzing Simultaneous Changes by Using the 100% Rule

Until now, we have analyzed the impact of a change in just a single parameter value on the optimal solution. That is, when we are studying the impact of one item of the input data (OFC or RHS value), we assume that all other input data in the model stay constant at their current values. What happens when there are *simultaneous* changes in more than one OFC value or more than one RHS value? Is it possible to analyze the impact of such simultaneous changes on the optimal solution with the information provided in the Sensitivity Report?

The answer is yes, albeit under only a specific condition, as discussed in the following section. It is important to note that the condition is valid only for analyzing simultaneous changes in either OFC values or RHS values, but not a mixture of the two types of input data.

Simultaneous Changes in Constraint RHS Values

Consider a situation in which Anderson Home Electronics realizes that it has only 4,200 available electronic components and, *at the same time*, it has an opportunity to obtain an additional 200 hours of assembly time. What is the impact of these *simultaneous* changes on the optimal solution? To answer this question, we first use a condition called the 100% rule. This condition can be stated as follows:

$$\sum_{\text{changes}} \text{change/allowable change} \leq 1 \qquad (4\text{–}1)$$

That is, we compute the ratio of each proposed change in a parameter's value to the maximum allowable change in its value, as given in the Sensitivity Report. The sum of these ratios must not exceed 1 (or 100%) in order for the information given in the current Sensitivity Report to be valid. If the sum of the ratios does exceed 1, the current information may still be valid; we just cannot guarantee its validity. However, if the ratio does not exceed 1, the information is definitely valid.

To verify this rule for the proposed change in Anderson's problem, consider each change in turn. First, there is a decrease of 500 units (i.e., from 4,700 to 4,200) in the number of electronic components. From the Sensitivity Report (see Figure 4.16), we see that the allowable decrease in this RHS value is 950. The ratio is therefore

$$500/950 = 0.5263$$

Next, there is an increase of 200 hours (from 2,500 to 2,700) in the assembly time available. From the Sensitivity Report, we see that the allowable increase for this RHS value is 466.67. This ratio is, therefore,

$$200/466.67 = 0.4285$$

The sum of these ratios is

$$\text{Sum of ratios} = 0.5263 + 0.4285 = 0.9548 < 1$$

Because this sum does not exceed 1, the information provided in the Sensitivity Report is valid for analyzing the impact of these changes. First, the decrease of 500 units in electronic component availability reduces the size of the feasible region and will therefore cause profit to decrease. The magnitude of this decrease is $1,000 (= 500 units of electronic components, at a shadow price of $2 per unit).

In contrast, the additional 200 hours of assembly time will result in a larger feasible region and a net increase in profit of $4,800 (= 200 hours of assembly time, at a shadow price of $24 per hour). The net impact of these simultaneous changes is, therefore, an increase in profit of $3,800 (= $4,800 − $1,000).

Simultaneous Changes in OFC Values

The 100% rule similarly can be used to analyze simultaneous changes in OFC values. For example, what is the impact on the optimal solution if Anderson decides to drop the selling price of Blu-ray DVD players by $3 per unit but, at the same time, increase the selling price of satellite radio tuners by $8 per unit?

Once again, we calculate the appropriate ratios to verify the 100% rule. For the current solution to remain optimal, the allowable decrease in the OFC for Blu-ray DVD players is $5, while the allowable increase in the OFC for satellite radio tuners is $40. The sum of ratios is therefore

$$\text{Sum of ratios} = (\$3/\$5) + (\$8/\$40) = 0.80 < 1$$

Because the sum of ratios does not exceed 1, the current production plan is still optimal. The $3 decrease in profit per Blu-ray DVD player causes total profit to decrease by $3,180 (= $3 × 1,060). However, the $8 increase in the unit profit of each satellite radio tuner results in an increase of $3,040 (= $8 × 380) in total profit. The net impact is, therefore, a decrease in profit of only $140, to a new value of $69,260.

4.6 Pricing Out New Variables

The information given in the Sensitivity Report also can be used to study the impact of the introduction of new decision variables (products, in the Anderson example) into the model. For example, if Anderson's problem is solved again with a new product also included in the model, will we recommend that the new product be made? Or will we recommend not to make the new product and continue to make the same products (i.e., satellite radio tuners and Blu-ray DVD players) Anderson is making now?

Anderson's Proposed New Product

Suppose Anderson Home Electronics wants to introduce a new product, the Digital Home Theater Speaker System (DHTSS), to take advantage of the hot market for that product. The design department estimates that each DHTSS will require five units of electronic components, four units of non-electronic components, and four hours of assembly time. The marketing department estimates that it can sell each DHTSS for $175, a higher selling price than any of the other four products being considered by Anderson.

The question now is whether the DHTSS will be a profitable product for Anderson to produce. That is, even though the new product would have a higher selling price per unit, is it worthwhile from an overall profit perspective to divert resources from Anderson's existing products to make this new product? Alternatively, we could pose the question as this: What is the minimum price at which Anderson would need to sell each DHTSS in order to make it a viable product?

The answer to such a question involves a procedure called pricing out. Assume that Anderson decides to make a single DHTSS. Note that the resources required to make this system (five units of electronic components, four units of non-electronic components, and four hours of assembly time) will no longer be available to meet Anderson's existing production plan (380 satellite radio tuners and 1,060 Blu-ray DVD players, for a total profit of $69,400).

Checking the Validity of the 100% Rule Clearly, the loss of these resources is going to reduce the profit that Anderson could have made from its existing products. Using the shadow prices of these resources, we can calculate the exact impact of the loss of these resources. However, we must first use the 100% rule to check whether the shadow prices are valid by calculating the ratio of the reduction in each resource's availability to the allowable decrease for that resource (given in Figure 4.16). The resulting calculation is as follows:

$$\text{Sum of ratios} = (5/950) + (4/560) + (4/1,325) = 0.015 < 1$$

Required Profit Contribution of Each DHTSS Because the total ratio is less than 1, the shadow prices are valid to calculate the impact on profit of using these resources to produce a DHTSS rather than the existing products. We can determine this impact as

$$\begin{aligned}
&= 5 \times \text{shadow price of electronic components constraint} + \\
&\quad 4 \times \text{shadow price of nonelectronic components constraint} + \\
&\quad 4 \times \text{shadow price of assembly time constraint} \\
&= 5 \times \$2 + 4 \times \$0 + 4 \times \$24 \\
&= \$106
\end{aligned}$$

Hence, for DHTSS to be a viable product, the profit contribution of each DHTSS has to at least make up this shortfall in profit. That is, the OFC for DHTSS must be at least $106 for the optimal solution to have a non-zero value for DHTSS. Otherwise, the optimal solution of Anderson's model with a decision variable for DHTSS included will be the same as the current one, with DHTSS having a value of zero.

Finding the Minimum Selling Price of Each DHTSS Unit The actual cost of the resources used to make one DHTSS unit can be calculated as

$$= 5 \times \text{unit price of electronic components constraint} +$$
$$4 \times \text{unit price of non-electronic components constraint} +$$
$$4 \times \text{unit price of assembly time constraint}$$
$$= 5 \times \$7 + 4 \times \$5 + 4 \times \$10$$
$$= \$95$$

The minimum selling price for DHTSS units is then calculated as the sum of the cost of making a DHTSS unit and the marginal worth of resources diverted from existing products. In Anderson's case, this works out to $201 (= $106 + $95). Because Anderson's marketing department estimates that it can sell each DHTSS unit for only $175, this product will not be profitable for Anderson to produce.

What happens if Anderson *does* include DHTSS as a variable in its model and solves the expanded formulation again? In this case, from the discussion so far, we can say that the optimal solution will once again recommend producing 380 satellite radio tuners and 1,060 Blu-ray DVD players, for a total profit of $69,400. DHTSS will have a final value of zero (just as MP3 players and LCD TVs do in the current solution). What will be the reduced cost of DHTSS in this revised solution? We have calculated that the minimum selling price required for DHTSS to be a viable product is $201, while the actual selling price is only $175. Therefore, the reduced cost will be −$26, indicating that each DHTSS unit produced will cause Anderson's profit to decrease by $26.

To verify our conclusions, let us revise the LP model for Anderson Home Electronics to include the new product, DHTSS. The Excel layout and Solver entries for this revised model are shown in Figure 4.17. The Sensitivity Report for this model is shown in Figure 4.18.

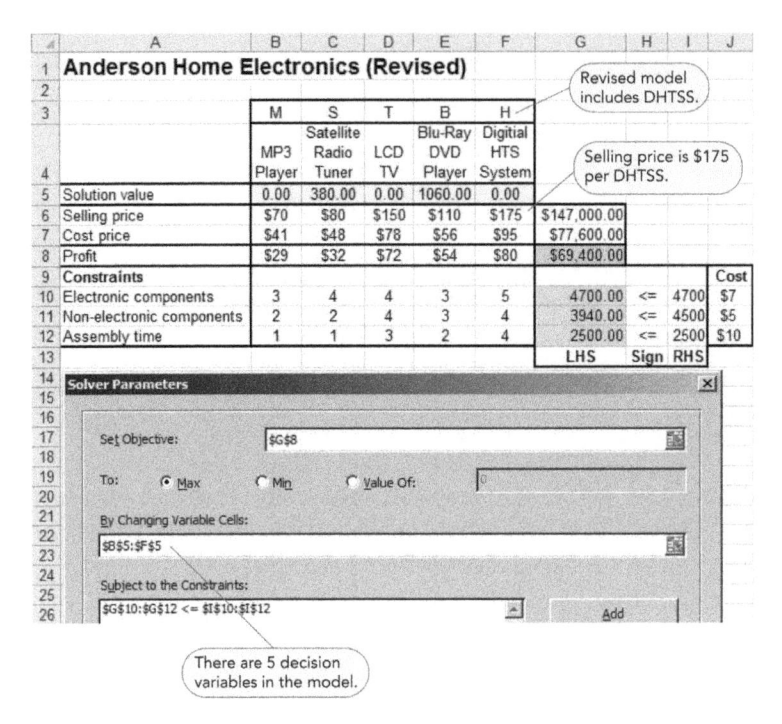

210 — Chapter 4: Linear Programming Sensitivity Analysis

Figure 4.17: Excel Layout and Solver Entries for Anderson Home Electronics—Revised Model

📊 File: Figure 4.17.xlsx, Sheet: Figure 4.17

Figure 4.18: Solver Sensitivity Report for Anderson Home Electronics—Revised Model

📊 File: Figure 4.17.xlsx, Sheet: Figure 4.18

The results show that it continues to be optimal for Anderson to produce 380 satellite radio tuners and 1,060 Blu-ray DVD players, for a total profit of $69,400. Further, the magnitude of the reduced cost for DHTSS is $26, as we had already calculated.

4.7 Sensitivity Analysis for a Minimization Example

Let us now analyze an example with a minimization objective. For such problems, we need to be aware that when a solution *improves*, the objective value decreases rather than increases.

Burn-Off Diet Drink Example

Burn-Off, a manufacturer of diet drinks, is planning to introduce a miracle drink that will magically burn away fat. The drink is a bit expensive, but Burn-Off guarantees that a person using this diet plan will lose up to 50 pounds in just three weeks. The drink is made up of four "mystery" ingredients (which we will call ingredients A, B, C, and D). The plan calls for a person to consume at least three 12-ounce doses per day (i.e., at least 36 ounces per day) but no more than 40 ounces per day.

Each of the four ingredients contains different levels of three chemical compounds (which we will call chemicals X, Y, and Z). Health regulations mandate that the dosage consumed per day should contain minimum prescribed levels of chemicals X and Y and should not exceed maximum prescribed levels for the third chemical, Z.

The composition of the four ingredients in terms of the chemical compounds (units per ounce) is shown in Table 4.2, along with the unit cost prices of the ingredients. Burn-Off wants to find the optimal way to mix the ingredients to create the drink, at minimum cost per daily dose.

Table 4.2: Data for Burn-Off Diet Drink

	Ingredient A	Ingredient B	Ingredient C	Ingredient D	Requirement
Chemical X	3	4	8	10	At least 280 units
Chemical Y	5	3	6	6	At least 200 units
Chemical Z	10	25	20	40	At most 1,050 units
Cost per ounce	$0.40	$0.20	$0.60	$0.30	

To formulate this problem, we let A, B, C, and D denote the number of ounces of ingredients A, B, C, and D to use, respectively. The problem can then be formulated as follows:

$$\text{Minimize daily dose cost} = \$0.40A + \$0.20B + \$0.60C + \$0.30D$$

subject to the constraints

$$
\begin{aligned}
A + B + C + D &\geq 36 &&\text{(daily dosage minimum)} \\
3A + 4B + 8C + 10D &\geq 280 &&\text{(chemical X requirement)} \\
5A + 3B + 6C + 6D &\geq 200 &&\text{(chemical Y requirement)} \\
10A + 25B + 20C + 40D &\leq 1{,}050 &&\text{(chemical Z max limit)} \\
A + B + C + D &\leq 40 &&\text{(daily dosage maximum)} \\
A, B, C, D &\geq 0 &&\text{(nonnegativity)}
\end{aligned}
$$

Burn-Off's Excel Solution

Figure 4.19 and Figure 4.20 show the Excel layout and Solver entries, and the Sensitivity Report, respectively, for Burn-Off's problem. The output shows that the optimal solution is to use 10.25 ounces of ingredient A, 4.125 ounces of ingredient C, and 21.625 ounces of ingredient D, to make exactly 36 ounces of the diet drink per day. Interestingly, ingredient B is not used, even though it is the least expensive ingredient. The total cost is $13.06 per day.

	A	B	C	D	E	F	G	H
1	**Burn-Off Diet Drink**							
2								
3		A	B	C	D			
4		Ingr A	Ingr B	Ingr C	Ingr D			
5	Number of ounces	10.250	0.000	4.125	21.625			
6	Cost	$0.40	$0.20	$0.60	$0.30	$13.06		
7	Constraints							
8	Daily dosage minimum	1	1	1	1	36.00	>=	36
9	Chemical X requirement	3	4	8	10	280.00	>=	280
10	Chemical Y requirement	5	3	6	6	205.75	>=	200
11	Chemical Z max limit	10	25	20	40	1050.00	<=	1050
12	Daily dosage maximum	1	1	1	1	36.00	<=	40
13						LHS	Sign	RHS

Solver Parameters (Make sure the Variables Non-Negative box is checked and Simplex LP is set as the solving method (not shown).)

Set Objective: $F$6

To: ○ Max ● Min ○ Value Of: 0 (Minimization objective.)

By Changing Variable Cells: $B$5:$E$5

Subject to the Constraints:
$F$11:$F$12 <= $H$11:$H$12
$F$8:$F$10 >= $H$8:$H$10
(Constraints include both ≤ and ≥ signs in this model.)

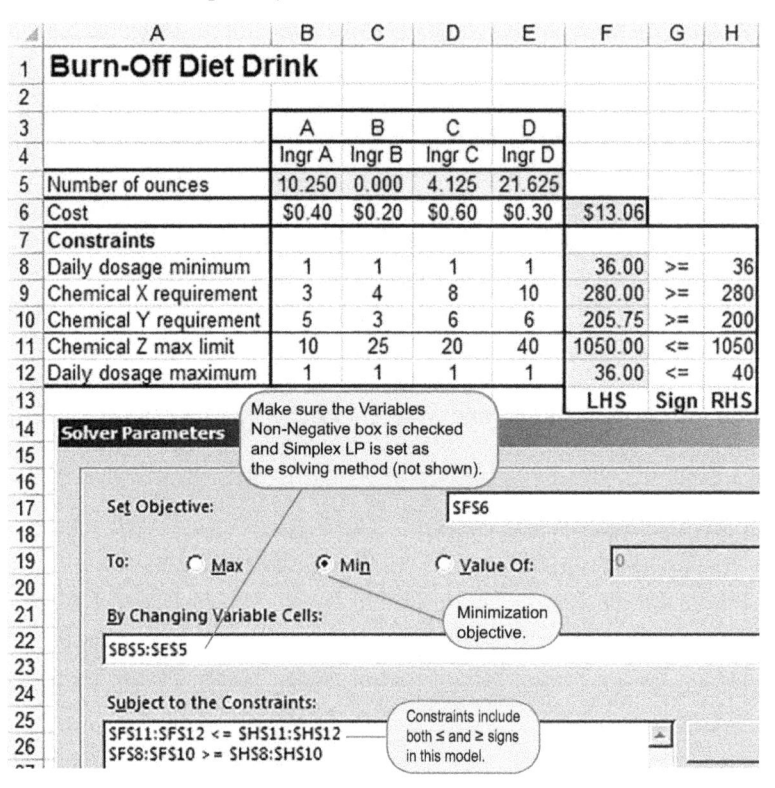

Figure 4.19: Excel Layout and Solver Entries for Burn-Off Diet Drink

File: Figure 4.19.xlsx, Sheet: Figure 4.19

The solution also indicates that the constraints for chemical Y and the maximum daily dosage are nonbinding. Although the minimum requirement is for only 200 units of chemical Y, the final drink actually provides 205.75 units of this chemical. The extra 5.75 units denote the level of oversatisfaction with this requirement. You may recall from Chapter 2 that we refer to this quantity as surplus, even though the Solver Answer Report always titles this value *slack*.

Sensitivity Analysis for a Minimization Example — 213

Microsoft Excel 14.0 Sensitivity Report
Worksheet: [Figure 4.19.xlsx]Burn-Off Diet Drink

Reduced cost shows increase in total cost if ingredient B is used.

Variable Cells

Cell	Name	Final Value	Reduced Cost	Objective Coefficient	Allowable Increase	Allowable Decrease
$B$5	Number of ounces Ingr A	10.250	0.000	0.400	0.061	0.250
$C$5	Number of ounces Ingr B	0.000	0.069	0.200	1E+30	0.069
$D$5	Number of ounces Ingr C	4.125	0.000	0.600	1.500	0.073
$E$5	Number of ounces Ingr D	21.625	0.000	0.300	0.085	1E+30

Constraints

Cell	Name	Final Value	Shadow Price	Constraint R.H. Side	Allowable Increase	Allowable Decrease
$F$8	Daily dosage minimum	36.000	0.375	36.00	16.500	1.278
$F$9	Chemical X requirement	280.000	0.088	280.000	41.000	11.000
$F$10	Chemical Y requirement	205.750	0.000	200.000	5.750	1E+30
$F$11	Chemical Z max limit	1050.000	-0.024	1050.000	47.143	346.000
$F$12	Daily dosage maximum	36.000	0.000	40.000	1E+30	4.000

Infinity

The shadow price for chemical X is positive, indicating that total cost increases as the requirement for chemical X increases.

The shadow price shows amount of decrease in total cost if chemical Z's limit is increased.

Figure 4.20: Solver Sensitivity Report for Burn-Off Diet Drink

X📄 File: Figure 4.19.xlsx, Sheet: Figure 4.20

Answering Sensitivity Analysis Questions for Burn-Off

As with the Anderson Home Electronics example, we use several questions to interpret the information given in the Sensitivity Report (Figure 4.20) for Burn-Off.

Q: What is the impact on cost if Burn-Off insists on using 1 ounce of ingredient B to make the drink?

A: The reduced cost indicates that each ounce of ingredient B used to make the drink will cause the total cost per daily dosage to increase by $0.069 (~ $0.07). The new cost will be $13.06 + $0.07 = $13.13.

Alternatively, if Burn-Off can find a way of reducing ingredient B's cost per ounce by at least $0.069 (to approximately $0.13 or less per ounce), then it becomes cost-effective to use this ingredient to make the diet drink.

Q: There is some uncertainty in the cost of ingredient C. How sensitive is the current optimal solution to this cost?

A: The current cost of ingredient C is $0.60 per ounce. The range for the cost coefficient of this ingredient shows an allowable increase of $1.50 and an allowable decrease of $0.073 for the current corner point solution to remain optimal. The cost per ounce of ingredient C could therefore fluctuate between $0.527 (= $0.60 − $0.073) and $2.10 (= $0.60 + $1.50) without affecting the current optimal mix.

The total cost will, however, change, depending on the actual unit cost of ingredient C. For example, if the cost of ingredient C increases to $1.00 per ounce, the new total cost will be

$$= \$13.06 + (\$0.40 \text{ extra per ounce} \times 4.125 \text{ ounces of C})$$
$$= \$13.06 + \$1.65$$
$$= \$14.71$$

Q: What do the shadow prices for chemical X and chemical Z imply in this problem?

A: The shadow price for chemical X is $0.088. Because the constraint for chemical X is a $\geq$ constraint, an increase by 1 unit in the RHS (from 280 to 281) makes the problem solution even more restrictive. That is, the feasible region becomes smaller. The optimal objective function value could, therefore, worsen. The shadow price indicates that for each additional unit of chemical X required to be present in the drink, the overall cost will increase by $0.088. This value is valid for an increase of up to 41 units and a decrease of up to 11 units in the requirement for chemical X.

In contrast, the constraint for chemical Z is a $\leq$ constraint. An increase in the RHS of the constraint (from 1,050 to 1,051) will cause the feasible region to become bigger. Hence, the optimal objective function value could possibly improve. The negative value of the shadow price for this constraint indicates that each unit increase in the maximum limit allowed for chemical Z will cause the total cost to decrease by $0.024. This value is valid for an increase of up to 47.143 units. Likewise, the total cost will *increase* by $0.024 for each unit *decrease* in the maximum limit allowed for chemical Z. This is valid for a decrease of up to 346 units in the maximum limit for chemical Z.

Q: Burn-Off can decrease the minimum requirement for chemical X by 5 units (from 280 to 275), provided that the maximum limit allowed for chemical Z is reduced to 1,000 units (i.e., reduced by 50 units). Is this trade-off cost-effective for Burn-Off to implement?

A: Because we are dealing with simultaneous changes in RHS values, we first verify whether the 100% rule is satisfied. To do so, we take the ratio of each proposed change to its maximum allowable change. The calculation is

$$\text{Sum of ratios} = (5/11) + (50/346) = 0.599 < 1$$

Because the sum does not exceed 1, we can use the shadow price information in the Sensitivity Report (Figure 4.20). The reduction of 5 units in the requirement for chemical X will cause the feasible region to increase in size. The total cost will therefore improve (i.e., go down) by $0.44 (= 5 units, at a shadow price of $0.088 per unit).

In contrast, the reduction of 50 units in the maximum allowable limit for chemical Z makes the feasible region shrink in size. The total cost will therefore be adversely affected (i.e., go up) by $1.20 (= 50 units, at a shadow price of $0.024 per unit).

The net impact of this trade-off, therefore, is an increase in total cost of $0.76 (= $1.20 − $0.44). The new cost will be $13.82. Clearly, this trade-off is not cost-effective from Burn-Off's perspective and should be rejected.

EXCEL EXTRA

Drop-Down Lists

Especially when you are creating spreadsheets for other people to use, it can pay off significantly to make the spreadsheets as mistake-proof as possible. A special form of data validation is the *drop-down list*, which forces the user to select an entry for a particular cell (or set of cells) from a prescribed list of choices. This can also be an effective way to ensure that words are entered with the correct spelling and capitalization. The choices are contained in a list somewhere in the workbook, usually in a column of cells.

Sometimes LP models are updated and solved, retaining their structure but potentially using not only different parameters, but even different decision variables. For example, in Figure 4.19, perhaps the firm can blend its diet drink from four out of six possible ingredients. In that case, the labels in cells B4:E4 could potentially change.

To create the drop-down list, first insert the list of options (say, Ingr A to Ingr F) somewhere in the spreadsheet. In this example, let's say we place these six values in cells T1 through T6, respectively. Then highlight cells B4:E4 and select:

Data|Data Validation

Under Settings|Allow:, choose List. Then under Settings|Source:, select the range T1:T6 (or manually enter =$T$1:$T$6), and click OK.

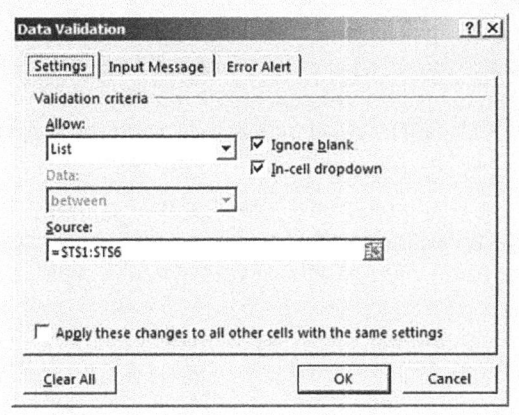

Once this drop-down list is created, a small box with a triangle will appear to the right of cells B4:E4 whenever any of them is selected. Clicking on that triangle will display the relevant prescribed list of choices from which you must select a value for that cell.

4.8 Summary

In this chapter, we present the important concept of sensitivity analysis. Sometimes referred to as postoptimality analysis, sensitivity analysis is used by management to answer a series of what-if questions about inputs to an LP model. It also tests just how sensitive the optimal solution is to changes in (1) objective function coefficients and (2) constraint RHS values.

We first explore sensitivity analysis graphically (i.e., for problems with only two decision variables). We then discuss how to interpret information in the Answer Report and Sensitivity Report generated by Solver. We also discuss how the information in these reports can be used to analyze simultaneous changes in model parameter values and determine the potential impact of a new variable in the model.

Key Points
- LP models are solved with deterministic assumptions, i.e., known and fixed values for all input parameters.
- But managers are often interested in studying the impact of changes in the values of input parameters via sensitivity analysis.
- If the change in an input data value is known for sure, the easiest approach is to change it in the formulation and resolve the model.
- Sensitivity analysis involves examining how sensitive the optimal solution is to changes in profits, resources, or other input parameters.
- Excel's Solver can be used to generate an LP model's Sensitivity Report.
- There is a range for each objective function coefficient (OFC) over which the current solution remains optimal.
- If an OFC changes too much, a new corner point could become optimal.
- Changes in OFC values do not affect the size of the feasible region.
- Changes in constraint right-hand-side (RHS) values could affect the size of the feasible region.
- The location of the optimal corner point changes if the RHS of a binding constraint changes.
- The feasible region becomes smaller if the RHS value of a binding ≤ constraint decreases.
- The shadow price is the change in objective function value for a one-unit increase in a constraint's RHS value.
- The shadow price is valid only for a certain range of change in a constraint's RHS value.
- Increasing the RHS of a ≤ constraint endlessly will eventually make it a redundant constraint.
- Decreasing the RHS of a ≤ constraint endlessly will eventually make some other constraint a redundant constraint.

- There is a range of values for each RHS for which the current corner points continue to exist.
- Increasing the RHS value of a nonbinding ≤ constraint does not affect the optimality of the current solution.
- The RHS value of a nonbinding ≤ constraint can be decreased up to its slack without affecting the optimality of the current solution.
- We must select the Simplex LP method as the solving method in the Solver Parameters window to obtain an LP's Sensitivity Report from Solver.
- The desired Solver reports must be explicitly selected in order for them to be created.
- The information in a Sensitivity Report analyzes only one change at a time.
- The Excel Sensitivity Report has two parts: Variable Cells and Constraints.
- If the size of the feasible region increases, the optimal objective function value could improve.
- The shadow price is valid only as long as the change in the RHS is within the Allowable Increase and Allowable Decrease values.
- The shadow price of a nonbinding constraint is zero.
- Solver displays infinity as 1E+30.
- Reduced cost is the minimum amount by which the OFC of a variable should change in order to affect the optimal solution.
- Changes beyond the values in the Allowable Increase or Allowable Decrease columns cannot be analyzed using the Sensitivity Report in Solver.
- Zeros in the Allowable Increase or Allowable Decrease columns for OFC values may indicate alternate optimal solutions.
- The 100% rule can be used to check whether simultaneous changes in RHS or OFC values can be analyzed by using the current Sensitivity Report.
- Using the 100% rule, if the sum of ratios (change / allowable change) does not exceed 1, the information in the Sensitivity Report is valid.
- Pricing out analyzes the impact of adding a new variable to the existing LP model.
- Minimization problems typically involve some ≥ constraints.
- The difference between the left-hand-side (LHS) and RHS values of a ≥ constraint is called surplus.
- A negative value for shadow price implies that cost will decrease if the RHS value increases.
- We can force Excel to identify alternate optimal solutions.

Glossary

Allowable Decrease for an OFC   The maximum amount by which the OFC of a decision variable can decrease for the current optimal solution to remain optimal.

Allowable Decrease for a RHS Value   The maximum amount by which the RHS value of a constraint can decrease for the shadow price to be valid.

Allowable Increase for an OFC   The maximum amount by which the OFC of a decision variable can increase for the current optimal solution to remain optimal.

Allowable Increase for a RHS Value The maximum amount by which the RHS value of a constraint can increase for the shadow price to be valid.

Answer Report A report created by Solver when it solves an LP model. This report presents the optimal solution in a detailed manner.

Objective Function Coefficient (OFC) The coefficient for a decision variable in the objective function. Typically, this refers to unit profit or unit cost.

100% Rule A rule used to verify the validity of the information in a Sensitivity Report when dealing with simultaneous changes to more than one RHS value or more than one OFC value.

Pricing Out A procedure by which the shadow price information in a Sensitivity Report can be used to gauge the impact of the addition of a new variable in an LP model.

Reduced Cost The minimum amount by which the OFC of a variable should change before it would have a non-zero optimal value.

Right-Hand Side (RHS) Value The amount of resource available (for a $\leq$ constraint) or the minimum requirement of some criterion (for a $\geq$ constraint). Typically expressed as a constant for sensitivity analysis.

Sensitivity Analysis The study of how sensitive an optimal solution is to model assumptions and to data changes. Also, referred to as postoptimality analysis.

Shadow Price The magnitude of the change in the objective function value for a one-unit increase in the RHS of a constraint.

Slack The difference between the RHS and LHS of a $\leq$ constraint. Typically represents the unused resource.

Surplus The difference between the LHS and RHS of a $\geq$ constraint. Typically represents the level of oversatisfaction of a requirement.

4.9 Exercises

Solved Problem

Solved Problem 4–1 Consider the Hong Kong Bank of Commerce and Industry example we first studied in Chapter 3 (section 3.5). How can we use the Sensitivity Report for that example to detect the presence of alternate optimal solutions for an LP problem? Also, how can we use Excel to possibly identify those alternate optimal solutions?

Solution For your convenience, we repeat the formulation portion of the Hong Kong Bank problem here. Define

F = number of full-time tellers to use (all starting at 9 A.M.)
P_1 = number of part-timers to use starting at 9 A.M. (leaving at 1 P.M.)
P_2 = number of part-timers to use starting at 10 A.M. (leaving at 2 P.M.)
P_3 = number of part-timers to use starting at 11 A.M. (leaving at 3 P.M.)
P_4 = number of part-timers to use starting at noon (leaving at 4 P.M.)
P_5 = number of part-timers to use starting at 1 P.M. (leaving at 5 P.M.)

Objective function:

$$\text{Minimize total daily personnel cost} = \$90F + \$28(P_1 + P_2 + P_3 + P_4 + P_5)$$

subject to the constraints:

$F + P_1$	≥ 10	(9 A.M. – 10 A.M. requirement)
$F + P_1 + P_2$	≥ 12	(10 A.M. – 11 A.M. requirement)
$0.5F + P_1 + P_2 + P_3$	≥ 14	(11 A.M. – 12 noon requirement)
$0.5F + P_1 + P_2 + P_3 + P_4$	≥ 16	(12 noon – 1 P.M. requirement)
$F + P_2 + P_3 + P_4 + P_5$	≥ 18	(1 P.M. – 2 P.M. requirement)
$F + P_3 + P_4 + P_5$	≥ 17	(2 P.M. – 3 P.M. requirement)
$F + P_4 + P_5$	≥ 15	(3 P.M. – 4 P.M. requirement)
$F + P_5$	≥ 10	(4 P.M. – 5 P.M. requirement)
F	≤ 12	(full-time tellers)
$4P_1 + 4P_2 + 4P_3 + 4P_4 + 4P_5 \leq 56$		(part-time workers limit)
$F, P_1, P_2, P_3, P_4, P_5$	≥ 0	(nonnegativity)

The Excel layout and Solver entries for this model are shown in Figure 4.21. The Sensitivity Report is shown in Figure 4.22.

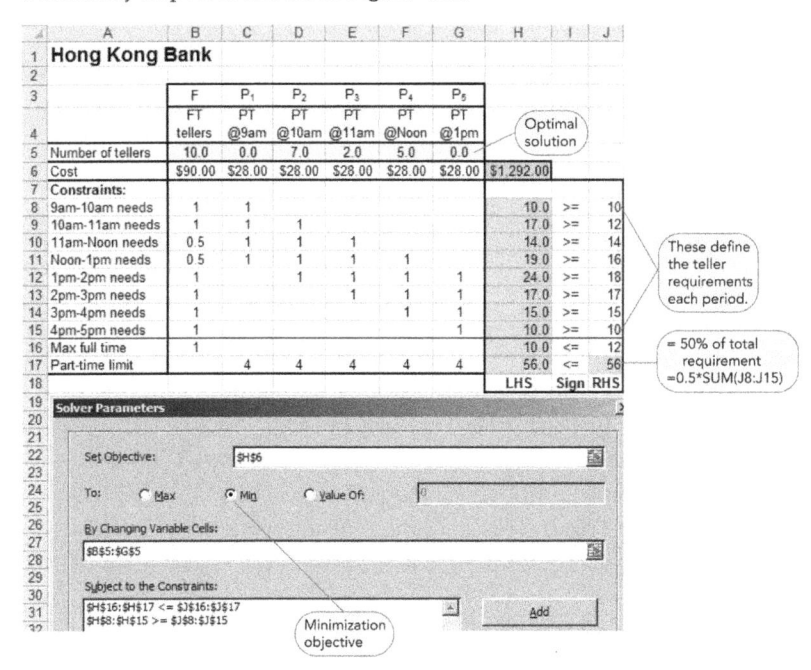

Figure 4.21: Excel Layout and Solver Entries for Hong Kong Bank

File: Figure 4.21.xlsx, Sheet: Figure 4.21

Microsoft Excel 14.0 Sensitivity Report
Worksheet: [Figure 4.21.xlsx]Hong Kong Bank

Reduced cost of zero indicates that a solution that uses part-time tellers at 9 A.M. exists, with no change in the optimal objective value.

Variable Cells

Cell	Name	Final Value	Reduced Cost	Objective Coefficient	Allowable Increase	Allowable Decrease
$B$5	Number of tellers FT tellers	10.00	0.00	90.00	1E+30	48.00
$C$5	Number of tellers PT @9am	0.00	0.00	28.00	48.00	0.00
$D$5	Number of tellers PT @10am	7.00	0.00	28.00	0.00	45.00
$E$5	Number of tellers PT @11am	2.00	0.00	28.00	60.00	0.00
$F$5	Number of tellers PT @Noon	5.00	0.00	28.00	0.00	60.00
$G$5	Number of tellers PT @1pm	0.00	0.00	28.00	48.00	0.00

These zeros indicate that there are alternate optimal solutions.

Constraints

Cell	Name	Final Value	Shadow Price	Constraint R.H. Side	Allowable Increase	Allowable Decrease
$H$8	9am-10am needs	10.00	0.00	10.00	6.00	0.00
$H$9	10am-11am needs	17.00	0.00	12.00	5.00	1E+30
$H$10	11am-Noon needs	14.00	60.00	14.00	0.00	3.00
$H$11	Noon-1pm needs	19.00	0.00	16.00	3.00	1E+30
$H$12	1pm-2pm needs	24.00	0.00	18.00	6.00	1E+30
$H$13	2pm-3pm needs	17.00	0.00	17.00	5.00	2.00
$H$14	3pm-4pm needs	15.00	60.00	15.00	0.00	3.00
$H$15	4pm-5pm needs	10.00	0.00	10.00	3.00	0.00
$H$16	Max full time	10.00	0.00	12.00	1E+30	2.00
$H$17	Part-time limit	56.00	-8.00	56.00	60.00	0.00

Figure 4.22: Solver Sensitivity Report for Hong Kong Bank

File: Figure 4.21.xlsx, Sheet: Figure 4.22

Figure 4.21 reveals that the optimal solution is to employ 10 full-time tellers, 7 part-time tellers at 10 A.M., 2 part-time tellers at 11 A.M., and 5 part-time tellers at noon, for a total cost of $1,292 per day.

In Figure 4.22, the shadow price of −$8 for the part-time limit of 56 hours indicates that each additional hour (over the 56-hour limit) that part-time tellers are allowed to work will allow the bank to reduce costs by $8. This shadow price is valid for a limit of 60 more hours (i.e., up to 116 hours).

Examining the Allowable Increase and Allowable Decrease columns for the OFCs, we see that there are several values of zero in these columns. This indicates that there are alternate optimal solutions to this problem.

Likewise, consider the reduced cost for variables P_1 (part-timers starting at 9 A.M.) and P_5 (part-timers starting at 1 P.M.). These are zero, even though these variables have values of zero (their lower limit). This implies that, for example, it is possible to force P_1 (or P_5) to have a non-zero value at optimality and not affect the total cost in any way. This is another indication of the presence of alternate optimal solutions to this problem.

How can we identify these optimal solutions by using Excel's Solver? There are at least a couple ways of doing so. First, simply rearranging the order in which the variables and/or constraints are included in the Excel layout may make Solver identify an alternate optimal solution. That is, we can just swap the order in which some of the rows and/or columns are included in the model. There is, however, no guarantee that this approach will always identify an alternate optimal solution.

The second approach, which definitely will find an alternate optimal solution (if one exists), is as follows. From the preceding discussion, we know that variable P_1 (which currently has a zero value) can have a non-zero value at an optimal solution. To force this to happen, we include the current objective function as a constraint, as follows:

$$\$90F + \$28(P_1 + P_2 + P_3 + P_4 + P_5) = \$1{,}292$$

This will force the new solution to have the same optimal cost (i.e., it is also an optimal solution). Then, the new objective for the model would be

$$\text{Max } P_1$$

Note that this will find a solution that costs $1,292, but has a non-zero value for P_1. We can repeat the same approach with the variable P_5 to find yet another optimal solution.

Using these approaches, we can identify two alternate solutions for Hong Kong Bank, as follows:

1. 10 full-time tellers, 6 part-time tellers at 9 A.M., 1 part-time teller at 10 A.M., 2 part-time tellers at 11 A.M., and 5 part-time tellers at noon.
2. 10 full-time tellers, 6 part-time tellers at 9 A.M., 1 part-time teller at 10 A.M., 2 part-time tellers at 11 A.M., 2 part-time tellers at noon, and 3 part-time tellers at 10 A.M.

The cost of each of these employment policies is also $1,292.

Discussion Questions

4–1. Discuss the role of sensitivity analysis in LP. Under what circumstances is it needed, and under what conditions do you think it is not necessary?

4–2. Is sensitivity analysis a concept applied to LP only, or should it also be used when analyzing other techniques (e.g., break-even analysis)? Provide examples to prove your point.

4–3. Explain how a change in resource availability can affect the optimal solution of a problem.

4–4. Explain how a change in an OFC can affect the optimal solution of a problem.

4–5. Are simultaneous changes in input data values logical? Provide examples to prove your point.

4–6. Explain the 100% rule and its role in analyzing the impact of simultaneous changes in model input data values.

4–7. How can a firm benefit from using the pricing out procedure?

4–8. How do we detect the presence of alternate optimal solutions from a Solver Sensitivity Report?

4–9. Why would a firm find information regarding the shadow price of a resource useful?

Problems

4–10. A graphical approach was used to solve the following LP model in Problem 2–16:

$$\text{Maximize profit} = \$4X + 5Y$$

subject to the constraints

$$5X + 2Y \le 40$$
$$3X + 6Y \le 30$$
$$X \quad \le 7$$
$$2X - Y \ge 3$$
$$X, Y \ge 0$$

Use the graphical solution to answer the following questions. Each question is independent of the others. Determine if (and how) the following changes would affect the optimal solution values and/or profit.
(a) A technical breakthrough raises the profit per unit of Y to $10.
(b) The profit per unit of X decreases to only $2.
(c) The first constraint changes to $5X + 2Y \le 54$.

4–11. A graphical approach was used to solve the following LP model in Problem 2–18:

$$\text{Minimize cost} = \$4X + \$7Y$$

subject to the constraints

$$2X + 3Y \ge 60$$
$$4X + 2Y \ge 80$$
$$X \quad \le 24$$
$$X, Y \ge 0$$

Use the graphical solution to answer the following questions. Each question is independent of the others. Determine if (and how) the following changes would affect the optimal solution values and/or cost.
(a) The cost per unit of Y increases to $9.
(b) The first constraint changes to $2X + 3Y \ge 90$.
(c) The third constraint changes to $X \le 15$.

4–12. A graphical approach was used to solve the following LP model in Problem 2–17:

$$\text{Maximize profit} = \$4X + \$3Y$$

subject to the constraints

$$2X + 4Y \le 72$$
$$3X + 6Y \ge 27$$
$$-3X + 10Y \ge 0$$
$$X, Y \ge 0$$

Use the graphical solution to answer the following questions. Each question is independent of the others. Determine if (and how) the following changes would affect the optimal solution values and/or profit.
(a) The profit per unit of X decreases to $1.
(b) The first constraint changes to $2X + 4Y \le 80$.
(c) The third constraint changes to $-3X + 10Y \le 0$.

4-13. Consider the Win Big Gambling Club media selection example discussed in section 3.3 of Chapter 3. Use the Sensitivity Report for this LP model (shown in Figure 4.23) to answer the following questions. Each question is independent of the others.

Microsoft Excel 14.0 Sensitivity Report
Problem 4-13. Win Big Gambling Club

Variable Cells

Cell	Name	Final Value	Reduced Cost	Objective Coefficient	Allowable Increase	Allowable Decrease
$B$5	Number of units TV spots	1.97	0.00	5000.00	1620.69	5000.00
$C$5	Number of units Newspaper ads	5.00	0.00	8500.00	1E+30	2718.75
$D$5	Number of units Prime-time radio spots	6.21	0.00	2400.00	1E+30	263.16
$E$5	Number of units Afternoon radio spots	0.00	-344.83	2800.00	344.83	1E+30

Constraints

Cell	Name	Final Value	Shadow Price	Constraint R.H. Side	Allowable Increase	Allowable Decrease
$F$8	Maximum TV	1.97	0.00	12.00	1E+30	10.03
$F$9	Maximum newspaper	5.00	2718.75	5.00	1.70	5.00
$F$10	Max prime-time radio	6.21	0.00	25.00	1E+30	18.79
$F$11	Max afternoon radio	0.00	0.00	20.00	1E+30	20.00
$F$12	Total budget	8,000.00	6.25	8000.00	8025.00	1575.00
$F$13	Maximum radio $	1,800.00	2.03	1800.00	1575.00	350.00
$F$14	Minimum radio spots	6.21	0.00	5.00	1.21	1E+30

Figure 4.23: Solver Sensitivity Report for Problem 4-13: Win Big Gambling Club

What is the impact on the audience coverage under the following scenarios?
(a) Management approves spending $200 more on radio advertising each week.
(b) The contractual agreement to place at least five radio spots per week is eliminated.
(c) The audience reached per ad increases to 9,100.
(d) There is some uncertainty in the audience reached per TV spot. For what range of values for this OFC will the current solution remain optimal?

4-14. Consider the MSA marketing research example discussed in Section 3.3. Use the Sensitivity Report for this LP model (shown in Figure 4.24) to answer the following questions. Each question is independent of the others.
(a) What is the maximum unit cost that will make it worthwhile to include in the survey persons 30 years of age or younger who live in a border state?
(b) What is the impact if MSA wants to increase the sample size to 3,000?
(c) What is the impact if MSA insists on including people 31–50 years of age who do not live in a border state?
(d) What is the impact if we can reduce the minimum 30 or younger persons required to 900, provided that we raise the persons 31–50 years of age to 650?

Chapter 4: Linear Programming Sensitivity Analysis

Microsoft Excel 14.0 Sensitivity Report
Problem 4-14. Management Science Associates

Variable Cells

Cell	Name	Final Value	Reduced Cost	Objective Coefficient	Allowable Increase	Allowable Decrease
$B$5	Number of households <= 30 and border	0.00	0.60	7.50	1E+30	0.60
$C$5	Number of households 31-50 and border	600.00	0.00	6.80	0.45	0.82
$D$5	Number of households >= 51 and border	140.00	0.00	5.50	0.6	29.90
$E$5	Number of households <= 30 and not border	1000.00	0.00	6.90	0.6	0.92
$F$5	Number of households 31-50 and not border	0.00	0.45	7.25	1E+30	0.45
$G$5	Number of households >= 51 and not border	560.00	0.00	6.10	1.025	0.60

Constraints

Cell	Name	Final Value	Shadow Price	Constraint R.H. Side	Allowable Increase	Allowable Decrease
$H$8	Total households	2300.00	5.98	2300.00	1E+30	700.00
$H$9	<= 30 households	1000.00	0.92	1000.00	700.00	1000.00
$H$10	31-50 households	600.00	0.82	600.00	700.00	493.75
$H$11	Border Mexico	740.00	0.00	0.00	395.00	1E+30
$H$12	<= 30 and not border	1000.00	0.00	0.00	500.00	1E+30
$H$13	>= 51 and border	140.00	-0.60	0.00	560.00	140.00

Figure 4.24: Solver Sensitivity Report for Problem 4–14: MSA Marketing Research

4-15. Consider the Whole Food Nutrition Center diet problem example discussed in Section 3.7 of Chapter 3. Use the Sensitivity Report for this LP model (shown in Figure 4.25) to answer the following questions. Each question is independent of the others.

Microsoft Excel 14.0 Sensitivity Report
Problem 4-15. Whole Food Nutrition Center

Variable Cells

Cell	Name	Final Value	Reduced Cost	Objective Coefficient	Allowable Increase	Allowable Decrease
$B$5	Number of pounds Grain A	0.025	0.000	0.330	0.063	1E+30
$C$5	Number of pounds Grain B	0.050	0.000	0.470	1E+30	0.190
$D$5	Number of pounds Grain C	0.050	0.000	0.380	1E+30	0.073

Constraints

Cell	Name	Final Value	Shadow Price	Constraint R.H. Side	Allowable Increase	Allowable Decrease
$E$8	Protein	3.000	0.038	3.000	0.000	0.250
$E$9	Riboflavin	2.350	0.000	2.000	0.350	1E+30
$E$10	Phosphorus	1.000	0.088	1.000	0.018	0.000
$E$11	Magnesium	0.425	0.000	0.425	0.000	1E+30
$E$12	Total Mix	0.125	-1.210	0.125	0.004	0.000

Figure 4.25: Solver Sensitivity Report for Problem 4–15: Whole Food Nutrition Center

(a) What is the impact if the daily allowance for protein can be reduced to 2.9 units?

(b) Whole Food Nutrition Center believes the unit price of grain A could be overestimated by 5% and the unit price of grain B could be underestimated by 10%. If these turn out to be true, what is the new optimal solution and optimal total cost?

(c) What is the impact if the reduction in the daily allowance for protein in (a) requires Whole Food Nutrition Center to simultaneously increase the daily allowance of riboflavin to 2.20 units?

4–16. Consider the cell phone manufacturing problem presented in Chapter 3 as Problem 3–6. Use Solver to create the Sensitivity Report for this LP problem. Use this report to answer the following questions. Each question is independent of the others.
  (a) Interpret the reduced costs for the products that are not currently included in the optimal production plan.
  (b) Another part of the corporation wants to take 35 hours of time on test device 3. How does this affect the optimal solution?
  (c) The company has the opportunity to obtain 20 additional hours on test device 1 at a cost of $25 per hour. Would this be worthwhile?
  (d) The company has the opportunity to give up 20 hours of time on device 1 and obtain 40 hours of time on device 2 in return. Would this be worthwhile? Justify your answer.

4–17. Consider the family farm planning problem presented in Chapter 3 as Problem 3–27. Use Solver to create the Sensitivity Report for this LP problem. Use this report to answer the following questions. Each question is independent of the others.
  (a) Is this solution a unique optimal solution? Why or why not?
  (b) If there are alternate solutions, use Solver to identify at least one other optimal solution.
  (c) Would the total profit increase if barley sales could be increased by 10%? If so, by how much?
  (d) Would the availability of more water increase the total profit? If so, by how much?

4–18. Consider the boarding stable feed problem presented in Chapter 3 as Problem 3–32. Use Solver to create the Sensitivity Report for this LP problem. Use this report to answer the following questions. Each question is independent of the others.
  (a) If the price of grain decreases by $0.01 per pound, will the optimal solution change?
  (b) Which constraints are binding? Interpret the shadow price for the binding constraints.
  (c) What would happen to the total cost if the price of mineral decreased by 20% from its current value?
  (d) For what price range of oats is the current solution optimal?

4–19. Consider Clint Hanks' problem presented in Chapter 3 as Problem 3–33. Use Solver to create the Sensitivity Report for this LP problem. Use this report to answer the following questions. Each question is independent of the others.
  (a) Interpret the shadow prices for the phosphorus and iron constraints.
  (b) What would happen to the total cost if Clint Hanks chooses to use oatmeal in the diet? Why?

(c) What would be the maximum amount Clint Hanks would be willing to pay for a serving of lasagna to make it a cost-effective item for inclusion in the diet?

(d) Is the solution to this problem a unique optimal solution? Justify your answer.

4-20. Consider the following LP problem, in which X and Y denote the number of units of products X and Y to produce, respectively:

$$\text{Maximize profit} = \$4X + \$5Y$$

subject to the constraints

$$X + 2Y \leq 10 \quad \text{(labor available, in hours)}$$
$$6X + 6Y \leq 36 \quad \text{(material available, in pounds)}$$
$$8X + 4Y \leq 40 \quad \text{(storage available, in square feet)}$$
$$X, Y \geq 0 \quad \text{(nonnegativity)}$$

The Excel Sensitivity Report for this problem is shown in Figure 4.26. Calculate and explain what happens to the optimal solution for each of the following situations. Each question is independent of the other questions.

Microsoft Excel 14.0 Sensitivity Report
Problem 4-20

Variable Cells

Cell	Name	Final Value	Reduced Cost	Objective Coefficient	Allowable Increase	Allowable Decrease
$B$4	Solution value X	2.00	0.00	4.00	1.00	1.50
$C$4	Solution value Y	4.00	0.00	5.00	3.00	1.00

Constraints

Cell	Name	Final Value	Shadow Price	Constraint R.H. Side	Allowable Increase	Allowable Decrease
$D$7	Labor	10.00	1.00	10.00	2.00	2.00
$D$8	Material	36.00	0.50	36.00	4.00	6.00
$D$9	Storage	32.00	0.00	40.00	1E+30	8.00

Figure 4.26: Solver Sensitivity Report for Problem 4-20

(a) You acquire 2 additional pounds of material.
(b) You acquire 1.5 additional hours of labor.
(c) You give up 1 hour of labor and get 1.5 pounds of material.
(d) The profit contributions for both products X and Y are changed to $4.75 each.
(e) You decide to introduce a new product that has a profit contribution of $2. Each unit of this product will use 1 hour of labor, 1 pound of material, and 2 square feet of storage space.

4-21. Consider the following LP problem, in which X and Y denote the number of units of products X and Y to produce, respectively:

$$\text{Maximize profit} = \$5X + \$5Y$$

subject to the constraints

$$2X + 3Y \leq 60 \quad \text{(resource 1)}$$
$$4X + 2Y \leq 80 \quad \text{(resource 2)}$$
$$X \quad \leq 18 \quad \text{(resource 3)}$$
$$X, Y \geq 0 \quad \text{(nonnegativity)}$$

The Excel Sensitivity Report for this problem is shown in Figure 4.27. Calculate and explain what happens to the optimal solution for each of the following situations. Each question is independent of the other questions.

Microsoft Excel 14.0 Sensitivity Report
Problem 4-21

Variable Cells

Cell	Name	Final Value	Reduced Cost	Objective Coefficient	Allowable Increase	Allowable Decrease
$B$4	Solution value X	15.00	0.00	5.00	5.00	1.67
$C$4	Solution value Y	10.00	0.00	5.00	2.50	2.50

Constraints

Cell	Name	Final Value	Shadow Price	Constraint R.H. Side	Allowable Increase	Allowable Decrease
$D$7	Resource 1	60.00	1.25	60.00	60.00	12.00
$D$8	Resource 2	80.00	0.63	80.00	8.00	40.00
$D$9	Resource 3	15.00	0.00	18.00	1E+30	3.00

Figure 4.27: Solver Sensitivity Report for Problem 4–21

(a) What is the optimal solution to this problem?
(b) For what ranges of values, holding all else constant, could each of the objective function coefficients be changed without changing the optimal solution?
(c) If we could obtain one additional unit of resource 1, how would it impact profit? Over what range of RHS values could we rely upon this value?
(d) If we were to give up one unit of resource 2, how would it impact profit? Over what range of RHS values could we rely upon this value?
(e) If we were to increase the profit for product X by $4, how would the solution change? What would be the new solution values and the new profit?
(f) If we were to decrease the profit for product Y by $2, how would the solution change? What would be the new solution values and the new profit?
(g) Suppose that two units of resource 3 were found to be unusable, how would the solution change?
(h) If we were able to obtain five more units of resource 3, would you be interested in the deal? Why or why not?
(i) If the profit for product X was increased to $7 while at the same time the profit for product Y was reduced to $4, what would be the new solution values and the new profit?
(j) Suppose you were to be offered 50 units of resource 1 at a premium of $1 each over the existing cost for that resource. Would you purchase this? If so, by how much would your profit increase?

4-22. The Good-to-Go Suitcase Company makes three kinds of suitcases: (1) Standard, (2) Deluxe, and (3) Luxury styles. Each suitcase goes through four production stages: (1) cutting and coloring, (2) assembly, (3) finishing, and (4) quality and packaging. The total number of hours available in each of these departments is 630, 600, 708, and 135, respectively.

Each Standard suitcase requires 0.7 hours of cutting and coloring, 0.5 hours of assembly, 1 hour of finishing, and 0.1 hours of quality and packaging. The corresponding numbers for each Deluxe suitcase are 1 hour, 5/6 hours, 2/3 hours, and 0.25 hours, respectively. Likewise, the corresponding numbers for each Luxury suitcase are 1 hour, 2/3 hours, 0.9 hours, and 0.4 hours, respectively.

The sales revenue for each type of suitcase is as follows: Standard $36.05, Deluxe $39.50, and Luxury $43.30. The material costs are Standard $6.25, Deluxe $7.50, and Luxury $8.50. The hourly cost of labor for each department is cutting and coloring $10, assembly $6, finishing $9, and quality and packaging $8.

The Excel layout and LP Sensitivity Report of Good-to-Go's problem are shown in Figure 4.28 and Figure 4.29, respectively. Each of the following questions is independent of the others.

	A	B	C	D	E	F	G	H
1	Good-to-Go Suitcase Company							
2								
3		Standard	Deluxe	Luxury				
4	Solution value	540.00	252.00	0.00				
5	Selling price per unit	$36.05	$39.50	$43.30	$29,421.00			
6	Material cost per unit	$6.25	$7.50	$8.50	$5,265.00			
7	Labor cost per unit	$19.80	$23.00	$25.30	$16,488.00			
8	Profit	$10.00	$9.00	$9.50	$7,668.00			
9	Constraints							Cost
10	Cutting & Coloring	0.70	1.00	1.00	630.00	<=	630	$10
11	Assembly	0.50	0.83	0.67	480.00	<=	600	$6
12	Finishing	1.00	0.67	0.90	708.00	<=	708	$9
13	Quality & Packaging	0.10	0.25	0.40	117.00	<=	135	$8
14					LHS	Sign	RHS	

Figure 4.28: Excel Layout for Good-to-Go Suitcase Company

(a) What is the optimal production plan? Which of the resources are scarce?

(b) Suppose Good-to-Go is considering including a polishing process, the cost of which would be added directly to the price. Each Standard suitcase would require 10 minutes of time in this treatment, each Deluxe suitcase would need 15 minutes, and each Luxury suitcase would need 20 minutes. Would the current production plan change as a result of this additional process if 170 hours of polishing time were available? Explain your answer.

(c) Now consider the addition of a waterproofing process where each Standard suitcase would use 1 hour of time in the process, each Deluxe suitcase would need 1.5 hours, and each Luxury suitcase would require 1.75

hours. Would this change the production plan if 900 hours were available? Why or why not?

Source: Professors Mark and Judith McKnew, Clemson University.

Microsoft Excel 14.0 Sensitivity Report
Problems P4-22&23. Good-to-Go Suitcase Company

Variable Cells

Cell	Name	Final Value	Reduced Cost	Objective Coefficient	Allowable Increase	Allowable Decrease
$B$4	Solution value Standard	540.00	0.00	10.00	3.50	2.56
$C$4	Solution value Deluxe	252.00	0.00	9.00	5.29	1.61
$D$4	Solution value Luxury	0.00	-1.12	9.50	1.12	1E+30

Constraints

Cell	Name	Final Value	Shadow Price	Constraint R.H. Side	Allowable Increase	Allowable Decrease
$E$10	Cutting & Coloring	630.00	4.38	630	52.36	134.40
$E$11	Assembly	480.00	0.00	600	1E+30	120.00
$E$12	Finishing	708.00	6.94	708	192.00	128.00
$E$13	Quality & Packaging	117.00	0.00	135	1E+30	18.00

Figure 4.29: Solver Sensitivity Report for Good-to-Go Suitcase Company

4–23. Suppose Good-to-Go (Problem 4–22) is considering the possible introduction of two new products to its line of suitcases: the Compact model (for teenagers) and the Kiddo model (for children). Market research suggests that Good-to-Go can sell the Compact model for no more than $30, whereas the Kiddo model would go for as much as $37.50 to specialty toy stores. The amount of labor and the cost of raw materials for each possible new product are as follows:

Cost Category	Compact	Kiddo
Cutting and coloring (hr.)	0.50	1.20
Assembly (hr.)	0.75	0.75
Finishing (hr.)	0.75	0.50
Quality and packaging (hr.)	0.20	0.20
Raw materials	$5.00	$4.50

Use a pricing-out strategy to check if either model would be economically attractive to make.

4–24. The Strollers-to-Go Company makes lightweight umbrella-type strollers for three different groups of children. The TiniTote is designed specifically for newborns who require extra neck support. The ToddleTote is for toddlers up to 30 pounds. Finally, the company produces a heavy-duty model called TubbyTote, which is designed to carry children up to 60 pounds. The stroller company is in the process of determining its production for each of the three types of strollers for the upcoming planning period.

The marketing department has forecast the following maximum demand for each of the strollers during the planning period: TiniTote 180, TubbyTote 70, and ToddleTote 160. Strollers-to-Go sells TiniTotes for $63.75, TubbyTotes for $82.50, and ToddleTotes for $66. As a matter of policy, it wants to produce no less than 50% of the forecast demand for each product. It also wants to keep production of ToddleTotes to a maximum of 40% of total stroller production.

The production department has estimated that the material costs for TiniTote, TubbyTote, and ToddleTote strollers will be $4, $6, and $5.50 per unit, respectively. The strollers are processed through fabrication, sewing, and assembly workstations. The metal and plastic frames are made in the fabrication station. The fabric seats are cut and stitched together in the sewing station. Finally, the frames are put together with the seats in the assembly station. In the upcoming planning period, there will be 620 hours available in fabrication, where the direct labor cost is $8.25 per hour. The sewing station has 500 hours available, and the direct labor cost is $8.50 per hour. The assembly station has 480 hours available, and the direct labor cost is $8.75 per hour.

The standard processing rate for TiniTotes is 3 hours in fabrication, 2 hours in sewing, and 1 hour in assembly. TubbyTotes require 4 hours in fabrication, 1 hour in sewing and 3 hours in assembly, whereas ToddleTotes require 2 hours in each station.

The Excel layout and LP Sensitivity Report for Strollers-to-Go's problem are shown in Figure 4.30 and Figure 4.31, respectively. Each of the following questions is independent of the others.

    a) How many strollers of each type should Strollers-to-Go make? What is the profit? Which constraints are binding?

    (b) How much labor time is being used in the fabrication, sewing, and assembly areas?

    (c) How much would Strollers-to-Go be willing to pay for an additional hour of fabrication time? For an additional hour of sewing time?

    (d) Is Strollers-to-Go producing any product at its maximum sales level? Is it producing any product at its minimum level?

    Source: Professors Mark and Judith McKnew, Clemson University.

4–25. Consider the Strollers-to-Go production problem (Problem 4–24).

    (a) Over what range of costs could the TiniTote materials vary and the current production plan remain optimal? (*Hint*: How are material costs reflected in the problem formulation?)

    (b) Suppose that Strollers-to-Go decided to polish each stroller prior to shipping. The process is fast and would require 10, 15, and 12 minutes, respectively, for TiniTote, TubbyTote, and ToddleTote strollers. Would this change the current production plan if 48 hours of polishing time were available?

	A	B	C	D	E	F	G	H
1	Strollers-to-Go Company							
2								
3		TiniTote	TubbyTote	ToddleTote				
4	Solution value	100.00	35.00	90.00				
5	Selling price per unit	$63.75	$82.50	$66.00	$15,202.50			
6	Material cost per unit	$4.00	$6.00	$5.50	$1,105.00			
7	Labor cost per unit	$50.50	$67.75	$51.00	$12,011.25			
8	Profit	$9.25	$8.75	$9.50	$2,086.25			
9	Constraints							Cost
10	Fabrication	3.0	4.0	2.0	620.00	<=	620	$8.25
11	Sewing	2.0	1.0	2.0	415.00	<=	500	$8.50
12	Assembly	1.0	3.0	2.0	385.00	<=	480	$8.75
13	Tinitote demand	1.0			100.00	<=	180	
14	Tubbytote demand		1.0		35.00	<=	70	
15	Toddletote demand			1.0	90.00	<=	160	
16	Toddletote max prod ratio	-0.4	-0.4	0.6	0.00	<=	0	
17	Tinitote min prod	1.0			100.00	>=	90	
18	Tubbytote min prod		1.0		35.00	>=	35	
19	Toddletote min prod			1.0	90.00	>=	80	
20					LHS	Sign	RHS	

Figure 4.30: Excel Layout for Strollers-to-Go Company

Microsoft Excel 14.0 Sensitivity Report
Problems 4-24to27. Strollers-to-Go Company

Variable Cells

Cell	Name	Final Value	Reduced Cost	Objective Coefficient	Allowable Increase	Allowable Decrease
$B$4	Solution value TiniTote	100.00	0.00	9.25	5.00	3.33
$C$4	Solution value TubbyTote	35.00	0.00	8.75	4.10	1E+30
$D$4	Solution value ToddleTote	90.00	0.00	9.50	1E+30	3.33

Constraints

Cell	Name	Final Value	Shadow Price	Constraint R.H. Side	Allowable Increase	Allowable Decrease
$E$10	Fabrication	620.00	3.60	620.00	110.50	43.33
$E$11	Sewing	415.00	0.00	500.00	1E+30	85.00
$E$12	Assembly	385.00	0.00	480.00	1E+30	95.00
$E$13	Tinitote demand	100.00	0.00	180.00	1E+30	80.00
$E$14	Tubbytote demand	35.00	0.00	70.00	1E+30	35.00
$E$15	Toddletote demand	90.00	0.00	160.00	1E+30	70.00
$E$16	Toddletote max prod ratio	0.00	3.85	0.00	13.00	8.67
$E$17	Tinitote min prod	100.00	0.00	90.00	10.00	1E+30
$E$18	Tubbytote min prod	35.00	-4.10	35.00	8.13	35.00
$E$19	Toddletote min prod	90.00	0.00	80.00	10.00	1E+30

Figure 4.31: Solver Sensitivity Report for Strollers-to-Go Company

4–26. Consider the Strollers-to-Go production problem (Problem 4–24).
  (a) Suppose that Strollers-to-Go could purchase additional fabrication time at a cost of $10.50 per hour. Should it be interested? Why or why not? What is the most that it would be willing to pay for an additional hour of fabrication time?
  (b) Suppose that Strollers-to-Go could purchase fabrication time only in multiples of 40-hour bundles. How many bundles should it be willing to purchase then?

4-27. Suppose that Strollers-to-Go (Problem 4–24) is considering the production of TwinTotes for families who are doubly blessed. Each TwinTote would require $7.10 in materials, 4 hours of fabrication time, 2 hours of sewing time, and 2 hours to assemble. Would this product be economically attractive to manufacture if the sales price were $86? Why or why not?

4-28. The Classic Furniture Company is trying to determine the optimal quantities to make of six possible products: tables and chairs made of oak, cherry, and pine. The products are to be made using the following resources: labor hours and three types of wood. Minimum production requirements are as follows: at least 3 each of oak and cherry tables, at least 10 each of oak and cherry chairs, and at least 5 pine chairs.

The Excel layout and LP Sensitivity Report for Classic Furniture's problem are shown in Figure 4.32 and 4.33, respectively. The objective function coefficients in the figures refer to unit profit per item. Each of the following questions is independent of the others.

(a) What is the profit represented by the objective function, and what is the production plan?
(b) Which constraints are binding?
(c) What is the range over which the unit profit for oak chairs can change without changing the production plan?
(d) What is the range over which the amount of available oak could vary without changing the combination of binding constraints?
(e) Does this Sensitivity Report indicate the presence of multiple optima? How do you know?
(f) After production is over, how many pounds of cherry wood will be left over?
(g) According to this report, how many more chairs were made than were required?

	A	B	C	D	E	F	G	H	I	J
1	Classic Furniture Company									
2										
3		Oak tables	Oak chairs	Cherry tables	Cherry chairs	Pine tables	Pine chairs			
4	Number of units	3.00	51.67	3.00	85.56	42.26	33.08			
5	Profit	$75	$35	$90	$60	$45	$20	$10,000.00		
6	Constraints									
7	Labor hours	7.5	3.5	9.0	6.0	4.5	2.0	1000.00	<=	1,000
8	Oak (pounds)	200	30					2150.00	<=	2,150
9	Cherry (pounds)			240	36			3800.00	<=	3,800
10	Pine (pounds)					180	27	8500.00	<=	8,500
11	Min oak tables	1						3.00	>=	3
12	Min cherry tables			1				3.00	>=	3
13	Min oak chairs		1					51.67	>=	10
14	Min cherry chairs				1			85.56	>=	10
15	Min pine chairs						1	33.08	>=	5
16								LHS	Sign	RHS

Figure 4.32: Excel Layout for Classic Furniture Company

Microsoft Excel 14.0 Sensitivity Report
Problems 4-28to32. Classic Furniture Company

Variable Cells

Cell	Name	Final Value	Reduced Cost	Objective Coefficient	Allowable Increase	Allowable Decrease
$B$4	Number of units Oak tables	3.00	0.00	75.00	0.00	1E+30
$C$4	Number of units Oak chairs	51.67	0.00	35.00	1E+30	0.00
$D$4	Number of units Cherry tables	3.00	0.00	90.00	0.00	1E+30
$E$4	Number of units Cherry chairs	85.56	0.00	60.00	1E+30	0.00
$F$4	Number of units Pine tables	42.26	0.00	45.00	88.33	0.00
$G$4	Number of units Pine chairs	33.08	0.00	20.00	0.00	13.25

Constraints

Cell	Name	Final Value	Shadow Price	Constraint R.H. Side	Allowable Increase	Allowable Decrease
$H$7	Labor hours	1000.00	10.00	1000.00	373.30	37.21
$H$8	Oak (pounds)	2150.00	0.00	2150.00	318.93	1250.00
$H$9	Cherry (pounds)	3800.00	0.00	3800.00	223.25	2239.78
$H$10	Pine (pounds)	8500.00	0.00	8500.00	1488.33	5039.50
$H$11	Min oak tables	3.00	0.00	3.00	6.25	2.35
$H$12	Min cherry tables	3.00	0.00	3.00	11.33	1.20
$H$13	Min oak chairs	51.67	0.00	10.00	41.67	1E+30
$H$14	Min cherry chairs	85.56	0.00	10.00	75.56	1E+30
$H$15	Min pine chairs	33.08	0.00	5.00	28.08	1E+30

Figure 4.33: Solver Sensitivity Report for Classic Furniture Company

4–29. Consider the Classic Furniture product mix problem (Problem 4–28). For each of the following situations, what would be the impact on the production plan and profit? If it is possible to compute the new profit or production plan, do so.
   (a) The unit profit for oak tables increases to $83.
   (b) The unit profit for pine chairs decreases to $13.
   (c) The unit profit for pine tables increases by $20.
   (d) The unit profit for cherry tables decreases to $85.
   (e) The company is required to make at least 20 pine chairs.
   (f) The company is required to make no more than 55 cherry chairs.

4–30. Consider the Classic Furniture product mix problem (Problem 4–28). For each of the following situations, what would be the impact on the production plan and profit? If it is possible to compute the new profit or production plan, do so.
   (a) The number of labor hours expands to 1,320.
   (b) The amount of cherry wood increases to 3,900.
   (c) The number of labor hours decreases to 950.
   (d) The company does not have a minimum requirement for cherry chairs.

4–31. Consider the Classic Furniture product mix problem (Problem 4–28). For each of the following situations, what would be the impact on the production plan and profit? If it is possible to compute the new profit or production plan, do so.
   (a) OFCs for oak tables and cherry tables each decrease by $15.
   (b) OFCs for oak tables and oak chairs are reversed.
   (c) OFCs for pine tables and pine chairs are reversed.
   (d) OFC for pine table increases by $20 while at the same time the OFC for pine chairs decreases by $10.
   (e) Unit profits for all three types of chairs are increased by $6 each.

4-32. Consider the Classic Furniture product mix problem (Problem 4–28). In answering each of the following questions, be as specific as possible. If it is possible to compute a new profit or production plan, do so.
   (a) A part-time employee who works 20 hours per week decided to quit his job. How would this affect the profit and production plan?
   (b) Classic has been approached by the factory next door, CabinetsRUs, which has a shortage of both labor and oak. CabinetsRUs proposes to take one full-time employee (who works 30 hours) plus 900 pounds of oak. It has offered $560 as compensation. Should Classic make this trade?
   (c) Classic is considering adding a new product, a cherry armoire. The armoire would consume 200 pounds of cherry wood and take 16 hours of labor. Cherry wood costs $9 per pound, and labor costs $12 per hour. The armoire would sell for $2,180. Should this product be made?
   (d) What would happen to the solution if a constraint were added to make sure that for every table made, at least two matching chairs were made?

4-33. The Tiger Catering Company is trying to determine the most economical combination of sandwiches to make for a tennis club. The club has asked Tiger to provide 70 sandwiches in a variety to include tuna, tuna and cheese, ham, ham and cheese, and cheese. The club has specified a minimum of 10 each of tuna and ham and 12 each of tuna/cheese and ham/cheese. Tiger makes the sandwiches using the following resources: bread, tuna, ham, cheese, mayonnaise, mustard, lettuce, tomato, packaging material, and labor hours.

The Excel layout and LP Sensitivity Report for Tiger Catering's problem are shown in Figure 4.34 and Figure 4.35, respectively. The objective function coefficients in the figures refer to unit cost per item. Each of the following questions is independent of the others.

	A	B	C	D	E	F	G	H	I
1	Tiger Catering Company								
2									
3		Tuna	Tuna/Ch	Ham	Ham/Ch	Cheese			
4	Number to make	10.00	30.00	10.00	12.00	8.00			
5	Cost	$2.42	$2.12	$3.35	$3.02	$2.36	$176.42		
6	Constraints								
7	Bread (slices)	2	2	2	2	2	140.00	<=	140
8	Tuna (oz.)	4	3				130.00	<=	130
9	Ham (oz.)			4	3		76.00	<=	100
10	Cheese (oz.)		1		1	4	74.00	<=	80
11	Mayo (oz.)	1.2	0.9	0.5	0.5	0.5	54.00	<=	72
12	Mustard (oz.)			0.2	0.2		4.40	<=	8
13	Lettuce (oz.)	0.25	0.25	0.25	0.25	0.25	17.50	<=	20
14	Tomato (oz.)	0.5	0.5	0.5	0.5	0.5	35.00	<=	40
15	Package (unit)	1	1	1	1	1	70.00	<=	72
16	Labor (hrs)	0.08	0.08	0.08	0.08	0.08	5.60	<=	8
17	Min total	1	1	1	1	1	70.00	>=	70
18	Min Tuna	1					10.00	>=	10
19	Min Tuna/Ch		1				30.00	>=	12
20	Min Ham			1			10.00	>=	10
21	Min Ham/Ch				1		12.00	>=	12
22							LHS	Sign	RHS

Figure 4.34: Excel Layout for Tiger Catering Company

Microsoft Excel 14.0 Sensitivity Report
Problems 4-33to37. Tiger Catering Company

Variable Cells

Cell	Name	Final Value	Reduced Cost	Objective Coefficient	Allowable Increase	Allowable Decrease
$B$4	Number to make Tuna	10.00	0.00	2.42	1E+30	0.38
$C$4	Number to make Tuna/Ch	30.00	0.00	2.12	0.24	1E+30
$D$4	Number to make Ham	10.00	0.00	3.35	1E+30	0.99
$E$4	Number to make Ham/Ch	12.00	0.00	3.02	1E+30	0.66
$F$4	Number to make Cheese	8.00	0.00	2.36	0.66	0.24

Constraints

Cell	Name	Final Value	Shadow Price	Constraint R.H. Side	Allowable Increase	Allowable Decrease
$G$7	Bread (slices)	140.00	0.00	140.00	1E+30	0.00
$G$8	Tuna (oz.)	130.00	-0.08	130.00	24.00	6.00
$G$9	Ham (oz.)	76.00	0.00	100.00	1E+30	24.00
$G$10	Cheese (oz.)	74.00	0.00	80.00	1E+30	6.00
$G$11	Mayo (oz.)	54.00	0.00	72.00	1E+30	18.00
$G$12	Mustard (oz.)	4.40	0.00	8.00	1E+30	3.60
$G$13	Lettuce (oz.)	17.50	0.00	20.00	1E+30	2.50
$G$14	Tomato (oz.)	35.00	0.00	40.00	1E+30	5.00
$G$15	Package (unit)	70.00	0.00	72.00	1E+30	2.00
$G$16	Labor (hrs)	5.60	0.00	8.00	1E+30	2.40
$G$17	Min total	70.00	2.36	70.00	0.00	8.00
$G$18	Min Tuna	10.00	0.38	10.00	13.50	10.00
$G$19	Min Tuna/Ch	30.00	0.00	12.00	18.00	1E+30
$G$20	Min Ham	10.00	0.99	10.00	6.00	1.50
$G$21	Min Ham/Ch	12.00	0.66	12.00	8.00	2.00

Figure 4.35: Solver Sensitivity Report for Tiger Catering Company

(a) What is the optimal cost represented by the objective function, and what is the optimal sandwich-making plan?
(b) Which constraints are binding?
(c) What is the range over which the cost for cheese sandwiches could vary without changing the production plan?
(d) What is the range over which the quantity of tuna could vary without changing the combination of binding constraints?
(e) Does this Sensitivity Report indicate the presence of multiple optimal solutions? How do you know?
(f) After the sandwiches are made, how many labor hours remain?

4-34. Consider the Tiger Catering problem (Problem 4-33). For each of the following situations, what would be the impact on the sandwich-making plan and total cost? If it is possible to compute the new cost or sandwich-making plan, do so.
(a) The unit cost for tuna sandwiches decreases by $0.30.
(b) The unit cost for tuna and cheese sandwiches increases to $2.40.
(c) The unit cost for ham sandwiches increases to $3.75.
(d) The unit cost for ham and cheese sandwiches decreases by $0.70.
(e) The club does not want any more than 12 ham sandwiches.
(f) The unit cost for cheese sandwiches decreases to $2.05.

4-35. Consider the Tiger Catering problem (Problem 4-33). For each of the following situations, what would be the impact on the sandwich-making plan and total cost? If it is possible to compute the new cost or sandwich-making plan, do so.
(a) The quantity of tuna available decreases to 120 ounces.

(b) The quantity of ham available increases to 115 ounces.
(c) The quantity of cheese available decreases to 72 ounces.
(d) Tiger is required to deliver a minimum of 13 tuna sandwiches.
(e) Tiger is required to deliver only a minimum of 10 tuna and cheese sandwiches.
(f) Tiger is asked to bring a minimum of only 66 sandwiches.

4-36. Consider the Tiger Catering problem (Problem 4–33). For each of the following situations, what would be the impact on the sandwich-making plan and total cost? If it is possible to compute the new cost or sandwich-making plan, do so.
(a) The cost of ham sandwiches and the cost of ham and cheese sandwiches each decreases by $0.35.
(b) The cost of both ham and cheese sandwiches and cheese sandwiches increases by $0.60.
(c) The cost of tuna decreases by $0.10 per ounce. (*Hint:* Note that tuna sandwiches use 4 ounces of tuna and tuna/cheese sandwiches use 3 ounces of tuna.)
(d) The availability of tuna increases by 10 ounces, and the availability of ham decreases by 10 ounces.
(e) A 16-ounce jar of mustard is sent by mistake instead of a 16-ounce jar of mayonnaise. (*Hint:* This would decrease the quantity of mayonnaise by 16 ounces and increase the quantity of mustard by 16 ounces.)

4-37. Consider the Tiger Catering problem (Problem 4–33). In answering each of the following questions, be as specific as possible. If it is possible to compute a new cost or sandwich-making plan, do so.
(a) An additional pound of tuna can be obtained for a premium of $1.50. Should this tuna be purchased?
(b) The tennis club is willing to accept fewer ham and ham and cheese sandwiches. How many of these sandwiches would Tiger try to substitute with other types before the firm would not be able to predict its new total cost?
(c) The tennis club wants to include a dill pickle slice with each meat sandwich order. If Tiger finds an average of 18 slices in a 2-pound pickle jar, how many jars should be included with the club's order?

4-38. Consider Figure 4.11, which shows the sensitivity report for the Flair Furniture example in Section 4.3. For each of the situations described below, check to see if the 100% rule can be used to determine the impact of the simultaneous changes described. If so, compute the total change in profit. Each question is independent of the other questions.
(a) Carpentry hours increase by 50, and painting hours increase by 400.
(b) The maximum tables decrease by 70, and painting hours increase by 100.
(c) The maximum chairs decrease by 100, and the maximum tables increase by 100.
(d) Carpentry hours decrease by 100, and painting hours decrease by 300.
(e) The profit contribution of chairs increases by $2.00 per unit, and maximum chairs allowed increases by 30.

(f) The profit contribution of chairs decreases by $1.00 per unit, and the profit contribution of tables increases by $2.00 per unit.

4–39. Consider Figure 4.20, which shows the Sensitivity Report for the Burn-Off Diet Drink example in Section 4.7. For each of the situations described below, check to see if the 100% rule can be used to determine the impact of the simultaneous changes described. If so, compute the total change in cost. Each question is independent of the other questions.
(a) The cost of ingredient B increases by $0.05, and the cost of ingredient A increases by $0.05.
(b) The cost of ingredient C decreases by $0.02, and the chemical Y requirement increases by 30.
(c) The cost of ingredient A increases by $0.02, and the cost of ingredient D increases by $0.03.
(d) The chemical X requirement decreases by 3, the chemical Y requirement increases by 1, and the chemical Z max limit increases by 6.
(e) The daily dosage minimum decreases by 1, and the daily dosage maximum decreases by 3.
(f) The daily dosage maximum increases by 20, and the chemical X requirement increases by 35.

4–40. Consider Figure 4.11, which shows the Sensitivity Report for the Flair Furniture Company example in Section 4.3. By examining this figure and the LP formulation, can you compute by hand the optimal product mix if carpentry hours increase by 200 units? If so, what is the answer?

4–41. Consider Figure 4.16, which shows the Sensitivity Report for the Anderson Home Electronics example in Section 4.4. Use the Sensitivity Report to answer the following questions, if possible. Each question is independent of the other questions.
(a) What is the impact of a 300-unit decrease in the supply of electronic components?
(b) What is the impact if the profit margin of the Satellite Radio Tuner decreases by $2.00?
(c) What is the impact if the profit margin of the Satellite Radio Tuner increases by $10.00?
(d) What is the impact if the profit margin of the LCD TV decreases by $2.00?
(e) What is the impact if the profit margin of the Blue-Ray DVD player decreases by $10.00?

4–42. Consider the Flair Furniture example from Sections 4.2 and 4.3. Suppose that the company is considering the option of making stools in addition to its tables and chairs. Stools take 1 hour of carpentry time and 0.5 hours of painting time. Each hour of carpentry time costs $20, and each hour of painting time costs $15. With the help of Figure 4.11 and using hand calculations, what would the minimum selling price of stools need to be to make offering them worthwhile financially?

4-43. Consider the Anderson Home Electronics example presented in Section 4.4. Suppose that the firm is considering the introduction of a new generation product to try to stay at the forefront of technology. The Blu-Ray TV is an LCD television with a built-in Blu-Ray DVD player. Each Blu-Ray TV will use 8 electronic components, 8 non-electronic components, and 4 hours of assembly time. With the help of Figure 4.16 and using hand calculations, what would the minimum selling price of the Blu-Ray TV need to be to make offering the new product worthwhile financially?

4-44. Consider Figure 4.22 from the Hong Kong Bank labor planning example presented in Solved Problem 4–1. Suppose that every day between 11:00 A.M. and noon, two tellers' worth of demand comes from employees from a nearby international company that requires a large number of teller transactions from the bank. The employees make these transactions and then go to lunch. How much money *per week* should the Hong Kong Bank be willing to offer its client to get the client to send all its employees over during the noon-1:00 P.M. time frame each day instead?

4-45. Consider Figure 4.22 from the Hong Kong Bank labor-planning example presented in Solved Problem 4–1. What would be the impact on daily cost if corporate policy changed to allow the part-time hours to increase to a maximum of 75% of the day's total requirement (instead of just 50%)?

Chapter 5
Transportation, Assignment, and Network Models

Have you ever looked at the map of a large amusement park and tried to determine the quickest route to the most popular roller coaster? There may be several paths to get there. Which one will allow you to start screaming as soon as possible? Or, have you coached a basketball team and tried to determine which starters are best for which positions? Cindy is fast, but she has a lot of turnovers. Julie is more careful with the ball, but she's not good at creating scoring opportunities. Who should be the point guard?

These are two examples of *network flow models*. Companies face problems like these all the time. The problems are related because they all can be represented by modeling flow through a system where there are choices regarding which paths to take. The examples that we cover in this chapter can all be formulated and solved as linear programs. Some of them always have the same structure for the same problem size (for example, a *transportation problem* with three plants and three distribution centers). In this case, the manager can design an Excel template to handle problems for that particular size, and subsequently only the parameters need to be updated when a new problem needs to be solved.

After describing the characteristics of network models, we provide examples for six different types of network problems in this chapter. They all have similar types of constraints that ensure that "flow" entering or leaving a *node* in the network needs to satisfy some condition. Some of these models may be particularly useful for organizations or governments operating physical networks; for example, roadways, pipelines, electric grids, or computer networks. Some of the models work well for managers of distribution networks (e.g., shipping decisions). As in Chapters 2 to 4, we can find *optimal* solutions to these problems because they are formulated as linear programs.

Chapter Objectives

After completing this chapter, you will be able to:
1. Structure special LP network flow models.
2. Set up and solve transportation models, using Excel's Solver.
3. Set up and solve transportation models with Max-Min and Min-Max objectives.
4. Extend the basic transportation model to include transshipment points.
5. Set up and solve maximal-flow network models, using Excel's Solver.
6. Set up and solve shortest-path network models, using Excel's Solver.
7. Connect all points of a network while minimizing total distance, using the minimal-spanning tree model.

5.1 Types of Network Models

In this chapter, we examine six different examples of special linear programming (LP) models, called *network flow models*: (1) transportation, (2) transshipment, (3) assignment, (4) maximal-flow, (5) shortest-path, and (6) minimal-spanning tree models. Networks consist of nodes (or points) and arcs (or lines) that connect the nodes together. Roadways, telephone systems, and citywide water systems are all examples of networks.

Transportation Model

The transportation model deals with the distribution of goods from several supply points (also called origins, or *sources*) to a number of demand points (also called destinations, or *sinks*). Usually, we have a given capacity of goods at each source and a given requirement for the goods at each destination. The most common objective of a transportation model is to schedule shipments from sources to destinations so that total production and transportation costs are minimized. Occasionally, transportation models can have a maximization objective (e.g., maximize total profit of shipping goods from sources to destinations).

Transportation models can also be used when a firm is trying to decide where to locate a new facility. Before opening a new warehouse, factory, or office, it is good practice to consider a number of alternative sites. Good financial decisions concerning facility location also involve minimizing total production and transportation costs for the entire system.

Transshipment Model

In a basic transportation model, shipments either leave a supply point or arrive at a demand point. An extension of the transportation model is called the transshipment model, in which a point can have shipments that both arrive and leave. An example would be a warehouse where shipments arrive from factories and then leave for retail outlets. It may be possible for a firm to achieve cost savings (economies of scale) by consolidating shipments from several factories at the warehouse and then sending them together to retail outlets. This type of approach is the basis for the *hub-and-spoke* system of transportation employed by most major U.S. airlines. For example, most travel on Delta Air Lines from the western U.S. to the eastern U.S. (or vice versa) involves a connection through Delta's hubs in Atlanta, Georgia, or Detroit, Michigan.

Assignment Model

The assignment model refers to the class of LP problems that involve determining the most efficient assignment of people to projects, salespeople to territories, contracts to bidders, jobs to machines, and so on. The typical objective is to minimize total cost or total time of performing the tasks at hand, although a maximization objective is also possible. An important characteristic of assignment models is that each job or worker can be assigned to at most one workstation or project, and vice versa.

Maximal-Flow Model
Consider a network that has a specific starting point (called the *origin*) and a specific ending point (called the *destination*). The arcs in the network have capacities that limit the amounts of flow that can occur on them. These capacities can be different for different arcs. The maximal-flow model finds the maximum flow that can occur from the origin to the destination through this network. This model can be used to determine, for example, the maximum number of vehicles (cars, trucks, and so forth) that can go through a network of roads from one location to another.

Shortest-Path Model
Consider a network that has a specified origin and a specified destination. The arcs in the network are such that there are many paths available to go from the origin to the destination. The shortest-path model finds the shortest path or route through this network from the origin to the destination. For example, this model can be used to find the shortest distance and route from one city to another through a network of roads. The *length* of each arc can be a function of its distance, travel time, travel cost, or any other measure.

Minimal-Spanning Tree Model
The minimal-spanning tree model determines the path through the network that connects all the points. The most common objective is to minimize total distance of all arcs used in the path. For example, when the points represent houses in a subdivision, the minimal-spanning tree model can be used to determine the best way to connect all the houses to electrical power, water systems, and so on, in a way that minimizes the total distance or length of power lines or water pipes.

Implementation Issues
All the examples used to describe the various network models in this chapter are rather small (compared to real problems), to make it easier for you to understand the models. In some cases, the small size of these network examples may make them solvable by inspection or intuition. For larger real-world problems, however, finding a solution can be very difficult and requires the use of computer-based modeling approaches, as discussed here.

For network models, we depart from our convention in previous chapters of using a separate column for each decision variable. As we shall see, double-subscripted variables accommodate many network models naturally. Excel provides an efficient tool for solving such problems because the decision variables can be set up in the form of a table. We often wish to add across rows or down columns (representing summing across one of the two subscripts), and Excel accomplishes this task easily. Furthermore, network models of a specific dimension (e.g., a transportation model with 3 origins and 4 destinations) are often formulated in the exact same way, where only the parameters differ from problem to problem. As such, managers can create

Excel templates for problems of a specific size (e.g., a 3×4 transportation problem) where all they have to do is enter new numbers and run Solver with all of its settings (objective function, constraints, etc.) pre-defined.

5.2 Characteristics of Network Models

Each of the circles (numbered 1 to 5) in Figure 5.1 is called a *node*. A node can be defined as the location of a specific point on the network. For example, nodes could represent cities on a road network, Ethernet ports on a campus computer network, houses in a city's water supply network, etc. An *arc* is a line that connects two nodes to each other. Arcs could represent roads that connect cities, computer network cables, pipes that carry water to each house, etc. Figure 5.1 shows a network that has 5 nodes and 10 arcs.

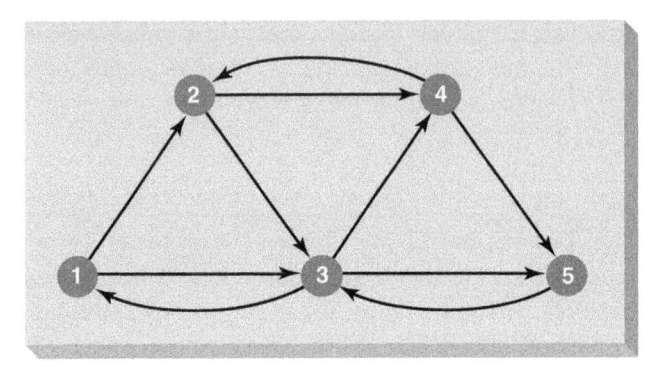

Figure 5.1: Example of a Network (Nodes are circles; arcs are lines.)

Types of Arcs

As shown in Figure 5.1, it is not necessary for an arc to exist between every pair of nodes in a network. A network that does have arcs between all pairs of nodes is called a *fully connected* network. Arcs can be either *unidirectional* (meaning that flow can occur only in one direction, as in a one-way road) or *bidirectional* (meaning that flow can occur in either direction). From a modeling perspective, it is convenient to represent a bidirectional arc with a pair of unidirectional arcs with opposite flow directions. This concept is illustrated in Figure 5.1 by the pairs of arcs between nodes 1 and 3, nodes 3 and 5, and nodes 2 and 4. Flows between all other pairs of nodes in Figure 5.1 are unidirectional.

Arcs can also be classified as capacitated or uncapacitated. A *capacitated* arc has a limited capacity, as in the case of a water pipe or a road. An *uncapacitated* arc, in contrast, can support an unlimited flow. In practice, this does not necessarily mean that the arc has infinite capacity. Rather, it means that the arc's capacity is so high that it is not a constraint in the model. An example could be a road in a small, rural area. The road rarely encounters traffic congestion because its capacity is far greater than the number of vehicles traveling on it at any one time.

Types of Nodes

Nodes can be classified as *supply nodes*, *demand nodes*, or *transshipment* nodes. A supply node, also known as an origin or a source, denotes a location such as a factory that creates goods. That is, goods enter the network at that node.

A demand node, also known as a destination or a sink, denotes a location such as a retail outlet that consumes goods. That is, goods leave the network at that node.

A transshipment node denotes a location through which goods pass on their way to or from other locations. In many practical networks, the same node can be a combination of a supply node, a demand node, and a transshipment node. For example, in the case of Delta Air Lines, Atlanta is a supply node for people starting their trip from Atlanta, a demand node for people ending their trip in Atlanta, and a transshipment node for people taking connecting flights through Atlanta.

Common Characteristics

Why are transportation models (and other network flow models) a special case of LP models? The reason is that many network models share some common characteristics, as follows:

1. In *all* network models, the decision variables represent the amounts of flows (or shipments) that occur on the unidirectional arcs in the network. For example, the LP model for the network shown in Figure 5.1 will have 10 decision variables representing the amounts of flows on the 10 unidirectional arcs.
2. The constraint coefficients (i.e., the coefficients in front of decision variables in a constraint) for all flow balance constraints and most other problem-specific constraints in network models equal either 0 or 1. That is, if a decision variable exists in a constraint in a network model, its constraint coefficient is usually 1. This special trait allows network flow models to be solved very quickly, using specialized algorithms. However, we use Solver in the same manner as in Chapters 2 and 3 to solve these models here.
3. If all supply values at the supply nodes and all demand values at the demand nodes are whole numbers (i.e., integer values), the solution to a network model will automatically result in integer values for the decision variables, even if we don't impose an explicit condition to this effect. This property is especially useful in modeling the assignment and shortest-path models discussed later in this chapter.

5.3 Transportation Model

Let's begin to illustrate the transportation model with an example dealing with the Executive Furniture Company. This company manufactures office desks at three locations: Des Moines, Evansville, and Fort Lauderdale. The firm distributes the desks through regional warehouses located in Albuquerque, Boston, and Cleveland (see Figure 5.2).

Decision Modeling In Action

Optimizing Daily Dray Operations Across an Intermodal Freight Network

Continuously increasing fuel prices and the geographic expansion of distribution networks have made intermodal freight transport systems a competitive alternative to single mode transportation services. Intermodal freight transport systems enable a trade-off between cost and efficiency.

In large metropolitan hub areas, an intermodal freight network may involve several hundred drivers and up to thousands of daily containers that move to or from several distinct rail ramps. The main objective related to an intermodal freight network is to maximize the driver's productivity and minimize the time and miles not directly associated with moving loaded containers to or from rail ramps.

Schneider National Inc., a $4 billion premier provider of truckload, logistics and intermodal services in North America and China, implemented a study to find a solution to optimize intermodal freight network transportation. Schneider has provided expert transportation and logistics solutions over the past 80 years.

Schneider formulated the problem using a set-partitioning model and solved it using column-generation heuristic techniques. The solution they developed integrates with a commercial transportation management system to provide real-time data to maintain status information related to shipments and drivers and accordingly send recommendations to a driver assignment process.

According to previous analysis done by Schneider, the cost of outsourcing a shipment to a foreign carrier is approximately 60% more expensive than covering the shipment with a company driver. After implementing the proposed solution, they have been able to realize a 5% decrease in their reliance on foreign carriers, resulting in a 3% reduction in overall dray cost.

Source: Based on X. Sun, et al. "Optimizing Transportation by Inventory Routing and Workload Balancing: Optimizing Daily Dray Operations across an Intermodal Freight Network," *Interfaces* 44, 6 (November – December 2014): 579–590.

Figure 5.2: Geographic Locations of Executive Furniture's Factories and Warehouses

Estimates of the monthly supplies available at each factory and the monthly desk demands at each of the three warehouses are shown in Figure 5.3.

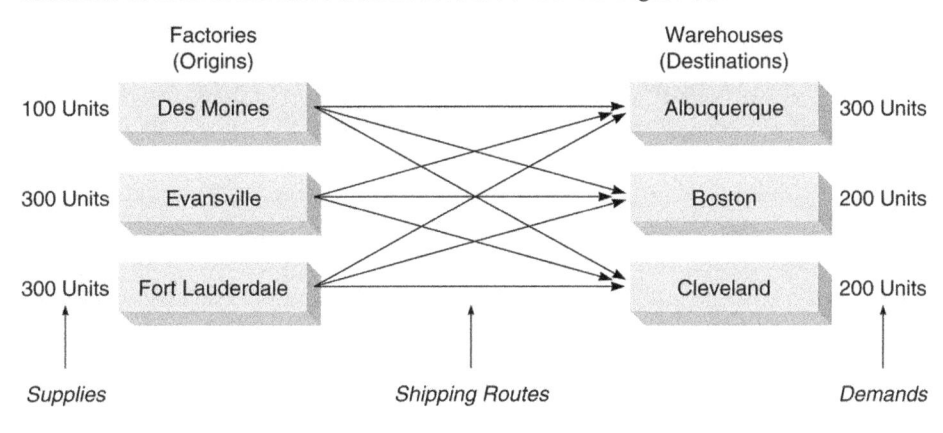

Figure 5.3: Network Model for Executive Furniture—Transportation

The firm has found that production costs per desk are identical at each factory, and hence the only relevant costs are those of shipping from each factory to each warehouse. These costs, shown in Table 5.1, are assumed to be constant, regardless of the volume shipped.[1] The transportation problem can now be described as *determi-*

---

[1] The other assumptions that held for LP problems (see Chapter 2) are still applicable to transportation problems.

ning the number of desks to be shipped on each route so as to minimize total transportation cost. This, of course, must be done while observing the restrictions regarding factory supplies and warehouse demands.

Table 5.1: Transportation Costs per Desk for Executive Furniture

	To		
From	Albuquerque	Boston	Cleveland
Des Moines	$5	$4	$3
Evansville	$8	$4	$3
Fort Lauderdale	$9	$7	$5

We see in Figure 5.3 that the total factory supply available (700) is exactly equal to the total warehouse demand (700). When this situation of equal total demand and total supply occurs (something that is rather unusual in real life), a balanced model is said to exist. Later in this section we look at how to deal with *unbalanced* models—namely, those in which total demands are greater than or less than total supplies.

LP Formulation for Executive Furniture's Transportation Model

Because there are three factories (Des Moines, Evansville, and Fort Lauderdale) and three warehouses (Albuquerque, Boston, and Cleveland), there are nine potential shipping routes. We therefore need nine decision variables to define the number of units that would be shipped from each supply node (factory) to each demand node (warehouse). In general, the number of decision variables in a basic transportation model is the number of supply nodes multiplied by the number of demand nodes.

Recall from section 5.2 that in the transportation model (as well as in other network flow models), decision variables denote the flow between two nodes in the network. Therefore, it is convenient to represent these flows by using double-subscripted decision variables. We let the first subscript represent the supply node and the second subscript represent the demand node of the flow. Hence, for the Executive Furniture example, let

$$X_{ij} = \text{number of desks shipped from factory } i \text{ to warehouse } j$$

where

$i = D$ (for Des Moines), E (for Evansville), or F (for Fort Lauderdale)
$j = A$ (for Albuquerque), B (for Boston), or C (for Cleveland)

Objective Function The objective function for this model seeks to minimize the total transportation cost and can be expressed as

$$\text{Minimize total shipping costs} = 5X_{DA} + 4X_{DB} + 3X_{DC} + 8X_{EA} + 4X_{EB} \\ + 3X_{EC} + 9X_{FA} + 7X_{FB} + 5X_{FC}$$

Constraints Because the Executive Furniture example is a balanced model, we know that all desks will be shipped from the factories and all demand will be satisfied at the warehouses. The number of desks shipped from each factory will therefore be equal to the number of desks available, and the number of desks received at each warehouse will be equal to the number of desks required.

Supply Constraints The *supply constraints* deal with the supplies available at the three factories. For each factory, the number of desks leaving the factory will equal the supply at that factory. These constraints are written as

$$X_{DA} + X_{DB} + X_{DC} = 100 \quad \text{(Des Moines supply)}$$
$$X_{EA} + X_{EB} + X_{EC} = 300 \quad \text{(Evansville supply)}$$
$$X_{FA} + X_{FB} + X_{FC} = 300 \quad \text{(Fort Lauderdale supply)}$$

Demand Constraints Now, let's model the *demand constraints* that deal with the warehouse demands. At each warehouse, the number of desks received will equal demand. These constraints are written as

$$X_{DA} + X_{EA} + X_{FA} = 300 \quad \text{(Albuquerque demand)}$$
$$X_{DB} + X_{EB} + X_{FB} = 200 \quad \text{(Boston demand)}$$
$$X_{DC} + X_{EC} + X_{FC} = 200 \quad \text{(Cleveland demand)}$$

In general, the number of constraints in the basic transportation model is the sum of the number of supply nodes and the number of demand nodes. There could, however, be other problem-specific constraints that restrict shipments in individual routes. For example, if we wished to ensure that no more than 100 desks are shipped from Evansville to Cleveland, an additional constraint in the model would be $X_{EC} \leq 100$. Moreover, if we wanted to prohibit *any* shipment along that route we could say $X_{EC} = 0$. Alternatively, we could assign a very large cost to that route so that there would be no way that Solver would allow that shipment. An advantage of this approach is that the basic Solver setup for the 3×3 transportation model would not have to be modified by adding another constraint.

Solving the Transportation Model Using Excel

For many network models, the number of arcs (and, hence, decision variables) could be quite large. For this reason, it is usually more convenient to model network flow models in Excel in such a way that decision variables are in a *tabular* form, with rows (for example) denoting supply nodes and columns denoting demand nodes. The formula view of the Excel layout for Executive Furniture's transportation model is shown in Figure 5.4, and the optimal solution is shown in Figure 5.5.

248 — Chapter 5: Transportation, Assignment, and Network Models

	A	B	C	D	E	F	G
1	Executive Furniture (Transportation)						
2							
3	Shipments:		To				
4	From	Albuquerque	Boston	Cleveland	Flow out		Capacity
5	Des Moines				=SUM(B5:D5)	=	100
6	Evansville				=SUM(B6:D6)	=	300
7	Fort Lauderdale				=SUM(B7:D7)	=	300
8	Flow in	=SUM(B5:B7)	=SUM(C5:C7)	=SUM(D5:D7)	LHS	Sign	RHS
9		=	=	=	Sign		
10	Demand	300	200	200	RHS		
11							
12	Unit costs:		To				
13	From	Albuquerque	Boston	Cleveland			
14	Des Moines	5	4	3			
15	Evansville	8	4	3			
16	Fort Lauderdale	9	7	5			
17							
18	Total cost =	=SUMPRODUCT(B14:D16,B5:D7)					

Callouts:
- Flow in = Sum of all entries in the column.
- Decision variables are modeled in a table.
- Flow out = Sum of all entries in the row.
- In this layout, factories are shown as rows, and warehouses are shown as columns. Alternatively, we could show factories as columns and warehouses as rows.
- All costs are also modeled in a table.
- Objective function value is SUMPRODUCT of all entries in cost table and decision variable table.

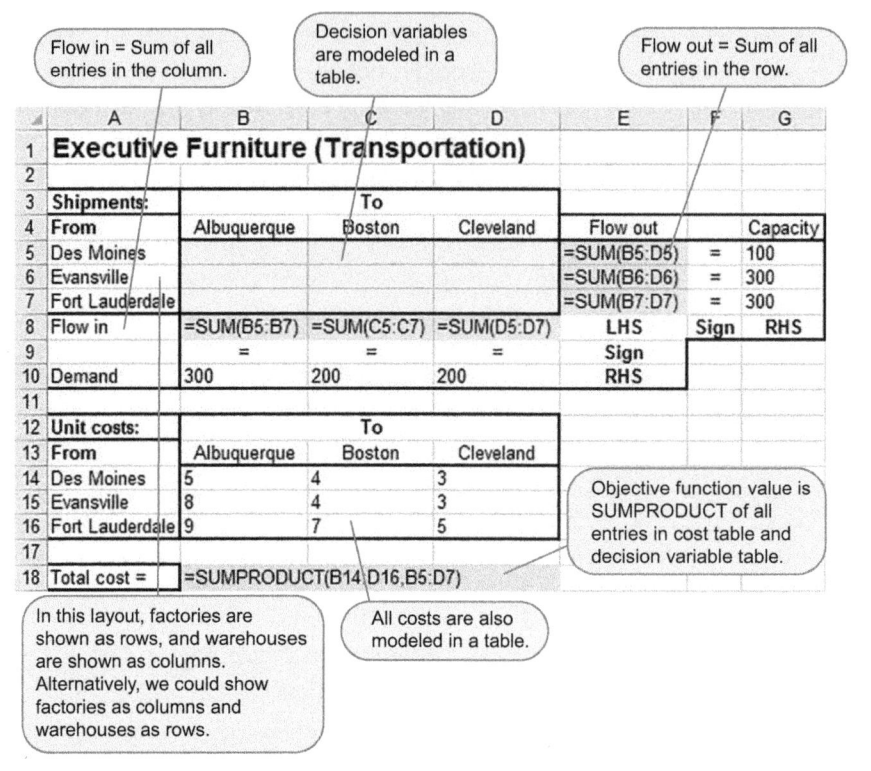

Figure 5.4: Formula View of Excel Layout for Executive Furniture—Transportation

File: Figure 5.4.xlsx, Sheet: Figure 5.4

EXCEL NOTES

- The Companion Website for this book, at *degruyter.com/view/product/486941*, contains the Excel file for each sample problem discussed here. The relevant file/sheet name is shown below the title of the corresponding figure in this book.

- In each of our Excel layouts, for clarity, changing variable cells are shaded yellow, the objective cell is shaded green, and cells containing the LHS formula for each constraint are shaded blue.

By adding the row entries, we can easily calculate the appropriate total flows coming out of each factory (the LHS of the supply constraints). The supply constraints are entered into Solver all at once as $E$5:$E$7 = $G$5:$G$7. Similarly, by adding the column entries, we can easily calculate the appropriate flows coming into each warehouse (demand constraint). The demand constraints are entered into Solver all at once as $B$8:$D$8 = $B$10:$D$10. Since this is a balanced transportation model, all supply and all demand constraints have = signs in the model.

Transportation Model — 249

Factories | **Warehouses** | All constraints are = since problem is balanced

	A	B	C	D	E	F	G
1	**Executive Furniture (Transportation)**						
2							
3	Shipments:		To				
4	From	Albuquerque	Boston	Cleveland	Flow out		Capacity
5	Des Moines	100.0	0.0	0.0	100.0	=	100.0
6	Evansville	0.0	200.0	100.0	300.0	=	300.0
7	Fort Lauderdale	200.0	0.0	100.0	300.0	=	300.0
8	Flow in	300.0	200.0	200.0	LHS	Sign	RHS
9		=	=	=		Sign	
10	Demand	300.0	200.0	200.0	RHS		
11							
12	Unit costs:		To				
13	From	Albuquerque	Boston	Cleveland			
14	Des Moines	$5	$4	$3			
15	Evansville	$8	$4	$3			
16	Fort Lauderdale	$9	$7	$5			
17							
18	Total cost =	$3,900					

Solver Parameters

Set Objective: $B$18

To: ○ Max ● Min ○ Value

By Changing Variable Cells:
$B$5:$D$7

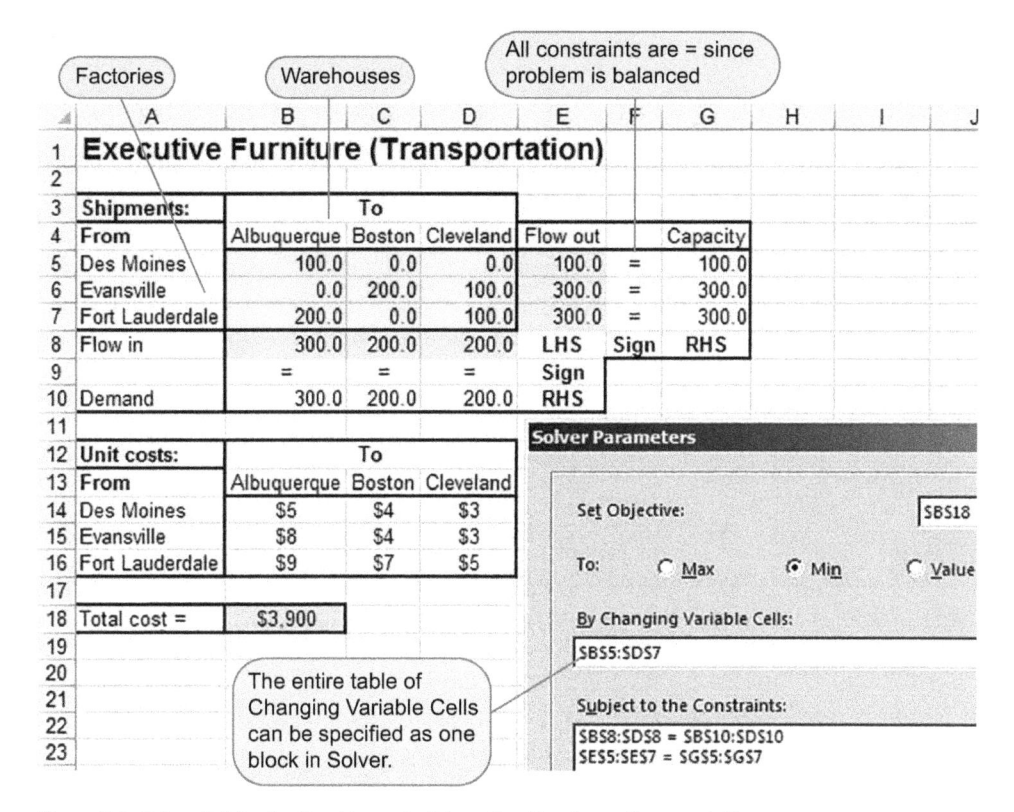

Subject to the Constraints:
$B$8:$D$8 = $B$10:$D$10
$E$5:$E$7 = $G$5:$G$7

The entire table of Changing Variable Cells can be specified as one block in Solver.

Figure 5.5: Solver Entries for Excel Layout of Executive Furniture—Transportation

📊 File: Figure 5.4.xlsx, Sheet: Figure 5.5

The optimum solution for the Executive Furniture Company is to ship 100 desks from Des Moines to Albuquerque, 200 desks from Evansville to Boston, 100 desks from Evansville to Cleveland, 200 desks from Fort Lauderdale to Albuquerque, and 100 desks from Fort Lauderdale to Cleveland. The total shipping cost is $3,900. Observe that because all supplies and demands were integer values, all shipments turned out to be integer values as well.

Unbalanced Transportation Models

In the Executive Furniture example, the total supply from the three factories equals the total requirements at the three warehouses. All supply and demand constraints could therefore be specified as equalities (i.e., using the = sign). But what if the total supply exceeds the total demand, or vice versa? In these cases, we have an **unbalanced model**, and the supply or demand constraints need to be modified accordingly.

There are two possible scenarios: (1) Total supply exceeds the total demand and (2) total supply is less than the total demand.

Total Supply Exceeds the Total Demand If total supply exceeds total demand, all demands will be fully satisfied at the demand nodes, but some of the supplies at one or more supply nodes will not need to be shipped out. That is, they will remain at the supply nodes. To allow for this possibility, the total flow *out* of each supply node should be permitted to be smaller than the supply at that node. The total flow *into* the demand nodes will, however, continue to be written with = signs.

Assume that the supply and demand values in the Executive Furniture example are altered so that the total supply at the three factories exceeds the total demand at the three warehouses. For example, assume that the monthly supply at Des Moines is 150 desks. The total supply is now 750 desks, while the total demand is only 700 desks. The total flow out of Des Moines (i.e., $X_{DA} + X_{DB} + X_{DC}$) should now be permitted to be smaller than the total supply. That is, the constraint needs to be written as an inequality, as follows:

$$X_{DA} + X_{DB} + X_{DC} \leq 150 \text{ (Des Moines supply)}$$

Likewise, the supply constraints at the Evansville and Fort Lauderdale factories would need to be revised as

$$X_{EA} + X_{EB} + X_{EC} \leq 300 \quad \text{(Evansville supply)}$$
$$X_{FA} + X_{FB} + X_{FC} \leq 300 \quad \text{(Fort Lauderdale supply)}$$

Because the demand constraints at the three warehouses will continue to be written as = constraints, the solution will show movement of 700 desks between the factories and the warehouses. The remaining supply of 50 desks will remain at their original locations at one or more of the factories.

Total Supply Is Less Than the Total Demand When total supply is less than total demand, all items at the supply nodes will be shipped out, but demands at one or more demand nodes will remain unsatisfied. To allow for this possibility, the total flow *in* at demand nodes should be permitted to be smaller than the requirement at those nodes. The total flow *out* of supply nodes will, however, continue to be written with = signs.

Assume that the supply and demand values in the Executive Furniture example are altered so that the total supply at the three factories is now *less* than the total demand at the three warehouses. For example, assume that the monthly demand at the Albuquerque warehouse is 350 desks. The total flow *into* Albuquerque (i.e., $X_{DA} + X_{EA} + X_{FA}$) should now be permitted to be smaller than the total demand. The demand constraint for this warehouse should therefore be written as

$$X_{DA} + X_{EA} + X_{FA} \leq 350 \quad \text{(Albuquerque demand)}$$

Likewise, the demand constraints at the Boston and Cleveland warehouses would need to be written as

$$X_{DB} + X_{EB} + X_{FB} \leq 200 \quad \text{(Boston demand)}$$
$$X_{DC} + X_{EC} + X_{FC} \leq 200 \quad \text{(Cleveland demand)}$$

In this case, because the supply constraints at the three factories will continue to be written as = constraints, the solution will show movements of 700 desks between the factories and the warehouses. The remaining demand of 50 desks will remain unsatisfied, and one or more of the warehouses will not get its full share of desks.

Alternate Optimal Solutions

Just as with regular LP problems, it is possible for a transportation model to have alternate or multiple optimal solutions. In fact, having multiple optimal solutions is quite common in transportation models. Practically speaking, multiple optimal solutions provide management with greater flexibility in selecting and using resources. Chapter 4 (section 4.4) indicates that if the allowable increase or allowable decrease for the objective coefficient of a variable has a value of zero (in the Variable Cells table of the Solver Sensitivity Report), this usually indicates the presence of alternate optimal solutions. In Solved Problem 4–1, we saw how Solver can be used to identify alternate optimal solutions.

An Application of the Transportation Model: Facility Location

The transportation model has proven to be especially useful in helping firms decide where to locate a new factory or warehouse. Because a new location has major financial implications for a firm, several alternative locations must usually be considered and evaluated. Even though a firm may consider a wide variety of subjective factors, including quality of labor supply, presence of labor unions, community attitude, utilities, and recreational and educational facilities, a final decision also involves minimizing total production and shipping costs. This means that the facility location analysis should analyze each location alternative within the framework of the overall distribution system. The new location that will yield the minimum cost for the entire system should be the one recommended.

How do we use the transportation model to help in this decision-making process? Consider a firm that is trying to decide between several competing locations for a new factory. To determine which new factory yields the lowest total systemwide cost, we solve separate transportation models: one for each of the possible locations. We illustrate this application of the transportation model in Solved Problem 5–1 at the end of this chapter, with the case of the Hardgrave Machine Company, which is trying to decide between Seattle, Washington, and Birmingham, Alabama, as a site to build a new factory.

Decision Modeling In Action

Walmart Optimizes the Carton Mix at Distribution Centers

To accommodate its continuous growth in online shopping, Walmart has launched distribution centers in different locations across the United States to effectively and efficiently fulfill online orders. One issue in order fulfillment is carton mix and usage, since customers could get annoyed by having their orders divided over several boxes.

Walmart's Carrollton distribution center in Georgia (CDC) handles a significant portion of the volume of products shipped directly to customers, and to stores for customer pickup. In spring 2011, the CDC executed a cost improvement project to optimize its carton mix. The goal of the project was to develop a process to create an optimal mix of carton sizes to reduce shipping, material, and labor costs of conveyable orders, and at the same time improve customer satisfaction.

The solution was developed using an Excel-based algorithm to determine the optimal carton sizes for four automated and six manual carton sizes. Walmart then implemented this solution into a decision support system for reconfiguring the carton mix at other distribution centers. Walmart achieved cost savings of $600,000 per year and has projected annual cost savings of $2 million across the entire Walmart.com network.

Source: Based on S. Ahire, M. Malhotra, and J. Jensen. "Carton-Mix Optimization for Walmart.com Distribution Centers," *Interfaces* 45, 4 (July – August 2015): 341–357.

5.4 Transportation Models with Max-Min and Min-Max Objectives

In all LP models discussed so far (starting in Chapter 2), the objective function has sought to either maximize or minimize some function of the decision variables. However, there are some situations, especially in transportation settings, where we may be interested in a special type of objective function. The objective in these situations may be to *maximize the minimum value* of the decision variables (Max-Min model), or, alternatively, *minimize the maximum value* of the decision variables (Min-Max model). These types of objective functions are applicable when we want to reduce the variability in the values of the decision variables. Let's illustrate this issue by revisiting Executive Furniture's transportation example and formulating it as a Min-Max model.

Managers at Executive Furniture noticed that the optimal solution to their transportation problem (Figure 5.5) recommends the use of only five of the nine available shipping routes. Further, the entire demand at Boston is being satisfied by the factory at Evansville. This means that if, for any reason, the Evansville factory has a production problem in a given month, the Boston warehouse is severely affected. To avoid this situation, the managers would like to distribute the shipments among all shipping routes, to the extent possible. They would like to achieve this by minimizing the maximum amount shipped on any specific route. Note that because the total number of desks available is fixed, if we reduce the number shipped on any route, shipments on some other route(s) will automatically increase. This implies that the difference between the largest and smallest shipments will be lowered to the extent allowed by the other constraints in the model.

To achieve this new objective, the managers are willing to allow an increase of up to 5% in the current total transportation cost. Because the current plan costs $3,900 (Figure 5.5), this implies that the maximum transportation cost allowed is $1.05 \times \$3,900 = \$4,095$.

Formulating the Problem To formulate this Min-Max model, we define a new decision variable as follows:

$$S = \text{maximum quantity shipped on any route}$$

The objective function is to minimize the value of S. We then set all the other decision variables (i.e., the nine shipping quantities) in the model to be less than or equal to S. Note that doing so implies that S will be at least as large as the largest of the nine shipping amounts. Further, because S is being minimized in the objective function, S will automatically equal the maximum quantity shipped on any route. The complete LP model may be written as

$$\text{Minimize } S$$

subject to the constraints

$$
\begin{array}{lll}
X_{DA} + X_{DB} + X_{DC} & = 100 & \text{(Des Moines supply)} \\
X_{EA} + X_{EB} + X_{EC} & = 300 & \text{(Evansville supply)} \\
X_{FA} + X_{FB} + X_{FC} & = 300 & \text{(Fort Lauderdale supply)} \\
X_{DA} + X_{EA} + X_{FA} & = 300 & \text{(Albuquerque demand)} \\
X_{DB} + X_{EB} + X_{FB} & = 200 & \text{(Boston demand)} \\
X_{DC} + X_{EC} + X_{FC} & = 200 & \text{(Cleveland demand)} \\
\end{array}
$$

$$5X_{DA} + 4X_{DB} + 3X_{DC}$$
$$+ 8X_{EA} + 4X_{EB} + 3X_{EC}$$
$$+ 9X_{FA} + 7X_{FB} + 5X_{FC} \leq 4{,}095 \quad \text{(Cost constraint)}$$

$$
\begin{array}{lll}
X_{DA} \leq S & X_{DB} \leq S & X_{DC} \leq S \\
X_{EA} \leq S & X_{EB} \leq S & X_{EC} \leq S \\
X_{FA} \leq S & X_{FB} \leq S & X_{FC} \leq S \\
\end{array}
$$

All variables ≥ 0

Solving the Problem The Excel layout and Solver entries for Executive Furniture's revised transportation model are shown in Figure 5.6. Notice that the objective cell (B18) is also a decision variable (i.e., changing variable cell). The supply and demand constraints are the same as in Figure 5.5. However, we now have a new constraint on the total cost. In addition, we have constraints specifying that each of the nine shipping routes (cells B5:D7) should be less than or equal to cell B18, and this can be entered as a single block in Solver.

Interpreting the Results The revised optimal solution costs $4,095 and uses seven of the nine available shipping routes. The maximum number shipped on any route drops from 200 (in Figure 5.5) to only 102.50. This solution reveals an interesting point. Recall that if all supply and demand values are integers, all flows are also integer values in network flow models. However, when we add additional constraints (i.e., other than supply and demand constraints), this integer solution property is destroyed, and the resulting solution can have fractional values. In Executive Furniture's case, the managers would need to round up and round down values appropriately to achieve an integer-valued shipping plan.

The LP model can be set up in a similar manner if the objective is to maximize the minimum value of the decision variables (i.e., Max-Min model). The only modifications needed to the Min-Max model discussed previously are to (1) change the objective from Max to Min and (2) change the sign in the constraints linking the decision variables to the variable S from $\leq$ to $\geq$.

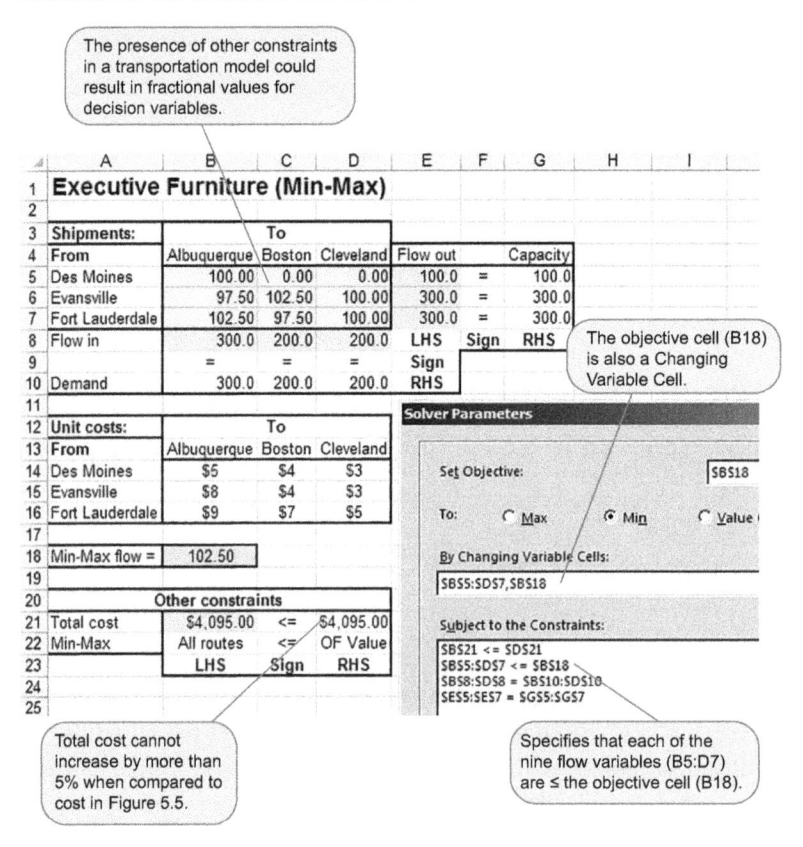

Figure 5.6: Excel Layout and Solver Entries for Executive Furniture—Min-Max

File: Figure 5.6.xlsx

EXCEL EXTRA

Creating Linked Charts

Visual tools can represent powerful means to communicate results to users. Business professionals often use *charts and graphs* to clearly present their data. Excel provides a wide variety of charting and graphing options that are relatively easy to create and that *link* directly to data from an Excel spreadsheet. When the data change, the chart automatically updates. For Excel models that are periodically updated and solved, linked charts can be especially useful communication tools. Once the chart is created, it automatically updates each time the model is solved.

For example, let's create a bar chart ("Column Chart") for the solution to the transportation model in Figure 5.6 (Excel file: Figure 5.6.xlsx).

1. Select the range A4:D7.

2. Click Insert|Recommended Charts. Select the first type and click OK.

3. Move and size the chart as desired.

4. Chart titles, axes titles, legends, etc. can be added. Select the chart, and the Chart Tools menu appears. Click Design|Add Chart Element. Add titles, legends, etc. as needed..

5. You may notice that the bars currently represent how much is being shipped to each warehouse. If you want to show how much is being shipped from each factory, you can easily switch the data accordingly as follows:

    a. Select The Chart, And The Chart Tools Menu Should Appear.

    b. Click Design|Switch Row/Column.

6. The chart can be saved as a separate sheet, or it can be embedded in the current sheet or even a different sheet. To save it as a separate sheet, select the chart and then click:

Design|Move Chart

The following chart is then generated.

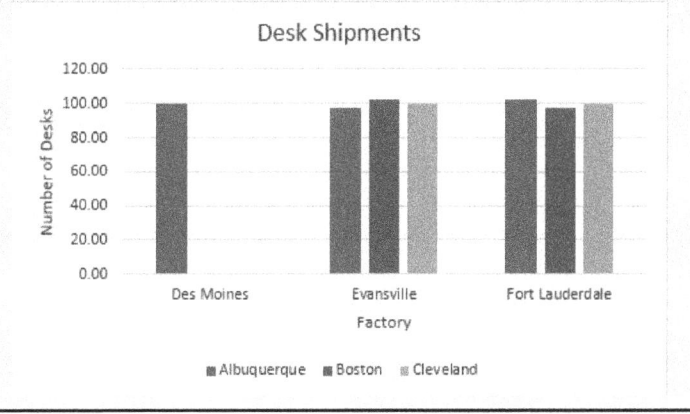

5.5 Transshipment Model

In the basic transportation model, shipments either flow *out* of supply nodes or flow *into* demand nodes. That is, it is possible to explicitly distinguish between supply nodes and demand nodes for flows. In the more general form of the transportation model, called the transshipment model, flows can occur both *out* of and *into* the same node. Such models are often needed when a firm uses warehouses or cross-docking depots to consolidate incoming shipments and ship from there to the final destinations.

We use two examples in the following sections to illustrate transshipment models. The first is a simple extension of the Executive Furniture Company's transportation model that allows one of the factories to receive goods from other factories before shipping out. The second is a larger example that includes some pure transshipment nodes where the number of units coming in equals the number of units going out.

Executive Furniture Company Example—Revisited

Let's consider a modified version of the Executive Furniture Company example from section 5.3. As before, the company has factories in Des Moines, Evansville, and Fort Lauderdale and warehouses in Albuquerque, Cleveland, and Boston. Recall that the supply at each factory and demand at each warehouse are shown in Figure 5.3.

Now suppose that due to a special contract with an Evansville-based shipping company, it is possible for Executive Furniture to ship desks from its Evansville factory to its three warehouses at very low unit shipping costs. These unit costs are so attractive that Executive Furniture is considering shipping all the desks produced at its other two factories (Des Moines and Fort Lauderdale) to Evansville and then using this new shipping company to move desks from Evansville to all its warehouses.

The revised unit shipping costs are shown in Table 5.2. Note that the Evansville factory now shows up both in the "From" and "To" entries because it is possible for this factory to receive desks from other factories and then ship them out to the warehouses. There are therefore two additional shipping routes available: Des Moines to Evansville and Fort Lauderdale to Evansville.

Table 5.2: Revised Transportation Costs per Desk for Executive Furniture

	Albuquerque	Boston	Cleveland	Evansville
Des Moines	$5	$4	$3	$2
Evansville	$3	$2	$1	—
Fort Lauderdale	$9	$7	$5	$3

LP Formulation for Executive Furniture's Transshipment Model

The LP formulation for this model follows the same logic and structure as the formulation for Executive Furniture's transportation model (see section 5.3). However, we now have two *additional* decision variables for the two new shipping routes. We define these as follows:

X_{DE} = number of desks shipped from Des Moines to Evansville
X_{FE} = number of desks shipped from Fort Lauderdale to Evansville

Objective Function The objective function for this transshipment model, including the two additional decision variables and using the unit costs shown in Table 5.2, can be written as follows:

$$\text{Minimize total shipping costs} = 5X_{DA} + 4X_{DB} + 3X_{DC} + 2X_{DE} + 3X_{EA} + 2X_{EB}$$
$$+ X_{EC} + 9X_{FA} + 7X_{FB} + 5X_{FC} + 3X_{FE}$$

Constraints Let's first consider the supply constraints for the Des Moines and Fort Lauderdale factories. After taking into account the new routes that allow desks to be shipped from either of these locations to the Evansville factory (rather than directly to the warehouses), the constraints are modified as

$$(X_{DA} + X_{DB} + X_{DC} + X_{DE}) = 100 \quad \text{(Des Moines supply)}$$
$$(X_{FA} + X_{FB} + X_{FC} + X_{FE}) = 300 \quad \text{(Fort Lauderdale supply)}$$

Now, let's model the supply constraint at Evansville:

$$\text{(Total flow } out \text{ of Evansville)} = \text{Capacity} + \text{(Total flow } into \text{ Evansville)}$$
$$(X_{EA} + X_{EB} + X_{EC}) = 300 + (X_{DE} + X_{FE})$$

There is no change in the demand constraints that represent the warehouse requirements. So, as discussed in section 5.3, they are

$$X_{DA} + X_{EA} + X_{FA} = 300 \quad \text{(Albuquerque demand)}$$
$$X_{DB} + X_{EB} + X_{FB} = 200 \quad \text{(Boston demand)}$$
$$X_{DC} + X_{EC} + X_{FC} = 200 \quad \text{(Cleveland demand)}$$

Excel Solution Figure 5.7 shows the Excel layout and Solver entries for Executive Furniture's transshipment model. Note that the modeler can incorporate the new transshipment option at Evansville in a variety of equivalent ways. We have chosen to keep the form of the LHS of the Evansville supply constraint the same as that for the other factories and have entered the RHS (cell H6) as a formula equal to the production capacity at Evansville plus the number of desks arriving from Des Moines and Albuquerque (=300+E8). We have colored cell H6 blue to designate that it contains a formula rather than just a number (similar to Figure 3.6). For the new Evansville demand column (column E), we calculate the flow of desks into Evansville like we do for the three warehouses (adding down the column); however, we do not need a new constraint to represent demand at Evansville, so cells E9 and E10 are left empty, and cell E8 is not colored.

	A	B	C	D	E	F	G	H
1	Executive Furniture (Transshipment)							
2								
3	Shipments:		To					
4	From	Albuquerque	Boston	Cleveland	Evansville	Flow out		Capacity
5	Des Moines	0.0	0.0	100.0	0.0	100.0	=	100.0
6	Evansville	300.0	200.0	100.0	0.0	600.0	=	600.0
7	Fort Lauderdale	0.0	0.0	0.0	300.0	300.0	=	300.0
8	Flow in	300.0	200.0	200.0	300.0	LHS	Sign	RHS
9		=	=	=		Sign		
10	Demand		300.0	200.0	200.0	RHS		
11								
12	Unit costs:		To					
13	From	Albuquerque	Boston	Cleveland	Evansville			
14	Des Moines	$5	$4	$3	$2			
15	Evansville	$3	$2	$1	$0			
16	Fort Lauderdale	$9	$7	$5	$3			
17								
18	Total cost =	$2,600						

Notes on figure:
- Evansville is now also included as a destination.
- These 300 desks are shipped from the Fort Lauderdale factory to the Evansville factory.
- Capacity for Evansville also reflects the transshipment flow.
- Cell B18 contains: =SUMPRODUCT(B5:E7,B14:E16)

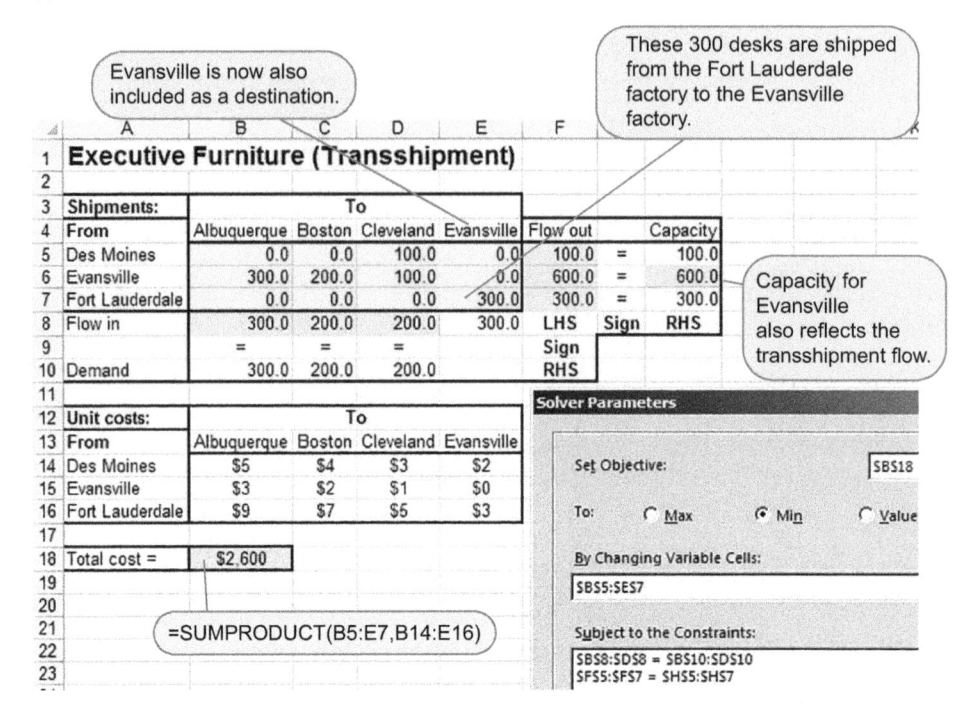

Solver Parameters:
- Set Objective: $B$18
- To: Min
- By Changing Variable Cells: $B$5:$E$7
- Subject to the Constraints:
  $B$8:$D$8 = $B$10:$D$10
  $F$5:$F$7 = $H$5:$H$7

Figure 5. 7: Excel Layout and Solver Entries for Executive Furniture—Transshipment

File: Figure 5.7.xlsx

In the revised solution, which now has a total transportation cost of $2,600, Executive Furniture should ship the 300 desks made at Fort Lauderdale to Evansville and then ship the consolidated load to the warehouses. It continues, though, to be cost beneficial to ship desks made at the Des Moines factory directly to a warehouse.

Lopez Custom Outfits—A Larger Transshipment Example

More general transshipment problems include transshipment nodes that neither create products nor are final destinations for products. For those transshipment nodes, we need to introduce *flow balance* equations into the model that ensure that the amount entering those nodes equals the amount leaving them. The Lopez Custom Outfits example illustrates this approach.

Paula Lopez makes and sells custom outfits for theme parties hosted by her wealthy clients. She uses three tailoring shops located in the Northeastern United States (in Albany, Boston, and Hartford) to make the outfits. These are then shipped to her finishing facilities in Charlotte and Richmond, where they are further customized to suit the clients' specifications and inspected before being shipped to the clients. Paula's clients are based primarily in four cities: Dallas, Louisville, Memphis, and Nashville.

Paula has received the following firm orders for custom outfits: 450 from Dallas, 300 from Louisville, 275 from Memphis, and 400 from Nashville. Her tailoring shop in Albany can make up to 450 outfits, the Boston shop can handle up to 500 outfits, and the Hartford shop has the capacity to make 580 outfits. Therefore, Paula's total tailoring capacity exceeds the total demand for outfits. She therefore knows that she will be able to fully satisfy all her clients' needs.

There is no production cost difference between the three tailoring shops, and Paula sells all her outfits at the same fixed price to her clients. There is also no cost difference between Charlotte and Richmond with regard to the customization and inspection processes at these locations. Further, since these processes do not consume too much time or space, Paula need not be concerned about both these locations with regard to capacity. Paula's cost difference between the various locations arises primarily from the shipping costs per outfit, which are summarized in Table 5.3

Table 5.3: Transportation Costs per Outfit for Lopez Custom Outfits

From	To Charlotte	To Richmond
Albany	$40	$55
Boston	$43	$46
Hartford	$50	$50

From	To Dallas	To Louisville	To Memphis	To Nashville
Charlotte	$38	$40	$51	$40
Richmond	$30	$47	$41	$45

LP Formulation for Lopez Custom Outfits Transshipment Model

Before we discuss the LP formulation for this model, it is useful to draw it as a network so that we can visualize the various flows that could occur. Figure 5.8 shows the network for Paula's transshipment model. We note that there are arcs both coming into and going out of the transshipment nodes, Charlotte and Richmond.

The LP formulation for this model involves 14 decision variables, 1 for each of the arcs shown in Figure 5.8. Let's define these decision variables as

X_{ij} = number of outfits shipped from location i to location j

where

$i = A$ (for Albany), B (for Boston), H (for Hartford), C (for Charlotte), or R (for Richmond)

$j = C$ (for Charlotte), R (for Richmond), D (for Dallas), L (for Louisville), M (for Memphis), or N (for Nashville)

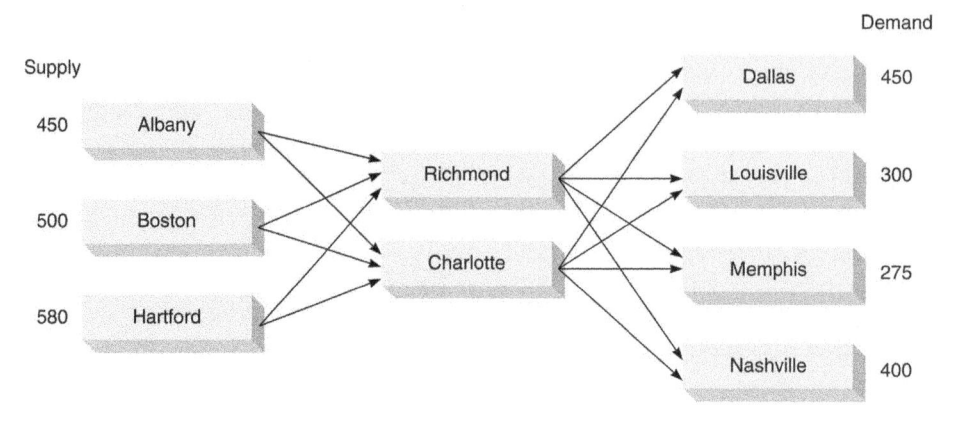

Figure 5.8: Network Model for Lopez Custom Outfits—Transshipment

Objective Function The objective function for this problem seeks to minimize the total transshipment cost and can be expressed as

$$\text{Minimize } \$40X_{AC} + \$55X_{AR} + \$43X_{BC} + \$46X_{BR} + \$50X_{HC} + \$50X_{HR} +$$
$$\$38X_{CD} + \$40X_{CL} + \$51X_{CM} + \$40X_{CN} + \$30X_{RD} + \$47X_{RL} + \$41X_{RM} + \$45X_{RN}$$

Constraints Here again, we need to write a constraint for each of the nine nodes in the network (see Figure 5.8). For the three tailoring shops, the supply constraints can be expressed as

$$X_{AC} + X_{AR} \leq 450 \quad \text{(Albany supply)}$$
$$X_{BC} + X_{BR} \leq 500 \quad \text{(Boston supply)}$$
$$X_{HC} + X_{HR} \leq 580 \quad \text{(Hartford supply)}$$

Because total supply exceeds total demand, this is an unbalanced model in which not all tailoring shops will be used to their full capacity. The supply constraints therefore need to be written as inequalities.

Now, let's model the flow equation at the two transshipment locations, Charlotte and Richmond. We formulate the constraints so that the amount entering each node equals the amount leaving:

$$X_{AC} + X_{BC} + X_{HC} = X_{CD} + X_{CL} + X_{CM} + X_{CN} \quad \text{(flow balance at Charlotte)}$$
$$X_{AR} + X_{BR} + X_{HR} = X_{RD} + X_{RL} + X_{RM} + X_{RN} \quad \text{(flow balance at Richmond)}$$

Finally, we model the four demand constraints as

$$X_{CD} + X_{RD} = 450 \quad \text{(Dallas demand)}$$
$$X_{CL} + X_{RL} = 300 \quad \text{(Louisville demand)}$$
$$X_{CM} + X_{RM} = 275 \quad \text{(Memphis demand)}$$
$$X_{CN} + X_{RN} = 400 \quad \text{(Nashville demand)}$$

Since all demands will be met in this model, we can express all four demand constraints using = signs.

Excel Solution Figure 5.9 shows the Excel layout and Solver entries for Lopez's transshipment model. Note that Charlotte and Richmond appear both in the rows and in the columns. Also, even though the table of flows contains 30 cells (i.e., cells B5:G9), only 14 of these are actual routes that exist (shown in yellow in Figure 5.9).

How do we enter these changing variable cells in Solver? There are two simple ways of doing this. First, we can specify only the 14 shaded cells as changing variable cells. Recall that to do this in Solver, we must separate entries for nonadjacent cells by using commas (i.e., B5:C7, D8:G9). Although this approach is quite straightforward, it could be cumbersome, especially if there are many nonadjacent decision variables in the model.

The second (and easier) approach is to specify the entire cell range B5:G9 in the By Changing Variable Cells box in Solver. Then, for all routes that do not exist (e.g., Albany to Dallas), we simply set the unit cost to artificially high values ($2,000 in this case). We have illustrated this approach in Figure 5.9.

The RHS values of the Charlotte and Richmond flow balance constraints are simple cell references to B10 and C10, respectively (which contain the amounts shipped into each of those two warehouses). Then the constraints for those two transshipment nodes are entered as a group: $H8:H9=$J8$J9. The other supply and demand constraints are entered as they would be for a regular transportation problem.

The optimal solution has a total transshipment cost of $116,775. Paula should use the Albany and Boston tailoring shops to full capacity but use the Hartford tailoring shop for only 475 units of their 580-unit capacity. Shipments from Albany and Hartford go to just one of the transshipment locations, but shipments from Boston are split between the two locations. Each demand location then receives all its outfits from one of the two transshipment locations.

Figure 5.9 — Lopez Custom Outfits (Transshipment)

	A	B	C	D	E	F	G	H	I	J
1	**Lopez Custom Outfits (Transshipment)**									
2										
3	Shipments:			To						
4	From	Charlotte	Richmond	Dallas	Louisville	Memphis	Nashville	Flow out		Capacity
5	Albany	450.0	0.0	0.0	0.0	0.0	0.0	450.0	<=	450.0
6	Boston	250.0	250.0	0.0	0.0	0.0	0.0	500.0	<=	500.0
7	Hartford	0.0	475.0	0.0	0.0	0.0	0.0	475.0	<=	580.0
8	Charlotte	0.0	0.0	0.0	300.0	0.0	400.0	700.0	=	700.0
9	Richmond	0.0	0.0	450.0	0.0	275.0	0.0	725.0	=	725.0
10	Flow in	700.0	725.0	450.0	300.0	275.0	400.0	LHS	Sign	RHS
11				=	=	=	=		Sign	
12	Demand			450.0	300.0	275.0	400.0	RHS		
13										
14	Unit costs:			To						
15	From	Charlotte	Richmond	Dallas	Louisville	Memphis	Nashville			
16	Albany	$40	$55	$2,000	$2,000	$2,000	$2,000			
17	Boston	$43	$46	$2,000	$2,000	$2,000	$2,000			
18	Hartford	$50	$50	$2,000	$2,000	$2,000	$2,000			
19	Charlotte	$2,000	$2,000	$38	$40	$51	$40			
20	Richmond	$2,000	$2,000	$30	$47	$41	$45			
21										
22	Total cost =	$116,775								

Callouts:
- Only the 16 shaded cells represent actual shipping routes.
- Charlotte and Richmond are pure transshipment nodes with no demand or supply.
- Harford is not being used to fill capacity.
- A high unit cost (like $2,000 in this case) prevents shipments on these routes.
- =SUMPRODUCT(B5:G9,B16:G20)
- The entire table B5:C9 can be entered as the Changing Variable Cells even though some of the routes (non-shaded) do not exist.

Solver Parameters
- Set Objective: $B$22
- To: Min
- By Changing Variable Cells: $B$5:$G$9
- Subject to the Constraints:
  - $D$10:$G$10 = $D$12:$G$12
  - $H$5:$H$7 <= $J$5:$J$7
  - $H$8:$H$9 = $J$8:$J$9

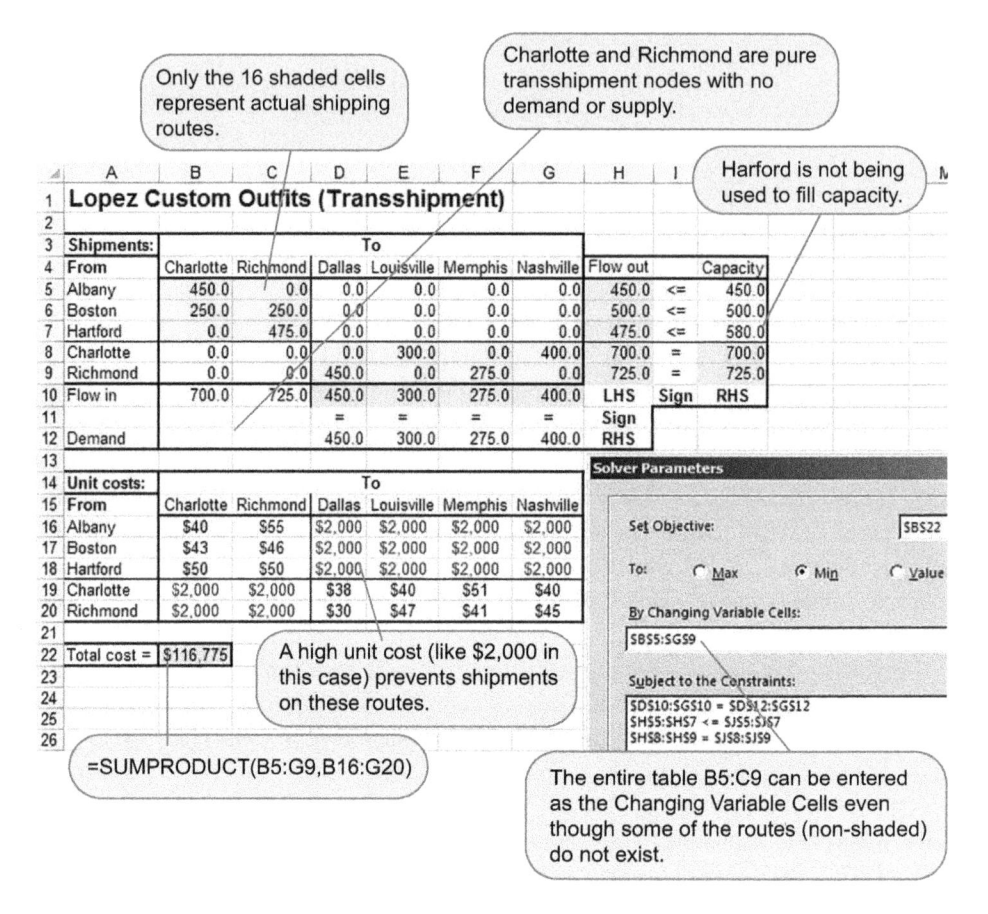

Figure 5.9: Excel Layout and Solver Entries for Lopez Custom Outfits—Transshipment

File: Figure 5.9.xlsx

5.6 Assignment Model

The next model we will study is the assignment model. Recall from section 5.1 that this model seeks to identify an optimal one-to-one assignment of people to tasks, jobs to machines, and so on. The typical objective is to minimize the total cost of the assignment, although a maximization objective is also possible. To represent each assignment model, we associate a table. Generally, the rows denote the people or jobs we want to assign, and the columns denote the tasks or machines to which we want them assigned. The numbers in the table are the costs (or benefits) associated with each particular one-to-one assignment.

Fix-It Shop Example

As an illustration of the assignment model, let's consider the case of Fix-It Shop, which has just received three new rush projects to repair: (1) a radio, (2) a toaster oven, and (3) a coffee table. Three workers, each with different talents and abilities, are available to do the jobs. The Fix-It Shop owner estimates what it will cost in wages to assign each of the workers to each of the three projects. The costs, which are shown in Table 5.4, differ because the owner believes that each worker will differ in speed and skill on these quite varied jobs.

Table 5.4: Estimated Project Repair Costs for Fix-It Shop

	Project		
Person	1	2	3
Adams	$11	$14	$ 6
Brown	$ 8	$10	$11
Cooper	$ 9	$12	$ 7

Decision Modeling In Action

University of Illinois Helps the National Science Foundation Automate their Panel Scheduling

The National Science Foundation (NSF) is an independent federal agency created by Congress to promote the progress of science. NSF funds research throughout the United States, and this is done through program directors who solicit requests for funding through calls for proposals and then create expert panels to review the requests.

One of the responsibilities of the program directors is to reserve meeting rooms for different panels. NSF has approximately 60 meeting rooms for hosting panel discussion at headquarters. Previously, NSF used a "First Come First Serve" approach to handle the scheduling process. The main problem was that the panel organizers used to make multiple reservations for the same panel and then decide later which room to use. So, some panels had multiple reservations while others could not find an empty slot. NSF found that the number of room reservations was about three times the number of actual panels. This led to an inefficient use of resources and an increased workload for the support staff who actually made the reservations and attempted to resolve scheduling conflicts.

The Department of Computer Science at the University of Illinois, implemented a study to automate the room reservation process of NSF by constructing and solving an optimization model that determined the assignment of panels to available rooms in order to maximize the utilization of available meeting rooms. The model included constraints related to multiday panels, the differences between the rooms in terms of size and the technology available in the rooms, whether the rooms were assigned to specific directorate or not, and finally double-booking for both rooms and panel experts.

The developed model enabled NSF to reduce the workload for both panel organizers and their support staff, allowing them to focus more on the primary aspects of their jobs.

Source: Based on J. Sauppe, D. Morrison, and S. Jacobson. "Assigning Panels to Meeting Rooms at the National Science Foundation," *Interfaces* 45, 6 (November – December 2015): 529–542.

The owner's objective is to assign the three projects to the workers in a way that will result in the lowest total cost to the shop. Note that the assignment of people to projects must be on a one-to-one basis; each project must be assigned to at most one worker only, and vice versa. If the number of rows in an assignment model is equal to the number of columns (as in the Fix-It example), we refer to this problem as a *balanced* assignment model.

Because the Fix-It Shop example consists of only three workers and three projects, one easy way to find the best solution is to list all possible assignments and their respective costs. For example, if Adams is assigned to project 1, Brown to project 2, and Cooper to project 3, the total cost will be $11 + $10 + $7 = $28 Table 5.5 summarizes all six assignment options. The table also shows that the least-cost solution would be to assign Cooper to project 1, Brown to project 2, and Adams to project 3, at a total cost of $25.

Table 5.5: Summary of Fix-It Shop's Assignment Alternatives and Costs

\multicolumn{3}{c}{Project Assignment}	Labor Costs ($)		Total Costs
1	2	3			
Adams	Brown	Cooper	$11 + $10 + $ 7	=	$28
Adams	Cooper	Brown	$11 + $12 + $11	=	$34
Brown	Adams	Cooper	$ 8 + $14 + $ 7	=	$29
Brown	Cooper	Adams	$ 8 + $12 + $ 6	=	$26
Cooper	Adams	Brown	$ 9 + $14 + $11	=	$34
Cooper	Brown	Adams	$ 9 + $10 + $ 6	=	$25

Obtaining solutions by enumeration works well for small models but quickly becomes inefficient as assignment models become larger. For example, a model involving the assignment of eight workers and eight tasks, which actually is not that large in a real-world situation, yields $8! (= 8 \times 7 \times 6 \times 5 \times 4 \times 3 \times 2 \times 1)$, or 40,320 possible solutions! Because it would clearly be impractical to individually examine so many alternatives, a more efficient solution approach is needed.

Solving Assignment Models

A straightforward approach to solving assignment models is to formulate them as a transportation model. To do so for the Fix-It Shop problem, let's view each worker as a supply node in a transportation network with a supply of one unit. Likewise, let's view each project as a demand node in the network with a demand of one unit. The arcs connecting the supply nodes to the demand nodes represent the possible assignment of a supply (worker) to a demand (project). The network model is illustrated in Figure 5.10.

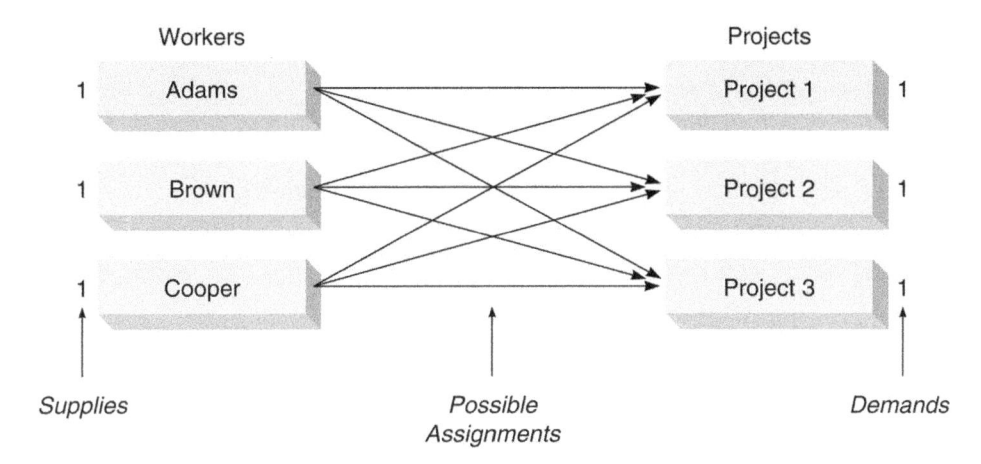

Figure 5.10: Network Model for Fix-It Shop—Assignment

We see that this network looks identical to a transportation model with three supply nodes and three demand nodes. But here, all supplies and demands are equal to one unit each. The objective is to find the least-costly solution that uses the one-unit supplies at the origin nodes to satisfy the one-unit demands at the demand nodes. However, we need to also ensure that each worker *uniquely* gets assigned to just one project, and vice versa. That is, the *entire* supply of one unit at an origin node (worker) should flow to the same demand node (project), indicating the assignment of a worker to a project. How do we ensure this? The answer lies in the special property of network models stated earlier: When all the supplies and demands in a network model are whole numbers (as in this case), the resulting solution will automatically have integer-valued flows on the arcs.

Consider the "flow" out of the supply node for Adams in the Fix-It Shop example. The three arcs (to projects 1, 2, and 3) denote the assignment of Adams to these projects. Due to the integer property of the resulting network flows, the only possible solutions will have a flow of 1 on one of the three arcs and a flow of 0 on the other two arcs. This is the only way in which a total flow of 1 (equal to the "supply" at the node representing Adams) can flow on these arcs and have integer values. The arc that has a flow of 1 in the optimal solution will indicate the project to which Adams should be assigned. Likewise, arcs that have flows of 1 and originate from the other two supply nodes will show the optimal assignments for those two workers.

Even without us constraining it to be so, the solution to the assignment model yields a solution in which the optimal values of the decision variables are either 1 (indicating the assignment of a worker to a project) or 0 (indicating that the worker should not be assigned to the project). In fact, there are several situations in which such decision variables, known as *binary*, or 0–1, variables must have values of zero or one in the formulation itself. We study these types of models in more detail in Chapter 6.

LP Formulation for Fix-It Shop's Assignment Model

We now develop the LP model for Fix-It Shop's example. Let

X_{ij} = "Flow" on arc from node denoting worker i to node denoting project j. The solution value will equal 1 if worker i is assigned to project j, and will equal 0 otherwise.

where

$i = A$ (for Adams), B (for Brown), C (for Cooper)
$j = 1$ (for project 1), 2 (for project 2), 3 (for project 3)

Objective Function The objective is to minimize the total cost of assignment and is expressed as

$$\text{Minimize total assignment costs} = \$11X_{A1} + \$14X_{A2} + \$6X_{A3} + \$8X_{B1} \\ + \$10X_{B2} + \$11X_{B3} + \$9X_{C1} + \$12X_{C2} + \$7X_{C3}$$

Constraints As in the transportation model, we have supply constraints at each of the three supply nodes (workers) and demand constraints at each of the three demand nodes (projects). Mirroring the transportation model approach, these can be written as

$$\begin{aligned}
X_{A1} + X_{A2} + X_{A3} &= 1 & \text{(Adams availability)} \\
X_{B1} + X_{B2} + X_{B3} &= 1 & \text{(Brown availability)} \\
X_{C1} + X_{C2} + X_{C3} &= 1 & \text{(Cooper availability)} \\
X_{A1} + X_{B1} + X_{C1} &= 1 & \text{(project 1 requirement)} \\
X_{A2} + X_{B2} + X_{C2} &= 1 & \text{(project 2 requirement)} \\
X_{A3} + X_{B3} + X_{C3} &= 1 & \text{(project 3 requirement)}
\end{aligned}$$

Excel Solution Figure 5.11 shows the Excel layout and Solver entries for Fix-It Shop's assignment model. The optimal solution identified by the model indicates that Adams should be assigned to project 3, Brown to project 2, and Cooper to project 1, for a total cost of $25.

Solving Maximization Assignment Models The model discussed here can be very easily modified to solve *maximization* assignment models, in which the objective coefficients represent profits or benefits rather than costs. The only change needed would be in the statement of the objective function (which would be set to maximize instead of minimize).

Fix-It Shop (Assignment)

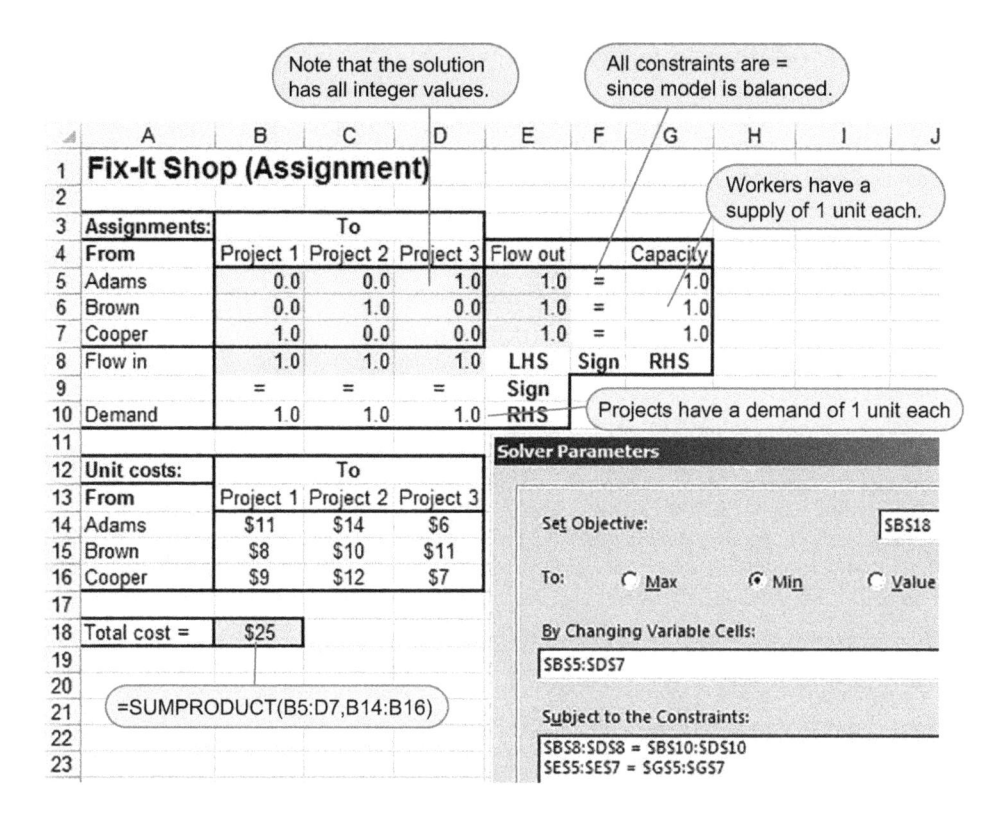

Note that the solution has all integer values.

All constraints are = since model is balanced.

Workers have a supply of 1 unit each.

	A	B	C	D	E	F	G
3	Assignments:		To				
4	From	Project 1	Project 2	Project 3	Flow out		Capacity
5	Adams	0.0	0.0	1.0	1.0	=	1.0
6	Brown	0.0	1.0	0.0	1.0	=	1.0
7	Cooper	1.0	0.0	0.0	1.0	=	1.0
8	Flow in	1.0	1.0	1.0	LHS	Sign	RHS
9		=	=	=	Sign		
10	Demand	1.0	1.0	1.0	RHS		

Projects have a demand of 1 unit each

	A	B	C	D
12	Unit costs:		To	
13	From	Project 1	Project 2	Project 3
14	Adams	$11	$14	$6
15	Brown	$8	$10	$11
16	Cooper	$9	$12	$7
18	Total cost =	$25		

=SUMPRODUCT(B5:D7,B14:B16)

Solver Parameters

Set Objective: $B$18

To: ○ Max ● Min ○ Value

By Changing Variable Cells:
$B$5:$D$7

Subject to the Constraints:
$B$8:$D$8 = $B$10:$D$10
$E$5:$E$7 = $G$5:$G$7

Figure 5.11: Excel Layout and Solver Entries for Fix-It Shop—Assignment

X📊 File: Figure 5.11.xlsx

Unbalanced Assignment Models In the Fix-It Shop example, the total number of workers equaled the total number of projects. All supply and demand constraints could therefore be specified as equalities (i.e., using the = sign). What if the number of workers exceeds the number of projects, or vice versa? In these cases, we have *unbalanced* assignment models and, just as in the case of unbalanced transportation models, the supply or demand constraints need to be modified accordingly. For example, if the number of workers exceeds the number of projects, the supply constraints would become inequalities, and the demand constraints would remain equality constraints. In contrast, if the number of projects exceeds the number of workers, the supply constraints would remain equality constraints, and the demand constraints would become inequalities. Solved Problem 5–2 at the end of this chapter shows an example of an unbalanced assignment model.

Decision Modeling In Action

Scheduling the Belgian Soccer League with the Assignment Model

Worldwide interest in soccer has increased significantly over the past several years, and Belgian soccer is no exception. Belgacom TV pays millions of Euros each year for the soccer broadcasting rights, and there is a great deal of interest in ensuring that the league's schedule is properly designed. In addition to the obvious influence on the results of the sports competition, the schedule also affects game attendance, public interest, and the league's profitability and attractiveness to broadcasters, sponsors, and advertisers in subsequent years.

Until the 2005–2006 season, schedules were created manually, which resulted in several teams viewing the schedules as being unbalanced and unfair. There were even accusations that the chairman of the calendar committee was favoring his own team. For the 2006–2007 season, the authors used an assignment model to develop the schedule for the Jupiler League, the highest division in Belgian Soccer. The league is organized as a double round-robin tournament with 18 teams, and it includes several constraints such as no team can play more than two consecutive home or away matches, the total number of breaks is minimal, and no team should start or end the season with a break. The authors expanded their model to a two-phased approach starting with the 2007–2008 season. In the first phase, each team is assigned a home-away pattern; in the second phase, the actual opponents are determined.

A spokesperson for the Belgian soccer league states that due to the use of this two-phased assignment model, "We have been able to come up with schedules that are much more satisfying for our partners (the police, Belgacom TV, and the clubs). In addition, the transparency of the process of agreeing upon a schedule has improved considerably as well."

Source: Based on D. Goossens and F. Spieksma. "Scheduling the Belgian Soccer League," *Interfaces* 39, 2 (March–April 2009): 109–118.

5.7 Maximal-Flow Model

The *maximal-flow* model allows us to determine the maximum amount that can flow from a given origin node to a given destination node in a network with capacitated arcs. It has been used, for example, to find the maximum number of automobiles that can flow through a state highway road system.

Road System in Waukesha, Wisconsin

Waukesha, a small town in Wisconsin, is in the process of developing a road system for the downtown area. Bill Blackstone, a city planner, would like to determine the maximum number of cars that can flow through the town from west to east. The road network is shown in Figure 5.12, where the arcs represent the roads.

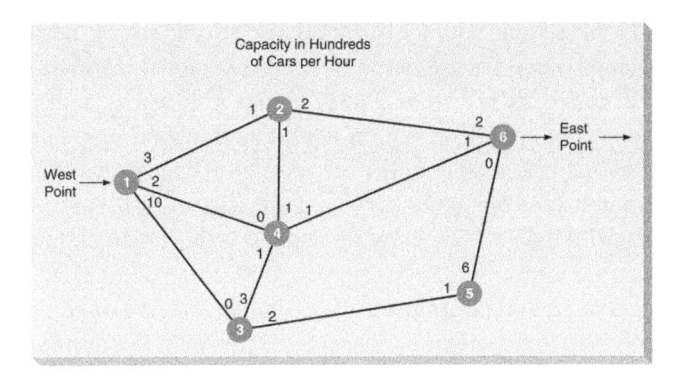

Figure 5.12: Road Network for Waukesha—Maximal-Flow

The numbers by the nodes indicate the maximum number of cars (in hundreds of cars per hour) that can flow (or travel) *from* the various nodes. For example, the number 3 by node 1 (on the road from node 1 to node 2) indicates that 300 cars per hour can travel from node 1 to node 2. Likewise, the numbers 1, 1, and 2 by node 2 indicate that 100, 100, and 200 cars can travel per hour on the roads from node 2 to nodes 1, 4, and 6, respectively. Note that traffic can flow in both directions down a road. A zero (0) means no flow in that direction, or a one-way road.

Unlike the transportation and assignment models, in which there are multiple origin nodes and multiple destination nodes, the typical maximal-flow model has a single starting node (origin) and a single ending node (destination).

LP Formulation for Waukesha Road System's Maximal-Flow Model

To formulate this example as an LP model, we first replace each two-way (bidirectional) road in the network with two one-way (unidirectional) roads with flows in opposite directions. Note that some of the unidirectional roads (e.g., the road from node 4 to node 1, the road from node 6 to node 5) are not needed because the maximum flow permissible in that direction is zero (i.e., it is a one-way road). The revised network for Waukesha therefore has 15 unidirectional roads (i.e., roads 1→2, 1→3, 1→4, 2→1, 2→4, 2→6, 3→4, 3→5, 4→2, 4→3, 4→6, 5→3, 5→6, 6→2 and 6→4).

As with the transportation and assignment models, the presence of 15 unidirectional arcs in the network implies that there are 15 decision variables in Waukesha's maximal-flow model—1 for each arc (road) in the network. Let

X_{ij} = Number of cars that flow (or travel) per hour on road from node i to node j

where i and j each equal 1, 2, 3, 4, 5, or 6. Of course, flow variables are defined only on roads that actually exist. For example, X_{12} (i.e., $i=1, j=2$) is defined, while X_{15} (i.e., $i=1, j=5$) is not defined.

We need to determine the maximum number of cars that can originate at node 1 and terminate at node 6. Hence, node 1 is the origin node in this model, and node 6 is the destination node. All other nodes (nodes 2 to 5) are transshipment nodes, where flows of cars neither start nor end. However, unlike in the transportation and assignment models, there is neither a known quantity of "supply" of cars available at node 1, nor is there a known quantity of "demand" for cars required at node 6. For this reason, we need to slightly modify the network to set up and solve the maximal-flow model using LP.

The modification consists of creating a unidirectional *dummy* arc (road) going *from* the destination node (node 6) *to* the origin node (node 1). We call this a dummy arc because the arc (road) really does not exist in the network and has been created only for modeling purposes. The capacity of this dummy arc is set at infinity (or any artificially high number, such as 1,000 for the Waukesha example). The modified network is shown in Figure 5.13.

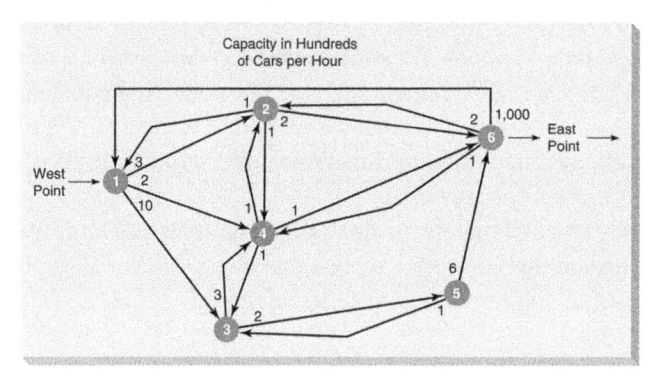

Figure 5.13: Modified Road Network for Waukesha—Maximal-Flow

Objective Function Let's consider the objective function first. The objective is to maximize the total number of cars flowing *into* node 6. Assume that there are an unknown number of cars flowing on the dummy road from node 6 to node 1. However, because there is no supply at node 6 (i.e., no cars are created at node 6), the entire number of cars flowing *out* of node 6 (on road 6 → 1) must consist of cars that flowed *into* node 6. Likewise, because there is no demand at node 1 (i.e., no cars are consumed at node 1), the entire number of cars on road 6 → 1 must consist of cars that originally flowed *out* of node 1 (to nodes 2, 3, and 4).

These two issues imply that if we maximize the number of cars flowing on the dummy road 6 → 1, this is equivalent to maximizing the total number of cars flowing *out* of node 1 as well as the total number of cars flowing *into* node 6. The objective for Waukesha's maximal-flow model can therefore be written as

$$\text{Maximize } X_{61}$$

Constraints Because all nodes in the network are transshipment nodes with no supplies or demands, flow balance equations are written to ensure that the number of cars flowing out of each of those nodes equals the number of cars flowing in. Hence,

$$X_{12} + X_{13} + X_{14} = X_{61} + X_{21} \quad \text{(flow balance at node 1)}$$
$$X_{21} + X_{24} + X_{26} = X_{12} + X_{42} + X_{62} \quad \text{(flow balance at node 2)}$$
$$X_{34} + X_{35} = X_{13} + X_{43} + X_{53} \quad \text{(flow balance at node 3)}$$
$$X_{42} + X_{43} + X_{46} = X_{14} + X_{24} + X_{34} + X_{64} \quad \text{(flow balance at node 4)}$$
$$X_{53} + X_{56} = X_{35} \quad \text{(flow balance at node 5)}$$
$$X_{61} + X_{62} + X_{64} = X_{26} + X_{46} + X_{56} \quad \text{(flow balance at node 6)}$$

Finally, we have capacity constraints on the maximum number of cars that can flow on each road. These are written as

$$X_{12} \le 3 \quad X_{13} \le 10 \quad X_{14} \le 2$$
$$X_{21} \le 1 \quad X_{24} \le 1 \quad X_{26} \le 2$$
$$X_{34} \le 3 \quad X_{35} \le 2$$
$$X_{42} \le 1 \quad X_{43} \le 1 \quad X_{46} \le 1$$
$$X_{53} \le 1 \quad X_{56} \le 6$$
$$X_{61} \le 1{,}000 \quad X_{62} \le 2 \quad X_{64} \le 1$$

Excel Solution Figure 5–4 shows the Excel layout and Solver entries for Waukesha's maximal-flow model. To be consistent with earlier models, flows on arcs have been modeled here using a tabular layout (cells B5:G10). As noted earlier, a big advantage of the tabular layout is that it greatly simplifies the calculations of the total flows in and total flows out of each node in the network.

However, of the 36 (= 6 × 6) arcs represented by cells B5:G10, only 16 of them actually exist in Waukesha's network. That is, the decision variables in this model refer only to selected entries in the table. These entries have been shaded yellow in Figure 5.14.

As with the Lopez Custom Outfits transshipment model we discussed in section 5.5, there are two ways of specifying the variables for a maximal-flow model in Solver. First, we could enter only the shaded cells, as illustrated in the By Changing Variable Cells box in Figure 5.14. Note that we separate entries for nonadjacent cells by using commas (i.e., $B$6,$B$10,$C$5, etc.). As you can see, this approach could be cumbersome especially if there are many nonadjacent decision variables in the model.

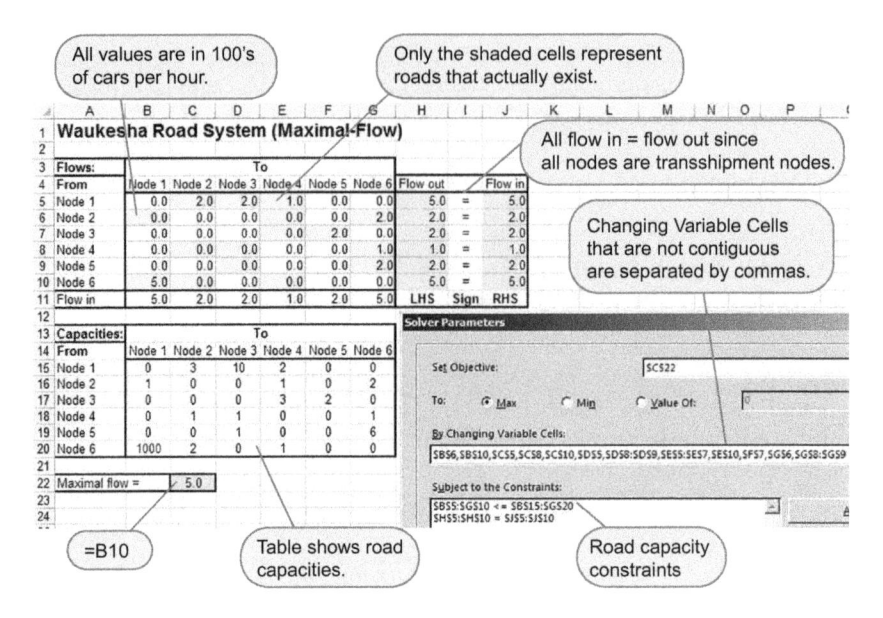

272 — Chapter 5: Transportation, Assignment, and Network Models

Figure 5.14: Excel Layout and Solver Entries for Waukesha Road System—Maximal-Flow

📊 File: Figure 5.14.xlsx

In the second (and easier) approach, we specify the entire cell range B5:G10 in the By Changing Variable Cells box in Solver.[2] Then, for all roads that do not exist (e.g., road $1 \to 5$, road $2 \to 3$), we set the flow capacity to zero. Solved Problem 5-3 at the end of this chapter shows an example of this approach for a maximal-flow model.

The solution to Waukesha's problem shows that 500 cars (recall that all numbers are in hundreds of cars) can flow through the town from west to east. The values of the decision variables indicate the actual car flow on each road. Total flow out (column H) and total flow in (column J) at each node are also shown. For example, the total flow out of node 1 is 500 cars, split as 200 cars on $1 \to 2$, 200 cars on $1 \to 3$, and 100 cars on $1 \to 4$.

5.8 Shortest-Path Model

The *shortest-path model* finds how a person, or an item, can travel from one location to another through a network while minimizing the total distance traveled, time taken, or some other measure. In other words, it finds the shortest path or route from an origin to a destination.

---

[2] If there are more than 14 nodes in the network, we cannot use this approach with the standard version of Solver (included with Excel) because that version can handle a maximum of only 200 decision variables.

Decision Modeling In Action

Maximal-Flow Model Facilitates Improved Natural Gas Production and Transport

Norwegian gas covered three percent of the worldwide production in 2007, and its export is expected to increase by nearly 50 percent within the next decade. With over 7,800 km of subsea pipelines, the natural gas transport network on the Norwegian Continental Shelf (NCS) is the world's largest offshore pipeline network. The network has an annual capacity of 120 billion standard cubic meters, which represents about 15 percent of European consumption.

In order to ensure the most effective usage of this complex network, StatoilHydro, Norway's main shipper of natural gas, and Gassco, an independent network operator, use a maximum flow model embedded within a decision support tool named GassOpt to optimize the network configuration and routing. The primary decision variables in this model are the total flow and component flow between different nodes in the network. The objective function is to maximize the gas flow with some penalty terms for pressure increases, etc. The constraints include such issues as field capacities, market demands, mass balance, and pressure and flow restrictions.

GassOpt has been used extensively for the development of the dry-gas network on the NCS for the past decade, and is expected to remain an important part of infrastructure development. StatoilHydro estimates that its accumulated savings related to the use of GassOpt were approximately US$2 billion during the period 1995–2008.

Source: Based on F. Rømo et al. "Optimizing the Norwegian Natural Gas Production and Transport," *Interfaces* 39, 1 (January–February 2009): 46–56.

Ray Design Inc. Example

Every day, Ray Design Inc. must transport beds, chairs, and other furniture items from the factory to the warehouse. This involves going through several cities (nodes). Ray would like to find the path with the shortest distance, in miles. The road network is shown in Figure 5.15.

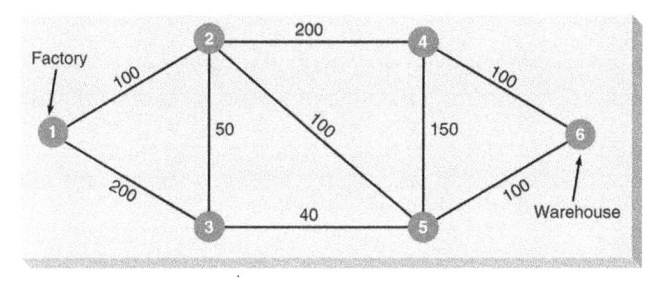

Figure 5.15: Roads from Ray Design's Factory to Warehouse—Shortest-Path

The shortest-path model is another example of a network model that has a unique starting node (origin) and a unique ending node (destination). If we assume that there is a supply of one unit at node 1 (factory) and a demand of one unit at node 6 (warehouse), the shortest-path model for the Ray Design example is identical to a transshipment model with a single origin node (node 1), a single destination node (node 6), and four transshipment nodes (node 2 through node 5).

Because the supply and demand both equal one unit, which is a whole number, the solution to the model will have integer-valued flows on all arcs. Hence, the supply of one unit at node 1 will flow in its entirety on either road 1→2 or road 1→3. Further, because the net flow is zero at each of the transshipment nodes (cities), a flow of one unit on an incoming arc (road) at any of these cities automatically has to result in a flow of one unit on an outgoing road from that city.

LP Formulation for Ray Design Inc.'s Shortest-Path Model

Because all 9 arcs (roads) in the network are bidirectional, we first replace each one with a pair of unidirectional roads. But we do not need to analyze any flows that enter the origin node or that leave the destination node. There are, therefore, 14 decision variables in the model. As usual, let

X_{ij} = Flow on road from node i to node j. The solution value will equal 1 if travel occurs on the road from node i to node j and will equal 0 otherwise.

where i equals 1, 2, 3, 4, or 5, and j equals 2, 3, 4, 5, or 6. As with the maximal-flow model, flow variables are defined only on roads that actually exist. For example, X_{12} (i.e., $i=1, j=2$) is defined, while X_{14} (i.e., $i=1, j=4$) is not defined.

Objective Function The objective is to minimize the distance between node 1 and node 6 and can be expressed as

$$\text{Minimize } 100X_{12} + 200X_{13} + 50X_{23} + 200X_{24} + 100X_{25}$$
$$+ 50X_{32} + 40X_{35} + 200X_{42} + 150X_{45} + 100X_{46}$$
$$+ 100X_{52} + 40X_{53} + 150X_{54} + 100X_{56}$$

The optimal value for each variable will be 0 or 1, depending on whether travel occurs on that road. So, the objective function is the sum of road distances on which travel (flow) actually occurs.

Constraints We write the constraints at each node as follows:

$$\begin{aligned}
X_{12} + X_{13} &= 1 & &\text{(supply of one unit at node 1)} \\
X_{23} + X_{24} + X_{25} &= X_{12} + X_{32} + X_{42} + X_{52} & &\text{(transshipment at node 2)} \\
X_{32} + X_{35} &= X_{13} + X_{23} + X_{53} & &\text{(transshipment at node 3)} \\
X_{42} + X_{45} + X_{46} &= X_{24} + X_{54} & &\text{(transshipment at node 4)} \\
X_{52} + X_{53} + X_{54} + X_{56} &= X_{25} + X_{35} + X_{45} & &\text{(transshipment at node 5)} \\
X_{46} + X_{56} &= 1 & &\text{(demand of one unit at node 6)}
\end{aligned}$$

Excel Solution Figure 5.16 shows the Excel layout and Solver entries for Ray Design's shortest-path model. Once again, we use the tabular layout to represent flows on roads. However, only 14 of the 36 cells in the range B5:F9 actually represent roads that exist as possible routes through the system (indicated by the cells shaded yellow in Figure 5.16). As with the maximal-flow model, roads that do not exist need to be excluded when specifying entries for the changing variable cells in Solver. One way of achieving this is to separate noncontiguous cell entries by using commas, as shown in Figure 5.16. That is, we specify only cells $B$5,$B$7:$B$9,$C$5:$C$6, etc. in the By Changing Variables Cells box in Solver.

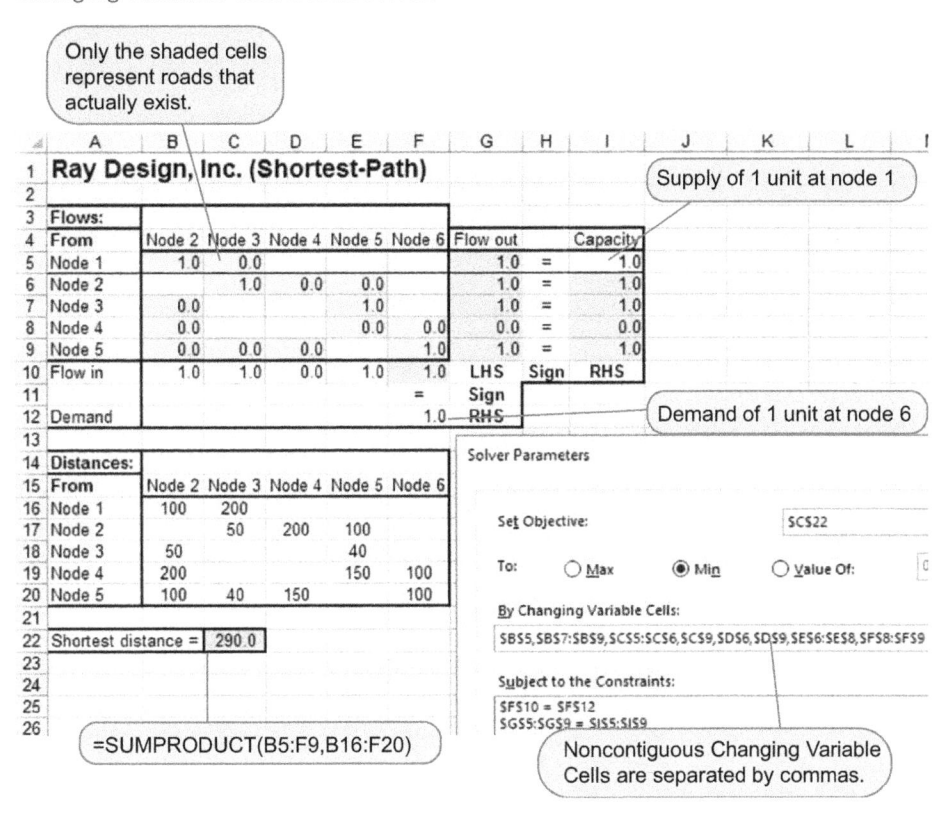

Figure 5.16: Excel Layout and Solver Entries for Ray Design Inc.—Shortest-Path

File: Figure 5.16.xlsx

Decision Modeling In Action

A Decision-Making Tool for a Regional Network of Clinical Laboratories in Spain

The operation of healthcare systems in large and geographically dispersed areas has a negative impact on the quality of the services provided if it is not managed in an effective and efficient manner. One of the factors that is considered a bottleneck in dispersed healthcare systems is the complexity of managing transportation-related problems.

The School of Engineering at the University of Seville in Spain developed a decision support system based on network flow modeling to help healthcare managers improve the delivery of biological samples collected from patients in hospitals and outpatient clinics to laboratories that test them. The problem formulation consisted of 47,000 variables and 36,000 constraints. In addition, a web-based tool was developed to provide planners with interactive functions, enabling them to explore solutions and interactively access data to analyze what-if scenarios.

The tool was tested on the Andalusian Healthcare System (AHS). Some of the results attained were the facilitation of cooperation between AHS and the laboratories it deals with, optimum usage of its fully equipped laboratories, and reduction in the number of outsourced tests.

Source: Based on J. Pineda, P. Gonzalez-R, and J. Framinan. "A Decision-Making Tool for a Regional Network of Clinical Laboratories," *Interfaces* 43, 4 (July – August 2013): 360–372.

Alternatively, we can specify the entire cell range (cells B5:F9) in the By Changing Variable Cells box in Solver.[3] However, to prevent travel on roads that do not exist (e.g., $1 \to 4, 1 \to 5$), the distance of these roads can be set to a large number (compared to other distances in the problem) in the corresponding cells in B16:F20. For example, we could specify a large distance such as 2,000 for road $1 \to 4$ in cell D16. Clearly, no travel will occur on this road because the objective is to minimize total distance. Solved Problem 5–4 at the end of this chapter shows an example of this approach.

The solution to Ray's problem shows that the shortest distance from the factory to the warehouse is 290 miles and involves travel through cities 2, 3, and 5.

5.9 Minimal-Spanning Tree Model

The *minimal-spanning tree model* can be used to connect all the nodes of a network to each other while minimizing the total distance of all the arcs used for this connection. It has been applied, for example, by telephone companies to connect a number of phones (nodes) together while minimizing the total length of telephone cable (arcs).

Lauderdale Construction Company Example

Let's consider the Lauderdale Construction Company, which is currently developing a luxurious housing project in Panama City, Florida. Melvin Lauderdale, owner of

---

[3] As with the maximal-flow model, the standard version of Solver cannot handle this approach on networks with more than 14 nodes.

Lauderdale Construction, must determine the minimum total length of water pipes needed to provide water to each house. The network of eight houses is shown in Figure 5.17, along with the distances between the houses (in hundreds of feet).

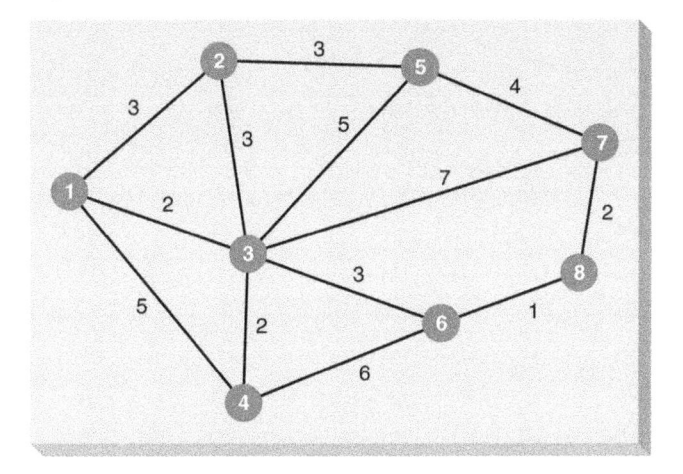

Figure 5.17: Network for Lauderdale Construction—Minimal-Spanning Tree

Unlike the other network flow models studied so far in this chapter, in a minimal-spanning tree model, it is difficult to classify nodes *a priori* as origins, destinations, and transshipment nodes. For this reason, we do not formulate these models as LP problems using the flow balance equations. However, the minimal-spanning tree model is very easy to solve by hand, using a simple four-step solution procedure. The procedure is outlined as follows:

Steps for Solving the Minimal-Spanning Tree Model
1. Select any node in the network.
2. Connect this node to its nearest node.
3. Considering all the connected nodes, find the nearest *unconnected* node and then connect it. If there is a tie, and two or more unconnected nodes are equally near, select one arbitrarily. A tie suggests that there may be more than one optimal solution.
4. Repeat step 3 until all the nodes are connected.

We can now solve the network in Figure 5.17 for Melvin Lauderdale. We start by arbitrarily selecting any node (house). Let's say we select house 1. Because house 3 is the nearest one to house 1, at a distance of 2 (200 feet), we connect these two houses. That is, we select arc $1 \rightarrow 3$ for inclusion in the spanning tree. This is shown in Figure 5.18.

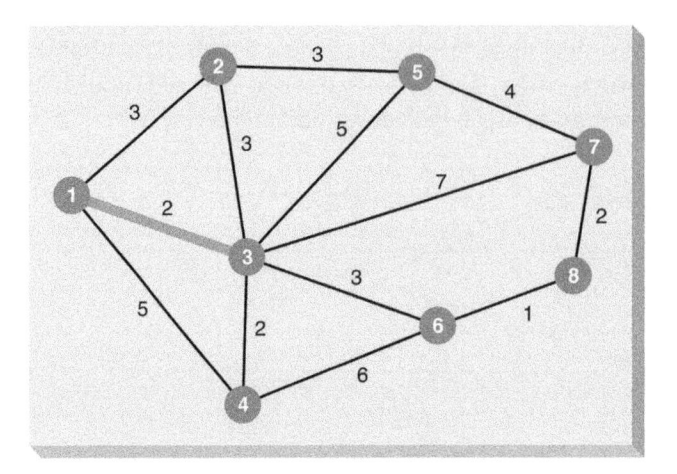

Figure 5.18: First Iteration for Lauderdale Construction

Next, considering connected houses 1 and 3, we look for the unconnected house that is closest to either house. This turns out to be house 4, which is 200 feet from house 3. We connect houses 3 and 4 by selecting arc $3 \rightarrow 4$ (see Figure 5.19(a)).

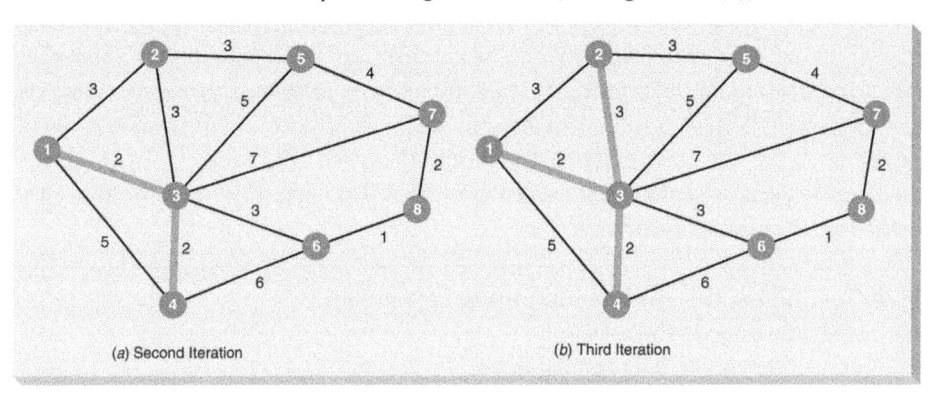

(a) Second Iteration

(b) Third Iteration

Figure 5.19: Second and Third Iterations for Lauderdale Construction

We continue, looking for the nearest unconnected house to houses 1, 3, and 4. This is either house 2 or house 6, both at a distance of 300 feet from house 3. We arbitrarily pick house 2 and connect it to house 3 by selecting arc $3 \rightarrow 2$ (see Figure 5.19(b)).

We continue the process. There is another tie for the next iteration, with a minimum distance of 300 feet (house 2 to house 5 and house 3 to house 6). Note that we do not consider house 1 to house 2, with a distance of 300 feet, at this iteration because both houses are already connected. We arbitrarily select house 5 and connect it to house 2 by selecting arc $2 \rightarrow 5$ (see Figure 5.20(a)). The next nearest house is house 6, and we connect it to house 3 by selecting arc $3 \rightarrow 6$ (see Figure 5.20(b)).

(a) Fourth Iteration

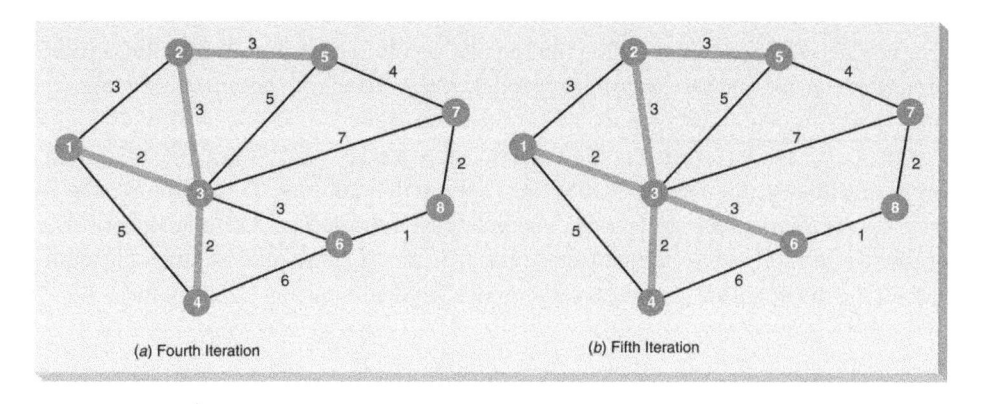

(b) Fifth Iteration

Figure 5.20: Fourth and Fifth Iterations for Lauderdale Construction

At this stage, we have only two unconnected houses left. House 8 is the nearest one to house 6, with a distance of 100 feet, and we connect it by using arc $6 \rightarrow 8$ (see Figure 5.21(a). Then the remaining house, house 7, is connected to house 8 using arc $8 \rightarrow 7$ (see Figure 5.21(b)).

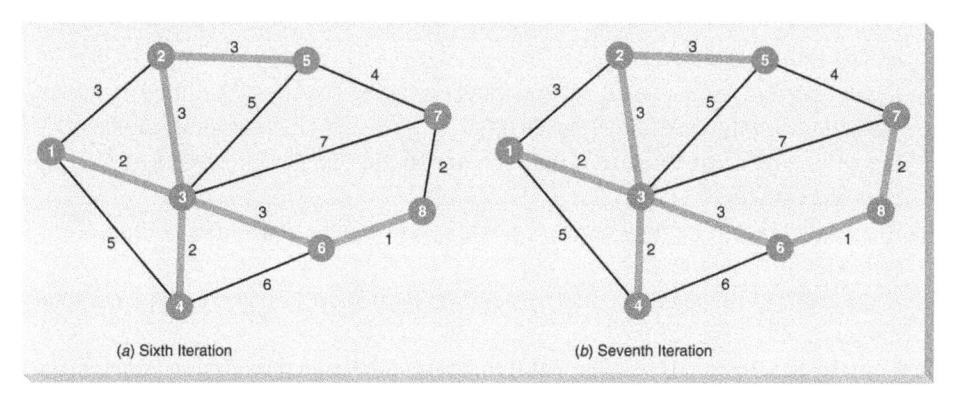

(a) Sixth Iteration

(b) Seventh Iteration

Figure 5.21: Sixth and Seventh (Final) Iterations for Lauderdale Construction

Because there are no more unconnected houses, Figure 5.21(b) shows the final solution. Houses 1, 2, 4, and 6 are all connected to house 3. House 2 is connected to house 5. House 6 is connected to house 8, and house 8 is connected to house 7. The total distance is 1,600 feet.

5.10 Summary

This chapter presents six important network flow models. First, we discuss the transportation model, which deals with the distribution of goods from several supply points to a number of demand points. We also consider transportation models with Max-Min and Min-Max objectives. We then extend the discussion to the transshipment model, which includes points that permit goods to both flow in and flow out of them. Next, we discuss the assignment model, which deals with determining the most efficient assignment of issues such as people to projects.

The fourth model covered is the maximal-flow model, which finds the maximum flow of any quantity or substance that can go through a network. This is followed by a discussion of the shortest-path model, which finds the shortest path through a network. Finally, we introduce the minimal-spanning tree model, which determines the path through the network that connects all the nodes while minimizing total distance.

Key Points
- A node is a specific point or location in a network.
- An arc connects two nodes to each other.
- Arcs can be one way or two way.
- A key property of network models is that if all supplies and demands are integers, all flows in the network will also be integers.
- Transportation models deal with distribution of goods from supply points to demand points at minimum cost.
- Balanced supply and demand in a transportation model occurs when total supply equals total demand.
- It is convenient to express all network flows by using double-subscripted variables.
- We write a supply constraint for each origin (e.g., factory) in a transportation model.
- We write a demand constraint for each destination (e.g., warehouse) in a transportation model.
- In an Excel layout for network flow models, it is convenient to use a tabular form to model the flows on each arc.
- A transportation model is unbalanced if the total supply does not equal the total demand.
- If total supply exceeds total demand in a transportation model, the supply constraints are written as inequalities.
- If total demand exceeds total supply in a transportation model, the demand constraints are written as inequalities.
- It is quite common for transportation models to have alternate optimal solutions.
- Deciding where to locate a new facility within an overall distribution system is aided by the transportation model. We solve a separate transportation model with each location to find the location with the lowest system cost.
- Max-Min and Min-Max models seek to reduce the variability in the values of the flows (i.e., decision variables) in the different arcs of a network.
- The addition of constraints other than supply and demand constraints may cause the optimal solution in network flow models to no longer be integers.
- Transshipment models include nodes that can have shipments arrive as well as leave.
- A pure transshipment point is one where no supply or demand exists, i.e., all flows simply pass through this point.

- For many network models, it is a good idea to first draw the network and visualize the various flows.
- The objective in a typical assignment problem is to find the one-to-one assignment of people to projects, jobs to machines, and so on, so that the total costs are minimized.
- Each supply and each demand in an assignment model equals one unit.
- The special integer flow property of network models automatically ensures unique assignments for the assignment problem.
- An assignment model can sometimes involve a maximization objective.
- A maximal-flow model finds the most flow that can occur through a network.
- In a maximal-flow model, we replace each two-way arc (e.g., road) with a pair of one-way arcs.
- In a maximal-flow model, there is a decision variable associated with each arc in the network.
- In a maximal-flow model, we add a one-way dummy arc from the destination node to the source node. The objective is to maximize the flow on the dummy arc.
- In a maximal-flow model, because all nodes are transshipment nodes with no supplies or demand, the net flow at each node is zero.
- Capacity constraints in a maximal-flow model limit the flows on the arcs.
- In Solver, entries for non-adjacent cells are separated by commas.
- In a network model, arc capacities of zero will prevent flows on arcs.
- A shortest-path model has a unique starting node (origin) and a unique ending node (destination), and seeks to find the shortest route between these two nodes.
- All flows in a shortest-path model will equal exactly one unit.
- To prevent flows on certain arcs, their distance (or cost) can be set to a large value.
- A minimal-spanning tree model connects all nodes in a network while minimizing total distance.
- Minimal-spanning tree models can be easily solved by hand using a simple solution procedure that involves four steps.

Glossary

Assignment Model A specific type of network model that involves determining the most efficient assignment of people to projects, salespeople to territories, contracts to bidders, jobs to machines, and so on.

Balanced Model A model in which total demand (at all destinations) is equal to total supply (at all origins).

Destination A demand location in a transportation model. Also called a *sink*.

Facility Location Analysis An application of the transportation model to help a firm decide where to locate a new factory, warehouse, or other facility.

Max-Min Model A model that maximizes the minimum value of some or all of the decision variables.

Maximal-Flow Model A problem that finds the maximum flow of any quantity or substance through a network.

Min-Max Model A model that minimizes the maximum value of some or all of the decision variables.

Minimal-Spanning Tree Model A model that determines the path through the network that connects all the nodes while minimizing total distance.

Origin A supply location or source in a transportation model. Also called a *source*.

Shortest-Path Model A model that determines the shortest path or route through a network.

Transportation Model A specific network model case that involves scheduling shipments from origins to destinations so that total shipping costs are minimized.

Transshipment Model An extension of the transportation model in which some points have both flows in and out.

Unbalanced Model A situation in which total demand is not equal to total supply.

5.11 Exercises

Solved Problems

Solved Problem 5–1 The Hardgrave Machine Company produces computer components at its factories in Cincinnati, Kansas City, and Pittsburgh. These factories have not been able to keep up with demand for orders at Hardgrave's four warehouses in Detroit, Houston, New York, and Los Angeles. As a result, the firm has decided to build a new factory to expand its productive capacity. The two sites being considered are Seattle, Washington, and Birmingham, Alabama. Both cities are attractive in terms of labor supply, municipal services, and ease of factory financing.

Table 5.6 presents the production costs and monthly supplies at each of the three existing factories, monthly demands at each of the four warehouses, and estimated production costs at the two proposed factories.

Table 5.6: Hardgrave Machine's Demand and Supply Data

Warehouse	Monthly Demand (units)	Production Plant	Monthly Supply	Cost to Produce One Unit
Detroit	10,000	Cincinnati	15,000	$48
Houston	12,000	Kansas City	6,000	$50
New York	15,000	Pittsburgh	14,000	$52
Los Angeles	9,000		35,000	
	46,000			

Supply needed from the new plant = 46,000 − 35,000 = 11,000 units per month.

Estimated Production Cost per Unit at Proposed Plants	
Seattle	$53
Birmingham	$49

Transportation costs from each factory to each warehouse are summarized in Table 5.7. Where should Hardgrave locate the new factory?

Table 5.7: Hardgrave Machine's Shipping Costs

		To		
From	Detroit	Houston	New York	Los Angeles
Cincinnati	$25	$55	$40	$60
Kansas City	$35	$30	$50	$40
Pittsburgh	$36	$45	$26	$66
Seattle	$60	$38	$65	$27
Birmingham	$35	$30	$41	$50

The total cost of each individual factory-to-warehouse route is found by adding the shipping costs (in the body of Table 5.7) to the respective unit production costs (from Table 5.6). For example, the total production plus shipping cost of one computer component from Cincinnati to Detroit is $73 (= $25 for shipping plus $48 for production).

To determine which new factory (Seattle or Birmingham) yields the lowest total system cost, we solve two transportation models: one for each of the two possible locations. In each case, there are 4 factories and 4 warehouses. Hence, there are 16 decision variables.

Figure 5.22 and Figure 5.23 show the resulting optimum solutions with the total cost for each of the two locations. From these solutions, it appears that Seattle should be selected as the new factory site. Its total cost of $3,704,000 is less than the $3,741,000 cost at Birmingham.

Solved Problem 5-2 Seccombe, Inc., a publisher headquartered in New York, wants to assign three recently hired college graduates, Jones, Smith, and Wilson, to regional sales offices in Omaha, Miami, and Dallas. But the firm also has an opening in New York and would send one of the three there if it were more economical than a move to Omaha, Miami, or Dallas. It will cost $1,000 to relocate Jones to New York, $800 to relocate Smith there, and $1,500 to move Wilson. The other relocation costs are as follows:

		Office	
Hiree	Omaha	Miami	Dallas
Jones	$800	$1,100	$1,200
Smith	$500	$1,600	$1,300
Wilson	$500	$1,000	$2,300

What is the optimal assignment of personnel to offices?

284 —— Chapter 5: Transportation, Assignment, and Network Models

Hardgrave Machine Company (Seattle)

The model includes new plant at Seattle.

Shipments: To

From	Detroit	Houston	NY	LA	Flow out		Capacity
Cincinnati	10,000	4,000	1,000	0	15,000	=	15,000
Kansas City	0	6,000	0	0	6,000	=	6,000
Pittsburgh	0	0	14,000	0	14,000	=	14,000
Seattle	0	2,000	0	9,000	11,000	=	11,000
Flow in	10,000	12,000	15,000	9,000	LHS	Sign	RHS
	=	=	=	=	Sign		
Demand	10,000	12,000	15,000	9,000	RHS		

Proposed capacity of Seattle plant.

Unit costs: To

From	Detroit	Houston	NY	LA
Cincinnati	$73	$103	$88	$108
Kansas City	$85	$80	$100	$90
Pittsburgh	$88	$97	$78	$118
Seattle	$113	$91	$118	$80

Total cost = $3,704,000

Optimal Cost

Solver Parameters

Set Objective: $B$20

To: ○ Max ● Min ○ Value

By Changing Variable Cells:
$B$5:$E$8

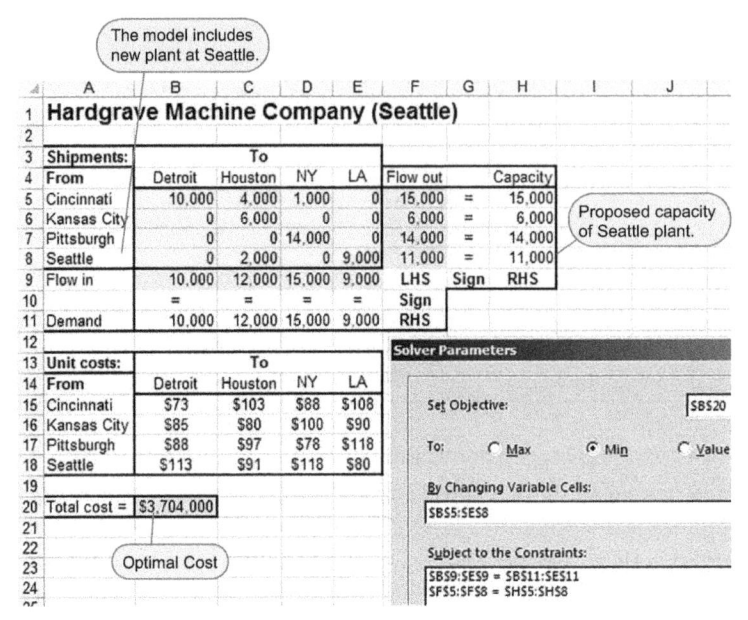

Subject to the Constraints:
$B$9:$E$9 = $B$11:$E$11
$F$5:$F$8 = $H$5:$H$8

Figure 5.22: Excel Layout and Solver Entries for Hardgrave Machine—New Facility in Seattle

📄 File: Figure 5.22.xlsx, Sheet: Figure 5.22

Hardgrave Machine Company (Birmingham)

The model includes new plant at Birmingham. *Proposed capacity of Birmingham plant.*

Shipments: To

From	Detroit	Houston	NY	LA	Flow out		Capacity
Cincinnati	10,000	0	1,000	4,000	15,000	=	15,000
Kansas City	0	1,000	0	5,000	6,000	=	6,000
Pittsburgh	0	0	14,000	0	14,000	=	14,000
Birmingham	0	11,000	0	0	11,000	=	11,000
Flow in	10,000	12,000	15,000	9,000	LHS	Sign	RHS
	=	=	=	=	Sign		
Demand	10,000	12,000	15,000	9,000	RHS		

Unit costs: To

From	Detroit	Houston	NY	LA
Cincinnati	$73	$103	$88	$108
Kansas City	$85	$80	$100	$90
Pittsburgh	$88	$97	$78	$118
Birmingham	$84	$79	$90	$99

Total cost = $3,741,000

Optimal Cost

Solver Parameters

Set Objective: $B$20

To: ○ Max ● Min ○ Value

By Changing Variable Cells:
$B$5:$E$8

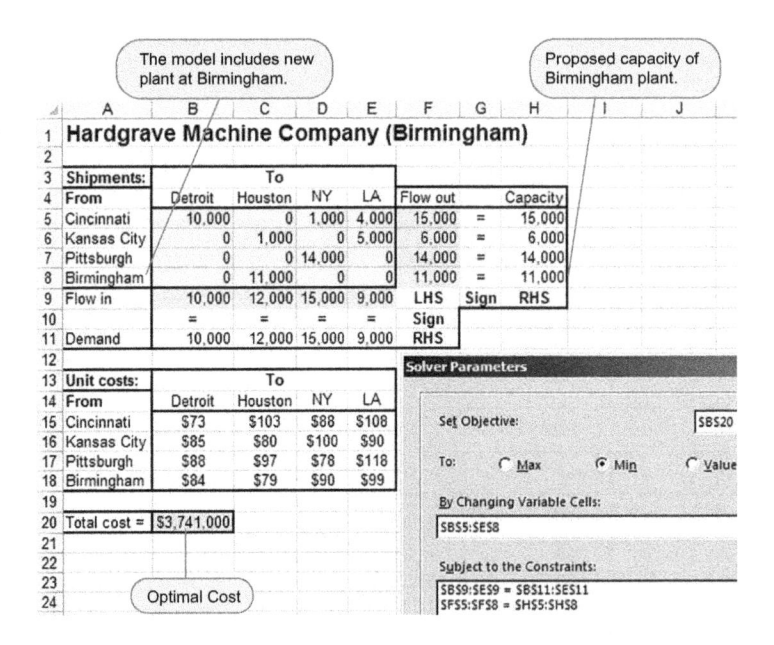

Subject to the Constraints:
$B$9:$E$9 = $B$11:$E$11
$F$5:$F$8 = $H$5:$H$8

Figure 5.23: Excel Layout and Solver Entries for Hardgrave Machine—New Facility in Birmingham

📄 File: Figure 5.22.xlsx, Sheet: Figure 5.23

Solution Because this is an unbalanced assignment model with three supply points (hirees) and four demand points (offices), the demand constraints should be expressed as inequalities (i.e., they should have ≤ signs).

Figure 5.24 shows the Excel layout and solution for Seccombe's assignment model. The optimal solution is to assign Wilson to Omaha, Smith to New York, and Jones to Miami. Nobody is assigned to Dallas. The total cost is $2,400.

Figure 5.24: Excel Layout and Solver Entries for Seccombe, Inc.—Assignment

File: Figure 5.24.xlsx

Solved Problem 5–3 PetroChem, an oil refinery located on the Mississippi River south of Baton Rouge, Louisiana, is designing a new plant to produce diesel fuel. Figure 5.25 shows the network of the main processing centers along with the existing rate of flow (in thousands of gallons of fuel). The management at PetroChem would like to determine the maximum amount of fuel that can flow through the plant, from node 1 to node 7.

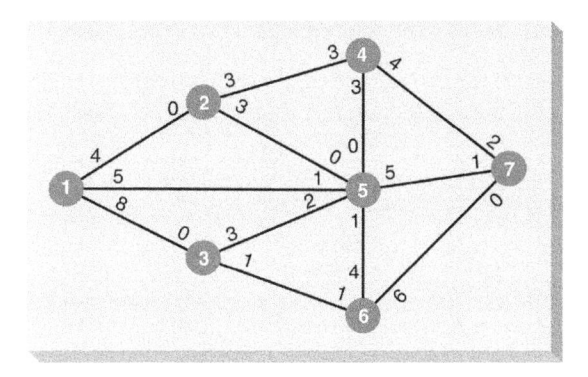

Figure 5.25: Network for PetroChem—Maximal-Flow

286 — Chapter 5: Transportation, Assignment, and Network Models

Solution Node 1 is the origin node, and node 7 is the destination node. As described in Section 5.7, we convert all bidirectional arcs into unidirectional arcs, and we introduce a dummy arc from node 7 to node 1. The modified network is shown in Figure 5.26. The capacity of the dummy arc from node 7 to node 1 is set at a large number such as 1,000.

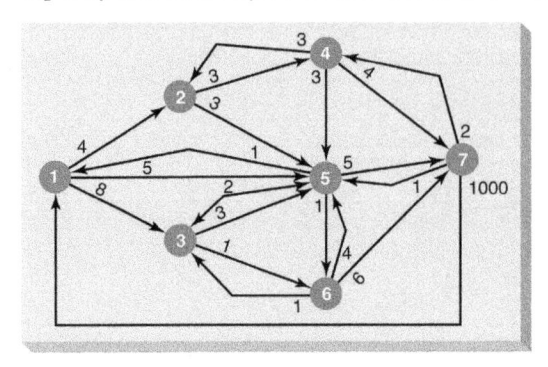

Figure 5.26: Modified Network for PetroChem—Maximal-Flow

Figure 5.27 shows the Excel layout and solution for this model. Unlike our earlier maximal-flow example in Figure 5.14, the entire cell range B5:H11 has been specified as the changing variable cells in Solver. However, the capacity of all arcs that do not exist (shown by the non-yellow cells in B5:H11) has been set to zero (in cells B16:H22) to prevent any fuel flows on these pipes (arcs).

Figure 5.27: Excel Layout and Solver Entries for PetroChem—Maximal-Flow

File: Figure 5.27.xlsx

The optimal solution shows that it is possible to have 10,000 gallons flow from node 1 to node 7 using the existing network.

Solved Problem 5-4 The network in Figure 5.28 shows the roads and cities surrounding Leadville, Colorado. Leadville Tom, a bicycle helmet manufacturer, must transport helmets to a distributor based in Dillon, Colorado. To do this, the shipment must go through several cities. Tom would like to find the shortest way to get from Leadville to Dillon. What do you recommend?

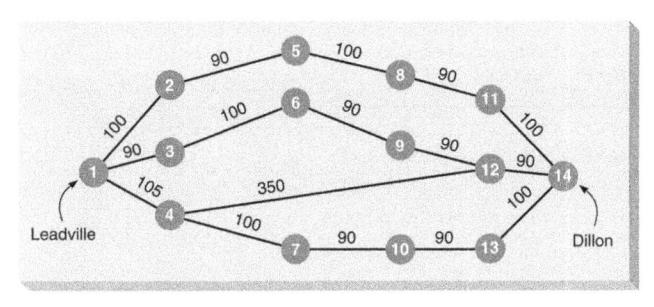

Figure 5.28: Network for Leadville Tom—Shortest-Path

Solution We associate a supply of one unit at Leadville (node 1) and a demand of one unit at Dillon (node 14). Figure 5.29 shows the Excel layout and solution for this model. Unlike our earlier shortest-path example in Figure 5.16, the entire cell range B5:N17 has been specified as the changing variable cells in Solver. However, we prevent flow (travel) on all roads that do not exist (shown by the non-yellow cells in B5:N17) by setting their distances to high values (in cells B24:N36).

The optimal solution shows that the shortest distance from Leadville to Dillon is 460 miles and involves travel through nodes 3, 6, 9, and 12.

Solved Problem 5-5 Roxie LaMothe, owner of a large horse breeding farm near Orlando, is planning to install a complete water system connecting all the various stables and barns. The locations of the facilities and the distances between them are given in the network shown in Figure 5.30. Roxie must determine the least expensive way to provide water to each facility. What do you recommend?

288 — Chapter 5: Transportation, Assignment, and Network Models

Only the shaded cells denote roads that actually exist.

Table shows the flow between all pairs of nodes.

Supply at node 1 = 1 unit.

	A	B	C	D	E	F	G	H	I	J	K	L	M	N	O	P	Q
1	Leadville Tom (Shortest-Path)																
2																	
3	Flows:																
4	From	N 2	N 3	N 4	N 5	N 6	N 7	N 8	N 9	N 10	N 11	N 12	N 13	N 14	Flow out		Capacity
5	Node 1	0.0	1.0	0.0	0.0	0.0	0.0	0.0	0.0	0.0	0.0	0.0	0.0	0.0	1.0	=	1.0
6	Node 2	0.0	0.0	0.0	0.0	0.0	0.0	0.0	0.0	0.0	0.0	0.0	0.0	0.0	0.0	=	0.0
7	Node 3	0.0	0.0	0.0	0.0	1.0	0.0	0.0	0.0	0.0	0.0	0.0	0.0	0.0	1.0	=	1.0
8	Node 4	0.0	0.0	0.0	0.0	0.0	0.0	0.0	0.0	0.0	0.0	0.0	0.0	0.0	0.0	=	0.0
9	Node 5	0.0	0.0	0.0	0.0	0.0	0.0	0.0	0.0	0.0	0.0	0.0	0.0	0.0	0.0	=	0.0
10	Node 6	0.0	0.0	0.0	0.0	0.0	0.0	0.0	1.0	0.0	0.0	0.0	0.0	0.0	1.0	=	1.0
11	Node 7	0.0	0.0	0.0	0.0	0.0	0.0	0.0	0.0	0.0	0.0	0.0	0.0	0.0	0.0	=	0.0
12	Node 8	0.0	0.0	0.0	0.0	0.0	0.0	0.0	0.0	0.0	0.0	0.0	0.0	0.0	0.0	=	0.0
13	Node 9	0.0	0.0	0.0	0.0	0.0	0.0	0.0	0.0	0.0	1.0	0.0	0.0	0.0	1.0	=	1.0
14	Node 10	0.0	0.0	0.0	0.0	0.0	0.0	0.0	0.0	0.0	0.0	0.0	0.0	0.0	0.0	=	0.0
15	Node 11	0.0	0.0	0.0	0.0	0.0	0.0	0.0	0.0	0.0	0.0	0.0	0.0	0.0	0.0	=	0.0
16	Node 12	0.0	0.0	0.0	0.0	0.0	0.0	0.0	0.0	0.0	0.0	0.0	0.0	1.0	1.0	=	1.0
17	Node 13	0.0	0.0	0.0	0.0	0.0	0.0	0.0	0.0	0.0	0.0	0.0	0.0	0.0	0.0	=	0.0
18	Flow in	0.0	1.0	0.0	0.0	1.0	0.0	0.0	1.0	0.0	0.0	1.0	0.0	0.0	1.0	LHS	
19																=	Sign
20	Demand														1.0	RHS	
21																	
22	Distances:																
23	From	N 2	N 3	N 4	N 5	N 6	N 7	N 8	N 9	N 10	N 11	N 12	N 13	N 14			
24	Node 1	100	90	105	1000	1000	1000	1000	1000	1000	1000	1000	1000	1000			
25	Node 2	1000	1000	1000	90	1000	1000	1000	1000	1000	1000	1000	1000	1000			
26	Node 3	1000	1000	1000	1000	100	1000	1000	1000	1000	1000	1000	1000	1000			
27	Node 4	1000	1000	1000	1000	1000	100	1000	1000	1000	1000	350	1000	1000			
28	Node 5	90	1000	1000	1000	1000	1000	100	1000	1000	1000	1000	1000	1000			
29	Node 6	1000	100	1000	1000	1000	1000	1000	90	1000	1000	1000	1000	1000			
30	Node 7	1000	1000	100	1000	1000	1000	1000	1000	90	1000	1000	1000	1000			
31	Node 8	1000	1000	1000	100	1000	1000	1000	1000	1000	90	1000	1000	1000			
32	Node 9	1000	1000	1000	1000	90	1000	1000	1000	1000	1000	90	1000	1000			
33	Node 10	1000	1000	1000	1000	1000	90	1000	1000	1000	1000	1000	90	1000			
34	Node 11	1000	1000	1000	1000	1000	1000	90	1000	1000	1000	1000	1000	100			
35	Node 12	1000	1000	350	1000	1000	1000	1000	90	1000	1000	1000	1000	90			
36	Node 13	1000	1000	1000	1000	1000	1000	1000	1000	90	1000	1000	1000	100			
37																	
38	Shortest distance		460														

Demand at node 14 = 1 unit.

Solver Parameters

Set Objective: $SDS38

To: ○ Max ● Min ○ Value

By Changing Variable Cells:
$B$5:$N$17

Subject to the Constraints:
$N$18 = $N$20
$O$5:$O$17 = $Q$5:$Q$17

=SUMPRODUCT(B5:N17,B24:N36)

Distances of roads that do not exist are set to very high values.

All cells in the decision variable table (B5:N17) are specified as Changing Variable Cells. No flow occurs on roads that do not exist since their distances are very high.

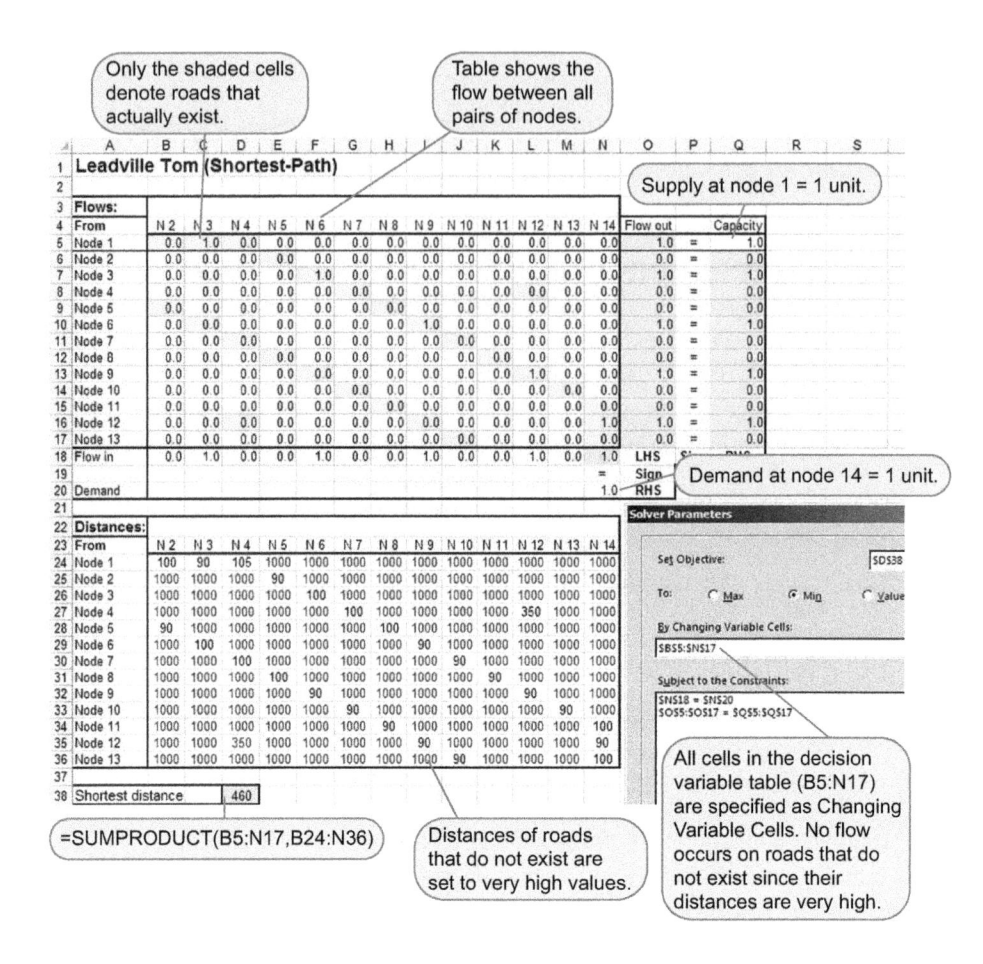

Figure 5.29: Excel Layout and Solver Entries for Leadville Tom—Shortest-Path

File: Figure 5.29.xlsx

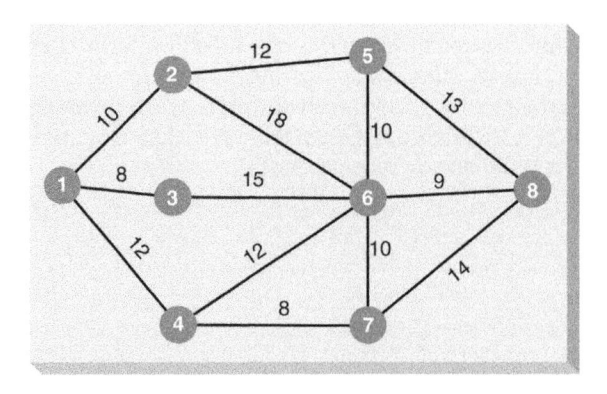

Figure 5.30: Network for Roxie LaMothe—Minimal-Spanning Tree

Solution This is a typical minimal-spanning tree problem that can be solved by hand. We begin by selecting node 1 and connecting it to the nearest node, which is node 3. Nodes 1 and 2 are the next to be connected, followed by nodes 1 and 4. Now we connect node 4 to node 7 and node 7 to node 6. At this point, the only remaining points to be connected are node 6 to node 8 and node 6 to node 5. The final solution is shown in Figure 5.31.

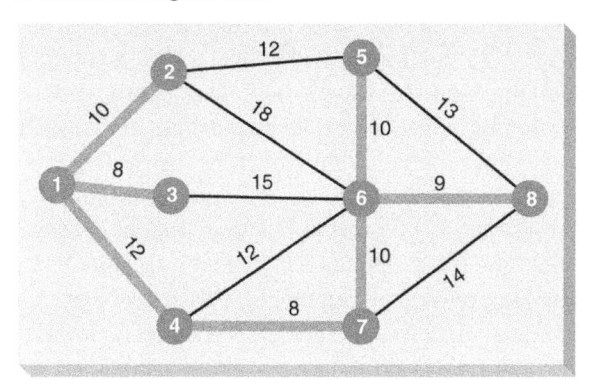

Figure 5.31: Minimal-Spanning Tree for Roxie LaMothe

Discussion Questions

5–1. Is the transportation model an example of decision making under certainty or decision making under uncertainty? Why?

5–2. What is a balanced transportation model? Describe the approach you would use to solve an unbalanced model.

5–3. What is the enumeration approach to solving assignment models? Is it a practical way to solve a 5 row × 5 column model? a 7 × 7 model? Why?

5–4. What is the minimal-spanning tree model? What types of problems can be solved using this type of model?

5–5. Give several examples of problems that can be solved using the maximal-flow model.

5–6. Describe a problem that can be solved by using the shortest-path model.

5–7. What is a flow balance constraint? How is it implemented in a network model?

5–8. How can we manipulate a maximal-flow network model in order to set it up as a linear program?

5–9. Why is it more convenient to set up network models in Excel by using a tabular form?

5–10. How can we manipulate a maximal-flow network model in order to specify all arcs between each pair of nodes (i.e., the entire table) as the changing variable cells in *Solver*?

5–11. How can we manipulate a shortest-path network model in order to specify all arcs between each pair of nodes (i.e., the entire table) as the changing variable cells in *Solver*?

Problems

Note: The networks for all problems given here involve no more than 14 nodes. If we arrange the decision variables in tabular form, the total number of entries will be no more than 196 (= 14 × 14). Therefore, it should be possible to specify the entire table in the By Changing Variable Cells box even in the standard version of Solver.

5-12. The Oconee County, South Carolina, superintendent of education is responsible for assigning students to the three high schools in his county. A certain number of students have to travel to and from school by bus, as several sectors of the county are beyond walking distance from a school. The superintendent partitions the county into five geographic sectors as he attempts to establish a plan that will minimize the total number of student miles traveled by bus. Of course, if a student happens to live in a certain sector and is assigned to the high school in that sector, there is no need to bus that student because he or she can walk to school. The three schools are located in sectors B, C, and E. The table for this problem reflects the number of high-school-age students living in each sector and the distance, in miles, from each sector to each school. Assuming that each high school has a capacity of 1,100 students, set up and solve Oconee County's problem as a transportation model.

	Distance to Schools, in Miles			
Sector	Sector B	Sector C	Sector E	Number of Students
A	6	7	11	800
B	0	3	10	600
C	9	0	6	400
D	8	3	5	700
E	15	8	0	500

5-13. Marc Hernandez's construction firm currently has three projects in progress. Each requires a specific supply of gravel. There are three gravel pits available to provide for Hernandez's needs, but shipping costs differ from location to location. The following table summarizes the transportation costs:

	To			
From	Job 1	Job 2	Job 3	Tonnage Allowance
Central pit	$9	$ 8	$ 7	3,000
Rock pit	$7	$11	$ 6	4,000
Acme pit	$4	$ 3	$12	6,000
Job requirements (tons)	2,500	3,750	4,850	

(a) Determine Hernandez's optimal shipping quantities so as to minimize total transportation costs.

(b) It is the case that Rock Pit and Central Pit can send gravel by rail to Acme for $1 per ton. Once the gravel is relocated, it can be trucked to the jobs. Reformulate this problem to determine how shipping by rail could reduce the transportation costs for the gravel.

5–14. The Southern Rail Company ships coal by rail from three coal mines to meet the demand requirements of four coal depots. The following table shows the distances from the mines to the various depots and the availabilities and requirements for coal. Determine the best shipment of coal cars to minimize the total miles traveled by the cars.

	To				
From	Columbia	Albany	Springfield	Pleasatanburg	Supply of Cars
Parris	50	30	60	70	35
Butler	20	80	10	90	60
Century	100	40	80	30	25
Demand for cars	30	45	25	20	

5–15. The Piedmont Investment Corporation has identified four small apartment buildings in which it would like to invest. The four banks generally used by Piedmont have provided quotes on the interest rates they would charge to finance each purchase. The banks have also advised Piedmont of the maximum amount of money they are willing to lend at this time. Piedmont would like to purchase as many buildings as possible while paying the lowest possible amount in total interest. More than one bank can be used to finance the same property. What should Piedmont do?

	Property (interest rates)				
Savings and Loan Company	Hill St.	Banks St.	Park Ave.	Drury Lane	Max Credit Line
First Homestead	8%	8%	10%	11%	$80,000
Commonwealth	9%	9%	12%	10%	$100,000
Washington Federal	9%	11%	10%	9%	$120,000
Loan required	$60,000	$40,000	$130,000	$70,000	

5–16. The manager of the O'Brian Glass Company is planning the production of automobile windshields for the next four months. The demand for the next four months is projected to be as shown in the following table.

Month	Demand for Windshields
1	130
2	140
3	260
4	120

O'Brian can normally produce 100 windshields in a month. This is done during regular production hours at a cost of $100 per windshield. If demand in any one month cannot be satisfied by regular production, the production manager has three other choices: (1) He can produce up to 50 more windshields per month in overtime but at a cost of $130 per windshield; (2) he can purchase a limited number of windshields from a friendly competitor for resale at a cost of $150 each (the maximum number of outside purchases over the four-month period is 450 windshields); or (3) he can fill the demand from his on-hand inventory. The inventory carrying cost is $10 per windshield per month. Back orders are not permitted. Inventory on hand at the beginning of month 1 is 40 windshields. Set up and solve this "production smoothing" problem as a transportation model to minimize cost. *Hint:* Set the various production options (e.g., regular production, outside purchase, etc.) as supply nodes and the monthly demands as the demand nodes.

5-17. Maurice's Pump Manufacturing Company currently maintains plants in Atlanta and Tulsa that supply major distribution centers in Los Angeles and New York. Because of an expanding demand, Maurice has decided to open a third plant and has narrowed the choice to one of two cities—New Orleans or Houston. The pertinent production and distribution costs, as well as the plant capacities and distribution center demands, are shown in the following table.

	Distribution Centers			
Plants	Los Angeles	New York	Capacity	Production Cost (per unit)
Atlanta (existing)	$8	$5	600	$6
Tulsa (existing)	$4	$7	900	$5
New Orleans (proposed)	$5	$6	500	$4 *(anticipated)*
Houston (proposed)	$4	$6	500	$3 *(anticipated)*
Forecast demand	800	1,200		

Which of the new possible plants should be opened?

5-18. A food distribution company ships fresh spinach from its four packing plants to large East-coast cities. The shipping costs per crate, the supply and demand are shown in the table for this problem.

			Markets		
Packing Plants	Atlanta	Boston	Charlestown	Dover	Supply
Eaglestown	$6.00	$7.00	$7.50	$7.50	8,000
Farrier	$5.50	$5.50	$4.00	$7.00	10,000
Guyton	$6.00	$5.00	$6.50	$7.00	5,000
Hayesville	$7.00	$7.50	$8.50	$6.50	9,000
Demand	8,000	9,000	10,000	5,000	

(a) Formulate a model that will permit the company to meet its demand at the lowest possible cost.

(b) The company wishes to spread out the source for each of its markets to the maximum extent possible. To accomplish this, it will accept a 5% increase in its total transportation cost from part (a). What is the new transportation plan, and what is the new cost?

5–19. The Lilly Snack Company is considering adding an additional plant to its three existing facilities in Wise, Virginia; Humboldt, Tennessee; and Cleveland, Georgia to serve three large markets in the Southeast. Two locations—Brevard, North Carolina, and Laurens, South Carolina—are being considered. The transportation costs per pallet are shown in the table for this problem.

	\multicolumn{5}{c	}{From}	
To	Wise	Humboldt	Cleveland	Brevard	Laurens	Demand
Charlotte	$20	$17	$21	$29	$27	250
Greenville	$25	$27	$20	$30	$28	200
Atlanta	$22	$25	$22	$30	$31	350
Capacity	300	200	150	150	150	

(a) Which site would you recommend? Why?

(b) Suppose that the Brevard location has been selected. Due to the perishable nature of the goods involved, management wishes to restrict the maximum number of pallets shipped from any one plant to any single market. To accomplish this, management is willing to accept a 10% surcharge on the optimal transportation costs from part (a). What is the new transportation plan, and what is the new cost?

5–20. Meg Bishop, vice president of supply chain at the Lilly Snack Company (see Problem 5–19) has been able to secure shipping from the proposed plant in Brevard to its plants in Wise and Cleveland for $6 and $5 per pallet, respectively. If Lilly chooses to place a new plant in Brevard, what would be the new shipping plan and cost? Ignore part (b) of Problem 5–19 in answering this question.

5–21. The distribution system for the Smith Company consists of three plants (A, B, and C), two warehouses (D and E), and four customers (W, X, Y, and Z). The relevant supply, demand, and unit shipping cost information are given in the table for Problem 5–21 near the top of the next page. Set up and solve the transshipment model to minimize total shipping costs.

					To			To			
Plant	Supply	Customer	Demand	From	D	E	From	W	X	Y	Z
A	450	W	450	A	$4	$7	D	$6	$4	$8	$4
B	500	X	300	B	$8	$5	E	$3	$6	$7	$7
C	380	Y	300	C	$5	$6					
		Z	400								

5-22. A supply chain consists of three plants (A, B, and C), three distributors (J, K, and L), and three stores (X, Y, and Z). The relevant supply, demand, and unit shipping cost information are given in the table for this problem. Set up and solve the transshipment model to minimize total shipping costs.

					To				To					
Plant	Supply	Store	Demand	From	J	K	L	From	X	Y	Z	J	K	L
A	400	X	400	A	$4	$7	$5	J	$6	$4	$8		$6	$5
B	500	Y	325	B	$8	$5	$4	K	$3	$6	$7	$6		$7
C	350	Z	400	C	$5	$6	$7	L	$2	$4	$5	$5	$7	

5-23. In a job shop operation, four jobs can be performed on any of four machines. The hours required for each job on each machine are presented in the following table:

	Machine			
JOB	W	X	Y	Z
A	16	14	10	13
B	15	13	12	12
C	12	12	9	11
D	18	16	14	16

The plant supervisor would like to assign jobs so that total time is minimized. Use the assignment model to find the best solution.

5-24. Greg Pickett, coach of a little-league baseball team, is preparing for a series of four games against four good opponents. Greg would like to increase the probability of winning as many games as possible by carefully scheduling his pitchers against the teams they are each most likely to defeat. Because the games are to be played back-to-back in less than one week, Greg cannot count on any pitcher to start in more than one game.

Greg knows the strengths and weaknesses not only of his pitchers but also of his opponents, and he believes he can estimate the probability of winning each of the four games with each of the four starting pitchers. Those probabilities are listed in the following table.

	Opponent			
Starting Pitcher	Des Moines	Davenport	Omaha	Peoria
Jones	0.40	0.80	0.50	0.60
Baker	0.30	0.40	0.80	0.70
Parker	0.80	0.80	0.70	0.90
Wilson	0.20	0.30	0.40	0.50

What pitching rotation should Greg set to provide the highest sum of the probabilities of winning each game for his team?

5-25. Cindy Jefferson, hospital administrator at Anderson Hospital must appoint head nurses to four newly established departments: urology, cardiology, orthopedics, and pediatrics. Believing in the decision modeling approach to problem solving, Cindy has interviewed four nurses—Morris, Richards, Cook, and Morgan—and developed an index scale ranging from 0 to 100 to be used in the assignment. An index of 0 implies that the nurse would be perfectly suited to that task. A value close to 100, on the other hand, implies that the nurse is not at all suited to head that unit. The following table gives the complete set of index scales that Cindy feels represent all possible assignments.

	Department			
Nurse	Urology	Cardiology	Orthopedics	Pediatrics
Morris	15	18	28	75
Richards	23	48	32	38
Cook	24	36	51	36
Morgan	55	38	25	12

Which nurse should be assigned to which unit?

5-26. A trauma center keeps ambulances at locations throughout the east side of a city in an attempt to minimize the response time in the event of an emergency. The times, in minutes, from the ambulance locations to the population centers are given in the following table.

	Population Centers			
Ambulance Locations	East	Northeast	Southeast	Central
Site 1	12	8	9	13
Site 2	10	9	11	10
Site 3	11	12	14	11
Site 4	13	11	12	9

Find the optimal assignment of ambulances to population centers that will minimize the total emergency response time.

5-27. The Central Police Department has five detective squads available for assignment to five open crime cases. The chief of detectives wishes to assign the squads so that the total time to conclude the cases is minimized. The average number of days, based on past performance, for each squad to complete each case is shown in following table.

	Case				
Squad	A	B	C	D	E
1	27	7	3	7	14
2	30	6	12	7	20
3	21	5	4	3	10
4	21	12	7	12	8
5	8	26	24	25	13

Use the assignment model to find the best solution.

5-28. Kelly Spaugh, course scheduler of a technical college's business department, needs to assign instructors to courses next semester. As a criterion for judging who should teach each course, Kelly reviews the student evaluations of teaching for the past two years. Because each of the four professors taught each of the four courses at one time or another during the two-year period, Kelly is able to determine a course rating for each instructor. These ratings are shown in the table for this problem.

	Course			
Professor	Statistics	Management	Finance	Economics
Strausbaugh	70	60	80	75
Kelley	80	60	80	75
Davidson	65	55	80	60
Merkle	95	40	65	55

Find the best assignment of professors to courses to maximize the overall teaching ratings.

5-29. Coogan Construction is in the process of installing power lines to a large housing development. Rob Coogan wants to minimize the total length of wire used, which will minimize his costs. The housing development is shown as a network in Figure 5.32. Each house has been numbered, and the distance between houses is given in hundreds of feet. What do you recommend?

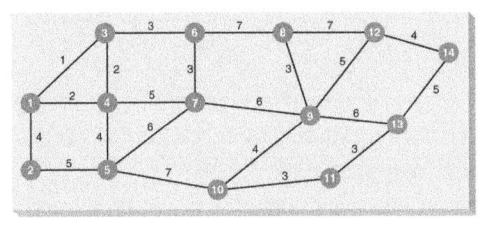

Figure 5.32: Network for Problem 5–29: Coogan Construction

5-30. The city of Six Mile, South Carolina, is considering making several of its streets one way. What is the maximum number of cars per hour that can travel from east (node 1) to west (node 8)? The network is shown in Figure 5.33.

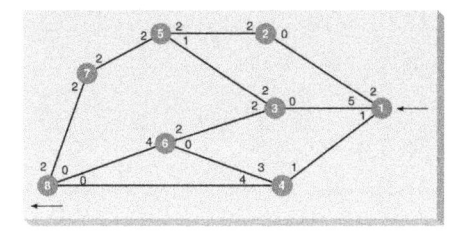

Figure 5.33: Network for Problem 5-30: Six Mile, South Carolina

5-31. Two Chaps and a Truck Movers have been hired to move the office furniture and equipment of Wray Properties to the company's new headquarters. What route do you recommend? The network of roads is shown in Figure 5.34.

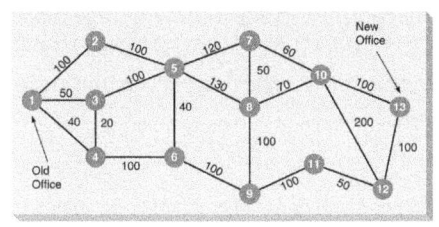

Figure 5.34: Network for Problem 5-31: Two Chaps and a Truck Movers

5-32. A security firm needs to connect alarm systems to the firm's main control site from five potential trouble locations. Since the systems must be fail-safe, the cables must be run in special pipes. These pipes are very expensive but large enough to simultaneously handle five cables (the maximum that might be needed). Use the minimal-spanning tree model to find the minimum total length of pipes needed to connect the locations shown in Figure 5.35. Node 6 represents the main control site.

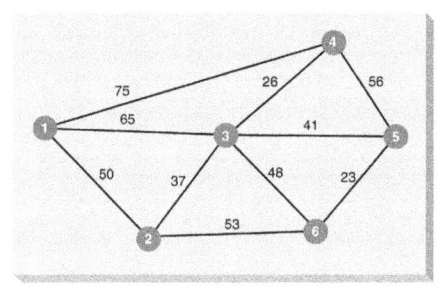

Figure 5.35: Network for Problem 5-32

5-33. Figure 5.36 shows a network of nodes. Any sequence of activities that takes a flow of one unit from node 1 to node 6 will produce a widget. For example, one unit flowing from node 1 to node 4 to node 6 would create a widget. Other paths are possible. Quantities given are numbers of widgets per day.

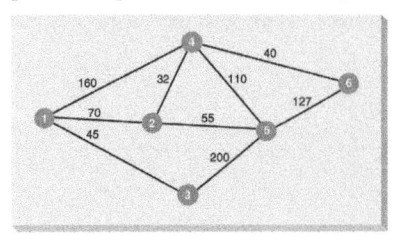

Figure 5.36: Network for Problem 5–33

(a) How many widgets could be produced in one day?
(b) Suppose we want to ensure that no more than 100 widgets are processed along any of the arcs in the production facility. How many widgets are now possible?

5-34. The road system around the hotel complex (node 1) near a large amusement park (node 11) is shown in Figure 5.37. The numbers by the nodes represent the traffic flow in hundreds of cars per hour. What is the maximum flow of cars from the hotel complex to the park?

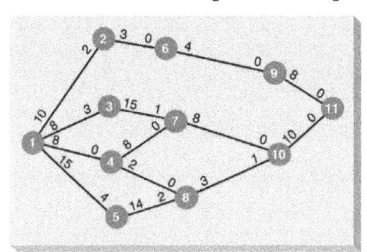

Figure 5.37: Network for Problem 5–34

5-35. The network in Figure 5.38 shows the pipeline transportation system for treated water from the treatment plant (node 1) to a city water supply system (node 14). The arc capacities represent millions of gallons per hour. How much water can be transported per hour from the plant to the city using this network?

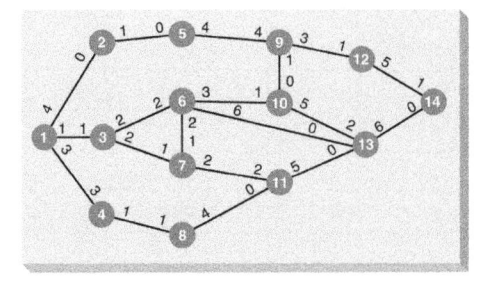

Figure 5.38: Network for Problem 5–35

5-36. In Problem 5-35, two of the terminals in the water supply network (see Figure 5.38), represented by nodes 10 and 11, are to be taken offline for routine maintenance. No material can flow into or out of these nodes. What impact does this have on the capacity of the network? By how much, if any, will the capacity of this network be decreased during the maintenance period?

5-37. The network shown in Figure 5.39 represents the major roads between Port Huron (node 1) and Dearborn (node 14). The values on the arcs represent the distance, in miles. Find the shortest route between the two cities.

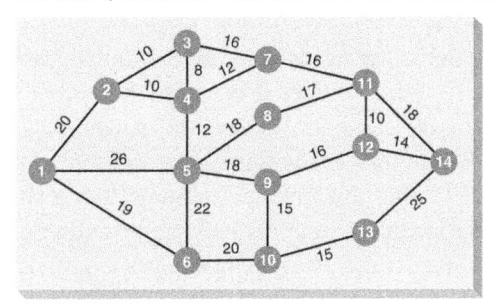

Figure 5.39: Network for Problem 5-37

5-38. In Problem 5-37, all roads leading into and out of nodes 4 and 9 (see Figure 5.39) have been closed because of bridge repairs. What impact (if any) will this have on the shortest route between Port Huron and Dearborn?

5-39. Solve the minimal-spanning tree model in the network shown in Figure 5.40. Assume that the numbers in the network represent distance in hundreds of yards.

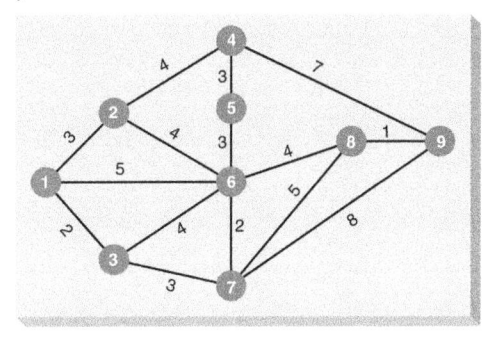

Figure 5.40: Network for Problem 5-39

5-40. A secure facility needs to run a hard-wired local area network to connect each of nine sectors. The possible routes the network could utilize, along with the expenses of running the cable between the sectors, in thousands of dollars, are shown in the table at the bottom of this page. Determine the least expensive way to route the network cable to connect all nine sectors. The blank boxes represent no feasible route between the sectors.

From/To	Sector 2	Sector 3	Sector 4	Sector 5	Sector 6	Sector 7	Sector 8	Sector 9
Sector 1	6			3	6			
Sector 2		7	6		4			4
Sector 3			4		5	3		8
Sector 4					8		9	3
Sector 5							7	
Sector 6						8	10	
Sector 7								9
Sector 8								2

5-41. The Kimten Manufacturing Company needs to process 18 jobs. Kimten can process each job on any of the six machines it has available. Iqbal Ahmed, production supervisor at Kimten, wants to allocate jobs to machines in such a manner that all machines have total loads that are as close as possible to each other. For purposes of solving this problem, assume that a single job can be split between multiple machines and that jobs can be moved from one machine to another with no loss of time. The machine hours required for each job are shown in the following table.

Job	Machine Hours
1	39.43
2	27.94
3	40.27
4	18.27
5	12.72
6	35.20
7	27.94
8	17.20
9	17.20
10	17.20
11	21.50
12	16.74
13	28.29
14	6.07
15	16.01
16	18.49
17	12.16
18	36.67

5-42. Create a template in Excel, including all of the appropriate Solver settings, that would accommodate a standard transportation problem with 5 origins and 4 destinations.

5-43. Managers sometimes make the mistake of trying to solve an assignment problem by hand by assigning workers to jobs according to a "best rating next" myopic decision rule, where the next assignment made is the one that has the lowest remaining cost (for a minimization problem) or highest remaining rating (for a maximization problem). Such an approach can lead to poor decisions because it doesn't consider the impact on the remaining assignments to be made. Consider a repair shop, similar to the Fix-It Shop example in Section 5.6, with three workers and three projects. Estimated project repair costs are provided in the following table.

	Project		
Person	1	2	3
Donovan	$20	$28	$30
Edwards	$26	$24	$25
Franklin	$18	$20	$22

(a) Use the "best rating next" rule described above to assign workers to projects. What is the total cost?

(b) Solve the problem optimally using Excel. What is the total cost?

5-44. Create a template in Excel, including all of the appropriate Solver settings, that would accommodate a standard transshipment problem with 2 origins, 3 transshipment nodes, and 3 destinations.

5-45. Modify the Executive Furniture example of Section 5.3 to include another potential factory in Little Rock, Arkansas. Unit costs from Little Rock are $4 to Albuquerque, $6 to Boston, and $4 to Cleveland. Capacity in Little Rock would be 150 units.

(a) Resolve the model, incorporating the new potential factory. What is the new solution, and what is the new total cost?

(b) What are the implications for the solution if the capacity in Little Rock rises to 300 units?

5-46. Create a template in Excel, including all of the appropriate Solver settings, that would accommodate a standard assignment problem with 6 people to be assigned to 6 jobs to *maximize* effectiveness.

5-47. Consider the Ray Design, Inc. shortest path problem in Section 5.8 (Figure 5.16). Suppose that a new road has opened between nodes 3 and 4 with a distance of 30 in either direction. Modify the model to incorporate this new route, and resolve the problem. What is the new route and total distance travelled?

5-48. Create a template in Excel, including all of the appropriate Solver settings, that would accommodate a standard shortest path problem with 8 nodes, where the objective is to find the shortest path through the network from node 1 to node 8. In Solver, specify all cells in the decision variable table in the By Changing Variable Cells box. Insert a large distance into all cells in the distance table. (The user can then insert the actual, i.e., smaller, distances into each cell that represents an actual route.)

5-49. Consider the Road System in Waukesha, Wisconsin, maximal-flow example in Section 5.7 (Figure 5.14).

(a) Suppose that the road between nodes 1 and 4 has been closed indefinitely due to mud slides. Resolve the problem. What is the new solution and maximal flow?

(b) Now suppose that due to the closing of the road between nodes 1 and 4, a new one-way road will be built between node 3 and a new node 4A. The capacity of this route will be 300 cars per hour. An additional one-way road will be built between node 4A and node 6 with a capacity of 400 cars per hour. Modify the model to incorporate this new option, and resolve the problem. What is the new solution and maximal flow?

Chapter 6
Integer, Goal, and Nonlinear Programming Models

Suppose that you are building a new house and need to make several interrelated choices. You would like to install a gas fireplace, a hot tub for the backyard, a whirlpool tub for the master bathroom, a backyard patio, and an outdoor barbecue pit. You would love to have all of these, but your budget won't allow it. And the available budget will depend in part on whether you choose either maple or cherry cabinets. After some deliberation, you have decided that you only need either the backyard hot tub or the indoor jet tub. You have also decided that you will only build the barbecue pit if the patio is built. How will you make your final selections? Modelers can incorporate yes-no decisions such as these for the many similar decisions that exist in organizations via the use of *binary variables*.

In this chapter, we examine mathematical programming models that do not satisfy the characteristics of the strictly linear programs (LPs) that we have seen so far in Chapters 2–5. We begin by investigating models whose solutions must have *integer* values, i.e., fractional answers are not allowable. Adding this condition to Excel's Solver is literally as easy as adding another constraint to the model. An important caveat, though, is that the size of problems with integer variables that Solver (or any other optimization software) can handle is not nearly as large. We will next see examples of a special type of integer variable called a *binary variable*, which can only take on the value of 0 or 1. The introduction of binary variables can significantly expand our modeling capabilities. These allow *yes-no* decisions and certain other types of logic (e.g., mutually exclusive choices or dependent decisions) that might at first appear to be nonlinear into our models. Again, these are relatively easy to handle using Solver. We devote a section to illustrating how binary variables allow us to introduce the notion of *fixed costs* into our models, which only kick in if any related activity takes place.

Another limitation of standard LPs is that they contain precisely one objective. However, there may be situations when organizations have multiple objectives that they wish to minimize or maximize. The next part of the chapter illustrates how to use *goal programming* to try to accommodate more than one goal. After some adjustments to the model, standard LP solution procedures can be applied. Finally, we move to *nonlinear programming* models. The model formulations look like standard LP, but the functions are *nonlinear* instead of linear. Unfortunately, *optimal* solutions are no longer guaranteed. However, Excel's Solver still has the capability to search for a good solution that *might* be the best one.

Chapter Objectives

After completing this chapter, you will be able to:
1. Formulate integer programming models.
2. Set up and solve IP models using Excel's Solver.
3. Understand the difference between general integer and binary integer variables.
4. Understand the use of binary integer variables in formulating problems involving fixed costs.
5. Formulate goal programming problems and solve them using Excel's Solver.
6. Formulate nonlinear programming problems and solve them using Excel's Solver.

6.1 Models That Relax Linear Programming Conditions

Earlier chapters focus on the linear programming (LP) category of mathematical programming models. These LP models have three characteristics:
- The decision variables can have fractional values.
- There is a unique objective function.
- All mathematical expressions (objective function and constraints) must be linear.

This chapter presents a series of other important mathematical models that allow us to relax each of these basic LP conditions. The new models—integer programming, goal programming, and nonlinear programming—are introduced here and then discussed in detail in the remainder of this chapter.

Integer Programming Models

Although fractional values such as $X = 0.33$ and $Y = 109.4$ may be valid for decision variables in many problems, a large number of business problems can be solved only if variables have *integer* values. For example, when an airline decides how many flights to operate on a given sector, it can't decide to operate 5.38 flights; it must operate 5, 6, or some other integer number.

In sections 6.2 and 6.3, we present two types of integer variables: general integer variables and binary variables. General integer variables are variables that can take on any integer value that satisfies all the constraints in a model (e.g., 5 submarines, 8 employees, 20 insurance policies). Binary variables are a special type of integer variable that can take on only either of two values: 0 or 1. They allow us to efficiently introduce "yes-no" decisions and certain logical conditions (for example, mutually exclusive alternatives or contingency decisions) into our math programming models that would otherwise be difficult or even impossible. In this chapter, we examine how problems involving both types of integer variables can be formulated and solved using Excel's Solver.

Integer programming (IP) problems can also be classified as *pure* and *mixed* types of problems, as follows:
- *Pure IP problems.* These are problems in which all decision variables must have integer solutions (general integer, binary, or a combination of the two).

– *Mixed IP problems.* These are problems in which some, but not all, decision variables must have integer solutions (i.e., general integer, binary, or a combination of the two). The noninteger variables can have fractional optimal values. We discuss an example of these types of problems in section 6.4.

Goal Programming Models

LP forces a decision maker to state only one objective. But what if a business has several objectives? Management may indeed want to minimize costs, but it might also simultaneously want to maximize market share, maximize machine utilization, maintain full employment, and minimize environmental impacts. These objectives often can conflict with each other. For example, minimizing costs may be in direct conflict with maintaining full employment. *Goal programming* is an extension to LP that permits multiple objectives such as these to be considered simultaneously. We discuss goal programming in detail in section 6.5.

Nonlinear Programming Models

Linear programming can be applied, of course, only to cases in which the objective function and all constraints are linear expressions. Yet in many situations, this may not be the case. For example, consider a simple demand function as seen in introductory microeconomics: $P = b - mQ$, where P is the unit price, b is the intercept, m is the slope, and Q is the quantity that we want to sell to the market. In this case, total revenue equals $P \times Q = bQ - mQ^2$. Hence, if X and Y denote the number of units of two products to sell to the market, the objective function could be something like

$$\text{Maximize revenue} = 25X - 0.4X^2 + 30Y - 0.5Y^2$$

Because of the squared terms, this is a nonlinear objective function. In a similar manner, we could have one or more nonlinear constraints in the model. We discuss *nonlinear programming* models in detail in section 6.6.

Now let's examine each of these extensions of LP—integer, goal, and nonlinear programming—one at a time.

6.2 Models with General Integer Variables

A model with general integer variables (which we will call an *IP model*) has an objective function and constraints identical to those of LP models. There is no real difference in the basic procedures for formulating an IP model and an LP model. The only additional requirement in an IP model is that one or more of the decision variables must take on integer values in the optimal solution. The actual value of this integer variable, however, is limited only by the constraints in the model. That is, values such as 0, 1, 2, 3, and so on are perfectly valid for these variables, as long as these values satisfy all constraints in the model.

Let's look at a simple two-variable example of an IP product mix problem and see how to formulate it. We recognize that you are unlikely to ever encounter such small problems in real-world situations. However, as discussed in Chapter 2, a primary advantage of two-variable models is that we can easily represent them on a two-dimensional graph and use them effectively to illustrate how IP models behave. Let's then also look at how this two-variable IP model can be set up and solved by using Excel's Solver. The Excel setup can be extended to handle much larger IP models. In fact, thanks to the continued significant advances in computing technology, researchers have successfully modeled and solved IP models involving thousands of decision variables and constraints in just a few minutes (or even seconds).

Harrison Electric Company

Harrison Electric Company, located in Chicago's Old Town area, produces two expensive products that are popular with renovators of historic old homes: ornate lamps and old-fashioned ceiling fans. Both lamps and ceiling fans require a two-step production process involving wiring and assembly time. It takes about 2 hours to wire each lamp and 3 hours to wire a ceiling fan. Final assembly of each lamp and fan requires 6 and 5 hours, respectively. The production capability in this period is such that only 12 hours of wiring time and 30 hours of assembly time are available. Each lamp produced nets the firm $600, and each fan nets $700 in profit.

Formulating the Problem If we let L denote the number of lamps to make and F denote the number of ceiling fans to make, Harrison's product mix decision can be formulated using LP as follows:

$$\text{Maximize profit} = \$600L + \$700F$$

subject to the constraints

$$2L + 3F \leq 12 \quad \text{(wiring hours)}$$
$$6L + 5F \leq 30 \quad \text{(assembly hours)}$$
$$L, F \geq 0$$

Solving the Problem Graphically Because there are only two decision variables, let's employ the graphical approach to visualize the feasible region. The shaded region in Figure 6.1 shows the feasible region for the LP problem. The optimal corner point solution turns out to be $L = 3.75$ lamps and $F = 1.50$ ceiling fans, for a profit of $3,300.

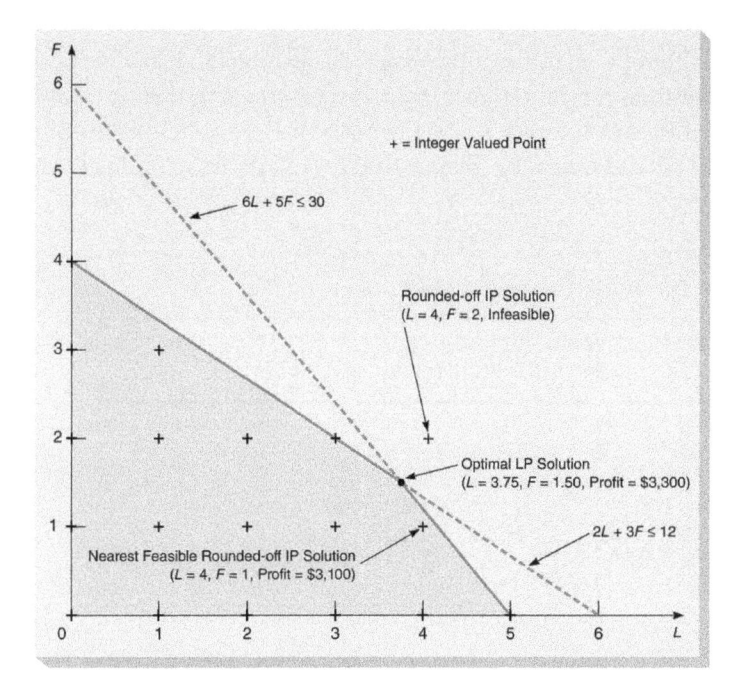

Figure 6.1: Graph for Harrison Electric—General IP

Interpreting the Results Because Harrison cannot produce and sell a fraction of a product, the production planner, Wes Wallace, recognized that he was dealing with an IP problem. It seemed to Wes that the simplest approach was to round off the optimal fractional LP solutions for L and F to integer values. Unfortunately, rounding can produce two problems. First, if we use the traditional rounding rule (i.e., round down if the fraction is below 0.5 and round up otherwise), the resulting integer solution may not even be in the feasible region. For example, using this rule, we would round Harrison's LP solution to $L = 4$ lamps and $F = 2$ fans. As we can see from Figure 6.1, that solution is not feasible. It is, hence, not a practical answer. Second, even if we manage to round the LP solution in such a way that the resulting integer solution is feasible, there is no guarantee that it is the optimal IP solution. For example, suppose Wes considers all possible integer solutions to Harrison's problem (shown in Figure 6.1) and rounds the LP solution to its nearest feasible IP solution (i.e., $L = 4$ lamps and $F = 1$ fan). As we will see later, it turns out that this IP solution is not the optimal solution. Also, note that because this problem involves only two variables, we can at least visualize which IP solutions are feasible and round off the LP solution appropriately. Obviously, even the process of rounding the LP solution to obtain a feasible IP solution could be very cumbersome to do if there are more variables in the model.

What is the optimal integer solution in Harrison's case? Table 6.1 lists the entire set of integer-valued solutions for this problem. By inspecting the right-hand column, we see that the optimal integer solution is $L = 3$ lamps and $F = 2$ ceiling fans, for a total profit = $3,200. The IP solution of $L = 4$ lamps and $F = 1$ fan yields a profit of only $3,100.

Table 6.1: Integer Solutions for Harrison Electric—General IP

Lamps (L)	Ceiling Fans (F)	Profit ($600L + $700F)
0	0	$ 0
1	0	$ 600
2	0	$1,200
3	0	$1,800
4	0	$2,400
5	0	$3,000
0	1	$ 700
1	1	$1,300
2	1	$1,900
3	1	$2,500
4	1	$3,100 ← Nearest feasible rounded-off IP solution
0	2	$1,400
1	2	$2,000
2	2	$2,600
3	2	$3,200 ← Optimal IP solution
0	3	$2,100
1	3	$2,700
0	4	$2,800

Properties of Optimal Integer Solutions We note two important properties of the optimal integer solution. First, the optimal point $L = 3$ and $F = 2$ is not a corner point (i.e., a point where two or more constraints intersect) in the LP feasible region. In fact, unlike LP problems, in which the optimal solution is always a corner point of the feasible region, the optimal solution in an IP model need not be a corner point. As we will discuss shortly, this is what makes it difficult to solve IP models in practice.

Second, the integer restriction results in an objective function value that is no better (and is usually worse) than the optimal LP solution. The logic behind this occurrence is quite simple. Notice that the feasible region for the IP problem is actually a finite set of disconnected points (see the + symbols in Figure 6.1) that lie within the feasible region for the LP problem. Consequently, the feasible region for the original LP problem includes *all* IP solution points, in addition to an infinite number of LP solution points. That is, the optimal IP solution will always be a feasible solution for the LP problem, *but not vice versa*. We call the LP equivalent of an IP problem (i.e., the IP model with the integer requirement deleted) the *relaxed* problem. As a rule, the IP solution can never produce a better objective value than its LP relaxed problem. At best, the two solutions can be equal (if the optimal LP solution turns out to be integer valued).

Although it is possible to solve simple IP problems such as Harrison Electric's by inspection or enumeration, larger problems cannot be solved in this manner. There would simply be too many points to enumerate. Fortunately, most LP software packages, including Excel's Solver, are capable of handling models with integer variables.

Decision Modeling In Action

Improving Disaster Response Times at CARE International Using Integer Programming

Each year natural disasters kill about 70,000 people and affect 200 million more worldwide. When a disaster strikes, large quantities of supplies are needed to provide relief aid to the affected areas. However, unavailability of supplies or slowness in mobilizing them may cause emergency responses to be ineffective, resulting in increased human suffering and loss of life.

CARE International, with programs in 65 countries, is one of the largest humanitarian organizations that provide relief aid to disaster survivors. To improve disaster response times, CARE collaborated with researchers from the Georgia Institute of Technology to develop a model that evaluates the effect of pre-positioning relief items on average response times.

The model focuses on upfront investment (initial inventory stocking and warehouse setup) and average response time and seeks to answer the following question: Given an initial investment, which network configuration minimizes the average response time? To answer this question, the researchers developed a mixed integer programming model. The model contained about 470,000 variables, including 12 binary variables, and about 56,000 constraints, and it yielded optimal solutions in less than four hours.

The model's results helped CARE determine a desired configuration for its pre-positioning network. Based in part on the results of the study, CARE has pre-positioned relief supplies in three facilities around the world—Dubai, Panama, and Cambodia.

Source: Based on S. Duran, M. A. Gutierrez, and P. Keskinocak. "Pre-Positioning of Emergency Items for CARE International," *Interfaces* 41, 3 (May–June 2011): 223–237.

Using Solver to Solve Models with General Integer Variables

We can set up Harrison Electric's IP problem in Excel in exactly the same manner as we have for several LP examples in Chapters 2 and 3. For clarity, we once again use the same Excel layout here as in those chapters; that is, all parameters (solution value, objective coefficients, and constraint coefficients) associated with a decision variable are modeled in the same column. The objective function and each constraint in the model are shown on separate rows of the worksheet.

EXCEL NOTES

- The Companion Website for this book, at *degruyter.com/view/product/486941*, contains the Excel file for each sample problem discussed here. The relevant file/sheet name is shown below the title of the corresponding figure in this book.

- In each of the Excel layouts, for clarity, changing variable cells are shaded yellow, the objective cell is shaded green, and cells containing the left-hand-side (LHS) formula for each constraint are shaded blue.

- Also, to make the equivalence of the *written* formulation and the Excel layout clear, the Excel layouts show the decision variable names used in the written formulation of the model. Note that these names have no role in using Solver to solve the model.

The Excel layout for Harrison Electric's problem is shown in Figure 6.2. As usual, we specify the objective cell (objective function), changing variable cells (decision variables), and constraint LHS and right-hand-side (RHS) cell references in the Solver Parameters window.

Specifying the Integer Requirement Before we solve the model, we need to specify the integer value requirement for the two decision variables. We specify this in Solver as a constraint, as follows:

- Use the Add option to include a new constraint. In the LHS entry for the new constraint (see Figure 6.2), enter the cell reference for a decision variable that must be integer valued. If there are several decision variables in the model that must be integer valued and they are in contiguous cells (i.e., next to each other), the entire cell range may be entered in the LHS entry. For Harrison's problem, the entry in this box would be B5:C5, corresponding to the number of lamps and fans to make, respectively.

- Next, click the drop-down box in the Add Constraint window. Note that this box has six choices, of which three (i.e.,<=, =, and >=) have been used so far. The remaining three are int (for Integer), bin (for Binary), and dif (for AllDifferent).[1] Click the choice int. The word integer is displayed automatically in the box for the RHS entry. This indicates to Solver that all variables specified in the LHS box must be integer valued in the optimal solution.

---

[1] We illustrate only the int and bin choices in this book. The third choice, dif, is relevant for special types of sequencing models that are not discussed here.

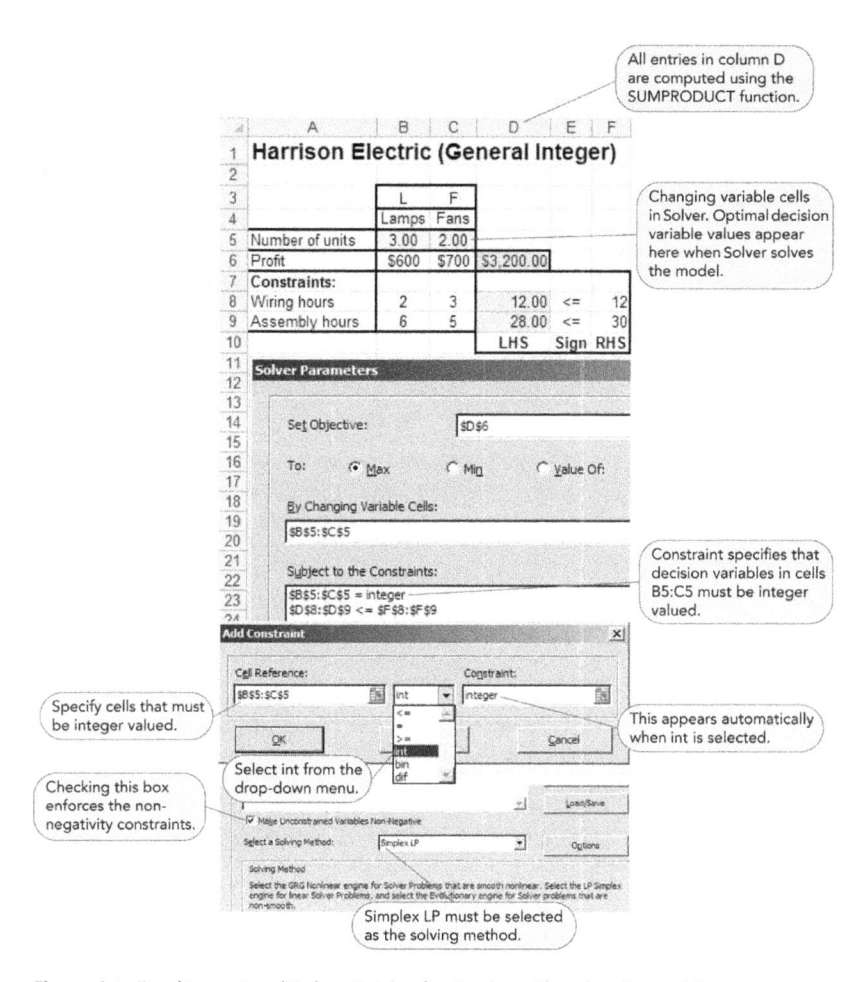

Figure 6.2: Excel Layout and Solver Entries for Harrison Electric—General IP

X🗐 File: Figure 6.2.xlsx

Solving the IP Model We are now ready to solve the IP model. Before we click Solve, we need to verify that the Make Unconstrained Variables Non-Negative box is checked and that Simplex LP is specified in the Select a Solving Method box, as shown in Figure 6.2. The result, also shown in Figure 6.2, indicates that 3 lamps and 2 fans, for a profit of $3,200, is identified as the optimal solution.

As noted previously, thanks to advances in computing technology, Solver (and other decision modeling software packages) can identify optimal solutions very quickly, even for IP models involving thousands of decision variables and constraints. However, when compared with an LP model, the computational effort required to solve an IP model (of the same size) grows rapidly with problem size. We now briefly discuss the reason for this phenomenon.

EXCEL EXTRA

Using VBA to Interact with the User

As a potential future modeler for your organization, you are being shown in this book how to build and solve your models in Excel. Oftentimes, however, the person who runs the model on a regular basis may not be the model creator. Ideally, models can be created such that users with little Excel knowledge can still run them—for example models that have users respond to questions and just click on buttons to obtain the results. Excel contains a powerful program behind the scenes called VBA (Visual Basic for Applications), which facilitates such automation.

We'll provide a simple example here to give a quick glance into the possibilities. Several good books on VBA programming are available for interested readers.

Let's take the example in Figure 6.2 and prompt the user to enter the respective profit margins for lamps and fans, as well as the hours available for both wiring and assembly. Then Solver will run automatically, and the solution will be displayed in a message box. This will all be activated after the user clicks on a button.

To insert a command button, you'll first need to have the Developer ribbon installed at the top of Excel. If you don't see Developer as one of your choices in the ribbon, add it by selecting:

File|Options|Customize Ribbon|Main Tabs: Developer|OK

To enter the VBA editor, press Alt F11 (or click on Developer|Visual Basic). To be able to run Solver with VBA, make sure that it is referenced by clicking Tools|References|Solver|OK.

Next, make sure that "Sheet1 (Figure 6.2)" is selected in the Project Explorer in the upper left of the screen. Select Insert|Module, and a white editing space should appear. Enter the following in the white editing space:

Public Sub Harrison()
   Range("B6") = InputBox("What is the unit profit for lamps?")
   Range("C6") = InputBox("What is the unit profit for fans?")
   Range("F8") = InputBox("How many wiring hours are available?")
   Range("F9") = InputBox("How many assembly hours are available?")
   SolverSolve UserFinish:=True
   MsgBox "Optimal Number of lamps = " & Range("B5") & vbNewLine _
     & "Optimal Number of Fans = " & Range("C5") & vbNewLine _
     & "Maximum Profit = " & FormatCurrency(Range("D6"), 2), , "Solution Results"
End Sub

Press Alt F11 to return to regular Excel. To create an activation button, select Developer|Controls: Insert, and then click on the first icon under Form Controls (looks like a rectangle). Go to the Excel sheet and drop and drag to draw the button to your desired size. A dialog box will automatically ask which macro to attach to the button. Choose the only option ("Harrison"). Finally, right-click on the button and click Edit Text to create your desired button label (for example, "Run Program"). Click on the button, and the program should run!

How Are IP Models Solved?

As shown in Figure 6.1, the optimal solution to an IP model need not be at a corner point of the feasible region. Unfortunately, the simplex method evaluates only corner points as candidates for the optimal solution. In order to use the simplex method to identify an integer-valued optimal point that may *not* be a corner point, we employ a procedure called the branch-and-bound (B&B) method. The B&B method is used by most software packages, including Solver, to solve IP models.

Although we do not discuss the details of the B&B procedure in this book, we provide a brief description of how it works. Essentially, the B&B procedure uses a "divide and conquer" strategy. Rather than try to search for the optimal IP solution over the entire feasible region at one time, the B&B procedure splits the feasible region into progressively smaller and smaller subregions. It then searches each subregion in turn. Clearly, the best IP solution over all subregions will be the optimal IP solution over the entire feasible region.

In creating each subregion, the B&B procedure forces a corner point of the new subregion to have integer values for at least one of the variables in the model. This procedure is called *branching*. Finding the optimal solution for each subregion involves the solution of an LP model, referred to in Solver as a subproblem. Hence, in order to solve a single IP model, we may have to solve several LP subproblems. Clearly, this could become computationally quite burdensome, depending on the number of subregions that need to be created and examined for an IP model. The computer memory needed could also become extensive, especially for models with a large number of integer variables, because we need to store detailed information regarding each subregion (e.g., the part of the LP feasible region that it occupies, whether or not it has been examined, and whether or not the optimal solution is integer). Stopping rules are used to efficiently conduct and stop the search process for different subregions.

Solver Options

Now let's return to how Solver handles IP problems and examine the options available when solving IP models. The Options window is shown in Figure 6.3. We have not concerned ourselves about these options so far while solving LP models because the default values are adequate to solve most, if not all, LP models considered here. However, for IP models, some of these options deserve additional attention.

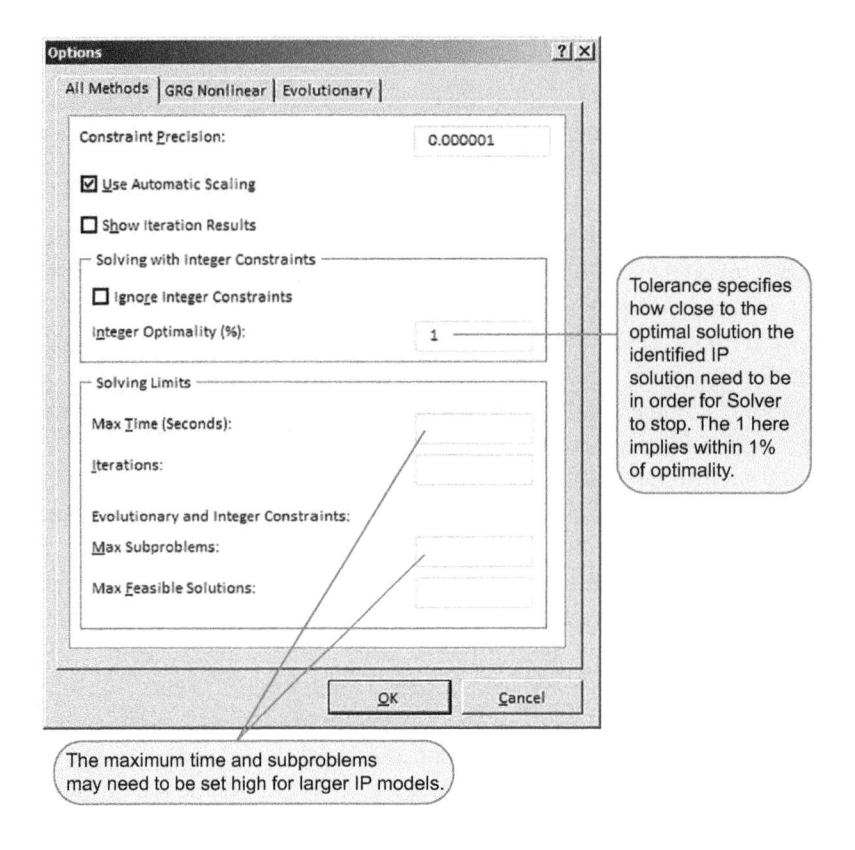

Figure 6.3: Solver Options Window for IP Models

Solving with Integer Constraints Checking the Ignore Integer Constraints box causes Solver to solve the problem as an LP model. As discussed earlier, the optimal objective value of an IP model will always be *worse* than that for the corresponding LP model (i.e., lower profit for a maximization problem and higher cost for a minimization problem). Hence, this option allows us to quickly get an idea about the best IP solution that we can find for the model.

The Integer Optimality (%) option is set at a default value of 1% (shown as 1 in Solver). (This default value may vary by computer.) A value of 1% implies that we are willing to accept an IP solution that is within 1% of the true optimal IP solution value. When Solver finds a solution within the allowable tolerance, it stops and presents that as the final solution. When this occurs, it is explicitly indicated by the message: "Solver found an integer solution within tolerance," as shown in Figure 6.4. If we wish to find the *true* optimal solution, we must set the tolerance to 0%. *We recommend that you always set the tolerance to 0% when first creating an IP model. Otherwise, the resulting solution may not be optimal for your problem. Then only if solution time is taking too long should you consider using a higher tolerance.*

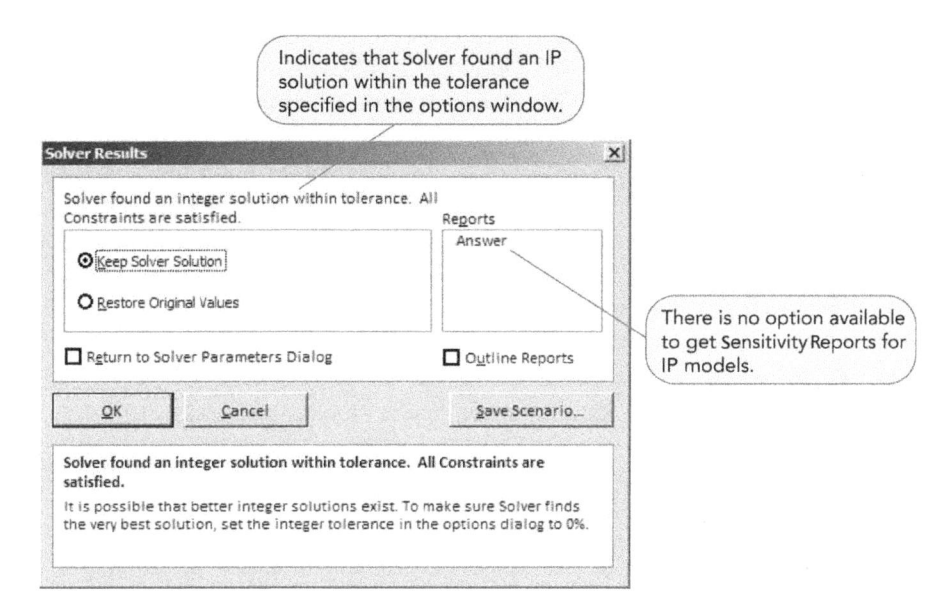

Figure 6.4: Solver Results Window for IP Models

Solving Limits In general, it should be sufficient to leave the Max Time (Seconds) option at its default value (shown as blank in Excel 2016) and run the problem. However, as the number of integer-valued decision variables increases in an IP model, this time limit may be exceeded and will need to be extended. Solver will warn you when the limit is reached and give you the opportunity to allow more time for an IP problem to solve.

Likewise, the default values for the Max Subproblems and Max Feasible Solutions options (shown as blank in Excel 2016) should be sufficient for most, if not all, IP models considered here. Recall from our brief discussion of the B&B method that in order to solve a single IP model, Solver may need to solve several LP subproblems.

Should We Include Integer Requirements in a Model?
We have already discussed one reason we should be cautious about including integer requirements in a model—namely, the possible computational burden involved in solving large IP models. A second reason for this caution has to do with sensitivity reports.

Recall from Chapter 4 that after solving an LP model, we can generate a Sensitivity Report that provides a wealth of information regarding how sensitive the current optimal solution is to changes in input data values. The information in this report even allows us to analyze issues such as the impact of acquiring additional resources, pricing out new products, etc. However, as soon as we specify that one or more decision variables in the model are integers, we lose the ability to obtain a Sensitivity Report. In fact, as shown in Figure 6.4, Solver does not even give you an option to get a Sensitivity Report for an IP model.

Do these two reasons mean that we should not include the integer requirements in a model? For many real-world IP models (and all the models discussed in this book), the computational issue is probably not relevant because of available computing technology. However, in practice, it is a good idea to ask ourselves the following question, especially when the model includes a large number of integer decision variables: "Do we definitely need to find the optimal integer solution, or would it be acceptable to solve the problem as an LP problem and then round off, even if that may lead to a slightly suboptimal solution?" Obviously, there is no single easy answer to this question, and the ultimate answer would depend on the cost (or profit) implications for that specific problem. The answer to this question also could be influenced by the desirability of being able to have a Sensitivity Report for the particular problem scenario.

Decision Modeling In Action

SPRINT Enables Hera to Optimize Staff Management Using Integer Programming

Hera Group is the second largest Italian multi-utility company that provides environmental services (collection, treatment, and disposal of urban and industrial wastes), water services (aqueducts, sewerage, and purification), and energy services (natural gas, electricity, and district heating) in northern Italy. Hera serves around 3.3 million citizens and handles more than 1.1 million requests annually. In such a demanding environment, the efficient assignment and management of staff members is a definite competitive advantage for Hera.

The main challenge that Hera faces is finding the best trade-off between the efficacy required to achieve appropriate service levels and the efficiency required to control the operational cost of the system. This trade-off should consider both the long-term design and the day-to-day management of the front office. To enable the optimization of its staff management for desk customer-relation services, Hera developed a decision support system called SPRINT (Sistema Previsionale Integrato Normalizzazione Tempi).

SPRINT is an integrated forecast and time normalization system that provides complete management and optimization of the desk staff employees who deliver Hera's services. The system helps determine the staffing required for each time slot using an innovative adaptive staffing approach that takes into consideration the constraints of congestion hours and service level agreement. The system computes, using an integer linear programming model, the shifts that minimize the staff required to serve the users.

Some of the benefits attained after using SPRINT for two years are planning and management processes improvement, significant improvement of desk customer services, and increased staff productivity. SPRINT handles about 75% of customers and 85% of requests in an efficient manner, and the system has enabled Hera to rank first for the quality of service provided among Italian utilities in 2011.

Source: Based on D. Vigo, C. Caremi, A. Gordini, S. Bosso, G. D'Aleo, B. Beleggia. "SPRINT: Optimization of Staff Management for Desk Customer Relations Services at Hera," *Interfaces* 44, 5 (September–October 2014): 461–479.

6.3 Models with Binary Variables

As discussed earlier, binary variables are restricted to values of 0 and 1. Recall that the assignment model and shortest-path model in Chapter 5 both involve variables that ultimately take on values of either 0 or 1 at optimality. However, in both of those models, we do not have to specify explicitly that the variables are binary. The integer property of network flow models, along with the supply and demand values of one unit each, automatically ensures that the optimal solution has a value of 0 or 1.

In contrast, we now examine models in which we will explicitly specify that the variables are binary. A binary variable is a powerful modeling tool that is applicable whenever we want to model a *yes* or *no* decision between exactly two choices. That is, the decision must select either choice 1 or choice 2 in its entirety, and partial or fractional selections are not allowed. When we are faced with such a decision, we associate a binary variable with it. With one of the two choices, we associate a value of 1 for the binary variable. A value of 0 for the binary variable is then associated with the other choice. Now, we write the objective function and constraints in a manner that is consistent with this definition of the binary variable.

A popular application of binary variables is in *selection* problems, which involve the selection of an optimal subset of items from a larger set of items. Typical examples include decisions such as introducing new products (e.g., introduce a specific product or not), building new facilities (e.g., build a specific facility or not), selecting team members (e.g., select a specific individual or not), and investing in projects (e.g., invest in a specific project or not). Another popular application of binary variables is in a class of problems known as *set-covering* problems. These problems typically deal with trying to identify the optimal set of locations to cover or serve a specified set of customers. Examples include locating fire stations, police precincts, or medical clinics to serve a community, locating cell phone towers to provide uninterrupted signal over a region, etc.

Let's consider simple examples to illustrate both types of problems—selection and set covering—that use binary variables.

Portfolio Selection at Simkin and Steinberg

The Houston-based investment firm of Simkin and Steinberg specializes in recommending oil stock portfolios for wealthy clients. One such client has up to $3 million available for investments and insists on purchasing large blocks of shares of each company in which he invests. Table 6.2 describes the various companies that are under consideration.

Table 6.2: Oil Investment Opportunities

Company Name (Location)	Expected Annual Return (thousands)	Cost For Block of Shares (thousands)
Trans-Texas Oil (Texas)	$ 50	$ 480
British Petro (Foreign)	$ 80	$ 540
Dutch Shell (Foreign)	$ 90	$ 680
Houston Drilling (Texas)	$120	$1,000
Lone Star Petro (Texas)	$110	$ 700
San Diego Oil (California)	$ 40	$ 510
California Petro (California)	$ 75	$ 900

The objective is to maximize annual return on investment, subject to the following specifications made by the client:
- At least two Texas companies must be in the portfolio.
- No more than one investment can be made in foreign companies.
- Exactly one of the two California companies must be included.
- If British Petro stock is included in the portfolio, then Trans-Texas Oil stock must also be included.

Formulating the Problem Note that the decision regarding each company has to be one of two choices. That is, the investment firm either buys a large block of shares in the company or it doesn't buy the company's shares. To formulate this problem, let's therefore associate a binary variable with each of the seven companies. For example, we define a binary variable, T, for Trans-Texas Oil as follows:

$$T = \begin{cases} 1 \text{ if Trans-Texas Oil is included in the portfolio} \\ 0 \text{ if Trans-Texas Oil is not included in the portfolio} \end{cases}$$

In a similar manner, we define binary variables B (British Petro), D (Dutch Shell), H (Houston Oil), L (Lone Star Petro), S (San Diego Oil), and C (California Petro).

We now need to express the objective function and constraints in a manner that is consistent with the previous definition of the binary variables. The objective function can be written as

$$\text{Maximize return on investment} = \$50T + \$80B + \$90D + \$120H + \$110L + \$40S + \$75C$$

All figures are in thousands of dollars. In the previous expression, if T has an optimal value of 1 (implying that we include Trans-Texas Oil in the portfolio), this would contribute $50,000 to the total return. In contrast, if T has an optimal value of 0 (implying that we *not* include Trans-Texas Oil in the portfolio), this would contribute $0 to the total return.

Next, we model the constraints. The constraint regarding the $3 million investment limit can be expressed in a similar manner to that of the objective function. That is,

$$\$480T + \$540B + \$680D + \$1{,}000H + \$700L + \$510S + \$900C \leq \$3{,}000$$

Again, all figures are in thousands of dollars. Depending on whether the optimal value of a binary variable is 0 or 1, the corresponding investment cost will be calculated in the LHS of the previous expression.

The other constraints in the problems are special ones that exploit the binary nature of these variables. These types of constraints are what make the use of binary variables a powerful modeling tool. We discuss these special constraints in the following sections.

k Out of *n* Choices The requirement that at least two Texas companies must be in the portfolio is an example of a "*k* out of *n* choices" constraint. There are three (i.e., $n = 3$) Texas companies (denoted by the variables T, H, and L), of which at least two (i.e., $k = 2$) must be selected. We can model this constraint as

$$T + H + L \geq 2$$

Mutually Exclusive Choices The condition that no more than one investment can be made in foreign companies is an example of a *mutually exclusive* constraint. Note that the inclusion of one foreign company means that the other must be excluded. We can model this constraint as

$$B + D \leq 1$$

The condition regarding the two California companies is also an example of having mutually exclusive variables. The sign of this constraint is, however, an equality rather than an inequality because Simkin and Steinberg *must* include a California company in the portfolio. That is,

$$S + C = 1$$

If–Then (or Linked) Choices The condition that, if British Petro is included in the portfolio then Trans-Texas Oil must also be included in the portfolio, is an example of an *if–then* constraint (sometimes called a *contingent decision*). We can model this relationship as

$$B \leq T$$

or, if you prefer to have only a constant on the RHS,

$$B - T \leq 0$$

Note that if B equals 0 (i.e., British Petro is not included in the portfolio), this constraint allows T to equal either 0 or 1. However, if B equals 1, then T must also equal 1.

The relationship discussed here is a one-way linkage in that Trans-Texas Oil must be included if British Petro is included, but not vice versa. If the relationship is two-way (i.e., either include both or include neither), we then rewrite the constraint as

$$B = T$$

or, once again, if you prefer to have only a constant on the RHS,

$$B - T = 0$$

Solving the Problem The complete formulation of Simkin and Steinberg's problem is as follows:

$$\text{Maximize return} = \$50T + \$80B + \$90D + \$120H + \$110L + \$40S + \$75C$$

subject to the constraints

$\$480T + \$540B + \$680D$		
$+ \$1{,}000H + \$700L$		
$+ \$510S + \$900C$	$\leq \$3{,}000$	(investment limit)
$T + H + L$	≥ 2	(Texas companies)
$B + D$	≤ 1	(foreign companies)
$S + C$	$= 1$	(California companies)
B	$\leq T$	(Trans-Texas and British Petro)
All variables	$= 0$ or 1	

The Excel layout and Solver entries for Simkin and Steinberg's 0–1 problem are shown in Figure 6.5. The specification of the objective cell, changing variable cells, and constraint LHS and RHS cell references in the Solver Parameters window is similar to that used for LP and general IP models.

Specifying the Binary Requirement To specify the binary requirement for all variables, we again use the Add option to include a new constraint. In the LHS entry for the new constraint (see Figure 6.5), we enter the cell reference for a decision variable that must be binary valued. If there are several decision variables that must be binary valued, we can enter the entire cell range, provided that these variables are in contiguous cells. For Simkin and Steinberg's problem, we enter B5:H5 in this box, corresponding to binary variables T through C, respectively.

We then click the drop-down box in the Add Constraint window and click the choice bin. The word binary is automatically displayed in the box for the RHS entry. This indicates to Solver that all variables specified in the LHS box are binary variables.

Models with Binary Variables — 321

	A	B	C	D	E	F	G	H	I	J	K
1	Simkin and Steinberg (Binary)										
2											
3		T	B	D	H	L	S	C			
		Trans-Texas Oil	British Petro	Dutch Shell	Houston Oil	Lone Star Petro	San Diego Oil	Calif Petro			
5	Invest? (1 = Yes, 0 = No)	0	0	1	1	1	1	0			
6	Exp annual return ('000)	$50	$80	$90	$120	$110	$40	$75	$360		
7	Constraints:										
8	Investment limit	480	540	680	1000	700	510	900	2890	<=	3000
9	Foreign companies		1	1					1	<=	1
10	British & Trans-Texas		1						0	<=	0
11	Texas companies	1				1	1		2	>=	2
12	California companies						1	1	1	=	1
13									LHS	Sign	RHS

All entries in column I are computed using the SUMPRODUCT function.

(=B5 annotation on row 10)

Solver Parameters

Set Objective: $I$6

To: ● Max ○ Min ○ Value Of: 0

By Changing Variable Cells:
$B$5:$H$5

Subject to the Constraints:
$B$5:$H$5 = binary
$I$11 >= $K$11
$I$12 = $K$12
$I$8:$I$10 <= $K$8:$K$10

Add Constraint

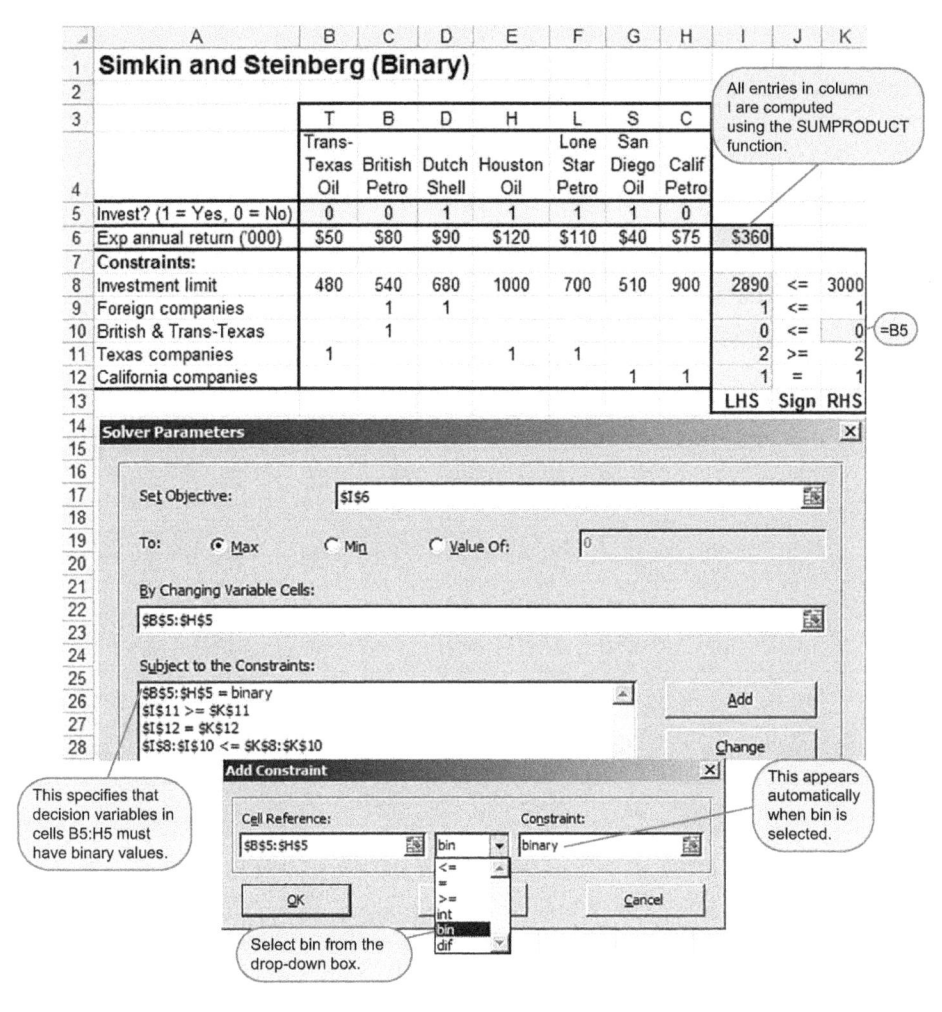

Cell Reference: $B$5:$H$5   bin   Constraint: binary

(Select bin from the drop-down box: <=, =, >=, int, bin, dif)

This specifies that decision variables in cells B5:H5 must have binary values.

This appears automatically when bin is selected.

Figure 6.5: Excel Layout and Solver Entries for Simkin and Steinberg—Binary IP

📄 File: Figure 6.5.xlsx

Interpreting the Results Figure 6.5 shows that the optimal solution is for Simkin and Steinberg to recommend that the client invest in Dutch Shell (D), Houston Oil (H), Lone Star Petro (L), and San Diego Oil (S). The expected return is $360,000 (all values are in units of $1,000). Note that the solution invests only $2.89 million of the available $3 million. Why did this happen? There are two reasons: (1) Company stocks can be bought only in fixed blocks, and (2) specifications made by the client are possibly too restrictive.

Set-Covering Problem at Sussex County

As noted earlier, set-covering problems typically deal with trying to identify the optimal set of locations to cover or serve a specified set of customers. Consider the case of Sussex County, which needs to build health care clinics to serve seven communities (named A to G) in the region. Each clinic can serve communities within a maximum radius of 30 minutes' driving time, and a community may be served by more than one clinic. Table 6.3 shows the times it takes to travel between the seven communities. What is the minimum number of clinics that would be needed, and in which communities should they be located?

Table 6.3: Sussex County Driving Times

				To			
From	A	B	C	D	E	F	G
A	0	15	20	35	35	45	40
B	15	0	35	20	35	40	40
C	20	35	0	15	50	45	30
D	35	20	15	0	35	20	20
E	35	35	50	35	0	15	40
F	45	40	45	20	15	0	35
G	40	40	30	20	40	35	0

Formulating and Solving the Problem The decision regarding each community has to be one of two choices—either locate a clinic in that community or not. To formulate this problem, therefore, let's associate a binary variable with each of the seven communities. For example, we define a binary variable, A, for community A as follows:

$$A = \begin{cases} 1 \text{ if a clinic is located in community A} \\ 0 \text{ if a clinic is not located in community A} \end{cases}$$

In a similar manner, we define binary variables B, C, D, E, F, and G for communities B to G, respectively. Because Sussex County would like to minimize the number of clinics needed, we write the objective function as

$$\text{Minimize total number of clinics} = A + B + C + D + E + F + G$$

We now need to identify which communities are served by a clinic at a given location. For example, a clinic located at community A would serve communities A, B, and C because all three of these are within the 30-minute driving time limit. Table 6.4 shows the communities covered by the clinics at all seven locations.

Table 6.4: Sussex County Community Coverage

Community	Communities within 30 Minutes
A	A, B, C
B	A, B, D
C	A, C, D, G
D	B, C, D, F, G
E	E, F
F	D, E, F
G	C, D, G

The constraints need to ensure that each community is served (or covered) by at least one clinic. For this reason, they are called *covering constraints*. For Sussex County's problem, these constraints are as follows:

$$A + B + C \geq 1 \quad \text{(community A is covered)}$$
$$A + B + D \geq 1 \quad \text{(community B is covered)}$$
$$A + C + D + G \geq 1 \quad \text{(community C is covered)}$$
$$B + C + D + F + G \geq 1 \quad \text{(community D is covered)}$$
$$E + F \geq 1 \quad \text{(community E is covered)}$$
$$D + E + F \geq 1 \quad \text{(community F is covered)}$$
$$C + D + G \geq 1 \quad \text{(community G is covered)}$$
$$\text{All variables} = 0 \text{ or } 1$$

There are no other constraints in Sussex County's problem. However, if necessary, we could use the three types of constraints described earlier—k out of n choices, mutually exclusive, and if–then—in Simkin and Steinberg's portfolio selection problem to model any other specifications. For example, if Sussex does not want to locate clinics at both B and D, this would be modeled as a mutually exclusive constraint (i.e., $B + D \leq 1$). Notice that this set-covering problem utilizes a form similar to a standard labor-planning problem (see section 3.5), except that the decision variables here are binary and the RHS terms all equal 1.

The Excel layout and Solver entries for Sussex County's set-covering problem are shown in Figure 6.6.

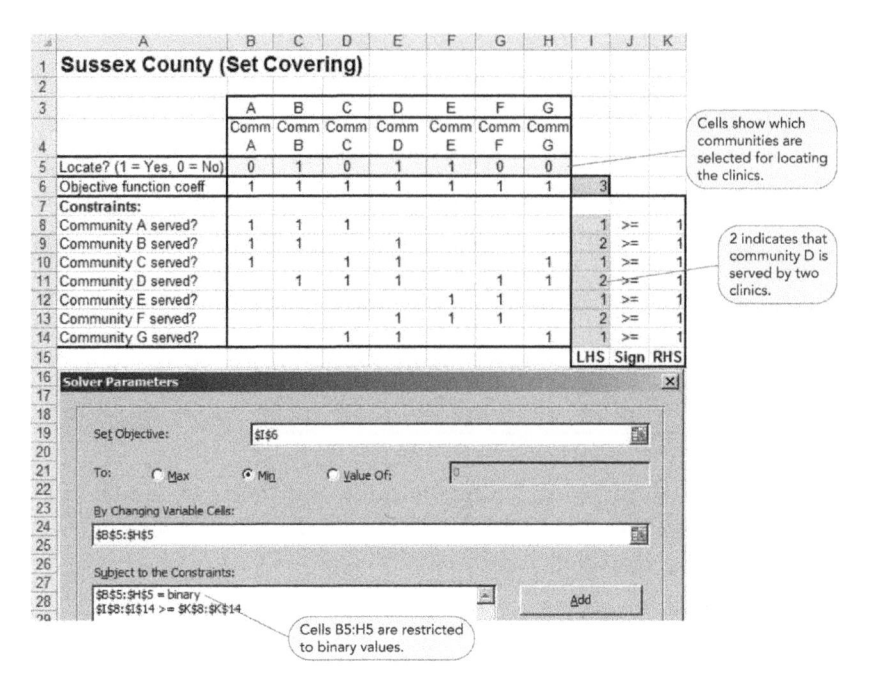

324 — Chapter 6: Integer, Goal, and Nonlinear Programming Models

Figure 6.6: Excel Layout and Solver Entries for Sussex County—Set Covering

📗 File: Figure 6.6.xlsx

Interpreting the Results The results indicate that Sussex County will need to open three clinics, one each at communities B, D, and E, to serve the seven communities. Residents of three of the seven communities (B, D, and F) will be served by two clinics each, while residents of the other four communities will be served by only one each.

Note that because Sussex County permits more than one clinic to serve a community, the constraints in our model included the ≥ sign. In contrast, if Sussex County wants each community to be served by exactly one clinic, the constraints would include the = sign. This specification may, however, cause the model to be infeasible in some cases. For example, the driving times could be such that it would be impossible to find a set of locations that uniquely serves all communities. In fact, this is the case in Sussex County's problem (see if you can verify this).

Alternate Optimal Solutions It turns out that there are multiple optimal solutions to Sussex County's model. For example, locating clinics in communities A, C, and F is also optimal (see if you can verify this solution). Recall that in Chapter 4 we studied how to use the Sensitivity Report in Solver to detect the presence of alternate optimal solutions. However, because we cannot obtain sensitivity reports for IP models, we cannot adopt that strategy here. In general, there is no easy way to detect the presence of alternate optimal solutions for IP models.

Decision Modeling in Action

Binary Integer Programming Facilitates Better Course Scheduling at the Universidad de Chile

In its simplest form, the course and examination scheduling problem can be defined as the assignment of a set of courses to different time slots and classrooms while satisfying certain requirements. These requirements can vary widely based on factors such as the institution's policies, room availabilities, level of classes being scheduled, etc.

The Executive Education Unit (EEU) of the Universidad de Chile offers courses primarily for professionals and high-level executives. Ensuring proper schedules for this high-profile audience is critical because any perception of disorganization would affect the EEU adversely. Between 2003 and 2008, about 7,000 students attended EEU courses.

The eClasSkeduler decision support system used at EEU consists of four modules: (1) an input information module that stores all information relating to courses, classrooms, and instructors, (2) a user interface module that transforms the input data to the format necessary for the binary integer programming (BIP) optimization model, (3) an optimization module that contains the source code for the BIP model, and (4) a report module that transforms the BIP model's results to a user-friendly management report with various performance indicators.

The use of eClasSkeduler has benefited all EEU participants by curtailing operating costs, lowering unused classroom capacity, and producing fewer schedule conflicts and off-premise classroom assignments.

Sources: Based on J. Miranda. "eClasSkeduler: A Course Scheduling System for the Executive Education Unit at the Universidad de Chile," *Interfaces* 40, 3 (May–June 2010): 196–207.

6.4 Mixed Integer Models: Fixed-Charge Problems

In all LP and general integer models studied so far, we typically deal with situations in which the total cost is directly proportional to the magnitude of the decision variable. For example, if X denotes the number of toasters we will be making, and if each toaster costs $10 to make, the total cost of making toasters is written as $10X$. Such costs per unit are referred to as *variable* costs.

In many situations, however, there are fixed costs in addition to the per-unit variable costs. These may include the costs to set up machines for the production run, construction costs to build a new facility, or design costs to develop a new product. Unlike variable costs, these fixed costs are independent of the volume of production. They are incurred whenever the decision to go ahead with a project or production run is made.

Problems that involve both fixed and variable costs are a classic example of mixed integer programming models. We call such problems fixed-charge problems.

We use binary variables to model the fixed-cost issue (e.g., whether we will incur the setup cost or not). Either linear or integer variables can be used to deal with the variable-cost issue, depending on the nature of these variables. In formulating the model, we need to ensure that whenever the decision variable associated with the variable cost is nonzero, the binary variable associated with the fixed cost takes on a value of 1 (i.e., the fixed cost is also incurred).

To illustrate this type of situation, let's revisit the Hardgrave Machine Company facility location example that we first studied as Solved Problem 5–1 in Chapter 5.

Locating a New Factory for Hardgrave Machine Company

Hardgrave Machine Company produces computer components at its factories in Cincinnati, Kansas City, and Pittsburgh. These factories have not been able to keep up with demand for orders at Hardgrave's four warehouses in Detroit, Houston, New York, and Los Angeles. As a result, the firm has decided to build a new factory to expand its productive capacity. The two sites being considered are Seattle, Washington, and Birmingham, Alabama. Both cities are attractive in terms of labor supply, municipal services, and ease of factory financing.

Table 6.5 presents the production costs and monthly supplies at each of the three existing factories, monthly demands at each of the four warehouses, and estimated production costs at the two proposed factories. Transportation costs from each factory to each warehouse are summarized in Table 6.6.

Table 6.5: Hardgrave Machine's Demand and Supply Data

Warehouse	Monthly Demand (units)	Production Plant	Monthly Supply	Cost To Produce One Unit
Detroit	10,000	Cincinnati	15,000	$48
Houston	12,000	Kansas City	6,000	$50
New York	15,000	Pittsburgh	14,000	$52
Los Angeles	9,000		35,000	
	46,000			

Supply needed from new plant = 46,000 − 35,000 = 11,000 units per month

	Estimated Production Cost per Unit at Proposed Plants
Seattle	$53
Birmingham	$49

Table 6.6: Hardgrave Machine's Shipping Costs

	To			
From	Detroit	Houston	New York	Los Angeles
Cincinnati	$25	$55	$40	$60
Kansas City	$35	$30	$50	$40
Pittsburgh	$36	$45	$26	$66
Seattle	$60	$38	$65	$27
Birmingham	$35	$30	$41	$50

In addition to this information, Hardgrave estimates that the monthly fixed cost of operating the proposed facility in Seattle would be $400,000. The Birmingham plant would be somewhat cheaper due to the lower cost of living at that location. Hardgrave estimates that the monthly fixed cost of operating the proposed facility in Birmingham would be $325,000. Note that the fixed costs at *existing* plants need not be considered here because they will be incurred regardless of which new plant Hardgrave decides to open—that is, they are sunk costs.

As in Chapter 5, the question facing Hardgrave is this: Which of the new locations, in combination with the existing plants and warehouses, will yield the lowest cost? Note that the unit cost of shipping from each plant to each warehouse is found by adding the shipping costs (Table 6.6) to the corresponding production costs (Table 6.5). In addition, the solution needs to consider the monthly fixed costs of operating the new facility.

Recall that we handled this problem in Solved Problem 5–1 by setting up and solving two separate transportation models—one for each of the two new locations. In the following pages, we show how we can use binary variables to model Hardgrave's problem as a single mixed integer programming model.

Decision Variables There are two types of decisions to be made in this problem. The first involves deciding which of the new locations (Seattle or Birmingham) to select for the new plant. The second involves trying to decide the shipment quantities from each plant (including the new plant) to each of the warehouses.

To model the first decision, we associate a binary variable with each of the two locations. Let

$$Y_S = \begin{cases} 1 \text{ if Seattle is selected for the new plant} \\ 0 \text{ otherwise} \end{cases}$$

$$Y_B = \begin{cases} 1 \text{ if Birmingham is selected for the new plant} \\ 0 \text{ otherwise} \end{cases}$$

To model the shipping quantities, we once again use double-subscripted variables, as discussed in Chapter 5. Note that there are 5 plants (3 existing and 2 proposed) and 4 warehouses in the problem. Therefore, the model will include 20 decision variables denoting the shipping quantities (one variable for each possible shipping route). Let

$$X_{ij} = \text{Number of units shipped from plant } i \text{ to warehouse } j$$

where

$i = C$ (Cincinnati), K (Kansas City), P (Pittsburgh), S (Seattle), or B (Birmingham)
$j = D$ (Detroit), H (Houston), N (New York), or L (Los Angeles)

Objective Function Let's first model the objective function. We want to minimize the total cost of producing and shipping the components and the monthly fixed costs of maintaining the new facility. This can be written as

$$\begin{aligned}
\text{Minimize total costs} = {} & \$73X_{CD} + \$103X_{CH} + \$88X_{CN} + \$108X_{CL} \\
& + \$85X_{KD} + \$80X_{KH} + \$100X_{KN} + \$90X_{KL} \\
& + \$88X_{PD} + \$97X_{PH} + \$78X_{PN} + \$118X_{PL} \\
& + \$113X_{SD} + \$91X_{SH} + \$118X_{SN} + \$80X_{SL} \\
& + \$84X_{BD} + \$79X_{BH} + \$90X_{BN} + \$99X_{BL} \\
& + \$400,000Y_S + \$325,000Y_B
\end{aligned}$$

The last two terms in the expression for the objective function represent the fixed costs. Note that these costs will be incurred only if the plant is built at the location (i.e., the variable Y_S or Y_B has a value of 1).

Constraints Because this is a balanced problem, all supply and demand constraints can be written as equalities. We begin with the supply constraints for the three existing plants:

$$\begin{aligned}
X_{CD} + X_{CH} + X_{CN} + X_{CL} &= 15,000 && \text{(Cincinnati supply)} \\
X_{KD} + X_{KH} + X_{KN} + X_{KL} &= 6,000 && \text{(Kansas City supply)} \\
X_{PD} + X_{PH} + X_{PN} + X_{PL} &= 14,000 && \text{(Pittsburgh supply)}
\end{aligned}$$

However, when writing the supply constraint for a new plant (Seattle or Birmingham), we need to ensure that a supply is available at that plant *only* if the plant is actually built. For example, the supply at Seattle is 11,000 units if the new plant is built there and 0 otherwise. We can model this as follows:

$$\begin{aligned}
X_{SD} + X_{SH} + X_{SN} + X_{SL} &= 11,000Y_S && \text{(Seattle supply)} \\
X_{BD} + X_{BH} + X_{BN} + X_{BL} &= 11,000Y_B && \text{(Birmingham supply)}
\end{aligned}$$

Note that if Seattle is selected for the new plant, Y_S equals 1. Hence, a supply of 11,000 is available there. In contrast, if Seattle is not selected for the new plant, Y_S equals 0. Hence, the supply in the constraint becomes 0; that is, all flows from Seattle have to equal 0. The supply constraint for Birmingham works in a similar manner.

The demand constraints at the four existing warehouses (Detroit, Houston, New York, and Los Angeles) can be written as

$$X_{CD} + X_{KD} + X_{PD} + X_{SD} + X_{BD} = 10{,}000 \quad \text{(Detroit demand)}$$
$$X_{CH} + X_{KH} + X_{PH} + X_{SH} + X_{BH} = 12{,}000 \quad \text{(Houston demand)}$$
$$X_{CN} + X_{KN} + X_{PN} + X_{SN} + X_{BN} = 15{,}000 \quad \text{(New York demand)}$$
$$X_{CL} + X_{KL} + X_{PL} + X_{SL} + X_{BL} = 9{,}000 \quad \text{(Los Angeles demand)}$$

Finally, we need to ensure that exactly one of the two sites is selected for the new plant. This is another example of the mutually exclusive variables discussed in section 6.3. We can express this as

$$Y_S + Y_B = 1$$

Solving the Problem and Interpreting the Results The formula view of the Excel layout for Hardgrave's fixed-charge problem is shown in Figure 6.7. The Solver entries and optimal solution are shown in Figure 6.8.

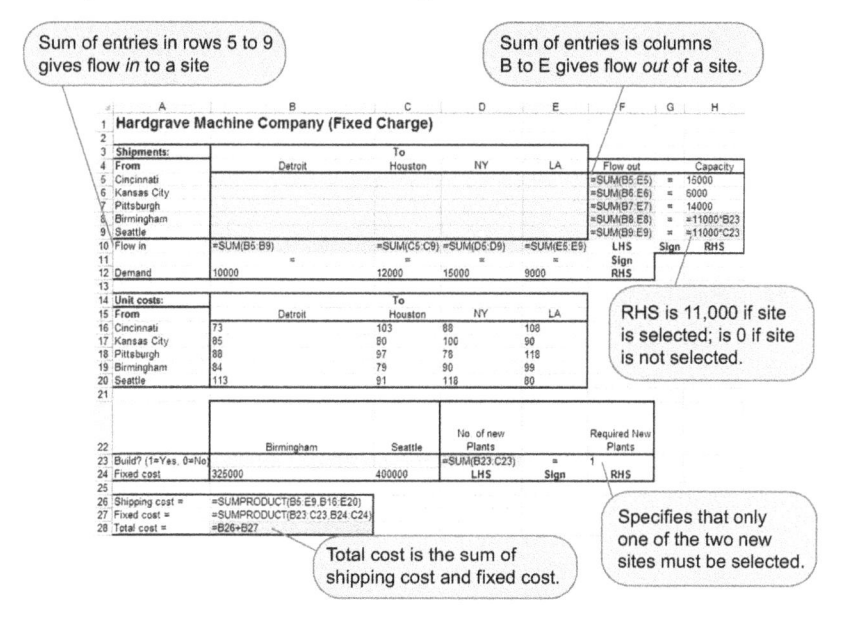

Figure 6.7: Formula View of Excel Layout for Hardgrave Machine—Fixed Charge

File: Figure 6.7.xlsx, Sheet: Figure 6.7

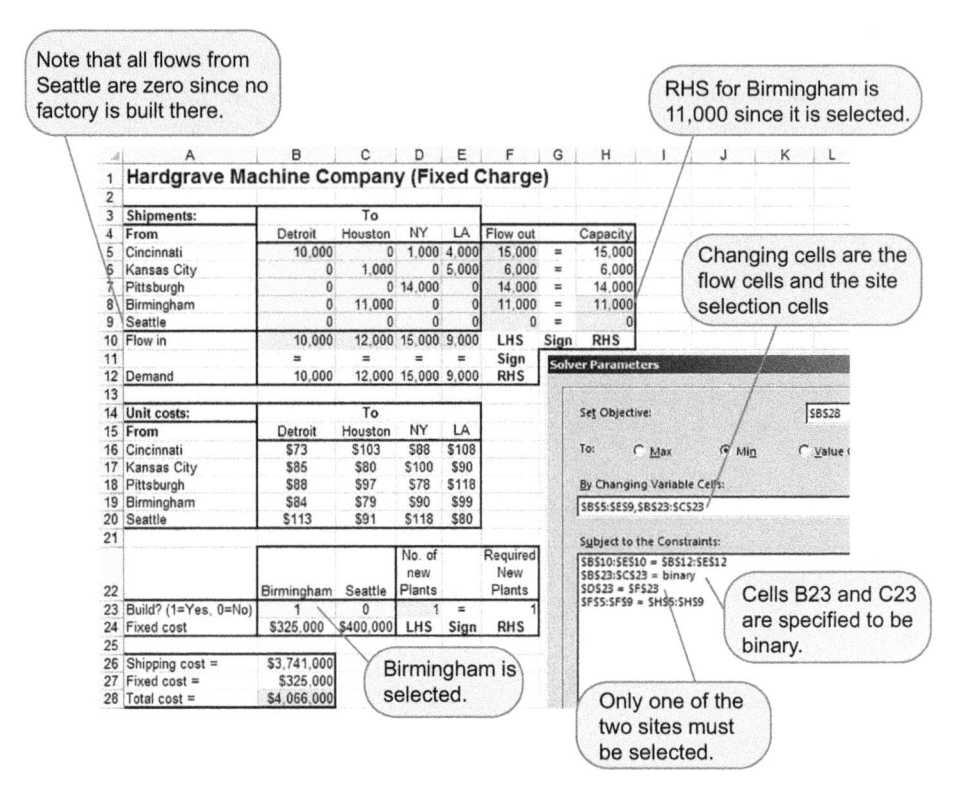

330 — Chapter 6: Integer, Goal, and Nonlinear Programming Models

Figure 6.8: Solver Entries and Solution for Hardgrave Machine—Fixed Charge

File: Figure 6.7.xlsx, Sheet: Figure 6.8

Referring to Solved Problem 5–1, we see that the cost of shipping was $3,704,000 if the new plant was built in Seattle. This cost was $3,741,000 if the new plant was built in Birmingham. With the fixed costs included, the total costs would be

Seattle: $3,704,000 + $400,000 = $4,104,000
Birmingham: $3,741,000 + $325,000 = $4,066,000

That is, Hardgrave should select Birmingham as the site for the new plant. Figure 6.8 shows this solution. Note that the shipping quantities in this solution are the same as those obtained in Solved Problem 5–1 for the solution with the Birmingham plant (as shown in Figure 5.23).

6.5 Goal Programming Models

In today's business environment, maximizing profit (or minimizing cost) is not always the only objective that a firm may specify. In many cases, maximizing profits is just one of several objectives that may include maximizing machine utilization, maintaining full employment, providing quality ecological management, minimizing noise level in the neighborhood, and meeting numerous other noneconomic targets. Often, some of these objectives are conflicting (i.e., it may not be possible to simultaneously achieve these objectives).

Mathematical programming techniques such as LP and IP have the shortcoming that their objective function can deal with only a single criterion, such as profit, cost, or some such measure. To overcome this shortcoming, an important technique that has been developed to handle decision models involving multiple objectives is called goal programming (GP).

How do LP/IP and GP models differ? In LP/IP models, we try to find the best possible value for a single objective. That is, the aim is to *optimize* a single measure. In GP models, on the other hand, we first set a goal (or desired target) for each objective. In most decision modeling situations, some of these goals may be achievable only at the expense of other goals. Therefore, we establish a hierarchy or rank of importance among these goals so that lower-ranked goals are given less prominence than higher-ranked goals. Based on this hierarchy, GP then attempts to reach a "satisfactory" level for each goal. That is, GP tries to satisfice the multiple objectives (i.e., come as close as possible to their respective goals) rather than optimize them.

How does GP satisfice the goals? Instead of trying to maximize or minimize the objective functions directly, as in LP/IP, with GP we try to minimize *deviations* between the specified goals and what we can actually achieve for the multiple objective functions within the given constraints. Deviations can be either positive or negative, depending on whether we overachieve or underachieve a specific goal. These deviations are not only real decision variables in the GP model, but they are also the only terms in the objective function. The objective is to minimize some function of these deviation variables.

Goal Programming Example: Wilson Doors Company

To illustrate the formulation of a GP problem, let's consider the product mix problem faced by the Wilson Doors Company. The company manufactures three styles of doors—exterior, interior, and commercial. Each door requires a certain amount of steel and two separate production steps: forming and assembly. Table 6.7 shows the material requirement, forming and assembly times, and selling price per unit of each product, along with the monthly availability of all resources.

Table 6 7: Data for Wilson Doors

	Exterior	Interior	Commercial	Availability
Steel (lbs./door)	4	3	7	9,000 pounds
Forming (hrs./door)	2	4	3	6,000 hours
Assembly (hrs./door)	2	3	4	5,200 hours
Selling price/door	$70	$110	$110	

Formulating and Solving the LP Model Let's denote E = number of exterior doors to make, I = number of interior doors to make, and C = number of commercial doors to make. If Wilson's management had just a single objective (i.e., to maximize total sales), the LP formulation for the problem would be written as

$$\text{Maximize total sales} = \$70E + \$110I + \$110C$$

subject to the constraints

$$4E + 3I + 7C \leq 9{,}000 \quad \text{(steel usage)}$$
$$2E + 4I + 3C \leq 6{,}000 \quad \text{(forming time)}$$
$$2E + 3I + 4C \leq 5{,}200 \quad \text{(assembly time)}$$
$$E, I, C \geq 0$$

The optimal LP solution turns out to be $E = 1{,}400$, $I = 800$, and $C = 0$, for total sales of $186,000. At this stage, you should be able to easily verify this yourself. However, for your convenience, this LP solution is included in the Excel file *Figure 6.9.xlsx, Sheet: LP* on the Companion Website for this book.

Specifying the Goals Now suppose that Wilson is not happy with this LP solution because it generates no sales from commercial doors. In contrast, exterior doors generate $98,000 (= $70 × 1,400), and interior doors generate $88,000 (= $110 × 800) in sales. This would imply that while the sales agents for exterior and interior doors get sales bonuses this month, the sales agent for commercial doors gets nothing. To alleviate this situation, Wilson would prefer that each type of door contribute a certain level of sales. Wilson, however, is not willing to compromise too much on *total* sales. Further, management does not want to be unduly unfair to the sales agents for exterior and interior doors by taking away too much of their sales potential (and, hence, their sales bonus). Considering all issues, suppose Wilson sets the following goals:

Goal 1: Achieve total sales of at least $180,000
Goal 2: Achieve exterior doors sales of at least $70,000
Goal 3: Achieve interior doors sales of at least $60,000
Goal 4: Achieve commercial doors sales of at least $35,000

Notice that these goals look similar to constraints. However, there is a key difference. Constraints are restrictions that *must* be satisfied by the solution. Goals, on the other hand, are specifications that we would *like* to satisfy. However, it is acceptable to leave one or more goals unsatisfied in the final solution if it is impossible to satisfy them (because of other, possibly conflicting, goals and constraints in the model). We now have a GP problem in which we want to find the product mix that achieves these four goals as much as possible, given the production resource constraints.

Decision modeling in Action

Goal Programming helps AMEDD Optimize Workforce Planning Decisions

The Medical Department of the U.S. Army (AMEDD) has a mission to provide healthcare delivery for the U.S. Army. One of the challenges that AMEDD faces is the large number of medical specialties in AMEDD, and so determining the appropriate number of hires and promotions for each medical specialty is a complicated task. Accordingly, AMEDD had an urgent need to optimize its workforce planning. AMEDD previously used a manual approach to project the number of hires, promotions, and personnel inventory for each medical specialty across AMEDD to support a 30-year life cycle.

An objective force model (OFM), which is a mixed integer linear weighted goal programming model, was applied to optimize AMEDD workforce planning given the deterministic continuation rates. In addition, a discrete-event simulation model was developed to verify and validate the results.

The OFM permitted better transparency for AMEDD decision makers, while effectively projecting the optimal number of officers to meet the demands of the workforce structure. Furthermore, the OFM provided tremendous value to AMEDD in terms of time, requiring only seconds to solve rather than months, which enabled AMEDD to conduct quick what-if analyses to support its decisions. In terms of personnel strategy and policy, OFM supported decisions related to recruiting goals for the Army's recruiting command, classroom capacity for specialty training, promotion requirements, and force-reduction objectives.

Source: Based on N. Bastian, P. McCurry, L. Fulton, P. Griffin, S. Cui, T. Hanson, S. Srinivas. "The AMEDD Uses Goal Programming to Optimize Workforce Planning Decisions," *Interfaces* 45, 4 (July–August 2015): 305–324.

Formulating the GP Model To formulate any problem as a GP problem, we must first define two deviation variables for each goal. These two deviation variables represent, respectively, the extent to which a goal is underachieved or overachieved. Because there are four goals in Wilson's problem, we define eight deviation variables, as follows:

d_T^- = amount by which the total sales goal is underachieved
d_T^+ = amount by which the total sales goal is overachieved
d_E^- = amount by which the exterior doors sales goal is underachieved
d_E^+ = amount by which the exterior doors sales goal is overachieved
d_I^- = amount by which the interior doors sales goal is underachieved
d_I^+ = amount by which the interior doors sales goal is overachieved
d_C^- = amount by which the commercial doors sales goal is underachieved
d_C^+ = amount by which the commercial doors sales goal is overachieved

Using these deviation variables, we express the four goals mathematically as follows:

$$70E + 110I + 110C + d_T^- - d_T^+ = 180{,}000 \quad \text{(total sales goal)}$$
$$70E + d_E^- - d_E^+ = 70{,}000 \quad \text{(exterior doors sales goal)}$$
$$110I + d_I^- - d_I^+ = 60{,}000 \quad \text{(interior doors sales goal)}$$
$$110C + d_C^- - d_C^+ = 35{,}000 \quad \text{(commercial doors sales goal)}$$

The first equation states that the total sales (i.e., $70E + \$110I + \$110C$) plus any underachievement of total sales minus any overachievement of total sales has to equal the goal of \$180,000. For example, the LP solution ($E = 1{,}400$, $I = 800$, and $C = 0$) yields total sales of \$186,000. Because this exceeds the goal of \$180,000 by \$6,000, d_T^+ would equal \$6,000, and d_T^- would equal \$0. Note that it is not possible for both d_T^+ and d_T^- to be nonzero at the same time because it is not logical for a goal to be both underachieved and overachieved at the same time (the appearance of deviation variables in the minimization objective function will assure this mathematically). The second, third, and fourth equations specify a similar issue with regard to sales from exterior, interior, and commercial doors, respectively.

Because all four of Wilson's goals specify that their targets should be *at least* met, we want to minimize only the level of underachievement in each goal. That is, we are not concerned if any or all goals are overachieved. With this background information, we can now formulate Wilson's problem as a single GP model, as follows:

$$\text{Minimize total underachievement of goals} = d_T^- + d_E^- + d_I^- + d_C^-$$

subject to the constraints

$$70E + 110I + 110C + d_T^- - d_T^+ = 180{,}000 \quad \text{(total sales goal)}$$
$$70E + d_E^- - d_E^+ = 70{,}000 \quad \text{(exterior doors sales goal)}$$
$$110I + d_I^- - d_I^+ = 60{,}000 \quad \text{(interior doors sales goal)}$$
$$110C + d_C^- - d_C^+ = 35{,}000 \quad \text{(commercial doors sales goal)}$$
$$4E + 3I + 7C \le 9{,}000 \quad \text{(steel usage)}$$
$$2E + 4I + 3C \le 6{,}000 \quad \text{(forming time)}$$
$$2E + 3I + 4C \le 5{,}200 \quad \text{(assembly time)}$$
$$E, I, C, d_T^-, d_T^+, d_E^-, d_E^+, d_I^-, d_I^+, d_C^-, d_C^+ \ge 0$$

If Wilson were just interested in *exactly* achieving all four goals, how would the objective function change? In that case, we would specify it to minimize the total underachievement and overachievement (i.e., the sum of all eight deviation variables). This, of course, is probably not a reasonable objective in practice because Wilson is not likely to be upset with an overachievement of any of its sales goals.

In general, once all the goals have been defined in a GP problem, management should analyze each goal to see if it wishes to include only one or both deviation variables for that goal in the minimization objective function. In some cases, the goals could even be one-sided in that it is not even feasible for one of the deviation variables to be nonzero. For example, if Wilson specifies that the $180,000 target for total sales is an absolute minimum (i.e., it cannot be violated), the underachievement deviation variable d_T^- can be eliminated from the GP model.

Now that we have formulated Wilson's GP model with the four goals, how do we solve it? There are two approaches commonly used in practice: (1) using weighted goals and (2) using ranked goals (or prioritized goals). Let's now discuss both of these approaches.

Solving Goal Programming Models with Weighted Goals

As currently formulated, Wilson's GP model assumes that all four goals are equally important to its managers. That is, because the objective function is just the sum of the four deviation variables $(d_T^-, d_E^-, d_I^-, \text{and } d_C^-)$ a unit underachievement in the total sales goal (d_T^-) has the same impact on the objective function value as a unit underachievement in any of the other three sales goals $(d_E^-, d_I^-, \text{or } d_C^-)$. If that is indeed the case in Wilson's problem, we can simply solve the model as currently formulated. However, as noted earlier, it is common in practice for managers to rank different goals in some hierarchical fashion.

Formulating the Weighted GP Model Suppose Wilson specifies that the total sales goal is five times as important as each of the other three sales goals. To include this specification in the weighted goal approach for solving GP models, we assign numeric weights to each deviation variable in the objective function. These weights serve as the objective coefficients for the deviation variables. The magnitude of the weight assigned to a specific deviation variable would depend on the relative importance of that goal. In Wilson's case, because minimizing d_T^- is five times as important as minimizing $d_E^-, d_I^-,$ or d_C^-, we can now write the objective function with weighted goals for Wilson's model as

$$\text{Minimize total } \textit{weighted} \text{ underachievement of goals} = 5d_T^- + d_E^- + d_I^- + d_C^-$$

The constraints are as listed earlier for the model. The problem now reduces to an LP model with a single objective function. Setting up this model in Excel and solving it by using Solver therefore become rather straightforward tasks.

Solving the Weighted GP Model The Excel layout and Solver entries for Wilson's problem with weighted goals are shown in Figure 6.9. Note that the model includes 11 decision variables (three product variables associated with the three types of doors and eight deviation variables associated with the four goals). The results also show the extent to which each goal has been achieved (shown in cells P8:P11).

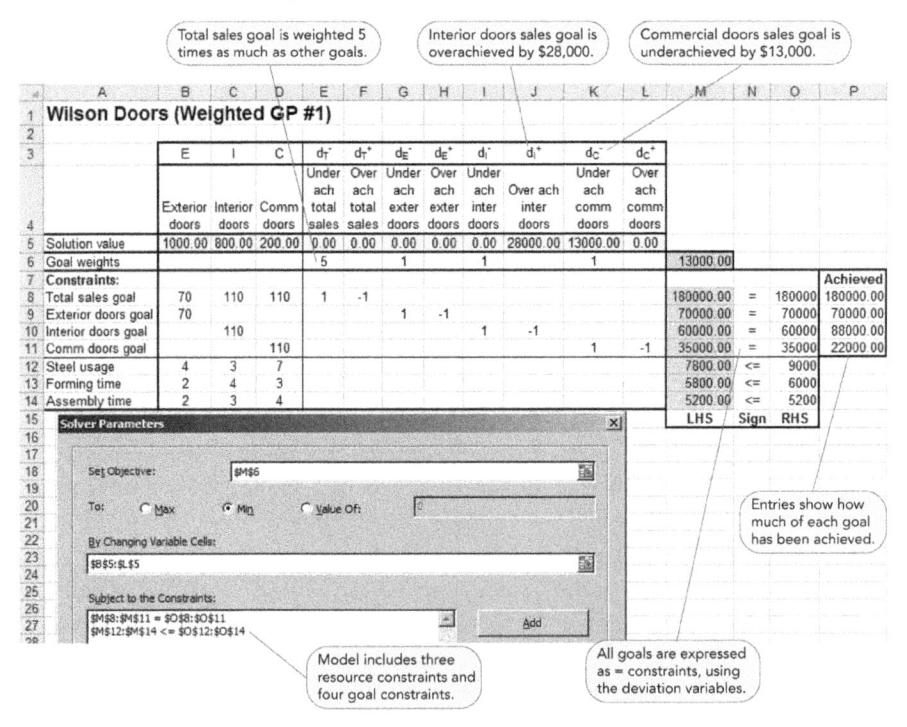

Figure 6.9: Excel Layout and Solver Entries for Wilson Doors—Weighted Goals Solution 1

File: Figure 6.9.xlsx, Sheet: Figure 6.9

Interpreting the Results The optimal weighted GP solution is for Wilson to produce 1,000 exterior doors, 800 interior doors, and 200 commercial doors. This results in total revenue of $180,000, which exactly satisfies that goal (i.e., d_T^+ and d_T^- are both equal to 0). Regarding the goals for the different types of doors, the exterior doors sales goal is also exactly satisfied, while the interior doors sales goal is overachieved by $28,000. In contrast, sales from commercial doors are only $22,000 (= $110 × 200), which underachieves the goal of $35,000 by $13,000. Wilson should, however, be willing to accept this result because management is more concerned about the total sales goal (hence, assigned it a larger weight) than with the commercial doors sales goal. That is, in trying to satisfy Wilson's *stronger* desire to generate at least $180,000 in total sales, the weighted GP solution continues to leave the commercial doors sales goal underachieved to a certain extent.

Drawbacks of the Weighted Goals Approach Although the weighted goals approach is rather easy to use, it suffers from two major drawbacks. First, it is appropriate to use only if all the goals (and, hence, the deviation variables) are measured in the same units (such as dollars). This is indeed the case in Wilson's problem, where all four goals are measured in dollars. However, what happens if different goals are measured in different units? For example, the first goal could be about sales (measured in dollars), and the second goal could be about steel usage (measured in pounds). In such cases, it is very difficult to assign appropriate weights because different deviation variables in the same objective function are measured in different units.

Second, even if all goals are measured in the same units, it is not always easy to assign suitable weights for the different deviation variables. For example, in Wilson's problem, how does management decide that the total sales goal is exactly 5 times as important as the other three goals? What if it is only 2.5 times as important? Clearly, this would affect the choice of weights, which, in turn, could affect the optimal solution.

In fact, as shown in Figure 6.10, if we assign a weight of only 2.5 (instead of 5) to the total sales goal in Wilson's weighted GP model and continue to assign a weight of 1 to each of the other three goals, the optimal solution changes completely. Interestingly, the total sales goal, which Wilson has specified as the most important goal, now turns out to be the only underachieved goal (by $4,333.33). The exterior and commercial doors sales goals are fully satisfied, while the interior doors sales goal is actually overachieved by $10,666.67. This clearly illustrates the importance of properly selecting weights.

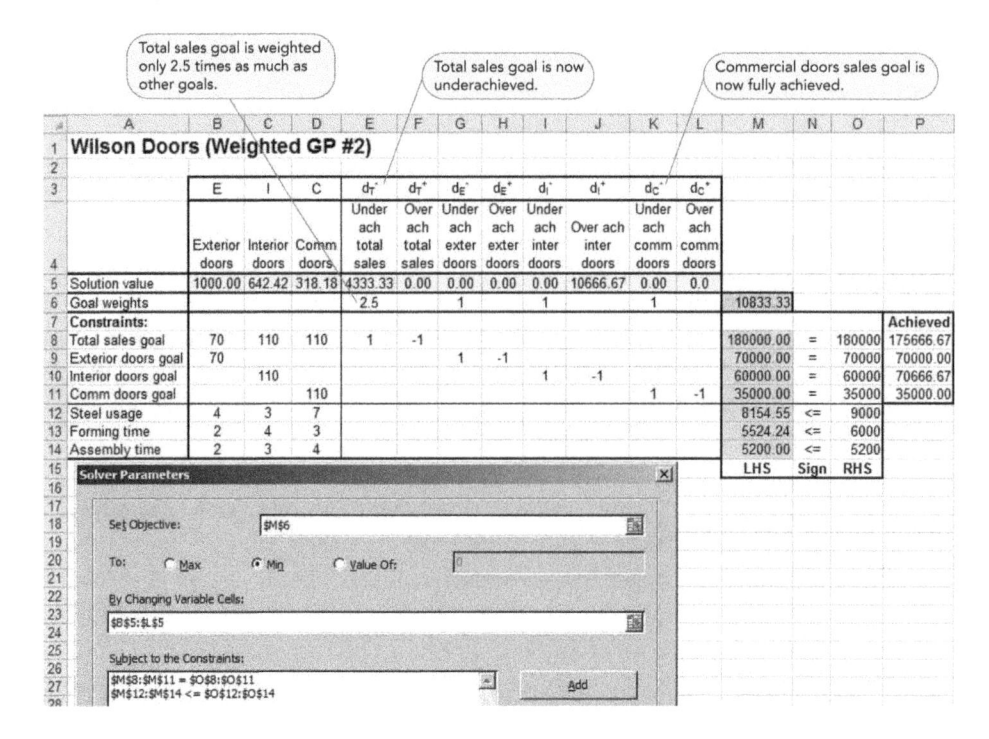

Figure 6.10: Excel Layout and Solver Entries for Wilson Doors—Weighted Goals Solution 2

File: Figure 6.9.xlsx, Sheet: Figure 6.10

By the way, the LP solution shown in Figure 6.10 has fractional solution values for interior and commercial doors. Wilson can fix this either by solving the problem as a general IP model or by rounding off the fractional values appropriately. For your convenience, the IP solution (obtained by constraining variables E, I, and C to be integer valued in Solver) for this problem is included in the Excel file *Figure 6.9.xlsx, Sheet: Figure 6.10 IP* on the Companion Website for this book. The total sales goal turns out to be underachieved by $4,290 in the IP solution.

To overcome these two drawbacks with the weighted GP approach, we examine an alternate approach—the ranked, or prioritized, goals approach—for solving GP problems.

Solving Goal Programming Models with Ranked Goals

In the ranked goals approach to solving GP models, we assign ranks (or priorities), rather than weights, to goals. The idea is that goals can be ranked based on their importance to management. Lower-ranked goals are considered only after higher-ranked goals are met. Note that it is possible to assign the same rank to two or more goals.

Decision Modeling In Action

General Electric Automates Bed Assignment for Mount Sinai Medical Center in New York

Bed management is one of the most important functions in any hospital because of its major impact on patient care and flow, patient and staff satisfaction, and, most important, on the hospital's operating performance. One of the challenges related to bed management is optimizing the bed assignment process, which is a complex process given the dynamics in the hospital's environment. Handling this challenge requires centralizing data and information, ensuring consideration of interdependencies between different units, and efficient and effective management of resources.

General Electric (GE) developed an analytical decision support system with embedded mathematical models to periodically recommend bed patient assignments. The decision support system was based on an innovative mixed integer goal programming modeling approach to accommodate the multiple goals and complex operating rules of different hospitals.

The developed bed-assignment solution was implemented and hosted as a cloud-based application for Mount Sinai Medical Center in New York. In order to evaluate the tool developed, experiments were run on historical data sets to analyze the runtime efficiency, assignment coverage, reduction in patient wait times, and quality of assignments.

The quality of the solution generated was satisfying for the team. More than 90% of the bed requests generated received an automated bed placement suggestion. The algorithm consistently suggested placing patients in better or the same tiers as the previously followed manual process, while for some cases the managers could place the patients in better tiers because of their long experience or judgmental knowledge that was not reflected in the algorithm. Experiments showed that 54% of the patients would experience a potential reduction of waiting time of one hour, while at least 23% of patience would see a three-hour reduction in waiting times.

Source: Based on B. Thomas, S. Bollapraga, K. Akbay, D. Toledano, P. Katlic, O. Dulgeroglu, D. Yang. "Automated Bed Assignments in a Complex and Dynamic Hospital Environment," *Interfaces* 43, 5 (September–October 2013): 435–448.

Let's discuss this approach by revisiting Wilson Doors Company's problem. Recall that Wilson's management has currently specified the following four goals:

Goal 1: Achieve total sales of at least $180,000
Goal 2: Achieve exterior doors sales of at least $70,000
Goal 3: Achieve interior doors sales of at least $60,000
Goal 4: Achieve commercial doors sales of at least $35,000

Because in the ranked goals approach we are no longer restricted to measuring all goals in the same units, let's expand Wilson's problem by adding another goal. Suppose Wilson plans to switch to a different type of steel for the next production period. Management would therefore like to ensure that the production plan this period uses up as much of the current availability of steel (9,000 pounds) as possible. This is formally stated in the following goal:

Goal 5: Achieve steel usage of as close to 9,000 pounds as possible

Wilson's management has examined these five goals and has decided to rank, them in decreasing order of rank, as follows:

Rank R_1: Goal 1
Rank R_2: Goal 5
Rank R_3: Goals 2, 3, and 4

This means, in effect, that meeting the total sales goal is much more important than meeting the steel usage goal, which, in turn, is much more important than meeting the sales goals for each of the three types of doors. If we wish, we can further distinguish between goals within the same rank by assigning appropriate weights. For example, we can assign appropriate weights to any of the three goals with rank R_3 (i.e., goals 2, 3, and 4) to make that goal more important than the other two.

Formulating the Ranked GP Model In addition to the eight deviation variables that we have already defined earlier (i.e., $d_T^-, d_T^+, d_E^-, d_E^+, d_I^-, d_I^+, d_C^-$, and d_C^+), we define a ninth deviation variable, as follows:

$$d_S^- = \text{amount by which the steel usage goal is underachieved}$$

Note that we do not have to define a deviation variable for overachievement of steel usage (i.e., d_S^+) because steel is a resource constraint. That is, steel usage can never exceed 9,000 pounds. Also, unlike the eight deviation variables associated with the four sales goals, which are measured in dollars, the deviation variable d_S^- is measured in pounds.

Using the deviation variable d_S^- we can express the steel usage goal mathematically, as follows, just as we expressed the other four goals:

$$4E + 3I + 7C + d_S^- = 9{,}000 \quad \text{(steel usage goal)}$$

Based on the specified ranking of goals (recall that goals with rank R_1 are the most important, goals with rank R_2 are the next most important, then R_3, and so on), Wilson's ranked GP problem can be stated as

$$\text{Minimize ranked deviations} = R_1(d_T^-) + R_2(d_S^-) + R_3(d_E^- + d_I^- + d_C^-)$$

subject to the constraints

$70E + 110I + 110C + d_T^- - d_T^+$	$= 180{,}000$	(total sales goal)
$4E + 3I + 7C + d_S^-$	$= 9{,}000$	(steel usage goal)
$70E + d_E^- - d_E^+$	$= 70{,}000$	(exterior doors sales goal)
$110I + d_I^- - d_I^+$	$= 60{,}000$	(interior doors sales goal)
$110C + d_C^- - d_C^+$	$= 35{,}000$	(commercial doors sales goal)
$2E + 4I + 3C$	$\leq 6{,}000$	(forming time)
$2E + 3I + 4C$	$\leq 5{,}200$	(assembly time)
$E, I, C, d_T^-, d_T^+, d_S^-, d_E^-, d_E^+, d_I^-, d_I^+, d_C^-, d_C^+ \geq$	0	(nonnegativity)

Note that within each rank, the objective function in this model includes only the underachievement deviation variable because all four sales goals specify that the goals should be "at least" met, and the steel usage goal can never be overachieved.

Solving the Rank R_1 GP Model and Interpreting the Results To find the optimal solution for a GP model with ranked goals, we need to set up and solve a series of LP models. In the first of these LP models, we consider only the highest-ranked (rank R_1) goals and ignore all other goals (ranks R_2 and R_3). The objective function then includes only the deviation variable with rank R_1. In Wilson's problem, the objective of the first LP model is

$$\text{Minimize rank } R_1 \text{ deviation} = d_T^-$$

Solving this LP model using Solver is a rather simple task, and Figure 6.11 shows the relevant information. The results demonstrate that it is possible to fully achieve the rank R_1 goal (i.e., the total sales goal can be fully satisfied, and the optimal value of d_T^- is 0). However, at the present time, the steel usage goal is underachieved by 1,200 pounds, the interior doors sales goal is overachieved by $28,000, and the commercial doors sales goal is underachieved by $13,000.

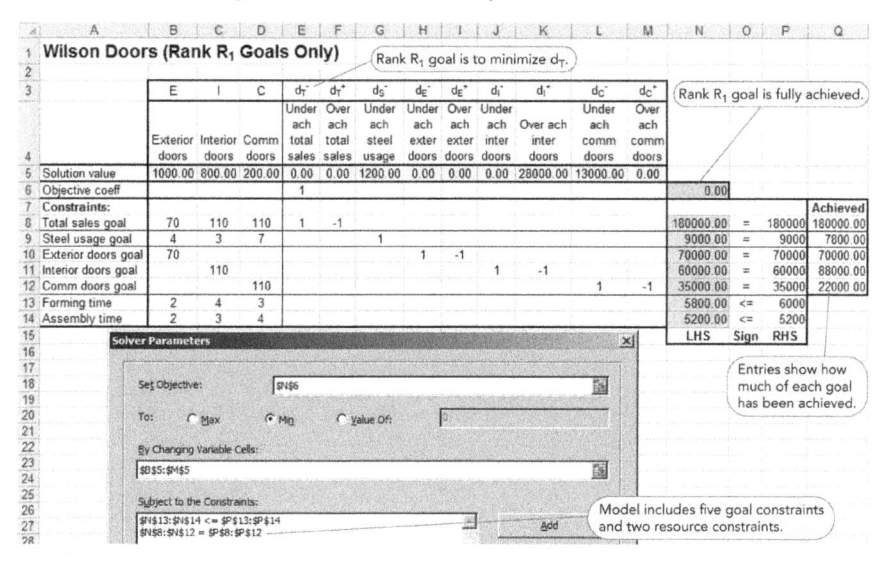

Figure 6.11: Excel Layout and Solver Entries for Wilson Doors—Rank R_1 Goals Only

File: Figure 6.11.xlsx, Sheet: Figure 6.11

Solving the Rank R_2 GP Model and Interpreting the Results Now that we have optimally solved the model with the rank R_1 goal, we consider all goals with the next-highest rank (R_2) in the second LP model. In Wilson's problem, this is the steel usage goal. However, in setting up this LP model, we explicitly specify the optimal value of the total sales goal from the rank R_1 model. To do so, we set the value of the relevant deviation variable (i.e., d_T^-) to its optimal value of 0 in the LP model.

For Wilson's second LP model, the objective function and *additional* constraint are as follows:

$$\text{Minimize rank } R_2 \text{ deviation} = d_S^-$$

and

$$d_T^- = 0 \quad \text{(optimal value of rank } R_1 \text{ goal)}$$

Figure 6.12 shows the Excel layout and Solver entries for this LP model. The results show that it is possible to fully achieve the rank R_2 goal also. That is, it is possible to reduce the value of the deviation variable d_S^- also to 0, while maintaining the value of the rank R_1 deviation variable d_T^- at its optimal value of 0. In fact, the total sales goal is now overachieved by $4,333.33, and the exterior doors sales goal is overachieved by $63,000.

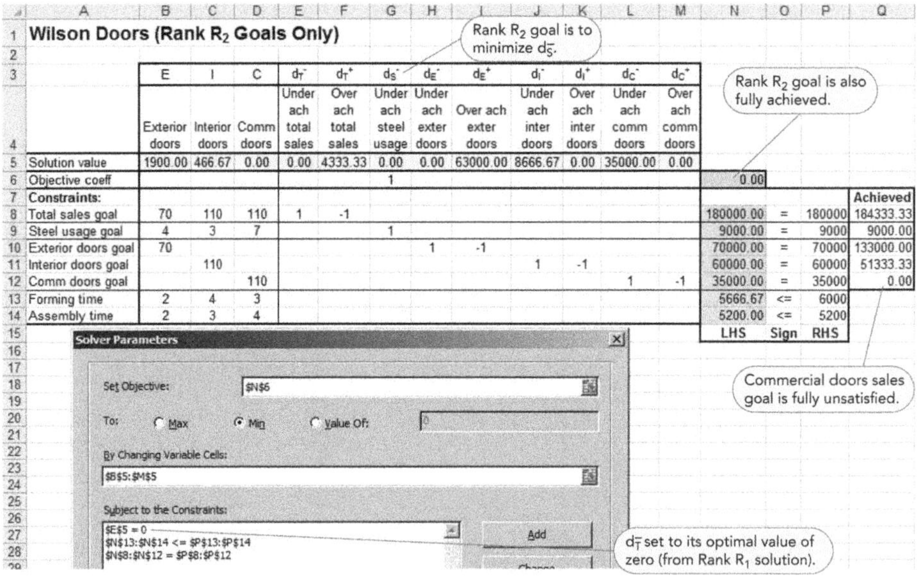

Figure 6.12: Excel Layout and Solver Entries for Wilson Door—Rank R_2 Goals Only

File: Figure 6.11.xlsx, Sheet: Figure 6.12

However, this emphasis on reducing the value of d_S^- results in the value of d_C^- ballooning up from $13,000 in the rank R_1 solution (Figure 6.11) to $35,000 in the rank R_2 solution (Figure 6.12). This implies that the commercial doors sales goal is fully unsatisfied and that no commercial doors should be made. Likewise, the interior doors sales goal is also underachieved by $8,666.67. While this solution may seem unfair to the sales agents for interior and commercial doors, it is still perfectly logical because Wilson has ranked the steel usage goal higher than the sales goals for all three door types.

The LP solution shown in Figure 6.12 has a fractional solution value for interior doors. Interestingly, the IP solution for this problem (included in the Excel file *Figure 6.11.xlsx, Sheet: Figure 6.12 IP* on the Companion Website for this book) is considerably different from the LP solution in Figure 6.12. The steel usage goal is still fully satisfied. However, while overachievements d_T^+ and d_E^+ along with underachievement d_C^- all decrease from their corresponding LP solution values, underachievement d_I^- increases from $8,666.67 to $13,580. That is, the IP solution pulls three of the four goals closer to their target while moving one further away from its target, when compared to the LP solution.

Solving the Rank R3 GP Model and Interpreting the Results Now that the goals with ranks R_1 and R_2 have been optimized, we proceed to consider all goals with the next-highest rank (R_3) in the third LP model. As before, in setting up this model, we explicitly specify the optimal values of the rank R_1 and R_2 goals obtained from the first two LP models.

For Wilson's third LP model, the objective function and *additional* constraints are as follows:

$$\text{Minimize rank } R_3 \text{ deviations} = d_E^- + d_I^- + d_C^-$$

and

$$d_T^- = 0 \quad \text{(optimal value of rank } R_1 \text{ goal)}$$
$$d_S^- = 0 \quad \text{(optimal value of rank } R_2 \text{ goal)}$$

Figure 6.13 shows the Excel layout and Solver entries for this LP model. The results show that after fully optimizing the rank R_1 and R_2 goals, the best we can do is to attain a total underachievement of $33,631.58 in the rank R_3 goals. In the final solution, the total sales goal is exactly satisfied, while the exterior doors sales goal is overachieved by $48,631.58. In contrast, the interior doors and commercial doors sales goals are underachieved by $13,684.21 and $19,947.37, respectively.

As with the second LP model, this solution too has fractional values for the production variables. The IP solution for this problem (included in the Excel file *Figure 6.11.xlsx, Sheet: Figure 6.13 IP* on the Companion Website for this book) turns out to be the same as the IP solution we obtained for the rank R_2 model. That is, if we solve Wilson's problem using IP models, the rank R_3 model is not able to improve on the solution obtained in the rank R_2 model.

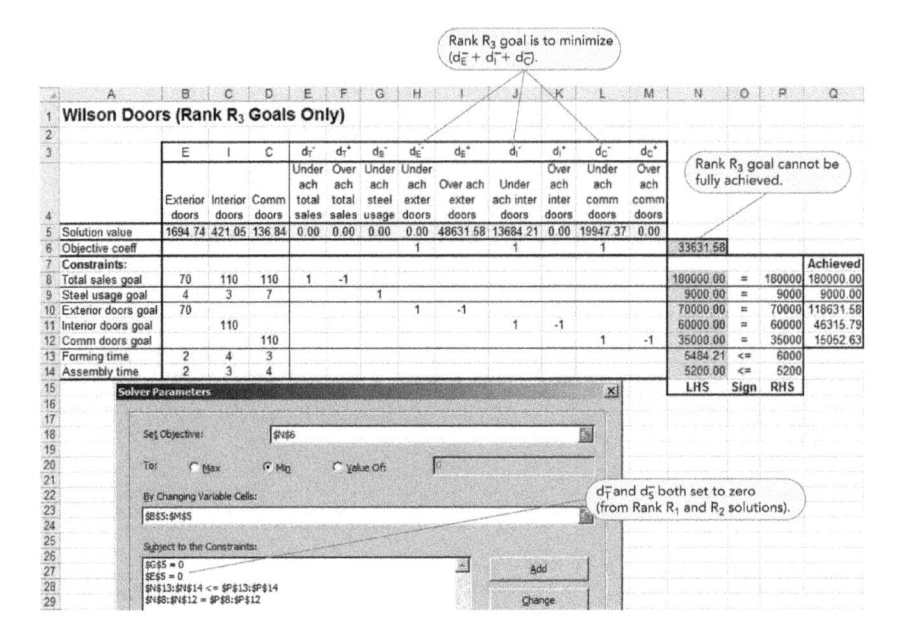

Figure 6.13: Excel Layout and Solver Entries for Wilson Doors—Rank R_3 Goals Only

File: Figure 6.11.xlsx, Sheet: Figure 6.13

Comparing the Two Approaches for Solving GP Models

The weighted goals approach considers all goals simultaneously, and the optimal solution depends to a great extent on the weights assigned for different goals. In contrast, the ranked goals approach considers goals in a hierarchical manner. Optimal values for all higher-ranked goal deviation variables are *explicitly* specified while considering LP models with lower-ranked goals as objective functions. Which approach should we then use for a specific problem? If all goals are measured in the same units, and if it is possible to assign appropriate weights for each goal, using the weighted goals approach is clearly the easier option. In all other situations, we would need to use the ranked goals approach.

6.6 Nonlinear Programming Models

LP, IP, and GP all assume that a problem's objective function and constraints are linear. That means that they cannot contain nonlinear terms, such as X^3, $1/X$, log X, or $5XY$. Yet in many real-world situations, the objective function and/or one or more constraints may be nonlinear. Here are two simple examples:

- We have assumed in all models so far that the profit contribution per unit of a product is fixed, regardless of how many units we sell of the product. That is, if Y denotes the number of units sold of a specific product and the product has a profit contribution of $6 per unit, the total profit is $6Y, for *all* values of Y. However, it may be that the unit profit contribution of a product decreases as its demand (i.e., number of units sold) increases (because the prices may need to decrease to entice more customers to purchase the product). Suppose this relationship turns out to be

$$\text{Profit contribution per unit} = \$6 - \$0.02Y$$

Then, the total profit from this product is given by the following nonlinear expression:

$$\text{Total profit} = (\$6 - \$0.02Y) \times Y = \$6Y - \$0.02Y^2$$

- Likewise, we have assumed in all models so far that the relationship between resource usage and production level is linear. For example, if each patient requires 5 minutes of nursing time and there are P patients, the total time needed is $5P$ minutes, for all values of P. This term would be included in the LHS of the nursing time constraint. However, it is quite possible that the efficiency of nurses decreases as the patient load increases. Suppose the time required per patient is actually $(5 + 0.25P)$. That is, the time per patient increases as the number of patients increases. The term to be included in the nursing time constraint's LHS would now be $(5 + 0.25P) \times P = (5P + 0.25P^2)$, which would make the constraint nonlinear.

In such situations, the resulting model is called a nonlinear programming (NLP) model. By definition, an NLP model has a nonlinear objective function or at least one nonlinear constraint, or both. In this section, we examine NLP models and illustrate how Excel's Solver can often be used to solve these models. In practice, NLP models are difficult to solve and should be used with a lot of caution. Let's first examine the reason for this difficulty.

Why Are NLP Models Difficult to Solve?

In every LP, IP, and GP model, the objective function and all constraints are linear. This implies, for example, that with two variables, each equation in the model corresponds to a straight line. In contrast, as shown in Figure 6.14, a nonlinear expression in two variables is a curve. Depending on the extent of nonlinearity in the expression, the curve could be quite pronounced in that it could have many twists and turns.

You may recall from Chapter 2 that a feature of all LP models is that an optimal solution always occurs at a corner point (i.e., point where two or more linear constraints intersect). Software packages (including Solver) exploit this feature to find optimal solutions quickly even for large linear models. Unfortunately, if one or more constraints are nonlinear, an optimal solution need not be at a corner point of the feasible region. Further, as you can see from Figure 6.14, if the objective function itself is nonlinear (as in the equation of an ellipse or a sphere), it is not even easy to visualize at which feasible point the solution is optimized. This is one major reason why many NLP models are so difficult to solve in practice. As you can well imagine, this issue becomes even more difficult for NLP models that involve many decision variables.

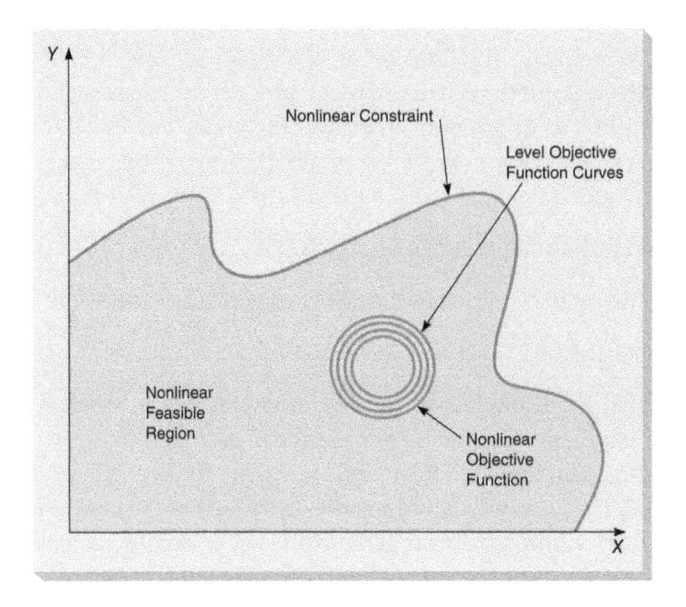

Figure 6.14: Model with Nonlinear Constraints and a Nonlinear Objective Function

Local versus Global Optimal Solutions A second reason for the difficulty in solving NLP models is the concept of local versus global optimal solutions. Perhaps a simple analogy will help you understand this concept. A local optimal solution is like the peak of a specific mountain in a mountain range. The global optimal solution, in contrast, is the peak of the highest mountain in that range. If you are on a specific mountain, it is likely that you can easily see the peak of that mountain—and possibly even find your way to it. However, unless you can see all the mountains in the entire range from your current location, you have no way of knowing if the peak of your specific mountain is just a local peak or whether it is the global peak.

Figure 6.15 illustrates this phenomenon with respect to NLP models. For the linear objective function shown in the figure, point Ⓐ is a local optimal solution, whereas point Ⓑ is a global optimal solution. The difficulty with all NLP solution procedures (including the procedure available in Solver) is that, depending on where the procedure starts the search process, it could terminate the search at either a global or a local optimal solution. For example, if the procedure starts at point Ⓓ, the search process could in fact lead it to the global optimal solution, point Ⓑ, first. In contrast, if it starts at point Ⓒ, the search process could find the local optimal solution, point Ⓐ, first. Because there are no better solutions in the immediate vicinity of point Ⓐ, the procedure will erroneously terminate and yield point Ⓐ as the optimal solution.

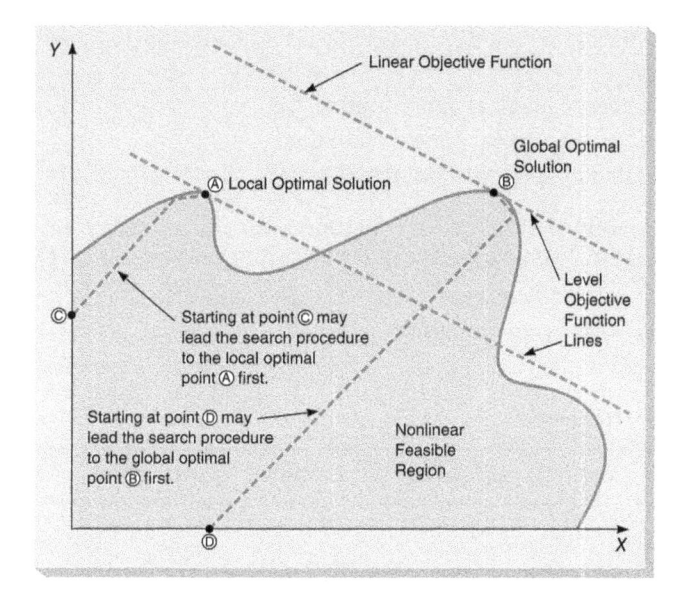

Figure 6.15: Local versus Global Optimal Solutions in an NLP Model

Unfortunately, there is no precise way of knowing where to start the search process for a given NLP problem. Hence, it is usually a good idea to try different starting solutions for NLP models. Hopefully, at least one of them will result in the global optimal solution.

Solving Nonlinear Programming Models Using Solver

To illustrate how NLP models can be set up and solved using Solver, let's consider an example in which the objective function and some of the constraints are nonlinear. The weekly profit at Pickens Memorial Hospital depends on the number of patients admitted in three separate categories: medical, surgical, and pediatric. The hospital can admit a total of 200 patients (regardless of category) each week. However, because Pickens Memorial serves a large community, patient demand in each category by itself far exceeds the total patient capacity.

Due to a fixed overhead, the profit per patient in each category actually increases as the number of patients increases. Further, some patients who are initially classified as medical patients then get reclassified as surgical patients. As a result, the profit per surgical patient also depends on the number of medical patients admitted. The accountants at Pickens Memorial have analyzed this situation and have identified the following information:

$$\text{Profit contribution per medical patient} = \$45 + \$2M$$
$$\text{Profit contribution per surgical patient} = \$70 + \$3S + \$2M$$
$$\text{Profit contribution per pediatric patient} = \$60 + \$3P$$

where

M = number of medical patients admitted
S = number of surgical patients admitted
P = number of pediatric patients admitted

Pickens Memorial has identified three main constraints for this model: X-ray capacity, marketing budget, and lab capacity. Table 6.8 shows the relevant weekly data for these three constraints for each category of patient. The table also shows the weekly availabilities of each of these three resources.

Table 6.8: Data for Pickens Memorial Hospital

	Medical	Surgical	Pediatric	Availability
Number of X-rays per patient	1	3	1	560 X-rays
Marketing budget per patient	$3	$5	$3.5	$1,000
Number of lab tests per patient	3	3	3	140 hours

The hospital's chief laboratory supervisor has noted that the time required per lab test increases as the total number of medical patients admitted (M) increases. Based on historical data, the supervisor estimates this relationship to be as follows

$$\text{Time required per lab test (in hours)} = 0.2 + 0.001M$$

Formulating the Problem The objective function for Pickens Memorial seeks to maximize the total profit and can be written as

$$\text{Maximize profit} = (\$45 + \$2M) \times M + (\$70 + \$3S + \$2M) \times S + (\$60 + \$3P) \times P$$
$$= \$45M + \$2M^2 + \$70S + \$3S^2 + \$2MS + \$60P + \$3P^2$$

Clearly, this is a nonlinear expression. The constraints correspond to the total patient capacity of 200 and to the three limiting resources (i.e., X-ray capacity, marketing budget, and lab capacity). They may be expressed as follows:

$$
\begin{aligned}
M + S + P &\leq 200 & &\text{(total patient capacity)} \\
M + 3S + P &\leq 560 & &\text{(x-ray capacity)} \\
3M + 5S + 3.5P &\leq 1{,}000 & &\text{(marketing budget, \$)} \\
(0.2 + 0.001M) \times (3M + 3S + 3P) &\leq 140 & &\text{(lab capacity, hours)} \\
M, S, P &\geq 0 & &
\end{aligned}
$$

The total patient capacity, X-ray capacity, and marketing budget constraints are linear. However, the lab capacity constraint is nonlinear because it includes terms involving multiplication of variables. We can simplify and rewrite this constraint as

$$0.6M + 0.6S + 0.6P + 0.003M^2 + 0.003MS + 0.003MP \leq 140$$

Decision modeling in Action

Using Quadratic Programming to Improve Water-Release Policies on the Delaware River

The Delaware River provides half of the drinking water for New York City (NYC). The water releases from three NYC dams on the river's headwaters impact the reliability of the water supply, the flood potential, and the quality of the aquatic habitat. Changes in release policies, however, are restricted by two US Supreme Court decrees and the need for unanimity among NYC as well as the four states (New York, New Jersey, Pennsylvania, and Delaware) affected by these changes.

In January 2006, a coalition of four conservation organizations undertook a decision modeling-based project to study and suggest revisions to the release policies. A key component of this analysis was a quadratic nonlinear programming allocation model. The primary objective was to benefit river habitat and fisheries without increasing NYC's drought risk. The strategy was to quantify the risk-benefit trade-offs from increased conservation releases and create a simple algorithm that would explicitly link release quantities to reservoir levels.

It is estimated that the use of this model has increased critical summertime fish habitats by about 200 percent, while increasing NYC's drought risk by only 3 percent. The new release rules also mitigate flood risk and are significantly simpler to administer than prior approaches.

Source: Based on P. Kolesar and J. Serio. "Breaking the Deadlock: Improving Water-Release Policies on the Delaware River Through Operations Research," *Interfaces* 41, 1 (January–February 2011): 18–34.

Solving the Problem Using Excel's Solver We now illustrate how Excel's Solver can be used to solve this NLP model. Solver uses the generalized reduced gradient (GRG) procedure, sometimes called the *steepest ascent* (or *steepest descent*) *procedure*. This is an iterative procedure that moves from one feasible solution to the next in improving the value of the objective function. The GRG procedure can handle problems with both nonlinear constraints and nonlinear objective functions.

There are only three decision variables (i.e., M, S, and P) in Pickens Memorial's NLP model. These are denoted by cells B5, C5, and D5, respectively, in Figure 6.16. However, the model includes several nonlinear terms involving these three variables: M^2, S^2, P^2, MS, and MP. There are several ways in which we can include these terms in our Excel layout. Here are two simple approaches (*Note:* Figure 6.16 illustrates the second approach):

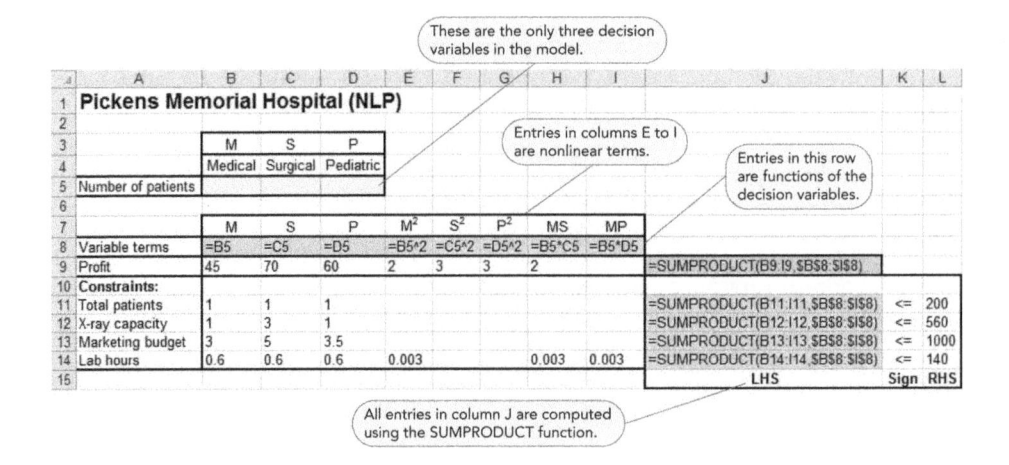

Chapter 6: Integer, Goal, and Nonlinear Programming Models

Figure 6.16: figure 6.16 Formula View of Excel Layout for Pickens Memorial—NLP

File: Figure 6.16.xlsx, Sheet: Figure 6.16

- We can directly type the nonlinear formula in the appropriate cell. For example, for the nonlinear objective function in this model, the formula in the objective cell can be directly entered as follows:

$$= 45*B5 + 2*B5^\wedge 2 + 70*C5 + 3*C5^\wedge 2 + 2*B5*C5 + 60*D5 + 3*D5^\wedge 2$$

In a similar manner, we can enter the nonlinear formula for the lab capacity constraint directly in the cell corresponding to the LHS of that constraint, as follows:

$$= 0.6*B5 + 0.6*C5 + 0.6*D5 + 0.003*B5^\wedge 2$$
$$+ 0.003*B5*C5 + 0.003*B5*D5$$

- Alternatively, as illustrated in Figure 6.16, we can use the same Excel layout that we have used in all LP and IP models so far. This means that (1) each decision variable is modeled in a separate column of the worksheet and (2) the objective function and LHS formulas for all constraints are computed using Excel's SUMPRODUCT function. To use this layout for NLP models, we create a cell entry for each linear or nonlinear term involving the decision variables. In Pickens Memorial's case, we need cells for M, S, P, M^2, S^2, P^2, MS, and MP. These terms are represented by cells B8 to I8, respectively, in Figure 6.16. (For clarity, we have shaded these cells blue in this NLP model.) The formulas for these cells are

= B5	(entry for M in cell B8)
= C5	(entry for S in cell C8)
= D5	(entry for P in cell D8)
= B5^2	(entry for M^2 in cell E8)
= C5^2	(entry for S^2 in cell F8)
= D5^2	(entry for P^2 in cell G8)
= B5*C5	(entry for MS in cell H8)
= B5*D5	(entry for MP in cell I8)

The layout for this model now looks similar to all other Excel layouts we have used so far. Hence, we can use the SUMPRODUCT function to model the objective function as well as the constraint LHS values. Note, however, that even though cells B8:I8 are used in computing the objective function and constraint LHS values in column J, only cells B5:D5 are specified in the By Changing Variable Cells box in Solver (as shown in Figure 6.17). The entries in row 8 are simply calculated from the final values for M, S, and P in cells B5:D5, respectively.

Figure 6.17 also shows the other Solver entries and solution for Pickens Memorial's NLP model. We note that in addition to ensuring that the Make Unconstrained Variables Non-Negative box is checked, we must now specify GRG Nonlinear in the Select a Solving Method, instead of Simplex LP, as we have done so far for all LP, IP, and GP models.

Interpreting the Results In obtaining the solution shown in Figure 6.17, we set the initial values of all three decision variables (i.e., cells B5:D5) to zero. The final result indicates that Pickens Memorial should admit 20 medical patients, 180 surgical patients, and no pediatric patients each week, for a total weekly profit of $118,700.

Is this a local optimal solution or a global optimal solution? As noted earlier, it is usually a good idea to try different starting solutions for NLP models. Hence, let's solve Pickens Memorial's NLP model again using Solver, but with different starting values for the decision variables. Figure 6.18 shows the final result obtained by Solver when we start with initial values of $M = 100$, $S = 0$, and $P = 100$. Interestingly, we get a different final solution now: Pickens Memorial should admit no medical and surgical patients but admit 200 pediatric patients each week, for a total weekly profit of $132,000.

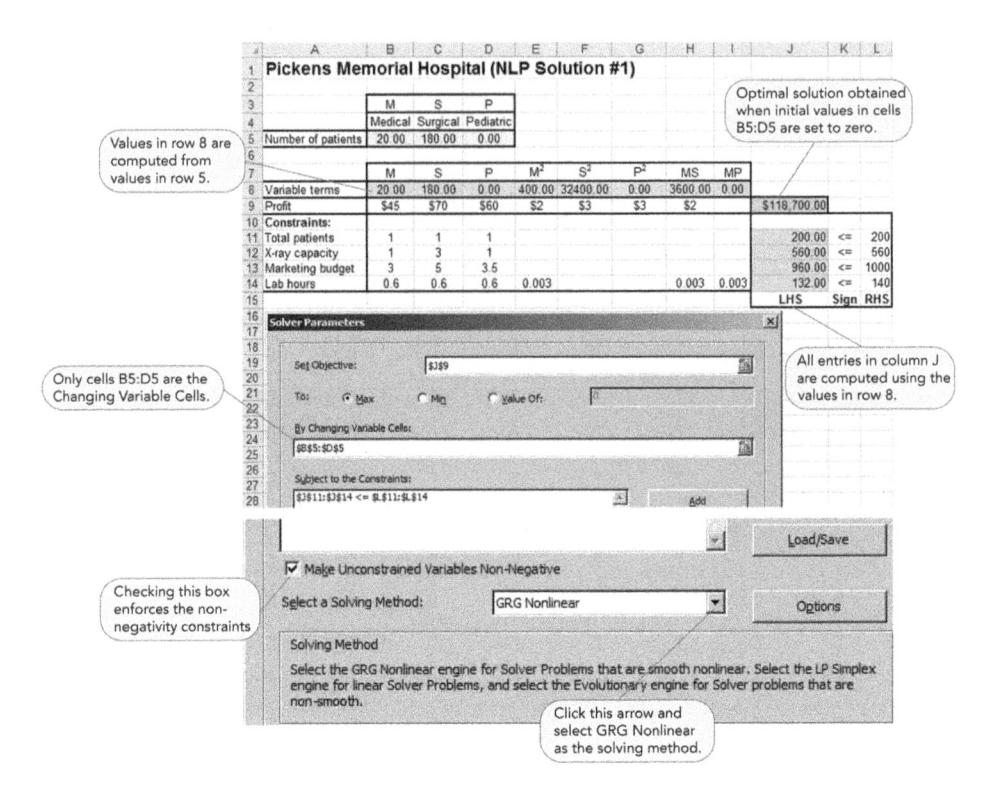

Figure 6.17: Excel Layout and Solver Entries for Pickens Memorial—NLP Solution 1

File: Figure 6.16.xlsx, Sheet: Figure 6.17

Figure 6.18: Excel Layout and Solver Entries for Pickens Memorial—NLP Solution 2

Because this profit is higher than the $118,700 profit shown in Figure 6.17, it is clear that the earlier solution is only a local optimal solution. We can of course manually experiment with other starting values for the decision variables to see if we can get a solution better than $132,000. Solver, however, has an option to automatically try different starting points. We should note, though, that while this approach will identify the best solution from a range of possible local optimal solutions, it does not guarantee that it will find the global optimal solution. In fact, as we will see later, when we use this approach, Solver will explicitly include the message "Solver converged in probability to a global solution" rather than say it found a global optimal solution (as it does when we use the Simplex LP method).

Solver Options for NLP Models We click the Options button in Solver and select the GRG Nonlinear tab to get the window shown in Figure 6.19. We focus our attention primarily on the box labeled Multistart. To get Solver to automatically try different starting values for the decision variables, we check not only the box labeled Use Multistart but also the box labeled Require Bounds on Variables. What are the bounds on the decision variables? Clearly, the nonnegativity constraints provide a lower bound for each variable. We can easily specify upper bounds for each decision variable by adding them as constraints in Solver. The likelihood of finding a global solution increases as the bounds we specify on variables become tighter and the longer Solver runs. We illustrate the use of bounds on variables in Solved Problem 6–3 at the end of this chapter.

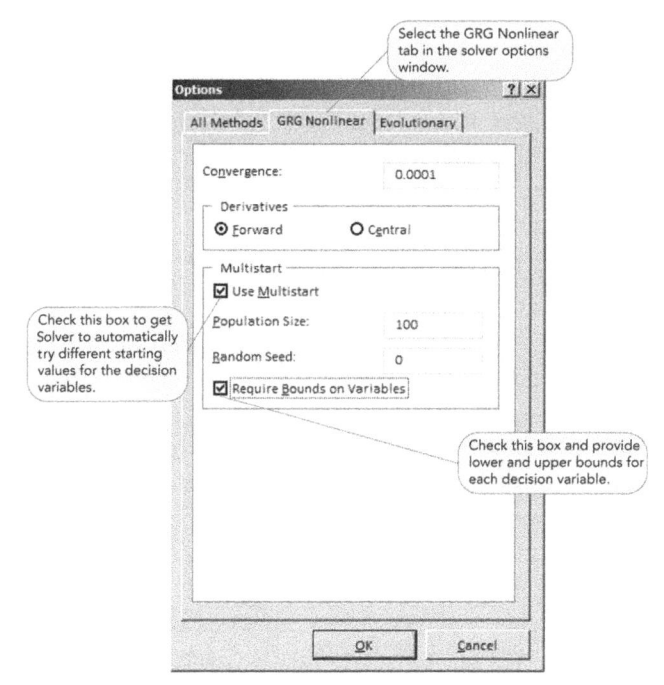

Figure 6.19: Solver Options Window for NLP Models

In the case of Pickens Memorial, it is clear that none of the variables can exceed a value of 200; therefore, we can specify this as the upper bound for all variables. If we do so and solve the model with the options specified as shown in Figure 6.19, we get the same solution shown in Figure 6.18. (We urge you to try this out yourself, using the Excel file *Figure 6.16.xlsx* on the Companion Website for this book.) It is therefore likely that this solution is, in fact, the global optimal solution. If so, perhaps Pickens Memorial should consider renaming itself the Pickens Memorial Pediatric Hospital!

Quadratic Programming Models When the only nonlinear terms in an objective function are squared terms (such as M^2) and the problem's constraints are all linear, this is a special type of NLP model called a quadratic programming (QP) model. A number of useful problems in the field of portfolio selection fall into this category. QP problems can be solved by using a modified version of the simplex method. Such work, however, is beyond the scope of this book.

Computational Procedures for Nonlinear Programming Problems
Although we have used Solver to find an optimal solution for Pickens Memorial's NLP example, there is no general method that guarantees an optimal solution for all NLP problems in a finite number of steps. As noted earlier, NLP problems are inherently more difficult to solve than LP problems.

Perhaps the best way to deal with nonlinear problems is to try to reduce them into a form that is linear or almost linear. One such approach, called *separable programming*, deals with a class of problems in which the objective and constraints are approximated by piecewise linear functions (i.e., continuous functions consisting of a set of connected straight lines with different slopes). In this way, the powerful procedures (such as the simplex algorithm) for solving LP problems can again be applied. In general, however, work in the area of NLP is the least charted and most difficult of all the decision models.

6.7 Summary

This chapter addresses three special types of LP problems. The first, integer programming, examines LP problems that cannot have fractional answers. We note that there are two types of integer variables: general integer variables, which can take on any nonnegative integer value that satisfies all the constraints in a model, and binary variables, which can take on only either of two values: 0 or 1. We illustrate how models involving both types of integer variables can be set up in Excel and solved using Solver.

The second special type of LP problem studied is goal programming. This extension of LP allows problems to have multiple objective functions, each with its own goal. We show how to model such problems using weighted goals as well as ranked goals. In either case, we use Excel's Solver to obtain optimal solutions.

Finally, we introduce the advanced topic of NLP as a special mathematical programming problem. Excel's Solver can be a useful tool in solving simple NLP models.

Key Points
- Integer Programming (IP) is an extension of LP that solves problems requiring integer solutions.
- Models with general integer variables are similar to LP models—except that variables must be integer valued.
- Rounding is one way to reach integer solution values, but it often does not yield the optimal IP solution.
- An important concept to understand is that an IP solution is usually worse in terms of higher cost or lower profit, when compared to the solution of the same LP problem.
- Although using enumeration is feasible for some small IP problems, it can be impossible for larger problems.
- The Excel layout for IP models is similar to that used for LP models.
- The general integer variable requirement is specified as an additional constraint in Solver, and it is enforced using the int option.
- Solver uses a procedure called branch-and-bound to solve IP problems.
- The branch-and-bound procedure to solve a single IP problem can involve solving multiple LP problems.
- Computer processing time and memory requirements may make it difficult to solve large IP models.
- The maximum time allowed in the Options box of Solver could become an issue for large IP problems.
- Reducing the tolerance (Integer Optimality (%) in the Options box of Solver) will yield a more accurate IP solution—but could take considerably more time.
- Sensitivity reports are not available for IP models.
- When a decision involves one of two choices, we utilize a special type of integer variable called a binary variable by associating a value of 1 with one of the choices and a value of 0 with the other choice.
- Two popular applications of binary models are selection and set covering.
- Binary variables can be used to write different types of constraints, such as selecting k out of n choices, avoiding incompatible selections, and enforcing dependencies.
- The binary requirement is specified as an additional constraint in Solver, and it is enforced using the bin option.
- A set-covering problem seeks to identify the optimal set of locations to cover a specified set of customers.
- In general, there is no easy way to detect the presence of alternate optimal solutions for IP models.
- Fixed-charge problems include fixed costs in addition to variable costs.
- Sunk costs are not considered in an optimization model.
- To model the opening of a new facility, a binary variable can be used to ensure that supply is available at a facility only if it is opened.

- Goal Programming (GP) is an extension of LP that permits more than one objective to be stated.
- Whereas LP optimizes, GP satisfices.
- In GP, we want to minimize deviation variables (i.e., deviations from the goals), which are the only terms in the objective function.
- Goals look similar to constraints except that goals may remain unsatisfied in the final solution.
- We must first define two deviation variables for each goal in a GP problem – one for underachieving and one for overachieving the goal.
- We then use these deviation variables to express goals as equations.
- Both deviation variables will have values of zero if a goal is fully satisfied.
- There are two common approaches to solving GP models: (1) weighted goals and (2) ranked goals.
- Weights can be used to distinguish between the importance of different goals.
- In the weighted goals approach, the problem reduces to an LP model with a single objective function.
- The weighted goals approach has two major drawbacks: (1) it only works if all goals are measured in the same units and (2) it is not always easy to assign suitable weights for the different deviation variables.
- In the ranked goals approach, lower-ranked goals are considered only after higher-ranked goals are satisfied to the extent possible.
- The ranked goals approach can handle goals that are measured in different units.
- Solving a model with ranked goals requires us to solve a series of LP models.
- Rank R_2 goals are considered after rank R_1 goals. Optimal values of rank R_1 goals are explicitly specified in the model as constraints.
- With Nonlinear Programming (NLP), the objective function and/or one or more constraints can be nonlinear.
- The optimal solution to an NLP model need not be at a corner point of the feasible region.
- An NLP model can have both local and global optimal solutions.
- There is no precise way to know where to start the solution search process for an NLP model.
- GRG Nonlinear must be selected as the solving method in Solver for an NLP model.
- It is usually a good idea to try different starting solutions for NLP models.
- We can use the Multistart option in Solver to automatically try different starting values for the decision variables in an NLP problem.
- Quadratic programming contains squared terms in the objective function.
- We cannot always find a global optimal solution to an NLP problem.

Glossary

Binary Variables Decision variables that are required to have integer values of either 0 or 1. Also called *0–1 variables*.

Branch-and-Bound (B&B) Method An algorithm used by Solver and other software to solve IP problems. It divides the set of feasible solutions into subregions that are examined systematically.

Deviation Variables Terms that are minimized in a goal programming problem. They are the only terms in the objective function.

Fixed-Charge Problem A problem in which there is a fixed cost in addition to variable costs. Fixed costs need to be modeled using binary (or 0–1) variables.

General Integer Variables Decision variables that are required to be integer valued. Actual values of these variables are restricted only by the constraints in the problem.

Generalized Reduced Gradient (GRG) Procedure A procedure used by Solver to solve NLP problems.

Goal Programming (GP) A mathematical programming technique that permits decision makers to set and rank multiple objective functions.

Integer Programming (IP) A mathematical programming technique that produces integer solutions to LP problems.

Mixed Integer Programming A category of problems in which some decision variables must have integer values (either general integer or binary) and other decision variables can have fractional values.

Nonlinear Programming (NLP) A category of mathematical programming techniques that allow the objective function and/or constraints to be nonlinear.

Quadratic Programming (QP) An NLP model in which the objective function includes only quadratic nonlinear terms and the constraints are all linear.

Ranked Goals An approach in which a decision maker ranks goals based on their relative importance to the decision maker. Lower-ranked goals are considered only after higher-ranked goals have been optimized. Also known as *prioritized goals*.

Satisfice To come as close as possible to reaching a set of objectives.

Weighted Goals An approach in which the decision maker assigns weights to deviation variables based on their relative importance to the decision maker.

6.8 Exercises

Solved Problems

Solved Problem 6–1 Consider the 0–1 integer programming problem that follows:

$$\text{Maximize profit} = 50X_1 + 45X_2 + 48X_3$$

subject to the constraints

$$19X_1 + 27X_2 + 34X_3 \leq 80$$
$$22X_1 + 13X_2 + 12X_3 \leq 40$$
$$X_1, X_2, X_3 = 0 \text{ or } 1$$

Now reformulate this problem with additional constraints so that no more than two of the three variables can take on a value equal to 1 in the solution. Further, make sure that if $X_1 = 1$, then $X_2 = 1$ also, and vice versa. Then solve the new problem using Excel.

Solution We need two new constraints to handle the reformulated problem:

$$X_1 + X_2 + X_3 \leq 2$$

and

$$X_1 - X_2 = 0$$

The Excel layout and Solver entries for this problem are shown in Figure 6.20. The optimal solution is $X_1 = 1$, $X_2 = 1$, $X_3 = 0$, with an objective value of 95.

	A	B	C	D	E	F	G
1	Solved Problem 6-1 (Binary)						
2							
3		X_1	X_2	X_3			
4	Solution value	1	1	0			
5	Objective coeff	50	45	48	95		
6	Constraints:						
7	Constraint 1	19	27	34	46	<=	80
8	Constraint 2	22	13	12	35	<=	40
9	Constraint 3	1	1	1	2	<=	2
10	Constraint 4	1	-1		0	=	0
11					LHS	Sign	RHS

Solver Parameters

Set Objective: $E$5

To: ● Max ○ Min ○ Value Of:

By Changing Variable Cells:
$B$4:$D$4

Subject to the Constraints:
$B$4:$D$4 = binary
$E$10 = $G$10
$E$7:$E$9 <= $G$7:$G$9

(If $X_1 = 1$, then $X_2 = 1$.)

(Select at most 2 of the 3 variables.)

(All decision variables are binary.)

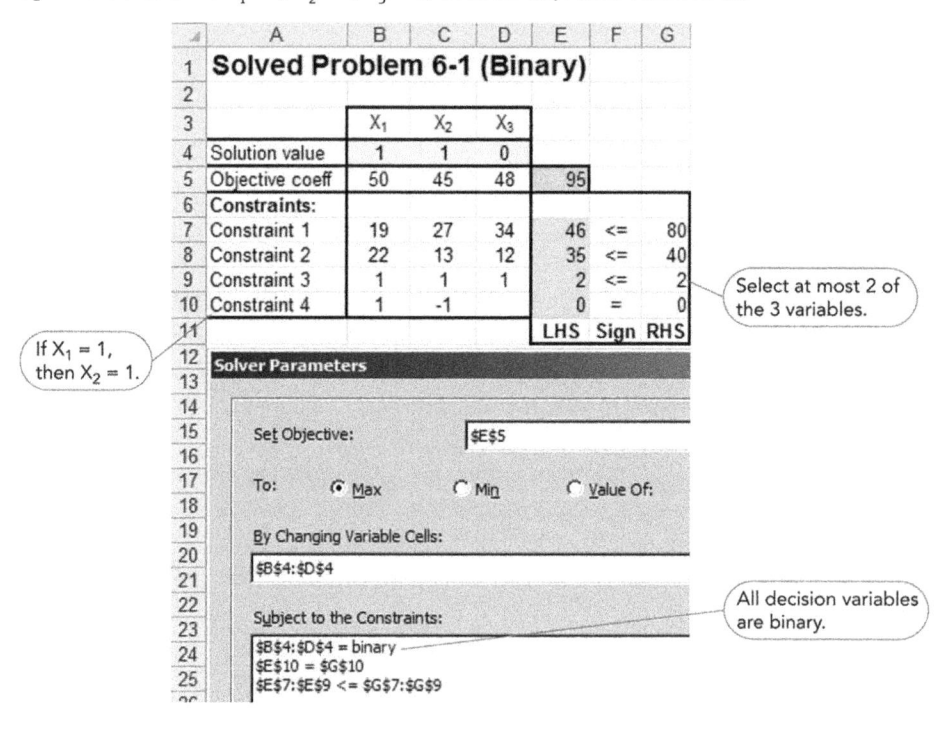

Figure 6.20: Excel Layout and Solver Entries for Solved Problem 6–1

X File: Figure 6.20.xlsx

Solved Problem 6-2 Recall the Harrison Electric Company general IP problem discussed in section 6.2. Its IP model is

Maximize profit = $600L + $700F

subject to the constraints

$$2L + 3F \leq 12 \quad \text{(wiring hours)}$$
$$6L + 5F \leq 30 \quad \text{(assembly hours)}$$
$$L, F \geq 0, \text{and integer}$$

where L = number of lamps produced and F = number of ceiling fans produced.

Reformulate and solve Harrison Electric's problem as a GP model, with the following goals in rank order. (Note that more than one goal has been assigned the same rank.) Remember that both L and F need to be integer valued.

Rank R_1: Produce at least 4 lamps (goal 1) and 3 ceiling fans (goal 2).
Rank R_2: Limit overtime in the assembly department to 10 hours (goal 3) and in the wiring department to 6 hours (goal 4).
Rank R_3: Maximize profit (goal 5).

Solution Let's define d_i^- and d_i^+ as the underachievement and overachievement deviation variables, respectively, for the ith goal. Then, the GP model can be formulated as follows:

$$\text{Minimize} = R_1(d_1^- + d_2^-) + R_2(d_3^+ + d_4^+) + R_3(d_5^-)$$

subject to the constraints

$$\left. \begin{array}{l} L + d_1^- - d_1^+ = 4 \\ F + d_2^- - d_2^+ = 3 \end{array} \right\} \text{Rank 1}$$

$$\left. \begin{array}{l} 2L + 3F + d_3^- - d_3^+ = 18 \\ 6L + 5F + d_4^- - d_4^+ = 40 \end{array} \right\} \text{Rank 2}$$

$$600L + 700F + d_5^- - d_5^+ = 99,999 \} \quad \text{Rank 3}$$

$$L, F, \text{all } d_i \geq 0$$
$$L, F \text{ integer}$$

The time availabilities in the wiring and assembly departments (rank R_2 goals) have been adjusted to include the permissible overtime. The target of $99,999 for the rank R_3 goal represents an unrealistically high profit. It is just a mathematical trick to use as a target so that we can get as close as possible to the maximum profit.

Note that for the rank R_1 goals, we need to minimize only the underachievement deviation variables d_1^- and d_2^-. Likewise, for the rank R_2 goals, we must minimize only the overachievement deviation variables d_3^+ and d_4^+. Finally, for the rank R_3 goal, we must minimize only the underachievement deviation variable d_5^-.

Figures 6.21, 6.22, and 6.23 show the Excel layout and Solver entries for this problem when each goal is considered in order of its rank. In each case, optimal values of the deviation variables for a higher-ranked goal are explicitly specified while solving the problem for a lower-ranked goal. For example, while solving the GP problem with the rank R_2 goals (Figure 6.22), the optimal values of the rank R_1 deviation variables (namely $d_1^- = 0$ and $d_2^- = 0$) from Figure 6.21 are explicitly specified in Solver.

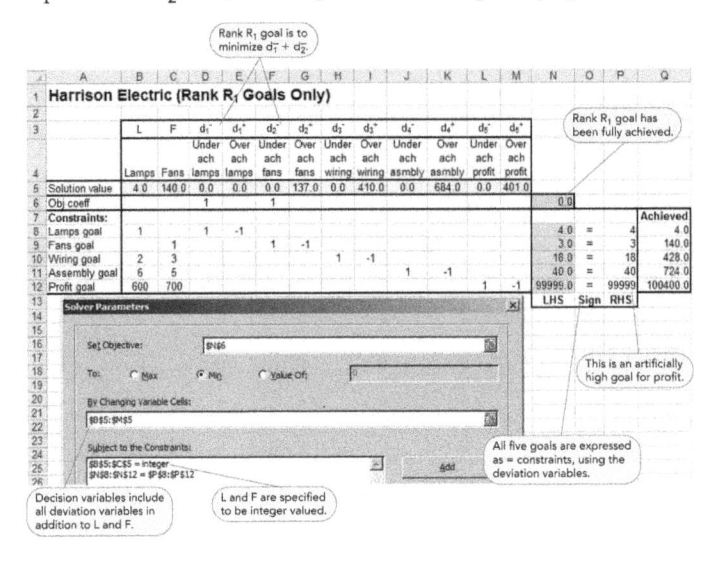

Figure 6.21: Excel Layout and Solver Entries for Harrison Electric—Rank R_1 Goals Only

File: Figure 6.21.xlsx, Sheet: Figure 6.21

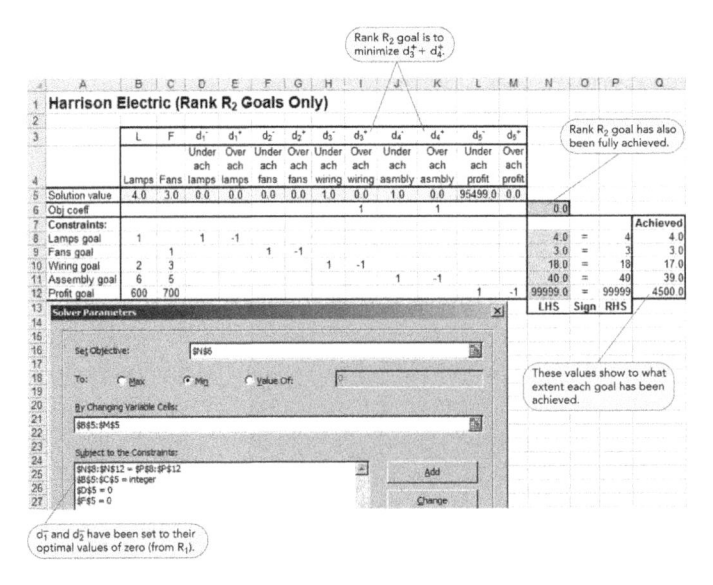

Figure 6.22: Excel Layout and Solver Entries for Harrison Electric—Rank R_2 Goals Only

File: Figure 6.21.xlsx, Sheet: Figure 6.22

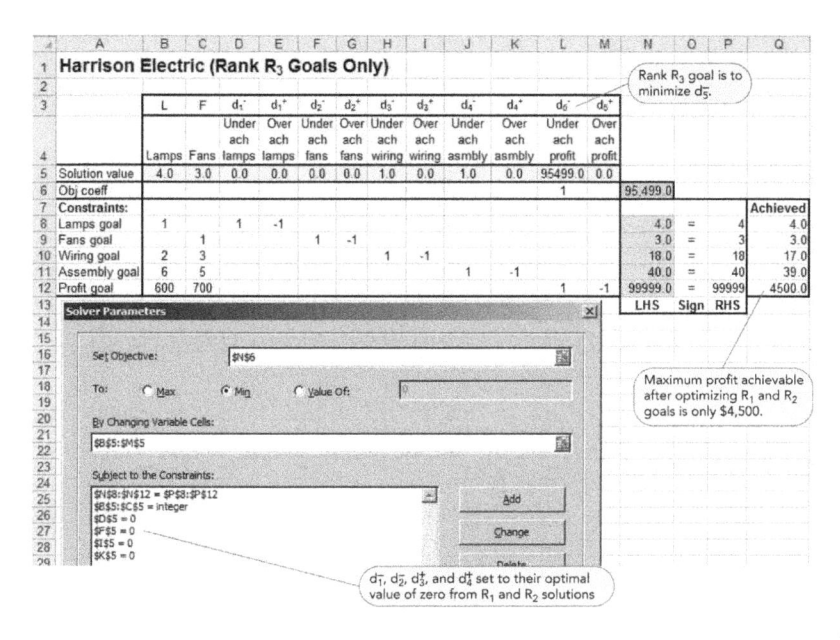

Figure 6.23: Excel Layout and Solver Entries for Harrison Electric—Rank R_3 Goals Only

X📄 File: Figure 6.21.xlsx, Sheet: Figure 6.23

The optimal solution shown in Figure 6.21 considers only the rank R_1 goals. Therefore, restricting overtime in assembly and wiring is not an issue in this problem. The solution, therefore, uses a large amount of overtime (note the values for d_3^+ and d_4^+ in Figure 6.21).

However, when we now solve the rank R_2 GP problem in Figure 6.22, the solution minimizes the use of excessive overtime. As a consequence, the deviation variable for underachieving profit (d_5^-) now has a large value (due to the artificially large value of $99,999 we used as the target for profit).

When we now try to minimize this deviation variable in the rank R_3 GP problem (Figure 6.23), we obtain the overall optimal solution for this GP problem. The optimal solution is $L = 4, F = 3, d_1^- = 0, d_2^- = 0, d_3^+ = 0$, and $d_4^+ = 0$, and $d_5^- = 95,499$. In effect, this means that the maximum profit we can get while achieving our higher-ranked goals is only $4,500 (= $600 × 4 + $700 × 3).

Solved Problem 6-3 Thermolock Corporation produces massive rubber washers and gaskets like the type used to seal joints on the NASA space shuttles. To do so, it combines two ingredients, rubber and oil. The cost of the industrial-quality rubber used is $5 per pound, and the cost of the high-viscosity oil is $7 per pound. Two of the three constraints Thermolock faces are nonlinear. If R and O denote the number of pounds used of rubber and oil, respectively, the firm's objective function and constraints can be written as follows:

Minimize cost = $5R + $7O

subject to the constraints

$$3R + 0.25R^2 + 4O + 0.3O^2 \geq 125 \quad \text{(hardness constraint)}$$
$$13R + R^3 \geq 80 \quad \text{(tensile strength constraint)}$$
$$0.7R + O \geq 17 \quad \text{(elasticity constraint)}$$
$$R, O \geq 0$$

Set up and solve Thermolock's NLP model using Solver.

Solution The Excel layout and Solver entries for Thermolock's problem are shown in Figure 6.24. As in the Pickens Memorial NLP example, the only decision variables (i.e., changing variable cells) are in cells B5 and C5. The entries in row 8 (cells B8:F8) represent all linear and nonlinear terms involving these decision variables. The formulas for these cells are

= B5	(entry for R in cell B8)
= C5	(entry for O in cell C8)
= B5^2	(entry for R^2 in cell D8)
= C5^2	(entry for O^2 in cell E8)
= B5^3	(entry for R^3 in cell F8)

Let's use the Multistart option available in the GRG Nonlinear method in Solver to solve this NLP model. Recall that for NLP models, we should select GRG Nonlinear as the solving method to use.

We then click the Options button in Solver and check the boxes labeled Use Multistart and Require Bounds on Variables in the GRG Nonlinear tab (refer to Figure 6.19). As noted previously, the nonnegativity constraints provide lower bounds for the variables. In Thermolock's case, we have specified a value of 50 as an upper bound for each of the two decision variables. When we now solve the model, we get the result shown in Figure 6.24, which specifies that Thermolock should use 3.325 pounds of rubber and 14.672 pounds of oil, at a total cost of $119.33.

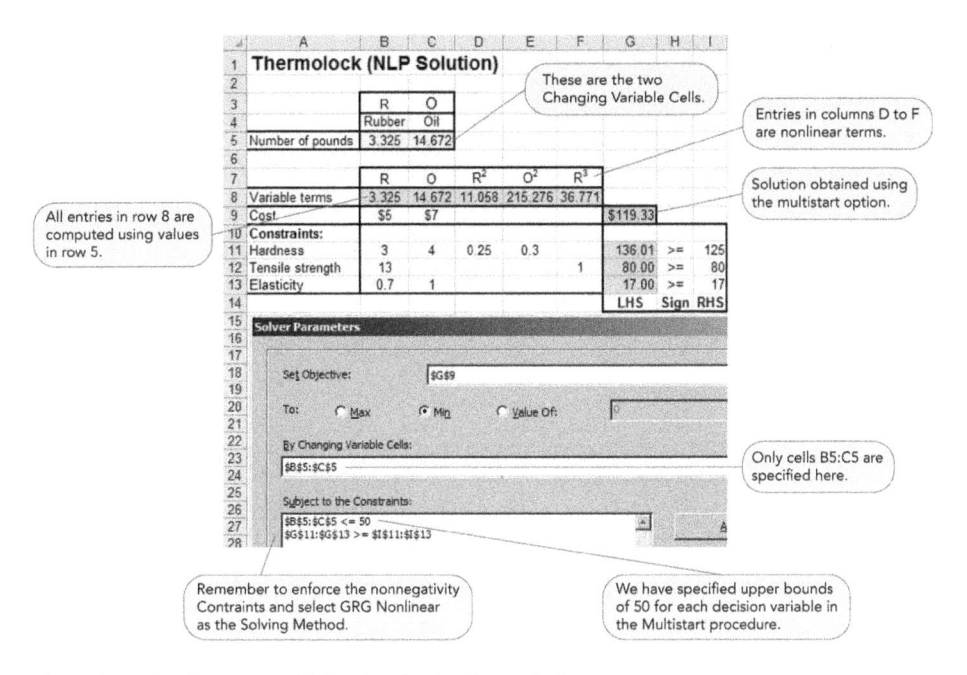

Figure 6.24: Excel Layout and Solver Entries for Thermolock

File: Figure 6.24.xlsx, Sheet: Figure 6.24

Here again, we ask whether this is a local or global optimal solution. Since we have used Solver to automatically try different starting values for the decision variables (within the bounds we have specified), it is probable, although not guaranteed, that this is a global optimal solution. As shown in Figure 6.25, Solver makes this fact clear in its message in the Solver Results window. By the way, to verify that other local optimal solutions are possible, we urge you to use the Excel file *Figure 6.24.xlsx* on the Companion Website for this book and experiment with different starting values for R and O. For example, when we start with values of 5 each for R and O, the final result (included in the Excel file *Figure 6.24.xlsx, Sheet: Figure 6.24 Alt* on the Companion Website of this book) obtained by Solver is to use 10 pounds each of rubber and oil, at a total cost of $120. Because this cost is higher than the $119.33 cost in the earlier solution (Figure 6.24), it is clear that this solution is a local optimal solution.

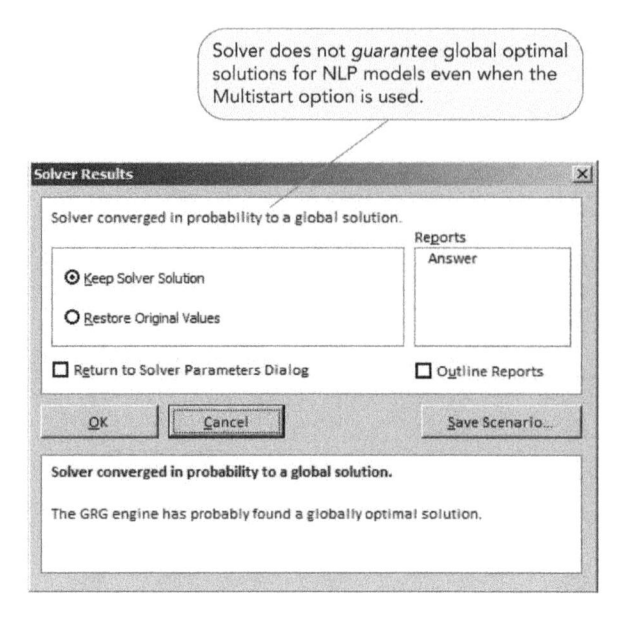

Figure 6.25: Solver Results Window When Using the Multistart Option for NLP Models

Discussion Questions

6–1. Compare the similarities and differences between LP and GP.
6–2. Provide your own examples of five applications of IP.
6–3. What is the difference between pure and mixed IP models? Which do you think is most common, and why?
6–4. What is meant by *satisficing*, and why is the term often used in conjunction with GP?
6–5. What are deviation variables? How do they differ from decision variables in traditional LP problems?
6–6. If you were the president of a college and were employing GP to assist in decision making, what might your goals be? What kinds of constraints would you include in your model?
6–7. What does it mean to rank goals in GP? How does this affect the problem's solution?
6–8. Provide your own examples of problems where (a) the objective is nonlinear and (b) one or more constraints are nonlinear.
6–9. Explain in your own words why IP problems are more difficult to solve than LP problems.
6–10. Explain the difference between assigning weights to goals and ranking goals.
6–11. What does the term *quadratic programming* mean?
6–12. Which of the following are NLP models, and why? Are any of these quadratic programming models? Assume that all variables are nonnegative in all problems.

(a) Maximize profit $= 3X_1 + 5X_2 + 99X_3$
subject to the constraints
$$X_1 \geq 10$$
$$X_2 \leq 5$$
$$X_3 \geq 18$$

(b) Maximize profit $= 25X_1 + 30X_2 + 8X_1X_2$
subject to the constraints
$$X_1 \geq 8$$
$$X_1 + X_2 \geq 12$$
$$X_1 - X_2 = 11$$

(c) Maximize profit $= 3X_1 + 4X_2$
subject to the constraints
$$X_1^2 - 5X_2 \geq 8$$
$$3X_1 + 4X_2 \geq 12$$

(d) Maximize profit $= 18X_1 + 5X_2 + X_2^2$
subject to the constraints
$$4X_1 - 3X_2 \geq 8$$
$$X_1 + X_2 \geq 18$$

Problems

6–13. A cleaning crew currently spends 6 hours per house cleaning eight houses every day, for a profit of $15 per hour. The crew now wants to offer its services to other houses, as well as small professional offices. The crew believes it will take 7 hours to clean the office of a lawyer and that the profit for doing so will be $19 per hour. It will take 10 hours to clean a doctor's office, and the profit for doing so will be $25 per hour. The crew can make 120 hours of labor available per day and does not want to cancel any of its existing house contracts. What is the best mix of homes and offices to clean per day to maximize profit? Remember that your solution must be in whole numbers.

6–14. An airline is preparing to replace its old planes with three new styles of jets. The airline needs 17 new planes to service its current routes. The decision regarding which planes to purchase should balance cost with capability factors, including the following: (1) The airline can finance up to $700 million in purchases; (2) each 7A7 jet will cost $38 million, each 7B7 jet will cost $27 million, and each 7C7 jet will cost $22 million; (3) at least one-third of the planes purchased should be the longer-range 7A7; (4) the annual maintenance budget is to be no more than $12 million; (5) the annual maintenance cost per 7A7 is estimated to be $800,000, $600,000 for each 7B7, and $500,000 for each 7C7; and (6) annually, each 7A7 can carry 125,000 passengers, each 7B7 can fly 95,000 passengers, and each 7C7 can fly 80,000 passengers. Formulate this as an IP problem to maximize the annual passenger-carrying capability. Solve it by using Excel.

6–15. The Gaubert Marketing Company needs the following number of telemarketers on the phones during the upcoming week: Monday 23, Tuesday 16, Wednesday 21, Thursday 17, Friday 20, Saturday 12, and Sunday 15. Each employee works five consecutive days followed by 2 days off per week. How many telemarketers should be scheduled each day of the week to begin their five-day work week? The objective is to minimize the total number of employees needed to fulfill the daily requirements.
(a) Solve as an IP model.
(b) Additional information is now available for Gaubert. Daily pay from Monday through Friday is $90, pay for Saturday is $110, and Sunday workers earn $125. In addition, up to four people can be hired who will work Friday, Saturday, and Sunday. Their pay for this three-day week is $250. The new objective is to minimize total weekly labor costs. Revise the IP model and solve it.

6–16. A hospital is planning an $8 million addition to its existing facility. The architect has been asked to consider the following design parameters: (1) There should be at least 10 and no more than 20 intensive care unit (ICU) rooms; (2) there should be at least 10 and no more than 20 cardiac care unit (CCU) rooms; (3) there should be no more than 50 double rooms; (4) there should be at least 35 single rooms; and (5) all patient rooms should fit inside the allotted 40,000-square-foot space (not including hallways). The following table summarizes the relevant room data:

	Single	Double	ICU	CCU
Cost per room to build and furnish ($ thousands)	$45	$54	$110	$104
Minimum square feet required	300	360	320	340
Profit per room per month ($ thousands)	$21	$28	$48	$41

How many rooms of each type should the architect include in the new hospital design?

6–17. A vending machine is programmed to count out the correct change for each transaction. Formulate and solve an IP model that will determine how change is to be made for a purchase of $4.43 when a $10 bill is inserted into the machine. The model's solution should be based on the availability of coins in the machine, with the objective of minimizing the total number of coins used to make the change.

Denomination	Availability
$1 coin	8
Quarter ($0.25)	9
Dime ($0.10)	7
Nickel ($0.05)	11
Penny ($0.01)	10

6–18. Stockbroker Susan Drexler has advised her client as shown in the following table.

Investment	Cost (thousands)	Expected Return (thousands)
Andover municipal bonds	$ 400	$ 35
Hamilton city bonds	$1,000	$100
East Power & Light Co.	$ 350	$ 30
Nebraska Electric Service	$ 700	$ 65
Southern Gas and Electric	$ 490	$ 45
Manuel Products Co.	$ 270	$ 20
Builders Paint Co.	$ 800	$ 90
Rest Easy Hotels Co.	$ 500	$ 50

The client agrees to this list but provides several conditions: (1) No more than $3,000,000 can be invested, (2) the money is to be spread among at least five investments, (3) no more than one type of bond can be purchased, (4) at least two utility stocks must be purchased, and (5) at least two regular stocks must be purchased. Formulate this as a 0–1 IP problem for Ms. Drexler to maximize expected return. Solve it by using Excel.

6–19. Porter Investments needs to develop an investment portfolio for Mrs. Singh from the following list of possible investments.

Investment	Cost	Expected Return
A	$ 10,000	$ 700
B	$ 12,000	$ 1,000
C	$ 3,500	$ 390
D	$ 5,000	$ 500
E	$ 8,500	$ 750
F	$ 8,000	$ 640
G	$ 4,000	$ 300

Mrs. Singh has a total of $60,000 to invest. The following conditions must be met: (1) If investment F is chosen, then investment G must also be part of the portfolio, (2) at least four investments should be chosen, and (3) of investment A and B, exactly one must be included. What stocks should be included in Mrs. Singh's portfolio?

6-20. A truck with the capacity to load 2,200 cubic feet of cargo is available to transport items selected from the following table.

Item	Value	Volume (cu. ft.)
A	$1,800	700
B	$1,400	600
C	$1,100	450
D	$ 900	400
E	$1,600	650
F	$1,100	350
G	$1,200	600

If selected, an item must be shipped in its entirety (i.e., partial shipments are not allowed). Of items B, C, and D, at least two items must be selected. If item B is selected, then item G cannot be selected. Which items should be selected to maximize the value of the shipment?

6-21. The Greenville Ride have $19 million available to sign free-agent pitchers for the next season. The following table provides the relevant information for eight pitchers who are available for signing, such as whether each throws right or left handed, whether each is a starter or reliever, the cost in millions of dollars to sign each, and the relative value of each on the market on a scale of 1 to 10 (10 = highest).

Pitcher	Throws	Start/Relief	Cost (millions)	Value
A	L	R	$9	8
B	R	S	$4	5
C	R	S	$5	6
D	L	S	$5	5
E	R	R	$6	8
F	R	R	$3	5
G	L	S	$8	7
H	R	S	$2	4

The Ride feel that the following needs exist for next season: (1) at least two right-handed pitchers, (2) at least one left-handed pitcher, (3) at least two starters, and (4) at least one right-handed reliever. Who should the Ride try to sign, if their objective is to maximize total value?

6-22. Allied Products has six R&D projects that are potential candidates for selection during the upcoming fiscal year. The table for this problem provides the expected net present value (NPV) and capital requirements over the next five years for each project.

The table also indicates the planned budget expenditures for the entire R&D program during each of the next five years. Which projects should be selected?

Project	NPV (thousands)	Capital Required (thousands)				
		Year 1	Year 2	Year 3	Year 4	Year 5
1	$140	$ 80	$25	$22	$18	$10
2	$260	$ 95	$40	$ 5	$10	$35
3	$ 88	$ 58	$17	$14	$12	$12
4	$124	$ 32	$24	$10	$ 6	$ 7
5	$176	$115	$25	$25	$10	$ 0
6	$192	$ 48	$20	$12	$32	$40
R&D Budget		$225	$80	$60	$50	$50

6–23. I-Go Airlines has operations in eight cities throughout the United States. It is searching for the best location(s) to designate as a hub, which would then serve other cities within a 1,400-mile radius. For economic reasons, I-Go would like to operate no more hubs than necessary to cover all eight cities. Which of the cities in the table for this problem should be designated as hubs?

	Atlanta	Boston	Chicago	Dallas	Denver	LA	Philadelphia	Seattle
Atlanta	—	1,108	717	783	1,406	2,366	778	2,699
Boston		—	996	1,794	1,990	3,017	333	3,105
Chicago			—	937	1,023	2,047	767	2,108
Dallas				—	794	1,450	1,459	2,112
Denver					—	1,026	1,759	1,313
Los Angeles						—	2,723	1,141
Philadelphia							—	2,872

6–24. Laurens County has six communities that need to be served by fire stations. The number of minutes it takes to travel between the communities is shown in the following table. The county would like to establish the minimum number of fire stations so that each community can get a response in five minutes or less. How many stations will be needed, and what communities will each station serve?

	A	B	C	D	E	F
A	—	4	6	3	5	8
B		—	4	10	6	5
C			—	9	3	5
D				—	6	3
E					—	10

6–25. Georgia Atlantic Corporation needs to decide on the locations for two new warehouses. The candidate sites are Philadelphia, Tampa, Denver, and Chicago. The following table provides the monthly capacities and the monthly fixed costs for operating warehouses at each potential site.

Warehouse	Monthly Capacity (units)	Monthly Fixed Cost
Philadelphia	250	$1,000
Tampa	260	$ 800
Chicago	280	$1,200
Denver	270	$ 700

The warehouses will need to ship to three marketing areas: North, South, and West. Monthly requirements are 200 units for North, 180 for South, and 120 for West. The following table provides the cost to ship one unit between each location and destination.

Warehouse	North	South	West
Philadelphia	$4	$ 7	$ 9
Tampa	$6	$ 3	$11
Chicago	$5	$ 6	$ 5
Denver	$8	$10	$ 2

In addition, the following conditions must be met by the final decision: (1) A warehouse must be opened in either Philadelphia or Denver, and (2) if a warehouse is opened in Tampa, then one must also be opened in Chicago. Which two sites should be selected for the new warehouses to minimize total fixed and shipping costs?

6–26. A manufacturer has acquired four small assembly plants, located in Charlotte, Tulsa, Memphis, and Buffalo. The plan is to remodel and keep two of the plants, while closing the other two. The table for this problem provides the anticipated monthly capacities and the monthly fixed costs for operating plants at each potential site. It is estimated that the costs to remodel and/or close the plants are equivalent.

	Charlotte	Tulsa	Memphis	Buffalo
Monthly capacity (units)	7,000	6,500	7,250	7,500
Monthly fixed cost ($)	$30,000	$35,000	$34,000	$32,000
Shipping to Region 1 ($/unit)	$5	$8	$3	$2
Shipping to Region 2 ($/unit)	$4	$5	$3	$9
Shipping to Region 3 ($/unit)	$5	$3	$4	$10

	Region 1	Region 2	Region 3
Monthly demand (units)	3,000	4,000	6,500

Because of union considerations, if the plant in Buffalo is kept open, the plant in Tulsa must also be kept open. If the objective is to minimize total fixed and shipping costs, which two sites should be selected to continue assembly?

6–27. A hospital in a large city plans to build two satellite trauma centers to provide improved emergency service to areas, such as highways and high-crime districts, that have historically demonstrated an increased need for critical care services. The city council has identified four potential locations for these centers. The table for this problem shows the locations (1–4), and the mileage from each center to each of the eight high-need areas (A–H).

	A	B	C	D	E	F	G	H
1	25	5	55	5	35	15	65	45
2	5	25	15	35	25	45	35	55
3	25	55	5	35	35	75	5	35
4	35	15	25	5	55	35	45	25

Assume that the cost of building the trauma centers will be the same, regardless of which locations are chosen.
(a) Which two locations will minimize the total mileage from the trauma centers to the high-need areas? Which locations should be designated to receive injured persons from each of the high-need locations?
(b) Now solve this as a set-covering model, assuming that the hospital wants to keep the distance between a high-need location and a trauma center to no more than 35 miles.

6–28. The Columbia Furniture Mart manufactures desks, tables, and chairs. In order to manufacture these products, Columbia must rent the appropriate equipment at a weekly cost of $2,000 for desks, $2,500 for tables, and $1,500 for chairs. The labor and material requirements for each product are shown in the following table, along with the selling price and variable cost to manufacture.

	Labor Hours	Lumber (sq. ft.)	Sales Price	Variable Cost
Desks	4	12	$135	$97
Tables	3	8	$110	$82
Chairs	2	6	$ 50	$32

There are 2,500 labor hours and 8,000 square feet of lumber available each week. Determine the product mix that maximizes weekly profit.

6–29. Rollins Publishing needs to decide what textbooks from the table for this problem to publish.

	Demand	Fixed Cost	Variable Cost	Selling Price
Book 1	9,000	$12,000	$19	$40
Book 2	8,000	$21,000	$28	$60
Book 3	5,000	$15,000	$30	$52
Book 4	6,000	$10,000	$20	$34
Book 5	7,000	$18,000	$20	$45

For each book, the maximum demand, fixed cost of publishing, variable cost, and selling price are provided. Rollins has the capacity to publish a total of

20,000 books. Which books should be selected, and how many of each should be published?

6–30. Sandy Edge is president of Edge File Works, a firm that manufactures two types of metal file cabinets. Demand for the two-drawer model is 650 cabinets per week; demand for the three-drawer cabinet is 400 per week. Edge has a weekly operating capacity of 1,600 hours, with the two-drawer cabinet taking 1.5 hours to produce and the three-drawer cabinet requiring 2 hours. Each two-drawer model sold yields a $12 profit, and the profit for the three-drawer model is $14. Edge has listed the following goals, in rank order:

Rank 1: Attain a profit as close as possible to $12,000 each week.
Rank 2: Avoid underutilization of the firm's production capacity.
Rank 3: Sell as many two- and three-drawer cabinets as demand indicates.

Set up and solve this problem as a goal programming model.

6–31. Eric Weiss, marketing director at Charter Power and Light, is about to begin an advertising campaign promoting energy conservation. Each TV ad costs $10,000, while each newspaper ad costs $4,000. Weiss has set the following goals, in rank order:

Rank 1: The total advertising budget of $240,000 should not be exceeded.
Rank 2: There should be at least 10 TV ads and at least 20 newspaper ads.
Rank 3: The total number of people reached by the ads should be at least 9 million.

Each television spot reaches approximately 300,000 people. A newspaper advertisement is read by about 150,000 people. Set up and solve this goal programming problem to find out how many of each type of ad Weiss should place.

6–32. Consider the staffing situation faced by the Gaubert Marketing Company in Problem 6–15. Ignore the salary and part-time information given in part (b) of that problem. Develop a schedule that meets the daily employee requirements and satisfices the following three weighted goals:

Goal 1: Use at most 27 total employees; weight = 50.
Goal 2: Minimize the excess employees scheduled on Saturday; weight = 30.
Goal 3: Minimize the excess employees scheduled on Sunday weight = 20.

6–33. White & Becker Tools (W&B) requires 2,000 electric motors next month for its product line of weed trimmers. Each motor is composed of three components: a coil, a shaft, and housing. W&B has the capability to produce these components or purchase them from an outside vendor. The costs of producing them and purchasing them are shown in the following table.

Component	Production Cost per Unit	Purchase Cost per Unit
Coil	$2.60	$3.12
Shaft	$1.80	$2.16
Housing	$1.40	$1.68

The components that are produced by W&B must pass through three departments: fabrication, molding, and inspection. The number of hours each component requires in each department and the total number of hours available next month in each department are shown in the following table.

Department	Coil (hr.)	Shaft (hr.)	Housing (hr.)	Availability (hr.)
Fabrication	0.5	0.2	0.6	3,000
Molding	0.4	0.7	0.3	3,000
Inspection	0.2	0.3	0.4	1,800

In order to determine the number of components that will be produced and the number that will be purchased, W&B has set the following goals, in rank order:

Rank 1: The total costs to produce and purchase components next month should not exceed $14,000.
Rank 2: Idle time in the fabrication department should be minimized.
Rank 3: At least 200 coils should be purchased from the vendor next month.

Determine the number of components produced and purchased next month, according to these ranked goals.

6-34. Pendelton County plans to develop several new recreational facilities that must be completed within the $3.5 million budget. A survey of county residents has resulted in information about the types of facilities that county residents would like to see built, as described in the following table. The table also shows the cost to construct and maintain each facility, the acres each facility will require, and the average monthly usage of each facility. The county has decided that at least 15 facilities will be built and has set aside 55 acres to be used for construction.

Facility	Cost per Facility	Acres per Facility	People per Month	Annual Maintenance
Basketball courts	$300,000	3	700	$3,000
Baseball fields	$250,000	5	1,000	$6,000
Playgrounds	$ 75,000	2	800	$3,000
Soccer fields	$175,000	3	1,200	$7,000

The county has also established the following list of ranked goals:

Rank 1: It would like to spend the entire budget.
Rank 2: It would like to build enough facilities so that 15,000 people or more each month can use them.
Rank 3: It wants to avoid using more than the 55 acres that have been set aside for the project.

Rank 4: It would like to avoid spending more than $80,000 per year on maintenance costs for the new facilities.

How many of each type of facility should be constructed?

6-35. Theo Harris earns $55,000 a year and has $9,000 to invest in a portfolio. His investment alternatives and their expected returns are shown in the following table.

Investment	Description	Expected Return
A	IRA (retirement)	3.5%
B	Employer's retirement plan	4.5%
C	Deferred income (retirement)	8.0%
D	Unity mutual fund	7.0%
E	Liberty mutual fund	7.5%
F	Money market	5.5%

Theo's investment goals are as follows and can be ranked according to the weights shown in parentheses. Which investments should be included in Theo's portfolio, and how much should he invest in each?

Goal 1: (25) Invest all funds available.

Goal 2: (20) Maximize the total annual return in dollars, with a target of $1,000.

Goal 3: (15) Invest at least 3% of salary in the employer's retirement plan.

Goal 4: (15) Invest at least 10% of the total investment in the money market.

Goal 5: (10) Invest at most 25% of the total investment in retirement plans.

Goal 6: (10) Invest at least 50% of the total investment in nonretirement plans.

Goal 7: (5) Invest at most 50% of the total investment in mutual funds.

6-36. A hospital kitchen needs to make a fruit salad that contains at least 6,500 units of vitamin A and 1,800 units of vitamin C. Data on five available fruits are shown in the following table.

Fruit Type	Vitamin A (units/lb.)	Vitamin C (units/lb.)	Cost per lb.	Maximum Available (lb.)
Apple	330	36	$1.49	No limit
Banana	367	41	$0.49	11
Grape	453	18	$1.69	8
Pear	91	18	$0.99	No limit
Strawberry	122	254	$2.99	14

It is estimated that at least 24 pounds, but no more than 32 pounds, of fruit salad will be necessary. The following goals (in rank order) need to be considered for the mix:

Rank 1: The salad should cost no more than $30.

Rank 2: At least 6 pounds of bananas should be in the salad.

Rank 3: At least 3 pounds of pears should be in the salad.

6–37. Consider the following NLP problem:

$$\text{Maximize } 10X_1 + 15X_2 + 25X_3$$

subject to the constraints

$$X_1 + X_2 + X_3 \leq 12$$
$$X_1^2 + X_2^2 \leq 32$$
$$2X_1 + X_3^3 \leq 44$$
$$X_1, X_2, X_3 \geq 0$$

(a) Set up and solve the model by using Solver. Use a starting value of zero for each decision variable.

(b) Is the solution that is obtained a local optimal or global optimal solution? How do you know?

6–38. Consider the following NLP problem:

$$\text{Maximize } 2X_1 + X_2 - 2X_3 + 3X_1X_2 + 7X_3^3$$

subject to the constraints

$$2X_1 + 4X_2 + 3X_3 \geq 34$$
$$3X_1 + X_2 \geq 10$$
$$X_1 + X_2 + X_3 \leq 12$$
$$X_1, X_2, X_3 \geq 0$$

(a) Set up and solve the model by using Solver. Use a starting value of zero for each decision variable.

(b) Is the solution that is obtained a local optimal or global optimal solution? How do you know?

6–39. Hinkel Rotary Engine, Ltd., produces four-, six-, and eight-cylinder models of automobile engines. The firm's profit for each four-cylinder engine sold during its quarterly production cycle is $1,800 − 50X_1$, where X_1 is the number of four-cylinder engines sold. Hinkel makes a profit of $2,400 − 70X_2$ for each of the six-cylinder engines sold, with X_2 equal to the number of six-cylinder engines sold. The profit associated with each eight-cylinder engine is $1,950 − 65X_3^2$, where X_3 is equal to the number of eight-cylinder engines sold. There are 5,000 hours of production time available during each production cycle. A four-cylinder engine requires 100 hours of production time, a six-cylinder engine takes 130 hours, and an eight-cylinder model takes 140 hours to manufacture. Formulate this production problem for Hinkel and solve it by using Excel. Use several different starting values for the decision variables to try to identify a global optimal solution.

6–40. A snowmobile manufacturer produces three models, the XJ6, the XJ7, and the XJ8. In any given production-planning week, the company has 40 hours available in its final testing bay. Each XJ6 requires 1 hour of testing, each XJ7 requires 1.5 hours, and each XJ8 takes 1.6 hours. The revenue (in $ thousands) per unit of each model is defined as ($4 − 0.1X_1$) for XJ6, ($5 − 0.2X_2$) for XJ7, and ($6 − 0.2X_3$) for XJ8, where X_1, X_2, and X_3 are the numbers of XJ6, XJ7, and XJ8 models made, respectively. Formulate this problem to maximize revenue and solve it by using Excel. Use several different starting values for the decision variables to try to identify a global optimal solution.

6–41. Susan Jones would like her investment portfolio to be selected from a combination of three stocks—Alpha, Beta, and Gamma. Let variables A, B, and G denote the percentages of the portfolio devoted to Alpha, Beta, and Gamma, respectively. Susan's objective is to minimize the variance of the portfolio's return, given by the following function:

$$3A^2 + 2B^2 + 2G^2 + 2AB - 1.1AG - 0.7BG$$

The expected returns for Alpha, Beta, and Gamma are 15%, 11%, and 9%, respectively. Susan wants the expected return for the total portfolio to be at least 10%. No individual stock can constitute more than 70% of the portfolio. Formulate this portfolio selection problem and solve using Excel. Use several different starting values for the decision variables to try to identify a global optimal solution.

6–42. Ashworth Industries would like to make a price and production decision on two of its products. Define Q_A and Q_B as the quantities of products A and B to produce and P_A and P_B as the price for products A and B. The weekly quantities of A and B that are sold are functions of the price, according to the following expressions:

$$Q_A = 5,500 - 200P_A$$
$$Q_B = 4,500 - 225P_B$$

The variable costs per unit of A and B are $18 and $12, respectively. The weekly production capacity for A and B are 275 and 350 units, respectively. Each unit of A requires 1 hour of labor, while each unit of B requires 2 hours. There are 700 hours of labor available each week. What quantities and price of products A and B will maximize weekly profit? (*Hint:* Set up the objective function in terms of profit per unit multiplied by the number of units produced for both products.) Use several different starting values for the decision variables to try to identify a global optimal solution.

6–43. The Kimten Manufacturing Company needs to process 18 jobs. Kimten can process each job on any of the six machines it has available, but each job must be allocated to only one machine. Iqbal Ahmed, production supervisor at Kimten, wants to allocate jobs to machines in such a manner that all machines have total loads that are as close as possible to each other. The machine hours required for each job are shown in the following table.

Job	Machine Hours
1	39.43
2	27.94
3	40.27
4	18.27
5	12.72
6	35.20
7	27.94
8	17.20
9	17.20
10	17.20
11	21.50
12	16.74
13	28.29
14	6.07
15	16.01
16	18.49
17	12.16
18	36.67

6-44. The "traveling salesperson problem" has a long history in operations research. A traveling salesperson must visit each of n cities exactly once, minimizing the total cost of travel and returning to the city of origin. What route should be taken? If the cities form a nice circle, the answer is obvious. However, in other cases the answer is not obvious at all, and, due to potential backtracking, it is often not best to go to the next-closest city upon leaving one. This problem applies to other decisions as well, such as vehicle routing problems and certain job scheduling problems.

We define d_{ij} as the distance (or cost) of going from city i to city j. We further define the following binary decision variables:

$$X_{ij} = \begin{cases} 1 \text{ if city } j \text{ is visited immediately following city } i \\ 0 \text{ otherwise} \end{cases}$$

At first glance, it would appear that this can be set up as an assignment model (section 5.6) because we need constraints ensuring that every city is entered exactly once and every city must be left exactly once. That's not enough, however. Formulating the traveling salesperson problem as an assignment model would not eliminate "subtours," meaning, for example, that an answer for a four-city problem might come back as $X_{12} = 1$, $X_{21} = 1$, $X_{34} = 1$, and $X_{43} = 1$, in which case there's nothing connecting cities 1 and 2 to cities 3 and 4. The ingenious answer to the subtour problem is to introduce a set of additional constraints that will eliminate any subtours. These constraints utilize regular nonnegative variables t_i, one for each city i except for city 1.

The formulation is provided below. Create a template in Excel, including all the appropriate Solver settings, that would accommodate a standard traveling salesperson problem with 5 cities. (*Note: The traveling salesperson formulation is computationally cumbersome. Adding each new city significantly increases solution time. After about 10 cities, more powerful software than Excel should probably be used.*)

$$\text{Minimize distance} = \sum_{i=1}^{n}\sum_{j=1}^{n} d_{ij} X_{ij}$$

Subject to the constraints

$$\sum_{j=1}^{n} X_{ij} = 1, \text{ for } i = 1,\ldots,n$$

$$\sum_{i=1}^{n} X_{ij} = 1, \text{ for } j = 1,\ldots,n$$

$$t_i - t_j + nX_{ij} \leq n-1, \text{ for } i,j = 2,\ldots,n \ (i \neq j)$$

$$t_i \geq 0, X_{ij} = 0 \text{ or } 1$$

6-45. A binary variable can be used to ensure that at least one out of two constraints must be satisfied, but not necessarily both. Define Y as a binary variable and incorporate it into the constraints below so that both constraints could be entered into a mixed IP model but only one of them would have to be satisfied in the optimal solution. (*Hint: Define M as a very large number and use it in both constraints.*)

$$\text{Either } 3A + 2B \leq 18$$
$$\text{or } A + 4B \leq 16$$

6-46. Binary variables can be used to provide a choice of RHS values for a constraint. For example, perhaps the amount of beer produced must fit into a 6-pack, a 12-pack, or a 24-pack. If there are T possible RHS values, introduce T binary variables Y_i, where

$$Y_i = \begin{cases} 1 \text{ if the } i^{th} \text{ RHS is activated} \\ 0 \text{ otherwise} \end{cases}$$

With that in mind, introduce two constraints that will ensure that

$$3A + 12B = 38 \text{ or } 50 \text{ or } 78 \text{ or } 90$$

6-47. The "knapsack problem" has a long history in operations research. The traditional version has a hiker getting ready to go camping, and she needs to determine which items to carry in her knapsack. Each item has a weight and a subjective value. There's a limit on the number of pounds that she can carry. Which items should she take?

The table for this problem presents potential items for the camping trip, how much they weigh, and a value for each on a scale from 1 to 10, with 10 being best. The hiker only wants to carry at most 18 pounds in her knapsack.

(*Note: The knapsack problem has number of other applications whenever there is a choice of options, each of which has a cost and a value. This includes certain portfolio selection problems such as the Simkin and Steinberg example in section 6.3 with only the investment limit constraint.*)

ITEM	WEIGHT (pounds)	VALUE
Machete	2	8
Junk food	10	7
Healthy food	12	9
Cooking equipment	6	8
Charcoal	4	6
Water	3	10
Textbook for studying	5	5
Laptop computer	3	6
Toiletries	3	5

(a) Formulate the binary program to solve this problem, and find the optimal solution using Excel. Is there anything odd about the solution? What constraint probably needs to be added?

(b) A common heuristic (or "rule-of-thumb") for knapsack-like problems is to take the ratio of value ÷ cost for each item and then place each item in the knapsack until the knapsack is full. Try that heuristic on this problem. How does it compare with the optimal solution?

6–48. A binary variable can be introduced to a mixed integer program to allow for a "threshold constraint." A threshold constraint says that if any units are used, at least a specified minimum amount must be used.

Define X as the number of students that will go on a planned field trip. The school will rent a bus only if at least 20 students plan to go on the trip. Define Y as a binary variable that equals 1 if X is nonzero, and equals 0 if X is zero (i.e., if nobody goes on the trip). If M represents a very large number, what two constraints can be added to the mixed integer program to ensure that if any students go on the field trip, at least 20 have to go?

6–49. Suppliers frequently offer quantity discounts to their customers to entice large orders. Consider the following all-units quantity discount schedule.

Units ordered	Price per unit
1–999	$50.00
1,000–4,999	$45.00
≥ 5,000	$40.00

With the help of binary variables, an all-units quantity discount schedule can be incorporated into a mixed integer program that determines order size. Let Q be a decision variable that represents the total amount purchased. Let q_i be a decision variable that represents the total amount purchased if Q lies in interval i of the price schedule. In other words, Q will equal q_1 or q_2 or q_3, depending on the quantity purchased. Also, let Y_i be a binary variable that equals 1 if Q lies in interval i of the price schedule, and 0 otherwise. For example, if 3,000 units are ordered, $Q = q_2 = 3{,}000$, and $Y_2 = 1$; meanwhile, $q_1 = q_3 = Y_1 = Y_3 = 0$.

Using these definitions, the purchasing cost in the objective function will then equal $50q_1 + 45q_2 + 40q_3$. One of the new constraints added to the program will be $Q = q_1 + q_2 + q_3$. In addition to nonnegativity and binary constraints, what additional four constraints need to be added to ensure that the correct price is charged for the amount purchased? (*Hint: Define M as a very large number, and use it in two of the new constraints.*)

6–50. Suppliers frequently offer quantity discounts to their customers to entice large orders. Consider the following incremental quantity discount schedule.

Units ordered	Price per unit
1–1,000	$50.00
1,001–5,000	$50.00 for the first 1000 units and $45.00 for units ordered between 1,001 and 5,000
≥ 5,000	$50.00 for the first 1000 units, $45.00 for the next 4,000 units, and $40.00 for any units ordered beyond 5,000

With the help of binary variables, an incremental quantity discount schedule can be incorporated into a mixed integer program that determines order size. Let Q be a decision variable that represents the total amount purchased. Let q_i be a decision variable that represents the total amount purchased within interval i of the price schedule. Thus, Q will equal $q_1 + q_2 + q_3$. Also, let Yi be a binary variable that equals 1 if Q lies in any higher interval than interval i of the price schedule (i.e., if Q would yield a lower marginal price than the price in interval i), and 0 otherwise. For example, if 5,200 units are ordered, $Q = 5{,}200$, $q_1 = 1{,}000$, $q_2 = 4{,}000$, $q_3 = 200$, $Y_1 = 1$, and $Y_2 = 1$. On the other hand, if only 3,200 units are purchased, $Q = 3{,}200$, $q_1 = 1{,}000$, $q_2 = 2{,}200$, $q_3 = 0$, $Y_1 = 1$, and $Y_2 = 0$.

Using these definitions, the purchasing cost in the objective function will then equal $50q_1 + 45q_2 + 40q_3$. One of the new constraints added to the program will be $Q = q_1 + q_2 + q_3$. In addition to nonnegativity and binary constraints, what additional four constraints need to be added to ensure that the correct price is charged for the amount purchased? (*Hint: Define M as a very large number, and use it in one of the new constraints.*)

6–51. A company is considering opening new stores in the United States. The potential new locations are contained in the following table, where each binary variable equals 1 if that location gets a new store, and 0 if not.

Location	Binary Variable	Location	Binary Variable
Pullman, WA	P	Houston, TX	H
Dearborn, MI	D	Orlando, FL	O
Tallahassee, FL	T	San Antonio, TX	S

Write out the necessary constraints to accommodate each situation described below. Consider each question independent of the others.
(a) At most one store can be opened in Florida.
(b) Exactly one store must be opened in Texas.
(c) No more than four stores can be opened.
(d) A store can be opened in Pullman only if another will be opened in Dearborn.
(e) If a store is opened in Houston, then a store must be opened in San Antonio.
(f) Either both Florida cities will have a new store, or neither will.
(g) At least three stores outside of Florida must be opened.

6–52. Indicate which of the following constraints are linear (or could be with the appropriate algebraic manipulation). In all cases, A, B, and C are continuous decision variables.
(a) $5A + B/C \leq 100$
(b) $2B \geq 63$
(c) $\dfrac{4A + 3B + 5C}{A + B + C} \geq 25$
(d) $A \leq -B$
(e) $10A - 4A2 = 2$
(f) $A + 1/B \geq 16$
(g) $\sqrt{6A} + 6B - 2C \leq 300$
(h) $4ABC = 60$

6–53. Consider the Greenberg Motors example from section 3.8. Retrieve file *Figure 3.14.xlsx, Sheet: Figure 3.14* from the Companion Website. Rerun the model (seen in Figure 3.14) by making all decision variables integer. (The solution will take a while to run, and you may need to answer "Continue" if you reach an iteration limit.) How much worse is the new cost? Did the new decision variable values round as you would have expected?

6–54. Dexter is taking 18 credit hours this semester, and he has 6 final exams on Monday. The first one starts at 8:00 a.m., and they run straight through until the last one is over at 8:00 p.m. It is 3:00 a.m. on Saturday morning and Dexter has not started studying yet. Right now, he has a C in every class. The following table gives Dexter's expected final grades if he studies the appropriate amount of time.

	Studying	
Subject	Expected Grade	Requirements
Math 202	B	6
Phil 101	B+	23
MgtOp 470	A	44
Anthro 216	B–	18
Psych 409	B+	8
Fin 416	A–	30

If Dexter does not study for a class at all, then he will get a C. No other amounts of studying will give him a different grade than the above table indicates. Dexter does not plan to sleep from now until the test begins, unless he can sleep for exactly 6 straight hours. If he does get the extra sleep, he projects that he will be able to have to study for Fin 416 only for 10 hours to get the A– (instead of studying for 30 hours). Dexter does plan to eat for a total of 2 hours and watch TV on Saturday night for a total of 1 more hour. He will devote the rest of the time to studying. Also, Dexter refuses to study more psychology unless he spends more time first studying philosophy. Furthermore, he refuses to study both anthropology and psychology. Each of these courses are three credit courses. Given his university's GPA system (i.e. A = 4.0, A– = 3.7, B+ = 3.3, B = 3.0, B– = 2.7, C+ = 2.3, C = 2.0, etc.), formulate a binary integer program to determine the courses for which Dexter should study in order to end up with the highest possible GPA. Model this in Excel's Solver to determine the solution. *(Hint: See problem 6–45 to learn how to use a binary variable to ensure that only one out of two constraints must be satisfied.)*

Chapter 7
Project Management

Have you ever been in charge of a big event? In high school, you might have been chair of the prom committee, director of the homecoming committee, or head of the graduation ceremony board. At work, you might have been the team leader for a new product introduction, facility expansion planning, or Enterprise Resource Planning implementation. As a volunteer, you might have been in charge of the annual charity fundraiser, the elementary school picnic, or the river cleanup project. And even if you have never managed people in such situations, you have certainly had your own personal projects to contend with, e.g., writing a paper, moving to a new apartment, applying to college, or selling a house. How did you schedule your activities? Did most of your projects end on time? How did you manage unexpected events? Did you complete your tasks within your budget? These are all important elements of *project management*.

Organizations manage projects all the time; hence, skilled project managers are valuable assets. A project differs from ongoing operations primarily because it has a specific, well-defined output, and the project essentially ends once that output has been attained. As such, many projects involve personnel from different departments that come together solely to complete the project, and subsequently they return to their regular activities. An employee who is a member of several project teams may at times be reporting to several "bosses." Project managers have the challenge of supervising some personnel who are not normally their direct subordinates. Project managers must be able to manage budgets, people, and schedules.

In this chapter, we primarily focus on creating and managing project schedules. If you have ever had a custom house built, you would be one of the lucky few if the house was actually finished on time. So many unexpected events can cause ripple effects throughout the schedule.

We begin by describing the three phases in project management: *planning, scheduling*, and *controlling*. Next, we illustrate how to construct project networks to visually display the various project activities and their precedence relationships. We then describe the *critical path analysis* technique, which is used to determine when the project is expected to be completed and which activities have no *slack*, i.e., which activities cannot be delayed in order to complete the project on time. Of course, a lot of things can go wrong (or right), so in most cases projected activity times may carry a lot of uncertainty. We describe how to use *PERT analysis* to incorporate uncertain activity times and make projections about the probability of completing the project within a stated time. We then present templates that can help managers monitor and control budgets and personnel needs throughout the course of the project. We end the chapter by describing how managers can *crash* their projects by shortening certain activities to ensure that a specified deadline is met. Linear programming can determine the best activities to crash.

Learning Objectives
After completing this chapter, you will be able to:
1. Understand how to plan, monitor, and control projects using PERT/CPM.
2. Determine earliest start, earliest finish, latest start, latest finish, and slack times for each activity.
3. Understand the impact of variability in activity times on the project completion time.
4. Develop resource loading charts to plan, monitor, and control the use of various resources during a project.
5. Use LP to find the least-cost solution to reduce total project time and solve these LP models using Excel's Solver.

7.1 Planning, Scheduling, and Controlling Projects

Every organization at one time or another will take on a large and complex project. For example, when Microsoft Corporation sets out to develop a major new operating system (e.g., Windows 10), a program costing hundreds of millions of dollars, and has hundreds of programmers working on millions of lines of code, immense stakes ride on delivering the project properly and on time. Likewise, whenever STX Europe AS, a leading builder of cruise and offshore vessels headquartered in Oslo, Norway, undertakes the construction of a cruise ship, this large, expensive project requires the coordination of tens of thousands of steps. Companies in almost every industry worry about how to manage similar large-scale complicated projects effectively.

Scheduling large projects is a difficult challenge for most managers, especially when the stakes are high. There are numerous press reports of firms that have incurred millions of dollars in cost overruns in their projects for various reasons; one prominent recent example is Boeing's Dreamliner project. Unnecessary delays have occurred in many projects due to poor scheduling, and companies have gone bankrupt due to poor controls. How can such problems be solved? The answers lie in a popular decision modeling approach known as project management.

Phases in Project Management
A *project* can be defined as a series of related tasks (or activities) directed toward a major well-defined output. A project can consist of thousands of specific activities, each with its own set of requirements of time, money, and other resources, such as labor, raw materials, and machinery. Regardless of the scope and nature of the project, the management of large projects involves the three phases discussed in the following sections (see Figure 7.1). Each phase addresses specific questions regarding the project.

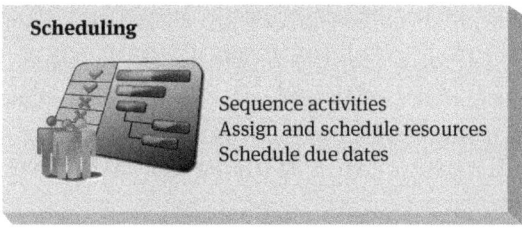

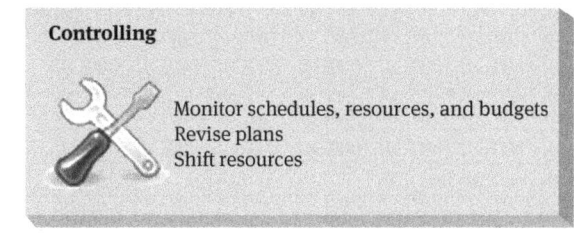

Figure 7.1: Project Planning, Scheduling, and Controlling

Project Planning   Project planning is the first phase of project management and involves considering issues such as goal setting, defining the project, and team organization. Specific questions to consider in this phase include the following:
1. What is the goal or objective of the project?
2. What are the various activities (or tasks) that constitute the project?
3. How are these activities linked? That is, what are the precedence relationships between the activities?
4. What is the time required for each activity?
5. What other resources (e.g., labor, raw materials, machinery) are required for each activity?

Project Scheduling   The second phase of project management involves developing the specific time schedule for each activity and assigning people, money, and supplies to specific activities. The questions addressed in this phase should be considered soon after the project has been planned but *before* it is actually started. These questions include the following:
1. When will the entire project be completed?

2. What is the schedule (start and finish time) for each activity?
3. What are the critical activities in the project? That is, what activities will delay the entire project if they are late?
4. What are the noncritical activities in the project? That is, what activities can run late without delaying the completion time of the entire project?
5. By how much can a noncritical activity be delayed without affecting the completion time of the entire project?
6. If we take the variability in activity times into consideration, what is the probability that a project will be completed by a specific deadline?

Managers frequently employ a Gantt chart to help them visualize project scheduling. For each activity, Gantt charts display a horizontal bar along a time line. As such, Gantt charts provide time estimates for each activity and establish a projected completion time. Gantt charts are easy to construct and understand, and they permit managers to plan and track the progress of each activity. For example, Figure 7.2 shows the Gantt chart for a school science fair project. In this example, the student performs some activities simultaneously, which allows the project to be completed quicker.

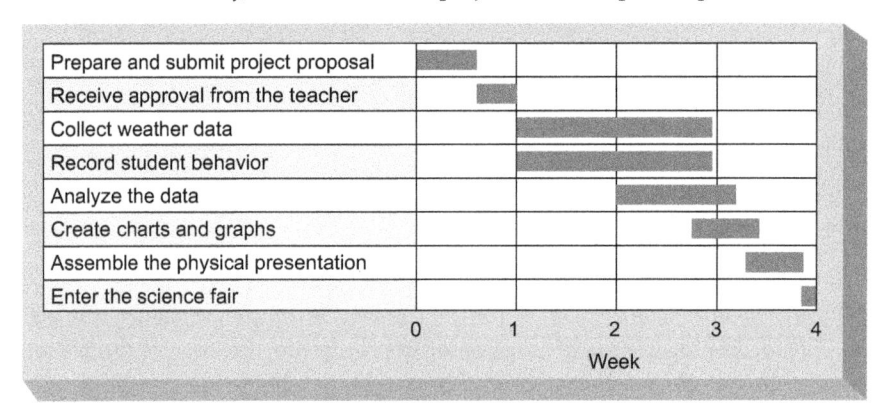

Figure 7.2: Gantt Chart of Activities for a Science Fair Project

Gantt charts such as the one in Figure 7.2 may suffice for simple projects; however, for more complicated projects they do not adequately address interrelationships between activities and resources. For this reason, on most large projects, Gantt charts are used mainly to provide summaries of a project's status. Managers generate detailed schedules using other network-based approaches, as discussed in subsequent sections.

Project Controlling The project manager's job is hardly finished once the project begins. At this point the control phase begins, where people must be properly managed, physical resources must be made available when needed, schedules must be maintained, and budgets must be tracked. Effective control helps to identify problem areas early and helps management revise plans and shift or add resources

as necessary. The questions addressed in this phase should be considered at regular intervals during the project to ensure that it meets all time and cost schedules. These questions include the following:
1. At any particular date or time, is the project on schedule, behind schedule, or ahead of schedule?
2. At any particular date or time, is the money spent on the project equal to, less than, or greater than the budgeted amount?
3. Are there enough resources available to finish the project on time?
4. What is the best way to finish the project in a shorter amount of time and at the least cost?

In this chapter, we investigate how project management techniques can be used to answer all these questions.

Use of Software Packages in Project Management
In recent times, managing large and complex projects has become considerably easier due to the availability and capabilities of specialized project management software packages. These programs typically have simple interfaces for entering the project data, and they automate many of the routine calculations required for effective project management. In addition, they are capable of efficiently presenting the status of a project, using comprehensive graphs and tables. Numerous sophisticated software programs are available on the market, including Microsoft Project, Oracle Primavera, ProChain Project Scheduling, and Turboproject.

These programs produce a broad variety of reports, including (1) detailed cost breakdowns for each task, (2) total program labor curves, (3) cost distribution tables, (4) functional cost and hour summaries, (5) raw material expenditure forecasts, (6) variance reports, (7) time analysis reports, and (8) work status reports.

Although it is possible to set up spreadsheets to perform many of the routine calculations involved, Excel is not usually the ideal choice for such tasks. Specialized software such as Microsoft Project can be better used to plan, schedule, and monitor projects.

There are, however, some issues that Microsoft Project does not handle. For example, one such issue is question 4 posed in the section "Project Controlling" (What is the best way to finish the project in a shorter amount of time and at the least cost?). We can best answer this question by setting up and solving the problem as a linear programming (LP) model. For this question, we describe using Excel's Solver to solve the LP model.

7.2 Project Networks

Once a project's mission or goal has been clearly specified, the first issues we need to address deal with *project planning*. That is, we need to identify the activities that constitute the project, the precedence relationships between those activities, and the time and other resources required for each activity.

Identifying Activities

Almost any large project can be subdivided into a series of smaller activities or tasks. Identifying the activities involved in a project and the precedence relationships that may exist between these activities is the responsibility of the project team. In subdividing a project into various activities, however, the project team must be careful to ensure the following:

- Each activity has clearly identifiable starting and ending points. In other words, we should be able to recognize when an activity has started and when it has ended. For example, if the project goal is to build a house, an activity may be to lay the foundation. It is possible to clearly recognize when we start this activity and when we finish this activity.
- Each activity is clearly distinguishable from every other activity. That is, we should be able to associate every action we take and every dollar we spend with a specific (and unique) activity. For example, while building a house, we need to be able to recognize which actions and expenses are associated with laying the foundation.

The number of activities in a project depends on the nature and scope of the project. It also depends on the level of detail with which the project manager wants to monitor and control the project. In a typical project, it is common for each activity in the project to be a project of its own. That is, a project may actually be a master project that, in turn, consists of several mini-projects. In practice, it is convenient to develop a work breakdown structure to identify the activities in a project.

Work Breakdown Structure A work breakdown structure (WBS) defines a project by dividing it into its major subcomponents, which are then subdivided into more detailed subcomponents, and so on. Gross requirements for people, supplies, and equipment are also estimated in this planning phase. The WBS typically decreases in size from top to bottom and is indented like this:

Level	
1	Project
2	Major tasks in the project
3	Subtasks in major tasks
4	Activities to be completed

This hierarchical framework can be illustrated with the process of preparing to move to a new house or apartment. As we see in Figure 7.3, the project, "Prepare to move," is labeled 1.0. The first step is to identify the major tasks in the project (level 2). Three examples would be soliciting movers or recruiting helpers if self-moving (1.1), packing belongings (1.2), and closing out the current house or apartment (1.3). The major subtasks for 1.3 would be either listing the house for sale or ending the lease (1.3.1), notifying utilities and the post office that you will no longer be living in your current location (1.3.2), and cleaning up the house or apartment (1.3.3). Then each major subtask is broken down into level 4 activities that need to be done, such as scrubbing the bathrooms (1.3.3.1), vacuuming, etc. There are usually many level 4 activities.

Level	Level ID Number	Activity
1	1.0	Prepare to move
2	1.1	Solicit movers/helpers
2	1.2	Pack belongings
2	1.3	Close out of current house/apartment
3	1.3.1	List house for sale/end lease
3	1.3.2	Notify utilities/post office
3	1.3.3	Clean house
4	1.3.3.1	Scrub bathrooms

Figure 7.3: Work Breakdown Structure

Identifying Activity Times and Other Resources

Once the activities of a project have been identified, the time required and other resources (e.g., money, labor, raw materials) for each activity are determined. In practice, identifying this input data is a complicated task involving a fair amount of expertise and competence on the project leader's part. For example, many individuals automatically present inflated time estimates, especially if their job is on the line if they fail to complete the activity on time. The project leader has to be able to recognize these types of issues and adjust the time estimates accordingly.

Project Management Techniques: PERT and CPM

When the questions in the project planning phase have been addressed, we move on to the project scheduling phase. The program evaluation and review technique (PERT) and the critical path method (CPM) are two popular decision modeling procedures that help managers answer the questions in the scheduling phase, even for large and complex projects. They were developed because there was a critical need for a better way to manage projects (see the *History* box).

Although some people still view PERT and CPM as separate techniques and refer to them by their original names, the two are similar in basic approach. The growing practice, therefore, is to refer to PERT and CPM simply as *project management* techniques.

HISTORY

How PERT and CPM Started

Managers have been planning, scheduling, monitoring, and controlling large-scale projects for hundreds of years, but it has only been in the past 60 years that decision modeling techniques have been applied to major projects. One of the earliest techniques was the *Gantt chart*. This type of chart displays the start and finish times of one or more activities, as shown in the accompanying chart.

In 1958, the Special Projects Office of the U.S. Navy developed the *program evaluation and review technique* (PERT) to plan and control the Polaris missile program. This project involved the coordination of thousands of contractors. Today, PERT is still used to monitor countless government contract schedules. At about the same time (1957), the *critical path method* (CPM) was developed by J. E. Kelly of Remington Rand and M. R. Walker of DuPont. Originally, CPM was used to assist in the building and maintenance of chemical plants at DuPont.

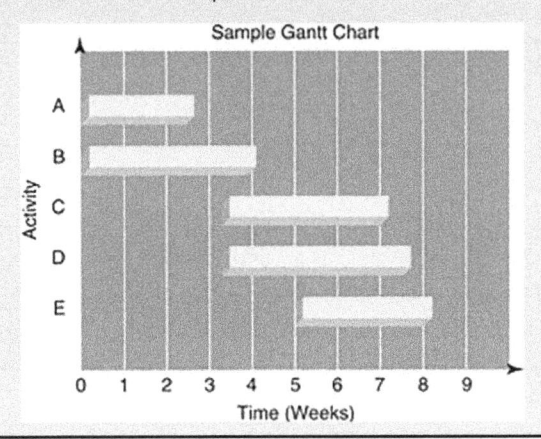

Sample Gantt Chart

PERT versus CPM The primary difference between PERT and CPM is in the way the time needed for each activity in a project is estimated. In PERT, each activity has three time estimates that are combined to determine the expected activity completion time and its variance. PERT is considered a *probabilistic* technique; it allows us to find the probability that the entire project will be completed by a specific due date.

In contrast, CPM is a *deterministic* approach. It estimates the completion time of each activity using a single time estimate. This estimate, called the *standard* or *normal* time, is the time we estimate it will take under typical conditions to complete the activity. In some cases, CPM also associates a second time estimate with each activity. This estimate, called the *crash time*, is the shortest time it would take to finish an activity if additional funds and resources were allocated to the activity.

As noted previously, identifying these time estimates is a complicated task in most real-world projects. In our discussions in this chapter, however, we will assume that the time estimates (a single time estimate in CPM and three time estimates in PERT) are available for each activity.

Project Management Example: General Foundry, Inc.

General Foundry, Inc., a metal works plant in Milwaukee, has long tried to avoid the expense of installing air pollution control equipment. The local environmental protection agency has recently given the foundry 16 weeks to install a complex air filter system on its main smokestack. General Foundry has been warned that it may be forced to close unless the device is installed in the allotted period. Lester Harky, the managing partner, wants to make sure that installation of the filtering system progresses smoothly and on time.

General Foundry has identified the eight activities that need to be performed for the project to be completed. When the project begins, two activities can be simultaneously started: building the internal components for the device (activity A) and making the modifications necessary for the floor and roof (activity B). The construction of the collection stack (activity C) can begin when the internal components are completed. Pouring the concrete floor and installing the frame (activity D) can be started as soon as the internal components are completed and the roof and floor have been modified.

After the collection stack has been constructed, two activities can begin: building the high-temperature burner (activity E) and installing the pollution control system (activity F). The air pollution device can be installed (activity G) after the concrete floor has been poured, the frame has been installed, and the high-temperature burner has been built. Finally, after the control system and pollution device have been installed, the system can be inspected and tested (activity H).

All these activities and precedence relationships seem rather confusing and complex when they are presented in a descriptive form, as here. It is therefore convenient to list all the activity information in a table, as shown in Table 7.1. We see in the table that activity A is listed as an immediate predecessor of activity C. Likewise, both activities D and E must be performed prior to starting activity G.

Table 7.1: Activities and Their Immediate Predecessors for General Foundry

Activity	Description	Immediate Predecessors
A	Build internal components	—
B	Modify roof and floor	—
C	Construct collection stack	A
D	Pour concrete and install frame	A, B
E	Build high-temperature burner	C
F	Install pollution control system	C
G	Install air pollution device	D, E
H	Inspect and test	F, G

Note that it is enough to list just the immediate predecessors for each activity. For example, in Table 7.1, because activity A precedes activity C and activity C precedes activity E, the fact that activity A precedes activity E is *implicit*. This relationship need not be explicitly shown in the activity precedence relationships.

When a project has many activities with fairly complicated precedence relationships, it is difficult for an individual to comprehend the complexity of the project from just the tabular information. In such cases, a visual representation of the project, using a project network, is convenient and useful. A project network is a diagram of all the activities and the precedence relationships that exist between these activities in a project. We now illustrate how to construct a project network for General Foundry, Inc.

Drawing the Project Network

Recall from the discussion in Chapter 5 that a network consists of nodes (or points) and arcs (or lines) that connect the nodes together. There are two approaches to drawing a project network: activity on node (AON) network and activity on arc (AOA) network. In the AON approach, we denote each activity with a node. Arcs represent precedence relationships between activities. In contrast, in the AOA approach, we represent each activity with an arc. Each node represents an event, such as the start or finish of an activity.

Although both approaches are popular in practice, many of the project management software packages, including Microsoft Project, use AON networks. For this reason, we focus only on AON networks in this chapter. For details on AOA project networks, we refer you to a project management book.

AON Network for General Foundry In the General Foundry example, two activities (A and B) do not have any predecessors. We draw separate nodes for each of these activities, as shown in Figure 7.4. Although not required, it is usually convenient to have a unique starting activity for a project. We have included, therefore, a dummy activity called Start in Figure 7.4. This dummy activity does not really exist and takes up zero time and resources. Activity Start is an immediate predecessor for both activities A and B, and it serves as the unique starting activity for the entire project.

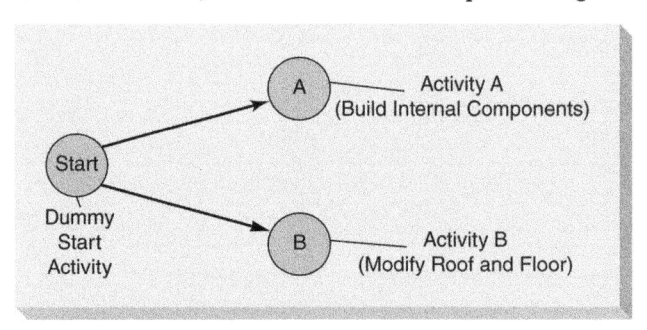

Figure 7.4: Beginning AON Network for General Foundry

We now show the precedence relationships by using arcs (shown with arrow symbols: →). For example, an arrow from activity Start to activity A indicates that Start is a predecessor for activity A. In a similar fashion, we draw an arrow from Start to B.

Next, we add a new node for activity C. Because activity A precedes activity C, we draw an arc from node A to node C (see Figure 7.5). Likewise, we first draw a node to represent activity D. Then, because activities A and B both precede activity D, we draw arcs from A to D and from B to D (see Figure 7.5).

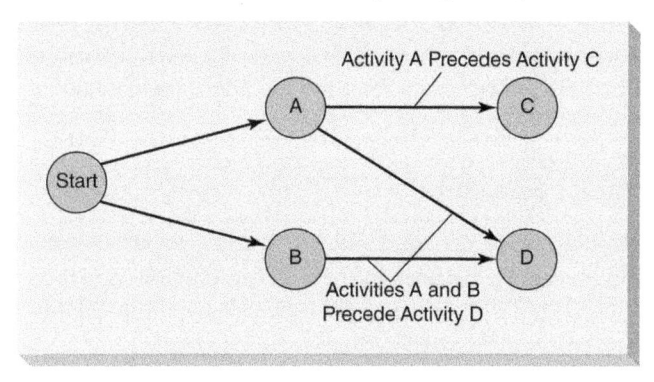

Figure 7.5: Intermediate AON Network for General Foundry

We proceed in this fashion, adding a separate node for each activity and a separate arc for each precedence relationship that exists. The complete AON project network for the General Foundry project example is shown in Figure 7.6.

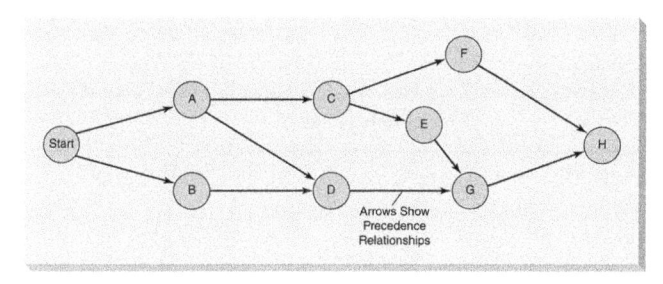

Figure 7.6: Complete AON Network for General Foundry

Drawing a project network properly takes some time and experience. When we first draw a project network, it is not unusual that we place our nodes (activities) in the network in such a fashion that the arcs (precedence relationships) are not simple straight lines. That is, the arcs could be intersecting each other and even facing in opposite directions. For example, if we switched the locations of the nodes for activities E and F in Figure 7.6, the arcs from F to H and E to G would intersect. Although such a project network is perfectly valid, it is good practice to have a well-drawn network. One rule that we especially recommend is to place the nodes in such a fashion that all arrows point in the same direction. To achieve this, we suggest that you first draw a rough draft version of the network to make sure all the relationships are shown. Then you can redraw the network to make appropriate changes in the location of the nodes.

As with the unique starting node, it is convenient to have the project network finish with a unique ending node. In the General Foundry example, it turns out that a unique activity, H, is the last activity in the project. We therefore automatically have a unique ending node here. However, in situations where a project has multiple ending activities, we include a dummy ending activity. This is an activity that does not exist and takes up zero time or resources. This dummy activity has all the multiple ending activities in the project as immediate predecessors. We illustrate this type of situation in Solved Problem 7–2 at the end of this chapter.

7.3 Determining the Project Schedule

Look back at Figure 7.6 for a moment to see General Foundry's completed AON project network. Once this project network has been drawn to show all the activities and their precedence relationships, the next step is to determine the project schedule. That is, we need to identify the planned starting and ending times for each activity.

Let us assume that General Foundry estimates the activity time required for each activity, in weeks, as shown in Table 7.2. The table indicates that the total time for all eight of General Foundry's activities is 25 weeks. However, because several activities can take place simultaneously, it is clear that the total project completion time may be much less than 25 weeks. To find out just how long the project will take, we perform critical path analysis for the network.

Table 7.2: Time Estimates for General Foundry

Activity	Description	Time (weeks)
A	Build internal components	2
B	Modify roof and floor	3
C	Construct collection stack	2
D	Pour concrete and install frame	4
E	Build high-temperature burner	4
F	Install pollution control system	3
G	Install air pollution device	5
H	Inspect and test	2
	Total time (weeks)	25

The critical path is the *longest* time path through the network. To find the critical path, we calculate two distinct starting and ending times for each activity. These are defined as follows:

Earliest start time (EST) = the earliest time at which an activity can start, assuming all predecessors have been completed
Earliest finish time (EFT) = the earliest time at which an activity can be finished
Latest start time (LST) = the latest time at which an activity can start so as to not delay the completion time of the entire project
Latest finish time (LFT) = the latest time by which an activity has to finish so as to not delay the completion time of the entire project

---

Decision Modeling In Action

Handling Complexity in Heathrow's Terminal 5 Construction Project

The construction of Terminal 5 at London's Heathrow airport was one of the largest projects in Europe. It involved diverting two rivers over 13 kilometers, constructing two terminal buildings, building a new road linking Terminal 5 to the M25, building a new air traffic control tower, making extensions to the existing above-ground and underground rail links and airfield infrastructure (including taxiways and aircraft stands), adding a new baggage handling system, and building a 4,000-space multilevel car park and a 600-bed hotel.

The duration of the project was 3 years and 10 months and involved more than 60,000 people over its life cycle. It had over 700 constraints, including, but not limited to, restrictions on delivery, working times, and the availability of one entrance/exit to the site through which all the vehicles and workers had to pass and be subjected to high security measures associated with an airport. At peak times, approximately 8,000 workers per day and 250 deliveries of materials per hour had to pass in and out of the site. The cost of the project exceeded $7 billion.

In order to handle this complex project, the British Airports Authority (BAA) broke it down into four main areas, 16 major projects, and 147 subprojects. They then developed an approach to ensure the project teams were integrated, and they used digital models for the project design and execution. Extensive use of preassembly techniques and off-site prefabrication was made to manufacture, assemble, and test components before they were brought on site. The BAA assumed full responsibility for any risks that might have arisen during the execution of the project.

Although the Terminal 5 construction project was successfully completed on time and within budget, the official opening was challenging due to numerous small problems that arose that day, leading to the cancellation of many flights and the loss of thousands of suitcases. The BAA admitted afterwards that perhaps they had failed to work closely enough with their airline customer British Airways in the handover of Terminal 5 post construction, and that they should have carried out the move to the new terminal in incremental steps.

Source: Based on T. Brady and A. Davies. "Managing Structural and Dynamic Complexity: A Tale of Two Projects," *Project Management Journal* 45, 4 (2014): 21–38.

We use a two-pass process, consisting of a *forward pass* and a *backward pass*, to determine these time schedules for each activity. The earliest times (EST and EFT) are determined during the forward pass. The latest times (LST and LFT) are determined during the backward pass.

Forward Pass

To clearly show the activity schedules on a project network, we use the notation shown in Figure 7.7. The EST of an activity is shown in the top-left corner of the node denoting that activity. The EFT is shown in the top-right corner. The latest times, LST and LFT, are shown in the bottom-left and bottom-right corners, respectively.

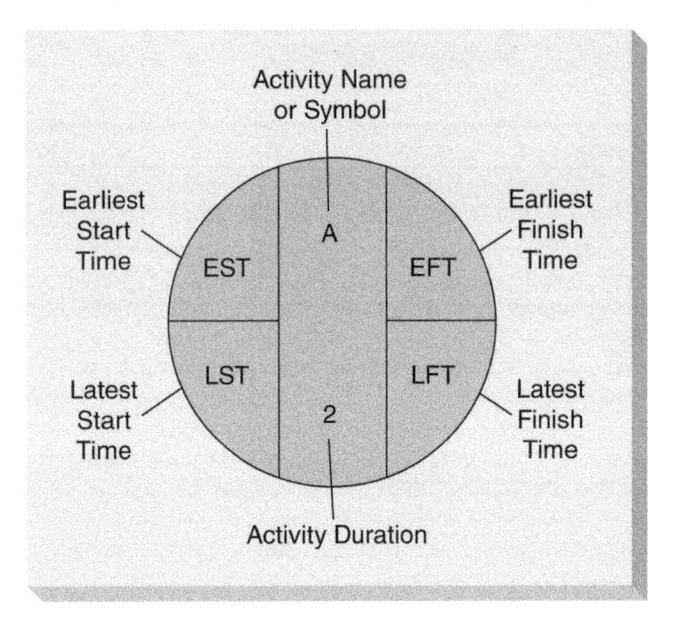

Figure 7.7: Notation Used in Nodes for Forward and Backward Passes

EST Rule Before an activity can start, *all* its immediate predecessors must be finished:
- If an activity has only a single immediate predecessor, its EST equals the EFT of the predecessor.
- If an activity has multiple immediate predecessors, its EST is the maximum of all EFT values of its predecessors. That is,

$$\text{EST} = \text{Maximum \{EFT value of all immediate predecessors\}} \quad (7\text{–}1)$$

EFT Rule The EFT of an activity is the sum of its EST and its activity time. That is,

$$\text{EFT} = \text{EST} + \text{Activity time} \quad (7\text{–}2)$$

Figure 7.8 shows the complete project network for General Foundry's project, along with the EST and EFT values for all activities. We next describe how these values have been calculated.

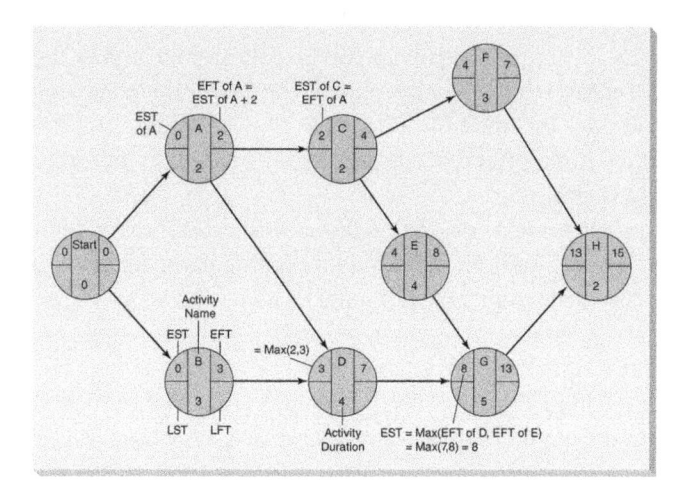

Figure 7.8: Earliest Start Times and Earliest Finish Times for General Foundry

Because activity Start has no predecessors, we begin by setting its EST to 0. That is, activity Start can begin at the *end* of week 0, which is the same as the beginning of week 1.[1] If activity Start has an EST of 0, its EFT is also 0 because its activity time is 0.

Next, we consider activities A and B, both of which have only Start as an immediate predecessor. Using the EST rule, the EST for both activities A and B equals zero, which is the EFT of activity Start. Now, using the EFT rule, the EFT for A is 2 (= 0 + 2), and the EFT for B is 3 (= 0 + 3). Because activity A precedes activity C, the EST of C equals the EFT of A (= 2). The EFT of C is therefore 4 (= 2 + 2).

We now come to activity D. Both activities A and B are immediate predecessors for D. Whereas A has an EFT of 2, activity B has an EFT of 3. Using the EST rule, we compute the EST of activity D as follows:

EST of D = Maximum (EFT of A, EFT of B) = Maximum (2, 3) = 3

The EFT of D equals 7 (= 3 + 4). Next, both activities E and F have activity C as their only immediate predecessor. Therefore, the EST for both E and F equals 4 (= EFT of C). The EFT of E is 8 (= 4 + 4), and the EFT of F is 7 (= 4 + 3).

Activity G has both activities D and E as predecessors. Using the EST rule, we know its EST is therefore the maximum of the EFT of D and the EFT of E. Hence, the EST of activity G equals 8 (= maximum of 7 and 8), and its EFT equals 13 (= 8 + 5).

---

[1] In writing all earliest and latest times, we need to be consistent. For example, if we specify that the EST value of activity *i* is week 4, do we mean the *beginning* of week 4 or the *end* of week 4? Note that if the value refers to the *beginning* of week 4, it means that week 4 is also available for performing activity *i*. In our discussions, *all* earliest and latest time values correspond to the *end* of a period. That is, if we specify that the EST of activity *i* is week 4, it means that activity *i* starts work only at the beginning of week 5.

Finally, we come to activity H. Because it also has two predecessors, F and G, the EST of H is the maximum EFT of these two activities. That is, the EST of H equals 13 (= maximum of 7 and 13). This implies that the EFT of H is 15 (= 13 + 2). Because H is the last activity in the project, this also implies that the earliest time in which the entire project can be completed is 15 weeks.

Although the forward pass allows us to determine the earliest project completion time, it does not identify the critical path. In order to identify this path, we need to now conduct the backward pass to determine the LST and LFT values for all activities.

Backward Pass

Just as the forward pass begins with the first activity in the project, the backward pass begins with the last activity in the project. For each activity, we first determine its LFT value, followed by its LST value. The following two rules are used in this process: the LFT rule and the LST rule.

LFT Rule This rule is again based on the fact that before an activity can start, all its immediate predecessors must be finished:
- If an activity is an immediate predecessor for just a single activity, its LFT equals the LST of the activity that immediately follows it.
- If an activity is an immediate predecessor to more than one activity, its LFT is the minimum of all LST values of all activities that immediately follow it. That is,

$$\text{LFT} = \text{Minimum \{LST of all immediate following activities\}} \qquad (7\text{--}3)$$

LST Rule The LST of an activity is the difference between its LFT and its activity time. That is,

$$\text{LST} = \text{LFT} - \text{Activity time} \qquad (7\text{--}4)$$

Figure 7.9 shows the complete project network for General Foundry's project, along with LST and LFT values for all activities. Next, we analyze how these values were calculated.

We begin by assigning an LFT value of 15 weeks for activity H. That is, we specify that the LFT for the entire project is the same as its EFT. Using the LST rule, we calculate that the LST of activity H is equal to 13 (= 15 − 2).

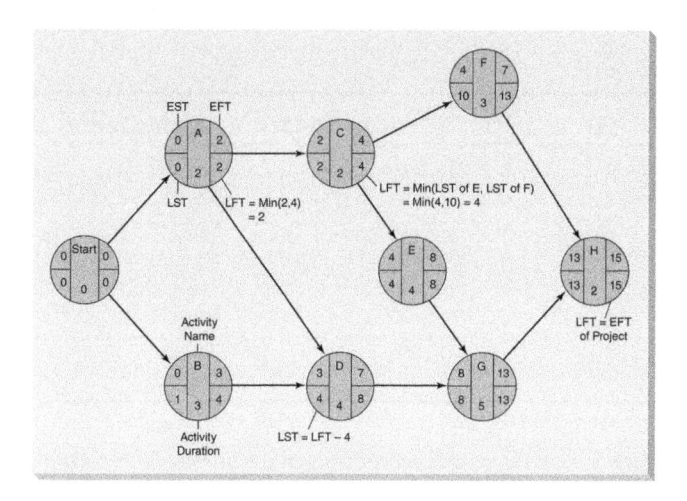

Figure 7.9: Latest Start Times and Latest Finish Times for General Foundry

Because activity H is the lone succeeding activity for both activities F and G, the LFT for both F and G equals 13. This implies that the LST of G is 8 (= 13 − 5), and the LST of F is 10 (= 13 − 3).

Proceeding in this fashion, we find that the LFT of E is 8 (= LST of G), and its LST is 4 (= 8 − 4). Likewise, the LFT of D is 8 (= LST of G), and its LST is 4 (= 8 − 4).

We now consider activity C, which is an immediate predecessor to two activities: E and F. Using the LFT rule, we compute the LFT of activity C as follows:

LFT of C = Minimum (LST of E, LST of F) = Minimum (4, 10) = 4

The LST of C is computed as 2 (= 4 − 2). Next, we compute the LFT of B as 4 (= LST of D) and its LST as 1 (= 4 − 3).

We now consider activity A. We compute its LFT as 2 (= Minimum of LST of C and LST of D). Hence, the LST of activity A is 0 (= 2 − 2). Finally, both the LFT and LST of activity Start are equal to 0.

Calculating Slack Time and Identifying the Critical Path(s)

After we have computed the earliest and latest times for all activities, it is a simple matter to find the amount of slack time, or free time, that each activity has. *Slack* is the length of time an activity can be delayed without delaying the entire project. Mathematically,

$$\text{Slack} = \text{LST} - \text{EST} \text{ or Slack} = \text{LFT} - \text{EFT} \tag{7-5}$$

Table 7.3 summarizes the EST, EFT, LST, LFT, and slack time for all of General Foundry's activities. Activity B, for example, has 1 week of slack time because its LST is 1 and its EST is 0 (alternatively, its LFT is 4 and its EFT is 3). This means that activity B can be delayed by up to 1 week, and the whole project can still finish in 15 weeks.

Table 7.3: General Foundry's Project Schedule and Slack Times

Activity	EST	EFT	LST	LFT	Slack, LST–EST	On Critical Path?
A	0	2	0	2	0	Yes
B	0	3	1	4	1	No
C	2	4	2	4	0	Yes
D	3	7	4	8	1	No
E	4	8	4	8	0	Yes
F	4	7	10	13	6	No
G	8	13	8	13	0	Yes
H	13	15	13	15	0	Yes

On the other hand, activities A, C, E, G, and H have *no* slack time. This means that none of them can be delayed without delaying the entire project. This also means that if Harky wants to reduce the total project time, he will have to reduce the length of one of these activities. These activities are called critical activities and are said to be on the *critical path*. The critical path is a continuous path through the project network that
- Starts at the first activity in the project (Start in our example)
- Terminates at the last activity in the project (H in our example)
- Includes only critical activities (i.e., activities with no slack time)

General Foundry's critical path, Start-A-C-E-G-H, is shown in the network in Figure 7.10. The total project completion time of 15 weeks corresponds to the longest path in the network.

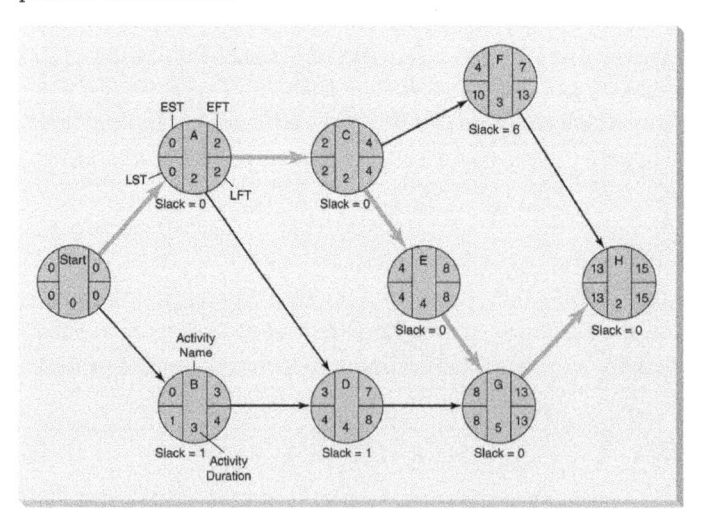

Figure 7.10: Critical Path and Slack Times for General Foundry

Multiple Critical Paths In General Foundry's case, there is just a single critical path. Can a project have multiple critical paths? The answer is yes. For example, in General Foundry's case, what if the time required for activity B were estimated as four weeks instead of three? Due to this change, the earliest and latest times for activities B and D would have to be revised, as shown in Figure 7.11.

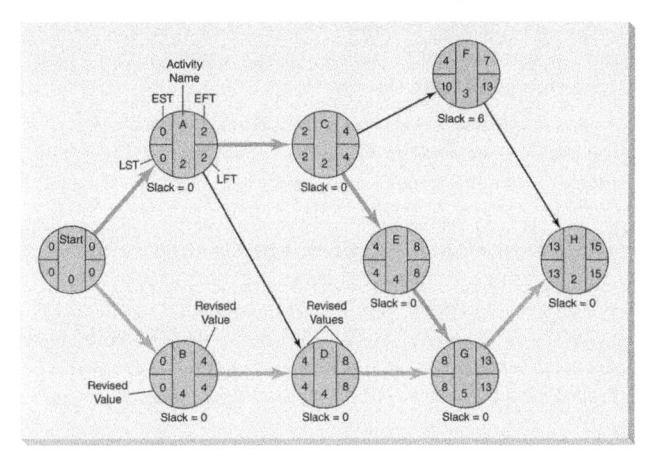

Figure 7.11: Modified Network with Multiple Critical Paths for General Foundry

Note that in addition to the original critical path (Start-A-C-E-G-H), there is now a second critical path (Start-B-D-G-H). Delaying an activity on either critical path will delay the completion of the entire project.

Total Slack Time versus Free Slack Time
Let us now refer to the project network in Figure 7.10. Consider activities B and D, which have slacks of one week each. Does it mean that we can delay *each* activity by one week and still complete the project in 15 weeks? The answer is no, as discussed next.

Let's assume that activity B is delayed by one week. It has used up its slack of one week and now has an EFT of 4. This implies that activity D now has an EST of 4 and an EFT of 8. Note that these are also its LST and LFT values, respectively. That is, activity D also has no slack time now. Essentially, the slack of one week that activities B and D had was *shared* between them. Delaying either activity by one week causes not only that activity but also the other activity to lose its slack. This type of a slack time is referred to as *total slack*. Typically, when two or more noncritical activities appear successively in a path, they share total slack.

In contrast, consider the slack time of 6 weeks in activity F. Delaying this activity decreases only its slack time and does not affect the slack time of any other activity. This type of a slack time is referred to as *free slack*. Typically, if a noncritical activity has critical activities on either side of it in a path, its slack time is free slack.

Decision Modeling In Action

Project Management Has Significant Impact on the Performance of Australian Small to Medium Enterprises

To test the assumption that using project management to achieve organizational objectives improves the overall performance of the organization, especially in small to medium enterprises, a study was conducted at the University of Technology in Sydney. The data were provided by the Australian Bureau of Statistics, which surveyed Australian businesses with fewer than 200 employees for five consecutive years to track changes in these enterprises.

A model was created to assess the relationship between productivity and business practices using binary logistic regression, and backward elimination was used to eliminate nonsignificant independent variables from the model. Further, the correlation of project management with other business practices was measured.

The model demonstrated that project management has a significant impact on the productivity of small to medium enterprises. About 15% more of the survey respondents who used project management reported an increase in productivity compared with those who did not use project management. In fact, project management turned out to have a higher impact on productivity than marketing skills. Accordingly, the research team suggested that a balancing of organizational budgets between marketing and project management may be a viable option for these organizations.

Source: Based on J. Pollack and D. Adler. "Does Project Management Affect Business Productivity? Evidence from Australian Small to Medium Enterprises," *Project Management Journal* 45, 6 (2014): 17–24

7.4 Variability in Activity Times

In identifying all earliest and latest times so far, and the associated critical path(s), we have adopted the CPM approach of assuming that all activity times are known and fixed constants. That is, there is no variability in activity times. However, in practice, it is likely that activity completion times vary depending on various factors.

For example, building internal components (activity A) for General Foundry is estimated to finish in two weeks. Clearly, factors such as late arrival of raw materials, absence of key personnel, and so on, could delay this activity. Suppose activity A actually ends up taking three weeks. Because activity A is on the critical path, the entire project will now be delayed by one week, to 16 weeks. If we had anticipated completion of this project in 15 weeks, we would obviously miss our deadline.

Although some activities may be relatively less prone to delays, others could be extremely susceptible to delays. For example, activity B (modify roof and floor) could be heavily dependent on weather conditions. A spell of bad weather could significantly affect its completion time.

The preceding discussion implies that we cannot ignore the impact of variability in activity times when deciding the schedule for a project. In general, there are three approaches that we can use to analyze the impact of variability in activity times on the completion time of the project:

- The first approach is to provide for variability by building in "buffers" to activity times. For example, if we know based on past experience that a specific activity has exceeded its time estimate by 20% on several occasions, we can build in a 20% time buffer for this activity by inflating its time estimate by 20%. There are, of course, a few obvious drawbacks to this approach. For example, if every activity has inflated time estimates due to these buffers, the entire project duration will be artificially large. Incidentally, practicing project managers will tell you that providing time buffers is not practical because the people concerned with the activity will just proceed more slowly than planned on the activity because they know that the buffer exists (i.e., the duration will stretch to fit the allotted time).
- The second approach, known as PERT analysis, employs a probability-based analysis of the project completion time. A primary advantage of this approach is that it is fairly easy to understand and implement. However, the drawback is that we have to make certain assumptions regarding the probability distributions of activity times. We discuss this approach in detail in this section.
- The third approach uses computer simulation, the topic of Chapter 10. This approach, while typically being the most difficult approach from an implementation point of view, is also likely to be the most comprehensive in terms of its capabilities and analysis. We illustrate this approach for a project management problem in Solved Problem 10–4.

PERT Analysis

Recall that in our study so far, we have estimated the duration for each activity by using a single time estimate (such as two weeks for activity A in General Foundry's project). In practice, such durations may be difficult to estimate for many activities. For example, think about the difficulty you would have if someone asked you to estimate exactly how long you will take to complete your income tax forms this year. (Remember, your estimate must be guaranteed to be sufficient and should not include any unnecessary buffers.) To correct for this difficulty, in PERT analysis we base the duration of each activity on three separate time estimates:

Optimistic time (a) = The time an activity will take, assuming favorable conditions (i.e., everything goes as planned). In estimating this value, there should be only a small probability (say, 1/100) that the activity time will be a or lower.

Most likely time (m) = The most realistic estimate of the time required to complete an activity.

Pessimistic time (b) = The time an activity will take, assuming unfavorable conditions (i.e., nothing goes as planned). In estimating this value, there should also be only a small probability that the activity time will be b or higher.

How do we use these three time estimates? It turns out that a probability distribution, known as the beta probability distribution, is very appropriate for approximating the distribution of activity times. As shown in Figure 7.12, one way to characterize the beta distribution is to use three parameters—which, in the case of activity durations, correspond to the optimistic, most likely, and pessimistic time estimates we have already defined for each activity.

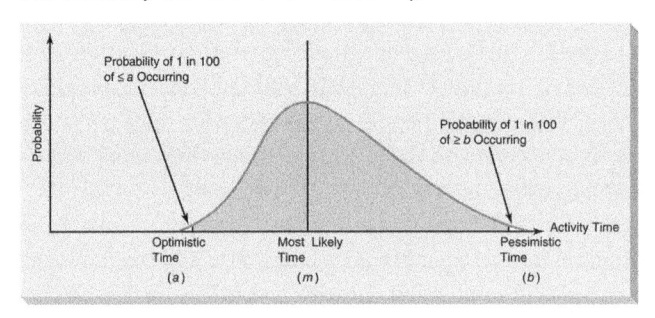

Figure 7.12: Beta Probability Distribution with Three Time Estimates

By using these three parameters for each activity, we can compute its expected activity time and variance. To find the expected activity time (t), the beta distribution weights the three time estimates as follows:

$$t = (a + 4m + b)/6 \qquad (7\text{-}6)$$

That is, the most likely time (m) is given four times the weight of the optimistic time (a) and pessimistic time (b). It is important to note that this expected activity time, t, computed using Equation 7–6 for each activity, is used in the project network to compute all earliest and latest times.

To compute the variance of activity completion time, we use this formula:[2]

$$\text{Variance} = \left[(b-a)/6\right]^2 \qquad (7\text{-}7)$$

The standard deviation of activity completion time is the square root of the variance. Hence,

$$\text{Standard deviation} = \sqrt{\text{Variance}} = (b-a)/6 \qquad (7\text{-}8)$$

---

[2] This formula is based on the statistical concept that from one end of the beta distribution to the other is 6 standard deviations (± 3 standard deviations from the mean). Because (b − a) is 6 standard deviations, the variance is [(b − a) / 6]².

EXCEL NOTE

The Companion Website for this book, at *degruyter.com/view/product/486941*, contains the Excel file for each sample problem discussed here. TThe relevant file/sheet name is shown below the title of the corresponding figure in this book.

For General Foundry's project, let us assume that Lester Harky has estimated the optimistic, most likely, and pessimistic times for each activity, as shown in columns C, D, and E, respectively, in Figure 7.13. Note that some activities (e.g., A, B) have relatively small variability, while others (e.g., F, G) have a large spread between their pessimistic and optimistic time estimates. On occasion, it is possible for an activity to have no variability at all (i.e., the activity's *a*, *m*, and *b* time estimates are all the same).

	A	B	C	D	E	F	G	H
1	PERT Time Estimates (in Weeks) for General Foundry							
2								
3	Activity	Description	Optimistic time (a)	Most likely time (m)	Pessimistic time (b)	Expected time	Variance	Standard deviation
4	A	Build internal components	1	2	3	2.0	0.11	0.33
5	B	Modify roof and floor	2	3	4	3.0	0.11	0.33
6	C	Construct collection stack	1	2	3	2.0	0.11	0.33
7	D	Pour concrete and install frame	2	4	6	4.0	0.44	0.67
8	E	Build high-temperature burner	1	4	7	4.0	1.00	1.00
9	F	Install pollution control system	1	2	9	3.0	1.78	1.33
10	G	Install air pollution device	3	4	11	5.0	1.78	1.33
11	H	Inspect and test	1	2	3	2.0	0.11	0.33

Column G = $\left(\dfrac{\text{Column E} - \text{Column C}}{6}\right)^2$

Three time estimates for each activity

Column F = $\dfrac{\text{Column C} + 4 \times \text{Column D} + \text{Column E}}{6}$

=SQRT (Column G)

Figure 7.13: Excel Layout to Compute General Foundry's Expected Times and Variances

File: Figure 7.13.xlsx

Using these estimates in Equations 7–6 through 7–8, we compute the expected time, variance, and standard deviation for each activity. These values are shown in columns F, G, and H, respectively, of Figure 7.13. Note that the expected times shown in column F are, in fact, the activity times we used in our earlier computation and identification of the critical path. Hence, the earliest and latest times we computed before (see Table 7.3) are valid for the PERT analysis of General Foundry's project.

EXCEL EXTRA

Sorting

It's easy to sort a data set in Excel for a field based on increasing or decreasing numeric values or based on alphabetical (or reverse alphabetical) order for text. Additional fields can be set as tiebreakers (called "adding a level").

For example, one could sort the activities in Figure 7.13 from highest-to-lowest variance, then from highest-to-lowest expected time, then alphabetically by activity name as follows.

First highlight the range to be sorted (A3:H11). If you include the column labels, be sure that the box My data has headers is checked in the Sort dialog box after it appears. Next select:

Data|Sort. Under Sort by, select "Variance." Then under Order, select "Largest to Smallest." Next click on the Add Level button to create the tiebreaker based on "Expected time" (Order "Largest to Smallest"). Finally, click on the Add Level button to create the tiebreaker based on "Activity" (Order|A to Z) and click OK. The data will now be sorted by activities G-F-E-D-B-A-C-H.

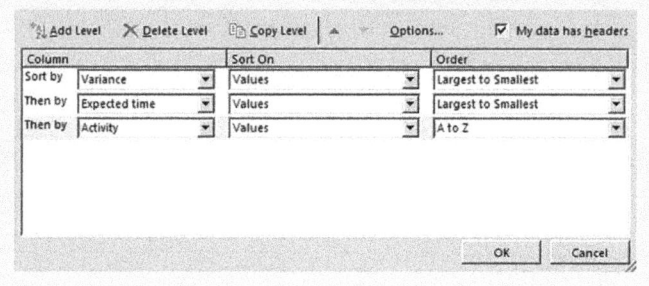

Column	Sort On	Order
Sort by Variance	Values	Largest to Smallest
Then by Expected time	Values	Largest to Smallest
Then by Activity	Values	A to Z

Note: You can select Options... to sort by columns instead of rows or to make the sorting case sensitive.

Tip: It can be good practice to have your original data file saved somewhere just in case you accidentally make a mistake while sorting (e.g., omitting a column) or if you need to recover the data in its original order.

Probability of Project Completion

Critical path analysis helped us determine that General Foundry's expected project completion time is 15 weeks. Lester Harky knows, however, that there is significant variation in the time estimates for several activities. Variation in activities that are on the critical path can affect the overall project completion time, possibly delaying it. This is one occurrence that worries Harky considerably.

PERT uses the variance of critical path activities to help determine the variance of the overall project. Project variance is computed by summing variances of critical activities:

$$\text{Project variance} = \sum(\text{Variances of activities on critical path}) \quad (7\text{–}9)$$

From Figure 7.13 we know that the variance of activity A is 0.11, variance of activity C is 0.11, variance of activity E is 1.00, variance of activity G is 1.78, and variance of activity H is 0.11. Hence, the total project variance and project standard deviation may be computed as

$$\text{Project variance }(\sigma_p^2) = 0.11 + 0.11 + 1.00 + 1.78 + 0.11 = 3.11$$

which implies

$$\text{Project standard deviation }(\sigma_p) = \sqrt{\text{Project variance}} = \sqrt{3.11} = 1.76$$

PERT now makes two assumptions: (1) Total project completion times follow a normal probability distribution, and (2) activity times are statistically independent. With these assumptions, the bell-shaped normal curve shown in Figure 7.14 can be used to represent project completion dates. This normal curve implies that there is a 50% chance that the project completion time will be less than 15 weeks and a 50% chance that it will exceed 15 weeks. That is, instead of viewing the computed project completion time as a guaranteed estimate (as we did earlier, when using the CPM approach), the PERT analysis views it as just the expected completion time, with only a 50% probability of completion within that time.

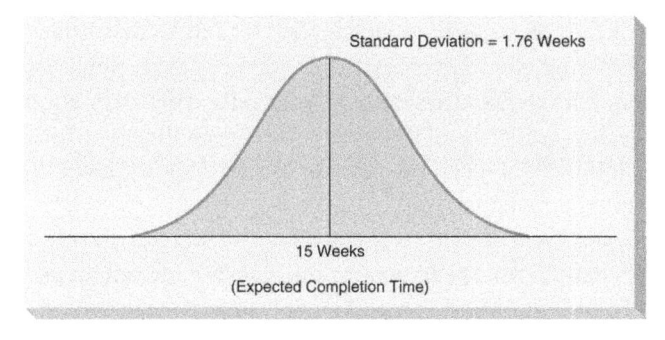

Figure 7.14: Probability Distribution for Project Completion Times

How can this information be used to help answer questions regarding the probability of finishing the project at different times? For example, what is the probability that Harky will finish this project on or before the 16-week deadline imposed by the environmental agency? To find this probability, Harky needs to determine the appropriate area under the normal curve. The standard normal equation can be applied as follows:

$$Z = (\text{Target completion time} - \text{Expected completion time})/\sigma_p \quad (7\text{--}10)$$
$$= (16 \text{ weeks} - 15 \text{ weeks})/1.76 \text{ weeks} = 0.57$$

where Z is the number of standard deviations the target completion time lies from the expected completion time.

Referring to the normal probability table in Appendix C or using the Excel formula =NORMSDIST(0.57), we find a probability of 0.7157. Thus, there is a 71.57% chance that the pollution control equipment can be put in place in 16 weeks or less. This is shown in Figure 7.15.

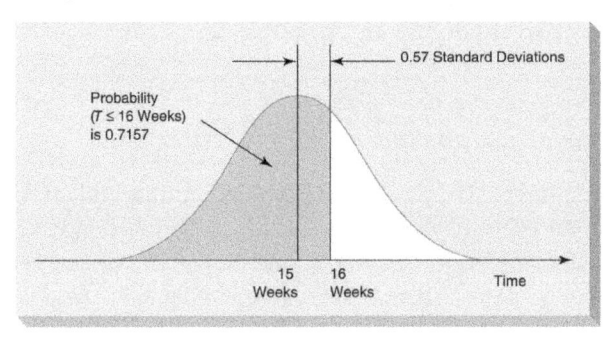

Figure 7.15: Probability of General Foundry Meeting the 16-Week Deadline

Determining Project Completion Time for a Given Probability

Lester Harky is extremely worried that there is only a 71.57% chance that the pollution control equipment can be put into place in 16 weeks or less. He thinks that it may be possible for him to plead with the environmental agency for more time. However, before he approaches the agency, he wants to arm himself with sufficient information about the project. Specifically, he wants to find the target completion time by which he has a 99% chance of completing the project. He hopes to use his analysis to persuade the agency to agree to this extended deadline.

Clearly, this target completion time would be greater than 16 weeks. However, what is the exact value of this new deadline? To answer this question, we again use the assumption that General Foundry's project completion time follows a normal probability distribution, with a mean of 15 weeks and a standard deviation of 1.76 weeks.

For Harky to find the target completion time under which the project has a 99% chance of completion, he needs to determine the Z value that corresponds to 99%, as shown in Figure 7.16.

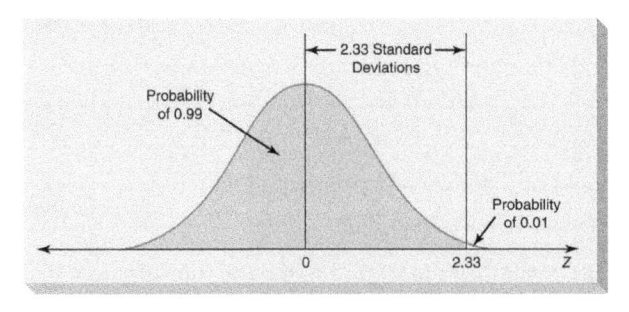

Figure 7.16: Z Value for 99% Probability of Project Completion

Referring again to the normal probability table in Appendix C or using the formula =NORMSDIST(2.33) in Excel, we identify a Z value of 2.33 as being closest to the probability of 0.99. That is, Harky's target completion time should be 2.33 standard deviations above the expected completion time. Starting with the standard normal equation (see Equation 7–10), we can solve for the target completion time and rewrite the equation as

$$\text{Target completion time} = \text{Expected completion time} + Z \times \sigma_P \qquad (7\text{–}11)$$
$$= 15 + 2.33 \times 1.76 = 19.1 \text{ weeks}$$

Hence, if Harky can get the environmental agency to give him a new target completion time of 19.1 weeks (or more), he can be 99% sure of finishing the project on time.

Decision Modeling in Action

Impact of Project Management Body of Knowledge on Construction Projects

National Taiwan University of Science and Technology implemented a study to examine the relationships and interactions between the Project Management Body of Knowledge (PMBOK), project performance, customer satisfaction, and project success in construction projects. Experienced interviewees from private engineering firms and public agencies in Taiwan were asked to complete a questionnaire, and the responses were analyzed using structural equation modeling, an effective statistical method for these types of research.

The PMBOK recommended the use of several project management techniques to improve project performance. However, searching case by case for the combination of project management techniques that obtain the largest improvement in project performance was very time consuming. Therefore, the study used a genetic algorithm (GA), an adaptive heuristic search procedure that can solve large-scale optimization problems, to identify the project management techniques that would help achieve the highest project performance.

The results suggested the use of "bidder's conference" and "procurement negotiations" techniques to minimize bidding and legal procurement problems. The study also recommended the use of "stakeholder analysis," "communication requirements analysis," and "communication methods" to perform effective communication management. The researchers believe that these empirical results will help practitioners improve the performance of construction projects.

Source: Based on J. Chou and J. Jang. "Project Management Knowledge and Effects on Construction Project Outcomes: An Empirical Study," *Project Management Journal* 43, 5 (2012): 47–67.

Variability in Completion Time of Noncritical Paths

In our discussion so far, we have focused exclusively on the variability in completion times of activities on the critical path. This seems logical because these activities are, by definition, the more important activities in a project network. However, when there is variability in activity times, it is important that we also investigate the variability in the completion times of activities on *noncritical* paths.

Consider, for example, activity D in General Foundry's project. Recall from Table 7.3 that this is a noncritical activity, with a slack time of one week. Therefore, we have not considered the variability in D's time in computing the probabilities of project completion times. We observe, however, that D has a variance of 0.44 (see Figure 7.13). In fact, the pessimistic completion time for D is 6 weeks. This means that if D ends up taking its pessimistic time to finish, the project will not finish in 15 weeks, even though D is not a critical activity.

For this reason, when we find probabilities of project completion times, it may be necessary for us to not focus only on the critical path(s). We may need to also compute these probabilities for noncritical paths, especially those that have relatively large variances. It is possible for a noncritical path to have a smaller probability of completion within a due date compared with the critical path. In fact, a different critical path can evolve because of the probabilistic situation.

7.5 Managing Project Costs and Other Resources

The techniques discussed so far are very good for planning, scheduling, and monitoring a project with respect to time. We have not, however, considered another very important factor—project *cost*. In this section, we begin by investigating how costs can be planned and scheduled. Then we see how costs can be monitored and controlled.

Planning and Scheduling Project Costs: Budgeting Process

The overall approach in the budgeting process of a project is to determine how much is to be spent every week or month. This is accomplished as follows:

Three Steps of the Budgeting Process
1. Identify all costs associated with each of the activities. Then add these costs together to get one estimated cost or budget for each activity. When dealing with a large project, several activities may be combined into larger work packages. A work package is simply a logical collection of activities. Because the General Foundry project is quite small, each activity can be a work package.
2. Identify when and how the budgeted cost for an activity will actually be spent. In practice, this would be specific to the activity in question. For example, in some cases the entire cost may be spent at the start of the activity. In others, the expense may occur only after the activity has been completed.
    In our discussion here, we assume that the cost of each activity is spent at a linear rate over time. Thus, if the budgeted cost for a given activity is $48,000, and the activity's expected time is four weeks, the budgeted cost per week is $12,000 (= $48,000 / 4 weeks).
3. Using the earliest and latest start and finish times for each activity, find out how much money should be spent during each period of the project to finish it by the target completion time.

Budgeting for General Foundry Let's apply the three-step budgeting process to the General Foundry problem. Lester Harky has carefully computed the costs associated with each of his eight activities. Assuming that the cost of each activity is spent at a linear rate over time, he has also divided the total budget for each activity by the activity's expected time to determine the weekly budget for the activity. The budget for activity A, for example, is $22,000 (see Table 7.4). Because its expected time (t) is 2 weeks, $11,000 is spent each week to complete the activity. Table 7.4 also provides two pieces of data we found earlier: the EST and LST for each activity.

Table 7.4: Activity Costs for General Foundry

Activity	Expected Time (t)	EST	LST	Total Budgeted Cost	Budgeted Cost Per Week
A	2	0	0	$22,000	$11,000
B	3	0	1	$30,000	$10,000
C	2	2	2	$26,000	$13,000
D	4	3	4	$48,000	$12,000
E	4	4	4	$56,000	$14,000
F	3	4	10	$30,000	$10,000
G	5	8	8	$80,000	$16,000
H	2	13	13	$16,000	$ 8,000
				Total $308,000	

Looking at the total of the budgeted activity costs, we see that the entire project will cost $308,000. Finding the weekly budget will help Harky determine how the project is progressing week to week.

The weekly budget for the project is developed from the data in Table 7.4. The EST for activity A is 0. Because A takes 2 weeks to complete, its weekly budget of $11,000 should be spent in weeks 1 and 2. For activity B, the EST is 0, the expected completion time is 3 weeks, and the budgeted cost per week is $10,000. Hence, $10,000 should be spent for activity B in each of weeks 1, 2, and 3. Using the EST, we can find the exact weeks during which the budget for each activity should be spent. These weekly amounts can be summed for all activities to arrive at the weekly budget for the entire project. For example, a total of $21,000 each should be spent during weeks 1 and 2. These weekly totals can then be added to determine the total amount that should be spent to date (total to date). All these computations are shown in Figure 7.17.

Chapter 7: Project Management

Budgeted Costs (in Thousands) for General Foundry, Using EST

Activity	1	2	3	4	5	6	7	8	9	10	11	12	13	14	15	Total Cost
A	$11	$11														$22
B	$10	$10	$10													$30
C			$13	$13												$26
D				$12	$12	$12	$12									$48
E					$14	$14	$14	$14								$56
F					$10	$10	$10									$30
G									$16	$16	$16	$16	$16			$80
H														$8	$8	$16
																$308
Total per week	$21	$21	$23	$25	$36	$36	$36	$14	$16	$16	$16	$16	$16	$8	$8	
Total to date	$21	$42	$65	$90	$126	$162	$198	$212	$228	$244	$260	$276	$292	$300	$308	

= Sum of all activity costs for the current week.

= Sum of weekly totals up to the current week.

= Sum of the total cost for each activity.

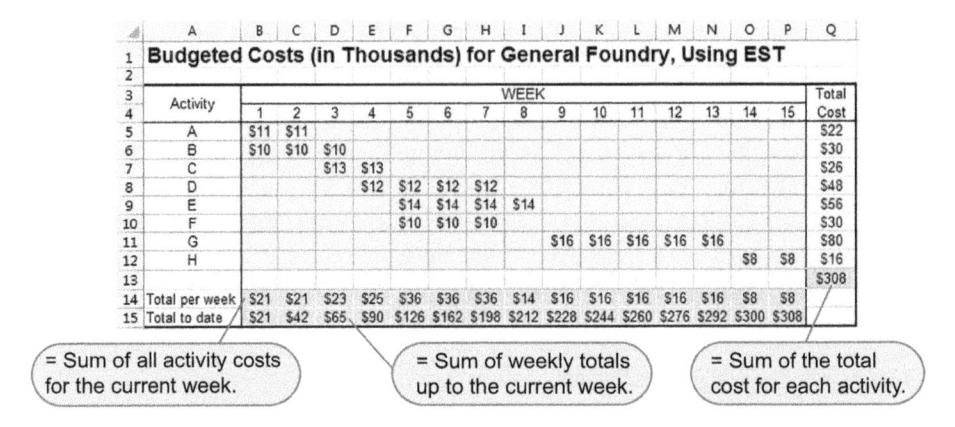

Figure 7.17: Excel Layout to Compute General Foundry's Weekly Budget Using Earliest Start Times

File: Figure 7.17.xlsx

The activities along the critical path (A-C-E-G-H) must spend their budgets at the times shown in Figure 7.17. The activities that are *not* on the critical path, however, can be started at a later date. This concept is embodied in the LST for each activity. Thus, if LST values are used, another budget can be obtained. This budget will delay the expenditure of funds until the last possible moment. The procedures for computing the budget when LST is used are the same as when EST is used. The results of the new computations are shown in Figure 7.18.

Budgeted Costs (in Thousands) for General Foundry, Using LST

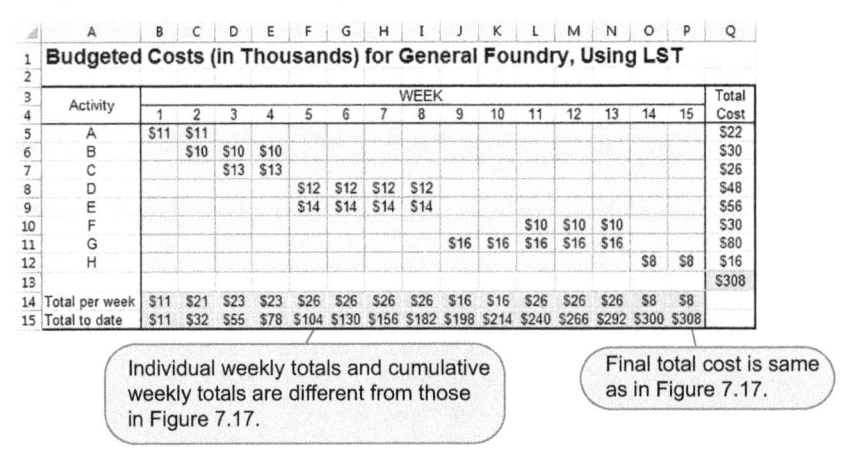

Activity	1	2	3	4	5	6	7	8	9	10	11	12	13	14	15	Total Cost
A	$11	$11														$22
B			$10	$10	$10											$30
C			$13	$13												$26
D					$12	$12	$12	$12								$48
E						$14	$14	$14	$14							$56
F										$10	$10	$10				$30
G									$16	$16	$16	$16	$16			$80
H														$8	$8	$16
																$308
Total per week	$11	$21	$23	$23	$26	$26	$26	$26	$16	$16	$26	$26	$26	$8	$8	
Total to date	$11	$32	$55	$78	$104	$130	$156	$182	$198	$214	$240	$266	$292	$300	$308	

Individual weekly totals and cumulative weekly totals are different from those in Figure 7.17.

Final total cost is same as in Figure 7.17.

Figure 7.18: Excel Layout to Compute General Foundry's Weekly Budget Using Latest Start Times

File: Figure 7.18.xlsx

Compare the budgets given in Figures 7.17 and 7.18. The amount that should be spent to date (total to date) for the budget in Figure 7.17 reveals the earliest possible time that funds can be expended. In contrast, the budget in Figure 7.18 uses fewer financial resources in the first few weeks because it was prepared using LST values. That is, the budget in Figure 7.18 shows the latest possible time that funds can be expended and have the project still finish on time. Therefore, Lester Harky can use any budget between these feasible ranges and still complete the air pollution project on time. These two figures form feasible budget ranges.

This concept is illustrated in Figure 7.19, which plots the total-to-date budgets for EST and LST.

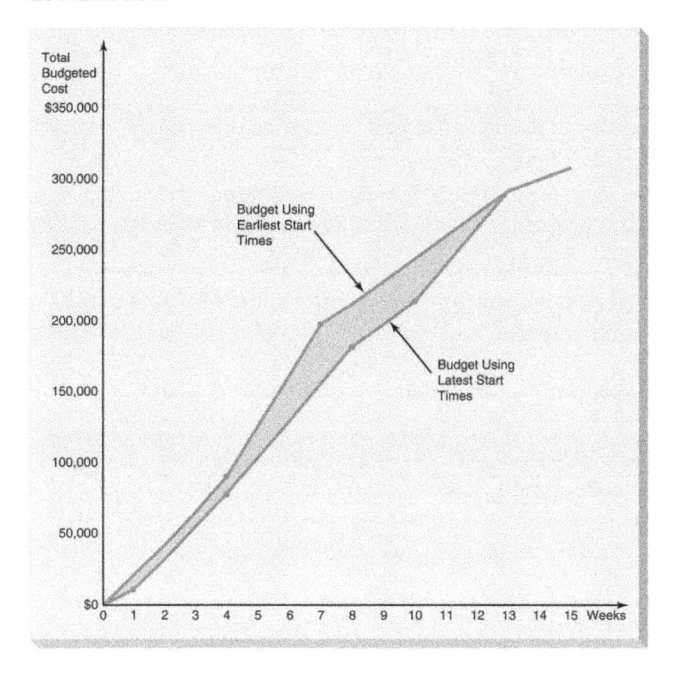

Figure 7.19: Budget Ranges for General Foundry

Monitoring and Controlling Project Costs

Budget charts like the ones shown in Figure 7.19 are typically developed before the project is started. Then, as the project is being completed, funds expended should be monitored and controlled. The purpose of monitoring and controlling project costs is to ensure that the project is progressing on schedule and that cost overruns are kept to a minimum. The status of the entire project should be checked periodically.

Lester Harky wants to know how his air pollution project is going. It is now the end of the sixth week of the 15-week project. Activities A, B, and C have been fully completed. These activities incurred costs of $20,000, $36,000, and $26,000, respectively. Activity D is only 10% complete, and so far the cost expended on it has been $6,000. Activity E is 20% complete, with an incurred cost of $20,000. Activity F is 20% complete, with an incurred cost of $4,000. Activities G and H have not been started. Is the air pollution project on schedule? What is the value of work completed? Are there any cost overruns?

One way to measure the value of the work completed (or the cost-to-date) for an activity is to multiply its total budgeted cost by the percentage of completion for that activity.[3] That is,

$$\text{Value of work completed} = \text{Percentage of work completed} \times \text{Activity budget} \quad (7\text{--}12)$$

To determine the cost difference (i.e., the amount of overrun or underrun) for an activity, the value of work completed is subtracted from the actual cost. Hence,

$$\text{Cost difference} = \text{Actual cost} - \text{Value of work completed} \quad (7\text{--}13)$$

If a cost difference is negative, it implies that there is a cost underrun. In contrast, if the number is positive, there has been a cost overrun.

Figure 7.20 summarizes this information for General Foundry's project. The second column shows the total budgeted cost (from Table 7.4), and the third column contains the percentage of completion for each activity. Using these data, and the actual cost expended for each activity, we can compute the value of work completed and the cost difference for every activity.

Column D = Column B × Column C   Column F = Column E − Column D

	A	B	C	D	E	F
1	Monitoring and Controlling Budgeted Costs for General Foundry					
2						
3	Activity	Total Budgeted Cost	Percentage Completed	Value of Work Completed	Actual Cost	Activity Difference
4	A	$22,000	100%	$22,000	$20,000	-$2,000
5	B	$30,000	100%	$30,000	$36,000	$6,000
6	C	$26,000	100%	$26,000	$26,000	$0
7	D	$48,000	10%	$4,800	$6,000	$1,200
8	E	$56,000	20%	$11,200	$20,000	$8,800
9	F	$30,000	20%	$6,000	$4,000	-$2,000
10	G	$80,000	0%	$0	$0	$0
11	H	$16,000	0%	$0	$0	$0
12			Total =	$100,000	$112,000	$12,000

Total cost overrun or underrun. Overrun of $12,000 in this case.

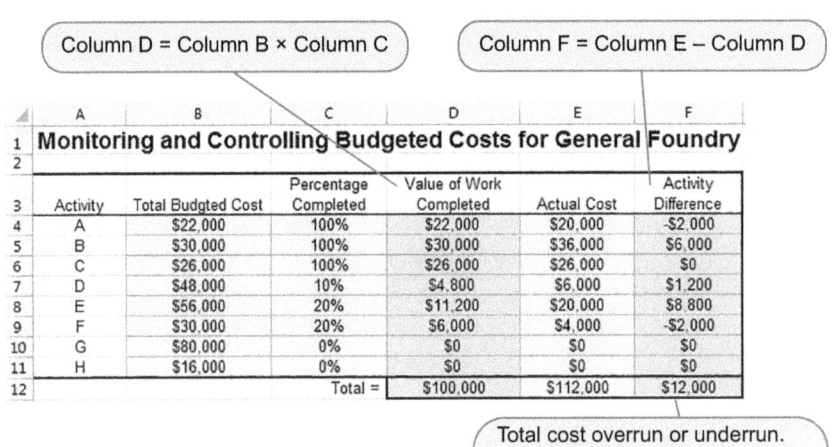

Figure 7.20: Excel Layout to Compute Current Expenditures Compared to the Budget for General Foundry

File: Figure 7.20.xlsx

---

[3] The percentage of completion for each activity can be measured in many ways. For example, we might use the ratio of labor hours expended to total labor hours estimated.

Activity D, for example, has a value of work completed of $4,800 (= $48,000 × 10%). The actual cost is $6,000, implying that there is a cost overrun of $1,200. The cost difference for all activities can be added to determine the total project overrun or underrun. In General Foundry's case, we can see from Figure 7.20 that there is a $12,000 cost overrun at the end of the sixth week. The total value of work completed so far is only $100,000, and the actual cost of the project to date is $112,000.

How do these costs compare with the budgeted costs for week 6? If Harky had decided to use the budget for ESTs (see Figure 7.17), we can see that $162,000 should have been spent. Thus, the project is behind schedule, and there are cost overruns. Harky needs to move faster on this project to finish on time. He must also control future costs carefully to try to eliminate the current cost overrun of $12,000. To monitor and control costs, the budgeted amount, the value of work completed, and the actual costs should be computed periodically.

Managing Other Resources

So far, we have focused on monitoring and controlling costs. Although this is clearly an important issue, there may be other resources (e.g., labor, machinery, materials) that also need to be carefully planned for and monitored in order for a project to finish on schedule. For example, activity E (build high-temperature burner) may need some specialized equipment in order to be performed. Likewise, installation of the air pollution device (activity G) may require a specialist to be present. It is important, therefore, that we be aware of such resource requirements and ensure that the right resources are available at the right time.

Just as we constructed a weekly budget using activity schedules and costs (see Figures 7.17 and 7.18), we can construct weekly requirement charts for any resource. Assume that Lester Harky has estimated the support staff requirement for each of the eight activities in the project, as shown in Table 7.5. For example, during each week that activity A is in progress, Harky needs four support staffers to be available.

Table 7.5: Support Staff Requirements for General Foundry

Activity	Description	Support Staff Needed Per Week
A	Build internal components	4
B	Modify roof and floor	5
C	Construct collection stack	6
D	Pour concrete and install frame	4
E	Build high-temperature burner	3
F	Install pollution control system	4
G	Install air pollution device	7
H	Inspect and test	2

Figure 7.21 shows the weekly support staff needed for General Foundry's project using EST values.

Support Staff Requirements for General Foundry, Using EST

Activity	1	2	3	4	5	6	7	8	9	10	11	12	13	14	15	Total Staff
A	4	4														8
B	5	5	5													15
C			6	6												12
D				4	4	4	4									16
E					3	3	3	3								12
F					4	4	4									12
G								7	7	7	7	7				35
H													2	2		4
																114
Total per week	9	9	11	10	11	11	11	3	7	7	7	7	7	2	2	
Total to date	9	18	29	39	50	61	72	75	82	89	96	103	110	112	114	

(Staff required on a weekly basis.) (Cumulative staff needed.) (Total staff needed over all activities.)

Figure 7.21: Excel Layout to Compute General Foundry's Weekly Staff Requirements Using Earliest Start Times

📊 File: Figure 7.21.xlsx

A graph that plots the total resource (such as labor) needed per period (*Y*-axis) versus time (*X*-axis) is called a resource loading chart. Figure 7.22 shows the support staff loading chart for General Foundry's project.

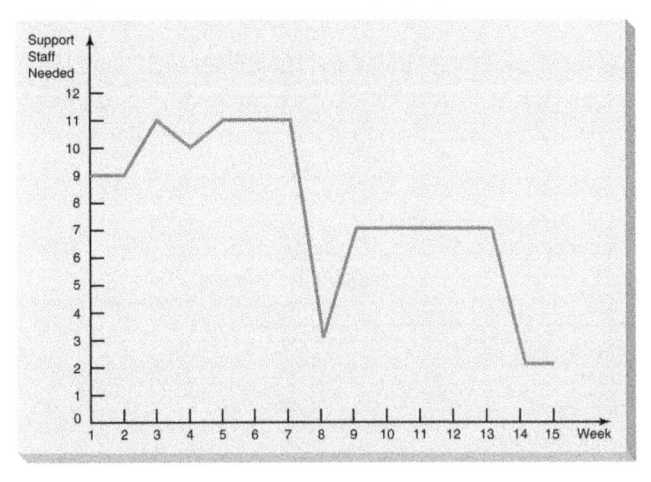

Figure 7.22: Support Staff Loading Chart for General Foundry

7.6 Project Crashing

While managing a project, it is not uncommon for a project manager to be faced with either (or both) of the following situations: (1) The project is behind schedule, and (2) the scheduled project completion time has been moved forward. In either situation, some or all of the remaining activities need to be speeded up in order to finish the project by the desired due date. The process of shortening the duration of a project in the least expensive manner possible is called crashing.

As noted in section 7.2, the CPM is a deterministic technique in which each activity has two estimates of time. The first is the *standard* or *normal* time that we used in our computation of earliest and latest times. Associated with this standard time is the *standard* or *normal cost* of the activity, which we used in section 7.5 to schedule and monitor the cost of the project.

Decision Modeling In Action

Turning Project Uncertainties into Business Opportunities

Although economists argue that uncertainties are necessary for the existence of opportunities, practitioners view uncertainties as risks that have a negative impact on a project's implementation. A study was conducted on 20 projects to identify the classes of opportunities and the contextual situations under which they occur.

The identified opportunities were grouped into four main categories: technology innovation, implementation process (i.e., outsourcing), business process (i.e., early market penetration), and future projects. In contrast, the 33 situations of project uncertainty defined by the project managers were grouped into six classes: contextual turbulences, stakeholders' uncertainties, technological uncertainties, organizational uncertainties, malpractice, and project environment uncertainties.

Mapping was conducted to see the linkage between opportunities and uncertainties, and it was found that all the identified opportunities were connected with at least one situation of uncertainty but not every situation of uncertainty related to opportunities. The study concluded that the lack of a clear distinction between risk and uncertainty during the project allows for misperceptions that lead to missed opportunities at the project and enterprise level.

Source: Based on T. Lechler, B. Edington, and T. Gao. "Challenging Classic Project Management: Turning Project Uncertainties into Business Opportunities," *Project Management Journal* 43, 6 (2012): 59–69.

The second time is the *crash time*, which is defined as the shortest duration required to complete an activity. Associated with this crash time is the *crash cost* of the activity. Usually, we can shorten an activity by adding extra resources (e.g., equipment, people) to it. Hence, it is logical for the crash cost of an activity to be higher than its standard cost.

The amount of time by which an activity can be shortened (i.e., the difference between its standard time and crash time) depends on the activity in question. We may not be able to shorten some activities at all. For example, if a casting needs to be heat-treated in a furnace for 48 hours, adding more resources does not help shorten the time. In contrast, we may be able to shorten some activities significantly (e.g., we may be able to frame a house in three days instead of 10 days by using three times as many workers).

Likewise, the cost of crashing (or shortening) an activity depends on the nature of the activity. Managers usually are interested in speeding up a project at the least additional cost. Hence, in choosing which activities to crash, and by how much, we need to ensure that all the following occur:

- The amount by which an activity is crashed is, in fact, permissible.
- Taken together, the shortened activity durations will enable us to finish the project by the due date.
- The total cost of crashing is as small as possible.

In the following pages, we first illustrate how to crash a small project using simple calculations that can even be performed by hand. Then, we describe an LP-based approach that can be used to determine the optimal crashing scheme for projects of any size.

Crashing General Foundry's Project (Hand Calculations)

Suppose that General Foundry has been given only 13 weeks (instead of 16 weeks) to install the new pollution control equipment or face a court-ordered shutdown. As you may recall, the length of Lester Harky's critical path was 15 weeks. Which activities should Harky crash, and by how much, in order to meet this 13-week due date? Naturally, Harky is interested in speeding up the project by two weeks, at the least additional cost.

Crashing a project using hand calculations involves four steps, as follows:

Four Steps of Project Crashing

1. Compute the crash cost per week (or other time period) for all activities in the network. If crash costs are assumed to be linear over time, the following formula can be used:

$$\text{Crash cost per period} = \frac{(\text{Crash cost} - \text{Standard cost})}{(\text{Standard time} - \text{Crash time})} \quad \quad (7\text{--}14)$$

2. Using the current activity times, find the critical path(s) in the project network. Identify the critical activities.
3. If there is only one critical path, select the activity on this critical path that (a) can still be crashed and (b) has the smallest crash cost per period. Crash this activity by one period.

    If there is more than one critical path, select one activity from each critical path such that (a) each selected activity can still be crashed, and (b) total crash cost per period of all selected activities is the smallest. Crash each activity by one period. Note that a single activity may be common to more than one critical path.
4. Update all activity times. If the desired due date has been reached, stop. If not, return to step 2.

General Foundry's standard and crash times and standard and crash costs are shown in Table 7.6. Note, for example, that activity B's standard time is three weeks (the estimate used in computing the current critical path), and its crash time is one week. This means that activity B can be shortened by up to two weeks if extra resources are provided. The cost of these additional resources is $4,000 (= Difference between the crash cost of $34,000 and the standard cost of $30,000). If we assume that the crashing cost is linear over time (i.e., the cost is the same each week), activity B's crash cost per week is $2,000 (= $4,000 / 2 weeks).

Table 7.6: Standard and Crash Times and Costs for General Foundry

Activity	Time (weeks) Standard	Crash	Cost Standard	Crash	Crash Cost Per Week
A	2	1	$22,000	$22,750	$ 750
B	3	1	$30,000	$34,000	$2,000
C	2	1	$26,000	$27,000	$1,000
D	4	3	$48,000	$49,000	$1,000
E	4	2	$56,000	$58,000	$1,000
F	3	2	$30,000	$30,500	$ 500
G	5	2	$80,000	$84,500	$1,500
H	2	1	$16,000	$19,000	$3,000

This calculation is shown in Figure 7.23. Crash costs for all other activities can be computed in a similar fashion.

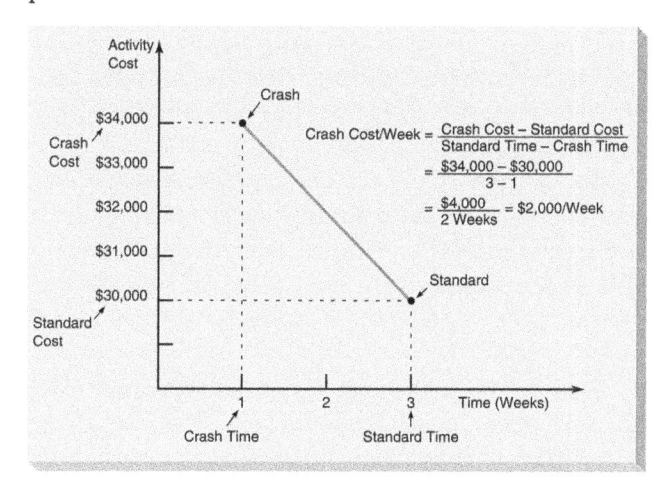

Figure 7.23: Standard and Crash Times and Costs for Activity B

Steps 2, 3, and 4 of the project-crashing process can now be applied to reduce General Foundry's project completion time at a minimum cost. For your convenience, we show the project network for General Foundry again in Figure 7.24.

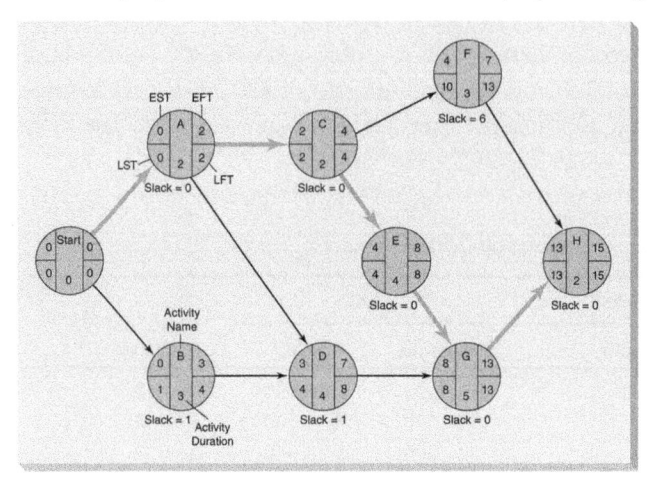

Figure 7.24: Critical Path and Slack Times for General Foundry

The current critical path (using standard times) is Start-A-C-E-G-H, in which Start is a dummy starting activity. Of these critical activities, activity A has the lowest crash cost per week, at $750. Harky, therefore, should crash activity A by one week to reduce the project completion time to 14 weeks. The cost is an additional $750. Note that activity A cannot be crashed any further because it has reached its crash limit of one week.

At this stage, the original path Start-A-C-E-G-H remains critical, with a completion time of 14 weeks. However, a new path Start-B-D-G-H is also critical now, with a completion time of 14 weeks. Hence, any further crashing must be done to both critical paths.

On each of these critical paths, we need to identify one activity that can still be crashed. We also want the total cost of crashing an activity on each path to be the smallest. We might be tempted to simply pick the activities with the smallest crash cost per period in each path. If we do this, we would select activity C from the first path and activity D from the second path. The total crash cost would then be $2,000 (= $1,000 + $1,000).

But we spot that activity G is common to both paths. That is, by crashing activity G, we will simultaneously reduce the completion time of both paths. Even though the $1,500 crash cost for activity G is higher than that for activities C or D, we would still prefer crashing G because the total cost is now only $1,500 (compared with the $2,000 if we crash C and D).

Hence, to crash the project down to 13 weeks, Lester Harky should crash activity A by one week and activity G by one week. The total additional cost is $2,250 (= $750 + $1,500).

Crashing General Foundry's Project Using Linear Programming

Although the preceding crashing procedure is simple for projects involving just a few activities, it can become extremely cumbersome to use for larger projects. Linear programming (LP) is an excellent technique for determining the optimal (i.e., least expensive) way to crash even larger projects. Let us examine how this technique may be used here.

The data needed for General Foundry's project crashing LP model are the standard and crash time and cost data (see Table 7.6) and the activity precedence information (see Figure 7.24). We develop the model as follows.

EXCEL NOTES

- In each of our Excel layouts, for clarity, changing variable cells are shaded yellow, the objective cell is shaded green, and cells containing the left-hand-side (LHS) formula for each constraint are shaded blue.

- Also, to make the equivalence of the written formulation and the Excel layout clear, our Excel layouts show the decision variable names used in the written formulation of the model. Note that these names have no role in using Solver to solve the model.

Decision Variables As with all the LP models we formulated in Chapters 2–5, we begin by defining the decision variables. For each activity i, we define the following two decision variables:

T_i = Time at which activity i starts
C_i = Number of periods (weeks, in this case) by which activity i is crashed

Because there are eight activities in General Foundry's project, there are 16 decision variables in the project crashing LP model.

Objective Function Next, we formulate the objective function. The objective function here is to minimize the total cost of crashing the project down to 13 weeks. Using the crash cost per week, computed in Table 7.6, we can express this as follows:

$$\text{Minimize total crash cost} = \$750C_A + \$2{,}000C_B + \$1{,}000C_C + \$1{,}000C_D \\ + \$1{,}000C_E + \$500C_F + \$1{,}500C_G + \$3{,}000C_H$$

Precedence Constraints Finally, we formulate the constraints. The first set of constraints in this LP model enforces the precedence relationships between activities (shown in the project network in Figure 7.24). We write one constraint for each precedence relationship (i.e., arc) in the project network. In writing these constraints, we must remember that the duration of each activity may be reduced by a crash amount (C_i). For example, consider the precedence relationship between activities A and C. Activity A starts at time T_A, and its duration is $(2 - C_A)$ weeks. Hence, activity A finishes at time $(T_A + 2 - C_A)$. This implies that the earliest start time of activity C (i.e., T_C) can be *no earlier* than $(T_A + 2 - C_A)$. We can express this mathematically as

$$T_C \geq T_A + (2 - C_A) \quad (\text{precedence } A \rightarrow C)$$

In a similar fashion, we can express all other activity precedence relationships as follows:

$$T_D \geq T_A + (2 - C_A) \quad (\text{precedence } A \rightarrow D)$$
$$T_D \geq T_B + (3 - C_B) \quad (\text{precedence } B \rightarrow D)$$
$$T_E \geq T_C + (2 - C_C) \quad (\text{precedence } C \rightarrow E)$$
$$T_F \geq T_C + (2 - C_C) \quad (\text{precedence } C \rightarrow F)$$
$$T_G \geq T_D + (4 - C_D) \quad (\text{precedence } D \rightarrow G)$$
$$T_G \geq T_E + (4 - C_E) \quad (\text{precedence } E \rightarrow G)$$
$$T_H \geq T_F + (3 - C_F) \quad (\text{precedence } F \rightarrow H)$$
$$T_H \geq T_G + (5 - C_G) \quad (\text{precedence } G \rightarrow H)$$

Crash Time Limit Constraints We need a second set of constraints to restrict the number of periods by which each activity can be crashed. Using the crash time limits given in Table 7.6, we can write these constraints as

$$C_A \leq 1 \quad C_B \leq 2 \quad C_C \leq 1 \quad C_D \leq 1$$
$$C_E \leq 2 \quad C_F \leq 1 \quad C_G \leq 3 \quad C_H \leq 1$$

Project Completion Constraint Finally, we specify that the project must be completed in 13 weeks or less. Activity H, the last activity in the project, starts at time T_H. The standard time for H is two weeks, and C_H denotes the number of weeks by which its duration can be crashed. Hence, the actual duration of activity H is $(2 - C_H)$, and its completion time is $(T_H + 2 - C_H)$. We write this constraint, and the nonnegativity constraints, as

$$T_H + 2 - C_H \leq 13$$

$$\text{All } T_i \text{ and } C_i \geq 0$$

Excel Solution Figure 7.25 shows the formula view of the Excel layout for General

Foundry's project crashing LP model. This layout follows the same structure and logic we have used in earlier chapters for all LP models. That is, we have modeled all parameters (solution value, objective coefficients, and constraint coefficients) associated with a decision variable in a separate column of the worksheet. We then have computed the objective function and LHS formulas for all constraints, using Excel's SUMPRODUCT function. In implementing this model in Excel, we have algebraically modified each constraint so that all variables are in the LHS of the equation, and only a constant appears on the right-hand side (RHS). For example, the precedence relationship between activities A and C has been modified from $[T_C \geq T_A + (2 - C_A)]$ to $[T_C - T_A + C_A \geq 2]$.

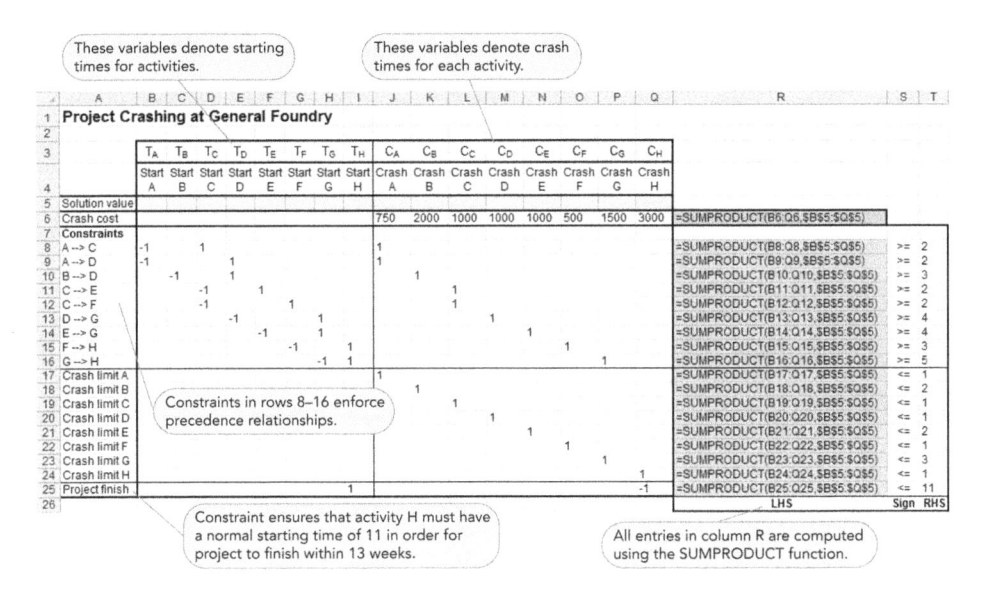

Figure 7.25: Formula View of Excel Layout for Project Crashing at General Foundry

File: Figure 7.25.xlsx, Sheet: Figure 7.25

Interpreting the Results The Solver entries and solution for this LP model are shown in Figure 7.26. The results show that the General Foundry project can be crashed to 13 weeks, at a cost of $2,250 (cell R6). To do so, activities A (cell J5) and G (cell P5) should be crashed by one week each. As expected, this is the same as the result we obtained earlier, using hand calculations. Cells B5:I5 show the revised starting times for activities A through H, respectively.

424 — Chapter 7: Project Management

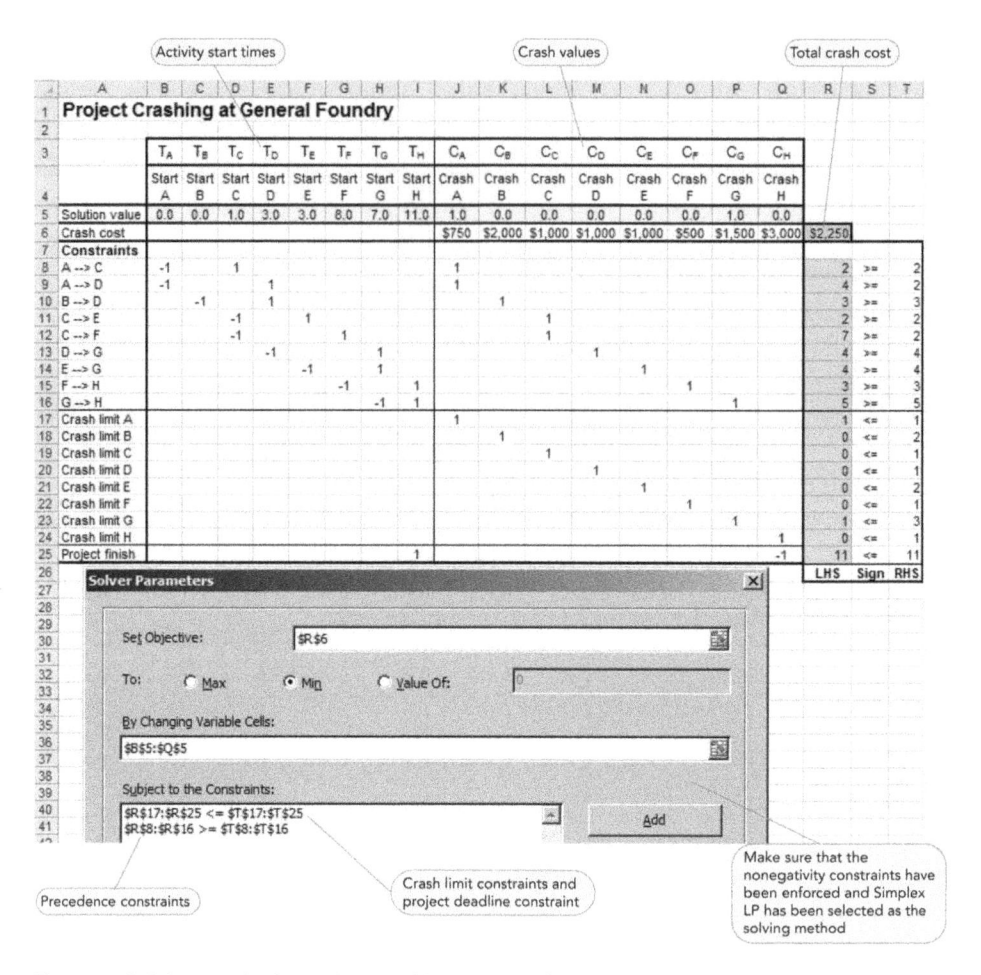

Figure 7.26: Solver Entries for Project Crashing at General Foundry

File: Figure 7.25.xlsx, Sheet: Figure 7.26

Using Linear Programming to Determine Earliest and Latest Starting Times

It turns out that we can make minor modifications to the project crashing LP model presented earlier to compute the EST and LST for each activity in a project. However, because the two-pass procedure we discussed in section 7.3 is rather straightforward, LP is seldom used in practice for this purpose. For this reason, we do not discuss these LP models in detail here and just briefly illustrate their construction.

We first modify the project crashing LP model by removing the project completion constraint and setting all crashing decision variables (C_i) to zero. All precedence constraints in this model remain as is. Then, we solve two LP models in sequence: the first to identify the earliest times and the second to identify the latest times. The

additional modifications needed to the project crashing LP model for each of these models are as follows:
- **LP model for earliest starting times.** In this LP model, we set the objective function to *minimize* the sum of all activity starting times. That is, the objective is

$$\text{Minimize sum of activity times} = T_A + T_B + \cdots + T_H$$

- **LP model for latest starting times.** In this LP model, we set the objective function to *maximize* the sum of all activity starting times. That is, the objective is

$$\text{Maximize sum of activity times} = T_A + T_B + \cdots + T_H$$

However, we need to ensure that the entire project finishes at its earliest completion time (as computed by the LP model for the EST). Hence, we add a constraint regarding the starting time of the *last activity* in the project. For example, in General Foundry's project, we set the LST of activity H at 13 weeks (i.e., $T_H = 13$).

7.7 Summary

This chapter presents the fundamentals of project management techniques. We discuss two techniques, PERT and CPM, both of which are excellent for controlling large and complex projects.

We first show how to express projects using project networks. Using a two-pass procedure, we can then identify the project schedule and the critical path(s). PERT is probabilistic and allows three time estimates for each activity; these estimates are used to compute the project's expected completion time and variance. We show how to use these parameters to find the probability that the project will be completed by a given date.

We discuss how project management techniques can also be used to plan, schedule, monitor, and control project costs. Using these techniques, we show how to determine at any point whether a project is on schedule and whether there are cost overruns or underruns.

Finally, we discuss how to crash projects by reducing their completion time through additional resource expenditures. We also illustrate how LP can be used to find the least-cost approach to crashing large projects.

Key Points
- Project management techniques can be used to manage large, complex projects.
- There are three phases in managing large projects: planning, scheduling, and controlling.
- Gantt charts are useful for project scheduling, and they are used in large projects mainly to provide project summaries.
- Projects must be monitored and controlled at regular intervals.

- Software packages automate many of the routine calculations in project management.
- Excel is not a convenient software tool to use for project management.
- A project can be subdivided into several activities.
- An activity in a project may be a project of its own.
- A work breakdown structure details the activities in a project.
- Activity times for a project need to be estimated.
- PERT, a probabilistic technique, and CPM, a deterministic technique, are two popular project management techniques.
- When drawing a project network, it is enough to list only the immediate predecessors for each activity.
- Networks consist of nodes that are connected by arcs.
- There are two types of project networks—Activity on Node (AON) and Activity on Arc (AOA).
- Nodes denote activities in an AON network.
- Arcs denote precedence relationships in an AON network.
- It is convenient, but not required, to have unique starting and ending activities in a project.
- Critical path analysis helps determine the project schedule.
- The critical path is the longest path in the network.
- In critical path analysis, we use a two-pass procedure to find the project schedule.
- The forward pass in critical path analysis identifies all the earliest times.
- All predecessor activities must be completed before an activity can begin.
- Earliest Finish Time (EFT) = Earliest Start Time (EST) + Activity time.
- EST of an activity = Maximum EFT of all predecessor activities.
- The backward pass in critical path analysis finds all the latest times.
- Latest Start Time (LST) = Latest Finish time (LFT) – Activity time.
- LFT of an activity = Minimum LST of all activities that follow.
- Slack time is free time for an activity.
- Critical activities have no slack time.
- A project can have multiple critical paths.
- Total slack time is shared among more than one activity, while free slack time is associated with a single activity.
- Activity times may be subject to variability.
- There are three approaches to studying the impact of variability in activity times: (1) adding "buffers" to activity times, (2) employing PERT analysis, and (3) using computer simulation.
- PERT uses three time estimates for each activity.
- The beta probability distribution is often used to describe activity times.
- With PERT, the expected activity time is used in the project network to compute all earliest and latest times.

- With PERT, we compute the project variance by summing variances of only those activities that are on the critical path.
- With PERT, we can compute the probability of project completion, or we can compute the due date for a given probability.
- With PERT, noncritical paths with large variances should be closely monitored.
- The budgeting process determines the budget per period of the project.
- We can form a weekly budget using EST values, LST values, or any start values in between.
- We can track costs to see if the project is on budget.
- We can compute the value of work completed for each activity and then compute cost underruns and overruns.
- Other resources besides costs can also be planned for and monitored.
- Reducing a project's duration is called crashing.
- Crash time is the shortest duration of an activity.
- With crashing, we want to find the cheapest way of crashing a project to the desired due date.
- Crashing assumes that crash costs are linear over time.
- Crashing activities common to more than one critical path may be cheapest.
- Linear programming (LP) can be used to determine the optimal crashing plan.
- The decision variables in an LP model for crashing are the activity start times and crash amounts.
- The objective in crashing is typically to minimize total crash cost.
- The constraints define the precedence relationships in the project network.
- Each activity can typically be crashed by only a finite amount, which may sometimes be zero (i.e., that activity cannot be crashed).
- In crashing models, there is usually one constraint that specifies the desired project due date.

Glossary

Activity A job or task that consumes time and is a key subpart of a total project.

Activity on Arc (AOA) Network A project network in which arcs denote activities and nodes denote events.

Activity on Node (AON) Network A project network in which nodes denote activities and arcs denote precedence relationships.

Activity Time The duration of an activity.

Backward Pass A procedure that moves from the end of the network to the beginning of the network and is used in determining an activity's LFT and LST.

Beta Probability Distribution A probability distribution that is often used in PERT to compute expected activity completion times and variances.

Crashing The process of reducing the total time it takes to complete a project by expending additional funds.

Critical Activities Critical activities have zero slack time.

Critical Path A series of activities that have zero slack. It is the longest time path through the network. A delay for any activity that is on the critical path will delay the completion of the entire project.

Critical Path Analysis An analysis that determines the total project completion time, the critical path for the project, slack, EST, EFT, LST, and LFT for every activity.

Critical Path Method (CPM) A deterministic network technique that is similar to PERT but uses only one time estimate. CPM is used for monitoring budgets and project crashing.

Dummy Activity A fictitious activity that consumes no time and is inserted into an AOA project network to display the proper precedence relationships between activities.

Earliest Finish Time (EFT) The earliest time that an activity can be finished without violation of precedence requirements.

Earliest Start Time (EST) The earliest time that an activity can start without violation of precedence requirements.

Event A point in time that marks the beginning or ending of an activity. It is used in AOA networks.

Expected Activity Time (t) The average time it should take to complete an activity. Expected time $= (a + 4m + b)/6$.

Forward Pass A procedure that moves from the beginning of a network to the end of the network. It is used in determining an activity's EST and EFT.

Gantt Chart An alternative to project networks for showing a project schedule.

Immediate Predecessor An activity that must be completed before another activity can be started.

Latest Finish Time (LFT) The latest time that an activity can be finished without delaying the entire project.

Latest Start Time (LST) The latest time that an activity can be started without delaying the entire project.

Most Likely Time (m) The amount of time that you would expect it would take to complete an activity. Used in PERT.

Optimistic Time (a) The shortest amount of time that could be required to complete an activity. Used in PERT.

Pessimistic Time (b) The greatest amount of time that could be required to complete an activity. Used in PERT.

Program Evaluation and Review Technique (PERT) A probabilistic modeling procedure that allows three time estimates for each activity in a project.

Project Management A decision modeling approach that allows managers to plan, schedule, and control projects.

Project Network A graphical display of a project that shows activities and precedence relationships.

Resource Loading Chart A graph that plots the resource needed per period versus time.

Slack Time The amount of time that an activity can be delayed without delaying the entire project. Slack = LST − EST or LFT − EFT.
Variance of Activity Completion Time A measure of dispersion of the activity completion time. Variance $=[(b-a)/6]^2$.
Work Breakdown Structure (WBS) A plan that details the activities in a project.

7.8 Exercises

Solved Problems

Solved Problem 7–1 To complete the wing assembly for an experimental aircraft, Scott DeWitte has laid out the seven major activities involved. These activities have been labeled A through G in the following table, which also shows their estimated times (in weeks) and immediate predecessors:

Activity	a	m	b	Immediate Predecessors
A	1	2	3	—
B	2	3	4	—
C	4	5	6	A
D	8	9	10	B
E	2	5	8	C, D
F	4	5	6	D
G	1	2	3	E

Determine the expected time and variance for each activity.

Solution For each activity, the expected time and variance can be computed using the formulas presented in Equations 7–6 and 7–7, respectively. The results are summarized in the following table:

Activity	Expected Time (weeks)	Variance
A	2	0.111
B	3	0.111
C	5	0.111
D	9	0.111
E	5	1.000
F	5	0.111
G	2	0.111

Solved Problem 7–2 Referring to Solved Problem 7–1, Scott now would like to determine the critical path for the entire wing assembly project, as well as the expected completion time for the total project. In addition, he would like to determine the probability that the project will finish in 21 weeks or less.

Solution The AON network for Scott DeWitte's project is shown in Figure 7.27. Note that this project has multiple activities (A and B) with no immediate predecessors and multiple activities (F and G) with no successors. Hence, in addition to a dummy unique starting activity (Start), we have included a dummy unique finishing activity (End) for the project.

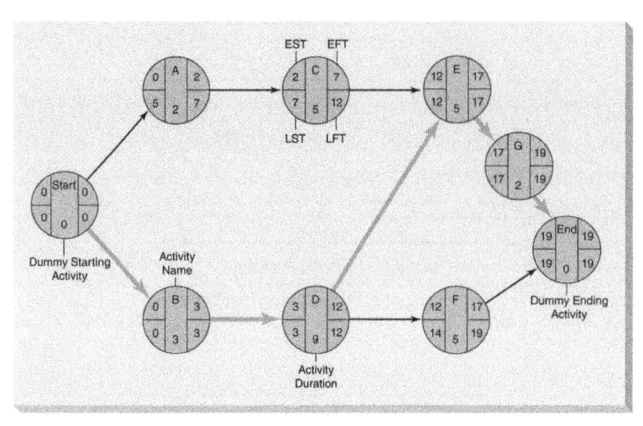

Figure 7.27: Critical Path for Solved Problem 7–2

Figure 7.27 shows the earliest and latest times for all activities. The activities along the critical path are B, D, E, and G. These activities have zero slack. The expected project completion time is 19 weeks. The sum of the variances of the critical activities is 1.333, which implies that the standard deviation of the project completion time is 1.155 weeks. Hence,

$$P(\text{Completion time} \leq 21 \text{ weeks}) = P(Z \leq (21-19)/1.155) = P(Z \leq 1.73)$$
$$= 0.9582 \text{ (from Appendix C)}$$

Discussion Questions

7–1. What are some of the questions that can be answered with project management?
7–2. What are the major differences between PERT and CPM?
7–3. What is an activity? What is an immediate predecessor?
7–4. Describe how expected activity times and variances can be computed in a PERT analysis.
7–5. Briefly discuss what is meant by critical path analysis. What are critical path activities, and why are they important?
7–6. What are the EST and LST? How are they computed?
7–7. Describe the meaning of slack and discuss how it can be determined.

7-8. How can we determine the probability that a project will be completed by a certain date? What assumptions are made in this computation?

7-9. Briefly describe how project budgets can be monitored.

7-10. What is crashing, and how is it done by hand?

7-11. Why is LP useful in project crashing?

Problems

7-12. A certification program consists of a series of activities that must be accomplished in a certain order. The activities, their immediate predecessors, and estimated durations appear in the following table.

Activity	Immediate Predecessors	Time (days)
A	—	2
B	—	5
C	—	1
D	B	10
E	A, D	3
F	C	6
G	E, F	8

(a) Develop a project network for the certification program.
(b) Determine the EST, EFT, LST, LFT, and slack for each activity. Also determine the total program completion time and the critical path(s).

7-13. A local political campaign must coordinate a number of necessary activities to be prepared for an upcoming election. The following table describes the relationships between these activities that need to be completed, as well as estimated times.

Activity	Immediate Predecessors	Time (weeks)
A	—	4
B	—	6
C	A	3
D	A	4
E	B, C	8
F	B	7
G	D, E	2
H	F	1

(a) Develop a project network for this problem.
(b) Determine the EST, EFT, LST, LFT, and slack for each activity. Also determine the total project completion time and the critical path(s).

7-14. The Pickett Marketing Firm is developing a new Web-based media campaign for a client. The following table describes the relationships between the activities that need to be completed.

Activity	Immediate Predecessors	Time (days)
A	—	4
B	A	6
C	B	12
D	B	11
E	D	9
F	D	8
G	D	10
H	C	5
I	C	7
J	E, F, G	4
K	H, I	9

(a) Develop a project network for this problem.
(b) Determine the EST, EFT, LST, LFT, and slack for each activity. Also determine the total project completion time and the critical path(s).

7–15. The activities required to design a prototype of an experimental machine are listed in the following table, along with their immediate predecessors and estimated durations.

Activity	Immediate Predecessors	Time (days)
A	—	5
B	—	4
C	A	2
D	A	1
E	B	5
F	B	7
G	C, E	9
H	D, F	6

(a) Develop a project network for this problem.
(b) Determine the EST, EFT, LST, LFT, and slack for each activity. Also determine the total project completion time and the critical path(s).

7–16. An office complex is to be renovated. Before the job can be completed, various tradespeople and skilled workers must install their materials. The table for this problem describes the relationships between the activities that need to be completed.

Activity	Immediate Predecessors	Time (days)
A1	—	5
A2	A1	6
A3	A1	2
A4	A1	9
A5	A2	9
A6	A3, A4	3
A7	A4	7
A8	A4	4
A9	A5, A6, A7	6
A10	A8	5

(a) Develop a project network for this problem.
(b) Determine the EST, EFT, LST, LFT, and slack for each activity. Also determine the total project completion time and the critical path(s).

7–17. An electrical contractor is examining the amount of time his crews take to complete wiring jobs. Some crews seem to take longer than others. For an upcoming job, a list of activities and their optimistic, most likely, and pessimistic completion times are given in the following table.

Activity	a	m	b	Immediate Predecessors
A	3	6	9	—
B	2	4	6	—
C	1	2	3	—
D	6	7	8	C
E	2	4	6	B, D
F	6	10	14	A, E
G	1	2	6	A, E
H	3	6	9	F
I	10	11	12	G
J	14	16	21	G
K	2	8	11	H, I

(a) Develop a project network for this problem.
(b) Determine the expected duration and variance for each activity.
(c) Determine the EST, EFT, LST, LFT, and slack for each activity. Also determine the total project completion time and critical path(s) for installing electrical wiring and equipment.
(d) What is the probability that this job will finish in 38 days or less?

7–18. A plant engineering group needs to set up an assembly line to produce a new product. The following table describes the relationships between the activities that need to be completed for this product to be manufactured.

	Days			
Activity	a	m	b	Immediate Predecessors
A	3	6	6	—
B	5	8	11	A
C	5	6	10	A
D	1	2	6	B, C
E	7	11	15	D
F	7	9	14	D
G	6	8	10	D
H	3	4	8	F, G
I	3	5	7	E, F, H

(a) Develop a project network for this problem.
(b) Determine the expected duration and variance for each activity.
(c) Determine the EST, EFT, LST, LFT, and slack for each activity. Also determine the total project completion time and the critical path(s).
(d) Determine the probability that the project will be completed in less than 34 days.
(e) Determine the probability that the project will take more than 29 days.

7–19. A plant is acquiring new production machinery. Before the machinery can be fully functional, a number of activities must be performed, including roughing out for power, placing the machinery, installing the equipment that will feed product to the machinery, etc. The activities, their precedence relationships, and their durations are shown in the following table.

	Days			
Activity	a	m	b	Immediate Predecessors
A	8	10	12	—
B	6	7	8	—
C	3	3	6	—
D	10	20	30	A
E	6	7	8	C
F	9	10	11	B, D, E
G	6	7	11	B, D, E
H	14	15	16	F
I	10	11	12	F
J	6	7	8	G, H
K	4	7	10	I, J
L	1	2	6	G, H

(a) Determine the expected times and variances for each activity.
(b) Construct a project network for this problem.

(c) Determine the EST, EFT, LST, LFT, and slack for each activity. Also determine the critical path and project completion time.
(d) What is the probability that the project will be finished in 70 days?
(e) What is the probability that the project will need at least 75 days?

7–20. A series of activities must be completed in a coordinated fashion to complete a landscaping overhaul. The following table shows the activities; their optimistic, most likely, and pessimistic durations; and their immediate predecessors.

Activity	Days a	Days m	Days b	Immediate Predecessors
A	4	8	12	—
B	4	10	13	A
C	7	14	18	B
D	9	16	20	B
E	6	9	12	B
F	2	4	6	D, E
G	4	7	13	C, F
H	3	5	7	G
I	2	3	4	G, H

(a) Determine the expected times and variances for each activity.
(b) Construct a project network for this problem.
(c) Determine the EST, EFT, LST, LFT, and slack for each activity. Also determine the critical path and project completion time.
(d) What is the probability that the project will be finished in less than 57 days?
(e) What is the probability that the project will need at least 50 days?

7–21. LeBron Woods is responsible for developing a leadership-training program for his organization. The following table describes the relationships between the activities that need to be completed.

Activity	Days a	Days m	Days b	Immediate Predecessors
A	3	7	14	—
B	5	10	15	—
C	3	5	10	A, B
D	5	12	13	C
E	2	5	8	C
F	2	5	14	E
G	5	8	11	F
H	6	10	14	D
I	3	4	8	F, H
J	4	7	10	G, I

(a) Determine the expected times and variances for each activity.
(b) Construct a project network for this problem.
(c) Determine the EST, EFT, LST, LFT, and slack for each activity. Also determine the critical path and project completion time.
(d) What is the probability that the project will be finished in less than 49 days?
(e) What is the probability that the project will need at least 54 days?

7–22. The expected project completion time for the construction of a pleasure yacht is 21 months, and the project variance is 6. What is the probability that the project will
(a) require at least 17 months?
(b) be completed within 20 months?
(c) require at least 23 months?
(d) be completed within 25 months?

7–23. The Coogan Construction Company has determined that the expected completion time for its most popular model home follows the normal probability distribution with a mean of 25 weeks and a standard deviation of four weeks.
(a) What is the probability that the next home will be completed within 30 weeks?
(b) What is the probability that the next home will be completed within 22 weeks?
(c) Find the number of weeks within which Coogan is 99% sure the next home will be completed.
(d) Find the number of weeks within which Coogan is 85% sure the next home will be completed.

7–24. The General Foundry air pollution project discussed in this chapter has progressed over the past several weeks, and it is now the end of week 8. Lester Harky would like to know the value of the work completed, the amount of any cost overruns or underruns for the project, and the extent to which the project is ahead of schedule or behind schedule by developing a table like the one in Figure 7.20. The current project status is shown in the following table.

Activity	Percentage Completed	Actual Cost
A	100	$20,000
B	100	$36,000
C	100	$26,000
D	100	$44,000
E	55	$29,000
F	55	$12,000
G	10	$ 5,000
H	13	$ 1,800

7-25. Fred Ridgeway has been given the responsibility of managing a training and development program. He knows the EST and LST (both in months), and the total costs for each activity. This information is given in the table for this problem.

Activity	EST	LST	t	Total Cost
A	0	0	6	$10,000
B	1	4	2	$14,000
C	3	3	7	$ 5,000
D	4	9	3	$ 6,000
E	6	6	10	$14,000
F	14	15	11	$13,000
G	12	18	2	$ 4,000
H	14	14	11	$ 6,000
I	18	21	6	$18,000
J	18	19	4	$12,000
K	22	22	14	$10,000
L	22	23	8	$16,000
M	18	24	6	$18,000

(a) Using ESTs, determine Fred's total monthly budget.
(b) Using LSTs, determine Fred's total monthly budget.

7-26. Fred Ridgeway's project (see Problem 7–25) has progressed over the past several months, and it is now the end of month 16. Fred would like to know the current status of the project with regard to schedule and budget by developing an appropriate table. The relevant data are shown in the following table.

Activity	Percentage Completed	Actual Cost
A	100	$13,000
B	100	$12,000
C	100	$ 6,000
D	100	$ 6,000
E	60	$ 9,000
F	10	$ 800
G	80	$ 3,600
H	15	$ 375

Assume that activities not shown in the table have not yet started and have incurred no cost to date. All activities follow their earliest time schedules.

7-27. Susan Roger needs to coordinate the opening of a new office for her company in Denver. The activity time and relationships for this project, as well as the total budgeted cost for each activity, are shown in the following table.

Activity	Immediate Predecessors	Time (weeks)	Total Cost
A	—	2	$2,200
B	A	3	$5,100
C	A	4	$6,000
D	B, C	2	$3,600
E	C	3	$2,700
F	D, E	3	$1,800

(a) Develop a weekly budget for this project, using the earliest start times.
(b) Develop a weekly budget for this project, using the latest start times.

7-28. Susan Roger's project (see Problem 7–27) has progressed over the past several weeks, and it is now the end of week 8. Susan would like to know the current status of the project with regard to schedule and budget by developing an appropriate table. Assume that all activities follow their earliest time schedules. The relevant data are shown in the following table.

Activity	Percentage Completed	Actual Cost
A	100	$1,900
B	100	$5,300
C	100	$6,150
D	40	$1,800
E	60	$1,755
F	0	$ 0

7-29. General Foundry's project crashing data are shown in Table 7.6. Crash this project by hand to 10 weeks. What are the final times for each activity after crashing, and what is the total cost associated with reducing the duration of this project from 15 to 10 weeks?

7-30. Bowman Builders manufactures steel storage sheds for commercial use. Joe Bowman, president of Bowman Builders, is contemplating producing sheds for home use. The activities necessary to build an experimental model and related data are given in the table for this problem. The project completion time using standard times is 14 weeks.

Activity	Immediate Predecessors	Standard Time (weeks)	Standard Cost	Crash Time (weeks)	Crash Cost
A	—	3	$1,000	2	$1,600
B	—	2	$2,000	1	$2,700
C	—	1	$300	1	$300
D	A	7	$1,300	3	$1,600
E	B	6	$850	3	$1,000
F	C	2	$4,000	1	$5,000
G	D, E	4	$1,500	2	$2,000

Set up and solve an LP model using Excel to crash this project to 10 weeks. How much does it cost to reduce the duration of this project from 14 to 10 weeks?

7–31. The table for this problem describes the various activities of a construction project in a chemical plant.

Activity	Immediate Predecessors	Standard Time (days)	Standard Cost	Crash Time (days)	Crash Cost
A	—	4	$2,000	2	$2,600
B	A	6	$3,500	5	$4,300
C	A	8	$3,300	6	$3,900
D	B	5	$1,200	4	$1,800
E	C, D	3	$1,700	2	$2,200
F	E	7	$2,200	5	$3,600
G	E	5	$ 900	4	$1,550
H	F, G	4	$1,200	3	$1,700

(a) Set up and solve an LP model using Excel to crash this project to 22 days. What is the total crashing cost?

(b) Assuming each activity can only be crashed in whole days, what is the earliest completion of this project? What is the total associated crash cost?

7–32. A new order filling system needs to be installed as soon as possible. The table for this problem lists the project's activities and their predecessors. Also provided is the cost information to reduce the standard activity times.

Activity	Immediate Predecessors	Standard Time (days)	Standard Cost	Crash Time (days)	Crash Cost
A	—	7	$2,000	5	$ 3,500
B	A	10	$3,000	8	$ 4,700
C	A	8	$3,400	7	$ 3,700
D	C	6	$1,600	4	$ 2,600
E	C	7	$1,900	4	$ 4,000
F	D, E	5	$1,200	3	$ 2,800
G	B, C	11	$8,200	8	$10,900
H	F, G	4	$2,600	3	$ 3,800

Set up and solve an LP model using Excel to crash this project to 24 days. What is the total crashing cost?

7-33. Software Development Specialists (SDS) is involved with developing software for customers in the banking industry. SDS breaks a large programming project into teams that perform the necessary steps. Team A is responsible for going from general systems design all the way through to actual systems testing. This involves 18 separate activities. Team B is then responsible for the final installation.

To determine cost and time factors, optimistic, most likely, and pessimistic time estimates have been made for all the 18 activities involved for team A. The first step that this team performs is general systems design. The optimistic, most likely, and pessimistic times are 3, 4, and 5 weeks. Following this, a number of activities can begin. Activity 2 is involved with procedures design. Optimistic, most likely, and pessimistic times for completing this activity are 4, 5, and 12 weeks. Activity 3 is developing detailed report designs. Optimistic, most likely, and pessimistic time estimates are 6, 8, and 10 weeks. Activity 4, detailed forms design, has optimistic, most likely, and pessimistic time estimates of 2, 5, and 5 weeks.

Activities 5 and 6 involve writing detailed program specifications and developing file specifications. The three time estimates for activity 5 are 6, 7, and 8 weeks, and the three time estimates for activity 6 are 3, 4, and 5 weeks. Activity 7 involves specifying system test data. Before this is done, activity 6, involving file specifications, must be completed. The time estimates for activity 7 are 2, 3, and 7 weeks. Activity 8 involves reviewing forms. Before activity 8 can be conducted, detailed forms design must be completed. The time estimates for activity 8 are 3, 3, and 9 weeks. The next activity, activity 9, is reviewing the detailed report design. This requires that the detailed report design, activity 3, be completed first. The time estimates for activity 9 are 1, 3, and 5 weeks, respectively.

Activity 10 involves reviewing procedures design. Time estimates are 1, 2, and 9 weeks. Of course, procedures design must be done before activity 10 can be started. Activity 11 involves the system design checkpoint review. A number of activities must be completed before this is done. These activities include reviewing the forms, reviewing the detailed report design, reviewing the procedures design, writing detailed program specs, and specifying system test data. The optimistic, most likely, and pessimistic time estimates for activity 11 are 3, 4, and 5 weeks. Performing program logic design is activity 12. This can be started only after the system design checkpoint review is completed. The time estimates for activity 12 are 4, 5, and 6 weeks.

Activity 13, coding the programs, is done only after the program logic design is completed. The time estimates for this activity are 6, 10, and 14 weeks. Activity 14 is involved in developing test programs. Activity 13 is the immediate predecessor. Time estimates for activity 14 are 3, 4, and 11 weeks. Developing a system test plan is activity 15. A number of activities must be completed before activity 15 can be started. These activities include specifying system test data, writing detailed program specifications, and reviewing procedure designs, the detailed report design, and forms. The time estimates for activity 15 are 3, 4, and 5 weeks.

Activity 16, creating system test data, has time estimates of 2, 4, and 6 weeks. Activity 15 must be done before activity 16 can be started. Activity 17 is reviewing program test results. The immediate predecessor to activity 17 is to test the programs (activity 14). The three time estimates for activity 17 are 2, 3, and 4 weeks. The final activity is conducting system tests. This is activity 18. Before activity 18 can be started, activities 16 and 17 must be complete. The three time estimates for conducting these system tests are 2, 6, and 7 weeks.

How long will it take for team A to complete its programming assignment?

7–34. Bradshaw Construction is involved in constructing municipal buildings and other structures that are used primarily by city and state municipalities. The construction process involves developing legal documents, drafting feasibility studies, obtaining bond ratings, and so forth. Recently, Bradshaw was given a request to submit a proposal for the construction of a municipal building. The first step is to develop legal documents and to perform all steps necessary before the construction contract is signed. This requires more than 20 separate activities that must be completed. These activities, their immediate predecessors, and optimistic (a), most likely (m), and pessimistic (b) time estimates are given in the table for this problem.

Determine the total project completion time for this preliminary step, the critical path, and slack time for all activities involved.

Activity	a	m	b	Description of Activity	Immediate Predecessors
1	1	4	7	Draft legal documents	—
2	2	3	4	Prepare financial statements	—
3	3	4	5	Draft history	—
4	7	8	9	Draft demand portion of feasibility study	—
5	4	4	7	Review and approval of legal documents	1
6	1	2	6	Review and approval of history	3
7	4	5	6	Review feasibility study	4
8	1	2	6	Draft final financial portion of feasibility study	7
9	3	4	5	Draft facts relevant to the bond transaction	5
10	1	1	4	Review and approve financial statements	2
11	18	20	22	Receive firm price of project	—

		Weeks			
Activity	a	m	b	Description of Activity	Immediate Predecessors
12	1	2	3	Review and complete financial portion of feasibility study	8
13	1	1	4	Complete draft statement	6, 9, 10, 11, 12
14	0.25	0.50	0.75	Send all materials to bond rating services	13
15	0.20	0.30	0.40	Print statement and distributed it to all interested parties	14
16	1	1	4	Make presentation to bond rating services	14
17	1	2	3	Receive bond rating	16
18	3	5	7	Market bonds	15, 17
19	0.10	0.20	0.30	Execute purchase contract	18
20	0.10	0.15	0.50	Authorize and complete final statement	19
21	2	3	7	Purchase contract	19
22	0.20	0.50	0.80	Make bond proceeds available	20
23	0	0.20	0.40	Sign construction contract	21, 22

7–35. Getting a degree from a college or university can be a long and difficult task. Certain courses must be completed before other courses may be taken. Develop a network diagram in which every activity is a particular course that you must take for your degree program. The immediate predecessors will be course prerequisites. Don't forget to include all university, college, and departmental course requirements. Then try to group these courses into semesters or quarters for your particular school. How long do you think it will take you to graduate? Which courses, if not taken in the proper sequence, could delay your graduation?

7–36. Dream Team Productions is in the final design phases of its new film, *Killer Worms*, to be released next summer. Market Wise, the firm hired to coordinate the release of *Killer Worms* toys, has identified 16 activities to be completed before the release of the film. These activities, their immediate predecessors, and optimistic (a), most likely (m), and pessimistic (b) time estimates are given in the following table.

		Weeks		
Activity	Immediate Predecessors	a	m	b
A	—	1	2	6
B	—	3	3.5	4
C	—	10	12	14
D	—	4	5	9
E	—	2	4	6
F	A	6	7	8
G	B	2	4	6
H	C	5	7	9
I	C	9	10	14
J	C	2	4	6
K	D	2	4	6
L	E	2	4	6
M	F, G, H	5	6	7
N	J, K, L	1	1.5	2
O	I, M	5	7	9
P	N	5	7	9

(a) How many weeks in advance of the film release should Market Wise start its marketing campaign? What are the critical paths?

(b) If activities I and J were unnecessary, what impact would this have on the critical path and the number of weeks needed to complete the marketing campaign?

7-37. Sager Products has been in the business of manufacturing and marketing toys for toddlers for the past two decades. Jim Sager, president of the firm, is considering the development of a new manufacturing line to allow it to produce high-quality plastic toys at reasonable prices. The development process is long and complex. Jim estimates that there are five phases involved and multiple activities for each phase.

Phase 1 of the development process involves the completion of four activities. These activities have no immediate predecessors. Activity A has an optimistic completion time of 2 weeks, a most likely completion time of 3 weeks, and a pessimistic completion time of 4 weeks. Activity B has estimated values of 5, 6, and 10 weeks for these three completion times. Similarly, activity C has estimated completion times of 1, 1, and 4 weeks; and activity D has expected completion times of 8, 9, and 13 weeks.

Phase 2 involves six separate activities. Activity E has activity A as an immediate predecessor. Time estimates are 1, 1, and 4 weeks. Activity F and activity G both have activity B as their immediate predecessor. For activity F, the time estimates are 3, 4, and 5 weeks. For activity G, the time estimates are 1, 3, and 5 weeks. The only immediate predecessor for activity H is activity C. All three time estimates for activity H are 5 weeks. Activity D must be performed before activity I and activity J can be started. Activity I has estimated completion times of 9, 10, and 11 weeks. Activity J has estimated completion times of 1, 2, and 6 weeks.

Phase 3 is the most difficult and complex of the entire development project. It also consists of six separate activities. Activity K has time estimates of 2, 3, and 4 weeks. The immediate predecessor for this activity is activity E. The immediate predecessor for activity L is activity F. The time estimates for activity L are 3, 4, and 8 weeks. Activity M has 2, 2, and 5 weeks for the estimates of the optimistic, most likely, and pessimistic times. The immediate predecessor for activity M is activity G. Activities N and O both have activity I as their immediate predecessor. Activity N has 8, 9, and 10 weeks for its three time estimates. Activity O has 1, 1, and 4 weeks as its time estimates. Finally, activity P has time estimates of 4, 4, and 10 weeks. Activity J is the only immediate predecessor.

Phase 4 involves five activities. Activity Q requires activity K to be completed before it can be started. All three time estimates for activity Q are 6 weeks. Activity R requires that both activity L and activity M be completed first. The three time estimates for activity R are 1, 2, and 3 weeks. Activity S requires activity N to be completed first. Its time estimates are 6, 6, and 9 weeks. Activity T requires that activity O be completed. The time estimates for activity T are 3, 4, and 5 weeks. The final activity for phase 4 is activity U. The time estimates for this activity are 1, 2, and 3 weeks. Activity P must be completed before activity U can be started.

Phase 5 is the final phase of the development project. It consists of only two activities. Activity V requires that activity Q and activity R be completed before it can be started. Time estimates for this activity are 9, 10, and 11 weeks. Activity W is the final activity of the process. It requires three activities to be completed before it can be started: activities S, T, and U. The estimated completion times for activity W are 2, 3, and 7 weeks.

(a) Given this information, determine the expected completion time for the entire process. Also determine which activities are along the critical path.
(b) Jim hopes that the total project will take less than 40 weeks. Is this likely to occur?
(c) Jim has just determined that activities D and I have already been completed and that they do not need to be part of the project. What is the impact of this change on the project completion time and the critical path?

7–38. As described at the end of Section 7.6, set up an Excel model to compute the EST and LST for the activities identified in Problem 7.14.

7–39. Complete the designated calculations for the following subsets of activities. Each subset is independent of the other subsets in the problem.

(a) Activity H has an EFT of 12 days. Activity I has an EFT of 15 days. Compute the EST for each activity in this table:

Activity	Immediate Predecessors	Time (days)
J	H	2
K	H	7
L	I	4
M	J, K, L	9

(b) Activity V has an EST of 13 days. Compute the EFT for each activity in this table:

Activity	Immediate Predecessors	Time (days)
V	U	3
W	V	12
X	V	14
Y	W, X	5
Z	Y	9

(c) Activity T has an LFT of 50 days. Compute the LFT for each activity in this table:

Activity	Immediate Predecessors	Time (days)
P	0	10
Q	0	10
R	P, Q	6
S	Q	8
T	R, S	10

(d) Activity E has an LST of 16 days. Compute the LST for each activity in this table:

Activity	Immediate Successors	Time (days)
A	B, C	4
B	D	3
C	D, E	6
D	E	5

7-40. Suppose that you are chair of the senior banquet planning committee at your college. Develop a list of activities for this project, including considerations such as entertainment, guest speaker, decorations, marketing, and food selection & preparation. Determine immediate predecessors and activity times. Draw the project network.

(a) How many days will the banquet preparation take?
(b) Which activities can be delayed and by how much?

7-41. Consider the data for a simple project as given in the following table.

Activity	a	m	b	Immediate Predecessors
A	8	10	12	–
B	1	6	23	–
C	9	12	15	A, B
D	2	5	8	C

(a) What is the critical path? What is the expected completion time of the project?
(b) What is the probability of all activities on the critical path being completed within 29 days?
(c) What is the probability of all activities on the other (noncritical) path being completed within 29 days?
(d) Is it safe to say that the probability of the project being completed with 29 days is equal to your answer from part (b)?

7-42. Draw the project network for the activities identified in the following table.

Activity	Immediate Predecessors
A	–
B	–
C	–
D	B
E	C
F	A
G	A
H	B, C
I	G
J	F
K	G
L	D
M	D, F
N	F
O	I, L, M

Activity	Immediate Predecessors
P	H
Q	I, J, K, N
R	M
S	O, Q, R
T	E, P, V
U	P
V	P
W	O
X	T, U
Y	S, U, W
Z	X, Y

7-43. Consider the data for a simple project as given in the following table.

	Days			Immediate
Activity	a	m	b	Predecessors
A	7	10	12	–
B	1	6	23	A
C	10	12	16	B
D	1	5	7	C

(a) Note that this project has only one path. What is the expected completion time of the project?
(b) What is the probability of the project being completed within 38 days?
(c) Suppose that the project manager can make some investments to reduce the pessimistic time for activity B. What would the new pessimistic time for activity B need to become (rounded to two decimal places) to ensure that the probability of the project being completed within 38 days is at least 90%? *Hint: Consider using Excel's* Goal Seek.

7-44. Consider the General Foundry project as described in this chapter. Suppose that a new ending activity I has been established that has H as an immediate predecessor. The standard time for I is 4 weeks, and the crash time for I is 1 week. The standard cost for I is $10,000, and the crash cost for I is $12,400.
(a) Modify the linear program shown in Figure 7.25 to incorporate this new activity.
(b) How much must each activity be crashed in order for the new project to be completed within 15 weeks?

7-45. Consider the budgeting problem for the General Foundry project as described in Section 7.5, using the information provided in Table 7.4. Suppose that cash flow is a big concern for the project manager. In particular, the following constraints have been imposed: (1) total expenditures for any week can never exceed $26,000; no more than five weeks can have a $26,000 expenditure, and (3) $26,000 spent two weeks in a row can occur only once over the life of the project. Find a feasible project schedule that would satisfy these constraints.

Chapter 8
Decision Analysis

How do you make major decisions in your life? Do you weigh the pros and cons? Do you use "gut feel?" Do you ask for advice from others? When do you "play it safe," and when do you "go for it?" If you have ever purchased a lottery ticket or gambled in Las Vegas, did you ask yourself why? We all know that the odds are stacked against us and the gamble is a losing proposition in expected value, yet countless millions of dollars are gambled and lost throughout the world every single day. Why do people take the risk when all gamblers, taken as a whole, are losing?

Organizations make major decisions with an uncertain future all the time, from the decision to introduce a new product, to the decision to hire a new CEO, to the decision to open up a plant overseas. Often financial analysis provides a key input into the decision process. Predictions of the probability of potential outcomes represent another very important input for organizations trying to make risk/return tradeoffs. Estimating those probabilities accurately can present a major challenge. A firm might know that a devastating tsunami would destroy its plant on the coast, but what is the chance of the next tsunami coming? Will the economy grow or shrink next year? Will a new government administration enact laws that will help or hurt the organization? What if we really have no idea about future probabilities? Can we still make rational decisions?

This chapter describes logical approaches to decision making, even when decision makers cannot make predictions about future likelihoods at all. We begin by describing the five steps involved in a systematic process. We then differentiate between the three types of decision-making environments: decision making under *certainty*, *uncertainty*, and *risk*. We next describe five different rational methods that decision makers can use to make decisions, under the assumption that they cannot estimate the probabilities of future events (decision making under uncertainty). Each of these methods can easily be set up and analyzed in Excel. Then we examine situations where decision makers do have probability estimates (decision making under risk). We describe how to maximize or minimize *expected monetary value*, and we explain how to compute how much it would be worth to the decision maker to know with certainty what the future outcomes will be (*expected value of perfect information*). We follow this discussion by showing how *decision trees* can often help to analyze larger decision making under risk problems, including how to calculate the *expected value of sample information*. We next show how to use Bayesian analysis to revise probability estimates as new information comes in. Finally, we describe *utility theory*, which is a way to incorporate a decision maker's attitudes toward risk (e.g. *risk avoider* vs. *risk seeker*) into decision analysis. In this way, the decision maker's *expected utility* is maximized, as opposed to the risk-neutral expected monetary value.

Chapter Objectives

After completing this chapter, you will be able to:
1. List the steps of the decision-making process and describe the different types of decision-making environments.
2. Make decisions under uncertainty and under risk.
3. Use Excel to set up and solve problems involving decision tables.
4. Develop accurate and useful decision trees.
5. Revise probability estimates using Bayesian analysis.
6. Understand the importance and use of utility theory in decision making.

8.1 What is Decision Analysis?

To a great extent, the successes and failures that a person experiences in life depend on the decisions that he or she makes. The development of the Mac computer, followed by the iPod, the iPhone, and the iPad, made Steve Jobs a very wealthy person. In contrast, the person who designed the flawed tires at Firestone (which caused so many accidents with Ford Explorers in the late 1990s) probably did not have a great career at that company. Why and how did these people make their respective decisions? A single decision can make the difference between a successful career and an unsuccessful one. *Decision analysis* is an analytic and systematic approach to the study of decision making. In this chapter, we present decision models that are useful in helping managers make the best possible decisions.

What makes the difference between good and bad decisions? In most practical situations, managers have to make decisions without knowing for sure which events will occur in the future. In such cases, a good decision can be defined as one that is based on logic, considers all possible decision alternatives, examines all available information about the future, and applies the decision modeling approach described in this chapter. Occasionally, due to the uncertainty of future events, a good decision could result in an unfavorable outcome. But if a decision is made properly, it is still a good decision.

In contrast, a bad decision is one that is not based on logic, does not use all available information, does not consider all alternatives, and does not employ appropriate decision modeling techniques. If you make a bad decision but are lucky enough that a favorable outcome occurs, you have still made a bad decision. Although occasionally good decisions yield bad results, in the long run, using decision analysis will result in successful outcomes.

8.2 The Five Steps in Decision Analysis

Whether you are deciding about signing up for next semester's classes, buying a new computer, or building a multimillion-dollar factory, the steps in making a good decision are basically the same:

Five Steps of Decision Making
1. Clearly define the problem at hand.
2. List *all* possible decision alternatives.
3. Identify the possible future outcomes for each decision alternative.
4. Identify the payoff (usually profit or cost) for each combination of alternatives and outcomes.
5. Select one of the decision analysis modeling techniques discussed in this chapter. Apply the decision model and make your decision.

Thompson Lumber Company Example

We use the case of Thompson Lumber Company as an example to illustrate the use of the five decision analysis steps. John Thompson is the founder and president of Thompson Lumber Company, a profitable firm located in Portland, Oregon.

STEP 1 In the first step, John identifies his decision-making problem as whether to expand his business by manufacturing and marketing a new product, backyard storage sheds.

STEP 2 The second step is to generate the complete list of decision alternatives available to the decision maker. In decision analysis, a decision alternative is defined as a course of action that is available to the decision maker. There is no limit to the number of decision alternatives that a problem can have. The decision maker has total control over which decision alternative he or she chooses and must choose exactly one of the alternatives listed in the problem.

In Thompson Lumber's case, let us assume that John decides that his alternatives are as follows: (1) build a large plant to manufacture the storage sheds, (2) build a small plant to manufacture the storage sheds, or (3) build no plant at all (i.e., not develop the new product line and keep his business at its current size).

One of the biggest mistakes that decision makers make in practice is to leave out important decision alternatives. For example, suppose John had left out the alternative to build no plant at all. It could well turn out that based on all the issues in the decision-making problem, the best decision for him would have been to not expand his business. However, by not including that alternative among his choices, John would have been unable to select that decision. In general, it is important to remember that while a particular decision alternative may sometimes appear to be inappropriate on the surface, it may turn out to be an excellent choice when all issues in the problem are considered.

STEP 3 The third step involves identifying all possible future outcomes for each decision alternative. In decision analysis, outcomes are also known as *states of nature*. There is no limit to the number of outcomes that can be listed for a decision alternative, and each alternative can have its own unique set of outcomes. Exactly one of the listed outcomes will occur for a specific decision alternative. However, the decision maker has little or no control over which outcome will occur.

In Thompson Lumber's case, suppose John determines that all three of his decision alternatives have the same three possible outcomes: (1) Demand for the sheds will be high, (2) demand for the sheds will be moderate, or (3) demand for the sheds will be low.

As with decision alternatives, a common mistake in practice is to forget about some of the possible outcomes. Optimistic decision makers may tend to ignore bad outcomes under the mistaken assumption that they will not happen, whereas pessimistic managers may discount a favorable outcome. If we don't consider all possibilities, we will not make a logical decision, and the results may be undesirable.

STEP 4 The fourth step is to define the measurable output resulting from each possible combination of decision alternative and outcome. That is, we need to identify the output that will result if we choose a specific decision alternative, and a particular outcome then occurs. In decision analysis, we call these outputs *payoffs*, regardless of whether they denote profit or cost. Payoffs can also be nonmonetary (e.g., number of units sold or number of workers needed).

In Thompson Lumber's case, let us assume that John wants to use net profits to measure his payoffs. He has already evaluated the potential profits associated with the various combinations of alternatives and outcomes, as follows:

- If John decides to build a large plant, he thinks that with high demand for sheds, the result would be a net profit of $200,000 to his firm. The net profit would, however, be only $100,000 if demand were moderate. If demand were low, there would actually be a net loss of $120,000. Payoffs are also called conditional values because, for example, John receiving a profit of $200,000 is conditional upon both his building a large factory and having high demand.
- If he builds a small plant, the results would be a net profit of $90,000 if there were high demand for sheds, a net profit of $50,000 if there were moderate demand, and a net loss of $20,000 if there were low demand.
- Finally, doing nothing would result in a $0 payoff in any demand scenario.

The easiest way to present payoff values is by constructing a *payoff table*, or decision table. A payoff table for John's conditional profit values is shown in Table 8.1. All the decision alternatives are listed down the left side of this table, and all the possible outcomes are listed across the top. The body of the table contains the actual payoffs (profits, in this case).

STEP 5 The last step is to select a decision analysis model and apply it to the data to help make the decision. The types of decision models available for selection depend on the environment in which we are operating and the amount of uncertainty and risk involved. The model specifies the criteria to be used in choosing the best decision alternative.

Table 8.1: Payoff Table for Thompson Lumber

	Outcomes		
Alternatives	High Demand	Moderate Demand	Low Demand
Build large plant	$200,000	$100,000	-$120,000
Build small plant	$ 90,000	$ 50,000	-$ 20,000
No plant	$ 0	$ 0	$ 0

8.3 Types of Decision-Making Environments

The types of decisions people make depend on how much knowledge or information they have about the problem scenario. There are three decision-making environments, as described in the following sections.

Type 1: Decision Making Under Certainty In the environment of decision making under certainty, decision makers know for sure (i.e., with certainty) the payoff for every decision alternative. Typically, this means that there is only one outcome for each alternative. Naturally, decision makers will select the alternative that will result in the best payoff. The mathematical programming approaches covered in Chapters 2–6 are all examples of decision modeling techniques suited for decision making under certainty.

Let's see how decision making under certainty could affect Thompson Lumber's problem. In this environment, we assume that John knows exactly what will happen in the future. For example, if he knows with certainty that demand for storage sheds will be high, what should he do? Looking at John's conditional profit values in Table 8.1, it is clear in this case that he should build the large plant, which has the highest profit, $200,000.

In real-world cases, however, few managers would be fortunate enough to have complete information and knowledge about the outcomes under consideration. In most situations, managers would either have no information at all about the outcomes, or, at best, have probabilistic information about future outcomes. These are the second and third types of decision-making environments, respectively.

Type 2: Decision Making Under Uncertainty In decision making under uncertainty, decision makers have no information at all about the various outcomes. That is, they do not know the likelihood (or probability) that a specific outcome will occur. For example, it is impossible to predict the probability that the Democratic Party will control the U.S. Congress 25 years from now. Likewise, it may be impossible in some cases to assess the probability that a new product or undertaking will be successful.

There are several decision models available to handle decision-making problems under uncertainty. These are explained in section 8.4.

Type 3: Decision Making Under Risk In decision making under risk, decision makers have some knowledge regarding the probability of occurrence of each outcome. The probability could be a precise measure (e.g., the probability of being dealt an ace from a deck of cards is exactly 1/13) or an estimate (e.g., the probability that it will rain tomorrow is 0.40). Regardless of how the probabilities are determined, in decision making under risk, decision makers attempt to identify the alternative that optimizes their *expected* payoff.

Decision Modeling In Action

Decision Analysis Helps American Airlines Assess Uncertainty of Bid Quotes

American Airlines, Inc. (AA) is the world's largest airline in passenger miles transported. Although its primary goal is to transport passengers, AA has to also manage ancillary functions such as full-truckload (FTL) freight shipment of maintenance equipment and in-flight service items. The inventory value of these goods as they move point to point worldwide can be more than $1 billion at any given time.

Each year AA has approximately 500 requests for quotes (RFQs) in the bid process for its FTL point-to-point freight shipment routes. AA needed a should-cost model to assess these quotes to ensure that it did not overpay its FTL suppliers. Working with researchers at North Carolina State University, AA developed a decision tree–based analysis that estimated reasonable costs for these shipments. The fully expanded decision tree for this problem had nearly 60,000 end points.

AA has now used this decision tree model on more than 20 RFQs to prioritize its contractual opportunities and obtain accurate assessments of the FTL costs, thus minimizing the risk of overpaying its FTL suppliers.

Source: Based on M. J. Bailey et al. "American Airlines Uses Should-Cost Modeling to Assess the Uncertainty of Bids for Its Full-Truckload Shipment Routes," *Interfaces* 41, 2 (March–April 2011): 194–196.

Decision analysis models for business problems in this environment typically employ one of two criteria: (1) maximization of expected monetary value or (2) minimization of expected opportunity loss. We study models using both criteria for decision making under risk in section 8.5.

8.4 Decision Making Under Uncertainty

As noted previously, an environment of decision making under uncertainty exists when a manager cannot assess the probabilities of the different outcomes with confidence or when virtually no probability data are available. In this section, we discuss the following five different decision-making criteria to handle such situations:

1. Maximax
2. Maximin
3. Criterion of realism
4. Equally likely
5. Minimax regret

Decision Making Under Uncertainty — 455

In discussing these criteria here, we assume that all payoffs represent profits. That is, we prefer higher payoffs to smaller ones. If the payoffs represent costs (i.e., we prefer smaller payoffs to higher ones), some of the criteria would need to be used differently. To avoid this confusion, an easy option is to convert costs in a payoff table to profits by multiplying all cost values by –1. This way, we can apply the criteria as discussed here for all problems, regardless of whether the payoffs represent profits or costs.

The first four criteria can be computed directly from the decision (payoff) table, whereas the minimax regret criterion requires use of the opportunity loss table (which we compute subsequently). Let us look at each of the five criteria and apply them to the Thompson Lumber example. Remember that the decision-making environment assumes that John has no probability information about the three outcomes—high demand, moderate demand, and low demand for storage sheds.

Maximax Criterion

The maximax criterion selects the decision alternative that *maxi*mizes the *max*imum payoff over all alternatives. We first locate the maximum payoff for each alternative and then select the alternative with the highest value among these maximum payoffs. Because this criterion takes an extremely rosy view of the future and locates the alternative with the overall highest possible payoff, it is also called the *optimistic* criterion.

In Table 8.2 we see that John's maximax choice is the first alternative, build large plant. The $200,000 payoff is the maximum of the maximum payoffs (i.e., $200,000, $90,000, and $0) for each decision alternative.

Table 8.2: Thompson Lumber's Maximax Decision

Alternatives	Outcomes			Maximum For Alternative
	High Demand	Moderate Demand	Low Demand	
Build large plant	$200,000	$100,000	–$120,000	$200,000 →Maximax
Build small plant	$ 90,000	$ 50,000	–$ 20,000	$ 90,000
No plant	$ 0	$ 0	$ 0	$ 0

Maximin Criterion

The opposite of the maximax criterion is the maximin criterion, which takes an extremely conservative view of the future. For this reason, it is also called the *pessimistic* criterion. The maximin criterion finds the alternative that *maxi*mizes the *min*imum payoff over all decision alternatives. We first locate the minimum payoff for each alternative and then select the alternative with the highest value among those minimum payoffs.

John's maximin choice, no plant, is shown in Table 8.3. The $0 payoff is the maximum of the minimum payoffs (i.e., −$120,000, −$20,000, and $0) for each alternative.

Table 8.3: Thompson Lumber's Maximin Decision

	Outcomes			
Alternatives	High Demand	Moderate Demand	Low Demand	Minimum for Alternative
Build large plant	$200,000	$100,000	−$120,000	−$120,000
Build small plant	$ 90,000	$ 50,000	−$ 20,000	−$ 20,000
No plant	$ 0	$ 0	$ 0	$ 0 →Maximax

Criterion of Realism (Hurwicz)

Decision makers are seldom extreme optimists or extreme pessimists. Because most tend to be somewhere in between the two extremes, the criterion of realism (or *Hurwicz*) decision criterion offers a compromise between optimistic and pessimistic decisions. In this criterion, we use a parameter called the coefficient of realism to measure the decision maker's level of optimism regarding the future. This coefficient, denoted by α, has a value between 0 and 1. An α value of 0 implies that the decision maker is totally pessimistic about the future, while an α value of 1 implies that the decision maker is totally optimistic about the future. The advantage of this approach is that it allows the decision maker to build in personal feelings about relative optimism and pessimism. The formula is as follows:

$$\text{Realism payoff for alternative} = \alpha \times (\text{Maximum payoff for alternative}) \\ + (1 - \alpha) \times (\text{Minimum payoff for alternative}) \quad (8\text{–}1)$$

Because the realism payoff is just a weighted average for the maximum and minimum payoffs (where α is the weight), this criterion is also called the *weighted average* criterion.

Suppose we identify John Thompson's coefficient of realism to be $\alpha = 0.45$. That is, John is a slightly pessimistic person (note that $\alpha = 0.5$ implies a strictly neutral person). Under this situation, his best decision would be to build a small plant. As shown in Table 8.4, this alternative has the highest realism payoff, at $29,500 [= 0.45 × $90,000 + 0.55 × (−$20,000)].

Table 8.4: Thompson Lumber's Criterion of Realism Decision ($\alpha = 0.45$)

	Outcomes			
Alternatives	High Demand	Moderate Demand	Low Demand	Wt. Avg. ($\alpha = 0.45$) for Alternative
Build large plant	$200,000	$100,000	-$120,000	$24,000
Build small plant	$ 90,000	$ 50,000	-$ 20,000	$29,500 →Realism
No plant	$ 0	$ 0	$ 0	$ 0

Equally Likely (Laplace) Criterion

The equally likely (or *Laplace*) criterion finds the decision alternative that has the highest average payoff. We first calculate the average payoff for each alternative and then pick the alternative with the maximum average payoff. Note that the Laplace approach essentially assumes that all the outcomes are equally likely to occur.

The equally likely choice for Thompson Lumber is the first alternative, build a large plant. This strategy, as shown in Table 8.5, has a maximum average payoff of $60,000 over all alternatives.

Table 8.5: Thompson Lumber's Equally Likely Decision

	Outcomes			
Alternatives	High Demand	Moderate Demand	Low Demand	Average for Alternative
Build large plant	$200,000	$100,000	-$120,000	$60,000 →Equally likely
Build small plant	$ 90,000	$ 50,000	-$ 20,000	$40,000
No plant	$ 0	$ 0	$ 0	$ 0

Minimax Regret Criterion

The final decision criterion that we discuss is based on opportunity loss, also called *regret*. Opportunity loss is defined as the difference between the optimal payoff and the actual payoff received. In other words, it's the amount lost by *not* picking the best alternative. Minimax regret finds the alternative that *mini*mizes the *max*imum opportunity loss within each alternative.

To use this criterion, we need to first develop the opportunity loss table. This is done by determining the opportunity loss of not choosing the best alternative for each outcome. To do so, we subtract each payoff for a specific outcome from the *best* payoff for that outcome. For example, the best payoff with high demand in Thompson

Lumber's payoff table is $200,000 (corresponding to building a large plant). Hence, we subtract all payoffs for that outcome (i.e., in that column) from $200,000. Likewise, the best payoffs with moderate demand and low demand are $100,000 and $0, respectively. We therefore subtract all payoffs in the second column from $100,000 and all payoffs in the third column from $0. Table 8.6 illustrates these computations and shows John's complete opportunity loss table.

Table 8.6: Opportunity Loss Table for Thompson Lumber

	Outcomes		
Alternatives	High Demand	Moderate Demand	Low Demand
Build large plant	$200,000 − $200,000 = $ 0	$100,000 − $100,000 = $ 0	$0 − (−$120,000) = $120,000
Build small plant	$200,000 − $ 90,000 = $110,000	$100,000 − $ 50,000 = $ 50,000	$0 − (−$ 20,000) = $ 20,000
No plant	$200,000 − $ 0 = $200,000	$100,000 − $ 0 = $100,000	$0 − $ 0 = $ 0

Once the opportunity loss table has been constructed, we locate the maximum opportunity loss (regret) for each alternative. We then pick the alternative with the smallest value among these maximum regrets. As shown in Table 8.7, John's minimax regret choice is the second alternative, build a small plant. The regret of $110,000 is the minimum of the maximum regrets (i.e., $120,000, $110,000, and $200,000) over all three alternatives.

Table 8.7: Thompson Lumber's Minimax Regret Decision

	Outcomes			
Alternatives	High Demand	Moderate Demand	Low Demand	Maximum for Alternative
Build large plant	$ 0	$ 0	$120,000	$120,000
Build small plant	$110,000	$ 50,000	$ 20,000	$110,000 →Minimax
No plant	$200,000	$100,000	$ 0	$200,000

Using Excel to Solve Decision-Making Problems under Uncertainty

As just demonstrated in the Thompson Lumber example, calculations for the different criteria in decision making under uncertainty are fairly straightforward. In most cases, we can perform these calculations quickly even by hand. However, if we wish, we can easily construct Excel spreadsheets to calculate these results for us. Figure

8.1 shows the relevant formulas for the different decision criteria in the Thompson Lumber example. The results are shown in Figure 8.2.

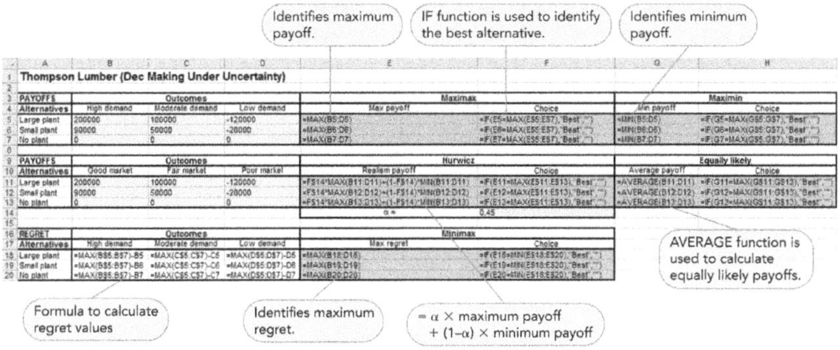

Figure 8.1: Formula View of Excel Layout for Thompson Lumber: Decision Making under Uncertainty

📊 File: Figure 8.1.xlsx, Sheet: Figure 8.1

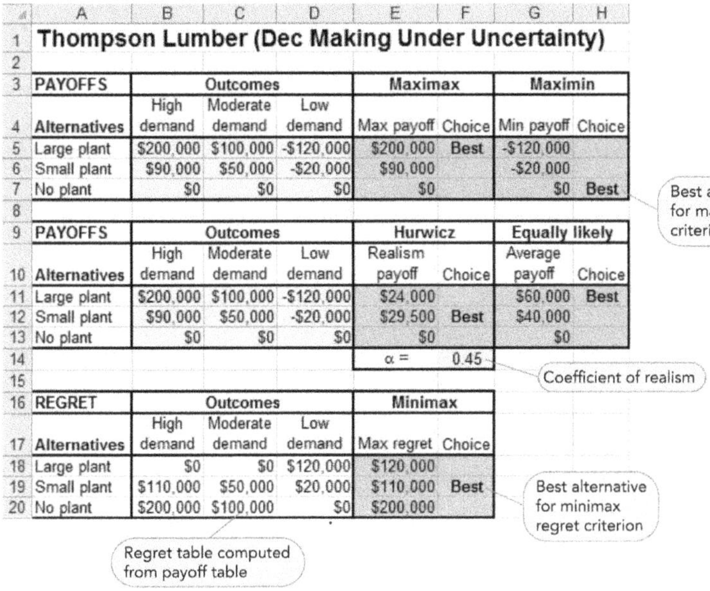

Figure 8.2: Excel Solution for Thompson Lumber: Decision Making under Uncertainty

📊 File: Figure 8.1.xlsx, Sheet: Figure 8.2

Note that the number of decision alternatives and the number of outcomes would vary from problem to problem. The formulas shown in Figure 8.1 can, however, easily be modified to accommodate any changes in these parameters.

EXCEL NOTES

- The Companion Website for this book, at *degruyter.com/view/product/486941*, contains the Excel file for each sample problem discussed here. The relevant file/sheet name is shown below the title of the corresponding figure in this book.

- For clarity, our Excel layouts in this chapter are color-coded as follows:

    - *Input cells*, where we enter the problem data, are shaded yellow.

    - *Output cells*, where the results are shown, are shaded green.

EXCEL EXTRA

Naming the "Winner" of a Max or Min Search

The Excel functions Max and Min can be used to identify the largest and smallest values in a list, respectively. Sometimes, however, we also want to identify the "owner" of that value, for example, the city that has the highest crime rate, not just the value of the highest crime rate. Combining Excel's Match and Index functions can achieve this.

The Match function returns the relative position of an item in a row or column that matches a value. Match has three arguments, separated by commas: (1) the value to be looked up, (2) the range that is covered, and (3) 0 for exact match (or 1 for the largest value ≤ the lookup value; or −1 for the smallest value ≥ the lookup value). Match returns a number, e.g., a "5" means that the fifth entry in the row or column matched the lookup value.

The one-dimensional Index function returns the ith value from a column or row, where the user specifies i. Index has two arguments, separated by a comma: (1) the range of the column or row and (2) the ith value desired.

For example, in Figure 8.2, a column called "Choice" has been added to the far right of each section, and the choice leading to the winning decision has been labeled "Best" in that column. Such an approach works fine; however, the user still has to glance back across to the first column to know the name of the decision that won.

Alternatively, the following reports the winners of each decision criterion in a single table:

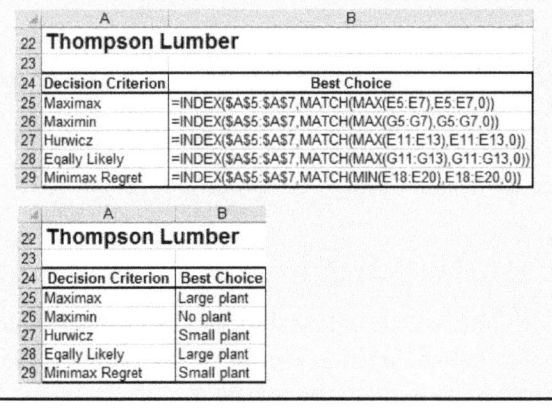

	A	B
22	**Thompson Lumber**	
23		
24	Decision Criterion	Best Choice
25	Maximax	=INDEX($A$5:$A$7,MATCH(MAX(E5:E7),E5:E7,0))
26	Maximin	=INDEX($A$5:$A$7,MATCH(MAX(G5:G7),G5:G7,0))
27	Hurwicz	=INDEX($A$5:$A$7,MATCH(MAX(E11:E13),E11:E13,0))
28	Eqally Likely	=INDEX($A$5:$A$7,MATCH(MAX(G11:G13),G11:G13,0))
29	Minimax Regret	=INDEX($A$5:$A$7,MATCH(MIN(E18:E20),E18:E20,0))

	A	B
22	**Thompson Lumber**	
23		
24	Decision Criterion	Best Choice
25	Maximax	Large plant
26	Maximin	No plant
27	Hurwicz	Small plant
28	Eqally Likely	Large plant
29	Minimax Regret	Small plant

Note that the number of decision alternatives and the number of outcomes would vary from problem to problem. The formulas shown in Figure 8.1 can, however, easily be modified to accommodate any changes in these parameters.

8.5 Decision Making Under Risk

In many real-world situations, it is common for the decision maker to have some idea about the probabilities of occurrence of the different outcomes. These probabilities may be based on the decision maker's personal opinions about future events or on data obtained from market surveys, expert opinions, and so on. As noted previously, when the probability of occurrence of each outcome can be assessed, the problem environment is called *decision making under risk*.

In this section, we consider one of the most popular methods of making decisions under risk: selecting the alternative with the highest expected monetary value. We also look at the concepts of expected opportunity loss and expected value of perfect information.

Expected Monetary Value

Given a decision table with payoffs and probability assessments, we can determine the expected monetary value (EMV) for each alternative. The EMV for an alternative is computed as the *weighted average* of all possible payoffs for that alternative, where the weights are the probabilities of the different outcomes. That is,

$$\begin{aligned}
\text{EMV (Alternative } i) = &\ (\text{Payoff of first outcome}) \\
&\times (\text{Probability of first outcome}) \\
&+ (\text{Payoff of second outcome}) \\
&\times (\text{Probability of second outcome}) \\
&+ \ldots + (\text{Payoff of last outcome}) \\
&\times (\text{Probability of last outcome})
\end{aligned} \quad (8\text{--}2)$$

In Thompson Lumber's case, let us assume that John has used his knowledge of the storage shed industry to specify that the probabilities of high demand, moderate demand, and low demand are 0.3, 0.5, and 0.2, respectively. Under this scenario, which alternative would give him the greatest EMV? To determine this, we compute the EMV for each alternative, as shown in Table 8.8. The largest EMV, $86,000, results from the first alternative, build a large plant.

Table 8.8: Thompson Lumber's EMV Decision

	Outcomes			
Alternatives	High Demand	Moderate Demand	Low Demand	EMV for Alternative
Build large plant	$200,000	$100,000	−$120,000	$200,000 × 0.3 + $100,000 × 0.5 + (−$120,000) × 0.2 = $86,000
Build small plant	$ 90,000	$ 50,000	−$ 20,000	$90,000 × 0.3 + $50,000 × 0.5 + (−$20,000) × 0.2 = $48,000
No plant	$ 0	$ 0	$ 0	$0 × 0.3 + $0 × 0.5 + $0 × 0.2 = $ 0
Probabilities	0.3	0.5	0.2	

Observe that the EMV represents the long-run *average* payoff, while the *actual* payoff from a decision will be one of the payoffs listed in the decision table. That is, the EMV of $86,000 does not mean that John will actually realize a profit of $86,000 if he builds a large plant. Nevertheless, the EMV is widely used as an acceptable criterion to compare decision alternatives in many business decisions because companies make similar decisions on a repeated basis over time.

Expected Opportunity Loss

An alternative approach in decision making under risk is to minimize expected opportunity loss (EOL). Recall from section 8.4 that opportunity loss, also called regret, refers to the difference between the optimal payoff and the actual payoff received. The EOL for an alternative is computed as the weighted average of all possible regrets for that alternative, where the weights are the probabilities of the different outcomes. That is,

$$\begin{aligned} \text{EOL (Alternative } i) = \ & \text{(Regret of first outcome)} \\ & \times \text{(Probability of first outcome)} \\ & + \text{(Regret of second outcome)} \\ & \times \text{(Probability of second outcome)} \\ & + \ldots + \text{(Regret of last outcome)} \\ & \times \text{(Probability of last outcome)} \end{aligned} \quad (8\text{--}3)$$

The EOL values for Thompson Lumber's problem are computed as shown in Table 8.9. Using minimum EOL as the decision criterion, the best decision would be the first alternative, build a large plant, with an EOL of $24,000. It is important to note that the minimum EOL will *always* result in the same decision alternative as the maximum EMV.

Table 8.9: Thompson Lumber's EOL Decision

Alternatives	High Demand	Moderate Demand	Low Demand	EOL for Alternative
Build large plant	$ 0	$ 0	$120,000	$0 × 0.3 + $0 × 0.5 + $120,000 × 0.2 = $ 24,000
Build small plant	$110,000	$ 50,000	$ 20,000	$110,000 × 0.3 + $50,000 × 0.5 + $20,000 × 0.2 = $ 62,000
No plant	$200,000	$100,000	$ 0	$200,000 × 0.3 + $100,000 × 0.5 + $0 × 0.2 = $110,000
Probabilities	0.3	0.5	0.2	

Expected Value of Perfect Information

John Thompson has been approached by Scientific Marketing, Inc., a market research firm, with a proposal to help him make the right decision regarding the size of the new plant. Scientific claims that its analysis will tell John with *certainty* whether the demand for storage sheds will be high, moderate, or low. In other words, it will change John's problem environment from one of decision making under risk to one of decision making under certainty. Obviously, this information could prevent John from making an expensive mistake. Scientific would charge $30,000 for the information. What should John do? Should he hire Scientific to do the marketing study? Is the information worth $30,000? If not, what is it worth?

We call the type of information offered by Scientific *perfect information* because it is certain (i.e., it is never wrong). Although such perfect information is almost never available in practice, determining its value can be very useful because it places an upper bound on what we should be willing to spend on *any* information. In what follows, we therefore investigate two related issues: the expected value with perfect information (EVwPI) and the expected value of perfect information (EVPI).

The EVwPI is the expected payoff if we have perfect information *before* a decision has to be made. Clearly, if we knew for sure that a particular outcome was going to occur, we would choose the alternative that yielded the best payoff for that outcome. Unfortunately, until we get this information, we don't know for sure which outcome is going to occur. Hence, to calculate the EVwPI value, we choose the best payoff for each outcome and multiply it by the probability of occurrence of that outcome. That is,

$$\begin{aligned}
\text{EVwPI} = \ & (\text{Best payoff of first outcome}) \\
& \times (\text{Probability of first outcome}) \\
& + (\text{Best payoff of second outcome}) \\
& \times (\text{Probability of second outcome}) \\
& + \ldots + (\text{Best payoff of last outcome}) \\
& \times (\text{Probability of last outcome})
\end{aligned} \quad (8-4)$$

We then compute the EVPI as the EVwPI minus the expected value *without* information, namely, the maximum EMV. That is,

$$\text{EVPI} = \text{EVwPI} - \text{Maximum EMV} \qquad (8\text{–}5)$$

By referring to Table 8.8, we can calculate the EVPI for John as follows:

1. The best payoff for the outcome high demand is $200,000, associated with building a large plant. The best payoff for moderate demand is $100,000, again associated with building a large plant. Finally, the best payoff for low demand is $0, associated with not building a plant. Hence,

   EVwPI = $200,000 × 0.3 + $100,000 × 0.5 + $0 × 0.20 = $110,000

   That is, if we had perfect information, we would expect an *average* payoff of $110,000 if the decision could be repeated many times.

2. Recall from Table 8.8 that the maximum EMV, or the best expected value *without* information, is $86,000. Hence,

   EVPI = EVwPI − Maximum EMV = $110,000 − $86,000 = $24,000

Thus, the most John should pay for perfect information is $24,000. Because Scientific Marketing wants $30,000 for its analysis, John should reject the offer. It is important to note that the following relationship always holds: EVPI = Minimum EOL. Referring to Thompson Lumber's example, we see that EVPI = Minimum EOL = $24,000.

Using Excel to Solve Decision-Making Problems under Risk

Just as with decision making under uncertainty, calculations for finding the EMV, EOL, EVwPI, and EVPI in decision making under risk are also fairly straightforward. In most small cases, we can perform these calculations quickly even by hand. However, if we wish, we can once again easily construct Excel spreadsheets to calculate these values for us. Figure 8.3 shows the relevant formulas to solve the Thompson Lumber example. The results are shown in Figure 8.4.

As with Figure 8.1, note that the number of decision alternatives and number of outcomes would vary from problem to problem. The formulas shown in Figure 8.3 can, however, be easily modified to accommodate any changes in these parameters.

Decision Making Under Risk — 465

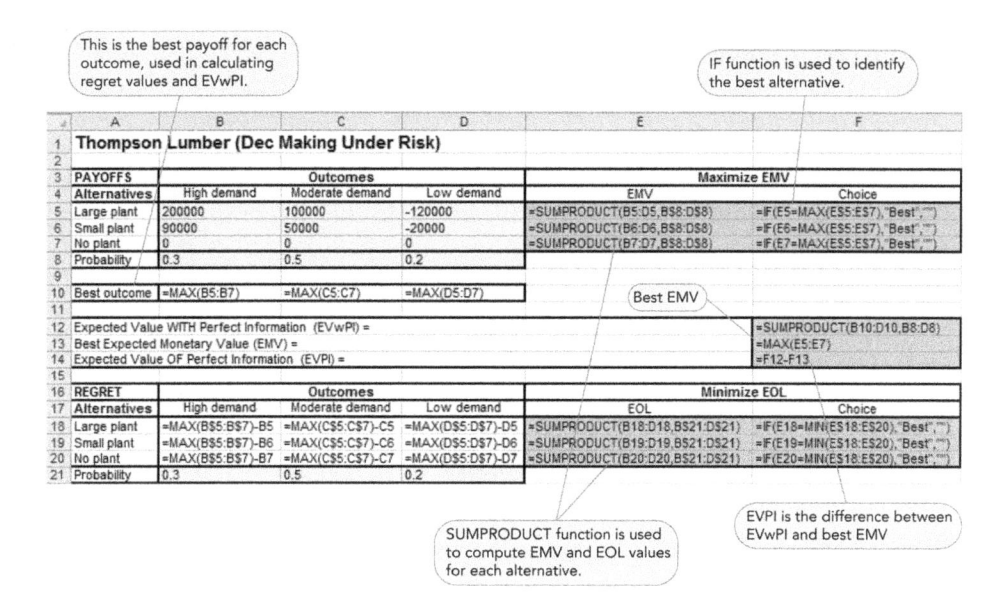

This is the best payoff for each outcome, used in calculating regret values and EVwPI.

IF function is used to identify the best alternative.

	A	B	C	D	E	F
1	Thompson Lumber (Dec Making Under Risk)					
2						
3	PAYOFFS		Outcomes		Maximize EMV	
4	Alternatives	High demand	Moderate demand	Low demand	EMV	Choice
5	Large plant	200000	100000	-120000	=SUMPRODUCT(B5:D5,B$8:D$8)	=IF(E5=MAX(E$5:E$7),"Best","")
6	Small plant	90000	50000	-20000	=SUMPRODUCT(B6:D6,B$8:D$8)	=IF(E6=MAX(E$5:E$7),"Best","")
7	No plant	0	0	0	=SUMPRODUCT(B7:D7,B$8:D$8)	=IF(E7=MAX(E$5:E$7),"Best","")
8	Probability	0.3	0.5	0.2		
9						
10	Best outcome	=MAX(B5:B7)	=MAX(C5:C7)	=MAX(D5:D7)		
11					Best EMV	
12	Expected Value WITH Perfect Information (EVwPI) =				=SUMPRODUCT(B10:D10,B8:D8)	
13	Best Expected Monetary Value (EMV) =				=MAX(E5:E7)	
14	Expected Value OF Perfect Information (EVPI) =				=F12-F13	
15						
16	REGRET		Outcomes		Minimize EOL	
17	Alternatives	High demand	Moderate demand	Low demand	EOL	Choice
18	Large plant	=MAX(B$5:B$7)-B5	=MAX(C$5:C$7)-C5	=MAX(D$5:D$7)-D5	=SUMPRODUCT(B18:D18,B$21:D$21)	=IF(E18=MIN(E$18:E$20),"Best","")
19	Small plant	=MAX(B$5:B$7)-B6	=MAX(C$5:C$7)-C6	=MAX(D$5:D$7)-D6	=SUMPRODUCT(B19:D19,B$21:D$21)	=IF(E19=MIN(E$18:E$20),"Best","")
20	No plant	=MAX(B$5:B$7)-B7	=MAX(C$5:C$7)-C7	=MAX(D$5:D$7)-D7	=SUMPRODUCT(B20:D20,B$21:D$21)	=IF(E20=MIN(E$18:E$20),"Best","")
21	Probability	0.3	0.5	0.2		

SUMPRODUCT function is used to compute EMV and EOL values for each alternative.

EVPI is the difference between EVwPI and best EMV

Figure 8.3: Formula View of Excel Layout for Thompson Lumber: Decision Making under Risk

File: Figure 8.3.xlsx, Sheet: Figure 8.3

	A	B	C	D	E	F
1	Thompson Lumber (Dec Making Under Risk)					
2						
3	PAYOFFS		Outcomes		Maximize EMV	
4	Alternatives	High demand	Moderate demand	Low demand	EMV	Choice
5	Large plant	$200,000	$100,000	-$120,000	$86,000	Best
6	Small plant	$90,000	$50,000	-$20,000	$48,000	
7	No plant	$0	$0	$0	$0	
8	Probability	0.3	0.5	0.2		
9						
10	Best outcome	$200,000	$100,000	$0		
11						
12	Expected Value WITH Perfect Information (EVwPI) =				$110,000	
13	Best Expected Monetary Value (EMV) =				$86,000	
14	Expected Value OF Perfect Information (EVPI) =				$24,000	
15						
16	REGRET		Outcomes		Minimize EOL	
17	Alternatives	High demand	Moderate demand	Low demand	EOL	Choice
18	Large plant	$0	$0	$120,000	$24,000	Best
19	Small plant	$110,000	$50,000	$20,000	$62,000	
20	No plant	$200,000	$100,000	$0	$110,000	
21	Probability	0.3	0.5	0.2		

Known probability for each outcome

Best EMV choice is large plant

EVPI = minimum EOL

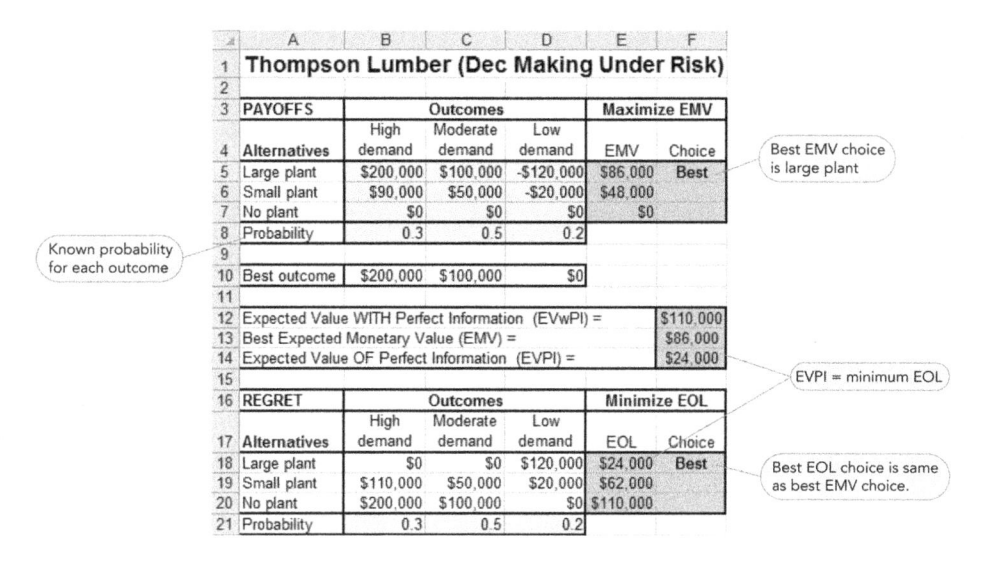

Best EOL choice is same as best EMV choice.

Figure 8.4: Excel Solution for Thompson Lumber: Decision Making under Risk

File: Figure 8.3.xlsx, Sheet: Figure 8.4

8.6 Decision Trees

Any problem that can be presented in a decision table also can be graphically illustrated in a *decision tree*. A decision tree consists of nodes (or points) and arcs (or lines), just like a network. (You may recall that we studied several network models in Chapter 5.) We illustrate the construction and use of decision trees using the Thompson Lumber example.

Decision Modeling In Action

Designing U.S. Army Installations Using Decision Analysis

Prior to 2002, army installations at about 100 major bases in the United States were managed by five U.S. Army organizations. In October 2002, the Installation Management Agency (IMA) was established to centrally manage all installations worldwide. The IMA's objective was to ensure a standard delivery of services and resources to all installations while reducing costs and redundancies.

Within the United States, the IMA was set up to use four regions to manage all continental U.S. installations. Based partly on concerns from Congress, the army wanted an analysis to verify if the IMA's use of four regions was indeed appropriate. Researchers from the U.S. Military Academy used decision analysis to evaluate several regional alternatives (i.e., using anywhere from just 1 up to 8 regions), measuring how well each alternative would perform the functions. The measures captured the effectiveness and efficiency of the regional organization for each function.

The analysis showed that four regions were an appropriate number to manage installations effectively. The use of a decision analysis framework to develop both qualitative and quantitative models of this problem helped provide a sound analysis to senior army decision makers.

Source: Based on T. E. Trainor et al. "The US Army Uses Decision Analysis in Designing Its US Installation Regions," *Interfaces* 37, 3 (May–June 2007): 253–264.

A decision tree presents the decision alternatives and outcomes in a sequential manner. All decision trees are similar in that they contain *decision nodes* and *outcome nodes*. These nodes are represented using the following symbols:

☐ = A *decision* node. Arcs (lines) originating from a decision node denote all decision alternatives available to the decision maker at that node. Of these, the decision maker must select only one alternative.

○ = An *outcome* node. Arcs (lines) originating from an outcome node denote all outcomes that could occur at that node. Of these, only one outcome will actually occur.

Although it is possible for a decision tree to begin with an outcome node, most trees begin with a decision node. In Thompson Lumber's case, this decision node indicates that John has to decide among his three alternatives: building a large plant, a small plant, or no plant. Each alternative is represented by an arc originating from this decision node. Once John makes this decision, one of three possible outcomes (high demand, moderate demand, or low demand) will occur. The simple decision tree to represent John's decision is shown in Figure 8.5.

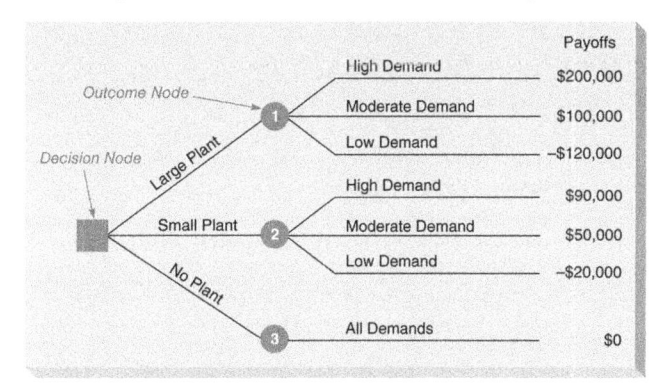

Figure 8.5: Decision Tree for Thompson Lumber

Observe that all alternatives available to John are shown as arcs originating from a decision node (□). Likewise, at each outcome node (O), all possible outcomes that could occur if John chooses that decision alternative are shown as arcs. The payoffs resulting from each alternative and outcome combination are shown at the end of each relevant path in the tree. For example, if John chooses to build a large plant and demand turns out to be high, the resulting payoff is $200,000.

Folding Back a Decision Tree

The process by which a decision tree is analyzed to identify the optimal decision is referred to as *folding back* the decision tree. We start with the payoffs (i.e., the right extreme of the tree) and work our way back to the first decision node. In folding back the decision tree, we use the following two rules:

– At each outcome node, we compute the expected payoff, using the probabilities of all possible outcomes at that node and the payoffs associated with those outcomes.
– At each decision node, we select the alternative that yields the better expected payoff. If the expected payoffs represent profits, we select the alternative with the largest value. In contrast, if the expected payoffs represent costs, we select the alternative with the smallest value.

The complete decision tree for Thompson Lumber is presented in Figure 8.6. For convenience, the probability of each outcome is shown in parentheses next to each outcome. The EMV at each outcome node is then calculated and placed by that node. The EMV at node 1 (if John decides to build a large plant) is $86,000, and the EMV at node 2 (if John decides to build a small plant) is $48,000. Building no plant has, of course, an EMV of $0.

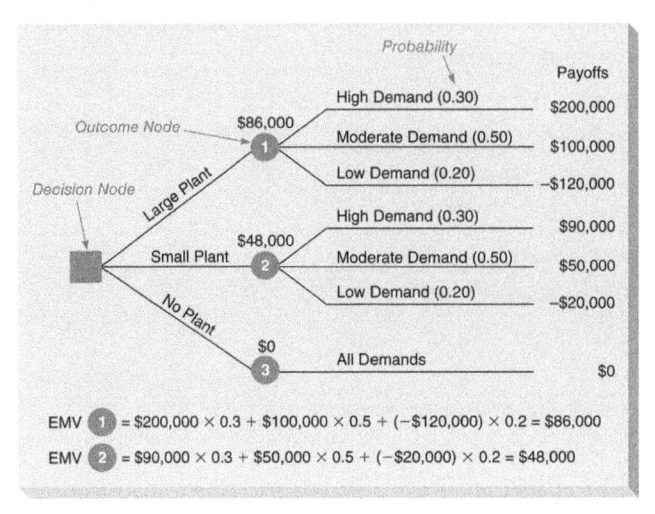

Figure 8.6: Complete Decision Tree for Thompson Lumber

At this stage, the decision tree for Thompson Lumber has been folded back to just the first decision node and the three alternatives (arcs) originating from it. That is, all outcome nodes and the outcomes from these nodes have been examined and collapsed into the EMVs. The reduced decision tree for Thompson Lumber is shown in Figure 8.7.

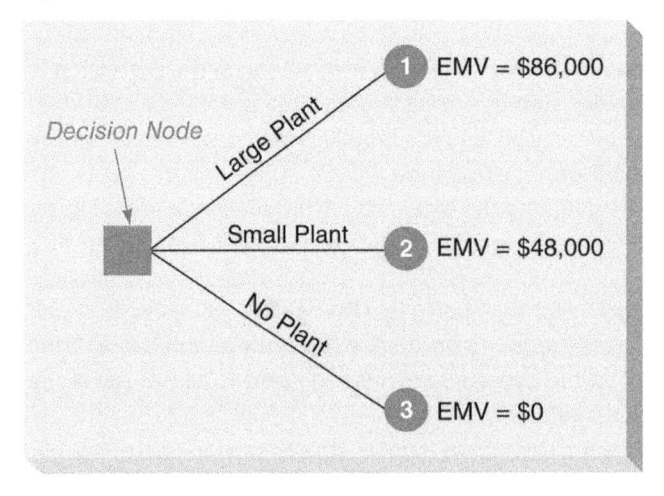

Figure 8.7: Reduced Decision Tree for Thompson Lumber

Using the rule stated earlier for decision nodes, we now select the alternative with the highest EMV. In this case, it corresponds to the alternative to build a large plant. The resulting EMV is $86,000.

8.7 Decision Trees for Multistage Decision-Making Problems

The Thompson Lumber problem discussed so far is a single-stage problem. That is, John has to choose a decision alternative, which is followed by an outcome. Depending on the alternative chosen and the outcome that occurs, John gets a payoff, and the problem ends there.

In many cases, however, the decision-making scenario is a multistage problem. In such cases, the decision maker must evaluate and make a set of sequential decisions up front (i.e., before the first decision is implemented). However, the decisions are actually implemented in a sequential manner, as follows. The problem usually begins with the decision maker implementing his or her initial decision. This is followed by an outcome. Depending on the initial decision and the outcome that occurs after it, the decision maker next implements his or her next decision. The alternatives for this follow-up decision may be different for different outcomes of the earlier decision. This decision, in turn, is followed by an outcome. The set of outcomes for this decision may be different from the set of outcomes for the earlier decision. This sequence could continue several more times, and the final payoff is a function of the sequence of decisions made and the outcomes that occurred at each stage of the problem.

At one or more stages in a problem, it is possible for a specific decision to have no outcomes following it. In such cases, the decision maker is immediately faced with the next decision. Likewise, at one or more stages in the problem, it is possible to have one outcome occur directly after another outcome without the decision maker facing a decision in between the two.

For multistage scenarios, decision tables are no longer convenient, and we are forced to analyze these problems using decision trees. Although we can, in theory, extend multistage scenarios to a sequence of as many decisions and outcomes as we wish, we will limit our discussion here to problems involving just two stages. To facilitate this discussion, let us consider an expanded version of the Thompson Lumber problem.

A Multistage Decision-Making Problem for Thompson Lumber
Before deciding about building a new plant, let's suppose John Thompson has been approached by Smart Services, another market research firm. Smart will charge John $4,000 to conduct a market survey. The results of the survey will indicate either positive or negative market conditions for storage sheds. What should John do?

John recognizes that Smart's market survey will not provide him with *perfect* information, but it may help him get a better feel for the outcomes nevertheless. The type of information obtained here is referred to either as *sample* information or *imperfect* information.

Recall from section 8.5 that we calculated John's EVPI as $24,000. That is, if the results of the market survey are going to be 100% accurate, John should be willing to pay up to $24,000 for the survey. Because Smart's survey will cost significantly less (only $4,000), it is at least worth considering further. However, given that it yields only imperfect information, how much is it actually worth? We determine this by extending the decision tree analysis for Thompson Lumber to include Smart's market survey.

Expanded Decision Tree for Thompson Lumber

John's new decision tree is represented in Figure 8.8. Let's take a careful look at this more complex tree. Note that all possible alternatives and outcomes are included in their logical sequence. This is one of the strengths of using decision trees in making decisions. The user is forced to examine all possible outcomes, including unfavorable ones. He or she is also forced to make decisions in a logical, sequential manner.

Examining the tree, we see that John's first decision point is whether to conduct Smart's market survey. If he chooses not to do the survey (i.e., the upper part of the tree), he is immediately faced with his second decision node: whether to build a large plant, a small plant, or no plant. The possible outcomes for each of these alternatives are high demand (0.3 probability), moderate demand (0.5 probability), and low demand (0.2 probability). The payoffs for each of the possible consequences are listed along the right side of the tree. As a matter of fact, this portion of John's tree in Figure 8.8 is identical to the simpler decision tree shown in Figure 8.6. Can you see why this is so?

The lower portion of Figure 8.8 reflects the decision to conduct the market survey. This decision has two possible outcomes—positive survey result or negative survey result—each with a specific probability. For now, let us assume that John knows these probabilities to be as follows: probability of 0.57 that the survey will indicate positive market conditions for storage sheds, and probability of 0.43 that the survey will indicate negative market conditions. An explanation of how these probabilities can be calculated in real-world situations is the topic of section 8.9.

Regardless of which survey outcome occurs, John is now faced with his next decision. Although the decision alternatives at this point could be different for different survey outcomes, let us assume in John's case that for both survey outcomes he has the same three alternatives: whether to build a large plant, a small plant, or no plant. Each alternative has the same three outcomes as before: high demand, moderate demand, and low demand. The key difference, however, is that the survey outcome (positive or negative) allows John to update the probabilities of the demand outcomes. For this reason, the probabilities shown in parentheses for these outcomes in Figure 8.8 are called *conditional probabilities*. An explanation of how these probabilities can be calculated in real-world situations is also presented in section 8.9. For now, let us assume that these probabilities have already been calculated and are available to John.

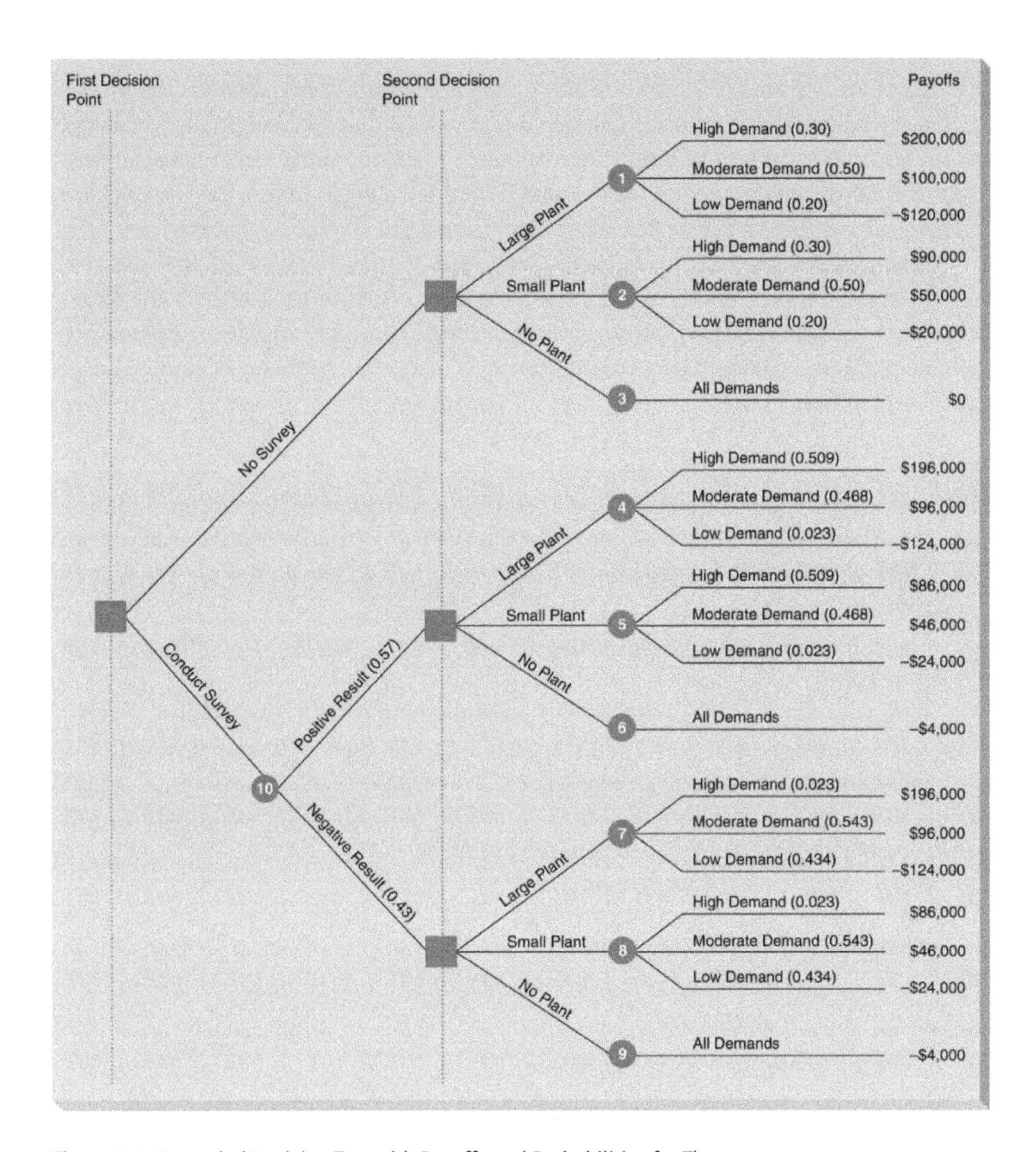

Figure 8.8: Expanded Decision Tree with Payoffs and Probabilities for Thompson

From Figure 8.8, we note, for example, that the probability of high demand for sheds, given a positive survey result, is 0.509. Note that this is higher than the 0.30 probability that John had estimated for high demand before the market survey. This increase in the probability is not surprising because you would, of course, expect a positive survey result to be a stronger indicator of high demand. Don't forget, however, that any market research study is subject to error. Therefore, it is possible that Smart's market survey didn't result in very reliable information. In fact, as shown in Figure 8.8, demand for sheds could be moderate (with a probability of 0.468) or low (with a probability of 0.023), even if Smart's survey results are positive.

Likewise, we note in Figure 8.8 that if the survey results are negative, the probability of low demand for sheds increases from the 0.20 that John originally estimated to 0.434. However, because Smart's survey results are not perfect, there are nonzero probabilities of moderate and high demand for sheds, even if the survey results are negative. As shown in Figure 8.8, these values are 0.543 and 0.023, respectively.

Finally, when we look to the payoff values in Figure 8.8, we note that the cost of the market survey ($4,000) has to be subtracted from every payoff in the lower portion of the tree (i.e., the portion with the survey). Thus, for example, the payoff for a large plant followed by high demand for sheds is reduced from the original value of $200,000 to $196,000.

Folding Back the Expanded Decision Tree for Thompson Lumber

With all probabilities and payoffs specified in the decision tree, we can start folding back the tree. We begin with the payoffs at the end (or right side) of the tree and work back toward the initial decision node. When we finish, the sequence of decisions to make will be known.

For your convenience, we have summarized the computations for John's problem in Figure 8.9.

A pair of slashes (/ /) through a decision branch indicates the alternative selected at a decision node. In Figure 8.9, all expected payoffs have been noted next to the relevant nodes on the decision tree. Although we explain each of these computations in detail below, you may find it easier to perform all computations on the tree itself after you have solved several decision tree problems.

1. If the market survey is *not* conducted.

    EMV (node 1) = EMV (Large plant)
    $$= \$200,000 \times 0.30 + \$100,000 \times 0.50 + (-\$120,000) \times 0.20$$
    $$= \$86,000$$
    EMV (node 2) = EMV (Small plant)
    $$= \$90,000 \times 0.30 + \$50,000 \times 0.50 + (-\$20,000) \times 0.20 = \$48,000$$
    EMV (node 3) = EMV (No plant)
    $$= \$0$$

    Thus, if the market survey is not conducted, John should build a large plant, for an expected payoff of $86,000. As expected, this is the same result we saw earlier, in Figure 8.6.

2. Now let us examine the portion of the tree where the market survey is conducted. Working backward from the payoffs, we first consider outcome nodes 4, 5, and 6. All calculations at these nodes are conditional on a positive survey result. The calculations are as follows:

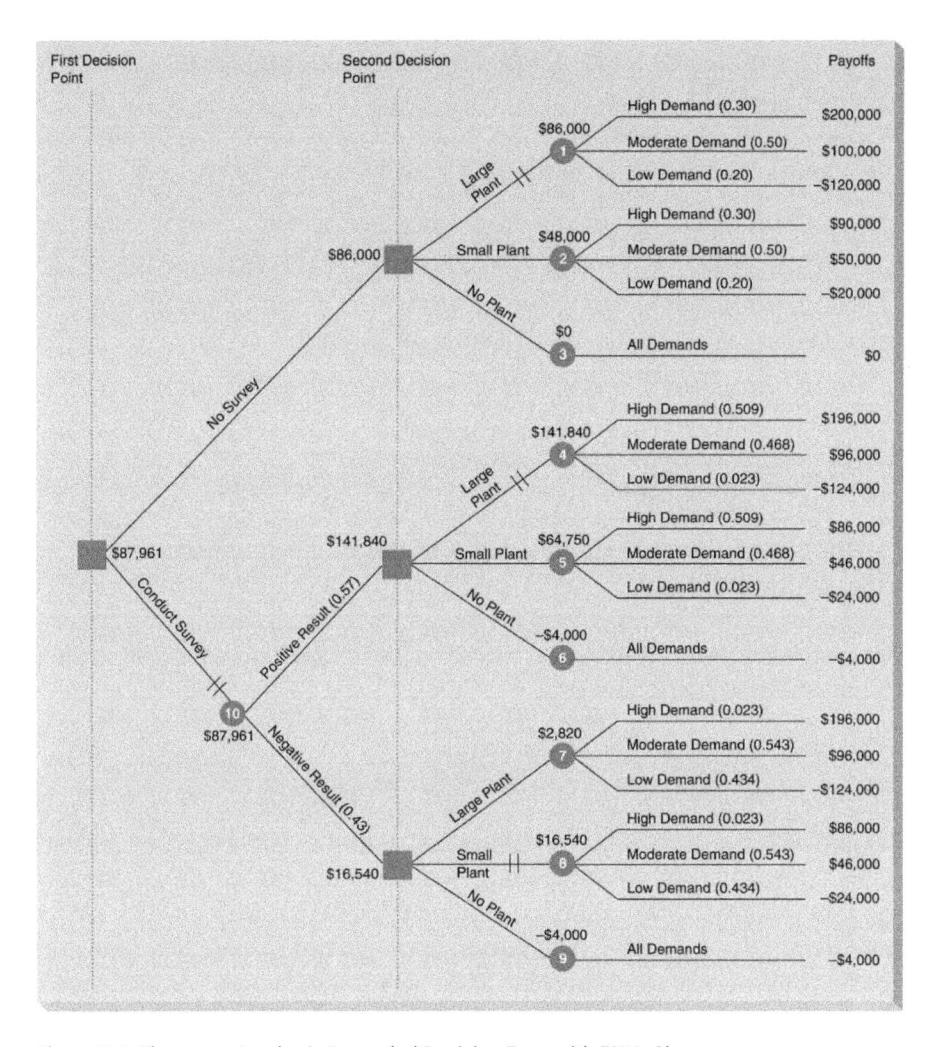

Decision Trees for Multistage Decision-Making Problems — 473

Figure 8.9: Thompson Lumber's Expanded Decision Tree, with EMVs Shown

EMV (node 4) = EMV (Large plant | Positive survey result)
    = $196,000 × 0.509 + $96,000 × 0.468 + (−$124,000) × 0.023
    = $141,840

EMV (node 5) = EMV (Small plant | Positive survey result)
    = $86,000 × 0.509 + $46,000 × 0.468 + (−$24,000) × 0.023
    = $64,750

EMV (node 6) = EMV (No plant | Positive survey result)
    = −$4,000

Thus, if the survey results are positive, a large plant should be built, for an expected payoff of $141,840.

3. Next, we consider outcome nodes 7, 8, and 9. All calculations at these nodes are conditional on a negative survey result. The calculations are as follows:

$$\text{EMV (node 7)} = \text{EMV (Large plant} | \text{Negative survey result)}$$
$$= \$196,000 \times 0.023 + \$96,000 \times 0.543 + (-\$124,000) \times 0.434$$
$$= \$2,820$$

$$\text{EMV (node 8)} = \text{EMV (Small plant} | \text{Negative survey result)}$$
$$= \$86,000 \times 0.023 + \$46,000 \times 0.543 + (-\$24,000) \times 0.434$$
$$= \$16,540$$

$$\text{EMV (node 9)} = \text{EMV (No plant} | \text{Negative survey result)}$$
$$= -\$4,000$$

Thus, given a negative survey result, John should build a small plant, with an expected payoff of $16,540.

4. Continuing on the lower portion of the tree and moving backward, we next consider outcome node 10. At this node, we compute the expected value if we conduct the market survey, as follows:

$$\text{EMV (node 10)} = \text{EMV (Conduct survey)}$$
$$= \$141,840 \times 0.57 + \$16,540 \times 0.43 = \$87,961$$

5. Finally, we consider the initial decision node. At this node, we compare the EMV of not conducting the survey with the EMV of conducting the survey. Because the EMV of $87,961 if we conduct the survey is higher than the $86,000 EMV if the survey is not conducted, John's decision should be to accept Smart's offer to conduct a survey and await the result. If the survey result is positive, John should build a large plant; but if the result is negative, John should build a small plant.

Expected Value of Sample Information

The preceding computations indicate that John Thompson should accept Smart's offer to conduct a survey at a cost of $4,000. However, what should John do if Smart wants $6,000 for the survey? In this case, the EMV if the survey is conducted will be only $85,961. (Can you see why this is so?) Because this is less than the $86,000 EMV without the survey, John should reject the survey and build a large plant right away.

We can perhaps pose an alternate question here: What is the actual value of Smart's survey information? An effective way of measuring the value of a market survey (which is typically imperfect information) is to compute the expected value of sample information (EVSI), as follows:

$$\text{EVSI} = (\text{EMV of best decision } with \text{ sample information, } assuming \text{ no cost to get it})$$
$$- (\text{EMV of best decision } without \text{ any information}) \quad (8\text{–}6)$$

In John's case, the EMV without any information (i.e., if the survey is not conducted) is $86,000. In contrast, if the survey is conducted, the EMV becomes $91,961. (Remember that we need to add the $4,000 survey cost to the EMV value at node 10 in Figure 8.9 because we are assuming that there is no survey cost here.) Thus,

$$\text{EVSI} = \$91,961 - \$86,000 = \$5,961$$

This means that John could have paid up to $5,961 for this *specific* market survey and still come out ahead. Because Smart charges only $4,000, it is indeed worthwhile. In contrast, if Smart charges $6,000, it is not worthwhile.

We address an interesting question at this point: If the cost of a proposed survey is less than its EVSI, does it mean we should immediately accept it? Although we recommended this decision in John's example, the answer to this question in many real-world settings could be no. The reason is as follows. Suppose John could approach *several* different market survey firms for help. Because each survey is different in terms of how imperfect its information is, each survey has its own EVSI. In John's example, the survey offered by Smart Services has an EVSI of only $5,961, much less than the EVPI of $24,000. Although paying $4,000 to get $5,961 worth of information may seem to be a good idea, the better question for John to ask could be whether there is some *other* survey available that perhaps costs more than $4,000 but yields considerably more than $5,961 worth of information. In this regard, a measure that may be useful to compute is the efficiency of sample information, as follows:

$$\text{Efficiency of sample information} = \text{EVSI/EVPI} \qquad (8\text{–}7)$$

In the case of the current survey, the efficiency is $5,961/$24,000 = 0.2484, or 24.84%. That is, the survey offered by Smart is only 24.84% as good as the best possible information. As noted earlier, if John can find a survey that is more efficient, it may be worthwhile to consider it, even if it costs more than the Smart Services survey.

8.8 Estimating Probability Values Using Bayesian Analysis

In discussing Thompson Lumber's multistage decision problem (see Figure 8.9), we assumed that the following event and conditional probabilities were available to John with regard to the survey offered by Smart Services:

$P(\text{Positive survey result}) = P(\text{PS}) = 0.570$
$P(\text{Negative survey result}) = P(\text{NS}) = 0.430$
$P(\text{High demand}|\text{Positive survey result}) = P(\text{HD}|\text{PS}) = 0.509$
$P(\text{Moderate demand}|\text{Positive survey result}) = P(\text{MD}|\text{PS}) = 0.468$
$P(\text{Low demand}|\text{Positive survey result}) = P(\text{LD}|\text{PS}) = 0.023$
$P(\text{High demand}|\text{Negative survey result}) = P(\text{HD}|\text{NS}) = 0.023$
$P(\text{Moderate demand}|\text{Negative survey result}) = P(\text{MD}|\text{NS}) = 0.543$
$P(\text{Low demand}|\text{Negative survey result}) = P(\text{LD}|\text{NS}) = 0.443$

In practice, as illustrated in this section, John would have computed these probabilities using Bayes' theorem on data regarding the performance of Smart Services on past surveys. Bayes' theorem allows decision makers to incorporate additional information (e.g., past performance) to revise their probability estimates of various outcomes. Before continuing further, you may wish to review Bayes' theorem in Appendix A.

Calculating Revised Probabilities

In order to evaluate the reliability of the survey, John asks Smart Services to provide him with information regarding its performance on past surveys. Specifically, he wants to know how many similar surveys the company has conducted in the past, what it predicted each time, and what the actual result turned out to be eventually in each case. Let's assume that Smart has data on 75 past surveys that it has conducted. In these 75 surveys, Smart had predicted high demand in 30 cases, moderate demand in 15 cases, and low demand in 30 cases. These data are summarized in Table 8.10.

Table 8.10: Reliability of the Smart Services Survey in Predicting Actual Outcomes

When Actual Outcome Was	Survey Result Was	
	Positive (PS)	Negative (NS)
High demand (HD)	$P(PS|HD) = 29/30 = 0.967$	$P(NS|HD) = 1/30 = 0.033$
Moderate demand (MD)	$P(PS|MD) = 8/15 = 0.533$	$P(NS|MD) = 7/15 = 0.467$
Low demand (LD)	$P(PS|LD) = 2/30 = 0.067$	$P(NS|LD) = 28/30 = 0.933$

Table 8.10 reveals, for example, that in 29 of 30 past cases where a product's demand subsequently turned out to be high, Smart's surveys had predicted positive market conditions. That is, the probability of positive survey results, given high demand, $P(PS|HD)$, is 0.967. Likewise, in 7 of 15 past cases where a product's demand subsequently turned out to be moderate, Smart's surveys had predicted negative market conditions. That is, the probability of negative survey results, given moderate demand, $P(NS|MD)$, is 0.467. How does John use this information to gauge the accuracy of Smart's survey in his specific case?

Recall that without any market survey information, John's current probability estimates of high, moderate, and low demand are $P(HD)=0.30$, $P(MD)=0.50$, and $P(LD)=0.20$, respectively. These are referred to as *prior* probabilities. Based on the survey performance information in Table 8.10, we compute John's revised, or *posterior*, probabilities—namely, $P(HD|PS)$, $P(MD|PS)$, $P(LD|PS)$, $P(HD|NS)$, $P(MD|NS)$, and $P(LS|NS)$. This computation, using the formula for Bayes' theorem (see Equation A-7 in Appendix A), proceeds as follows:

$$P(HD|PS) = \frac{P(PS \text{ and } HD)}{P(PS)} = \frac{P(PS|HD) \times P(HD)}{P(PS)}$$

$$= \frac{P(PS|HD) \times P(HD)}{P(PS|HD) \times P(HD) + P(PS|MD) \times P(MD) + P(PS|LD) \times P(LD)}$$

$$= \frac{0.967 \times 0.30}{0.967 \times 0.30 + 0.533 \times 0.50 + 0.067 \times 0.20} = \frac{0.290}{0.570} = 0.509$$

The other five revised probabilities (i.e., P(MD|PS), P(LD|PS), etc.) can be computed in a similar manner. However, as you can see, Bayes' formula is rather cumbersome and somewhat difficult to follow intuitively. For this reason, it is perhaps easier in practice to compute these revised probabilities by using a probability table. We show these calculations in Table 8.11 for the case where the survey result is positive and in Table 8.12 for the case where the survey result is negative.

Table 8.11: Probability Revisions, Given a Positive Survey Result (PS)

Outcome	Conditional Prob. P(PS | Outcome)	Prior Prob.	Joint Prob.	Revised Prob. P(Outcome|PS)
High demand (HD)	0.967 × 0.30 =		0.290	0.290/0.57 = 0.509
Moderate demand (MD)	0.533 × 0.50 =		0.267	0.267/0.57 = 0.468
Low demand (LD)	0.067 × 0.20 =		0.013	0.013/0.57 = 0.023
	P(PS) = P(Positive Survey) =		0.570	1.000

Table 8.12: Probability Revisions, Given a Negative Survey Result (NS)

Outcome	Conditional Prob. P(NS|Outcome)	Prior Prob.	Joint Prob.	Revised Prob. P(Outcome|NS)
High demand (HD)	0.033 × 0.30 =		0.010	0.010/0.43 = 0.023
Moderate demand (MD)	0.467 × 0.50 =		0.233	0.233/0.43 = 0.543
Low demand (LD)	0.933 × 0.20 =		0.187	0.187/0.43 = 0.434
	P(NS) = P(Negative Survey) =		0.430	1.000

The calculations in Table 8.11 are as follows. For any outcome, such as high demand (HD), we know the conditional probability, P(PS|HD), and the prior probability, P(HD). Using Equation A-6 in Appendix A, we can compute the joint probability, P(PS and HD), as the product of the conditional and prior probabilities. After we repeat this computation for the other two outcomes (moderate demand and low demand), we add the three joint probabilities— P(PS and HD) + P(PS and MD) + P(PS and LD) —to determine P(PS). Observe that this computation is the same as that in the denominator of the Bayes' theorem formula. After we have computed P(PS), we can use Equation A-5 in Appendix

A to compute the revised probabilities $P(HD|PS)$, $P(MD|PS)$, and $P(LD|PS)$. Table 8.12 shows similar calculations when the survey result is negative. As you can see, the probabilities obtained here are the same ones we used earlier in Figure 8.9.

Potential Problems in Using Survey Results

In using past performance to gauge the reliability of a survey's results, we typically base our probabilities only on those cases in which a decision to take some course of action is actually made. For example, we can observe demand only in cases where the product was actually introduced after the survey was conducted. Unfortunately, there is no way to collect information about the demand in situations in which the decision after the survey was to not introduce the product. This implies that conditional probability information is not quite always as accurate as we would like it to be. Nevertheless, calculating conditional probabilities helps to refine the decision-making process and, in general, to make better decisions. For this reason, the use of Bayesian analysis in revising prior probabilities is very popular in practice.

8.9 Utility Theory

So far we have used monetary values to make decisions in all our examples. In practice, however, using money to measure the value of a decision could sometimes lead to bad decisions. The reason for this is that different people value money differently at different times. For example, having $100 in your pocket may mean a lot to you today, if you are a student, but may be relatively unimportant in a few years when you are a wealthy businessperson having read this book. This implies that while you may be unwilling to bet $100 on a risky project today, you may be more than willing to do so in a few years. Unfortunately, when we use monetary values to make decisions, we do not account for these perceptions of risk in our model.

Here's another example to drive home this point. Assume that you are the holder of a lottery ticket. In a few moments, a fair coin will be flipped. If it comes up tails, you win $100,000. If it comes up heads, you win nothing. Now suppose a wealthy person offers you $35,000 for your ticket before the coin is flipped. What should you do? According to a decision based on monetary values, as shown in the decision tree in Figure 8.10, you should reject the offer and hold on to your ticket because the EMV of $50,000 is greater than the offer of $35,000.

In reality, what would you do? It is likely that many people would take the guaranteed $35,000 in exchange for a risky shot at $100,000. (In fact, many would probably be willing to settle for a lot less than $35,000.) Of course, just how low a specific individual would go is a matter of personal preference because, as noted earlier, different people value money differently. This example, however, illustrates how basing a decision on EMV may not be appropriate.

Utility Theory — 479

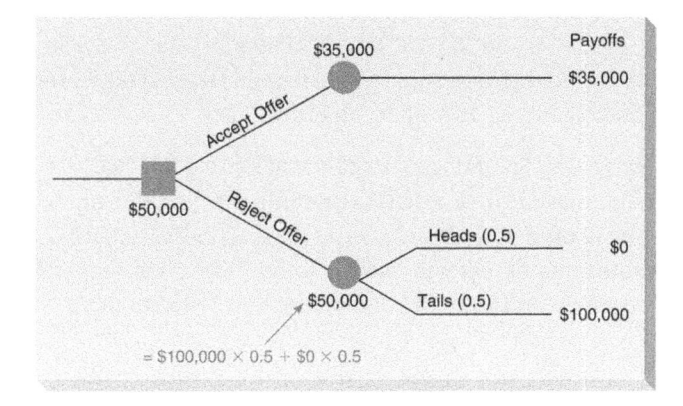

```
                    $35,000                    Payoffs
                       ●──────────────────── $35,000
              Accept Offer
        ■
  $50,000    Reject Offer
                           Heads (0.5)
                       ●──────────────────── $0
                    $50,000   Tails (0.5)
                                            $100,000
         ↗
   = $100,000 × 0.5 + $0 × 0.5
```

Figure 8.10: Decision Tree for a Lottery Ticket

One way to get around this problem and incorporate a person's attitude toward risk in the model is through utility theory. In the next section, we explore first how to measure a person's utility function and then how to use utility measures in decision making.

Measuring Utility and Constructing a Utility Curve

Using a utility function is a way of converting a person's value for money and attitudes toward risk into a dimensionless number between 0 and 1. There are three important issues to note at this stage:

- Each person has his or her own utility function. It is therefore critical in any problem to determine the utility function for the decision maker in that problem.
- A person's utility function could change over time as his or her economic and other conditions change. Recall the earlier example about how important $100 is to you today as opposed to how important it may be to you in a few years. A person's utility function should therefore be updated periodically.
- A person may have different utility functions for different magnitudes of money. For example, most people tend to be very willing to take risks when the monetary amounts involved are small. (After all, we're all willing to buy a $1 lottery ticket, even when we know very well that we're unlikely to win anything.) However, the same people tend to be unwilling to take risks with larger monetary amounts. (Would you be willing to buy a $1,000 lottery ticket even if the potential top prize were $1 billion?) This implies that we should consider a person's utility function only over the relevant range of monetary values involved in the specific problem at hand.

Let us use an example to study how we can determine a person's utility function.

Jane Dickson's Utility Function Jane Dickson would like to construct a utility function to reveal her preference for monetary amounts between $0 and $50,000. We start assessing Jane's utility function by assigning a utility value of 0 to the worst payoff and a utility value of 1 to the best payoff. That is, $U(\$0) = 0$ and $U(\$50,000) = 1$. Monetary values between these two payoffs will have utility values between 0 and 1. To determine these utilities, we begin by posing the following gamble to Jane, as outlined in Figure 8.11:

> You have a 50% chance at getting $0 and a 50% chance at getting $50,000. That is, the EMV of this gamble is $25,000. What is the minimum guaranteed amount that you will accept in order to walk away from this gamble? In other words, what is the minimum amount that will make you indifferent between alternative 1 (gamble between $0 and $50,000) and alternative 2 (obtain this amount for sure).

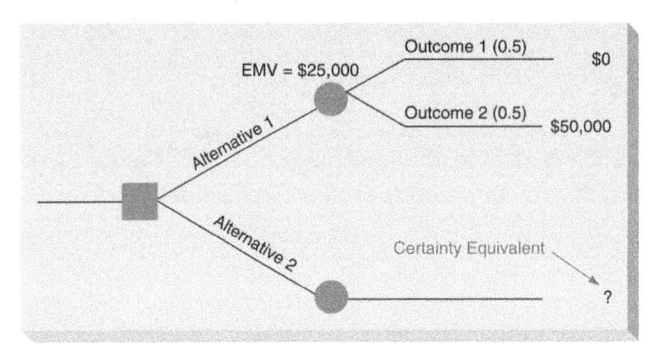

Figure 8.11: Gamble Posed to Jane for Utility Assessment

The answer to this question may vary from person to person, and it is called the *certainty equivalent* between the two payoff values ($0 and $50,000, in this case). Let's suppose Jane is willing to settle for $15,000. (Some of you may have settled for less, while others may have wanted more.) That is, Jane is willing to accept a guaranteed payoff of $15,000 to avoid the risk associated with a potential payoff of $50,000. The implication is that from a utility perspective (i.e., with respect to Jane's attitudes toward risk and value for money), the expected value between $0 and $50,000 is only $15,000, and not the $25,000 we calculated in Figure 8.11. In other words, $U(\$15,000) = U(\$0) \times 0.5 + U(\$50,000) \times 0.5 = 0 \times 0.5 + 1 \times 0.5 = 0.5$ for Jane.

We repeat the gamble in Figure 8.11, except that the two monetary amounts presented to Jane in the gamble are $15,000 and $50,000. The EMV is $32,500. Let's suppose Jane is willing to settle for a certainty equivalent of $27,000. This implies that for Jane, $U(\$27,000) = U(\$15,000) \times 0.5 + U(\$50,000) \times 0.5 = 0.5 \times 0.5 + 1 \times 0.5 = 0.75$.

We repeat the gamble in Figure 8.11 again, this time with monetary amounts of $0 and $15,000. The EMV is $7,500. Let's suppose Jane is willing to settle for a certainty equivalent of $6,000. This implies that for Jane, $U(\$6,000) = U(\$0) \times 0.5 + U(\$15,000) \times 0.5 = 0 \times 0.5 + 0.5 \times 0.5 = 0.25$.

At this stage, we know the monetary values associated with utilities of 0, 0.25, 0.5, 0.75, and 1 for Jane. If necessary, we can continue this process several more times to find additional utility points. For example, we could present the gamble between $27,000 (with a utility of 0.75) and $50,000 (with a utility of 1) to determine the monetary value associated with a utility of $0.875 = (0.75 \times 0.5 + 1 \times 0.5)$. However, the five assessments shown here are usually enough to get an idea of Jane's feelings toward risk. Perhaps the easiest way to view Jane's utility function is to construct a utility curve that plots utility values (Y-axis) versus monetary values (X-axis). This is shown in Figure 8.12. In the figure, the assessed utility points of $0, $6,000, $15,000, $27,000, and $50,000 are obtained from the preceding discussion, while the rest of the curve is eyeballed in. As noted earlier, it is usually enough to know five points on the curve in order to get a reasonable approximation.

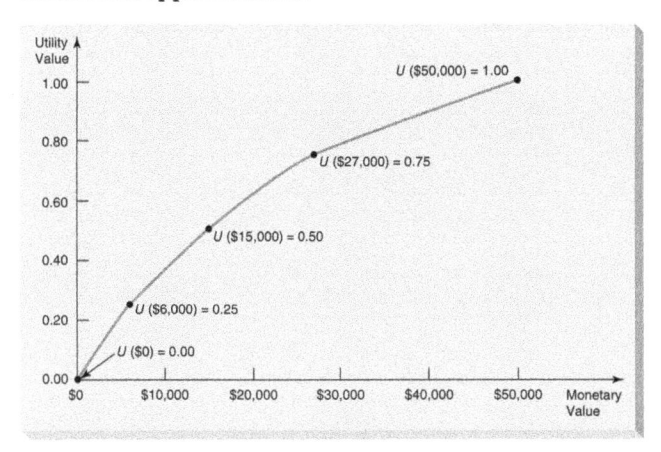

Figure 8.12: Utility Curve for Jane Dickson

Jane's utility curve is typical of a risk avoider. A risk avoider is a decision maker who gets less utility or pleasure from a greater risk and tends to avoid situations in which high losses might occur. As monetary value increases on her utility curve, the utility increases at a slower rate. Another way to characterize a person's attitude toward risk is to compute the risk premium, defined as

$$\text{Risk premium} = (\text{EMV of gamble}) - (\text{Certainty equivalent}) \qquad (8-8)$$

The risk premium represents the monetary amount that a decision maker is willing to give up in order to avoid the risk associated with a gamble. For example, Jane's risk premium in the first gamble between $0 and $50,000 is computed as $25,000 − $15,000 = $10,000. That is, Jane is willing to give up $10,000 to avoid the uncertainty associated with a gamble. Likewise, she is willing to give up $5,500 (= $32,500 − $27,000) to avoid the risk of gambling between $15,000 and $50,000.

Clearly, a person who is more averse to risk will be willing to give up an even larger amount to avoid the uncertainty. In contrast, a person who is a risk seeker will insist on getting a certainty equivalent that is greater than the EMV in order to walk away from a gamble. Such a person will therefore have a negative risk premium.

Finally, a person who is risk neutral will always specify a certainty equivalent that is exactly equal to the EMV. Based on the preceding discussion, we can now define the following three preferences for risk:
- Risk avoider or risk-averse person: Risk premium > 0
- Risk indifferent or risk-neutral person: Risk premium = 0
- Risk seeker or risk-prone person: Risk premium < 0

Figure 8.13 illustrates the utility curves for all three risk preferences. As shown in the figure, a person who is a risk seeker has an opposite-shaped utility curve to that of a risk avoider. This type of decision maker gets more utility from a greater risk and a higher potential payoff. As monetary value increases on his or her utility curve, the utility increases at an increasing rate. A person who is risk neutral has a utility curve that is a straight line.

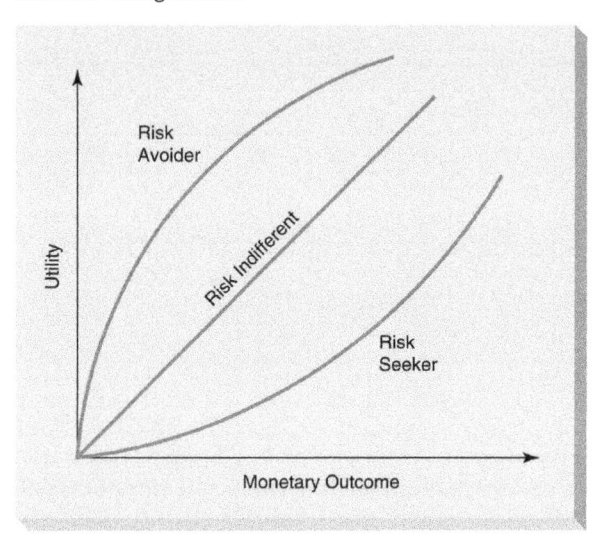

Figure 8.13: Utility Curves for Different Risk Preferences

The shape of a person's utility curve depends on the specific decision being considered, the person's psychological frame of mind, and how the person feels about the future. As noted earlier, it may well be that a person has one utility curve for some situations and a completely different curve for others. In practice, most people are likely to be risk seekers when the monetary amounts involved are small (recall the earlier comment about buying a $1 lottery ticket) but tend to become risk avoiders as the monetary amounts increase. The exact monetary amount at which a specific individual switches from being a risk seeker to a risk avoider is, of course, a matter of personal preference.

Exponential Utility Function If a person is a risk avoider, it is possible to use curve-fitting techniques to fit an equation to the utility curve. This makes it convenient to determine the person's utility for any monetary value within the appropriate range. Looking at the utility curve in Figure 8.13 for a risk avoider, it is apparent that the curve can be approximated by an exponential function. The equation would be as follows:

$$U(X) = 1 - e^{-X/R} \qquad (8\text{-}9)$$

where e is the exponential constant (equal to 2.7182), X represents the monetary value, and R is a parameter that controls the shape of the person's utility curve. As R increases, the utility curve becomes flatter (corresponding to a decision maker who is less risk averse).

Utility as a Decision-Making Criterion

Once we have determined a decision maker's utility curve, how do we use it in making decisions? We construct the decision tree and make all prior and revised probability estimates and computations as before. However, instead of using monetary values as payoffs, we now replace all monetary payoffs with the appropriate utility values. We then fold back the decision tree, using the criterion of maximizing expected utility values. Let's look at an example.

Mark Simkin has an opportunity to invest in a new business venture. If the venture is a big success, Mark will make a profit of $40,000. If the venture is a moderate success, Mark will make a profit $10,000. If the venture fails, Mark will lose his investment of $30,000. Mark estimates the venture's chances as 20% for big success, 30% for moderate success, and 50% for failure. Should Mark invest in the venture?

Mark's alternatives are displayed in the tree shown in Figure 8.14. Using monetary values, the EMV at node 1 is $40,000 × 0.2 + $10,000 × 0.3 + (−$30,000) × 0.5 = −$4,000.

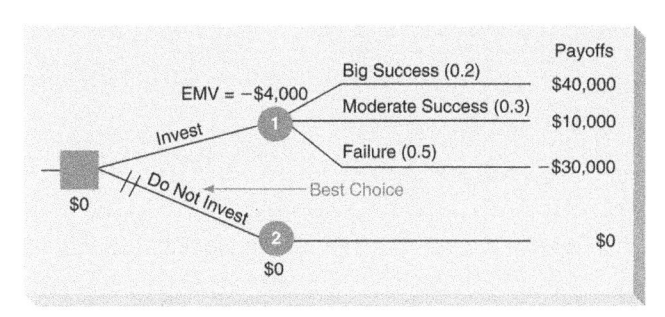

Figure 8.14: Decision Tree Using EMV for Mark Simkin

Because this is smaller than the EMV of $0 at node 2, Mark should turn down the venture and invest his money elsewhere.

Now let's view the same problem from a utility perspective. Using the procedure outlined earlier, Mark is able to construct a utility curve showing his preference for monetary amounts between $40,000 and −$30,000 (the best and worst payoffs in his problem). This curve, shown in Figure 8.15, indicates that within this monetary range Mark is a risk seeker (i.e., a gambler).

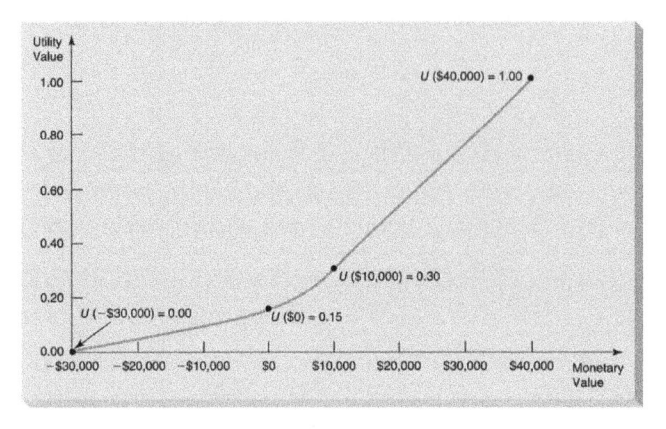

Figure 8.15: Utility Curve for Mark Simkin

From Figure 8.15, we note the following utility values for Mark: $U(-\$30,000) = 0$, $U(\$0) = 0.15$, $U(\$10,000) = 0.30$, and $U(\$40,000) = 1$. Substituting these values in the decision tree in Figure 8.14 in place of the monetary values, we fold back the tree to maximize Mark's expected utility. The computations are shown in Figure 8.16.

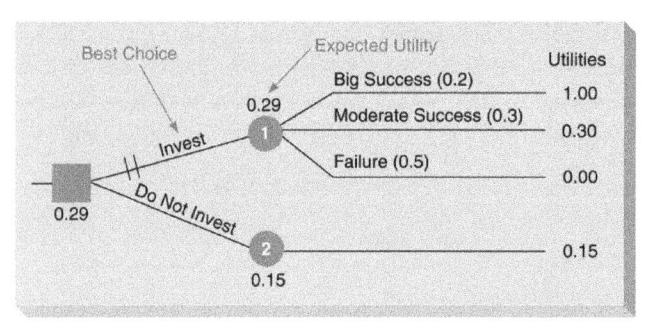

Figure 8.16: Decision Tree Using Utility Values for Mark Simkin

Using utility values, the expected utility at node 1 is 0.29, which is greater than the utility of 0.15 at node 2. This implies that Mark should invest his money in the venture. As you can see, this is the opposite of the decision suggested if EMV had been used, and it clearly illustrates how using utilities instead of monetary values may lead to different decisions in the same problem. In Mark's case, the utility curve indicates that he is a risk seeker, and the choice of investing in the venture certainly reflects his preference for risk.

8.10 Summary

This chapter introduces the topic of decision analysis, which is an analytic and systematic approach to studying decision making. We first indicate the steps involved in making decisions in three different environments: (1) decision making under certainty, (2) decision making under uncertainty, and (3) decision making under risk. For decision problems under uncertainty, we identify the best alternatives, using criteria such as maximax, maximin, criterion of realism, equally likely, and minimax regret. For decision problems under risk, we discuss the computation and use of the expected monetary value (EMV), expected opportunity loss (EOL), and expected value of perfect information (EVPI). We also illustrate the use of Excel to solve decision analysis problems.

Decision trees are used for larger decision problems in which decisions must be made in sequence. In this case, we compute the expected value of sample information (EVSI). Bayesian analysis is used to revise or update probability values.

When it is inappropriate to use monetary values, utility theory can be used to assign a utility value to each decision payoff. In such cases, we compute expected utilities and select the alternative with the highest utility value.

Key Points
- Decision analysis is an analytic and systematic way to tackle decision problems.
- A good decision is based on logic.
- A bad decision does not consider all alternatives.
- Decision analysis involves five steps: (1) define the problem, (2) list alternatives, (3) identify possible outcomes, (4) identify payoffs, and (5) select and apply a decision analysis model.
- During the fourth step of decision analysis, the decision maker can construct decision or payoff tables.
- In decision making under certainty, the consequence of each alternative and the outcome that will occur are known for sure. This scenario is obviously very unlikely in real-world settings.
- In decision making under uncertainty, we do not have probability estimates of the occurrence of each outcome.
- In decision making under risk, we know probability estimates of the occurrence of each outcome.
- Maximax is an optimistic approach.
- Maximin is a pessimistic approach.
- The criterion of realism uses a weighted average approach.
- The equally likely criterion selects the alternative yielding the highest average payoff.
- Minimax regret is based on opportunity loss.
- With minimax regret, we first develop the opportunity loss table from the payoff table.
- Excel worksheets can be created easily to solve decision-making problems under uncertainty.

- Expected Monetary Value (EMV) is the weighted average of possible payoffs for each alternative.
- Expected Opportunity Loss (EOL) is the expected cost of not picking the best solution.
- Minimum EOL will always result in the same decision as the maximum EMV.
- Expected Value of Perfect Information (EVPI) places an upper bound on what to pay for any information.
- EVPI is the expected value with perfect information minus the maximum EMV.
- EVPI = Minimum EOL.
- Decision problems involving alternatives and outcomes can be effectively represented as decision trees.
- Decision trees present decision alternatives and outcomes in a sequential manner.
- A decision tree usually begins with a decision node, and it contains both decision nodes and outcome nodes.
- We fold back a decision tree from the end toward the beginning to identify the best decision.
- The EMV is calculated at each outcome node of a decision tree.
- The best alternative is selected at a decision node of a decision tree.
- Multistage decision problems involve a sequence of decision outcomes or alternatives. It is possible for one outcome to directly follow another outcome.
- Multistage decision problems are analyzed using decision trees.
- EVPI is an upper bound on the value of sample information.
- All outcomes and alternatives must be considered in a multistage decision-making problem.
- Many of the probabilities in a multistage decision-making problem are conditional probabilities.
- Expected Value of Sample Information (EVSI) measures the value of imperfect or sample information.
- Comparing EVSI to EVPI may provide a good measure of the relative value of a current sample or survey.
- Bayes' theorem allows decision makers to revise probability values.
- Prior probabilities are estimates before a market survey.
- Revised probabilities are determined using the prior probabilities and market survey information.
- We can calculate conditional probabilities using a probability table.
- EMV is not always the best criterion to use to make decisions.
- A utility function converts a person's value for money and attitudes toward risk into a dimensionless number between 0 and 1.
- We assign the worst payoff a utility of 0 and the best payoff a utility of 1.
- The certainty equivalent is the minimum guaranteed amount you are willing to accept to avoid the risk associated with a gamble.
- A utility curve plots utility values versus monetary values.

- Risk premium is the EMV that a person is willing to give up in order to avoid the risk associated with a gamble.
- A risk neutral person has a utility curve that is a straight line.
- Utility values replace monetary values when using utility as a decision-making criterion.
- Using expected utility may lead to a decision that is different from the one suggested by EMV.

Glossary

Certainty Equivalent The minimum guaranteed amount one is willing to accept to avoid the risk associated with a gamble.

Coefficient of Realism (α) A number from 0 to 1 such that when α is close to 1, the decision criterion is optimistic, and when α is close to zero, the decision criterion is pessimistic.

Conditional Value A consequence or payoff, normally expressed in a monetary value, that occurs as a result of a particular alternative and outcome. Also known as a *payoff*.

Criterion of Realism A decision criterion that represents a weighted average of optimistic and pessimistic decisions. Also known as *Hurwicz*.

Decision Alternative A course of action or a strategy that can be chosen by a decision maker.

Decision Making under Certainty A decision-making environment in which the future outcomes are known.

Decision Making under Risk A decision-making environment in which several outcomes can occur as a result of a decision or an alternative. Probabilities of the outcomes are known.

Decision Making under Uncertainty A decision-making environment in which several outcomes can occur. Probabilities of these outcomes are not known.

Decision Table A table in which decision alternatives are listed down the rows and outcomes are listed across the columns. The body of the table contains the payoffs. Also known as a *payoff table*.

Efficiency of Sample Information A ratio of the expected value of sample information to the expected value of perfect information.

Equally Likely A decision criterion that places an equal weight on all outcomes. Also known as *Laplace*.

Expected Monetary Value (EMV) The average or expected monetary outcome of a decision if it can be repeated many times. This is determined by multiplying the monetary outcomes by their respective probabilities. The results are then added to arrive at the EMV.

Expected Opportunity Loss (EOL) The average or expected regret of a decision.

Expected Value of Perfect Information (EVPI) The average or expected value of information if it is completely accurate.

Expected Value of Sample Information (EVSI) The average or expected value of imperfect or survey information.

Expected Value with Perfect Information (EVwPI) The average or expected value of the decision if the decision maker knew what would happen ahead of time.

Maximax An optimistic decision-making criterion. This is the alternative with the highest possible return.

Maximin A pessimistic decision-making criterion that maximizes the minimum outcome. It is the best of the worst possible outcomes.

Minimax Regret A decision criterion that minimizes the maximum opportunity loss.

Opportunity Loss The amount you would lose by not picking the best alternative. For any outcome, this is the difference between the consequences of any alternative and the best possible alternative. Also called *regret*.

Outcome An occurrence over which a decision maker has little or no control. Also known as a state-of-nature.

Risk Avoider A person who avoids risk. As the monetary value increases on the utility curve, the utility increases at a decreasing rate. This decision maker gets less utility for a greater risk and higher potential returns.

Risk Neutral A person who is indifferent toward risk. The utility curve for a risk-neutral person is a straight line.

Risk Premium The monetary amount that a person is willing to give up in order to avoid the risk associated with a gamble.

Risk Seeker A person who seeks risk. As the monetary value increases on the utility curve, the utility increases at an increasing rate. This decision maker gets more pleasure for a greater risk and higher potential returns.

Sequential Decisions Decisions in which the outcome of one decision influences other decisions.

Utility Curve A graph or curve that illustrates the relationship between utility and monetary values. When this curve has been constructed, utility values from the curve can be used in the decision-making process.

Utility Theory A theory that allows decision makers to incorporate their risk preference and other factors into the decision-making process.

8.11 Exercises

Solved Problems

Solved Problem 8–1 Cal Bender and Becky Addison are undergraduates in business at Central College. To make extra money, Cal and Becky have decided to look into starting a small company that would provide word-processing services to students who need term papers or other reports prepared in a professional manner. They have identified three strategies. Strategy 1 is to invest in a fairly expensive microcomputer system with a high-quality laser printer. In a good market, they should be able to obtain a net profit of $10,000 over the next two years. If the market is bad, they could lose $8,000. Strategy 2 is to purchase a cheaper system. With a good market, they could get a return during the next two years of $8,000. With a bad market, they could incur a loss of $4,000. Their final strategy, strategy 3, is to do nothing. Cal is basically a risk taker, whereas Becky tries to avoid risk.

a. Which decision criterion should Cal use? What would Cal's decision be?
b. Which decision criterion should Becky use? What decision would Becky make?
c. If Cal and Becky were indifferent to risk, which decision criterion should they use? What would be the decision?

Solution The problem is one of decision making under uncertainty. To answer the specific questions, it is helpful to construct a decision table showing the alternatives, outcomes, and payoffs, as follows:

Alternative	Good Market	Bad Market
Expensive system	$10,000	-$8,000
Cheaper system	$ 8,000	-$4,000
Do nothing	$ 0	$ 0

a. Cal should use the maximax, or optimistic, decision criterion. The maximum payoffs for the three alternatives are $10,000, $8,000, and $0, respectively. Hence, Cal should select the expensive system.
b. Becky should use the maximin, or pessimistic, decision criterion. The minimum payoffs for the three alternatives are -$8,000, -$4,000, and $0, respectively. Hence, Becky should choose to do nothing.
c. If Cal and Becky are indifferent to risk, they should use the equally likely criterion. The average payoffs for the three alternatives are $1,000, $2,000, and $0, respectively. Hence, their decision would be to select the cheaper system.

Solved Problem 8–2 Maria Rojas is considering the possibility of opening a small dress shop on Fairbanks Avenue, a few blocks from the university. She has located a good mall that attracts students. Her options are to open a small shop, a medium-sized shop, or no shop at all. The market for a dress shop can be good, average, or bad. The probabilities for these three possibilities are 0.2 for a good market, 0.5 for an average market, and 0.3 for a bad market. The net profit or loss for the medium-sized and small shops for the various market conditions are given in the following payoff table:

	Outcomes		
Alternative	Good Market	Average Market	Bad Market
Small shop	$ 75,000	$25,000	-$40,000
Medium-sized shop	$100,000	$35,000	-$60,000
No shop	$ 0	$ 0	$ 0
Probabilities	0.2	0.5	0.3

Building no shop at all yields no loss and no gain. What do you recommend?

Solution The problem can be solved by computing the EMV for each alternative, as follows:

EMV (Small shop) = $75,000 × 0.2 + $25,000 × 0.5 + (−$40,000) × 0.3 = $15,500
EMV (Medium shop) = $100,000 × 0.2 + $35,000 × 0.5 + (−$60,000) × 0.3 = $19,500
EMV (No shop)   = $0

As can be seen, the best decision is to build the medium-sized shop. The EMV for this alternative is $19,500.

Solved Problem 8–3 Monica Britt has enjoyed sailing small boats since she was 7 years old, when her mother started sailing with her. Today Monica is considering the possibility of starting a company to produce small sailboats for the recreational market. Unlike other mass-produced sailboats, however, these boats will be made specifically for children between the ages of 10 and 15. The boats will be of the highest quality and extremely stable, and the sail size will be reduced to prevent problems with capsizing.

Because of the expense involved in developing the initial molds and acquiring the necessary equipment to produce fiberglass sailboats for young children, Monica has decided to conduct a pilot study to make sure that the market for the sailboats will be adequate. She estimates that the pilot study will cost her $10,000. Furthermore, the pilot study can be either successful or not successful. Her basic decisions are to build a large manufacturing facility, a small manufacturing facility, or no facility at all. With a favorable market, Monica can expect to make $90,000 from the large facility or $60,000 from the smaller facility. If the market is unfavorable, however, Monica estimates that she would lose $30,000 with a large facility, whereas she would lose only $20,000 with the small facility. Monica estimates that the probability of a favorable market, given a successful pilot study result, is 0.8. The probability of an unfavorable market, given an unsuccessful pilot study result, is estimated to be 0.9. Monica feels there is a 50–50 chance that the pilot study will be successful. Of course, Monica could bypass the pilot study and simply make the decision whether to build a large plant, a small plant, or no facility at all. Without doing any testing in a pilot study, she estimates the probability of a successful market is 0.6. What do you recommend?

Solution The decision tree for Monica's problem is shown in Figure 8.17. The tree shows all alternatives, outcomes, probability values, payoffs, and EMVs. The expected value computations at the various nodes are as follows:

EMV (Node 1) = $60,000 × 0.6 + (−$20,000) × 0.4 = $28,000
EMV (Node 2) = $90,000 × 0.6 + (−$30,000) × 0.3 = $42,000
EMV (Node 3) = $0
EMV (Node 4) = $50,000 × 0.8 + (−$30,000) × 0.2 = $34,000
EMV (Node 5) = $80,000 × 0.8 + (−$40,000) × 0.2 = $56,000
EMV (Node 6) = −$10,000

EMV (Node 7) = $50,000 × 0.1 + (−$30,000) × 0.9 = −$22,000
EMV (Node 8) = $80,000 × 0.1 + (−$40,000) × 0.9 = $28,000
EMV (Node 9) = −$10,000
EMV (Node 10) = $56,000 × 0.5 + (−$10,000) × 0.5 = $23,000

Monica's optimal solution is to *not* conduct the pilot study and construct the large plant directly. The EMV of this decision is $42,000.

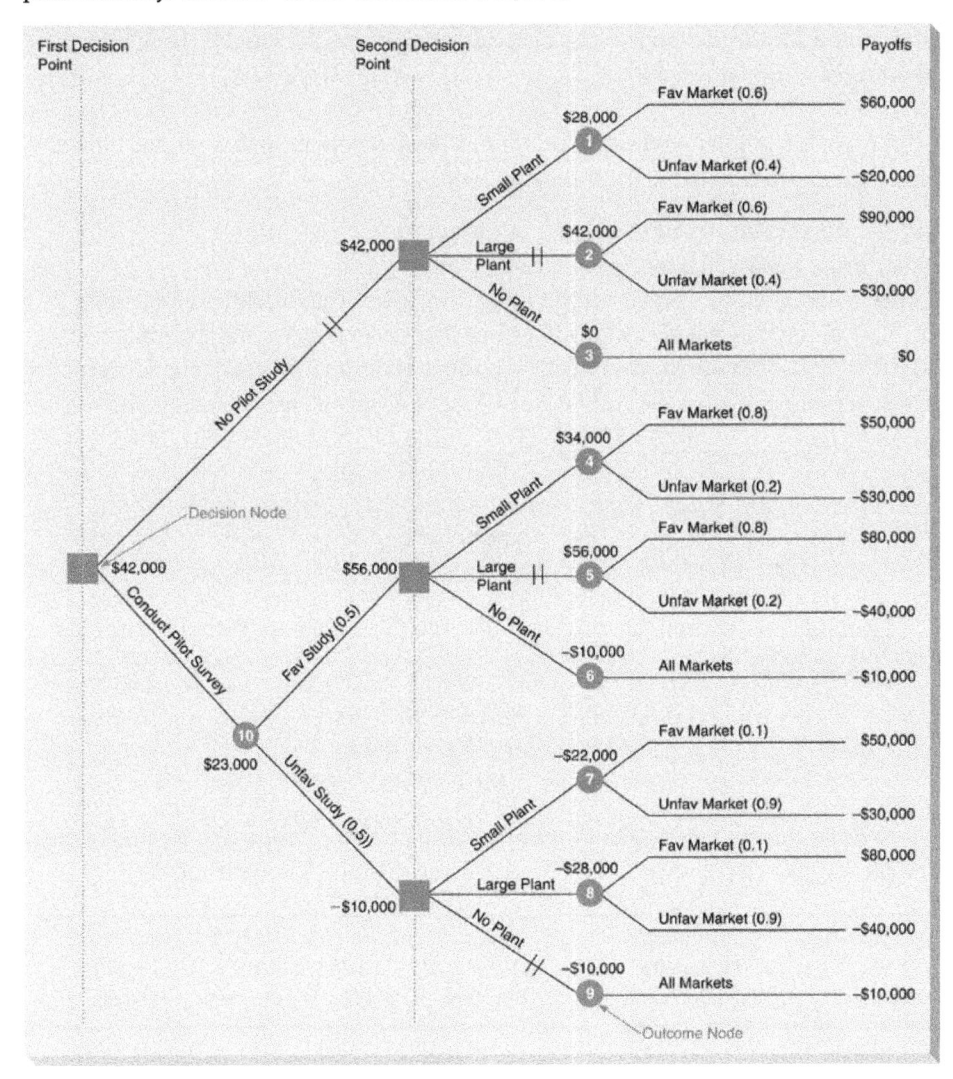

Figure 8.17: Complete Decision Tree for Monica Britt

Solved Problem 8-4 Developing a small driving range for golfers of all abilities has long been a desire of John Jenkins. John, however, believes that the chance of a successful driving range is only about 40%. A friend of John's has suggested that he conduct a survey in the community to get a better feel for the demand for such a facility. There is a 0.9 probability that the survey result will be positive if the driving range will be successful. Furthermore, it is estimated that there is a 0.8 probability that the survey result will be negative if indeed the driving range will be unsuccessful. John would like to determine the chances of a successful driving range, given a positive result from the survey.

Solution This problem requires the use of Bayes' theorem. Before we start to solve the problem, we will define the following terms:

$P(S)$ = probability of successful driving range
$P(U)$ = probability of unsuccessful driving range
$P(P|S)$ = probability survey result will be positive given a successful driving range
$P(N|S)$ = probability survey result will be negative given a successful driving range
$P(P|U)$ = probability survey result will be positive given an unsuccessful driving range
$P(N|S)$ = probability survey result will be negative given an unsuccessful driving range

Now, we can summarize what we know:

$$P(S) = 0.4$$
$$P(P|S) = 0.9$$
$$P(N|U) = 0.8$$

From this information, we can compute three additional probabilities needed to solve the problem:

$$P(U) = 1 - P(S) = 1 - 0.4 = 0.6$$
$$P(U|S) = 1 - P(P|S) = 1 - 0.9 = 0.9$$
$$P(P|U) = 1 - P(N|U) = 1 - 0.8 = 0.2$$

Now we can put these values into Bayes' theorem to compute the desired revised probability given a positive survey result, as shown in the following table:

Outcome	Conditional Probability $P(P \mid \text{Outcome})$	Prior Probability of Outcome	Joint Probability $P(P \text{ and Outcome})$	Posterior Probability
Successful driving range (S)	0.9 ×	0.4 =	0.36	0.36/0.48 = 0.75
Unsuccessful driving range (U)	0.2 ×	0.6 =	0.12	0.12/0.48 = 0.25
			0.48	

The probability of a successful driving range, given a positive survey result is $P(S|P) = P(P \text{ and } S)/P(S) = 0.36/0.48$, or 0.75.

Discussion Questions

8–1. Give an example of a good decision that you made that resulted in a bad outcome. Also give an example of a bad decision that you made that had a good outcome. Why was each decision good or bad?

8–2. Describe what is involved in the decision-making process.

8–3. What is an alternative? What is an outcome?

8–4. Discuss the differences between decision making under certainty, decision making under risk, and decision making under uncertainty.

8–5. State the meanings of EMV and EVPI.

8–6. Under what conditions is a decision tree preferable to a decision table?

8–7. What is the difference between prior and posterior probabilities?

8–8. What is the purpose of Bayesian analysis? Describe how you would use Bayesian analysis in the decision-making process.

8–9. What is the purpose of utility theory?

8–10. Briefly discuss how a utility function can be assessed. What is a standard gamble, and how is it used in determining utility values?

8–11. How is a utility curve used in selecting the best decision for a particular problem?

8–12. What is a risk seeker? What is a risk avoider? How do the utility curves for these types of decision makers differ?

Problems

8–13. In the environment of increased competition, a fitness club executive is considering the purchase of additional equipment. His alternatives, outcomes, and payoffs (profits) are shown in the following table:

Equipment	Favorable Market	Unfavorable Market
Acme	$400,000	−$175,000
Standard	$280,000	−$ 90,000
High Pro	$ 95,000	−$ 15,000

(a) If the executive is an optimistic decision maker, which alternative will he likely choose?

(b) If the executive is a pessimistic decision maker, which alternative will he likely choose?

(c) Market research suggests the chance of a favorable market for fitness clubs is 76%. If the executive uses this analysis, which alternative will he likely choose?

8-14. Steve's Mountain Bicycle Shop is considering three options for its facility next year. Steve can expand his current shop, move to a larger facility, or make no change. With a good market, the annual payoff would be $76,000 if he expands, $90,000 if he moves, and $40,000 if he does nothing. With an average market, his payoffs will be $30,000, $41,000, and $15,000, respectively. With a poor market, his payoff will be −$17,000, −$28,000, and $4,000, respectively.
(a) Which option should Steve choose if he uses the maximax criterion?
(b) Which option should Steve choose if he uses the maximin criterion?
(c) Which option should Steve choose if he uses the equally likely criterion?
(d) Which option should Steve choose if he uses the criterion of realism with $\alpha = 0.4$?
(e) Which option should Steve choose if he uses the minimax regret criterion?

8-15. Steve (see Problem 8–14) has gathered some additional information. The probabilities of good, average, and poor markets are 0.25, 0.45, and 0.3, respectively.
(a) Using EMVs, what option should Steve choose? What is the maximum EMV?
(b) Using EOL, what option should Steve choose? What is the minimum EOL?
(c) Compute the EVPI and show that it is the same as the minimum EOL.

8-16. Debbie Gibson is considering three investment options for a small inheritance that she has just received—stocks, bonds, and money market. The return on her investment will depend on the performance of the economy, which can be strong, average, or weak. The returns for each possible combination are shown in the following table:

Investment	Strong	Average	Weak
Stocks	12%	6%	−10%
Bonds	7%	4%	1%
Money market	4%	3%	2%

Assume that Debbie will choose only one of the investment options.
(a) Which investment should Debbie choose if she uses the maximax criterion?
(b) Which investment should Debbie choose if she uses the maximin criterion?
(c) Which investment should Debbie choose if she uses the equally likely criterion?
(d) Which investment should Debbie choose if she uses the criterion of realism with $\alpha = 0.5$?

(e) Which investment should Debbie choose if she uses the minimax regret criterion?

8-17. After reading about economic predictions, Debbie Gibson (see Problem 8-16) has assigned the probability that the economy will be strong, average, and weak at 0.2, 0.35, and 0.45, respectively.
   (a) Using EMVs, what option should Debbie choose? What is the maximum EMV?
   (b) Using EOL, what option should Debbie choose? What is the minimum EOL?
   (c) Compute the EVPI and show that it is the same as the minimum EOL.

8-18. A hospital administrator in Portland is trying to determine whether to build a large wing onto the existing hospital, a small wing, or no wing at all. If the population of Portland continued to grow, a large wing could return $225,000 to the hospital each year. If the small wing were built, it would return $90,000 to the hospital each year if the population continued to grow. If the population of Portland remained the same, the hospital would encounter a loss of $125,000 if the large wing were built. Furthermore, a loss of $65,000 would be realized if the small wing were constructed and the population remained the same. It is unknown whether Portland's population will grow in the near future.
   (a) Construct a decision table.
   (b) Using the equally likely criterion, determine the best alternative.
   (c) The chairman of the hospital's board has advised using a coefficient of realism of 0.7 in determining the best alternative. What is the best decision according to this criterion?

8-19. Shaq Bryant sells newspapers on Sunday mornings in an area surrounded by three busy churches. Assume that Shaq's demand can either be for 100, 300, or 500 newspapers, depending on traffic and weather. Shaq has the option to order 100, 300, or 500 newspapers from his supplier. Shaq pays $1.25 for each newspaper he orders and sells each for $2.50.
   (a) How many papers should Shaq order if he chooses the maximax criterion?
   (b) How many papers should Shaq order if he chooses the maximin criterion?
   (c) How many papers should Shaq order if he chooses the equally likely criterion?
   (d) How many papers should Shaq order if he chooses the criterion of realism with $\alpha = 0.45$?
   (e) How many papers should Shaq order if he chooses the minimax regret criterion?

8-20. Shaq (see Problem 8-19) has done some research and discovered that the probabilities for demands of 100, 300, and 500 newspapers are 0.4, 0.35, and 0.25, respectively.
   (a) Using EMVs, how many papers should Shaq order?

(b) Using EOL, how many papers should Shaq order?
(c) Compute Shaq's EVwPI and EVPI.

8-21. The Boatwright Sauce Company is a small manufacturer of several different sauces to use in food products. One of the products is a blended sauce mix that is sold to retail outlets. Joy Boatwright must decide how many cases of this mix to manufacture each month. The probability that the demand will be six cases is 0.1, for seven cases is 0.5, for eight cases is 0.3, and for nine cases is 0.1. The cost of every case is $55, and the price that Joy gets for each case is $90. Unfortunately, any cases not sold by the end of the month are of no value, due to spoilage. How many cases of sauce should Joy manufacture each month?

8-22. Waldo Books needs to decide how many copies of a new hardcover release to purchase for its shelves. The store has assumed that demand will be 50, 100, 150, or 200 copies next month, and it needs to decide whether to order 50, 100, 150, or 200 books for this period. Each book costs Waldo $20 and can be sold for $30. Waldo can sell any unsold books back to the supplier for $4.
(a) Which option should Waldo choose if it uses the maximax criterion?
(b) Which option should Waldo choose if it uses the maximin criterion?
(c) Which option should Waldo choose if it uses the equally likely criterion?
(d) Which option should Waldo choose if it uses the criterion of realism with $\alpha = 0.7$?
(e) Which option should Waldo choose if it uses the minimax regret criterion?

8-23. After researching the market, Waldo Books (see Problem 8-22) has concluded that the probabilities of selling 50, 100, 150, and 200 books next month are 0.2, 0.35, 0.25, and 0.2, respectively.
(a) Using EMVs, how many books should Waldo order?
(b) Using EOL, how many books should Waldo order?
(c) Compute Waldo's EVwPI and EVPI.

8-24. A souvenir retailer has an opportunity to establish a new location inside a large airport. The annual returns will depend primarily on the size of the space she rents and if the economy will be favorable. The retailer has worked with the airport concession commission and has projected the following possible annual earnings associated with renting a small, medium, large, or very large space:

Size	Good Economy	Fair Economy	Poor Economy
Small	$ 70,000	$28,000	-$ 14,000
Medium	$112,000	$42,000	-$ 28,000
Large	$140,000	$42,000	-$ 56,000
Very large	$420,000	$35,000	-$224,000

(a) What is the souvenir retailer's maximax decision?
(b) What is her maximin decision?

(c) What is her equally likely decision?
(d) What is her criterion of realism decision, using $\alpha = 0.8$?
(e) What is her minimax regret decision?

8-25. An ambulance driver has three major routes from the hospital base station to the university, to which he makes several trips weekly. The traffic patterns are, however, very complex. Under good conditions, Broad Street is the fastest route. When Broad is congested, one of the other routes, either Drexel Avenue or the expressway, is usually preferable. Over the past two months, the driver has tried each route several times under different traffic conditions. This information is summarized (in minutes of travel time to work) in the following table:

Route	No Congestion	Mild Congestion	Severe Congestion
Broad Street	10	21	30
Drexel Avenue	13	17	23
Expressway	20	21	20

In the past 50 days, the driver has encountered severe traffic congestion 10 days and mild traffic congestion 20 days. Assume that the past 50 days are typical of traffic conditions.

(a) Which route should the driver take? Remember that we want to find the fastest route.
(b) If the ambulance had a traffic scanner to accurately inform the driver of the level of congestion in this part of town, how much time could he potentially save?

8-26. A group of medical professionals is considering constructing a private clinic. If patient demand for the clinic is high, the physicians could realize a net profit of $100,000. If the demand is low, they could lose $40,000. Of course, they don't have to proceed at all, in which case there is no cost. In the absence of any market data, the best the physicians can guess is that there is a 50–50 chance that demand will be good.

(a) Construct a decision tree to help analyze this problem. What should the medical professionals do?
(b) The physicians have been approached by a market research firm that offers to perform a study of the market at a fee of $5,000. The market researchers claim that their experience enables them to use Bayes' theorem to make the following statements of probability:

probability of high demand given a positive study result = 0.82
probability of low demand given a positive study result = 0.18
probability of high demand given a negative study result = 0.11
probability of low demand given a negative study result = 0.89
probability of a positive study result = 0.55
probability of a negative study result = 0.45

Expand the decision tree in part (a) to reflect the options now open with the market study. What should the medical professionals do now?

(c) What is the maximum amount the physicians would be willing to pay for the market study?

(d) What is the efficiency of the market study's information?

8–27. In Problem 8–26, you helped a group of medical professionals analyze a decision, using EMV as the decision criterion. This group has also assessed its utility for money: $U(-\$45{,}000) = 0$, $U(-\$40{,}000) = 0.1$, $U(-\$5{,}000) = 0.7$, $U(\$0) = 0.9$, $U(\$95{,}000) = 0.99$, and $U(\$100{,}000) = 1$.

(a) Are the medical professionals risk seekers or risk avoiders? Justify your answer.

(b) Use expected utility as the decision criterion and determine the best decision for the medical professionals (including the option to use the market research firm).

8–28. Jerry Young is thinking about opening a bicycle shop in his hometown. Jerry loves to take his own bike on 50-mile trips with his friends, but he believes that any small business should be started only if there is a good chance of making a profit. Jerry can open a small shop, a large shop, or no shop at all. Because there will be a five-year lease on the building that Jerry is thinking about using, he wants to make sure that he makes the correct decision.

Jerry has done some analysis about the profitability of the bicycle shop. If Jerry builds the large bicycle shop, he will earn $60,000 if the market is good, but he will lose $40,000 if the market is bad. The small shop will return a $30,000 profit in a good market and a $10,000 loss in a bad market. At the present time, he believes that there is a 59% chance that the market will be good.

Jerry also has the option of hiring his old marketing professor for $5,000 to conduct a marketing research study. If the study is conducted, the results could be either favorable or unfavorable. It is estimated that there is a 0.6 probability that the survey will be favorable. Furthermore, there is a 0.9 probability that the market will be good, given a favorable outcome from the study. However, the marketing professor has warned Jerry that there is only a probability of 0.12 of a good market if the marketing research results are not favorable.

(a) Develop a decision tree for Jerry and help him decide what he should do.

(b) How much is the marketing professor's information worth? What is the efficiency of this information?

8–29. A manufacturer buys valves from two suppliers. The quality of the valves from the suppliers is as follows:

Percentage Defective	Probability for Supplier A	Probability for Supplier B
1	0.60	0.30
3	0.25	0.40
5	0.15	0.30

For example, the probability of getting a batch of valves that are 1% defective from supplier A is 0.60. Because the manufacturer orders 10,000 valves per order, this would mean that there is a 0.6 probability of getting 100 defective valves out of the 10,000 valves if supplier A is used to fill the order. A defective valve can be repaired for 60 cents. Although the quality of supplier B is lower, it will sell an order of 10,000 valves for $37 less than supplier A.

(a) Develop a decision tree to help the manufacturer decide which supplier it should use.

(b) For how much less would supplier B have to sell an order of 10,000 valves than supplier A for the manufacturer to be indifferent between the two suppliers?

8–30. After observing the heavy snow that his town received the previous winter, Ajay Patel plans to offer a snow-clearing service in his neighborhood this winter. If he invests in a new heavy-duty blower, Ajay forecasts a profit of $700 if snowfall this winter is heavy, a profit of $200 if it is moderate, and a loss of $900 if it is light. As per the current weather forecasts, the probabilities of heavy, moderate, and light snowfall this winter are 0.4, 0.3, and 0.3, respectively.

Rather than purchase a new blower, Ajay could get his father's blower repaired and just accept smaller jobs. Under this option, Ajay estimates a profit of $350 for a heavy snowfall, a profit of $100 for a moderate snowfall, and a loss of $150 for a light snowfall. Ajay, of course, has the option of choosing neither of these alternatives.

The local weather expert, Samantha Adams, is Ajay's good friend. For $50, she is willing to run sophisticated weather models on her computer and tell Ajay whether she expects this winter to be unseasonably cold. For the sake of solving this problem, assume that the following information is available. There is a 45% chance that Samantha will predict this winter to be unseasonably cold. If she does say this, the probabilities of heavy, moderate, and light snowfall are revised to 0.7, 0.25, and 0.05, respectively. On the other hand, if she predicts that this winter will not be unseasonably cold, these probabilities are revised to 0.15, 0.33, and 0.52, respectively.

Draw the decision tree for the situation faced by Ajay. Fold back the tree and determine the strategy you would recommend he follow. What is the efficiency of Samantha's information?

8–31. Oscar Weng is planning to raise funds to pay for a scouting trip by running a concession stand during tomorrow's high school soccer game. Oscar needs to decide whether to rent a large insulated thermos from the local rental store and sell cocoa at the game or to rent a large refrigerated container and sell lemonade. Unfortunately, Oscar does not have the resources to rent both items. Sales depend on whether it is sunny or rainy during the game. If the weather is sunny, Oscar will make a profit of $60 from lemonade but only $20 from cocoa. If, however, it is rainy, Oscar will make a profit of $80 from cocoa but only break even if he brings lemonade. Based on the local newspaper's prediction, Oscar thinks there is a 60% chance of it being sunny tomorrow.

Oscar's older brother Elmo, who has earned the Meteorology Badge, claims he can predict the weather more accurately than the newspaper. For only $4, he offers to study the weather and tell Oscar if there is a "good chance" or "bad chance" of it being sunny tomorrow. Assume that the following data are available about the accuracy of the brother's information:

- The probability that he will say "good chance" is 0.7.
- If he says "good chance," then there is a 0.83 probability that it will actually be sunny tomorrow.
- If he says "bad chance," then there is only a 0.25 probability that it will actually be sunny tomorrow.

(a) Draw the complete decision tree for Oscar's problem and fold it back to help him decide what he should do.
(b) How much is his brother's information actually worth to Oscar?

8–32. You have been hired by the No Flight Golf Company, and your first task is to decide whether to market a new golf ball utilizing breakthrough technology and, if so, determine the price. The payoff of your decision will be affected by whether your competitor will market similar balls and the price of their golf balls after you go to market. The cost to market the golf balls is $80,000, and the probability that your competitor will enter the market is 0.75. The following table describes the payoffs of each pricing combination, assuming that No Flight will have competition:

	Competitor's Price		
Our Price	High	Medium	Low
High	$400,000	$250,000	$ 25,000
Medium	$475,000	$325,000	$175,000
Low	$350,000	$250,000	$125,000

If No Flight sets its price high, the probability that the competition will set its price high, medium, and low is 0.3, 0.55, and 0.15, respectively. If No Flight sets its price medium, the probability that the competition will set its price high, medium, and low is 0.2, 0.7, and 0.1, respectively. Finally, if No Flight sets its price low, the probability that the competition will set its price high, medium, and low is 0.15, 0.25, and 0.6, respectively.

If No Flight has no competition for its new golf balls, its expected payoff for setting the price high, medium, and low is $600,000, $500,000, and $400,000, respectively, excluding marketing costs. Do you recommend marketing the new golf balls? If so, what is your pricing recommendation?

8-33. Your regular tennis partner has made a friendly wager with you. The two of you will play out one point in which you can serve. The loser pays the winner $100. If your first serve is not in play, you get a second serve. If your second serve is not in play, you lose the point. You have two kinds of serves: a hard one and a soft one. You know that your hard serve is in play 65% of the time and, when it is in play, you win the point 75% of the time. You put your soft serve in play 88% of the time and, when it is in play, you win the point 27% of the time. Should you accept the wager? If so, should you use your hard or soft serve?

8-34. Rob Johnson is a product manager for Diamond Chemical. The firm is considering whether to launch a new product line that will require building a new facility. The technology required to produce the new product is yet untested. If Rob decides to build the new facility and the process is successful, Diamond Chemical will realize a profit of $675,000. If the process does not succeed, the company will lose $825,000. Rob estimates that there is a 0.6 probability that the process will succeed.

Rob can also decide to build a pilot plant for $60,000 to test the new process before deciding to build the full-scale facility. If the pilot plant succeeds, Rob feels the chance of the full-scale facility succeeding is 85%. If the pilot plant fails, Rob feels the chance of the full-scale facility succeeding is only 20%. The probability that the pilot plant will succeed is estimated at 0.6. Structure this problem with a decision tree and advise Rob what to do.

8-35. Rob Johnson (see Problem 8-34) has some revised information concerning the accuracy of the pilot plant probabilities. According to his new information, the probability that the pilot plant will be successful, given that the full-scale facility will work, is 0.8. The probability that the pilot plant will fail, given that the full-scale facility will fail, is 0.85. Calculate the posterior probabilities and reevaluate the decision tree from Problem 8-34. Does this new information affect Diamond Chemical's original decision?

8-36. You are reconsidering your analysis of the tennis wager between you and your partner (see Problem 8-33) and have decided to incorporate utility theory into the decision-making process. The following table describes your utility values for various payoffs:

Monetary Value	Utility
−$100	0.00
−$ 50	0.50
$ 0	0.80
$ 50	0.95
$100	1.00

(a) Redo Problem 8–33 using this information.
(b) How can you best describe your attitude toward risk? Justify your answer.

8–37. Shamrock Oil owns a parcel of land that has the potential to be an underground oil field. It will cost $500,000 to drill for oil. If oil does exist on the land, Shamrock will realize a payoff of $4,000,000 (not including drilling costs). With current information, Shamrock estimates that there is a 0.2 probability that oil is present on the site. Shamrock also has the option of selling the land as is for $400,000, without further information about the likelihood of oil being present. A third option is to perform geological tests at the site, which would cost $100,000. There is a 30% chance that the test results will be positive, after which Shamrock can sell the land for $650,000 or drill the land, with a 0.65 probability that oil exists. If the test results are negative, Shamrock can sell the land for $50,000 or drill the land, with a 0.05 probability that oil exists. Using a decision tree, recommend a course of action for Shamrock Oil.

8–38. Shamrock Oil (see Problem 8–37) has some revised information concerning the accuracy of the geological test probabilities. According to this new information, the probability that the test will be positive, given that oil is present in the ground, is 0.85. The probability that the test will be negative, given that oil is not present, is 0.75. Calculate the posterior probabilities and reevaluate the decision tree from Problem 8–37. Does this new information affect Shamrock Oil's original decision?

8–39. Shamrock Oil (see Problem 8–37) has decided to rely on utility theory to assist in the decision concerning the oil field. The following table describes its utility function; all monetary values are in thousands of dollars:

Monetary Value	Utility
−$ 600	0.00
−$ 500	0.03
−$ 50	0.10
$ 400	0.15
$ 550	0.17
$3,400	0.90
$3,500	1.00

(a) Redo Problem 8–37 using this information.
(b) How can you best describe Shamrock Oil's attitude toward risk? Justify your answer.

8-40. Jim Sellers is thinking about producing a new type of electric razor for men. If the market is good, he would get a return of $140,000, but if the market for this new type of razor is poor, he would lose $84,000. Because Ron Bush is a close friend of Jim Sellers, Jim is considering the possibility of using Bush Marketing Research to gather additional information about the market for the razor. Ron has suggested two options to Jim. The first alternative is a sophisticated questionnaire that would be administered to a test market. It will cost $5,000. The second alternative is to run a pilot study. This would involve producing a limited number of the new razors and trying to sell them in two cities that are typical of American cities. The pilot study is more accurate but is also more expensive. It would cost $20,000. Ron has suggested that it would be a good idea for Jim to conduct either the questionnaire or the pilot before making the decision concerning whether to produce the new razor. But Jim is not sure if the value of either option is worth the cost.

For the sake of solving this problem, assume that Jim has the following probability estimates available: the probability of a successful market without performing the questionnaire or pilot study is 0.5, the probability of a successful market given a positive questionnaire result is 0.78, the probability of a successful market given a negative questionnaire result is 0.27, the probability of a successful market given a positive pilot study result is 0.89, and the probability of a successful market given a negative pilot study result is 0.18. Further, the probability of a positive questionnaire result is 0.45, and the probability of a positive pilot study result is also 0.45.

(a) Draw the decision tree for this problem and identify the best decision for Jim.
(b) What is the value of the questionnaire's information? What is its efficiency?
(c) What is the value of the pilot study's information? What is its efficiency?

8-41. Jim Sellers (see Problem 8-40) has been able to estimate his utility for a number of different values, and he would like to use these utility values in making his decision. The utility values are $U(-\$104,000) = 0$, $U(-\$89,000) = 0.5$, $U(-\$84,000) = 0.55$, $U(-\$20,000) = 0.7$, $U(-\$5,000) = 0.8$, $U(\$0) = 0.81$, $U(\$120,000) = 0.9$, $U(\$135,000) = 0.95$, and $U(\$140,000) = 1$.

(a) Solve Problem 8–40(a) again using utility values.
(b) Is Jim a risk avoider or risk seeker? Justify your answer.

8-42. Jason Scott has applied for a mortgage to purchase a house, and he will go to settlement in two months. His loan can be locked in now at the current market interest rate of 7% and a cost of $1,000. He also has the option of waiting one month and locking in the rate available at that time at a cost of $500. Finally, he can choose to accept the market rate available at settlement in two months at no cost. Assume that interest rates will either increase by 0.5% (0.3 probability), remain unchanged (0.5 probability), or decrease by 0.5% (0.2 probability) at the end of one month.

Rates can also increase, remain unchanged, or decrease by another 0.5% at the end of the second month. If rates increase after one month, the probabilities that they will increase, remain unchanged, and decrease at the end of the second month are 0.5, 0.25, and 0.25, respectively. If rates remain unchanged after one month, the probabilities that they will increase, remain unchanged, and decrease at the end of the second month are 0.25, 0.5, and 0.25, respectively. If rates decrease after one month, the probabilities that they will increase, remain unchanged, and decrease at the end of the second month are 0.25, 0.25, and 0.5, respectively.

Assuming that Jason will stay in the house for 5 years, each 0.5% increase in the interest rate of his mortgage will cost him $2,400. Each 0.5% decrease in the rate will likewise save him $2,400. What strategy would you recommend?

8-43. Jason Scott (see Problem 8-42) has decided to incorporate utility theory into his decision with his mortgage application. The following table describes Jason's utility function:

Monetary Value	Utility
−$4,800	0.00
−$2,900	0.10
−$2,400	0.12
−$1,000	0.15
−$ 500	0.19
$ 0	0.21
$1,900	0.26
$2,400	0.30
$4,800	1.00

(a) How can you best describe Jason's attitude toward risk? Justify your answer.
(b) Will the use of utilities affect Jason's original decision in Problem 8-42?

8-44. An investor is deciding whether to build a retail store. If she invests in the store and it is successful, she expects a return of $100,000 in the first year. If the store is not successful, she will suffer a loss of $80,000. She guesses that the probability that the store will be a success is 0.6.

To remove some of the uncertainty from this decision, the investor tries to establish more information, but this market research will cost $20,000. If she spends this money, she will have more confidence in her investment. There is a 0.6 probability that this information will be favorable; if it is, the likelihood that the store will be a success increases to 0.9. If the information is not favorable, the likelihood that the store will be a success reduces to only 0.2. Of course, she can elect to do nothing.

(a) What do you recommend?
(b) How much is the information worth? What is its efficiency?

8-45. Replace all monetary values in Problem 8-44 with the following utilities:

Monetary Value	Utility
$100,000	1.00
$ 80,000	0.40
$ 0	0.20
-$ 20,000	0.10
-$ 80,000	0.05
-$100,000	0.00

(a) What do you recommend, based on expected utility?

(b) Is the investor a risk seeker or a risk avoider? Justify your answer.

8-46. The Jamis Corporation is involved with waste management. During the past 10 years, it has become one of the largest waste disposal companies in the Midwest, serving primarily Wisconsin, Illinois, and Michigan. Bob Jamis, president of the company, is considering the possibility of establishing a waste treatment plant in northern Mississippi. From past experience, Bob believes that a small plant would yield a $500,000 profit, regardless of the demand for the plant. The success of a medium-sized plant would depend on demand. With a low demand for waste treatment, Bob expects a $200,000 profit. A fair demand would yield a $700,000 profit, and a high demand would return $800,000. Although a large plant is much riskier than a medium-sized one, the potential rewards are much greater. With a high demand, a large plant would return $1,000,000. However, the plant would yield a profit of only $400,000 with a fair demand, and it would actually lose $200,000 with a low demand. Looking at the current economic conditions in northern Mississippi, Bob estimates that the probabilities of low, fair, and high demands are 0.15, 0.4, and 0.45, respectively.

Because of the large potential investment and the possibility of a loss, Bob has decided to hire a market research team that is based in Jackson, Mississippi. This team will perform a survey to get a better feel for the probability of a low, medium, or high demand for a waste treatment facility. The cost of the survey is $50,000, and the survey could result in three possible outcomes—low, fair, and high. To help Bob determine whether to go ahead with the survey, the marketing research firm has provided Bob with the following information regarding the conditional probabilities, i.e., P(Survey results|Possible outcomes):

	Survey Results		
Possible Outcome	Low	Fair	High
Low demand	0.7	0.2	0.1
Fair demand	0.4	0.5	0.1
High demand	0.1	0.3	0.6

For example, P(Low survey result | Low demand) = 0.7. What should Bob do?

8-47. Before market research was done, Peter Martin believed that there was a 50–50 chance that his food store would be a success. The research team determined that there was a 0.75 probability that the market research would be favorable, given a successful food store. Moreover, there was a 0.65 probability that the market research would be unfavorable, given an unsuccessful food store. This information is based on past experience.
   (a) If the market research is favorable, what is Peter's revised probability of a successful food store?
   (b) If the market research is unfavorable, what is Peter's revised probability of a successful food store?

8-48. A market research company has approached you about the possibility of using its services to help you decide whether to launch a new product. According to its customer portfolio, it has correctly predicted a favorable market for its clients' products 14 out of the last 16 times. It has also correctly predicted an unfavorable market for its clients' products 9 out of 11 times. Without this research company's help, you have estimated the probability of a favorable market at 0.55. Calculate the posterior probabilities, using the track record of the research firm.

8-49. Lathum Consulting is an econometrics research firm that predicts the direction of the gross national product (GNP) during the next quarter. More specifically, it forecasts whether the GNP will grow, hold steady, or decline. The following table describes Lathum's track record from past predictions by displaying the probabilities of its predictions, given the actual outcome:

	GNP Prediction		
Actual GNP	Growth	Steady	Decline
Growth	0.75	0.08	0.05
Steady	0.18	0.80	0.12
Decline	0.07	0.12	0.83

For example, the chance that Lathum will predict that the GNP will grow when it actually is steady is 18%. Your company is considering a contract with Lathum Consulting to assist in predicting the direction of next quarter's GNP. Prior to enlisting Lathum's services, you have assessed the probabilities of the GNP growing, holding steady, and declining at 0.3, 0.45, and 0.25, respectively. Calculate the posterior probabilities, using the services of Lathum Consulting.

8-50. In the past few years, the traffic problems in Lynn McKell's hometown have gotten worse. Now, Broad Street is congested about half the time. The normal travel time to work for Lynn is only 15 minutes when she takes Broad Street and there is no congestion. With congestion, however, it takes Lynn 40 minutes to get to work using Broad Street. If Lynn decides to take the expressway, it takes

30 minutes, regardless of the traffic conditions. Lynn's utility for travel time is $U(15 \text{ minutes}) = 0.9$, $U(30 \text{ minutes}) = 0.7$, and $U(40 \text{ minutes}) = 0.2$.
(a) Which route will minimize Lynn's expected travel time?
(b) Which route will maximize Lynn's utility?
(c) When it comes to travel time, is Lynn a risk seeker or a risk avoider? Justify your answer.

8–51. The decision tree in Figure 8.18 is designed to choose the cost-minimizing strategy set. What is the expected monetary value of the best solution?

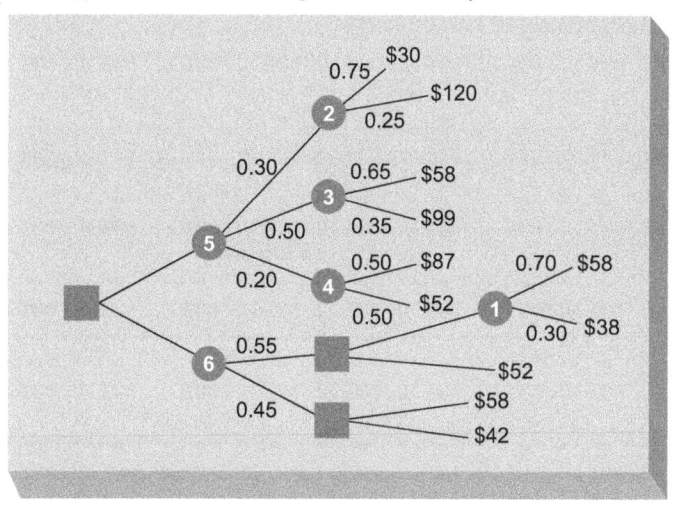

Figure 8.18: Decision tree for Problem 8–51

8–52. Create your own new decision criterion for decision making under uncertainty that is logical but not exactly the same as the five criteria described in Section 8.4.
(a) Describe the rule in complete detail.
(b) Apply it to Thompson Lumber's decision (see Table 8.1).
(c) Modify the spreadsheet from Figure 8.1 to incorporate your new rule.

8–53. Xun Xu's Aeronautics is comparing market research proposals from two different companies. If both research reports were free, the EMV using the report from Jackson Analytics would be $240,000, while the EMV using the report from Witt Consulting would be $265,000. The report from Jackson Analytics would cost $15,000, and the report from Witt Consulting would cost $50,000. With no market research, the EMV would be $180,000. With perfect information, the EMV would be $300,000.
(a) What is the expected value of sample information for both proposals?
(b) What is the efficiency of sample information for both proposals?
(c) Which proposal, if either, should be chosen?

8-54. Revise the Excel spreadsheet in Figure 8.1 to create a template for a decision with four alternatives and four outcomes.

8-55. Consider the Thompson Lumber EMV decision from Table 8.8. Suppose that the utility function for Thompson Lumber can be expressed as $1 - 1.2^{-[(X + 120{,}000) / 30{,}000]}$ for monetary value X.
   (a) Compute the expected utility of each decision for Thompson Lumber.
   (b) Which choice maximizes expected utility?

8-56. Revise the Excel spreadsheet in Figure 8.3 to create a template for a decision with four alternatives and four outcomes.

8-57. The "equally likely" decision criterion is equivalent to a "maxi-mean" rule. A related, but not necessarily equivalent rule would be "maxi-median". Apply a "maxi-median" rule to the following payoff table. Which alternative is best under this rule? Is it the same as the best alternative under the "equally likely" rule?

		Outcomes		
Alternatives	Alpha	Beta	Gamma	Delta
A	$ 600	$800	$900	$100
B	$1500	$600	$500	$400
C	$ 850	$850	$ 50	$750

8-58. Create an Excel spreadsheet to automate the calculations in Tables 8.10, 8.11, and 8.12.

Chapter 9
Queuing Models

Have you ever been so frustrated by waiting in a long line that you vowed to boycott that company? (This is not an option, of course, at the Division of Motor Vehicles.) We all have experienced long lines, whether at the amusement park, the security line at the airport, or the local grocery store. A 20-minute line at a fast-food restaurant brings into question the primary mission of that restaurant! Long lines can induce stress quickly. They can cause customers to give up and leave (*reneging*) or even decide not to join the line in the first place (*balking*). And customer frustration may not stop there. A single negative post on social media complaining about long lines may be read by dozens or hundreds of other potential customers. When we consider all the things that a company can do to provide excellent customer service, providing short waiting times must assuredly be near the top of the list.

To keep happy customers and minimize complaints, managers must take active measures to keep lines at a reasonable length. Often the primary trade-off is between the cost of additional servers versus longer waiting times for customers. Fortunately, managers have access to powerful analytical and computer tools that can indicate important measures such as the average time waiting in line and the average length of the line for a given number of servers.

We begin this chapter by describing the major queuing system costs of service and waiting. We then describe the characteristics of a queuing system that properly categorize it based on the arrival pattern, the line itself, and the service facility. The bulk of the chapter is divided into five sections that each analyze waiting lines that address a specific queuing system category: (1) one server, (2) multiple servers, (3) one server with no variation in service times, (4) one server with service times that are not exponentially distributed, and (5) finite population of arriving customers. Each of these sections includes formulas that can compute important waiting line measures. These formulas are all coded into the ExcelModules program that is available from the companion website. The important performance characteristics of the waiting line are determined after entering just a few numbers that describe that queuing system into ExcelModules. Especially with the help of ExcelModules, many queueing problems are relatively easy to solve as long as you can identify the appropriate model to use and you express the inputs in the appropriate time units. We end the chapter by briefly describing how modelers can develop computer simulations to analyze more complex queuing environments.

Chapter Objectives

After completing this chapter, readers will be able to:
1. Discuss the trade-off curves for cost of waiting time and cost of service.
2. Understand the three parts of a queuing system: the arrival population, the queue, and the service facility.
3. Describe basic queuing system configurations.
4. Understand the assumptions of common queuing models discussed in this chapter.
5. Use Excel to analyze a variety of operating characteristics of queuing systems.
6. Understand more complex queuing systems.

9.1 The Importance of Queuing Theory

The study of queues,[1] also called *waiting lines*, is one of the oldest and most widely used decision modeling techniques. Queues are an everyday occurrence, affecting people shopping for groceries, buying gasoline, making bank deposits, and waiting on the telephone for the first available customer service person to answer. Queues can also take the form of machines waiting to be repaired, prisoners to be processed in a jail system, or airplanes lined up on a runway for permission to take off.

Most queuing problems focus on finding the ideal level of service that a firm should provide. Supermarkets must decide how many cash register checkout positions should be opened. Gasoline stations must decide how many pumps should be available. Manufacturing plants must determine the optimal number of mechanics to have on duty each shift to repair machines that break down. Banks must decide how many teller windows to keep open to serve customers during various hours of the day. In most cases, this level of service is an option over which management has control. An extra teller, for example, can be borrowed from another chore or can be hired and trained quickly if demand warrants it. This may, however, not always be the case. For example, a plant may not be able to locate or hire skilled mechanics to repair sophisticated electronic machinery.

Approaches for Analyzing Queues

In practice, there are two principal approaches that managers can use to analyze the performance of a queuing system and evaluate its cost-effectiveness. The first approach is based on *analytical modeling*. For several different queuing systems that satisfy certain properties, decisions modelers have derived explicit formulas to calculate various performance measures. These formulas, although rather cumbersome in some cases, are quite straightforward to use, especially if they are coded in a computer software program. In this chapter, we discuss analytical models for a few simple

---
1 The word *queue* is pronounced like the letter Q (i.e., "kew").

queuing systems. Although we show the mathematical equations needed to compute the performance measures of these queuing systems, we will actually use Excel worksheets (included on the Companion Website) to calculate these values in each case. From a managerial perspective, therefore, the use of these analytical models will be very easy and straightforward.

Many real-world queuing systems can be so complex, however, that they cannot be modeled analytically at all. When this happens, decision modelers usually turn to the second approach—computer simulation—to analyze the performance of these systems. We discuss simulation in Chapter 10 and also illustrate how this technique can be used to analyze queuing systems.

9.2 Queuing System Costs

As noted earlier, a primary goal of queuing analysis is to find the best level of service that a firm should provide. In deciding this ideal level of service, managers have to deal with two types of costs:

1. *Cost of providing the service.* This is also known as the service cost. Examples of this type of cost include wages paid to servers, the cost of buying an extra machine, and the cost of constructing a new teller window at a bank. As a firm increases the size of its staff and provides added service facilities, the result could be excellent customer service with seldom more than one or two customers in a queue. While customers may be happy with the quick response, the cost of providing this service can, however, become very expensive.

HISTORY

How Queuing Models Began

Queuing theory began with the research work of a Danish engineer named A. K. Erlang. In 1909 Erlang experimented with fluctuating demand in telephone traffic. Eight years later, he published a report addressing the delays in automatic dialing equipment. At the end of World War II, Erlang's early work was extended to more general problems and to business applications of waiting lines.

---

2. *Cost of not providing the service.* This is also known as the waiting cost and is typically the cost of customer dissatisfaction. If a facility has just a minimum number of open checkout lines, pumps, or teller windows, the service cost is kept low, but customers may end up with long waiting times in the queue. How many times would you return to a large department store that had only one cash register open every time you shop? As the average length of the queue increases and poor service results, customers and goodwill may be lost.

Most managers recognize the trade-off that must take place between the cost of providing good service and the cost of customer waiting time, and they try to achieve a happy medium between the two. They want queues that are short enough so that customers don't become unhappy and either storm out without buying or buy but never return. But they are willing to allow some waiting in line if this wait is balanced by a significant savings in service costs.

One means of evaluating a service facility is thus to look at a total expected cost, a concept illustrated in Figure 9.1. Total expected cost is the sum of expected waiting costs and expected costs of providing service.

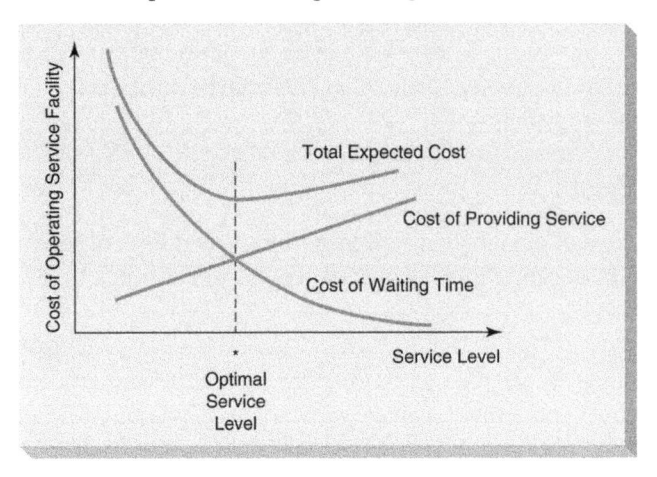

Figure 9.1: Queuing Costs and Service Levels

Service costs increase as a firm attempts to raise its level of service. For example, if three teams of stevedores, instead of two, are employed to unload a cargo ship, service costs are increased by the additional price of wages. As service improves in speed, however, the cost of time spent waiting in lines decreases. This waiting cost may reflect lost productivity of workers while their tools or machines are awaiting repairs or may simply be an estimate of the costs of customers lost because of poor service and long queues.

Three Rivers Shipping Company Example As an illustration of a queuing system, let's look at the case of the Three Rivers Shipping Company. Three Rivers runs a huge docking facility on the Ohio River near Pittsburgh. Approximately five ships arrive to unload their cargoes of steel and ore during every 12-hour work shift. Each hour that a ship sits idle in line, waiting to be unloaded, costs the firm a great deal of money, about $1,000 per hour. From experience, management estimates that if one team of stevedores is on duty to handle the unloading work, each ship will wait an average of 7 hours to be unloaded. If two teams are working, the average waiting time drops to 4 hours; for three teams, it is 3 hours; and for four teams of stevedores, only 2 hours. But each additional team of stevedores is also an expensive proposition, due to union contracts.

The Three Rivers superintendent would like to determine the optimal number of teams of stevedores to have on duty each shift. The objective is to minimize total expected costs. This analysis is summarized in Table 9.1. To minimize the sum of service costs and waiting costs, the firm makes the decision to employ two teams of stevedores each shift.

Table 9.1: Three Rivers Shipping Company Waiting Line Cost Analysis

	Number of Teams of Stevedores			
	1	2	3	4
(a) Average number of ships arriving per shift	5	5	5	5
(b) Average time each ship waits to be unloaded (hours)	7	4	3	2
(c) Total ship hours lost per shift $(a \times b)$	35	20	15	10
(d) Estimated cost per hour of idle ship time	$1,000	$1,000	$1,000	$1,000
(e) Value of ship's lost time or waiting cost $(c \times d)$	$35,000	$20,000	$15,000	$10,000
(f) Stevedore team salary,* or service cost	$6,000	$12,000	$18,000	$24,000
(g) Total expected cost $(e + f)$	$41,000	$32,000 ↑ Optimal cost	$33,000	$34,000

*Stevedore team salaries are computed as the number of people in a typical team (assumed to be 50) multiplied by the number of hours each person works per day (12 hours) multiplied by an hourly salary of $10 per hour. If two teams are employed, the rate is just doubled.

9.3 Characteristics of a Queuing System

In this section, we discuss the three components of a queuing system that are critical for the development of analytical queuing models: (1) the arrivals or inputs to the system (sometimes referred to as the *calling population*), (2) the queue or the waiting line itself, and (3) the service facility. Together, these three components define the type of queuing system under consideration.

Arrival Characteristics

Regarding the input source that generates arrivals or customers for a queuing system, it is important to consider the following: (1) size of the arrival population, (2) pattern of arrivals (or the arrival distribution) at the queuing system, and (3) behavior of the arrivals.

Size of the Arrival Population Population sizes are considered to be either *infinite (unlimited)* or *finite (limited)*. When the number of customers or arrivals on hand at any given moment is just a small portion of potential arrivals, the arrival population is considered an infinite, or unlimited population. For practical purposes, examples of unlimited populations include cars arriving at a highway tollbooth, shoppers arriving at a supermarket, or students arriving to register for classes at a large university. Most queuing models assume such an infinite arrival population. When this is not the case, modeling becomes much more complex. An example of a finite, or limited population is a shop with only eight machines that might break down and require service.

Arrival Distribution Arrivals can be characterized either by an average *arrival rate* or by an average *arrival time*. Because both measures occur commonly in practice, it is important to distinguish between the two. An average arrival rate denotes the average number of arrivals in a given interval of time. Examples include two customers per hour, four trucks per minute, two potholes per mile of road, and five typing errors per printed page. In contrast, an average arrival time denotes the average time between successive arrivals. Examples include 30 minutes between customers, 0.25 minutes between trucks, 0.5 miles between potholes, and 0.2 pages between typing errors. It is important to remember that for analytical queuing models, we typically use the average arrival *rate*.

Customers can arrive at a service facility either according to some known constant schedule (e.g., one patient every 15 minutes, one student for advising every half hour), or they can arrive in a random manner. Arrivals are considered random when they are independent of one another and their occurrence cannot be predicted exactly.

It turns out that in many real-world queuing problems, even when arrivals are random, the actual number of arrivals per unit of time can be estimated by using a probability distribution known as the Poisson distribution. The Poisson distribution is applicable whenever the following assumptions are satisfied: (1) The average arrival rate over a given interval of time is known, (2) this average rate is the same for all equal-sized intervals, (3) the actual number of arrivals in one interval has no bearing on the actual number of arrivals in another interval, and (4) there cannot be more than one arrival in an interval as the size of the interval approaches zero. For a given average arrival rate, a discrete Poisson distribution can be established by using the following formula:[2]

$$P(X) = \frac{e^{-\lambda} \lambda^X}{X!} \text{ for } X = 0, 1, 2, \cdots \qquad (9\text{--}1)$$

where

X = number of arrivals per unit of time (e.g., hour)
$P(X)$ = probability of exactly X arrivals
λ = average arrival *rate* (i.e., average number of arrivals per unit of time)
e = 2.7183 (known as the exponential constant)

---

[2] The term $X!$, called X *factorial*, is defined as $(X)(X-1)(X-2)\ldots(3)(2)(1)$. For example, $5! = (5)(4)(3)(2)(1) = 120$. By definition, $0! = 1$.

These values are easy to compute with the help of a calculator or Excel. Figure 9.2 illustrates the shape of the Poisson distribution for $\lambda = 2$ and $\lambda = 4$. This means that if the average arrival rate is $\lambda = 2$ customers per hour, the probability of 0 customers arriving in any random hour is 0.1353, the probability of 1 customer is 0.2707, 2 customers is 0.2707, 3 customers is 0.1804, 4 customers is 0.0902, and so on. The chance that 9 or more will arrive in any hour is virtually zero.

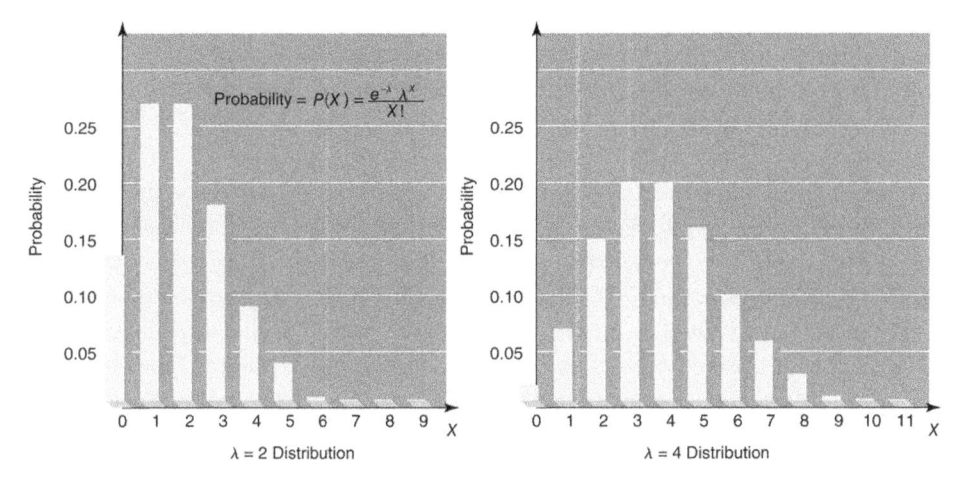

Figure 9.2: Two Examples of the Poisson Distribution for Arrival Times

All the analytical models discussed in this chapter assume Poisson arrivals. However, in practice, arrivals in queuing systems need not always be Poisson and could follow other probability distributions. The use of statistical goodness-of-fit tests to identify these distributions and analytical queuing models to analyze such systems are topics discussed in more advanced texts. Of course, as we will discuss in Chapter 10, we can also analyze such queuing systems by using computer simulation.

Behavior of Arrivals Most queuing models assume that an arriving customer is a patient customer. Patient customers are people or machines that wait in the queue until they are served and do not switch between lines. Unfortunately, life and decision models are complicated by the fact that people have been known to balk or renege. Balking refers to customers refusing to join a queue because it is too long to suit their needs or interests. Reneging customers are those who enter the queue but then become impatient and leave without completing their transaction. Actually, both situations serve to accentuate the need for queuing models. How many times have you seen a shopper with a basket full of groceries, including perishables such as milk, frozen food, or meats, simply abandon the shopping cart before checking out because the queue was too long? This occurrence, which is expensive for the store, makes managers acutely aware of the importance of service-level decisions.

Queue Characteristics

The queue itself is the second component of a queuing system. The *length* of a queue can be either limited (finite) or unlimited (infinite). A queue is said to be limited when it cannot increase to an infinite length due to physical or other restrictions. For example, the queue at a bank's drive-up window may be limited to 10 cars because of space limitations. Or, the number of people waiting for service in an airline's phone reservation system may be limited to 30 due to the number of telephone lines available. In contrast, a queue is defined as unlimited when its size is unrestricted, as in the case of the tollbooth serving arriving automobiles. In all the analytic queuing models we discuss in this chapter, we assume that queue lengths are *unlimited*.

A second waiting line characteristic deals with queue discipline. This refers to the rule by which customers in the line are to receive service. Most systems use a queue discipline known as the first-in, first-out (FIFO) rule. However, in places such as a hospital emergency room or an express checkout line at a supermarket, various assigned priorities may preempt FIFO. Critically injured patients will move ahead in treatment priority over patients with broken fingers or noses. Shoppers with fewer than 10 items may be allowed to enter the express checkout queue but are then treated as first-come, first-served. Computer programming runs are another example of queuing systems that operate under priority scheduling. In many large companies, when computer-produced paychecks are due out on a specific date, the payroll program has highest priority over other runs.[3]

Service Facility Characteristics

The third part of a queuing system is the service facility itself. It is important to examine two basic properties: (1) the configuration of the service facility and (2) the pattern of service times (or the service distribution) at the facility.

Configuration of the Service Facility Service facilities are usually classified in terms of the number of servers (or channels) and the number of phases (or service stops) that must be made. A single-server queuing system is typified by the drive-in bank that has only one open teller or by the type of a drive-through fast-food restaurant that has a similar setup. If, on the other hand, the bank has several tellers on duty and each customer waits in one common line for the first available teller, we would have a multiple-server queuing system at work. Many banks today are multiple-server service systems, as are most post offices and many airline ticket counters.

A single-phase system is one in which the customer receives service from only one station and then exits the system. A fast-food restaurant in which the person who takes your order also brings you the food and takes your money is a single-phase

---

[3] The term FIFS (*first-in, first-served*) is often used in place of FIFO. Another discipline, LIFS (*last-in, first-served*), is commonly used when material is stacked or piled and the items on top are used first.

system. So is a driver's license bureau in which the person taking your application also grades your test and collects the license fee. But if a fast-food restaurant requires you to place your order at one station, pay at a second, and pick up the food at a third service stop, it is a multiphase system. Similarly, if the driver's license bureau is large or busy, you will probably have to wait in line to complete the application (the first service stop), queue again to have the test graded (the second service stop), and finally go to a third service counter to pay the fee. To help you relate the concepts of servers and phases, Figure 9.3 presents four possible service facility configurations.

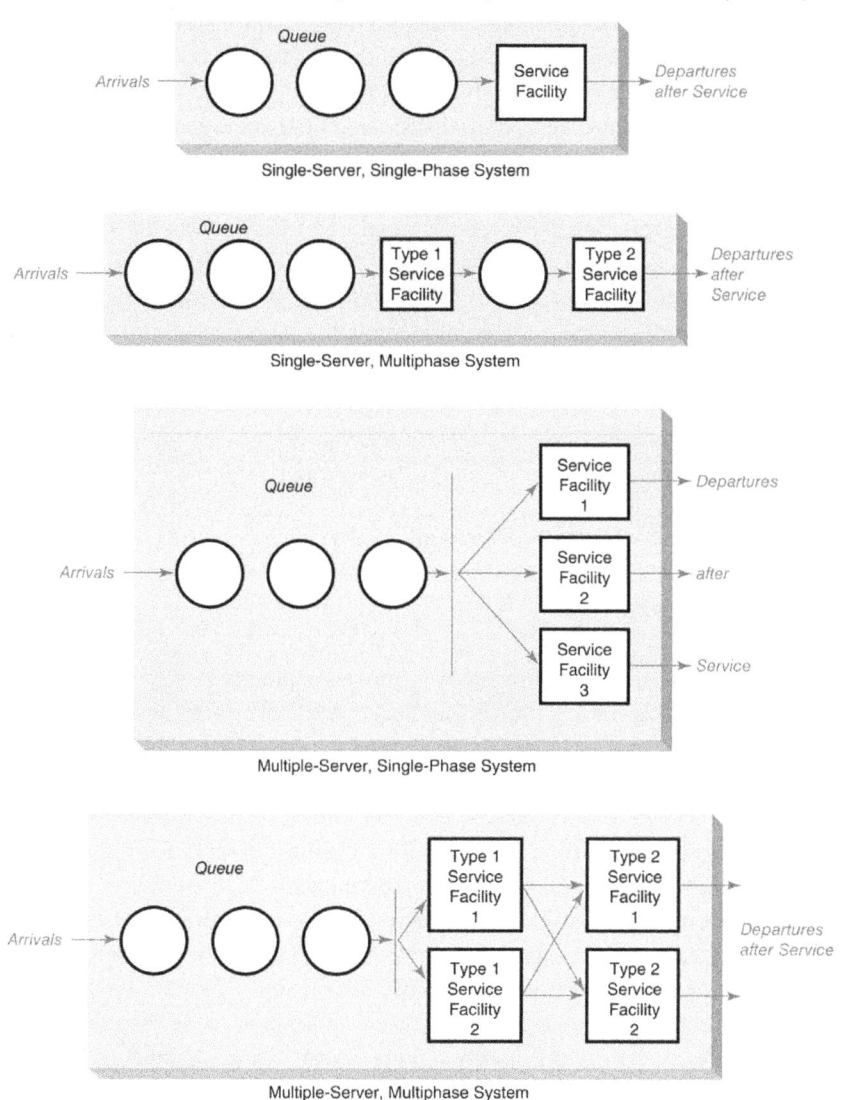

Figure 9.3: Four Basic Queuing System Configurations

Service Distribution Service patterns are like arrival patterns in that they can be either constant or random. If the service time is constant, it takes the same amount of time to take care of each customer. This is the case, for example, in a machine-performed service operation such as an automatic car wash. More often, however, service times are randomly distributed. Even in such situations, it turns out that we can estimate service times in many real-world queuing problems by using a probability distribution known as the *exponential distribution*.

The Poisson and exponential probability distributions are directly related to each other. If the number of arrivals follows a Poisson distribution, it turns out that the time between successive arrivals follows an exponential distribution. Processes that follow these distributions are commonly referred to as *Markovian* processes.

Just as we did with arrivals, we need to distinguish here between service rate and service time. While the service rate denotes the number of units served in a given interval of time, the service time denotes the length of time taken to perform the service. Although the exponential distribution estimates the probability of service times, the parameter used in this computation is the average service rate. For any given average service rate, such as two customers per hour, or four trucks per minute, the exponential distribution can be established using the formula

$$P(t) = e^{-\mu t} \quad \text{for } t \geq 0 \tag{9-2}$$

where

t = service time
$P(t)$ = probability that service time will be greater than t
μ = average service rate (i.e., average number of customers served per unit of time)
e = 2.7183 (exponential constant)

Figure 9.4 illustrates that if service times follow an exponential distribution, the probability of any very long service-time is low. For example, when the average service *rate* is 3 customers per hour (i.e., the average service *time* is 20 minutes per customer), seldom, if ever, will a customer require more than 1.5 hours (= 90 minutes). Likewise, if the average service rate is one customer per hour (i.e., $\mu = 1$), the probability of the customer spending more than 3 hours (= 180 minutes) in service is quite low.

Before the exponential distribution is used in a queuing model, the decision modeler can and should observe, collect, and plot service time data to determine whether they fit the distribution. Of course, in practice, service times in queuing systems need not always be exponential and could follow other probability distributions. As with arrivals, the use of statistical goodness-of-fit tests to identify these distributions is discussed in more advanced texts. In this chapter, while most of our analytical models assume exponential service times, we also will discuss models for queuing systems involving constant service times and general service times (i.e., service times follow some arbitrary distribution with mean μ and standard deviation σ). The use of computer simulation (the topic of Chapter 10) is another approach for analyzing such queuing systems.

[Figure: graph showing Probability That Service Time ≥ t vs Time t in Hours, with two exponential curves labeled "Average Service Rate = 3 Customers per Hour ⇒ Average Service Time = 20 Minutes (or 1/3 Hours) per Customer" and "Average Service Rate = 1 Customer per Hour"; curve equation: Probability That Service Time $\geq t = e^{-\mu t}$ for $t \geq 0$; μ = Average Service Rate]

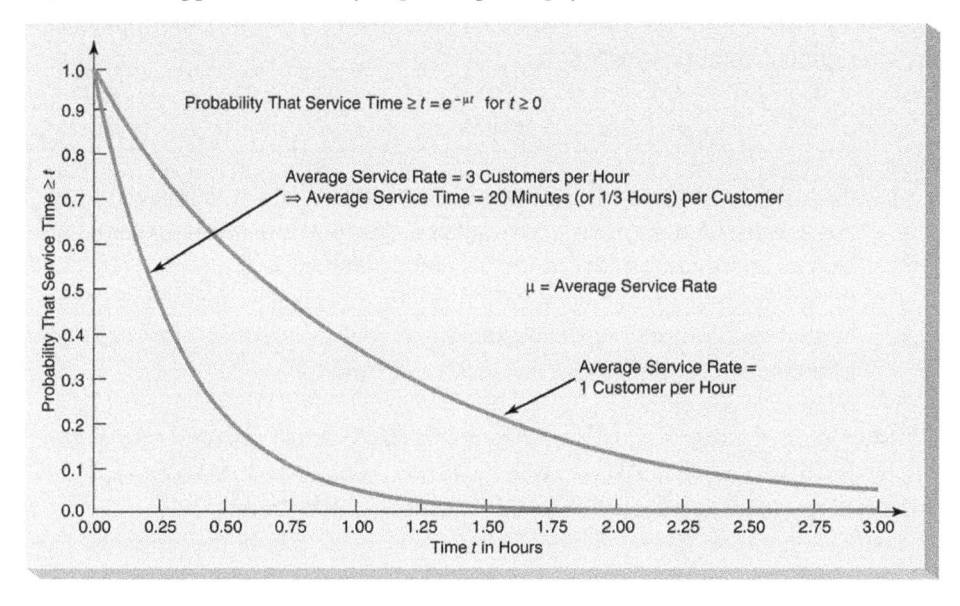

Figure 9.4: Two Examples of the Exponential Distribution for Service Times

Measuring the Queue's Performance

Queuing models can help a manager obtain many performance measures (also known as operating characteristics) of a waiting line system. We list here some of the measures commonly used in practice. For each performance measure, we also list the standard notation that is used:

- ρ = utilization factor of the system (i.e., the probability that all servers are busy)
- L_q = average length (i.e., the number of customers) of the queue
- L = average number of customers in the system (i.e., the number in the queue plus the number being served)
- W_q = average time that each customer spends in the queue
- W = average time that each customer spends in the system (i.e., the time spent waiting plus the time spent being served)
- P_0 = probability that there are no customers in the system (i.e., the probability that the service facility will be idle)
- P_n = probability that there are exactly n customers in the system

Kendall's Notation for Queuing Systems

In queuing theory, we commonly use a three-symbol notation, known as *Kendall's notation*, to classify the wide variety of queuing models that are possible in practice. The three-symbol notation is as follows:

$$A/B/s$$

where
- A = the arrival probability distribution. Typical choices are M (Markovian) for a Poisson distribution, D for a constant or deterministic distribution, or G for a general distribution with known mean and variance.
- B = the service time probability distribution. Typical choices are M for an exponential distribution, D for a constant or deterministic distribution, or G for a general distribution with known mean and variance.
- s = number of servers.

Using Kendall's notation, we would denote a single-server queuing system with Poisson arrival and exponential service time distributions as an M/M/1 system. If this system had two servers, we would then classify it as an M/M/2 system.

Kendall's notation has sometimes been extended to include five symbols. The first three symbols are the same as just discussed. The fourth symbol denotes the maximum allowable length of the queue. It is used in systems in which there is a finite, or limited, queue length. The fifth symbol denotes the size of the arrival population. It is used in systems in which the size of the arrival population is finite. By default, if these two symbols are omitted, their values are assumed to be infinity. Hence, the M/M/1 notation discussed previously corresponds to an M/M/1/∞/∞ queuing system.

Variety of Queuing Models Studied Here

Although a wide variety of queuing models can be applied in practice, we introduce you to five of the most widely used models in this chapter. These are outlined in Table 9.2, and examples of each follow in the next few sections. More complex models are described in queuing theory textbooks or can be developed through the use of computer simulation (which is the focus of Chapter 10). Note that all five of the queuing models in Table 9.2 have five characteristics in common. They all assume the following:

1. Arrivals that follow the Poisson probability distribution.
2. FIFO queue discipline.
3. A single-phase service facility.
4. Infinite, or unlimited, queue length. That is, the fourth symbol in Kendall's notation is ∞.
5. Service systems that operate under steady, ongoing conditions. This means that both arrival rates and service rates remain stable during the analysis.

Table 9.2: Queuing Models Described in This Chapter

Name (Kendall Notation)	Example	Number of Servers	Number of Phases	Arrival Rate Pattern	Service Time Pattern	Population Size	Queue Discipline
Simple system (M/M/1)	Information counter at department store	Single	Single	Poisson	Exponential	Unlimited	FIFO
Multiple-server (M/M/s)	Airline ticket counter	Multiple	Single	Poisson	Exponential	Unlimited	FIFO
Constant service (M/D/1)	Automated car wash	Single	Single	Poisson	Constant	Unlimited	FIFO
General service (M/G/1)	Auto repair shop	Single	Single	Poisson	General	Unlimited	FIFO
Limited population (M/M/s/∞/N)	Shop with exactly ten machines that might break	Multiple	Single	Poisson	Exponential	Limited	FIFO

9.4 M/M/1 Queuing System

In this section, we present a decision model to determine the operating characteristics of an M/M/1 queuing system. After these numeric measures have been computed, we then add in cost data and begin to make decisions that balance desirable service levels with queuing costs.

Assumptions of the M/M/1 Queuing Model

The single-server, single-phase model we consider here is one of the most widely used and simplest queuing models. It assumes that seven conditions exist:

1. Arrivals are served on a FIFO basis.
2. Every arrival waits to be served, regardless of the length of the line; that is, there is no balking or reneging.
3. Arrivals are independent of preceding arrivals, but the average number of arrivals (the arrival rate) does not change over time.
4. Arrivals are described by a Poisson probability distribution and come from an infinite or very large population.
5. Service times also vary from one customer to the next and are independent of one another, but their average rate is known.
6. Service times occur according to the exponential probability distribution.
7. The average service rate is greater than the average arrival rate; that is, $\mu > \lambda$. If this condition does not hold (and $\mu \leq \lambda$), the queue length will grow indefinitely because the service facility does not have the capacity to handle the arriving customers (on average).

When these seven conditions are met, we can develop equations that define the system's operating characteristics. The mathematics used to derive each equation is rather complex and beyond the scope of this book, so we will just present the resulting equations here.

Although we could calculate the operating characteristic equations for *all* the queuing systems discussed in this chapter by hand, doing so can be quite cumbersome. An easier approach is to develop Excel worksheets for these formulas and use them for all calculations. This allows us to focus on what is really important for managers: the interpretation and use of the results of queuing models. Therefore, we adopt this approach in our discussions in this chapter.

Decision Modeling In Action

IBM Uses Queuing Analysis to Improve Semiconductor Production

IBM's 300 mm fabrication (fab) facility in East Fishkill, New York, cost more than $4 billion to build. High capacity utilization and short lead times are keys to reducing the cost per wafer, expediting time to market, and improving profitability and yield. IBM's managers and engineers therefore maintain constant focus on balancing future demand, equipment utilization, bottlenecks, and lead times.

To help in this effort, IBM developed an advanced queuing network model called Enterprise Production Planning and Optimization System (EPOS) to address both short-term tactical capacity planning and long-term strategic capital investment planning. EPOS enhances prior queuing network models by not only adding the ability to model product-specific batch arrivals and service, but also by embedding a linear program to help decide which lot to allocate to which queue when route choices are present.

Since its implementation, EPOS has become an integral part of IBM's efforts to improve factory performance by predicting bottlenecks, managing lead times, prioritizing continuous-improvement efforts, and planning capital equipment investments, thus helping IBM reduce expenses by tens of millions of dollars.

Source: Based on S. M. Brown et al. "Queuing Model Improves IBM's Semiconductor Capacity and Lead-Time Management," *Interfaces* 40, 5 (September–October 2010): 397–407.

Operating Characteristic Equations for an M/M/1 Queuing System
We let

λ = average number of arrivals per time period (e.g., per hour)

μ = average number of people or items served per time period

It is very important to note two issues here. First, both λ and μ must be rates. That is, they must denote the average number of occurrences per a given time interval. Second, both λ and μ must be defined for the *same time interval*. That is, if λ denotes the average number of units arriving *per hour*, then μ must denote the average number of units served *per hour*. As noted earlier, it is necessary for the average service rate to be greater than the average arrival rate (i.e., $\mu > \lambda$). The operating characteristic equations for the M/M/1 queuing system are as follows:

1. Average server utilization in the system:

$$\rho = \lambda/\mu \tag{9-3}$$

2. Average number of customers or units waiting in line for service:

$$L_q = \frac{\lambda^2}{\mu(\mu - \lambda)} \tag{9-4}$$

3. Average number of customers or units in the system:

$$L = L_q + \lambda/\mu \tag{9-5}$$

4. Average time a customer or unit spends waiting in line for service:

$$W_q = \frac{L_q}{\lambda} = \frac{\lambda}{\mu(\mu - \lambda)} \tag{9-6}$$

5. Average time a customer or unit spends in the system (namely, in the queue or being served):

$$W = W_q + 1/\mu \tag{9-7}$$

6. Probability that there are zero customers or units in the system:

$$P_0 = 1 - \lambda/\mu \tag{9-8}$$

7. Probability that there are *n* customers or units in the system:

$$P_n = (\lambda/\mu)^n P_0 \tag{9-9}$$

Arnold's Muffler Shop Example

We now apply these formulas to the queuing problem faced by Arnold's Muffler Shop in New Orleans. Customers needing new mufflers arrive at the shop on the average of two per hour. Arnold's mechanic, Reid Blank, can perform this service at an average rate of three per hour, or about one every 20 minutes. Larry Arnold, the shop owner, studied queuing models in an MBA program and feels that all seven of the conditions for a single-server queuing model are met. He proceeds to calculate the numeric values of the operating characteristics of his queuing system.

Using ExcelModules for Queuing Model Computations

> **EXCEL NOTES**
>
> – The Companion Website for this textbook, at *degruyter.com/view/product/486941*, contains a set of Excel worksheets, bundled together in a software package called ExcelModules. The procedure for installing and running this program, as well as a brief description of its contents, is given in Appendix B.
>
> – The Companion Website also provides the Excel file for each sample problem discussed here. The relevant file/sheet name is shown below the title of the corresponding figure in this book.
>
> – For clarity, all worksheets for queuing models in ExcelModules are color coded as follows:
>
>   – *Input cells*, where we enter the problem data, are shaded yellow.
>
>   – *Output cells*, which show results, are shaded green.

When we run the ExcelModules program, we see a new tab titled ExcelModules in Excel's Ribbon. We select this tab and then click the Modules icon followed by the Queuing Models menu. The choices shown in Figure 9.5 are displayed. From these choices, we select the appropriate queuing model.

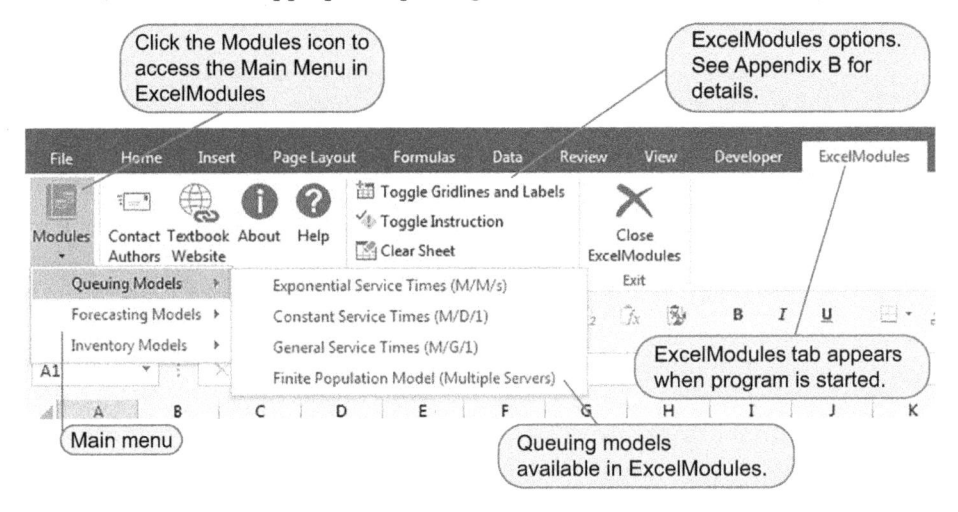

Figure 9.5: Queuing Models Menu in ExcelModules

When *any* of the queuing models is selected in ExcelModules, we are first presented with an option to specify a title for the problem (see Figure 9.6). The default title is Problem Title.

M/M/1 Queuing System — 525

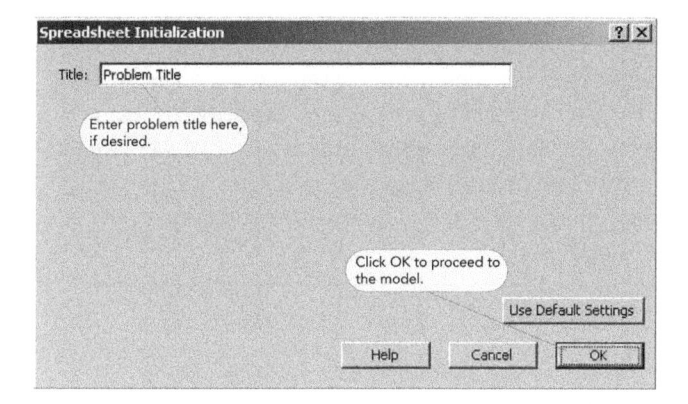

Figure 9.6: Input Window for Optional Problem Title

ExcelModules Solution for Arnold's Muffler Shop The M/M/1 queuing model is included in ExcelModules as a special case of the M/M/s model with s = 1. Hence, to analyze Arnold's problem, we select the choice labeled Exponential Service Times (M/M/s), shown in Figure 9.5. When we click OK after entering the problem title, we get the screen shown in Figure 9.7. Each queuing worksheet in ExcelModules includes one or more messages specific to that model. It is important to note and follow the messages. For example, the M/M/s worksheet includes the following two messages:

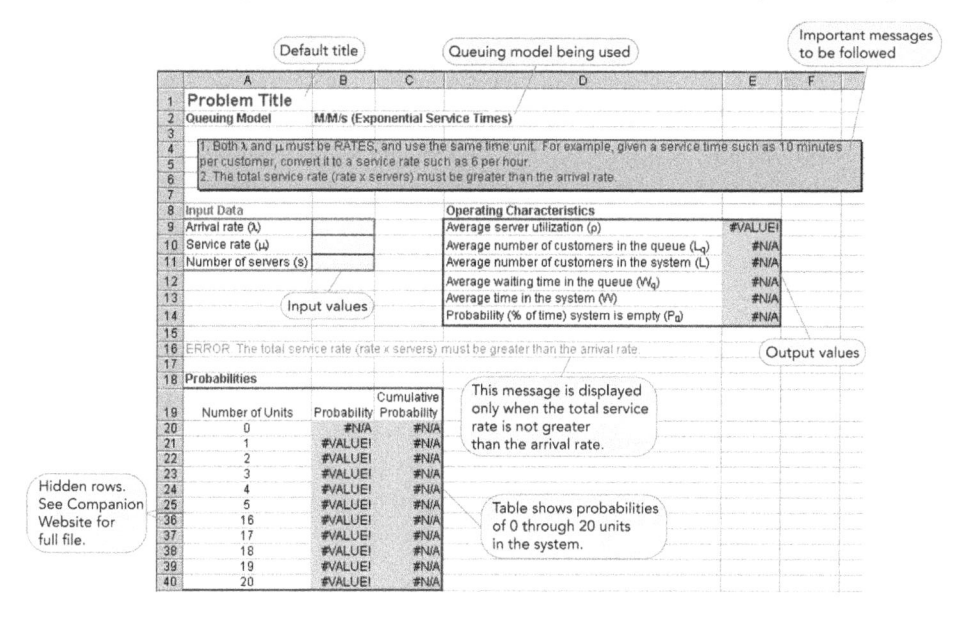

Figure 9.7: M/M/s Worksheet in ExcelModules

File: Figure 9.7.xlsx, Sheet: Figure 9.7

1. Both λ and μ must be RATES and use the same time unit. For example, given a service time of 10 minutes per customer, convert it to a service rate of six per hour.
2. The total service rate (rate × servers) must be greater than the arrival rate.

If the total average service rate ($\mu \times s$) does *not* exceed the average arrival rate (λ), the worksheet will automatically print the error message shown in row 16. This message is seen in Figure 9.7 because the values of λ, μ, and number of servers have not been input yet and have defaulted to zero values.

EXCEL NOTES

- The worksheets in ExcelModules contain formulas to compute the operating characteristics for different queuing models. The default values of zero for input data such as (λ) and (μ) cause the results of these formulas to initially appear as #N/A, #VALUE!, or #DIV/0! (see Figure 9.7). However, as soon as we enter valid values for these input data, the worksheets display the formula results.

- Once ExcelModules has been used to create an Excel worksheet for a particular queuing model (such as M/M/s), the resulting worksheet can be used to compute the operating characteristics with several different input parameter values. For example, we can enter different input values in cells B9:B11 of Figure 9.7 and compute the resulting operating characteristic values without having to create a *new* M/M/s worksheet each time.

In Larry Arnold's case, the average arrival rate (λ) is two cars per hour. The average service rate (μ) is three mufflers per hour. We therefore enter these values in cells B9 and B10, respectively, as shown in Figure 9.8. The number of servers (cell B11) equals one here because there is only one mechanic.

The worksheet now displays the operating characteristics of this queuing system in cells E9:E14. In addition, the worksheet computes the probability that there are exactly *n* customers in the system, for $n = 0$ through 20. Cumulative probabilities (i.e., the probability that there are *n* or *fewer* customers) are also calculated. These values are shown in cells A19:C40.

The results show that there are, on average, two cars in the system (i.e., $L = 2$), and each car spends an average of one hour in the system (i.e., $W = 1$ hour). The corresponding values for the waiting line alone (not including the server) are $L_q = 1.33$ cars, and $W_q = 0.667$ hours (or 40 minutes). The mechanic (server) is busy 67% of the time (i.e., the utilization factor $\rho = 0.67$). The fact that there is only one mechanic implies that an arriving car has a 33% chance of not having to wait ($P_0 = 0.33$).

M/M/1 Queuing System

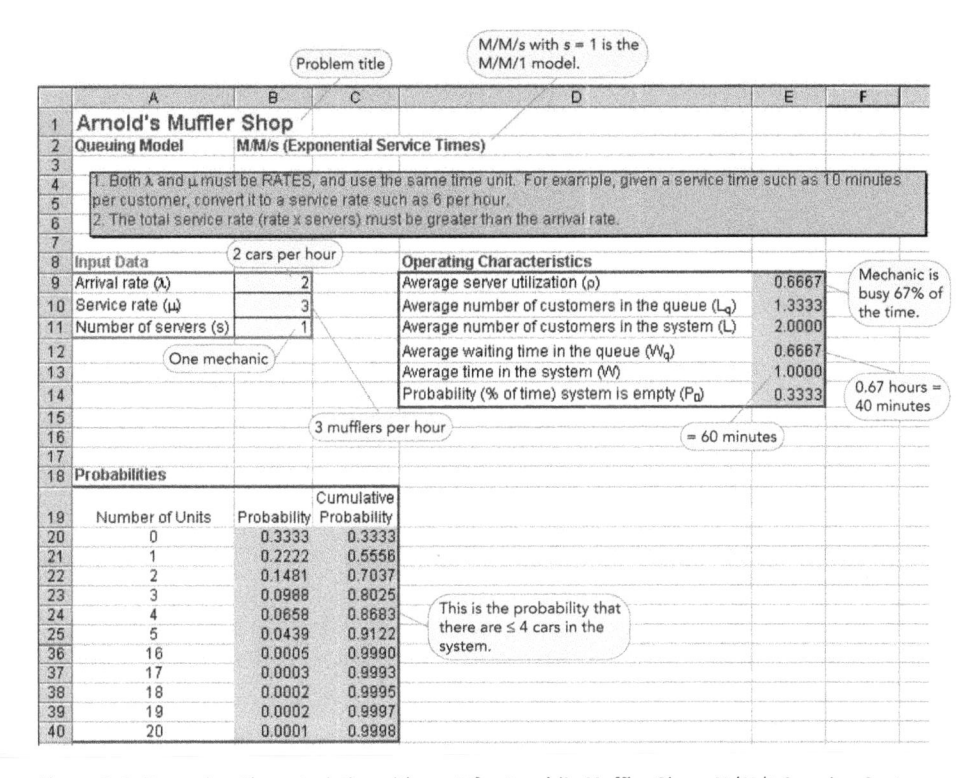

	A	B	C	D	E	F
1	Arnold's Muffler Shop		*(Problem title)*	*(M/M/s with s = 1 is the M/M/1 model.)*		
2	Queuing Model	M/M/s (Exponential Service Times)				
3						
4	1. Both λ and μ must be RATES, and use the same time unit. For example, given a service time such as 10 minutes per customer, convert it to a service rate such as 6 per hour.					
5						
6	2. The total service rate (rate × servers) must be greater than the arrival rate.					
7						
8	Input Data		*(2 cars per hour)*	Operating Characteristics		
9	Arrival rate (λ)	2		Average server utilization (ρ)	0.6667	*Mechanic is busy 67% of the time.*
10	Service rate (μ)	3		Average number of customers in the queue (L_q)	1.3333	
11	Number of servers (s)	1		Average number of customers in the system (L)	2.0000	
12		*(One mechanic)*		Average waiting time in the queue (W_q)	0.6667	
13				Average time in the system (W)	1.0000	*0.67 hours = 40 minutes*
14				Probability (% of time) system is empty (P_0)	0.3333	
15						
16			*(3 mufflers per hour)*		= 60 minutes	
17						
18	Probabilities					
19	Number of Units	Probability	Cumulative Probability			
20	0	0.3333	0.3333			
21	1	0.2222	0.5556			
22	2	0.1481	0.7037			
23	3	0.0988	0.8025			
24	4	0.0658	0.8683	*This is the probability that there are ≤ 4 cars in the system.*		
25	5	0.0439	0.9122			
36	16	0.0005	0.9990			
37	17	0.0003	0.9993			
38	18	0.0002	0.9995			
39	19	0.0002	0.9997			
40	20	0.0001	0.9998			

Figure 9.8: Operating Characteristics with $\mu = 3$ for Arnold's Muffler Shop: M/M/1 Queuing System

📄 File: Figure 9.7.xlsx, Sheet: Figure 9.8

Cost Analysis of the Queuing System

Now that the operating characteristics of the queuing system have been computed, Arnold decides to do an economic analysis of their impact. The queuing model was valuable in predicting potential waiting times, queue lengths, idle times, and so on. But it did not identify optimal decisions or consider cost factors. As stated earlier, the solution to a queuing problem may require a manager to make a trade-off between the increased cost of providing better service and the decreased waiting costs derived from providing that service.

Arnold estimates that the cost of customer waiting time, in terms of customer dissatisfaction and lost goodwill, is $10 per hour spent in his shop. Observe that this time includes the time a customer's car is waiting in the queue for service as well as the time when the car is actually being serviced. The only cost of providing service that Arnold can identify is the salary of Reid Blank, the mechanic, who is paid $12 per hour.

The total cost, defined as the sum of the waiting cost and the service cost, is calculated as follows:

$$\text{Total cost} = C_w \times L + C_s \times s \tag{9-10}$$

where

C_w = customer waiting cost per unit time period
L = average number of customers in the system
C_s = cost of providing service per server per unit time period
s = number of servers in the queuing system

In Arnold's case, $C_w = \$10$ per hour, $L = 2$ (see Figure 9.8), $C_s = \$12$ per hour, and $s = 1$ (because there is only one mechanic). Hence, Arnold computes his total cost as $\$10 \times 2 + \$12 \times 1 = \$32$ per hour.

Increasing the Service Rate

Now Arnold faces a decision. He finds out through the muffler business grapevine that Rusty Muffler Shop, a crosstown competitor, employs a mechanic named Jimmy Smith who can install new mufflers at an average rate of four per hour. Larry Arnold contacts Smith and inquires as to his interest in switching employers. Smith says that he would consider leaving Rusty Muffler Shop but only if he were paid a $15 per hour salary. Arnold, being a crafty businessman, decides to check whether it would be worthwhile to fire Blank and replace him with the speedier but more expensive Smith.

Arnold first recomputes all the operating characteristics, using a new average service rate (μ) of four mufflers per hour. The average arrival rate (λ) remains at two cars per hour. The revised characteristic values if Smith is employed are shown in Figure 9.9.

It is quite evident that Smith's higher average rate (four mufflers per hour compared with Blank's three per hour) will result in shorter queues and waiting times. For example, a customer would now spend an average of only 0.5 hours in the system (i.e., $W = 0.5$) and 0.25 hours waiting in the queue ($W_q = 0.25$) as opposed to 1 hour in the system and 0.67 hours in the queue with Blank as the mechanic. The average number of customers in the system (L) decreases from two units to one unit.

Arnold revises his economic analysis with the new information. The revised values are $C_w = \$10$ per hour, $L = 1$ (see Figure 9.9), $C_s = \$15$ per hour, and $s = 1$ (because there is still only one mechanic). Hence, Arnold's revised total cost with Smith as the mechanic is $\$10 \times 1 + \$15 \times 1 = \$25$ per hour. Because the total cost with Blank as the mechanic was $32 per hour, Arnold may very well decide to hire Smith and reduce his cost by $7 per hour (or $56 per 8-hour day).

M/M/s Queuing System

	A	B	C	D	E	F
1	Arnold's Muffler Shop					
2	Queuing Model	M/M/s (Exponential Service Times)				
3						
4	1. Both λ and μ must be RATES, and use the same time unit. For example, given a service time such as 10 minutes					
5	per customer, convert it to a service rate such as 6 per hour.					
6	2. The total service rate (rate x servers) must be greater than the arrival rate.					
7						
8	Input Data			Operating Characteristics		
9	Arrival rate (λ)	2		Average server utilization (ρ)	0.5000	
10	Service rate (μ)	4		Average number of customers in the queue (L_q)	0.5000	
11	Number of servers (s)	1		Average number of customers in the system (L)	1.0000	
12				Average waiting time in the queue (W_q)	0.2500	
13		(New service rate)		Average time in the system (W)	0.5000	
14				Probability (% of time) system is empty (P_0)	0.5000	
15						0.25 hours =
16					= 30 minutes	15 minutes
17						
18	Probabilities					
19	Number of Units	Probability	Cumulative Probability			
20	0	0.5000	0.5000			
21	1	0.2500	0.7500			
22	2	0.1250	0.8750			
23	3	0.0625	0.9375			
24	4	0.0313	0.9688			
25	5	0.0156	0.9844			
36	16	0.0000	1.0000			
37	17	0.0000	1.0000			
38	18	0.0000	1.0000			
39	19	0.0000	1.0000			
40	20	0.0000	1.0000			

Figure 9.9: Revised Operating Characteristics with $\mu = 4$ for Arnold's Muffler Shop: M/M/1 Queuing System

■ File: Figure 9.7.xlsx, Sheet: Figure 9.9

9.5 M/M/s Queuing System

The next logical step is to look at a multiple-server queuing system, in which two or more servers are available to handle arriving customers. Let us still assume that customers awaiting service form one single line and then proceed to the first available server. An example of such a multiple-server, single-phase waiting line is found in many banks or post offices today. A common line is formed, and the customer at the head of the line proceeds to the first free teller or clerk. (Refer to Figure 9.3 for a typical multiple-server configuration.)

The multiple-server system presented here again assumes that arrivals follow a Poisson probability distribution and that service times are distributed exponentially. Service is first come, first served, and all servers are assumed to perform at the same average rate.[4] Other assumptions listed earlier for the single-server model apply as well.

---

[4] Analytical models for multi-server queuing systems where different servers perform at different average rates are beyond the scope of this book.

Operating Characteristic Equations for an M/M/s Queuing System
We let

λ = average number of arrivals per time (e.g., per hour)
μ = average number of customers served per time *per server*
s = number of servers

As with the M/M/1 system, it is very important in an M/M/s system that we define both λ and μ for the *same time interval*. It is also important to note that the average service rate μ is defined *per server*. That is, if there are two servers and each server can handle an average of three customers per hour, μ is defined as three per hour, *not* six per hour ($=2\times 3$). Finally, as noted earlier, it is necessary for the average total service rate to be greater than the average arrival rate (that is, $s\mu > \lambda$).

The operating characteristic equations for the M/M/s queuing system are as follows:

1. Average server utilization in the system:

$$\rho = \lambda/(s\mu) \tag{9-11}$$

2. Probability that there are zero customers or units in the system:

$$P_0 = \frac{1}{\left[\sum_{k=0}^{s-1}\frac{1}{k!}\left(\frac{\lambda}{\mu}\right)^k\right] + \frac{1}{s!}\left(\frac{\lambda}{\mu}\right)^s \frac{s\mu}{(s\mu-\lambda)}} \tag{9-12}$$

3. Average number of customers or units waiting in line for service:

$$L_q = \frac{(\lambda/\mu)^s \lambda\mu}{(s-1)!(s\mu-\lambda)^2} P_0 \tag{9-13}$$

4. Average number of customers or units in the system:

$$L = L_q + \lambda/\mu \tag{9-14}$$

5. Average time a customer or unit spends waiting in line for service:

$$W_q = L_q/\lambda \tag{9-15}$$

6. Average time a customer or unit spends in the system:

$$W = W_q + 1/\mu \tag{9-16}$$

7. Probability that there are *n* customers or units in the system:

$$P_n = \frac{(\lambda/\mu)^n}{n!} P_0 \quad \text{for } n \le s \tag{9-17}$$

$$P_n = \frac{(\lambda/\mu)^n}{s!\, s^{(n-s)}} P_0 \quad \text{for } n > s \tag{9-18}$$

These equations are more complex than the ones used in the single-server model. Yet they are used in exactly the same fashion and provide the same type of information as those in the simpler M/M/1 model.

Arnold's Muffler Shop Revisited

For an application of the multiple-server queuing model, let us return to Arnold's Muffler Shop problem. Earlier, Larry Arnold examined two options. He could retain his current mechanic, Reid Blank, at a total system cost of $32 per hour, or he could fire Blank and hire a slightly more expensive but faster worker named Jimmy Smith. With Smith on board, the system cost could be reduced to $25 per hour.

Arnold now explores a third option. He finds that at minimal after-tax cost, he can open a second service bay in which mufflers can be installed. Instead of firing his first mechanic, Blank, he would hire a second mechanic, Joel Simpson. The new mechanic would be able to install mufflers at the same average rate as Blank ($\mu = 3$ per hour) and be paid the same salary as Blank ($12 per hour). Customers, who would still arrive at the average rate of $\lambda = 2$ per hour, would wait in a single line until one of the two mechanics became available. To find out how this option compares with the old single-server queuing system, Arnold computes the operating characteristics for the M/M/2 system.

ExcelModules Solution for Arnold's Muffler Shop with Two Mechanics Once again, we select the choice titled Exponential Service Times (M/M/s) from the Queuing Models menu in ExcelModules (see Figure 9.5). After entering the optional title, we enter the input data as shown in Figure 9.10. For Arnold's problem, observe that the average arrival rate (λ) is two cars per hour. The average service rate (μ) is three mufflers per hour *per mechanic*. We enter these values in cells B9 and B10, respectively. The number of servers (cell B11) is two because there are now two mechanics.

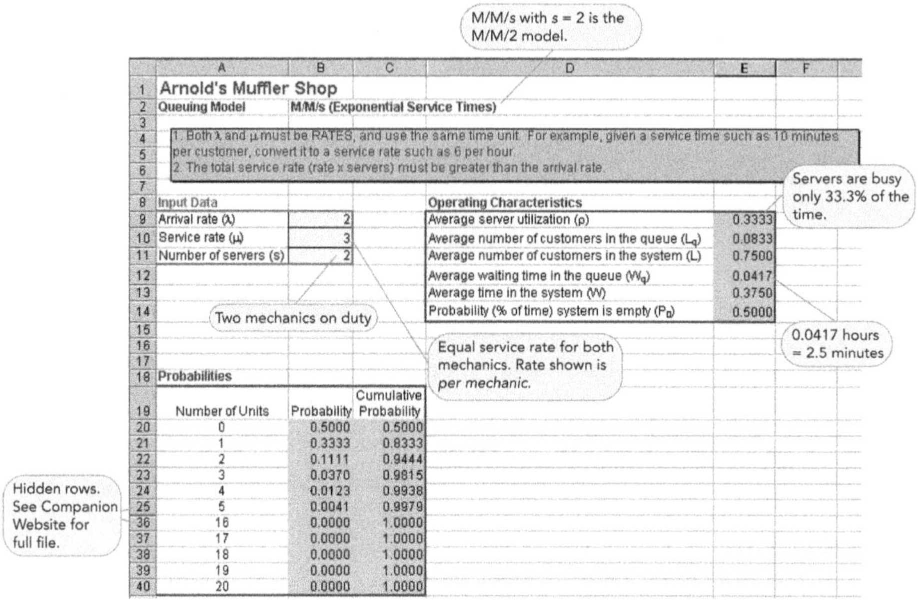

Figure 9.10: Revised Operating Characteristics for Arnold's Muffler Shop: M/M/2 Queuing System

File: Figure 9.10.xlsx

The worksheet now displays the operating characteristics of this queuing system in cells E9:E14. Probabilities of having a specific number of units in the system are shown in cells A19:C40. Arnold first compares these results with the earlier results. The information is summarized in Table 9.3. The increased service from opening a second bay has a dramatic effect on almost all results. In particular, average time spent waiting in line (W_q) drops down from 40 minutes with only Blank working or 15 minutes with only Smith working, to only 2.5 minutes with Blank and Simpson working! Similarly, the average number of cars in the system (L) falls to 0.75.[5] But does this mean that a second bay should be opened?

---

[5] Note that adding a second mechanic cuts queue waiting time and length by more than half; that is, the relationship between the number of servers and queue characteristics is *nonlinear*. This is because of the random arrival and service processes. When there is only one mechanic, and two customers arrive within a minute of each other, the second will have a long wait. The fact that the mechanic may have been idle for 30 minutes before they both arrive does not change the average waiting time. Thus, single-server models often have high wait times compared to multiple-server models.

Table 9.3: Effect of Service Level on Arnold's Operating Characteristics

Operating Characteristic	Level of Service		
	One Mechanic ($\mu = 3$)	Two Mechanics ($\mu = 3$ each)	One Faster Mechanic ($\mu = 4$)
Probability that the system is empty (P_o)	0.33	0.50	0.50
Average number of cars in the system (L)	2 cars	0.75 cars	1 car
Average time spent in the system (W)	60 minutes	22.5 minutes	30 minutes
Average number of cars in the queue (L_q)	1.33 cars	0.083 cars	0.50 cars
Average time spent in the queue (W_q)	40 minutes	2.5 minutes	15 minutes

Cost Analysis of the Queuing System

To complete his economic analysis of the M/M/2 queuing system, Arnold notes that the relevant values are $C_w = \$10$ per hour, $L = 0.75$ (see Figure 9.10), $C_s = \$12$ per hour, and $s = 2$ (because there are two mechanics). The total cost is, therefore, $\$10 \times 0.75 + \$12 \times 2 = \$31.50$ per hour.

As you recall, total cost with just Blank as the mechanic was found to be \$32 per hour. Total cost with just the faster but more expensive Smith was \$25 per hour. Although opening a second bay would be likely to have a positive effect on customer goodwill and hence lower the cost of waiting time (i.e., lower C_w), it does mean an increase in the total cost of providing service. Look back to Figure 9.1 and you will see that such trade-offs are the basis of queuing theory. Based on his analysis, Arnold decides to replace his current worker Blank with the speedier Smith and not open a second service bay.

9.6 M/D/1 Queuing System

When customers or equipment are processed according to a fixed cycle, as in the case of an automatic car wash or an amusement park ride, constant service rates are appropriate. Because constant service rates are certain, the values for L_q, W_q, L, and W in such a queuing system are always less than they would be in an equivalent M/M/s system, which has variable service times. As a matter of fact, both the average queue length and the average waiting time in the queue are *halved* with the constant service rate model.

Decison Modeling In Action

Queueing Model to Determine Vaccine Prioritization for Effective Pandemic Response

One of the primary goals of public policy makers is to determine the best strategies to protect the population from pandemic disease. The foremost way to curtail pandemics effectively is through prophylactic vaccination. However, because of the limited supply of vaccines, the most efficient way is to prioritize populations based upon their level of risk to the infection.

In that capacity, the Center for Disease Control and Prevention and the Georgia Institute of Technology worked together to derive a mathematical decision framework to track the effectiveness of prioritized vaccination over the course of a pandemic in order to minimize both infection and mortality rates.

The team developed a solution, based on the disease-propagation process (susceptible, exposed and infected but not infectious, infectious but not yet symptomatic, infectious and asymptomatic, infectious and symptomatic, recovered and immune), with a vaccine queueing model and an optimization engine to determine optimal prioritized coverage. Some of the constraints included in the model were vaccine inventory levels, individual risk factors, and the estimated outbreak characteristics. The model was based on the 2009 H1N1 vaccine supply data. The team analyzed the vaccination effectiveness under different start times, as well as on different infection percentages of the population.

The model developed has been in use since 2011 in Georgia for advising on vaccine distribution and prioritization. The developed system empowered policy makers to make the right decisions at the right time to save more lives, better utilize limited resources, and reduce the health-service burden during a pandemic event.

Source: Based on E. Lee, F. Yaun, F. Pietz, B. Benecke, G. Burel. "Vaccine Prioritization for Effective Pandemic Response," *Interfaces* 45, 5 (September–October 2015): 425–443.

Operating Characteristic Equations for an M/D/1 Queuing System

In the M/D/1 queuing system we let

λ = average number of arrivals per time (e.g., per hour)

μ = constant number of people or items served per time period

The operating characteristic equations for the M/D/1 queuing system are as follows:
1. Average server utilization in the system:

$$\rho = \lambda/\mu \tag{9-19}$$

2. Average number of customers or units waiting in line for service:

$$L_q = \frac{\lambda^2}{2\mu(\mu - \lambda)} \tag{9-20}$$

3. Average number of customers or units in the system:

$$L = L_q + \lambda/\mu \qquad (9\text{--}21)$$

4. Average time a customer or unit spends waiting in line for service:

$$W_q = L_q/\lambda = \frac{\lambda}{2\mu(\mu-\lambda)} \qquad (9\text{--}22)$$

5. Average time a customer or unit spends in the system (namely, in the queue or being served):

$$W = W_q + 1/\mu \qquad (9\text{--}23)$$

6. Probability that there are zero customers or units in the system:

$$P_0 = 1 - \lambda/\mu \qquad (9\text{--}24)$$

Garcia-Golding Recycling, Inc.

Garcia-Golding Recycling, Inc., collects and compacts aluminum cans and glass bottles in New York City. Its truck drivers, who arrive to unload these materials for recycling, wait an average of 15 minutes before emptying their loads. The cost of the driver and truck time wasted while in queue is valued at $60 per hour. Garcia-Golding is considering purchasing a new automated compactor. The new compactor will be able to process truckloads at a constant rate of 12 trucks per hour (i.e., 5 minutes per truck), and its cost will be amortized at a rate of $3 per truck unloaded. Trucks arrive according to a Poisson distribution at an average rate of 8 per hour. Should Garcia-Golding purchase the new compactor?

ExcelModules Solution for Garcia-Golding Recycling We select the choice titled Constant Service Times (M/D/1) from the Queuing Models menu in ExcelModules (see Figure 9.5. After entering the optional title, we enter the input data as shown in Figure 9.11. For Garcia-Golding's problem, the average arrival rate (λ) is 8 trucks per hour. The constant service rate (μ) is 12 trucks per hour. We enter these values in cells B9 and B10, respectively. The worksheet now displays the operating characteristics of this queuing system in cells E9:E14.

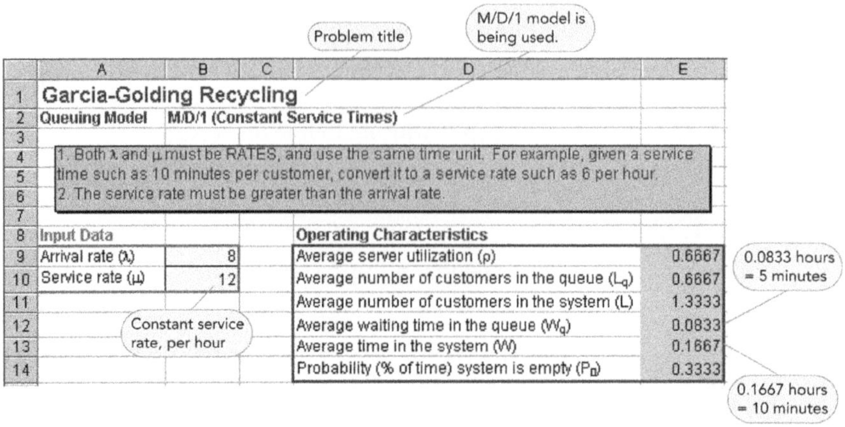

Figure 9.11: Operating Characteristics for Garcia-Golding Recycling: M/D/1 Queuing System

File: Figure 9.11.xlsx

Cost Analysis of the Queuing System

The *current* system makes drivers wait an average of 15 minutes before they empty their trucks. The waiting cost per trip is

$$\text{Current waiting cost per trip} = (0.25 \text{ hours waiting}) \times \$60/\text{hour}$$
$$= \$15 \text{ per trip}$$

The average waiting time in the queue (W_q) with the new automated compactor is only 0.0833 hours, or 5 minutes. Therefore, the revised waiting cost per trip is

$$\text{Revised waiting cost per trip} = (0.0833 \text{ hours waiting}) \times \$60/\text{hour}$$
$$= \$5 \text{ per trip}$$
$$\text{Savings with new equipment} = \$15 - \$5 = \$10 \text{ per trip}$$
$$\text{Amortized cost of equipment} = \$3 \text{ per trip}$$
$$\text{Hence, net savings} = \$10 - \$3 = \$7 \text{ per trip}$$

Garcia-Golding should therefore purchase the new compactor.

9.7 M/G/1 Queuing System

So far, we have studied systems in which service times are either exponentially distributed or constant. In many cases, however, service times could follow some arbitrary, or general distribution with mean μ and standard deviation σ. In such cases, we refer to the model as a *general* service time model. Real-world examples of general service times include time required to service vehicles at an auto repair shop (e.g., an oil change service) and time required by a store clerk to complete a sales transaction.

M/G/1 Queuing System

The single-server system presented here assumes that arrivals follow a Poisson probability distribution. As in earlier models, with the M/G/1 model we also assume that (1) service is on a first-come, first-served basis, (2) there is no balking or reneging, and (3) the average service rate is greater than the average arrival rate.

Operating Characteristic Equations for an M/G/1 Queuing System

For the M/G/1 system we let

λ = average number of arrivals per time (e.g., per hour)
μ = average number of people or items served per time period
σ = standard deviation of service time

As with the M/M/s models, with the M/G/1 model, λ and μ must be defined for the *same time interval*. Also, it is important to note that while λ and μ are rates (i.e., number of occurrences in a specified time interval), σ is the standard deviation of the service time. The units for σ should, however, be consistent with λ and μ. For example, if λ and μ are expressed as average rates per hour, σ should also be measured in hours.

The operating characteristic equations for the M/G/1 model are as follows:

1. Average server utilization in the system:

$$\rho = \lambda/\mu \qquad (9\text{-}25)$$

2. Average number of customers or units waiting in line for service:

$$L_q = \frac{\lambda^2 \sigma^2 + (\lambda/\mu)^2}{2(1-(\lambda/\mu))} \qquad (9\text{-}26)$$

3. Average number of customers or units in the system:

$$L = L_q + \lambda/\mu \qquad (9\text{-}27)$$

4. Average time a customer or unit spends waiting in line for service:

$$W_q = L_q/\lambda \qquad (9\text{-}28)$$

5. Average time a customer or unit spends in the system:

$$W = W_q + 1/\mu \qquad (9\text{-}29)$$

6. Probability that there are zero customers or units in the system:

$$P_0 = 1 - \lambda/\mu \qquad (9\text{-}30)$$

Meetings with Professor Crino

Professor Michael Crino advises all honors students at Central College. During the registration period, students meet with Professor Crino to decide courses for the following semester and to discuss any other issues of concern. Rather than have students set up specific appointments to see him, Professor Crino prefers setting aside two hours each day during the registration period and having students drop by informally. This approach, he believes, makes students feel more at ease with him.

Based on his experience, Professor Crino thinks that students arrive at an average rate of one every 12 minutes (or five per hour) to see him. He also thinks the Poisson distribution is appropriate to model the arrival process. Advising meetings last an average of 10 minutes each; that is, Professor Crino's service rate is six per hour. However, because some students have concerns that they wish to discuss with Professor Crino, the length of these meetings varies. Professor Crino estimates that the standard deviation of the service time (i.e., the meeting length) is 5 minutes.

ExcelModules Solution for Professor Crino's Problem We select the choice titled General Service Times (M/G/1) from the Queuing Models menu in ExcelModules (see Figure 9.5). After entering the optional title, we enter the input data in the screen as shown in Figure 9.12. For Professor Crino's problem, the average arrival rate (λ) is five students per hour. The average service rate (μ) is six students per hour. Observe that, as required, μ exceeds λ, and both are for the same time interval (per hour, in this case). The standard deviation (σ) of the service time is 5 minutes. However, because λ and μ are expressed per hour, we also express σ in hours and write it as 0.0833 hours (= 5 minutes).

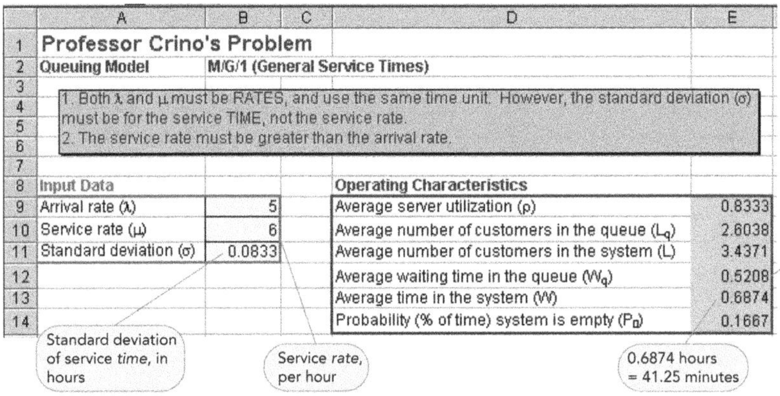

	A	B	C	D	E
1	Professor Crino's Problem				
2	Queuing Model		M/G/1 (General Service Times)		
3					
4	1. Both λ and μ must be RATES, and use the same time unit. However, the standard deviation (σ)				
5	must be for the service TIME, not the service rate.				
6	2. The service rate must be greater than the arrival rate.				
7					
8	Input Data			Operating Characteristics	
9	Arrival rate (λ)	5		Average server utilization (ρ)	0.8333
10	Service rate (μ)	6		Average number of customers in the queue (L_q)	2.6038
11	Standard deviation (σ)	0.0833		Average number of customers in the system (L)	3.4371
12				Average waiting time in the queue (W_q)	0.5208
13				Average time in the system (W)	0.6874
14				Probability (% of time) system is empty (P_0)	0.1667

Standard deviation of service *time*, in hours

Service rate, per hour

0.5208 hours = 31.2 minutes

0.6874 hours = 41.25 minutes

Figure 9.12: Operating Characteristics for Professor Crino's Problem: M/G/1 Queuing System

File: Figure 9.12.xlsx, Sheet: Figure 9.12

We enter the values of λ, μ, and σ in cells B9, B10, and B11, respectively, as shown in Figure 9.12. The worksheet now displays the operating characteristics of this queuing system in cells E9:E14.

The results indicate that, on average, Professor Crino is busy during 83.3% of his advising period. There are 2.60 students waiting to see him on average, and each student waits an average of 0.52 hours (or approximately 31 minutes).

Using Excel's Goal Seek to Identify Required Model Parameters

Looking at the results in Figure 9.12, Professor Crino realizes that making students wait an average of 31 minutes is unacceptable. Ideally, he would like to speed up these meetings so that students wait no more than 15 minutes (or 0.25 hours) on average. He realizes that he has little control over the standard deviation of the service time. However, by insisting that students come prepared (e.g., decide ahead of time which courses they want to take) for these meetings, Professor Crino thinks he can decrease the average meeting length. The question is this: What should be the average meeting length that will enable Professor Crino to meet his goal of a 15-minute average waiting time?

One way to solve this problem is to plug in different values for the average service rate μ in cell B10 of Figure 9.12 and keep track of the W_q value in cell E12 until it drops below 0.25. An alternate, and preferred, approach is to use a procedure in Excel called Goal Seek to automate the search process for the value of μ. You may recall that we used Goal Seek in Chapter 1 to find the break-even point. The Goal Seek procedure allows us to specify a desired value for a *target cell*. This target cell should contain a formula that involves a different cell, called the *changing cell*. Once we specify the target cell, its desired value, and the changing cell in Goal Seek, the procedure automatically manipulates the changing cell value to try to make the target cell achieve its desired value.

In our model, the changing cell is the average service rate μ (cell B10). The target cell is the average waiting time W_q (cell E12). We want the target cell to achieve a value of 15 minutes (which we specify as 0.25 hours because μ and λ are per hour). After bringing up the General Service Times (M/G/1) worksheet in ExcelModules (see Figure 9.12), we invoke the Goal Seek procedure by clicking the Data tab on Excel's Ribbon, followed by the What-If Analysis button (found in the Data Tools group within the Data tab), and then finally on Goal Seek. The window shown in Figure 9.13 is now displayed.

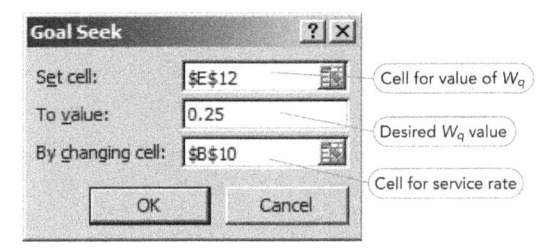

Figure 9.13: Goal Seek Input Window in Excel

We specify cell E12 as the target cell in the Set cell box, a desired value of 0.25 for this cell in the To value box, and cell B10 in the box labeled By changing cell. When we click OK, we get the windows shown in Figure 9.14. The results indicate that if Professor Crino can increase his service rate to 6.92 students per hour, the average waiting time drops to around 15 minutes. That is, Professor Crino needs to reduce his average meeting length to approximately 8.67 minutes (=6.92 students per 60 minutes).

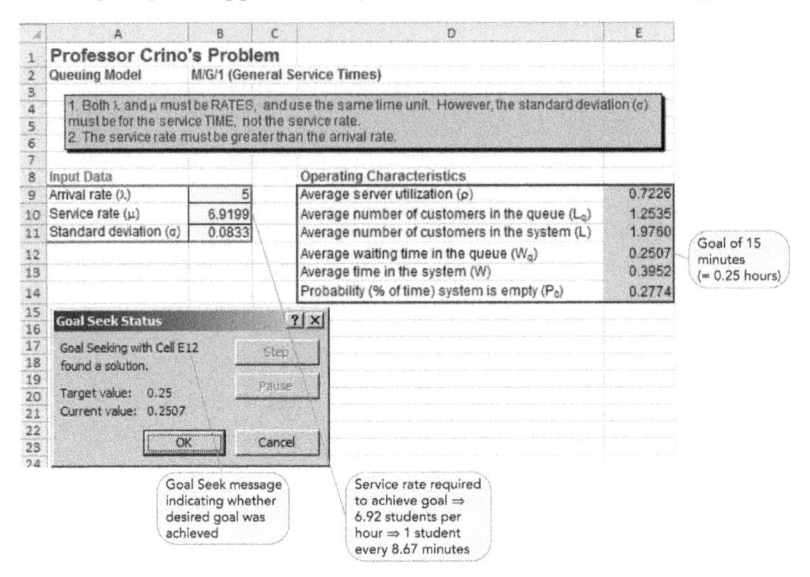

Figure 9.14: Goal Seek Status Window and Revised Operating Characteristics for Professor Crino's Problem: M/G/1 Queuing System

File: Figure 9.12.xlsx, Sheet: Figure 9.14

We can use Goal Seek in any of the queuing models discussed here to determine the value of an input parameter (e.g., μ or λ) that would make an operating characteristic reach a desired value. For example, we could use it in the M/M/1 worksheet (section 9.4) to find the value of μ that would allow Arnold to offer his customers a guarantee of having to wait no more than 5 minutes (or 0.0833 hours). The answer turns out to be six mufflers per hour. See if you can verify this by using Goal Seek and the Exponential Service Times (M/M/s) queuing model in ExcelModules.

9.8 M/M/S/∞/N Queuing System

All the queuing models we have studied so far have assumed that the size of the calling population is infinite. Hence, as customers arrive at the queuing system, the potential number of customers left in the population is still large, and the average arrival rate does not change. However, when there is a limited population of potential customers for a service facility, we need to consider a different queuing model. This model would be used, for example, if we were considering equipment repairs in a factory that has 5 machines, if we were in charge of maintenance for a fleet of 10 commuter airplanes, or if we ran a hospital ward with 20 beds. The limited population model permits any number of servers to be considered.

Decision Modeling In Action

Designing Guest Flow and Operations Logistics for the "Dolphin Tales" Show in Georgia Aquarium

The Georgia Aquarium partnered with the Georgia Institute of Technology to enhance the experience of the guests of the "Dolphin Tales" show by designing the guest movement in order to limit congestion. A decision support system (DSS) was developed to optimize the "Dolphin Tales" show. The DSS was based on a heuristic algorithm to find good feasible solutions for intractable nonlinear mixed integer program resource allocation instances. Then, the team integrated simulation and optimization technology into a unified software framework for realistic modeling of large-scale applications with human cognitive and behavioral elements. Finally, they developed software to automatically interpret computer-rendered drawings of processes and tasks into system process maps to enable animation of processes and allow decision makers to review the efficiency of the system operations and customer experience.

Some of the constraints that were put into consideration during the study were maximum limits on wait time, queue length, range of utilization desired at each station, assignability and availability for each of station, and maximum limit on the cycle time of an individual.

Although the main objective was to mitigate congestion to enhance the guests' experience, the DSS provided value on both strategic and operational levels.

In addition to reduced congestion and enhanced guest experience, some of the benefits attained from implementing the DSS were reduced operational and logistics costs, as well as improved wellness of the dolphins. The total dollar value of improvements was estimated to be about $1.5 million per year.

Source: Based on E. Lee, C. Chen, N. Brown, J. Handy, A. Desiderio, R. Lopez, B. Davis. "Designing Guest Flow and Operations Logistics for the Dolphin Tales," *Interfaces* 42, 5 (September–October 2012): 492–506.

The reason the $M/M/s/\infty/N$ model differs from the earlier queuing models is that there is now a dependent relationship between the length of the queue and the arrival rate. To illustrate this situation, we can assume that our factory has five machines. If all five are broken and awaiting repair, the arrival rate drops to zero. In general, as the waiting time becomes longer in a limited population queuing system, the arrival rate of customers drops lower.

In this section, we describe a finite arrival population model that has the following assumptions:
1. There are *s* servers with *identical* service time distributions.

2. The population of units seeking service is finite, of size N.[6]
3. The arrival distribution of *each customer* in the population follows a Poisson distribution, with an average rate of λ.
4. Service times are exponentially distributed, with an average rate of μ.
5. Both λ and μ are specified for the same time period.
6. Customers are served on a first-come, first-served basis.

Operating Characteristic Equations for the Finite Population Queuing System

For the $M/M/s/\infty/N$ model we let

λ = average number of arrivals per time (e.g., per hour)

μ = average number of people or items served per time period

s = number of servers

N = size of the population

The operating characteristic equations for the $M/M/s/\infty/N$ model are as follows:

1. Probability that there are zero customers or units in the system:

$$P_0 = \frac{1}{\sum_{n=0}^{s-1} \frac{N!}{(N-n)!n!} \left(\frac{\lambda}{\mu}\right)^n + \sum_{n=s}^{N} \frac{N!}{(N-n)!s!s^{n-s}} \left(\frac{\lambda}{\mu}\right)^n} \quad (9\text{–}31)$$

2. Probability that there are exactly n customers in the system:

$$P_n = \frac{N!}{(N-n)!n!} \left(\frac{\lambda}{\mu}\right)^n P_0, \quad \text{if } 0 \le n \le s \quad (9\text{–}32)$$

$$P_n = \frac{N!}{(N-n)!s!s^{n-s}} \left(\frac{\lambda}{\mu}\right)^n P_0, \quad \text{if } s < n \le N \quad (9\text{–}33)$$

$$P_n = 0, \quad \text{if } n > N \quad (9\text{–}34)$$

3. Average number of customers or units in line, waiting for service:

$$L_q = \sum_{n=s}^{N} (n-s) P_n \quad (9\text{–}35)$$

---

[6] Although there is no definite number that we can use to divide finite from infinite arrival populations, the general rule of thumb is this: If the number in the queue is a significant proportion of the arrival population, we should use a finite queuing model.

4. Average number of customers or units in the system:

$$L = \sum_{n=0}^{s-1} nP_n + L_q + s\left(1 - \sum_{n=0}^{s-1} P_n\right) \qquad (9\text{--}36)$$

5. Average time a customer or unit spends in the queue waiting for service:

$$W_q = \frac{L_q}{\lambda(N-L)} \qquad (9\text{--}37)$$

6. Average time a customer or unit spends in the system:

$$W = \frac{L}{\lambda(N-L)} \qquad (9\text{--}38)$$

Department of Commerce Example
The U.S. Department of Commerce (DOC) in Washington, DC, uses five high-speed printers to print all documents. Past records indicate that each of these printers needs repair after about 20 hours of use. Breakdowns have been found to be Poisson distributed. The one technician on duty can repair a printer in an average of 2 hours, following an exponential distribution.

ExcelModules Solution for the DOC's Problem We select the choice titled Finite Population Model (Multiple Servers) from the Queuing Models menu in ExcelModules (see Figure 9.5). After entering the optional title, we get the screen shown in Figure 9.15. For the DOC's problem, the average arrival rate (λ) for *each printer* is $1/20 = 0.05$ per hour. The average service rate (μ) is one every two hours, or 0.50 printers per hour. As before, both μ and λ are expressed for the same time period (per hour, in this case). The number of servers (s) is one because there is only one technician on duty. Finally, the population size (N) is five because there are five printers at the DOC.

We enter the values of λ, μ, s, and N in cells B9, B10, B11, and B12, respectively, as shown in Figure 9.15. The worksheet now displays the operating characteristics of this queuing system in cells E9:E15. Probability values (P_n) are shown in cells B19:B24.

Chapter 9: Queuing Models

	A	B	C	D	E
1	Department of Commerce				
2	Queuing Model	M/M/s with a finite population			
3	1. Both λ and μ must be RATES, and use the same time unit.				
4	2. The arrival rate is for each member of the population. For example, if each member of the				
5	population goes for service once every 20 minutes, then enter λ = 3 (per hour).				
6					
7					
8	Input Data			Operating Characteristics	
9	Arrival rate per customer (λ)	0.05		Average server utilization (ρ)	0.4380
10	Service rate (μ)	0.5		Average number of customers in the queue (L_q)	0.2035
11	Number of servers (s)	1		Average number of customers in the system (L)	0.6395
12	Population size (N)	5		Average waiting time in the queue (W_q)	0.9333
13				Average time in the system (W)	2.9333
14		1 technician	5 printers	Probability (% of time) system is empty (P_0)	0.5640
15				Effective arrival rate	0.2180
16					
17	Probabilities				
18	Number of Units	Probability	Cumulative Probability	Number waiting	Arrival rate(n)
19	0	0.5640	0.5640	0	0.25
20	1	0.2820	0.8459	0	0.2
21	2	0.1128	0.9587	1	0.15
22	3	0.0338	0.9926	2	0.1
23	4	0.0068	0.9993	3	0.05
24	5	0.0007	1.0000	4	0
25	6				
26	7				
27	8				
28	9				
29	10				
48	29				
49	30				
50	31				

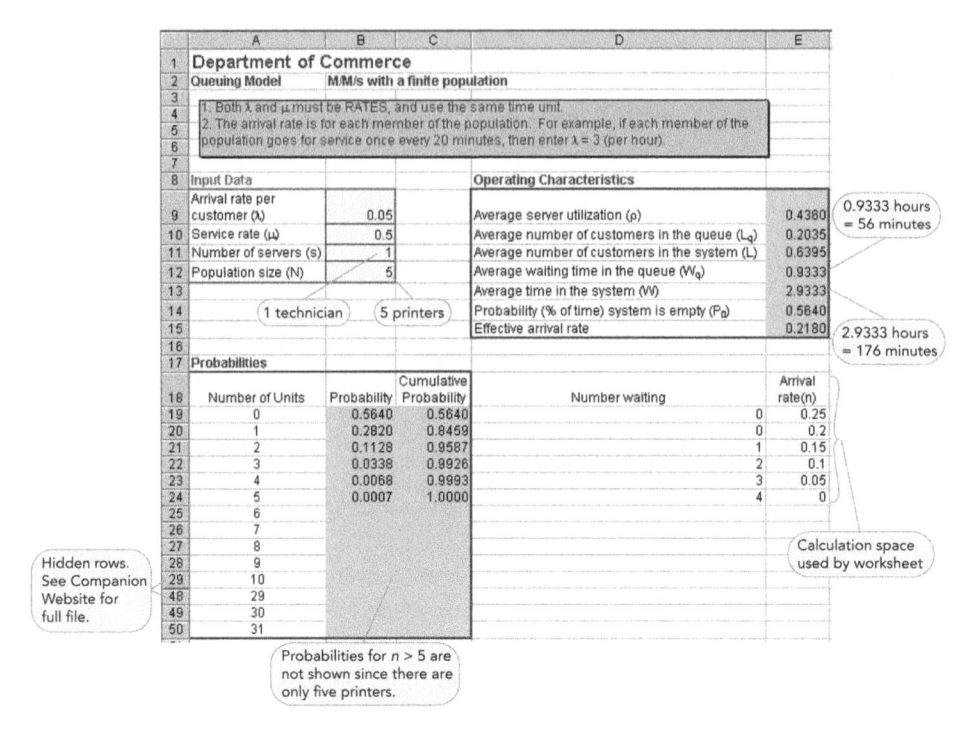

0.4380 → 0.9333 hours = 56 minutes

0.2180 → 2.9333 hours = 176 minutes

Hidden rows. See Companion Website for full file.

Probabilities for n > 5 are not shown since there are only five printers.

Calculation space used by worksheet

Figure 9.15: Operating Characteristics for the Department of Commerce Problem: M/M/1 Queuing System with Finite Population

X File: Figure 9.15.xlsx, Sheet: Figure 9.15

Cost Analysis of the Queuing System

The results indicate that there are 0.64 printers down, on average, in the system. If printer downtime is estimated at $120 per hour, and the technician is paid $25 per hour, we can compute the total cost per hour as

$$\text{Total cost} = (\text{Average number of printers down}) \times (\text{Cost of downtime hour})$$
$$+ (\text{Cost of technician hour})$$
$$= 0.64 \times \$120 + \$25 = \$101.80 \text{ per hour}$$

The office manager is willing to consider hiring a second printer technician, provided that doing so is cost-effective. To check this, we compute the DOC queue's operating characteristics again. However, the number of servers this time (cell B11) is two. The results are shown in Figure 9.16.

M/M/S/∞/N Queuing System — 545

	A	B	C	D	E
1	Department of Commerce				
2	Queuing Model	M/M/s with a finite population			
3	1. Both λ and μ must be RATES, and use the same time unit.				
4	2. The arrival rate is for each member of the population. For example, if each member of the				
5	population goes for service once every 20 minutes, then enter λ = 3 (per hour).				
6					
7					
8	Input Data			Operating Characteristics	
9	Arrival rate per customer (λ)	0.05		Average server utilization (ρ)	0.2268
10	Service rate (μ)	0.5		Average number of customers in the queue (L_q)	0.0113
11	Number of servers (s)	2		Average number of customers in the system (L)	0.4648
12	Population size (N)	5		Average waiting time in the queue (W_q)	0.0497
13				Average time in the system (W)	2.0497
14		(2 technicians)		Probability (% of time) system is empty (P_0)	0.6186
15				Effective arrival rate	0.2268
16					
17	Probabilities				
18	Number of Units	Probability	Cumulative Probability	Number waiting	Arrival rate(n)
19	0	0.6186	0.6186	0	0.25
20	1	0.3093	0.9279	0	0.2
21	2	0.0619	0.9897	0	0.15
22	3	0.0093	0.9990	1	0.1
23	4	0.0009	1.0000	2	0.05
24	5	0.0000	1.0000	3	0
25	6				
26	7			Calculation space used by worksheet.	
27	8				
28	9				
29	10				
48	29				
49	30				
50	31				

L drops to 0.46 with two technicians.

System is empty 62% of the time—that is, no printers are broken.

Hidden rows. See Companion Website for full file.

Figure 9.16: Revised Operating Characteristics for the Department of Commerce Problem: M/M/2 Queuing System with Finite Population

File: Figure 9.15.xlsx, Sheet: Figure 9.16

Figure 9.16 indicates that there are now only 0.46 printers, on average, in the system. We can compute the revised total cost per hour as

Total cost = (Average number of printers down) × (Cost of downtime hour)
+ (Cost of technician hour) × (Number of technicians)
= 0.46 × $120 + $25 × 2 = $105.20 per hour

Because the total cost is higher in this case ($105.20 versus $101.80 per hour), the office manager should not hire a second technician.

EXCEL EXTRA

Hiding Rows, Columns, Sheets, and Formulas

As shown in Figure 9.16, sometimes we want to hide rows (or columns) either to show certain rows (or columns) together on the same screen or perhaps to simply hide information from users that they typically would not need to see.

- To hide consecutive rows (columns), select the rows (columns), then right click and choose Hide.
- To display hidden rows (columns), select the row (column) above (left of) *and* below (right of) the hidden set, then right click and choose Unhide.

Sometimes you may wish to hide an entire sheet from the user. For example, there might be a sheet that contains a model and a lot of formulas that you do not want to confuse users with by showing the sheet to them. Note that at least one sheet must always be visible.

- To hide a sheet, place the cursor over the sheet tab, then right click and choose Hide.
- To display a hidden sheet, place the cursor over any remaining visible sheet tab, then right click and choose Unhide. Now select your sheet and click OK.

Finally, you can hide a formula from appearing in the formula bar when you place the cursor into a cell. The result of the formula will still appear in the cell, but the user will be unable to see the formula that generated it.

- To hide a formula, place the cursor in the cell of interest and select:

    Home|Font|Protection|Hidden|OK

- To unhide a formula, repeat and uncheck the Protection|Hidden option.
- The formula can only be hidden if the sheet is protected:

    Home|Format|Protect Sheet...|OK (optional password)

- To unprotect the sheet:

    Home|Format|Unprotect Sheet...|OK

9.9 More Complex Queuing Systems

Many queuing systems that occur in real-world situations have characteristics like those of Arnold's Muffler Shop, Garcia-Golding Recycling, Inc., Professor Crino's advising meetings, and the Department of Commerce examples. This is true when the situation calls for issues such as (1) single or multiple servers, (2) Poisson arrivals, (3) exponential, constant, or arbitrary service times, (4) a finite or an infinite arrival population, (5) infinite queue length, (6) no balking or reneging, and/or (7) first-in, first-out service.

Often, however, *variations* of this specific case are present in a queuing system. Arrival times, for example, may not be Poisson distributed. A college registration system in which seniors have first choice of courses and hours over all other students is an example of a first-come, first-served model with a preemptive priority queue discipline. A physical examination for military recruits is an example of a multiphase system—one that differs from the single-phase models discussed in this chapter. Recruits first line up to have blood drawn at one station, then wait to take an eye exam at the next station, talk to a psychiatrist at the third, and are examined by a doctor for medical problems at the fourth. At each phase, the recruits must enter another queue and wait their turn. An airline reservation system with a finite number of phone lines is an example of a system with a limited queue length.

It turns out that for many of these more complex queuing systems also, decision modelers have developed analytical models to compute their operating characteristics. Not surprisingly, the mathematical expressions for these computations are somewhat more cumbersome than the ones covered in this chapter.[7] However, as noted previously, real-world queuing systems can often be so complex that they cannot be modeled analytically at all. When this happens, decision modelers usually turn to a different approach—*computer simulation*—to analyze the performance of these systems. We discuss simulation in Chapter 10.

9.10 Summary

Queuing systems are an important part of the business world. This chapter describes several common queuing situations and presents decision models for analyzing systems that follow certain assumptions: (1) The queuing system involves just a single phase of service, (2) arrivals are Poisson distributed, (3) arrivals are treated on a first-in, first-out basis and do not balk or renege, (4) service times follow the exponential distribution, an arbitrary distribution, or are constant, and (5) the average service rate is faster than the average arrival rate.

The models illustrated in this chapter are for single-server, single-phase and for multiple-server, single-phase problems. We show how to compute a series of operating characteristics in each case using Excel worksheets and then study total expected costs. Total cost is the sum of the cost of providing service plus the cost of waiting time.

Key operating characteristics for a system are (1) utilization rate, (2) percentage of idle time, (3) average time spent waiting in the system and in the queue, (4) average number of customers in the system and in the queue, and (5) probabilities of various numbers of customers in the system.

---

[7] Often, the qualitative results of queuing models are as useful as the quantitative results. Results show that it is inherently more efficient to pool resources, use central dispatching, and provide single multiple-server systems rather than multiple single-server systems.

We emphasize that a variety of queuing situations exist that do not meet all the assumptions of the traditional models considered here. In such cases, we need to use more complex analytical models or turn to a technique called computer simulation, which is the topic of Chapter 10.

Key Points
- A primary goal of queuing analysis is to find the best level of service for an organization.
- Sophisticated models exist to handle variations of basic assumptions of queuing theory.
- When the model becomes too complex, we can use computer simulation (topic of Chapter 10) to analyze queues.
- Managers must deal with the trade-off between the cost of providing service and the cost of customer waiting time. The latter may be hard to quantify.
- Total expected cost in queuing theory is the sum of service plus waiting costs.
- The goal in queuing theory is to find the service level that minimizes total expected cost.
- Unlimited (or infinite) populations are assumed for most queuing models.
- Analytical queuing models typically use the average arrival rate per unit or customer.
- Arrivals are random when they are independent of one another and cannot be predicted exactly.
- The Poisson distribution is used in many queuing models to represent arrival patterns.
- Balking refers to customers who do not join a queue.
- Reneging customers join a queue but leave before being served.
- The models in this chapter assume unlimited queue length.
- Most queuing models use the first-in, first-out rule. This is obviously not appropriate in all service systems, especially those dealing with emergencies.
- Service facilities can either have a single server or multiple servers.
- Single-phase means the customer receives service at only one station before leaving the system. Multiphase implies two or more stops before leaving the system.
- Service times often follow the exponential distribution.
- It is important to verify that the assumption of exponential service times is valid before applying a model that makes that assumption.
- Key operating characteristics of a queuing system are: system utilization factor, average queue length, average number in the system, average queue waiting time, average time in the system, probability there are no customers in the system, and probability there are exactly n customers in the system.
- Kendall's three-symbol notation (sometimes extended to include five symbols) is used to classify queuing systems.

- Seven assumptions must be met if the single-server, single-phase model is to be applied.
- Both λ (average arrival rate) and μ (average service rate) must be rates and be defined for the same time interval.
- ExcelModules includes worksheets for all the queuing models discussed in this chapter.
- To analyze M/M/1 systems, we use the M/M/s worksheet in ExcelModules and set $s = 1$.
- Important: The total service rate in a queuing model must exceed the arrival rate.
- Conducting an economic analysis is the next step following the calculation of the key operating characteristics of a queuing system. It permits cost factors to be included.
- Customer waiting time is often considered the most important factor in queuing analysis.
- The multiple-server model (M/M/s) also assumes Poisson arrivals and exponential service times.
- In the M/M/s model, the average service rate is μ per server.
- Typically, we dramatically lower waiting time results by adding a second server to a single-line queuing system.
- Constant service rates speed up the process compared to exponentially distributed service times with the same value of μ.
- General service time models assume arbitrary distributions for service times.
- With general service time models, λ and μ are rates and must be for the same time interval. The standard deviation, σ, must also be measured in the same time unit.
- Excel's Goal Seek procedure allows us to find the required value of a queue parameter to achieve a stated goal.
- In the finite population model, the arrival rate is dependent on the length of the queue.

Glossary

Arbitrary, or General, Distribution A probability distribution that is sometimes used to describe random service times in a queuing system.

Arrival Population The population from which arrivals at the queuing system come. Also known as the *calling population*.

Balking The case in which arriving customers refuse to join the waiting line.

Computer Simulation A technique for representing queuing models that are complex and difficult to model analytically.

Exponential Distribution A probability distribution that is often used to describe random service times in a queuing system.

Finite, or Limited, Population A case in which the number of customers in the system is a significant proportion of the calling population.

Finite, or Limited, Queue Length A queue that cannot increase beyond a specific size.

First-In, First-Out (FIFO) A queue discipline in which the customers are served in the strict order of arrival.

Goal Seek A procedure in Excel that can be used to identify the value of a queuing system parameter required to achieve a desired value of an operating characteristic.

Infinite, or Unlimited, Population A calling population that is very large relative to the number of customers currently in the system.

Infinite, or Unlimited, Queue Length A queue that can increase to an infinite size.

M/D/1 Kendall's notation for the constant service time model.

M/G/1 Kendall's notation for the arbitrary, or general, service time model.

M/M/1 Kendall's notation for the single-server model with Poisson arrivals and exponential service times.

M/M/s Kendall's notation for the multiple-server queuing model (with *s* servers), Poisson arrivals, and exponential service times.

Multiphase System A system in which service is received from more than one station, one after the other.

Multiple-Server Queuing System A system that has more than one service facility, all fed by the same single queue.

Operating Characteristics Descriptive characteristics of a queuing system, including the average number of customers in a line and in the system, the average waiting times in a line and in the system, and the percentage of idle time.

Poisson Distribution A probability distribution that is often used to describe random arrivals in a queue.

Queue One or more customers or units waiting to be served. Also called a *waiting line*.

Queue Discipline The rule by which customers in a line receive service.

Queuing Model A mathematical model that studies the performance of waiting lines or queues.

Reneging The case in which customers enter a queue but then leave before being served.

Service Cost The cost of providing a particular level of service.

Single-Phase System A queuing system in which service is received at only one station.

Single-Server Queuing System A system with one service facility fed by one queue. Servers are also referred to as *channels*.

Utilization Factor (ρ) The proportion of time that a service facility is in use.

Waiting Cost The cost to a firm of having customers or units waiting in line to be served.

9.11 Exercises

Solved Problems

Solved Problem 9–1 The Maitland Furniture store gets an average of 50 customers per shift. The manager of Maitland wants to calculate whether she should hire one, two, three, or four salespeople. She has determined that average waiting times will be seven minutes with one salesperson, four minutes with two salespeople, three minutes with three salespeople, and two minutes with four salespeople. She has estimated the cost per minute that customers wait at $1. The cost per salesperson per shift (including fringe benefits) is $70. How many salespeople should be hired?

Solution The manager's calculations are as follows:

	Number of Salespeople			
	1	2	3	4
(a) Average number of customers per shift	50	50	50	50
(b) Average waiting time (minutes) per customer	7	4	3	2
(c) Total waiting time (minutes) per shift (a × b)	350	200	150	100
(d) Cost per minute of waiting time (estimated)	$1	$1	$1	$1
(e) Value of lost time per shift (c × d)	$350	$200	$150	$100
(f) Salary cost per shift	$70	$140	$210	$280
(g) Total cost per shift	$420	$340	$360	$380

Because the minimum total cost per shift relates to two salespeople, the manager's optimum strategy is to hire two salespeople.

Solved Problem 9–2 Marty Schatz owns and manages a chili dog and soft drink store near the campus. Although Marty can service 30 customers per hour on the average (μ), he gets only 20 customers per hour (λ). Because Marty could wait on 50% more customers than actually visit his store, it doesn't make sense to him that he should have any waiting lines.

Marty hires you to examine the situation and to determine some characteristics of his queue. After looking into the problem, you make the seven assumptions listed in section 9.4. What are your findings?

Solution For this problem, we use the Exponential Service Times (M/M/s) queuing worksheet in ExcelModules. The arrival rate (λ) is 20 customers per hour, the service rate (μ) is 30 customers per hour, and there is one server. We enter these values in cells B9, B10, and B11, respectively, as shown in Figure 9.17.

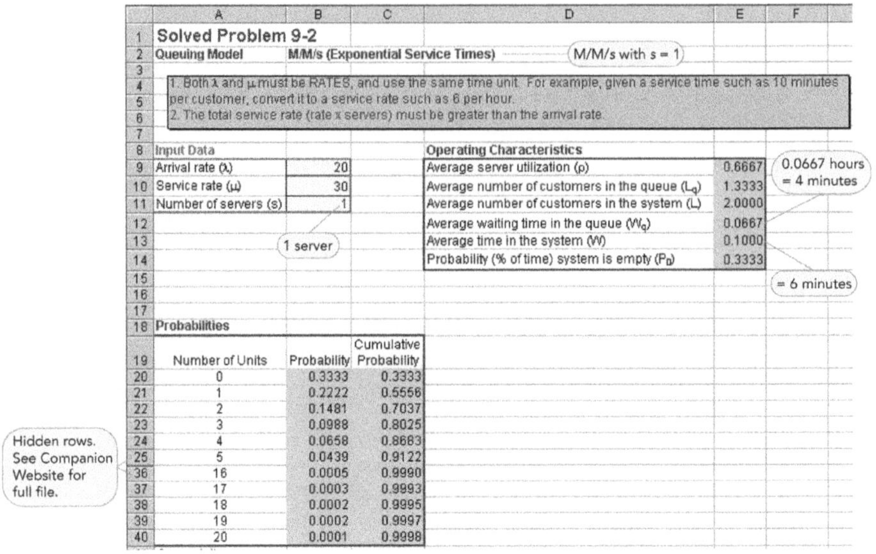

Figure 9.17: Operating Characteristics for Solved Problem 9–2: M/M/1 Queuing System

	A	B	C	D	E	F
1	Solved Problem 9-2					
2	Queuing Model	M/M/s (Exponential Service Times)		(M/M/s with s = 1)		
3						
4	1. Both λ and μ must be RATES, and use the same time unit. For example, given a service time such as 10 minutes					
5	per customer, convert it to a service rate such as 6 per hour.					
6	2. The total service rate (rate x servers) must be greater than the arrival rate.					
7						
8	Input Data			Operating Characteristics		
9	Arrival rate (λ)	20		Average server utilization (ρ)	0.6667	0.0667 hours
10	Service rate (μ)	30		Average number of customers in the queue (L_q)	1.3333	= 4 minutes
11	Number of servers (s)	1		Average number of customers in the system (L)	2.0000	
12				Average waiting time in the queue (W_q)	0.0667	
13		(1 server)		Average time in the system (W)	0.1000	
14				Probability (% of time) system is empty (P_0)	0.3333	
15						
16						= 6 minutes
17						
18	Probabilities					
19	Number of Units	Probability	Cumulative Probability			
20	0	0.3333	0.3333			
21	1	0.2222	0.5556			
22	2	0.1481	0.7037			
23	3	0.0988	0.8025			
24	4	0.0658	0.8683			
25	5	0.0439	0.9122			
36	16	0.0005	0.9990			
37	17	0.0003	0.9993			
38	18	0.0002	0.9995			
39	19	0.0002	0.9997			
40	20	0.0001	0.9998			

(Hidden rows. See Companion Website for full file.)

Figure 9.17: Operating Characteristics for Solved Problem 9–2: M/M/1 Queuing System

File: Figure 9.17.xlsx

The operating characteristics of this queuing system are displayed in cells E9:E14. The probabilities that there are exactly *n* customers in the system, for *n* = 0 through 20, are shown in cells B20:B40.

Solved Problem 9-3 Refer to Solved Problem 9–2. Marty agreed that these figures seemed to represent his approximate business situation. You are quite surprised at the length of the lines and elicit from him an estimated value of the customer's waiting time (in the queue, not being waited on) at 10 cents per minute. During the 12 hours that Marty is open, he gets 12 × 20 = 240 customers. The average customer is in a queue four minutes, so the total customer waiting time is 240 × 4 minutes = 960 minutes. The value of 960 minutes is $0.10 × 960 minutes = $96. You tell Marty that not only is 10 cents per minute quite conservative, but he could probably save most of that $96 of customer ill will if he hired another salesclerk. After much haggling, Marty agrees to provide you with all the chili dogs you can eat during a week-long period in exchange for your analysis of the results of having two clerks wait on the customers.

Assuming that Marty hires one additional salesclerk whose service rate equals Marty's rate, complete the analysis.

Solution We once again use the Exponential Service Times (M/M/s) queuing worksheet in ExcelModules. The arrival rate (λ) is 20 customers per hour, and the service rate (μ) is 30 customers per hour. There are, however, two servers now. We enter these values in cells B9, B10, and B11, respectively, as shown in Figure 9.18.

Figure 9.18: Operating Characteristics for Solved Problem 9–3: M/M/2 Queuing System

	A	B	C	D	E	F
1	Solved Problem 9-3					
2	Queuing Model	M/M/s (Exponential Service Times)				
3						
4	1. Both λ and μ must be RATES, and use the same time unit. For example, given a service time such as 10 minutes					
5	per customer, convert it to a service rate such as 6 per hour.					
6	2. The total service rate (rate x servers) must be greater than the arrival rate.					
7						
8	Input Data			Operating Characteristics		
9	Arrival rate (λ)	20		Average server utilization (ρ)	0.3333	
10	Service rate (μ)	30		Average number of customers in the queue (L_q)	0.0833	
11	Number of servers (s)	2		Average number of customers in the system (L)	0.7500	
12				Average waiting time in the queue (W_q)	0.0042	
13		2 servers		Average time in the system (W)	0.0375	
14				Probability (% of time) system is empty (P_0)	0.5000	
15						
16						W_q drops from
17						0.0667 hours to
18	Probabilities					0.0042 hours
19	Number of Units	Probability	Cumulative Probability			(= 0.25 minutes) with two servers.
20	0	0.5000	0.5000			
21	1	0.3333	0.8333			
22	2	0.1111	0.9444			
23	3	0.0370	0.9815			
24	4	0.0123	0.9938			
25	5	0.0041	0.9979			
36	16	0.0000	1.0000			
37	17	0.0000	1.0000			
38	18	0.0000	1.0000			
39	19	0.0000	1.0000			
40	20	0.0000	1.0000			

Hidden rows. See Companion Website for full file.

X File: Figure 9.18.xlsx

The operating characteristics of this queuing system are displayed in cells E9:E14. The probabilities that there are exactly n customers in the system, for $n = 0$ through 20, are shown in cells B20:B40.

You now have (240 customers) × (0.0042 hours) = 1 hour total customer waiting time per day. The total cost of 1 hour of customer waiting time is (60 minutes × ($0.10 per minute) = $6.

You are ready to point out to Marty that hiring one additional clerk will save $96 − $6 = $90 of customer ill will per 12-hour shift. Marty responds that the hiring should also reduce the number of people who look at the line and leave, as well as those who get tired of waiting in line and leave. You tell Marty that you are ready for two chili dogs, extra hot.

Discussion Questions

9–1. What is a queuing problem? What are the components in a queuing system?
9–2. What are the assumptions underlying common queuing models?
9–3. Describe the important operating characteristics of a queuing system.
9–4. Why must the service rate be greater than the arrival rate in a single-server queuing system?
9–5. Briefly describe three situations in which the FIFO discipline rule is not applicable in queuing analysis.

9-6. Provide examples of four situations in which there is a limited, or finite, waiting line.

9-7. What are the components of the following systems? Draw and explain the configuration of each.
(a) Barbershop
(b) Car wash
(c) Laundromat
(d) Small grocery store

9-8. Do doctors' offices generally have random arrival rates for patients? Are service times random? Under what circumstances might service times be constant?

9-9. Do you think the Poisson distribution, which assumes independent arrivals, is a good estimation of arrival rates in the following queuing systems? Defend your position in each case.
(a) Cafeteria in your school
(b) Barbershop
(c) Hardware store
(d) Dentist's office
(e) College class
(f) Movie theater

Problems

9-10. The Edge Convenience Store has approximately 300 customers shopping in its store between 9 A.M. and 5 P.M. on Saturdays. In deciding how many cash registers to keep open each Saturday, Edge's manager considers two factors: customer waiting time (and the associated waiting cost) and the service costs of employing additional checkout clerks. Checkout clerks are paid an average of $10 per hour. When only one is on duty, the waiting time per customer is about 10 minutes (or $\frac{1}{6}$ hour); when two clerks are on duty, the average checkout time is 6 minutes per person; 4 minutes when three clerks are working; and 3 minutes when four clerks are on duty.

Edge's management has conducted customer satisfaction surveys and has been able to estimate that the store suffers approximately $13 in lost sales and goodwill for every *hour* of customer time spent waiting in checkout lines. Using the information provided, determine the optimal number of clerks to have on duty each Saturday to minimize the store's total expected cost.

9-11. From historical data, Harry's Car Wash estimates that dirty cars arrive at a rate of 10 per hour all day Saturday. With a crew working the wash line, Harry figures that cars can be cleaned at a rate of one every five minutes. One car at a time is cleaned in this example of a single-server waiting line. Assuming Poisson arrivals and exponential service times, find the
(a) average number of cars in line

(b) average time a car waits before it is washed
(c) average time a car spends in the service system
(d) utilization rate of the car wash
(e) probability that no cars are in the system

9-12. Rockwell Electronics Corporation retains a service crew to repair machine breakdowns that occur on an average of $\lambda = 3$ per day (approximately Poisson in nature). The crew can service an average of $\mu = 8$ machines per day, with a repair time distribution that resembles the exponential distribution.
(a) What is the utilization rate of this service system?
(b) What is the average downtime for a broken machine?
(c) How many machines are waiting to be serviced at any given time?
(d) What is the probability that more than one machine is in the system? What is the probability that more than two machines are broken and waiting to be repaired or being serviced? More than three? More than four?

9-13. The people staffing the ticket booth at an aquarium can distribute tickets and brochures to 440 patrons every hour, according to an exponential distribution. On a typical day, an average of 352 people arrive every hour to gain entrance to the aquarium. The arrivals have been found to follow a Poisson distribution. The aquarium's manager wants to make the arrival process as convenient as possible for the patrons and so wishes to examine several queue operating characteristics.
(a) Find the average number of patrons waiting in line to purchase tickets.
(b) What percentage of the time is the ticket window busy?
(c) How much time, on average, does an aquarium visitor spend in the system?
(d) What is the average time spent waiting in line to get to the ticket window?
(e) What is the probability that there are more than two people in the system? More than three people?
(f) What is the probability that there are more than two people in line? More than three people?

9-14. A computer processes jobs on a first-come, first-served basis in a time-sharing environment. The jobs have Poisson arrival rates, with an average of six minutes between arrivals. The objective in processing these jobs is that they spend no more than eight minutes, on average, in the system. How fast does the computer have to process jobs, on average, to meet this objective?

9-15. An agent in a train station sells tickets and provides information to travelers. An average of two travelers approach the agent for assistance each minute. Their arrival is distributed according to a Poisson distribution. The agent is able to meet the travelers' needs in approximately 20 seconds, distributed exponentially.

(a) What is the probability that there are more than two travelers in the system? More than three? More than four?
(b) What is the probability that the system is empty?
(c) How long will the average traveler have to wait before reaching the agent?
(d) What is the expected number of travelers in the queue?
(e) What is the average number in the system?
(f) If a second agent is added (who works at the same pace as the first), how will the operating characteristics computed in parts (b), (c), (d), and (e) change? Assume that travelers wait in a single line and go to the first available agent.

9–16. The wheat harvesting season in the U.S. Midwest is short, and most farmers deliver their truckloads of wheat to a giant central storage bin within a two-week span. Because of this, wheat-filled trucks waiting to unload and return to the fields have been known to back up for a block at the receiving bin. The central bin is owned cooperatively, and it is to every farmer's benefit to make the unloading/storage process as efficient as possible. The cost of grain deterioration caused by unloading delays and the cost of truck rental and idle driver time are significant concerns to the cooperative members. Although farmers have difficulty quantifying crop damage, it is easy to assign a waiting and unloading cost for truck and driver of $18 per hour. The storage bin is open and operating 16 hours per day, seven days per week during the harvest season and is capable of unloading 35 trucks per hour, according to an exponential distribution. Full trucks arrive during the hours the bin is open, at a rate of about 30 per hour, following a Poisson pattern.

To help the cooperative get a handle on the problem of lost time while trucks are waiting in line or unloading at the bin, find the
(a) average number of trucks in the unloading system
(b) average time per truck in the system
(c) utilization rate for the bin area
(d) probability that there are more than three trucks in the system at any given time
(e) total daily cost to the farmers of having their trucks tied up in the unloading process
(f) The cooperative, as mentioned, uses the storage bin only two weeks per year. Farmers estimate that enlarging the bin would cut unloading costs by 50% next year. It will cost $9,000 to do so during the off-season. Would it be worth the cooperative's while to enlarge the storage area?

9–17. A restaurant's reservation agent takes reservations for dinner by telephone. If he is already on the phone when a patron calls to make a reservation, the incoming call is answered automatically, and the customer is asked to wait for the agent. As soon as the agent is free, the patron who has been on hold the

longest is transferred to the agent to be served. Calls for reservations come in at a rate of about 15 per hour. The agent can make a reservation in an average of three minutes. Calls tend to follow a Poisson distribution, and the times to make a reservation tend to be exponential. The agent is paid $15 per hour. The restaurant estimates that every minute a customer must wait to speak to the agent costs the restaurant $1.
- (a) What is the average time that diners must wait before their calls are transferred to the agent?
- (b) What is the average number of callers waiting to make a reservation?
- (c) The restaurant is considering adding a second agent, who would be paid the same $15 per hour, to take calls. Should it hire another agent? Explain.

9–18. Sal's International Barbershop is a popular haircutting and styling salon near the campus of the University of New Orleans. Four barbers work full time and spend an average of 15 minutes on each customer. Customers arrive all day long, at an average rate of 12 per hour. When they enter, they take a number to wait for the first available barber. Arrivals tend to follow the Poisson distribution, and service times are exponentially distributed.
- (a) What is the probability that the shop is empty?
- (b) What is the average number of customers in the barbershop?
- (c) What is the average time spent in the shop?
- (d) What is the average time that a customer spends waiting to be called to a chair?
- (e) What is the average number of customers waiting to be served?
- (f) What is the shop's utilization factor?
- (g) Sal's is thinking of adding a fifth barber. How will this affect the utilization rate?

9–19. Sal (see Problem 9–18) is considering changing the queuing characteristics of his shop. Instead of selecting a number for the first available barber, a customer will be able to select which barber he or she prefers upon arrival. Assuming that this selection does not change while the customer is waiting for his or her barber to become available and that the requests for each of the four barbers are evenly distributed, answer the following:
- (a) What is the average number of customers in the barber shop?
- (b) What is the average time spent in the shop?
- (c) What is the average time a customer spends waiting to be called to a chair?
- (d) What is the average number of customers waiting to be served?
- (e) Explain why the results from Problems 9–18 and 9–19 differ.

9–20. Carlos Gomez is the receiving supervisor for a large grocery store. Trucks arrive to the loading dock at an average rate of four per hour, according to a Poisson distribution, for 8 hours each day. The cost of operating a truck is estimated to be $80 per hour. Trucks are met by a three-person crew, which can unload a truck in an average of 12 minutes, according to an exponential distribution. The payroll cost associated with hiring a crew member, including benefits, is $22 per hour. Carlos is now considering the installation of new equipment to help the crew, which would decrease the average unloading time from 12 minutes to 9 minutes. The cost of this equipment would be about $500 per day. Is the installation of the new equipment economically feasible?

9-21. A local office of the Department of Motor Vehicles (DMV) wishes to overcome the reputation of making citizens wait in line for extremely long times before being able to conduct their business. Accordingly, the DMV is analyzing how best to serve the driving public. Its goal is to make sure that citizens will not have to wait more than five minutes before they are engaged in service with a clerk. The DMV currently has eight clerks to serve people. If a clerk is not busy with customers, he can fill his time with filing or processing mailed-in requests for service. On a typical day, drivers come into the DMV according to the following pattern:

Time	Arrival Rate (Customers/Hour)
8 A.M.–10 A.M.	20
10 A.M.–2 P.M.	40
2 P.M.–5 P.M.	25

Arrivals follow a Poisson distribution. Service times follow an exponential distribution, with an average of 10 minutes per customer. How many clerks should be on duty during each period to maintain the desired level of service? *Hint: Use Excel's* Goal Seek *procedure to find the answer.*

9-22. Julian Argo is a computer technician in a large insurance company. He responds to a variety of complaints from agents regarding their computers' performance. He receives an average of one computer per hour to repair, according to a Poisson distribution. It takes Julian an average of 50 minutes to repair any agent's computer. Service times are exponentially distributed.

(a) Determine the operating characteristics of the computer repair facility. What is the probability that there will be more than two computers waiting to be repaired?

(b) Julian believes that adding a second repair technician would significantly improve his office's efficiency. He estimates that adding an assistant, but still keeping the department running as a single-server system, would double the capacity of the office from 1.2 computers per hour to 2.4 computers per hour. Analyze the effect on the waiting times for such a change and compare the results with those found in part (a).

(c) Insurance agents earn $30 for the company per hour, on average, while computer technicians earn $18 per hour. An insurance agent who does not have access to his or her computer is unable to generate revenue for the company. What would be the hourly savings to the firm associated with employing two technicians instead of one?

9–23. Julian (see Problem 9–22) is considering putting the second technician in another office on the other end of the building, so that access to a computer technician is more convenient for the agents. Assume that the other agent will also have the ability to repair a computer in 50 minutes and that each faulty computer will go to the next available technician. Is this approach more cost-effective than the two approaches considered in Problem 9–22?

9–24. Bru-Thru is a chain of drive-through beer and wine outlets where customers arrive, on average, every five minutes. Management has a goal that customers will be able to complete their transaction, on average, in six minutes with a single server. Assume that this system can be described as an M/M/1 configuration. What is the average service time that is necessary to meet this goal?

9–25. Recreational boats arrive at a single gasoline pump located at the dock at Trident Marina at an average rate of 10 per hour on Saturday mornings. The fill-up time for a boat is normally distributed, with an average of 5 minutes and a standard deviation of 1.5 minutes. Assume that the arrival rate follows the Poisson distribution.
(a) What is the probability that the pump is vacant?
(b) On average, how long does a boat wait before the pump is available?
(c) How many boats, on average, are waiting for the pump?

9–26. A chemical plant stores spare parts for maintenance in a large warehouse. Throughout the working day, maintenance personnel go to the warehouse to pick up supplies needed for their jobs. The warehouse receives a request for supplies, on average, every 2 minutes. The average request requires 1.7 minutes to fill. Maintenance employees are paid $20 per hour, and warehouse employees are paid $12 per hour. The warehouse is open 8 hours each day. Assuming that this system follows the M/M/s requirements, what is the optimal number of warehouse employees to hire?

9–27. During peak times the entry gate at a large amusement park experiences an average arrival of 500 customers per minute, according to a Poisson distribution. The average customer requires four seconds to be processed through the entry gate. The park's goal is to keep the waiting time less than five seconds. How many entry gates are necessary to meet this goal?

9–28. Customers arrive at Valdez's Real Estate at an average rate of one per hour. Arrivals can be assumed to follow the Poisson distribution. Juan Valdez, the agent, estimates that he spends an average of 30 minutes with each customer. The standard deviation of service time is 15 minutes, and the service time distribution is arbitrary.
(a) Calculate the operating characteristics of the queuing system at Valdez's agency.

(b) What is the probability that an arriving customer will have to wait for service?

9–29. If Valdez wants to ensure that his customers wait an average of around 10 minutes, what should be his average service time? Assume that the standard deviation of service time remains at 15 minutes.

9–30. Customers arrive at an automated coffee vending machine at a rate of 4 per minute, following a Poisson distribution. The coffee machine dispenses a cup of coffee at a constant rate of 10 seconds.
(a) What is the average number of people waiting in line?
(b) What is the average number of people in the system?
(c) How long does the average person wait in line before receiving service?

9–31. Chuck's convenience store has only one gas pump. Cars pull up to the pump at a rate of one car every eight minutes. Depending on the speed at which the customer works, the pumping time varies. Chuck estimates that the pump is occupied for an average of five minutes, with a standard deviation of one minute. Calculate Chuck's operating characteristics. Comment on the values obtained. What, if anything, would you recommend that Chuck should do?

9–32. Get Connected, Inc., operates several Internet kiosks in Atlanta, Georgia. Customers can access the Web at these kiosks, paying $2 for 30 minutes or a fraction thereof. The kiosks are typically open for 10 hours each day and are always full. Due to the rough usage these PCs receive, they break down frequently. Get Connected has a central repair facility to fix these PCs. PCs arrive at the facility at an average rate of 0.9 per day. Repair times take an average of 1 day, with a standard deviation of 0.5 days.

Calculate the operating characteristics of this queuing system. How much is it worth to Get Connected to increase the average service rate to 1.25 PCs per day?

9–33. A construction company owns six backhoes, which each break down, on average, once every 10 working days, according to a Poisson distribution. The mechanic assigned to keeping the backhoes running is able to restore a backhoe to sound running order in 1 day, according to an exponential distribution.
(a) How many backhoes are waiting for service, on average?
(b) How many are currently being served?
(c) How many are in running order, on average?
(d) What is the average waiting time in the queue?
(e) What is the average wait in the system?

9–34. A technician monitors a group of five computers in an automated manufacturing facility. It takes an average of 15 minutes, exponentially distributed, to adjust any computer that develops a problem. The computers run for an average of 85 minutes, Poisson distributed, without requiring adjustments. Compute the following measures:

(a) average number of computers waiting for adjustment
(b) average number of computers not in working order
(c) probability the system is empty
(d) average time in the queue
(e) average time in the system

9–35. A copier repair person is responsible for servicing the copying machines for seven companies in a local area. Repair calls come in at an average of one call every other day. The arrival rate follows the Poisson distribution. Average service time per call, including travel time, is exponentially distributed, with a mean of two hours. The repair person works an eight-hour day.
(a) On average, how many hours per day is the repair person involved with service calls?
(b) How many hours, on average, does a customer wait for the repair person to arrive after making a call?
(c) What is the probability that more than two machines are out of service at the same time?

9–36. The Johnson Manufacturing Company operates six identical machines that are serviced by a single technician when they break down. Breakdowns occur according to the Poisson distribution and average 0.03 breakdowns per machine operating hour. Average repair time for a machine is five hours and follows the exponential distribution.
(a) What percentage of the technician's time is spent repairing machines?
(b) On average, how long is a machine out of service because of a breakdown?
(c) On average, how many machines are out of service?
(d) Johnson wants to investigate the economic feasibility of adding a second technician. Each technician costs the company $18 per hour. Each hour of machine downtime costs $120. Should a second technician be added?

9–37. A typical subway station in Washington, DC, has six turnstiles, each of which can be controlled by the station manager to be used for either entrance or exit control—but never for both. The manager must decide at different times of the day how many turnstiles to use for entering passengers and how many to use to allow passengers to exit.

At the Washington College Station, passengers enter the station at a rate of about 84 per minute between the hours of 7 and 9 A.M. Passengers exiting trains at the stop reach the exit turnstile area at a rate of about 48 per minute during the same morning rush hour. Each turnstile can allow an average of 30 passengers per minute to enter or exit. Arrival rates and service times have been thought to follow Poisson and exponential distributions, respectively. Assume that riders form a common queue at both entry and exit turnstile areas and proceed to the first empty turnstile.

The Washington College Station manager does not want the average passenger at his station to have to wait in a turnstile line for more than six seconds, nor does he want more than eight people in any queue at any average time.
(a) How many turnstiles should be opened in each direction every morning?
(b) Discuss the assumptions underlying the solution of this problem, using queuing theory.

9-38. A court clerk is responsible for receiving and logging legal documents that are to be placed before the various judges to review and sign. She receives these documents on a first-come, first-served basis. Lawyers' couriers arrive before the clerk at an average rate of eight per hour, according to a Poisson distribution. The time it takes the clerk to process the documents is normally distributed, with an average of six minutes and a standard deviation of two minutes.
(a) What is the probability that a courier will have to wait for service?
(b) On average, how many couriers will be waiting for service?
(c) How long is the average wait for service?

9-39. County General Hospital's cardiac care unit (CCU) has seven beds, which are virtually always occupied by patients who have just undergone heart surgery. Two registered nurses are on duty at the CCU in each of the three 8-hour shifts. On average, a patient requires a nurse's attention every 66 minutes. The arrival rate follows a Poisson distribution. A nurse will spend an average of 19 minutes (exponentially distributed) assisting a patient and updating medical records regarding the care provided.
(a) What percentage of the nurses' time is spent responding to these requests?
(b) What is the average time a patient spends waiting for one of the nurses to arrive at bedside?
(c) What is the average number of patients waiting for a nurse to arrive?
(d) What is the probability that a patient will not have to wait for a nurse to arrive?

9-40. Consider the Arnold's Muffler Shop example in Figure 9.8. Arnold has three chairs in the waiting room area.
(a) If all customers who bring their cars into the shop want to wait in the waiting room, what is the probability that someone will not have a seat?
(b) Arnold wants to provide a comfortable waiting room experience, so he would prefer that the probability that a customer has to stand is no more than 3%. How many more chairs will he need to purchase? *Hint: You may need to re-run the model in Excel to find out.*

9-41. A unique feature of the exponential distribution is that the standard deviation of its service *time* is equal to the mean of its service *time*.

(a) Run the M/M/1 model with an arrival rate of 15 customers per hour and a service rate of 20 customers per hour. What is the average waiting time in the queue (in minutes)?

(b) Now run the M/G/1 model with the same parameters as in part (a). Assume when running that model that the service time is exponentially distributed. What is the average waiting time in the queue (in minutes)? Is your answer the same as for part (a)?

9-42. A unique feature of the exponential distribution is that the standard deviation of its service *time* is equal to the mean of its service *time*.

(a) Run the M/M/1 model with an arrival rate of 20 customers per hour and a service rate of 25 customers per hour. What is the average waiting time in the queue (in minutes)?

(b) Now consider the M/G/1 model with the same parameters as in part (a). Assume when running that model that the service time is not exponentially distributed, and its standard deviation is .03 hours (= 1.8 minutes per customer). Before running the model, do you expect the waiting time to be greater than or less than that in part (a)? Run the model—what is the average waiting time in the queue (in minutes)? Did your answer confirm your intuition?

9-43. Lizao Zhang, owner of Lizao Zhang's Treats, is considering the purchase of three alternative self-serve sundae machines to serve customers. The average service time for all three machines is normally distributed with a mean of 40 seconds. However, the machines differ with regard to the consistency of their service times due to stalling, resetting, etc. Machine A is so consistent that it effectively has no variability. Machine B is less reliable and has a standard deviation of 20 seconds. Machine C is the least reliable with a standard deviation of 60 seconds. Customers love their ice cream in the hot summertime and arrive in the store about every 50 seconds (Poisson arrivals). Lizao estimates the cost of waiting due to lost goodwill as 10 cents per minute of waiting. The amortized cost per customer of operating Machine A is 50 cents, Machine B is 45 cents, and Machine C is 40 cents.

(a) How long will customers wait in line (in minutes) for each machine?

(b) Calculate the total cost per customer of using each machine. Which should be purchased?

9-44. Richard Muszynski's Gas and Wash has an automatic car wash, and customers purchasing gas at the station receive a discounted car wash, depending on the number of gallons of gas they buy. The car wash can accommodate one car at a time, and it takes exactly 5 minutes to wash each car. In addition, it is known that the average number of vehicles waiting in the line is 2.

(a) Use Goal Seek and the M/D/1 model to estimate the average arrival rate of vehicles to the car wash.

(b) How long does each vehicle wait in line on average (in minutes)?

9-45. Consider a standard M/M/1 queuing system at a bank with a single teller. You know that customers arrive at a rate of 40 per hour (Poisson distributed). If you also know that the teller is idle on average 2 hours out of her 8-hour day, estimate the average service time of this teller (in minutes). *Hint: You should be able to solve this problem by hand.*

9-46. If you look carefully at the formulas in this chapter for all four unlimited population models, you can verify that for each one, $L = \lambda W$ and $L_q = \lambda W_q$. These are instances of the more general relationship known as *Little's Law*, which states that for any steady state system, inventory equals average flow rate times average flow time. An advantage of using Little's Law is that we don't need to know the distributions of either the arrival process or the service process, the number of servers, or even the service priority rules. Given the relationship, if you know two of the values, then it is straightforward to solve for the third. For example, suppose that on average, Freddie's Fast Fish has approximately 500 pounds of fish in cold storage. Freddie cooks and serves about 150 pounds of fish each day. Using Little's Law, how long does the fish stay in storage on average?

9-47. During the evening hours, an average of 40 customers can be found in Gihan's Sports Bar. About 32 customers arrive each hour. Using Little's Law (see Problem 9-46), how long does each customer stay at Gihan's?

Chapter 10
Simulation Modeling

Have you ever played a video game? If so, you have experienced a computer *simulation*. Whether you're defending the earth from alien invaders, helping to save the princess, matching up against the NBA's best players, or being chased by annoying ghosts, each of these games presents some sort of model of reality into which we all can escape. And we are just now discovering the limitless potential of virtual reality simulators that transform our experience from simply looking at a screen into becoming enveloped within a full-sensory environment that feels like we're really there.

Organizations make extensive use of computer simulation to help analyze business processes. Most of the techniques in other chapters of this book apply well for very specific environments under very specific assumptions. As a general rule, the more complicated the environment becomes, the more likely it is that simulation will be the tool of choice to analyze it. An important feature of computer simulation is the ability to incorporate uncertain events and randomness into the model. Excel can handle many different kinds of computer simulation models. For even more complicated models, managers can write simulations using specialized Excel add-ins or powerful simulation-specific software packages.

We begin this chapter by defining simulation and describing its advantages and disadvantages. We next describe the steps involved in *Monte Carlo simulation*, which is the primary focus of this chapter. Generating random numbers for unknown variables plays a key role in Monte Carlo simulation. We illustrate random number generation for several common probability distributions using Excel. We then show how Excel's Data Table feature can be used to replicate the model numerous times and record the results. We further illustrate how Excel's Scenario Manager feature can be used to incorporate decisions into the simulation model by automatically running it for several combinations of input parameter values. The chapter includes four sections that illustrate a specific simulation example: (1) expected profit based on random demand, sales price, and cost; (2) inventory analysis based on random demand and lead time; (3) a waiting line problem based on random customer arrival times and service times according to discrete distributions; and (4) a revenue management model to help fill van seats for a limousine service with random reservation requests, walk-up customers, and no-shows. We end the chapter by briefly describing the two other major categories of simulation models: *operational gaming* and *systems simulation*.

Chapter Objectives

After completing this chapter, you will be able to:
1. Understand the basic steps of conducting a simulation.
2. Explain the advantages and disadvantages of simulation.
3. Tackle a wide variety of problems by using simulation.
4. Set up and solve simulation models by using Excel's standard functions.
5. Explain other types of simulation models.

10.1 Why Create a Simulation?

We are all aware to some extent of the importance of simulation models in our world. Boeing Corporation and Airbus Industries, for example, commonly build simulation models of their proposed jet airplanes and then test the aerodynamic properties of the models. Your local civil defense organization may carry out rescue and evacuation practices as it simulates the natural disaster conditions of a hurricane or tornado. The U.S. Army simulates enemy attacks and defense strategies in war games played on computers. Business students take courses that use management games to simulate realistic competitive business situations. And thousands of organizations develop simulation models to assist in making decisions involving their supply chain, inventory control, maintenance scheduling, plant layout, investments, and sales forecasting. Simulation is one of the most widely used decision modeling tools. Various surveys of the largest U.S. corporations reveal that most use simulation in corporate planning.

Simulation sounds like it may be the solution to all management problems. This is, unfortunately, by no means true. Yet we think you may find it one of the most flexible and fascinating of the decision modeling techniques in your studies. Let's begin our discussion of simulation with a simple definition.

Simulation Basics

To *simulate* is to try to duplicate the features, appearance, and characteristics of a real system. In this chapter, we show how to simulate a business or management system by building a *mathematical model* that comes as close as possible to representing the reality of the system. We won't build any *physical* models, as might be used in airplane wind tunnel simulation tests. But just as physical model airplanes are tested and modified under experimental conditions, we need to experiment with our mathematical models to estimate the effects of various actions. The idea behind simulation is to imitate a real-world situation mathematically, to then study its properties and operating characteristics, and, finally, to draw conclusions and make action decisions based on the results of the simulation. In this way, the real-life system is not touched until the advantages and disadvantages of what may be a major policy decision are first measured on the system's model.

To use simulation, a manager should (1) define a problem, (2) introduce the variables associated with the problem, (3) construct a mathematical model, (4) set up possible courses of action for testing, (5) run the experiment, (6) consider the results (possibly deciding to modify the model or change data inputs), and (7) decide what course of action to take. These steps are illustrated in Figure 10.1.

```
Define Problem
      ↓
Introduce Important Variables
      ↓
Construct Simulation Model
      ↓
Specify Values of Variables to Be Tested
      ↓
Conduct the Simulation
      ↓
Examine the Results
      ↓
Select Best Course of Action
```

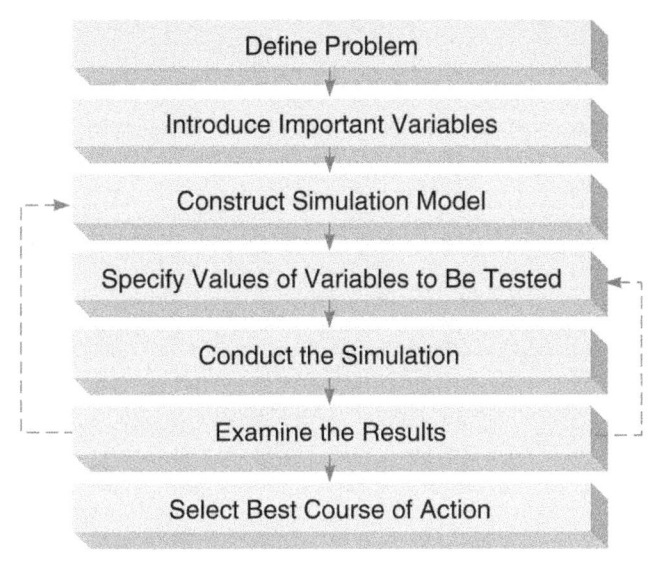

Figure 10.1: Process of Simulation

The problems tackled by simulation can range from very simple to extremely complex, from bank teller lines to an analysis of the U.S. economy. Although very small simulations can be conducted by hand, effective use of this technique requires some automated means of calculation—namely, a computer. Even large-scale models, simulating perhaps years of business decisions, can be handled in a reasonable amount of time by computer. Though simulation is one of the oldest decision modeling tools (see the *History* box), it was not until the introduction of computers in the mid-1940s and early 1950s that it became a practical means of solving management and military problems.

In this chapter, we explain the *Monte Carlo simulation* method and use it to model a variety of problems. For each simulation model, we show how the problem can be set up in Excel and solved using Excel's standard built-in functions. There are, however, several available add-ins (e.g., Crystal Ball and @Risk) that make setting up and solving simulation models on Excel even easier. We end this chapter by briefly discussing two other types of simulation models besides the Monte Carlo approach.

HISTORY

Simulation

The history of simulation goes back 5,000 years to Chinese war games, called *weich'i*, and continues through 1780, when the Prussians used the games to help train their army. Since then, all major military powers have used war games to test military strategies under simulated environments.

From military or operational gaming, a new concept, *Monte Carlo simulation*, was developed as a decision modeling technique by the great mathematician John von Neumann during World War II. Working with neutrons at the Los Alamos Scientific Laboratory, von Neumann used simulation to solve physics problems that were too complex or expensive to analyze by hand or with physical models. The random nature of the neutrons suggested the use of a roulette wheel in dealing with probabilities. Because of the gaming nature, von Neumann called it the Monte Carlo model of studying laws of chance.

With the advent and common use of business computers in the 1950s, simulation grew as a management tool. Specialized computer languages (GPSS and SIMSCRIPT) were developed in the 1960s to handle large-scale problems more effectively. Since the 1980s, prewritten simulation programs to handle situations ranging from queuing to inventory have been developed. A few of them are Arena, ProModel, SLAM, and WITNESS.

Advantages and Disadvantages of Simulation

Simulation is a tool that has become widely accepted by managers for several reasons. The main advantages of simulation are as follows:

1. It is relatively straightforward and flexible. Properly implemented, a simulation model can be made flexible enough to easily accommodate several changes to the problem scenario.
2. It can be used to analyze large and complex real-world situations that cannot be solved by using conventional decision models. For example, it may not be possible to build and solve a purely mathematical model of a city government system that incorporates important economic, social, environmental, and political factors. But simulation has been used successfully to model urban systems, hospitals, educational systems, national and state economies, and even world food systems.
3. Simulation allows what-if types of questions. With a simulation model, a manager can try out several policy decisions within a matter of minutes.
4. Simulations perform *risk analysis* by generating many possible results based on factors with inherent uncertainty. In addition to reporting average outcomes, simulations produce *distributions* of possible outcomes. This facilitates best case/worst case analysis, along with estimating probabilities of certain desirable or undesirable outcomes occurring.
5. Simulations do not interfere with the real-world system. It may be too disruptive, for example, to experiment with new policies or ideas in a hospital, school, or

manufacturing plant. With simulation, experiments are done with the model, not on the system itself.
6. Simulation allows us to study the interactive effects of individual components or variables to determine which ones are important. In any given problem scenario, not all inputs are equally important. We can use simulation to selectively vary each input (or combination of inputs) to identify the ones that most affect the results.
7. "Time compression" is possible with simulation. The effects of ordering, advertising, or other policies over many months or years can be obtained by a computer simulation model in a short time.
8. Simulation allows for the inclusion of real-world complications that most decision models cannot permit. For example, some of the queuing models discussed in Chapter 9 require exponential or Poisson distributions; the PERT analysis covered in Chapter 7 requires normal distributions. But simulation can use any probability distribution that the user defines.

The main disadvantages of simulation are as follows:

1. Good simulation models can be very expensive. It is often a long, complicated process to develop a model. A corporate planning model, for example, can take months or even years to develop.
2. Simulation does not generate optimal solutions to problems, as do other decision modeling techniques, such as linear programming or integer programming. It is a trial-and-error approach that can produce different solutions in repeated runs.
3. Managers must generate all the conditions and constraints for solutions that they want to examine. The simulation model does not produce answers by itself.
4. Each simulation model is unique. Its solutions and inferences are not usually transferable to other problems.

10.2 Monte Carlo Simulation

When a problem contains elements that exhibit chance or probability in their behavior, Monte Carlo simulation may be applied. The basic idea in Monte Carlo simulation is to randomly generate values for the unknown elements (i.e., variables) in the model through random sampling. The technique breaks down into simple steps. This section examines each of these steps in turn.

Steps of Monte Carlo Simulation
1. Establish a probability distribution for each variable in the model that is subject to chance.
2. Using random numbers, simulate values from the probability distribution for each variable in step 1.
3. Repeat the process for a series of replications (also called *runs*, or *trials*).

Step 1: Establish a Probability Distribution for Each Variable

Many variables in real-world systems are probabilistic in nature, and we might want to simulate them. A few of these variables are as follows:
- Product demand
- Lead time for orders to arrive
- Time between machine breakdowns
- Time between arrivals at a service facility
- Service time
- Time to complete a project activity
- Number of employees absent from work on a given day
- Stock market performance

There are several ways in which we can establish a *probability distribution* for a given variable. One common approach is to examine the historical outcomes of that variable. Then, we can compute the probability of each possible outcome of the variable by dividing the frequency of each observation by the total number of observations. Alternatively, we can use statistical goodness-of-fit tests to identify a commonly known probability distribution (e.g., normal, uniform, exponential, Poisson, binomial) that best characterizes the behavior of the variable. In practice, there are hundreds of probability distributions available to characterize the behavior of the various variables in a simulation model. In our study here, however, we will examine only a few of these probability distributions.

Harry's Auto Shop Example To illustrate how to establish a probability distribution for a variable, let us consider, for example, the monthly demand for radial tires at Harry's Auto Shop over the past 60 months. The data are shown in the first two columns of Table 10.1. If we assume that past demand rates will hold in the future, we can convert these data to a probability distribution for tire demand. To do so, we divide each demand frequency by the total number of months, 60. This is illustrated in the third column of Table 10.1.

Table 10.1: Historical Monthly Demand for Radial Tires at Harry's Auto Shop

Demand	Frequency	Probability
300	3	$3/60 = 0.05$
320	6	$6/60 = 0.10$
340	12	$12/60 = 0.20$
360	18	$18/60 = 0.30$
380	15	$15/60 = 0.25$
400	6	$6/60 = 0.10$

Step 2: Simulate Values from the Probability Distributions

Once we have established the probability distribution for a variable, how do we simulate random values from this distribution? As we shall see shortly, the procedure to do so varies, based on the type of probability distribution. In this section, let us see how we can use the probability distribution identified in Table 10.1 to simulate Harry's tire demand for a *specific* month in the future. Note that in simulating the demand for any given month, we need to ensure the following:

- The actual monthly demand value is 300, 320, 340, 360, 380, or 400.
- There is a 5% chance that the monthly demand is 300, 10% chance that it is 320, 20% chance that it is 340, 30% chance that it is 360, 25% chance that it is 380, and 10% chance that it is 400.

These probability values, however, reflect only the long-term behavior. That is, if we simulate tire demand for many months (several hundred, or, better yet, several thousand), the demand will be 300 for exactly 5% of the months, 320 for exactly 10% of the months, and so on. Based on our knowledge of probability distributions, we can also use these probability values to compute Harry's expected value (or average) of monthly demand, as follows:

$$\text{Expected monthly demand} = \sum_i (i\text{th demand value}) \times (\text{Probability of } i\text{th demand value})$$
$$= 300 \times 0.05 + 320 \times 0.10 + 340 \times 0.20 + 360 \times 0.30$$
$$+ 380 \times 0.25 + 400 \times 0.10$$
$$= 358 \text{ tires}$$

In the short term, however, the occurrence of demand may be quite different from these probability values. For example, if we simulate demand for just five months, it is entirely possible (and logical) for the demand to be 320 tires per month for *all* five months. The average demand for these five months would then be 320 tires per month, which is quite different from the expected value of 358 tires per month we just calculated. Hence, what we need is a procedure that will achieve the following objectives:

- Generate, in the *short term*, random demand values that do not exhibit any specific pattern. The expected value need not necessarily equal 358 tires per month.
- Generate, in the *long term*, random demand values that conform exactly to the required probability distribution. The expected value must equal 358 tires per month.

In simulation, we achieve these objectives by using a concept called *random numbers*.

Random Numbers A random number is a number that has been selected through a totally random process. For example, assume that we want to generate a series of random numbers from a set consisting of 100 integer-valued numbers: 0, 1, 2, ..., 97, 98, 99. There are several ways to do so. One simple way would be as follows:
1. Mark each of 100 identical balls with a unique number between 0 and 99. Put all the balls in a large bowl and mix thoroughly.
2. Select *any* ball from the bowl. Write down the number.
3. Return the ball to the bowl and mix again. Go back to step 2.

Instead of balls in a bowl, we could have accomplished this task by using the spin of a roulette wheel with 100 slots, or by using tables of random digits that are commonly available.[1] Also, as we shall see shortly, it turns out that most computer software packages (including Excel) and many handheld calculators have built-in procedures for generating an endless set of random numbers.

Using Random Numbers to Simulate Demand in Harry's Auto Shop How do we use random numbers to simulate Harry's tire demand? We begin by converting the probability distribution in Table 10.1 to a *cumulative probability* distribution. As shown in Table 10.2, the cumulative probability for each demand value is the sum of the probability of that demand and all demands *less than* that demand value. For example, the cumulative probability for a demand of 340 tires is the sum of the probabilities for 300, 320, and 340 tires. Obviously, the cumulative probability for a demand of 400 tires (the maximum demand) is 1.

Table 10.2: Cumulative Probabilities for Radial Tires at Harry's Auto Shop

Demand	Probability	Cumulative Probability
300	0.05	0.00 + 0.05 = 0.05
320	0.10	0.05 + 0.10 = 0.15
340	0.20	0.15 + 0.20 = 0.35
360	0.30	0.35 + 0.30 = 0.65
380	0.25	0.65 + 0.25 = 0.90
400	0.10	0.90 + 0.10 = 1.00

Consider the set of 100 integer-valued numbers ranging from 0 to 99. We now use the cumulative probabilities computed in Table 10.2 to create *random number intervals* by assigning these 100 numbers to represent the different possible demand values. Because there is a 5% probability that demand is 300 tires, we assign 5% of the numbers (i.e., 5 of the 100 numbers between 0 and 99) to denote this demand value.

---

[1] See, for example, *A Million Random Digits with 100,000 Normal Deviates*. New York: The Free Press, 1955, p. 7.

For example, we could assign the first 5 numbers possible (i.e., 0, 1, 2, 3, and 4) to denote a demand of 300 tires. Every time the random number drawn is one of these five numbers, the implication is that the simulated demand that month is 300 tires. Likewise, because there is a 10% chance that demand is 320 tires, we could let the next 10 numbers (i.e., 5 to 14) represent that demand—and so on for the other demand values. The complete random number intervals for the Harry's Auto Shop problem are shown in Table 10.3. It is important to note that the specific random numbers assigned to denote a demand value are not relevant, as long as the assignment is unique and includes the right proportion of numbers. That is, for example, we can use any set of 5 random numbers between 0 and 99 to denote a demand value of 300 tires, as long as these numbers are not assigned to denote any other demand level.

Table 10.3: Random Number Intervals for Radial Tires at Harry's Auto Shop

Demand	Probability	Cumulative Probability	Random Number Interval
300	0.05	0.05	0 to 4
320	0.10	0.15	5 to 14
340	0.20	0.35	15 to 34
360	0.30	0.65	35 to 64
380	0.25	0.90	65 to 89
400	0.10	1.00	90 to 99

To simulate demand using the random number intervals, we need to generate random numbers between 0 and 99. Suppose we use a computer for this purpose (we will see how to do so shortly). Assume that the first random number generated is 52. Because this is between 35 and 64, it implies that the simulated demand in month 1 is 360 tires. Now assume that the second random number generated is 6. Because this is between 5 and 14, it implies that the simulated demand in month 2 is 320 tires. The procedure continues in this fashion.

Step 3: Repeat the Process for a Series of Replications

As noted earlier, although the long-term average demand is 358 tires per month in Harry's example, it is likely that we will get different average values from a short-term simulation of just a few months. It would be very risky to draw any hard-and-fast conclusion regarding any simulation model from just a few simulation replications. We need to run the model for several thousand replications (also referred to as *runs*, or *trials*) in order to gather meaningful results.

Decision Modeling In Action

Simulating a Production Line at Delphi

Delphi Corporation, a major supplier of fuel injectors to automobile manufacturers, was considering a new line that would produce the next generation of fuel injectors. In order for the line to be financially viable, it needed to have a high throughput, be cost effective to build, and be able to fit in the available space. To address this issue, Delphi used a simulation model at a very early design stage to serve as a test bed for several candidate line designs.

Simulating a line design involves fully specifying various details, such as which machines to use, in what order, conveyor lengths, machine process rates, failure and repair distributions for each machine, etc. Although such detailed information is typically not available at the concept stage of a line design, this is precisely when simulation helps to assess a line's potential performance characteristics. A major advantage of using simulation at such an early stage is that implementing the model's recommendations is inexpensive because the equipment has not yet been built. In contrast, the model's recommendations may be more difficult to cost justify after the equipment has been built since much of the cost has already been sunk.

The simulation analysis has provided and continues to provide Delphi with valuable guidance for the layout, loading, and staffing of the new production line.

Source: Based on M. H. Tongarlak et al. "Using Simulation Early in the Design of a Fuel Injector Production Line," *Interfaces* 40, 2 (March–April 2010): 105–117.

10.3 Role of Computers in Simulation

Although it is possible to simulate small examples such as the Harry's Auto Shop problem by hand, it is easier and much more convenient to conduct most simulation exercises by using a computer. Three of the primary reasons for this follow:

1. It is quite cumbersome to use hand-based random-number generation procedures for even common probability distributions, such as the normal, uniform, and exponential distributions. As noted earlier, most computer software packages (including Excel) have built-in procedures for generation of random numbers. It is quite easy to simulate values from many probability distributions by using a software package's random-number generator.
2. For the simulation results to be valid and useful, it is necessary to replicate the process hundreds (or even thousands) of times. Doing this by hand is laborious and time-consuming. In contrast, it is possible to simulate thousands of replications for a model in just a matter of seconds by using most software packages.
3. During the simulation process, depending on the complexity and scope of the model, we may need to manipulate many input parameters and keep track of several output measures. Here again, doing so by hand could become very cumbersome. Software packages, on the other hand, can be used to easily change multiple input values and track as many output measures as required in any simulation model.

Types of Simulation Software Packages

Three types of software packages are available to help set up and run simulation models on computers, as discussed in the following sections.

General-Purpose Programming Languages General-purpose programming languages that can be used to set up and run simulation models include standard programming languages such as Visual Basic, C++, and Fortran. The main advantage of these languages is that an experienced programmer can use them to develop simulation models for many diverse situations. The big disadvantage, however, is that a program written for a simulation model is specific to that model and is not easily portable. That is, a simulation model developed for one problem or situation may not be easily transferable to a different situation.

Special-Purpose Simulation Languages and Programs Languages such as GPSS, Simscript III, and Visual SLAM and programs such as Arena, Extend, MicroSaint Sharp, BuildSim, AweSim, ProModel, and Xcell can be used to set up and run simulation models. Using such special-purpose languages and programs has three advantages compared with using general-purpose languages: (1) They require less programming time for large simulations, (2) they are usually more efficient and easier to check for errors, and (3) they have built-in procedures to automate many of the tasks in simulation modeling. However, because of the significant learning curve associated with these languages, they are typically likely to be most useful to experienced modelers dealing with extremely complex simulation models.

Spreadsheet Models The built-in ability to generate random numbers and use them to select values from several probability distributions makes spreadsheets excellent tools for conducting simple simulations. Spreadsheets are also very powerful for quickly tabulating results and presenting them using graphs. In keeping with the focus of this book, we therefore use Excel in this chapter to develop several simulation models.

Random Generation from Some Common Probability Distributions Using Excel

In the following pages, we discuss how we can use Excel's built-in functions to generate random values from seven commonly used probability distributions in simulation models: (1) continuous uniform, (2) discrete uniform, (3) normal, (4) exponential, (5) binomial, (6) discrete general with two outcomes, and (7) discrete general with more than two outcomes.

Generating Random Numbers in Excel Excel uses the RAND function to generate random numbers. The format for using this function is

$$= \text{RAND}()$$

Note that the = sign before the RAND function implies that the cell entry is a formula. Also, there is no argument within the parentheses—that is, the left parenthesis is immediately followed by the right parenthesis.

If we enter =RAND() in any cell of a spreadsheet, it will return a random value between 0 and 1 (actually, between 0 and 0.9999 ...) *each time you press the calculate key* (i.e., the F9 key). The RAND function can be used either by itself in a cell or as part of a formula. For example, to generate a random number between 0 and 4.9999 ..., the appropriate formula to use would simply be

$$= 5*\text{RAND}()$$

Continuous Uniform Distribution A variable follows a continuous uniform distribution between a lower limit a and an upper limit b if all equally sized intervals between a and b are equally likely. The variable from a continuous distribution can take on a fractional value. To simulate a variable that follows this distribution, we use the following formula:

$$= a + (b-a)*\text{RAND}()$$

For example, if $a=3$ and $b=9$, we know that $=(9-3)*\text{RAND}()$ will generate a random value between 0 and 5.9999.... If we add this to 3, we will get a random value between 3 and 8.999 ... (which, for all practical purposes, is 9).

Discrete Uniform Distribution If all values between a and b are equally likely, but the variable is allowed to take on only *integer* values between a and b (inclusive), we refer to this as a discrete uniform distribution. To generate values randomly from this distribution, there are two different approaches we can use in Excel. First, we can extend the preceding formula for continuous uniform distributions by including Excel's INT function. The resulting formula is

$$= \text{INT}(a + (b-a+1)*\text{RAND}())$$

Note that we need to add 1 to the $(b-a)$ term in this formula because the INT function always rounds down (that is, it just drops the fractional part from the value).

Alternatively, Excel has a built-in function called RANDBETWEEN that we can use to generate random values from discrete uniform distributions between a and b. The format for this function is

$$= \text{RANDBETWEEN}(a, b)$$

So, for example, if we want to generate random integers between 0 and 99 (as we did in the Harry's Auto Shop example earlier), we can use either of these two Excel formulas:

$$= \text{INT}(100*\text{RAND}()) \quad \text{or} \quad = \text{RANDBETWEEN}(0,99)$$

Normal Distribution   The normal distribution is probably one of the most commonly used distributions in simulation models. The normal distribution is always identified by two parameters: mean μ and standard deviation σ (or variance σ^2). To simulate a random value from a normal distribution with mean μ and standard deviation σ, we use the NORMINV function in Excel as follows:

$$=\text{NORMINV}(\text{RAND}(),\mu,\sigma)$$

For example, the formula =NORMINV(RAND(),30,5) will generate a random value from a normal distribution with a mean of 30 and a standard deviation of 5. If we repeat this process several thousand times, 50% of the values will be below 30 and 50% will be above 30, 68.26% will be between 25 and 35 (= mean ± 1 standard deviation), and so on. Note that a normally distributed random value will include fractions because the normal distribution is a continuous distribution. If we need to convert normally distributed random values to integers, we can do so by using Excel's ROUND function as follows:

$$=\text{ROUND}(\text{NORMINV}(\text{RAND}(),\mu,\sigma),0)$$

The argument of 0 in the ROUND function specifies that we want to round off fractional values to the nearest number with zero decimal places (i.e., integer). In this case, fractional values of 0.5 and above are rounded up, while fractional values below 0.5 are rounded down.

In some situations, we may need to truncate the value generated from a normal distribution. For example, if we randomly generate demand values from a normal distribution with a mean of 10 and a standard deviation of 4, it is possible that the generated value is sometimes negative. Because demand cannot be negative, we may need to truncate the generated demand by setting any negative value to zero. A simple way of doing so is to use Excel's MAX function, as follows:

$$=\text{MAX}(0,\text{NORMINV}(\text{RAND}(),10,4))$$

Exponential Distribution   The exponential distribution is commonly used to model arrival and service times in queuing systems. (You may recall that we saw a few examples of this in Chapter 9.) The exponential distribution can be described by a single parameter, μ, which describes the average *rate* of occurrences. (Alternatively, $1/\mu$ describes the mean time between successive occurrences.) To simulate a random value from an exponential distribution with average rate μ, we use the following formula in Excel:

$$=-(1/\mu)*LN(RAND())$$

where LN in the formula refers to the natural logarithmic function.

For example, if the average service rate in a queuing system is 10 customers per hour, the service *time* (in hours) for a specific customer may be randomly generated by using the following formula:

$$=-(1/10)*LN(RAND())$$

Binomial Distribution The binomial distribution models the probability of the number of successes occurring in *n* independent events (called trials), where each event has the same two outcomes, which we will label success and failure, and the probability of success in each event is the same value, *p*. To simulate a random number of successes in the *n* trials, we use the CRITBINOM function in Excel as follows:[2]

$$=CRITBINOM(n,p,RAND())$$

Discrete General Distribution with Two Outcomes If the outcomes of a probability distribution are discrete but the probabilities of the various outcomes are *not* the same, we refer to this as a discrete general distribution (as opposed to a discrete uniform distribution, where all outcomes have the same probability).

Let us first consider a discrete general distribution with only two outcomes. Suppose we want to randomly select individuals from a population where there are 55% males and 45% females. This implies that in the long term, our selected group will have exactly 55% males and 45% females. However, in the short term, any combination of males and females is possible and logical. To simulate these random draws in Excel, we can use the IF function as follows:

$$=IF(RAND()<0.55,\text{"Male"},\text{"Female"})$$

Note that the quotes are needed in the IF function because Male and Female are both text characters. If we use numeric codes (e.g., 1 = Male, 2 = Female) instead of text characters, the formula is then

$$=IF(RAND()<0.55,1,2)$$

Because RAND() has a 55% chance of returning a value between 0 and 0.55 (which implies it has a 45% chance of returning a value between 0.55 and 0.999...), the preceding formula is logical. Note that we could have set up the IF function such that *any* 55% of values between 0 and 1 denotes male and the other 45% denotes female. For example, we could have expressed the formula as follows:

---

[2] Starting with Excel 2010, an additional function called BINOM.INV is available, which is an improved version of CRITBINOM and uses the same arguments.

=IF(RAND()<0.45,"Female","Male")

If we replicate the simulation enough times, the male-to-female split will be the same (i.e., 55% male and 45% female), regardless of how the IF function is set up.

Discrete General Distribution with More Than Two Outcomes Let us now consider a discrete general distribution with more than two outcomes by revisiting the Harry's Auto Shop example. The demand for tires is one of six values: 300, 320, 340, 360, 380, or 400. However, unlike with the discrete uniform distribution, in this case the probability of demand for each value is not the same.

We want to use Excel to simulate demands randomly from this distribution, just as we did manually in Table 10.3 using random number intervals. To do so, a more experienced Excel user could use a *nested* IF function (i.e., IF function within IF function). However, it is probably more convenient to use Excel's LOOKUP, VLOOKUP, or HLOOKUP functions to randomly select values from this type of probability distribution. In our discussion here, we illustrate the use of the LOOKUP function.

Figure 10.2 shows the Excel layout showing the formulas for setting up a LOOKUP function. We begin by arranging all the demand values in a column (say, column A). Titles, like the ones shown in row 1, are optional. We then list the probability of each demand in another column (say, column B). In Figure 10.2, we have shown the demand values in cells A2:A7 and the corresponding probabilities in cells B2:B7.

Just as we did in Table 10.3, we now create the *random number intervals*. The only difference is that instead of using two-digit random numbers from 0 to 99, we use continuous-valued random numbers from 0 to 0.9999. The formulas to compute the random number intervals for Harry's example are shown in cells C2:D7 of Figure 10.2. The actual values are shown in Figure 10.3. Notice that the lower-limit numbers in cells C2:C7 are identical to the ones we developed in Table 10.3. The upper-limit numbers are slightly different because we used discrete random numbers in Table 10.3 and we are using continuous random numbers here. Although we have shown the random number intervals in columns that are adjacent to the demand and probability values here, these could be in any location of the spreadsheet.

EXCEL NOTES

- The Companion Website for this book, at *degruyter.com/view/product/486941*, contains the Excel file for each sample problem discussed here. The relevant file/sheet name is shown below the title of the corresponding figure in this book.

- For clarity, our simulation worksheets are color coded as follows:
  - *Input cells*, where we enter known data, are shaded yellow.
  - *Simulation cells*, which show simulated values, are shaded blue.
  - *Output cells*, where the results are shown, are shaded green.

- When you open any of the Excel files for the examples in this chapter, if the Calculation options in Excel is set to automatic (click Formulas|Calculation options|Automatic), Excel will automatically recalculate all random numbers in the model. This, in turn, may cause all simulated values in the worksheet to change. Hence, the values you see in the Excel file may not be the same as those shown in the screenshots included in the book.

- *Tip:* After creating a simulation model, if you wish to save your results in such a way that the values do *not* change each time you open the Excel file, you can set the Calculation options in Excel to manual (click Formulas|Calculation options|Manual). Alternatively, you can use the Paste Values feature in Excel (see Appendix B for details). You can copy the cells showing the results and use Paste Values to save your answers as values rather than as formulas. Remember, however, that any cell overwritten in this manner will no longer contain the formula.

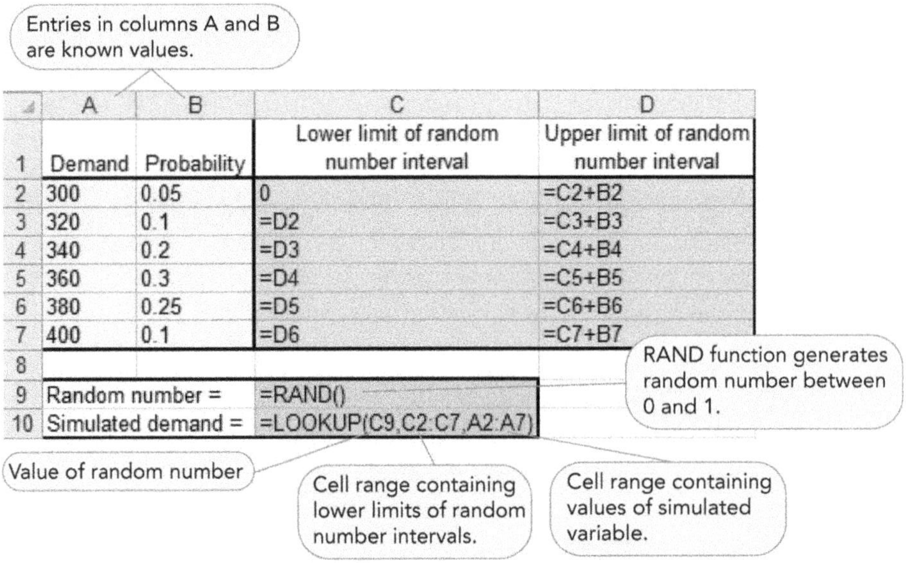

Entries in columns A and B are known values.

	A	B	C	D
1	Demand	Probability	Lower limit of random number interval	Upper limit of random number interval
2	300	0.05	0	=C2+B2
3	320	0.1	=D2	=C3+B3
4	340	0.2	=D3	=C4+B4
5	360	0.3	=D4	=C5+B5
6	380	0.25	=D5	=C6+B6
7	400	0.1	=D6	=C7+B7
8				
9	Random number =		=RAND()	
10	Simulated demand =		=LOOKUP(C9,C2:C7,A2:A7)	

Value of random number

Cell range containing lower limits of random number intervals.

Cell range containing values of simulated variable.

RAND function generates random number between 0 and 1.

Figure 10.2: Excel Layout and Formulas for a LOOKUP Function

File: Figure 10.2.xlsx, Sheet: Figure 10.2

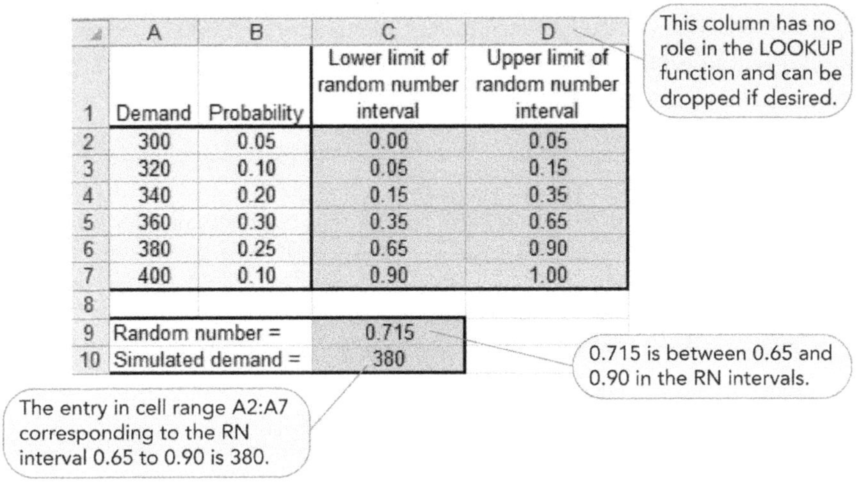

	A	B	C	D
1	Demand	Probability	Lower limit of random number interval	Upper limit of random number interval
2	300	0.05	0.00	0.05
3	320	0.10	0.05	0.15
4	340	0.20	0.15	0.35
5	360	0.30	0.35	0.65
6	380	0.25	0.65	0.90
7	400	0.10	0.90	1.00
8				
9	Random number =		0.715	
10	Simulated demand =		380	

Column D: *This column has no role in the LOOKUP function and can be dropped if desired.*

0.715 is between 0.65 and 0.90 in the RN intervals.

The entry in cell range A2:A7 corresponding to the RN interval 0.65 to 0.90 is 380.

Figure 10.3: Simulation Using a LOOKUP Function

File: Figure 10.2.xlsx, Sheet: Figure 10.3

The format for the LOOKUP function is

$$=\text{LOOKUP}(\text{RAND}(),\text{C2:C7},\text{A2:A7})$$

The first cell range in the LOOKUP function must contain the *lower limits* of the random number intervals (i.e., cells C2:C7). Excel takes the value generated by the RAND() function and proceeds down this column to identify the entry where the RAND() value exceeds the lower limit. It then moves to the other range specified in the LOOKUP function (i.e., cells A2:A7) and selects the corresponding entry shown there. In our case, this range has the demand value that we wish to simulate.[3]

Let's suppose the random number generated is 0.715 (shown in cell C9 of Figure 10.3). Using the preceding logic, the LOOKUP function compares this number to the entries in the cell range C2:C7. Having recognized that 0.715 exceeds the fifth entry (0.65) in the range but not the sixth (0.90), it returns the fifth entry in the cell range A2:A7. This is cell A6 (also shown in cell C10), which corresponds to a demand value of 380 tires.[4]

---

[3] Note that the upper limit of the random number interval (cells D2:D7) plays no role in the LOOKUP function. In fact, it is not necessary to even show this column, and we can safely delete it. However, we have included these entries in all our models here to make it easier to understand the use of the LOOKUP function.

[4] In this example, we have shown the value of the random number separately in cell C9 and used this number in the formula in cell C10. Note that the RAND() function could have been directly embedded in the LOOKUP formula itself. Except for the simulation model discussed in section 10.4, we do not show the random number values separately in our models.

For your convenience, Table 10.4 presents a summary of the Excel formulas we have presented so far for simulating random values from various probability distributions. In the following sections, we describe four simulation models that use these formulas for their implementation.

Table 10.4: Simulation from Various Probability Distributions Using Excel's Built-in Formulas

To Simulate	Use Built-in Excel Formula
Random number	=RAND()
Continuous uniform distribution	=a+(b−a)*RAND()
Between a and b	
Discrete uniform distribution	=INT(a+(b−a+1)*RAND()) or
Between a and b	=RANDBETWEEN(a,b)
Normal distribution	=NORMINV(RAND(), μ, σ)
Mean = μ; Standard deviation = σ	
Exponential distribution	=−(1/μ)*LN(RAND())
Mean rate = μ	
Binomial distribution	=CRITBINOM(n, p, RAND())
Number of events = n	
Probability of success in each event = p	
Discrete general distribution with two outcomes only: A and B	=IF(RAND()<p, A, B)
Probability of outcome A = p	
Discrete general distribution with more than two outcomes:	=LOOKUP(RAND(), Range1, Range2)
Range1 = Cell range containing lower limits of the random number intervals	
Range2 = Cell range containing the variable values	

10.4 Simulation Model to Compute Expected Profit

Let us set up the Harry's Auto Shop example as our first simulation model. Recall from Table 10.1 that Harry's monthly demand of tires is 300, 320, 340, 360, 380, or 400, with specific probabilities for each value. Now let us assume that the following additional information is known regarding Harry's operating environment:

- Depending on competitors' prices and other market conditions, Harry estimates that his average selling price per tire each month follows a discrete uniform distribution between $60 and $80 (in increments of $1).
- Harry's variable cost per tire also varies each month, depending on material costs and other market conditions. This causes Harry's average profit margin per tire (calculated as a percentage of the selling price) to vary each month. Using past data, Harry estimates that his profit margin per tire follows a continuous uniform distribution between 20% and 30% of the selling price.

- Harry estimates that his fixed cost of stocking and selling tires is $2,000 per month.

Using this information, let us simulate and calculate Harry's *average profit* per month from the sale of auto tires.

Setting Up the Model

In any simulation model, the first issue we need to understand is what we mean by *one replication* of the model. In Harry's case, each replication corresponds to simulating one month of tire sales. That is, we will set up the model to simulate one month of tire sales at Harry's Auto Shop and then run the model repeatedly for as many replications as desired. The logic of Harry's simulation process is presented in Figure 10.4. Such flow diagrams, or flowcharts, are very useful in understanding the logical sequence of events in simulation models, especially in complex problem scenarios.

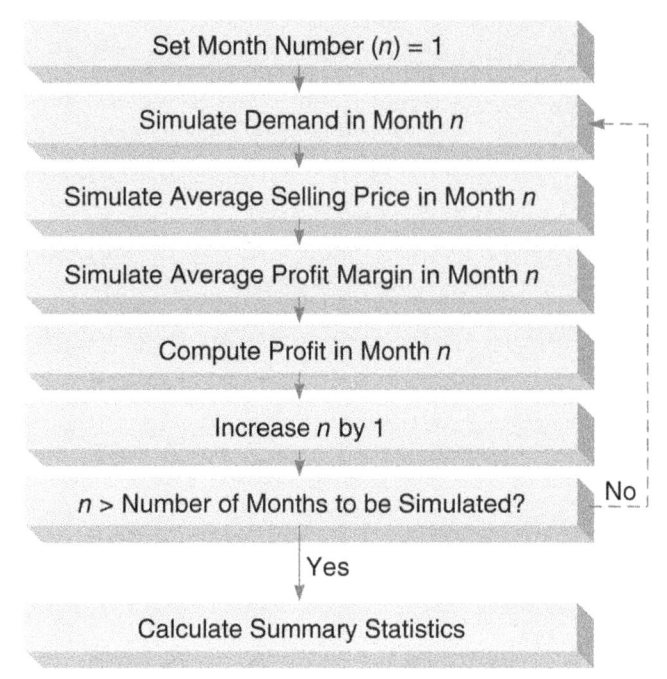

```
Set Month Number (n) = 1
          ↓
Simulate Demand in Month n  ←---
          ↓                    |
Simulate Average Selling Price in Month n
          ↓                    |
Simulate Average Profit Margin in Month n
          ↓                    |
Compute Profit in Month n      |
          ↓                    |
Increase n by 1                |
          ↓                    |
n > Number of Months to be Simulated?  --No--
          ↓ Yes
Calculate Summary Statistics
```

Figure 10.4: Flowchart for Harry's Auto Shop Simulation Model

Let us now translate the flowchart in Figure 10.4 into a simulation model, using Excel. Figure 10.5 shows the formula view of the Excel layout for Harry's model. All titles, like the ones shown in rows 1 and 3, are optional. For a given replication, the spreadsheet is organized as follows:
- Cell A4 generates the random number used to simulate the demand that month. For this model alone, we show the actual value of the random number used to simulate each variable value.

- The random number in cell A4 is used in a LOOKUP function to simulate the monthly demand in cell B4. The data (demands, probabilities, and random number intervals) of the LOOKUP function are shown in cells I4:L9.
- In cell C4, we simulate the average selling price per tire by using the RANDBETWEEN function (with $a = 60$ and $b = 80$). The formula is =RANDBETWEEN(60,80).
- Cell D4 generates the random number used to simulate the average profit margin per tire.
- The random number in cell D4 is used in cell E4 to simulate the average profit margin per tire. For this, we use the continuous uniform distribution formula, with $a = 0.2$ and $b = 0.3$. The formula is = 0.2 + (0.3−0.2)* D4.
- Cell F4 shows the fixed cost, equal to $2,000 per month.
- Using these simulated values, Harry's monthly profit is calculated in cell G4 as

$$\text{Profit} = (\text{Demand for tires}) \times (\text{Average selling price per tire})$$
$$\times (\text{Average profit margin per tire}) - (\text{Monthly fixed cost})$$

That is, the formula in cell G4 is =B4*C4*E4-F4.

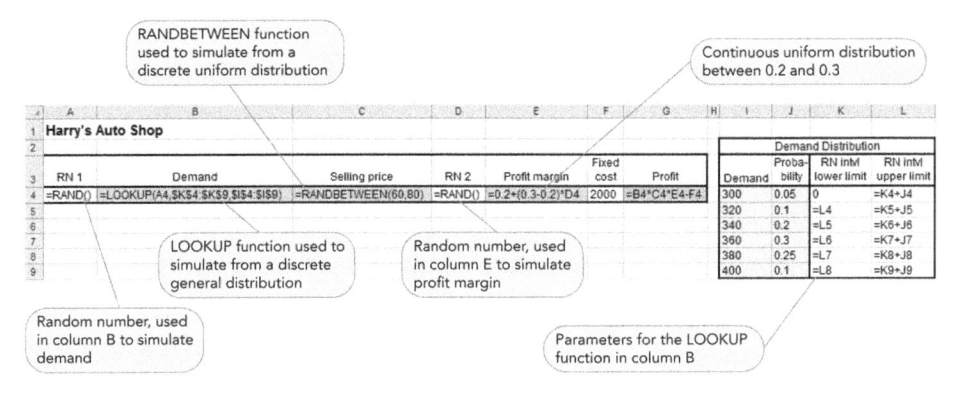

Figure 10.5: Excel Layout and Formulas for Harry's Auto Shop

File: Figure 10.5.xlsx, Sheet: Figure 10.5

Figure 10.6 shows the result for a single replication of Harry's simulation model. This result indicates that Harry will earn a profit of $4,125.52 per month. It is important to remember, however, that each randomly simulated value only represents something that *could* occur. As such, there is no guarantee that the specific values simulated in Figure 10.6 will actually occur. Due to the presence of random numbers, these simulated values will change each time the model is replicated (i.e., they will change each time the F9 key is pressed in Excel). Hence, it would be incorrect to estimate Harry's profit based on just one replication (month).

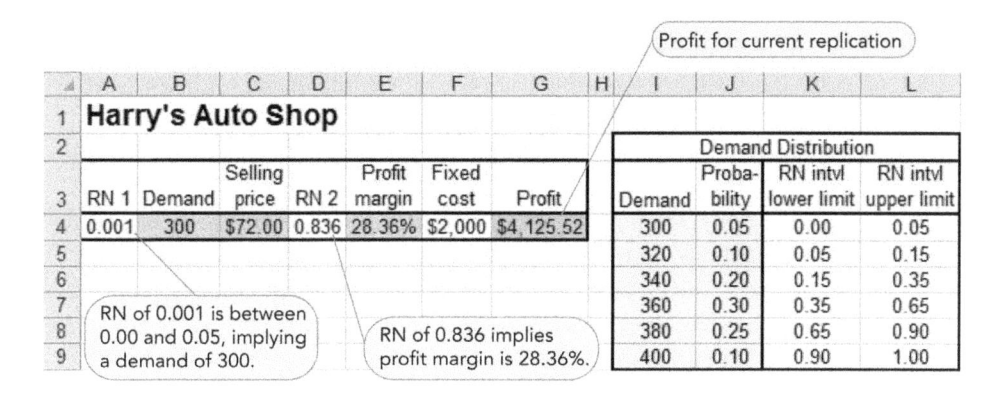

Simulation Model to Compute Expected Profit — 585

	A	B	C	D	E	F	G	H	I	J	K	L
1	Harry's Auto Shop											
2										Demand Distribution		
3	RN 1	Demand	Selling price	RN 2	Profit margin	Fixed cost	Profit		Demand	Proba-bility	RN intvl lower limit	RN intvl upper limit
4	0.001	300	$72.00	0.836	28.36%	$2,000	$4,125.52		300	0.05	0.00	0.05
5									320	0.10	0.05	0.15
6									340	0.20	0.15	0.35
7	RN of 0.001 is between								360	0.30	0.35	0.65
8	0.00 and 0.05, implying			RN of 0.836 implies					380	0.25	0.65	0.90
9	a demand of 300.			profit margin is 28.36%.					400	0.10	0.90	1.00

Cell G4 annotation: Profit for current replication

Figure 10.6: Results for the Simulation Model of Harry's Auto Shop

File: Figure 10.5.xlsx, Sheet: Figure 10.6

To calculate Harry's *average* monthly profit, we need to replicate the simulation model several thousand times. However, in order to keep the computation times reasonable (especially in a classroom setting) and to keep the size of the resulting Excel files relatively small, we illustrate only 200 replications in most of our models in this chapter. We then compute summary statistics just from these 200 replications. It is important to note that 200 replications are not enough for a simulation model to yield consistent summary results. That is, an average based on just 200 replications, for example, will be different each time we run the simulation model. Therefore, in practice, we should replicate a model as many times as convenient.

Replication by Copying the Model

In simulation models where each replication consists of just a single row of computations in Excel (such as in Harry's model), an easy way to perform 200 replications is to copy all formulas and values in that row to 199 other rows. For example, we can copy cells A4:G4 in Figure 10.6 to cells A5:G203. (*Note:* For your convenience, a worksheet illustrating this way of replicating Harry's model is included in the Excel file *Figure 10.5.xlsx* on the Companion Website; see the sheet named *Figure 10.6 Alt*.) Due to the use of random numbers in the formulas, the values of the simulated variables will be different in each replication. Hence, each of the 200 entries computed in cells G4:G203, which represents the monthly profit that *could* result in a given month, will be different. Once we have simulated these 200 monthly profit values, we can compute the average monthly profit by using the Excel formula =AVERAGE(G4:G203).

A clear drawback of this approach for replicating a simulation model is that it could make the resulting Excel file quite large and unwieldy. In fact, for models where each replication consists of computations spanning several rows in Excel (as we will see shortly), it is impractical to even consider copying the entire model 200 or more times. For this reason, we next illustrate a different approach—one that replicates a model multiple times without requiring us to copy the entire model each time.

Replication Using Data Table

For replicating a simulation model, we can use an Excel procedure called Data Table. The primary use of this procedure in Excel is to plug in different values for a variable in a formula and compute the result each time. For example, if the formula is (2a + 5), we can set up Data Table to plug in several values for the variable *a* and report the result of the formula each time. In a simulation model, however, we don't really have a "variable" and a "formula" to use in Data Table. So, as explained next, we make Data Table plug in multiple values for a dummy variable in a dummy formula (both of which have nothing to do with the simulation model) and report the "result" each time. The key here is that each time Data Table computes the formula's result, it automatically updates all calculations on the Excel sheet (i.e., it activates the F9 key). As a consequence, all random numbers in the simulation model change, and the result is a new replication of the model, with new values for all simulated entries.

We illustrate in Figure 10.7 the use of Data Table to replicate Harry's simulation model 200 times. Here again, we have chosen 200 replications just for convenience. The procedure is as follows:

1. We first use 200 cells in an empty column in the spreadsheet to represent the 200 values of the *dummy* variable. If we wish, we can leave these cells blank because they have no real role to play in the simulation model. However, as we have done in cells N4:N203 in Figure 10.7, it is convenient to fill these cells with numbers from 1 to 200, to indicate we are performing 200 replications. If we wish, we can title this column *Replication* or *Run* (as shown in cell N3). *Note:* A convenient way to enter a series of numbers in Excel is to click Fill|Series found within the Home tab.
2. In the cell adjacent to the *first* cell in the range N4:N203 (i.e., in cell O4), we specify the cell reference for the output measure we want replicated 200 times. In Harry's model, this corresponds to cell G4, the monthly profit value. Hence, the formula in cell O4 would be =G4. We can title this column *Profit* if we wish (as shown in cell O3). We leave cells O5:O203 blank. Data Table will fill in these cells automatically when we run it.
3. We now use the mouse or keyboard to select the range N4:O203 (i.e., both columns). *After* selecting this range, we click the Data tab and choose What-If Analysis | Data Table. The window titled Data Table, shown in Figure 10.7, is now displayed.
4. Because our table is arranged in columns, we leave the Row input cell box blank. We then select any arbitrary cell that has nothing to do with the simulation model and enter this cell reference in the Column input cell box. It is important to make sure this selected cell (AA1, in Figure 10.7) has no role to play in the simulation

model. In effect, we are telling Data Table that cell AA1 contains our *dummy* formula.

5. Finally, we click OK to run Data Table. The procedure now takes the 200 entries in cells N4:N203, plugs them one at a time in cell AA1, and reports the value of cell G4 each time in cells O4:O203. As noted earlier, even though the variable values in cells N4:N203 and the formula in cell AA1 are dummies, Excel generates new random numbers for each replication of the model. The simulated results in cells O4:O203 are therefore different for each replication.

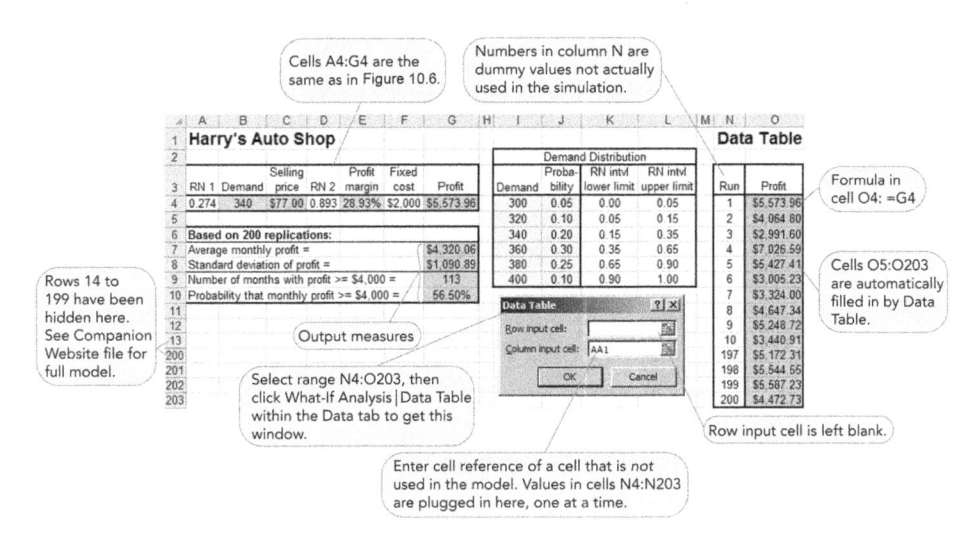

Figure 10.7: Data Table for Harry's Auto Shop

X File: Figure 10.5.xlsx, Sheet: Figure 10.7

Analyzing the Results

Cells O4 to O203 show the monthly profit for 200 replications (months). We can now calculate the following statistics:

Cell G7: =AVERAGE(O4:O203) Average monthly profit = $4,320.06

Cell G8: =STDEV(O4:O203) Standard deviation of monthly profit = $1,090.89

Note: Values in your file will be different if you recalculate the model because the random numbers will change, and we are using only 200 replications.

Alternatively, if the Analysis ToolPak add-in is installed and enabled, we can use Excel's Descriptive Statistics procedure to compute these and other statistics, such as confidence intervals. We invoke this procedure by clicking Data Analysis | Descriptive Statistics, found within the Data tab. The window shown in Figure 10.8 appears. We enter the information as shown and press OK. The summary statistics shown in Figure 10.8(b) are then displayed. The results indicate, for example, that the 95% confidence interval for the average monthly profit would extend from $4,167.95 to $4,472.17 (=$4,320.06 ± $152.11).

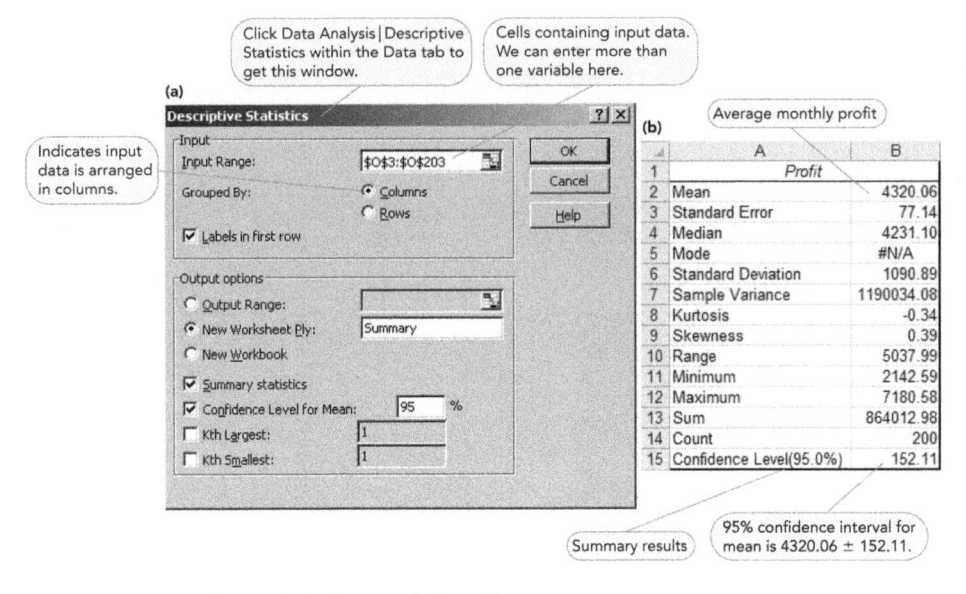

Figure 10.8: Descriptive Statistics for Harry's Auto Shop

File: Figure 10.5.xlsx, Sheet: Figure 10.8

We can also calculate several other measures of performance. For example, suppose Harry estimates that in order for tire sales to be financially viable, he needs to earn a monthly profit of at least $4,000 from tires. What is the probability that Harry will earn this amount of profit? To answer this question, we first need to count the number of months (of the 200 months) in which Harry's profit exceeds $4,000. We can use Excel's COUNTIF function to do this, as shown in cell G9 of Figure 10.7. The relevant formula is

Cell G9: =COUNTIF(O4:O203,">=4000")   Number of months with profit ≥ $4,000 = 113

Then, we divide this count by 200 to get the probability value (shown in cell G10). Figure 10.7 shows that Harry has a 56.5% chance of earning a monthly profit exceeding $4,000. Here again, the values will be different if you recalculate the model because the random numbers will change, and we are using only 200 replications.

Now suppose Harry decides that if his profit from tire sales is below $3,000 per month, he will stop selling tires. Using an approach similar to the one discussed here, see if you can calculate the probability of this event.

EXCEL NOTES

- All entries in a simulation model, including columns in Data Table, can be formatted in any manner desired. For example, the profit value can be formatted to display as currency.

- It is usually a good idea to change the Calculation options in Excel to Manual or Automatic Except for Data Tables when using Data Table (click Calculation options, found within the Formulas tab). Otherwise, Excel will recalculate the entire Data Table each time we make *any* change in the spreadsheet. Depending on the size of the simulation model and the table, this could be time-consuming.

- For the same reason, it is a good idea to set up each simulation model in a separate Excel file rather than in a different sheet of the same file.

- If we change the Calculation options to manual, remember that Excel will recalculate values only when we press the F9 key. Likewise, Data Table will initially show the same result value for every replication. We need to press F9 to get the final values.

- Once we have set up and run Data Table, we cannot edit parts of it (if we try to change any entry in the table, Excel will return the message "Cannot change part of a data table."). To edit a Data Table, we select all cells that were automatically filled in by the Data Table procedure (e.g., cells O5:O203 in Figure 10.7) and delete those cells. Now we make any changes we wish to the table (such as changing the number of replications) and run the Data Table procedure again.

- Although Data Table shows the value of the final output measure for each replication, the simulation model itself does not show details (e.g., monthly demand, selling price) for these replications. If we want to see complete details for each replication, we need to copy the entire model as many times as desired.

EXCEL EXTRA

Automating with Macros

Working with Excel sheets can become quite laborious if the same sequence of entries must be repeated many times. Macros can automate sequences of keystrokes and mouse clicks used for repeated tasks. For example, you may wish to apply a favorite formatting style to data as you move from sheet to sheet. Macros are *recorded*. Once you turn the macro recorder on, the system converts all of your keystrokes to Visual Basic for Applications (VBA) code and stores it for later use. To record a macro:

1. Rehearse the necessary commands and steps.
2. Activate the macro recorder by clicking View|Macros|Record Macro....
3. In the Record Macro dialog box, name the macro. To run the macro by pressing a keyboard shortcut key, enter a letter in the Shortcut key box. You can use Ctrl + *letter* (for lowercase letters) or Ctrl + Shift + *letter* (for uppercase letters), where letter is any letter key on the keyboard. Finally choose the storage location for the macro. Select the Personal Macro Workbook if you want to use the macro in other workbooks.

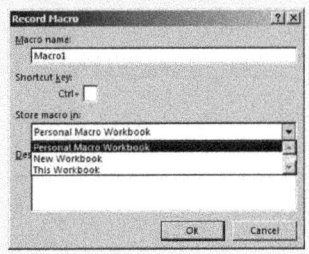

4. After possibly entering an optional Description, click OK, and perform the steps to be included in the macro (using the keyboard and/or the mouse). *Important: if you select cells while running a macro, the macro records <u>absolute cell references</u> unless you prefer <u>relative cell references</u>* (turned on and off by View|Macros|Use Relative References).
5. To stop: View|Macros|Stop Recording.

An alternative to creating a predefined Data Table to record simulation results as seen earlier in Figure 10.7 would be to build a column of outputs by having the user run a macro each time. The column would contain output *values* that would not change each time the sheet is recalculated. We'll have the cursor start well below the bottom of the table, then use the End key followed by the Up arrow key to reach the bottom of the table, and finally go one row below that to paste the result.

For example, instead of having the Data Table in Figure 10.7, just have the "Profit" heading in Cell O3. Then start the recorder as described above and complete these steps:

    Press the F5 key; type G4; click OK
    Select Home|Copy
    Press the F5 key; type O1000; click OK
    Select View|Macros|Use Relative References
    Press the End key; press the Up arrow key; press the Down arrow key
    Select Home|Paste|Paste Values
    Press the Esc key
    Select View|Macros|Stop Recording

10.5 Simulation Model of an Inventory Problem

There are two main factors to consider in most inventory problems: (1) how much to order and (2) when to order. Under specific assumptions, it is possible to develop precise analytical models to answer these questions.[5]

In many real-world inventory situations, though, several inventory parameters are random variables. For example, the demand for an item could be random, implying that the rate at which its inventory is depleted is uncertain. Likewise, the time between when we place an order for an item with our supplier and when we receive it (known as the *lead time*) could be random. This implies that we may run out of inventory for the item before we receive the next shipment, causing a *stockout*.

Although it may be possible for us to express the behavior of parameters, such as demand and lead time, by using probability distributions, developing analytical models becomes extremely difficult. In such situations, simulation represents the best means to answer the kind of inventory questions noted here.

In Solved Problem 10–1 at the end of this chapter, we simulate a fairly simple inventory problem in which only the demand is random. In the following pages, we illustrate a more comprehensive inventory problem in which both the demand and lead time are random variables.

Simkin's Hardware Store

Simkin's Hardware Store sells the Ace model electric drill. Daily demand for the drill is relatively low but subject to some variability. Over the past 300 days, Barry Simkin has observed the demand frequency shown in column 2 of Table 10.5. He converts this historical frequency into a probability distribution for the variable daily demand (column 3).

Table 10.5: Distribution of Daily Demand for Ace Electric Drills

Demand	Frequency	Probability
0	15	15/300 = 0.05
1	30	30/300 = 0.10
2	60	60/300 = 0.20
3	120	120/300 = 0.40
4	45	45/300 = 0.15
5	30	30/300 = 0.10

---

[5] We discuss some of these models in Chapter 12.

Decision Modeling In Action

Kroger Uses Simulation-Optimization to Improve Pharmacy Inventory Management

The Kroger Co. is one of the largest grocery retailers in the United States, covering 34 states and operating 2,422 supermarkets and 1,950 in-store pharmacies. Sales in 2014 totaled about $108 billion. In 2012, its pharmacies filled more than 160 million prescriptions, with a total retail value of approximately $8 billion.

Improving customer service is at the heart of Kroger's business strategy. Toward that end, Kroger's operations research team, in collaboration with faculty from Wright State University, developed an innovative simulation-optimization system for pharmacy inventory management. The main objective was to improve the accuracy of predicting demand to ensure that future prescriptions will be in stock. The simulation model was designed to mimic the pharmacy's periodic inventory system, and it was designed to provide end users with a visual intuitive experience and deliver near-optimal results in milliseconds through local search heuristics. Challenges faced by the team included business resistance to complicated inventory formulas along with complex demand distributions and cost structures that made it difficult to apply traditional inventory models.

The system was implemented in October 2011 in all Kroger pharmacies in the United States, and it has reduced out-of-stocks by 1.6 million per year, ensuring greater patient access to medications. That has resulted in a revenue increase of $80 million per year, a reduction in inventory cost of more than $120 million, and an annual reduction in labor cost equivalent to $10 million.

Source: Based on X. Zhang, et al. "Kroger Uses Simulation-Optimization to Improve Pharmacy Inventory Management," *Interfaces* 44, 1 (January–February 2014): 70–84.

When Simkin places an order to replenish his inventory of drills, the time between when he places an order and when it is received (i.e., the *lead time*) is a probabilistic variable. Based on the past 100 orders, Simkin has found that lead time follows a discrete uniform distribution between one and three days. He currently has seven Ace electric drills in stock, and there are no orders due.

Simkin wants to identify the order quantity, Q, and reorder point, R, that will help him reduce his total monthly costs. The *order quantity* is the fixed size of each order that is placed. The *reorder point* specifies the inventory level at which an order is triggered. That is, if the inventory level at the end of a day is at or below the reorder point, an order is placed. The total cost includes the following three components:
- A fixed order cost that is incurred each time an order is placed
- A holding cost for each drill held in inventory from one period to the next
- A stockout cost for each drill that is not available to satisfy demand

Simkin estimates that the fixed cost of placing an order with his Ace drill supplier is $20. The cost of holding a drill in stock is $0.02 per drill per day. Each time Simkin is unable to satisfy a demand (i.e., he has a stockout), the customer buys the drill elsewhere, and Simkin loses the sale. He estimates that the cost of a stockout is $8 per drill. Assume that the shop operates 25 days each month on average.

Note that there are two decision variables (order quantity, Q and reorder point, R) and two probabilistic components (demand and lead time) in Simkin's inventory problem. Using simulation, we can try different (Q, R) combinations to see which combination yields the lowest total cost. As an illustration, let us first examine a policy that has $Q = 10$ and $R = 5$; that is, each time the inventory at the end of a day drops to 5 or fewer, we place an order for 10 drills with the supplier.

Setting Up the Model

In Simkin's problem, each replication corresponds to tracking the inventory position and orders for electric drills over a month (i.e., 25 days), on a day-by-day basis. Hence, unlike Harry's Auto Shop problem in section 10.4, where we could model each replication by using just a single row in Excel, Simkin's simulation model will be much larger. If we represent the inventory operations of each day as a single row, the model will consist of 25 rows.

The Excel layout for Simkin's problem is shown in Figure 10.9. Wherever necessary, we have shown the Excel formula used in a column.

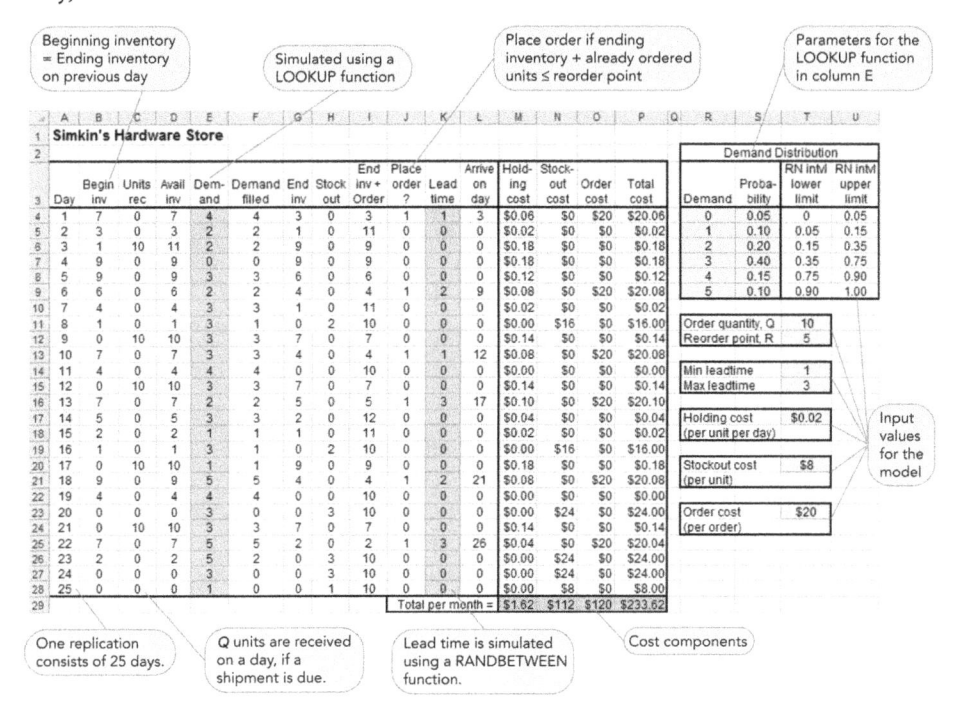

Figure 10.9: Excel Layout and Results for Simkin's Hardware Store

📊 File: Figure 10.9.xlsx, Sheet: Figure 10.9

In Figure 10.9, all input parameters for the simulation model (e.g., the order quantity, reorder point, lead time range, all unit costs) are shown in separate cells (in column T). All formulas in the model use these cell references, rather than the values directly. This is a good practice to follow, especially if we want to use the simulation model to run several what-if scenarios using different values for these parameters (as we shall see shortly). The model in Figure 10.9 is organized as follows:

- Column A shows the day number (1 to 25).
- Column B shows the beginning inventory at the start of a day. On day 1, this equals 7 (given). On all other days, the beginning inventory equals the ending inventory of the previous day. For example, cell B5 = cell G4, cell B6 = cell G5, and so on.
- Column C shows the units received (if any) that day from a prior order. Because there are no outstanding orders on day 1, cell C4 shows a value of 0. The formula for the remaining cells in this column uses Excel's COUNTIF function. In column L (discussed shortly), we simulate the arrival day for each order that is placed. We use the COUNTIF formula to check the number of times the current day number matches the arrival day number. The formula used to calculate the number of units arriving each day is then as follows:

$$\text{Units received} = \text{Number of orders due that day} \times \text{Order size}$$

For example, the formula in cell C5 is

$$=\text{COUNTIF}(\$L\$4:L4, A5) * \$T\$11$$

The COUNTIF portion of the formula checks to see how many orders are due for arrival on day 2 (specified by cell A5). This number is then multiplied by the order quantity, Q, specified in cell T11. Note that the use of a $ to anchor cell references in this formula allows us to directly copy it to cells C6:C28.

- The total *available* inventory each day, shown in column D, is then the sum of the values in columns B and C:

$$\text{Column D} = \text{Column B} + \text{Column C}$$

- Column E shows the demand each day. These values are simulated from the discrete general probability distribution shown in Table 10.5, using Excel's LOOKUP function. The parameters (demands, probabilities, and random number intervals) of the LOOKUP function are shown in cells R4:U9. Hence, the formula in cells E4:E28 is

$$=\text{LOOKUP}(\text{RAND}(), \$T\$4:\$T\$9, \$R\$4:\$R\$9)$$

Here again, the use of $ to anchor cell references in the formula allows us to create it in cell E4 and then copy it to cells E5:E28.

- Column F shows the actual demand filled. If the demand is less than or equal to the available inventory, the entire demand is satisfied. In contrast, if the demand exceeds the available inventory, then only the demand up to the inventory level is satisfied. We can use Excel's MIN function to model this, as follows:

$$\text{Demand satisfied} = \text{MIN (Available inventory, Demand)}$$

Hence, column F = MIN(column D, column E).
- Column G calculates the ending inventory. If the demand is less than the available inventory, there is some ending inventory. However, if the demand is greater than or equal to the available inventory, the ending inventory is zero. We can use Excel's MAX function to model this, as follows:

$$\text{Ending inventory} = \text{MAX (Available inventory} - \text{Demand, 0)}$$

Hence, column G = MAX(column D − column E, 0).
- We now calculate the stockout (or lost sales) in column H. If the demand exceeds the available inventory, there is a stockout. However, if the demand is less than or equal to the available inventory, there is no stockout. Once again, we can use the MAX function to model this, as follows:

$$\text{Stockout} = \text{MAX (Demand} - \text{Available inventory, 0)}$$

Hence, column H = MAX(column E − column D, 0).
- If the ending inventory is at or below the reorder point, an order needs to be placed with the supplier. Before we place an order, however, we need to check whether there are outstanding orders. The reason for this is as follows. If the ending inventory level has already triggered an order on an earlier day, but that order has not yet been received due to the delivery lead time, a duplicate order should not be placed. Hence, in column I, we calculate the inventory position; that is, we add the *actual* ending inventory (shown in column G) and any orders that have already been placed. The logic behind the formula in column I is as follows:

> Inventory position at end of period $t =$
> Inventory position at end of period $(t-1)$
> $-$ Demand satisfied in period $t +$ Order size, if
> an order was placed at the end of period $(t-1)$

For example, the formula in cell I5 is

$$=I4-F5+IF(J4=1,\$T\$11,0)$$

- If the inventory position at the end of any day is at or below the reorder point (cell T12), an order is to be placed that day. We denote this event in column J by using an IF function (1 implies place an order, 0 implies don't place an order). For example, the formula in cell J5 is

$$=IF(I5<=\$T\$12,1,0)$$

- If an order is placed, the delivery lead time for this order is simulated in column K by using a RANDBETWEEN function (between 1 and 3). For example, the formula in cell K5 is

    =IF(J5=1,RANDBETWEEN($T$14,$T$15),0)

- Finally, in column L, we calculate the arrival day of this order as follows:

    Arrive on day = Current day + Lead time + 1

    For example, the formula in cell L5 is

    =IF(J5=1,A5+K5+1,0)

    Note that this formula includes +1 because the order is actually placed at the end of the current day (or, equivalently, the start of the next day).

Computation of Costs

Columns M through P show the cost computations for Simkin's inventory model each day of the month. The relevant formulas are as follows:

    Column M: Holding Cost   = $T$17 × Ending inventory in column G
    Column N: Stockout Cost   = $T$20 × Shortage in Column H
    Column O: Order Cost   = $T$23 (if value in Column J = 1)
    Column P: Total Cost   = Column M + Column N + Column O

The totals for each cost component for the entire month are shown in row 29 (cells M29:P29). For instance, the replication in Figure 10.9 shows a holding cost of $1.62 (cell M29), stockout cost of $112 (cell N29), order cost of $120 (cell O29), and total cost of $233.62 (cell P29).

Replication Using Data Table

To compute Simkin's average monthly cost, we need to replicate the model as many times as possible. Each time, due to the presence of random variables, all simulated values in the spreadsheet will change. Hence, the inventory costs will change.

We have already seen how we can use Data Table to easily replicate a simulation model multiple times. In Harry's Auto Shop example, we replicated only a single output measure (i.e., monthly profit) by using Data Table (see Figure 10.7).

In contrast, suppose we would like to replicate each of the four costs—holding cost, stockout cost, order cost, and total cost—in Simkin's example. It turns out that we can expand the use of Data Table to replicate all four measures at the same time. The procedure, illustrated in Figure 10.10, is as follows:

1. Here again, we illustrate only 200 replications of the model. We first enter numbers 1 to 200 in cells W4:W203, corresponding to these 200 replications.
2. In cells X4 to AA4 (i.e., adjacent to the *first* cell in the range W4:W203), we specify the cell references for the four output measures we want replicated. Hence, the

formula in cell X4 is =M29, in cell Y4 is = N29, in cell Z4 is = O29, and in cell AA4 is = P29. We leave cells X5:AA203 blank. As before, Data Table will fill in these cells when we run it.

3. We now use the mouse or keyboard to select the entire range W4:AA203 (i.e., all five columns). *After* selecting this range, we choose Data | What-If Analysis | Data Table from Excel's menu.

4. We leave the row input cell box blank and enter some arbitrary cell reference in the column input box. As before, we need to make sure the selected cell (AA1, in this case) is not used anywhere in the simulation model.

5. Finally, we click OK to run Data Table. The procedure computes and displays 200 simulated values of the monthly holding, stockout, order, and total costs in columns X, Y, Z, and AA, respectively.

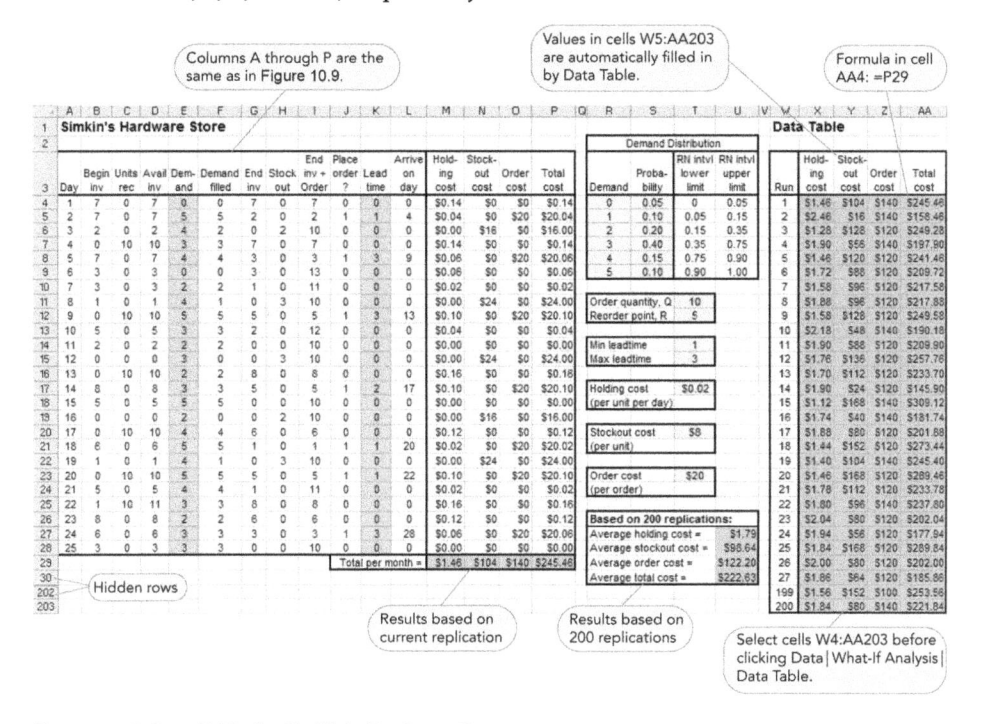

Figure 10.10: Data Table for Simkin's Hardware Store

Analyzing the Results

We can now use the 200 cost values to conduct statistical analyses, as before. For example, if $Q = 10$ and $R = 5$, Figure 10.10 indicates that Simkin's average monthly costs of holding, stockout, and order are $1.79 (cell U27), $98.64 (cell U28), and $122.20 (cell U29), respectively. The average total cost, shown in cell U30, is $222.63.

As an exercise, see if you can set up Data Table to calculate Simkin's average demand fill rate per month. That is, what percentage of monthly demand received does Simkin satisfy on average? *Hint:* The fill rate for each replication is the ratio of demand satisfied (sum of entries in column F) to demand received (sum of entries in column E).

Using Scenario Manager to Include Decisions in a Simulation Model

In simulating Simkin's inventory model so far, we have assumed a fixed order quantity, Q, of 10, and a fixed reorder point, R, of 5. Recall, however, that Simkin's objective was to identify the Q and R values that will help him reduce his total monthly costs. To achieve this objective, suppose Simkin wants to try four different values for Q (i.e., 8, 10, 12, and 14) and two different values for R (i.e., 5 and 8). One approach to run this extended simulation would be to run the model and Data Table (see Figure 10.10) eight times—once for each combination of Q and R values. We could then compare the average total cost (cell U30) in each case to determine which combination of Q and R is best. This approach, of course, could become quite cumbersome, especially if we wanted to vary several different input parameters and try multiple values for each parameter.

It turns out that we can use an Excel procedure called Scenario Manager to automatically run a simulation model for several combinations of input parameter values. To do so, we first assume *any* combination of values for the input parameters and set up the complete simulation model (including Data Table) to replicate the desired output measures. After we have done so, we next define multiple scenarios—one for each combination of input parameter values. When we then run Scenario Manager, Excel will automatically run the model and the Data Table replications for each scenario and report the desired results.

We illustrate the construction and use of Scenario Manager by using the simulation model we have already constructed for Simkin (shown in Figure 10.10 for $Q = 10$ and $R = 5$). The procedure is as follows:

1. Invoke Scenario Manager by clicking What-If Analysis | Scenario Manager, found within the Data tab. The window shown in Figure 10.11 is displayed.

Simulation Model of an Inventory Problem — 599

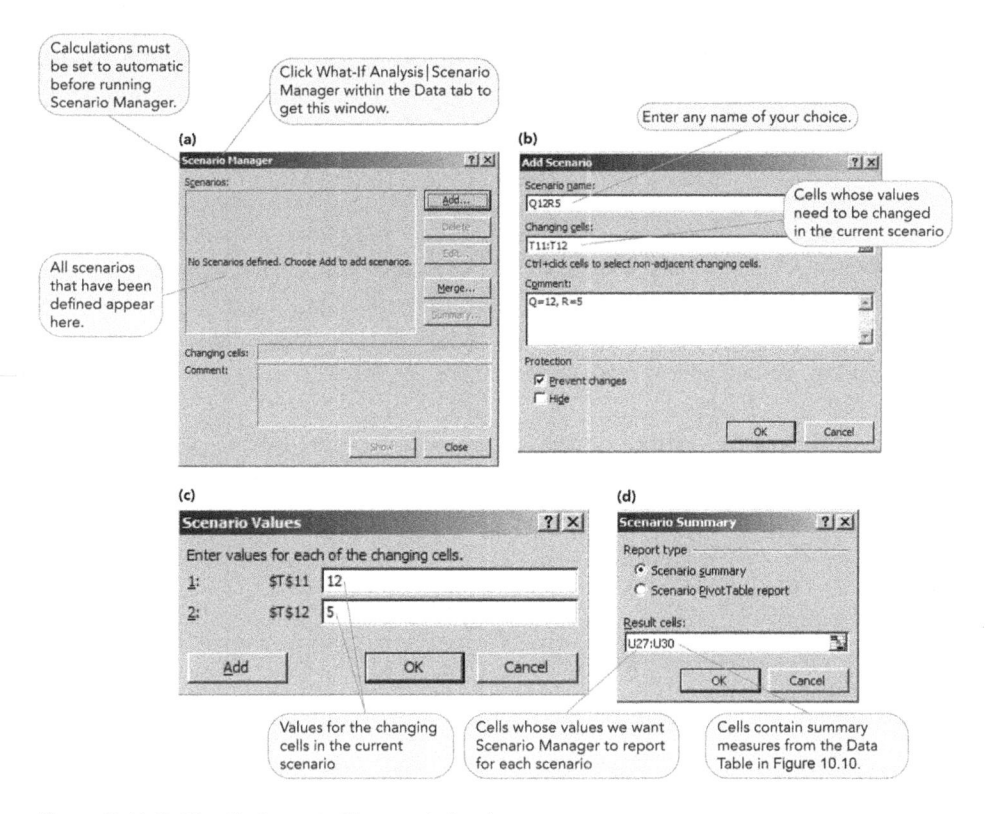

Figure 10.11: Setting Up Scenario Manager in Excel

2. Click Add to create a new scenario. The Add Scenario window shown in Figure 10.11(b) is displayed. In the box titled Scenario name, enter any name of your choice for the scenario. (In Simkin's model, we have used names such as Q8R5, Q8R8, and Q12R5 to make the scenarios self-explanatory.) In the Changing cells box, enter the cell references for the cells whose values you wish to change. In Simkin's model, these would be cells T11 and T12, corresponding to the input parameters Q and R, respectively. If the changing cells are not contiguous in the model, separate the cell references with commas. Next, if desired, enter a comment to describe the scenario. Checking the Prevent changes option protects the scenario from being accidentally edited or deleted, while the Hide option hides the scenario.

   Click OK to get the Scenario Values window, as shown in Figure 10.11(c). For each changing cell, enter the appropriate value. For example, for the scenario shown in Figure 10.11(c), the values of Q and R are 12 and 5, respectively.

3. Repeat step 2 for as many scenarios as desired. In Simkin's model, you define eight scenarios corresponding to the eight combinations (Q, R): (8, 5), (8, 8), (10, 5), (10, 8), (12, 5), (12, 8), (14, 5), and (14, 8). You can also edit or delete a scenario after it has been created (assuming that the Prevent changes option is unchecked).

4. When all scenarios have been defined, click Summary (see Figure 10.11(a)) to run Scenario Manager. The Scenario Summary window shown in Figure 10.11(d) appears. In the box titled Result cells, enter the cell references for the output measures you would like Scenario Manager to report for each scenario. In Simkin's model, these would be cells U27:U30, corresponding to the four average cost measures—holding cost, stockout cost, order cost, and total cost (see Figure 10.10). Here again, use commas to separate cell references that are not contiguous.

   The results can be shown either as a Scenario summary table (preferred in most cases) or as a PivotTable report. (Choose the latter option if there are many changing cells and scenarios, and if you are comfortable analyzing results using PivotTables in Excel.)
5. Click OK. Scenario Manager runs the simulation model (including Data Table) for each scenario and presents the results in a separate worksheet, as shown in Figure 10.12. (We have added grid lines to the summary table to make it clearer.)

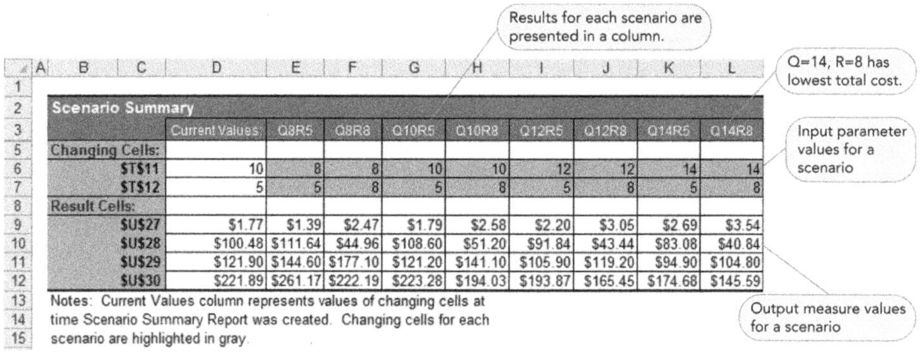

Scenario Summary									
	Current Values:	Q8R5	Q8R8	Q10R5	Q10R8	Q12R5	Q12R8	Q14R5	Q14R8
Changing Cells:									
$T$11	10	8	8	10	10	12	12	14	14
$T$12	5	5	8	5	8	5	8	5	8
Result Cells:									
$U$27	$1.77	$1.39	$2.47	$1.79	$2.58	$2.20	$3.05	$2.69	$3.54
$U$28	$100.48	$111.64	$44.96	$108.60	$51.20	$91.84	$43.44	$83.08	$40.84
$U$29	$121.90	$144.60	$177.10	$121.20	$141.10	$105.90	$119.20	$94.90	$104.80
$U$30	$221.89	$261.17	$222.19	$223.28	$194.03	$193.87	$165.45	$174.68	$145.59

Notes: Current Values column represents values of changing cells at time Scenario Summary Report was created. Changing cells for each scenario are highlighted in gray.

Figure 10.12: Scenario Manager Results for Simkin's Hardware Store

File: Figure 10.9.xlsx, Sheet: Figure 10.12

EXCEL NOTES

- The Calculation options in Excel must not be set to Manual *before* you run Scenario Manager. If this option is set to Manual, Scenario Manager will report the same summary results for all scenarios.
- The standard version of Excel can accommodate up to 32 changing cells for each scenario.
- Although the number of scenarios allowed in Excel is limited only by your computer's memory, note that Scenario Manager may take a long time to execute if you include too many scenarios, especially if running each scenario involves running Data Table with many replications.

Analyzing the Results

For each combination of order quantity and reorder point, Figure 10.12 shows the average monthly holding, stockout, order, and total costs. Note that because all these values are based on only 200 replications of the simulation model, they could change each time we run Scenario Manager. Looking at the values in Figure 10.12, it appears that Simkin's lowest total cost of $145.59 per month is obtained when he uses an order quantity of 14 units and a reorder point of 8 units.

As an exercise, see if you can compute other output measures (e.g., demand fill rate, probability that total monthly cost exceeds $200) in the simulation model. Then, include these measures also in the Results cell for each scenario and run Scenario Manager. Likewise, see if you can analyze the impact on total cost when you vary the values of other input parameters, such as the minimum and maximum delivery lead times.

10.6 Simulation Model of a Queuing Problem

In Chapter 9, using analytical models, we computed performance measures for several simple queuing systems. However, as noted in that chapter, many real-world queuing systems can be difficult to model analytically. In such cases, we usually turn to simulation to analyze the performance of these systems. To study this issue, in this section we illustrate an example of a queuing model in which both the arrival times of customers and the service times at the facility follow discrete general distributions. Then, in Solved Problem 10–2 at the end of this chapter, we discuss the simulation of another queuing model in which arrival times are exponentially distributed and service times are normally distributed.

Denton Savings Bank

Sanjay Krishnan, manager at the Denton Savings Bank, is attempting to improve customer satisfaction by offering service such that (1) the average customer waiting time does not exceed 2 minutes and (2) the average queue length is 2 or fewer customers. The bank gets an average of 150 customers each day. Given the existing situation for service and arrival times, as shown in Table 10.6, does the bank meet Sanjay's criteria?

Table 10.6: Distribution of Service Times and Time between Arrivals at Denton Savings Bank

Service Time	Probability	Time Between Arrivals	Probability
1	0.25	0	0.10
2	0.20	1	0.15
3	0.40	2	0.10
4	0.15	3	0.35
		4	0.25
		5	0.05

602 —— Chapter 10: Simulation Modeling

Note that in simulating this queuing model, we need to keep track of the passage of time to record the specific arrival and departure times of customers. We refer to such models, in which events (e.g., customer arrivals and departures) occur at discrete points in time, as discrete-event simulation models.

Setting Up the Model

Each replication of this simulation model corresponds to a day's operation at the bank (i.e., the arrival and service of 150 customers). The Excel layout for this problem is presented in Figure 10.13.

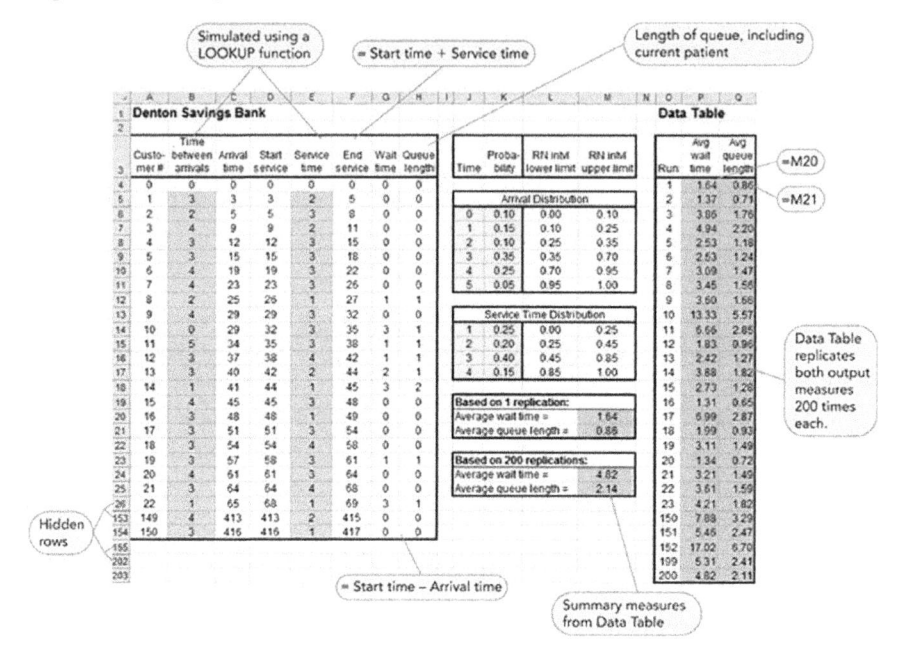

Figure 10.13: Excel Layout and Results for Denton Savings Bank

📊 File: Figure 10.13.xlsx

To keep track of the passage of time in this model, we monitor a clock that starts at zero and continually counts time (in minutes, in Denton's model). Observe that in row 4, we have included customer number 0, with zero values for all columns, to *initialize* this simulation clock. This is a good practice in all discrete-event simulation models. Rows 5 through 154 in the spreadsheet are organized as follows:

- Column A lists the customer number (1 through 150).
- Column B shows the time between arrivals of successive customers, simulated using a LOOKUP function. The parameters (i.e., arrival times, probabilities, and random number intervals) for this LOOKUP function are shown in cells J6:M11. The formula in cells B5:B154 is

$$=LOOKUP(RAND(), \$L\$6:\$L\$11, \$J\$6:\$J\$11)$$

The $ symbol in the formula anchors the cell references so that we can create the formula in cell B5 and then copy it to cells B6:B154.

- Column C calculates the actual arrival time of the current customer as the sum of the arrival time of the previous customer and the time between arrivals (simulated in column B). This type of computation is an example of the use of the simulation clock, which records the actual elapsed clock time in a simulation model. For example, the formula in cell C5 is

$$=C4+B5$$

- The actual time at which this customer starts service is calculated in column D as the maximum of the customer's arrival time and the time the previous customer finishes service. For example, the formula in cell D5 is

$$=MAX(C5, F4)$$

- Column E shows the service time for this customer, simulated using a LOOKUP function. The parameters of this LOOKUP function are shown in cells J14:M17. The formula in cells E5:E154 is

$$=LOOKUP(RAND(), \$L\$14:\$L\$17, \$J\$14:\$J\$17)$$

- The clock time at which this customer ends service is shown in column F as the sum of the start time (shown in column D) and the service time (shown in column E). For example, the formula in cell F5 is

$$=D5+E5$$

- Column G calculates the wait time of this customer as the difference between the customer's start time (shown in column D) and arrival time (shown in column C). For example, the formula in cell G5 is

$$=D5-C5$$

- Finally, column H calculates the queue length by using Excel's MATCH function. The MATCH function is used to determine how many customers (up to the current customer) have start times that are sooner than the arrival time of the current customer. Clearly, all customers (including the current one) who do not meet this criterion are in the queue. For example, the formula in cell H5 is

$$=A5-MATCH(C5, \$D\$5:D5, 1)$$

Using the wait times and queue lengths shown in cells G5:H154 for the 150 customers, we can determine the following two performance measures for the bank each day: (1) average wait time per customer (shown in cell M20) and (2) average queue length (shown in cell M21).

Replication Using Data Table

Based on the average wait time and queue length values in cells M20 and M21, respectively, of Figure 10.13, it may seem to appear that Denton is meeting both of Sanjay's desired targets. The average wait time is only 1.64 minutes, and there are only 0.86 customers on average in the queue.

However, note that these values are based on just one replication and will change each time we recalculate the model. Hence, to determine more precise values for these averages, we now replicate each performance measure 200 times. Figure 10.13 shows how we can use Data Table to do so, in columns O through Q. Note that Data Table has been used here to replicate both performance measures at the same time.

Analyzing the Results

Based on the average values computed from 200 replications in Figure 10.13, it appears that the system does *not* meet either criterion. The average wait time of 4.82 minutes per customer (cell M24) is more than double Sanjay's desired target of 2 minutes per customer. The average queue length of 2.14 customers (cell M25) is, however, close to Sanjay's desired target of 2 customers. Sanjay should, perhaps, focus on initiating training programs to improve the average service rate of his tellers.

Decision Modeling In Action

Simulation Model Helps Grady Memorial Hospital in Atlanta Transform Emergency Department and Patient Care

A hospital's Emergency Department (ED) performs a vital function, and improving its timeliness of care, quality of care, and operational efficiency is crucial for its impact on patient lives. A joint team from Emory University School of Medicine, Grady Health System, Rockdale Medical Center, and Health Ivy Tech Community College collaborated to create an ED decision support system that couples machine learning, simulation, and optimization to improve the performance of EDs in hospitals. The system enables healthcare administrators to optimize the ED workflow, starting from patient registration to discharge, and to reduce the patient's length of stay in the ED. One of the main challenges was predicting the care required for patients, given the uncertainty in the number of incoming injuries and diseases. The system facilitated analyzing the entire patient flow, enabling decision makers to understand the complexities and interdependencies of the different steps in the process.

The system was tested at Grady Memorial Hospital in Atlanta, and it reduced the length of stay by almost 33%. The savings gained from the system were used to establish a clinical decision unit that assures the quality of the related administrative work. The creation of that unit led to a 28% reduction in ED readmissions. Further, 32% of nonurgent care cases were eliminated after creating a walk-in center. These improvements enabled the ED to reduce the average ED stay to around 7 hours, improve the performance of its ED and trauma by more than 16%, and reduce the number of patients who left without being seen by more than 30%. The resulting savings were approximately $190 million. After the success achieved at Grady, the model was implemented successfully in EDs of ten other hospitals.

Source: Based on E. Lee, et al. "Transforming Hospital Emergency Department Workflow and Patient Care," *Interfaces* 45, 1 (January–February 2015): 58–82.

10.7 Simulation Model of a Revenue Management Problem

Another popular application of simulation is in *revenue management* problems, first introduced by the airline and hotel industries as *yield management* problems. This type of problem focuses on trying to identify the most efficient way of using an existing capacity (usually fixed) to manage revenues in situations where customer demand and behavior are uncertain.[6] To study this type of problem, in this section we consider an example in which the owner of a limousine service wants to find the optimal number of reservations she should accept for a trip. Then, in Solved Problem 10-3 at the end of this chapter, we illustrate the simulation of another revenue management problem, involving room reservations at a hotel.

Judith's Airport Limousine Service

Judith McKnew is always on the lookout for entrepreneurial opportunities. Living in Six Mile, South Carolina, she recognizes that the nearest airport is 50 miles away. Judith estimates that, on average, there are about 45 people from Six Mile (and its vicinity) who need rides to or from the airport each day. To help them, Judith is considering leasing a 10-passenger van and offering a limousine service between Six Mile and the airport. There would be four trips per day: a morning trip and an evening trip to the airport, and a morning trip and an evening trip from the airport.

After researching the issue carefully, Judith sets some operating guidelines for her problem and estimates the following parameters for each trip:

- Reservations for a trip can be made up to 12 hours in advance by paying a nonrefundable $10 deposit. Judith will accept reservations up to her reservation limit (which this simulation model will help her decide).
- The ticket price is $35 per passenger per trip. Passengers with reservations must pay the $25 balance at the start of the trip.
- The number of reservations requested each trip follows a discrete uniform distribution between 7 and 14. Judith will, of course, reject a reservation request if she has reached her reservation limit.
- The probability that a person with a reservation shows up for the trip is 0.80. In other words, 20% of people with reservations do not show up. Anyone who does not show up forfeits the $10 deposit.
- If the number of passengers who show up exceeds 10 (the passenger capacity of the van), alternate arrangements must be made to get these extra people to the airport. This will cost Judith $75 per person. That is, Judith will lose $40 (=$75−$35) per overbooked person.

---

[6] A good description of *yield management* can be found in B. C. Smith, J. F. Leimkuhler, and R. M. Darrow, "Yield Management at American Airlines," *Interfaces* 22, 1 (January–February 1992): 8–31.

606 —— Chapter 10: Simulation Modeling

- The number of walk-up passengers (i.e., passengers without reservations) for a trip has the following discrete general distribution: probability of zero walk-ups is 0.30, probability of one walk-up is 0.45, and probability of two walk-ups is 0.25. Judith does not anticipate that there will ever be more than two walk-ups per trip.
- Walk-up passengers pay $50 per trip. However, Judith does not have to make alternate arrangements for these passengers if her van is full.
- The total cost per trip (to or from the airport) to Judith is $100. Note that due to the possibility of walk-up passengers on the return trip, Judith has to make a trip to the airport even if she has no passengers on that trip.

Judith wants to find out how many reservations she should accept in order to maximize her average profit per trip. Specifically, she is considering accepting 10, 11, 12, 13, or 14 reservations.

Setting Up the Model

Each replication in Judith's problem corresponds to one trip. The Excel layout for this problem, shown in Figure 10.14, is organized as follows:

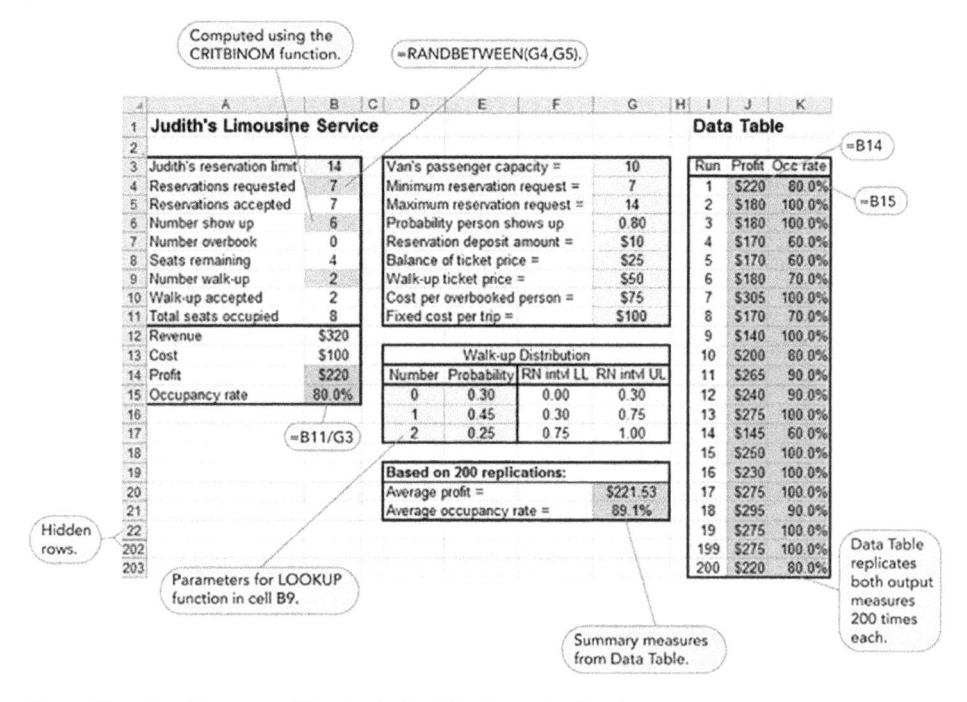

Figure 10.14: Excel Layout and Results for Judith's Limousine Service

File: Figure 10.14.xlsx, Sheet: Figure 10.14

- Cell B3 shows the number of reservations accepted for the trip. Note that this is a decision that is specified by Judith. Let us first set up the model assuming that

- Judith accepts 14 reservations for each trip. Later, we will use Scenario Manager to run this model automatically for all reservation limits (i.e., 10 to 14).
- Cell B4 shows the number of reservations requested for a trip. We simulate this value from a discrete uniform distribution by using the RANDBETWEEN function with parameters $a = 7$ (specified in cell G4) and $b = 14$ (specified in cell G5). The formula in cell B4 is

    =RANDBETWEEN(G4,G5)

- In cell B5, we set the actual number of reservations accepted by Judith for the trip as the *smaller* of Judith's reservation limit (cell B3) and the number of reservations requested (cell B4). The formula in cell B5 is

    =MIN(B3,B4)

- Next, we simulate the number of people with reservations who actually show up. This can be modeled as a binomial distribution where the number of independent events (n) corresponds to the number of people with reservations (i.e., cell B5), and the probability of success in each event (p) is the probability the person will actually show up (0.80 here, shown in cell G6). The relevant formula in cell B6 is[7]

    =CRITBINOM(B5,G6,RAND())

- If the number of passengers showing up (cell B6) exceeds the van's passenger capacity (specified in cell G3), we have overbooked passengers. Otherwise, we have no overbooked passengers. In cell B7, we calculate the number of overbooked passengers by using the MAX function, as follows:

    =MAX(B6−G3,0)

- Likewise, if the van capacity exceeds the number of passengers showing up, we have some seats remaining. Otherwise, we are full. In cell B8, we calculate this number as follows:

    =MAX(G3−B6,0)

- Next, in cell B9, we simulate the number of walk-up passengers by using a LOOKUP function. The parameter values for this function are specified in cells D15:G17. The formula in cell B9 is

    =LOOKUP(RAND(),F15:F17,D15:D17)

---

[7] As noted previously, we can use either the CRITBINOM function or the BINOM.INV function starting with Excel 2010.

- The number of walk-ups that can be accommodated in the van is obviously limited by the seats remaining (cell B8). Hence, in cell B10, we calculate the number of walk-ups accepted by using a MIN function, as follows:

$$=MIN(B8,B9)$$

- In cell B11, we compute the total number of seats occupied for the trip. The formula is

$$=G3-B8+B10$$

- The total revenue and cost for the trip are now calculated in cells B12 and B13, respectively, as

Revenue = $10 × Reservations accepted + $25 × Number of people who show up
 + $50 × Walk-ups accepted
 = G7*B5 + G8*B6 + G9*B10
Cost = $75 × Number overbooked + $100
 = G10*B7 + G11

- In cell B14, we calculate the trip profit as (Revenue − Cost).
- Another performance measure that is popular in many revenue management problems is the percentage of capacity that has been actually utilized. Airlines and hotels refer to this measure as the *load factor*. To illustrate this measure, we compute Judith's occupancy rate for the trip in cell B15 as

$$=B11/G3$$

Replicating the Model Using Data Table and Scenario Manager
The profit of $220 (shown in cell B14) and occupancy rate of 80% (shown in cell B15) in Figure 10.14 are based on just one replication of the model. Hence, they should not be used to make any conclusive statements about Judith's problem. To determine more precise values, we now replicate each performance measure 200 times. Columns I through K show how we can use Data Table to do so. The formula in cell J4 is =B14, while the formula in cell K4 is =B15. Cells J5:K203 are left blank and will be automatically filled in by the Data Table procedure when it is run. Based on these 200 replicated values, we calculate the average values of both measures (shown in cells G20 and G21, respectively). With a reservation limit of 14, Figure 10.14 indicates that Judith can expect a profit of $221.53 per trip and an occupancy rate of 89.1%.

Now that we have set up Judith's simulation model and Data Table for a specific reservation limit, we can use Scenario Manager to try different values for this parameter. The procedure is as follows (here again, remember to make sure that Calculations options is set to Automatic in Excel before running Scenario Manager):
1. Invoke Scenario Manager by clicking Data|What-If Analysis|Scenario Manager.

2. Define five scenarios, corresponding to the five reservation limits that Judith wants to try (i.e., 10 to 14). For each scenario, specify cell B3 as the cell reference in the Changing cells box and enter the appropriate reservation limit in the Scenario Values window.
3. Once all scenarios have been defined, click Summary. In the box titled Result cells, specify cells G20 and G21 as the cells to track.
4. Click OK to run Scenario Manager. The results appear in a separate worksheet, as shown in Figure 10.15.

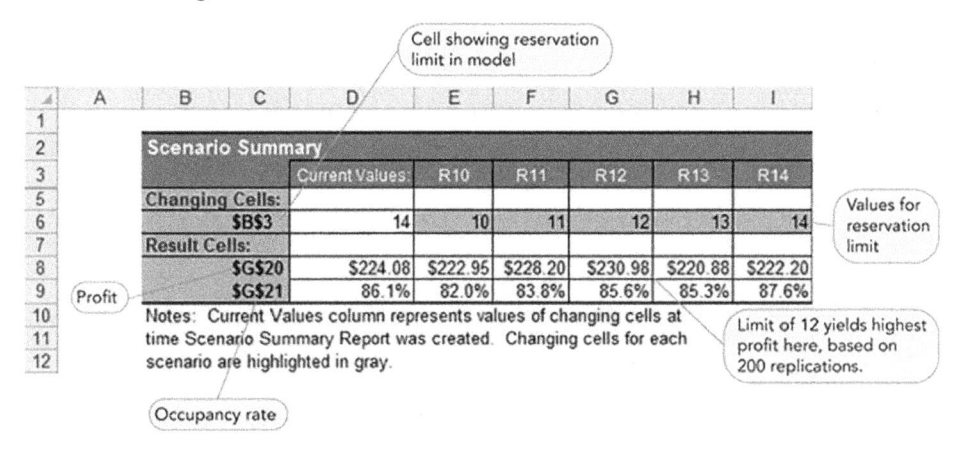

Figure 10.15: Scenario Manager Results for Judith's Limousine Service

File: Figure 10.14.xlsx, Sheet: Figure 10.15

Analyzing the Results

Comparing the profit values in Figure 10.15, it appears that Judith's best choice would be to accept 12 reservations per trip. (Remember that this result is based on only 200 replications.) The resulting average profit is $230.98 per trip. Not surprisingly, the occupancy rate is highest when Judith accepts 14 reservations, even though the rate does not seem to exceed 90% in any scenario.

So far, we have developed four simulation models using Excel's built-in functions. We have also used Data Table to replicate the output measures in each model and Scenario Manager to automatically try different values for one or more input parameters. Solved Problems 10–1 to 10–4 at the end of this chapter discuss four additional simulation models using only Excel's built-in functions. As previously noted, there are several available add-in programs (e.g., Crystal Ball) that make it even easier to develop and replicate simulation models using Excel.

10.8 Other Types of Simulation Models

Simulation models are often broken into three categories. The first, the Monte Carlo method discussed in this chapter, uses the concepts of probability distributions and random numbers to evaluate system responses to various policies. The other two categories are operational gaming and systems simulation. Although in theory the three methods are distinctly different from one another, the growth of computerized simulation has tended to create a common basis in procedures and blur these differences.[8]

Operational Gaming

Operational gaming refers to simulation involving two or more competing players. The best examples are military games and business games. Both allow participants to match their management and decision-making skills in hypothetical situations of conflict.

Military games are used worldwide to train a nation's top military officers, to test offensive and defensive strategies, and to examine the effectiveness of equipment and armies. Business games, first developed by the firm Booz, Allen, and Hamilton in the 1950s, are popular with both executives and business students. They provide an opportunity to test business skills and decision-making ability in a competitive environment. The person or team that performs best in the simulated environment is rewarded by knowing that his or her company has been most successful in earning the largest profit, grabbing a high market share, or perhaps increasing the firm's trading value on the stock exchange.

During each period of competition, be it a week, month, or quarter, teams respond to market conditions by coding their latest management decisions with respect to inventory, production, financing, investment, marketing, and research. The competitive business environment is simulated using a computer, and a new printout summarizing current market conditions is presented to players. This allows teams to simulate years of operating conditions in a matter of days, weeks, or a semester.

Systems Simulation

Systems simulation is similar to business gaming in that it allows users to test various managerial policies and decisions to evaluate their effect on the operating environment. This variation of simulation models the dynamics of large systems. Such systems are corporate operations, the national economy, a hospital, or a city government system.

---

[8] Theoretically, random numbers are used only in Monte Carlo simulation. However, in some complex gaming or systems simulation problems in which relationships cannot be defined exactly, it may be necessary to use the probability concepts of the Monte Carlo method.

In a corporate operating system, sales, production levels, marketing policies, investments, union contracts, utility rates, financing, and other factors are all related in a series of mathematical equations that are examined through simulation. In a simulation of an urban government, systems simulation could be employed to evaluate the impact of tax increases, capital expenditures for roads and buildings, housing availability, new garbage routes, immigration and out-migration, locations of new schools or senior citizen centers, birth and death rates, and many more vital issues. Simulations of *economic systems*, often called *econometric* models, are used by government agencies, bankers, and large organizations to predict inflation rates, domestic and foreign money supplies, and unemployment levels. Inputs and outputs of a typical economic system simulation are illustrated in Figure 10.16.

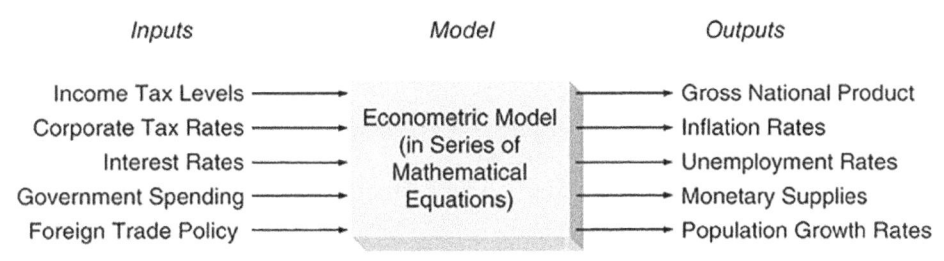

Inputs	Model	Outputs
Income Tax Levels	Econometric Model (in Series of Mathematical Equations)	Gross National Product
Corporate Tax Rates		Inflation Rates
Interest Rates		Unemployment Rates
Government Spending		Monetary Supplies
Foreign Trade Policy		Population Growth Rates

Figure 10.16: Inputs and Outputs of a Typical Economic System Simulation

The value of systems simulation lies in its allowance of what-if questions to test the effects of various policies. A corporate planning group, for example, can change the value of any input, such as an advertising budget, and examine the impact on sales, market share, or short-term costs. Simulation also can be used to evaluate different research and development projects or to determine long-range planning horizons.

10.9 Summary

This chapter discusses the concept and approach of simulation as a problem-solving tool. Simulation involves building a mathematical model that attempts to describe a real-world situation. The model's goal is to incorporate important variables and their interrelationships in such a way that we can study the impact of managerial changes on the total system. The approach has many advantages over other decision modeling techniques and is especially useful when a problem is too complex or difficult to solve by other means.

The Monte Carlo method of simulation uses random numbers to generate random variable values from probability distributions. The simulation procedure is conducted for many time periods to evaluate the long-term impact of each policy value being studied.

We first illustrate how to set up Monte Carlo simulations by using Excel's built-in functions. We also show how Excel's Data Table can be used to run several replications of simulation models and how Scenario Manager can be used to try different values for input parameters.

We conclude this chapter with a brief discussion of operational gaming and systems simulation, two other categories of simulation.

Key Points
- To simulate means to duplicate the features of a real system. The idea is to imitate a real-world situation with a mathematical model that does not affect operations.
- The advantages of simulation make it one of the most widely used decision modeling techniques in corporations.
- The disadvantages of simulation include cost, its trial-and-error nature, and the fact that each model is unique and not necessarily transferrable to other problems.
- Monte Carlo simulation can be used when we have decision variables that are probabilistic.
- Since very little in life is certain, there are plenty of decision variables in business problems that we may want to simulate.
- To establish a probability distribution for a variable, we often assume that historical behavior is a good indicator of future outcomes.
- Since probabilities reflect behavior over the long-term, simulated results can differ from analytical results in a short-term simulation.
- A random number is a number that has been selected through a totally random process.
- There are several ways to pick random numbers—using a computer, a table, a roulette wheel, and so on.
- Cumulative probabilities are found by summing all the previous probabilities up to the current demand.
- When developing a table for random number generation, we create a random number interval for each value of the variable. The specific numbers assigned to an interval are not relevant as long as the right proportion of unique numbers is assigned to the interval.
- When using a table for random number generation, we simulate values by comparing random numbers against the random number intervals.
- A simulation process must be repeated numerous times to get meaningful results.
- Simulation software packages have built-in procedures for simulating from several different probability distributions.
- Simulation software packages also allow us to easily replicate a model and keep track of several output measures.
- The use of simulation has been broadened by the availability of computing technology.
- Special-purpose simulation languages have several advantages over general-purpose languages.
- Excel's RAND function generates random decimal numbers between 0 and 1.

Summary

- Uniform distributions can be either discrete or continuous.
- Excel's RANDBETWEEN function can be used to simulate from a discrete uniform distribution.
- Excel's NORMINV function can be used to simulate from a normal distribution.
- Excel's LN function can be used to simulate from an exponential distribution.
- Excel's CRITBINOM function can be used to simulate from a binomial distribution
- Excel's IF function can be used to select from two (or more) possible outcomes.
- Excel's LOOKUP function can be used to simulate from a discrete general distribution.
- The first range in the LOOKUP function for simulating from a discrete general distribution must contain the lower limits of the random number intervals.
- The first issue to understand in any simulation model is what we mean by one replication of the model.
- We need to replicate a simulation model at least a few thousand times to get consistent summary results.
- If the simulation model is very compact, we can perform replications by simply copying the model several times. But this could make the Excel file very large.
- Using Data Table in Excel is a convenient way of replicating a large model several times.
- Excel's Descriptive Statistics procedure can be used to compute summary statistics.
- Simulation results can be used to compute several performance measures.
- Simulation is useful in inventory problems when demand and lead time (the time between order placement and order receipt) are probabilistic.
- To run several what-if scenarios using the same model, it is good to make parameter values cell references in all formulas.
- We use a $ symbol to anchor cell references while copying formulas in Excel.
- We use Scenario Manager when we want to try several values for one or more input parameters in a model.
- Results from Scenario Manager can be shown either as a Scenario Summary table or as a PivotTable.
- Simulation is an effective technique for modeling many real-world queuing systems that cannot be analyzed analytically.
- In discrete-event simulation models, we need to keep track of the passage of time by using a simulation clock.
- In a queuing simulation, we can use Excel's MATCH function to calculate the queue length.
- Revenue and yield management problems are popular in the airline and hotel industries.
- Business simulation games are popular educational tools in many colleges.
- Econometric models are huge simulations involving thousands of regression equations tied together by economic factors. They use what-if questions to test various policies.
- Simulation is a popular technique for analyzing uncertainty in projects.

Glossary

CRITBINOM An Excel function that can be used to randomly generate values from binomial probability distributions. Starting with Excel 2010, an improved version of this function, called BINOM.INV, is available.

Data Table A procedure in Excel that allows simulation models to be replicated several times.

Discrete-Event Simulation A simulation model in which we need to keep track of the passage of time by using a simulation clock.

Discrete General Distribution A distribution in which a variable can take on one of several discrete values, each with its own probability.

Flow Diagram, or Flowchart A graphical means of presenting the logic of a simulation model. It is a tool that helps in writing a simulation computer program.

Inventory Position On-hand inventory plus any outstanding orders that have not yet arrived.

LOOKUP An Excel function that can be used to randomly generate values from discrete general probability distributions.

Monte Carlo simulation A simulation that experiments with probabilistic elements of a system by generating random numbers to create values for those elements.

NORMINV An Excel function that can be used to randomly generate values from normal probability distributions.

Operational Gaming The use of simulation in competitive situations, such as military games and business or management games.

RAND An Excel function that generates a random number between 0 and 1 each time it is computed.

RANDBETWEEN An Excel function that can be used to randomly generate values from discrete uniform probability distributions.

Random Number A number whose value is selected completely at random.

Replication A single run of a simulation model. Also known as a *run* or *trial*.

Simulation A technique that involves building a mathematical model to represent a real-world situation. The model is then experimented with to estimate the effects of various actions and decisions.

Systems Simulation A simulation model that deals with the dynamics of large organizational or governmental systems.

10.10 Exercises

Solved Problems

Solved Problem 10–1

Higgins Plumbing and Heating maintains a supply of eight water heaters in any given week. Owner Jerry Higgins likes the idea of having this large supply on hand to meet customer demand, but he also recognizes that it is expensive to do so. He examines water heater sales over the past 50 weeks and notes the following data:

Water Heater Sales Per Week	Number of Weeks This Number Was Sold
4	6
5	5
6	9
7	12
8	8
9	7
10	3

a. Set up a model to simulate Higgins' weekly sales over a two-year (104-week) period and compute the following measures (based on a single replication):
   - Average weekly sales
   - Number of weeks with stockouts over a two-year period

   Replicate your model 200 times, using Data Table, to determine (1) the average weekly sales and (2) probability that Higgins will have more than 20 weeks with stockouts over a two-year period.

b. Use the probability distribution for sales to determine the expected value of sales. Explain any differences between this value and the average value computed using Data Table in part (a).

Solution The Excel layout to answer all the questions in this problem is presented in Figure 10.17. The spreadsheet is organized as follows:
- Column A shows the week number.
- We use a LOOKUP function to simulate the weekly sales in column B. The parameters (random number intervals, sales, and probabilities) for the LOOKUP function are shown in cells E4:H10.
- In column C, we use an IF function to determine the occurrence of a stockout (0 = no stockout, 1 = stockout). For example, the formula in cell C4 is =IF(B4>$H$12,1,0).

616 —— Chapter 10: Simulation Modeling

Parameters for LOOKUP function used to simulate sales

	A	B	C	D	E	F	G	H	I	J	K	L
1	Higgins Plumbing and Heating									Data Table		
2						Sales Distribution						
3	Week	Sales	Stockout? (1 = Yes)		Sales	Prob- ability	RN intM lower limit	RN intM upper limit		Run	Avg sales	Stockou t weeks
4	1	8	0		4	0.12	0.00	0.12		1	7.14	24
5	2	8	0		5	0.10	0.12	0.22		2	6.81	21
6	3	4	0		6	0.18	0.22	0.40		3	7.14	23
7	4	9	1		7	0.24	0.40	0.64		4	6.94	22
8	5	6	0		8	0.16	0.64	0.80		5	6.75	21
9	6	7	0		9	0.14	0.80	0.94		6	6.88	23
10	7	8	0		10	0.06	0.94	1.00		7	6.83	21
11	8	7	0							8	7.03	23
12	9	7	0		Supply each week =			8		9	6.84	17
13	10	7	0							10	6.76	23
14	11	9	1		(a)					11	6.76	18
15	12	9	1		Based on 1 replication:					12	6.76	21
16	13	8	0		Average sales =			7.14		13	6.95	23
17	14	9	1		No. of stockout weeks =			24		14	6.80	18
18	15	8	0							15	6.77	21
19	16	8	0		Based on 200 replications:					16	7.12	25
20	17	9	1		Average sales =			6.90		17	6.93	20
21	18	9	1		P(>20 stockout weeks) =			54.5%		18	6.77	22
22	19	7	0							19	7.01	20
23	20	9	1		(b)					20	6.65	19
24	21	8	0		Expected sales =			6.88		21	6.95	27
25	22	7	0							22	6.88	20
106	103	7	0							103	6.99	22
107	104	8	0							104	6.92	26
108										105	7.08	21
202										199	6.84	19
203										200	6.94	23

=H16
=H17

COUNTIF function is used to count number of weeks with >20 stockouts.

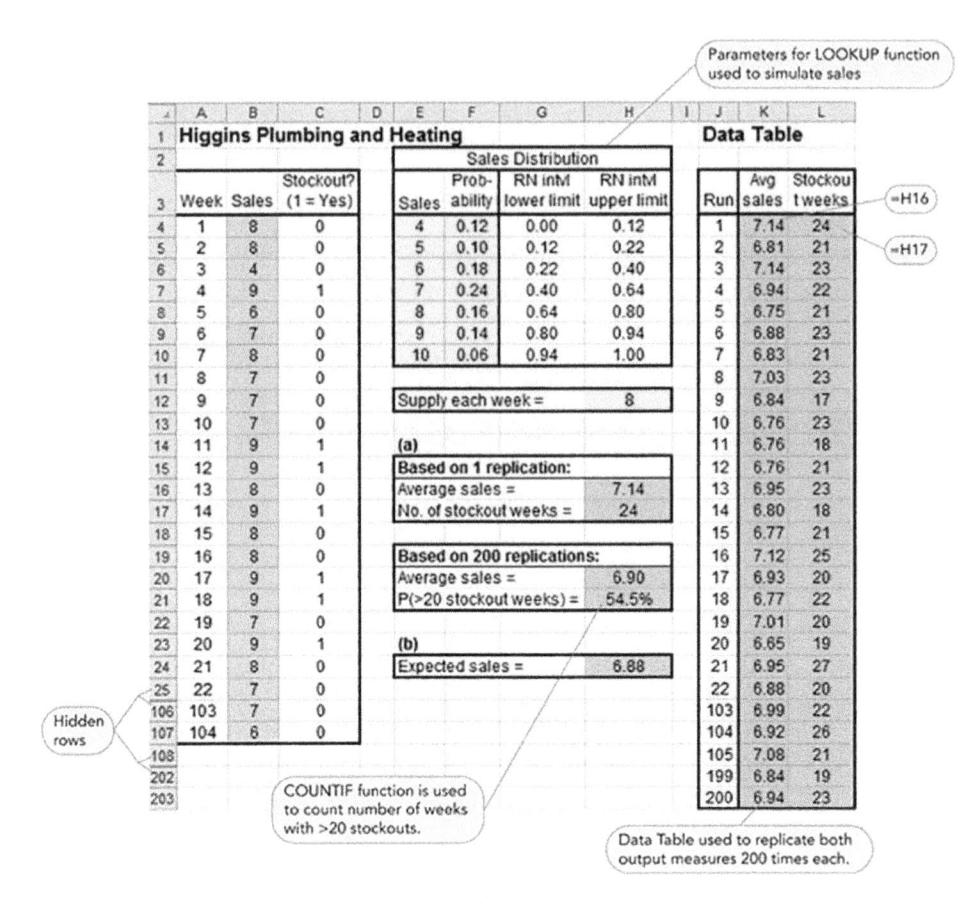

Data Table used to replicate both output measures 200 times each.

Figure 10.17: Excel Layout and Results for Higgins Plumbing and Heating

File: Figure 10.17.xlsx

a. The average sales over the two-year period is the average of the sales values in cells B4:B107. This value, shown in cell H16 in Figure 10.17, is 7.14 units per week. Next, we can add the 104 stockout indicators in cells C4:C107 to determine the number of stockouts over the two-year period. This value, shown in cell H17, is 24 stockout weeks. (Remember that these values will change each time you recalculate the model.)

We now set up Data Table to run 200 replications of the values in cells H16 and H17. The table is shown in columns J to L in Figure 10.17. From the 200 replicated values in cells K4:K203, we compute the average sales to be 6.90 units per week (shown in cell H20). We then use Excel's COUNTIF function on the 200 replicated values in cells L4:L203 to compute the probability that Higgins will have more than 20 weeks with stockouts over a two-year period. The formula used is

=COUNTIF(L4:L203,">20")/200. The value, shown in cell H21, indicates that there is a 54.5% chance that this event will occur.

b. Using expected values, we find the following:

$$\text{Expected heater sales} = 0.12 \times 4 + 0.10 \times 5 + 0.18 \times 6 + 0.24 \times 7$$
$$+ 0.16 \times 8 + 0.14 \times 9 + 0.06 \times 10$$
$$= 6.88 \text{ heaters}$$

We can compute this value by using the following formula:

=SUMPRODUCT(E4:E10,F4:F10)

This value is shown in cell H24 in Figure 10.17. The simulated average (6.90 in Figure 10.17) is based on just 200 replications of the model. Hence, although this value is close to the expected value of 6.88, the two values need not necessarily be the same. With a longer simulation, the two values will become even closer.

Solved Problem 10–2 Norris Medical Clinic is staffed by a single physician who, on average, requires 15 minutes to treat a patient. The distribution of this service time follows a "truncated" normal distribution with a standard deviation of 4 minutes, but with a minimum service time of 5 minutes. Patients arrive at an average rate of 2.5 customers per hour, according to the exponential distribution. Simulate 100 patient arrivals and replicate the model 200 times, using Data Table, to answer the following questions:

a. What percentage of time is the queue empty?
b. How many patients, on average, are in the queue?
c. What is the average wait time per patient in the queue?

Solution This is an example of a discrete-event simulation model. The model simulates a queuing system in which arrival times follow an exponential distribution and service times follow a normal distribution. Each replication of the model corresponds to the arrival and service of 100 patients at the clinic. The Excel layout for this problem is presented in Figure 10.18. We have included patient number 0, with zero values for all columns, to *initialize* the simulation clock that keeps track of the passage of time. Rows 5 through 104 in the spreadsheet are organized as follows:
- Column A shows the patient number (1 through 100).
- Column B shows the time between arrivals of successive patients, simulated from an exponential distribution by using the LN function. From Table 10.4, the Excel formula is =−(1/μ)*LN(RAND()). Note that the average arrival rate, μ, in this case is 2.5 patients per hour. However, because all other times in this problem are counted in minutes, we convert the interarrival time between successive patients to minutes also. The formula in cells B5:B104 is therefore

$$= -60 * (1/\$K\$6) * (LN(RAND()))$$

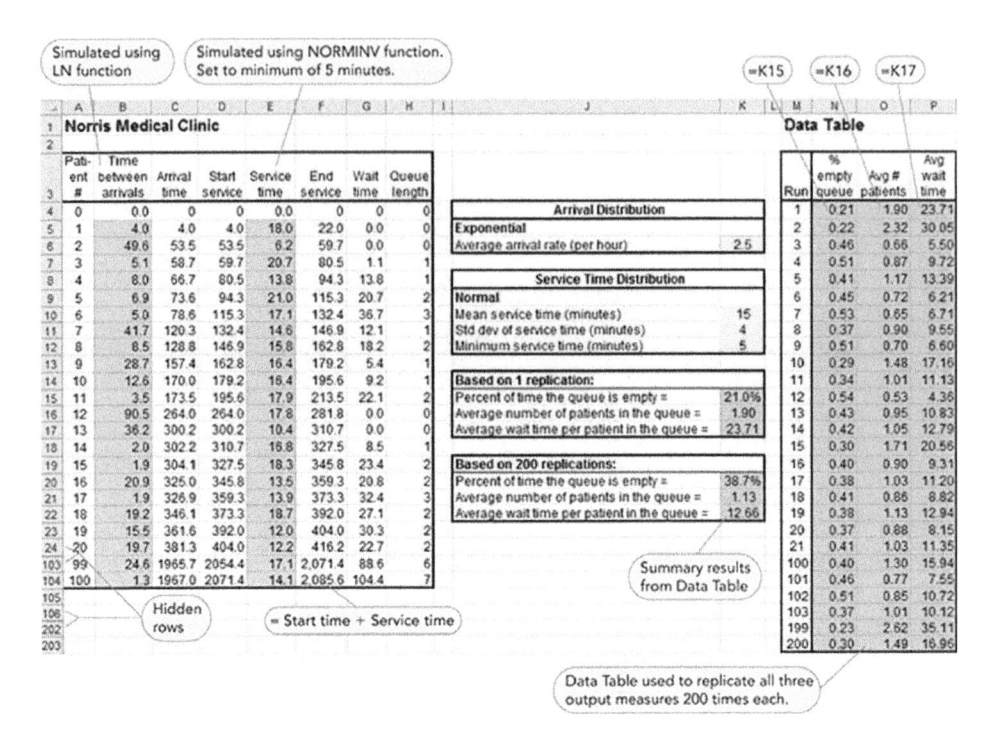

Figure 10.18: Excel Layout and Results for Norris Medical Clinic

📊 File: Figure 10.18.xlsx

- In column C, we calculate the arrival time of the current patient as the sum of the arrival time of the previous patient and the time between arrivals (column B). For example, the formula in cell C5 is

$$=C4+B5$$

- The time this patient actually starts service is calculated in column D as the maximum of the arrival time and the time the previous patient finishes service. For example, the formula in cell D5 is

$$=MAX(C5,F4)$$

- Column E shows the service time for this patient, simulated using a NORMINV function. The parameters of this NORMINV function are shown in cells K10:K11. We use a MAX function to ensure that the minimum service time per patient is 5 minutes. The formula in cells E5:E104 is

$$=MAX(\$K\$12, NORMINV(RAND(), \$K\$10, \$K\$11))$$

- The time at which this patient ends service is shown in column F as the sum of the start time (shown in column D) and the service time (shown in column E).
- In column G, we calculate the wait time of this patient as the difference between the patient's start time (shown in column D) and arrival time (shown in column C).
- Finally, in column H, we calculate the queue length, using Excel's MATCH function. For example, the formula in cell H5 is

$$=A5-MATCH(C5,\$D\$5:D5,1)$$

Using the 100 wait time and queue length values in cells G5:H104, we determine the following three performance measures for the queuing system each day:

a. Percentage of time the queue is empty (cell K15)

$$=COUNTIF(H5:H104,"=0")/100=21\%$$

b. Average number of patients in the queue (cell K16)

$$=AVERAGE(H5:H104)=1.90$$

c. Average wait time per patient in the queue (cell K17)

$$=AVERAGE(G5:G104)=23.71 \text{ minutes}$$

The values in cells K15:K17 represent results from just one replication of the model. To determine more precise values for these measures, we now replicate all three measures 200 times each. The Data Table procedure to do so is shown in columns M through P in Figure 10.18. Based on the 200 replicated values in this Data Table procedure, the queue at the clinic is empty 38.7% of the time, there are 1.13 patients on average in the queue at any time, and each patient in the queue waits for an average of 12.66 minutes.

Solved Problem 10–3 Heartbreak Hotel routinely experiences no-shows (people who make reservations for a room and don't show up) during the peak season, when the hotel is always full. No-shows follow the distribution shown in the following table:

No-shows	Probability
0	0.10
1	0.13
2	0.31
3	0.16
4	0.21
5	0.09

To reduce the number of vacant rooms, the hotel overbooks three rooms; that is, the hotel accepts three more reservations than the number of rooms available. On a day when the hotel experiences fewer than three no-shows, there are not enough rooms for those who have reservations. The hotel's policy is to send these guests to a competing hotel down the street, at Heartbreak's expense of $125. If the number of no-shows is more than three, the hotel has vacant rooms, resulting in an opportunity cost of $50 per room.

a. Simulate one month (30 days) of operation to calculate the hotel's total monthly cost due to overbooking and opportunity loss. Replicate this cost 200 times to compute the average monthly cost.
b. Heartbreak Hotel would like to determine the most desirable number of rooms to overbook. Of these six choices—0, 1, 2, 3, 4, or 5 rooms—what is your recommendation? Why?

Solution This is an example of a revenue management problem where the number of no-shows follows a discrete general distribution. Each replication of the simulation model corresponds to 30 days of operations at the hotel. The Excel layout for this model is presented in Figure 10.19.

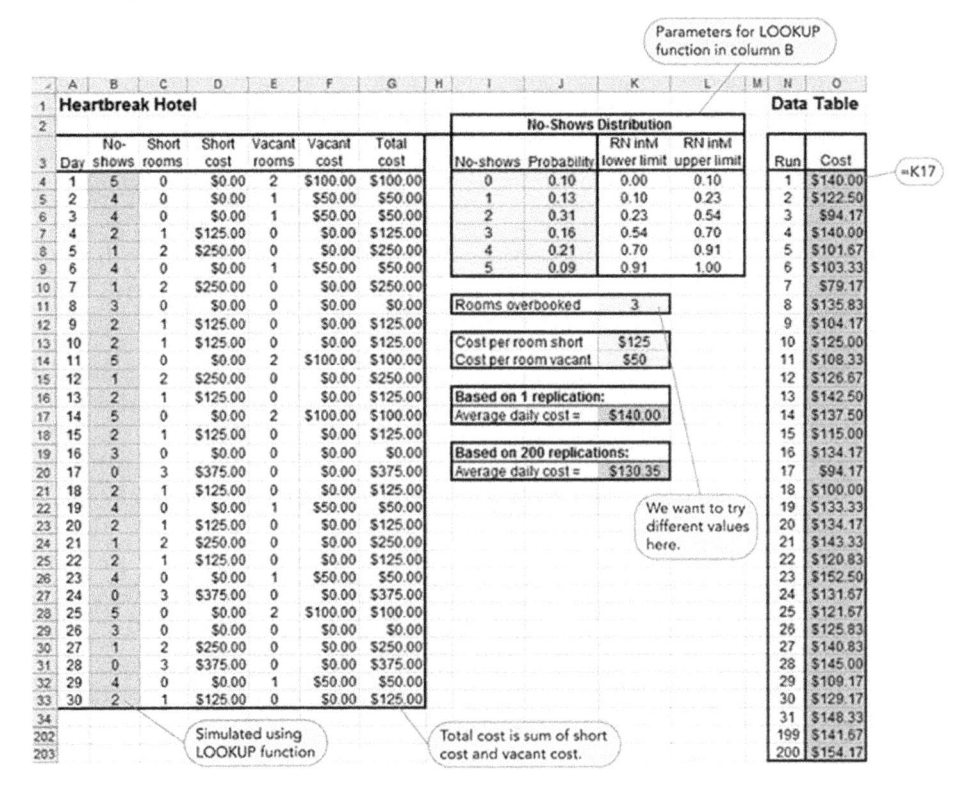

Figure 10.19: Excel Layout and Results for Heartbreak Hotel

File: Figure 10.19.xlsx, Sheet: Figure 10.19

The spreadsheet is organized as follows:
- Column A shows the day number (1 through 30).
- In column B, we use a LOOKUP function to simulate the number of no-shows. The parameters for this LOOKUP function are shown in cells I4:L9.
- In column C, we compute the number of short rooms (i.e., rooms that are unavailable for guests) by comparing the number of no-shows with the number of rooms we decide to overbook (shown in cell K11). For example, the formula in cell C4 is

$$=\text{MAX}(\$K\$11-B4,0)$$

- Short cost in column $D = \$K\$13 \times$ column C.
- In column E, we compute the number of vacant rooms by once again comparing the number of no-shows with the number of rooms we decide to overbook (shown in cell K11). For example, the formula in cell E4 is

$$=\text{MAX}(B4-\$K\$11,0)$$

- Vacant cost in column $F = \$K\$14 \times$ column E.
- Total cost in column $G =$ column $D +$ column E.

a. The average total cost of $140 per day shown in cell K17 is based on only one replication. Hence, to get a more precise estimate of this average, we replicate this measure by using Data Table, as shown in column N and O in Figure 10.19. Based on 200 replications, the average total cost at Heartbreak Hotel appears to be $130.35 per day (shown in cell K20).

b. To determine the number of rooms that Heartbreak Hotel should overbook each day, we set up Scenario Manager to automatically try the six choices—0, 1, 2, 3, 4, and 5. For each scenario, cell K11 is the Changing Cell and cell K20 is the Result Cell. The results of the Scenario Manager procedure, shown in Figure 10.20, indicate that Heartbreak Hotel should overbook two rooms each day. The total cost of $83.55 at this level is the lowest among all scenarios.

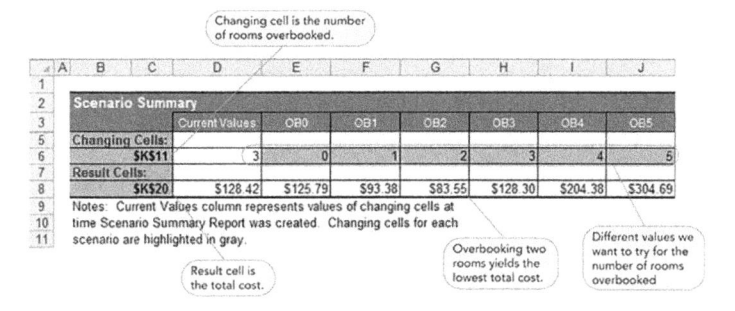

Figure 10.20: Scenario Manager Results for Heartbreak Hotel

File: Figure 10.19.xlsx, Sheet: Figure 10.20

Solved Problem 10-4 General Foundry, Inc., a metalworks plant in Milwaukee, has long been trying to avoid the expense of installing air pollution control equipment. The local environmental protection agency (EPA) recently gave the foundry 16 weeks to install a complex air-filter system on its main smokestack. General Foundry has been warned that it may be forced to close unless the device is installed in the allotted period. Lester Harky, the managing partner, wants to make sure that installation of the filtering system progresses smoothly and on time. General Foundry has identified the eight activities that need to be performed in order for the project to be completed. For each activity, the following table shows the immediate predecessors and three time estimates—-optimistic, most likely, and pessimistic:

Activity	Description	Immediate Predecessors	Optimistic Time (a)	Most Likely Time (m)	Pessimistic Time (b)
A	Build internal components	—	1	2	3
B	Modify roof and floor	—	2	3	4
C	Construct collection stack	A	1	2	3
D	Pour concrete and install frame	A, B	2	4	6
E	Build high-temperature burner	C	1	4	7
F	Install pollution control system	C	1	2	9
G	Install air pollution device	D, E	3	4	11
H	Inspect and test	F, G	1	2	3

Lester wants to find the probability that the project will meet the EPA's 16-week deadline. Round off all activity times to two decimal places.

Solution This is an example of analyzing uncertainty in a project management problem. Recall that in Chapter 7, we studied this issue analytically using probability distributions. In that analysis, we first computed the expected value and variance of the project completion time, assuming that the activity time of each activity followed a beta distribution. We then used a normal distribution to compute various probabilities for the project completion time (see section 7.4 for details). As noted in that chapter, another popular way to analyze uncertainty in projects is by using simulation. Let us simulate General Foundry's project here.

It is convenient to first express the activities in the project as a project network. We show this in Figure 10.21, where the nodes represent the activities and the arcs represent the precedence relationships between activities.

Exercises — 623

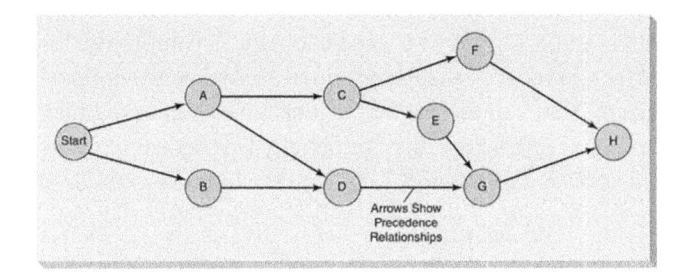

Figure 10.21: Project Network for General Foundry

The Excel layout for this simulation model is presented in Figure 10.22.

	A	B	C	D	E	F	G	H	I	J	K	L	M	N
1	General Foundry's Project												Data Table	
2	Calculations set to Manual. Press F9 to recalculate.													
3	Activity	Description	Immed. pred.	Optimistic time (a)	Most likely time (m)	Pessimistic time (b)	Expected Time	St. Dev. Time	Activity time	Start time	Finish time		Run	Finish Time
4	A	Build internal components	—	1	2	3	2.00	0.33	2.13	0.00	2.13		1	17.08
5	B	Modify roof and floor	—	2	3	4	3.00	0.33	3.56	0.00	3.56		2	15.87
6	C	Construct collection stack	A	1	2	3	2.00	0.33	2.64	2.13	4.77		3	15.61
7	D	Pour concrete and install frame	A, B	2	4	6	4.00	0.67	3.79	3.56	7.35		4	15.76
8	E	Build high-temperature burner	C	1	4	7	4.00	1.00	3.71	4.77	8.48		5	19.02
9	F	Install pollution control system	C	1	2	9	3.00	1.33	3.50	4.77	8.27		6	17.40
10	G	Install air pollution device	D, E	3	4	11	5.00	1.33	6.73	8.48	15.21		7	16.32
11	H	Inspect and test	F, G	1	2	3	2.00	0.33	1.87	15.21	17.08		8	16.82
12													9	13.54
13		Average Completion Time (Weeks) =		15.18									10	13.71
14		P(Completion Time <= 16 Weeks) =		70.00%									11	15.05
15													12	15.35
16													13	17.32
17													14	17.00
18													15	16.38
19		= (a + 4m + b) / 6											16	13.29
20													17	16.81
21													18	12.20
22													19	15.14
23													20	15.23

Annotations:
- = (b − a) / 6
- Activity times simulated using the NORM.INV function.
- = Start time + Activity time
- Start time of an activity must satisfy all precedence relationships.
- = (a + 4m + b) / 6

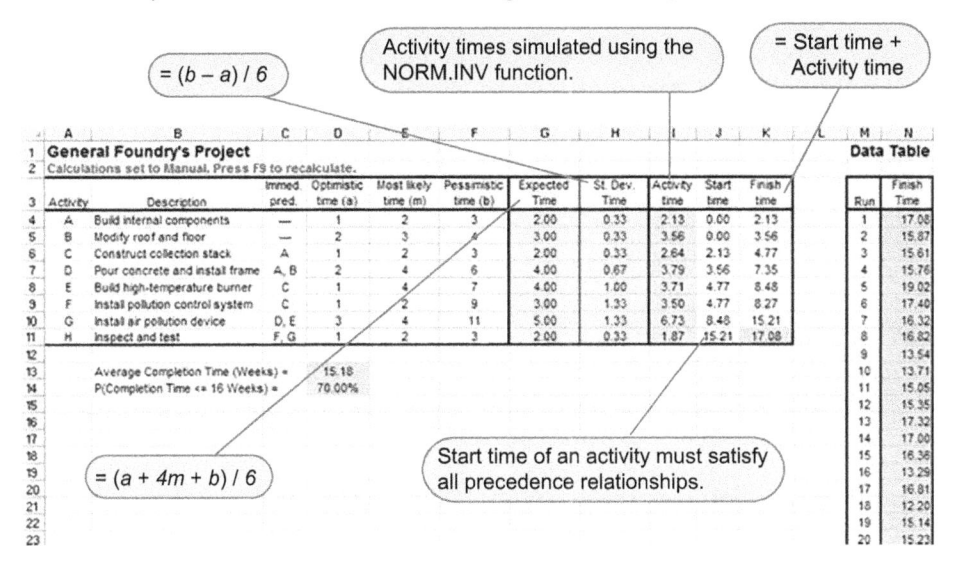

Figure 10.22: Excel Layout and Results Using Crystal Ball for General Foundry

X📄 File: Figure 10.22.xlsx

The spreadsheet is organized as follows:
- Columns A through F show the name, description, immediate predecessors, and three time estimates for each activity (activities A through H).
- In Columns G and H, we compute the expected time and standard deviation of each activity using Equations 7–6 and 7–8, respectively.
- In column I, we simulate the actual duration of each activity by using the NORM.INV function in Excel. We then round this value to two decimal places, using the ROUND function. For example, the formula in cell I4 is

=ROUND(NORM.INV(RAND(),G4,H4),2)

- In column J, we calculate the actual start time for each activity. In computing this time, we need to ensure that all predecessors for an activity have been completed before that activity can begin. For example, both activities A and B have to finish before activity D can start. Hence, the start time for activity D is set equal to the maximum of the finish times of activities A and B. That is, the formula in cell J7 is

$$=MAX(K4,K5)$$

- In column K, we compute the finish time of each activity as the sum of the start time of that activity (column J) and the actual duration of that activity (column I).

In General Foundry's project, the project completion time is the completion time of activity H, shown in cell K11. Based on the single replication shown in Figure 10.22 it appears that the project will finish in only 17.08 weeks. However, in order to get a more precise value of this output measure, we use Data Table to replicate the model 200 times in cells M4:N203.

Based on the 200 replications, it appears that the average completion time of the project is 15.18 weeks. More important for General Foundry, the simulation indicates that there is a 70.00% chance that the project will finish in less than 16 weeks. Note that this probability is consistent with the analytical result we obtained in section 7.4 using normal probability analysis.

Discussion Questions

10-1. What are the advantages and limitations of simulation models?
10-2. Why might a manager be forced to use simulation instead of an analytical model in dealing with a problem of
  (a) inventory ordering policy?
  (b) ships docking in a port to unload?
  (c) bank teller service windows?
  (d) the U.S. economy?
10-3. What types of management problems can be solved more easily by using decision modeling techniques other than simulation?
10-4. What are the major steps in the simulation process?
10-5. What is Monte Carlo simulation? What principles underlie its use, and what steps are followed in applying it?
10-6. Why is a computer necessary in conducting a real-world simulation?
10-7. What is operational gaming? What is systems simulation? Give examples of how each may be applied.
10-8. Do you think the application of simulation will increase strongly in the next 10 years? Why or why not?
10-9. Would the average output value in a simulation problem change appreciably if a longer period were simulated? Why or why not?
10-10. How might drawing a flow diagram help in developing a simulation model?

10–11. Perform an Internet search for the two popular Excel Add-In programs for simulation called Crystal Ball and @RISK. Describe some of the useful features of these programs that increase the capabilities of standard Excel. Be sure to comment specifically on their distribution-fitting capabilities.

10–12. What does Scenario Manager allow you to accomplish in an Excel-based simulation model?

10–13. Do you think we can use Excel's Solver to solve simulation models? Why or why not?

Problems

Notes:
- Simulation models for all the following problems can be set up by using Excel.
- Wherever necessary, replications can be done using Data Table.
- In all problems, we have specified the number of replications to use simply as N. In general, we recommend that you try to replicate each simulation model as many times as is convenient. If you are using Data Table, 200 to 300 replications should be appropriate to keep the computation time reasonable and the resulting Excel file relatively small (even though the average values may vary from simulation to simulation).
- Wherever a decision is involved, you can use Scenario Manager.

10–14. Weekly demand for tennis balls at The Racquet Club is normally distributed, with a mean of 35 cases and a standard deviation of 5 cases. The club gets a profit of $50 per case.
(a) Simulate 52 weeks of demand and calculate the average weekly profit. Make all demand values integers in your model.
(b) What is the probability that weekly profit will be $2,000 or more?

10–15. Edward Owen is responsible for the maintenance, rental, and day-to-day operation of several large apartment complexes on the upper east side of New York City. Owen is especially concerned about the cost projections for replacing air conditioner (A/C) compressors. He would like to simulate the number of A/C failures each month. Using data from similar apartment buildings he manages in a New York City suburb, Clark establishes the probability of failures during a month as follows:

Number of A/C Failures	Probability
0	0.10
1	0.17
2	0.21
3	0.28
4	0.16
5	0.07
6	0.01

(a) Simulate Owen's monthly A/C failures for a period of three years. Compute the average number of failures per month.
(b) Explain any difference between the simulated average failures and the expected value of failures computed by using the probability distribution.

10-16. Jay's Appliances sells microfridges according to the monthly demand distribution shown in the following table:

Demand	Probability
10	0.02
15	0.07
20	0.11
25	0.12
30	0.21
35	0.18
40	0.21
45	0.06
50	0.02

Simulate six years of demand and compare theoretical and simulated results for the following measures:
(a) Average demand.
(b) Probability that demand will be less than or equal to 30 microfridges.

10-17. Shawn Bishop, a neuroscience PhD student at Clarksville University, has been having problems balancing his checkbook. His monthly income is derived from a graduate research assistantship; however, he also makes extra money in most months by tutoring undergraduates in their introductory neurobiology course. His chances of various income levels are shown here (assume that this income is received at the beginning of each month):

Monthly Income	Probability
$ 850	0.35
$ 900	0.25
$ 950	0.25
$1,000	0.15

Bishop has expenditures that vary from month to month, and he estimates that they will follow this distribution:

Monthly Expenses	Probability
$ 800	0.05
$ 900	0.20
$1,000	0.40
$1,100	0.35

Bishop begins his final year with $1,500 in his checking account. Simulate the cash flow for 12 months and replicate your model N times to identify Bishop's (a) ending balance at the end of the year and (b) probability that he will have a negative balance in any month.

10-18. Chelsea Truman sells celebrity magazines on Sunday morning in an area surrounded by three busy shopping centers. Demand for the magazines is distributed as shown in the following table:

Demand	Probability
50	0.05
75	0.10
100	0.25
125	0.30
150	0.20
175	0.10

Chelsea has decided to order 100 magazines from her supplier. Chelsea pays $2 for each magazine she orders and sells each magazine for $3. Unsold magazines can be returned to the supplier for $0.75.

(a) Simulate one year (52 Sundays) of operation to calculate Chelsea's total yearly profit. Replicate this calculation N times. What is the average yearly profit?

(b) Chelsea would like to investigate the profitability of ordering 50, 100, 150, and 175 magazines at the start of each Sunday. Which order quantity would you recommend? Why?

10-19. The Paris Bakery has decided to bake 30 batches of its famous beignets at the beginning of the day. The store has determined that daily demand will follow the distribution shown in the following table:

Daily Demand	Probability
15	0.08
20	0.12
25	0.25
30	0.20
35	0.20
40	0.15

Each batch costs the Paris Bakery $50 and can be sold for $100. The Paris Bakery can sell any unsold batches for $25 the next day.

(a) Simulate one month (25 days) of operation to calculate the bakery's total monthly profit. Replicate this calculation N times to compute the average total monthly profit.

(b) The Paris Bakery would like to investigate the profitability of baking 25, 30, 35, or 40 batches at the start of the day. Which quantity would you recommend? Why?

10–20. Lionel's Life Jacket Rentals leases life jackets each day from a supplier and rents them to customers who use them when they raft down the Delaware River. Each day, Lionel leases 30 life jackets from his supplier at a cost of $4 per life jacket. He rents them to his customers for $15 per day. Rental demand follows the normal distribution, with a mean of 30 life jackets and a standard deviation of 6 life jackets. (In your model use integers for all demands.)

(a) Simulate this leasing policy for a month (30 days) of operation to calculate the total monthly profit. Replicate this calculation N times. What is the average monthly profit?

(b) Lionel would like to evaluate the average monthly profit if he leases 25, 30, 35, and 40 life jackets. What is your recommendation? Why?

10–21. Kirkpatrick Aircrafts operates a large number of computerized plotting machines. For the most part, the plotting devices are used to create line drawings of complex wing airfoils and fuselage part dimensions. The engineers operating the automated plotters are called loft lines engineers.

The computerized plotters consist of a minicomputer system connected to a 4×5-foot flat table with a series of ink pens suspended above it. When a sheet of clear plastic or paper is properly placed on the table, the computer directs a series of horizontal and vertical pen movements until the desired figure is drawn.

The plotting machines are highly reliable, with the exception of the four sophisticated ink pens that are built in. The pens constantly clog and jam in a raised or lowered position. When this occurs, the plotter is unusable.

Currently, Kirkpatrick Aircrafts replaces each pen as it fails. The service manager has, however, proposed replacing all four pens every time one fails. This should cut down the frequency of plotter failures. At present, it takes one hour to replace one pen. All four pens could be replaced in two hours. The total cost of a plotter being unusable is $500 per hour. Each pen costs $80. The following breakdown data are thought to be valid:

One Pen Replaced		Four Pens Replaced	
Hours Between Failures	Probability	Hours Between Failures	Probability
10	0.05	70	0.10
20	0.15	100	0.15
30	0.15	110	0.25
40	0.20	120	0.35
50	0.20	130	0.20
60	0.15	140	0.05

(a) For each option (replacing one pen at a time and replacing all four pens at a time), simulate the average total time a plotter would operate before it would have 20 failures. Then compute the total cost per hour for each option to determine which option Kirkpatrick Aircrafts should use. Use N replications.

(b) Compute the total cost per hour analytically for each option. How do these results compare with the simulation results?

10-22. A high school guidance counselor has scheduled one-on-one meetings today with 10 seniors to discuss their college plans. Each meeting is scheduled for 20 minutes, with the first meeting set to start at 9:00 A.M. Due to their hectic class and extracurricular schedules, not every student arrives on time, and not every meeting lasts exactly 20 minutes. The counselor knows the following from past experience: A student will be 10 minutes early 5% of the time, 5 minutes early 20% of the time, exactly on time 35% of the time, 5 minutes late 30% of the time, and 10 minutes late 10% of the time. The counselor further estimates that there is a 15% chance that a meeting will take only 15 minutes, 50% chance it will take exactly the planned time, 25% chance it will take 25 minutes, and 10% chance it will take 30 minutes.

Students are seen in the order in which they have been scheduled, regardless of when they arrive. However, a student arriving early can see the counselor as soon as the previous meeting ends. Use N replications to determine when the counselor will complete the last meeting.

10-23. Dr. Carter Logue practices dentistry in Santa Fe, New Mexico. Logue tries hard to schedule appointments so that patients do not have to wait beyond their appointment time. His October 20 schedule is shown in the following table:

Patient	Scheduled Appointment	Time Needed (min.)
Adams	9:30 A.M.	20
Brown	9:45 A.M.	15
Crawford	10:15 A.M.	15
Dannon	10:30 A.M.	10
Erving	10:45 A.M.	20
Fink	11:15 A.M.	15
Graham	11:30 A.M.	30
Hinkel	11:45 A.M.	15

Unfortunately, not every patient arrives exactly on schedule. Also, some examinations take longer than planned, and some take less time than planned. Logue's experience dictates the following: 20% of the patients will be 20 minutes early, 10% of the patients will be 10 minutes early, 40% of the patients will be on time, 25% of the patients will be 10 minutes late, and 5% of the patients will be 20 minutes late.

He further estimates that there is a 15% chance that an appointment will take 20% less time than planned, 50% chance it will take exactly the planned time, 25% chance it will take 20% more time than planned, and 10% chance it will take 40% more time than planned.

Dr. Logue has to leave at 12:15 P.M. on October 20 to catch a flight to a dental convention in Rio de Janeiro. Assuming that he is ready to start his workday at 9:30 A.M. and that patients are treated in order of their scheduled exam (even if one late patient arrives after an early one), will he be able to make the flight? Use N replications.

10–24. Lee Appliances knows that weekly demand for high-end microwaves is normally distributed, with a mean of 25 units and a standard deviation of 7 units. (In your model use integers for all demands.) Lee replenishes its inventory by ordering 300 units from the distributor whenever its current inventory reaches 70 units. The lead time (in weeks) to receive an order from the distributor follows the distribution shown in the following table:

Lead Time	Probability
1	0.15
2	0.25
3	0.30
4	0.15
5	0.10
6	0.10

The cost to hold one unit in inventory for one week is $20. The cost to place an order with the factory is $300. Stockout costs are estimated at $100 per unit. The initial inventory level is 140 units.

(a) Simulate 52 weeks of operation to calculate the total semiannual cost and the percentage of stockouts for the period. Replicate these calculations N times each to calculate the average values for these measures.

(b) Lee would like to evaluate the economics of ordering 250, 275, 300, 325, and 350 units, with a reorder point of 70 units. Based on the average total semiannual cost, which order quantity would you recommend?

(c) Lee would like to evaluate the economics of ordering 300 units, with reorder points of 60, 70, 80, 90, and 100 tires. Based on the average total semiannual cost, which reorder point would you recommend?

10–25. Mattress Heaven orders a certain brand of mattress from its supplier and sells the mattresses at its retail location. The store currently orders 400 mattresses whenever the inventory level drops to 200. The cost to hold one mattress in inventory for one day is $0.75. The cost to place an order with the supplier is $75, and stockout costs are $150 per mattress. Beginning inventory is 150 mattresses. The daily demand probabilities are shown in the following table:

Daily Demand	Probability
20	0.08
30	0.14
40	0.20
50	0.26
60	0.22
70	0.10

Lead time follows a discrete uniform distribution between 2 and 5 days (both inclusive). Simulate this inventory policy for a quarter (90 days) and calculate the total quarterly cost. Also calculate the percentage of stockouts for the quarter. Replicate these calculations N times each to calculate the average values for these measures.

10–26. Consider the Mattress Heaven problem described in Problem 10–25.
  (a) Mattress Heaven would like to evaluate ordering 350, 400, 450, and 500 mattresses when the reorder point of 200 is reached. Based on the average total quarterly cost, which order quantity would you recommend?
  (b) Mattress Heaven would like to evaluate reorder points of 150, 200, 250, and 300 mattresses, with an order quantity of 400 mattresses. Based on the average total quarterly cost, which reorder point would you recommend?

10–27. Music Mania sells MP3 players to its customers. Music Mania orders 300 MP3 players from its supplier when its inventory reaches 80 units. Daily demand for MP3 players is discrete, uniformly distributed between 30 and 60 (both inclusive). The lead time from the supplier also varies for each order and is discrete, uniformly distributed between 1 and 3 days (both inclusive). The cost to hold one unit in inventory for one day is $0.50. The cost to place an order is $100. Stockout cost per unit is estimated at $20. Initial inventory is 300 units.

Simulate this inventory policy for a quarter (90 days) and calculate the total quarterly cost. Also calculate the percentage of stockouts for the quarter. Replicate these calculations N times each to calculate the average values for these measures.

10–28. Consider the Music Mania problem described in Problem 10–27.
  (a) Music Mania would like to evaluate ordering 250, 300, 350, and 400 MP3 players when the reorder point of 80 is reached. Based on the average total quarterly cost, which order quantity would you recommend?
  (b) Music Mania would like to evaluate reorder points of 60, 80, and 100 MP3 players, with an order quantity of 300 players. Based on the average total cost for the quarter, which reorder point would you recommend?

10–29. Troy's Tires sells a certain brand tire that has a daily demand that is normally distributed, with a mean of 15 tires and a standard deviation of 4 tires. (In your model use integers for all demands.) Troy's Tires replenishes its inventory by ordering 250 tires from the factory whenever its current inventory reaches 40 tires. The lead time (in days) to receive an order from the factory follows the distribution shown in the following table:

Lead Time	Probability
1	0.10
2	0.22
3	0.28
4	0.15
5	0.15
6	0.10

The cost to hold one tire in inventory for one day is $0.20. The cost to place an order with the factory is $100. Stockout costs are estimated at $10 per tire. The initial inventory level is 100 tires.

(a) Simulate 6 months (180 days) of operation to calculate the total semiannual cost and the percentage of stockouts for the period. Replicate these calculations N times each to calculate the average values for these measures.

(b) Troy's Tires would like to evaluate the economics of ordering 150, 200, 250, 300, and 350 tires, with a reorder point of 40 tires. Based on the average total semiannual cost, which order quantity would you recommend?

(c) Troy's Tires would like to evaluate the economics of ordering 250 tires, with reorder points of 40, 50, 60, 70, and 80 tires. Based on the average total semiannual cost, which reorder point would you recommend?

10–30. Ashcroft Airlines flies a six-passenger commuter fight once a day to Gainesville, Florida. A nonrefundable one-way fare with a reservation costs $129. The daily demand for this flight is given in the following table, along with the probability distribution of no-shows (where a no-show has a reservation but does not arrive at the gate and forfeits the fare):

Demand	Probability	No-shows	Probability
5	0.05	0	0.15
6	0.11	1	0.25
7	0.20	2	0.26
8	0.18	3	0.23
9	0.16	4	0.11
10	0.12		
11	0.10		
12	0.08		

Ashcroft currently overbooks three passengers per flight. If there are not enough seats for a passenger at the gate, Ashcroft Airlines refunds his or her fare and provides a $150 voucher good on any other trip. The fixed cost for each flight is $450, regardless of the number of passengers.
(a) Set up a simulation model and calculate Ashcroft's profit per flight. Replicate the calculation N times each to calculate the average profit per flight.
(b) Ashcroft Airlines would like to investigate the profitability of overbooking 0, 1, 2, 3, 4, and 5 passengers. What is your recommendation? Why?

10-31. Winston-Salem's general hospital has an emergency room that is divided into six departments: (1) the initial exam station to treat minor problems and make diagnoses; (2) an x-ray department; (3) an operating room; (4) a cast-fitting room; (5) an observation room for recovery and general observation before final diagnosis or release; and (6) an out-processing department where clerks check out patients and arrange for payment or insurance forms. The probabilities that a patient will go from one department to another are presented in the following table:

From	To	Probability
Initial exam station	X-ray department	0.45
	Operating room	0.15
	Observation room	0.10
	Out-processing clerk	0.30
X-ray department	Operating room	0.10
	Cast-fitting room	0.25
	Observation room	0.35
	Out-processing clerk	0.30
Operating room	Cast-fitting room	0.25
	Observation room	0.70
	Out-processing clerk	0.05
Cast-fitting room	Observation room	0.55
	X-ray department	0.05
	Out-processing clerk	0.40
Observation room	Operating room	0.15
	X-ray department	0.15
	Out-processing clerk	0.70

Simulate the trail followed by 200 emergency room patients. Process one patient at a time, from entry at the initial exam station until leaving through out-processing. Note that a patient can enter the same department more than once. Based on your simulation, what is the probability that a patient enters the x-ray department more than once?

10-32. Management of Charlottesville Bank is concerned about a loss of customers at its main office downtown. One solution that has been proposed is to add one or more drive-through teller windows to make it easier for customers in cars to obtain quick service without parking. Neha Patel, the bank president, thinks the bank should risk the cost of installing only one drive-through window. She is informed by her staff that the cost (amortized over a 20-year period) of building a drive-through window is $36,000 per year. It also costs $48,000 per year in wages and benefits to staff each new drive-through window.

The director of management analysis, Robyn Lyon, believes that two factors encourage the immediate construction of two drive-through windows, however. According to a recent article in *Banking Research* magazine, customers who wait in long lines for drive-through service will cost banks an average of $3 per minute in loss of goodwill. Also, adding a second drive-through window will cost an additional $48,000 in staffing, but amortized construction costs can be cut to a total of $60,000 per year if the two drive-through windows are installed together instead of one at a time. To complete her analysis, Lyon collected arrival and service rates at a competing downtown bank's drive-through windows for one month. These data are shown in the following table:

Time Between Arrivals (min.)	Occurrences	Service Time (min.)	Occurrences
1	200	1	100
2	250	2	150
3	300	3	350
4	150	4	150
5	100	5	150
		6	100

(a) Simulate a one-hour time period for a system with one drive-through window. Replicate the model N times.
(b) Simulate a one-hour time period for a system with two drive-through windows. Replicate the model N times.
(c) Conduct a cost analysis of the two options. Assume that the bank is open 7 hours per day and 200 days per year.

10–33. Erik Marshall owns and operates one of the largest BMW auto dealerships in St. Louis. In the past 36 months, his weekly sales of Z3s have ranged from a low of 6 to a high of 12, as reflected in the following table:

Z3 Sales per Week	Frequency
6	3
7	4
8	6
9	12
10	9
11	1
12	1

Erik believes that sales will continue during the next 24 months at about the same rate and that delivery lead times will also continue to follow this pace (stated in probability form):

Delivery Time (weeks)	Probability
1	0.44
2	0.33
3	0.16
4	0.07

Erik's current policy is to order 14 autos at a time (two full truckloads, with 7 autos on each truck) and to place a new order whenever the stock on hand reaches 12 autos. Beginning inventory is 14 autos. Erik establishes the following relevant costs: (i) The carrying cost per Z3 per week is $400, (ii) the cost of a lost sale averages $7,500, and (iii) the cost of placing an order is $1,000.
(a) Simulate Erik's inventory policy for the next two years. What is the total weekly cost of this policy? Also, what is the average number of stockouts per week? Use N replications of your model.
(b) Erik wishes to evaluate several different ordering quantities—12, 14, 16, 18, and 20. Based on the total weekly cost, what would you recommend? Why? Set $R = 12$ in each case.

10–34. Jesse's Plumbing Service's monthly demand follows a discrete uniform distribution between 40 and 55 jobs. The probability that a specific job will be for minor service (e.g., clogged sink) is 0.65, and the probability that it will be for a major service (e.g., flooded basement) is 0.35. Revenues for minor service follow a normal distribution, with a mean of $100 and a standard deviation of $15. For major projects, Jesse estimates that revenues will be $600 with 30% chance, $900 with 40% chance, or $1,200 with 30% chance. Set up a simulation model for Jesse's problem and replicate it N times to calculate his average monthly revenue.

10–35. Sydney Garner is considering building a 300-seat amphitheater in a popular park. After studying the market, Sydney has drawn the following conclusions:
- There will be one show every night during summer months.
- The theater will make a profit of $1 on each occupied seat and suffer a loss of $0.25 on each unoccupied seat.
- The probability that it rains on any given night is 0.2.
- The number of customers on a dry night is normally distributed, with a mean of 275 and a standard deviation of 30.
- The number of customers on a cold night is normally distributed, with a mean of 200 and a standard deviation of 50.

Set up Sydney's problem and simulate total profit for one month (30 days). In your model use integers for all demands. Replicate your model N times and calculate Sydney's average monthly profit.

10-36. Wang's Concrete Service notes that the number of jobs each month follows this distribution: 10 with probability 0.15, 11 with probability 0.20, 12 with probability 0.20, 13 with probability 0.20, 14 with probability 0.15, and 15 with probability 0.10. The probability that a specific job will be for a residential driveway is 70%, and the probability that it will be for a commercial project is 30%. Revenues for residential driveways follow a normal distribution, with a mean of $500 and a standard deviation of $50. Commercial projects, although more lucrative, also have larger variability. Wang estimates that revenues here follow a normal distribution, with a mean of $1,500 and a standard deviation of $400. Set up a simulation model for Wang's problem and replicate it N times to calculate the average monthly revenue.

10-37. The Decatur Fire Department makes annual door-to-door solicitations for funds. Residents of each visited house are asked to contribute $15 (and receive a free family portrait package), $25 (and receive two free family portrait packages), or $35 (and receive three free family portrait packages). An analysis from previous years' solicitations indicates the following:

- Only 80% of the homes visited have someone at home.
- When someone is at home, there is only a 40% chance that he or she will make a donation.
- Of the people making donations, there is a 50% chance they will contribute $15, a 25% chance they will contribute $25, and a 15% chance they will contribute $35. Occasionally (10% chance), a person makes a donation in excess of $35. Such distributions follow a discrete uniform distribution between $40 and $50 (in increments of $1).

The fire chief plans to visit 30 houses tomorrow. Set up a simulation model and replicate it N times to determine the probability that the chief will receive more than $300 in donations from these 30 houses.

10-38. A local bank has a single drive-through window with arrival times and service times that follow the distributions from the following table:

Time Between Arrivals (min.)	Probability	Service Time (min.)	Probability
1	0.15	1	0.15
2	0.24	2	0.35
3	0.27	3	0.22
4	0.22	4	0.28
5	0.12		

Simulate the arrival of 200 customers to compute each of the following measures: (a) average time a customer waits for service, (b) average time a customer is in the system (wait plus service time), and (c) percentage of time the server is busy with customers. Replicate each measure N times to compute the average.

10-39. Colin sells pretzels at the local high school basketball games. For an upcoming game, Colin has to decide how many pretzels to order (170, 190, or 210), at a cost of $0.50 each. Colin sells pretzels for $1.50 each. However, any unsold pretzels must be thrown away.

If the game is interesting, Colin thinks that fewer people will visit his stand. In such a case, Colin estimates that demand will be normally distributed, with a mean of 140 and a standard deviation of 20. However, if the game is a blowout, he expects more people to visit the stand. Demand in this case follows a discrete uniform distribution between 180 and 200. Based on his familiarity with the two teams, he estimates that there is only a 40% chance that the game will be a blowout.

Set up a simulation model and replicate it N times for each order size to determine Colin's expected profit and expected percentage of unsold pretzels. What do you recommend that Colin do?

10-40. The Diego Street Convenience Store has a single checkout register, with customer arrival distribution shown in the following table:

Time Between Arrivals (min.)	Probability
1	0.18
2	0.20
3	0.22
4	0.25
5	0.15

Service time follows a discrete uniform distribution between 1 and 4 minutes. Simulate the arrival of 200 customers to compute the average time a customer waits for service and the probability that a customer waits 3 minutes or longer for service.

Replicate each measure N times to compute its average.

10-41. Zodiac Chemical manufactures chlorine gas by passing electricity through saltwater in a diaphragm cell. The plant has 88 diaphragm cells that operate in parallel. Each cell can produce 5 tons of chlorine gas per day, and each ton of chlorine gas has a profit contribution of $15. Due to the harsh environment, cell failures occur, causing the cell to be taken offline for maintenance. A cell fails, on average, every 30 hours, according to the exponential probability distribution. Only one cell can be repaired at any given time. Using the current maintenance procedure, the repair time follows a normal probability distribution, with a mean of 21 hours and a standard deviation of 6 hours, but with a minimum value of 5 hours. A new maintenance procedure is being considered that will require a significant capital investment. If this new procedure is implemented, the repair time will still follow a normal distribution, but the mean time will be 14 hours, the standard deviation will be 4 hours, and the minimum time will be 3 hours. Simulate 200 failures to determine the annual savings in downtime with the new method.

10-42. Make a Splash T-Shirts is planning to print and sell specially designed T-shirts for the upcoming World Series. The shirts will cost $12 each to produce and can be sold for $30 each until the World Series. After the World Series, the price will be reduced to $20 per shirt. The demand at the $30 price is expected to be normally distributed, with a mean of 12,000 shirts and a standard deviation of 2,500 shirts. The demand for the $20 price is expected to be normally distributed, with a mean of 5,000 shirts and a standard deviation of 1,000 shirts. Any shirts left over will be discarded. Because of the high setup costs, Make a Splash T-Shirts is planning to produce one run of 17,000 shirts. In your model use integers for all demands.
   (a) Simulate N setups to calculate the average profit for this quantity of shirts.
   (b) Make a Splash T-Shirts would like to evaluate producing 16,000, 17,000, 18,000, 19,000, and 20,000 shirts. Which would you recommend? Why?

10-43. Phillip Florrick is responsible for the warehouse operation for a local discount department store chain. The warehouse has only one unloading dock, which is currently operated by a single three-person crew. Trucks arrive at an average rate of five per hour and follow the exponential probability distribution. The average time for one of the crews to unload a truck tends to follow a normal distribution, with a mean of 9 minutes and standard deviation of 3 minutes (minimum time is 1 minute). Phillip has estimated the cost of operating a truck at $40 per hour. Phillip pays each person on the unloading crew $11 per hour. The unloading dock operates 8 hours each day. Simulate 100 days of this operation to calculate the total daily cost. Replicate this calculation N times to compute the expected total cost per day of this operation.

10-44. A customer service counter at a local bookstore is normally staffed by a single employee. The probabilities of arrival times and service times are shown in the following table:

Time Between Arrivals (min.)	Probability	Service Time (min.)	Probability
1	0.07	1	0.07
2	0.25	2	0.24
3	0.23	3	0.28
4	0.26	4	0.28
5	0.19	5	0.13

Simulate the arrival of 100 customers to compute the average number of customers in line and the probability that a customer will have to wait 3 or more minutes for service to begin. Replicate each measure N times to compute its average.

10-45. Timberwolves Electric and Wiring Company installs wiring and electrical fixtures in residential construction. Andrew Dickel, the owner of Timberwolves, has been concerned with the amount of time it takes to complete wiring jobs because some of his workers are very unreliable. For each wiring job, a list of activities, their mean duration times, standard deviation of duration times, and immediate predecessors are given in the following table:

| | Days | | |
Activity	Mean	Standard Deviation	Immediate Predecessors
A	5.83	0.83	—
B	3.67	0.33	—
C	2.00	0.33	—
D	7.00	0.33	C
E	4.00	0.67	B, D
F	10.00	1.33	A, E
G	2.17	0.50	A, E
H	6.00	1.00	F
I	11.00	0.33	G
J	16.33	1.00	G
K	7.33	1.33	H, I

Assume that all activity durations follow a normal distribution, with the means and standard deviations shown. Use simulation to determine the probability that Timberwolves will finish the project in 40 days or less.

10-46. A plant engineering group needs to set up an assembly line to produce a new product. The following table describes the relationships between the activities that need to be completed for this product to be manufactured:

| | Days | | | |
Activity	a	m	b	Immediate Predecessors
A	3	6	8	—
B	5	8	10	A
C	5	6	8	A
D	1	2	4	B, C
E	7	11	17	D
F	7	9	12	D
G	6	8	9	D
H	3	4	7	F, G
I	3	5	7	E, F, H

Assume that each activity time is normally distributed with expected time and standard deviation computed as shown in equations 7–6 and 7–8, respectively. Round off all activity times to two decimal places.
(a) Use simulation to determine the probability that the project will finish in 37 days or less.
(b) Use simulation to determine the probability that the project will take more than 32 days.

10-47. Luna Martinez, director of personnel at Management Resources, Inc., is designing a program that customers can use when searching for jobs. Some of the activities include preparing résumés, writing letters, making appointments to see prospective employers, researching companies and industries, and so on. Information on the activities is shown in the following table:

Activity	Mean	Standard Deviation	Immediate Predecessors
A	10.00	0.67	—
B	7.17	0.50	—
C	3.17	0.17	—
D	20.00	3.33	A
E	7.00	0.33	C
F	10.00	0.33	B, D, E
G	7.33	0.67	B, D, E
H	15.00	0.33	F
I	11.17	0.50	F
J	7.00	0.33	G, H
K	6.67	0.67	I, J
L	2.17	0.50	G, H

Assume that all activity durations follow a normal distribution, with the means and standard deviations shown. Round off all activity times to two decimal places. Use simulation to determine the average project completion time and the probability that the project will take at least 75 days.

10-48. Lamont Henri needs to plan and manage a local construction project. The following table describes the relationships between the activities that need to be completed:

| | | Days | | |
Activity	a	m	b	Immediate Predecessors
A	4	8	13	—
B	4	10	15	A
C	7	14	20	B
D	9	16	19	B
E	6	9	11	B
F	2	4	5	D, E
G	4	7	11	C, F
H	3	5	9	G
I	2	3	4	G, H

Assume that each activity time is normally distributed with expected time and standard deviation computed as shown in equations 7–6 and 7–8, respectively. Round off all activity times to one decimal place. Use simulation to determine the probability that the project will take at least 50 days.

10-49. Elena Wilhelm is responsible for developing a comprehensive sales training program for her organization. The following table describes the relationships between the activities that need to be completed:

| | Days | | |
Activity	Minimum	Maximum	Immediate Predecessors
A	7	13	—
B	5	11	—
C	3	8	A, B
D	5	9	C
E	2	9	C
F	3	5	E
G	5	12	F
H	9	12	D
I	6	8	F, H
J	7	10	G, I

Assume that the actual duration of each activity follows a discrete uniform distribution between the minimum and maximum times shown for that activity. Use simulation to determine the probability that the project will be finished in less than 49 days. Round off each activity time to the nearest whole number.

10-50. Lynn Rogers (who just turned 30) currently earns $60,000 per year. At the end of each calendar year, she plans to invest 10% of her annual income in a tax-deferred retirement account. Lynn expects her salary to grow between 0% and 8% each year, following a discrete uniform distribution between these two rates. Based on historical market returns, she expects the tax-deferred account to return between –5% and 20% in any given year, following a conti-

nuous uniform distribution between these two rates. Use N replications of a simulation model to answer each of the following questions.
(a) What is the probability that Lynn will have in excess of $1 million in this account when she turns 60 (i.e., in 30 years)?
(b) If Lynn wants this probability to be over 95%, what should be her savings rate each year?

10-51. Adams College has a self-insured employee healthcare plan. Each employee pays a monthly premium of $100. Adams pays the rest of the healthcare costs. The number of covered employees is 1,000 this year. Each year, the number of employees who have major health claims follows a continuous uniform distribution between 10% and 15%, and the number of employees who have minor health claims follows a continuous uniform distribution between 60% and 65%. The rest have no health claims. Round off all numbers of claims to integers.

For this year, major health claims are expected to follow a normal distribution, with a mean of $5,000 and a standard deviation of $1,000. Minor health claims are expected to follow a normal distribution, with a mean of $1,500 and a standard deviation of $300. For purposes of simulating this model, assume that every minor health claim is the same amount simulated above. Assume likewise for major health clams. Use N replications of a simulation model to answer each of the following questions.
(a) What is the probability that Adams College's total out-of-pocket cost will exceed $300,000 this year?
(b) The number of employees from year to year follows a continuous uniform distribution between a 3% decrease and a 4% increase. Round off all numbers of employees to integers. Also, due to rising health costs, the mean of minor health claims is expected to rise in a discrete uniform manner between 2% and 5% each year, and the mean of major health claims is expected to rise in a discrete uniform manner between 4% and 7% each year. What is the probability that Adams College's total out-of-pocket cost will exceed $2,000,000 over the next five years?

10-52. Consider Figure 10.10 for Simkin's Hardware Store. Column J in the spreadsheet indicates a value of 1 if an order is placed and a value of 0 if an order is not placed. Modify the spreadsheet to make it more "manager-friendly" by having "Yes" indicate that an order is placed and "No" indicate that an order is not placed. Make all necessary adjustments to other formulas in the spreadsheet to accommodate this change.

10-53. The *newsvendor model* is a classic inventory problem based on the situation of newsstand owner who must determine how many newspapers to order early in the morning to satisfy that day's demand. She has one chance to purchase. At the end of the day, unsold newspapers are thrown away. On the other hand, if demand exceeds the order size, then the newsvendor loses potential sales.

So the question is, with uncertain demand and a single chance to purchase, how many units should be purchased? The answer is typically *not* to order expected demand. Instead, the optimal order size should represent a trade-off between the cost of ordering too much and the opportunity cost of not ordering enough.

We let Q = order size (the decision), U = cost per unit of unmet demand (underage), and O = cost per unit of excess inventory (overage). It turns out that for any distribution function of demand, $F()$, the best order decision is to select Q such that $F() = U / (O+U)$.

For some distributions, we can solve this general equation for the best order size Q^* directly. In particular, (1) for the uniform distribution between a and b, $Q^* = a + (b-a)[U/(O+U)]$, and (2) for the normal distribution with mean μ and standard deviation σ, $Q^* = \mu + z\sigma$, where z comes from the Standard Normal Distribution table for the "critical ratio" value of $U/(O+U)$. Using Excel, z = NORMSINV(U/(O+U)).

Create simulations to test these policies. Using Excel, analyze the uniform distribution in sheets 1 through 5, and analyze the normal distribution in sheets 6 through 10. The cost to buy the units is $60 each (this represents the overage cost). The items can be sold for $100 each. (Thus, the underage cost is the margin on a sale of $100 − $60 = $40.) Enter the revenue and cost per unit at the top of sheet 1 (and use cell references on the other sheets to retrieve those). For the uniform distribution, assume that demand is uniformly distributed between 1000 and 5000 units (integers only). For the normal distribution, assume that demand is normally distributed with a mean of 5,000 and a standard deviation of 1,000. On each sheet, enter the appropriate distribution parameters at the top of the sheet, somewhere near the costs. Use 10,000 trials for each analysis. Indicate the trial number in column A. In column B, compute the random demand. Place the order size in column C, and calculate the revenue in column D. Revenue equals the sales price per unit times the minimum of the demand (column B) and the order size (column C). Place the actual cost in column E, which equals the cost per unit times the order size (column C). In column F compute the profit for that trial (column D minus column E). Note that it is possible for the profit to be negative for any given trial.

For both of your distributions, test the following strategies (put each in a separate sheet): (a) order the optimal strategy given by the formulas above; (b) order the average demand (this equals $(a + b) / 2$ for the uniform distribution, and it equals μ for the normal distribution); (c) order randomly each time (use the same formula in column C as you have in column B); (d) order the previous trial's demand (use a random order size for the first trial); and (e) order 4,000 for the uniform, or order 6,000 for the normal. Record your average profit, minimum profit, and maximum profit (over the 10,000 trials) for each of your strategies, and put the results in a small table. Did the optimal solutions from part (a) perform best?

10-54. Complete the exercise that asks you to compute other output measures for Simkin's Hardware Store and include them in the Scenario Manager as described under "Analyzing the Results" for the Scenario Manager for Figure 10.12.

10-55. Complete the exercise that asks you to compute the average fill rate for Simkin's Hardware Store as described under "Analyzing the Results" for the Data Table for Figure 10.10.

10-56. An alternative to using Excel's built-in functions to generate "live" random numbers that change each time that a model is recalculated is to use Excel's Random Number Generator tool found under Data | Data Analysis. This tool generates random numbers according to a specified distribution and then pastes them to a range in Excel. An advantage of using such "static" random numbers is that you can use the same set of random numbers in a model when comparing different decisions. In this way, differences in outputs can be more fully attributed to the decisions themselves rather than differences in the random numbers generated between runs of the model.

For the Simkin's Hardware Store model in Figure 10.9, use Excel's Random Number Generator to generate 10 "Variables" of 25 "Random Numbers" each for both the Demand in column E and the Lead Time in column K. Use a discrete distribution to generate both sets of numbers. Now you have enough random numbers to plug into the model to run it for 10 trials. For each trial, copy/paste new sets of your generated random numbers into the respective Demand and Lead Time columns and record the Total Cost per month. Then change your policy to $Q = 20$ and $R = 8$ and record the Total Cost per month for that set of decisions. Repeat this procedure for all 10 trials. Compute the average cost for each policy ($Q = 10$, $R = 5$ vs. $Q = 20$, $R = 8$), averaged over the 10 trials. Which policy performed better? *(Note: This problem illustrates the more general approach of using the same random number "seed" when using simulation to compare policies. If you wanted to have 200 or more trials, you might consider utilizing macros or VBA code to assist.)*

10-57. In the old game show "Let's Make a Deal," contestants chose one of three curtains, behind which were either fabulous prizes or nothing, or worse (sometimes "booby prizes" would be behind a curtain). First, a contestant chose a curtain, numbered 1, 2, or 3. Then the host, Monty Hall, would open one of the remaining curtains to show that it did not contain the grand prize. Finally, the contestant was offered the opportunity to switch to the remaining unopened curtain and take whatever was behind it, or to stay with the original curtain chosen and take whatever was behind that one. Despite the emotions involved and whatever is behind the curtain that is shown (which will never be the grand prize), the question actually just boils down to whether the contestant should stay with the original door or switch.

Create a Monte Carlo simulation of the game in Excel that compares the two strategies (stay and switch). Run the game for 1000 rounds, with 2 players each round, a "Stayer" and a "Switcher." Put the trial numbers in column A. Label column B "Prize," and label column C "Choice." Both columns B and C should use the formula =RANDBETWEEN(1,3). This represents both a random door for the prize and a random choice for the player. Then label columns D, E, F, and G "Stayer's Choice," "Stayer Correct?", "Switcher's Choice," "Switcher Correct?," respectively. The Stayer's Choice would simply cell-reference column C. The Switcher's Choice would simply cell-reference column B. (Note that if the Switcher were originally incorrect, then he or she will receive the grand prize after switching because the other incorrect door will have already been opened.) For columns E and G, you can use an IF function to insert a 1 if the choice matches the prize and a 0 if it does not. (Thus, in each round either the Stayer will have a 1 and the Switcher will have a 0, or vice versa.) Calculate the percent correct at the bottom of the spreadsheet. How often is the Stayer correct, and how often is the Switcher correct?

10-58. Rockin' Jon's Apparel is planning to sell T-shirts at an upcoming rock concert. Jon has three decisions to make: (1) the number of shirts to produce (Q), (2) the selling price (P), and (3) the level of advertising (A). Because the shirts are specific to this concert at this venue, any unsold shirts must be thrown out with no salvage value. Customer demand D follows the formula $D = a - bP + c(A/100)$, where a is the demand intercept, b is the demand price slope per dollar, and c is the demand advertising slope per 100 dollars.

Create an Excel model for this problem. Inputs include a, b, c, and the unit variable cost C. The outputs are the demand and the profit (loss). The demand should include a MAX function to ensure that if the result of the formula for D is negative, then demand will just equal 0. The profit (loss) equals $P \times \text{MIN}(Q, D) - CQ - A$.

The four model inputs vary as follows.
- Variable cost: There's a 35% chance that the supplier will be unable to deliver on time, in which case an expedited supplier must be used, costing $15 per shirt instead of the usual $5 per shirt.
- Intercept: The intercept a is assumed to follow a normal distribution with a mean of 5,000 and a standard deviation of 500.
- Advertising slope: Historical data suggests that c is exponentially distributed with a mean of 6.7.
- Price slope: The effect of price on demand depends upon a variety of factors. Historical observations of b for similar situations include 202, 182, 222, 204, 198, 192, 190, 202, 187, 186. Assume that these 10 values are equally likely in the future.

Using a sample size of 200, run a simulation using Data Table to compare two different options. Option 1 is a purchase quantity of 800, advertising of

$400, and a price of $23.00. Option 2 (more conservative) is a purchase quantity of 600, advertising of $200, and a price of $19.00. Write up a summary paragraph that compares your two scenarios. What are the risk/return trade-offs? Which option would you recommend?

10-59. Consider the model for Harry's Auto Shop in Figure 10.7. Modify the spreadsheet to consider the following changes to the inputs. First, average selling price is now normally distributed with mean $72 and standard deviation $10 (rounded to the nearest penny). Second, profit margin is now uniformly distributed between 22% and 35%. Finally, demand now has the following distribution:

Demand	Probability
310	0.02
330	0.03
350	0.20
375	0.20
390	0.30
400	0.15
425	0.10

Run the simulation using these new input distributions for 500 trials. What is the mean profit? The median profit? The minimum profit? The maximum profit?

Chapter 11
Forecasting Models

Have you ever entered an NCAA basketball tournament pool where you had to select the winners of all 67 games? Did you use "gut feel," did you select your favorite teams, or did you base some of your choices on results from previous tournaments? Whichever approach you used, you were *forecasting* the game winners. We make forecasts in our personal lives on a regular basis. We try to predict monthly expenses when establishing a household budget. We estimate weekly food consumption from our family when we shop at the grocery store. We estimate travel time when we determine when to leave home for that night's concert.

Organizations also make forecasts regularly. They may need to predict future employee turnover rates, upcoming changes in their industry, or regulatory impacts on their operations. Perhaps the most important forecast that they make is for future customer demand because demand forecasts drive so many operational decisions. Many of the inputs to the various models that we have presented in this book are actually predictions of the future. As the saying goes, "garbage-in, garbage-out," implying that poor forecasts will lead to poor decisions, even if the model being used is very sophisticated and powerful. The importance of accurate forecasting as a first step to many decisions cannot be overstated.

We begin this chapter by outlining the seven steps in forecasting. We then describe the three categories of forecasting models: *qualitative, time-series,* and *causal*. Next, we briefly define four popular qualitative forecasting methods: *Delphi method, jury of executive opinion, sales force composite,* and *consumer market survey*. Prior to moving into our study of quantitative methods, we present the three major ways that firms measure forecast error: *mean absolute deviation, mean squared error,* and *mean absolute percent error*. Time-series models base forecasts of the future on data patterns from the past. We illustrate the standard time-series models of *moving average, weighted moving average,* and *exponential smoothing*. We then show how to incorporate into our forecasts increasing or decreasing *trends* in data, as well as data that exhibit *seasonal* fluctuations. Causal forecasting models base forecasts of the future on the levels of certain inputs that are thought to *cause* the level of our output of interest. For example, attendance at a football game might be thought to be caused by the respective records of both teams, the weather that day, the price of the tickets, star players on the visiting team, and the chances of making the playoffs. We illustrate how to estimate the impact of such causes via *regression* analysis. All of our quantitative models are coded into the ExcelModules program that is available from the companion website. In all cases, you need to input historical data into the spreadsheets to generate predictions about the future. We predict that you'll find these models useful!

Chapter Objectives

After completing this chapter, you will be able to:
1. Understand and know when to use various types of forecasting models.
2. Compute a variety of forecasting error measures.
3. Compute moving averages, weighted moving averages, and exponential smoothing time-series models.
4. Decompose time-series data to identify and analyze trends and seasonality.
5. Identify variables and use them in causal simple and multiple linear regression models.
6. Use Excel to analyze a variety of forecasting models.

11.1 What is Forecasting?

Every day, managers make decisions without knowing exactly what will happen in the future. Inventory is ordered even though no one knows what sales will be, new equipment is purchased even though no one knows the demand for products, and investments are made even though no one knows what profits will be. Managers are constantly trying to reduce this uncertainty and to make better estimates of what will happen in the future. Accomplishing this objective is the main purpose of forecasting.

There are many ways to try to forecast the future. In many firms (especially small ones), the forecasting models may be qualitative or subjective, involving "expert" opinions based on intuition and years of experience. The more reliable forecasting models, however, are usually *quantitative* models, such as moving averages, exponential smoothing, trend analysis, seasonality analysis, decomposition models, and causal regression analysis, that rely on numeric data.

There is seldom a single superior forecasting model. One may find regression models effective, another may use several quantitative models, and a third may combine both quantitative and qualitative techniques. Whichever model works best for a firm is the one that should be used. In this chapter, we discuss several different forecasting models that are commonly used in practice. For each model, we show the equations needed to compute the forecasts and provide examples of how they are analyzed.

Regardless of the model used to make the forecast, the following steps that present a systematic overall way of initiating, designing, and implementing a forecast system are used:

Steps to Forecasting
1. Determine the use of the forecast; what is the objective we are trying to obtain?
2. Identify the items that need to be forecasted.
3. Determine the time horizon of the forecast: Is it 1 to 30 days (short time horizon), 1 month to 1 year (medium time horizon), or more than 1 year (long time horizon)?
4. Select the forecasting model or models.
5. Gather the data needed to make the forecast.

6. Validate the forecasting model.
7. Make the forecast and implement the results.

When the forecasting model is used to generate forecasts regularly over time, data must be collected routinely, and the actual computations must be repeated. In this age of technology and computers, however, forecast calculations are seldom performed by hand. Computers and forecasting software packages simplify these tasks to a great extent. Numerous statistical programs, such as R, SAS, SPSS, and Minitab, are readily available to handle various forecasting models. However, in keeping with the spreadsheet focus of this book, we use Excel add-ins such as Analysis ToolPak and worksheets (included on this book's Companion Website) to actually calculate the forecast values for each model. Several other spreadsheet-based forecasting software programs (such as Crystal Ball Predictor by Oracle Corporation and StatTools by Palisade Corporation) are also popular in practice.

11.2 Types of Forecasts

The forecasting models we consider here can be classified into three categories. These categories, shown in Figure 11.1, are qualitative models, time-series models, and causal models. Although we provide a brief description of a few qualitative models in section 11.3, the focus of this chapter is on time-series and causal models.

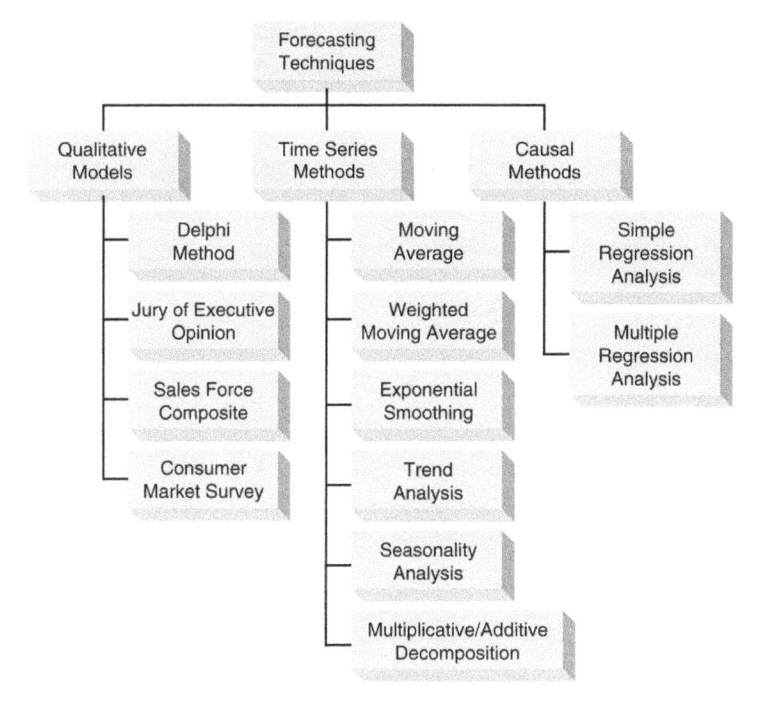

Figure 11.1: Forecasting Models Discussed

Qualitative Models

Qualitative models attempt to incorporate judgmental or subjective factors into the forecasting model. Opinions by experts, individual experiences and judgments, and other subjective factors may be considered. Qualitative models are especially useful when subjective factors are expected to be very important or when accurate quantitative data are difficult to obtain. Qualitative models are also useful for long-term forecasting.

Time-Series Models

Whereas qualitative models rely on judgmental or subjective data, time-series models rely on quantitative data. Time-series models attempt to predict the future by using historical data. These models assume that what happens in the future is a function of what has happened in the past. In other words, time-series models look at what has happened over a period of time and use a series of past data to make a forecast. Thus, if we are forecasting weekly sales for lawn mowers, we use the past weekly sales for lawn mowers in making the forecast. The time-series models we examine in this chapter are (1) moving averages, (2) weighted moving averages, (3) exponential smoothing, (4) linear trend analysis, (5) seasonality analysis, and (6) multiplicative and additive decomposition.

Causal Models

Like time-series models, causal models also rely on quantitative data. Causal models incorporate the variables or factors that might influence the quantity being forecasted into the forecasting model. For example, daily sales of a cola drink might depend on the season, the average temperature, the average humidity, whether it is a weekend or a weekday, and so on. Thus, a causal model would attempt to include factors for temperature, humidity, season, day of the week, and so on. Causal models can also include past sales data as time-series models do.

11.3 Qualitative Forecasting Models

Here is a brief overview of four different qualitative forecasting techniques commonly used in practice:

1. *Delphi method.* The Delphi iterative group process allows experts, who may be in different places, to make forecasts. There are three different types of participants in the Delphi process: decision makers, staff personnel, and respondents. The decision-making group usually consists of 5 to 10 experts who will be making the actual forecast. The *staff personnel* assist the decision makers by preparing, distributing, collecting, and summarizing a series of questionnaires and survey results. The *respondents* are a group of people whose judgments are valued and are being sought. This group provides inputs to the decision makers before the forecast is made.

2. *Jury of executive opinion.* This method begins with the opinions of a small group of high-level managers, often in combination with statistical models, and results in a group estimate of demand.
3. *Sales force composite.* In this approach, each salesperson estimates what sales will be in his or her region; these forecasts are reviewed to ensure that they are realistic and are then combined at the district and national levels to reach an overall forecast.
4. *Consumer market survey.* This method solicits input from customers or potential customers regarding their future purchasing plans. It can help not only in preparing a forecast but also in improving product design and planning for new products.

Decision Modeling In Action

Digital platforms, supported by cloud computing capabilities, are experiencing increasing demand due to the rapid growth of mobile technologies. Cloud platforms are currently reactive in that they require human intervention to adjust computing resources to meet demand. IBM's Global Technology Services (GTS), which is responsible for the design, build, and delivery of enterprise systems, used advanced analytics to develop a Progressive Cloud Computing (PCC) system. PCC uses innovative numerical analysis techniques, as well as advanced forecasting models, to predict demand in near real-time. The solution method employed by PCC combines time-series forecasting models, discrete-event simulation, and predictive models.

GTS successfully applied the PCC system to various sporting tournaments in 2014. The system reduced the cloud-computing hours needed by about 50 percent, and it required less labor due to automation. IBM expects that PCC will have widespread application to businesses in various sectors, and that PCC can be used to address complexities in a rapidly expanding digital world.

Source: Based on A.K. Baughman, et al. "IBM Predicts Cloud Computing Demand for Sports Tournaments," *Interfaces* 46, 1 (January–February 2017): 33–48.

11.4 Measuring Forecast Error

The overall accuracy of a forecasting model can be determined by comparing the forecasted values with the actual or observed values. If F_t denotes the forecast in period t and A_t denotes the actual value in period t, the forecast error (or forecast deviation) is defined as

$$\text{Forecast error} = \text{Actual value} - \text{Forecast value}$$
$$= A_t - F_t \qquad (11\text{–}1)$$

Several measures are commonly used in practice to calculate the overall forecast error. These measures can be used to compare different forecasting models as well as to monitor forecasts to ensure that they are performing well. Three of the most popular measures are covered in the following sections.

Mean Absolute Deviation Mean absolute deviation (MAD) is computed as the average of the *absolute* values of the individual forecast errors. That is, if we have forecasted and actual values for T periods, MAD is calculated as

$$\text{MAD} = \sum_{t=1}^{T} |\text{Forecast error}|/T = \sum_{t=1}^{T} |A_t - F_t|/T \quad (11\text{–}2)$$

Mean Squared Error The mean squared error (MSE) is computed as the average of the *squared* values of the individual forecast errors. That is, if we have forecasted and actual values for T periods, MSE is calculated as

$$\text{MSE} = \sum_{t=1}^{T} (\text{Forecast error})^2/T = \sum_{t=1}^{T} (A_t - F_t)^2/T \quad (11\text{–}3)$$

A characteristic of using MSE is that it tends to accentuate large deviations due to the squared term. For example, if the forecast error for period 1 is twice as large as the error for period 2, the squared error in period 1 is four times as large as that for period 2. Hence, using MSE as the measure of forecast error typically indicates that we prefer several smaller deviations rather than even one large deviation.

Mean Absolute Percent Error A problem with both MAD and MSE is that their values depend on the magnitude of the item being forecast. If the forecast item is measured in thousands, the MAD and MSE values can be very large. To avoid this problem, we can use the mean absolute percent error (MAPE). This is computed as the average of the absolute difference between the forecasted and actual values, expressed as a percentage of the actual values. That is, if we have forecasted and actual values for T periods, MAPE is calculated as

$$\text{MAPE} = 100 \sum_{t=1}^{T} [|A_t - F_t|/A_t]/T \quad (11\text{–}4)$$

MAPE is perhaps the easiest measure to interpret. For example, a result that MAPE is 2% is a clear statement that is not dependent on issues such as the magnitude of the input data. For this reason, although we calculate all three measures in our analyses, we focus primarily on MAPE in our discussions.

11.5 Basic Time-Series Forecasting Models

A time series is based on a sequence of evenly spaced (e.g., weekly, monthly, quarterly) data points. Examples include weekly sales of Dell personal computers, quarterly earnings reports of Cisco Systems stock, daily shipments of Energizer batteries, and annual U.S. consumer price indices. Forecasting time-series data implies that future values are predicted *only* from past values. Other variables, no matter how potentially valuable, are ignored.

Components of a Time Series

We can view a long-term time series (i.e., data for over one year) as being made up of four distinct components. Analyzing a time series means breaking down the data to identify these four components and then projecting them forward. The process of identifying the four components is referred to as *decomposition*. The four components are as follows:

1. *Trend.* A trend is the upward or downward movement of data over time. For example, prices for many consumer goods exhibit an upward trend over time due to the presence of inflation. Although it is possible for the relationship between time and the data to have any form (linear or nonlinear), we focus only on linear trend relationships in this chapter.
2. *Seasonality.* Seasonality is the pattern of demand fluctuations that occur every year above or below the average demand. That is, the same seasonal pattern repeats itself every year over the time horizon. For example, lawn mower sales are always above average each year in spring and below average in winter.
3. *Cycles.* Just as seasonality is the pattern that occurs each year, cycles are patterns that occur over several years. Cycles are usually tied to the business cycle. For example, the economies of most countries experience cycles of high growth followed by a period of relatively low growth or even recession.
4. *Random variations.* Random variations are "blips" in the data caused by chance and unusual situations. They follow no discernible pattern. For this reason, we cannot really capture this component and use it to forecast future values.

Figure 11.2 shows a time series and its components.

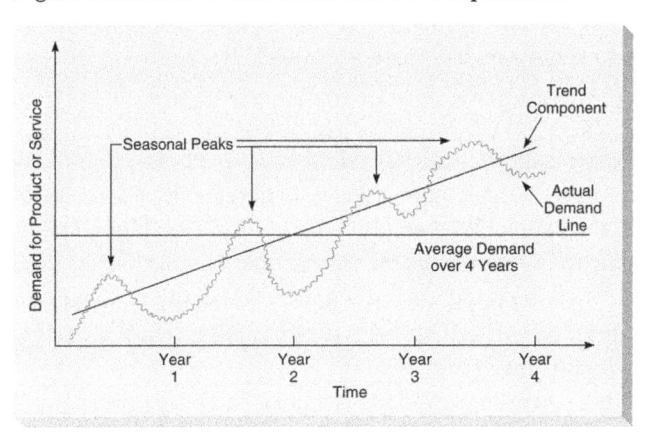

Figure 11.2: Components of a Time Series (Charted over Four Years)

There are two general approaches to decomposing a time series into its components. The most widely used is a multiplicative decomposition model, which assumes that the forecasted value is the product of the four components. It is stated as

$$\text{Forecast} = \text{Trend} \times \text{Seasonality} \times \text{Cycles} \times \text{Random variations} \quad (11\text{–}5)$$

An additive decomposition model that adds the components together to provide an estimate is also available. It is stated as

$$\text{Forecast} = \text{Trend} + \text{Seasonality} + \text{Cycles} + \text{Random variations} \quad (11\text{–}6)$$

We study the multiplicative model in section 11.7 and the additive model in Solved Problem 11–4 at the end of this chapter. As noted earlier, the random variations follow no discernible pattern. In most real-world models, forecasters assume that these variations are averaged out over time. They then concentrate on only the seasonal component and a component that is a combination of the trend and cyclical factors.

Stationary and Nonstationary Time-Series Data

Time-series data are said to be stationary data if there is no significant upward or downward movement (or trend) in the data over time. That is, the average value for the time-series data remains constant over the time horizon considered in the model. Stationary time-series data are typically encountered when the time horizon is short term (1–30 days) or medium term (1 month to 1 year). For time horizons that are long term (1 year or greater), time-series data tend to typically exhibit some trend. In such cases, we refer to the data as *nonstationary*.

In the remainder of this section, we discuss three popular forecasting models used for stationary time-series data: (1) moving averages, (2) weighted moving averages, and (3) exponential smoothing. Although we show the equations needed to compute the forecasts for each model, we use Excel worksheets (included on this book's Companion Website) to actually calculate these values.

Moving Averages

Moving averages are useful if we can assume that the item we are trying to forecast will stay fairly steady over time. We calculate a three-period moving average by summing the actual value of the item for the past three periods and dividing the total by 3. This three-period moving average serves as the forecast for the next period. With each passing period, the most recent period's actual value is added to the sum of the previous two periods' data, and the earliest period is dropped. This tends to smooth out short-term irregularities in the time series.

The moving average for the preceding k periods (where k can be any integer > 2) serves as the forecast for the following period. Mathematically, the k-period moving average can be expressed as

$$k\text{-period moving average} = \sum(\text{Actual values in previous } k \text{ periods})/k \quad (11\text{–}7)$$

Wallace Garden Supply Example Monthly sales of storage sheds at Wallace Garden Supply are shown in the middle column of Table 11.1. A three-month moving average is shown in the rightmost column. As discussed next, we can also use the ExcelModules program to calculate these moving averages.

Table 11.1: Three-Month Moving Averages Forecast for Wallace Garden Supply

Month	Actual Sales	Three-Month Moving Averages
January	10	
February	12	
March	16	
April	13	$(10+12+16)/3 = 12.67$
May	17	$(12+16+13)/3 = 13.67$
June	19	$(16+13+17)/3 = 15.33$
July	15	$(13+17+19)/3 = 16.33$
August	20	$(17+19+15)/3 = 17.00$
September	22	$(19+15+20)/3 = 18.00$
October	19	$(15+20+22)/3 = 19.00$
November	21	$(20+22+19)/3 = 20.33$
December	19	$(22+19+21)/3 = 20.67$

EXCEL NOTES

- The Companion Website for this book, at *degruyter.com/view/product/486941*, contains a set of Excel worksheets, bundled together in a software package called ExcelModules. The procedure for installing and running this program, as well as a brief description of its contents, is given in Appendix B.

- The Companion Website also provides the Excel file for each sample problem discussed here. The relevant file/sheet name is shown below the title of the corresponding figure in this book.

- For clarity, all worksheets for forecasting models in ExcelModules are color coded as follows:

  - *Input cells*, where we enter the problem data, are shaded yellow.

  - *Output cells*, which show forecasts and measures of forecast error, are shaded green.

Using ExcelModules for Forecasting Model Computations

When we run the ExcelModules program, we see a new tab titled ExcelModules in Excel's Ribbon. We select this tab and then click the Modules icon, followed by the Forecasting Models menu. The choices shown in Figure 11.3 are displayed. From these choices, we select the appropriate forecasting model.

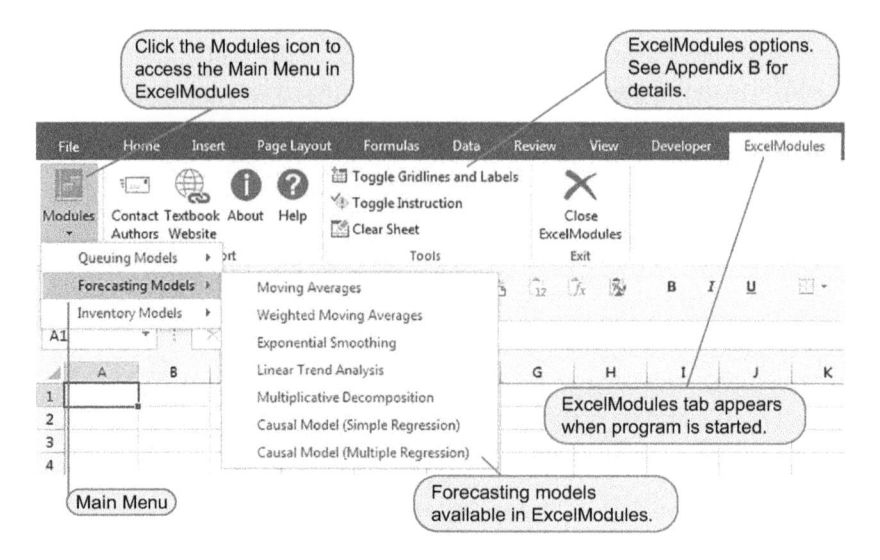

Figure 11.3: Forecasting Models Menu in ExcelModules

When *any* of the forecasting models are selected in ExcelModules, we are first presented with a window that allows us to specify several options. Some of these options are common for all models, whereas others are specific to the forecasting model selected. For example, Figure 11.4 shows the Spreadsheet Initialization window when we select the Moving Averages forecasting model. The options here include the following:

1. The title of the problem. The default value is Problem Title.
2. The number of past periods for which we have data regarding the item (e.g., demand, sales) being forecast. The default value is 3.
3. The name for the period (e.g., Week, Month). The default value is Period.
4. The number of periods to average (i.e., the value of k in Equation 11–7). The default value is 2.
5. Graph. Checking this box results in line graphs of the actual and forecast values.

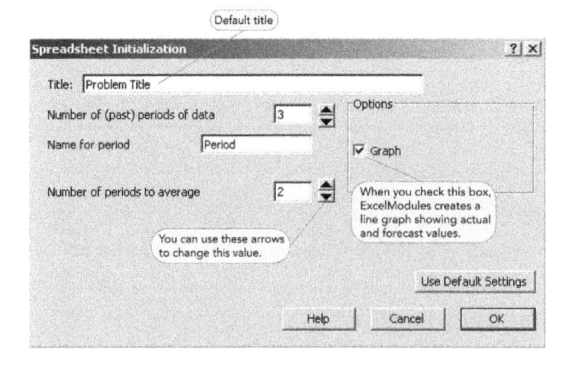

Figure 11.4: Sample Options Window for Forecasting Models in ExcelModules

Decision Modeling In Action

Forecasting Sales at Sun Microsystems

Sun Microsystems Inc., a worldwide supplier of enterprise computing products, employs about 33,500 people and has revenues of over $14 billion. Although Sun's products range from microprocessors to information technology services, the bulk of its income is from the sales of computer servers and storage systems.

Sun's strategy involves extensive outsourcing, which presents significant supply chain management challenges due to the short life cycle of its computer products. Sun therefore relies on accurate demand forecasts over a quarterly time horizon to effectively manage its supply chain. Sun's sales forecasting had historically relied on judgmental forecasts, which are subject to distortion. To address this deficiency, Sun's supply chain managers worked with researchers to develop statistical forecasting techniques that could be used to enhance—but not supplant—the company's judgmental forecasts. The result of this project was a suite of software called the Sun Labs Forecasting System.

This forecasting system operates almost entirely unattended and provides an effective combination of judgmental and statistical forecasting information that consistently improves upon the forecast accuracy of both constituents. The system has been received very favorably by Sun's supply chain managers.

Source: Based on P. M. Yelland, S. Kim, and R. Stratulate. "A Bayesian Model for Sales Forecasting at Sun Microsystems," *Interfaces* 40, 2 (March–April 2010): 118–129.

Using ExcelModules for Moving Averages Figure 11.5 shows the options we select for the Wallace Garden Supply example.

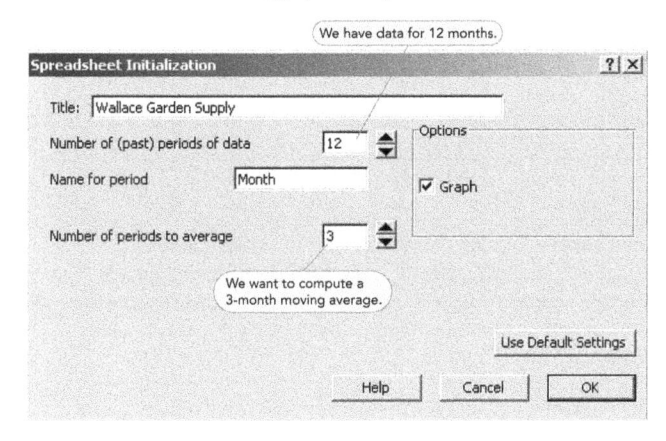

Figure 11.5: Options Window for Moving Averages Worksheet in ExcelModules

When we click OK on this screen, we get the screen shown in Figure 11.6, where we enter the actual shed sales for the 12 months (see Table 11.1) in cells B7:B18.

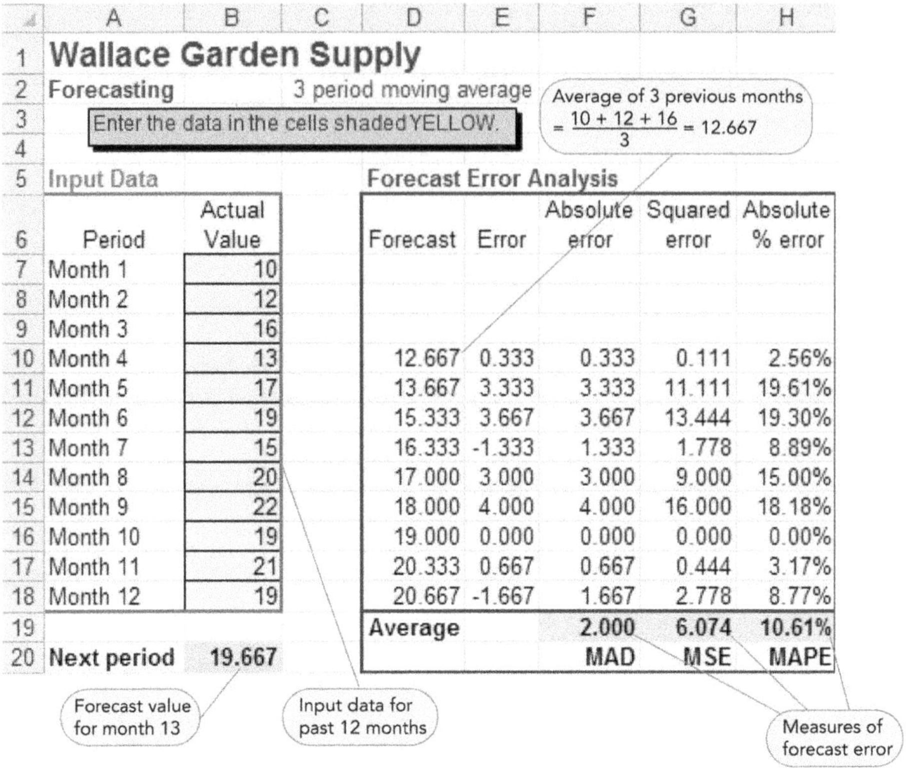

Wallace Garden Supply

Forecasting — 3 period moving average

Enter the data in the cells shaded YELLOW.

Average of 3 previous months = $\dfrac{10 + 12 + 16}{3} = 12.667$

Input Data

Period	Actual Value		Forecast	Error	Absolute error	Squared error	Absolute % error
Month 1	10						
Month 2	12						
Month 3	16						
Month 4	13		12.667	0.333	0.333	0.111	2.56%
Month 5	17		13.667	3.333	3.333	11.111	19.61%
Month 6	19		15.333	3.667	3.667	13.444	19.30%
Month 7	15		16.333	-1.333	1.333	1.778	8.89%
Month 8	20		17.000	3.000	3.000	9.000	15.00%
Month 9	22		18.000	4.000	4.000	16.000	18.18%
Month 10	19		19.000	0.000	0.000	0.000	0.00%
Month 11	21		20.333	0.667	0.667	0.444	3.17%
Month 12	19		20.667	-1.667	1.667	2.778	8.77%
			Average		2.000	6.074	10.61%
Next period	19.667				MAD	MSE	MAPE

Forecast value for month 13

Input data for past 12 months

Measures of forecast error

Figure 11.6: Moving Averages Model for Wallace Garden Supply

File: Figure 11.6.xlsx, Sheet: Figure 11.6

EXCEL NOTES

- The worksheets in ExcelModules contain formulas to compute the forecasts and forecast errors for different forecasting models. The default zero values for the input data cause the results of these formulas to initially appear as #N/A, #VALUE!, or #DIV/0!. However, as soon as we enter valid values for the input data, the worksheets will display the formula results.

- Once ExcelModules has been used to create the Excel worksheet for a particular forecasting model (e.g., a three-period moving averages model), the resulting worksheet can be used to compute the forecasts with several different input data. For example, we can enter different input data in cells B7:B18 of Figure 11.6 and compute the results without having to create a new three-period moving averages worksheet each time.

The worksheet now displays the three-month moving averages (shown in cells D10:D18), and the forecast for the next month (i.e., January of the next year), shown in cell B20. In addition, the following measures of forecast error are also calculated and reported: MAD (cell F19), MSE (cell G19), and MAPE (cell H19).

The output indicates that a three-month moving average model results in a MAPE of 10.61%. The forecast for the next period is 19.667 storage sheds. The line graph (if Graph is checked in the options in Figure 11.5) is shown in a separate worksheet. We show the graph for the Wallace Garden Supply example in Figure 11.7.

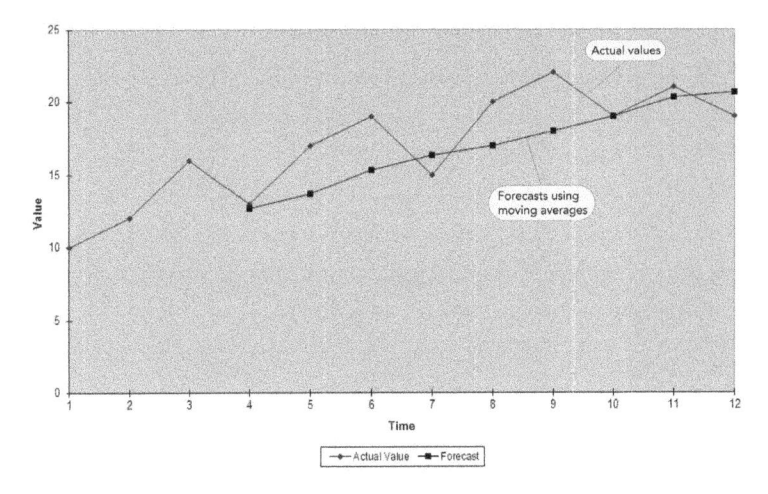

Figure 11.7: Chart of Three-Period Moving Averages Forecast for Wallace Garden Supply

File: Figure 11.6.xlsx, Sheet: Figure 11.7

Interpreting Forecast Errors As noted earlier, the measures of forecast error allow us to compare different forecasting models to see which one provides the best forecast. For example, instead of a three-month moving average, we can try a four-month moving average for the Wallace Garden Supply example. See if you can repeat the procedure described in Figures 11.5 and 11.6 for a four-month moving average. You should see that the MAPE with $k=4$ is 14.22%. This implies that, at least in this example, the three-month moving average model provides a better forecast than the four-month model. We can try other values for k in a similar fashion.

Weighted Moving Averages

In the regular moving average approach, all the input data are assumed to be equally important. For example, in a three-period model, data for all three previous periods are given equal importance, and a simple average of the three values is computed. In some cases, however, data for some periods (e.g., recent periods) may be more important than data for other periods (e.g., earlier periods). This is especially true if there is a trend or pattern in the data. In such cases, we can use weights to place more emphasis on some periods and less emphasis on others.

The choice of weights is somewhat arbitrary because there is no set formula to determine them. Therefore, deciding which weights to use requires some experience and a bit of luck. For example, if the latest period is weighted too heavily, the model might reflect a large unusual change in the forecast value too quickly.

Mathematically, the *k*-period weighted moving average, which serves the forecast for the next period, can be expressed as

$$k\text{-period weighted moving average} = \frac{\sum_{i=1}^{k} (\text{Weight for period } i) \times (\text{Actual value in period } i)}{\sum_{i=1}^{k} (\text{Weights})} \quad (11-8)$$

Wallace Garden Supply Revisited—Part I Instead of using a three-month moving average, let us assume that Wallace Garden Supply would like to forecast sales of storage sheds by weighting the past three months, as follows:

Period	Weight
Last month	3
Two months ago	2
Three months ago	1

The results of the Wallace Garden Supply weighted average forecast using these weights are shown in Table 11.2. Let us now see how we can also use ExcelModules to compute these weighted moving averages.

Table 11.2: Three-Month Weighted Moving Averages Forecast for Wallace Garden Supply

Month	Actual Sales	Weighted Moving Averages
January	10	
February	12	
March	16	
April	13	$(1 \times 10 + 2 \times 12 + 3 \times 16)/6 = 13.67$
May	17	$(1 \times 12 + 2 \times 16 + 3 \times 13)/6 = 13.83$
June	19	$(1 \times 16 + 2 \times 13 + 3 \times 17)/6 = 15.50$
July	15	$(1 \times 13 + 2 \times 17 + 3 \times 19)/6 = 17.33$
August	20	$(1 \times 17 + 2 \times 19 + 3 \times 15)/6 = 16.67$
September	22	$(1 \times 19 + 2 \times 15 + 3 \times 20)/6 = 18.17$
October	19	$(1 \times 15 + 2 \times 20 + 3 \times 22)/6 = 20.17$
November	21	$(1 \times 20 + 2 \times 22 + 3 \times 19)/6 = 20.17$
December	19	$(1 \times 22 + 2 \times 19 + 3 \times 21)/6 = 20.50$

Using ExcelModules for Weighted Moving Averages When we select the choice titled Weighted Moving Averages from the Forecasting Models menu in ExcelModules (see Figure 11.3), the window shown in Figure 11.8 is displayed. The option entries in this window are similar to those for moving averages (see Figure 11.5). The only additional choice is the box labeled Weights sum to 1. Although not required, it is common practice to assign weights to various periods such that they sum to one (note, for example, that the sum of weights in the Wallace Garden Supply example is 6). Our specific entries for Wallace Garden Supply's problem are shown in Figure 11.8.

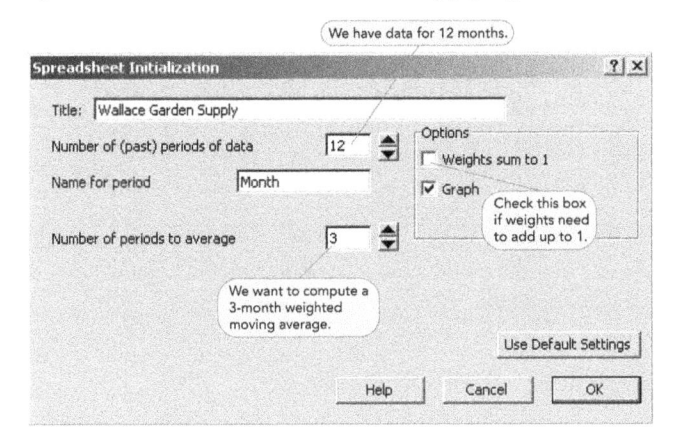

Figure 11.8: Options Window for Weighted Moving Averages Worksheet in ExcelModules

When we click OK on this screen, we get the screen shown in Figure 11.9, where we enter the actual shed sales for the 12 months (see Table 11.2) in cells B7:B18 and the weights for the past 3 months in cells C7:C9.

The worksheet now displays the three-month weighted moving averages (shown in cells E10:E18), and the forecast for the next month (i.e., January of the next year), shown in cell B20. In addition, the following measures of forecast error are also calculated and reported: MAD (cell G19), MSE (cell H19), and MAPE (cell I19). The line graph, if asked for, is shown on a separate worksheet (included in file *Figure 11.9.xlsx*).

In this particular example, you can see that weighting the latest month more heavily actually provides a less accurate forecast. That is, the MAPE value is now 12.20%, compared with a MAPE value of only 10.61% for the three-month simple moving average.

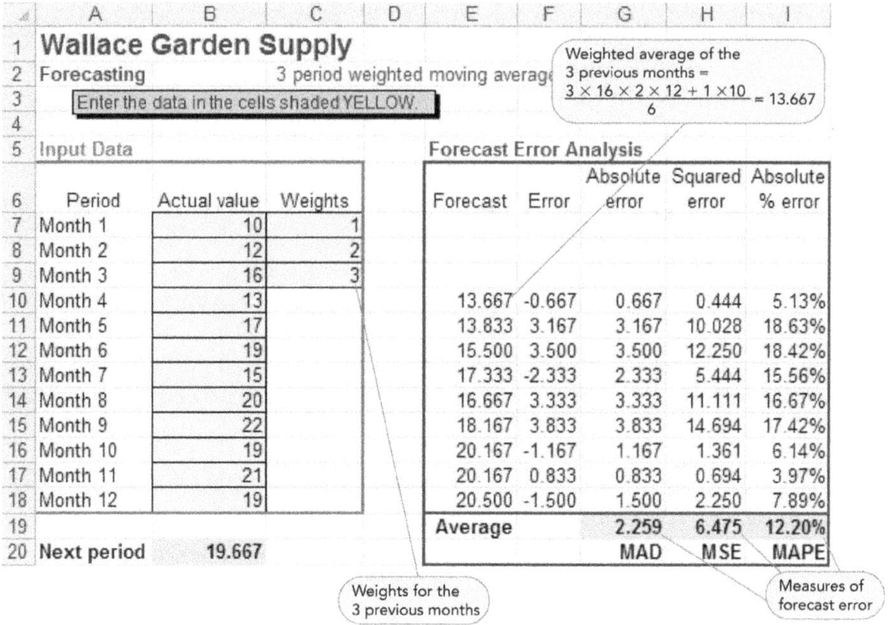

Figure 11.9: Weighted Moving Averages Model for Wallace Garden Supply

	A	B	C	D	E	F	G	H	I
1	**Wallace Garden Supply**					Weighted average of the			
2	Forecasting		3 period weighted moving average			3 previous months =			
3	Enter the data in the cells shaded YELLOW.					$\frac{3 \times 16 \times 2 \times 12 + 1 \times 10}{6} = 13.667$			
4									
5	Input Data					Forecast Error Analysis			
6	Period	Actual value	Weights			Forecast	Error	Absolute error	Squared error	Absolute % error
7	Month 1	10	1							
8	Month 2	12	2							
9	Month 3	16	3							
10	Month 4	13				13.667	-0.667	0.667	0.444	5.13%
11	Month 5	17				13.833	3.167	3.167	10.028	18.63%
12	Month 6	19				15.500	3.500	3.500	12.250	18.42%
13	Month 7	15				17.333	-2.333	2.333	5.444	15.56%
14	Month 8	20				16.667	3.333	3.333	11.111	16.67%
15	Month 9	22				18.167	3.833	3.833	14.694	17.42%
16	Month 10	19				20.167	-1.167	1.167	1.361	6.14%
17	Month 11	21				20.167	0.833	0.833	0.694	3.97%
18	Month 12	19				20.500	-1.500	1.500	2.250	7.89%
19						Average		2.259	6.475	12.20%
20	Next period	19.667						MAD	MSE	MAPE

(Weights for the 3 previous months; Measures of forecast error)

Figure 11.9: Weighted Moving Averages Model for Wallace Garden Supply

File: Figure 11.9.xlsx, Sheet: Figure 11.9

Using Solver to Determine the Optimal Weights As noted earlier, the choice of weights is somewhat arbitrary because there is no set formula to determine them. However, for a specified value of k (i.e., number of periods to use in computing the weighted moving average), we can use Excel's Solver to find the optimal weights to use in the forecasting model.

Recall that we used Solver to solve linear, integer, and nonlinear programming problems in Chapters 2 through 6. Setting up a problem in Solver requires three components:

- *Changing variable cells.* These cells denote the decision variables for which we are trying to identify optimal values.
- *Objective cell.* This cell contains the formula for the measure we are trying to either maximize or minimize.
- *Constraints.* These are one or more restrictions on the values that the decision variables are allowed to take.

In our case, the decision variables are the weights to be used in computing the weighted moving average. Hence, we specify cells C7:C9 as our changing variable cells. The objective is to minimize some measure of forecast error, such as MAD, MSE, or MAPE. Let us assume that we want to minimize the MAPE here. Cell I19 is, therefore, the objective cell.

If we want to specify that the weights must add up to one, we must include this as a constraint in the model. The only other constraint is the nonnegativity constraint on the decision variables (weights). Recall that we can easily enforce this constraint by checking the Make Unconstrained Variable Non-Negative box in the Solver Parameters window. It is important to note that we should select GRG Nonlinear as the solving method to solve this problem because the formula for the objective function (MAPE, in this case) is *nonlinear*.

Figure 11.10 shows the Solver entries and results for the Wallace Garden Supply problem. For illustration purposes, we have chosen to include the constraint that the sum of weights must equal one. The formula to model this constraint is shown in Figure 11.10.

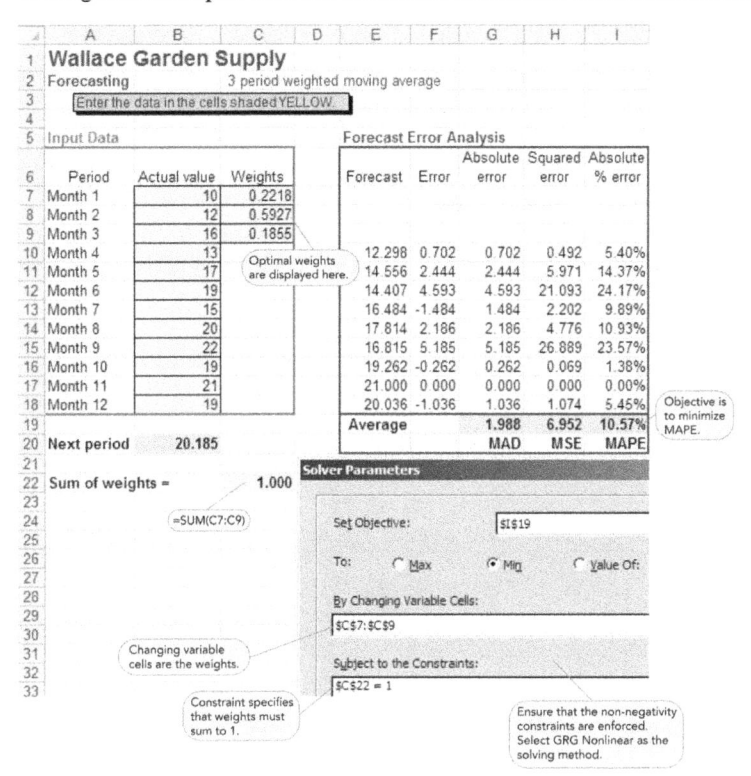

Figure 11.10: Optimal Weights, Using Solver, for Wallace Garden Supply

File: Figure 11.9.xlsx, Sheet: Figure 11.10

The results indicate that MAPE decreases to 10.57% when weights of 0.185, 0.593, and 0.222 are associated with the latest period, the period before that, and two periods before that, respectively. Observe that MSE actually increases from 6.475 in Figure 11.9 to 6.952 in Figure 11.10. That is, the weights that minimize MAPE need not necessarily minimize the MSE value also.

Exponential Smoothing

Both moving averages and weighted moving averages are effective in smoothing out sudden fluctuations in the demand pattern in order to provide stable estimates. In fact, increasing the size of k (i.e., the number of periods averaged) smooths out fluctuations even better. However, doing so requires us to keep extensive records of past data.

An alternate forecasting approach that is also a type of moving average technique, but requires little record keeping of past data, is called exponential smoothing. Let F_t denote the forecast in period t and A_t denote the actual value in period t. The basic exponential smoothing formula is as follows:

Forecast for period $(t+1)$ = Forecast for period t +
$\alpha \times$ (Actual value in period t − Forecast for period t)

or

$$F_{t+1} = F_t + \alpha \times (A_t - F_t) \tag{11-9}$$

where α is a weight (called a smoothing constant) that has a value between 0 and 1, inclusive. The forecast for a period is equal to the forecast for the previous period, adjusted by a fraction (specified by α) of the forecast error in the previous period. Observe that in Equation 11–9, F_t can be written as

$$F_t = F_{t-1} + \alpha \times (A_{t-1} - F_{t-1})$$

Likewise, F_{t-1} can be expressed in terms of F_{t-2} and A_{t-2}, and so on. Substituting for F_t, F_{t-1}, F_{t-2}, and so on in Equation 11–9, we can show that

$$F_{t+1} = \alpha A_t + \alpha(1-\alpha) A_{t-1} + \alpha(1-\alpha)^2 A_{t-2} + \alpha(1-\alpha)^3 A_{t-3} + \cdots \tag{11-10}$$

That is, the forecast in period $(t+1)$ is just a weighted average of the actual values in period t, $(t-1)$, $(t-2)$, and so on. Observe that the weight associated with a period's actual value decreases exponentially over time. For this reason, the term *exponential smoothing* is used to describe the technique.

The actual value of α can be changed to give more weight to recent periods (when α is high) or more weight to past periods (when α is low). For example, when $\alpha = 1$, the forecast in period $t+1$ is equal to the actual value in period t. That is, the entire new forecast is based just on the most recent period. When $\alpha = 0.5$, it can be shown mathematically that the new forecast is based almost entirely on values in just the past three periods. When $\alpha = 0.1$, the forecast places relatively little weight on recent periods and takes many periods of values into account.

Wallace Garden Supply Revisited—Part II Suppose Wallace Garden Supply would like to forecast sales of storage sheds by using an exponential smoothing model. To get the model started, we need to know the forecast for the first period, January. In Wallace's problem, let us assume that the forecast for sales of storage sheds in January equals the actual sales that month (i.e., 10 sheds). The exponential smoothing forecast calculations are shown in Table 11.3 for $\alpha = 0.1$ and $\alpha = 0.9$. Next, we show how we can use ExcelModules to perform these calculations.

Table 11.3: Exponential Smoothing Forecasts for Wallace Garden Supply ($\alpha = 0.1$ and $\alpha = 0.9$)

Month	Actual Sales	Forecast ($\alpha = 0.1$)	$\alpha = 0.9$
January	10	10.0 (assumed value)	10.0
February	12	10.0 + 0.1 (10− 10.0) = 10.0	10.0
March	16	10.0 + 0.1 (12− 10.0) = 10.2	11.8
April	13	10.2 + 0.1 (16− 10.2) = 10.8	15.6
May	17	10.8 + 0.1 (13 − 10.8) = 11.0	13.3
June	19	11.0 + 0.1 (17 − 11.0) = 11.6	16.6
July	15	11.6 + 0.1 (19 − 11.6) = 12.3	18.8
August	20	12.3 + 0.1 (15 − 12.3) = 12.6	15.4
September	22	12.6 + 0.1 (20 − 12.6) = 13.4	19.5
October	19	13.4 + 0.1 (22 − 13.4) = 14.2	21.7
November	21	14.2 + 0.1 (19 − 14.2) = 14.7	19.3
December	19	14.7 + 0.1 (21 − 14.7) = 15.3	20.8

Using ExcelModules for Exponential Smoothing When we select the choice titled Exponential Smoothing from the Forecasting Models menu in ExcelModules (see Figure 11.3), the window shown in Figure 11.11 is displayed. The option entries in this window are similar to those for moving averages (as we saw in Figure 11.5).

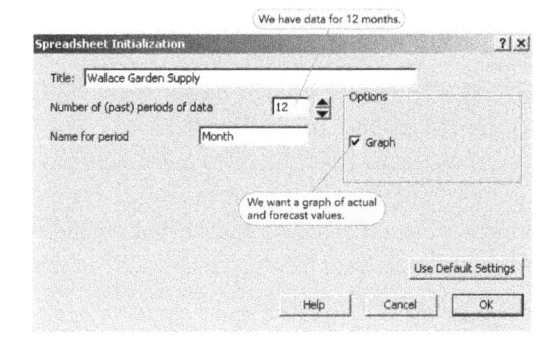

Figure 11.11: Options Window for Exponential Smoothing Worksheet in ExcelModules

When we click OK on this screen, we get the screen shown in Figure 11.12. We now enter the actual shed sales for the 12 months (see Table 11.3) in cells B7:B18 and the value of α in cell B20. We use $\alpha = 0.1$ for this sample computer run. By default, ExcelModules assumes that the forecast for the first period equals the actual sales in that period (i.e., cell D7 = cell B7). In cases where this forecast is a different value, we can just type that entry into cell D7.

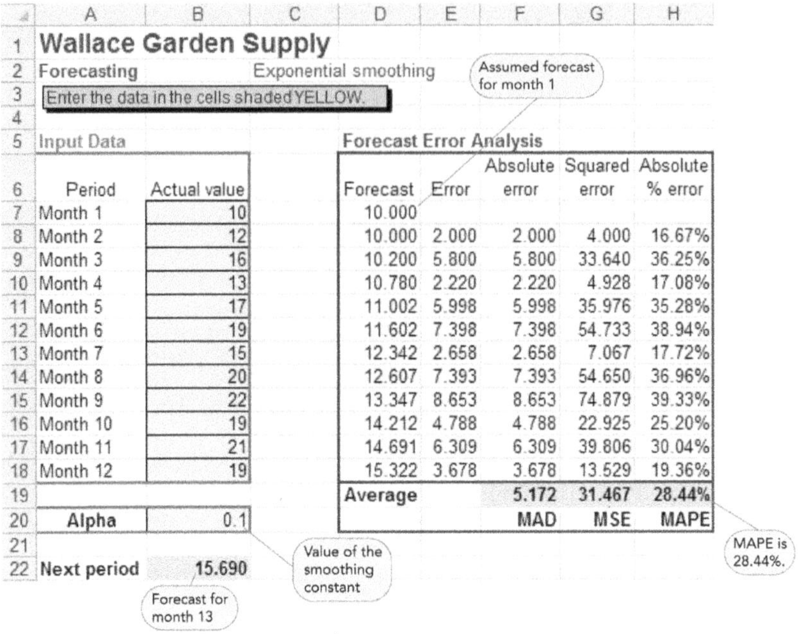

Wallace Garden Supply

	A	B	C	D	E	F	G	H
1	Wallace Garden Supply							
2	Forecasting		Exponential smoothing			Assumed forecast for month 1		
3	Enter the data in the cells shaded YELLOW.							
4								
5	Input Data				Forecast Error Analysis			
6		Period	Actual value		Forecast	Error	Absolute error	Squared error	Absolute % error
7		Month 1	10		10.000				
8		Month 2	12		10.000	2.000	2.000	4.000	16.67%
9		Month 3	16		10.200	5.800	5.800	33.640	36.25%
10		Month 4	13		10.780	2.220	2.220	4.928	17.08%
11		Month 5	17		11.002	5.998	5.998	35.976	35.28%
12		Month 6	19		11.602	7.398	7.398	54.733	38.94%
13		Month 7	15		12.342	2.658	2.658	7.067	17.72%
14		Month 8	20		12.607	7.393	7.393	54.650	36.96%
15		Month 9	22		13.347	8.653	8.653	74.879	39.33%
16		Month 10	19		14.212	4.788	4.788	22.925	25.20%
17		Month 11	21		14.691	6.309	6.309	39.806	30.04%
18		Month 12	19		15.322	3.678	3.678	13.529	19.36%
19					Average		5.172	31.467	28.44%
20		Alpha	0.1				MAD	MSE	MAPE
21					Value of the smoothing constant				MAPE is 28.44%.
22		Next period	15.690						

Forecast for month 13

Figure 11.12: Exponential Smoothing Model for Wallace Garden Supply, Using $\alpha = 0.1$

X▦ File: Figure 11.12.xlsx, Sheet: Figure 11.12

The worksheet now displays the exponential smoothing forecasts (shown in cells D7:D18) and the forecast for the next month (i.e., January of the next year), shown in cell B22. In addition, the following measures of forecast error are also calculated and reported: MAD (cell F19), MSE (cell G19), and MAPE (cell H19). The line graph, if asked for, is shown on a separate worksheet (included in file *Figure 11.12.xlsx*).

With $\alpha = 0.1$, MAPE turns out to be 28.44%. Note that all error values here have been computed using months 2 through 12, compared with earlier cases (see Figures 11.6 and 11.9) where only months 4 through 12 were used. (Whenever making direct comparisons among methods or among parameter values for a given method, be sure to cover the same set of periods when computing error values.)

See if you can repeat the exponential smoothing calculations for $\alpha = 0.9$ and obtain a MAPE of 17.18%.

Using Solver to Determine the Optimal Value of α Just as we used Solver to find the optimal weights in the weighted moving average technique, we can use it to find the optimal smoothing constant in the exponential smoothing technique. The lone changing variable cell here is the value of α (cell B20, as shown in Figure 11.13). The objective cell is the measure of forecast error (i.e., MAD, MSE, or MAPE) that we want to minimize. In Figure 11.13, we have chosen to minimize the MAPE (cell H19). The only constraint (other than the nonnegativity constraint) is that the value of α must be less than or equal to one. Here again, the solving method selected in Solver should be GRG Nonlinear.

	A	B	C	D	E	F	G	H
1	Wallace Garden Supply							
2	Forecasting		Exponential smoothing					
3	Enter the data in the cells shaded YELLOW.							
4								
5	Input Data			Forecast Error Analysis				
						Absolute	Squared	Absolute
6	Period	Actual value		Forecast	Error	error	error	% error
7	Month 1	10		10.000				
8	Month 2	12		10.000	2.000	2.000	4.000	16.67%
9	Month 3	16		10.838	5.162	5.162	26.649	32.26%
10	Month 4	13		13.000	0.000	0.000	0.000	0.00%
11	Month 5	17		13.000	4.000	4.000	16.000	23.53%
12	Month 6	19		14.675	4.325	4.325	18.702	22.76%
13	Month 7	15		16.487	-1.487	1.487	2.211	9.91%
14	Month 8	20		15.864	4.136	4.136	17.106	20.68%
15	Month 9	22		17.596	4.404	4.404	19.391	20.02%
16	Month 10	19		19.441	-0.441	0.441	0.194	2.32%
17	Month 11	21		19.256	1.744	1.744	3.041	8.30%
18	Month 12	19		19.987	-0.987	0.987	0.973	5.19%
19				Average		2.608	9.842	14.70%
20	Alpha	0.419				MAD	MSE	MAPE
22	Next period	19.573						

Optimal value of α is displayed here.

Changing variable cell is α.

Constraint specifies $\alpha \leq 1$.

Solver Parameters: Set Objective: $H$19; Min; By Changing Variable Cells: $B$20; Subject to the Constraints: $B$20 <= 1

Objective is to minimize MAPE.

Minimum MAPE is 14.70%.

Ensure that the non-negativity constraints are enforced. Select GRG Nonlinear as the solving method.

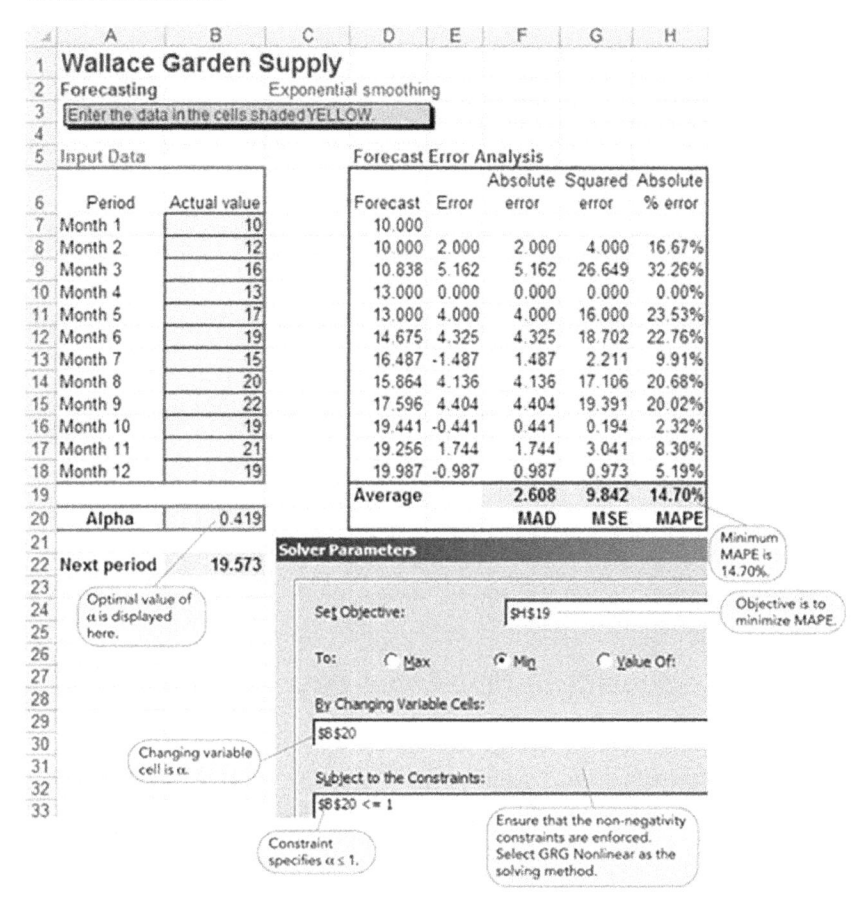

Figure 11.13: Optimal Smoothing Constant, Using Solver, for Wallace Garden Supply

X▦ File: Figure 11.12.xlsx, Sheet: Figure 11.13

Figure 11.13 shows the Solver entries and results for the Wallace Garden Supply problem. The optimal value of α turns out to be 0.419, yielding a MAPE value of 14.70%. Compare this with a MAPE of 28.44% when $\alpha = 0.1$ and a MAPE of 17.18% when $\alpha = 0.9$.

The value of MSE is 9.842 when $\alpha = 0.419$. However, the minimum value of MSE is 8.547 and is obtained when $\alpha = 0.646$. (See if you can verify this for yourself by using Solver.) That is, the same value of α need not necessarily minimize both the MAPE and MSE measures.

Decision Modeling In Action

New-Product Forecasting at Intel

When a new product is introduced, its adoption rate can be severely impacted by any production shortage. In contrast, excess inventory of the product erodes profits and wastes production capacity that could have been better used elsewhere. Since this capacity is often shared by many products, life-cycle forecasting is critical not only for demand management but also for effective operations management.

Intel's microprocessor marketing and business planning (MMBP) team is responsible for forecasting demand for critical products in the desktop, mobile, and server markets. Each month, the team generates updated 12-month demand forecasts for each active product using historical data, collective mental models, and current market news. These forecasts serve as crucial inputs to Intel's three-month production cycle, as well as to production, materials, inventory, and logistics planning activities in later months.

Working with researchers from Lehigh University, Intel's MMBP team tested a new integrated forecasting model that perpetually reduces forecast variance as new market information is acquired over time. The new method shows a 9.7 percent reduction in MAPE over the 12-month horizon on average and an impressive 33 percent reduction in the MAPE for the fourth month (which Intel views as a critical month for production planning purposes). The new process also generates the forecast in about two hours, far less than the three days needed by the old process.

Source: Based on S. D. Wu et al. "Improving New-Product Forecasting at Intel Corporation," *Interfaces* 40, 5 (September-October 2010): 385–396.

11.6 Trend and Seasonality in Time-Series Data

Although moving average models smooth out fluctuations in a time series, they are not very good at picking up trends in data. Likewise, they are not very good at detecting seasonal variations in data. In this section, we discuss how trend and seasonal variations can be detected and analyzed in time-series data. Here again, although we show the equations needed to compute the forecasts for each model, we use worksheets (included in ExcelModules) to actually calculate these values.

Linear Trend Analysis

The *trend analysis* technique fits a trend equation (or curve) to a series of historical data points. It then projects the curve into the future for medium- and long-term forecasts. Several mathematical trend equations can be developed (e.g., linear, exponential, quadratic equations). However, in this section, we discuss only linear trends. In other words, the mathematical trend equation we develop will be a straight line.

Midwestern Electric Company Example Let's consider the case of Midwestern Electric Company. The firm's demand for electrical generators over the period 2002–2011 is shown in Table 11.4.

Table 11.4: Demand at Midwestern Electric

Year	Demand
2002	64
2003	68
2004	72
2005	74
2006	79
2007	80
2008	90
2009	105
2010	142
2011	122

The goal here is to identify a straight line that describes the relationship between demand for generators and time. The variable to be forecasted or predicted (demand, in this case) is called the dependent variable and is denoted by Y. The variable used in the prediction (year, in this case) is called the independent variable, and is denoted by X.

Scatter Chart

To quickly get an idea whether any relationship exists between two variables, a scatter chart (also called a scatter diagram or plot) can be drawn on a two-dimensional graph. The independent variable (e.g., time) is usually measured on the horizontal (X) axis, and the dependent variable (e.g., demand) is usually measured on the vertical (Y) axis.

Scatter Chart Using Excel Although we can draw a scatter chart by using ExcelModules (discussed shortly), we can also use Excel's built-in charting capabilities to draw such charts. The input data for Midwestern Electric's problem is shown in Figure 11.14. The steps for creating a scatter chart in Excel are as follows:

1. Enter the time (year) and demand data in two columns (preferably adjacent, with the year in the first column), as shown in Figure 11.14.
2. Highlight the two columns of data (i.e., cells A3:B12). Select the Insert tab in Excel's Ribbon and then select the desired option among the different Scatter charts that are available (see Figure 11.14). Excel will immediately draw the selected scatter chart using the variable in the first column as the X-axis and the variable in the second column as the Y-axis. If the column titles (row 2) were highlighted prior to selecting the chart, Excel automatically makes the title of the second column the chart title.

    To swap the X- and Y-axes (if necessary), click on the scatter chart. A new tab titled Chart Tools is now available (see Figure 11.15). Select Design and then select Switch Row/Column.

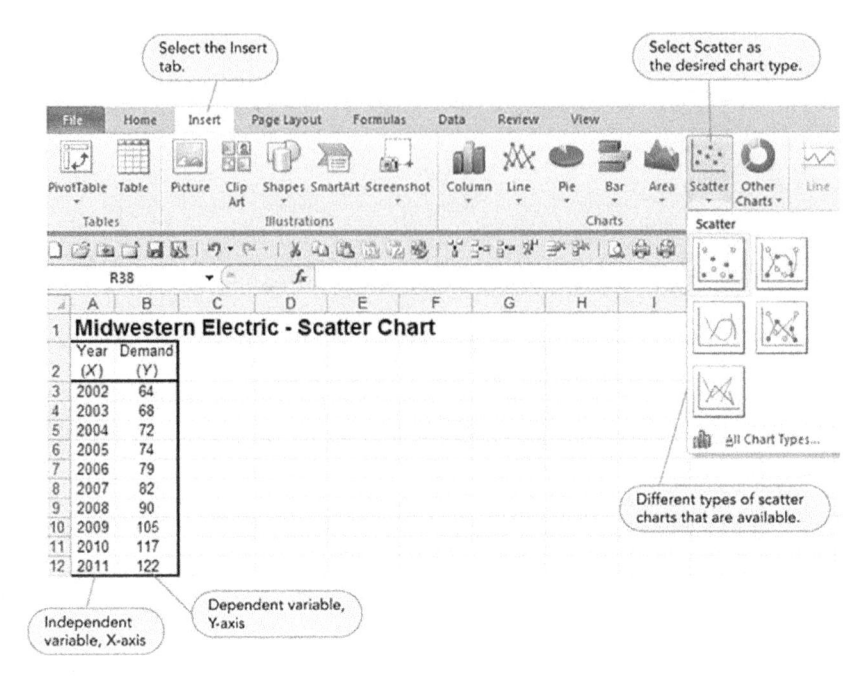

Figure 11.14: Creating a Scatter Chart in Excel

File: Figure 11.14.xlsx

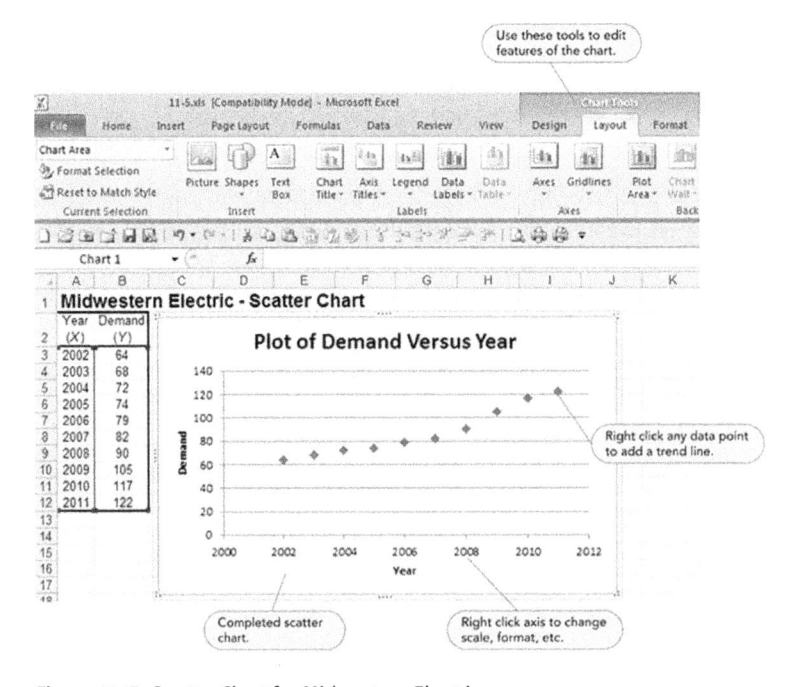

Figure 11.15: Scatter Chart for Midwestern Electric

3. To further customize the scatter chart, select the Layout tab within Chart Tools to reveal the various options shown in Figure 11.15. Also, if you want to display a linear trend line directly on the scatter chart, you can do so by right-clicking any of the data points on the chart and selecting the option Add Trendline.

It appears from the chart in Figure 11.15 that it may be reasonable to approximate the relationship between time and demand for generators in Midwestern Electric's problem by using a linear trend line.

EXCEL EXTRA

Conditional Formatting

Conditional Formatting represents a powerful, yet easy-to-use, tool that helps to visually identify characteristics of data via formatting (especially colors or icons) applied only to data possessing certain characteristics. When the data change, the formatting may automatically change along with them. This can be a great way to emphasize unusual values or identify large and/or small values. Conditional Formatting could be used, for example, to find out which salesperson had the highest sales last month or to identify which products had sales decreases of at least 10%.

Perhaps the most important visual formats available are (1) Color Scales for the whole data set, (2) Icon Sets for the whole data set, and (3) coloring the cells that meet certain conditions.

Some of the options include: Format all cells based on their values, Format only cells that contain, Format only top or bottom ranked values, Format only unique or duplicate values, and Use a formula to determine which cells to format. The various options under the Home|Conditional Formatting button are relatively self-explanatory.

As one example, we could apply Conditional Formatting to the demand amounts appearing in column B in Figure 11.15 to color the cells light red for any demands that exceed 99. First, select the range B3:B12, and then click:

> Home|Conditional Formatting|Highlight Cells Rules|Greater Than...

Type 99 in the first box, and click and choose Light Red Fill for the second box. Click OK.

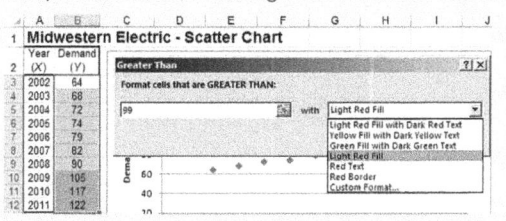

If, for example, new figures came in, and it turns out that demand in 2007 was actually 101, cell B8 would automatically turn light red after you entered the new sales amount.

To edit or delete a rule, click Home|Conditional Formatting|Manage Rules... .

Least-Squares Procedure for Developing a Linear Trend Line

A linear trend line between an independent variable (which always denotes time in a trend analysis) and a dependent variable (demand, in Midwestern Electric's example) is described in terms of its Y-intercept (i.e., the Y value at which the line intersects the Y-axis) and its slope (i.e., the angle of the line). The slope of a linear trend line can be interpreted as the average change in Y for a unit increase in the value of time (X). The line can be expressed by using the following equation:

$$\hat{Y} = b_0 + b_1 X \tag{11-11}$$

where

$\hat{Y}$ = forecasted average value of the dependent variable (demand) (pronounced "Y-hat")

X = value of the independent variable (time)

b_0 = Y- intercept of the line, based on the current sample

b_1 = slope of the line, based on the current sample

Note that we refer to $\hat{Y}$ as the forecasted *average* value because it is, in fact, the average (or expected value) of a probability distribution of possible values of Y for a given value of X.

To develop a linear trend line between Y and X, there are essentially an infinite number of values that we could assign to b_0 and b_1. Therefore, we cannot determine the best values for b_0 and b_1 either by eyeballing the scatter chart or by manually trying out different values. Note that we want to find values of b_0 and b_1 that make the forecasted demand (estimated from the trend line) for a specific year as close as possible to the actual demand that year. For example, if we had used the linear trend line to forecast demand for 2011, we would have wanted its forecast to be as close to 122 as possible. To achieve this objective, we use a precise statistical method known as the least-squares procedure. The goal of this procedure is to identify the linear trend line that minimizes the sum of the squares of the vertical differences from the line to each of the actual observations. That is, it minimizes the sum of the squared errors between the forecasted and actual values. Figure 11.16 illustrates the error terms.

Mathematically, we can express the least-squares procedure as follows: Find the values of b_0 and b_1 that minimize the sum of squared errors (SSE), defined as

$$SSE = \sum_{i=1}^{n}(Y_i - \hat{Y}_i)^2 = \sum_{i=1}^{n}[Y_i - (b_0 + b_1 X_i)]^2 \tag{11-12}$$

where n = number of observations (10, in Midwestern Electric's example).

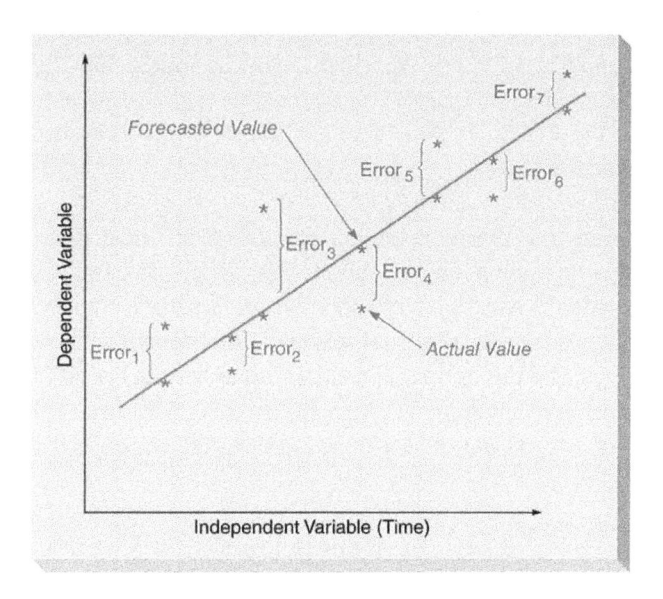

Figure 11.16: Least-Squares Method for Finding the Best-Fitting Straight Line

We can use calculus to solve Equation 11–12 and develop the following equations to compute the values of b_0 and b_1 and minimize SSE:[1]

$$b_1 = \frac{\sum XY - n\overline{XY}}{\sum X^2 - n\overline{X}^2} \qquad (11\text{–}13)$$

and

$$b_0 = \overline{Y} - b_1 \overline{X} \qquad (11\text{–}14)$$

where

$\overline{X}$ = average of the values of the Xs

$\overline{Y}$ = average of the values of the Ys

Even though the formulas for b_0 and b_1 may look somewhat cumbersome, they are fairly easy to use. In fact, most handheld calculators today have built-in functions to compute these values for a given data set. Of course, in keeping with our focus on using spreadsheets in this book, we will use Excel for these computations. There are two approaches available in Excel for this purpose:

---

[1] Essentially, we take the first derivative of Equation 1–12 with respect to b_0 and b_1, set both equations equal to zero, and solve for b_0 and b_1. See a statistics book for more details.

- *Least-squares procedure using* ExcelModules. We will discuss this approach in the following pages.
- *Least-squares procedure using* Excel's *Analysis ToolPak add-in*. We will discuss this approach in detail in section 11.8.

Transforming Time Values Recall that the independent variable X in linear trend analysis always denotes time. Depending on the manner in which this time is measured, the independent variable can be stated in months, such as January, February, etc., or in years, such as 2002, 2003, etc. (as in Midwestern Electric's example). Hence, in order to facilitate the trend line computations, we may need to transform the time values to a simpler numeric scheme. In the case of Midwestern Electric's data, a convenient way to do so would be to code the year 2002 as $X = 1$, the year 2003 as $X = 2$, and so on.

Using ExcelModules for Linear Trend Analysis Equations 11–13 and 11–14 have been coded in ExcelModules, along with formulas for computing the usual measures of forecast error. To run these computations, we select the choice titled Linear Trend Analysis from the Forecasting Models menu in ExcelModules (see Figure 11.3). The window shown in Figure 11.17 is displayed. The option entries in this window are similar to those for moving averages (as we saw in Figure 11.5). Note that if we check Graph in the options shown in Figure 11.17, ExcelModules will automatically draw a scatter chart, along with the linear trend line, as part of the output.

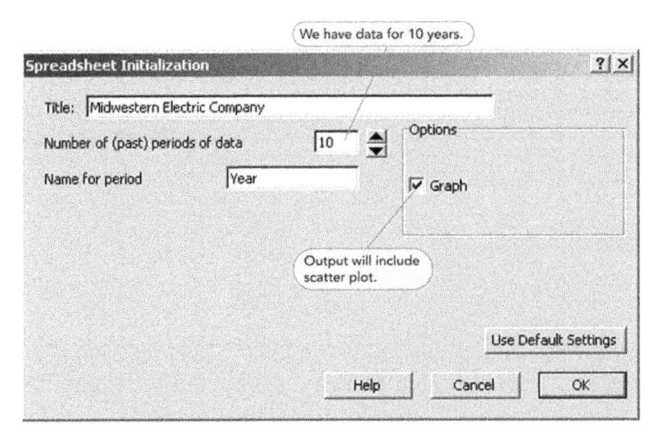

Figure 11.17: Options Window for Linear Trend Analysis Worksheet in ExcelModules

When we click OK on this screen, we get the screen shown in Figure 11.18. We now enter the actual demand for generators in 2002 to 2011 (refer to Table 11.4) in cells B7:B16 (*Y* values). The corresponding values for the time periods (*X*) are automatically input by ExcelModules into cells C7:C16. We also enter the time period for the forecast needed ($X = 11$, corresponding to the year 2012) into cell C21. Finally, if desired, we can enter the actual names of the periods (i.e., the years 2002 to 2011) into cells A7:A16.

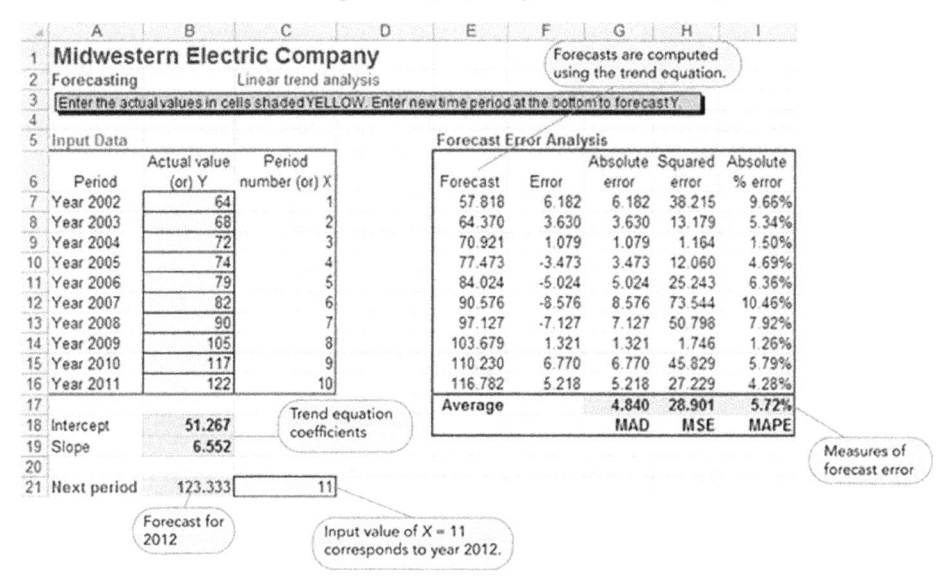

	A	B	C	D	E	F	G	H	I
1	Midwestern Electric Company					Forecasts are computed using the trend equation.			
2	Forecasting		Linear trend analysis						
3	Enter the actual values in cells shaded YELLOW. Enter new time period at the bottom to forecast Y.								
4									
5	Input Data				Forecast Error Analysis				
6	Period	Actual value (or) Y	Period number (or) X		Forecast	Error	Absolute error	Squared error	Absolute % error
7	Year 2002	64	1		57.818	6.182	6.182	38.215	9.66%
8	Year 2003	68	2		64.370	3.630	3.630	13.179	5.34%
9	Year 2004	72	3		70.921	1.079	1.079	1.164	1.50%
10	Year 2005	74	4		77.473	-3.473	3.473	12.060	4.69%
11	Year 2006	79	5		84.024	-5.024	5.024	25.243	6.36%
12	Year 2007	82	6		90.576	-8.576	8.576	73.544	10.46%
13	Year 2008	90	7		97.127	-7.127	7.127	50.798	7.92%
14	Year 2009	105	8		103.679	1.321	1.321	1.746	1.26%
15	Year 2010	117	9		110.230	6.770	6.770	45.829	5.79%
16	Year 2011	122	10		116.782	5.218	5.218	27.229	4.28%
17					Average		4.840	28.901	5.72%
18	Intercept	51.267		Trend equation coefficients			MAD	MSE	MAPE
19	Slope	6.552							
20									
21	Next period	123.333	11						

Figure 11.18: Linear Trend Analysis Model for Midwestern Electric

File: Figure 11.18.xlsx, Sheet: Figure 11.18

The worksheet now computes and reports the values of b_0 and b_1 (shown in cells B18 and B19, respectively, in Figure 11.18) for the least-squares linear trend line between time and demand. In Midwestern Electric's case, the equation of this relationship is

$$\text{Forecasted demand} = 51.267 + 6.552 \times \text{year}$$

Based on this equation, demand forecasts for 2002 through 2011 are displayed in cells E7:E16. The forecast for 2012 (i.e., time $X = 11$) is shown in cell B21 to be 123 generators (rounded). In addition, the following measures of forecast error are also calculated and reported: MAD (cell G17), MSE (cell H17), and MAPE (cell I17).

If specified in the options (see Figure 11.17), ExcelModules shows the scatter chart between X and Y on a separate worksheet, along with the least-squares linear trend line. We show this chart in Figure 11.19. We can compare the chart of actual demand values and the trend line to check the validity of the trend line model. In Midwestern Electric's case, the linear trend line seems to approximate the demand values reasonably well. The relatively low MAPE value of 5.72% also supports this conclusion.

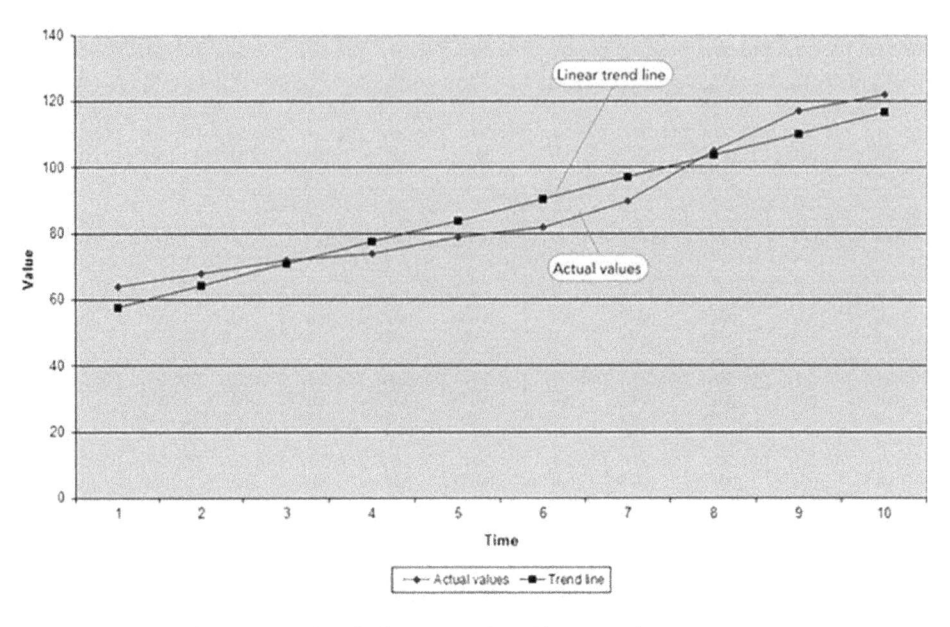

Figure 11.19: Chart of Linear Trend Analysis Forecast for Midwestern Electric

File: Figure 11.18.xlsx, Sheet: Figure 11.19

Seasonality Analysis

Time-series forecasting such as that in the example of Midwestern Electric involves looking at the *trend* of data over a series of time observations. Sometimes, however, recurring variations at certain periods (i.e., months) of the year make a seasonal adjustment in the time-series forecast necessary. Demand for coal and oil fuel, for example, usually peaks during cold winter months. Demand for golfing equipment and sunscreen may be highest in summer.

Analyzing time-series data in monthly or quarterly terms usually makes it easy to spot seasonal patterns. A seasonal *index*, which can be defined as the ratio of the average value of the item in a season to the overall annual average value, can then be computed for each season.

Several methods are available for computing seasonal indices. One such method, which bases these indices on the *average* value of the item over all periods (e.g., months, quarters), is illustrated in the following example. A different method, which uses a concept called *centered moving average* to compute seasonal indices, is illustrated in section 11.7.

Eichler Supplies Example Monthly demands of a brand of telephone-answering machines at Eichler Supplies are shown in cells C3:C26 of Figure 11.20 for the two most recent years.

Trend and Seasonality in Time-Series Data — 677

	A	B	C	D	E	F
1	Eichler Supplies					
2	Year	Month	Demand	Average Demand	Ratio	Seasonal Index
3	1	January	80	94	0.851	0.957
4		February	75	94	0.798	0.851
5		March	80	94	0.851	0.904
6		April	90	94	0.957	1.064
7		May	115	94	1.223	1.309
8		June	110	94	1.170	1.223
9		July	100	94	1.064	1.117
10		August	90	94	0.957	1.064
11		September	85	94	0.904	0.957
12		October	75	94	0.798	0.851
13		November	75	94	0.798	0.851
14		December	80	94	0.851	0.851
15	2	January	100	94	1.064	
16		February	85	94	0.904	
17		March	90	94	0.957	
18		April	110	94	1.170	
19		May	131	94	1.394	
20		June	120	94	1.277	
21		July	110	94	1.170	
22		August	110	94	1.170	
23		September	95	94	1.011	
24		October	85	94	0.904	
25		November	85	94	0.904	
26		December	80	94	0.851	

Callouts:
- Average of seasonal ratios for each month: $= \frac{0.851 + 1.064}{2}$
- Average demand for all 24 months
- Ratio = $\frac{\text{Demand}}{\text{Average demand}}$

Figure 11.20: Computation of Seasonal Indices for Eichler Supplies

File: Figure 11.20.xlsx

To compute the monthly seasonal indices, using the average demand value over the two years, we can create an Excel worksheet, as follows:

1. *Column D.* Compute the average monthly demand, using all the available data. In Eichler's case, we do this by taking the average of the demand values for all 24 months. The formula is =AVERAGE(C3:C26).
2. *Column E.* Compute the seasonal ratio for each month by dividing the actual demand that month by the average demand (i.e., column E = column C/column D). For example, the seasonal ratio for January of year 1 is 80/94 = 0.851.
3. *Column F.* Observe that because we have two years of time-series data, we have two seasonal ratios for each month. For example, January has ratios of 0.851 and 1.064, as shown in cells E3 and E15, respectively. We compute the seasonal index for January as the average of these two ratios. Hence, the seasonal index for January is equal to (0.851 + 1.064)/2 = 0.957. Similar computations for all 12 months of the year are shown in column F of Figure 11.20.

A seasonal index with value below 1 indicates that demand is below average that month, and an index with value above 1 indicates that demand is above average that month. Using these seasonal indices, we can adjust the monthly demand for any future month appropriately. For example, if we expect the third year's average demand for answering machines to be 100 units per month, we can forecast January's monthly demand as $100 \times 0.957 \approx 96$ units, which is below average. Likewise, we can forecast May's monthly demand as $100 \times 1.309 \approx 131$ units, which is above average.

11.7 Decomposition of a Time Series

Now that we have analyzed both trend and seasonality, we can combine these two issues to decompose time-series data. Recall from section 11.5 that a time series is composed of four components: trend, seasonality, cycles, and random variations. Recall also that we defined two types of time-series decomposition models in that section: (1) multiplicative models and (2) additive models. In this section, we use an example to illustrate how we can use a multiplicative decomposition model to break down a time series into two components: (1) a seasonal component and (2) a combination of the trend and cycle components (we refer to this combined component simply as *trend*). In Solved Problem 11–4 at the end of this chapter, we use the same example to illustrate how an additive decomposition model would break down the data. As discussed earlier, it is not possible to discern the random component in any decomposition model.

Multiplicative Decomposition Example: Sawyer Piano House

Sandy Sawyer's family has been in the piano business for three generations. The Sawyers stock and sell a wide range of pianos, from console pianos to grand pianos. Sandy's father, who currently runs the business, forecasts sales for different types of pianos each year by using his experience. Although his forecasts have been reasonably good, Sandy (who has recently completed her undergraduate degree in management) is highly skeptical of such a seat-of-the-pants approach. She feels confident that she can develop a quantitative model that will do a much better job of forecasting piano sales.

To convince her father that she is correct, Sandy decides to develop a model to forecast sales for grand pianos. She hopes to show him how good the model could be in capturing patterns in past sales. For this purpose, she collects sales data for the past five years, broken down by quarters each year. That is, she collects data for the past 20 quarters, as shown in Table 11.5. Because sales of grand pianos are seasonal and there has been an upward trend in sales each year, Sandy believes a decomposition model would be appropriate here. More specifically, she decides to use a multiplicative decomposition model.

Table 11.5: Sales of Grand Pianos at Sawyer Piano House

	2012	2013	2014	2015	2016
Quarter 1	4	6	10	12	18
Quarter 2	2	4	3	9	10
Quarter 3	1	4	5	7	13
Quarter 4	5	14	16	22	35

Although the computations for decomposing a time series using a multiplicative model are fairly simple, we illustrate them by using an Excel worksheet that is included for this purpose in ExcelModules.

Using ExcelModules for Multiplicative Decomposition

When we select the choice titled Multiplicative Decomposition from the Forecasting Models menu in ExcelModules (see Figure 11.3), the window shown in Figure 11.21 is displayed. We specify the number of periods for which we have past data (20, in Sandy's example), the name for the period (Quarter, because we have quarterly data), and the number of seasons each year (4, in Sandy's example). In addition, we see an option for the procedure to use in computing the seasonal indices.

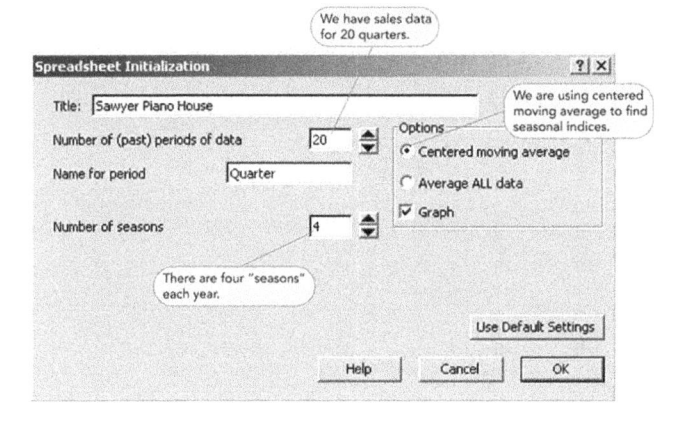

Figure 11.21: Options Window for Multiplicative Decomposition Worksheet in ExcelModules

The Average ALL Data option uses the procedure discussed in section 11.6 to compute the seasonal indices. In Sandy's example, this implies that we would first compute the average sales for all 20 quarters for which we have data. We would then divide the sales each quarter by the average sales to compute that quarter's seasonal ratio. Note that this will yield five ratios for each quarter (one for each year). Finally, we would average the five ratios for each quarter to compute that quarter's seasonal index.

The Centered Moving Average option uses a slightly more complicated procedure to compute the seasonal indices. Recall from section 11.5 that moving averages smooth out fluctuations in a time series. Hence, using this option could help us obtain more precise estimates of the seasonal indices. In the following pages, we illustrate this procedure for computing seasonal indices, using Sandy's example.

When we click OK on the screen in Figure 11.21, we get the screen shown in Figure 11.22. We now enter the actual pianos sold during the past 20 quarters (see Table 11.5) in cells B7:B26. The corresponding time periods (i.e., the X variable values) are automatically specified in cells C7:C26 by the worksheet.

$$\text{Seasonal ratio} = \frac{\text{Actual value}}{\text{Centered moving average}} \qquad \text{Unseasonalized value} = \frac{\text{Actual value}}{\text{Seasonal index}}$$

	A	B	C	D	E	F	G	H	I	J	K	L	M
1	Sawyer Piano House												
2	Forecasting		Multiplicative decomposition										
3	4 seasons	Enter the actual values in the cells shaded YELLOW. Do not change the time period numbers!											
4													
5	Input Data			Seasonal Index Computation			Forecast Error analysis						
6	Period	Actual value (Y)	Time period (X)	Centered average	Seasonal ratio	Seasonal index	Unseasonalized value	Unseasonalized Forecast	Seasonal ized Forecast	Error	Absolute error	Squared error	Absolute % error
7	Quarter 1	4	1			1.239	3.227	0.658	0.815	3.185	3.185	10.144	79.62%
8	Quarter 2	2	2			0.596	3.353	1.680	1.002	0.998	0.998	0.996	49.89%
9	Quarter 3	1	3	3.250	0.308	0.485	2.061	2.703	1.311	-0.311	0.311	0.097	31.13%
10	Quarter 4	5	4	3.750	1.333	1.577	3.170	3.725	5.876	-0.876	0.876	0.768	17.53%
11	Quarter 5	6	5	4.375	1.371	1.239	4.841	4.748	5.884	0.116	0.116	0.013	1.93%
12	Quarter 6	4	6	5.875	0.681	0.596	6.706	5.770	3.442	0.558	0.558	0.311	13.95%
13	Quarter 7	4	7	7.500	0.533	0.485	8.244	6.793	3.296	0.704	0.704	0.496	17.60%
14	Quarter 8	14	8	7.875	1.778	1.577	8.875	7.816	12.328	1.672	1.672	2.795	11.94%
15	Quarter 9	10	9	7.875	1.270	1.239	8.069	8.838	10.954	-0.954	0.954	0.910	9.54%
16	Quarter 10	3	10	8.250	0.364	0.596	5.029	9.861	5.882	-2.882	2.882	8.305	96.06%
17	Quarter 11	5	11	8.750	0.571	0.485	10.305	10.883	5.280	-0.280	0.280	0.079	5.61%
18	Quarter 12	16	12	9.750	1.641	1.577	10.143	11.906	18.780	-2.780	2.780	7.730	17.38%
19	Quarter 13	12	13	10.750	1.116	1.239	9.682	12.928	16.023	-4.023	4.023	16.186	33.53%
20	Quarter 14	9	14	11.750	0.766	0.596	15.088	13.951	8.322	0.678	0.678	0.460	7.54%
21	Quarter 15	7	15	13.250	0.528	0.485	14.427	14.973	7.265	-0.265	0.265	0.070	3.78%
22	Quarter 16	22	16	14.125	1.558	1.577	13.947	15.996	25.232	-3.232	3.232	10.447	14.69%
23	Quarter 17	18	17	15.000	1.200	1.239	14.523	17.019	21.093	-3.093	3.093	9.564	17.18%
24	Quarter 18	10	18	17.375	0.576	0.596	16.765	18.041	10.761	-0.761	0.761	0.580	7.61%
25	Quarter 19	13	19			0.485	26.794	19.064	9.249	3.751	3.751	14.067	28.85%
26	Quarter 20	35	20			1.577	22.188	20.086	31.684	3.316	3.316	10.994	9.47%
27									Average		1.722	4.751	23.74%
28						Intercept	-0.365				MAD	MSE	MAPE
29						Slope	1.023						

Input data for 20 quarters.

	A	B	C	D	E
30					
31	Seasonal Ratios				
32		Season 1	Season 2	Season 3	Season 4
33				0.308	1.333
34		1.371	0.681	0.533	1.778
35		1.270	0.364	0.571	1.641
36		1.116	0.766	0.528	1.558
37		1.200	0.576		
38	Average	1.239	0.596	0.485	1.577
39					
40	Forecasts for future periods				
41	Period	Unseasonalized forecast	Seasonal index	Seasonalized forecast	
42	21.000	21.109	1.239	26.162	
43	22.000	22.131	0.596	13.201	
44	23.000	23.154	0.485	11.234	
45	24.000	24.176	1.577	38.136	

Regression (trend line) parameters

Seasonal ratios in column E have been collected here.

Seasonal indices, also shown in column F

Measures of forecast error

Forecast using trend equation

Forecasts multiplied by seasonal index

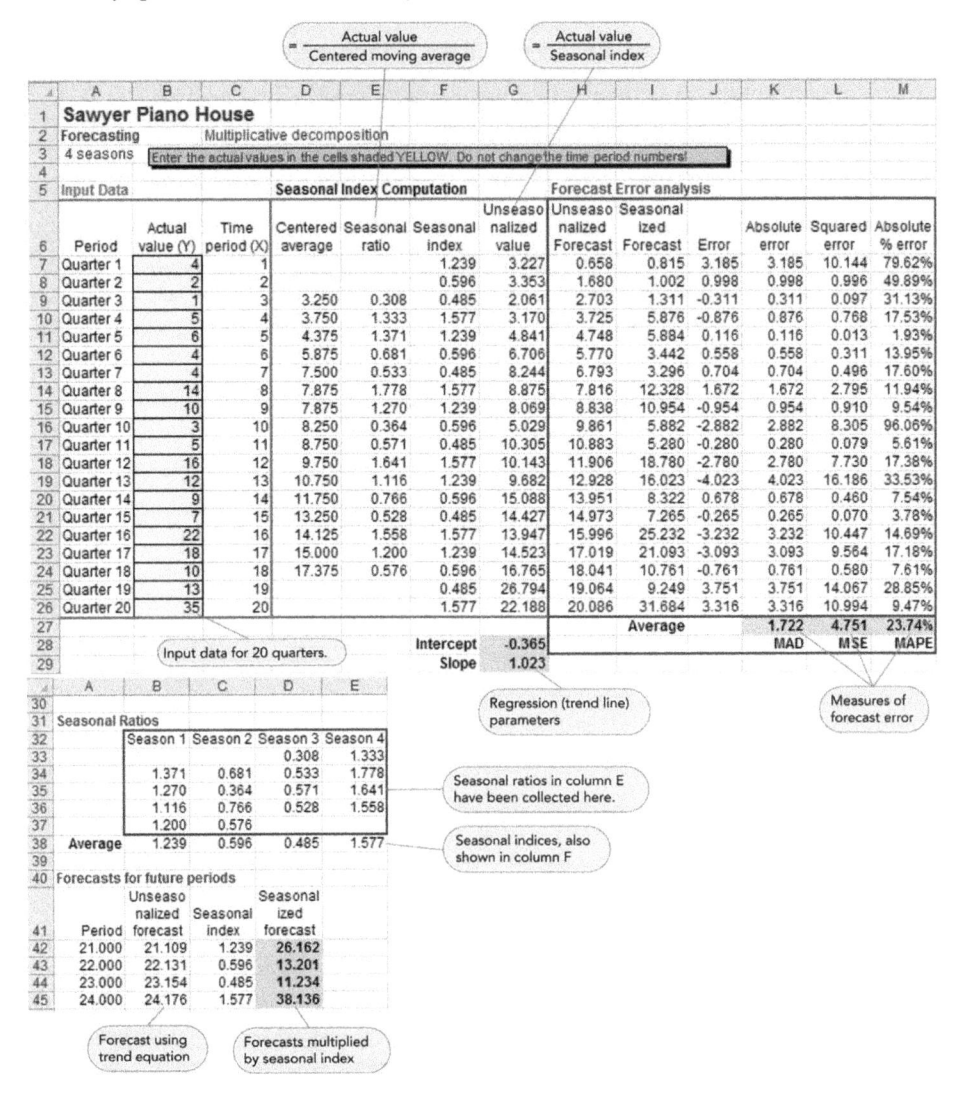

Figure 11.22: Multiplicative Decomposition Model for Sawyer Piano House

File: Figure 11.22.xlsx, Sheet: Figure 11.22

The worksheet now displays the results shown in Figure 11.22. The calculations are as follows:
1. *Computation of the seasonal indices, columns D–G.* First, we compute the seasonal indices:
   - In column D, we first smooth out fluctuations in each quarter's sales data by computing the moving average sales for k quarters, centered on that quarter. Because there are four seasons (quarters) in Sandy's time-series data, we use $k = 4$ here. Then, in cell D9 (for example), we compute the average sales for four quarters, where these four quarters are centered on the third quarter of year 1 (i.e., quarter number 3). *Note:* In cases in which k is even (such as here, in which $k = 4$), it is not possible to directly center k quarters of data around a quarter. We therefore modify the computations as follows (e.g., when $k = 4$):

   $$\text{Centered average for quarter } t = [0.5 \times \text{Sales in quarter } (t-2)$$
   $$+ \text{Sales in quarter } (t-1) + \text{Sales in quarter } t$$
   $$+ \text{Sales in quarter } (t+1) + 0.5 \times \text{Sales in quarter } (t+2)]/4$$

   - Next, we compute the seasonal ratio for each quarter by dividing the actual sales (column B) in that quarter by its centered average (column D). That is, column E = column B/column D.
   - The seasonal ratios for each quarter (four for each quarter, in Sandy's case) are collected in cells B33:E37. The seasonal index for each quarter is computed as the average of all the ratios for that quarter. These seasonal indices are shown in cells B38:E38 and repeated in column F, next to the appropriate quarters each year.
   - Finally, in column G, we compute the unseasonalized sales in each quarter as the actual sales (column B) in that quarter divided by the seasonal index (column F) for that quarter. That is, column G = column B/column F.
2. *Computation of the trend equation.* Now that we have the unseasonalized sales data, we can analyze the trend. Because the purpose of the linear trend equation is to minimize the least-squares error (as shown in section 11.6), it is important to remove the seasonal effects from the data before we develop the trend line. Otherwise, the presence of seasonal variations may severely affect the linear trend equation.

   Using the unseasonalized sales in column G as the dependent variable (Y) and the time period number in column C as the independent variable (X), we compute the linear trend equation. The resulting Y-intercept (a) and slope (b) for this straight line are shown in cells G28 and G29, respectively. In Sandy's case, the linear trend equation is

   $$\text{Unseasonalized sales forecast} = -0.365 + 1.023 \times \text{Quarter number}$$

3. *Computation of forecast, columns H and I.* The forecast is now calculated as the product of the composite trend and seasonality components. The computations are as follows:
   - In column H, we use the trend equation to compute the unseasonalized forecast for each quarter. For example, for the fourth quarter of year 2 (i.e., quarter number 8), this value is computed in cell H14 as $[-0.365 + 1.023 \times 8] = 7.816$. These values are also computed for the next year (i.e., quarters 21 to 24, denoting the four quarters in year 2017) in cells B42:B45.
   - We multiply the unseasonalized forecasts by the appropriate seasonal indices to get the seasonalized forecast for each quarter in column I. That is, column I = column H × column F. Cells D42:D45 show the seasonal forecasts for quarter numbers 21 to 24.
4. *Computation of forecast error measures, columns J through M.* As with all the other forecasting models in ExcelModules discussed so far, we compute the forecast error (i.e., Actual value − Forecast value) in column J, the absolute error in column K, the squared error in column L, and the absolute percentage error in column M for each quarter. We then use these error values to compute the MAD (cell K27), MSE (cell L27), and MAPE (cell M27) values.

Using Charts to Check the Validity of the Model How good is Sandy's multiplicative decomposition model at forecasting piano sales? One approach, of course, is to use the measures of forecasting error we have computed as indicators. As discussed earlier, however, these measures are difficult to interpret by themselves and are better suited for purposes of comparing different models. An alternative approach is to draw line charts of the actual and forecast values (columns B and I, respectively, in Figure 11.22) against the quarter number. These line charts are automatically drawn by ExcelModules and presented on a separate worksheet. The graph is shown in Figure 11.23.

The line charts show that there are a few quarters (e.g., quarters 1, 10, 13, 19, and 20) in which there are sizable errors in the forecast. Overall, however, Sandy's decomposition model seems to do a good job of replicating the pattern of piano sales over the past few years. There is no consistent under- or overforecast seen, and the forecast errors appear to be randomly distributed.

Using this analysis as evidence, it looks like Sandy will be able to convince her father that such quantitative forecasting decision models are the way to go in the future.

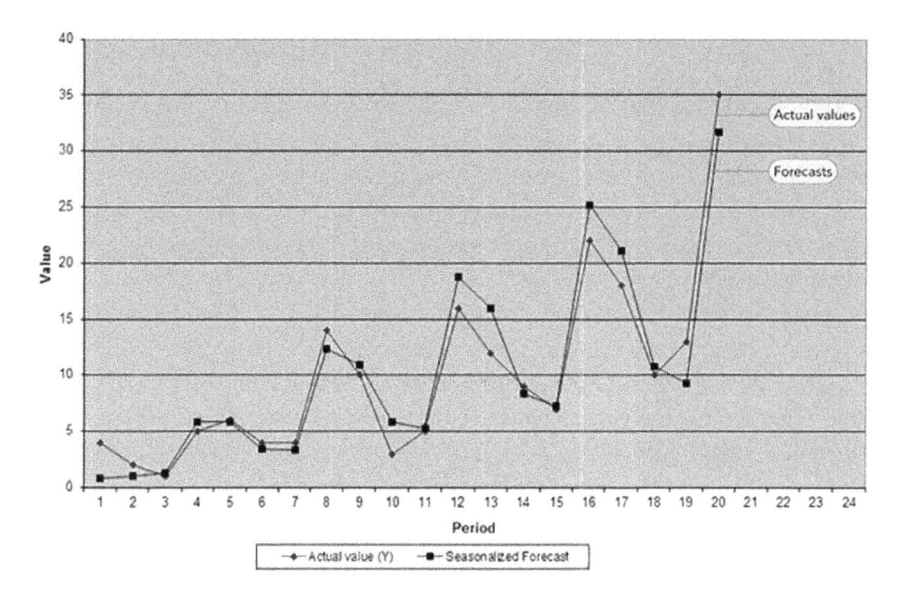

Figure 11.23: Chart of Multiplicative Decomposition Forecast for Sawyer Piano House

File: Figure 11.22.xlsx, Sheet: Figure 11.23

Decision Modeling In Action

Predicting Advertising Demand at NBCUniversal

NBCUniversal (NBCU), a world leader in the production, distribution, and marketing of entertainment, news, and information, had revenues of more than $14 billion in 2005. NBCU owns a television network and several stations in the United States, an impressive portfolio of cable networks, a major motion picture company, and very popular theme parks. More than 60 percent of NBCU's revenues are from the sales of on-air advertising time on its television networks and stations.

Each year, the upfront market is a brief period in late May when the television networks sell a majority of their on-air advertising inventory, right after announcing their program schedules for the upcoming broadcast year. To address the challenging problem of forecasting upfront market demand, NBCU initially relied primarily on judgment models and then tried time-series forecasting models. These models proved, however, to be rather unsatisfactory due to the unique nature of the demand population. NBCU now estimates upfront demand using a novel procedure that combines the Delphi forecasting method with grass-roots forecasting.

The system, which has been in place since 2004, has been used to support sales decisions each year worth more than $4.5 billion. The system enables NBCU to easily analyze pricing scenarios across all of its television properties, while predicting demand with a high level of accuracy. NBCU's sales leaders have credited the forecast system with giving them a unique competitive advantage over its competitors.

Source: Based on S. Bollapragada et al. "NBC-Universal Uses a Novel Qualitative Forecasting Technique to Predict Advertising Demand," *Interfaces* 38, 2 (March–April, 2008): 103–111.

11.8 Causal Forecasting Models: Simple and Multiple Regression

Consider an apparel firm that wishes to forecast the sales of its line of swimwear. It is likely that sales are related to variables such as the selling price, competitors' prices, average daily temperature, whether schools are in session, and advertising budgets. The purpose of a *causal forecasting model* is to develop the best statistical relationship between one or more of these variables and the variable being forecast (swimwear sales, in this case).

In a causal model for the apparel firm, swimwear sales would be the *dependent* (predicted or forecasted) variable, and the variables used to forecast swimwear sales would be *independent* (or predictor) variables. Note that unlike in the linear trend model we studied in section 11.6, there can be more than one independent variable in a causal model. Further, although time could be an independent variable in a causal model, it does not necessarily need to be one. That is, the data need not be time-series data.

The most common causal model used in practice is regression analysis. Several types of regression equations can be developed (e.g., linear, quadratic, cubic, logarithmic). In this section, however, we discuss only linear regression models.

In causal forecasting models, when we try to forecast the dependent variable by using just a single independent variable, the model is called a *simple* regression model. When we use more than one independent variable to forecast the dependent variable, the model is called a *multiple* regression model. We illustrate both types of models in the following sections, using simple examples. As with all models so far in this chapter, although we present a few key equations, we perform the actual calculations by using worksheets provided in ExcelModules.

Causal Simple Regression Model

Sue Taylor works for a home appraisal company that is used by several local banks to appraise the price of homes as part of the mortgage approval process. Based on her extensive experience with home appraisals, Sue knows that one factor that has a direct relationship to the selling price of a home is its size. Sue therefore wants to establish a mathematical relationship that will help her forecast the selling price of a home, based on its size. Table 11.6 provides information on the last 12 homes that have been sold in a specific neighborhood in the city where Sue lives.

As a first step toward developing this mathematical relationship, we should draw a scatter chart that shows selling price and home size. (Refer to section 11.6 to see how this chart can be drawn using Excel, if necessary.) We will, in fact, draw such a chart by using ExcelModules shortly. For now, let us proceed under the assumption that the scatter chart reveals a linear relationship between a home's selling price and its size. That is, the mathematical equation between these variables denotes a straight line.

Table 11.6: Home Sales Data for the Simple Regression Model

Home	Selling Price (thousands)	Home Size (thousands of sq. ft.)
1	$182.5	2.01
2	$227.3	2.65
3	$251.9	2.43
4	$325.2	2.89
5	$225.1	2.55
6	$315.0	3.00
7	$367.5	3.22
8	$220.8	2.37
9	$266.5	2.91
10	$261.0	2.56
11	$177.5	2.25
12	$235.9	3.41

Just as we did with linear trend analysis, we use the least-squares procedure here to establish the equation of this straight line. Once again, we let Y represent the dependent variable that we want to forecast (selling price, in this example). But unlike in the trend models, here the independent variable, X, is not time; instead, it is the size of each home. The same basic model discussed in section 11.6 applies. That is,

$$\hat{Y} = b_0 + b_1 X$$

where

$\hat{Y}$ = forecasted average value of the dependent variable, based on the current sample

X = value of the independent variable

b_0 = Y-intercept of the line, based on the current sample

b_1 = slope of the line, based on the current sample

Recall from section 11.6 that the objective of the least-squares procedure is to determine the values of b_0 and b_1 that minimize the sum of the squared errors between the forecasted ($\hat{Y}$) and actual (Y) values. The formulas to compute these values were given in Equations 11–13 and 11–14. However, rather than manually use these formulas, we next discuss the following two approaches to using Excel to develop this regression equation, as well as accompanying statistical measures:

- *Regression using ExcelModules.* In addition to computing the regression equation, ExcelModules computes the forecast for each observation and the three usual measures of forecast error (i.e., MAD, MSE, and MAPE).

– *Regression using Excel's* Analysis ToolPak *add-in.* An advantage of using this procedure is that it provides detailed information regarding the significance of the regression equation.

Causal Simple Regression Using ExcelModules

When we select the choice titled Causal Model (Simple Regression) from the Forecasting Models menu in ExcelModules (see Figure 11.3), the window shown in Figure 11.24 is displayed. The option entries in this window are similar to those for earlier procedures. If we check the Graph option, ExcelModules draws the scatter chart as part of the results, along with the least-squares regression line.

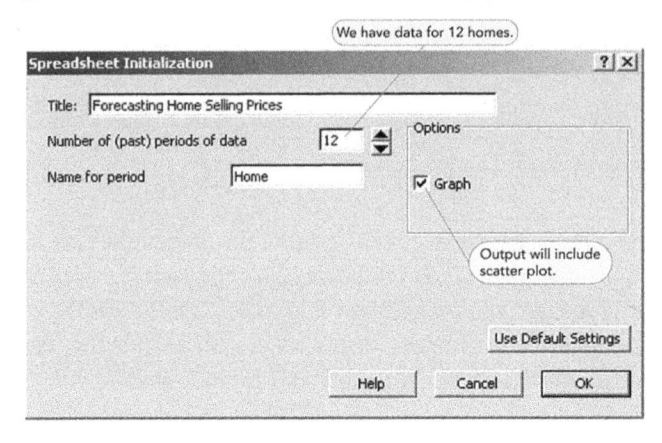

Figure 11.24: Options Window for Causal Model (Simple Regression) Worksheet in ExcelModules

When we click OK on this screen, we get the screen shown in Figure 11.25. We now enter the selling prices (dependent variable, *Y*) for the 12 homes in cells B7:B18 and the corresponding sizes (independent variable, *X*) in cells C7:C18.

The worksheet now computes and displays the regression equation. For Sue's problem, the *Y*-intercept b_0 is shown in cell B20, and the slope b_1 is shown in cell B21. The causal simple regression model is

$$\text{Forecasted average selling price} = -8.125 + 97.789 \times \text{Home size}$$

Typically, we can interpret the *Y*-intercept as the forecasted value of the dependent variable when the independent variable has a value of zero. However, in Sue's example, the *Y*-intercept of -8.125 has no practical meaning because a home with size zero does not exist. Further, because the data set does not include observations with $X = 0$, it would be inappropriate to interpret the *Y*-intercept at this *X* value. On the other hand, the slope of 97.789 implies that the average selling price of a home increases by $97,789 for every 1,000 square feet increase in size. (Remember that the selling price is in thousands of dollars and the sizes are in thousands of square feet.)

Causal Forecasting Models: Simple and Multiple Regression — 687

	A	B	C	D	E	F	G	H	I
1	**Forecasting Home Selling Prices**								
2	Forecasting		Causal regression analysis						
3	Enter the (Y,X) pairs in cells shaded YELLOW. Enter new value of X at the bottom to forecast Y.								
4									Forecasts are computed using the regression equation.
5	Input Data				Forecast Error Analysis				
6	Period	Dep Variable (or) (Y)	Indep Variable (or) (X)		Forecast	Error	Absolute error	Squared error	Absolute % error
7	Home 1	182.5	2.01		188.431	-5.931	5.931	35.178	3.25%
8	Home 2	227.3	2.65		251.016	-23.716	23.716	562.460	10.43%
9	Home 3	251.9	2.43		229.503	22.397	22.397	501.644	8.89%
10	Home 4	325.2	2.89		274.486	50.714	50.714	2571.944	15.59%
11	Home 5	225.1	2.55		241.237	-16.137	16.137	260.413	7.17%
12	Home 6	315.0	3.00		285.242	29.758	29.758	885.510	9.45%
13	Home 7	367.5	3.22		306.756	60.744	60.744	3689.818	16.53%
14	Home 8	220.8	2.37		223.635	-2.835	2.835	8.039	1.28%
15	Home 9	266.5	2.91		276.441	-9.941	9.941	98.832	3.73%
16	Home 10	261.0	2.56		242.215	18.785	18.785	352.869	7.20%
17	Home 11	177.5	2.25		211.901	-34.401	34.401	1183.396	19.38%
18	Home 12	235.9	3.41		325.336	-89.436	89.436	7998.816	37.91%
19					Average		30.400	1512.410	11.73%
20	Intercept	-8.125		Regression			MAD	MSE	MAPE
21	Slope	97.789		coefficients					
22							SE	42.602	
23	Forecast	295.0	3.10				Correlation	0.702	
24							r-squared	0.493	

Forecasted average selling price for house size of 3,100 square feet

Measures of forecast error

Standard error of the regression estimate

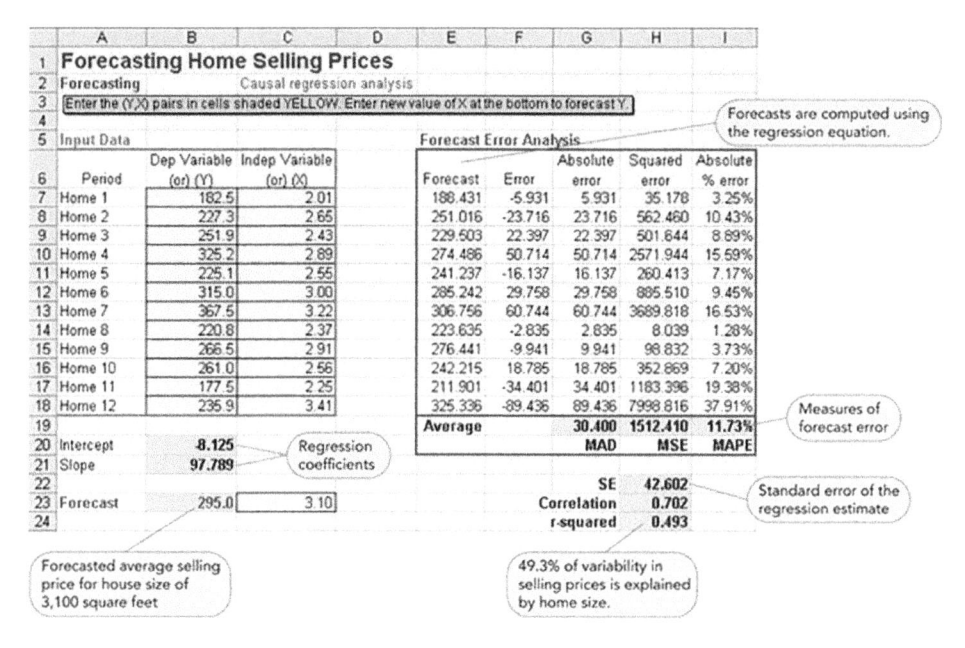

49.3% of variability in selling prices is explained by home size.

Figure 11.25: Causal Model (Simple Regression) for Forecasting Home Selling Prices

📊 File: Figure 11.25.xlsx, Sheet: Figure 11.25

In addition to computing the regression equation, ExcelModules plugs the size values for all homes into this equation to compute the forecasted selling price for each home. These forecasts are shown in cells E7:E18. The following measures of forecast error are then calculated and reported: MAD (30.40, in cell G19), MSE (1,512.41, in cell H19), and MAPE (11.73%, in cell I19).

Regression Charts Now that we have identified the equation for the causal simple regression model, how do we determine its validity and accuracy? One way to do so is to use the scatter chart of selling price versus size. Recall from section 11.6 that we can draw a scatter chart using Excel. However, ExcelModules automatically provides this chart if specified in the options (see Figure 11.24). The scatter chart for Sue's example is shown in Figure 11.26, along with the linear regression line, so we can see how well the model fits the data. From this chart, it appears that while there is a reasonable linear relationship between selling price and size, there are sizable differences between the actual values and the fitted line (forecast values) in a few cases.

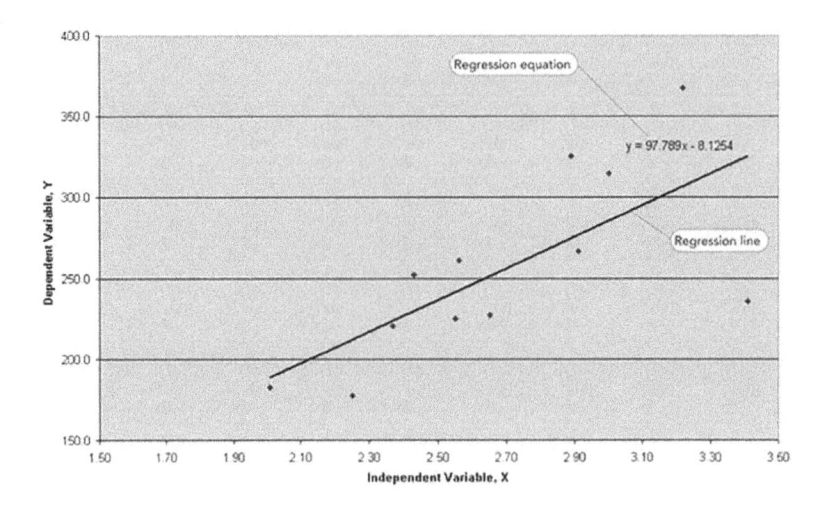

Figure 11.26: Scatter Chart with Regression Line for Forecasting Home Selling Prices

File: Figure 11.25.xlsx, Sheet: Figure 11.26

An alternative way to check the validity and accuracy of the causal model is to draw line charts of the actual and forecasted values (cells B7:B18 and E7:E18, respectively, in Figure 11.25) against the observation number. If the Graph option is checked in Figure 11.24, ExcelModules automatically draws these line charts also (in addition to the scatter chart) and presents them in a separate worksheet. The line charts for Sue's example, shown in Figure 11.27, indicate that the causal model she has developed does replicate the pattern of selling prices. However, these charts also confirm the presence of a few sizable forecast errors (e.g., homes 4, 7, 11, and 12). Sue may therefore want to consider including other independent variables in her causal model to improve the forecast accuracy.

Standard Error of the Regression Estimate   Another way of measuring the accuracy of the regression estimates is to compute the standard error of the regression estimate, $S_{Y.X}$, also called the *standard deviation of the regression*. The equation for computing the standard error is

$$S_{Y.X} = \sqrt{\Sigma(Y_i - \hat{Y}_i)^2 / (n-2)} \qquad (11\text{--}15)$$

where

Y_i = actual value of the dependent variable for the ith observation

$\hat{Y}_i$ = regression (forecasted) value of the dependent variable for the ith observation

n = number of observations

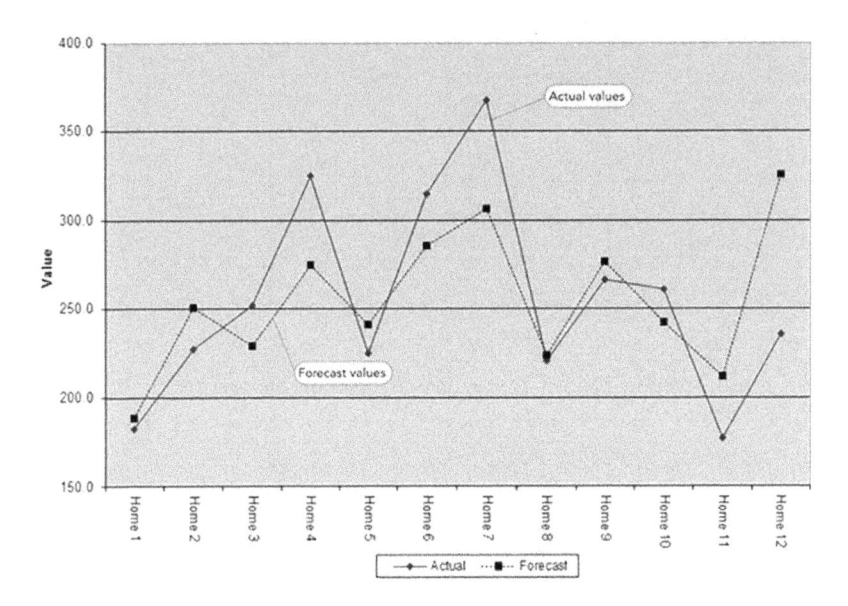

Figure 11.27: Chart of Causal Model (Simple Regression) Forecast for Forecasting Home Selling Prices

File: Figure 11.25.xlsx, Sheet: Figure 11.27

ExcelModules automatically computes and reports the standard error. The value for Sue's example, shown in cell H22 of Figure 11.25, is 42.602. This implies that the standard deviation of the distribution of home selling prices around the regression line, for a given value of home size, is $42,602. As we will see shortly, the standard error can be used in setting up confidence intervals around the average forecasted values.

Correlation Coefficient (r) The regression equation is one way of expressing the nature of the relationship between two variables.[2] The equation shows how one variable relates to the value and changes in another variable. Another way to evaluate the linear relationship between two variables is to compute the **correlation coefficient**. This measure expresses the degree or strength of the linear relationship. It is usually denoted by r and can be any number between and including +1 and −1. Figure 11.28 illustrates what different values of r might look like for different types of relationships between an independent variable X and a dependent variable Y.

The rather cumbersome equation for the correlation coefficient r is

$$r = \frac{n\Sigma XY - \Sigma X \Sigma Y}{\sqrt{[n\Sigma X^2 - (\Sigma X)^2][n\Sigma Y^2 - (\Sigma Y)^2]}} \quad (11\text{–}16)$$

---

[2] Regression lines do not always show cause-and-effect relationships. In general, they describe the relationship between the movement of variables.

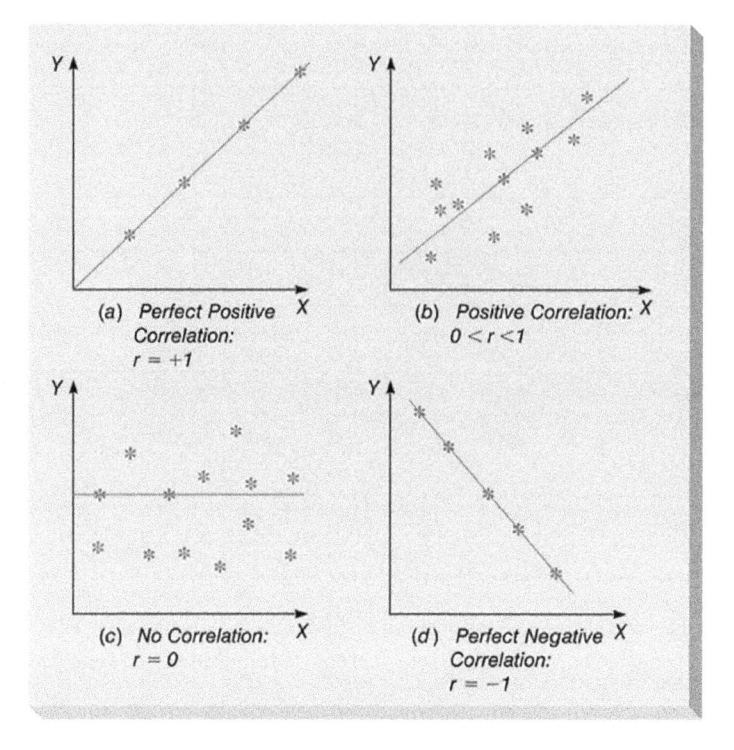

Figure 11.28: Four Values of the Correlation Coefficient

ExcelModules, however, also calculates and reports the value of the correlation coefficient. Although there is no specific rule to decide when two variables can be deemed to be highly correlated, in general, correlation coefficient magnitudes of 0.6 and greater are indicative of a strong relationship. In Sue's example, therefore, the *r* value of 0.702 (shown in cell H23 of Figure 11.25) indicates the presence of a strong positive linear relationship between selling price and home size.

Coefficient of Determination (R^2) Another measure that is used often to describe the strength of the linear relationship between two variables is the coefficient of determination. This is simply the square of the coefficient of correlation and is denoted by R^2. The value of R^2 will always be a positive number in the range $0 \le R^2 \le 1$. The coefficient of determination is defined as the amount of the variability in the dependent variable (*Y*) that is explained by the regression equation. In Sue's example, the value of R^2 is 0.493 (shown in cell H24 in Figure 11.25), which is just the square of 0.702, the correlation coefficient. This indicates that only 49.3% of the total variation in home selling prices is explained by size, leaving 51.7% unexplained (or explained by other variables). For this reason, as noted earlier, Sue may want to consider including other independent variables in her causal model.

Using the Causal Simple Regression Model Suppose Sue wants to estimate the average selling price of a home that is 3,100 square feet in size. We enter this value in cell C23 as shown in Figure 11.25 (note that we should enter 3,100 as 3.10). The model forecasts an average selling price of 295.0 (shown in cell B23), or $295,000. This forecast of $295,000 is called a *point estimate* of Y. As noted earlier, the forecasted value (point estimate) is actually the average, or expected value, of a distribution of possible values of home selling prices for a given value of size.

This computation of the forecasted selling price illustrates two potential weaknesses of causal forecasting methods such as regression. First, we see that even after the regression equation has been computed, it is necessary to provide an estimate of the independent variable before forecasting the corresponding value of the dependent variable. This may not be a problem in Sue's example (after all, she can always find out the size of any home for which she wants to forecast the selling price). However, consider a causal model that uses, for example, the unemployment rate to forecast stock market performance. In this case, imagine the difficulty of estimating the unemployment rate in the next period. As you can clearly see, any error in estimating this rate will result in a corresponding error in the forecasted stock market performance, even if the causal model itself is very good.

Second, even if we know the value of X for which we want to forecast Y, the regression line forecasts only the *average* value of Y. Depending on the variability of the distribution of Y values around the regression line (measured by the standard error of the regression estimate, $S_{Y,X}$), the actual value of Y for a given value of X could be quite far from the forecasted average value. Statistically, we can use the following formula to calculate an approximate confidence interval for *all* values of Y for a given value of X:[3]

$$\hat{Y} \pm Z_{\alpha/2} \times S_{Y,X} \quad \text{(or)} \quad (b_0 + b_1 X) \pm Z_{\alpha/2} \times S_{Y,X} \tag{11-17}$$

where $Z_{\alpha/2}$ is the standard normal value (see Appendix C) for a confidence level of $(1-\alpha)\%$. For example, an approximate 95% confidence interval for the selling price of *all* homes of size 3,100 square feet can be computed to be $295.0 \pm 1.96 \times 42.602 = 211.5$ to 378.5, or $211,500 to $378,500. As you can see, this is a fairly broad interval, which is consistent with the fact that the size of a home is able to explain only 49.3% of the variability in its selling price.

Would it be logical to use the causal model developed here to forecast the average selling price of a home of size 5,000 square feet? What about a home of size 1,400 square feet? We note that the sizes of both these homes are not within the range of

---

[3] We refer to this as an *approximate* formula for the confidence interval because the exact formula varies slightly, depending on the value of X for which the interval is computed. Also, when the sample size is large ($n > 30$), the confidence interval can be computed using normal (Z) tables. However, when the number of observations is small, the *t*-distribution is appropriate. For details, see any forecasting or statistics book.

sizes for the homes in Sue's data set (see Table 11.6). It is entirely possible, for example, that the relationship between selling price and home size follows a different causal relationship for large homes (i.e., home sizes in excess of 4,500 square feet). Hence, we cannot guarantee the validity of the causal model developed here in forecasting the selling prices of these homes.

Causal Simple Regression Using Excel's Analysis ToolPak (Data Analysis)

As noted earlier, Excel's Analysis ToolPak add-in includes a procedure for regression. (See section B.6 in Appendix B for details on how to install and enable this add-in in Excel.) When enabled, this add-in is called Data Analysis and appears as part of the Analysis group within the Data tab in Excel's Ribbon. To invoke the regression procedure, we click Data | Data Analysis and then select Regression from the list of choices, as shown in Figure 11.29. The window shown in Figure 11.29 is displayed.

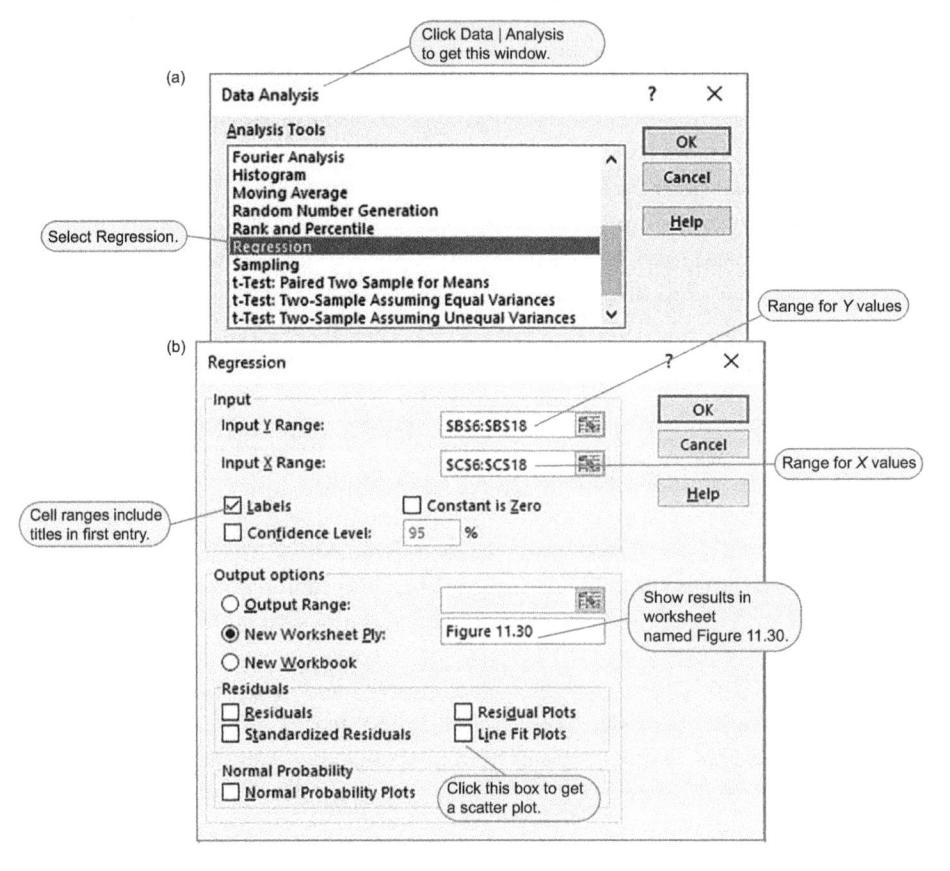

Figure 11.29: Simple Regression Using Excel's Analysis ToolPak

Running the Regression Procedure in Data Analysis We need to specify the cell ranges for the selling prices (Y) and sizes (X), and indicate where we want the output of the regression to be displayed. For example, in Figure 11.29, we have specified the Y-range as cells B6:B18 (from the Excel worksheet shown in Figure 11.25) and the X-range as cells C6:C18. We have asked for the output of the regression analysis to be presented in a new worksheet named *Figure 11.30*. If we check the box named Labels, the first entry in the cell range for a variable should include the name of that variable. Checking the box named Line Fit Plots will result in a scatter chart like the one in Figure 11.26.

All other options (i.e., Residuals, Standardized Residuals, Residual Plots, and Normal Probability Plot) deal with verifying the validity of assumptions made when using the least-squares procedures to develop a regression model. These options are usually more relevant for *explanatory* models, where the intent is to explain the variability in the dependent variable using the independent variable. Although still relevant, they are relatively less important in *predictive* regression models (such as in causal forecasting models), where the objective is mainly to obtain a good forecast of the dependent variable using the independent variable. For this reason, we do not discuss these topics here and refer you to any statistics book for a detailed discussion.

Results of the Regression Procedure When we click OK, Data Analysis runs the regression procedure, and the results shown in Figure 11.30 are displayed. Just as in the earlier results we obtained using ExcelModules (see Figure 11.25), the results here too show a Y-intercept of −8.125 (cell B18), slope of 97.989 (cell B19), correlation coefficient of 0.702 (cell B5; named Multiple R by Data Analysis), coefficient of determination R^2 of 0.493 (cell B6), and standard error of the regression estimate of 42.602 (cell B8). The adjusted R^2 measure in cell B7 is relevant only for multiple regression models, which we will discuss shortly.

The table labeled ANOVA details how well the regression equation fits the data. The total sum of squares (SS) value of 35,819.197 (cell C15) is a measure of the total variability in the dependent variable (home selling prices). Of this, 17,670.281 (cell C13) is explained by the regression equation, leaving 18,148.916 unexplained (cell C14, also known as the residual sum of squares). Recall that we defined the R^2 as the percentage of variation in Y that is explained by the regression equation. From the values in the ANOVA table, R^2 can be computed as $17{,}670.281/35{,}819.197 = 0.493$, or 49.3%, which is the same value reported in cell B6.

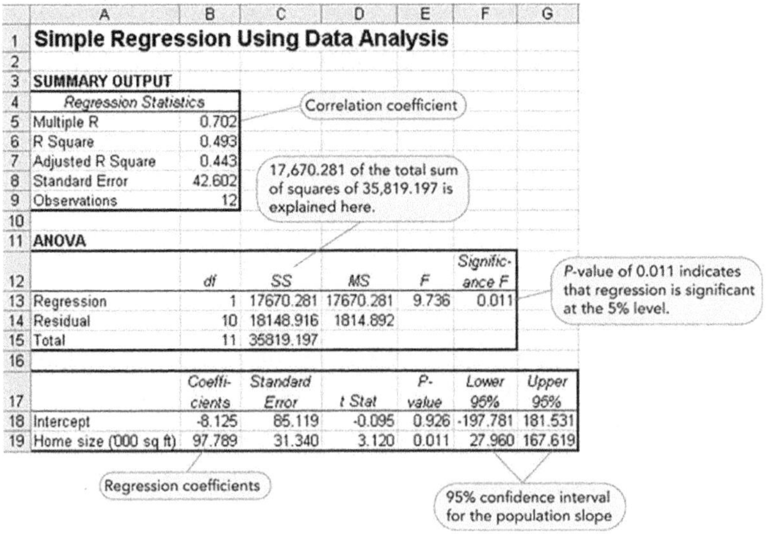

Simple Regression Using Data Analysis

SUMMARY OUTPUT

Regression Statistics	
Multiple R	0.702
R Square	0.493
Adjusted R Square	0.443
Standard Error	42.602
Observations	12

Correlation coefficient

17,670.281 of the total sum of squares of 35,819.197 is explained here.

ANOVA

	df	SS	MS	F	Signific-ance F
Regression	1	17670.281	17670.281	9.736	0.011
Residual	10	18148.916	1814.892		
Total	11	35819.197			

P-value of 0.011 indicates that regression is significant at the 5% level.

	Coeffi-cients	Standard Error	t Stat	P-value	Lower 95%	Upper 95%
Intercept	-8.125	85.119	-0.095	0.926	-197.781	181.531
Home size ('000 sq ft)	97.789	31.340	3.120	0.011	27.960	167.619

Regression coefficients

95% confidence interval for the population slope

Figure 11.30: Simple Regression Output from Excel's Analysis ToolPak

File: Figure 11.25.xlsx, Sheet: Figure 11.30

Statistical Significance of the Regression Equation The output from Data Analysis also provides information on the statistical significance of the regression equation. That is, it indicates whether the linear relationship obtained between Y and X is, in fact, a true reflection of the real situation or whether it is just a random occurrence based on this specific data set. Recall from Equation 11–11 that we expressed the regression equation as $\hat{Y} = b_0 + b_1 X$. Note that the two coefficients b_0 and b_1 are sample statistics because they are both estimated based on a specific sample. In Sue's model, for example, b_0 and b_1 have been estimated based on just 12 homes. Now suppose the true population relationship between Y and X (i.e., the relationship if our data set consisted of *all* homes in the population) can be expressed as follows:

$$\mu_{Y|X} = \beta_0 + \beta_1 X \qquad (11\text{–}18)$$

where

$\mu_{Y|X}$ = forecasted average value of Y for a given value of X, based on the entire population

β_0 = Y-intercept of the line, based on the entire population

β_1 = slope of the line, based on the entire population

Does a nonzero value of the slope b_1 based on a specific sample immediately imply that the true population slope β_1 is also nonzero? That is, is the slope between

Y and X significantly different from zero, from a statistical perspective? To test this issue, we set up the following null and alternate hypotheses:

H_0: $\beta_1 = 0$ (i.e., the regression between Y and X is not statistically significant)
H_1: $\beta_1 \neq 0$ (i.e., the regression between Y and X is statistically significant)

Using the information provided in the Data Analysis regression output, there are two ways to conduct this hypothesis test: (1) F-test and (2) t-test. We refer you to any statistics book for the details and rationale behind these tests. In our discussion here, we simply interpret the test results provided in the Data Analysis output.

The result of the F-test is included in the ANOVA table. The computed F-statistic of 9.736, shown in cell E13 in Figure 11.30, is F-distributed with 1 numerator degrees of freedom (cell B13) and 10 denominator degrees of freedom (cell B14). The P-value associated with this F-statistic is shown in cell F13 (Data Analysis labels this P-value as Significance F). In Sue's case, the P-value of the test is 0.011, implying that the null hypothesis can be rejected at the 5% significance level but not at the 1% level. Another way of stating this is that we are 98.9% ($= 1 - P$-value) confident that the relationship between Y and X is statistically significant.

The result of the t-test is included in the regression coefficients table. The computed t-statistic of 3.12, shown in cell D19 in Figure 11.30, is t-distributed with 10 degrees of freedom (cell B14). The P-value associated with this t-statistic is 0.011, shown in cell E19. Note that this is the same P-value we obtained in the F-test, which leads to the same conclusion as in that test. In fact, in simple regression models, the P-value will always be the same for both the F-test and the t-test. It is therefore not necessary to conduct both tests, although all statistical software packages, including Data Analysis, automatically report the results for both tests.

Data Analysis also provides information regarding the statistical significance of the Y-intercept. The computed t-statistic is shown in cell D18, and the associated P-value is shown in cell E18 in Figure 11.30. However, as noted earlier, the Y-intercept does not have a practical meaning in many causal regression models. For example, it is meaningless in Sue's model because a home cannot have a size of zero. For this reason, it is quite common for the result of this significance test to be ignored, even though most statistical software packages report it by default.

Confidence Intervals for the Population Slope In addition to testing for the statistical significance of the slope, we can also compute confidence intervals for the population slope (i.e., β_1). By default, Data Analysis always reports a 95% confidence interval for this parameter (shown in cells F19:G19 in Figure 11.30). The interval implies that while we have obtained a point estimate of 97.989 for the regression slope based on the current sample of 12 homes, we are 95% confident that the true population slope between home selling prices and sizes is somewhere between 27.960 and 167.619. Here again, the interval is fairly broad because the R^2 value of the regression model is only 49.3%.

We can also obtain intervals for other confidence levels by checking the appropriate option (see Figure 11.30) and specifying the desired confidence level. By the way, note that Data Analysis also reports the confidence interval for the Y-intercept. However, for the same reasons discussed previously, we typically ignore these types of computations regarding the Y-intercept.

Causal Multiple Regression Model

A *multiple regression* model is a practical extension of the simple regression model. It allows us to build a model with more than one independent variable. The general form of the multiple regression equation is

$$\hat{Y} = b_0 + b_1 X_1 + b_2 X_2 + \ldots + b_p X_p \tag{11-19}$$

where

b_0 = Y-axis intercept, based on the current sample

b_i = slope of the regression for the *i*th independent variable (X_i), based on the current sample

p = number of independent variables in the model

The mathematics of multiple regression becomes quite complex, based on the number of independent variables, and the computations are therefore best left to a computer. As with simple regression, we discuss two approaches here. The first approach uses a worksheet included in ExcelModules, and the second approach uses the regression procedure in Excel's Analysis ToolPak. Next, we illustrate both approaches for causal multiple regression models, using an expanded version of Sue Taylor's home selling price example.

Forecasting Home Selling Prices—Revisited Sue Taylor is not satisfied with the R^2 value of 0.493 obtained from her causal simple regression model. She thinks she can forecast home selling prices more precisely by including a second independent variable in her regression model. In addition to the size of a home, she believes that the area of the land (in acres) would also be a good predictor of selling prices. Sue has updated the information for the 12 homes in her input data, as shown in Table 11.7. What is the effect of including this additional independent variable?

Causal Multiple Regression Using ExcelModules

Let us first use ExcelModules to develop a regression model to predict the selling price of a home based both on its size and land area. When we select the choice titled Causal Model (Multiple Regression) from the Forecasting Models menu in ExcelModules (see Figure 11.3), the window shown in Figure 11.31 is displayed. The option entries in this window are similar to those for the simple regression model, with the additional choice to specify the number of independent variables. The entries for Sue's example are shown in Figure 11.31.

Table 11.7: Home Sales Data for the Multiple Regression Model

Home	Selling Price (thousands)	Home Size (thousands sq. ft.)	Land Area (acres)
1	$182.5	2.01	0.40
2	$227.3	2.65	0.60
3	$251.9	2.43	0.65
4	$325.2	2.89	1.10
5	$225.1	2.55	0.75
6	$315.0	3.00	1.50
7	$367.5	3.22	1.70
8	$220.8	2.37	0.45
9	$266.5	2.91	0.80
10	$261.0	2.56	1.00
11	$177.5	2.25	0.50
12	$235.9	3.41	0.70

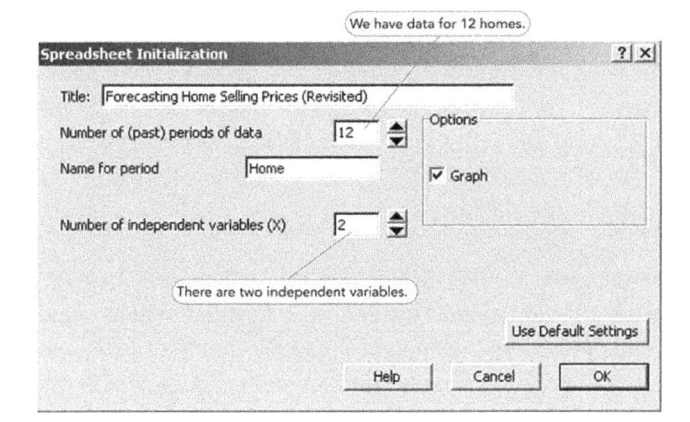

Figure 11.31: Options Window for Causal Model (Multiple Regression) Worksheet in ExcelModules

When we click OK on this screen, we get the screen shown in Figure 11.32. We now enter the selling prices (dependent variable, Y) for the past 12 years in cells B8:B19 and the corresponding home sizes (independent variable X_1) and land areas (independent variable X_2) in cells C8:C19 and D8:D19, respectively. Note that the values in cells B3:B19 and C3:C19 are the same as the ones we entered in the simple regression model earlier.

698 —— Chapter 11: Forecasting Models

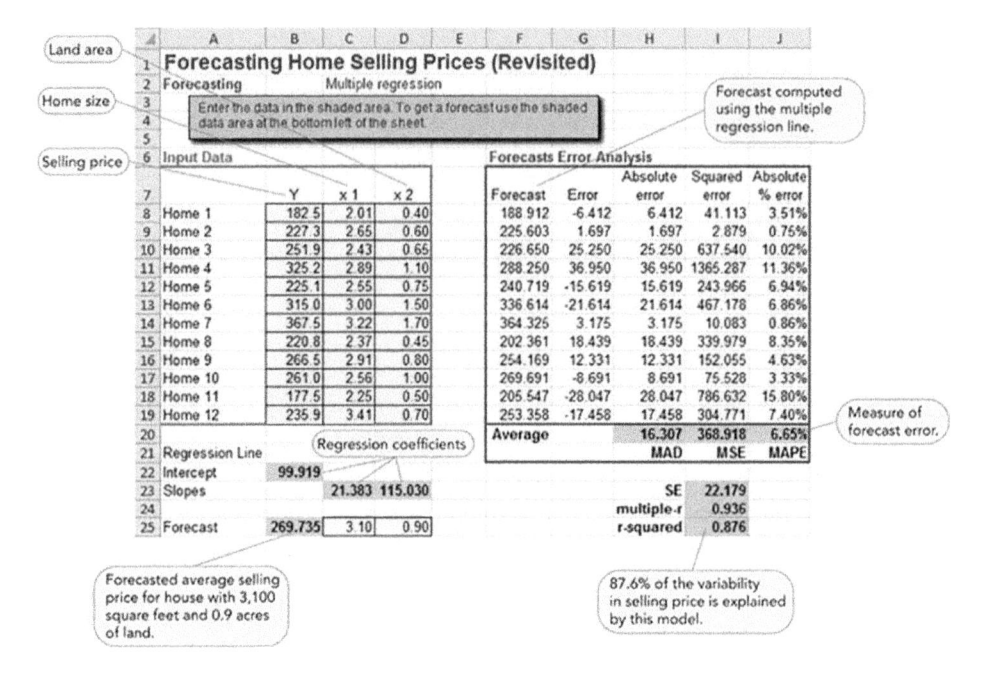

	A	B	C	D	E	F	G	H	I	J
1	Forecasting Home Selling Prices (Revisited)									
2	Forecasting		Multiple regression							
3	Enter the data in the shaded area. To get a forecast use the shaded									
4	data area at the bottom left of the sheet.									
5										
6	Input Data					Forecasts Error Analysis				
7		Y	x 1	x 2		Forecast	Error	Absolute error	Squared error	Absolute % error
8	Home 1	182.5	2.01	0.40		188.912	-6.412	6.412	41.113	3.51%
9	Home 2	227.3	2.65	0.60		225.603	1.697	1.697	2.879	0.75%
10	Home 3	251.9	2.43	0.65		226.650	25.250	25.250	637.540	10.02%
11	Home 4	325.2	2.89	1.10		288.250	36.950	36.950	1365.287	11.36%
12	Home 5	225.1	2.55	0.75		240.719	-15.619	15.619	243.966	6.94%
13	Home 6	315.0	3.00	1.50		336.614	-21.614	21.614	467.178	6.86%
14	Home 7	367.5	3.22	1.70		364.325	3.175	3.175	10.083	0.86%
15	Home 8	220.8	2.37	0.45		202.361	18.439	18.439	339.979	8.35%
16	Home 9	266.5	2.91	0.80		254.169	12.331	12.331	152.055	4.63%
17	Home 10	261.0	2.56	1.00		269.691	-8.691	8.691	75.528	3.33%
18	Home 11	177.5	2.25	0.50		205.547	-28.047	28.047	786.632	15.80%
19	Home 12	235.9	3.41	0.70		253.358	-17.458	17.458	304.771	7.40%
20						Average		16.307	368.918	6.65%
21	Regression Line							MAD	MSE	MAPE
22	Intercept	99.919								
23	Slopes		21.383	115.030				SE	22.179	
24								multiple-r	0.936	
25	Forecast	269.735	3.10	0.90				r-squared	0.876	

Callouts:
- Land area (points to column D header)
- Home size (points to column C header)
- Selling price (points to column B header)
- Forecast computed using the multiple regression line.
- Regression coefficients
- Measure of forecast error.
- Forecasted average selling price for house with 3,100 square feet and 0.9 acres of land.
- 87.6% of the variability in selling price is explained by this model.

Figure 11.32: Causal Model (Multiple Regression) for Forecasting Home Selling Prices

X🗐 File: Figure 11.32.xlsx, Sheet: Figure 11.32

The worksheet computes the multiple regression equation and displays the results. For Sue's example, the Y-intercept (b_0) is shown in cell B22, and the slopes b_1 for home size and b_2 for land area are shown in cells C23 and D23, respectively. The causal regression model is:

Forecasted average selling price = 99.919 + 21.383 × Home size + 115.030 × Land area

Note the huge difference between the regression coefficients here and the coefficients obtained in the simple regression model between selling price and home size. That is, the addition of the third variable in the model completely changes the regression equation, even though the data remain unchanged for selling price and home size. As it turns out, this is a fairly common occurrence in regression models.

The home size and land area values for the 12 homes in the sample are now plugged into this regression equation to compute the forecasted selling prices. These forecasts are shown in cells F8:F19. The following measures of forecast error are then calculated and reported: MAD (cell H20), MSE (cell I20), and MAPE (cell J20).

If the Graph option is checked in Figure 11.31, ExcelModules creates line charts of the actual and forecasted values against the observation number, and it shows the chart on a separate worksheet. We present the chart for Sue's example in Figure 11.33.

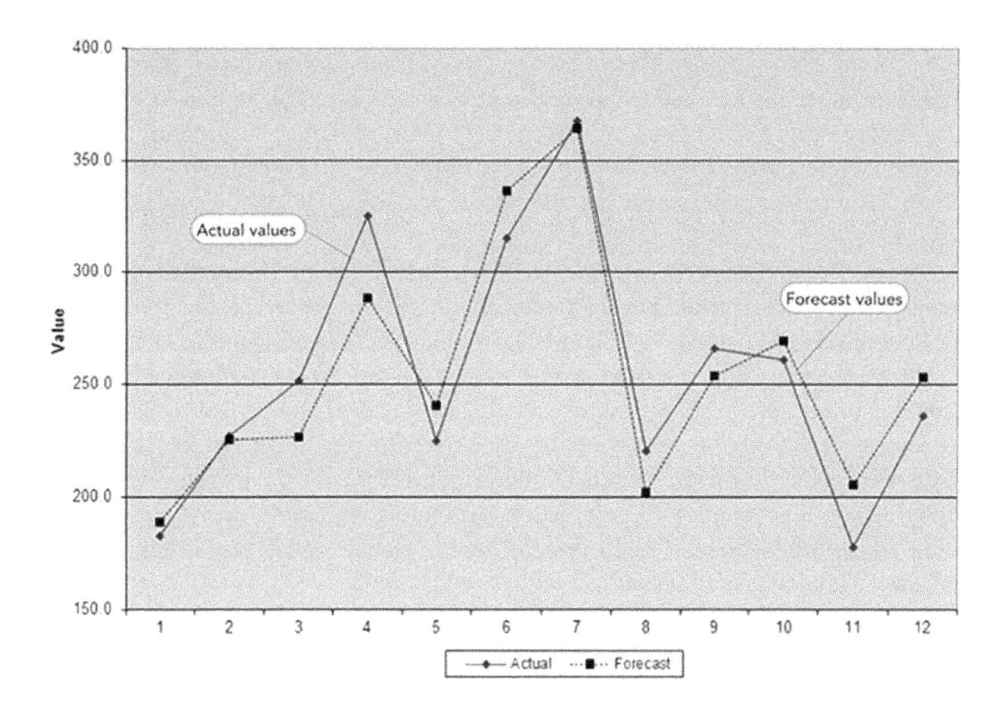

Figure 11.33: Chart of Causal Model (Multiple Regression) Forecast for Home Selling Prices

File: Figure 11.32.xlsx, Sheet: Figure 11.33

Analyzing the Results Is this multiple regression model better than the original simple regression model? The R^2 value increases from just 0.493 in the simple regression model to 0.876 with the addition of the second variable, land area. That is, home size and land area together are able to explain 87.6% of the variability in home selling prices. In addition, all three measures of forecast error show sizable drops in magnitude. For example, the MAPE decreases from 11.73% in the simple regression model to just 6.65% in the multiple regression model. Likewise, the MAD decreases from 30.40 in the simple regression model to just 16.307 with the second independent variable.

To further study the effect of adding land area as an independent variable, let us compare the multiple regression model's line chart (shown in Figure 11.33) with the simple regression model's chart (shown in Figure 11.27). It appears that most of the points in Figure 11.33 (especially homes 2, 6, 7, and 12) show a sizable improvement in terms of the forecast error.

All these issues seem to indicate that the addition of the second independent variable does help Sue in being able to forecast home selling prices more accurately. However, as we will see shortly when we study multiple regression analysis using Data Analysis, we need to be cautious in deciding which independent variable to add in a multiple regression model.

Using the Causal Multiple Regression Model Recall that we used the simple regression model to forecast the average selling price of a 3,100-square-foot home. Now suppose this home has a land area of 0.90 acres. We enter these values in cells C23 and D23, respectively, as shown in Figure 11.32 (recall that we should enter 3,100 as 3.10). The model forecasts an average selling price of 269.735 (shown in cell B25), or $269,735.

As with the simple regression model, we can use this point estimate in conjunction with the standard error of the regression estimate (given in cell I23 in Figure 11.32) to calculate an approximate 95% confidence interval for the selling price of *all* homes of size 3,100 square feet and with a land area of 0.9 acres. This confidence interval turns out to be $269.733 \pm 1.96 \times 22.179 = 226.262$ to 313.204, or \$226.262 to \$313,204. Because the standard error here is smaller than the corresponding value in the simple regression model, the width of this confidence interval is also narrower. However, while the confidence interval computed in the simple regression model was for *all* homes of size 3,100 square feet, the interval here is relevant only for those homes that also have a land area of 0.9 acres.

Causal Multiple Regression Using Excel's Analysis ToolPak (Data Analysis)
Just as we did in simple regression, we can also use Excel's Analysis ToolPak for multiple regression. To invoke the procedure, we once again click Data | Data Analysis and select Regression from the list of choices. The window shown in Figure 11.34 is displayed.

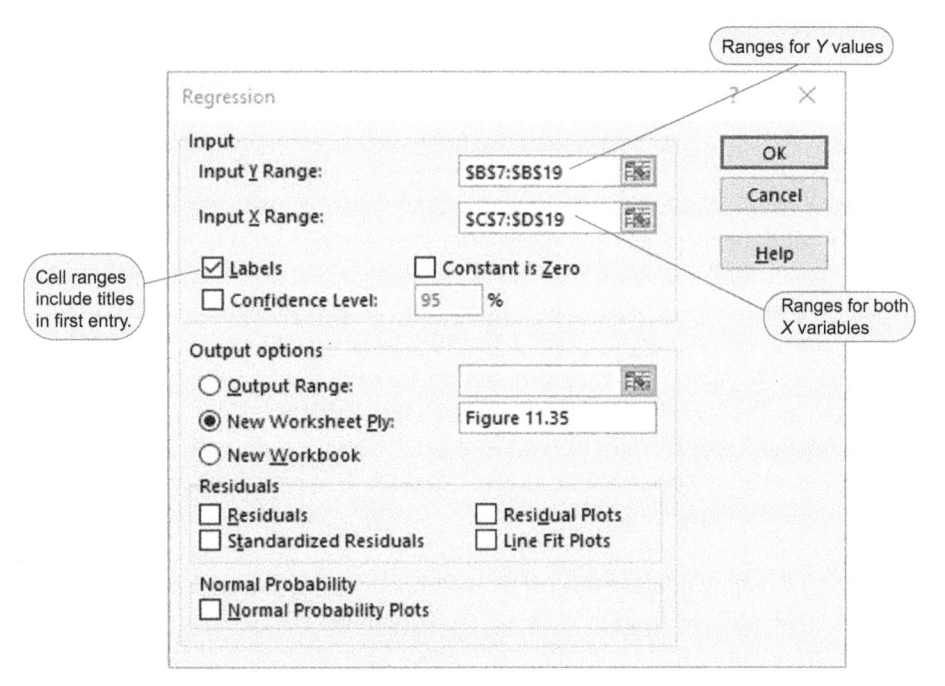

Figure 11.34: Multiple Regression Using Excel's Analysis ToolPak

Before we use Data Analysis for multiple regression, we need to ensure that the independent variables in the model are adjacent to each other in an Excel worksheet. In Sue's case, for example, we have entered the selling prices in cells B7:B19, as shown in Figure 11.32, and the two independent variables (home size and land area) in adjacent columns in cells C7:C19 and D7:D19, respectively. We now specify these cell ranges in the appropriate boxes, as shown in Figure 11.34. (Note that the cell ranges for both independent variables are specified as one entry: C7:D19.) The Labels box is checked to indicate that the cell ranges include the name of each variable as the first entry. We then indicate that we want the output of the regression to be displayed in a new worksheet named *Figure 11.35*. The rest of the entries and their implications are the same as in the simple regression procedure.

Results of the Regression Procedure When we click OK, Data Analysis runs the multiple regression procedure, and the results shown in Figure 11.35 are displayed. Here again, just as in the earlier results we obtained using ExcelModules (Figure 11.32), the results show a Y-intercept of 99.919 (cell B18), slope of 21.383 for home size (cell B19), slope of 115.030 for land area (cell B20), coefficient of determination R^2 of 0.876 (cell B6), and standard error of the regression estimate of 22.179 (cell B8). The adjusted R^2 value in cell B7 is an empirical measure that applies a correction factor to the R^2 value based on the number of independent variables and the number of observations. It is commonly used to compare multiple regression models with different numbers of independent variables (as opposed to the original R^2 value, which will always be higher for a model with a larger number of independent variables).

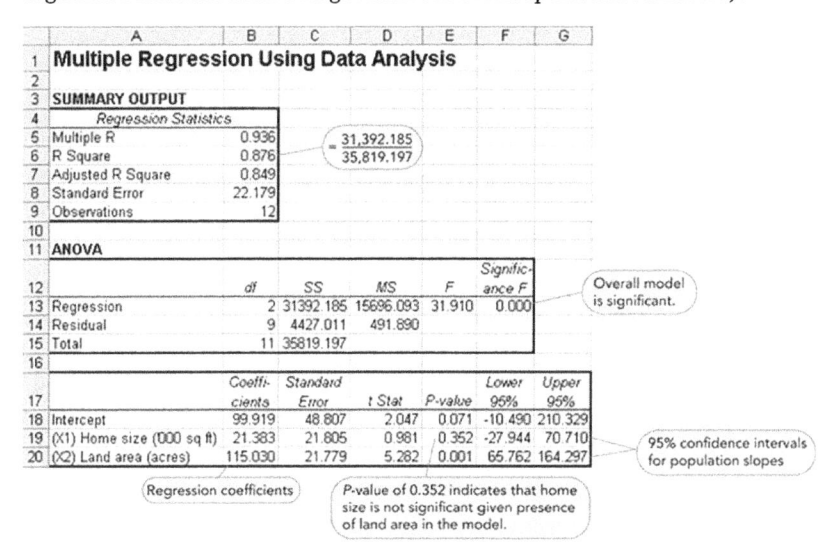

Figure 11.35: Multiple Regression Output from Excel's Analysis ToolPak

File: Figure 11.32.xlsx, Sheet: Figure 11.35

Notice that the total *SS* value of 35,819.197 (in cell C15 of the ANOVA table) is the same value we saw in the simple regression model. Of this, the multiple regression model explains 31,382.185, leaving only 4,427.011 unexplained. The R^2 value can therefore be computed as $31,382.185/35,819.197 = 0.876$, or 87.6%, which is the same value reported in cell B6.

Statistical Significance of the Regression Equation Just as we did in simple regression, if our data set consists of the entire population of homes, the true population relationship between *Y* and the two independent variables X_1 and X_2 can be expressed as

$$\mu_{Y|Xs} = \beta_0 + \beta_1 X_1 + \beta_2 X_2 \qquad (11\text{--}20)$$

where

$\mu_{Y|Xs}$ = forecasted average value of *Y* for a given values of X_1 and X_2, based on the entire population

β_0 = *Y*-intercept of the line, based on the entire population

β_1 = slope with respect to X_1, based on the entire population

β_2 = slope with respect to X_2, based on the entire population

Unlike simple regression, where we could test the significance of the regression relationship by using either the *F*-test or the *t*-test, in multiple regression these two tests deal with different issues. As before, we refer you to any statistics book for the details of these tests, and we only interpret their results in our discussion here.

In multiple regression, the *F*-test tests the overall significance of the regression model. That is, the null and alternate hypotheses for this test are as follows:

H_0: $\beta_1 = \beta_2 = 0$ (i.e., the overall regression model is not significant)

H_1: At least one of β_1 and $\beta_2 \neq 0$ (i.e., at least one variable in the model is significant)

In Sue's example, the computed *F*-statistic for this test is 31.910, as shown in cell E13 in Figure 11.35. This statistic is *F*-distributed with 2 numerator degrees of freedom (cell B13) and 9 denominator degrees of freedom (cell B14). The *P*-value associated with this *F*-statistic, shown in cell F13, is essentially zero, implying that the null hypothesis can be rejected at virtually any level of significance. That is, we can clearly conclude that there is a statistically significant relationship between *Y* and at least one of the two *X* variables. It is important to note that this result of the *F*-test should not be interpreted as an indication that both *X* variables are significant.

The *t*-test, in contrast, tests the significance of each of the regression slopes, given the presence of all the other independent variables. This previous condition illustrates an important issue about multiple regression: The relationship of each independent variable with the dependent variable in a multiple regression model is affected by all the other independent variables in the model. To illustrate this issue, let us first test the slope for the land area. The null and alternate hypotheses for this test are as follows:

H_0: $\beta_2 = 0$ (i.e., slope of land area is not significant, given presence of home size)

H_1: $\beta_2 \neq 0$ (i.e., slope of land area is significant, given presence of home size)

The computed *t*-statistic for this test is 5.282, as shown in cell D20 in Figure 11.35. This statistic is *t*-distributed with 9 degrees of freedom (cell B14). The *P*-value associated with this *t*-statistic, shown in cell E20, is 0.001, implying that there is a statistically significant relationship between *Y* and X_2 (land area), given the presence of the independent variable X_1 (home size) in the model.

Now let us test the slope for the home size. The null and alternate hypotheses for this test are as follows:

H_0: $\beta_1 = 0$ (i.e., slope of home size is not significant, given presence of land area)

H_1: $\beta_1 \neq 0$ (i.e., slope of home size is significant, given presence of land area)

The computed *t*-statistic for this test is 0.981, as shown in cell D19 in Figure 11.35. This statistic is also *t*-distributed with 9 degrees of freedom (cell B14). The *P*-value for this test, shown in cell E20, is 0.352, implying that there is *no* statistically significant relationship between *Y* and X_1 (home size), given the presence of the independent variable X_2 (land area) in the model. Are we concluding here that home size is not a relevant variable to predict home selling prices? The answer is an emphatic no. In fact, recall from the simple regression model that we did establish a statistically significant relationship between home selling prices and home size. All we are concluding in the multiple regression model is that home size adds little incremental value to the model when land area has already been included. In other words, when land area has been included in the regression model, we should perhaps not include home size in the model also, and we should possibly look for other independent variables.

Multicollinearity If home size was a statistically significant predictor in the simple regression model, why did it become nonsignificant when we added land area as a second independent variable? One possible explanation for this could be a phenomenon called *multicollinearity*. This occurs whenever two or more independent variables in a model are highly correlated with each other. When this happens, the relationship between each independent variable and the dependent variable is affected in an unpredictable manner by the presence of the other highly correlated independent variable.

How can we detect multicollinearity? We can use a simple correlation analysis to detect highly correlated pairs of independent variables.[4] To invoke the procedure in the Analysis ToolPak add-in, we click Data | Data Analysis and select Correlation from the list of choices that is presented. The window shown in Figure 11.36 is displayed. We enter the cell ranges for all variables, which must be arranged in adjacent columns or rows. (In Sue's example, we have included the cell ranges for Y, X_1, and X_2 from the worksheet shown in Figure 11.32.) When we now run the procedure, the results shown in Figure 11.35 (b) are displayed.

(a)

Click Data | Data Analysis and select Correlation to get this window.

Enter cell ranges for all variables.

Correlation

Input
Input Range: $SB$7:$D$19
Grouped By: ● Columns
○ Rows
☑ Labels in First Row

Data is arranged in columns.

Output options
○ Output Range:
● New Worksheet Ply: Figure 11.36
○ New Workbook

(b)

	A	B	C	D
1		(Y) Selling price ($'000)	(X1) Home size ('000 sq ft)	(X2) Land area (acres)
2	(Y) Selling price ($'000)	1.000		
3	(X1) Home size ('000 sq ft)	0.702	1.000	
4	(X2) Land area (acres)	0.929	0.663	1.000

Land area and selling price have a correlation coefficient of 0.929.

Home size and land area have a correlation coefficient of

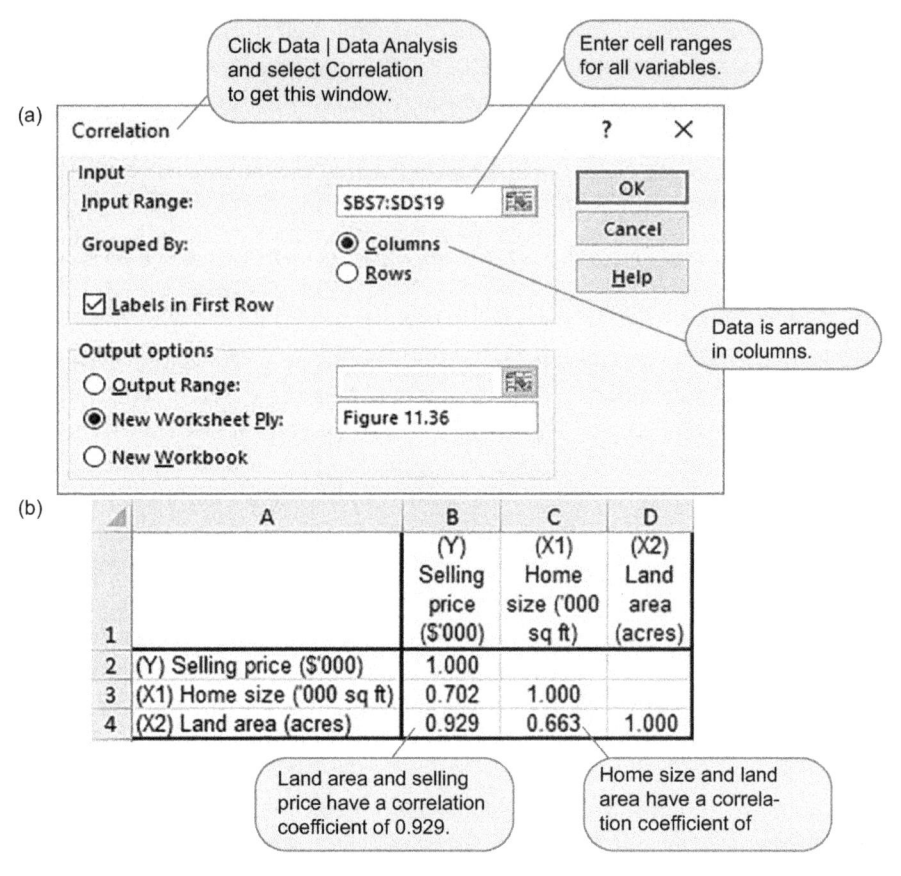

Figure 11.36: Correlation Analysis Using Excel's Analysis ToolPak

File: Figure 11.32.xlsx, Sheet: Figure 11.36

---

[4] Multicollinearity can also exist between more than just a pair of variables. For example, independent variables X_1 and X_2 may together be highly correlated with a third independent variable, X_3. We can detect such situations by using a measure called the variance inflationary factor. We refer to you any statistics book for details on this measure and its use.

The results indicate that both independent variables are individually highly correlated with the dependent variable. The correlation coefficient between Y and X_1 is 0.702 (cell B3), and it is 0.929 (cell B4) between Y and X_2. This explains why each variable, by itself, is significantly related to Y. However, the results also indicate that the X_1 and X_2 are correlated at a level of 0.663 (cell C4). As noted earlier, while there is no clear cutoff to decide when two variables are highly correlated, in general, correlation coefficient magnitudes of 0.6 or greater are indicative of a strong relationship. If two independent variables exhibit this level of relationship, they should not be included in a multiple regression model at the same time. If they are both included, the effect of each independent variable on the other can be unpredictable, as we saw in Sue's example in Figure 11.35.

Confidence Intervals for the Population Slopes Just as we did in simple regression, we can compute intervals at various levels of confidence for each population slope (i.e., β_1 and β_2). By default, Data Analysis always reports 95% confidence intervals for both these parameters (shown in cells F19:G19 and F20:G20, respectively, in Figure 11.35). Note that the confidence interval for β_1 extends from a negative value to a positive value (i.e., it spans a value of zero). This is consistent with our earlier finding that the slope of home size is not significantly different from zero, given the presence of land area in the model.

In this model also, the Y-intercept is not relevant for any practical interpretation. (After all, we cannot have a home of size zero with no land area.) For this reason, we ignore the hypothesis test and confidence interval information for the Y-intercept, even though Data Analysis provides that information by default.

11.9 Summary

Forecasts are a critical part of a manager's function. Demand forecasts drive the production, capacity, and scheduling systems in a firm and affect the financial, marketing, and personnel planning functions.

This chapter introduces three types of forecasting models: judgmental, time series, and causal. Four qualitative models are discussed for judgmental forecasting: Delphi method, jury of executive opinion, sales force composite, and consumer market survey. We then discuss moving averages, weighted moving averages, exponential smoothing, trend projection, seasonality, and multiplicative decomposition models for time-series data. Finally, we illustrate a popular causal model, regression analysis. In addition, we discuss the use of scatter charts and provide an analysis of forecasting accuracy. The forecast measures discussed include mean absolute deviation (MAD), mean squared error (MSE), and mean absolute percent error (MAPE).

As we demonstrate in this chapter, no forecasting method is perfect under all conditions. Even when management has found a satisfactory approach, it must still monitor and control its forecasts to make sure errors do not get out of hand. Forecasting can be a very challenging but rewarding part of managing.

Key Points
- No single forecasting method is superior; whatever works best should be used.
- There are seven steps in forecasting: (1) determine the use of the forecast, (2) identify items needed to be forecasted, (3) determine the time horizon of the forecast, (4) select the forecasting model or models, (5) gather necessary data, (6) validate the forecasting model, and (7) make the forecast and implement the results.
- The three categories of forecasting models are qualitative, time-series, and causal models.
- Qualitative forecasting models incorporate subjective factors.
- Time-series forecasting models assume that the past is an indication of the future.
- Causal forecasting models incorporate factors that influence the quantity being forecasted.
- Four qualitative or judgmental forecasting approaches are Delphi, jury of executive opinion, sales force composite, and consumer market survey.
- The forecast error tells us how well the model performed against itself using past data.
- Mean squared error (MSE) accentuates large deviations.
- Mean absolute percent error (MAPE) expresses the error as a percentage of the actual values.
- Stationary data have no trend, while nonstationary data exhibit trend.
- Moving averages smooth out variations when forecasting demands that are fairly steady.
- Forecast error measures permit comparison of different models.
- Weights can be used to put more emphasis on some periods in a weighted moving averages model.
- Weights in a weighted moving averages model usually add up to 1.
- Solver can be used to determine the optimal weights in a weighted moving averages model.
- The same weights in a weighted moving averages model need not minimize both MAPE and MSE.
- Exponential smoothing is a type of moving averages model.
- The smoothing constant α in an exponential smoothing model allows managers to assign weight to recent data.
- Linear trend analysis fits a straight line to time-series data.
- A scatter chart helps obtain ideas about a relationship.
- The slope of a linear trend line is the average change in Y for a unit increase in the value of time (X).
- The least-squares method finds a straight line that minimizes the sum of the squares of vertical differences from the line to each of the data points.

- We need to solve for the Y-intercept and the slope to find the equation of the least-squares line.
- Decomposition breaks down a time series into its components.
- Four components of a time series are trend, seasonality, cycles, and random variations.
- A multiplicative decomposition model is: Forecast = Trend × Seasonality × Cycles × Random variations.
- An additive decomposition model is: Forecast = Trend + Seasonality + Cycles + Random variations.
- The centered moving average approach helps smooth out fluctuations in the data.
- Multiplicative decomposition includes the following steps: (1) compute the seasonal indices, (2) convert the seasonalized time-series data to unseasonalized data, (3) compute the linear trend equation, (4) compute the forecast, (5) seasonalize the forecasts, and (6) compute measures of forecast error.
- We use line charts of the actual and forecast values to check the validity of the model.
- In a causal forecasting model, the dependent variable is the item we are trying to forecast, and the independent variable is an item (or items) we think might have a causal effect on the dependent variable.
- We determine the Y-intercept (b_0) and slope (b_1) of a causal forecasting model by using the least-squares formulas.
- The Y-intercept may not have a practical meaning in many causal models. The slope indicates the average change in Y for a unit increase in X.
- The standard error of a regression model is useful in creating confidence intervals around the regression line.
- The correlation coefficient helps measure the strength of the linear relationship between two variables.
- The coefficient of determination of a regression model tells us how much of the variability in the dependent variable is explained by the independent variable.
- Weakness of regression: (1) need to know the values of the independent variable, and (2) individual values of Y can be quite far from the forecasted average value.
- A causal model is typically valid only for the range of X values in the data set for which it was developed.
- Excel's Analysis ToolPak add-in includes a procedure for regression.
- Residual plots and the normal probability plot are used to verify the validity of assumptions in a regression model.
- Statistical significance tests check whether the regression relationship really exists for the entire population or whether it is just a random occurrence based on the current sample.
- There are two tests for testing statistical significance in simple regression models: F-test and t-test.

- Significance tests involving the *Y*-intercept for a regression model are often not relevant and are ignored.
- Adding additional independent variables turns a simple regression model into a multiple regression model.
- Calculations in multiple regression are very complex and best left to a computer.
- ExcelModules includes a worksheet for causal forecasting models using multiple regression.
- The effect of each independent variable in a multiple regression model is affected by all the other independent variables in the model.
- Forecast measures will typically improve in multiple regression models when compared to a simple regression model.
- Independent variables must be arranged adjacently in order to use the regression procedure in Excel's Data Analysis for multiple regression.
- The *F*-test tests the overall significance of the model in multiple regression.
- The *t*-test tests the significance of an individual independent variable in a multiple regression model, given the presence of all the other independent variables.
- Multicollinearity exists when two or more independent variables in a multiple regression model are highly correlated with each other.
- Pairwise multicollinearity can be detected by using correlation analysis.
- Confidence intervals can be constructed for the population slopes in a multiple regression model.
- In additive decomposition models, unseasonalize the data by *subtracting* the seasonal indices from the seasonalized data. Seasonalize forecasts by *adding* back the appropriate seasonal indices.

Glossary

Additive Decomposition Model A decomposition model in which the forecasted value is the sum of the four components: trend, seasonality, cycles, and random variations.

Causal Models Models that forecast using variables and factors, in addition to time.

Correlation Coefficient A measure of the strength of the linear relationship between two variables.

Coefficient of Determination A measure that indicates what percentage of the variability in the dependent variable is explained by the independent variables.

Cycles Patterns that occur over several years. Cycles are usually tied to the business cycle.

Decision-Making Group A group of experts in a Delphi technique who have the responsibility of making the forecast.

Delphi A judgmental forecasting technique that uses decision makers, staff personnel, and respondents to determine a forecast.

Dependent Variable The variable to be forecasted or predicted. Denoted by *Y*.

Exponential Smoothing A forecasting technique that is a combination of the last forecast and the last actual value.

Forecast Error The difference between the actual and forecasted values is also known as *forecast deviation.*

Independent Variable A variable used in a prediction. Denoted by X.

Least-Squares Procedure A procedure used in trend projection and regression analysis to minimize the squared distances between the estimated straight line and the actual values.

Mean Absolute Deviation (MAD) The average of the absolute forecast errors.

Mean Absolute Percent Error (MAPE) The average of the absolute forecast errors as a percentage of the actual values.

Mean Squared Error (MSE) The average of the squared forecast errors.

Moving Averages A forecasting technique that averages past values in computing the forecast.

Multiplicative Decomposition Model A decomposition model in which the forecasted value is the product of the four components trend, seasonality, cycles, and random variation.

Qualitative Models Models that forecast using judgments, experience, and qualitative and subjective data.

Random Variations "Blips" in the data that are caused by chance and unusual situations. They follow no discernible pattern.

Regression Analysis A forecasting procedure that uses the least-squares procedure on one or more independent variables to develop a forecasting model.

Scatter Chart A chart or diagram of the variable to be forecasted or predicted, drawn against another variable, such as time. Also called a *scatter diagram* or *plot*.

Seasonality A pattern of demand fluctuations above or below the trend line that occur every year.

Smoothing Constant A value between 0 and 1 that is used in an exponential smoothing forecast.

Standard Error of the Regression Estimate A measure of the accuracy of regression estimates. Also called *standard deviation of the regression*.

Stationary Data Time-series data in which there is no significant upward or downward movement (or trend) over time.

Time-Series Models Models that forecast by using historical data.

Trend The upward or downward movement of the data over time.

Weighted Moving Averages A moving average forecasting method that places different weights on different past values.

11.10 Exercises

Solved Problems

Solved Problem 11–1 Demand for outpatient surgery at Washington General Hospital has increased steadily in the past few years, as shown in the following table:

Year	Surgeries
1	45
2	50
3	52
4	56
5	58

The director of medical services predicted six years ago that demand in year 1 would be 42 surgeries. Using exponential smoothing with $\alpha = 0.20$, develop forecasts for years 2 through 6. What is the MAD value?

Solution To solve this problem, we use the Forecasting Models|Exponential Smoothing choice in ExcelModules. Figure 11.37 shows the computations. The input entries are shown in cells B7:B11, and the α value is shown in cell B13. The MAD value is calculated to be 8.98 (cell F12). The rounded forecast for year 6 is 50 (cell B15).

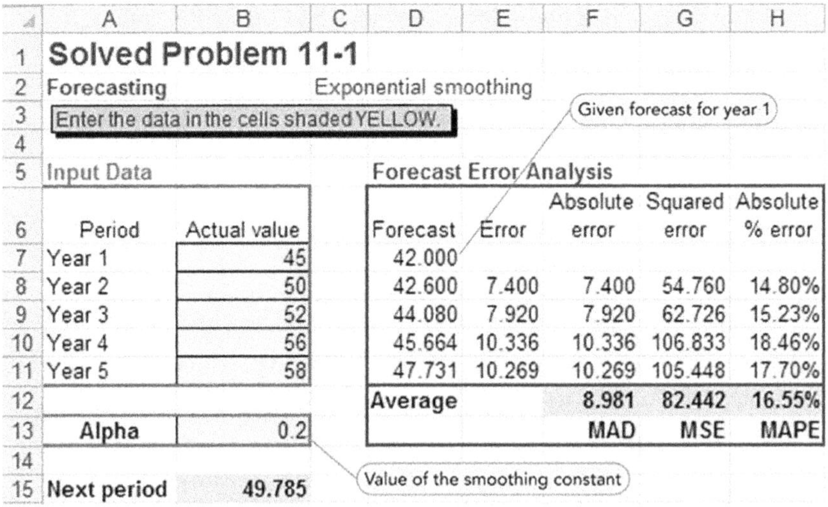

	A	B	C	D	E	F	G	H
1	**Solved Problem 11-1**							
2	Forecasting			Exponential smoothing				
3	Enter the data in the cells shaded YELLOW.					Given forecast for year 1		
4								
5	Input Data				Forecast Error Analysis			
6							Absolute	Squared	Absolute
6	Period	Actual value		Forecast	Error	error	error	% error
7	Year 1	45		42.000				
8	Year 2	50		42.600	7.400	7.400	54.760	14.80%
9	Year 3	52		44.080	7.920	7.920	62.726	15.23%
10	Year 4	56		45.664	10.336	10.336	106.833	18.46%
11	Year 5	58		47.731	10.269	10.269	105.448	17.70%
12				Average		8.981	82.442	16.55%
13	Alpha	0.2				MAD	MSE	MAPE
14								
15	Next period	49.785		Value of the smoothing constant				

Figure 11.37: Exponential Smoothing Model for Solved Problem 11–1

File: Figure 11.37.xlsx

Solved Problem 11–2 Room registrations (in thousands) at the Toronto Towers Plaza Hotel for the past nine years are as follows (earliest year is shown first): 17, 16, 16, 21, 20, 20, 23, 25, and 24. Management would like to determine the mathematical trend of guest registration in order to project future occupancy. This estimate would help the hotel determine whether a future expansion will be needed. Develop the linear trend equation and forecast year 11's registrations.

Solution To solve this problem, we use the Forecasting Models | Linear Trend Analysis choice in ExcelModules. Figure 11.38 shows the computations. The input entries are shown in cells B7:B15. The period values are automatically entered by ExcelModules in cells C7:C15.

The regression equation is Registrants = 14.556 + 1.133 × Year number. MAPE is calculated to be 5.88% (cell I16). The projected average registration for year 11 is 27,022 guests (cell B20).

	A	B	C	D	E	F	G	H	I
1	Solved Problem 11-2								
2	Forecasting		Linear trend analysis						
3	Enter the actual values in cells shaded YELLOW. Enter new time period at the bottom to forecast Y.								
4									
5	Input Data				Forecast Error Analysis				
6	Period	Actual value (or) Y	Period number (or) X		Forecast	Error	Absolute error	Squared error	Absolute % error
7	Year 1	17	1		15.689	1.311	1.311	1.719	7.71%
8	Year 2	16	2		16.822	-0.822	0.822	0.676	5.14%
9	Year 3	16	3		17.956	-1.956	1.956	3.824	12.22%
10	Year 4	21	4		19.089	1.911	1.911	3.652	9.10%
11	Year 5	20	5		20.222	-0.222	0.222	0.049	1.11%
12	Year 6	20	6		21.356	-1.356	1.356	1.838	6.78%
13	Year 7	23	7		22.489	0.511	0.511	0.261	2.22%
14	Year 8	25	8		23.622	1.378	1.378	1.898	5.51%
15	Year 9	24	9		24.756	-0.756	0.756	0.571	3.15%
16					Average		1.136	1.610	5.88%
17	Intercept	14.556	Regression coefficients				MAD	MSE	MAPE
18	Slope	1.133							
19									
20	Next period	27.022	11						

Forecast for year 11, in thousands

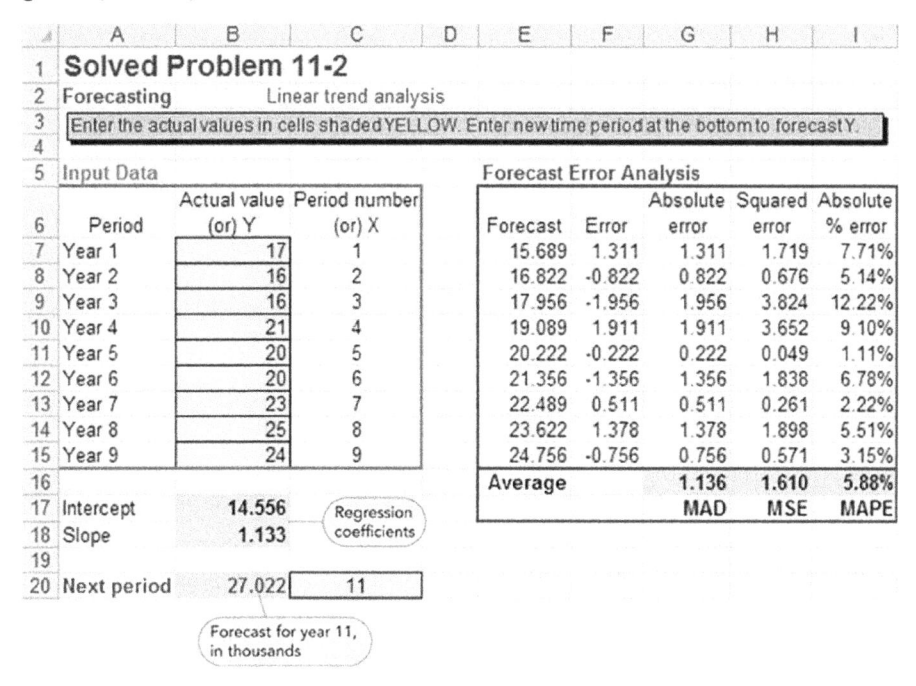

Figure 11.38: Trend Analysis Model for Solved Problem 11–2

X File: Figure 11.38.xlsx

Solved Problem 11–3 Quarterly demand for Jaguar XJ8s at a New York auto dealership is forecast using the equation

$$\hat{Y} = 10 + 3X$$

where X = quarter number ($X=1$ is quarter 1 of year 2015, $X=2$ is quarter 2 of year 2015, and so on), and $\hat{Y}$ = quarterly demand. The demand for luxury sedans is seasonal, and the indices for quarters 1, 2, 3, and 4 of each year are 0.80, 1.00, 1.30, and 0.90, respectively. Forecast the seasonalized demand for each quarter of year 2017.

Solution Using the coding scheme for X, quarters 1 to 4 of year 2017 are coded $X=9$ to 12, respectively. Hence,

$\hat{Y}$(quarter 1 of year 2017) = 10 + 3×9 = 37 Seasonalized forecast = 37×0.80 = 29.6
$\hat{Y}$(quarter 2 of year 2017) = 10 + 3×10 = 40 Seasonalized forecast = 40×1.00 = 40.0
$\hat{Y}$(quarter 3 of year 2017) = 10 + 3×11 = 43 Seasonalized forecast = 43×1.30 = 55.9
$\hat{Y}$(quarter 4 of year 2017) = 10 + 3×12 = 46 Seasonalized forecast = 40×0.90 = 41.0

Solved Problem 11-4 In section 11.7, we helped Sandy Sawyer decompose Sawyer Piano House's time-series data using a multiplicative decomposition model. Repeat the computations now, using an additive decomposition model. For your convenience, the data for this model (showing grand piano sales for the past 20 quarters) are repeated in Table 11.8.

Table 11.8: Sales of Grand Pianos at Sawyer Piano House

	2012	2013	2014	2015	2016
Quarter 1	4	6	10	12	18
Quarter 2	2	4	3	9	10
Quarter 3	1	4	5	7	13
Quarter 4	5	14	16	22	35

Solution Recall from Equation 11-6 that the additive decomposition model can be specified as

Forecast = Trend + Seasonality + Cycles + Random variations

Although ExcelModules does not include a worksheet for additive decomposition, the worksheet provided for multiplicative decomposition can easily be modified to suit an additive model. We first select the choice titled Multiplicative Decomposition from the Forecasting Models menu in ExcelModules. Then, as we did in Figure 11.21, we specify the number of periods for which we have past data (20), the name for the period (Quarter), and the number of seasons each year (4). In addition, we select the Centered Moving Average option to compute seasonal indices. We click OK, and in the resulting screen, we enter the actual number of pianos sold during the past 20 quarters in cells B7:B26. The corresponding time periods (i.e., the *X* variable values) are automatically specified in cells C7:C26 by the worksheet.

The worksheet displays the results of the multiplicative decomposition model. We now modify this worksheet as follows to transform it to an additive mode (unless specified here, the computations in a column are the same as in the multiplicative model). The results for the additive model are shown in Figure 11.39).

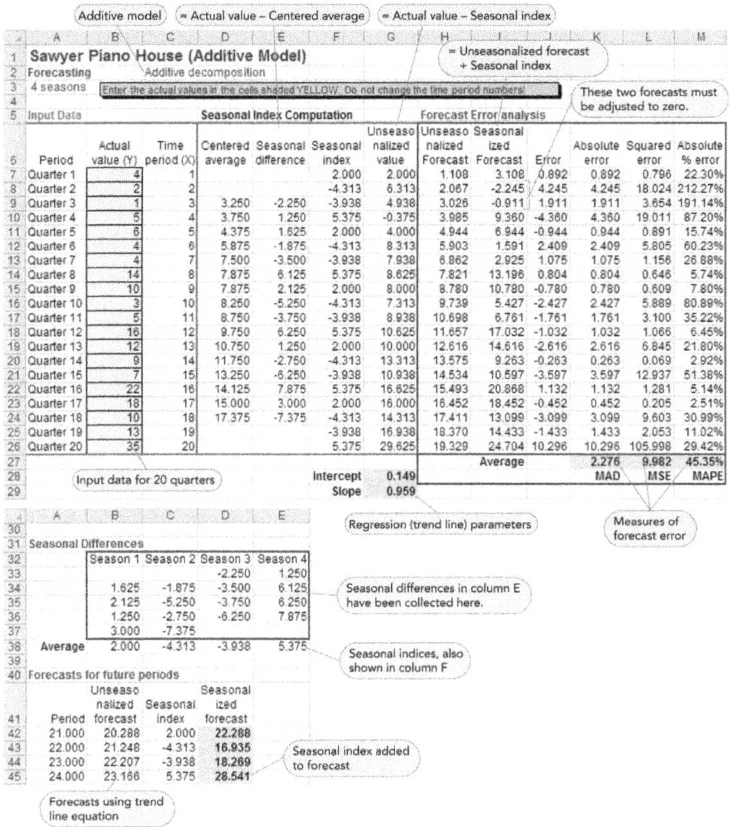

Period	Actual value (Y)	Time period (X)	Centered average	Seasonal difference	Seasonal index	Unseasonalized value	Unseasonalized Forecast	Seasonalized Forecast	Error	Absolute error	Squared error	Absolute % error
Quarter 1	4	1			2.000	2.000	1.108	3.108	0.892	0.892	0.796	22.30%
Quarter 2	2	2			-4.313	6.313	2.067	-2.245	4.245	4.245	18.024	212.27%
Quarter 3	1	3	3.250	-2.250	-3.938	4.938	3.026	-0.911	1.911	1.911	3.654	191.14%
Quarter 4	5	4	3.750	1.250	5.375	-0.375	3.985	9.360	-4.360	4.360	19.011	87.20%
Quarter 5	6	5	4.375	1.625	2.000	4.000	4.944	6.944	-0.944	0.944	0.891	15.74%
Quarter 6	4	6	5.875	-1.875	-4.313	8.313	5.903	1.591	2.409	2.409	5.805	60.23%
Quarter 7	4	7	7.500	-3.500	-3.938	7.938	6.862	2.925	1.075	1.075	1.156	26.88%
Quarter 8	14	8	7.875	6.125	5.375	8.625	7.821	13.196	0.804	0.804	0.646	5.74%
Quarter 9	10	9	7.875	2.125	2.000	8.000	8.780	10.780	-0.780	0.780	0.609	7.80%
Quarter 10	3	10	8.250	-5.250	-4.313	7.313	9.739	5.427	-2.427	2.427	5.889	80.89%
Quarter 11	5	11	8.750	-3.750	-3.938	8.938	10.698	6.761	-1.761	1.761	3.100	35.22%
Quarter 12	16	12	9.750	6.250	5.375	10.625	11.657	17.032	-1.032	1.032	1.066	6.45%
Quarter 13	12	13	10.750	1.250	2.000	10.000	12.616	14.616	-2.616	2.616	6.845	21.80%
Quarter 14	9	14	11.750	-2.750	-4.313	13.313	13.575	9.263	-0.263	0.263	0.069	2.92%
Quarter 15	7	15	13.250	-6.250	-3.938	10.938	14.534	10.597	-3.597	3.597	12.937	51.38%
Quarter 16	22	16	14.125	7.875	5.375	16.625	15.493	20.868	1.132	1.132	1.281	5.14%
Quarter 17	18	17	15.000	3.000	2.000	16.000	16.452	18.452	-0.452	0.452	0.205	2.51%
Quarter 18	10	18	17.375	-7.375	-4.313	14.313	17.411	13.099	-3.099	3.099	9.603	30.99%
Quarter 19	13	19			-3.938	16.938	18.370	14.433	-1.433	1.433	2.053	11.02%
Quarter 20	35	20			5.375	29.625	19.329	24.704	10.296	10.296	105.998	29.42%
								Average		2.276	9.982	45.35%
					Intercept	0.149				MAD	MSE	MAPE
					Slope	0.959						

Seasonal Differences

	Season 1	Season 2	Season 3	Season 4
			-2.250	1.250
	1.625	-1.875	-3.500	6.125
	2.125	-5.250	-3.750	6.250
	1.250	-2.750	-6.250	7.875
	3.000	-7.375		
Average	2.000	-4.313	-3.938	5.375

Forecasts for future periods

Period	Unseasonalized forecast	Seasonal index	Seasonalized forecast
21.000	20.288	2.000	**22.288**
22.000	21.248	-4.313	**16.935**
23.000	22.207	-3.938	**18.269**
24.000	23.166	5.375	**28.541**

Figure 11.39: Additive Decomposition Model for Sawyer Piano House

File: Figure 11.39.xlsx

1. *Computation of the seasonal indices, Columns D–G.* We compute the following:
   - In column D, we compute the centered moving average sales for each quarter.
   - Next, we compute the seasonal difference for each quarter by *subtracting* from the actual sales (column B) in that quarter its centered average (column D). That is, column E = column B – column D. Note that instead of dividing by the centered moving average (as in a multiplicative model), we subtract it in an additive model.

- The seasonal differences for each quarter are collected in cells B33:E37, and we compute the seasonal index for each quarter as the average of all the differences for that quarter. These seasonal indices are shown in cells B38:E38 and repeated in column F, next to the appropriate quarters each year. Seasonal index values in an additive model are positive or negative. A positive index indicates that the actual value in that period is above average, while a negative index indicates that the actual value is below average.
   - Finally, in column G, we compute the unseasonalized sales in each quarter as the actual sales (column B) in that quarter minus the seasonal index (column F) for that quarter. That is, column G = column B − column F.
2. *Computation of the trend equation.* Using the unseasonalized sales in column G as the dependent variable (Y) and the time period number in column C as the independent variable (X), we compute the linear trend equation. The resulting Y-intercept (a) and slope (b) for this straight line are shown in cells G28 and G29, respectively. In Sandy's case, the linear trend equation for the additive model is

$$\text{Unseasonalized sales forecast} = 0.149 + 0.959 \times \text{Quarter number}$$

3. *Computation of forecast, columns H and I.* We now calculate the forecast by adding the appropriate seasonal indices to the unseasonalized sales forecasts. Note that instead of multiplying by the seasonal index (as in a multiplicative model), we add it in an additive model. The computations are as follows:
   - In column H, we use the trend equation to compute the unseasonalized forecast for each quarter. For example, for the fourth quarter of year 2 (i.e., quarter 8), this value is computed in cell H14 as $(0.149 + 0.959 \times 8) = 7.821$. These values are also computed for the next year (i.e., quarters 21 to 24, denoting the four quarters in year 2017) in cells B42:B45.
   - The appropriate seasonal indices are added to the unseasonalized forecasts to get the seasonalized forecast for each quarter in column I. That is, column I = column H + column F Cells D42:D45 show the seasonal forecasts for quarters 21 to 24.

   Notice that the seasonal forecasts for quarters 2 and 3, shown in cells I8 and I9, respectively, are negative (because both quarters have negative seasonal indices that exceed their unseasonalized sales forecasts). Clearly, this is illogical in practice, and we should adjust these seasonal forecasts to zero. *Note: We have not adjusted these values in Figure 11.39 to facilitate this discussion.*
4. *Computation of forecast error measures, columns J through M.* We compute the MAD, MSE, and MAPE values in cells K27, L27, and M27, respectively.

The MAPE value of 45.35% in this case is much worse than the MAPE value of 23.74% obtained using the multiplicative model. Sandy may therefore be better off staying with the multiplicative model. If desired, we can ask ExcelModules to also draw line charts of the actual and forecasted values for the additive model. Although

Discussion Questions

11-1. Briefly describe the steps used to develop a forecasting system.
11-2. What is a time-series forecasting model?
11-3. What is the difference between a causal model and a time-series model?
11-4. What is a qualitative forecasting model, and when is using it appropriate?
11-5. What is the meaning of least squares in a regression model?
11-6. What are some of the problems and drawbacks of the moving average forecasting model?
11-7. What effect does the value of the smoothing constant have on the weight given to the past forecast and the past observed value?
11-8. Briefly describe the Delphi technique.
11-9. What is MAPE, and why is it important in the selection and use of forecasting models?
11-10. Describe how you can use charts to determine whether a forecasting model is valid.
11-11. What is a correlation coefficient? Why is it useful?
11-12. Explain how Solver can be used to identify the optimal weights in the weighted moving averages model.
11-13. In the decomposition model, how are seasonal indices used to adjust the forecast calculated using the trend equation?
11-14. What would be the result if the exponential smoothing model is used with a smoothing constant of zero? Smoothing constant of 0.5? Smoothing constant of one.?

Problems

11-15. McCall's Garden Supply has seen the following annual demand for lime bags over the past 11 years:

Year	Bags (thousands)	Year	Bags (thousands)
1	4	7	7
2	8	8	9
3	6	9	13
4	6	10	14
5	9	11	16
6	8		

(a) Develop 2-year, 3-year, and 4-year moving averages to forecast demand in year 12.

(b) Forecast demand with a 3-year weighted moving average in which demand in the most recent year is given a weight of 2 and demands in the other two years are each given a weight of 1.

(c) Forecast demand by using exponential smoothing with a smoothing constant of 0.4. Assume that the forecast for year 1 is 6,000 bags to begin the procedure.

(d) Which of the methods analyzed here would you use? Explain your answer.

11–16. Jeannette Phan is a college student who has just completed her junior year. The following table summarizes her grade point average (GPA) for each of the past nine semesters:

Year	Semester	GPA
Freshman	Fall	2.4
	Winter	2.9
	Spring	3.1
Sophomore	Fall	3.2
	Winter	3.0
	Spring	2.9
Junior	Fall	2.8
	Winter	3.6
	Spring	3.2

(a) Forecast Jeannette's GPA for the fall semester of her senior year by using a three-period moving average.

(b) Forecast Jeannette's GPA for the fall semester of her senior year by using exponential smoothing with $\alpha = 0.3$.

(c) Which of the two methods provides a more accurate forecast? Justify your answer.

(d) If you decide to use a three-period weighted moving average, find the optimal weights that would minimize MAPE. Is this method an improvement over the previous two methods?

11–17. Daily sales volume for Nilgiris Convenience Store is shown in the following table:

Day	Sales	Day	Sales
1	$622	6	$656
2	$418	7	$689
3	$608	8	$675
4	$752	9	$706
5	$588	10	$725

Develop two-day, three-day, and four-day moving averages to forecast the sales for each day. What is the forecast for day 11 in each case?

11–18. Consider the data given in Problem 11–17 for Nilgiris Convenience Store.

(a) If the store wants to use exponential smoothing to forecast the sales volume, what is the optimal value of α that would minimize MAPE? What is the forecast for day 11 using this model?

(b) If the store wants to use linear trend analysis to forecast the sales volume, what is the linear equation that best fits the data? What is the forecast for day 11 using this model?

(c) Which of the methods analyzed here and in Problem 11–17 would you use? Explain your answer.

11–19. The following table shows the number of Blu-ray DVD players that Electronic Depot has sold during the past 12 weeks:

Week	Sales	Week	Sales
1	22	7	24
2	27	8	25
3	30	9	22
4	21	10	30
5	33	11	38
6	28	12	37

Develop 2-week, 3-week, and 4-week moving averages to forecast the sales for each week. What is the forecast for week 13 in each case?

11–20. Consider the data given in Problem 11–19 for Blu-ray DVD player sales at Electronic Depot.

(a) If Electronic Depot decides to forecast sales by using a three-period weighted moving average, what are the optimal weights that minimize MAPE? What would be the week 13 forecast using these weights?

(b) If Electronic Depot decides to forecast sales by using exponential smoothing, what is the optimal value of α that minimizes MAPE? What would be the week 13 forecast using this procedure?

(c) Which of the methods analyzed here and in Problem 11–19 would you use? Explain your answer.

11–21. Sales of Hot-Blast heaters have grown steadily during the past five years, as shown in the following table:

Year	Sales
1	480
2	525
3	548
4	593
5	614

(a) Using exponential smoothing constants of 0.35, 0.65, and 0.95, develop forecasts for years 2 through 6. The sales manager had predicted, before the business started, that year 1's sales would be 440 air conditioners. Which smoothing constant gives the most accurate forecast?

(b) Use a three-year moving average forecasting model to forecast sales of heaters.

(c) Using linear trend analysis, develop a forecasting model for the sales of heaters.

(d) Which of the methods analyzed here would you use? Explain your answer.

11–22. Highland Automotive wishes to forecast the number of new cars that will be sold next week. The following table summarizes the number of new cars sold during each of the past 12 weeks:

Week	Number Sold	Week	Number Sold
1	22	7	28
2	26	8	26
3	23	9	29
4	27	10	29
5	21	11	27
6	25	12	31

(a) Provide a forecast by using a 3-week weighted moving average technique with weights 5, 3, and 1 (5 = most recent).

(b) Forecast sales by using an exponential smoothing model with $\alpha = 0.45$.

(c) Highland would like to forecast sales by using linear trend analysis. What is the linear equation that best fits the data?

(d) Which of the methods analyzed here would you use? Explain your answer.

11–23. The operations manager of a musical instrument distributor feels that demand for bass drums may be related to the number of television appearances by the popular rock group Green Shades during the preceding month. The manager has collected the data shown in the following table:

Demand	TV Appearances
3	4
6	5
7	8
5	7
10	9
9	6
8	6

(a) Graph these data to see whether a linear equation might describe the relationship between the group's television shows and bass drum sales.

(b) Use the least-squares regression method to derive a forecasting equation.

(c) What is your estimate for bass drum sales if Green Shades performed on TV four times last month?

11-24. Sales of industrial vacuum cleaners at Overholt Supply Co. over the past 13 months were as follows:

Month	Sales (thousands)	Month	Sales (thousands)
January	9	August	12
February	12	September	15
March	14	October	10
April	8	November	12
May	13	December	14
June	15	January	9
July	9		

(a) Using a moving average with three periods, determine the demand for vacuum cleaners for next February.
(b) Using a three-period weighted moving average with weights 3, 2, and 1 (3 = most recent), determine the demand for vacuum cleaners for February.
(c) Evaluate and comment on the accuracy of each of these models.

11-25. Calls to a college emergency hotline for the past 29 months are as follows (with the earliest month shown first): 50, 35, 25, 40, 45, 35, 20, 30, 35, 20, 15, 40, 55, 35, 25, 55, 55, 40, 35, 60, 75, 50, 40, 42, 51, 22, 38, 45, and 65.
(a) Assuming an initial forecast of 55 calls for month 1, use exponential smoothing with $\alpha = 0.15$, 0.65, and 0.95 to forecast calls for each month. What is the forecast for the 30th month in each case?
(b) Actual calls during the 30th month were 85. Which smoothing constant provides a superior forecast?

11-26. Passenger miles flown on I-Go Airlines, a commuter firm serving the Boston hub, are as follows for the past 12 weeks:

Week	Miles (thousands)	Week	Miles (thousands)
1	21	7	24
2	25	8	22
3	23	9	26
4	27	10	24
5	22	11	19
6	20	12	26

(a) Assuming an initial forecast of 22,000 miles for week 1, use exponential smoothing with $\alpha = 0.3$, 0.6, and 0.8 to forecast miles for weeks 2 through 12. What is the forecast for week 13 in each case?

(b) Evaluate and comment on the accuracy of each of these models.

11–27. Rental income at the Walsh Real Estate Company for the period February-July has been as follows:

Month	Income (thousands)
February	$83.0
March	$81.5
April	$77.8
May	$84.7
June	$84.3
July	$85.8

(a) Use exponential smoothing with α = 0.2 and 0.4 to forecast August's income. Assume that the initial forecast for February is $78,000.
(b) Which smoothing constant provides a better forecast? Justify your answer.
(c) Determine the optimal value of α that minimizes MAPE.

11–28. Commuter ridership in Athens, Greece, during the summer months is believed to be heavily tied to the number of tourists visiting the city. During the past 12 years, the data in the table for this problem have been obtained.

(a) Use trend analysis to forecast ridership in years 13, 14, and 15. How well does the model fit the data?
(b) Draw the relationship between the number of tourists and ridership. Is a linear model reasonable?
(c) Develop a linear regression relationship between the number of tourists and ridership.
(d) What is the expected ridership if 10 million tourists visit the city next year?

Year	Number of Tourists (millions)	Ridership (hundreds of thousands)
1	11	14
2	6	9
3	10	12
4	8	14
5	18	24
6	19	26
7	20	23
8	16	19
9	18	26
10	24	43
11	19	33
12	11	16

11–29. Becky Schalkoff, a New Orleans criminal psychologist, specializes in treating patients who are phobic, afraid to leave their homes. The following table indicates how many patients Dr. Schalkoff has seen each year for the past 10 years. It also indicates the crime rate (robberies per 1,000 population) in New Orleans during each year.

Year	Number of Patients	Crime Rate
1	30	67.3
2	27	70.6
3	34	82.4
4	35	84.7
5	34	90.1
6	49	98.0
7	54	110.1
8	48	103.8
9	52	112.3
10	55	125.2

Using trend analysis, how many patients do you think Dr. Schalkoff will see in years 11, 12, and 13? How well does the model fit the data?

11–30. Consider the patient data for Dr. Schalkoff given in Problem 11–29.
(a) Draw the relationship between the crime rate and Dr. Schalkoff's patient load. Is a linear model between these two variables reasonable?
(b) Apply linear regression to study the relationship between the crime rate and Dr. Schalkoff's patient load.
(c) If the crime rate increases to 140.2 in year 11, how many patients will Dr. Schalkoff treat?
(d) If the crime rate drops to 98.6, what is the patient projection?

11–31. In the past two years at William Middleton's tire dealership, 125 and 175 high-performance radials, respectively, were sold in fall, 225 and 275 were sold in winter, 75 and 90 were sold in spring, and 210 and 225 were sold in summer. With a major expansion planned, Mr. Middleton projects sales next year to increase to 900 high-performance radials. What will the seasonalized demand be each season for these tires?

11–32. Management of Remington's Department Store has used time-series extrapolation to forecast retail sales for the next four quarters. The sales estimates are $130,000, $150,000, $170,000, and $190,000 for the respective quarters. Seasonal indices for the four quarters have been found to be 1.25, 0.95, 0.75, and 1.05, respectively. Compute the seasonalized sales forecast for each quarter.

11–33. Charles Brandon is thinking about investing in the Purple Arrow Company, which makes central air conditioning units. The company has been in business for over 50 years, and Charles believes it is very stable. Based on his investing knowledge and experience, Charles believes that the dividend paid out by the company is a function of earnings per share (EPS). Using the Internet, Charles has been able to find the EPS and dividend per share paid by Purple Arrow for each of the past 10 years, as shown in the following table:

Year	EPS	Dividend Per Share
1	$2.34	$0.29
2	$1.70	$0.14
3	$1.89	$0.19
4	$1.94	$0.16
5	$1.51	$0.05
6	$2.04	$0.39
7	$1.72	$0.11
8	$1.98	$0.27
9	$1.89	$0.19
10	$1.57	$0.09

(a) Develop a regression model to predict the dividend per share based on EPS.
(b) Identify and interpret the R^2 value.
(c) The EPS next year is projected be $1.33. What is the expected dividend?

11–34. Thirteen students entered the undergraduate business program at Longstreet College two years ago. The table for this problem indicates what their GPAs were after they were in the program for two years and what each student scored on the SAT math exam when he or she was in high school.

(a) Is there a meaningful relationship between GPAs and SAT math scores? Justify your answer.
(b) If Gwen gets a 490 SAT math score, what is her predicted GPA?
(c) If Jarvis gets a perfect 800 SAT math score, what is his predicted GPA? Is it appropriate to use this model to predict Jarvis's score? Why or why not?

Student	Sat Math	GPA
A	460	3.00
B	440	3.03
C	630	3.10
D	730	3.55
E	650	3.76
F	430	3.98
G	460	2.25
H	520	2.63
I	770	3.32
J	540	2.09
K	650	2.85
L	750	4.00
M	410	1.70

11-35. Sruti Singh is shopping for a used Volkswagen Golf and feels that there is a relationship between the mileage and market value of the car. The following table provides data on previous car sales from the local area:

Car	Mileage	Market Value	Age (years)
1	11,600	$14,200	1
2	22,800	$14,000	1
3	35,000	$10,500	3
4	42,700	$ 9,300	3
5	54,500	$12,800	4
6	58,200	$10,900	5
7	66,800	$ 9,500	7
8	73,100	$ 7,900	6
9	77,500	$ 6,200	8
10	85,700	$ 7,500	9

(a) Develop a simple regression model to predict the market value of a Volkswagen Golf based on its mileage.
(b) What percentage of the market value variation is explained by the mileage variable?
(c) Sruti has found a car with 46,700 miles. Construct a 95% confidence interval for the market value of this car.

11-36. Sruti Singh (see Problem 11-35) would like to investigate the effect of adding the age of the car (in years) to the regression model. The table in Problem 11-35 includes the ages of the original 10 cars.
(a) Develop a multiple regression model to predict the market value of a Volkswagen Golf based on its mileage and age.
(b) What percentage of the selling price variation is explained by this expanded model?
(c) The car that Sruti found with 46,700 miles is 5 years old. What is the revised 95% confidence interval for the market value of this car? Explain why this interval is different from the one in Problem 11-35(c).

11-37. Callaway College is a small business school that offers an MBA program. The main entrance criterion for admission to the MBA program is the Common Business Admission Test (CBAT) score. The following table provides the GPAs of 12 students who have graduated recently, along with their CBAT scores and ages:

Student	GPA	CBAT	Age
1	3.70	690	34
2	3.00	610	29
3	3.25	480	24
4	4.00	740	39
5	3.52	580	30

Student	GPA	CBAT	Age
6	2.83	460	27
7	3.80	570	35
8	4.00	620	42
9	3.65	750	24
10	3.47	510	30
11	3.33	550	27
12	3.75	700	28

(a) Develop a simple regression model to predict the GPA of a student based on his or her CBAT score
(b) Identify and interpret the R^2 value.
(c) A new graduate student has a CBAT score of 630. Construct a 90% confidence interval for this student's predicted GPA.

11–38. Callaway College (see Problem 11–37) would like to investigate the effect of adding the age of the student to the regression model. The table in Problem 11–37 includes the ages of the original 12 students.
(a) Develop a multiple regression model to predict the GPA of a student based on his or her CBAT score and age.
(b) Identify and interpret the R^2 value for this expanded regression model.
(c) The new student with a CBAT score of 630 is 29 years old. What is the revised 90% confidence interval for this student's predicted GPA? Explain why this interval is different from the one in Problem 11–37(c).

11–39. Kurt's Hardware Store advertises and sells snow blowers each season. The following table provides the annual demand, level of advertising, in dollars, and snowfall, in inches, for the past eight years:

Year	Demand (units)	Advertising	Snowfall (inches)
1	41	$4,000	82
2	38	$3,500	64
3	26	$1,800	52
4	43	$2,800	60
5	33	$3,000	58
6	30	$2,400	50
7	34	$2,600	60
8	37	$2,200	53

(a) Develop a simple regression model to predict the demand for snow blowers based on the number of advertising dollars spent.
(b) What percentage of the demand variation is explained by the level of advertising?
(c) Next year's advertising budget is $2,600. What is the predicted demand for snow blowers?

11-40. Kurt's Hardware Store (see Problem 11-39) would like to investigate the effect of adding annual snowfall to the regression model. The table in Problem 11-39 includes the annual snowfall (in inches) for the past eight years.
 (a) Develop a multiple regression model to predict the demand for snow blowers based on the advertising budget and the amount of snowfall.
 (b) What percentage of the demand variation is explained by this expanded model?
 (c) What is the predicted demand for snow blowers with an advertising budget of $2,600 and expected snowfall of 65 inches?

11-41. The Fowler Martial Arts Academy trains young boys and girls in self-defense. Joan Fowler, the owner of the academy, notes that monthly revenue is higher when school is in session but quite low when school is out (because many children are away on vacation or at summer camp). She has researched revenues for the past four years and obtained the information shown in the following table:

Month	Year 1	Year 2	Year 3	Year 4
January	$59,042	$57,495	$56,583	$55,658
February	$62,659	$62,622	$66,438	$67,164
March	$22,879	$24,273	$27,766	$27,795
April	$29,946	$30,492	$31,600	$30,667
May	$26,839	$28,237	$29,589	$31,962
June	$19,134	$17,893	$20,115	$21,096
July	$20,051	$21,126	$19,324	$22,778
August	$19,625	$22,876	$23,486	$23,144
September	$19,925	$22,641	$24,719	$26,601
October	$58,435	$60,796	$60,666	$61,385
November	$87,705	$87,815	$86,693	$88,581
December	$77,430	$78,711	$80,056	$81,048

Decompose Joan's data by using a multiplicative model. Use the model to forecast revenues for year 5. Comment on the validity of the model.

11-42. In addition to his day job as an engineer, Luis Garcia runs a small ethnic grocery store. The shop stocks food items from southeast Asian countries and caters to the large population of people from this region who live in Luis's community. Luis wants to develop a quantitative model to forecast sales. His sales data (in thousands) for the past 16 quarters are as shown in the following table:

Quarter	Year 1	Year 2	Year 3	Year 4
Quarter 1	$42.9	$43.8	$49.0	$51.3
Quarter 2	$48.5	$50.3	$54.2	$58.2
Quarter 3	$54.1	$57.8	$59.3	$62.9
Quarter 4	$74.1	$79.8	$83.3	$88.5

Develop a multiplicative decomposition model for Luis's sales data. Use the model to forecast revenues for year 4. Comment on the validity of the model.

11–43. The GNP for each quarter of the past four years is shown in the following table:

Year	Quarter	GNP (BILLIONS)
1	1	$ 9,027
	2	$ 9,092
	3	$ 9,194
	4	$ 9,367
2	1	$ 9,505
	2	$ 9,588
	3	$ 9,726
	4	$ 9,938
3	1	$10,063
	2	$10,238
	3	$10,285
	4	$10,375
4	1	$10,430
	2	$10,473
	3	$10,501
	4	$10,580

(a) Find the optimal value of α that would minimize MAPE for the exponential smoothing model.
(b) What is the linear trend equation that best fits the data? Forecast the GNP for the first quarter of year 5 by using this equation.
(c) Forecast the GNP for the first quarter of year 5 by using a four-period moving average.
(d) Which of these methods is most appropriate to use? Justify your answer.

11–44. Using the data from Problem 11–43, forecast the GNP for each quarter of year 5 by using the multiplicative decomposition model. What is the MAPE value for this model?

11–45. The average price per gallon of gasoline in major U.S. cities for each month during a three-year period are shown in the following table:

Month	Year 1	Year 2	Year 3
January	$2.972	$3.301	$3.472
February	$2.955	$3.369	$3.484
March	$2.991	$3.541	$3.447
April	$3.117	$3.506	$3.564
May	$3.178	$3.498	$3.729
June	$3.148	$3.617	$3.640
July	$3.189	$3.593	$3.482
August	$3.255	$3.510	$3.427
September	$3.280	$3.582	$3.531

Month	Year 1	Year 2	Year 3
October	$3.274	$3.559	$3.362
November	$3.264	$3.555	$3.263
December	$3.298	$3.489	$3.131

(a) Using exponential smoothing with $\alpha = 0.45$, what is the gasoline price forecast for January of year 4?

(b) What is the linear trend equation that best fits the data? Forecast the average gasoline price for January of year 4 by using this equation.

(c) Which method is more accurate?

11-46. Using the data from Problem 11-45, forecast the average gasoline price for each month in year 4 by using the multiplicative decomposition model. What is the MAPE value for this model?

11-47. Quarterly sales figures for the Cavill Pump Company, in thousands, for the past four years are shown in the following table:

Quarter	Year 1	Year 2	Year 3	Year 4
1	$263	$312	$283	$319
2	$300	$323	$320	$303
3	$245	$298	$365	$339
4	$381	$390	$398	$368

(a) Forecast the demand for the first quarter of year 5 by using a four-period moving average model.

(b) What is the linear trend equation that best fits the data? Forecast the demand for the first quarter of year 5 by using this equation.

(c) Which method is more accurate?

11-48. Consider the data from Problem 11-47.

(a) Develop a sales forecast for each quarter in year 5 by using the multiplicative decomposition model.

(b) Repeat the computations by using an additive decomposition model.

(c) Which decomposition model is more accurate? Explain your answer.

11-49. The following table shows the quarterly demand, in thousands of cases, for a national beer distributor over the past 4 years:

Quarter	Year 1	Year 2	Year 3	Year 4
1	294	335	433	280
2	499	507	516	524
3	437	529	501	515
4	344	285	482	530

(a) Forecast the demand for the first quarter of year 5 by using a four-period moving average model.

(b) Forecast the demand for the first quarter of year 5 by using an exponential smoothing model with $\alpha = 0.4$.

(c) Which method is more accurate?

11–50. Consider the data from Problem 11–49.

(a) Forecast the demand for beer for each quarter in year 5 by using the multiplicative decomposition model.

(b) Repeat the computations by using an additive decomposition model.

(c) Which decomposition model is more accurate? Explain your answer.

11–51. You can compute the simple linear regression values of slope and intercept for a data set by using explicit Excel functions SLOPE and INTERCEPT. In fact, you can even use the single function FORECAST to make a forecast into the future along a regression line without the need of typing in a formula for $\hat{Y} = b_0 + b_1 X$. The respective syntax for these three functions are: SLOPE(range of known Y_s, range of known X_s), INTERCEPT(range of known Y_s, range of known X_s), and FORECAST(F, range of known Y_s, range of known X_s), where the Y_s are the dependent variables, the X_s are the independent variables, and F is the input for which you want a forecast.

Jianli Hu Flowers has experienced a demand for roses (in dozens) of 50, 52, 69, 74, 79, and 80 for January through June of this year.

(a) Use Excel's SLOPE and INTERCEPT functions to estimate the slope and intercept, respectively, of this demand pattern.

(b) Use Excel's FORECAST function to predict the demand for September of this year. Verify your prediction by using your slope and intercept values.

11–52. Suppose that you are using exponential smoothing method described in this chapter to forecast sales, and you know that sales will be decreasing every period for the foreseeable future. What value of alpha would be best (produce the smallest errors)?

11–53. In Figure 11.35, we discovered a potential multicollinearity problem. It appeared that home size was no longer a significant input given the presence of land area.

(a) Run a single regression based on just land area. What are the coefficients?

(b) What is the R^2 value for this model? How does it compare with the adjusted R^2 value for the multiple regression model shown in Figure 11.35? Which model appears to be a better predictor of the future of housing prices for this data set?

11–54. A limitation of using ExcelModules for some of the forecasting models described in this chapter is that the program creates a custom spreadsheet that covers a specific length of time. Thus, as actual values for new months into the future are realized, a new spreadsheet would need to be created, and all the old data would need to be reentered.

Consider Figure 11.12. Modify the program to account for 24 more future periods. Use an IF function to have the cells in the error columns appear only if the cell containing the actual value in column B for that particular month is not empty. For example, you could check to see if cell B19 has a value by using the ISBLANK(B19) function. Then if the cell is blank, place "" into the error cell; otherwise place the answer to the applicable error formula. Note that by doing this, the AVERAGE formulas at the bottom of your sheet will still be valid because they will ignore all cells containing "". Finally, eliminate the "Next period" cells (currently in row 22) because the reference would need to change with each new month. Instead, have the forecast (column D) value appear for the month following the latest month that has an actual value in column B by using a similar IF function as just described.

11–55. You can compute the multiple linear regression values for the intercept and each slope for a data set by using explicit Excel function LINEST. The syntax for this function is: LINEST(range of known Y_s, range of known X_s), where the Y_s are the dependent variables and the X_s are the independent variables. LINEST is an example of an "array function" in Excel because it returns more than one value (in this case the intercept plus one or more slopes). An array function in Excel is entered by selecting a set of contiguous cells across a row and pressing <Ctrl><Shift><Enter> instead of just <Enter>. For the LINEST function, select the number of cells equal to the number of independent variables + 1. The values will appear in reverse order; that is, the first cell will contain the slope of the last variable from the input range, continuing until the next-to-last cell that contains the slope of the first variable from the input range, finishing with the value of the intercept placed in the last cell.

(a) Use the LINEST function to calculate the regression coefficients for the data from the first 10 students in the table from Problem 11–37. CBAT and AGE are the independent variables, and GPA is the dependent variable.

(b) By cell-referencing your coefficients from part (a) enter an Excel formula to predict the GPA of a 31-year-old student with a CBAT of 720 and a 45-year-old student with a CBAT of 590.

11–56. Jacquie Welkener owns a company that manufactures sailboats. Actual demand for Jacquie's sailboats during each of the past two years was as follows:

	YEAR	
SEASON	1	2
Winter	1,400	1,200
Spring	1,500	1,400
Summer	1,000	2,100
Fall	600	750

Jacquie has forecasted that annual demand for her sailboats in year 3 will equal 5,600 sailboats. Based on this data and the seasonality model based on *average* value as described at the end of Section 11.6, what will the demand level be for Jacquie's sailboats in the spring of year 3?

11-57. Suppose that you use a weighted moving average forecasting method with weights of 12, 30, and 20, for one period ago, two periods ago, and three periods ago, respectively. If January's demand was 100 units, February's demand was 150 units, March's demand was 200 units, and April's demand was 300 units, what should be the forecast for May?

11-58. Consider the sales data from Problem 11-24.
  (a) Prepare separate moving average forecasts using 2, 3, 4, 5, 6, 7, and 8 months.
  (b) Compare your methods from part (a) based on MAD. *Note: For a valid comparison, the MAD should be based only on the months for which all your methods can make a forecast. For example, forecast errors in June should not be included in the MAD calculations because, with the given data, a moving average forecast can only be made for June based on 5 or fewer months included in the moving average.*

Appendix A
Probability Concepts and Applications

A.1 Fundamental Concepts

There are two basic principles in the mathematics of probability:
1. The probability, P, of any event or state of nature occurring is greater than or equal to 0 and less than or equal to 1. That is,

$$0 \leq P(\text{event}) \leq 1 \tag{A–1}$$

A probability of 0 indicates that an event is never expected to occur. A probability of 1 means that an event is always expected to occur.

2. The sum of the simple probabilities for all possible outcomes of an activity must equal 1. Both of these concepts are illustrated in Example 1.

Example 1: Two Laws of Probability Demand for white latex paint at Diversey Paint and Supply has always been 0, 1, 2, 3, or 4 gallons per day. (There are no other possible outcomes, and when one occurs, no other can.) Over the past 200 working days, the owner notes the following frequencies of demand:

Demand (gallons)	Number of Days
0	40
1	80
2	50
3	20
4	10
	Total 200

If this past distribution is a good indicator of future sales, we can find the probability of each possible outcome occurring in the future by converting the data into percentages of the total:

Demand	Probability
0	$0.20 \, (= 40/200)$
1	$0.40 \, (= 80/200)$
2	$0.25 \, (= 50/200)$
3	$0.10 \, (= 20/200)$
4	$0.05 \, (= 10/200)$
	Total $1.00 \, (= 200/200)$

Thus, the probability that sales are 2 gallons of paint on any given day is $P(2 \text{ gallons}) = 0.25 = 25\%$. The probability of any level of sales must be greater than or equal to 0 and less than or equal to 1. Since 0, 1, 2, 3, and 4 gallons exhaust all possible events or outcomes, the sum of their probability values must equal 1.

Types of Probability

There are two different ways to determine probability: the objective approach and the subjective approach.

Objective Probability Example 1 provides an illustration of objective probability assessment. The probability of any paint demand level is the relative frequency of occurrence of that demand in a large number of trial observations (200 days, in this case). In general:

$$P(\text{event}) = \frac{\text{Number of occurrences of the event}}{\text{Total number of trials or outcomes}}$$

Objective probability can also be set using what is called the classical, or logical, approach. Without performing a series of trials, we can often logically determine what the probabilities of various events should be. For example, the probability of tossing a fair coin once and getting a head is

$$P(\text{head}) = \frac{1}{2} \quad \begin{array}{l} \leftarrow \text{number of ways of getting a head} \\ \leftarrow \text{number of possible outcomes (head or tail)} \end{array}$$

Similarly, the probability of drawing a spade out of a deck of 52 playing cards can be logically set as

$$P(\text{spade}) = \frac{13}{52} \quad \begin{array}{l} \leftarrow \text{number of chances of drawing a spade} \\ \leftarrow \text{number of possible outcomes} \end{array}$$

$$= \frac{1}{4} = 0.25 = 25\%$$

Subjective Probability When logic and past history are not appropriate, probability values can be assessed *subjectively*. The accuracy of subjective probabilities depends on the experience and judgment of the person making the estimates. A number of probability values cannot be determined unless the subjective approach is used. What is the probability that the price of gasoline will be more than $4 in the next few years? What is the probability that the U.S. economy will be in a severe depression in 2030? What is the probability that you will be president of a major corporation within 20 years?

There are several methods for making subjective probability assessments. Opinion polls can be used to help in determining subjective probabilities for possible election returns and potential political candidates. In some cases, experience and judgment must be used in making subjective assessments of probability values. A production manager, for example, might believe that the probability of manufacturing a new product without a single defect is 0.85. In the Delphi method, a panel of experts is assembled to make their predictions of the future. This approach is discussed in Chapter 11.

A.2 Mutually Exclusive and Collectively Exhaustive Events

Events are said to be *mutually exclusive* if only one of the events can occur on any one trial. They are called *collectively exhaustive* if the list of outcomes includes every possible outcome. Many common experiences involve events that have both of these properties. In tossing a coin, for example, the possible outcomes are a head or a tail. Because both of them cannot occur on any one toss, the outcomes head and tail are mutually exclusive. Since obtaining a head and a tail represent every possible outcome, they are also collectively exhaustive.

Example 2: Rolling a Die Rolling a die is a simple experiment that has six possible outcomes, each listed in the following table with its corresponding probability:

Outcome of Roll	Probability
1	1/6
2	1/6
3	1/6
4	1/6
5	1/6
6	1/6
	Total 1

These events are both mutually exclusive (on any roll, only one of the six events can occur) and also collectively exhaustive (one of them must occur and hence they total in probability to 1).

Example 3: Drawing a Card You are asked to draw one card from a deck of 52 playing cards. Using a logical probability assessment, it is easy to set some of the relationships, such as

$$P(\text{drawing a 7}) = \frac{4}{52} = \frac{1}{13}$$

$$P(\text{drawing a heart}) = \frac{13}{52} = \frac{1}{4}$$

We also see that these events (drawing a 7 and drawing a heart) are *not* mutually exclusive because a 7 of hearts can be drawn. They are also *not* collectively exhaustive because there are other cards in the deck besides 7s and hearts.

You can test your understanding of these concepts by going through the following cases:

Draws	Mutually Exclusive?	Collectively Exhaustive?
1. Draw a spade and a club	Yes	No
2. Draw a face card and a number card	Yes	Yes
3. Draw an ace and a 3	Yes	No
4. Draw a club and a nonclub	Yes	Yes
5. Draw a 5 and a diamond	No	No
6. Draw a red card and a diamond	No	No

Adding Mutually Exclusive Events

Often, we are interested in whether one event *or* a second event will occur. When these two events are mutually exclusive, the law of addition is simply as follows:

$$P(\text{event } A \text{ or event } B) = P(\text{event } A) + P(\text{event } B)$$

or, more briefly,

$$P(A \text{ or } B) = P(A) + P(B) \tag{A-2}$$

For example, we just saw that the events of drawing a spade or drawing a club out of a deck of cards are mutually exclusive. Since $P(\text{spade}) = \frac{13}{52}$ and $P(\text{club}) = \frac{13}{52}$, the probability of drawing either a spade or a club is

$$\begin{aligned} P(\text{spade or club}) &= P(\text{spade}) + P(\text{club}) \\ &= \frac{13}{52} + \frac{13}{52} \\ &= \frac{26}{52} = \frac{1}{2} = 0.50 = 50\% \end{aligned}$$

The *Venn diagram* in Figure A.1 depicts the probability of the occurrence of mutually exclusive events.

$P(A \text{ or } B) = P(A) + P(B)$

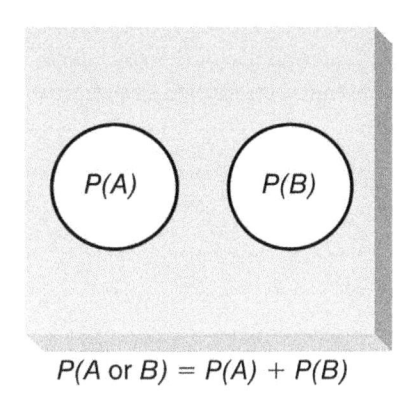

Figure A.1: Addition Law for Events that Are Mutually Exclusive

Law of Addition for Events that Are Not Mutually Exclusive
When two events are not mutually exclusive, Equation A–2 must be modified to account for double counting. The correct equation reduces the probability by subtracting the chance of both events occurring together:

$$P(\text{event } A \text{ or event } B) = P(\text{event } A) + P(\text{event } B)$$
$$- P(\text{event } A \text{ and event } B \text{ both occurring})$$

This can be expressed in shorter form as

$$P(A \text{ or } B) = P(A) + P(B) - P(A \text{ and } B) \qquad \textbf{(A–3)}$$

Figure A.2 illustrates this concept of subtracting the probability of outcomes that are common to both events. When events are mutually exclusive, the area of overlap, called the *intersection*, is 0, as shown in Figure A.1.

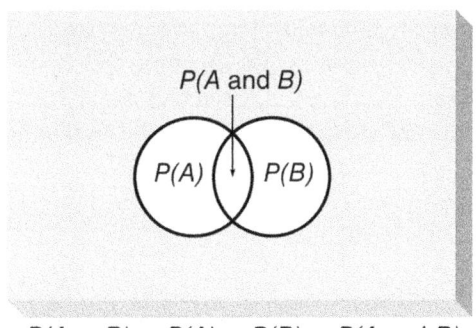

$P(A \text{ or } B) = P(A) + P(B) - P(A \text{ and } B)$

Figure A.2: Addition Law for Events that Are Not Mutually Exclusive

Let us consider the events drawing a 5 and drawing a diamond out of the card deck. These events are not mutually exclusive, so Equation A-3 must be applied to compute the probability of either a 5 or a diamond being drawn:

$$P(\text{five or diamond}) = P(\text{five}) + P(\text{diamond}) - P(\text{five and diamond})$$

$$= \frac{4}{52} + \frac{13}{52} - \frac{1}{52}$$

$$= \frac{16}{52} = \frac{4}{13}$$

A.3 Statistically Independent Events

Events can either be independent events or dependent events. When they are *independent*, the occurrence of one event has no effect on the probability of occurrence of the second event. Let us examine four sets of events and determine which are independent:

1. (a) Your education
   (b) Your income level } Dependent events. Can you explain why?
2. (a) Draw a jack of hearts from a full 52-card deck
   (b) Draw a jack of clubs from a full 52-card deck } Independent events
3. (a) Chicago Cubs win the National League pennant
   (b) Chicago Cubs win the World Series } Dependent events
4. (a) Snow in Santiago, Chile
   (b) Rain in Tel Aviv, Israel } Independent events

The three types of probability under both statistical independence and statistical dependence are (1) marginal, (2) joint, and (3) conditional. When events are independent, these three are very easy to compute, as we shall see.

A marginal (or a *simple*) probability is just the probability of an event occurring. For example, if we toss a fair die, the marginal probability of a 2 landing face up is $P(\text{die is a 2}) = \frac{1}{6} = 0.166$. Because each separate toss is an independent event (i.e., what we get on the first toss has absolutely no effect on any later tosses), the marginal probability for each possible outcome is $\frac{1}{6}$.

The joint probability of two or more independent events occurring is the product of their marginal or simple probabilities. This can be written as

$$P(AB) = P(A) \times P(B) \tag{A-4}$$

where

$P(AB)$ = joint probability of events A and B occurring together, or one after the other

$P(A)$ = marginal probability of event A

$P(B)$ = marginal probability of event B

The probability, for example, of tossing a 6 on the first roll of a die and a 2 on the second roll is

$$P(6 \text{ on first and 2 on second roll})$$
$$= P(\text{tossing a 6}) \times P(\text{tossing a 2})$$
$$= \frac{1}{6} \times \frac{1}{6} = \frac{1}{36}$$
$$= 0.028$$

The third type, conditional probability, is expressed as $P(B|A)$, or "the probability of event B, given that event A has occurred." Similarly, $P(A|B)$ would mean "the conditional probability of event A, given that event B has taken place." Since events are independent, the occurrence of one in no way affects the outcome of another, $P(A|B) = P(A)$ and $P(B|A) = P(B)$.

Example 4: Probabilities When Events Are Independent A bucket contains three black balls and seven green balls. We draw a ball from the bucket, replace it, and draw a second ball. We can determine the probability of each of the following events occurring:

1. A black ball is drawn on the first draw:

$$P(B) = 0.30$$

(This is a marginal probability.)

2. Two green balls are drawn:

$$P(GG) = P(G) \times P(G) = (0.7)(0.7) = 0.49$$

(This is a joint probability for two independent events.)

3. A black ball is drawn on the second draw if the first draw is green:

$$P(B|G) = P(B) = 0.30$$

(This is a conditional probability but equal to the marginal probability because the two draws are independent events.)

4. A green ball is drawn on the second draw if the first draw was green:

$$P(G|G) = P(G) = 0.70$$

(This is a conditional probability as above.)

A.4 Statistically Dependent Events

When events are statistically dependent, the occurrence of one event affects the probability of occurrence of some other event. Marginal, conditional, and joint probabilities exist under dependence as they did under independence, but the form of the latter two are changed.

A marginal probability is computed exactly as it was for independent events. Again, the marginal probability of the event A occurring is denoted as $P(A)$.

Calculating a conditional probability under dependence is somewhat more involved than it is under independence. The formula for the conditional probability of A, given that event B has taken place, is now stated as

$$P(A|B) = \frac{P(AB)}{P(B)} \tag{A-5}$$

The use of this important formula, often referred to as *Bayes' law*, or Bayes' theorem, is best understood with an example.

Example 5: Probabilities When Events Are Dependent Assume that we have an urn containing 10 balls, as follows:
- 4 are white (W) and lettered (L)
- 2 are white (W) and numbered (N)
- 3 are yellow (Y) and lettered (L)
- 1 is yellow (Y) and numbered (N)

You randomly draw a ball from the urn and see that it is yellow. What, then, we may ask, is the probability that the ball is lettered? (See Figure A.3.)

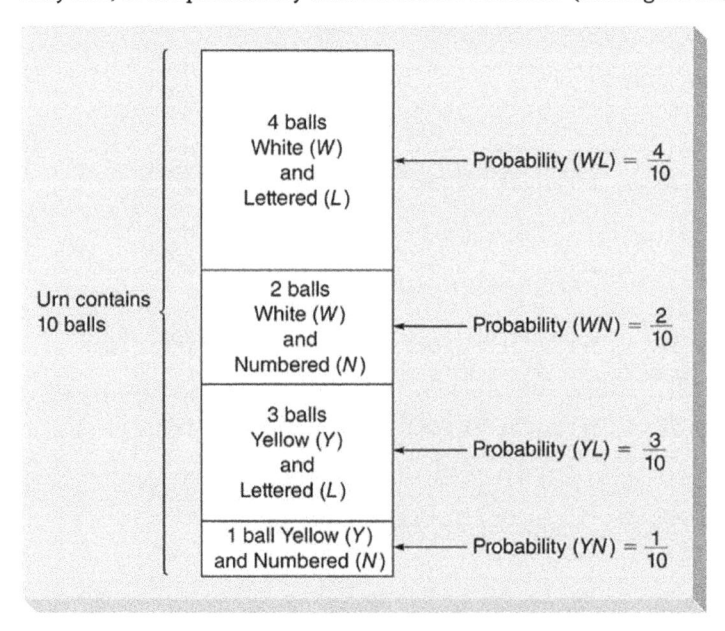

Figure A.3: Dependent Events of Example 5

Because there are 10 balls, it is a simple matter to tabulate a series of useful probabilities:

$$P(WL) = \frac{4}{10} = 0.4 \qquad P(YL) = \frac{3}{10} = 0.3$$

$$P(WN) = \frac{2}{10} = 0.2 \qquad P(YN) = \frac{1}{10} = 0.1$$

$$P(W) = \frac{6}{10} = 0.6, \text{ or } P(W) = P(WL) + P(WN) = 0.4 + 0.2 = 0.6$$

$$P(L) = \frac{7}{10} = 0.7, \text{ or } P(L) = P(WL) + P(YL) = 0.4 + 0.3 = 0.7$$

$$P(Y) = \frac{4}{10} = 0.4, \text{ or } P(Y) = P(YL) + P(YN) = 0.3 + 0.1 = 0.4$$

$$P(N) = \frac{3}{10} = 0.3, \text{ or } P(N) = P(WN) + P(YN) = 0.2 + 0.1 = 0.3$$

We can now apply Bayes' law to calculate the conditional probability that the ball drawn is lettered, given that it is yellow:

$$P(L|Y) = \frac{P(YL)}{P(Y)} = \frac{0.3}{0.4} = 0.75$$

This equation shows that we divided the probability of yellow and lettered balls (3 out of 10) by the probability of yellow balls (4 out of 10). There is a 0.75 probability that the yellow ball that you drew is lettered.

Recall that the formula for a joint probability under statistical independence was simply $P(AB) = P(A) \times P(B)$. When events are *dependent*, however, the joint probability is derived from Bayes' conditional formula. Equation A-6 reads "the joint probability of events A and B occurring is equal to the conditional probability of event A, given that B occurred, multiplied by the probability of event B":

$$P(AB) = P(A|B) \times P(B) \tag{A-6}$$

We can use this formula to verify the joint probability that $P(YL) = 0.3$, which was obtained by inspection in Example 5, by multiplying $P(L|Y)$ times $P(Y)$:

$$P(YL) = P(L|Y) \times P(Y) = (0.75)(0.4) = 0.3$$

Example 6: Joint Probabilities When Events Are Dependent Your stockbroker informs you that if the stock market reaches the 25,000-point level by January, there is a 0.70 probability that Tubeless Electronics will go up in value. Your own feeling is that there is only a 40% chance of the market average reaching 25,000 points by January. Can you calculate the probability that *both* the stock market will reach 25,000 points *and* the price of Tubeless Electronics will go up?

Let M represent the event of the stock market reaching the 25,000 level, and let T be the event that Tubeless goes up in value. Then

$$P(MT) = P(T|M) \times P(M) = (0.70)(0.40) = 0.28$$

Thus, there is only a 28% chance that *both* events will occur.

A.5 Revising Probabilities with Bayes' Theorem

Bayes' theorem can also be used to incorporate additional information as it is made available and to help create revised, or posterior, probabilities. This means that we can take new or recent data and then revise and improve upon our prior probability estimates for an event (see Figure A.4).

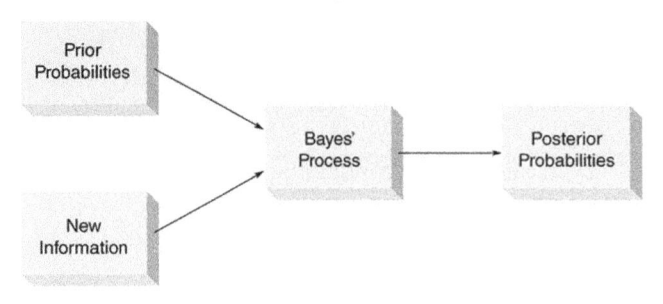

Figure A.4: Using Bayes' Process

Let's consider the following example.

Example 7: Posterior Probabilities A cup contains a pair of dice that are identical in appearance. One, however, is fair (unbiased) and the other is loaded (biased). The probability of rolling a 3 on the fair die is $\frac{1}{6}$, or 0.166. The probability of tossing the same number on the loaded die is 0.60.

We have no idea which die is which, but we select one by chance and toss it. The result is a 3. Given this additional piece of information, can we find the (revised) probability that the die rolled was fair? Can we determine the probability that it was the loaded die that was rolled?

The answer to these questions is yes, and we do so by using the formula for joint probability under statistical dependence and Bayes' theorem. First, we take stock of the information and probabilities available. We know, for example, that because we randomly selected the die to roll, the probability of it being fair or loaded is 0.50:

$$P(\text{fair}) = 0.50 \qquad P(\text{loaded}) = 0.50$$

We also know that

$$P(3|\text{fair}) = 0.166 \qquad P(3|\text{loaded}) = 0.60$$

Next, we compute joint probabilities $P(3 \text{ and fair})$ and $P(3 \text{ and loaded})$ using the formula $P(AB) = P(A|B) \times P(B)$:

$$P(3 \text{ and fair}) = P(3|\text{fair}) \times P(\text{fair})$$
$$= (0.166)(0.50) = 0.083$$
$$P(3 \text{ and loaded}) = P(3|\text{loaded}) \times P(\text{loaded})$$
$$= (0.60)(0.50) = 0.300$$

A 3 can occur in combination with the state "fair die" or in combination with the state "loaded die." The sum of their probabilities gives the unconditional or marginal probability of a 3 on the toss, namely, $P(3) = 0.083 + 0.300 = 0.383$.

If a 3 does occur, and if we do not know which die it came from, the probability that the die rolled was the fair one is

$$P(\text{fair}|3) = \frac{P(\text{fair and 3})}{P(3)} = \frac{0.083}{0.383} = 0.22$$

The probability that the die rolled was loaded is

$$P(\text{loaded}|3) = \frac{P(\text{loaded and 3})}{P(3)} = \frac{0.300}{0.383} = 0.78$$

These two conditional probabilities are called the *revised*, or *posterior*, *probabilities* for the next roll of the die.

Before the die was rolled in the preceding example, the best we could say was that there was a 50–50 chance that it was fair (0.50 probability) and a 50–50 chance that it was loaded. After one roll of the die, however, we are able to revise our prior probability estimates. The new posterior estimate is that there is a 0.78 probability that the die rolled was loaded and only a 0.22 probability that it was not.

General Form of Bayes' Theorem

Revised probabilities can also be computed in a more direct way using a general form for Bayes' theorem. Recall from Equation A-5 that Bayes' law for the conditional probability of event A, given event B, is

$$P(A|B) = \frac{P(AB)}{P(B)}$$

However, we can show that

$$P(A|B) = \frac{P(B|A)P(A)}{P(B|A)P(A) + P(B|\bar{A})P(\bar{A})} \tag{A-7}$$

where

$\bar{A}$ = the complement of the event A; for example,
if A is the event "fair die," then $\bar{A}$ is the event "unfair" or "loaded die"

Now let's return to Example 7.

Although it may not be obvious to you at first glance, we used this basic equation to compute the revised probabilities. For example, if we want the probability that the fair die was rolled given the first toss was a 3, namely, $P(\text{fair die}|3 \text{ rolled})$, we can let

- event "fair die" replace A in Equation A-7.
- event "loaded die" replace $\bar{A}$ in Equation A-7.
- event "3 rolled" replace B in Equation A-7.

We can then rewrite Equation A-7 and solve as follows:

$$P(\text{fair die}|3 \text{ rolled}) = \frac{P(3|\text{fair})P(\text{fair})}{P(3|\text{fair})P(\text{fair}) + P(3|\text{loaded})P(\text{loaded})}$$

$$= \frac{(0.166)(0.50)}{(0.166)(0.50) + (0.60)(0.50)}$$

$$= \frac{0.083}{0.383} = 0.22$$

This is the same answer that we computed in Example 7. Can you use this alternative approach to show the $P(\text{loaded die}|3 \text{ rolled}) = 0.78$? Either method is perfectly acceptable when we deal with probability revisions in Chapter 8.

A.6 Further Probability Revisions

Although one revision of prior probabilities can provide useful posterior probability estimates, additional information can be gained from performing the experiment a second time. If it is financially worthwhile, a decision maker may even decide to make several more revisions.

Example 8: A Second Probability Revision Returning to Example 7, we now attempt to obtain further information about the posterior probabilities as to whether the die just rolled is fair or loaded. To do so, let's toss the die a second time. Again, we roll a 3. What are the further revised probabilities?

To answer this question, we proceed as before, with only one exception. The probabilities $P(\text{fair}) = 0.50$ and $P(\text{loaded}) = 0.50$ remain the same, but now we must compute $P(3,3|\text{fair}) = (0.166)(0.166) = 0.027$ and $P(3,3|\text{loaded}) = (0.6)(0.6) = 0.36$. With these joint probabilities of two 3s on successive rolls, given the two types of dice, we can revise the probabilities:

$$P(3,3 \text{ and fair}) = P(3,3|\text{fair}) \times P(\text{fair})$$
$$= (0.027)(0.5) = 0.013$$
$$P(3,3 \text{ and loaded}) = P(3,3|\text{loaded}) \times P(\text{loaded})$$
$$= (0.36)(0.5) = 0.18$$

Thus, the probability of rolling two 3s, a marginal probability, is $0.013 + 0.18 = 0.193$, the sum of the two joint probabilities:

$$P(\text{fair}|3,3) = \frac{P(3,3 \text{ and fair})}{P(3,3)}$$
$$= \frac{0.013}{0.193} = 0.067$$
$$P(\text{loaded}|3,3) = \frac{P(3,3 \text{ and loaded})}{P(3,3)}$$
$$= \frac{0.18}{0.193} = 0.933$$

What has this second roll accomplished? Before we rolled the die the first time, we knew only that there was a 0.50 probability that it was either fair or loaded. When the first die was rolled in Example 7, we were able to revise these probabilities:

probability the die is fair = 0.22
probability the die is loaded = 0.78

Now, after the second roll in Example 8, our refined revisions tell us that

probability the die is fair = 0.067
probability the die is loaded = 0.933

This type of information can be extremely valuable in business decision making.

A.7 Random Variables

The preceding section discusses various ways of assigning probability values to the outcomes of an experiment. Let us now use this probability information to compute the expected outcome, variance, and standard deviation of the experiment. This can help select the best decision among a number of alternatives.

A random variable assigns a real number to every possible outcome or event in an experiment. It is normally represented by a letter such as X or Y. When the outcome itself is numerical or quantitative, a random variable can be assigned to the outcome numbers. For example, consider refrigerator sales at an appliance store. The number of refrigerators sold during a given day can be the random variable. Using X to represent this random variable, we can express this relationship as follows:

X = number of refrigerators sold during the day

In general, whenever the experiment has quantifiable outcomes, it is beneficial to define these quantitative outcomes as the random variable. Examples are given in Table A.1.

Table A.1: Examples of Random Variables

Experiment	Outcome	Random Variables	Range of Random Variables
Stock 50 Christmas trees	Number of Christmas trees sold	X = number of Christmas trees sold	0, 1, 2, ..., 50
Inspect 600 items	Number of acceptable items	Y = number of acceptable items	0, 1, 2, ..., 600
Send out 5,000 sales letters	Number of people responding to the letters	Z = number of people responding to the letters	0, 1, 2, ..., 5,000
Build an apartment building	Percent of building completed after 4 months	R = percent of building completed after 4 months	$0 \leq R \leq 100$
Test the lifetime of a lightbulb (minutes)	Length of time the bulb lasts up to 80,000 minutes	S = time the bulb burns	$0 \leq S \leq 80,000$

When the outcome itself is not numerical or quantitative, it is necessary to define a random variable that associates each outcome with a unique real number. Several examples are given in Table A.2.

Table A.2: Random Variables for Outcomes that Are Not Numbers

Experiment	Outcome	Random Variables	Range of Random Variables
Students respond to a questionnaire	Strongly agree (SA) Agree (A) Neutral (N) Disagree (D) Strongly disagree (SD)	$X = \begin{cases} 5 \text{ if SA} \\ 4 \text{ if A} \\ 3 \text{ if N} \\ 2 \text{ if D} \\ 1 \text{ if SD} \end{cases}$	1, 2, 3, 4, 5
One machine is inspected	Defective Not defective	$Y = \begin{cases} 0 \text{ if defective} \\ 1 \text{ if not defective} \end{cases}$	0, 1
Consumers respond to how they like a product	Good Average Poor	$Z = \begin{cases} 3 \text{ if good} \\ 2 \text{ if average} \\ 1 \text{ if poor} \end{cases}$	1, 2, 3

There are two types of random variables: discrete random variables and continuous random variables. Developing probability distributions and making computations based on these distributions depends on the type of random variable.

A random variable is a *discrete random variable* if it can assume only a finite or limited set of values. Which of the random variables in Table A.1 are discrete random variables? Looking at Table A.1, we can see that stocking 50 Christmas trees, inspecting 600 items, and sending out 5,000 letters are all examples of discrete random variables. Each of these random variables can assume only a finite or limited set of values. The number of Christmas trees sold, for example, can only be integer numbers from 0 to 50. There are 51 values that the random variable X can assume in this example.

A *continuous random variable* is a random variable that has an infinite or an unlimited set of values. Are there any examples of continuous random variables in Tables A.1 or A.2? Looking at Table A.1, we can see that testing the lifetime of a lightbulb is an experiment that can be described with a continuous random variable. In this case, the random variable, S, is the time the bulb burns. It can last for 3,206 minutes, 6,500.7 minutes, 251.726 minutes, or any other value between 0 and 80,000 minutes. In most cases, the range of a continuous random variable is stated as: lower value $\leq S \leq$ upper value, such as $0 \leq S \leq 80,000$. The random variable R in Table A.1 is also continuous. Can you explain why?

A.8 Probability Distributions

Earlier we discussed the probability values of an event. We now explore the properties of probability distributions. We see how popular distributions, such as the normal, Poisson, and exponential probability distributions, can save us time and effort. Since selection of the appropriate probability distribution depends partially on whether the random variable is *discrete* or *continuous*, we consider each of these types separately.

Probability Distribution of a Discrete Random Variable

When we have a discrete random variable, there is a probability value assigned to each event. These values must be between 0 and 1, and they must sum to 1. Let's look at an example.

The 100 students in Pat Shannon's statistics class have just completed the instructor evaluations at the end of the course. Dr. Shannon is particularly interested in student response to the textbook because he is in the process of writing a competing statistics book. One of the questions on the evaluation survey was: "The textbook was well written and helped me acquire the necessary information."

5. Strongly agree
4. Agree
3. Neutral
2. Disagree
1. Strongly disagree

The students' response to this question in the survey is summarized in Table A.3. Also shown is the random variable X and the corresponding probability for each possible outcome. This discrete probability distribution was computed using the relative frequency approach presented previously.

Table A.3: Probability Distribution for Textbook Question

Outcome	Random Variable (X)	Number Responding	Probability P(X)
Strongly agree	5	10	$0.1 = 10/100$
Agree	4	20	$0.2 = 20/100$
Neutral	3	30	$0.3 = 30/100$
Disagree	2	30	$0.3 = 30/100$
Strongly disagree	1	10	$0.1 = 10/100$
		Total 100	$1.0 = 100/100$

The distribution follows the three rules required of all probability distributions: (1) the events are mutually exclusive and collectively exhaustive, (2) the individual probability values are between 0 and 1 inclusive, and (3) the total of the probability values sum to 1.

Although listing the probability distribution as we did in Table A.3 is adequate, it can be difficult to get an idea about characteristics of the distribution. To overcome this problem, the probability values are often presented in graphical form. The graph of the distribution in Table A.3 is shown in Figure A.5.

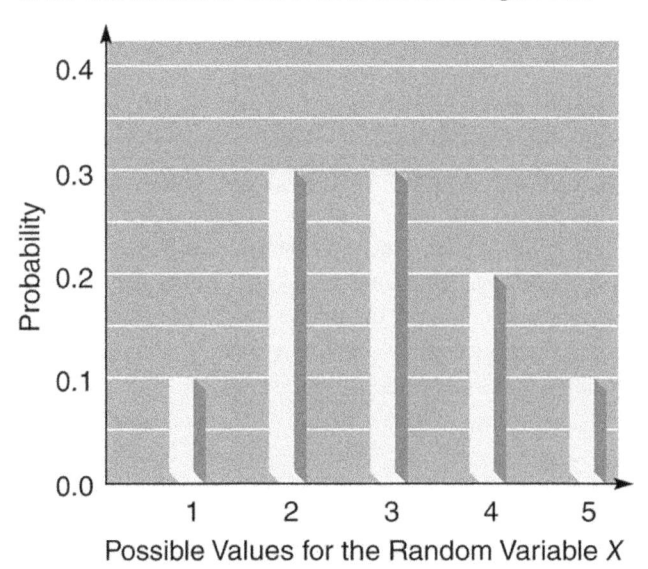

Figure A.5: Probability Function for Dr. Shannon's Class

The graph of this probability distribution gives us a picture of its shape. It helps us identify the central tendency of the distribution, called the expected value, and the amount of variability or spread of the distribution, called the variance.

Expected Value of a Discrete Probability Distribution

Once we have established a probability distribution, the first characteristic that is usually of interest is the *central tendency*, or average of the distribution. The *expected value*, a measure of central tendency, is computed as a weighted average of the values of the random variable:

$$E(X) = \sum_{i=1}^{n} X_i P(X_i) \qquad \text{(A-8)}$$
$$= X_1 P(X_1) + X_2 P(X_2) + \cdots + X_n P(X_n)$$

where

X_i = random variable's possible values

$P(X_i)$ = probability of each of the random variable's possible values

$\sum_{i=1}^{n}$ = summation sign indicating we are adding all n possible values

$E(X)$ = expected value of the random variable

The expected value of any discrete probability distribution can be computed by multiplying each possible value of the random variable, X_i, times the probability, $P(X_i)$, that outcome will occur, and summing the results, $\sum$. Here is how the expected value can be computed for the textbook question:

$$E(X) = \sum_{i=1}^{5} X_i P(X_i)$$
$$= X_1 P(X_1) + X_2 P(X_2) + X_3 P(X_3) + X_4 P(X_4) + X_5 P(X_5)$$
$$= (5)(0.1) + (4)(0.2) + (3)(0.3) + (2)(0.3) + (1)(0.1)$$
$$= 2.9$$

The expected value of 2.9 implies that the mean response is between disagree (2) and neutral (3), and that the average response is closer to neutral, which is 3. Looking at Figure A.5, this is consistent with the shape of the probability function.

Variance of a Discrete Probability Distribution

In addition to the central tendency of a probability distribution, most people are interested in the variability or the spread of the distribution. If the variability is low, it is much more likely that the outcome of an experiment will be close to the average or expected value. On the other hand, if the variability of the distribution is high, which means that the probability is spread out over the various random variable values, there is less chance that the outcome of an experiment will be close to the expected value.

The *variance* of a probability distribution is a number that reveals the overall spread or dispersion of the distribution. For a discrete probability distribution, it can be computed using the following equation:

$$\text{Variance} = \sum_{i=1}^{n} [X_i - E(X)]^2 P(X_i) \qquad \text{(A-9)}$$

where

X_i = random variable's possible values

$E(X)$ = expected value of the random variable

$[X_i - E(X)]$ = difference between each value of the random variable and the expected value

$P(X_i)$ = probability of each possible value of the random variable

To compute the variance, denoted by σ^2, each value of the random variable is subtracted from the expected value, squared, and multiplied times the probability of occurrence of that value. The results are then summed to obtain the variance. Here is how this procedure is done for Dr. Shannon's textbook question:

$$\text{Variance} = \sum_{i=1}^{5} [X_i - E(X)]^2 P(X_i)$$

$$\text{Variance} = (5-2.9)^2(0.1) + (4-2.9)^2(0.2) + (3-2.9)^2(0.3) + (2-2.9)^2(0.3)$$
$$+ (1-2.9)^2(0.1)$$
$$= (2.1)^2(0.1) + (1.1)^2(0.2) + (0.1)^2(0.3) + (-0.9)^2(0.3) + (-1.9)^2(0.1)$$
$$= 0.441 + 0.242 + 0.003 + 0.243 + 0.361$$
$$= 1.29$$

A related measure of dispersion or spread is the standard deviation. This quantity is also used in many computations involved with probability distributions. The standard deviation, denoted by σ, is just the square root of the variance:

$$\sigma = \sqrt{\text{variance}} \qquad \text{(A-10)}$$

The standard deviation for the textbook question is

$$\sigma = \sqrt{1.29} = 1.14$$

Probability Distribution of a Continuous Random Variable

There are many examples of *continuous random variables*. The time it takes to finish a project, the number of ounces in a barrel of butter, the high temperature during a given day, the exact length of a given type of lumber, and the weight of a railroad car of coal are all examples of continuous random variables. Since random variables can take on an infinite number of values, the fundamental probability rules for continuous random variables must be modified.

As with discrete probability distributions, the sum of the probabilities over all values of the random variable must equal 1. However, because there is an infinite number of values of the random variable, the probability of the random variable taking on an exact value must be 0. Why is this true? Note that if the probability of the random variable taking on an exact value was greater than 0, the sum of probabilities over all values would be infinitely large. For this reason, when we deal with a continuous random variable, we always talk about the probability of the random variable being within an interval, as opposed to being an exact value.

With a continuous probability distribution, there is a continuous mathematical function that describes the probability distribution. This function is called the probability density function or simply the *probability function*. It is usually represented by $f(X)$.

We now look at the sketch of a sample density function in Figure A.6. This curve represents the probability density function for the weight of a particular machined part. The weight could vary from 5.06 to 5.30 grams, with weights around 5.18 grams being the most likely. The shaded area represents the probability that the weight is between 5.22 and 5.26 grams.

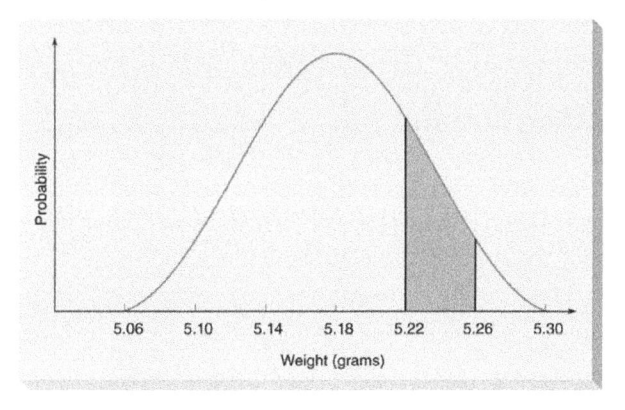

Figure A.6: Sample Density Function

If we wanted to know the probability of a part weighing exactly 5.1300000 grams, for example, we would have to compute the area of a slice of width 0. Of course, this would be 0. This result may seem strange, but if we insist on enough decimal places of accuracy, we are bound to find that the weight differs from 5.1300000 grams *exactly*, be the difference ever so slight.

In this section, we investigated the fundamental characteristics and properties of probability distributions in general. In the next three sections, we introduce two important continuous distributions—the normal distribution and the exponential distribution—and a useful discrete probability distribution—the Poisson distribution.

A.9 The Normal Distribution

One of the most popular and useful continuous probability distributions is the normal distribution. The probability density function of this distribution is given by the rather complex formula

$$f(X) = \frac{1}{\sigma\sqrt{2\pi}} e^{\left[\frac{-(X-\mu)^2}{2\sigma^2}\right]} \quad \text{(A–11)}$$

The normal distribution is specified completely when values for the mean, μ, and the standard deviation, σ, are known. Figure A.7 shows several different normal distributions with the same standard deviation and different means.

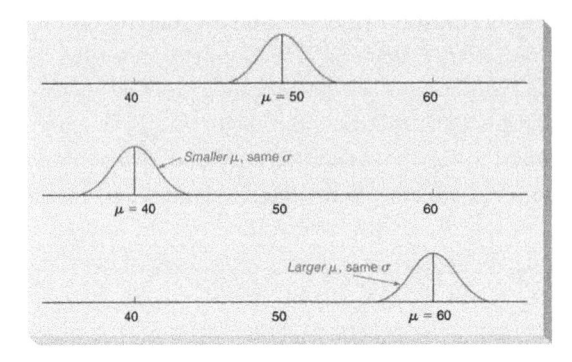

Figure A.7: Normal Distribution with Different Values for μ

As shown, differing values of μ will shift the average or center of the normal distribution. The overall shape of the distribution remains the same. On the other hand, when the standard deviation is varied, the normal curve either flattens out or becomes steeper. This is shown in Figure A.8.

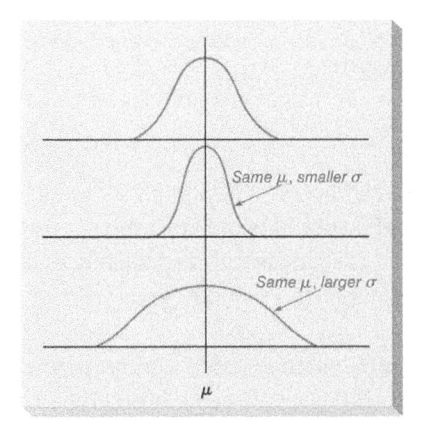

Figure A.8: Normal Distribution with Different Values for σ

As the standard deviation, σ, becomes smaller, the normal distribution becomes steeper. When the standard deviation becomes larger, the normal distribution has a tendency to flatten out or become broader.

Area under the Normal Curve

Because the normal distribution is symmetrical, its midpoint (and highest point) is at the mean. Values on the X axis are then measured in terms of how many standard deviations they lie from the mean. Recall that the area under the curve (in a continuous distribution) describes the probability that a random variable has a value within a specified interval. The normal distribution requires mathematical calculations beyond the scope of this book, but tables that provide areas or probabilities are readily available. For example, Figure A.9 illustrates three commonly used relationships that have been derived from standard normal tables (discussed in the next section). The area from point a to point b in the top drawing represents the probability, 68.26%, that the random variable will be within 1 standard deviation of the mean. In the middle graph, we see that about 95.44% of the area lies within ± 2 standard deviations of the mean. The third graph shows that 99.74% lies between $\pm 3\sigma$.

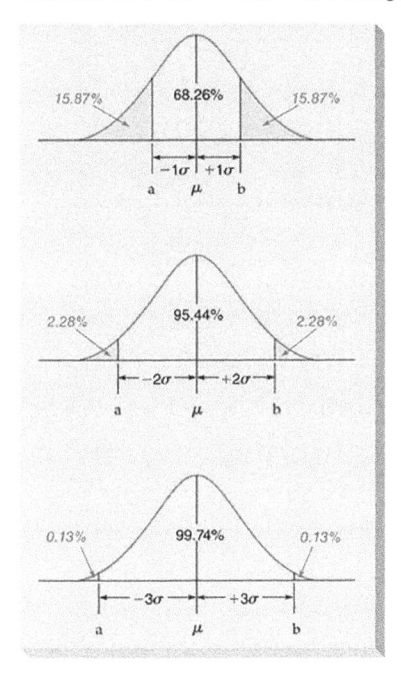

Figure A.9: Three Common Areas under Normal Curves

Translating Figure A.9 into an application implies that if the mean IQ in the United States is $\mu = 100$ points and if the standard deviation is $\sigma = 15$ points, we can make the following statements:

1. 68.26% of the population have IQs between 85 and 115 points (±1σ).
2. 95.44% of the people have IQs between 70 and 130 points (±2σ).
3. 99.74% of the population have IQs in the range from 55 to 145 points (±3σ).
4. Only 15.87% of the people have IQs greater than 115 points (from first graph, the area to the right of +1σ).

Many more interesting remarks could be drawn from these data. Can you tell the probability that a person selected at random has an IQ of less than 70? greater than 145? less than 130?

Using the Standard Normal Table

To use a table to find normal probability values, we follow two steps.

Step 1 Convert the normal distribution to what we call a *standard normal distribution*. A standard normal distribution is one that has a mean of 0 and a standard deviation of 1. All normal tables are set up to handle random variables with $\mu = 0$ and $\sigma = 1$. Without a standard normal distribution, a different table would be needed for each pair of μ and σ values. We call the new standard random variable Z. The value for Z for any normal distribution is computed from this equation:

$$Z = \frac{X - \mu}{\sigma} \qquad \text{(A–12)}$$

where

X = value of the random variable we want to measure

μ = mean of the distribution

σ = standard deviation of the distribution

Z = number of standard deviations from X to the mean, μ

For example, if $\mu = 100$, $\sigma = 15$, and we are interested in finding the probability that the random variable X is less than 130, we want $P(X < 130)$:

$$Z = \frac{X - \mu}{\sigma} = \frac{130 - 100}{15}$$
$$= \frac{30}{15} = 2 \text{ standard deviations}$$

This means that the point X is 2.0 standard deviations to the right of the mean. This is shown in Figure A.10.

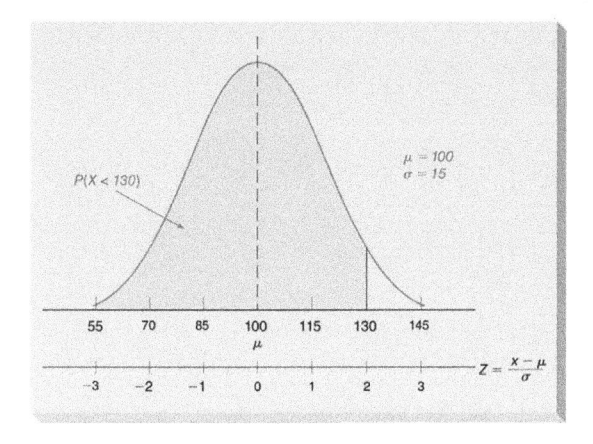

Figure A.10: Normal Distribution Showing the Relationship between Z Values and X Values

Step 2 Look up the probability from a table of normal curve areas. Appendix C is such a table of areas for the standard normal distribution. It is set up to provide the area under the curve to the left of any specified value of Z.

Let's see how Appendix C can be used. The column on the left lists values of Z, with the second decimal place of Z appearing in the top row. For example, for a value of Z = 2.00 as just computed, find 2.0 in the left-hand column and 0.00 in the top row. In the body of the table, we find that the area sought is 0.9772, or 97.72%. Thus,

$$P(X < 130) = P(Z < 2.00) = 0.9772$$

This suggests that if the mean IQ score is 100, with a standard deviation of 15 points, the probability that a randomly selected person's IQ is less than 130 is 0.9772. By referring back to Figure A.9, we see that this probability could also have been derived from the middle graph. (Note that $1.0 - 0.9772 = 0.0228 = 2.28$, which is the area in the right-hand tail of the curve.)

To feel comfortable with the use of the standard normal probability table, we need to work a few more examples. We now use the Haynes Construction Company as a case in point.

Haynes Construction Company Example

Haynes Construction Company builds primarily three- and four-unit apartment buildings (called triplexes and quadraplexes) for investors, and it is believed that the total construction time in days follows a normal distribution. The mean time to construct a triplex is 100 days, and the standard deviation is 20 days. Recently, the president of Haynes Construction signed a contract to complete a triplex in 125 days. Failure to complete the triplex in 125 days would result in severe penalty fees. What is the probability that Haynes Construction will not be in violation of their construction contract? The normal distribution for the construction of triplexes is shown in Figure A.11.

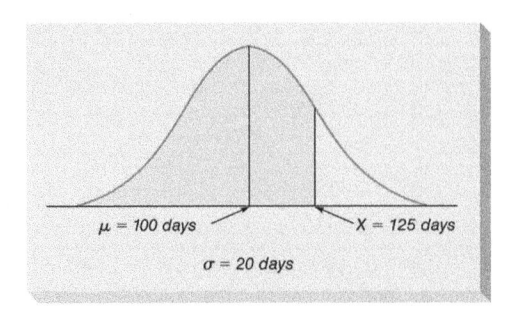

![Figure A.11]

Figure A.11: Normal Distribution for Haynes Construction

To compute this probability, we need to find the shaded area under the curve. We begin by computing Z for this problem:

$$Z = \frac{X - \mu}{\sigma}$$
$$= \frac{125 - 100}{20}$$
$$= \frac{25}{20} = 1.25$$

Looking in Appendix C for a Z value of 1.25, we find an area under the curve of 0.8944. (We do this by looking up 1.2 in the left-hand column of the table and then moving to the 0.05 column to find the value of $Z = 1.25$.) Therefore, the probability of not violating the contract is 0.8944, or an 89.44% chance.

Now let's look at the Haynes problem from another perspective. If the firm finishes this triplex in 75 days or less, it will be awarded a bonus payment of $5,000. What is the probability that Haynes will receive the bonus?

Figure A.12 illustrates the probability we are looking for in the shaded area.

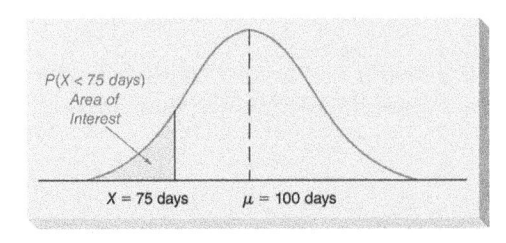

![Figure A.12]

Figure A.12: Probability that Haynes Will Receive the Bonus by Finishing in 75 Days

The first step is again to compute the Z value:

$$Z = \frac{X - \mu}{\sigma}$$
$$= \frac{75 - 100}{20}$$
$$= \frac{-25}{20} = -1.25$$

This Z value indicates that 75 days is −1.25 standard deviations to the left of the mean. But the standard normal table is structured to handle only positive Z values. To solve this problem, we observe that the curve is symmetric. The probability that Haynes will finish in *less than 75 days is equivalent* to the probability that it will finish in *more than 125 days*. In Figure A.11, we found that the probability that Haynes will finish in less than 125 days was 0.8944. So, the probability that it takes more than 125 days is

$$P(X > 125) = 1.0 - P(X < 125)$$
$$= 1.0 - 0.8944 = 0.1056$$

Thus, the probability of completing the triplex in 75 days or less is 0.1056, or 10.56%.

One final example: What is the probability that the triplex will take between 110 and 125 days? We see in Figure A.13 that

$$P(110 < X < 125) = P(X < 125) - P(X < 110)$$

That is, the shaded area in the graph can be computed by finding the probability of completing the building in 125 days or less *minus* the probability of completing it in 110 days or less.

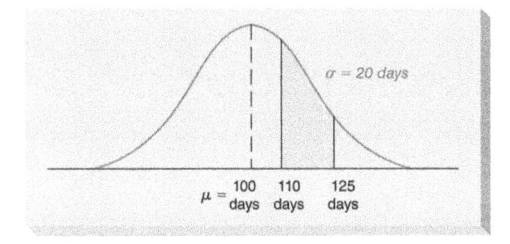

Figure A.13: Probability of Haynes' Finishing in 110 to 125 Days

Recall that $P(X < 125 \text{ days})$ is equal to 0.8944. To find $P(X < 110 \text{ days})$, we follow the two steps developed earlier:

1. $Z = \dfrac{X - \mu}{\sigma} = \dfrac{110 - 100}{20} = \dfrac{10}{20}$
   = 0.5 standard deviations
2. From Appendix C, we find that the area for $Z = 0.50$ is 0.6915. So, the probability that the triplex can be completed in less than 110 days is 0.6915. Finally,

$$P(110 < X < 125) = 0.8944 - 0.6915 = 0.2029$$

The probability that it will take between 110 and 125 days is 0.2029.

A.10 The Exponential Distribution

The *exponential distribution*, also called the negative exponential distribution, is used in dealing with queuing models. The exponential distribution describes the number of customers serviced in a time interval. The exponential distribution is a continuous distribution. Its probability function is given by

$$f(X) = \mu e^{-\mu X} \tag{A-13}$$

where

X = random variable (service times)

μ = average number of units the service facility can handle in a specific period of time

e = 2.718, the base of natural logarithms

The general shape of the exponential distribution is shown in Figure A.14.

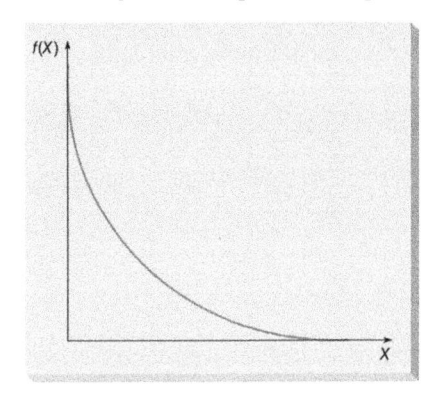

Figure A. 14: Negative Exponential Distribution

Its expected value and variance can be shown to be

$$\text{Expected value} = \frac{1}{\mu} \tag{A-14}$$

$$\text{Variance} = \frac{1}{\mu^2} \tag{A-15}$$

The exponential distribution is illustrated in Chapter 9.

A.11 The Poisson Distribution

An important *discrete probability distribution* is the Poisson distribution.[1] We examine it because of its key role in complementing the exponential distribution in queuing models in Chapter 9. The distribution describes situations in which customers arrive independently during a certain time interval, and the number of arrivals depends on the length of the time interval. Examples are patients arriving at a health clinic, customers arriving at a bank window, passengers arriving at an airport, and telephone calls going through a central exchange.

The formula for the Poisson distribution is

$$P(X) = \frac{\lambda^x e^{-\lambda}}{X!} \qquad \text{(A–16)}$$

where

$P(X)$ = probability of exactly X arrivals or occurrences

λ = average number of arrivals per unit of time (the mean arrival rate), pronounced "lambda"

e = 2.718, the base of the natural logarithms

X = specific value (0, 1, 2, 3, and so on) of the random variable

The mean and variance of the Poisson distribution are equal and are computed simply as

$$\text{expected value} = \lambda \qquad \text{(A–17)}$$

$$\text{variance} = \lambda \qquad \text{(A–18)}$$

A sample distribution for $\lambda = 2$ arrivals is shown in Figure A.15.

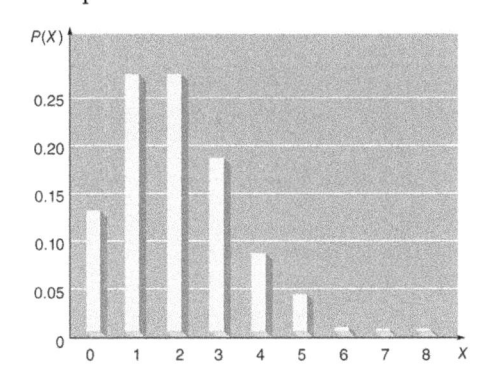

Figure A.15: Sample Poisson Distribution with $\lambda = 2$

---

1 This distribution, derived by Simeon Poisson in 1837, is pronounced "pwah-sahn."

A.12 Summary

Key Points
- People often misuse the two basic rules of probabilities by making such statements as "I'm 110% sure we're going to win the big game."
- Probabilities are sometimes subjective and based on personal experiences.
- Other times they are objective and based on logical observations such as the roll of a die.
- Often, probabilities are derived from historical data.
- Events are mutually exclusive if only one can occur on any single trial.
- Events are collectively exhaustive if the list of outcomes includes every possible outcome.
- If the events are mutually exclusive, then $P(A \text{ or } B) = P(A) + P(B)$.
- If events are not mutually exclusive, then $P(A \text{ or } B) = P(A) + P(B) - P(A \text{ and } B)$.
- A marginal probability is the probability of a single event occurring.
- Two events are statistically independent if the occurrence of one event has no effect on the probability of occurrence of the other event.
- The joint probability of independent events is the product of their marginal probabilities.
- The conditional probability, $P(A|B)$, is the probability of an event A occurring given that another event B has occurred.
- For independent events, the conditional probability $P(A|B)$ is equal to the marginal probability $P(A)$.
- Bayes' theorem can be used to compute revised probabilities.
- A random variable assigns a real number to every possible outcome or event in an experiment.
- There are two types of random variables: discrete and continuous.
- The expected value of a discrete probability distribution is a weighted average of the values of the random variable.
- A probability distribution is often described by its mean and variance.
- A probability density function $f(X)$ is a mathematical way of describing the probability distribution.
- The normal distribution affects a large number of processes in our lives, and it is specified by its mean and standard deviation.
- A 95% confidence is actually ± 1.96 standard deviations, whereas ± 3 standard deviations is a 99.74% spread.
- Managers often speak of 95% and 99% confidence intervals, which roughly refer to ± 2 and ± 3 standard deviation graphs, respectively, under normal distribution curves.
- The exponential distribution, also called the negative exponential distribution, is used in queuing models to describe the number of customers serviced in a time interval.
- The Poisson distribution, a discrete probability distribution, is used in queuing to model customer arrivals.

Glossary

Bayes' Theorem A formula that allows us to compute conditional probabilities when dealing with statistically dependent events.

Classical, or Logical, Approach An objective way of assessing probabilities based on logic.

Collectively Exhaustive Events A collection of all possible outcomes of an experiment.

Conditional Probability The probability of one event occurring given that another has taken place.

Continuous Probability Distribution A probability distribution with a continuous random variable.

Continuous Random Variable A random variable that can assume an infinite or unlimited set of values.

Dependent Events The situation in which the occurrence of one event affects the probability of occurrence of some other event.

Discrete Probability Distribution A probability distribution with a discrete random variable.

Discrete Random Variable A random variable that can only assume a finite or limited set of values.

Expected Value The (weighted) average of a probability distribution.

Independent Events The situation in which the occurrence of one event has no effect on the probability of occurrence of a second event.

Joint Probability The probability of events occurring together (or one after the other).

Marginal Probability The simple probability of an event occurring.

Mutually Exclusive Events A situation in which only one event can occur on any given trial or experiment.

Negative Exponential Distribution A continuous probability distribution that describes the time between customer arrivals in a queuing situation.

Normal Distribution A continuous bell-shaped distribution that is a function of two parameters, the mean and standard deviation of the distribution.

Objective Approach A method of determining probability values by observing a large number of trials or by basing it on logic.

Poisson Distribution A discrete probability distribution used in queuing theory.

Prior Probability A probability value determined before new or additional information is obtained. It is sometimes called an *a priori* probability estimate.

Probability A statement about the likelihood of an event occurring. It is expressed as a numeric value between 0 and 1, inclusive.

Probability Density Function The mathematical function that describes a continuous probability distribution. It is represented by $f(X)$.

Probability Distribution The set of all possible values of a random variable and their associated probabilities.

Random Variable A variable that assigns a number to every possible outcome of an experiment.

Relative Frequency Approach An objective way of determining probabilities based on observing frequencies over a number of trials.

Revised, or Posterior, Probability A probability value that results from new or revised information and prior probabilities.

Standard Deviation The square root of the variance.

Subjective Approach A method of determining probability values based on experience or judgment.

Variance A measure of dispersion or spread of the probability distribution.

A.13 Exercises

Discussion Questions

A–1. What are the two basic laws of probability?
A–2. What is the meaning of mutually exclusive events? What is meant by collectively exhaustive? Give an example of each.
A–3. Describe the various approaches used in determining probability values.
A–4. Why is the probability of the intersection of two events subtracted in the sum of the probability of two events?
A–5. What is the difference between events that are dependent and events that are independent?
A–6. What is Bayes' theorem, and when can it be used?
A–7. How can probability revisions assist in managerial decision making?
A–8. What is a random variable? What are the various types of random variables?
A–9. What is the difference between a discrete probability distribution and a continuous probability distribution? Give your own example of each.
A–10. What is the expected value, and what does it measure? How is it computed for a discrete probability distribution?
A–11. What is the variance, and what does it measure? How is it computed for a discrete probability distribution?
A–12. Name three business processes that can be described by the normal distribution.
A–13. After evaluating student response to a question about a case used in class, the instructor constructed the following probability distribution:

Response	Random Variable, X	Probability
Excellent	5	0.05
Good	4	0.25
Average	3	0.40
Fair	2	0.15
Poor	1	0.15

What kind of probability distribution is it?

Problems

A–14. A student taking Management Science 301 at East Haven University will receive one of five possible grades for the course: A, B, C, D, or E. The distribution of grades over the past two years is shown in the following table.

Grade	Number of Students
A	80
B	75
C	90
D	30
F	25
	Total 300

If this past distribution is a good indicator of future grades, what is the probability of a student receiving a C in the course?

A–15. A silver dollar is flipped twice. Calculate the probability of each of the following occurring:
(a) A head on the first flip
(b) A tail on the second flip given that the first toss was a head
(c) Two tails
(d) A tail on the first and a head on the second
(e) A tail on the first and a head on the second or a head on the first and a tail on the second
(f) At least one head on the two flips

A–16. An urn contains 8 red chips, 10 green chips, and 2 white chips. A chip is drawn and replaced, and then a second chip drawn. What is the probability of
(a) a white chip on the first draw?
(b) a white chip on the first draw and a red on the second?
(c) two green chips being drawn?
(d) a red chip on the second, given that a white chip was drawn on the first?

A–17. Evertight, a leading manufacturer of quality nails, produces 1-, 2-, 3-, 4-, and 5-inch nails for various uses. In the production process, if there is an overrun or if the nails are slightly defective, they are placed in a common bin. Yesterday, 651 of the 1-inch nails, 243 of the 2-inch nails, 41 of the 3-inch nails, 451 of the 4-inch nails, and 333 of the 5-inch nails were placed in the bin.
(a) What is the probability of reaching into the bin and getting a 4-inch nail?
(b) What is the probability of getting a 5-inch nail?
(c) If a particular application requires a nail that is 3 inches or shorter, what is the probability of getting a nail that will satisfy the requirements of the application?

A–18. Last year, at Northern Manufacturing Company, 200 people had colds during the year. One hundred fifty-five people who did no exercising had colds, whereas the remainder of the people with colds were involved in a weekly exercise program. Half of the 1,000 employees were involved in some type of exercise.

(a) What is the probability that an employee will have a cold next year?
(b) Given that an employee is involved in an exercise program, what is the probability that he or she will get a cold?
(c) What is the probability that an employee who is not involved in an exercise program will get a cold next year?
(d) Are exercising, and getting a cold, independent events? Explain your answer.

A–19. The Springfield Kings, a professional basketball team, has won 12 of its last 20 games and is expected to continue winning at the same percentage rate. The team's ticket manager is anxious to attract a large crowd to tomorrow's game but believes that depends on how well the Kings perform tonight against the Galveston Comets. He assesses the probability of drawing a large crowd to be 0.90 should the team win tonight. What is the probability that the team wins tonight and that there will be a large crowd at tomorrow's game?

A–20. David Mashley teaches two undergraduate statistics courses at Kansas College. The class for Statistics 201 consists of 7 sophomores and 3 juniors. The more advanced course, Statistics 301, has 2 sophomores and 8 juniors enrolled. As an example of a business sampling technique, Professor Mashley randomly selects, from the stack of Statistics 201 registration cards, the class card of one student and then places that card back in the stack. If that student was a sophomore, Mashley draws another card from the Statistics 201 stack; if not, he randomly draws a card from the Statistics 301 group. Are these two draws independent events? What is the probability of

(a) a junior's name on the first draw?
(b) a junior's name on the second draw, given that a sophomore's name was drawn first?
(c) a junior's name on the second draw, given that a junior's name was drawn first?
(d) a sophomore's name on both draws?
(e) a junior's name on both draws?
(f) one sophomore's name and one junior's name on the two draws, regardless of order drawn?

A–21. The oasis outpost of Abu Ilan, in the heart of the Negev desert, has a population of 20 Bedouin tribesmen and 20 Farima tribesmen. El Kamin, a nearby oasis, has a population of 32 Bedouins and 8 Farima. A lost Israeli soldier, accidentally separated from his army unit, is wandering through the desert and arrives at the edge of one of the oases. The soldier has no idea which oasis he has found, but the first person he spots at a distance is a Bedouin. What is the probability that he wandered into Abu Ilan? What is the probability that he is in El Kamin?

A–22. The lost Israeli soldier mentioned in Problem A-21 decides to rest for a few minutes before entering the desert oasis he has just found. Closing his eyes, he dozes off for 15 minutes, wakes, and walks toward the center of the oasis. The first person he spots this time he again recognizes as a Bedouin. What is the posterior probability that he is in El Kamin?

A–23. Ace Machine Works estimates that the probability their lathe tool is properly adjusted is 0.8. When the lathe is properly adjusted, there is a 0.9 probability that the parts produced pass inspection. If the lathe is out of adjustment, however, the probability of a good part being produced is only 0.2. A part randomly chosen is inspected and found to be acceptable. At this point, what is the posterior probability that the lathe tool is properly adjusted?

A–24. The Boston South Fifth Street Softball League consists of three teams: Mama's Boys, team 1; the Killers, team 2; and the Machos, team 3. Each team plays the other teams just once during the season. The win–loss record for the past five years is as follows:

Winner	(1)	(2)	(3)
Mama's Boys (1)	X	3	4
The Killers (2)	2	X	1
The Machos (3)	1	4	X

Each row represents the number of wins over the past five years. Mama's Boys beat the Killers three times, beat the Machos four times, and so on.

(a) What is the probability that the Killers will win every game next year?
(b) What is the probability that the Machos will win at least one game next year?
(c) What is the probability that Mama's Boys will win exactly one game next year?
(d) What is the probability that the Killers will win less than two games next year?

A–25. The schedule for the Killers next year is as follows (refer to Problem A-24):
  Game 1: The Machos
  Game 2: Mama's Boys

(a) What is the probability that the Killers will win their first game?
(b) What is the probability that the Killers will win their last game?
(c) What is the probability that the Killers will break even—win exactly one game?
(d) What is the probability that the Killers will win every game?
(e) What is the probability that the Killers will lose every game?
(f) Would you want to be the coach of the Killers?

A–26. The Northside Rifle team has two markspersons, Dick and Sally. Dick hits a bull's-eye 90% of the time, and Sally hits a bull's-eye 95% of the time.

(a) What is the probability that either Dick or Sally or both will hit the bull's-eye if each takes one shot?
(b) What is the probability that Dick and Sally will both hit the bull's-eye?
(c) Did you make any assumptions in answering the preceding questions? If you answered yes, do you think that you are justified in making the assumption(s)?

A–27. In a sample of 1,000 representing a survey from the entire population, 650 people were from Laketown, and the rest of the people were from River City. Out of the sample, 19 people had some form of cancer. Thirteen of these people were from Laketown.
(a) Are the events of living in Laketown and having some sort of cancer independent?
(b) Which city would you prefer to live in, assuming that your main objective was to avoid having cancer?

A–28. Compute the probability of "loaded die, given that a 3 was rolled," as shown in Example 7, this time using the general form of Bayes' theorem from Equation A-7.

A–29. Which of the following are probability distributions? Why?

(a)

Random Variable X	Probability
−2	0.1
−1	0.2
0	0.3
1	0.25
2	0.15

(b)

Random Variable Y	Probability
1	1.1
1.5	0.2
2	0.3
2.5	0.25
3	−1.25

(c)

Random Variable Z	Probability
1	0.1
2	0.2
3	0.3
4	0.4
5	0.0

A–30. Harrington Health Food stocks 5 loaves of Neutro-Bread. The probability distribution for the sales of Neutro-Bread is listed in the following table:

Number of Loaves Sold	Probability
0	0.05
1	0.15
2	0.20
3	0.25
4	0.20
5	0.15

How many loaves will Harrington sell, on average?

A–31. What are the expected value and variance of the following probability distribution?

Random Variable X	Probability
1	0.05
2	0.05
3	0.10
4	0.10
5	0.15
6	0.15
7	0.25
8	0.15

A–32. Sales for Fast Kat, a 16-foot catamaran sailboat, have averaged 250 boats per month over the past five years, with a standard deviation of 25 boats. Assuming that the demand is about the same as past years and follows a normal curve, what is the probability sales will be less than 280 boats?

A–33. Refer to Problem A-32. What is the probability that sales will be more than 265 boats during the next month? What is the probability that sales will be less than 250 boats next month?

A–34. Precision Parts is a job shop that specializes in producing electric motor shafts. The average shaft size for the E300 electric motor is 0.55 inch, with a standard deviation of 0.10 inch. It is normally distributed. What is the probability that a shaft selected at random will be between 0.55 and 0.65 inch?

A–35. Refer to Problem A-34. What is the probability that a shaft size will be greater than 0.65 inch? What is the probability that a shaft size will be between 0.53 and 0.59 inch? What is the probability that a shaft size will be under 0.45 inch?

A–36. An industrial oven used to cure sand cores for a factory that manufactures engine blocks for small cars is able to maintain fairly constant temperatures. The temperature range of the oven follows a normal distribution with a mean of 450°F and a standard deviation of 25°F. Leslie Larsen, president of the factory, is concerned about the large number of defective cores that have been produced in the last several months. If the oven gets hotter than 475°F, the core is defective. What is the probability that the oven will cause a core to be defective? What is the probability that the temperature of the oven will range from 460° to 470°F?

A-37. Steve Goodman, production foreman for the Florida Gold Fruit Company, estimates that the average sale of oranges is 4,700 and the standard deviation is 500 oranges. Sales follow a normal distribution.
- (a) What is the probability that sales will be greater than 5,500 oranges?
- (b) What is the probability that sales will be greater than 4,500 oranges?
- (c) What is the probability that sales will be less than 4,900 oranges?
- (d) What is the probability that sales will be less than 4,300 oranges?

A-38. Susan Williams has been the production manager of Medical Suppliers, Inc., for the past 17 years. Medical Suppliers, Inc., is a producer of bandages and arm slings. During the past 5 years, the demand for No-Stick bandages has been fairly constant. On average, sales have been about 87,000 packages of No-Stick. Susan has reason to believe that the distribution of No-Stick follows a normal curve, with a standard deviation of 4,000 packages. What is the probability that sales will be less than 81,000 packages?

A-39. Armstrong Faber produces a standard number two pencil called Ultra-Lite. Since Chuck Armstrong started Armstrong Faber, sales had grown steadily. With the increase in the price of wood products, however, Chuck has been forced to increase the price of the Ultra-Lite pencils. As a result, the demand for Ultra-Lite has been fairly stable over the past six years. On average, Armstrong Faber has sold 457,000 pencils each year. Furthermore, 90% of the time, sales have been between 454,000 and 460,000 pencils. It is expected that the sales follow a normal distribution with a mean of 457,000 pencils. Estimate the standard deviation of this distribution. (*Hint:* Work backward from the normal table to find Z. Then apply Equation A-12.)

A-40. Patients arrive at the emergency room of Costa Valley Hospital at an average of 5 per day. The demand for emergency room treatment at Costa Valley follows a Poisson distribution.
- (a) Compute the probability of exactly 0, 1, 2, 3, 4, and 5 arrivals per day.
- (b) What is the sum of these probabilities, and why is the number less than 1?

A-41. Using the data in Problem A-40, determine the probability of more than 3 visits for emergency room service on any given day.

A-42. Cars arrive at Carla's Muffler shop for repair work at an average of 3 per hour, following an exponential distribution.
- (a) What is the expected time between arrivals?
- (b) What is the variance of the time between arrivals?

Appendix B
Useful Excel 2016 Commands and Procedures for Installing ExcelModules

B.1 Introduction

Excel, Microsoft Office's spreadsheet application program, lets us embed hidden formulas that perform calculations on visible data. The main document (or file) used in Excel to store and manipulate data is a *workbook*. A workbook can consist of a number of worksheets, each of which can be used to list and analyze data. Excel allows us to enter and modify data on several worksheets simultaneously. We can also perform calculations based on data from multiple worksheets and/or workbooks.

This appendix provides a brief overview of some basic Excel commands and procedures, as applied to Excel 2016. It also discusses how add-ins, such as Solver and Data Analysis, can be installed and enabled in Excel. We should note that the fundamental appearance of a workbook as well as the syntax and use of functions, interface, and many menu commands has remained more or less the same since Excel 2007; the interface (in terms of the appearance of toolbars, menus, etc.) changed significantly in Excel 2007 when compared to Excel 2003 and prior versions. Likewise, Solver's appearance and menu options changed significantly in Excel 2010 compared to previous versions of Excel.

Finally, this appendix describes the installation and usage procedures for ExcelModules, a software package provided on the Companion Website for this book.[1] We use this software to develop and solve decision models for queuing (Chapter 9), forecasting (Chapter 11), and inventory control (Chapter 12).

In addition to the extensive help features built into Excel, for more detailed information on Excel, there are hundreds of books and there are thousands of online tutorials available to help us learn to use specific Excel features. To get a current listing of these online tutorials, simply type "Excel tutorial" in the search box of any Web browser.

B.2 Getting Started

When we start Excel, it opens an empty file (called a workbook) named Book1, as shown in Figure B.1. We can also start Excel by directly clicking on any Excel file accessible on the computer. In that case, Excel opens that file when it starts.

---

[1] The Companion Website for this book is at *degruyter.com/view/product/486941*.

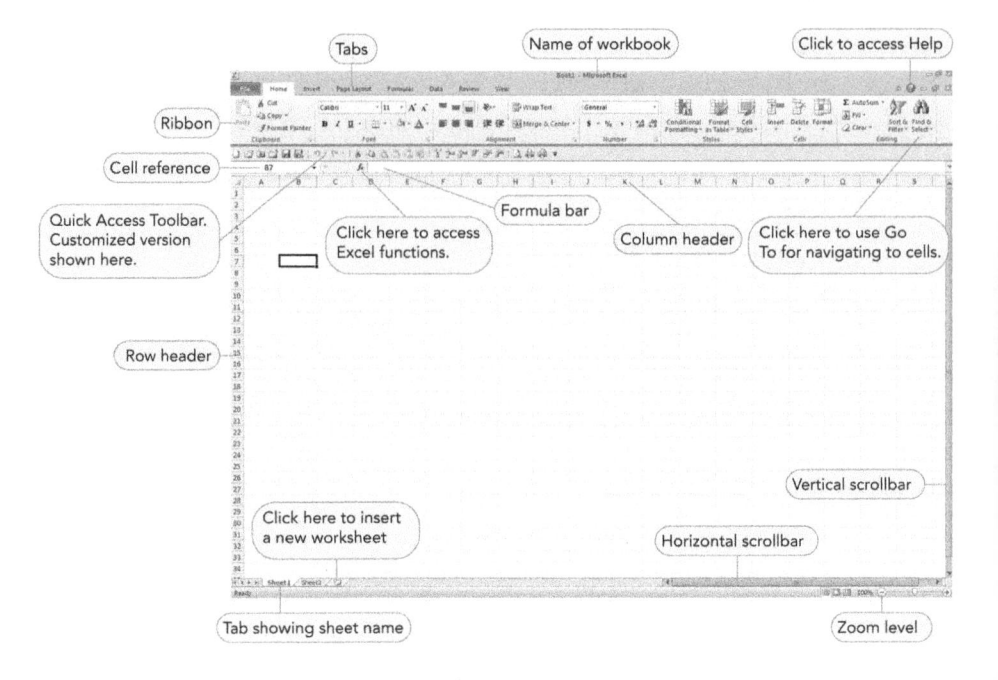

Figure B.1: General Layout of an Excel Worksheet

A workbook consists of a number of pages called *worksheets*. The number of blank worksheets in a new workbook is set in Excel's main options (click File | Options | General to view and/or change this number). We can easily insert more worksheets or delete existing ones, as illustrated later in this appendix. The sheet tabs at the bottom of each worksheet help us identify and move to each worksheet in the workbook. We can rename any sheet by double-clicking its tab and typing in the new name.

Organization of a Worksheet
A worksheet consists of columns and rows, as shown in Figure B.1. Columns are identified by headers with letters (e.g., A, B, C), and rows are identified by headers with numbers (e.g., 1, 2, 3). Excel files stored in Excel 2007 (and beyond) format (with the file extension *.xlsx*) have 1,048,576 rows by 16,384 columns per worksheet. In contrast, files stored under prior versions of Excel (with the file extension *.xls*) are restricted to only 65,536 rows and 256 columns. Where a row and a column intersect is known as a cell. Each cell has a reference based on the intersection of the row and column. For example, the reference of the cell at the intersection of column B and row 7 is referred to as cell B7 (as shown in Figure B.1).

A *cell* is the fundamental storage unit for Excel data, including both values and labels. A *value* is a number or a hidden formula that performs a calculation, and a *label* is a heading or some explanatory text. We can enter different types of entries (e.g., text, numbers, formulas, dates, and times) into cells.

Navigating through a Worksheet

We can navigate through a worksheet by using either the mouse or the keys on the keyboard. To select a cell by using the mouse, click the cell (e.g., B7, as shown in Figure B.1). To move anywhere on a worksheet, we can also use the arrow keys or the Page Up and Page Down keys on the keyboard.

We can also use the Go To menu option to navigate between cells. This option is useful if we want to modify the contents of a cell. To go to a specific cell, click Find & Select | Go To (see Figure B.1). In the Go To dialog box, we can even click the Special button to go to cells with special features. For example, we can choose to go to cells with comments, to blank cells, or to the last cell in the worksheet.

B.3 The Ribbon, Toolbars, and Tabs

A *toolbar* consists of commands (usually represented by icons) that provide shortcuts to common tasks. Excel 2016 has a single supersized toolbar called the Ribbon (see Figure B.1). The Ribbon consists of the following default tabs: File, Home, Insert, Page Layout, Formulas, Data, Review, and View. Additional tabs may be present in the Ribbon if we have installed additional add-ins (e.g., ExcelModules), as illustrated later in this appendix.

As with previous versions of Microsoft Office, many of the commands (and associated icons) in Excel's tabs are identical to the ones in other Microsoft Office programs such as PowerPoint and Word. We can customize any of the tabs in the Ribbon by right-clicking anywhere on them and selecting Customize the Ribbon or through Excel's options settings (illustrated later in this appendix).

File Tab The File tab, shown in Figure B.2, includes commands for many file-related tasks such as saving and printing. It also provided access to the numerous default options that may be set in Excel.

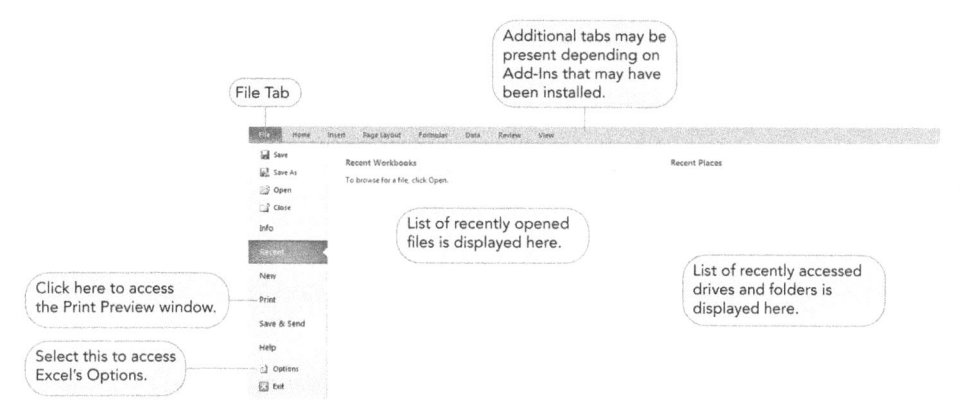

Figure B.2: Menu Commands in the File Tab in Excel 2016

The following list indicates the menu commands available on this tab, along with brief descriptions of each command. Many of the menu commands in this tab (as well as in other tabs) can be added to the Quick Access Toolbar for ease of access and use. This toolbar can be placed either above or below the Ribbon and customized as desired. For example, a customized version of the Quick Access Toolbar in shown below the Ribbon in Figure B.1.

1. *Save*. Save the current workbook (or file).
2. *Save As*. Save the current workbook under a different name, location or file type (e.g., .xls, .txt, .pdf).
3. *Open*. Open an existing workbook.
4. *Close*. Close the current workbook.
5. *Info*. Display information about the current workbook (e.g., properties, permissions, revision history).
6. *Recent*. Display a list of recently opened workbooks and places (folders). This is illustrated in Figure B.2.
7. *New*. Open a new blank workbook or other templates available in Microsoft Office.
8. *Print*. Print part or all of the current worksheet. This feature is discussed in more detail in section B.6.
9. *Save & Send*. Save the current workbook and send using e-mail, to the Web, etc.
10. *Help*. Access the extensive help built into Microsoft Excel. More detail on this feature is provided later in this appendix.
11. *Options*. Change the default workbook or worksheet options (e.g., font, number of worksheets). This feature is discussed in more detail in section B.7.
12. *Exit*. Exit Microsoft Excel.

Home Tab   The Home tab, shown in Figure B.3, includes commands for many editing and formatting related tasks. By default, this is the tab that is visible when Excel starts. The following list describes the primary menu commands on this tab. Note that on this tab (and all other tabs) in the Ribbon, icons representing commands associated with similar tasks are typically located together to form groups. For example, the groups in the Home tab are called Clipboard, Font, Alignment, Number, Styles, etc.

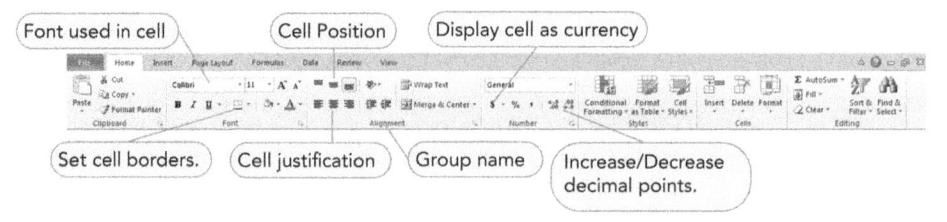

Figure B.3: Menu Commands in the Home Tab in Excel 2016

1. *Clipboard group*. Contains the standard editing tools Cut, Copy, and Paste. Click the arrow under the Paste command to access specialized paste options such as

Paste Values, Paste Formats, Paste Formulas, Paste Comments, Transpose, etc. Click the arrow next to Copy to copy the entire selected contents as a picture rather than as individual formulas, values, or text.

2. *Font group.* Contains commands to set the font type and size, as well as formatting features such as bold, italic, underline, font color, and fill color. We can also define borders for the selected cell(s).
3. *Alignment group.* Contains commands to set cell alignment features such as justification, position within the cell, wrap text, merge (or un-merge) cells, increase (or decrease) cell indent, and change text orientation (e.g., vertical, angular).
4. *Number group.* Contains commands to change the display mode (e.g., number, text, date, time, custom) and format (e.g., number of decimal points shown, display values as currency, display values as percentage) of the contents of a cell (or multiple cells).
5. *Style group.* Contains commands to change cell styles and set conditional formatting rules for cells. Click on Cell Styles to see the numerous styles that are built into Excel.
6. *Cells group.* Contains commands to insert, delete, or format entire worksheets, as well as individual cells, rows, or columns. To insert a new worksheet, click Insert | Insert Sheet or click the Insert Worksheet icon next to the Sheet tab (see Figure B.1 for illustration). To delete an existing worksheet, click Delete | Delete Sheet or right-click on the Sheet tab and select Delete.
   - To insert new row(s), click on the row header(s) above where we want the new row(s) to be inserted. Then click Insert | Insert Sheet Rows. To delete row(s), select the row(s) that we want to delete. Then click Delete | Delete Sheet Rows.
   - To change the height of a row, move the mouse to the bottom edge of the row heading. The cursor will change to a plus sign with arrows on the top and bottom. Click and drag to the new desired height. Double-clicking will automatically adjust the row height to the tallest entry in the row. Alternatively, click Format | Row Height or Format | AutoFit Row Height.
   - To hide a row(s), first select the row(s) to hide. Then click Format | Hide & Unhide | Hide Rows (or right-click the mouse and select the Hide option). To unhide hidden row(s), first select the row before and after the hidden row(s). Then click Format | Hide & Unhide | Unhide Rows (or right-click the mouse and select the Unhide option).
   - All of these actions (insert, delete, hide, unhide, and change column width) can also be done for columns, using similar procedures.
7. *Editing group.* Contains commands to perform editing tasks such as search, replace, sort, filter, etc. This group also includes the Fill command that can be used to automatically enter a series in a worksheet (e.g., numbers from 1 to 100, days of the week, months of the year) rather than typing these entries manually.

Insert Tab The Insert tab, shown in Figure B.4, includes commands for creating and/or inserting different objects such as tables, charts, pictures, clip art, hyperlinks (to other documents or Web links), text boxes, headers and/or footers, equations, symbols, etc. As with the Home tab, similar commands are arranged together within groups, such as Tables, Illustrations, Charts, Text, etc. Chapter 11 provides a detailed explanation of how to create a scatter chart in Excel.

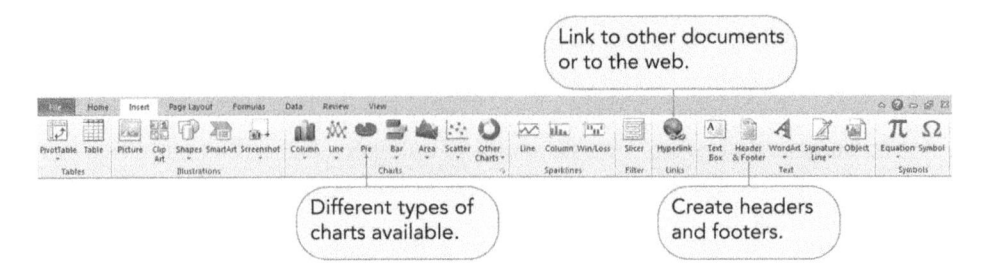

Figure B.4: Menu Commands in the Insert Tab in Excel 2016

Page Layout Tab The Page Layout tab, shown in Figure B.5, includes commands for setting print options such as margins, page orientation, size, print area, titles, page breaks, etc. In addition, it includes commands for displaying options such as view gridlines, view row and column headings, and themes. We discuss some of these commands in greater detail in section B.6.

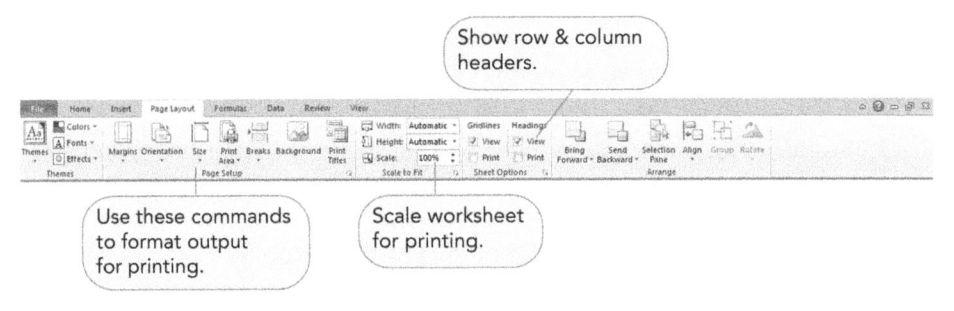

Figure B.5: Menu Commands in the Page Layout Tab in Excel 2016

Formulas Tab The Formulas tab, shown in Figure B.6, includes commands to access and select the numerous mathematical functions that are built into Excel for computational purposes.

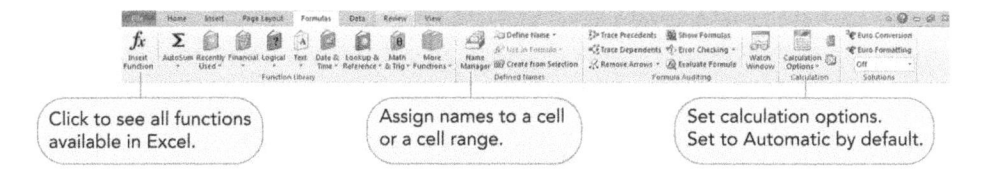

Figure B.6: Menu Commands in the Formulas Tab in Excel 2016

- Click to see all functions available in Excel.
- Assign names to a cell or a cell range.
- Set calculation options. Set to Automatic by default.

The icons representing these commands are arranged in the following default groups.
1. *Function Library group.* Click the Insert Function icon (represented by f_x) to access all functions available in Excel. Alternatively, click any of the other icons in this group (e.g., Financial, Logical, Math & Trig) to access only the functions under that subcategory.
2. *Defined Names group.* Use these commands to define names for an individual cell or a cell range. For example, if we define cell range B5:D10 using the name Table1, we can then refer to this cell range as Table1 in all formulas.
1. *Formula Auditing group.* These commands are useful for tracing and verifying cell relationships in formulas. They are especially useful when we encounter formula errors such as circular references.
2. *Calculation group.* Excel has three different options available for how it performs calculations:
    - *Automatic (default).* All calculations in all open worksheets and workbooks are performed automatically as soon as a cell entry is completed.
    - *Manual.* All calculations in the workbook are performed only when the F9 key is pressed.
    - *Automatic Except for Data Tables.* All calculations are performed automatically except for data tables, which are executed only when the F9 key is pressed. As discussed in Chapter 10, this option is very useful when running large simulation models.

Data Tab   The Data tab, shown in Figure B.7, includes commands to access data from external sources as well as several data tools to organize, manipulate, and analyze data. Of special interest in this book are the following: (1) the Sort and Filter options which allow us to sort data using multiple criteria, or filter it so that only selected entries are displayed, (2) the What-If Analysis command that includes three procedures (Scenario Manager, Goal Seek, and Data Table) that are discussed in this book, and (3) Excel add-ins such as Data Analysis and Solver found in the Analysis group. The Solver add-in forms the basis for all modeling applications discussed in Chapters 2 through 6, and the Data Analysis statistical tool is used in Chapters 10 and 11.

Figure B.7: Menu Commands in the Data Tab in Excel 2016

Review Tab The Review tab, shown in Figure B.8, includes commands for proofing text (e.g., spell check, thesaurus), creating and editing comments in cells, and using password options to protect individual cells, worksheets, or workbooks to prevent changes to their contents.

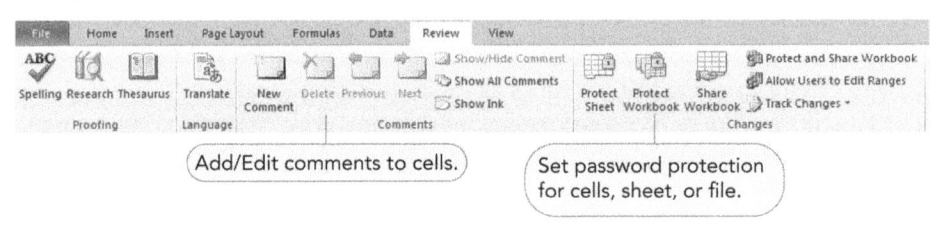

Figure B.8: Menu Commands in the Review Tab in Excel 2016

View Tab The View tab, shown in Figure B.9, includes various options to view the current worksheet, freeze rows and/or columns when scrolling, zoom in or out to specific content, and arrange multiple workbooks when more than one workbook is open. We can also record macros to automate repetitive tasks.

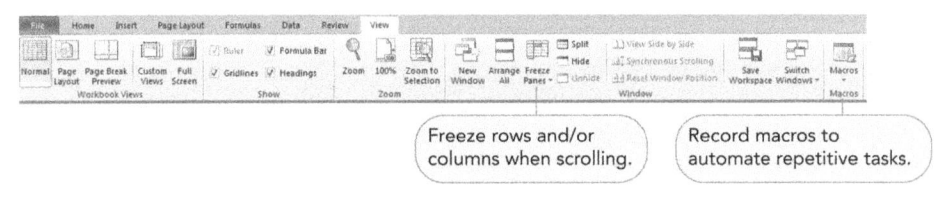

Figure B.9: Menu Commands in the View Tab in Excel 2016

Excel Help

If we are unsure about how to perform any action in Excel (or any other Microsoft Office program), we can use the extensive built-in help feature to get assistance. The help feature can display tips and detailed instructions (including examples) on how to use different Excel functions and procedures or provide help on the specific task we are performing. To start this feature, click the Help icon (which looks like a question mark) on the top-right side of the Ribbon (see Figure B.1) or click Help | Microsoft Excel Help, found within the File tab.

We can use common constructions to query the help database. For example, we can type "How do I format a cell?" and click the Search button. The program then responds with links to various help topics. If none of the suggestions match the query, click Next. When the response that best matches the query has been located, click that item. The help text is then displayed.

B.4 Working with Worksheets

To enter data or information in a worksheet, we first click the cell in which we want to enter the data. Then, we simply type in the data. We can enter numbers, text, dates, times, or formulas. (These are discussed in section B.5.) When we are done, we press the Enter key, and the next cell in the column is automatically selected.

Selecting a Group of Adjacent Cells Click the first cell to be selected. Hold down the Shift key and click the last cell to be selected. All cells in between these two cells will automatically be selected. Alternatively, after clicking the first cell, hold the left mouse button down and drag until we have selected all the cells needed.

Selecting a Group of Nonadjacent Cells Left-click the first cell to be selected. Hold down the Ctrl key and click each of the other cells to be selected. Only the cells clicked will be selected.

Selecting an Entire Row or Column Click the header (number) of the row that we want to select in its entirety. To select more than one entire row, keep either the Shift or the Ctrl key pressed (as discussed in the preceding item for selecting cells), depending on whether the rows are adjacent or nonadjacent. We can use a similar procedure to select one or more columns in their entirety.

Editing Data To edit the existing information in a cell, double-click the cell to be edited (or click once on the cell and press the F2 function key on the keyboard). We can now simply type over or modify the contents as desired.

Clearing Data To clear the data in selected cells, first select the cells that we want to clear. Next, press the Delete key on the keyboard.

B.5 Using Formulas and Functions

Formulas allow us to perform calculations on our worksheet data. A formula must start with an "equal to" (=) sign in Excel. To enter a formula, we click the cell where we want to enter the formula. Next type an = sign, followed by the formula. A formula can consist of mathematical operations involving numbers or cell references that point to cells with numerical values. After typing in a formula, press Enter to perform the calculation. If the Formulas | Calculation Options setting is set to Automatic (the default;

see Figure B.6), Excel will automatically recalculate the formula when we change any of the input values used in the formula.

Functions are formulas that are already built into Excel. As noted in section B.3, to see the full list of built-in functions in Excel, click the Insert Function command, found within the Formulas tab (or the f_x icon next to the formula bar on a worksheet, as shown in Figure B.1). A partial list is shown in Figure B.10. We can view subsets of these functions by selecting the category (e.g., Statistical, Financial) or click the appropriate category in the Function Library group.

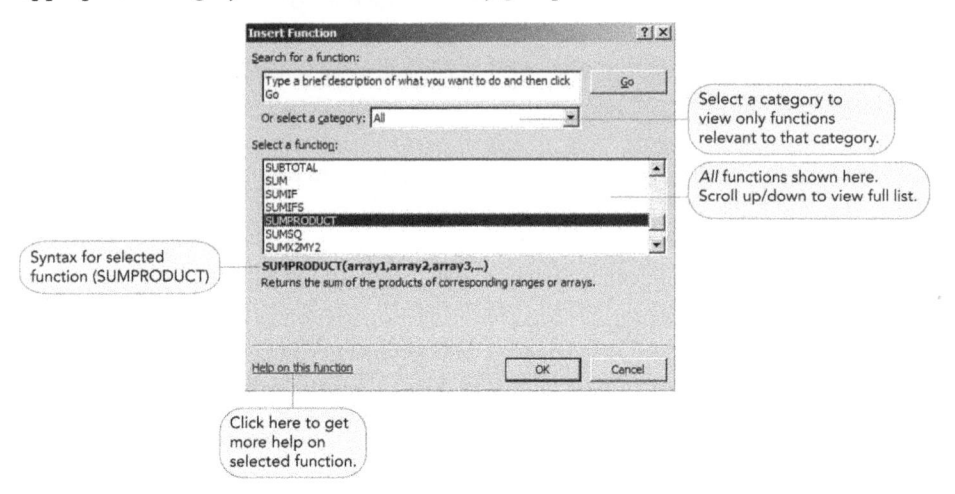

Figure B.10: Functions Available in Excel

When we select a specific function, the syntax for that function is displayed at the bottom of the window. For example, Figure B.10 shows the syntax for the SUMPRODUCT function that is used extensively in Chapters 2 through 6. For more detailed help on the selected function, click on Help on this function, in the bottom left of the window.

When using functions in Excel, we can prefix the function with an = sign and directly type in the function using the required syntax. Alternatively, we can select the cell in which we want to use a particular function. Then, we can call up the list of available functions (as described previously) and select the desired function. A window that shows the required input entries for the selected function is now displayed to guide us through the creation of the cell entry using the function.

Although Excel includes an extensive list of functions, Table B-1 presents a list of Excel functions that are the more commonly used based on our experience.

Table B.1: List of Common Excel Functions

Excel Function	Result
=1E+307	Can represent infinity, i.e., approximately the largest number that Excel can hold
=ABS(B6)	Returns the absolute value of the number in cell B6
=AND(B2=6,C2="Mary")	Returns "TRUE" (which has a value of 1) if both the value 6 is in cell B2 and the word Mary is in cell C2, and it returns "FALSE" (which has a value of 0) if both conditions are not true
=AVERAGE(A1:B6)	Calculates the mean of all numbers in the range A1 to B6, excluding blanks
=AVERAGEIF(A1:B6,">0")	Calculates the mean of all numbers in the range A1 to B6 that are positive
=CEILING(3.4, 1)	Rounds 3.4 up to the nearest whole integer (4)
=COLUMNS(B1:N7)	Counts the number of columns in the range B1:N7
=CONCATENATE("Mary"," ","Sanders")	Puts those three strings together as one string: "Mary Sanders"
=COUNT(A1:B6)	Counts all cells within the range that contain numbers
=COUNTIF(B4:M12,"<=60")	Counts all cells within the range with a value less than or equal to 60
=EXP(4)	Returns e raised to the power 4
=FV(0.12,5,1000)	Returns the future value of $1000 received every year for 5 years at 12% interest
=IF(A1=6,5,2)	If the value in cell A1 is 6, then a 5 is put in the cell; otherwise, a 2 is put there
=INDEX(B2:B12,3)	Returns the value in cell B4); =INDEX(B2:G5,2,3) (returns the value in cell D3
=INT(7.6)	Rounds 7.6 down to the nearest whole integer (7)
=INTERCEPT(y-range, x-range)	Provides the y-intercept of a regression line of dependent variables in the y-range with independent variables in the x-range
=ISBLANK(G2)	Returns "TRUE" (which = 1) if cell G2 is empty, and returns "FALSE" (which = 0) if not empty
=LARGE(B4:M7,2)	Returns the 2nd largest number from the range B4:M7
=LEFT("Darth Vader",3)	Returns the first 3 characters from the string "Darth Vader": "Dar"
=LEN("Luke Skywalker")	Returns the number of characters in the string "Luke Skywalker"
=LN(6)	Returns the natural log of the number 6
=MATCH(4,B2:B14,0)	Returns the relative position (index number) of the cell in the range B2:B14 containing 4
=MAX(A1:B6)	Returns the largest of all numbers in the range A1 to B6, excluding blanks
=MEDIAN(A1:B6)	Returns the median of all numbers in range A1 to B6, excluding blanks
=MIN(A1:B6)	Returns the smallest of all numbers in the range A1 to B6, excluding blanks

Excel Function	Result
=NORMSDIST(2.8)	Returns the standard normal cumulative distribution function of 2.8 standard deviations
=NORMSINV(0.92)	Returns the z-value for 92% from the standard normal distribution function
=NOT(A5=7)	Returns "TRUE" (which = 1) if A5 does not equal 7, and it returns "FALSE" (which = 0) if it does
=NOW()	Returns the date and time
=NPV(0.15,-1000,2000,3000)	Returns the net present value of $1000 paid after 1 year, $2000 received after 2 years, and $3000 received after 3 years, discounted at 15% per year
=OR(B2=6,C2="Mary")	Returns "TRUE" (which has a value of 1) if either the value 6 is in cell B2 or the word Mary is in cell C2, and it returns "FALSE" (which has a value of 0) if both conditions are not true
=PI()	Returns the value of Pi, 3.1459265358979
=PV(0.12,5,1000)	Returns the (negative of) present value of $1000 received every year for 5 years at 12% interest
=RAND()	Returns a random fractional number between 0 and 1 inclusive
=RANDBETWEEN(1,6)	Returns a random integer number between 1 and 6, i.e. rolls a die
=REPLACE(„Bob Jones",5,2,"BO")	Replaces the two characters beginning with the 5th ("J") with the letters "BO": "Bob BOnes"
=RIGHT(„Darth Vader",4)	Returns the last 4 characters from the string "Darth Vader": "ader"
=ROUND(5.4, 0)	Rounds the number 5.4 to 0 decimal places (rounds to 5)
=ROWS(B1:N7)	Counts the number of rows in the range B1:N7
=SLOPE(y-range, x-range)	Provides the y-intercept of a regression line of dependent variables in the y-range with independent variables in the x-range
=SMALL(B4:M7,2)	Returns the 2nd smallest number from the range B4:M7
=SQRT(7)	Calculates the square root of 7
=STDEV(A1:B6)	Calculates the standard deviation of numbers in the range A1 to B6, excluding blanks
=SUM(A1:B6)	Adds all numbers in the range A1 to B6
=SUMPRODUCT(A1:B2,D2:E3)	Multiplies corresponding components in the given arrays, and returns the sum of those products, e.g., A1*D2+A2*D3+B1*E2+B2*E3
=TODAY()	Returns the date
=VLOOKUP(40,A1:B3,2)	Searches for the largest number ≤ 40 in A1:A3 & returns that row's column B value

Copying Formulas

The mathematical symbols and numbers contained in formulas will copy directly. However, cell references are treated differently. Default cell referencing in formulas is actually recorded by Excel as distance relative to the current cell, as opposed to being recorded as an actual (unchanging) absolute cell name. For example, suppose that the formula in cell B4 is "=A2+6". Excel actually reads that formula as "Take the value from the cell located one column to the left and two rows above, and add that to the number 6." Thus, if cell B4 were then copied to cell D7, the new formula in cell D7 would be "=C5+6". In other words, the new cell referencing has the same relative distance as it did in the original cell. This type of feature is very useful, for example, with a table containing 12 columns representing each month and the formula at the bottom of each column sums the numbers in that respective column. In this case, the user would simply have to enter the formula once and then copy it over 11 times.

There are cases, however, where the user desires absolute, as opposed to, relative cell referencing for copying. An example might be a net present value analysis that references the same rate of return for each period. The user would prefer to just enter the rate of return once and have all copied formulas continue to reference that cell. To create absolute referencing, place a dollar sign ($) in front of the column and row label within the formula. (This is called "anchoring" the cell.) For example, if the formula in cell B4 is "=$A$2+6", then when the formula is copied to cell D7 is will still be "=$A$2+6". Note that it is also possible to anchor only the column or only the row. To complete the example, if the formula in cell B4 is "=$A2+6", then when the formula is copied to cell D7 it will become "=$A5+6". Alternatively, if the formula in cell B4 is "=A$2+6", then when the formula is copied to cell D7 it will become "=C$2+6".

Errors in Using Formulas and Functions

Sometimes, when we use a function or formula, the resulting output indicates an error in the entry. The following is a list of common errors when using formulas or functions and their possible causes:

1. #DIV/0! indicates that the formula or function involves division by zero.
2. #Name? indicates that the formula or function is not recognized by Excel. This is usually caused by a typographical error.
3. #VALUE indicates that one or more cell references used in a formula or function are invalid.
4. #### indicates that the cell is not wide enough to display the number. This can be easily remedied by increasing the width of the cell.

B.6 Printing Worksheets

If we wish to print the part or all of a worksheet, we can go directly to the print menu by clicking either File | Print (see Figure B.2) or the Print icon on the Quick Access Toolbar (see Figure B.1). The print interface window shown in Figure B.11 is displayed. A preview of the printed output is shown in the right side window. Before clicking Print, it is a good idea to verify that the output appears exactly the way we want it to print. Excel has numerous options available to make modifications to the printed output, as discussed in the following sections.

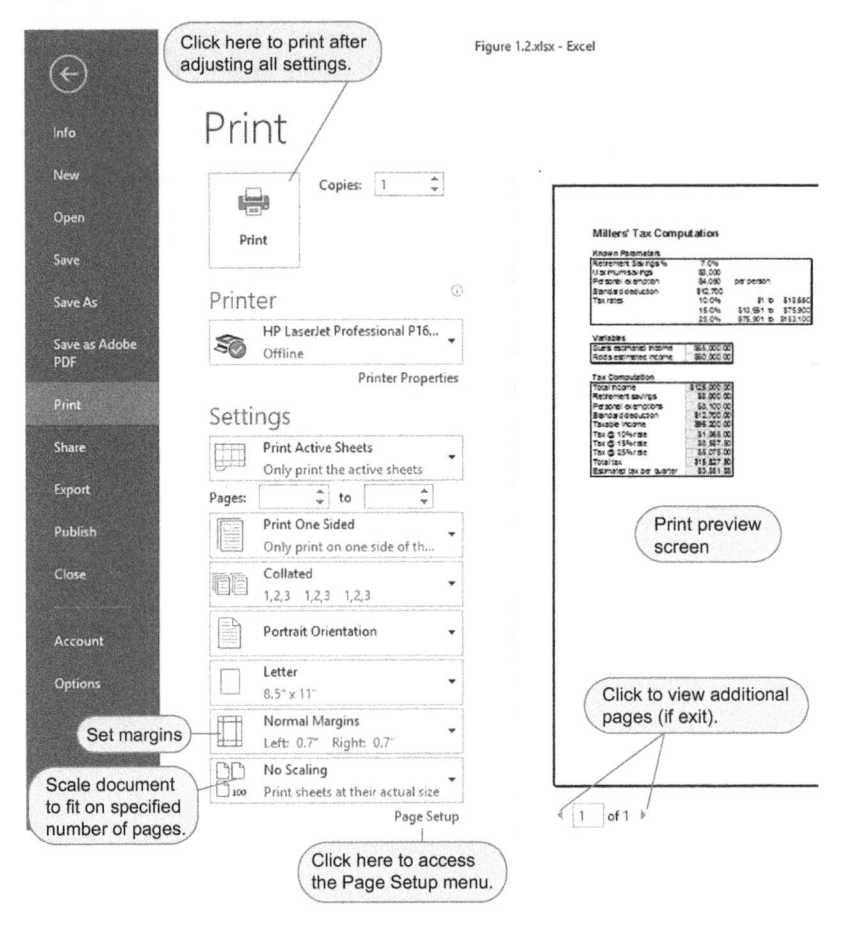

Figure B.11: Options Available in the Print Preview Window

Setting the Number of Copies, Paper Size, Orientation, and Scaling We can change the number of copies, paper size, page orientation, and print mode (one-sided or two-sided) using the options shown in Figure B.11. We can also scale the output so that the entire contents can be made to fit within a specified number of printed pages.

Setting the Print Area
If we wish to print only a portion of the current worksheet, first select the desired region of cells to print. Then click Print Area | Set Print Area, found in the Page Setup group within the Page Layout tab. We can clear a selected print area by clicking Print Area | Clear Print Area.

Setting Print Margins To change the print margins, click the arrow next to Normal Margins in Figure B.11 (or, alternatively, click Margins, found within the Page Layout tab) and adjust the margins as desired.

Page Breaks To insert a page break, first click on the row or column where we want the page break to be. For rows, the break will be above the selected row. For columns, it will be to the left of the selected column. Then click Breaks | Insert Page Break, found within the Page Layout tab. To remove an existing page break, first select the rows (or columns) on either side of the page break. Then click Breaks | Remove Page Break.

Centering Data on a Page To center data on a page, click Page Setup, as shown in Figure B.11 (or click Print Titles, found within the Page Layout tab). Select the tab named Margin and then check the boxes corresponding to whether we want the data centered horizontally, vertically, or both.

Inserting a Header or Footer To add a header and/or a footer, click Page Setup, as shown on Figure B.11 (or click Print Titles, found within the Page Layout tab). Then select the tab named Header/Footer and enter the text and format the header or footer.

Printing the Worksheet After making all adjustments, to print the worksheet click Print from within the Print Preview window in Figure B.11.

B.7 Excel Options and Add-Ins

As noted in section B.3, Excel has numerous options available with regard to how worksheets and workbooks are managed. To access these options, click Options, found within the File tab. The window shown in Figure B.12 is displayed.

As shown on the left pane of this screenshot, there are several categories of options available. Most are self-explanatory, and almost all can be left at their default values for most users. Note that two of the choices available here deal with customizing the Ribbon and Quick Access Toolbar, which we have already addressed. In the remainder of this section, we discuss in a bit more detail the last two option categories—Add-Ins and Trust Center—since they are of particular relevance in this book. Figure B.12 shows the contents of the right window pane when we select Add-Ins from the option categories.

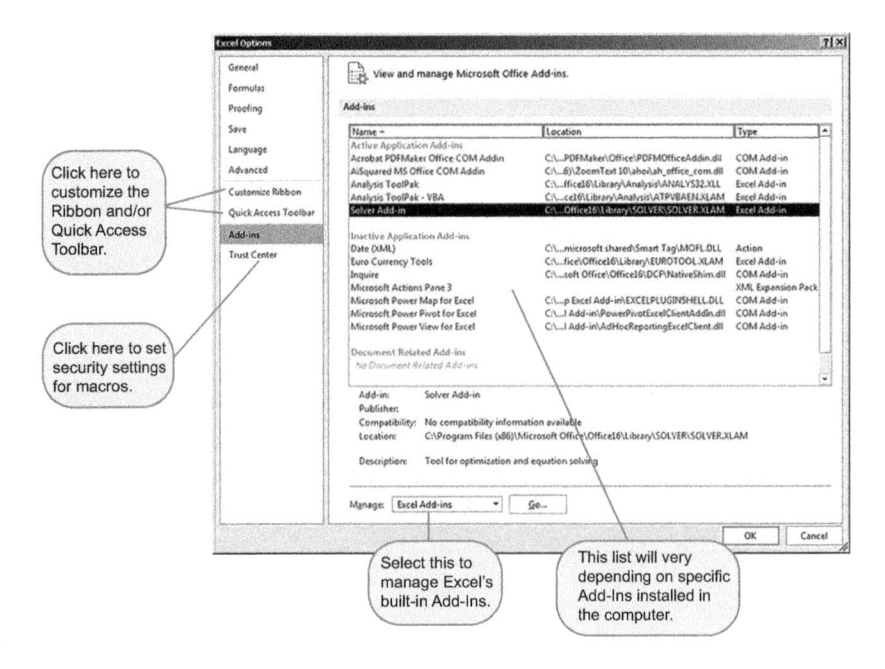

Figure B.12: Excel Options and Managing Add-ins

Add-Ins Add-ins are special programs that are designed to perform specific tasks in Excel. Typically, an add-in has the file extension *.xla*. Although Excel includes several add-ins, we focus here on only two, Solver and Data Analysis, that are useful in decision modeling.

Both Solver and Data Analysis are included with all recent versions of Excel. However, if we choose to install Excel using the default options, only Data Analysis may be installed during the installation process. To ensure that Solver is also installed, we need to change the installation defaults for Excel by clicking on the Excel options during the installation process and then choosing Add-Ins. Make sure the box next to the Solver option is checked.

Even after these add-ins have been installed, they need to be enabled (or switched on) in order for them to be available in Excel. To check if these add-ins have been enabled, start Excel and select the Data tab. If Data Analysis and/or Solver are seen as menu options in the Analysis group, the add-in has been enabled on that personal computer. However, if we do not see either (or both) add-ins, click File | Add-Ins to get the window shown in Figure B.12. Select Excel Add-Ins in the box labeled Manage and click Go.

The list of available Excel add-ins is now displayed, as shown in Figure B.13. To enable Data Analysis, make sure the boxes next to Analysis ToolPak and Analysis ToolPak – VBA are both checked. Likewise, to enable Solver, make sure the box next to Solver Add-In is checked.

Excel Options and Add-Ins — 783

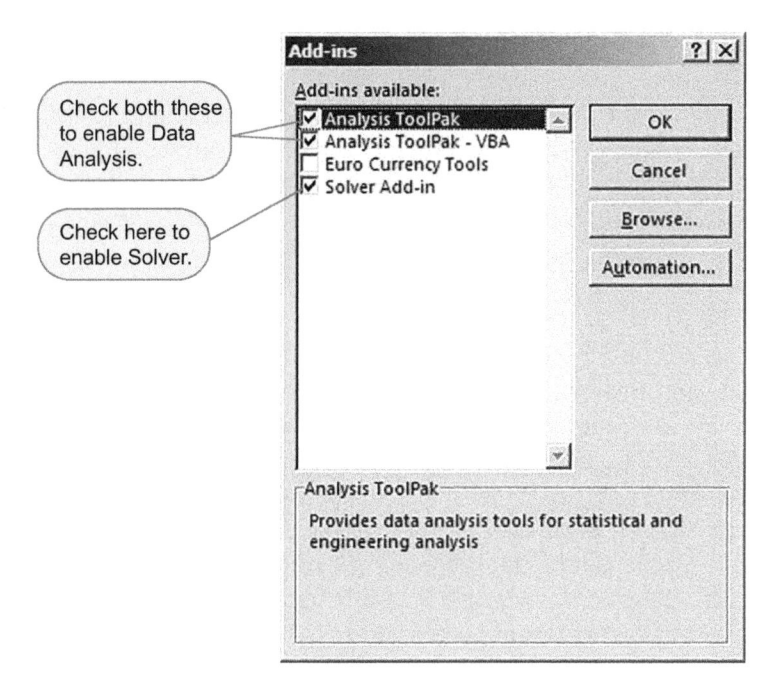

[Add-ins dialog box with callouts: "Check both these to enable Data Analysis." pointing to Analysis ToolPak and Analysis ToolPak - VBA; "Check here to enable Solver." pointing to Solver Add-in. Euro Currency Tools is unchecked. Description box reads: "Analysis ToolPak — Provides data analysis tools for statistical and engineering analysis"]

Figure B.13: List of Available Excel Add-ins

Depending on the boxes checked, the corresponding add-in should now be shown as an option under the Analysis group within the Data tab. For example, Figure B.7 shows that both Data Analysis and Solver add-ins have been enabled. From here onward, these add-ins will be available each time we start Excel on that computer. To access either add-in, simply click the Data tab and select the appropriate choice in the menu.

Trust Center Some add-ins (such as ExcelModules that we use in Chapters 9, 11, and 12) involve macros. By default, macros are disabled in Excel to prevent unauthorized programs for corrupting documents. To ensure that these add-ins function properly, we need to ensure that the macros embedded in them are enabled. To do so, click Trust Center in Excel's options window (see Figure B.12). Then click Trust Center Settings and select Macro Settings from the choices in the left side window. If we select Disable All Macros with Notification, Excel will ask for permission to run the macros each time the add-in is started. However, if we select Disable All Macros Without Notification, the add-in may not function properly since the macros are automatically disabled. As noted in Excel itself, selecting Enable All Macros is not recommended (unless we are sure of all the programs with macros that are being run).

B.8 ExcelModules

The Companion Website for this book contains a customized Excel add-in called ExcelModules. This program has been designed to help us better learn and understand decision models in queuing (Chapter 9), forecasting (Chapter 11), and inventory control (Chapter 12, which is available for free download from the Companion Website).

Installing ExcelModules

To install the current version (i.e., version 4) of ExcelModules on a Microsoft Windows based computer, locate and click the file named *ExcelModules4.exe* on the Companion Website. Then follow the setup instructions on the screen. Alternatively, download this executable file to the computer and install the program from there.

Default values have been assigned for most installation parameters in the setup program, but these can be changed as needed. For example, on most machines the program will be installed by default to a directory on the C: drive named *C:\Program Files (x86)\ExcelModules4*. Generally speaking, it is only necessary to simply click Next each time that the installation program asks a question. The program automatically creates a shortcut called *ExcelModules v4* on the desktop.

To install the current version of ExcelModules on a Mac, download the relevant ZIP file from the Companion Website. Unzip the file and follow the instructions in the ReadMe file that is included in the ZIP file.

Running ExcelModules

Once the program has been installed, we can start it by clicking the *ExcelModules v4* shortcut on the desktop. When ExcelModules is started, it automatically also starts Excel. Alternatively, if Excel is already open, we can add ExcelModules to it by clicking the *ExcelModules v4* icon on the desktop or by clicking the file named *ExcelModules4.xlam*, which is located in the directory where the software was installed. (The default is *C:\Program Files (x86)\ExcelModules4* if this was not changed at the time of installation.)

It is also possible to set ExcelModules to load automatically each time we start Excel, although we do not recommend this option. To do this, we follow the process described for add-ins in section B.6 and select the file named *ExcelModules4.xlam*.

As noted previously, ExcelModules requires the use of macros in Excel. Unless the computer has been set to always automatically allow macros (which is not recommended), Excel will generate a security notice, as shown in Figure B.14, asking for permission to enable macros each time we start ExcelModules. We must allow macros to be enabled in order for the program to function properly.

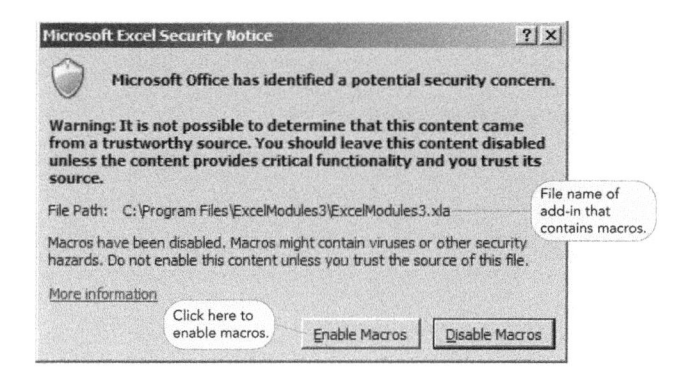

Figure B.14: Security Notice Regarding Macros in Excel

When the program starts, a new tab named ExcelModules appears on Excel's Ribbon, as shown in Figure B.15. When we click this tab, we see the ExcelModules ribbon with the following four groups: a group named Menu that includes a single icon named Modules, a group named Support that includes various way to get help for the program, a group named Tools with several program options, and a group named Exit that includes a single icon to close the program.

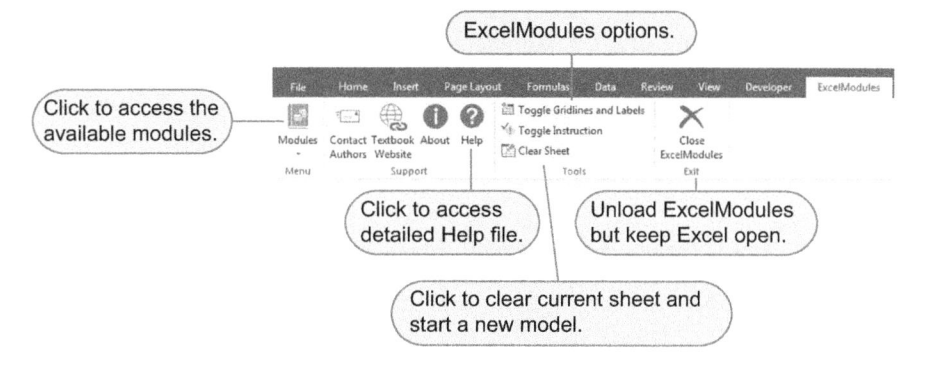

Figure B.15: ExcelModules Ribbon

When we click the Modules icon in the Menu group, we see the main menu as shown in Figure B.16. The main menu shows the three categories of decision models—Queuing, Forecasting, and Inventory—that are included in ExcelModules. Figure B.16 also lists the specific forecasting models that are included in the program. Instructions for using each decision model in ExcelModules are provided at appropriate places in Chapters 9, 11, and 12 (downloadable from the Companion Website) of this book.

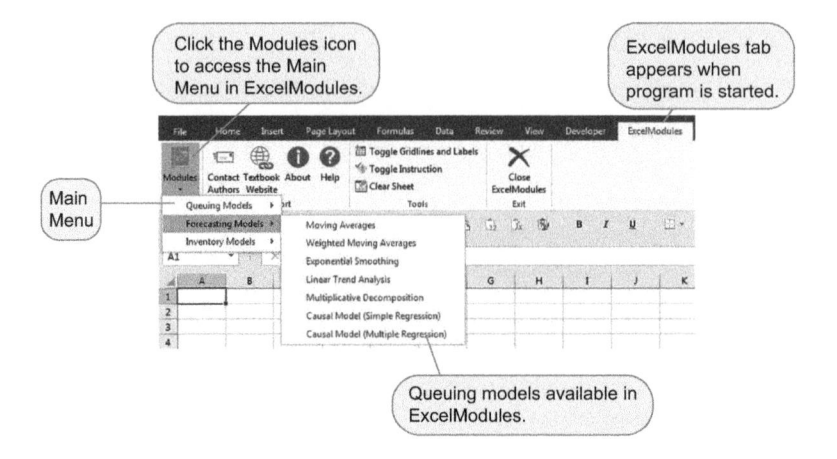

Figure B.16: Decision Models Available In Excelmodules

ExcelModules Help and Options

As shown in Figure B.15, the ExcelModules ribbon also includes a group named Support that includes the following four choices:

1. *Contact Authors.* Click this icon to email the authors for technical support if needed. When contacting the authors for help, please be sure to include the version number of the program (i.e., ExcelModules v4), the specific decision model in which the problem is occurring, and a detailed explanation of the problem. If appropriate, please attach the data file for which the problem occurs.
2. *Book Website.* Click to open the dedicated web page for this book on the browser.
3. *About.* Click to view a screen displaying details of this software.
4. *Help.* Click to access detailed help file for ExcelModules.

The group named Tools includes the following three choices:

5. *Toggle Gridlines and Labels.* Click to toggle the appearance of the spreadsheet by turning grid lines and row/column headers on or off.
6. *Toggle Instruction.* Click to remove the model-specific instruction textbox that is generated at the top of the worksheet for each model.
7. *Clear Sheet.* Click to erase the current worksheet (use with caution).

Finally, the group named Exit includes a single icon labeled Close ExcelModules. Clicking this icon unloads the ExcelModules add-in but leaves Excel open.

ExcelModules serves two purposes in the learning process. First, it can help us solve homework problems. We enter the appropriate data, and the program provides numerical solutions. In addition, ExcelModules allows us to note the Excel formulas used to develop solutions and modify them to deal with a wider variety of problems. This "open" approach allows us to observe, understand, and even change the formulas underlying the Excel calculations, conveying Excel's power as a decision modeling tool.

Appendix C
Areas Under The Standard Normal Curve

To find the area under a normal curve, we must know the Z score, which defines how many standard deviations we are from the mean of the distribution. For positive valued Z scores up to 3.59, the area under the normal curve can be read directly from the table below.

Example: For example, the area under the normal curve for a normal value that is 1.51 standard deviations above the mean (i.e., to the right of the mean, as shown in Figure C.1) is 0.9345. To find the area under (to the left of) negative valued Z scores, we use the symmetric property of the normal distribution. For example, the area under $Z = -1.51$ is the same as the area above $Z = 1.51$, equal to $1 - 0.9345 = 0.0655$.

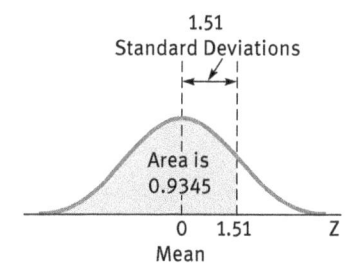

Figure C.1: Area Under Normal Curve for $Z = 1.51$.

Z	.00	.01	.02	.03	.04	.05	.06	.07	.08	.09
0.0	0.5000	0.5040	0.5080	0.5120	0.5160	0.5199	0.5239	0.5279	0.5319	0.5359
0.1	0.5398	0.5438	0.5478	0.5517	0.5557	0.5596	0.5636	0.5675	0.5714	0.5753
0.2	0.5793	0.5832	0.5871	0.5910	0.5948	0.5987	0.6026	0.6064	0.6103	0.6141
0.3	0.6179	0.6217	0.6255	0.6293	0.6331	0.6368	0.6406	0.6443	0.6480	0.6517
0.4	0.6554	0.6591	0.6628	0.6664	0.6700	0.6736	0.6772	0.6808	0.6844	0.6879
0.5	0.6915	0.6950	0.6985	0.7019	0.7054	0.7088	0.7123	0.7157	0.7190	0.7224
0.6	0.7257	0.7291	0.7324	0.7357	0.7389	0.7422	0.7454	0.7486	0.7517	0.7549
0.7	0.7580	0.7611	0.7642	0.7673	0.7704	0.7734	0.7764	0.7794	0.7823	0.7852
0.8	0.7881	0.7910	0.7939	0.7967	0.7995	0.8023	0.8051	0.8078	0.8106	0.8133
0.9	0.8159	0.8186	0.8212	0.8238	0.8264	0.8289	0.8315	0.8340	0.8365	0.8389
1.0	0.8413	0.8438	0.8461	0.8485	0.8508	0.8531	0.8554	0.8577	0.8599	0.8621
1.1	0.8643	0.8665	0.8686	0.8708	0.8729	0.8749	0.8770	0.8790	0.8810	0.8830
1.2	0.8849	0.8869	0.8888	0.8907	0.8925	0.8944	0.8962	0.8980	0.8997	0.9015
1.3	0.9032	0.9049	0.9066	0.9082	0.9099	0.9115	0.9131	0.9147	0.9162	0.9177
1.4	0.9192	0.9207	0.9222	0.9236	0.9251	0.9265	0.9279	0.9292	0.9306	0.9319
1.5	0.9332	0.9345	0.9357	0.9370	0.9382	0.9394	0.9406	0.9418	0.9429	0.9441
1.6	0.9452	0.9463	0.9474	0.9484	0.9495	0.9505	0.9515	0.9525	0.9535	0.9545
1.7	0.9554	0.9564	0.9573	0.9582	0.9591	0.9599	0.9608	0.9616	0.9625	0.9633
1.8	0.9641	0.9649	0.9656	0.9664	0.9671	0.9678	0.9686	0.9693	0.9699	0.9706
1.9	0.9713	0.9719	0.9726	0.9732	0.9738	0.9744	0.9750	0.9756	0.9761	0.9767
2.0	0.9772	0.9778	0.9783	0.9788	0.9793	0.9798	0.9803	0.9808	0.9812	0.9817
2.1	0.9821	0.9826	0.9830	0.9834	0.9838	0.9842	0.9846	0.9850	0.9854	0.9857
2.2	0.9861	0.9864	0.9868	0.9871	0.9875	0.9878	0.9881	0.9884	0.9887	0.9890
2.3	0.9893	0.9896	0.9898	0.9901	0.9904	0.9906	0.9909	0.9911	0.9913	0.9916
2.4	0.9918	0.9920	0.9922	0.9925	0.9927	0.9929	0.9931	0.9932	0.9934	0.9936
2.5	0.9938	0.9940	0.9941	0.9943	0.9945	0.9946	0.9948	0.9949	0.9951	0.9952
2.6	0.9953	0.9955	0.9956	0.9957	0.9959	0.9960	0.9961	0.9962	0.9963	0.9964
2.7	0.9965	0.9966	0.9967	0.9968	0.9969	0.9970	0.9971	0.9972	0.9973	0.9974
2.8	0.9974	0.9975	0.9976	0.9977	0.9977	0.9978	0.9979	0.9979	0.9980	0.9981
2.9	0.9981	0.9982	0.9982	0.9983	0.9984	0.9984	0.9985	0.9985	0.9986	0.9986
3.0	0.9987	0.9987	0.9987	0.9988	0.9988	0.9989	0.9989	0.9989	0.9990	0.9990
3.1	0.9990	0.9991	0.9991	0.9991	0.9992	0.9992	0.9992	0.9992	0.9993	0.9993
3.2	0.9993	0.9993	0.9994	0.9994	0.9994	0.9994	0.9994	0.9995	0.9995	0.9995
3.3	0.9995	0.9995	0.9995	0.9996	0.9996	0.9996	0.9996	0.9996	0.9996	0.9997
3.4	0.9997	0.9997	0.9997	0.9997	0.9997	0.9997	0.9997	0.9997	0.9997	0.9998
3.5	0.9998	0.9998	0.9998	0.9998	0.9998	0.9998	0.9998	0.9998	0.9998	0.9998

Appendix D
Brief Solutions to All Odd-Numbered End-Of-Chapter Problems

Chapter 1
- 1–19 (a) 375,000. (b) $22,500.
- 1–21 (a) Make major modifications. (b) $45,500.
- 1–23 $10,500.
- 1–25 10,550 units.
- 1–27 Yes. The profit will increase by $1,000.
- 1–29 (a) $BEP_A = 6,250$. $BEP_B = 7,750$. (b) Choose A. (c) 3,250 widgets, but both machines lose money at this production level.
- 1–31 (b) $140,000. (c) The $100 price appears to be too low. (d) $115.00.
- 1–33 (c) $4,122.50.
- 1–37 (b) 30.85%. (c) 10.329 ounces.

Chapter 2
- 2–15 $X = 2.3, Y = 3.9$, Objective $= 8.50$.
- 2–17 $X = 22.50. Y = 6.75$, Objective $= 110.25$.
- 2–19 $X = 3, Y = 5.6$, Objective $= 48.20$.
- 2–21 $A = 3.33, B = 1.67, C = 1.67$, Objective $= 158.33$.
- 2–23 Painting $= 624$, Glazing $= 300$, Revenue $= \$3,858$.
- 2–25 Internet $= 10$, Print $= 50$, Exposure $= 6$ million people.
- 2–27 Make 24 A motors and 84 B motors. Profit $= \$1,572$.
- 2–29 Invest $401.72 in Carolina Solar and $2,750.79 in South West. Total investment $= \$3,152.52$.
- 2–31 Regular $= 52$, Low Fat $= 48$, Profit $= \$161.36$.
- 2–33 Build 344 small boxes and 80 large boxes. Profit $= \$13,520$.
- 2–35 Make 175 benches and 50 tables. Profit $= \$2,575$.
- 2–37 Schedule 35 core courses and 25 electives. Faculty salaries $= \$166,000$.
- 2–39 16 pounds of Feed Mix X and 16 pounds of Feed Mix Y. Total cost $= \$112$ per day.
- 2–41 Build 284 small boxes, 80 large boxes, and 100 mini boxes. Profit $= \$13,420$.
- 2–43 EC221 $= 20,650$, EC496 $= 100$, NC455 $= 2,750$ and NC791 $= 400$. Profit $= \$232,700$.
- 2–45 Invest $2,555.25 in BBC and $1,139.50 in CBC
- 2–47 $2X + 2.5Y \leq 100$
- 2–49 (a) Infeasible solution. (b) Remove $8X + 4Y \leq 160$. Optimal cost $= \$286.67$.
- 2–51 $X = 48, Y = 16$, Objective $= 2,720$.
- 2–53 $X = 31.6418, Y = 10.4478, Z = 37.0149$, Objective $= 831.881$.
- 2–55 $A = 10, B = 0, C = 25, D = 0$, Optimal profit $= \$10,100$.

Chapter 3
- 3–1 Make 20 canvas, 40 plastic, 25 nylon, and 40 leather backpacks. Profit $= \$2,483.58$.
- 3–3 Make 1,200 Junior, 750 Travel, and 300 Deluxe pillows. Profit $= \$3,340.50$.
- 3–5 Make 116.67 Italian, 60 French, and 350 Caribbean. Profit $= \$39,600$.
- 3–7 In-house: W111 $= 1,864$, W222 $= 2,250$, W333 $= 1,020$.
  Out-source: W111 $= 136$, W222 $= 1,500$, W333 $= 680$. Total cost $= \$150,964.20$.
- 3–9 Interview 1,175 male Democrats and 525 female Democrats; 1,125 male Republicans and 675 female Republicans; and 450 male independents and 550 female independents. Total cost to poll $= \$49,100$.
- 3–11 Issue 4,000 $1 coupons, 6,500 $0.85 coupons, 1,500 $0.70 coupons, 1,500 $0.55 coupons, and 1,500 $0.40 coupons. Total cost $= \$37,234.50$.
- 3–13 Invest $100,000 in Miami, $191,666.67 in American Smart Car, $75,000 in Green Earth Energy, $50,000 in Rosslyn Drugs, and $83,333.33 in RealCo. Total Return $= \$38,708.33$.
- 3–15 Invest $30,000 in T-bills, $60,000 in international mutual funds, $20,000 in school bonds, $20,000 in certificates of deposit, $30,000 in tax-free municipal bonds, and $40,000 in the stock market. Total return $= \$19,075$.
- 3–17 Have 4 nurses begin work at 1 a.m., 9 at 5 a.m., 8 at 9 a.m., 7 at 1 p.m., 5 at 5 p.m., and none at 9 p.m. Total nurses needed is 33. Alternate solutions may exist.
- 3–19 Assign 12 nurses each to A and A(alt), 4 nurses each to B and B(alt), 10 nurses each to C and C(alt), and no nurses to either D or D(alt). Cost for each half shift $= \$21,252$. Total cost $= \$42,504$.

DOI 10.1515/9781501506208-015

3–21	Ship 210 pounds of Cargo A, 150 pounds of B, 125.45 pounds of E, and 250 pounds of G. Freight = $5,921.82
3–23	Ship 10 tons of A, 12 tons of B, and 5.78 tons of C. Revenue = $19,657.78.
3–25	Plant 32.5 acres of corn and 25 acres of okra. Total revenue = $151,775.
3–27	Plant 2,200 acres of wheat, 165.52 acres of alfalfa, and 1,000 acres of barley. Profit = $339,931.03.
3–29	Hire 15 union, 12 non-union, and 3 temporary workers. Total cost = $4,218.
3–31	Each pound of feed is comprised of 0.167 pounds of beef, 0.459 pounds of lamb, 0.066 pounds of rice, and 0.309 pounds of chicken. Cost = $0.40 per pound.
3–33	The diet should include 1.655 servings of chicken patty, 2.077 cups of milk, 9.348 cups of fruit cocktail, and 7.892 cups of orange juice. Cost = $8. *Note:* Alternate optimal solutions may exist.
3–35	The hotdog is comprised of 0.0313 pounds of beef, 0.0313 pounds of pork, and 0.0625 pounds of turkey. Cost = $0.086.
3–37	*Tuffcoat:* Base A = 320 gallons, Base B = 1,280 gallons, Cost = $6.10 per gallon. *Satinwear:* Base A = 625 gallons, Base B = 625 gallons, Cost = $5.50 per gallon. Total Cost = $16,635.
3–39	Feed A = 8 lb., Feed B = 2 lb., Feed C = 2 lb., Feed D = 12 lb., Feed E = 16 lb. Cost = $22.33 per bag.
3–41	*Unrounded solution:* IC341: September = 1,525, October = 0, November = 1,690, December = 1,000. IC256: September = 900, October = 1,989.42, November = 460.58, December = 1,250. Total cost: $12,429. Alternate solutions may exist.
3–43	*Unrounded solution:* January: 175 agents and 9.39 trainees; February: 175.64 agents and 21.28 trainees; March: 189.90 agents and 16.79 trainees; April: 200.99 agents and 2.68 trainees; May: 199.65 agents and 0 trainees. Salary = $3,236,250.53.
3–45	Total cost = $16,420.
3–47	Each school will have 1,120 students. Total mileage = 20,114.
3–49	*Unrounded solution:* 0.52 TV spots, 5 newspaper ads, 6.21 prime time radio spots, and 0 afternoon radio spots. Budget = $6,841.55.
3–51	Produce 700 units with regular production in all three months. Produce 50 units during overtime during all three months. Use no subcontracting in January, 60 units of subcontracting in February, and 130 units of subcontracting in March. Total cost = $105,220.
3–53	Purchase 20,000 units of A from the overseas supplier. Purchase 2,000 units of B from the overseas supplier. Purchase 4,000 units of C from the local supplier. Purchase 266.51 units of D from the local supplier and 733.49 units of D from the overseas supplier. Purchase 1,000 units of E from the local supplier. Total cost = $170,197.67.
3–55	*Unrounded solution:* $B_1 = 22.5$, $B_2 = 300$, $B_3 = 22.5$, $N_1 = 977.5$, $N_2 = 300$, $N_3 = 677.5$. Interview cost = $15,385.

Chapter 4

4–11	Solution to original problem: (24,4) $124: (a) No change in corner point; objective = $132. (b) New corner point: (24,14); objective increases to $194. (c) New corner point (15,10); objective = $130.
4–13	(a) Total audience would increase by 406. (b) No. They are already over this contract level. (c) No. Need to increase exposure to at least 3,144.83 for optimal solution to change. (d) 0 to 6,620.69.
4–15	(a) Total cost decreases by $0.0038. (b) 100% rule satisfied, same mix, total cost is $0.0529. (c) 100% rule satisfied, total cost decreases by $0.0038.
4–17	(a) Alternate optimal solutions exist. (b) Profit increases by $3,758.60, to $341,620.67. (c) Profit increases by $20.69 for each additional acre-foot of water.
4–19	(a) Phosphorus is a non-binding constraint and therefore has a shadow price of zero. Cost increases by $1 for each additional mg of iron required in the diet. (b) Cost does not change since the reduced cost for oatmeal is zero. (c) $0.55. (d) Multiple optimal solutions exist. Several OFC have zero allowable increase/decrease.
4–21	(a) Optimal solution = (15,10), profit = $125. (b) $\{3.33 \leq C_X \leq 10\}, \{2.5 \leq C_Y \leq 7.5\}$. (c) Profit would increase by $1.25; between 48 and 120. (d) Profit would decrease by $0.63; between 40 and 88. (e) Same corner point, new profit = $185. (f) Same corner point, new profit = $105. (g) No change. (h) No. The shadow price is zero. (i) Same corner point, new profit = $145. (j) Yes. Profit increases by $12.50.
4–23	Compact model is not attractive. Kiddo model is attractive.
4–25	(a) $0 to $7.33. (b) No.
4–27	No. Profit would decrease by $3.225 for each TwinTote made if TwinTotes are not included in the 40% limit for ToddleTotes. If it is included in the 40% limit, profit would decrease by $1.685.
4–29	(a) New production plan and increased profit unknown from current report. New plan would include more oak tables. (b) Production plan would not change. Profit decreases by $231.56. (c) Production plan would not change. Profit increases by $845.20. (d) Same production plan, profit decreases by $15. (e) No impact. Already making 33.08. (f) Currently making 85.56. Profit would decrease.
4–31	(a) Production plan will not change. Profit decreases by $90. (b) Production plan will not change. Profit increases by $1,946.80. (c) 100% rule not satisfied. New production plan and profit unknown from current report. (d) Production plan will not change. Profit increases by $514.40. (e) 100% rule not satisfied. New production plan and profit unknown from current report.
4–33	(a) Cost = $176.42, tuna = 10, tuna/cheese = 30, ham = 10, ham/cheese = 12, cheese = 8.

Appendix D: Brief Solutions to All Odd-Numbered End-Of-Chapter Problems — 791

4–35 (b) *Binding:* bread, tuna, minimum total, minimum tuna, minimum ham, and minimum ham/cheese. (c) Between $2.12 and $3.02. (d) Between 124 and 154 ounces. (e) No. (f) 2.4 hours.
(a) New production plan with higher cost. (b) No change. Current plan uses only 76 ounces. (c) New production plan with higher cost. (d) New production plan with higher cost. (e) No impact. Currently delivering 30 tuna and cheese. (f) Cost will decrease; currently delivering 70 sandwiches.
4–37 (a) No. This purchase would increase cost by $0.22. (b) Substitute at most 3.5 ham-type sandwiches. (c) 4 jars.
4–39 (a) Sum of ratios = .82 < 1, so the 100% rule can be used. Cost increase = $0.5125. (b) This is a mixture of OFC and RHS changes, so the 100% rule cannot be used. (c) Sum of ratios = .68 < 1, so the 100% rule can be used. Cost increase = $0.8538. (d) Sum of ratios = .57 < 1, so the 100% rule can be used. Cost decrease = $0.408. (e) Sum of ratios = 1.53 > 1, so the 100% rule cannot be used. (f) Sum of ratios = .85 < 1, so the 100% rule can be used. Cost increase = $3.08.
4–41 (a) Profit decrease = $600. (b) Beyond the allowable decrease. Profit impact unknown. (c) Profit increase = $3,800. (d) No impact, profit change = $0. (e) Beyond the allowable decrease. Profit impact unknown.
4–43 $248.
4–45 Cost decrease = $224.

Chapter 5

Note: Alternate optimal solutions could exist for some of these problems.

5–13 (a) Total cost = $52,200. (b) Total cost with transshipment = $51,450.
5–15 Total interest = $28,300, or an average rate of 9.43%.
5–17 Cost with New Orleans = $20,000, Cost with Houston = $19,500. Houston should be selected.
5–19 Cost with Brevard = $17,400, Cost with Laurens = $17,250. Laurens should be selected. (b) Maximum shipped on any route = 100, Cost = $18,650.
5–21 Total cost = $11,740.
5–23 Assign Job A to Machine Y, B to Z, C to W, and D to X. Total hours = 50.
5–25 Assign Morris to Cardiology, Richards to Orthopedics, Cook to Urology, and Morgan to Pediatrics. Total index = 86.
5–27 Assign Squad 1 to Case C, 2 to B, 3 to D, 4 to E, and 5 to A. Total days = 28.
5–29 Total length = 4,500 feet (use 1–2, 1–3, 1–4, 3–6, 4–5, 6–7, 7–9, 8–9, 9–10, 9–12, 10–11, 11–13, 12–14); Other solutions are available.
5–31 1–3–5–7–10–13, Distance = 430 miles.
5–33 (a) 167 widgets. (b) 140 widgets.
5–35 3 million gallons per hour.
5–37 Shortest distance = 74. The path is 1–5–9–12–14.
5–39 Distance = 2,100 yards (use 1–2, 1–3, 3–7, 4–5, 5–6, 6–7, 6–8, 8–9); Other solutions are available.
5–41 Load on each machine = 68.22 hours.
5–43 (a) Donovan assigned to Project 3, Edwards assigned to Project 2, and Franklin assigned to Project 1. Total cost = $72. (b) Donovan assigned to Project 1, Edwards assigned to Project 3, and Franklin assigned to Project 2. Total cost = $65.
5–45 (a) Ship 100 desks from Des Moines to Albuquerque, 200 desks from Evansville to Boston, 100 desks from Evansville to Cleveland, 150 desks from Little Rock to Albuquerque, 50 desks from Fort Lauderdale to Albuquerque, and 100 desks from Fort Lauderdale to Cleveland. Total cost = $3,150. (b) All of Albuquerque's demand is now satisfied from Little Rock. Des Moines now supplies its 100 desks to Cleveland. Fort Lauderdale produces nothing. New total cost = $2,600.
5–47 1–2–3–4–6, Distance = 280 miles.
5–49 (a) The 100 cars originally going on 1–4 now flow from 1–2 and then from 2–4. Maximal flow remains 500 cars. (b) Now 300 more cars (500 total) flow from 1–3, and those 300 cars flow across 3–4A–6. New Maximal flow = 800 cars.

Chapter 6

6–13 Clean 8 houses and 10 lawyer offices. Profit = $2,050.
6–15 (a) Total workers = 27. (b) Total pay = $12,345.
6–17 Need 10 coins.
6–19 Include all but investment A. Total return will be $3,580.
6–21 Sign pitchers B, C, D, F, and H. Total value = 25.
6–23 Select Atlanta and Los Angeles. Alternate solutions are possible.
6–25 Choose Philadelphia and Denver. Total cost = $4,390.
6–27 (a) Locations 1 and 3; 130 miles total. (b) Open trauma centers at locations 2 and 4.
6–29 Publish 8,000 copies of Book 2, 5,000 copies of Book 3, and 7,000 copies of Book 5. Profit = $487,000.
6–31 TV = 10, Newspaper = 35. Goals R_1 and R_2 fully satisfied. Goal R_3 underachieved by 750,000 people.
6–33 *Unrounded Solution:* Make 1,938.67 coils, 350.94 shafts, and 3,267.46 housings. Buy 61.33 coils, 1,649.06 shafts, and no housings. Goals R_1 and R_2 are fully satisfied. Goal R_3 is underachieved by 138.67 coils.

6–35	Invest $1,650 in investment B, $600 in investment C, $4,500 in investment E and $2,250 in investment F. Return is $583.50. Goals 1, 3, 5 and 7 are fully met. Goal 2 is underachieved by $416.50. Goal 4 is overachieved by $1,350. Goal 6 is overachieved by $2,250.
6–37	$X_1 = 2.80, X_2 = 4.92, X_3 = 3.37$. Objective = 186.07 Solution appears to be global optimal.
6–39	Produce 38.46 six-cylinder engines. Profit = $89,615.38. Solution appears to be global optimal.
6–41	Invest 21% of funds in A, 33% of funds in B, and 46% of funds in G. Solution appears to be global optimal.
6–43	Load on each machine = 68.56 hours.
6–45	$3A + 2B \le 18 + MY$ and $A + 4B \le 16 + M(1 - Y)$
6–47	(a) Carry the machete, the cooking equipment, the charcoal, the water, and the laptop. Total value = 38. Problem: no food—could add a constraint forcing at least one food package to be taken. (b) Toiletries replace cooking equipment. The total value drops by 3. There is room for 3 more pounds, but nothing else will fit.
6–49	$Q \ge 1000Y_2, Q \ge 5000Y_3, q_2 \le MY_2$, and $q_3 \le MY_3$.
6–51	(a) $T + O \le 1$. (b) $H + S = 1$. (c) $P + D + T + H + O + S \le 4$. (d) $D \ge P$. (e) $S \ge H$. (f) $T = O$. (g) $P + D + H + S \ge 3$.
6–53	The new solution was only 25 cents worse. Rounding was not always to the nearest whole unit.

Chapter 7

7–13	Critical path = A–C–E–G, Project length = 17 weeks.
7–15	Critical path B–E–G, Project length = 18 days.
7–17	(c) Critical path = C–D–E–F–H–K, Project length = 36.5 days. (d) 0.7352.
7–19	(c) Critical path = A–D–F–H–J–K, Project length = 69 days. (d) 0.6097. (e) 0.0473.
7–21	(c) Critical path = B–C–D–H–I–J, Project length = 48 days. (d) 0.6279. (e) 0.0251.
7–23	(a) 0.8944. (b) 0.2266. (c) 34.31 weeks. (d) 29.15 weeks.
7–25	(a) *EST totals for months 1–36*: $1,667, $8,667, $8,667, $2,381, $4,381, $4,381, $4,114, $2,114, $2,114, $2,114, $1,400, $1,400, $3,400, $3,400, $3,127, $3,127, $1,727, $1,727, $10,727, $10,727, $10,727, $10,727, $10,442, $10,442, $4,442, $2,714, $2,714, $2,714, $2,714, $2,714, $714, $714, $714, $714, and $714. (b) *LST totals for months 1–36*: $1,667, $1,667, $1,667, $2,381, $9,381, $9,381, $2,114, $2,114, $2,114, $4,114, $3,400, $3,400, $1,400, $1,400, $1,945, $3,127, $1,727, $1,727, $3,727, $6,727, $4,727, $7,727, $8,442, $7,442, $10,442, $9,896, $8,714, $5,714, $5,714, $5,714, $2,714, $714, $714, $714, $714, and $714.
7–27	(a) *EST totals for weeks 1–12*: $1,100, $1,100, $3,200, $3,200, $3,200, $1,500, $2,700, $2,700, $900, $600, $600, and $600. (b) *LST totals for weeks 1–12*: $1,100, $1,100, $1,500, $1,500, $3,200, $3,200, $2,600, $2,700, $2,700, $600, $600, and $600.
7–29	Total crash cost = $7,250. New durations for A = 1, C = 1, D = 3, and G = 2.
7–31	(a) Crash A by 2, D by 1, E by 1, F by 2, and H by 1. Total crash cost = $3,600. (b) Possible to crash project to 21 days. Total cost = $4,400.
7–33	Critical path = 1–3–9–11–12–13–14–17–18. Completion time = 47.5 weeks.
7–35	Answer will vary based on student. First, list all courses including electives to get a degree. Then list all prerequisites for every course. Develop network diagram. Potential difficulties include incorporating min/max number of courses to take during a given semester, and scheduling electives.
7–37	(a) Critical path = D–I–N–S–W. Project length = 38.5 weeks. (b) Probability = 0.8642. (c) Critical path = B–F–L–R–V. Project length = 27 weeks.
7–39	(a) J = 12, K = 12, L = 15, M = 19. (b) V = 16, W = 28, X = 30, Y = 35, Z = 44. (c) P = 34, Q = 32, R = 40, S = 40, T = 50. (d) A = 1, B = 8, C = 5, D = 11.
7–41	(a) Critical path = A–C–D. Project length = 27 days. (b) 89.96%. (c) 84.56%. (d) No.
7–43	(a) 34.83 days. (b) 78.47%. (c) 17.44 days.
7–45	A = weeks 1–2, B = weeks 1–3, C = weeks 3–4, D = weeks 4–6 & 8, E = weeks 5–8, F = weeks 7 & 10 & 13, G = weeks 9–13, H = weeks 14–15.

Chapter 8

8–13	(a) Maximax; Acme; $400,000. (b) Maximin; High Pro; –$15,000. (c) Acme, EMV = $262,000.
8–15	(a) Move shop, EMV = $32,550. (b) Move shop, EOL = $7,200. (c) EVPI = $7,200.
8–17	(a) Bonds, EMV = 3.25%. (b) Bonds, EOL = 2.15%. (c) EVPI = 2.15%.
8–19	(a) 500. (b) 100. (c) 300. (d) 100. (e) 300.
8–21	7 cases.
8–23	(a) 100. (b) 100. (c) EVwPI = $1,225. EVPI = $485.
8–25	(a) Drexel. (b) 0.60 minutes.
8–27	(a) Risk avoiders. (b) Expected utility = 0.90.
8–29	(a) Supplier A, Expected cost = $126. (b) $54.
8–31	(a) Expected profit = $50.36. Hire Elmo. (b) $10.36.

8–33	Expected payoff = $31.63. Accept wager.
8–35	Expected profit = $246,000. Build pilot.
8–37	Expected payoff = $565,000. Test land.
8–39	(a) Expected utility = 0.246. Test land. (b) Risk seeker.
8–41	(a) Expected utility = 0.823. Conduct questionnaire. (b) Risk avoider.
8–43	(a) Risk seeker. (b) No. Expected utility = 0.261.
8–45	(a) Expected utility = 0.62. Get information. (b) Risk seeker.
8–47	(a) 0.682. (b) 0.278.
8–49	Given growth prediction: 0.696, 0.250, 0.054. Given steady prediction: 0.058, 0.870, 0.072. Given decline prediction: 0.054, 0.195, 0.751.
8–51	$47.50.
8–53	(a) Jackson Analytics = $60,000, Witt Consulting = $85,000. (b) Jackson Analytics = 50%, Witt Consulting = 70.83%. (c) Choose Jackson Analytics because the proposal cost is $35,000 less while the EMV difference is only $25,000.
8–55	(a) Build large plant = 0.6258, Build small plant = 0.6294, No plant = 0.5177. (b) Build small plant.
8–57	Alternative C is best with a median of $800. This is not the same as the equally likely best choice of Alternative B.

Chapter 9

9–11	(a) 4.1667. (b) 25 minutes. (c) 30 minutes. (d) 0.8333. (e) 0.1667.
9–13	(a) 3.2 patrons. (b) 0.8. (c) 0.0114 hours. (d) 0.0091 hours. (e) 0.5120, 0.4096,
9–15	(a) 0.2963, 0.1975, 0.1317. (b) 0.3333. (c) 0.6667 minutes. (d) 1.333 travelers. (e) 2 travelers. (f) $P_0 = 0.5$, $W_q = 0.0417$ minutes, $L_q = 0.08333$ travelers, $L = 0.75$ travelers.
9–17	(a) 0.15 hours (9 minutes). (b) 2.25. (c) Do not add second server. Costs increase by $6.49 per hour.
9–19	(a) 12 total (3 per queue). (b) 1 hour. (c) 0.75 hours. (d) 9 total (2.25 per queue). (e) Single M/M/4 system is more efficient than 4 parallel independent M/M/1 systems.
9–21	8 a.m.–10 a.m.: 5 clerks, 10 a.m.–2 p.m.: 8 clerks, 2 p.m.–5 p.m.: 6 clerks.
9–23	Cost is $8.82 higher than the single-server system with two servers.
9–25	(a) 0.1667. (b) 0.2271 hours. (c) About 2 boats.
9–27	7 gates.
9–29	About 23 minutes per customer.
9–31	$L_q = 0.5417$ cars, $L = 1.1667$ cars, $W_q = 4.33$ minutes, $W = 9.33$ Consider adding a second pump.
9–33	(a) 0.3297. (b) 0.8431. (c) 5.1569. (d) 0.6395 days. (e) 1.6355 days.
9–35	(a) 5.53 hours. (b) 2.236 hours. (c) 0.22.
9–37	4 entry, 2 exit.
9–39	(a) 71.90%. (b) 0.1249 hours. (c) 0.5673 patients. (d) 57.79%.
9–41	(a) 0.15 hours = 9 minutes. (b) 9 minutes (same answer).
9–43	(a) Machine A = 1.33 min., Machine B = 1.67 min., Machine C = 4.33 min. (b) Machine A = 63 cents, Machine B = 62 cents, Machine C = 83 cents. Machine B is cheapest.
9–45	1.125 minutes.
9–47	1.25 hours.

Chapter 10

Note: All answers given here are based on only around 200 replications of the simulation model and are, hence, rather approximate. Your answers may therefore vary.

10–15	Expected failures = 2.48 per month. Simulation average is around the same value. Difference is due to the small number of replications in simulation.
10–17	(a) $359. (b) 0.0204.
10–19	(a) $30,649. (b) Order 35.
10–21	(a) 1 pen = $14 per hour; 4 pens = $11.25 per hour. (b) 1 pen = $13.81 per hour; 4 pens = $11.23 per hour. Compares very favorably.
10–23	Average time needed = 175 minutes, Probability finish in ≤ 165 minutes = 0.135.
10–25	$49,229; 5.51%.
10–27	$15,271; 10.67%.
10–29	(a) $6,899; 7.15%. (b) 200. (c) 70.
10–31	0.056.
10–33	$28,664 per month; 3.67 cars. (b) 20 cars.
10–35	$7,368.
10–37	0.14.
10–39	Order 190 pretzels. Profit = $145. Unsold = 16%.
10–41	$23,960.
10–43	$1,054.
10–45	0.94.
10–47	0.035.
10–49	0.45.

10–51	(a) 0.62. (b) 0.88.
10–53	Uniform Distribution: (a) Avg = $71,963, Min = −$56,000, Max = $104,000; (b) Avg = $69,612, Min = −$80,000, Max = $120,000; (c) Avg = $52,694, Min = −$196,140, Max = $197,460; (d) Avg = $52,913, Min = −$198,680, Max = $198,400; (e) Avg = $46,790, Min = −$140,000, Max = $160,000. Normal Distribution: (a) Avg = $161,010, Min = −$150,380, Max = $189,880; (b) Avg = $159,925, Min = −$175,492, Max = $200,000; (c) Avg = $143,148, Min = −$276,675, Max = $281,142; (d) Avg = $143,675, Min = −$256,509, Max = $285,718; (e) Avg = $131,437, Min = −$216,350, Max = $240,000. Yes, the optimal solutions performed best on average for both distributions.
10–55	82.29%
10–57	Stayer = 33.3%, Switcher = 66.7%.
10–59	Mean = $5,862, Median = $5,762, Minimum = $2,063, and Maximum = $10,061.

Chapter 11

11–15	(a) $\text{MAPE}_{2-MA} = 18.87\%$, $\text{MAPE}_{3-MA} = 19.18\%$, $\text{MAPE}_{4-MA} = 23.75\%$. (b) $\text{MAPE}_{3-WMA} = 17.76\%$. (c) $\text{MAPE}_{EXP} = 20.57\%$. (d) Three-period WMA seems to be best.
11–17	$\text{MAPE}_{2-MA} = 10.29\%$, 715.5, $\text{MAPE}_{3-MA} = 6.6\%$, 702, $\text{MAPE}_{4-MA} = 5.27\%$, 698.75.
11–18	$\text{MAPE}_{2-MA} = 18.41\%$, 37.5, $\text{MAPE}_{3-MA} = 18.11\%$, 35, $\text{MAPE}_{4-MA} = 18.27\%$, 31.75.
11–21	(a) $\text{MAPE}_{0.35} = 13.56\%$, $\text{MAPE}_{0.65} = 9.06\%$, $\text{MAPE}_{0.95} = 6.29\%$. (b) $\text{MAPE}_{3-MA} = 11.13\%$. (c) $Y = 451.2 + 33.60X$ if years are coded 1 to 5. MAPE = 1.02%. (d) Linear trend analysis.
11–23	(a) Graph indicates an approximate linear relationship. (b) $Y = 0.352 + 0.971X$. (c) 4.
11–25	$\text{Forecast}_{0.15} = 49$, $\text{Forecast}_{0.65} = 58$, $\text{Forecast}_{0.95} = 64$. (b) 0.95.
11–27	(a) $\text{MAPE}_{0.2} = 4.42\%$, $\text{MAPE}_{0.4} = 3.70\%$. (b) 0.4. (c) 0.7, MAPE = 3.08%.
11–29	Average patients = 23.733 + 3.285 × Year. 60 in year 11, 63 in year 12, and 66 in year 13. Fits very well.
11–31	193, 321, 106, and 280.
11–33	(a) Average dividend = −0.464 + 0.351 × EPS. (b) $R^2 = 0.69$. (c) Average dividend = $0.003.
11–35	(a) Average value = 15,322.82 − 0.096 × Mileage. (b) 72.2%. (c) $8,342 to $13,382.
11–37	(a) Average GPA = 2.019 + 0.002 × CBAT. (b) 43.9%. (c) 3.22 to 3.96.
11–39	(a) Average demand = 29.351 + 0.003 × Advertising. (b) 18.4%. (c) 36.
11–41	Demand for periods 49 to 60 = 60,493, 69,902, 28,402, 33,014, 31,973, 21,062, 22,124, 24,141, 24,595, 96,132, and 86,586, respectively. The model fits the data very well.
11–43	(a) 1.0. (b) Average GNP = 8,942.825 + 112.476 × Quarter; 10,855. (c) 10,496.
11–45	(a) $3.259. (b) Average price = 3.156 + 0.012 × Month; $3.598. (c) Exponential smoothing has a lower MAPE.
11–47	(a) 332. (b) Average Sales = 288.775 + 4.313 × Quarter; 362. (c) Four-period moving average has a lower MAPE.
11–49	(a) 462.25. (b) 482.88. (c) Four-period moving average has a lower MAPE.
11–51	(a) Slope = 6.7429, intercept = 43.7333. (b) 104.4190.
11–53	(a) Intercept = 145.403, slope = 129.199. (b) R^2 for the single regression model = 0.863, adjusted R^2 for the multiple regression model = 0.849, so the single regression model appears to be preferable.
11–55	(a) Intercept = 1.320937, slope of CBAT = 0.001702, slope of age = 0.03753. (b) First student = 3.71, second student = 3.83.
11–57	203.

Appendix A

A–15	(a) 0.5. (b) 0.5. (c) 0.25. (d) 0.25. (e) 0.50. (f) 0.75.
A–17	(a) 0.26. (b) 0.19. (c) 0.54.
A–19	0.54.
A–21	0.385, 0.615.
A–23	0.947.
A–25	(a) 0.2. (b) 0.4. (c) 0.44. (d) 0.08. (e) 0.48. (f) Not a good team.
A–27	(a) No. (b) River City.
A–29	(a) and (c).
A–31	$E(X) = 5.45, \sigma^2 = 4.047$.
A–33	0.2743, 0.5.
A–35	0.1587, 0.2347, 0.1587.
A–37	(a) 0.0548. (b) 0.6554. (c) 0.6554. (d) 0.2120.
A–39	1829.27 ≈ 1,830.
A–41	0.7365.

Index

A
Activities
– critical 400, 401, 418, 420, 426, 427, 430
– time estimates for 440, 441, 443, 444
Activity Immediate Predecessors Time 431, 432, 433
Activity on Arc. See AOA
Activity on Node. See AON
Activity Start 392, 393, 397, 399
Activity times 396, 402, 403, 425, 426, 640, 641
– expected 404, 426, 428, 430
– variability in 386, 402, 403, 405, 407, 409
Add Constraint 69, 70, 82, 310, 320
Add-ins 6, 25, 692, 781, 782, 783, 784
Advertising 38, 92, 93, 112, 645, 646, 724
Agents 166, 176, 555, 556, 557, 559, 791
AHS (Andalusian Healthcare System), 276
Airline 93, 166, 240, 365, 605, 608, 613
Albuquerque 244, 246, 249, 250, 256, 257, 794
Allocation 122, 132, 133, 178, 179
Allocation problems 132, 153
Allowable Decrease 196, 197, 199, 203, 205, 217, 220
Allowable Increase 197, 203, 205, 217, 218
All-polyester ties 103, 105, 107, 110
– month number of 104, 109
Alternate Model 123, 130, 147
Alternate Optimal Solutions 61, 83, 324
Alternatives 451, 455, 457, 458, 462, 486, 489
Alternatives High Demand 456, 457, 458
AMEDD 333
Amount 40, 119, 137, 138, 139, 149, 334
– guaranteed 480, 486, 487
– total 118, 138, 139, 161, 162, 379, 380
Analytical models 6, 510, 511, 515, 518, 591, 601
Andalusian Healthcare System (AHS), 276
Anderson 200, 203, 204, 205, 207, 208, 209
Anderson Home Electronics 200, 201, 202, 205, 206, 207, 210
Anderson's problem 201, 205, 206, 207
Answer Report 73, 74, 82, 83, 195, 201, 203
AOA (Activity on Arc), 392, 426, 427
AOA approach 392
AOA networks 428
AOA project networks 392, 428
AON (Activity on Node), 392, 426, 427
AON networks 392, 426, 430
Appendix 476, 477, 753, 754, 767, 768, 769
Applications 117, 251, 517, 731, 732, 750, 761
– blending 134, 135, 137, 139, 153
Area, shaded 48, 749, 754, 755
Arnold 527, 528, 531, 532, 533, 540, 562
Arrangements 605, 606
Arrival rate 520, 521, 541, 549, 551, 552, 563
Arrival times 601, 602, 603, 617, 618, 619, 636
Arrivals 513, 514, 518, 521, 555, 602, 757
– average number of 514, 521, 522, 530, 534, 537, 542
Arrows 86, 393, 770, 771, 781
Assembly 92, 96, 97, 228, 229, 331, 332
– hours in 230
Assembly time 200, 201, 204, 206, 331, 332, 335
– hours of 92, 96, 204, 206, 207, 208, 238
Assembly time constraint 208, 209
Assignment 127, 239, 262, 264, 265, 266, 295
Assignment model 240, 262, 263, 264, 265, 268, 281
– unbalanced 267, 285
Assignment problem 127, 134, 153, 281, 300
Assumptions 3, 4, 23, 88, 407, 548, 764
Atlanta 240, 243, 292, 293, 369, 560, 604
Availability of Painting Hours 188, 189, 190, 191
Available inventory 594, 595
Average, weighted 456, 461, 462, 486, 487, 664, 747
Average arrival rate 514, 515, 526, 530, 531, 537, 538
Average demand 571, 626, 643, 653, 677, 799
Average gasoline price 727
Average number 522, 548, 555, 556, 557, 562, 563
Average queue length 533, 548, 601, 603, 604
Average rate 528, 529, 531, 542, 557, 559, 577
Average risk score 94, 118, 120, 122, 178
Average sales 616, 679, 681, 766, 799
Average service rate 518, 530, 531, 537, 538, 539, 549
Average service time 518, 559, 560, 561, 563, 564
Average time 530, 533, 555, 557, 561, 562, 636
Average values 604, 608, 625, 630, 631, 632, 676
Average wait time 603, 604, 617, 619

B
BAA (British Airports Authority), 395
Basic Time-Series Forecasting Models 652, 653, 655, 657, 659, 661, 663
Bayes' theorem 476, 492, 740, 741, 758, 759, 760
Bayesian Analysis 449, 450, 475, 477, 485, 493
BBC (British Broadcasting Company), 97, 789
BEP (break-even point), 16, 18, 19, 26, 28, 29, 789
Binary integer programming (BIP), 109, 325
Binary variables 303, 317, 318, 319, 322, 355, 380
Binding 76, 82, 83, 188, 189, 190, 203
Binding constraints 107, 111, 188, 191, 196, 232, 235
– current 191, 196
BIP (binary integer programming), 109, 325

Birmingham 282, 283, 284, 326, 327, 328, 330
Blu-ray DVD players 200, 201, 205, 207, 208, 209, 210
Border state 115, 116, 117, 118, 223
Boston 244, 246, 251, 252, 258, 259, 261
Boston demand 247, 251, 253, 257
Break-even point. See BEP
Brief Solutions 789, 790, 792, 794, 796, 798, 799
British Airports Authority (BAA), 395
British Broadcasting Company (BBC), 97, 789
Budget 383, 411, 412, 413, 415, 427, 438
– marketing 348
Budgeted cost 410, 411, 415
Budgeting process 410, 427
Business decisions 24, 462, 567, 743

C
Calculation options in Excel to manual 580, 589
Calculations 472, 474, 477, 627, 631, 767, 773
Canadian Broadcasting Company (CBC), 97, 789
Capacity 29, 241, 259, 284, 286, 299, 302
– lab 348
– total patient 347, 348, 349
Capacity constraints 271, 281
Cardiac care unit (CCU), 366, 562
CARE International 309
Carpentry 38, 40, 47, 50, 184, 185, 188
Carpentry constraint 42, 44, 45, 46, 185, 190, 191
Carpentry constraint equation 44, 45
Carpentry hours 38, 73, 185, 236, 237
Carpentry time 38, 40, 42, 43, 44, 58, 197
Carpentry time constraint 44, 67, 76
Cars 269, 270, 272, 291, 526, 533, 794
– average number of 532, 533, 554
– maximum number of 268, 269, 270, 271, 297
Causal Forecasting Models 684, 685, 687, 693, 706, 707, 708
Causal models 649, 650, 684, 686, 688, 691, 707
Causal Multiple Regression Model 696
CBAT (Common Business Admission Test), 723, 729, 799
CBC (Canadian Broadcasting Company), 97, 789
CCU (cardiac care unit), 366, 562
Cell A1, 20, 777
Cell references 65, 66, 67, 69, 599, 600, 779
Cells 14, 64, 66, 131, 729, 769, 775
– changing 18, 20, 330, 539, 599, 600
– diaphragm 637
– first 586, 596, 729, 775
– fuel 170
– target 18, 539
– unique 64, 67
Cells A2, 579, 581
Cells A19, 526, 532
Cells B5, 64, 66, 69, 73, 271, 349, 351
Cells B7, 657, 658, 686, 688, 710, 711, 713
Cells B9, 526, 531, 535, 538, 543, 551, 552
Cells C2, 579, 581
Cells C7, 661, 662, 674, 680, 686, 711, 713
Cells C23, 698, 700

DOI 10.1515/9781501506208-016

Index

Cells E9, 526, 532, 535, 538, 543, 552, 553
Cells J7, 110, 624
Cells N4, 586, 587
Cells O4, 586, 587
Cereal 101, 134, 135, 136
Chairs 38, 39, 40, 44, 52, 186, 199
– cherry 232, 233
– profit contribution of 52, 236, 237
Chance 407, 408, 571, 629, 630, 635, 636
– bad 500
– good 23, 498, 500
Changing 46, 182, 183, 227, 232, 235, 589
Changing variable cells 63, 64, 65, 69, 82, 310, 662
Changing variable cells box 193, 271, 290, 301
Changing Variable Cells box in Solver 261, 272, 275, 276, 351
Choices 148, 149, 150, 151, 310, 317, 355
Cities 161, 274, 287, 369, 377, 378, 720
Classic Furniture product mix problem 233, 234
Cleveland 244, 246, 247, 249, 253, 293, 794
Click 74, 312, 769, 771, 775, 785, 786
– right 14, 546
Click Data 692, 700, 704
Clients 238, 259, 317, 318, 321, 367, 506
Coefficients 130, 185, 690, 693, 694, 707, 708
– correlation 689, 690, 693, 704, 705, 707, 708
Column 594, 595, 596, 621, 681, 682, 714
– first 460, 669
– second 414, 458, 669
Commands 63, 769, 770, 771, 772, 773, 774
– basic Excel 6, 767
Commands and Procedures for Installing ExcelModules 767, 768, 770, 772, 774, 776, 778
Commas 66, 271, 272, 275, 460, 599, 600
Commerce Problem 544, 545
Commercial doors sales goal 334, 335, 337, 340, 341, 342, 343
Common Business Admission Test. See CBAT
Compact model 229, 792
Companion Website 343, 363, 524, 655, 767, 784, 785
Company 1, 2, 29, 159, 170, 233, 318
Completed Actual Cost 436, 437, 438
Completion time 386, 395, 402, 403, 408, 409, 420
– estimated 443, 444
– expected 407, 409, 411, 443, 444, 446, 447
Components 180, 372, 373, 513, 653, 654, 707
Computations 472, 476, 477, 681, 696, 713, 714
Compute Expected Profit 582, 583, 585, 587, 589
Computer Analyses in Excel 101, 102, 104, 106, 108, 110, 112
Computer Methods 33, 34, 36, 38, 40, 42, 44
Computers 33, 34, 182, 558, 559, 560, 567
Conditional probabilities 477, 478, 486, 737, 738, 758, 759

Conditions 88, 137, 138, 206, 319, 367, 521
Confidence intervals 587, 691, 695, 700, 705, 723, 724
Connect 239, 240, 241, 276, 277, 278, 299
Consecutive days 154, 155
Constant service rates 533, 535, 549
Constraint coefficients 64, 71, 76, 102, 181, 185, 243
Constraint equations 50, 56, 88
– linear 84
Constraint LHS 67, 83, 310, 320
Constraint LHS Values 67, 121, 351
Constraint line 45, 46, 48, 55, 56, 60, 83
Constraint RHS 67, 70, 83, 116
Constraint RHS Values 67, 73, 122, 195, 206, 216
Constraint window and click 320
Constraint window in Solver 82
Constraints 40, 42, 67, 70, 76, 82, 83
– additional 178, 180, 247, 342, 343, 355, 358
– balance 143, 144, 145, 149, 153
– binary 380
– blending 139, 153
– carpentry and painting 46, 47, 53, 58, 188, 189, 190
– chairs limit 70, 197
– equality 178, 267
– lab capacity 349, 350
– nonbinding 188, 192, 196, 197, 217
– nonlinear 305, 345, 346, 349
– problem's 44, 47, 83, 84, 354
– redundant 58, 59, 82, 84, 88, 187, 190
– risk 118, 120, 150, 152, 178
– supply and demand 249, 253, 254, 261, 267, 280, 328
Construction projects 395, 409, 439
Continuous random variables 744, 745, 748, 749, 759
Contracts 141, 142, 170, 172, 177, 753, Corner point 50, 51, 83, 186, 191, 192, 199
– current optimal 187, 191, 192, 196
– identifiable 56, 57, 58, 62
– locations of 188, 189
– new 186, 187, 190, 192, 196, 197, 791
– optimal 50, 56, 58, 79, 80, 85, 86
Corner point method 51, 58, 83
Corner point property 50
Corner point solution 199
– current 213
– current optimal 187
– identifiable optimal 61
– optimal 50, 53, 56, 184, 306
Cost 410, 419, 503, 511, 643, 791, 793
– actual 209, 414, 415, 643
– amortized 536, 563
– carrying 141, 143, 179, 292, 635
– controlling project 413
– current 132, 204, 213
– estimated 410, 513
– higher 314, 355, 793
– holding 22, 142, 175, 592, 596, 600
– incurred 413
– least 54, 387
– new 177, 213, 214, 235, 236, 293, 381
– optimal 221, 235, 284, 513, 789
– standard 417, 418, 419, 438, 439, 447
– stockout 592, 596, 600, 630, 631, 632
– total 214, 528, 533, 790, 791, 792, 794
– total quarterly 631
– total semiannual 630, 632
– total transshipment 260, 261
Cost Analysis 527, 533, 536, 544, 634

Cost difference 259, 414, 415
Cost information, unit shipping 293, 294
Cost overruns 384, 413, 414, 415, 425, 436
Courses 296, 325, 382, 442, 537, 539, 796
CPM (critical path method), 389, 390, 417, 425, 426, 428, 430
Crash cost 417, 418, 419, 420, 421, 438, 439
– smallest 418, 420
– total 418, 420, 421, 427, 795
Crashing 417, 418, 420, 421, 425, 427, 431
Crashing cost, total 418, 420, 421, 439
Crashing decision variables 424
Crashing General Foundry's Project 418, 421
Credit hours 94, 381
Crino's Problem 538, 540
Criteria
– decision-making 454, 483, 487, 488
– likely 485, 489, 494, 495, 496
– maximax 455, 494, 495, 496
– maximin 455, 494, 495, 496
– minimax regret 455, 457, 494, 495, 496
Critical path 400, 406, 410, 418, 428, 795, 796
– multiple 401, 426
Critical path analysis 394, 406, 426, 428, 430
Critical path method. See CPM
Customer waits 516, 561, 636, 637
Customers 515, 518, 551, 552, 557, 563, 603
– average number of 518, 519, 523, 530, 534, 537, 557
– cost of 511, 527, 548
– current 603
– total 552, 553
– zero 523, 530, 535, 537, 542

D

Daily demand 591, 627, 631, 632
Data set 671, 692, 694, 702, 707, 728, 729
Data tab 18, 68, 586, 587, 773, 782, 783
Data Table 586, 587, 589, 596, 597, 604, 773
Data Table procedure 589, 608, 619
Date 131, 387, 411, 412, 418, 427, 778
Days 165, 435, 439, 445, 560, 594, 755
– arrival 594, 596
– average number of 8, 296
DB DC 247, 250, 253, 257
Decimal points 64, 195, 771
Decision alternatives 451, 452, 461, 462, 466, 486, 487
– possible 450, 451
Decision Analysis 449, 450, 451, 452, 454, 466, 485
Decision analysis models 452, 454, 485
Decision analysts 21, 22, 23, 24, 26, 27, 60
Decision criterion 459, 460, 462, 487, 488, 489, 498
Decision makers 357, 449, 451, 453, 456, 469, 488
Decision Making 453, 454, 455, 459, 461, 465, 487
Decision modelers 27, 510, 511, 518, 547
Decision modeling 1, 2, 5, 6, 9, 24, 25
Decision modeling approach 7, 21, 22, 24, 27, 295, 428
Decision modeling process 5, 6, 24, 25, 27, 52

Index — 797

Decision modeling techniques 2, 3, 5, 6, 34, 568, 569
Decision modeling tools 566, 567, 786
Decision models 3, 11, 12, 14, 16, 24, 26
Decision node 466, 467, 469, 472, 486
Decision support system. *See* DSS
Decision tree for Problem 507
Decision trees 466, 467, 470, 483, 484, 486, 498
– complete 467, 491, 500
Decision Trees for Multistage Decision-Making Problems 469, 471, 473
Decision variable cells 74
Decision variable values 120, 186, 187
Decision-making problem 4, 5, 6, 451, 453, 485, 486
Decision-making process 2, 5, 251, 478, 488, 493, 501
Decision-Making Tool 1, 276
Decisions 1, 449, 450, 451, 469, 478, 485
– bad 450, 478, 485, 493
– best 10, 451, 452, 490, 493, 495, 498
– good 450, 485, 493
– initial 469
– investment 34, 119, 149
– major 449
– making 5, 461, 470, 483, 485, 566
– managerial 2, 26, 760
– next 469, 470
– optimal 16, 141, 467, 527
– original 501, 502, 504
– pessimistic 456, 487
– poor 1, 301, 647
– yes-no 303, 304
Decomposition 653, 678, 679, 681, 683
Decomposition model 648, 678, 708, 709, 715, 727, 728
– additive 654, 678, 707, 708, 712, 727, 728
– multiplicative 678, 705, 712, 713, 726, 727, 728
Demand 280, 292, 452, 572, 591, 594, 595
– actual 594, 672, 674, 677, 729
– annual 715, 724, 730, 799
– customer 605, 615, 645, 647
– – random 565, 643
Demand constraints 110, 138, 247, 248, 249, 250, 267
Demand Fixed Cost Variable Cost Selling Price 371
Demand fluctuations 653, 709
Demand forecasts 647, 657, 668, 675, 705
Demand frequency 570, 591
Demand Frequency Probability 570
Demand level 573, 730
Demand locations 134, 261, 281
Demand nodes 243, 246, 247, 250, 256, 264, 265
Demand pattern 664, 728
Demand Probability Cumulative Probability Random Number Interval 573
Demand values 250, 571, 572, 573, 577, 579, 581
Department of Motor Vehicles (DMV), 558
Departments 21, 97, 158, 228, 295, 373, 633
Dependent variable 684, 685, 686, 688, 693, 707, 708
Destinations 134, 240, 241, 272, 273, 280, 281
Developing decision models 2, 21, 22, 23, 27
Development projects 444, 611
Deviation variables 333, 334, 335, 336, 337, 340, 356

– overachievement 359
– rank R1, 342, 360
– underachievement 335, 341, 359
Device 8, 159, 225, 391, 622
DHTSS (Digital Home Theater Speaker System), 207, 208, 209, 210
DHTSS unit 209
Difference 27, 76, 84, 218, 364, 450, 493
– absolute 76, 652
Digital Home Theater Speaker System. *See* DHTSS
Direction 60, 61, 62, 86, 242, 269, 506
Discrete uniform distribution 576, 578, 579, 582, 635, 637, 641
Distances 276, 277, 278, 287, 290, 299, 793
– shortest 241, 273, 276, 287, 793
Distribution 518, 549, 576, 577, 636, 746, 747
DMV (Department of Motor Vehicles), 558
DOC (Department of Commerce), 543
Driving range 492
– successful 492, 493
– unsuccessful 492
DSS (decision support system), 252, 276, 316, 339, 541, 604
Duration 403, 417, 422, 427, 434, 438, 439

E
Earliest finish time. *See* EFT
Earnings per share. *See* EPS
EEU (Executive Education Unit), 325
EFT (Earliest finish time), 395, 396, 397, 398, 399, 428, 431
Electronic components 200, 201, 203, 204, 206, 238
– additional unit of 203, 204
– five units of 208
– units of 204, 207
Employee Staffing Applications 123, 125
Employees 124, 125, 142, 155, 238, 642, 762
– total number of 54, 366
EMV (expected monetary value), 461, 462, 474, 487, 490, 491, 507
Ending inventory 142, 143, 144, 146, 594, 595
Entries 131, 193, 248, 351, 362, 581, 589
– first 66, 692, 693, 700, 701
Environment 2, 3, 452, 453, 454, 485, 565
– decision-making 8, 449, 450, 453, 455, 487
Environmental protection agency (EPA), 391, 622
EOL (expected opportunity loss), 461, 462, 485, 486, 487, 496, 796
EPS (earnings per share), 721, 722, 799
Equations 37, 46, 47, 48, 522, 673, 687
Error 23, 98, 652, 682, 691, 706, 779
– squared 652, 672, 682, 685, 706
– standard 688, 689, 691, 693, 700, 701, 707
Error values 73, 120, 666, 682
Estimated Production Cost 282, 326
Estimates 390, 403, 490, 558, 647, 691, 766
Estimating Probability Values 475, 477
Evansville 246, 247, 249, 256, 257, 258, 794
Events 733, 734, 735, 736, 737, 758, 759
– conditional probability of 737, 739, 741
– dependent 736, 738, 759
– exclusive 734, 759, 760
– probability of 736, 737, 739, 759
– second 734, 736, 759

EVPI (Expected Value of Perfect Information), 463, 464, 485, 486, 487, 496, 796
EVSI (Expected Value of Sample Information), 449, 474, 475, 485, 486, 487, 507
EVwPI (expected value with perfect information), 463, 464, 486, 488, 796
Excel 1, 63, 580, 589, 600, 767, 782
– functions in 623, 776
– install 782
– model in 102, 117, 312, 336, 423, 562
– regular 312
– scatter chart in 669, 670, 772
Excel Add-Ins 84, 649, 773, 782
– customized 784
– specialized 565
Excel Decision Model 15, 17
Excel file 12, 248, 580, 585, 589, 767, 768
Excel file Figure 332, 338, 343, 354, 363, 585, 715
Excel formulas 116, 139, 408, 577, 582, 585, 593
– simple 121
Excel formulas and Solver entries 73
Excel functions 84, 614, 776, 777, 778
Excel Layout 65, 103, 194, 248, 310, 350, 421
Excel layout and LP Sensitivity Report 232
Excel layout and solution 129, 285, 286, 287
Excel layout and Solver entries 85, 86, 135, 136, 201, 342, 360
Excel Layout and Solver Entries for Excel layout and Solver entries for Simkin 320
Excel Layout and Solver Entries for Simkin and Steinberg 321
Excel Layout and Solver Entries for Solved Problem 86, 87, 358
Excel model 12, 25, 30, 31, 180, 197, 199
Excel Options 782
Excel Options and Add-Ins 781, 783
Excel procedure 586, 598
Excel Sensitivity Report 217, 226, 227
Excel sheets 312, 586, 590
Excel Solution Figure 257, 261, 266, 271, 274, 422
Excel Solution for Thompson Lumber 459, 465
Excel spreadsheets 255, 458, 464, 508
Excel templates 239, 242
Excel worksheets 522, 524, 526, 654, 655, 677, 679
Excel-based simulation model 625
ExcelModules 524, 525, 656, 674, 696, 784, 786
Excel-Modules 665, 767
ExcelModules
– named 784, 785
– titled 524, 655
– worksheet in 526, 539, 658, 686, 697
ExcelModules for Forecasting Model Computations 655
ExcelModules for Linear Trend Analysis Equations 674
ExcelModules for Queuing Model Computations 524
ExcelModules in cells C7, 711
ExcelModules options 524, 656, 785
ExcelModules program 509, 524, 647, 655
ExcelModules Ribbon 785, 786
ExcelModules Solution 525, 531, 535, 538, 543
Excel's Analysis ToolPak 692, 694, 696, 700, 701, 704, 707

798 — Index

Excel's COUNTIF function 588, 594, 616
Excel's MATCH function 603, 613, 619
Excel's Solver 63, 77, 80, 181, 239, 303, 304
Excel's SUMPRODUCT function 66, 78, 82, 423
Executive Education Unit (EEU), 325
Executive Furniture 245, 246, 247, 249, 250, 256, 258
Executive Furniture's Transportation Model 246, 247, 256
Exit 272, 516, 561, 770, 780, 797
Expected costs 486, 512, 796
– total 512, 513, 547, 548, 554
Expected monetary value. See EMV
Expected opportunity loss. See EOL
Expected Value of Perfect Information. See EVPI
Expected Value of Sample Information. See EVSI
Expected value with perfect information. See EVwPI
Experiment 20, 339, 566, 567, 568, 743, 759
Exponential distribution 518, 555, 558, 561, 577, 617, 756
– negative 756, 758, 759
Exponential probability distributions 518, 521, 637, 638, 745
Exponential smoothing 647, 648, 664, 665, 716, 717, 719
Exponential smoothing forecasts 664, 665, 666, 709
Exponential smoothing model 664, 666, 706, 715, 718, 726, 728
Expression 33, 42, 44, 53, 81, 83, 138
Extended Flair Furniture Company Problem 53
Exterior 331, 332, 334, 337
Exterior doors sales goal 334, 335, 337, 340, 342, 343

F

Facility 287, 327, 373, 374, 490, 492, 494
Factories 245, 246, 247, 248, 250, 256, 326
– new 251, 281, 282, 283, 326
Feasible region 48, 56, 83, 191, 196, 308, 313
File Tab 769, 774, 781
Finish 387, 388, 410, 415, 417, 624, 755
First equation 51, 57, 334
First outcome 461, 462, 463
First quarter of year 726, 727, 728
Fixed costs 16, 18, 28, 29, 325, 326, 357
– monthly 30, 327, 328, 369, 370, 584
Fixed costs in addition 325, 355, 357
Fixed-Charge Problems 325, 327, 329, 355, 357
Flair Furniture 38, 39, 42, 43, 58, 66, 195
Flair's model 39, 52, 53, 185
Flair's problem 40, 41, 43, 48, 49, 50, 188
Flights 243, 304, 500, 501, 630, 632, 633
Flows 256, 265, 269, 272, 274, 280, 281
– amounts of 241, 243
Forecast 648, 664, 684, 707, 717, 727, 728
– initial 719, 720
– moving average 730
– new 664
– seasonal 682, 714
– seasonalized 682, 712, 714

Forecast demand 175, 230, 292, 672, 715, 716
Forecast error 651, 652, 655, 658, 682, 706, 709
– absolute 709
– measures of 658, 659, 661, 662, 666, 674, 675
Forecast Jeannette's GPA 716
Forecast revenues 725, 726
Forecast sales 678, 717, 718, 725, 728
Forecast Trend Seasonality Cycles Random variations 654, 712
Forecast values 649, 656, 660, 682, 687, 707
Forecasting 647, 648, 691, 692, 706, 784, 785
Forecasting Home Selling Prices 687, 688, 689, 696, 698
Forecasting Model Computations 655
Forecasting Models 648, 649, 650, 651, 656, 658, 706
– time-series 20, 651, 706, 715
– tried time-series 683
Forecasting Models menu in ExcelModules 656, 661, 665, 674, 679, 686, 696
Forecasting system 657, 715
Forecasting technique 708, 709
Foreign companies 318, 319, 320
Format 66, 74, 195, 546, 576, 671, 771
Formulas 546, 576, 586, 594, 603, 775, 779
Formulas tab 589, 772, 773, 776
Formulation 7, 8, 25, 26, 35, 90, 91
– model's 25
– written 65, 103, 122, 130, 194, 310, 421
Formulation process 9, 35
Fort Lauderdale 246, 249, 250, 256, 257, 258, 794
Foundry's project crashing LP model 423
Fractional values 41, 111, 113, 254, 304, 576, 577
F-test 695, 702, 707
Full-time tellers 124, 125, 126, 218, 219, 220, 221
Functions 13, 576, 578, 579, 729, 776, 779

G

Gasoline 101, 137, 138, 139, 510, 726, 732
Gasoline grades 137, 138, 139, 140, 153
General distribution 520, 536
– discrete 578, 579, 582, 601, 606, 613, 614
General Foundry 391, 392, 393, 394, 411, 416, 622
– project network for 392, 420, 623
General Foundry's case 401, 415
Global optimal solution 346, 347, 353, 356, 363, 375, 376
Global Technology Services (GTS), 651
GM3A motors 142, 143, 144
GM3A motors in February 144, 145
GM3As 142, 143, 144, 146
GM3B motors 143, 144
GM3Bs 142, 143, 144, 146
GNP (gross national product), 506, 726
Goal programming. See GP
Goal Programming Models 331, 333, 335, 337, 339, 341, 343
Goal Seek 18, 19, 20, 31, 32, 539, 540
Goal Seek procedure 18, 19, 20, 539
Goals 333, 335, 337, 339, 340, 356, 374
– decision maker ranks 357

– higher-ranked 331, 338, 356, 357, 359, 361
– lower-ranked 331, 338, 344, 356, 357, 360
– primary 103, 454, 511, 534, 548
– prioritized 335, 357
– ranked 335, 338, 341, 354, 356, 357, 373
– steel usage 340, 341, 343
– total underachievement of 334, 336
– weighted 335, 336, 354, 356, 357, 372
Goals approach
– ranked 338, 339, 344, 356
– weighted 335, 337, 344, 356
Goals R1, 794
GP (goal programming), 303, 305, 331, 333, 356, 357, 364
GP models 331, 333, 335, 341, 345, 351, 359
GP problem 331, 333, 335, 356, 360, 361
GPAs (grade point average), 716, 722, 723, 724, 729
GPAs, predicted 722, 724
Grade point average. See GPAs
Grades 137, 138, 173, 382, 517, 761
– regular 139
Grand pianos 678, 679, 712
Graphical and Computer Methods 33, 34, 36, 38, 40, 42, 44
Graphical solution approach 41, 80
Graphs 43, 44, 45, 46, 48, 183, 659
– middle 751, 753
– revised 59, 60, 188, 189
Graphs for Solved Problem 85, 87
Greenberg Motors problem in Excel 145
GRG (generalized reduced gradient), 349, 357
GRG Nonlinear 70, 71, 351, 356, 362, 663, 667
Gross national product. See GNP
Group 650, 770, 771, 772, 773, 785, 786

H

Hardgrave Machine 284, 329, 330
Hardgrave Machine Company 251, 282, 326
Harky 407, 408, 409, 411, 415, 418, 420
– Lester 405, 406, 408, 411, 413, 415, 418
Harry's Auto Shop 570, 572, 573, 574, 582, 583, 584
Harry's Auto Shop Simulation Model 583, 585
Harry's model 583, 585, 586
Hartford 258, 259, 261
HD. See High demand
Hepatitis B virus (HBV), 15, 16
Hewlett Packard. See HP
High demand (HD), 452, 457, 458, 471, 476, 477, 505
Holiday Meal Turkey Ranch Problem 56, 57, 77, 99
Home size 684, 685, 686, 692, 698, 701, 703
– slope of 703, 705
Homes 74, 546, 684, 686, 691, 695, 696
– next 436
Homes of size 691, 700, 705
Hong Kong Bank 124, 125, 126, 218, 219, 220, 238
Hospitals 8, 165, 339, 370, 495, 568, 604
Hours 157, 197, 228, 230, 528, 538, 797
– additional 189, 190, 204, 220, 225, 226, 230
– agent 176
– available 76, 158, 159

Index — 799

- downtime 544, 545
- extra 176
- machine 300, 376, 377
- part-time 124, 238
- regular production 292
- technician 544, 545
- total 125, 179, 793
- total number of 228, 373
Hours of assembly 92, 96, 228, 306, 312, 359
Hours of carpentry time 38, 40, 44, 197, 237
Hours of time 225, 228
House 241, 277, 278, 279, 365, 388, 636
Houston 282, 292, 326, 328, 329, 381, 793
HP (Hewlett Packard), 20

I

IBM 2, 6, 522, 651
IC256, 175, 176
IC341, 175, 176, 791
ICT (International City Trust), 118, 119, 121, 123, 178
ICT's problem 120, 122
IMA (Installation Management Agency), 466
Immediate predecessors 391, 397, 398, 435, 441, 443, 444
Impact 203, 206, 207, 223, 233, 237, 611
Impact of changes 181, 185, 187, 195, 196, 197, 198
Impact of Changes in RHS Value 188, 192
Impact of Project Management Body of Knowledge 409
Implementation 1, 24, 25, 27, 146, 150, 152
Independent events 578, 736, 737, 738, 758, 759, 762
Independent variables 684, 696, 697, 701, 703, 705, 708
- additional 696, 708
- second 696, 699, 703
Inequalities 37, 45, 46, 53, 83, 267, 280
Information 4, 5, 195, 196, 463, 475, 504
- new 52, 449, 501, 5
Ingredients 135, 136, 137, 173, 174, 211, 213
- cost of 213, 237
- ounces of 211, 212, 213
In-house 29, 108, 109, 110, 159, 790
Input data 9, 10, 25, 26, 206, 526, 658
Input data values 4, 25, 181, 182, 183, 216, 221
Input parameter values 185, 526, 565, 598
Inspection 89, 97, 241, 309, 373, 739
Installation Management Agency (IMA), 466
Installing ExcelModules 767, 768, 770, 772, 774, 776, 784
Integer 280, 310, 316, 338, 359, 577, 642
- general 304, 305, 357
Integer numbers 304, 745
Integer programming, See IP
- binary 325
Integer programming models 111, 152, 304
Integer requirements 41, 111, 309, 310, 315, 316
Integer solutions 304, 305, 307, 308, 314, 355, 357
Integer values 41, 243, 249, 303, 304, 305, 356

Integer variables 303, 304, 305, 309, 313, 325, 354
- binary 304
- general 304, 305, 307, 309, 311, 354, 355
- special type of 303, 304, 355
Integer-valued numbers ranging 572
Interest rates 291, 503, 504
Interior doors sales goal 334, 335, 337, 340, 341
Intermodal freight transport systems 244
International City Trust. See ICT
Intersection 50, 83, 188, 189, 190, 760, 768
Interval 380, 514, 612, 691, 695, 696, 723
Introduction 1, 2, 4, 6, 8, 10, 12
Inventory 21, 141, 143, 146, 591, 592, 630
- beginning 594, 630, 635
- on-hand 143, 292, 614
Inventory items 9
Inventory level 117, 592, 595, 630
Inventory position 593, 595, 614
Inventory Problem 21, 22, 591, 593, 595, 597, 599
Investment choices 119, 122, 148, 152, 163, 176
Investment conditions 119, 121
Investments 118, 150, 162, 163, 176, 367, 494
IP (integer programming), 41, 304, 343, 344, 345, 355, 357
IP model solutions 41
IP models 305, 311, 313, 314, 315, 355, 366
- large 315, 355
- mixed 364, 378
IP problems 307, 308, 309, 313, 315, 366, 367
IP solution 307, 308, 309, 314, 338, 343, 355
- optimal 307, 308, 313, 355
IQs 751, 752
Items 127, 128, 129, 130, 132, 368, 799
Items Number 744

J

Jobs 127, 262, 263, 290, 294, 300, 376
Judgments 9, 650, 709, 732, 733, 760
Judith 605, 606, 607, 608, 609
Judith's simulation model and Data Table 608

K

Kansas City 282, 283, 326, 327, 328
Kiddo model 229, 792
Knowledge 5, 6, 453, 454, 461, 571, 721

L

Labor costs 34, 252, 264
- direct 93, 230
Labor hours 38, 94, 95, 142, 144, 233, 234
Labor Planning Problem 123, 127
Labor staffing problems 123, 152
Land area 697, 698, 699, 700, 701, 703, 705
Large projects 384, 386, 388, 410, 425
Larger Maximization Example 200, 201, 203, 205
Latest finish time. See LFT
Latest start time. See LST
Latest times 395, 396, 397, 401, 402, 426, 428
LD. See Low demand
Left-hand-side. See LHS

Letters 510, 590, 743, 744, 745, 768, 778
Level 84, 143, 388, 389, 647, 705, 724
Level cost line 56, 57, 86
Level Cost Line Method 57
Level lines 48, 49, 53, 57, 86
Level profit 60, 61, 185
Level profit line 49, 53, 60, 85, 184, 186
Level profit lines approach 188, 189, 190
LFT (Latest finish time), 395, 398, 399, 426, 428, 431, 432
LFT values 398, 401
LG Display 117
LHS (left-hand-side), 66, 67, 75, 76, 82, 116, 217
LHS and RHS cells 67, 70
LHS cells 67, 75, 139
LHS formulas 67, 73, 248, 350, 423
LHS formulas of constraints 67
LHS input box 70
LHS values 73, 76, 78, 107
Lilly Snack Company 293
Limited value 4, 43
Line 44, 46, 47, 48, 509, 550, 672
Line charts 682, 688, 698, 707, 714
Line design 574
Line graph 656, 659, 661, 666
Linear equation 37, 44, 717, 718
Linear programming. See LP
Linear programming formulation 98, 99
Linear Programming Modeling Applications 101, 102, 104, 106, 108, 110, 112
Linear Programming Models 33, 34, 35, 36, 37, 54, 84
Linear Programming Problem 38, 39, 41, 43, 45, 47, 79
Linear Programming Sensitivity Analysis 181, 182, 184, 186, 188, 190, 192
Linear programs 33, 84, 89, 96, 99, 101, 239
Linear relationship 684, 687, 689, 690, 694, 707, 708
Load values 130, 131, 133
Local suppliers 180, 791
Locations 243, 259, 280, 290, 297, 327, 371
- transshipment 260, 261
Lock Cell 74
LOOKUP function 579, 581, 584, 602, 603, 615, 621
Low demand 455, 461, 462, 470, 476, 477, 505
Low demand (LD), 457, 458, 470, 476, 477, 497, 505
Low demand, probability of 472, 497
LP (linear programming), 33, 34, 35, 80, 101, 102, 152
LP formulation 35, 38, 41, 183, 185, 256
LP model in Problem 222
LP model solutions 41
LP models 36, 38, 41, 71, 183, 341, 343
- large 58, 62, 63
- multiperiod 153
- project crashing 421, 424, 425
- second 341, 342, 343
- single 40, 42, 183
LP problems 34, 37, 63, 88, 90, 225, 354
- large 62, 83
- maximization 77
- two-variable 81
LP problems in Excel 82
LP Sensitivity Report 228, 230, 232, 234
LP solution 307, 332, 334, 338, 343
- optimal 308, 309, 332

LP subproblems 313, 315
LSL 31
LST (Latest start time), 395, 398, 399, 412, 426, 428, 437
LST and LFT values 398, 401
LST Rule 398
LST values 398, 412, 413, 427

M

Machines 29, 300, 376, 555, 561, 563, 797
MAD (Mean absolute deviation), 652, 661, 662, 666, 705, 709, 730
Make Unconstrained Variables Non-Negative box 311, 351, 663
Make Unconstrained Variables Non-Negative box in Solver 82
Make Unconstrained Variables Non-Negative option 194
Management problems 566, 605, 613, 624
Management science 2, 26, 761
Management Sciences Associates. *See* MSA
Managerial Decision Modeling 1, 2, 4, 6, 8, 10, 12
Managers 11, 22, 23, 24, 27, 34, 252
– office 544, 545
Managing Project Costs 410, 411, 413, 415
Manufacturing Applications 103, 105, 107, 109, 111
MAPE (mean absolute percent error), 652, 659, 663, 666, 706, 717, 799
Market research 463, 493, 497, 498, 504, 506, 507
Market survey 461, 469, 470, 471, 472, 474, 475
Marketing Applications 112, 113, 115, 117
Material cost components 105, 106, 110
Material costs 103, 105, 106, 109, 110, 159, 230
– total 107, 110
Mathematical programming models 69, 83, 303, 304
Mathematical relationships 8, 88, 684
Maximal-flow model 241, 268, 269, 270, 271, 272, 281
Maximin 454, 485, 488, 489, 796
Maximization 181, 183, 240, 262, 281, 454
Maximize 38, 91, 93, 127, 167, 168, 270
Maximize profit 36, 37, 89, 98, 222, 226, 365
Maximum amount 217, 218, 252, 268, 285, 291, 498
Maximum demand 105, 229, 371, 572
Maximum EMV 462, 464, 486, 494, 495
Maximum number 112, 241, 254, 268, 292, 293
Maximum payoffs 455, 489
Maximum profit 38, 312, 359, 361, 643, 646
Max-Min Model 252, 254, 281
MBA program 523, 723
M/D/1 Queuing System 533, 534, 535, 536
Mean absolute deviation. *See* MAD
Mean absolute percent error. *See* MAPE
Mean squared error. *See* MSE
Mechanics 510, 526, 527, 528, 531, 532, 533
Mexico, border 114, 180
M/G/1 model 537, 563
M/G/1 Queuing System 536, 537, 538, 539, 540
Microsoft Excel 1, 5, 6, 34, 35, 770
Microsoft Project 387, 392

Minimal-spanning tree model 239, 240, 241, 276, 277, 280, 281
Minimization Linear Programming Problem 54, 55, 57
Minimum cost 135, 137, 161, 170, 171, 174, 177
Minimum number 96, 164, 165, 322, 369, 511
Minimum payoffs 455, 456, 489
Minimum value 252, 254, 281, 637, 667
Min-Max model 252, 253, 254, 280, 282
Minutes 533, 551, 559, 560, 563, 629, 797
– five 369, 554, 558, 559, 560
Mix 95, 167, 170, 171, 173, 174, 572
Mixed Integer Models 325, 327, 329
M/M/1 model 531, 563
M/M/1 Queuing Model 521, 525
M/M/1 Queuing System 521, 522, 523, 525, 527, 529, 544
M/M/2 Queuing System 532, 533, 545, 553
M/M/s Queuing System 529, 530, 531
M/M/s Worksheet in ExcelModules 525
Model 8, 9, 10, 22, 26, 94, 102
– additive 654, 678, 712, 713, 714
– balanced 246, 247, 281
– complex 22, 23, 520
– decision tree 454
– deterministic 3, 4, 24, 25, 26, 34
– general service time 536, 549
– linear 720, 721
– multiple-server 532, 549
– multiplicative 654, 678, 679, 713, 714, 725
– new 304, 785
– original 58, 130
– physical 8, 566, 568
– probabilistic 2, 3, 4, 5, 24, 25, 26
– qualitative 649, 650, 705, 709
– quantitative 466, 647, 648, 678, 725
– rank R2, 343
– real-world 182, 654
– revenue management 565
– revised 132, 209, 210
– scale 8, 72
– scaled 72
– schematic 8
– simple 11, 22
– single-phase 521, 547, 549
– single-server 529, 531, 532, 550
– system's 566
– transshipment 240, 256, 257, 259, 261, 293, 294
– two-drawer 372
– two-variable 38, 306
– unbalanced 246, 249, 260, 282, 289
Model assumptions 10, 25, 26, 218
Model customer arrivals 758
Model fit 720, 721
Model forecasts 691, 700
Modelers 257, 303, 312, 509, 575
Modeling 1, 3, 12, 243, 514, 541, 613
Modeling process 1, 9, 24
Modeling techniques 2, 5, 8, 34
Modeling tool 317, 319
Moderate demand 455, 461, 462, 463, 470, 476, 477
Monetary amounts 479, 480, 481, 482, 483, 488
Monetary values 478, 480, 481, 483, 484, 487, 488
Monte Carlo Simulation 565, 568, 569, 571, 610, 611, 612
Monthly costs 596, 597, 620
– total 592, 598, 601, 620

Monthly demand 282, 326, 570, 571, 582, 677, 678
Monthly profit 29, 30, 584, 585, 587, 588, 628
– total 627, 628
Mortgage-backed securities 118, 121, 122
Motors 92, 141, 142, 143, 144, 789, 799
Moving average models 668, 727
Moving averages 647, 648, 654, 655, 656, 716, 799
– three-month 655, 658, 659, 660
Moving averages model 658, 706, 715
– weighted 662, 706
Moving Averages Worksheet in ExcelModules 657
MP 349, 350, 351
MP3 players 200, 201, 204, 205, 631
MS 348, 349, 350, 351
MSA (Management Sciences Associates), 114, 115, 116, 223
MSE (mean squared error), 652, 661, 666, 667, 705, 706, 709
Mufflers 526, 528, 531, 540
Multiperiod Applications 141, 143, 145, 147, 149
Multiple regression 696, 697, 699, 700, 701, 702, 708
Multiple regression model 696, 697, 699, 701, 702, 703, 708
Multistage Decision-Making Problems 469, 471, 473

N

Names 64, 65, 75, 599, 770, 773, 779
– relevant file/sheet 12, 64, 103, 194, 248, 310, 405
National Science Foundation. *See* NSF
NBCU 683
NBDoT (New Brunswick Department of Transportation), 104
NCS (Norwegian Continental Shelf), 273
Nearest 277, 278, 279, 307, 308, 641, 777
Net impact 204, 205, 207, 214
Net present value. *See* NPV
Network 241, 242, 243, 280, 281, 299, 394
– intermodal freight 244
– road 241, 242, 268, 273, 297
Network flow models 3, 239, 243, 246, 254, 277, 280
Network for Problem 296, 297, 298, 299
Network models 239, 241, 243, 264, 265, 280, 281
– characteristics of 239, 242, 243
– maximal-flow 239, 289
New Brunswick Department of Transportation. *See* NBDoT
New constraints 53, 54, 76, 253, 310, 320, 380
New locations 188, 189, 191, 203, 251, 327, 496
New product 207, 208, 209, 315, 317, 449, 451
New production plan and profit 792
New Variables 181, 207, 209, 216, 217, 218
New York 282, 283, 285, 326, 328, 329, 339
Newspaper ads 112, 113, 372, 791
Newspapers 177, 372, 495, 500, 642, 794
Next month 372, 373, 496, 658, 661, 666, 765
Next year 118, 163, 720, 721, 722, 724, 763
NLP. *See* Nonlinear Programming
NLP models 345, 347, 350, 353, 356, 362, 364

Index — 801

NLP problems 354, 356, 357, 375
Nodes 242, 269, 270, 271, 273, 274, 289
- activity on 392, 426, 427
- outcome 466, 467, 468, 472, 474, 486
- pairs of 242, 286, 288, 289
- unconnected 277
- unique ending 273, 281, 394
- unique starting 273, 281, 394
Nonbinding 76, 188, 212, 217
Noncritical paths 409, 410, 427
Non-electronic components 200, 201, 238
- supply of 203
- units of 203, 208
Nonlinear objective function 305, 345, 346, 349, 350
Nonlinear Programming (NLP) 303, 304, 305, 344, 345, 354, 356
Nonlinear Programming Models 303, 304, 305, 306, 344, 345, 346
Nonnegativity constraints 44, 45, 68, 70, 81, 82, 847
Normal distribution 577, 636, 638, 643, 750, 751, 753
- standard 31, 752, 753
Normal tables, standard 751, 752, 755
NPV (net present value), 43, 368, 778, 779
NS 476, 477
NSF (National Science Foundation), 263
Number 39, 155, 246, 247, 607, 621, 777
- infinite 88, 308, 672, 749
- large 313, 316, 378, 379, 380, 758, 759
- largest 158, 777, 778
- quarter 681, 682, 714
- total 109, 115, 267, 268, 290, 366, 570
Nurses 164, 295, 345, 562, 790
Nutrients 55, 95, 171

O

Oak tables 233, 792
Objective cell 65, 66, 73, 82, 254, 310, 662
Objective force model (OFM), 333
Objective function 48, 61, 65, 66, 81, 106, 252
Objective function and constraints 37, 84, 141, 304, 305, 317, 318
Objective function coefficient. *See* OFC
Objective function coefficients 181, 185, 216, 218, 227, 232, 234
Objective function formula 67
Objective function line 48, 49, 51
Objective function value 51, 82, 99, 187, 196, 216, 218
- optimal 61, 189, 196, 214, 217
Objective value 68, 80, 84, 211, 309, 358
Objectives 8, 305, 331, 571, 789, 790, 794
OC 799
Occurrence 461, 485, 732, 736, 737, 758, 759
Occurring 731, 735, 736, 737, 738, 758, 759
Odd-Numbered End-Of-Chapter Problems 789, 790, 792, 794, 796, 798, 799
OFC (Objective function coefficient), 185, 187, 198, 199, 216, 217, 218
Offices 240, 283, 285, 365, 554, 558, 559
OFM (objective force model), 333
Oil 8, 137, 140, 361, 362, 363, 502
Operating characteristic equations 522, 523, 530, 534, 537, 542
Operating characteristics 521, 526, 527, 538, 544, 547, 560
Operations research 2, 6, 20, 26, 104, 377, 378
Opportunity loss table 455, 457, 458, 485

Optimal Integer Solutions 308, 316
Optimal solution 51, 52, 76, 83, 205, 220, 221
- current 182, 183, 187, 197, 205, 213, 217
- local 346, 351, 352, 363
- multiple 140, 205, 235, 251, 324, 792
- new 53, 197, 224
- unique 90, 225, 226
Optimal solution values 83, 107, 110, 123, 222
Optimal values 318, 319, 341, 342, 343, 344, 717
Optimistic 404, 405, 440, 441, 442, 456, 487
Optimization Models for Production Planning in LG Display 117
Options box of Solver 82, 355
Order 592, 594, 595, 596, 630, 642, 643
- large 31, 379, 380
Order cost 596, 600
Order quantity 592, 593, 594, 601, 630, 631, 632
Order size 31, 379, 380, 637, 642, 643
Ordering 569, 627, 630, 631, 632, 643
- economics of 630, 632
Ordering costs 22
Organizations 303, 383, 384, 402, 449, 565, 566
Origin node 265, 270, 274, 286
Origins 133, 134, 240, 241, 272, 281, 282
Ounces 31, 157, 211, 212, 213, 235, 236
Outcomes 451, 453, 457, 463, 469, 477, 487
Output 31, 611, 644, 645, 693, 694, 780
Outsource 109, 159, 160
Outsourcing cost 109, 110, 152

P

Painting constraint equations 50, 60
Painting constraints 46, 47, 53, 188, 189, 190, 196
Painting hours 188, 189, 190, 191, 236
Painting time 40, 42, 43, 47, 189, 190, 196
- hours of 38, 40, 46, 189, 197, 237
Painting time availability 188, 189, 190, 191, 196, 197
Parameter values 65, 607, 666
Parameters 9, 24, 25, 30, 404, 563, 594
- input 216, 598, 599, 601, 609, 612, 613
Part-time tellers 125, 126, 220, 221
Passengers 54, 365, 561, 605, 606, 607, 633
Paste Values 580, 590, 771
Patients 345, 347, 562, 617, 619, 629, 633
- medical 347, 348, 351
- pediatric 347, 348, 351
- surgical 347, 348, 351
Payoffs 452, 455, 458, 461, 467, 472, 487
- best 453, 457, 458, 463, 464, 480, 486
- expected 454, 463, 467, 472, 474, 501, 796
PCC (Progressive Cloud Computing), 651
PCs 3, 560
Pens 628, 629, 798
Perfect information 463, 464, 469, 507
- expected value of 449, 461, 463, 485, 486, 487
Performance 402, 476, 510, 511, 547, 550, 604
Performance measures 510, 511, 519, 603, 604, 608, 613
Periods, actual value in 651, 660, 664
Person 115, 479, 480, 481, 482, 488, 605
Personal exemptions 11, 13, 30
Personnel 36, 38, 54, 283, 383, 640

PERT (Program Evaluation and Review Technique), 389, 390, 406, 425, 426, 427, 428
Pessimistic times 403, 404, 405, 410, 440, 444, 447
Phases 383, 384, 385, 443, 444, 516, 517
Pickens Memorial 347, 348, 350, 351, 352, 353, 354
Pickens Memorial's NLP model 349, 351
Pictures 8, 101, 747, 771, 772
Pine chairs 232, 233
Pine tables 233
Pipes 242, 286, 297
Plant 168, 177, 292, 293, 327, 328, 370
- existing 327, 328
- large 453, 455, 457, 458, 462, 464, 474
- new 284, 285, 326, 327, 328, 329, 330
- pilot 8, 501
- small 451, 456, 457, 458, 470, 474, 797
Plots 44, 48, 56, 169, 413, 416, 428
- normal probability 693, 707
Point estimate 691, 695, 700
Points 44, 46, 47, 48, 49, 50, 346
Poisson probability distribution 520, 521, 529, 537
Pollution project, air 413, 414
Poly-cotton blend 105, 107, 109, 110
- month number of 104, 109
Population 540, 542, 549, 550, 694, 702, 762
- arrival 510, 513, 520, 542, 549
Population slopes 694, 695, 705, 708
Portfolio selection problem 118, 121, 129, 139, 162, 376, 379
Possible outcomes 452, 467, 470, 731, 732, 733, 759
Possible Problems in Developing Decision Models 21, 23
Possible values 10, 187, 196, 672, 691, 747, 748
Precedence relationships 387, 388, 391, 392, 393, 422, 427
Predecessors 392, 393, 395, 396, 397, 398, 446
Premium 137, 138, 165, 204, 227, 236
Premium grade gasoline 138, 139, 140
Press 33, 576, 588, 589, 590, 775
Price 30, 31, 180, 376, 500, 638, 646
Probability 470, 503, 636, 732, 755, 763, 766
- cumulative 526, 572, 612
- joint 477, 736, 737, 739, 740, 742, 758
- marginal 736, 737, 738, 741, 742, 758, 759
- posterior 492, 493, 501, 502, 506, 740, 763
- prior 476, 477, 486, 742, 759, 760
Probability Concepts and Applications 731, 732, 734, 736, 738, 740, 742
Probability density function 749, 750, 758, 759
Probability distributions 569, 570, 571, 745, 747, 748, 759
- beta 404, 426, 427
- common 565, 574, 575
- continuous 749, 750, 759
- discrete 746, 747, 748, 749, 758, 759, 760
- discrete general 594, 614
- normal 407, 408, 436, 614, 637
Probability estimates 449, 450, 476, 485, 503
- prior 740, 741
Probability function 746, 747, 749, 756
Probability of first outcome 461, 462, 463

802 — Index

Probability of occurrence 454, 461, 463, 736, 737, 758, 759
Probability of second outcome 461, 462, 463
Probability of winning 163, 164, 294
Probability revisions 477, 742, 760
Probability values 571, 732, 733, 745, 746, 759, 760
Problem 8, 21, 39, 81, 183, 304, 469
- blending 33, 135, 136, 153
- complex 2, 3, 22
- diet 35, 54, 134, 136, 137
- goal programming 304, 357, 372
- integer programming 37, 112, 357
- marketing research 113, 120, 121
- maximization 56, 62, 82, 84, 119, 301, 314
- minimization 54, 56, 69, 77, 82, 84, 181
- multiperiod 141, 143, 146, 147, 153
- network flow 34, 127, 134
- nonlinear programming 63, 304, 354, 662
- queuing 523, 527, 553, 601, 603
- real 8, 241
- revenue management 605, 607, 609, 620
- sample 12, 64, 103, 248, 310, 405, 460
- set-covering 317, 322, 323, 355
- two-variable 33, 95, 183
Problem parameter 9, 26, 27, 78
Problem scenario 7, 25, 26, 35, 40, 42, 80
Problem solving 22, 151, 295
Problem title 524, 525, 656
Procedures
- graphical 34, 43, 89, 90, 99
- least-squares 672, 674, 685, 693, 709
Product mix 102, 104, 109, 111, 158, 159, 333
Product mix problems 81, 103, 104, 111, 113, 135, 152
Production 141, 142, 143, 160, 204, 232, 325
- regular 179, 292, 791
Production costs 21, 93, 142, 143, 176, 282, 292
Production cycle 93, 375
Production decision choices 141
Production limit 192, 197
Production plan 3, 40, 41, 232, 233, 234, 792
- current 188, 199, 205, 207, 230
Production problems 21, 252, 375
Production process 38, 103, 104, 160, 761
Production time 93, 158, 182, 375
Production variables 111, 146, 343
Productivity 6, 402
Products 37, 38, 137, 200, 208, 226, 227
- existing 208, 209
- final 136, 180
Profit 16, 18, 189, 197, 203, 789, 792
- expected 28, 565, 637, 796
- highest 48, 49, 51, 85, 92, 453
- maximizing 101, 331
- net 105, 107, 110, 452, 488, 489, 497
- new 203, 227, 233, 234, 792
Profit coefficients 105, 106, 199
Profit contribution 38, 52, 182, 199, 200, 345, 347
Profit contribution of tables 185, 186, 187, 237
Profit impact 30, 793
Profit margin 237, 582, 646
Profit value 49, 50, 53, 74, 85, 184, 589
Profitability 498, 627, 628, 633
Program Evaluation and Review Technique. See PERT

Programming models 3, 35, 84
Programs 312, 380, 387, 575, 784, 785, 786
- mixed integer 379, 380
Progressive Cloud Computing. See PCC
Project 264, 265, 266, 383, 384, 388, 417
- complex 384, 387, 389, 395, 425
- simple 386, 446, 447
- total 427, 430, 444
Project completion, probability of 406, 408, 427
Project completion time 406, 407, 410, 435, 436, 438, 622
Project Controlling 384, 385, 386, 387
Project Crashing 417, 418, 419, 421, 423, 424, 428
Project length 795, 796
Project management 383, 384, 385, 402, 426, 428, 430
Project Management Body of Knowledge (PMBOK), 409
Project Management Journal 395, 402, 409, 417
Project management techniques 387, 389, 409, 425
Project managers 383, 388, 403, 417, 447
Project network 392, 393, 426, 427, 428, 431, 432
Project schedule 394, 395, 397, 399, 401, 425, 426
Project teams 383, 388, 395
Project variance 406, 407, 427, 436
Protein 55, 78, 134, 135, 171, 174, 224
Purchase 28, 29, 231, 291, 292, 365, 791
P-value 695, 702, 703

Q

QP. See quadratic programming
Quadratic programming (QP) 349, 354, 356, 357
Qualitative Forecasting Models 650, 706, 715
Quantities 30, 36, 55, 117, 157, 236, 376
Quantity discounts 30, 31, 379, 380
Quarter of year 681, 682, 712, 714, 726
Quarters 631, 679, 681, 682, 712, 714, 725
Queue 510, 511, 515, 516, 550, 563, 619
Queue discipline 516, 550
Queue length 516, 520, 521, 527, 549, 550, 603
Queuing models 520, 522, 524, 526, 540, 548, 549
- analytical 513, 514, 515, 548
Queuing Models menu in ExcelModules 524, 531, 535, 538, 543
Queuing system 510, 511, 513, 515, 516, 549, 553
- complex 510, 546, 547

R

Radial Tires 570, 572, 573
RAND 576, 577, 578, 581, 582, 603, 617
RAND function 576
RANDBETWEEN 576, 577, 582, 584, 596, 607, 614
Random number generation 565, 574, 612
Random number intervals 572, 573, 579, 581, 582, 612, 613
Random numbers 572, 573, 576, 581, 584, 612, 644
Random values 571, 575, 576, 577
Random variables 743, 744, 745, 747, 748, 749, 759
- discrete 744, 745, 759
- examples of continuous 745, 748
Range 196, 216, 312, 581, 582, 692, 728

Range A1, 777, 778
Rank goal, optimal value of 342, 343
Rank order 359, 372, 373, 374
Rank R1 goals 341, 356, 359, 360, 361
Rank R2 Goals 342, 356, 359, 360
Rank R3 Goals 343, 344, 359, 361
Rates 13, 504, 526, 549, 554, 560, 5615
Ray Design Inc 273, 274, 275
Realism, criterion of 454, 456, 485, 487, 494, 495, 496
Real-world situations 43, 52, 182, 183, 470, 611, 612
Reduced cost 199, 203, 204, 205, 209, 210, 217
Region 44, 45, 47, 83, 115, 370, 466
- feasible solution 47, 56, 59, 82, 84, 185
Regression 685, 686, 688, 692, 695, 707, 709
- simple 686, 687, 689, 692, 700, 702, 705
Regression equation 684, 685, 686, 687, 693, 694, 698
Regression estimate 688, 691, 693, 700, 701, 709
Regression line 688, 689, 691, 707, 728, 777, 778
Regression model 695, 696, 702, 703, 707, 708, 722
- causal simple 684, 686, 687, 696
Relationships 149, 320, 345, 431, 669, 689, 721
Reorder point 592, 593, 595, 601, 630, 631, 632
Repair 16, 510, 512, 541, 543, 558, 559
Replicate 585, 596, 627, 631, 634, 636, 637
Replications 583, 585, 586, 587, 589, 596, 625
Requirements 125, 148, 211, 214, 219, 237, 325
Reservations 556, 557, 605, 606, 607, 609, 619
Resources 3, 34, 37, 208, 227, 385, 415
- limited 35, 36, 38, 84, 534
Return 20, 94, 162, 163, 312, 495, 505
- expected 118, 164, 321, 367, 374, 376
- rate of 5, 779
- total 122, 318, 790, 794
Revenues 16, 28, 109, 159, 160, 168, 643
- total 16, 26, 97, 107, 109, 110, 168
Revised probabilities 477, 478, 486, 506, 741, 742, 758
RHS (right-hand-side), 66, 76, 82, 116, 216, 217, 218
RHS input boxes 70
RHS values 185, 188, 191, 192, 196, 206, 217
Right-hand-side. See RHS
Risk 150, 449, 454, 461, 481, 482, 488
Risk avoider 481, 482, 483, 503, 505, 507, 796
Risk premium 481, 482, 487, 488
Risk seeker 481, 482, 484, 503, 505, 507, 796
Roads 242, 269, 270, 272, 274, 275, 276
Role of Computers in Simulation 574, 575, 577, 579, 581
Rows 248, 460, 546, 585, 768, 771, 781
Rule 206, 207, 217, 218, 397, 792, 793

S

Sales 332, 615, 634, 681, 717, 765, 766
- unseasonalized 681, 714
Sales agents 332, 343
Sales force 6, 647, 651, 705, 706
Sales goals 335, 340, 341, 343
Sales price 30, 232, 565, 643

Salespeople 127, 240, 281, 551
Sample information, expected value
 of 449, 474, 485, 486, 487, 507
Satellite radio tuners 200, 201, 205, 207, 208, 209, 237
Saturday 127, 154, 155, 165, 178, 366, 554
Sawyer Piano House 678, 679, 680, 683, 712, 713
Scatter chart 669, 671, 672, 674, 684, 687, 688
Scenario Manager 598, 600, 601, 608, 609, 613, 625
Scenario summary table 600, 613
Scenario Values 599, 609
Scenarios 188, 598, 599, 600, 601, 609, 621
Schalkoff's patient load 721
Schedule 155, 268, 383, 386, 387, 415, 436
– all-units quantity discount 30, 379
Scheduling 96, 141, 268, 383, 384, 385, 390
Schools 28, 178, 276, 290, 379, 442, 725
Screen 657, 661, 665, 674, 680, 686, 697
SD (Strongly disagree), 744, 745, 746
Season 268, 650, 676, 679, 681, 721, 724
Seasonal index 676, 677, 681, 714
Seasonal indices 676, 677, 679, 680, 681, 707, 708
Seasonality 653, 668, 669, 677, 678, 707, 709
Seattle 282, 283, 284, 327, 328, 329, 330
Second outcome 461, 462, 463
Selection problems 178, 317
Selling price 29, 200, 684, 686, 691, 696, 698
Sensitivity analysis 10, 25, 181, 182, 183, 200, 216
Sensitivity Report 181, 195, 206, 218, 225, 237, 315
Servers 509, 520, 526, 528, 529, 530, 550
Service 510, 511, 523, 548, 550, 560, 561
– excellent customer 509, 511
– providing 512, 527, 528, 533, 547, 548
Service costs 510, 511, 512, 513, 528, 550, 554
Service facility 509, 510, 511, 512, 513, 516, 550
Service levels 510, 512, 521, 533, 548, 550
Service rate 518, 520, 526, 528, 552, 553, 563
Service systems 520, 548, 555
Service times 518, 536, 538, 558, 562, 563, 601
– exponential 540, 548, 549, 550, 551, 552, 554
– standard deviation of 537, 559, 560
Set 239, 286, 314, 372, 373, 572, 636
Shadow price 191, 196, 203, 204, 208, 214, 217
Shafts 372, 373, 765, 794
Shaq order 495, 496
Sheet 14, 202, 255, 343, 546, 590, 643
Sheet tab 546, 768, 771
Shifts 127, 164, 165, 166, 180, 513, 551
Ship 127, 256, 258, 370, 512, 513, 790
Shipments 240, 243, 244, 247, 252, 261, 262
Shipping 130, 291, 293, 327, 328, 330, 370
Shipping costs 251, 283, 290, 292, 327, 329, 370
– total 54, 134, 246, 249, 257, 293, 294
Shortest-path model 241, 272, 273, 274, 275, 280, 281
Sign 67, 70, 81, 82, 250, 368, 775

Significance 686, 695, 702, 708
– statistical 694, 695, 702, 707
Significant relationship, statistically 702, 703
Simkin 317, 319, 320, 321, 592, 596, 598
Simkin's model 599, 600
Simple and Multiple Regression 684, 685, 687, 689, 691, 693, 695
Simple regression model 684, 696, 699, 700, 703, 708, 724
Simulate 566, 583, 584, 607, 613, 627, 638
Simulate demand 571, 572, 573, 579
Simulate values 569, 571, 574, 612
Simulation 566, 567, 568, 569, 611, 613, 624
– computer 509, 519, 520, 547, 548, 549, 565
– systems 565, 610, 611, 612, 614, 624
Simulation clock 602, 603, 613, 614, 617
– computer 565, 569
– discrete-event 333, 602, 613, 617
Simulation Modeling 565, 566, 568, 570, 574, 575, 576
Simultaneous changes 181, 206, 207, 216, 217, 218, 236
Sites 293, 295, 329, 330, 370, 395, 502
Slack time 399, 400, 401, 410, 420, 426, 429
Slope 199, 672, 694, 707, 728, 729, 799
Smart Services 469, 475, 476
Smart's surveys 470, 476
Smoothing constant 706, 709, 715, 716, 718, 719, 720
Solution 9, 10, 21, 23, 25, 265, 330
– current 183, 205, 207, 209, 216, 217, 223
– final 24, 26, 46, 47, 343, 351, 356
– finite 61, 82
– graphical 43, 45, 47, 49, 56, 57, 222
– new 11, 180, 186, 197, 199, 301, 302
– possible 33, 83, 264, 265
– unbounded 33, 58, 61, 62, 84, 88, 90
Solution procedure, graphical 36, 41, 43, 187
Solution step 9, 25, 35
Solution value 64, 78, 102, 266, 274, 309, 423
Solved Problem 85, 86, 429, 551, 552, 710, 711
Solver 63, 72, 73, 82, 314, 353, 355
– changing variable cells in 146, 261, 275, 286, 287, 289
– constraints in 82, 83, 353
Solver add-ins 6, 68, 782, 783
Solver and Data Analysis 767, 782
Solver Entries 86, 116, 133, 284, 342, 358, 360
Solver Options 71, 313, 782
Solver Parameters Window 68, 70, 71, 78, 194, 310, 320
Solver Reports 82, 193, 194, 195, 197, 199
Solver Results 72, 73, 82, 194, 363
Solver Results Window 72, 73, 194, 364
Solver Sensitivity Report for Problem 205, 223, 224, 226, 227
Solving 34, 35, 55, 81, 315, 336, 341
Solving assignment models 264, 289
Solving Linear Programming Problems 58, 59, 61, 62, 63, 65, 67
Solving LP models 34, 36, 80, 313
Solving LP problems 58, 63, 80, 82, 84, 88, 102
Special Situations in Solving Linear Programming Problems 58, 59, 61

Specifications 166, 167, 172, 173, 320, 321, 323
Spreadsheet Example 11, 13, 15, 16, 17, 19
Spreadsheets 12, 64, 65, 107, 215, 575, 642
Springs 16, 18, 19, 716, 721, 729, 730
Square feet 93, 94, 226, 686, 691, 692, 700
Standard deviation 404, 407, 563, 577, 638, 751, 752
Standard time 417, 419, 420, 422, 438, 439, 447
Start 124, 147, 148, 149, 392, 393, 395
Start Excel 767, 782, 783, 784
Start of year 147, 148, 149, 150, 151, 176
Start time 534, 603, 619, 623, 624
– earliest 395, 412, 416, 422, 426, 428, 438
Stations 369, 516, 517, 541, 547, 550, 683
Statistically Dependent Events 737, 739, 759
Statistics 402, 587, 702, 703, 762
Statistics book 673, 691, 693, 695, 702, 704
Steps 6, 7, 10, 24, 25, 451, 452
Stockouts 591, 592, 595, 597, 615, 616, 631
Stocks 92, 93, 94, 162, 376, 494, 592
Stop 131, 313, 314, 418, 509, 589, 590
Storage sheds 451, 453, 455, 469, 470, 659, 660
Strollers-to-Go 229, 230, 231, 232
Strongly disagree (SD), 744, 745, 746
Student GPA CBAT Age 723, 724
Students 178, 290, 538, 629, 722, 724, 761
Styles 93, 104, 131, 158, 159, 770, 771
Subject 89, 90, 91, 98, 99, 222, 365
Success 483, 504, 505, 506, 578, 604, 607
Suitcases 33, 228, 229, 395
Sum 37, 206, 207, 248, 412, 425, 672
Summary 151, 279, 425, 485, 547, 611, 705
SUMPRODUCT 66, 67, 248, 258, 262, 267, 275
SUMPRODUCT function 66, 67, 116, 121, 133, 152, 156
Sunday 127, 154, 155, 157, 366, 627
Supplier 30, 498, 499, 627, 628, 630, 631
– overseas 180, 791
Supplies 247, 249, 250, 264, 265, 270, 274
– monthly 245, 250, 282, 326
– total 246, 249, 250, 260, 280, 281, 282
Supply constraints 247, 248, 250, 257, 260, 267, 328
Supply nodes 243, 246, 247, 250, 256, 264, 265
Supply points 240, 279, 280, 285
Support staff 153, 263, 415, 416
Surplus 76, 78, 82, 84, 88, 217, 218
Survey 114, 470, 474, 475, 476, 478, 505
Survey results 472, 474, 476, 477, 478, 492, 505
– negative 470, 474, 476, 477
– positive 470, 471, 472, 476, 477, 492, 493
Sussex County 322, 323, 324
Symbols 66, 67, 308, 466, 520, 603, 613
System 519, 523, 547, 548, 550, 555, 556
System test data, specifying 440, 441

T

Tables 39, 40, 52, 186, 199, 371, 745
– decision 461, 462, 466, 487, 489, 493, 495

- decision variable 248, 286, 288, 301
- payoff 452, 455, 485, 487, 489, 508
Tables and chairs 38, 39, 52, 63, 74, 232, 237
Tabs 768, 769, 770, 771, 772, 773, 781
Target completion time 407, 408, 409, 410
Tasks 240, 241, 262, 383, 384, 387, 770
Tax Computation 11, 12, 13, 15, 30
Taxable income 11, 13, 14, 15
Teams 268, 440, 512, 513, 610, 762, 763
Teams of stevedores 512, 513
Technicians 543, 544, 545, 559
Techniques 4, 6, 425, 548, 549, 565, 567
- mathematical programming 34, 35, 331, 357
Technology 2, 5, 402, 409, 500, 501, 534
Tellers 123, 125, 126, 238, 516, 564, 604
Template 300, 301, 378, 383, 508, 770
Terms 22, 35, 37, 42, 66, 81, 349
Test 501, 502, 517, 643, 695, 702, 703
Test device 159, 225
Thompson Lumber 457, 458, 459, 464, 465, 469, 470
Ties, all-silk 103, 104, 105, 106, 107, 109, 110
Ties Unlimited 109, 110
Time estimates 390, 403, 404, 440, 441, 443, 444
Time interval 530, 537, 538, 549, 756, 757, 758
Time periods 127, 166, 522, 542, 543, 634, 674
Time-series data 654, 668, 669, 675, 676, 677, 678
Tires 179, 571, 572, 573, 582, 584, 632
Titles 524, 579, 580, 583, 586, 655, 656
Total production 96, 240, 283
Total profit 39, 199, 204, 205, 207, 225, 345
Total sales goal 334, 335, 337, 338, 340, 341, 342
Total transportation cost 246, 258, 290, 293
Totals 129, 411, 412, 596, 795
Track 574, 602, 609, 612, 613, 614, 617
Transportation 102, 239, 240, 244, 248, 269, 270
Transportation Applications 127, 129, 131, 133
Transportation costs 240, 246, 259, 283, 290, 291, 293
Transportation models 239, 240, 244, 247, 251, 280, 282
- basic 239, 240, 246, 247, 256
Transportation problem 133, 134, 153, 239, 242, 245, 252
Transshipment nodes 243, 258, 259, 261, 262, 270, 271
Trend 653, 654, 668, 678, 706, 707, 709
Trend equation 668, 681, 682, 714, 715
- linear 681, 707, 711, 714, 726, 727
Trend line, linear 671, 672, 674, 675, 706
Trials 578, 643, 644, 732, 733, 759, 760
Trip 243, 536, 605, 606, 607, 608, 609
Triplex 753, 754, 755
Troy's Tires 631, 632
Trucks 127, 128, 129, 132, 535, 556, 638
- single 132, 133
- volume limit of 128, 132
- weight limit of 128, 132
T-statistic, computed 695, 703
T-test 695, 702, 707
Tuesday 127, 154, 155, 157, 165, 366
Turkey 55, 57, 61, 62, 78, 173, 791
Types 3, 117, 134, 159, 160, 185, 453

U
Uncertainty 4, 5, 185, 417, 453, 459, 485
Unconnected houses 278, 279
Unidirectional arcs 242, 243, 286
Uniform distribution 613, 642, 643, 798
- continuous 576, 582, 642
Unit costs 143, 218, 234, 235, 256, 257, 261
Unit price 16, 209, 305
Unit profit 96, 97, 199, 205, 232, 233, 312
Units 16, 31, 203, 214, 380, 630, 799
- additional 203, 204, 214, 227
University 263, 276, 402, 442, 489, 497, 557
Unrounded Solution 791, 794
Unseasonalized sales forecast 681, 714
Use Excel 99, 450, 510, 648
Use Excel's FORECAST function 728
Use simulation 639, 640, 641
Use Solver 225
Useful Excel 767, 768, 770, 772, 774, 776, 778
Users 24, 74, 131, 312, 460, 546, 779
Utilities 480, 481, 482, 484, 486, 488, 504
- expected 484, 485, 487, 498, 505, 508, 796
Utility curve 481, 482, 483, 484, 487, 488, 493
Utility function 479, 486, 493, 502, 508
- person's 479
Utility theory 449, 450, 478, 479, 481, 501, 502
Utility values 479, 480, 484, 485, 487, 488, 503
Utilization rate 547, 555, 556, 557

V
Validity 22, 23, 206, 687, 688, 725, 726
Values 598, 614, 617, 672, 745, 777, 778
- absolute 76, 652, 777
- actual 651, 652, 654, 664, 709, 714, 729
- current 80, 196, 197, 199, 205, 206, 225
- default 71, 313, 314, 315, 656, 781, 784
- desired 18, 539, 540, 550
- exact 408, 749
- forecasted 651, 686, 688, 689, 691, 708, 709
- given 31, 672, 689, 691, 694, 702
- high 261, 287, 288
- known 3, 12, 25, 26
- large 281, 361
- largest 460, 467
- non-zero 199, 208, 220, 221
- payoff 452, 472, 480
- replicated 608, 616, 619
- right-hand-side 181
- simulated 580, 584, 596, 597
- smallest 458, 460, 467
- starting 351, 352, 353, 356, 363, 375, 376
- total 127, 128, 129, 133, 368, 794, 795
Valves 96, 498, 499
Variability 402, 403, 409, 410, 426, 691, 747
Variable Cells table 195, 198, 205, 251
Variable costs 16, 18, 28, 29, 30, 325, 371
- total 16, 26
Variable values 152, 582, 583, 587, 680, 713
Variables 9, 353, 570, 586, 669, 684, 689
Variance 404, 405, 406, 429, 430, 748, 760
Variations, random 653, 654, 678, 707, 708, 709

VBA (Visual Basic for Applications), 312, 590, 782
Visual Basic for Applications. See VBA
Vitamin 36, 55, 77, 78, 101, 374
Volume 28, 29, 128, 130, 168, 245, 252
Volume capacity 127, 128, 132

W
Wait 512, 547, 555, 556, 557, 558, 562
Waiting 509, 512, 555, 556, 557, 562, 563
Waiting cost 511, 512, 513, 528, 536, 548, 550
- revised 536
Waiting lines 509, 510, 511, 513, 549, 550, 551
Waiting time 532, 539, 548, 551, 552, 553, 563
Wallace Garden Supply 655, 657, 659, 660, 661, 663, 667
Warehouse employees 559
Warehouses 245, 246, 247, 250, 256, 326, 370
Waukesha 268, 269, 270, 271, 301
WBS. See work breakdown structure
Weight capacity 127, 132, 167, 168
Weighted Goals Solution 336, 338
Weighted GP Model 336, 337
Weighted moving averages 647, 648, 659, 660, 661, 662, 716
Weighting 660, 661
Weights 132, 337, 660, 663, 664, 706, 749
- choice of 337, 659, 662
- optimal 662, 663, 666, 706, 715, 716, 717
- total 132, 133, 167, 174
Widgets 29, 297, 298, 789, 793
Wilson 283, 332, 335, 336, 337, 338, 343
Wilson's problem 333, 334, 335, 336, 337, 339, 341
Window 634, 661, 665, 692, 696, 704, 776
Winning 163, 164, 294, 295, 762
Winter 499, 653, 716, 721, 729
Wiring 92, 97, 306, 312, 359, 361, 639
Wiring hours 92, 306, 312, 359
WL 739
Work 23, 157, 165, 175, 176, 177, 414
- value of 414, 415, 427
Work breakdown structure (WBS), 388, 389, 429
Work schedules 54, 127, 154
Workbooks 215, 590, 767, 768, 773, 774, 781
- current 770
Workers 154, 157, 263, 264, 265, 266, 267
Worksheet 526, 658, 698, 713, 768, 769, 775
- queuing 525, 551, 552
Worthwhile 38, 208, 223, 225, 238, 475, 528

X
Xlsx 202, 284, 343, 360, 363, 585, 666
X-range 693, 777, 778
X-ray capacity 348, 349

Y
Year number 711, 721
Y-intercept 685, 686, 693, 695, 696, 705, 707
YL 739
Y-range 693, 777, 778

Z
Zero values 139, 221, 526, 602, 617